Learning just got more exciting!
Interactive Companion
Home
Companion Website
Select a Chapter:
The World of Psychology, 4/e
by Samuel E. Wood, Lindenwood University, and Ellen Green Wood, St. Louis Community College, Meramec
Welcome to the Interactive Companion Website for The World of Psychology, 4/e. Feel free to look around the demo chapter to see all that it has to offer.
In order to fully utilize the features of this site, we recommend downloading the latest version of FLASH PLAYER from www.macromedia.com and the latest version of QuickTime from www.quicktime.com
THE World OF PSYCHOLOGY
SAMUEL E. WOOD ELLEN GREEN WOOD
It all starts here.
Activate your PIN!*
*Your PIN is provided on the inside cover of every NEW copy of this textbook.

Introducing the Interactive Companion Web site for *The World of Psychology, 4/e*

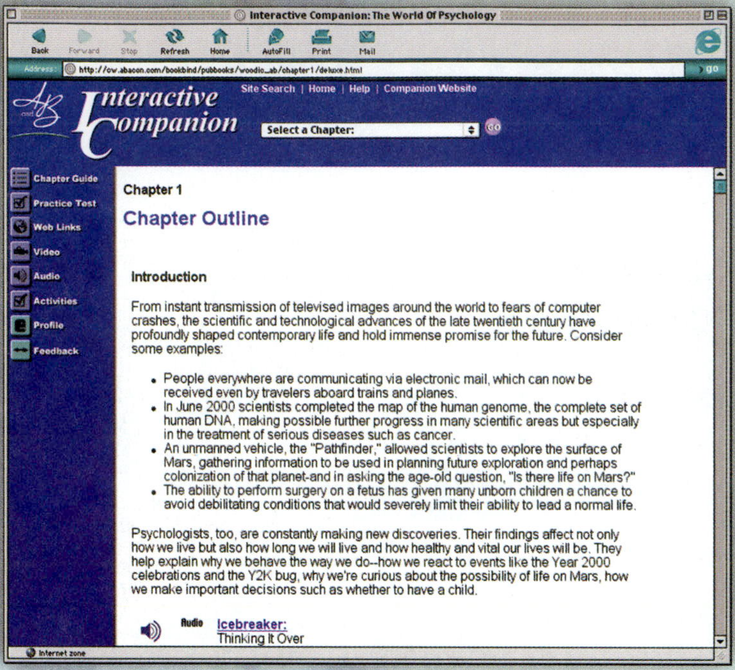

Learning has reached a whole new level with the Interactive Companion Web site – *by encouraging you to apply what you've learned through audio and video clips, Web sites, activities and practice tests.*

With the purchase of Wood & Wood's *The World of Psychology, 4/e*, you'll get access to this PIN-code protected Web site FREE of charge. The Allyn & Bacon Interactive Companion Web site represents an exciting new study tool that uses the latest in multimedia to review, enrich, and expand upon key concepts presented in its companion textbook.

Using chapter highlights as its organizing structure, the Interactive Companion helps you apply what you've learned by presenting you with hundreds of links to audio and video clips, Web sites, activities, and practice tests. These links are annotated with brief descriptions that help you understand the value and purpose of each type of media in the context of the chapter.

Everything you need is right here at your fingertips!

ACTIVATE YOUR PIN.

How will you benefit from using the Interactive Companion Web site?

- ✓ **Provides you with frequent feedback on your learning progress to perform better on tests.**
- ✓ **Offers highly interactive ways for you to engage with the textbook content.**
- ✓ **Adds variety to course materials and helps you study more effectively.**
- ✓ **Helps you to think critically about the information presented to you in the textbook and on the Web site.**
- ✓ **Gives you access to the latest information related to the textbook topics via the Web.**

> "*A major advantage of the Web site is that it allows students to connect with a wealth of learning support any time and any place. Professors can create a vast array of assignments and projects, knowing that all students – those in dorms and those commuting from home miles away, those with easy access to libraries and those who are more isolated – have the resources to complete the assignments and projects.*"
>
> ***Anita Woolfolk***
> ***Educational Psychology Professor***
> ***The Ohio State University***

Easy navigation that lets you study the way you want to!

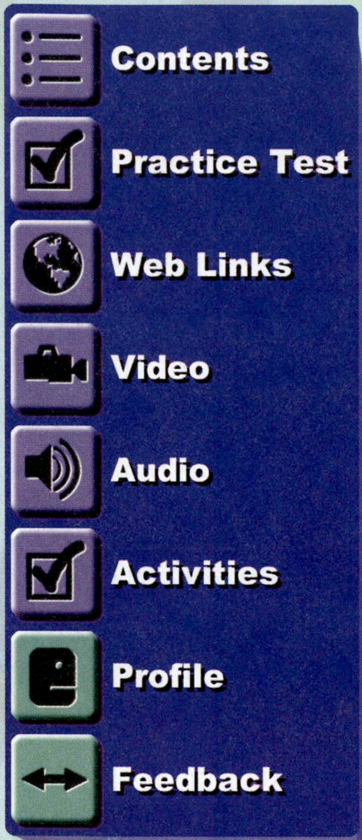

1. Each chapter begins with an attention-grabbing opener. **Click on the associated audio icon and you'll hear questions or issues framed around the chapter opener;** this allows you to hear as well as read about new concepts.
2. **Chapter learning objectives are linked to the various topic areas**, allowing you to go directly from what you need to learn in the chapter to the media assets that will help you learn this new information.
3. **Each topic area ends with an activity** that is a review of key terms. These are created as flash card exercises – allowing you to reinforce the information that you've learned from that section of the book.
4. **Every chapter ends with three items:**
   a. **Concept Check Activity** which asks you to match terms and concepts in the chapter with their definitions.
   b. **"Closing Thoughts"** in which you revisit the opening scenario and consider the situation in light of what you've learned in the chapter.
   c. **Practice Test,** which promotes self-regulation and self-monitoring, two key elements of successful learning.

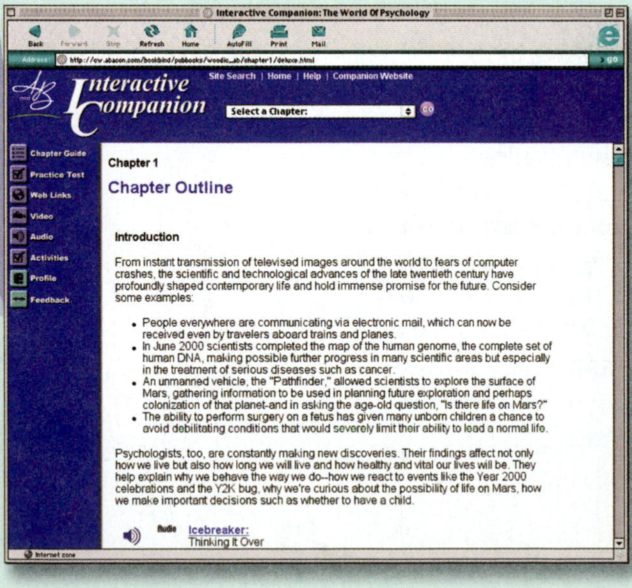

Everything you need is right here at your fingertips!

ACTIVATE YOUR PIN.

Interactive ways to prepare for that in-class exam and research paper!

Practice Test

Click on a **"Practice Test"** icon and you'll be able to test your understanding of the chapter material by completing a self-scoring practice test. You'll receive immediate results and feedback from your test, allowing you to review your weak areas in preparation for the actual in-class exam.

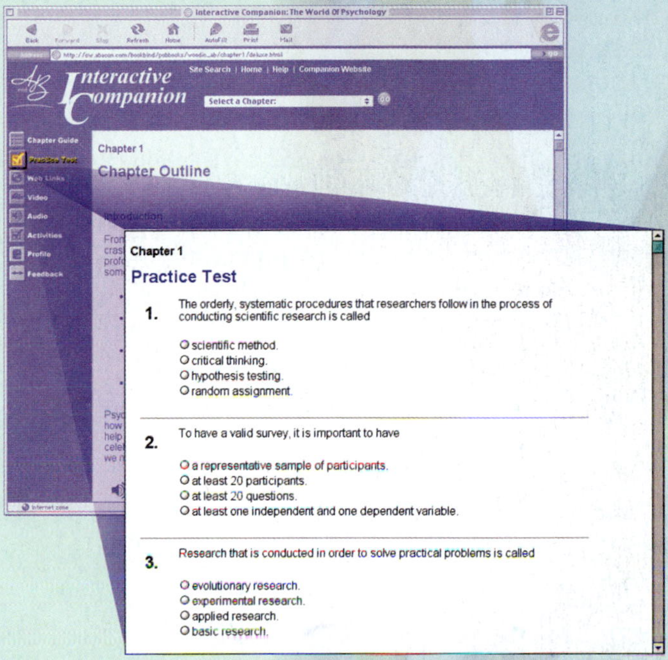

> *I think it's great. You can take practice tests so that when you really get tested, you already know what to expect. I think it really contributes to your learning.*
> ***Gloria, age 27***

Web links

With the benefit of an Internet connection, by clicking on the **"Web links"** icon you'll jump to current Web sites that provide you with additional information about the specific topics you're studying. Web links are continuously monitored and updated by Allyn & Bacon, so you'll always have the most current sites to access. This is a great resource for you to utilize when writing a research paper!

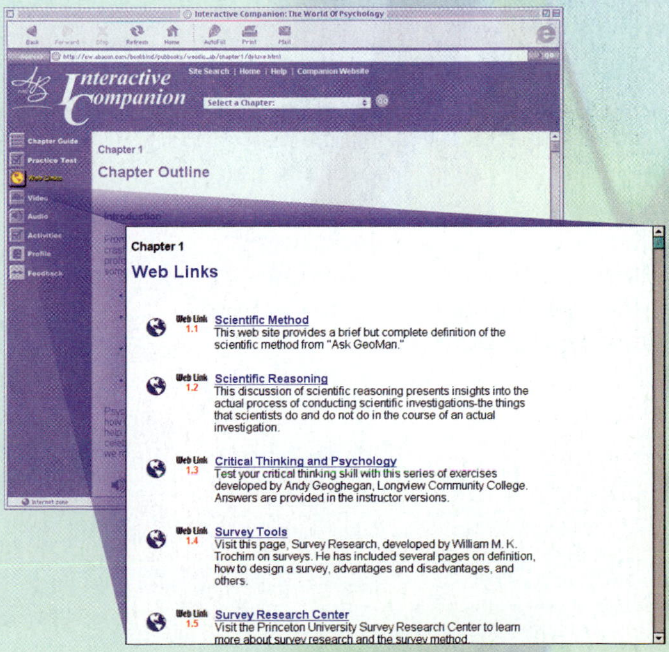

> *These Web links help me find quality Internet resources for the types of assignments required for class.*
> ***Debra, age 22***

Information comes alive when you see it and hear it!

Video

Click on a **"Video"** icon and you'll be captivated by the **sights and sounds of video segments directly related to the material you just read.** For some textbooks, these segments come from leading news sources. For others, they are part of custom videos developed to demonstrate concepts in the discipline.

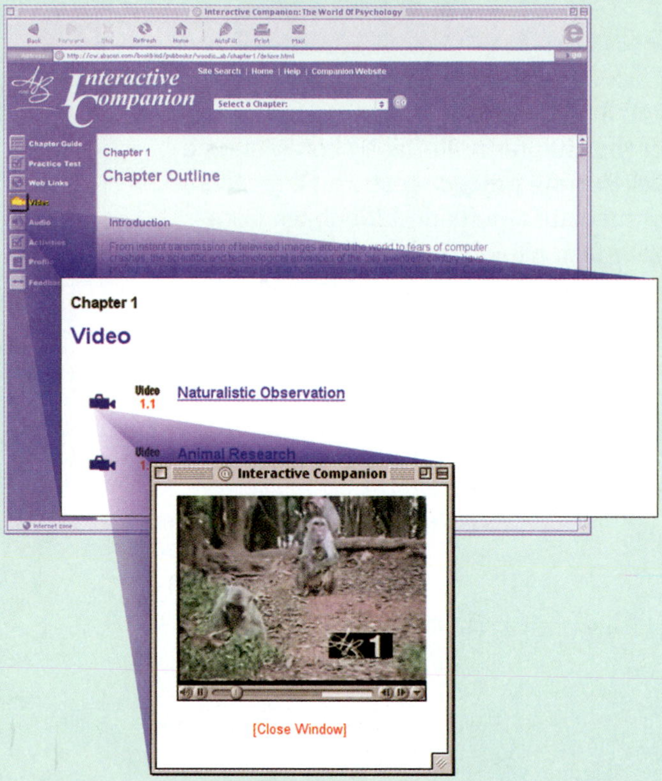

The audio, feedback, and videos help me understand each chapter.
Janel, age 40

Audio

Click on an **"Audio"** icon and you'll hear either the author of the textbook or a specialist in the field speaking directly about concepts in the book. Often **the "voice" will add background information or give examples – material that enhances and extends the chapter material.**

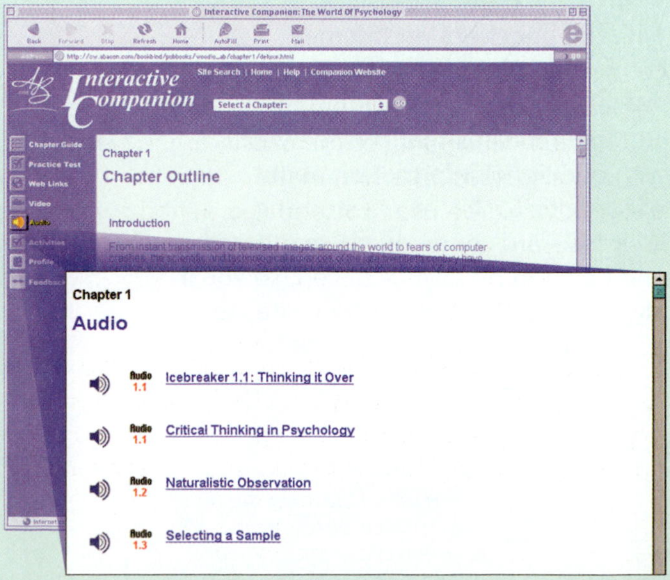

Everything you need is right here at your fingertips!

ACTIVATE YOUR PIN.

Activities can be used as extra credit to boost that grade even higher!

Activities

Click on an **"Activities"** icon and you can complete interesting activities directly related to the information presented in the textbook.

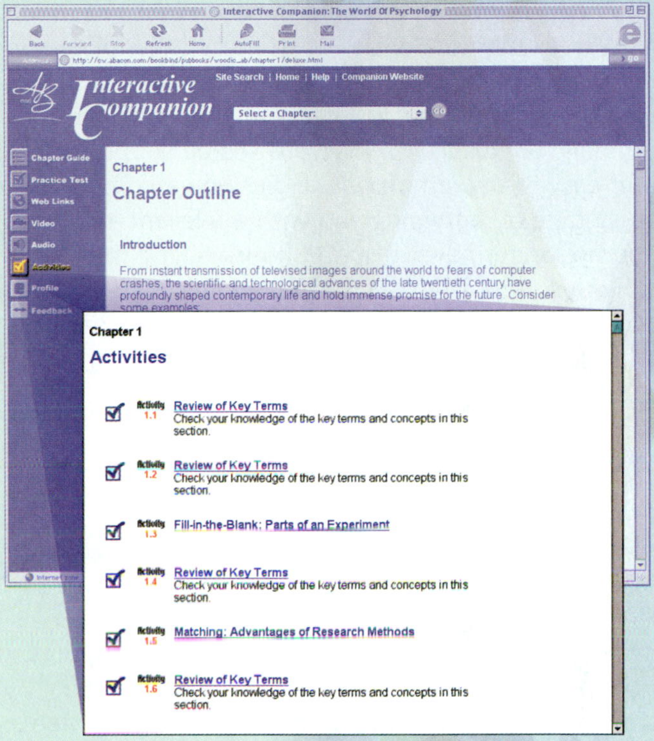

> *"I enjoyed using the Web site! The matching games and the vocabulary terms helped me the most.*
> ***Andy, age 18"***

Profile

By entering your profile on the site, you can avoid retyping it every time you need to submit homework. Once saved, the information will appear automatically whenever it's required. You can also subscribe to a mailing list for the Web site. This mailing list will be used to send you periodic updates on materials relevant to the topical area covered by this Web site.

Feedback

We are always looking to improve and expand upon the information and technology we offer you. If you have any suggestions, questions or technical difficulties, please contact us through the feedback feature on the site.

The World of Psychology

Fourth Edition

Samuel E. Wood
Lindenwood University
Ellen Green Wood

ALLYN AND BACON
BOSTON LONDON TORONTO SYDNEY TOKYO SINGAPORE

To our children:
Liane Kelly, Susan Benson, Alan Wood,
Bart Green, and Julie Kalina

Executive Editor: Carolyn Merrill
Development Editor: Kelly Perkins
Senior Marketing Manager: Caroline Croley
Senior Editorial–Production Administrator: Michael Granger
Editorial–Production Service: Lifland et al., Bookmakers
Composition and Prepress Buyer: Linda Cox
Manufacturing Buyer: Megan Cochran
Cover Administrator: Linda Knowles
Interior Design: Shelley Davidson
Illustrations: LMY Studio
Electronic Composition: Monotype Composition Company, Inc.

A Pearson Education Company
75 Arlington Street
Boston, MA 02116

Internet: www.ablongman.com

Library of Congress Cataloging-in-Publication Data

Wood, Samuel E.
The world of psychology / Samuel E. Wood, Ellen Green Wood. — 4th ed.
p. cm.
Includes bibliographical references and index.
ISBN 0-205-33427-X
1. Psychology. I. Wood, Ellen R. Green. II. Title.
BF121. W657 2002
150—dc21 2001022715

Printed in the United States of America
10 9 8 7 6 5 4 3 2 VHP 06 05 04 03 02 01

Credits appear on pages C-1 and C-2, which constitute a continuation of the copyright page.

Contents

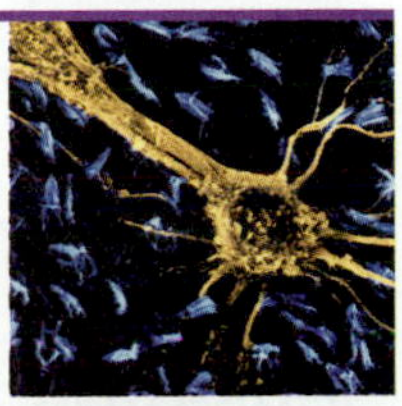

CHAPTER 4

States of Consciousness 123

CHAPTER 5

Learning 163

CHAPTER 6

Memory 203

CHAPTER 12

Human Sexuality and Gender 425

CHAPTER 13

Health and Stress 461

Just for Students: How This Textbook Can Help You Study

We all learn best when we can apply new concepts to the world we know. *The World of Psychology* allows you to do just that. Highly interactive *and* active, clearly written, and thoroughly up to date, this textbook will encourage you to think for yourself as you learn about, relate to, and apply the principles of psychology that affect your life.

So that you can make the most of all the material in the following pages, this textbook package incorporates a number of helpful features and supplementary items.

A Clear, Engaging Writing Style

This may sound crazy, but you will actually enjoy reading this textbook. It has received very positive responses from students and has been praised first and foremost for its writing style. The style is conversational, and the text uses numerous everyday examples and realistic analogies to help you grasp even the most complex concepts. A chapter opening vignette introduces each chapter's topics with a dramatic real-life story—one that is memorable and directly related to the chapter's content.

You'll be especially interested in the stories of:

- Michael J. Fox, who for 7 years kept the secret of his affliction with Parkinson's disease and then made the decision to retire from acting to spend more time with his family
- Ronald Cotton, who was sent to jail for a rape he didn't commit, based on the faulty memory of the victim
- Christopher Reeve, who works every day to turn the tragedy of his paralysis into a blessing
- S.B., a blind man who had surgery to regain his sight but then couldn't function in his new vision-based world
- The Milgram study, in which volunteers for an experiment demonstrated sadistic tendencies when asked to deliver electric shocks to others
- Robert, a child raised by monkeys who was found in the African jungle
- Bill, who has a phobia of popping balloons

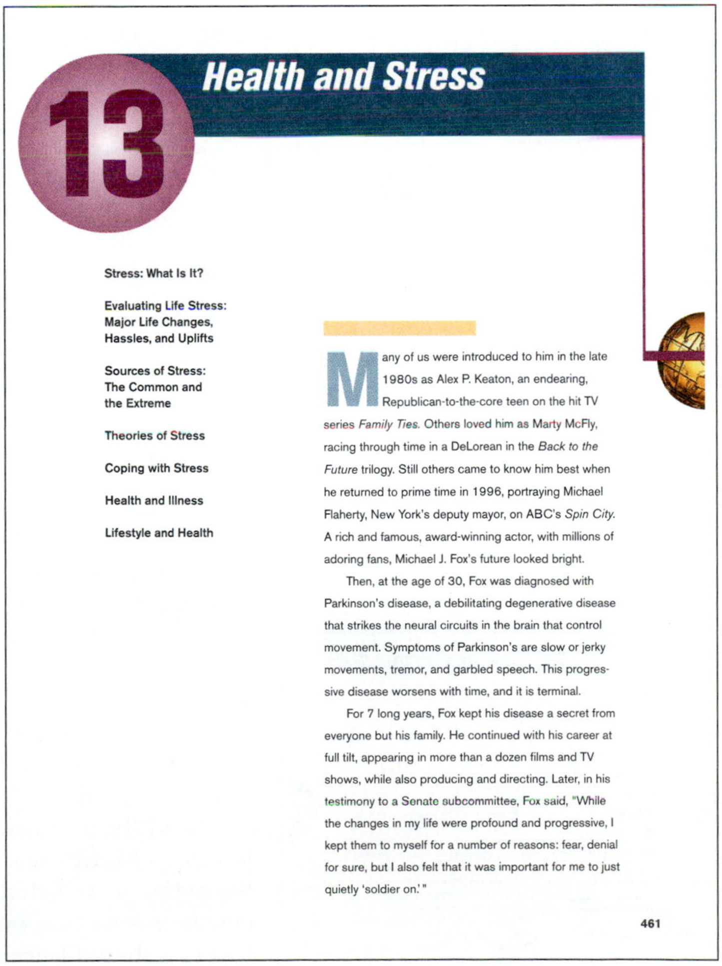
13 Health and Stress

Stress: What Is It?

Evaluating Life Stress: Major Life Changes, Hassles, and Uplifts

Sources of Stress: The Common and the Extreme

Theories of Stress

Coping with Stress

Health and Illness

Lifestyle and Health

Many of us were introduced to him in the late 1980s as Alex P. Keaton, an endearing, Republican-to-the-core teen on the hit TV series *Family Ties.* Others loved him as Marty McFly, racing through time in a DeLorean in the *Back to the Future* trilogy. Still others came to know him best when he returned to prime time in 1996, portraying Michael Flaherty, New York's deputy mayor, on ABC's *Spin City.* A rich and famous, award-winning actor, with millions of adoring fans, Michael J. Fox's future looked bright.

Then, at the age of 30, Fox was diagnosed with Parkinson's disease, a debilitating degenerative disease that strikes the neural circuits in the brain that control movement. Symptoms of Parkinson's are slow or jerky movements, tremor, and garbled speech. This progressive disease worsens with time, and it is terminal.

For 7 long years, Fox kept his disease a secret from everyone but his family. He continued with his career at full tilt, appearing in more than a dozen films and TV shows, while also producing and directing. Later, in his testimony to a Senate subcommittee, Fox said, "While the changes in my life were profound and progressive, I kept them to myself for a number of reasons: fear, denial for sure, but I also felt that it was important for me to just quietly 'soldier on.' "

461

Interact with Your Textbook

What better way to learn new material—to make it fresh, interesting, and memorable—than to demonstrate for yourself the principles discussed? The unique *Try It!* features encourage you to learn by doing. The highly praised *Try Its!* provide simple experiments, self-assessments, and activities that you can perform without elaborate equipment, usually as you read.

Research has shown that checking your progress at key points as you study helps you remember what you have read. Another way you can interact with this textbook is by taking the *Remember It!* quizzes at the ends of the main text sections.

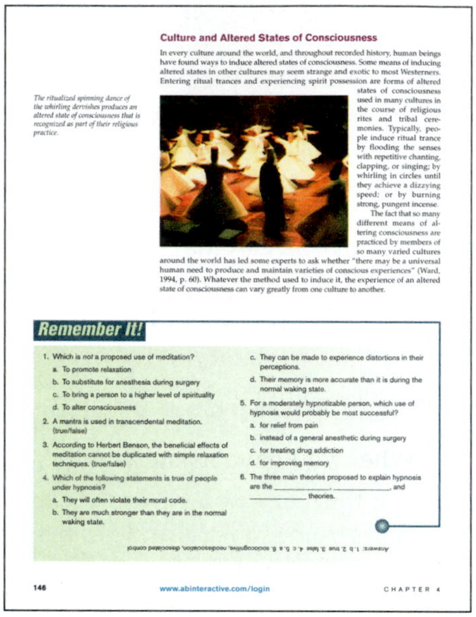

Finally, you'll have a chance to relate psychological principles to your own life in the *Apply It!* section at the end of each chapter. Each *Apply It!* helps you apply psychology to problems and issues that may affect your personal life. Among the wide range of topics addressed are these:

- Kicking your caffeine habit
- Beating procrastination
- Dealing with road rage
- Practicing good prenatal care
- Improving your creativity
- Overcoming the fear of public speaking
- Practicing good study habits
- Improving date-seeking skills
- Building good relationships
- Avoiding bad decisions
- Improving your memory

A Formula for Success

This textbook is organized to help you maximize your learning by following five steps: Survey, Question, Read, Recite, and Review. Together, these are known as the *SQ3R* method. You will learn and remember more if, instead of simply reading each chapter, you follow these steps. Here's how they work.

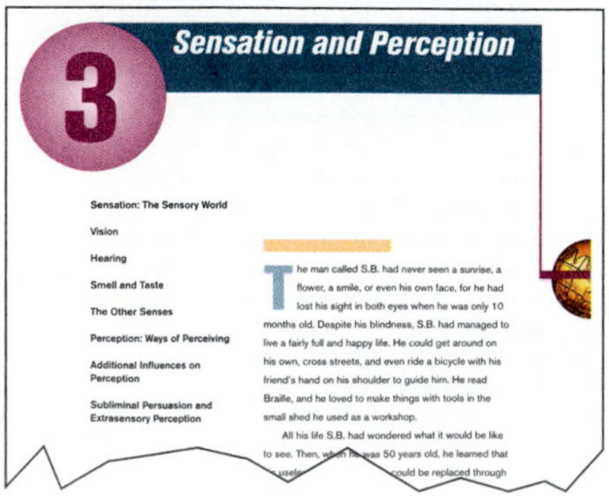

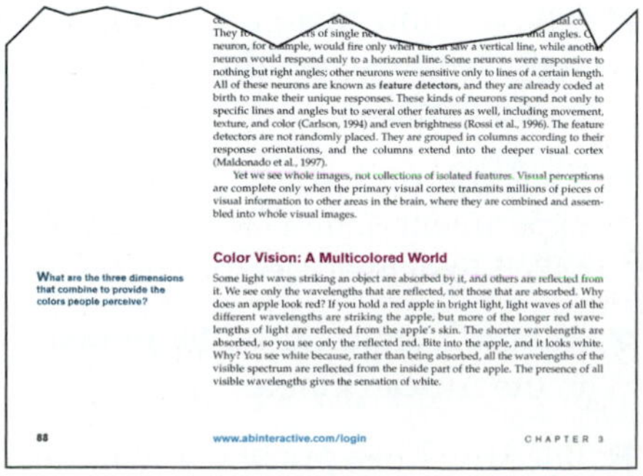

1. Survey First, scan the chapter you are going to read. The chapter outline helps you preview the content and its organization.

Read the section headings and the *learning objective questions*, (located in the margins), which are designed to focus your attention on key information that you should learn and remember.

Glance at the illustrations and tables, including the *Review & Reflect* tables, which organize, review, and summarize key concepts.

Then read the *Summary and Review*, located at the end of each chapter. This survey process gives you an overview of the chapter.

2. Question Before you actually read each section in a chapter, turn its heading into one or more questions. Some sections provide one or more learning objective questions, but you can also jot down questions of your own. For example, one heading in Chapter 1 is "The Goals of Psychology." The learning objective question is "What are the four goals of psychology?" You might add this question: "What is meant by 'control' as a goal of psychology?" Asking such questions helps focus your reading.

3. Read Read the section. As you read, try to answer the learning objective question(s) *and* your own question(s). After reading the section, stop. If the section is very long or if the material seems especially difficult or complex, you should pause after reading only one or two paragraphs.

4. Recite After reading part or all of a section, try to answer the learning objective question(s) and your own question(s). To better grasp each topic, write a short summary of the material. If you have trouble summarizing a topic or answering the questions, scan or read the section once more before trying again.

When you have mastered one section, move on to the next. If the text does not include a learning objective question, formulate your own. Then read and recite, answering your question or writing a brief summary as before.

5. Review Each major section in the book ends with a *Remember It!* that consists of a few questions about the preceding topics. Interspersed throughout each chapter, these quizzes cover the material emphasized by the learning objective questions. Answer the *Remember It!* questions, and check your answers against those provided. If you make errors, quickly review the preceding material until you know the answers.

When you have finished a chapter, revisit the *Remember Its!* and then turn to the *Summary and Review.* Review the *Key Terms.* If you don't know the meaning of a term, turn to the page where that term is defined in the margin. The *marginal definitions* provide a ready reference for important key terms that appear in boldface print in the text. All of these terms and definitions also appear in the *Glossary* at the end of the book.

Next, review each learning objective question in the *Summary and Review* and answer it in your own words. The answers provided are only condensed reminders, and you should be able to expand on them.

Finally, consider the thought-provoking questions in the *Thinking Critically* section under the three headings *Evaluation, Point/Counterpoint,* and *Psychology in Your Life.* Answering these questions requires more than simple memorization. These critical thinking questions give you the chance to reassure yourself that you really understand the information presented in the chapter.

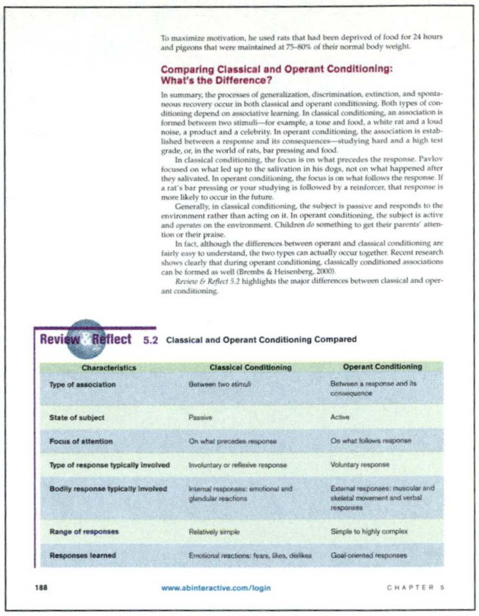
To maximize motivation, he used rats that had been deprived of food for 24 hours and pigeons that were maintained at 75–80% of their normal body weight.

Comparing Classical and Operant Conditioning: What's the Difference?

In summary, the processes of generalization, discrimination, extinction, and spontaneous recovery occur in both classical and operant conditioning. Both types of conditioning depend on associative learning. In classical conditioning, an association is formed between two stimuli—for example, a tone and food, a white rat and a loud noise, a product and a celebrity. In operant conditioning, the association is established between a response and its consequences—studying hard and a high test grade, or, in the world of rats, bar pressing and food.

In classical conditioning, the focus is on what precedes the response. Pavlov focused on what led up to the salivation in his dogs, not on what happened after they salivated. In operant conditioning, the focus is on what follows the response. If a rat's bar pressing or your studying is followed by a reinforcer, that response is more likely to occur in the future.

Generally, in classical conditioning, the subject is passive and responds to the environment rather than acting on it. In operant conditioning, the subject is active and *operates* on the environment. Children *do* something to get their parents' attention or their praise.

In fact, although the differences between operant and classical conditioning are fairly easy to understand, the two types can actually occur together. Recent research shows clearly that during operant conditioning, classically conditioned associations can be formed as well (Brembs & Heisenberg, 2000).

Review & Reflect 5.2 highlights the major differences between classical and operant conditioning.

Review & Reflect 5.2 Classical and Operant Conditioning Compared

Characteristics	Classical Conditioning	Operant Conditioning
Type of association	Between two stimuli	Between a response and its consequence
State of subject	Passive	Active
Focus of attention	On what precedes response	On what follows response
Type of response typically involved	Involuntary or reflexive response	Voluntary response
Bodily response typically involved	Internal responses: emotional and glandular reactions	External responses: muscular and skeletal movement and verbal responses
Range of responses	Relatively simple	Simple to highly complex
Responses learned	Emotional reactions: fears, likes, dislikes	Goal-oriented responses

188 www.abinteractive.com/login CHAPTER 5

Remember It!

1. Many people take aspirin to relieve painful headaches. Taking aspirin is a behavior that is likely to continue because of the effect of (positive, negative) reinforcement.
2. (Partial, Continuous) reinforcement is most effective in conditioning a new response; once a response is acquired, (partial, continuous) reinforcement results in greater resistance to extinction.
3. Glen and Megan are both employed raking leaves. Glen is paid $1 for each bag of leaves he rakes; Megan is paid $4 per hour. Glen is paid according to the ____________ schedule; Megan is paid according to the ____________ schedule.
   a. fixed-interval; fixed-ratio
   b. variable-ratio; fixed-interval
   c. variable-ratio; variable-interval
   d. fixed-ratio; fixed-interval
4. Which schedule of reinforcement yields the highest response rate and the greatest resistance to extinction?
   a. variable-ratio schedule
   b. fixed-ratio schedule
   c. variable-interval schedule
   d. fixed-interval schedule
5. Logan's parents have noticed that he has been making his bed every day, and they would like this to continue. Because they understand the partial-reinforcement effect, they will want to reward him *every* time he makes the bed. (true/false)
6. People often engage in behavior that is reinforcing in the short term but is not in their long-term interest. This reflects the influence of
   a. the magnitude of reinforcement.
   b. their level of motivation.
   c. the immediacy of reinforcement.
   d. the schedule of reinforcement.
7. Recall what you have learned about classical and operant conditioning. Which of the following is descriptive of operant conditioning?
   a. An association is formed between a response and its consequence.
   b. The responses acquired are usually emotional reactions.
   c. The subject is usually passive.
   d. The response acquired is usually an involuntary or reflexive response.

Answers: 1. negative 2. Continuous, partial 3. d 4. a 5. false 6. c 7. a

Punishment: That Hurts!

How does punishment differ from negative reinforcement?

In many ways **punishment** is the opposite of reinforcement. Punishment tends to lower the probability of a response by following it with an aversive or unpleasant consequence. And punishment can be accomplished by either adding an unpleasant stimulus or removing a pleasant stimulus. The added unpleasant stimulus might take the form of criticism, a scolding, a disapproving look, a fine, or a prison sentence. The removal of a pleasant stimulus might consist of withholding affection and attention, suspending a driver's license, or taking away a privilege such as watching television.

It is common to confuse punishment and negative reinforcement because both involve an unpleasant condition, but there is a big difference between the two. Punishment may involve adding a negative condition, but with negative reinforcement, a negative condition is terminated or avoided. Moreover, the two are designed to have opposite effects: Punishment is applied to discourage a behavior; negative reinforcement is used to encourage or strengthen a behavior. Unlike punishment, negative reinforcement *increases* the probability of a desired response by removing an unpleasant stimulus when the correct response is made. "Grounding" can be

punishment: The removal of a pleasant stimulus or the application of an unpleasant stimulus, which tends to suppress a response.

LEARNING 189

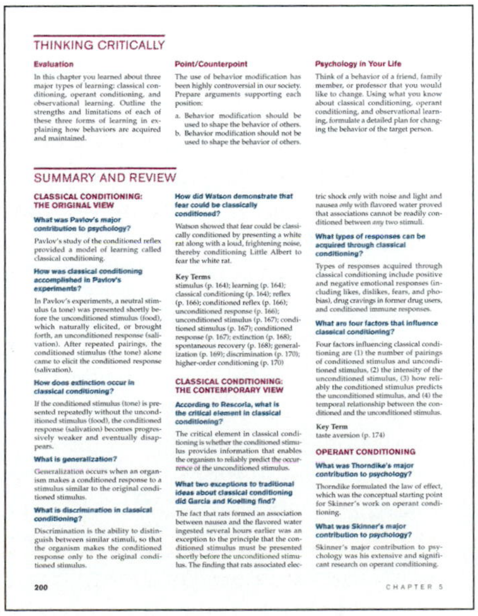
THINKING CRITICALLY

Evaluation

In this chapter you learned about three major types of learning: classical conditioning, operant conditioning, and observational learning. Outline the strengths and limitations of each of these three forms of learning in explaining how behaviors are acquired and maintained.

Point/Counterpoint

The use of behavior modification has been highly controversial in our society. Prepare arguments supporting each position:

a. Behavior modification should be used to shape the behavior of others.
b. Behavior modification should not be used to shape the behavior of others.

Psychology in Your Life

Think of a behavior of a friend, family member, or professor that you would like to change. Using what you know about classical conditioning, operant conditioning, and observational learning, formulate a detailed plan for changing the behavior of the target person.

SUMMARY AND REVIEW

CLASSICAL CONDITIONING: THE ORIGINAL VIEW

What was Pavlov's major contribution to psychology?

Pavlov's study of the conditioned reflex provided a model of learning called classical conditioning.

How was classical conditioning accomplished in Pavlov's experiments?

In Pavlov's experiments, a neutral stimulus (a tone) was presented shortly before the unconditioned stimulus (food), which naturally elicited, or brought forth, an unconditioned response (salivation). After repeated pairings, the conditioned stimulus (the tone) alone came to elicit the conditioned response (salivation).

How does extinction occur in classical conditioning?

If the conditioned stimulus (tone) is presented repeatedly without the unconditioned stimulus (food), the conditioned response (salivation) becomes progressively weaker and eventually disappears.

What is generalization?

Generalization occurs when an organism makes a conditioned response to a stimulus similar to the original conditioned stimulus.

What is discrimination in classical conditioning?

Discrimination is the ability to distinguish between similar stimuli, so that the organism makes the conditioned response only to the original conditioned stimulus.

How did Watson demonstrate that fear could be classically conditioned?

Watson showed that fear could be classically conditioned by presenting a white rat along with a loud, frightening noise, thereby conditioning Little Albert to fear the white rat.

Key Terms
stimulus (p. 164); learning (p. 164); classical conditioning (p. 164); reflex (p. 166); conditioned reflex (p. 166); unconditioned response (p. 166); unconditioned stimulus (p. 167); conditioned stimulus (p. 167); conditioned response (p. 167); extinction (p. 168); spontaneous recovery (p. 168); generalization (p. 169); discrimination (p. 170); higher-order conditioning (p. 170)

CLASSICAL CONDITIONING: THE CONTEMPORARY VIEW

According to Rescorla, what is the critical element in classical conditioning?

The critical element in classical conditioning is whether the conditioned stimulus provides information that enables the organism to reliably predict the occurrence of the unconditioned stimulus.

What two exceptions to traditional ideas about classical conditioning did Garcia and Koelling find?

The fact that rats formed an association between nausea and the flavored water ingested several hours earlier was an exception to the principle that the conditioned stimulus must be presented shortly before the unconditioned stimulus. The finding that rats associated electric shock *only* with noise and light and nausea *only* with flavored water proved that associations cannot be readily conditioned between *any* two stimuli.

What types of responses can be acquired through classical conditioning?

Types of responses acquired through classical conditioning include positive and negative emotional responses (including likes, dislikes, fears, and phobias), drug cravings in former drug users, and conditioned immune responses.

What are four factors that influence classical conditioning?

Four factors influencing classical conditioning are (1) the number of pairings of conditioned stimulus and unconditioned stimulus, (2) the intensity of the unconditioned stimulus, (3) how reliably the conditioned stimulus predicts the unconditioned stimulus, and (4) the temporal relationship between the conditioned and the unconditioned stimulus.

Key Term
taste aversion (p. 174)

OPERANT CONDITIONING

What was Thorndike's major contribution to psychology?

Thorndike formulated the law of effect, which was the conceptual starting point for Skinner's work on operant conditioning.

What was Skinner's major contribution to psychology?

Skinner's major contribution to psychology was his extensive and significant research on operant conditioning.

200 CHAPTER 5

And for Some Extra Practice . . .

Several items that supplement this textbook (listed below) may be available at your school's bookstore. Check with your instructor.

Study Guide The comprehensive and innovative *Study Guide,* written by Dan Kelts and Guy Aylward of Illinois Central College, incorporates the tried-and-tested SQ3R learning technique in a variety of exercises for each chapter.

Practice Tests Your instructor may require that the *Practice Tests* booklet be bundled with your text. Multiple-choice, true/false, and essay questions from the book's *Test Bank* help you practice for the real thing.

Web Site Allyn and Bacon provides access to this textbook's Web Site (*www.abacon.com/wood*) via a PIN code found in the front of a new textbook. Whether you're studying or just surfing the web, be sure to visit this Web Site for a wealth of helpful and fun material related to introductory psychology, including free practice tests, flashcards, personality-assessment quizzes, a psychology career corner, activities, and web links. The PIN code also gives you access to Content Select, Allyn and Bacon's premiere research tool for accessing articles on the web.

Psych Tutor This service of Allyn and Bacon provides free tutoring for students who purchase a new text. Qualified college psychology instructors tutor students on all material covered in the text, including art and figures. The Tutor Center provides tutoring assistance by four methods: phone, fax, e-mail, and the Internet, during Tutor Center hours. Students who bought used books can purchase the Psych Tutor for $25 at *www.aw.com/tutorcenter.*

Other Resources Available from Allyn and Bacon *Cross-Cultural Explorations: Activities in Culture and Psychology,* by Susan Goldstein; *Diversity Activities for Psychology,* by Valerie Whittlesy; *How to Think Straight About Psychology,* Sixth Edition, by Keith E. Stanovich; *How to Write Psychology Papers,* Second Edition, by Les Parrott, III; *Research Stories for Introductory Psychology,* by Matthew R. Merrens and Lary Shaffer; *Writing for Psychology,* by Christopher Thaiss and James Sanford; *Introduction to Cross-Cultural Psychology: Critical Thinking and Contemporary Applications,* by Eric Shiraev and David Levy.

Use It! How to Use the Internet in Introductory Psychology

Welcome to Introductory Psychology! You are about to begin one of the most fascinating and useful educational journeys of your college career. The authors of your textbook have provided you with a wealth of information on psychology to get you started on this exciting trip.

To help you round out your travels into the human psyche, your exploration of the emotions and actions that define us as human beings, we wish to introduce you to using the Internet to access additional resources about psychology. The Internet contains more information about psychology and related disciplines than could be covered in 10 or even 20 textbooks. You will find that having almost instantaneous access to this information will be a powerful aid to your study of psychology.

What is the Internet? The **Internet** is an incredibly vast network that connects millions of computers worldwide. The Internet is organized in such a way that it is possible to search for and retrieve information from the thousands of computer servers of which it is composed. A **server** is a computer system that provides individual computers access to information available on the Internet. The **World Wide Web,** often abbreviated **www** and sometimes referred to as "the Web," is the whole system of Internet servers. The World Wide Web links your computer to other computers so that you can search for, find, and retrieve information on any topic. This may seem a bit confusing to you now, but as you read what follows and actually begin "surfing the Net," you will soon get the hang of it.

So what does all this fancy techno-jargon have to do with psychology? A lot! Let's assume you have access to a personal computer that is connected to the Internet. This means that somewhere on the computer monitor, you will see an icon for the Internet provider (a private company) to which this computer has access. In this case, an **icon** is a symbol representing the name of the Internet provider. When you click or double-click on this icon, the provider's **home page,** a page containing information about the resources available through the Internet provider, will appear on the monitor. Depending on the Internet provider, the home page may ask you to do different things in order to access the Internet. For example, the home page of my Internet provider asks me to enter my password and then click on a button labeled *Connect* (to the Internet) in order to access the Internet. Other Internet providers may ask you to "log on" by going through a similar procedure.

Somewhere on the Internet provider's home page, once you have accessed the Internet, you will see the word *Search.* Next to it is a blank space. Here's where things get interesting. By typing a word or words in this blank space and then clicking on the word *Search* (or, in some cases, the word *Go*), you open a **search engine**—software capable of looking up every source of information about anything that is accessible on the Internet. Suppose the word you typed in the blank space was "Freud." In this case, every bit of information on the Internet related to Sigmund Freud—his work, his family, and what hundreds of authors have written about his life—would appear for your inspection and use, all in a matter of seconds!

I just opened the search engine on my personal computer and typed in the words "Sigmund Freud." Guess what I found?—18,440 web sites devoted to some aspect of Freud and his work. When I typed in the word "psychology," I found 2,452,593 web sites. Talk about having the world at your fingertips!

A **web site** is a specific location on the World Wide Web that contains information about some particular topic. Each web site has its own address, or **URL (Universal Resource Locator),** which is sometimes referred to as a **link.** For example, the first web site listed for "psychology" on my search engine is for the American Psychological Association (APA). Its URL is *www.apa.org*. The APA is one of the two predominant professional organizations for psychologists in the United States (the other is the American Psychological Society, or APS; its URL is *www.psychologicalscience.org*). These two web sites are among the most important ones for psychologists—both researchers and practitioners—because they provide hundreds of links to some of the best psychological information available on the web. Another useful URL is *www.psichi.org*. Clicking on this URL, which I found among the links generated by my search for "psychology," takes me to the home page for Psi Chi, the National Honor Society for students in psychology. Alternatively, if you already know the URL for the web site you wish to visit—as you do for APA, APS, and Psi Chi—you can simply type it into the search engine, click *Search* or *Go*, and be whisked immediately to that web site.

Among the nearly 2.5 million web sites related to psychology are those devoted to other professional organizations, departments of psychology at colleges and universities around the world, journals in psychology, and numerous psychological disorders and phenomena. In short, probably anything you want to know about psychology can be found on the Internet. Let's walk through an example.

Suppose you are studying Chapter 15 in your text (Psychological Disorders) and you become interested in phobias. You decide to check out what information the Internet offers on phobias. You begin by clicking or double-clicking on the icon of your Internet provider. Once its home page opens, you type the word "phobia" in the blank space and click on *Search* or *Go*. In a few seconds, you have before you all the information on phobias that is currently on the web. When I did this, I found 5,480 web sites related to phobias! I didn't stop there, though.

I scrolled down the list of URLs until I came across one that caught my eye—one on social phobias. I clicked on this URL (*www.mentalhealth.com/dis/p20-an03.html*). What I found was a nicely designed home page that gave me access to all sorts of information about social phobias, including a complete description of the disorder, its diagnosis and treatment, research on it, and a listing of other related links. In just a few seconds, I had at my disposal a tremendous amount of information on a topic in which I am interested. Suppose, though, that while studying phobias, I become interested in learning more about anxiety disorders in general. What I can do in this case is to go back and type "anxiety disorders" into the blank space and then click *Search* or *Go*. That's right—I can easily broaden my search for information.

Now that you know something about the Internet and how to access it, you, too, can have information about virtually any subject in the world at your disposal anytime you desire! This could be especially useful to you if your professor assigns a research paper on a certain topic. You should know, though, there is a downside to accessing information on the Internet. The Internet is not like your textbook, in which you can be confident that the information is accurate and up-to-date. Your textbook was written by two individuals who are highly knowledgeable about psychology and is published by a publisher with a reputation for publishing high-quality textbooks.

The Internet is different. Anybody who wants to—regardless of whether he or she is an amateur or an expert at psychology (or, for that matter, anything else)—can place information on the Internet. So, as they say in economics: "Buyer beware!" How can you tell if you are getting accurate information from a web site? That's a tricky question. Perhaps the best advice is to begin your Internet journey at URLs that are known to be both reliable and valid, such as those for the APA and APS. Both of these contain hundreds of links to other reliable and valid web sites. Keep in mind that the most valid and reliable sites—regardless of topic—were created and maintained by genuine authorities in their fields.

Now, have fun on your quest to learn more about psychology—may it never end!

To the Instructor

Our goals for the fourth edition of this book remain the same as for the first three editions: to introduce the world of psychology accurately and clearly to students via an interesting and memorable format. We present the principles of psychology using a clear and engaging writing style and a pedagogically sound learning format that is both accessible and appealing to students.

Having taught many thousands of students their first course in psychology, we are sensitive to the complexities and the subtleties of the teaching/learning process. Over the years we have witnessed tremendous changes in the field, in our students, and in ourselves as well. Thus, we also sought to create a textbook that is sensitive to the changing needs of modern students and their professors while providing a context in which students may learn about psychology's past, its present, and its probable future.

To accomplish our goals, we set the following objectives.

To Maintain a Clear, Understandable Writing Style That Students Will Find Interesting

First and foremost, a textbook is a teaching instrument. It cannot be a novel; nor should it be an esoteric, academic treatise. A good psychology textbook must communicate clearly to a diverse audience of various ages and levels of academic ability. Our text is appealing to accomplished students, yet accessible to students whose academic skills are yet to be fully developed.

We seek to achieve this objective by explaining concepts in much the same way as we do in our own psychology classes. This text is filled with everyday examples pertinent to students' lives.

To Write a Textbook That Encourages Students to Become Active Participants in the Learning Process

Reading about psychology is not enough. Students should be able to practice what they have learned, when appropriate. Many of the principles we teach can be demonstrated without elaborate equipment and sometimes as the student reads. What better way to teach new material and make it fresh, interesting, and memorable than to have students demonstrate principles for themselves using an important and innovative element of the book: *Try It!* boxes.

To Make Psychology Come Alive through the *Try It!* Boxes

The popular *Try Its!* personalize psychology, making it simple for students to actively link psychology with their everyday lives. Because the response from professors and students to the *Try It!* features in previous editions has been so positive, we have added 30% more *Try Its!* to this edition, for a total of 64 woven throughout the book, to get students excited about psychology. New *Try Its!* include:

- *Self-Assessment:* Are You a Jealous Mate? (evolutionary psychology)
- *Experiment:* Taste Receptors' Response to Temperature Change
- *Self-Assessment:* Are You a Lark or an Owl? (sleep patterns)

- *Practice Quiz:* How Might You Score on an IQ Test?
- *Self-Assessment:* Rate Your Emotional Intelligence (EQ)
- *Quiz:* Test Your Knowledge of Infant Development
- *Experiment:* Child Development and Class Inclusion
- *Activity:* What Motivates You to Eat?
- *Quiz:* How Much Do You Know about STDs?
- *Quiz:* Facts vs. Myths about AIDS
- *Activity:* Stress-Inoculation Training
- *Self-Assessment:* Evaluate Your Locus of Control
- *Self-Assessment:* Test Your Level of Self-Esteem
- *Quiz:* Does Anyone You Know Exhibit Signs of Anxiety Disorder?
- *Self-Assessment:* Are You an Aggressive Driver?

To Provide a Series of High-Interest Features That Will Appeal to Today's Students

Every chapter opens with a real-life vignette to capture student interest and build motivation. More than half of the chapter vignettes are new to this fourth edition, and they include a good mix of topics students can relate to—from timely events and issues, to popular personalities, to recent scientific advances, to classic psychological experiments. New vignette topics include:

- Psychological implications of the turn of the millennium
- Rave dances and the use of the drug Ecstasy (MDMA)
- Michael J. Fox's battle with Parkinson's disease
- A real-life case of faulty memory that sent the wrong man to prison for rape
- Recent developments in artificial intelligence that allow blind people to "see"
- Olympic gold medalist Rafer Johnson and his daughter Jenny Johnson Jordan, who competed in the 2000 Olympic Games
- Cybersex addiction
- The Milgram experiment
- Christopher Reeve's daily life after his paralyzing accident

The *Apply It!* section at the end of every chapter shows the practical applications of the principles of psychology and demonstrates the role of psychology in daily life. Forty percent of the *Apply Its!* in this edition are new, covering caffeine addiction, prenatal care, dating, road rage, positive psychology, fear of public speaking, and e-therapy.

To Promote and Nurture Critical Thinking

Critical thinking does not consist of being critical of all viewpoints other than one's own. Rather, critical thinking is a process of evaluating claims, propositions, or conclusions objectively to determine whether they follow logically from the evidence presented. Critical thinkers are open-minded, objective, and unbiased, and they maintain a skeptical attitude that leads them to search for alternative explanations.

Critical thinking is too important to leave to chance. The first *Apply It!* section, "Study Skills and Critical Thinking," provides students with an understanding of what critical thinking entails. In addition to promoting critical thinking throughout the text, we have also developed a systematic method of nurturing it. A *Thinking Critically* section at the end of each chapter features three categories of critical thinking questions:

1. *Evaluation* questions teach students to think critically as they evaluate psychological theories, techniques, approaches, perspectives, and research studies.
2. *Point/Counterpoint* questions require students to comprehend, to analyze, and to formulate convincing arguments on both sides of important issues in psychology.
3. *Psychology in Your Life* questions allow students to apply psychological principles and concepts to their own lives and the everyday world.

Instructors can use the *Thinking Critically* questions as a basis for essay questions or research paper topics.

To Help Students Understand and Appreciate Human Diversity and to Comprehend More Fully the Part Played by Multicultural Issues in Modern Psychology

We remain dedicated to the goal of promoting understanding of human diversity. Rather than emphasizing diversity only in special sections, we have responded to reviewers' preferences by expanding coverage of diversity issues and integrating it throughout the book. Human diversity is considered in relation to dozens of topics throughout the text, such as depression, extraversion, personality, schizophrenia, and intelligence testing.

To Provide an Accurate and Thoroughly Researched Textbook That Features Original Sources

To accomplish our goal of introducing the world of psychology accurately and clearly, we have gone back to original sources and have read and reread the basic works of the major figures in psychology and the classic studies in the field. For each revision this has meant more than 10,000 pages of photocopied research (and a basement approaching fire hazard status!). This reading has enabled us to write with greater clarity and assurance, rather than having to hedge or write tentatively when discussing what experts in the field have actually said. This book is one of the most carefully researched, up-to-date, and extensively referenced of all introductory psychology textbooks.

To Meet the Needs of Instructors by Adding New Topics

In response to valuable suggestions from our reviewers, we have made many additions to the fourth edition, including the following:

- In Chapter 1, "Introduction to Psychology," a new section on evolutionary psychology has been added to reflect the emergence of this fascinating field. Evolutionary psychology is also covered more extensively in Chapters 11, 12, and 14 and mentioned appropriately throughout the book.
- Chapter 2, "Biology and Behavior," features a new discussion on neurons' recently discovered ability to regenerate.

- In Chapter 4, "States of Consciousness," several new sections discuss the findings of up-to-date brain research on sleep, such as "Sleep Research and the Brain," "REM Sleep, Dreaming, and the Brain," and "REM Sleep and Dreaming: Are They the Same?"
- Chapter 7, "Cognition and Language," features an extensive section on high-tech applications of cognition. Artificial intelligence and robotics are discussed at length, with fascinating examples of how they are being used today.
- In Chapter 12, "Human Sexuality and Gender," a new section discusses gender bias in the workplace—a topic of increasing relevance as more and more women enter the workforce.

To Provide Instructors with a Complete, Coordinated Teaching Package of the Highest Quality

Allyn and Bacon offers the following supplements for the adopter of this textbook:

The **Instructor's Resource Manual (IRM),** prepared by Fred Whitford of Montana State University, provides lecture examples, demonstrations, diversity topics, and content lists of the transparencies and the Digital Media Archive. Fully updated, the *IRM* contains dozens of new lecture examples, marked with an icon and keyed to newly referenced material in the book. Classroom demonstrations have been updated and referenced to important Internet sites that contain the most current information available.

A comprehensive **Test Bank** contains approximately 2,300 questions and a computerized test item file (for Windows, Macintosh, and DOS), prepared by Rebecca Walker-Sands of Central Oregon Community College and Ron Walker-Sands. A separate booklet of practice tests is available free when bundled with the textbook.

A student **Study Guide** prepared by Dan Kelts and Guy Aylward of Illinois Central College contains multiple, varied learning aids sure to fit every student's needs. The *Study Guide* provides chapter overviews, timelines, chapter outlines, learning objectives, quizzes, fill-in-the-blank activities, matching activities, complete-the-diagram activities, key terms and concepts, study enhancement exercises, and comprehensive practice tests.

Psychology on the Net, 2002 is an Internet guide that shows students the basics of using the Internet, with activities and hundreds of psychology-related URLs (free when packaged with the text).

More than 200 new full-color **transparency acetates** are available upon adoption of the text. Allyn and Bacon also offers the **Digital Media Archive,** Version 3.0, which provides electronic images, video clips, and audio clips, as well as lecture outlines, on one cross-platform CD-ROM for integration into your lecture. A text-specific **PowerPoint presentation** is available, as well.

Allyn and Bacon provides a service called **Psych Tutor** for students enrolled in basic psychology courses who have purchased a new copy of this text. Qualified college psychology instructors tutor students on all material covered in the text. The Tutor Center provides tutoring assistance by four methods: phone, fax, e-mail, and the Internet during Tutor Center hours. Visit *www.abacon.com/wood* for more information.

The **PIN-coded Web Site** (*www.abacon.com/wood*) is an extensive site offering chapter overviews, online practice test questions, web links, *Try It!* games and activities, audio and video clips, electronic flashcards, personality tests, career information, and information for instructors about how to use the Web Site, all available via a PIN code found in the front of a new textbook. A new feature of the Web Site, **Content Select,** provides students with a wealth of journal articles that they can access to assist in their research.

The **Allyn and Bacon Interactive Video** is a 90-minute video available to adopters of the text. It contains brief video clips that coordinate with the chapter content, as well as critical thinking questions to help generate classroom discussion. A wide variety of additional videos are also available upon adoption of the text (enrollment restrictions may apply).

Course Compass™ is a dynamic, interactive online course management tool powered by Blackboard™. This exciting product allows you to teach with text-specific content in an easy-to-use, customizable format.

Acknowledgments

We are indebted to an incredible group of people at Allyn and Bacon for their contributions to *The World of Psychology.* First, we thank Carolyn Merrill, executive editor, for her inspiration, her unwavering support, and her standards of excellence. Carolyn is the prime mover of *The World of Psychology,* and her good taste and editorial excellence are in evidence throughout the book. In publishing, in particular, there is so much to do and so little time in which to do it. Carolyn does it all, and we have been moved (literally) by her power to motivate. Added to that are Carolyn's exceptional personal qualities, her great warmth, good humor, intelligence, integrity, and ability to empathize, all of which have made her someone whom we greatly admire and also cherish as a friend. We thank Carolyn also for bringing a new development editor, Kelly Perkins, to the book.

Kelly has devoted her full time to the project, and her excellent work has been instrumental in the making of this fourth edition. Bright, thoroughly knowledgeable in our field, and a virtually tireless worker, Kelly has added her own unique mark of excellence to the book. A pleasure to work with, she possesses in great depth the finest attributes of an ideal development editor.

We express our appreciation to Jodi Devine, developmental editor during the early stages of the fourth edition, who returned to graduate school during the summer semester of 2000. Between the time Jodi left for graduate school and Kelly Perkins came to us, executive editor Carolyn Merrill provided a seamless flow of development editing by retaining consulting development editor Mark Palmer. Mark is a seasoned professional who, with a writer's ear and an artist's eye, has obviously mastered his craft. We are grateful for Mark's excellent contributions.

The production process that transforms a manuscript into a finished book is long and incredibly complex. So we were delighted that our book was placed in the capable hands of Michael Granger, editorial production administrator.

We were also exceedingly fortunate to have Jane Hoover of Lifland et al., Bookmakers with us again in production of this fourth edition. Jane is a consummate professional who carefully read all the text revisions and scrutinized every figure, table, and feature to make sure they came together with clarity and precision. More broadly, Jane skillfully and painstakingly coordinated and guided the daily activities of the production process.

We express our appreciation to Lara Zeises, editorial assistant, for handling the review process and many other varied details of the project with great care. Thank you, Lara, for preparing the new manuscript for the text in such an excellent fashion and in a timely manner, and for being so pleasant to work with.

Production is one component of a successful book; marketing is another. And we are indeed fortunate to have a superior, talented marketing team. Our continuing enthusiastic appreciation goes to Sandi Kirshner, president of Allyn and Bacon. Sandi, one of the most creative people we know, is a virtual fountain of innovative ideas, which she always expresses with great style and animation. She has done a wonderful job with *The World of Psychology* over the years.

We also owe a large debt of gratitude to Joyce Nilsen, vice president, director of marketing. In our travels with Joyce, we have seen her competence firsthand and learned some of the secrets of her success. Joyce is a master of human relations who is also quite sincere. She has a great capacity to empathize with professors and sales representatives alike, and to truly understand their wants and needs. Another person in marketing who has made a major contribution to this edition is Caroline Croley, marketing manager. We are grateful for her efforts, as well as the efforts of Marcie Mealia, field marketing specialist.

All of the professionals at Allyn and Bacon work hard to maintain a standard of excellence in producing fine books. This certainly includes Bill Barke, president of Addison-Wesley Higher Education, who has kept in close touch with our book from its inception. We again express our deep appreciation to Bill, and we are ever grateful for his strong commitment to this project and for his continuing confidence in us.

No psychology text is considered complete without an accompanying package of ancillary materials. We are grateful to Dan Kelts and Guy Aylward of Illinois Central College for the outstanding and creative *Study Guide*. We again thank Fred Whitford at Montana State University for his work on the *Instructor's Resource Manual*, and Rebecca Walker-Sands of Central Oregon Community College and Ron Walker-Sands for their work on the *Test Bank*.

To Our Reviewers

We want to thank the conscientious and knowledgeable reviewers whose suggestions have helped shape this book. The following survey respondents provided feedback for the fourth edition:

Jeffrey S. Anastasi, Francis Marion University
Kathleen Bey, Palm Beach Community College
Robert Brownstein, Delaware Technical & Community College
Samuel Clay, Heartland Community College
Helen Doane, University of Minnesota at Duluth
James W. Downing, Sul Ross State University
Fred Fernandez, Modesta Junior College
Phil Finney, Southeast Missouri State University
Kenneth J. Good, Minnesota State University, Mankato
Audrey Guild, Houston Community College
Toni Haynes, Palm Beach Community College
Curt S. Ickes, Ashland University
R. Martin Lobdell, Pierce College
Karla Miley, Black Hawk College
Terri Morrow, Illinois Central College
Suzanne Nickeson, Umpqua Community College
Sam Olive, Henry Ford Community College
Ellen Pastorino, Valencia Community College
Michael P. Phillips, Metropolitan State College of Denver
Melissa Polusny, Minnesota State University, Mankato
Sally Ponce-O'Rourke, Moorpark College
William F. Price, North Country Community College
Sandra Prince-Madison, Delgado Community College
Joan Ratz, Minnesota State University, Mankato
George E. Riday, Citrus College
Barry J. Ries, Minnesota State University, Mankato
Susan Ringer, Hinds Community College

Vicki Ritts, St. Louis Community College–Meramec

Harold I. Siegel, Rutgers University

William E. Snell, Southeast Missouri State University

Jeanne Spaulding, Houston Community College

Jack Spaun, Citrus College

Maria Straus, Houston Community College

William E. Threlfall, Chabot College

Dennis Underwood, Henry Ford Community College

Rene Verry, Millikin University

Rebecca L. Walker, Central Oregon Community College

Janel Weigel, Black Hawk College

Clair Wiederholt, Madison Area Technical College

Marie Wiederholt, St. Charles County Community College

We also want to thank those who reviewed the third edition, who gave us many invaluable suggestions for improvement in this fourth edition:

Frank M. Bagrash, California State University at Fullerton

Mitchell E. Berman, University of Southern Mississippi

John Best, Eastern Illinois University

Thomas E. Billimek, San Antonio College

Cari B. Cannon, Santiago Canyon College

Helen Joan Crawford, Virginia Polytechnic Institute

David Diamond, University of South Florida

Michael K. Garza, Brookhaven College

Perilou Goddard, Northern Kentucky University

Gina M. Grimshaw, California State University at San Marcos

Eddie Harmon-Jones, University of Wisconsin–Madison

Barbara A. Hunter, Southwestern Illinois College

Brian M. Kelly, Bridgewater College

Robert Kuzendorf, University of Massachusetts, Lowell

Fred Leavitt, California State University at Hayward

Martin Marino, Atlantic Cape Community College

Linda Mealey, College of St. Benedict

Yozan Dirk Mosig, University of Nebraska at Kearney

Deanna R. Riviera, College of the Canyons

Cynthia J. Schellenbach, Oakland University

Howard A. Starr, Austin College

Finally, we extend our sincere thanks to the other reviewers of the first three editions, who offered comprehensive and valuable insight into what an introductory psychology text should be. The book could not exist without them:

George Armstrong, Bucks County Community College

Norma Baker, Belmont University

Michael L. Bell, Marlboro, MA

Joyce Bishop, Golden West College
Tim C. Bockes, Sul Ross State University
Ann Brandt-Williams, Glendale Community College
Allen Branum, South Dakota State University
Andre Cedras, Macomb Community College
Samuel Church, Fairmont State College
Pat Crane, San Antonio College
William Dwyer, University of Memphis
Thomas Fitzpatrick, Rockland Community College
Linda E. Flickinger, St. Clair Community College
Sally Foster, Mira Costa College
Laura Freberg, California Polytechnic State University
Katherine Fuhs, J. Sargeant Reynolds Community College
Wayne Hall, San Jacinto College
Jack Hartnett, Virginia Commonwealth University
Barbara Honhart, Baker College of Flint
Steven Hoyer, Pittsburg State University
Clixie L. Larson, Utah Valley Community College
John T. Long, Mt. San Antonio College
Maria Elena Lopez-Treviño, Mt. San Antonio College
Claire Lowder, Illinois Central College
Rick Lowe, Salt Lake City Community College
Lynn McCutcheon, Northern Virginia Community College
James Nelson, Parkland College
Jesse B. Newkirk III, Grossmont College
Diane Owsley, Elizabethtown Community College
Robert J. Pellegrini, San Jose State University
William E. Pelz, Herkimer County Community College
Gregory Pezzetti, Rancho Santiago College
Pennie Seibert, Boise State University
Harold Siegel, Rutgers University–Newark
Pamela Stewart, Northern Virginia Community College
Jonathan Stone, Dutchess Community College
Patti Thompson, Liberty University
June Vess, Liberty University
Rene Villa, Hillsborough Community College
Ken Vincent, Houston Community College
Everett Wagner, San Antonio College
Phyllis Walrad, Macomb Community College
Douglas Wessel, Black Hill State University
Diane E. Wille, Indiana University Southeast
Patrick Williams, University of Houston–Downtown

About the Authors

Samuel E. Wood received his doctorate from the University of Florida. He has taught at West Virginia University and the University of Missouri–St. Louis and was a member of the doctoral faculty at both universities. From 1984 to 1996, he served as president of the Higher Education Center, a consortium of 14 colleges and universities in the St. Louis area. He was a co-founder of the Higher Education Cable TV channel (HEC-TV) in St. Louis and served as its president and CEO from its founding in 1987 until 1996. Dr. Wood is currently an adjunct professor of psychology at Lindenwood University.

Ellen Green Wood received her doctorate in educational psychology from St. Louis University and was an adjunct professor of psychology at St. Louis Community College at Meramec. She has also taught in the clinical experiences program in education at Washington University and at the University of Missouri–St. Louis. In addition to her teaching, Dr. Wood has developed and taught seminars on critical thinking. She received the Telecourse Pioneer Award from 1982 through 1988 for her contributions to the field of distance learning.

Together, Sam and Evie Wood have more than 30 years of experience teaching introductory psychology to thousands of students of all ages, backgrounds, and abilities. *The World of Psychology* is the direct result of their teaching experience.

1 Introduction to Psychology

Where were you at midnight on December 31, 1999, as people around the world welcomed the arrival of the year 2000? Were you among the millions watching the spectacular fireworks displays in Sydney, Paris, London, Washington, and many other cities? Or were you one of those hunkered down in basements and bunkers, convinced that the Y2K bug (the software glitch that might mean that some computers wouldn't be able to handle the change from 1999 to 2000) would send planes crashing to the ground, jam elevators, and cause nuclear missiles to be launched without authorization?

The scientific and technological advances of the late 20th century profoundly shape contemporary life and hold immense promise for the future. Consider some examples:

- People everywhere are communicating via electronic mail, which can be received even by travelers aboard trains and planes. E-mail enables friends and relatives to keep in touch across great distances, allows students at widely scattered locations to take college courses, makes it possible to carry out many business-related tasks at home, and much more.

- In June 2000, scientists completed the map of the human genome, the sequencing of the complete set of human DNA, making possible advances in many areas, including the treatment of serious diseases such as cancer.
- An unmanned vehicle, the Pathfinder, explored the surface of Mars, gathering information for scientists to use in planning future exploration and perhaps colonization of that planet–and in answering the age-old question "Is there life on Mars?"
- The ability to perform microsurgery on fetuses has freed many unborn children from debilitating conditions that would have severely limited their ability to lead a normal life.

Psychologists, too, are constantly making new discoveries. Their findings affect not only how we live but also how healthy and vital we will be. They help explain why we behave the way we do–how we react to events like the Year 2000 celebrations and the Y2K bug, why we're curious about the possibility of life on Mars, how we make important decisions such as whether to have a child. Throughout this book we will explore what new discoveries in psychology mean for us as we enter the exciting world of the new millennium.

Now, let's begin our journey into the world of psychology.

A psychologist could ask a number of questions about the Year 2000 celebrations, for example: Why were some people so excited by this event? Why did others display such extreme fear of the Y2K bug? What childhood experiences might have shaped the personalities of people in both of these groups, leading them to respond in such different ways? These questions have to do with emotion and personality, two important areas of psychological research. But psychologists are also interested in many other aspects of human behavior—sensation and perception, learning, memory, intelligence and creativity, social interactions, and much more.

In this chapter we will explore how psychologists go about answering the many questions they ask. We will see that psychology is a science, based on research conducted according to the scientific method. We will look at the major methods psychologists use to do research on humans and other animals, as well as the ethical principles that govern that research. We will also examine the history of psychology and some key aspects of the field today.

PSYCHOLOGY: AN INTRODUCTION

Many people who consider the field of psychology conjure up images of mental disorders and abnormal behavior. Psychologists do study the strange and unusual, but they are interested in the normal and commonplace as well.

Just what is psychology? Psychology has changed over the years, and so has its definition. In the late 19th century, mental processes were considered to be the appropriate subject matter of psychology. Later there was a movement to restrict psychology to the study of observable behavior alone. Today the importance of both areas is recognized, and **psychology** is now defined as the scientific study of behavior and mental processes.

Answer true or false for each statement in the *Try It!* to see how much you already know about some of the topics we will explore in *The World of Psychology*. (You'll find the answers in the text below.)

Try It!

Indicate whether each statement is true (T) or false (F).

____ 1. Once damaged, brain cells never work again.

____ 2. All people dream during a night of normal sleep.

____ 3. As the number of bystanders at an emergency increases, the time it takes for the victim to get help decreases.

____ 4. Humans do not have a maternal instinct.

____ 5. It's impossible for human beings to hear a watch ticking 20 feet away.

____ 6. Eyewitness testimony is often unreliable.

____ 7. Chimpanzees have been taught to speak.

____ 8. Creativity and high intelligence do not necessarily go together.

____ 9. When it comes to close personal relationships, opposites attract.

____ 10. The majority of teenagers have a good relationship with their parents.

Psychology: Science or Common Sense?

What is the scientific method?

When students begin their first course in psychology, many of them consider it more common sense than science. Will you be studying a collection of common-sense notions this semester? Or can we make a valid claim that psychology is a science? For the *Try It!* common sense might have led you astray. All of the odd-numbered items are false, and all of the even-numbered items are true. So, common sense, alone, will not take you very far in your study of psychology.

Many people also believe that whether a field of study is considered a science depends on the nature of its body of knowledge. Physics, for example, is a science, and so is chemistry. But neither qualifies as a science solely because of its subject matter. A science is a science not because of the nature of its body of knowledge, but because the scientific method is used to acquire that body of knowledge.

The Scientific Method: A Method for All Sciences The **scientific method** consists of the orderly, systematic procedures that researchers follow as they identify a research problem, design a study to investigate the problem, collect and analyze data, draw conclusions, and communicate their findings.

Scientists do not simply pull a research problem out of thin air. In most cases they have a well-established body of theory to guide their research. A **theory** is a general principle or set of principles proposed to explain how a number of separate facts are related. A theory enables researchers to fit many separate facts into a larger

psychology: The scientific study of behavior and mental processes.

scientific method: The orderly, systematic procedures researchers follow as they identify a research problem, design a study to investigate the problem, collect and analyze data, draw conclusions, and communicate their findings.

theory: A general principle or set of principles proposed to explain how a number of separate facts are related.

framework and thereby impose order on what would otherwise be a disconnected jumble of data. The value of a theory rests on how well it accounts for the accumulated research findings in a given area and how accurately it can predict new findings.

The scientific method is the best method known for acquiring knowledge because the information derived from it is least compromised by biases, preconceptions, personal beliefs, and emotions (Christensen, 2001). The knowledge gained is dependable because it is based on empirical evidence—data collected and measurements made directly by the researcher. The results of scientific studies are usually published in a professional journal in the field so that they can be evaluated by other researchers.

Important, as well, are the values and attitudes scientists hold as they conduct their research. Researchers must strive to be open-minded—ready to consider new and variant explanations of behavior and mental processes. But they must also be skeptical, refusing to accept the ideas or conclusions of others in the absence of convincing evidence. Researchers must even be willing to alter or abandon their own deeply held beliefs and conclusions when faced with substantial evidence to the contrary.

What are the goals researchers in psychology seek to accomplish as they apply the scientific method in their research?

The Goals of Psychology

What are the four goals of psychology?

The goals of psychology are the description, explanation, prediction, and control of behavior and mental processes. Psychological researchers always seek to accomplish one or more of these goals when they plan and conduct their studies.

Description is usually the first step in understanding any behavior or mental process and is therefore more important in a very new area of research or in the early stages of research. To attain this goal, researchers describe the behavior or mental process of interest as accurately and completely as possible. A description tells *what* occurred.

The second goal, *explanation*, requires an understanding of the conditions under which a given behavior or mental process occurs. Such an understanding often enables researchers to state the causes of the behavior or mental process they are studying. But researchers do not reach the goal of explanation until their results have been tested, retested, and confirmed. The way researchers confirm an explanation is by eliminating or ruling out other competing explanations. An explanation tells *why* a given event or behavior occurred.

The goal of *prediction* is met when researchers can specify the conditions under which a behavior or event is likely to occur. Then, if researchers can identify all the antecedent (prior) conditions required for a behavior or event to occur, they can predict the behavior or event.

The goal of *control* is accomplished when researchers know how to apply a principle or change a condition to prevent unwanted occurrences or to bring about desired outcomes. A therapy could be designed to prevent anxiety attacks; a technique could be employed to improve memory.

To achieve the goal of explaining road violence—and perhaps eventually controlling it—psychological researchers might observe and describe the behavior of motorists under stressful conditions.

The two types of research psychologists pursue to accomplish their goals are (1) basic, or pure, research and (2) applied research. The purpose of **basic research** is to seek new knowledge and to explore and advance general scientific understanding. Basic research explores such topics as the nature of memory, brain function, motivation, and emotional expression.

Applied research is conducted specifically for the purpose of solving practical problems and improving the quality of life. Applied research focuses on such concerns as methods to improve memory or increase motivation, therapies to treat psychological disorders, ways to decrease stress, and so on. Applied research is primarily concerned with the fourth goal—control—because it specifies ways and means of changing behavior.

Critical Thinking: Thinking Like a Scientist

Living in the "information age," we are bombarded daily with information on every conceivable subject. The critical thinking skills scientists use are necessary to sift through all this information, pick out the true and useful, discard the false and misleading, and make intelligent decisions. **Critical thinking** is the process of objectively evaluating claims, propositions, or conclusions to determine whether they follow logically from the evidence presented.

Critical thinkers share some important characteristics:

- They are independent thinkers. Critical thinkers do not automatically accept and believe what they read or hear. They carefully analyze and evaluate the evidence and the reasoning presented. They are able to recognize manipulative emotional appeals, spot unsupported assumptions, and detect faulty logic.
- They are willing to suspend judgment. Critical thinkers do not make snap judgments; they gather and consider the most relevant and up-to-date information on all sides of an issue before taking a position.
- They are willing to modify or abandon prior judgments, including deeply held beliefs. Critical thinkers evaluate new evidence or experience that contradicts their existing beliefs. If they find it valid, they modify their beliefs to accommodate it.

To think critically about information you encounter in this text and in the popular media, it is important to (1) understand the various research methods psychologists use to achieve their goals, (2) know the advantages and limitations of these methods, and (3) be able to identify the elements that distinguish good research.

basic research: Research conducted to advance knowledge rather than for its practical application.

applied research: Research conducted to solve practical problems.

critical thinking: The process of objectively evaluating claims, propositions, or conclusions to determine whether they follow logically from the evidence presented.

descriptive research methods: Research methods that yield descriptions of behavior rather than causal explanations.

naturalistic observation: A research method in which the researcher observes and records behavior in its natural setting, without attempting to influence or control it.

DESCRIPTIVE RESEARCH METHODS

What are naturalistic observation and laboratory observation, and what are some of their advantages and limitations?

The goals of psychological research—description, explanation, prediction, and control—are typically accomplished in stages. In the early stages of research, descriptive research methods are usually the most appropriate. **Descriptive research methods** yield descriptions rather than explanations of the causes of behavior. Naturalistic and laboratory observation, the case study, and the survey are examples of descriptive research methods.

Naturalistic and Laboratory Observation

Naturalistic observation is a research method in which the researchers observe and record behavior in its natural setting without attempting to influence or control it. Ethologists are researchers who study the behavior patterns of animals in their natural environment. They might observe their subjects through high-powered telescopes or from blinds that they build to conceal themselves.

Often human subjects are not aware that they are being observed. This can be accomplished by means of one-way mirrors, a technique researchers often use to observe children in nursery schools or special classrooms. You may have seen episodes of *60 Minutes, 20/20,* or *Candid Camera* in which hidden cameras or tape recorders were used to gather information from unsuspecting subjects "caught in the act of being themselves."

A kind of naturalistic observation occurs on a large scale in England; about a million closed-circuit TV cameras like this one monitor activity in streets and shopping centers.

laboratory observation: A research method in which behavior is studied in a laboratory setting, where researchers can exert more control and take more precise measurements.

case study: An in-depth study of one or a few individuals consisting of information gathered through observation, interview, and perhaps psychological testing.

survey: A method in which researchers use interviews and/or questionnaires to gather information about the attitudes, beliefs, experiences, or behaviors of a group of people.

The major advantage of naturalistic observation is the opportunity to study behavior in normal settings. Here behavior occurs more naturally and spontaneously than it would under artificial and contrived laboratory conditions. Sometimes naturalistic observation is the only feasible way to study certain phenomena that would be either impossible or unethical to set up as an experiment, such as how people typically react during disasters like earthquakes or fires.

Naturalistic observation has its limitations, however. Researchers must wait for events to occur; they cannot speed up or slow down the process. And because they have no control over the situation, researchers cannot reach conclusions about cause-and-effect relationships. Another potential problem in naturalistic observation is *observer bias,* which is a distortion in researchers' observations. Observer bias can result when researchers' expectations about a situation cause them to see what they expect to see or to make incorrect inferences about the behavior they observe. The accuracy of observations can be improved substantially when two or more observers view the same behavior or when the behavior is videotaped.

Another method of studying behavior involves observation that takes place not in its natural setting, but in the laboratory. There researchers can exert more control and use more precise equipment to measure responses. Much of what is known about sleep or the human sexual response, for example, has been learned through **laboratory observation.**

The Case Study Method: Studying a Few Individuals in Depth

What is the case study method, and for what purposes is it particularly well suited?

The **case study,** or case history, is another descriptive research method used by psychologists. In a case study, a single individual or a small number of persons are studied in great depth, usually over an extended period of time. A case study involves the use of observation, interviews, and sometimes psychological testing. The case study is exploratory in nature, and its purpose is to provide a detailed description of some behavior or disorder. This method is particularly appropriate for studying people who have uncommon psychological or physiological disorders or brain injuries. Often case studies emerge during the course of treatment of these disorders. You may have read the book or seen the movie *Sybil,* the case study of a young woman who had multiple personalities. Much of what is known about unusual psychological disorders such as multiple personality, now known as dissociative identity disorder, comes from the in-depth analyses provided by case studies.

In some instances the results of detailed case studies have provided the foundation for psychological theories. The theory of Sigmund Freud was based primarily on case studies of his own patients.

Although the case study has proven useful in advancing knowledge in several areas of psychology, it has certain limitations. Researchers cannot establish the cause of behaviors observed in a case study, and observer bias is a potential problem. Moreover, because so few individuals are studied, researchers do not know how applicable, or generalizable, their findings may be to larger groups or to different cultures.

Survey Research: The Art of Sampling and Questioning

What are the methods and purposes of survey research?

Psychologists are interested in many questions that would not be possible to investigate using naturalistic observation or the case study. The **survey** is a method in which researchers use interviews and/or questionnaires to gather information about the attitudes, beliefs, experiences, or behaviors of a group of people. The results of carefully conducted surveys have provided much of the information available about the incidence of drug use, about sexual behaviors of particular segments of the population, and about the incidence of various mental disorders.

What is a representative sample, and why is it essential in a survey?

Selecting a Sample: More Than Numbers to Consider Researchers in psychology rarely conduct experiments or surveys using all members of the group they would like to study. For example, researchers interested in studying the sexual behavior of American women do not attempt to study every woman in the United States. Instead of studying the whole **population** (the entire group of interest to researchers and to which they wish to apply their findings), the researchers select a sample for study. A **sample** is a part of a population that is selected and studied in order to reach conclusions about the entire population of interest.

The results of carefully conducted surveys have provided valuable information about a wide variety of human behaviors.

Perhaps you have seen a carton of ice cream that contains three separate flavors packed side by side—chocolate, strawberry, and vanilla. To properly sample the carton, you would need a small amount of ice cream containing all three flavors in the same proportions as in the whole carton—a representative sample. A **representative sample** is one that mirrors the population of interest—that is, it includes important subgroups in the same proportions as they are found in that population. A *biased sample,* on the other hand, does not adequately reflect the larger population.

The most common method for obtaining a sample that is representative is to select a *random sample* from a list of all members of the population of interest. Participants are selected in such a way that every member of the larger population has an equal chance of being included in the sample. To obtain random samples, researchers use a procedure based on chance, such as pulling names out of a hat or using a table of random numbers generated by a computer. By using highly sophisticated polling techniques, organizations such as Gallup and Roper can accurately represent the views of the American public with carefully chosen samples as small as 1,000 people (O'Brien, 1996).

Interviews and Questionnaires: The Tools of Survey Researchers Researchers using the survey method rely on information gathered through interviews, questionnaires, or some combination of the two. Skilled interviewers asking well-worded questions of a carefully selected sample of people can gather accurate information. Survey results can be strongly affected by the questions' wording, context, and format (Schwartz, 1999). The validity or truthfulness of the responses can also be affected by personal characteristics of the interviewers, such as their gender, age, racial or ethnic background, religion, social class, accent, and vocabulary. In general, male interviewers obtain less information than do female interviewers. And people are most inhibited when they give personal information to interviewers who are of the same age but the opposite sex. Skilled survey researchers, therefore, must select interviewers who have personal characteristics that are appropriate for the intended respondents.

Surveys that use questionnaires can be completed more quickly and less expensively than those involving interviews. The largest survey ever taken of the sexual behavior of American women was conducted by *Cosmopolitan* magazine (Wolfe, 1981). About 106,000 women—3.5% of *Cosmopolitan* readers—completed and returned a questionnaire that had appeared in the magazine. Two-thirds of the respondents claimed to have had 5 to 25 sexual partners, and a high percentage reported having had intercourse with more than one partner on the same day. Do these results reflect the sexual behavior of American women in general?

The number of people who respond to a survey is not the most critical element. A researcher can generalize findings from a sample *only* if it is representative of the entire population of interest. The *Cosmopolitan* survey was a biased sample: Because the readers of *Cosmopolitan* magazine are mostly *young* women, they do not represent a cross-section of American women. Furthermore, the response rate was only 3.5% of the magazine's readers and, therefore, probably didn't even reflect the behavior of that group as a whole. It is possible that those women who chose to respond to the survey were more sexually active—or less sexually active, but more imaginative—than the average reader.

population: The entire group that is of interest to researchers and to which they wish to generalize their findings; the group from which a sample is selected.

sample: The portion of any population that is selected for study and from which generalizations are made about the larger population.

representative sample: A sample of participants selected from the larger population in such a way that important subgroups within the population are included in the sample in the same proportions as they are found in the larger population.

The critical point to remember is that surveys based on questionnaires appearing in magazines or on phone-in responses by TV viewers are not scientific. If a sample is not representative, it doesn't matter how many people are in that sample.

Advantages and Disadvantages of Survey Research If conducted properly, surveys can provide highly accurate information. They can also track changes in attitudes or behavior over time. For example, Johnston and others (2001) have tracked drug use among high school students since 1975. But such large-scale surveys can be costly and time-consuming.

The major limitation of the survey is that the respondents may provide inaccurate information. False information can result from a faulty memory or a desire to please the interviewer. Respondents may try to present themselves in a good light (called the *social desirability response*), or they may even deliberately attempt to mislead the researcher. Finally, when respondents answer questions about sensitive subjects, such as sexual behavior and the use of alcohol and drugs, they are often less candid in face-to-face interviews than in self-administered or computerized questionnaires (Tourangeau et al., 1997).

Remember It!

1. The orderly, systematic procedures scientists follow in acquiring a body of knowledge is the ______________ ______________.
2. The four goals of psychology are ______________, ______________, ______________, and ______________.
3. Basic research is designed to solve practical problems. (true/false)
4. Which descriptive research method would be best for studying each topic?

    ____ (1) attitudes toward exercise

    ____ (2) gender differences in how people position themselves and their belongings in a library

    ____ (3) physiological changes that occur during sleep

    ____ (4) the physical and emotional effects of a rare brain injury

    a. naturalistic observation

    b. laboratory observation

    c. case study

    d. survey
5. When conducting a survey, a researcher can compensate for a sample that is not representative by using a sample that is very large. (true/false)

Answers: 1. scientific method 2. description, explanation, prediction, and control 3. false 4. (1) d (2) a (3) b (4) c 5. false

THE EXPERIMENTAL METHOD: SEARCHING FOR CAUSES

What is the main advantage of the experimental method?

The descriptive research methods (naturalistic and laboratory observation, the case study, and the survey) are all well suited for satisfying the first goal of psychology—description. But at some point researchers usually seek to determine the causes of behavior and various other psychological phenomena. What, for example, are the causes of depression, insomnia, stress, forgetting, and aggression?

The **experimental method,** or the experiment, is the *only* research method that can be used to identify cause–effect relationships. An experiment is designed to test a **hypothesis**—a prediction about a cause–effect relationship between two or more conditions or variables. A *variable* is any condition or factor that can be manipulated, controlled, or measured. One variable of interest to you is the grade you will receive in this psychology course. Another variable that probably interests you is the amount of time you will spend studying for this course. Do you suppose there is a cause–effect relationship between the amount of time students spend studying and the grades they receive?

Under what conditions might the happy, party mood of these young drinkers turn aggressive?

Consider two other variables—alcohol consumption and aggression. Does the consumption of alcohol cause people to behave more aggressively? Alcohol consumption and aggressive behavior are often observed together. We can assume that there is likely to be more aggression among drinkers in a lively bar than among a gathering of nondrinkers in a discussion group. But can we assume that the alcohol consumption itself *causes* the aggressive behavior?

Alan Lang and his colleagues (1975) conducted an experiment to determine if alcohol consumption itself increases aggression or if the beliefs or expectations about the effects of alcohol cause the aggressive behavior. Participants in the experiment were 96 male college students who were classified as heavy social drinkers. Half the students were given plain tonic to drink; the other half were given a vodka-and-tonic drink in amounts sufficient to raise their blood alcohol level to .10, which is higher than the .08 level that is the legal limit for intoxication in most states. Participants were assigned to four groups:

Group 1: Expected alcohol/Received only tonic
Group 2: Expected alcohol/Received alcohol mixed with tonic
Group 3: Expected tonic/Received alcohol mixed with tonic
Group 4: Expected tonic/Received only tonic

You might think that heavy social drinkers could detect the difference between plain tonic and a one-to-five mixture of vodka and tonic. But during pilot testing, drinkers could distinguish between the two with no more than 50% accuracy (Marlatt & Rohsenow, 1981).

After the students had consumed the designated amount, the researchers had an accomplice, who posed as a participant, purposely provoke half the students by belittling their performance on a difficult task. All the students then participated in a learning experiment in which the same accomplice posed as the learner. The subjects were told to administer an electric shock to the accomplice each time he made a mistake on a decoding task. Each participant was allowed to determine the intensity and duration of the "shock." (Although the students believed they were shocking the accomplice, no shocks were actually delivered.) The researchers measured the aggressiveness of the students in terms of the duration and the intensity of the shocks they chose to deliver.

What were the results of the experiment? As you might imagine, the students who had been provoked gave the accomplice stronger shocks than those who had not been provoked. But the students who drank the alcohol were not necessarily the most aggressive. Regardless of the actual content of their drinks, the participants who thought they were drinking alcohol gave significantly stronger shocks, whether provoked or not, than those who assumed they were drinking only tonic (see Figure 1.1 on page 12). The researchers concluded that it was the expectation of drinking alcohol, not the alcohol itself, that caused the students to be more aggressive.

experimental method: The research method in which researchers randomly assign participants to groups and control all conditions other than one or more independent variables, which are then manipulated to determine their effect on some behavioral measure—the dependent variable in the experiment.

hypothesis: A prediction about the relationship between two or more variables.

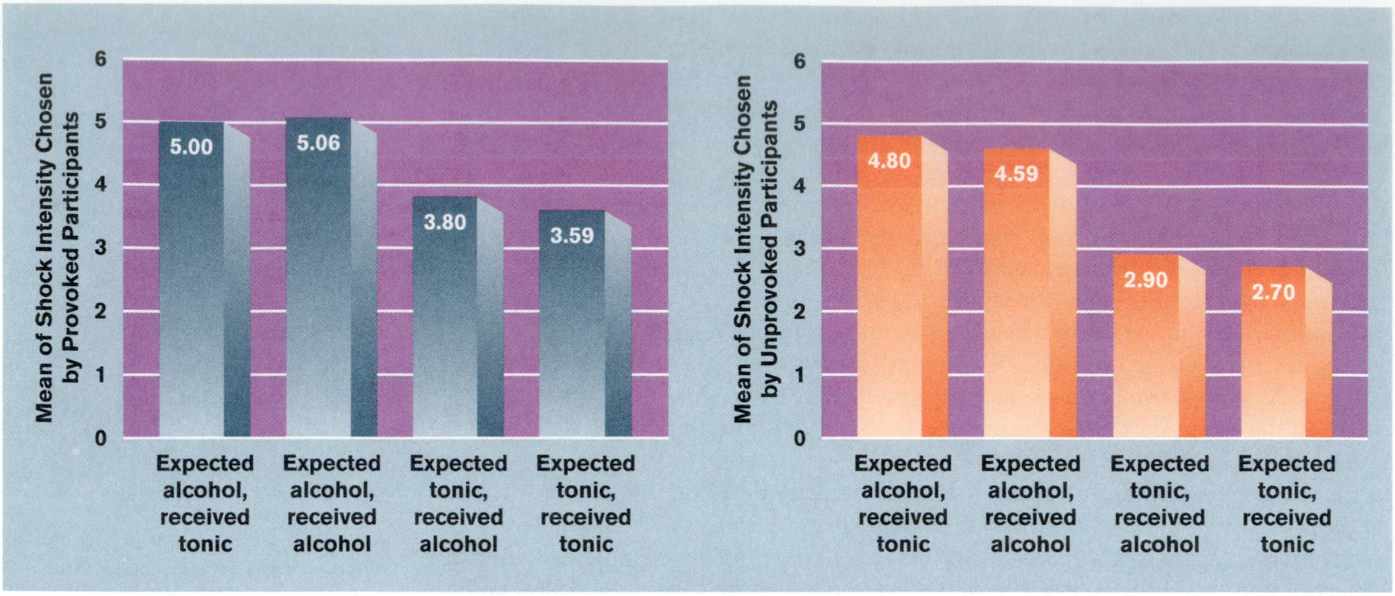

Figure 1.1

The Mean Shock Intensity Chosen by Provoked and Unprovoked Participants

In the Lang experiment, participants who thought they were drinking alcohol chose to give significantly stronger shocks, whether provoked or not, than those who believed they were drinking only tonic. (Data from Lang et al., 1975.)

Independent and Dependent Variables

What is the difference between the independent variable and the dependent variable?

In all experiments there are two types of variables. First, there are one or more **independent variables**—variables that the researcher manipulates in order to determine whether they cause any change in another behavior or condition. Sometimes the independent variable is referred to as the *treatment*. In the Lang experiment there were two independent variables—the alcoholic content of the drink and the expectation of drinking alcohol.

The second type of variable found in all experiments is the **dependent variable.** It is measured at the end of the experiment and is presumed to vary (increase or decrease) as a result of the manipulations of the independent variable(s). The dependent variable is presumed to depend on or to be affected by changes in the independent variable. Researchers must provide operational definitions of all variables in an experiment—that is, they must specify precisely how the variables will be observed and measured. In the Lang study the dependent variable—aggression—was operationally defined as the intensity and duration of the "shocks" the participants chose to deliver to the accomplice.

Experimental and Control Groups: The Same Except for the Treatment

How do the experimental and control groups differ?

Most experiments are conducted using two or more groups of participants. There must always be at least one **experimental group**—a group of participants who are exposed to the independent variable, or the treatment. The Lang experiment used three experimental groups:

Group 1: Expected alcohol/Received only tonic
Group 2: Expected alcohol/Received alcohol mixed with tonic
Group 3: Expected tonic/Received alcohol mixed with tonic

In most experiments it is desirable to have a **control group**—a group that is similar to the experimental group and used for purposes of comparison. The control group is exposed to the same experimental environment as the experimental group but is not given the treatment. The fourth group in the Lang study was exposed to neither of the two independent variables; that is, this group did not expect alcohol and did not receive alcohol. Because this group was similar to the experimental groups and was exposed to the same experimental environment, it served as a control group. In an experiment, all groups, including the control group, are measured on the dependent variable at the end of the experiment.

Sometimes an experiment is affected by **confounding variables**—factors or conditions other than the independent variable that are not equivalent across groups and that could cause differences among the groups with respect to the dependent variable. By conducting their experiment in a laboratory, Lang and his colleagues were able to control the experimental environment to eliminate such possible confounding variables as frustration, pain, and extreme noise or heat, which could have increased aggressive responses. The researchers altered only the independent variables—the students' expectations and the content of their drinks. That way, the researchers could be reasonably sure that the manipulation of those independent variables caused the differences in the degree of aggression among the groups.

independent variable: In an experiment, the factor or condition that the researcher manipulates in order to determine its effect on another behavior or condition known as the dependent variable.

dependent variable: The variable that is measured at the end of an experiment and is presumed to vary as a result of manipulations of the independent variable.

experimental group: In an experiment, the group that is exposed to the independent variable, or the treatment.

control group: In an experiment, a group that is similar to the experimental group and is exposed to the same experimental environment but is not exposed to the independent variable; used for purposes of comparison.

confounding variables: Any factors or conditions other than the independent variable that could cause observed changes in the dependent variable.

selection bias: The assignment of participants to experimental or control groups in such a way that systematic differences among the groups are present at the beginning of the experiment.

random assignment: In an experiment, the assignment of participants to experimental and control groups by using a chance procedure, which guarantees that each has an equal probability of being placed in any of the groups; a control for selection bias.

Generalizing the Experimental Findings: Do the Findings Apply to Other Groups?

What should be concluded from the Lang experiment? Can we conclude that people in general tend to be more aggressive when they believe they are under the influence of alcohol? Before reaching such a conclusion, we must consider several factors: (1) All participants in this experiment were male college students. We cannot be sure that the same results would have occurred if females or males of other ages had been included. (2) The participants in this experiment were classified as heavy social drinkers. Would the same results have occurred if nondrinkers, moderate social drinkers, or alcoholics had been included? To apply this experiment's findings to other groups, researchers would have to replicate, or repeat, the experiment using different populations of subjects. (3) The amount of alcohol given to the students was just enough to bring their blood alcohol level to .10. We cannot be sure that the same results would have occurred if they had consumed more or less alcohol.

Potential Problems in Experimental Research

If an experiment is properly designed and conducted, the researcher should be able to attribute changes in the dependent variable to the manipulations of the independent variable. But several factors other than the independent variables can cause changes in the dependent variable and, therefore, destroy the validity of an experiment. Three of these potential problems (confounding variables) are selection bias, the placebo effect, and experimenter bias. Researchers must design experiments to control for these and other problems that could invalidate their results.

What is selection bias, and what technique do researchers use to control for it?

Selection Bias: Bias from the Start **Selection bias** occurs when participants are assigned to groups in such a way that systematic differences among the groups are present at the beginning of the experiment. If selection bias occurs, then differences at the end of the experiment may not reflect the manipulation of the independent variable but may be due to preexisting differences in the groups.

To control for selection bias, researchers must use **random assignment.** This process consists of selecting participants by using a chance procedure (such as drawing the names of participants out of a hat) to guarantee that all participants have an equal probability of being assigned to any of the groups. Random assignment maximizes the likelihood that the groups will be as similar as possible at the beginning of the experiment. If there were preexisting differences in the level of aggressiveness of students in Lang's alcohol experiment, random assignment should have spread those differences across groups.

What is the placebo effect, and how do researchers control for it?

The Placebo Effect: The Power of Suggestion (for the Participant) Another factor that can influence the outcome of an experiment is the placebo effect. The **placebo effect** occurs when a participant's response to a treatment is due to his or her expectations about the treatment rather than to the treatment itself. Suppose a drug is prescribed for a patient and the patient reports improvement. The improvement could be a direct result of the drug, or it could be a result of the patient's expectation that the drug will work. Studies have shown that sometimes remarkable improvement in patients can be attributed solely to the power of suggestion—the placebo effect.

A researcher must use a control group to test whether results in an experiment are due to the treatment or to the placebo effect. So participants in the control group are given a fake treatment. In drug experiments, the control group is usually given a **placebo**—an inert, or harmless, substance such as a sugar pill or an injection of saline solution. To control for the placebo effect, researchers do not let participants know whether they are in the experimental group (receiving the treatment) or in the control group (receiving the placebo). If participants getting the real drug or treatment show a significantly greater improvement than those receiving the placebo, then the improvement can be attributed to the drug rather than to the power of suggestion. In the Lang experiment, some students who expected alcohol mixed with tonic were given only tonic. The tonic without alcohol functioned as a placebo. This enabled the researchers to measure the effect of the power of suggestion alone in producing aggression.

The placebo effect can invalidate the results of experiments when researchers do not take participants' expectations into account. But what about the expectations of those who conduct the experiments—the researchers themselves?

What is experimenter bias, and how is it controlled?

Experimenter Bias: The Power of Suggestion (for the Experimenter) The expectations of the experimenter are a third factor that can influence the outcome of an experiment. **Experimenter bias** occurs when researchers' preconceived notions or expectations become a self-fulfilling prophecy and cause the researchers to find what they expect to find. A researcher's expectations can be communicated to participants, perhaps unintentionally, through tone of voice, gestures, or facial expression. These communications can influence the participants' behavior. Expectations can also influence a researcher's interpretation of the experimental results, even if no influence occurred during the experiment.

Robert Rosenthal (1973) tested the effect of teacher expectations on student test scores. A group of 100 students were assigned randomly to five mathematics classes. However, the math instructors were told that the students had been assigned to their classes according to high or low ability in math. Even though math achievement scores for the five classes should have been about the same, the students who had been labeled as high in math ability outperformed the students who had been labeled low in math ability. More recently, Madon and others (1997) reported that this type of self-fulfilling prophecy is most powerful when teachers *overestimate* the ability of lower achievers. It seems amazing that nothing more than a belief held by teachers or experimenters can make a difference in the actual performance of students or participants. But more amazing is the finding that the participants don't even have to be human. The effects of experimenter bias have been observed in research with animal subjects as well.

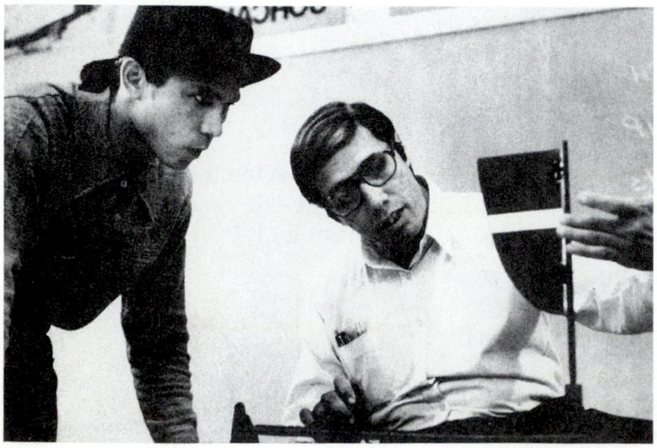

The movie Stand and Deliver *featured Edward James Olmos in the lead role. He played a real-life math teacher whose unwavering belief in the potential of his economically disadvantaged students inspired them to excel in math.*

To control for experimenter bias, researchers must not know which participants are assigned to the experimental and control groups until after the research data are collected and recorded. (Obviously, someone assisting the researcher does know.) When neither the participants nor the experimenter knows which participants are getting the treatment and which are in the control group, the experiment is using the **double-blind technique.**

placebo effect: The phenomenon that occurs when a person's response to a treatment or response on the dependent variable in an experiment is due to expectations regarding the treatment rather than to the treatment itself.

placebo (pluh-SEE-bo): Some inert substance, such as a sugar pill or an injection of saline solution, given to the control group in an experiment as a control for the placebo effect.

experimenter bias: A phenomenon that occurs when the researcher's preconceived notions in some way influence the participants' behavior and/or the interpretation of experimental results.

double-blind technique: An experimental procedure in which neither the participants nor the experimenter knows who is in the experimental or control groups until after the results have been gathered; a control for experimenter bias.

Advantages and Limitations of the Experimental Method

The overwhelming advantage of the experiment is its ability to reveal cause–effect relationships. This benefit is possible because researchers are able to exercise strict control over the experimental setting. This allows them to rule out factors other than the independent variable as possible reasons for differences in the dependent variable. But often the more control the experimenter exercises, the more unnatural and contrived the research setting becomes and the less generalizable findings may be to the real world. When participants know that they are taking part in an experiment, their behavior may be different from what it would be in a more natural setting. When a natural setting is considered to be an important factor in a study, researchers may choose to use a *field experiment*—an experiment conducted in a real-life setting. Although some control over the experimental environment is sacrificed, the advantage is more natural behavior on the part of the participants.

A major limitation of the experimental method is that in many areas of interest to psychologists this method is either unethical or not possible. Some treatments cannot be given to human participants because their physical or psychological health would be endangered, or their constitutional rights violated.

Remember It!

1. The experimental method is the *only* research method that can be used to identify cause–effect relationships between variables. (true/false)
2. A researcher investigates the effectiveness of a new antidepressant drug. She randomly assigns depressed patients to two groups. Group 1 is given the drug, and Group 2 is given a placebo. At the end of the experiment, the level of depression of all participants is measured as a score on a test called a depression inventory. Match the elements of this experiment with the appropriate term.
   - ___ (1) score on depression inventory
   - ___ (2) the antidepressant drug
   - ___ (3) Group 1
   - ___ (4) Group 2

   a. experimental group
   b. control group
   c. independent variable
   d. dependent variable
3. The placebo effect occurs when a participant responds according to
   a. the hypothesis.
   b. the actual treatment.
   c. how other subjects behave.
   d. his or her expectations.
4. The results of an experiment can be influenced by the expectations of either the participants or the researcher. (true/false)
5. Random assignment is used to control for
   a. experimenter bias.
   b. the placebo effect.
   c. selection bias.
   d. participant bias.

Answers: 1. true 2. (1) d (2) c (3) a (4) b 3. d 4. true 5. c

OTHER RESEARCH METHODS

The Correlational Method: Discovering Relationships, Not Causes

What is the correlational method, and when is it used?

Does stress cause illness? Does smoking cause cancer? Does echinacea reduce the risk of catching a cold? Researchers would like to have answers to these questions, but none of them can be studied using the experimental method. It is often illegal and always unethical to assign people randomly to experimental conditions that could be harmful. For example, to find out if smoking marijuana causes a decline in academic achievement, no researcher would randomly assign high school students to an experimental study that would require students in the experimental groups to smoke marijuana. Can you imagine a principal notifying parents that their son or daughter had been chosen to smoke marijuana for 2 years in order to further scientific knowledge?

Much knowledge about the effects on human health of marijuana, medicines, cigarette smoking, and stress has been gained through experiments on animals or through other research methods. When, for ethical reasons, an experimental study cannot be performed to determine cause–effect relationships, the **correlational method** is usually used. This research method determines the *correlation*, or degree of relationship, between two characteristics, events, or behaviors. A group is selected for study, and the variables of interest are measured for each participant in the study. For example, the variables might be amount of marijuana previously used and grade point average. Then the researcher applies a statistical formula to obtain a correlation coefficient.

What is a correlation coefficient?

The Correlation Coefficient: How Variables Relate A **correlation coefficient** is a numerical value indicating the degree and direction of the relationship between two variables. A correlation coefficient ranges from +1.00 (a perfect positive correlation) to .00 (no relationship) to −1.00 (a perfect negative correlation). The number in a correlation coefficient indicates the relative *strength* of the relationship between two variables—the higher the number, the stronger the relationship. Therefore, a correlation of −.85 is higher than a correlation of +.64.

The sign of a correlation coefficient (+ or −) indicates whether the two variables vary in the same or opposite directions. A positive correlation indicates that two variables vary in the same direction. For example, there is a positive though weak correlation between stress and illness. When stress increases, illness is likely to increase; when stress decreases, illness tends to decrease. A negative correlation means that an increase in the value of one variable is associated with a decrease in the value of the other variable. There is a negative correlation between the number of cigarettes people smoke and the number of years they can expect to live.

Correlation and Prediction Correlations are useful in making predictions—the stronger the relationship between the variables, the better the prediction. A perfect correlation (+1.00 or −1.00) would enable one to make completely accurate predictions.

A correlation is more useful for predicting the probable performance of a group than for predicting that of an individual. Because there is a correlation between cigarette smoking and lung cancer, it can be predicted that a group of 1,000 nonsmokers will experience a lower incidence of lung cancer than a group of 1,000 two-pack-a-day smokers. But from the correlation coefficient alone we cannot accurately predict which individuals in either group will develop cancer.

But the fact that there is a correlation between two variables does not necessarily mean that one variable causes the other. Only the experimental method can lead

correlational method: A research method used to establish the degree of relationship (correlation) between two characteristics, events, or behaviors.

correlation coefficient: A numerical value that indicates the strength and direction of the relationship between two variables; ranges from +1.00 (a perfect positive correlation) to −1.00 (a perfect negative correlation).

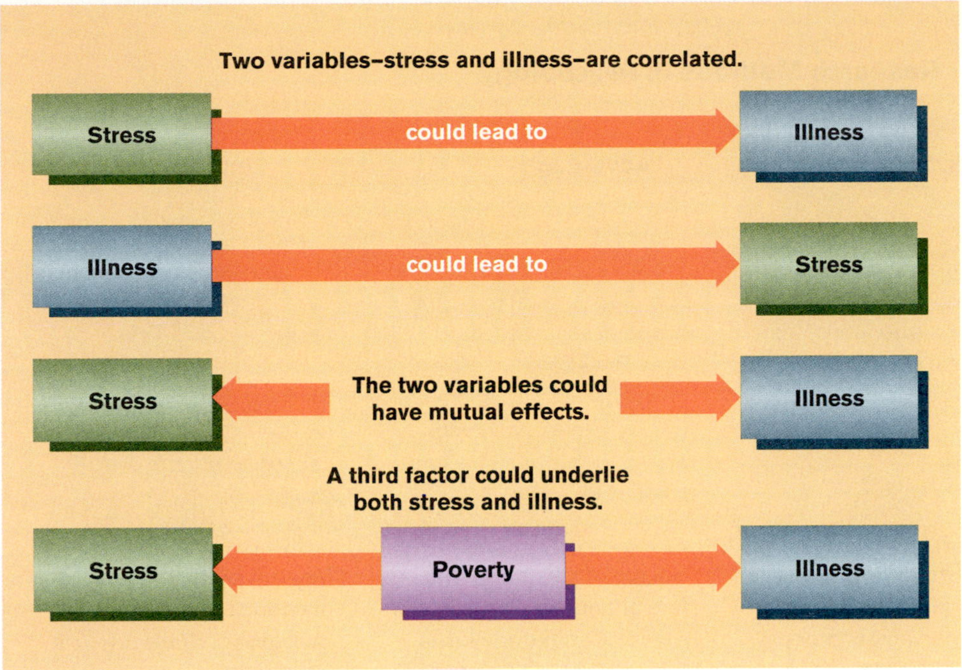

Figure 1.2

Correlation Does Not Prove Causation

A correlation between two variables does not prove that a cause–effect relationship exists between them. There is a correlation between stress and illness, but that does not mean that stress necessarily causes illness. Both stress and illness may result from another factor, such as poverty or poor general health.

to conclusions about cause and effect. When two variables such as stress and illness are correlated, we cannot conclude that stress makes people sick. It might be that illness causes stress, or that a third factor such as poverty or poor general health causes susceptibility to both illness and stress, as shown in Figure 1.2.

For more information on the correlation coefficient, see the Appendix on statistical methods, which follows Chapter 17.

Meta-Analysis: Combining the Results of Many Studies

To verify research findings, it is necessary that studies be replicated. **Replication** is the repeating of studies with the same procedures, but with different participants and preferably different investigators. If the results of a study are scientifically valid (that is, they measure what they were supposed to), a careful replication of the study should yield similar results.

But what if some replications find evidence of strong support for a hypothesis, others find no support, and still others find evidence to the contrary? Fortunately, there is a way researchers can average or combine the results of all such studies and reach conclusions about what the weight of evidence shows in the particular area of research.

Using a complex statistical technique known as **meta-analysis,** researchers can combine the results from many separate studies on the same topic to determine the strength of support for a hypothesis. For example, Janet Hyde and Marcia Lynn (1988) used meta-analysis to examine 165 studies reporting test results on verbal ability for about 1.5 million males and females. Their meta-analysis revealed no significant gender differences in verbal ability.

Review & Reflect 1.1 (on page 18) summarizes the different types of research methods we've discussed in this chapter.

replication: The process of repeating a study with different participants and preferably a different investigator to verify research findings.

meta-analysis: A complex statistical procedure used to combine the results from many studies on the same topic in order to determine the degree to which a hypothesis can be supported.

Review & Reflect 1.1 Research Methods in Psychology

Method	Description	Advantages	Limitations
DESCRIPTIVE METHODS			
Naturalistic and laboratory observation	Observation and recording of behavior in its natural setting or in a laboratory. With naturalistic observation, subjects may or may not know that they are being observed.	Provides descriptive information. Can provide basis for hypotheses to be tested later. Behavior studied in everyday setting is more natural. A laboratory setting allows for precise measurement of variables.	Researchers' expectations can distort observations (observer bias). Presence of researcher may influence behavior of subjects. In natural setting, researcher has little or no control over conditions.
Case study	In-depth study of one or a few individuals using observation, interview, and/or psychological testing.	Source of information for rare or unusual conditions or events. Can provide basis for hypotheses to be tested later.	May not be representative of condition or event. Time-consuming. Subject to misinterpretation by researcher.
Survey	Interviews and/or questionnaires used to gather information about attitudes, beliefs, experiences, or behaviors of a group of people.	Can provide accurate information about large numbers of people. Can track changes in attitudes and behavior over time.	Responses may be inaccurate. Sample may not be representative. Characteristics of interviewer may influence responses.
OTHER METHODS			
Experimental method	Random assignment of participants to groups. Manipulation of the independent variable(s) and measurement of its effect on the dependent variable.	Enables identification of cause–effect relationships.	Laboratory setting may inhibit natural behavior of participants. Findings may not be generalizable to the real world. In some cases, experiment is unethical.
Correlational method	Method used to determine the relationship (correlation) between two events, characteristics, or behaviors.	Can assess strength of relationship between variables. Provides basis for prediction.	Does not demonstrate cause and effect.
Meta-analysis	Statistical method of combining the results from many research studies to determine whether a hypothesis is supported.	Provide an overall estimate of the combined effects of many studies on the same topic.	Findings can be no more reliable than the research on which they are based.

Remember It!

1. The correlational method is used to demonstrate cause–effect relationships. (true/false)
2. Which of the following correlation coefficients indicates the strongest relationship?

   a. +.65 b. −.78 c. .00 d. +.25
3. There is a (positive, negative) correlation between the amount of exercise overweight people engage in and their body weight.
4. There is a (positive, negative) correlation between the amount of fat people eat and their body weight.
5. Test X has turned out to be a poor predictor of college GPA. Therefore, you can say that Test X is not (reliable, valid) for predicting GPA in college.
6. What is the term for a statistical procedure used to combine the results from many research studies to determine whether a specific hypothesis is supported?

   a. combinatorial analysis
   b. multiple analysis
   c. statistical summation
   d. meta-analysis

Answers: 1. false 2. b 3. negative 4. positive 5. valid 6. d

PARTICIPANTS IN PSYCHOLOGICAL RESEARCH

Ethics in Research: Protecting the Participants

What are some ethical guidelines governing the use of human participants in research?

In 1992 the American Psychological Association (APA) adopted a new set of ethical standards governing research with human participants so as to safeguard their rights while supporting the goals of scientific inquiry. Following are some of the main provisions of the code: Participation in research must be strictly voluntary, and participants must give *informed consent.* This means that they must be informed in advance about (1) the nature of the research, (2) any factors—risks, discomfort, or unpleasant emotional experiences—that might affect their willingness to participate, and (3) their freedom to decline to participate or to withdraw from the research at any time.

Most people would agree that research must be conducted to advance scientific knowledge and that research must be an ethical enterprise. But what about deception? Is it ethical for researchers to lie to participants or otherwise mislead them in order to conduct their studies? Clearly, without deception some research, such as the Lang experiment, could not be conducted, or the knowledge gained.

But some psychologists strictly oppose the use of deception under any circumstances. Diane Baumrind (1985) opposes research using deception because of the potential harm to the participants. She also believes that such practices will damage the reputation of psychology and psychologists and cause people to lose confidence in the profession. Even so, deception is used in many research studies, particularly in the field of social psychology.

Today the APA's code of ethical standards allows deception (1) if it is justified by the value of the potential findings, provided that equally effective procedures that do not involve deception cannot be used; (2) if participants are not deceived about "physical risks, discomfort, or unpleasant emotional experiences" that might affect their willingness to participate; and (3) if participants are debriefed as soon as possible after the experiment. The debriefing sessions provide information about the nature of the research and clear up any misconceptions about what occurred during the study. Researchers want to ensure that the participants understand that no one was actually harmed. In the Lang study, debriefing interviews informed students of the deception and revealed to them that no electric shocks were actually used.

Human Participants in Psychological Research: The Challenge of Diversity

Each year the population of the United States becomes more diverse, and this trend will continue. Projections by the U.S. Bureau of the Census (2000) indicate that the percentage of non-Hispanic Whites in the United States is expected to decrease from 71.5% in the year 2000 to 53% in 2050. During this same period the percentage of Asian Americans in the overall population is projected to increase from 3.8% to 11.3%; that of African Americans, from 12.2% to 13.2%; and that of Hispanic Americans, from 11.8% to 22.5%. Because of a longer life expectancy, the percentage of older adults in the U.S. population is also rising.

Is this diversity reflected in the participants in psychological studies? The answer is no. For practical reasons, the majority of studies with human participants in the last 30 years have used college students. Students are a convenient group for college professors to study, and professors often encourage their participation by offering pay or points toward a course grade (Kadzin, 1999). Psychology studies have also used disproportionate numbers of males (Gannon et al., 1992) and of Whites (Graham, 1992).

Because college students are a convenient group for professors to study, research results often do not reflect the characteristics of the more diverse general population.

Heavy reliance on college students presents a problem. College students are a relatively select group in terms of age, socioeconomic class, and educational level. Thus, they are not representative of the general population. But how generalizable the findings of a study using college students are to the general population depends on the nature of the study. Studies that investigate basic psychological processes such as sensation, perception, and memory are likely to be relatively generalizable, because these processes probably function in similar ways in most adults. But there is great cultural and individual variation in human social behavior and thus a problem in generalizing the results of many studies with college students to other segments of the population. To adequately understand human behavior, researchers must not only know how people are alike but also understand and appreciate how they differ (Kadzin, 1999).

Bias in Psychological Research

Several researchers have cited evidence of bias in psychological research, including gender bias (Gannon et al., 1992), age bias, and racial and ethnic bias (Sue, 1999).

In their studies of gender bias in psychological research, Ader and Johnson (1994) found that bias is still very much in evidence in reports of research findings and in discussion of single-sex studies. When conducting research in which all of the participants are of one sex, these authors ask, why do researchers consider it important to specify the gender of the sample clearly when it is female, but not when the sample is exclusively male? Such a practice, say Ader and Johnson, reveals a "tendency to consider male participants 'normative,' and results obtained from them generally applicable, whereas female participants are somehow 'different,' and results obtained from them are specific to female participants" (pp. 217–218). On a positive note, however, these researchers report that over the decades, gender bias in the sampling and selection of research subjects has decreased.

Investigating race bias, Sandra Graham (1992) reported finding a decline in research on African Americans in psychological journals. And prominent among the research articles that she did find was what she termed a methodological flaw—failure to include socioeconomic status—in research comparing White and African Americans. Graham points out that African Americans are overrepresented among those who are economically disadvantaged. She maintains that socioeconomic status should be incorporated into research designs "to disentangle race and social class effects" in studies that compare White and African Americans (p. 634).

Ageism is another continuing source of bias, especially apparent in the language used in psychological research (Schaie, 1993). For example, the titles of research on aging tend to focus heavily on loss, deterioration, decline, and dependency. Moreover, researchers are too likely to understate the great diversity among the older adults they study. According to Schaie (1993), "most research on adulthood shows that differences between those in their 60s and those in their 80s are far greater than those between 20- and 60-year-olds" (p. 50). Researchers should guard against descriptions or conclusions implying that all members of a given age group are defined by deterioration, forgetfulness, and deficits.

The Use of Animals in Research

Why are animals used in research?

Where would psychology be today without the laboratory rat, Pavlov's salivating dogs, the pigeon, and the many other species of animals used to advance scientific knowledge? Yet animals are used in only 7–8% of psychological experiments, and 95% of the animals used are rodents (Gallup & Suarez, 1985).

Why are animals used in research? There are at least six reasons. Animals are used in experimental studies because (1) they provide a simpler model for studying processes that operate similarly in humans; (2) researchers can exercise far more control over animal subjects and thus be more certain of their conclusions; (3) a wider range of medical and other manipulations can be used with animals; (4) it is easier to study the entire life span and even multiple generations in some animal species; (5) animals are more economical to use and are available at the researchers' convenience; and (6) some researchers simply want to learn more about the animals themselves.

Most psychologists recognize that many scientific advances would not have been possible without animal research. Where do you stand on this issue?

Psychologists recognize the tremendous contributions that laboratory animals have made and continue to make to science. Animal research has yielded much knowledge about the brain and the physiology of vision, hearing, and the other senses (Domjan & Purdy, 1995). It has also increased knowledge in the areas of learning, motivation, stress, memory, and the effects on the unborn of various drugs ingested during pregnancy. Almost half of the research funded by the National Institutes of Health is conducted on animals (Cork et al., 1997). Virtually all of the marvels of modern medicine are due at least in part to experimentation using animals.

The APA has always supported the use of animals in research, and its code of ethics supports the humane treatment of animals. According to the association's guidelines governing animal research, researchers must do everything possible to minimize discomfort, pain, and illness in animal subjects (APA, 1992b).

Nevertheless, a storm of controversy surrounds the research use of animals. Many animal rights advocates want all animal research stopped immediately. Some have even broken into laboratories, freed laboratory animals, destroyed records, and wrecked equipment and other property. Books on animal rights devote an average of 63.3% of their content to the use of animals in research (Nicholl & Russell, 1990). Yet, of the 6,309 million animals killed each year in the United States, only 0.3% are used in research and education, while 96.5% are used for food, 2.6% are killed by hunters, 0.4% are killed in animal shelters, and 0.2% are used for fur garments (Christensen, 1997).

In a survey of almost 4,000 randomly selected members of the APA, "80% of respondents expressed general support for psychological research on animals" (Plous, 1996, p. 1177). Among the general public, support for animal research is higher when the research is tied to human health and highest when the animals involved in such research are rats and mice rather than dogs, cats, or primates (Plous, 1996).

Overall, the animal rights controversy has served to increase concern for the treatment of animals as research subjects and to stimulate a search for alternative research methods that will decrease the numbers of animals needed. "The number of animals used in laboratory experiments is going down" (Mukerjee, 1997, p. 86).

Remember It!

1. Psychologists are required to debrief participants thoroughly after a research study when the study
   a. violates participants' rights to privacy.
   b. deceives participants about the true purpose of the research.
   c. exposes participants to unreasonable risk or harm.
   d. wastes taxpayers' money on trivial questions.
2. Which of the following groups has *not* been overrepresented as participants in psychological research?
   a. whites b. males c. females d. college students
3. Which of the following has *not* been identified as a source of bias in psychological research, according to the text?
   a. age b. gender c. race d. religion
4. Investigators use animals in psychological research to learn more about humans. (true/false)
5. The American Psychological Association (APA) has guidelines for ethical treatment for human participants but not for animal subjects. (true/false)

Answers: 1. b 2. c 3. d 4. true 5. false

EXPLORING PSYCHOLOGY'S ROOTS

If you were to trace the development of psychology from the beginning, you would need to stretch far back to the earliest pages of recorded history, even beyond the early Greek philosophers, such as Aristotle and Plato. People have always had questions about human nature, and they have always tried to understand human behavior. For centuries these questions were the subject of speculation and were considered to be in the realm of philosophy. It was not until experimental methods were applied to the study of psychological processes that psychology became recognized as a formal academic discipline.

Wundt and the Founding of Psychology

What was Wundt's contribution to psychology?

Three German physiologists—Ernst Weber, Gustav Fechner, and Hermann von Helmholtz—pioneered in the application of experimental methods to the study of psychological processes, and they profoundly influenced the early development of psychology. But it is Wilhelm Wundt (1832–1920) who is generally thought of as the "father of psychology."

Wundt established a psychological laboratory at the University of Leipzig in Germany in 1879. This event is considered to mark the birth of psychology as a formal academic discipline. Wundt's primary purpose was to identify the elements of consciousness and to discover the laws that govern how those elements are connected. He believed that consciousness could be reduced to its basic elements, just as water (H_2O) can be broken down into its constitutent elements—hydrogen (H) and oxygen (O). For Wundt pure sensations—such as sweetness, coldness, or redness—were the basic elements of consciousness. And these pure sensations, he believed, combined to form perceptions.

Even though these children experience the same sensations (sweetness and coldness) as they enjoy eating their ice cream, their reported introspections of the experience would probably differ.

But conscious experience can be observed only by the person having that experience. Therefore, research on the experience necessarily involves self-observation, or introspection. *Introspection* as a research method involves looking inward to examine one's own conscious experience and then reporting that experience. Wundt's advanced psychology students were rigorously trained in introspection. It is said that they had to introspect their way through some 10,000 separate practice experiences before their reports could be considered valid. But, of course, introspection is strictly subjective.

Using introspection, Wundt and his associates studied the perception of a variety of visual, tactile, and auditory stimuli, including rhythm patterns produced by metronomes set at different speeds. They also conducted experiments on reaction time and on attention span.

What is Wundt's legacy? Wundt put great emphasis on the use of precise measurements and the necessity of replicating research findings (Viney, 1993). And although his laboratory work lacked objectivity and was limited to the study of subjective sensory processes, perception, and reaction time, he did have a larger vision of the field of psychology—a vision that included studies of social and cultural influences on human thought (Benjafield, 1996). Wundt clearly earned a place as a major figure in psychology. In fact, he was placed first by historians of the field in a ranking of the most eminent psychologists of all time (Korn et al., 1991).

Titchener and Structuralism

What were the goals and method of structuralism, the first school of psychology?

Wundt's most famous student, Englishman Edward Bradford Titchener (1867–1927), took the new field to the United States, where he set up a psychological laboratory at Cornell University. He gave the name **structuralism** to this first school of thought in psychology, which aimed at analyzing the basic elements, or the structure, of conscious mental experience.

Just as Wundt's work was, structuralism was most severely criticized for its primary method, introspection. Introspection was not objective, even though it involved observation, measurement, and experimentation. When different introspectionists were exposed to the same stimulus, such as the click of a metronome, they frequently reported different experiences. Structuralism was not long considered to be a viable approach. Later schools of thought in psychology were established, partly in reaction against structuralism, which did not survive after the death of its most ardent spokesperson, E. B. Titchener.

Functionalism: The First American School of Psychology

What was the goal of the early school of psychology known as functionalism?

As structuralism was losing its influence in the United States in the early 20th century, a new school of psychology called functionalism was taking shape. **Functionalism** was concerned not with the structure of consciousness, but with how mental processes function—that is, how humans and animals use mental processes in adapting to their environment.

The influential work of Charles Darwin (1809–1882), especially his ideas about evolution and the continuity of species, was largely responsible for an increasing use of animals in psychological experiments. Even though Darwin contributed important seeds of thought that helped give birth to the new school of psychology, functionalism was primarily American in character and spirit.

The famous American psychologist William James (1842–1910) was an advocate of functionalism even though he did much of his writing before this school of psychology appeared. James's best-known work is his highly regarded and frequently quoted textbook *Principles of Psychology*, published more than a century ago (1890). James taught that mental processes are fluid and that they have continuity, rather than a rigid or fixed structure as the structuralists suggested. James spoke of the "stream of consciousness," which he said functioned to help humans adapt to their environment.

Functionalism broadened the scope of psychology to include the study of behavior as well as mental processes. It also allowed the study of children, animals, and the mentally impaired, groups that could not be studied by the structuralists because they could not be trained to use introspection. Functionalism also focused on an applied, more practical use of psychology by encouraging the study of

structuralism: The first formal school of psychology, aimed at analyzing the basic elements, or structure, of conscious mental experience through the use of introspection.

functionalism: An early school of psychology that was concerned with how mental processes help humans and animals adapt to their environments.

educational psychology, individual differences, and industrial psychology (adaptation in the workplace).

Gestalt Psychology: The Whole Is More Than the Sum of Its Parts

What is the emphasis of Gestalt psychology?

Gestalt psychology made its appearance in Germany in 1912. The Gestalt psychologists, notably Max Wertheimer, Kurt Koffka, and Wolfgang Köhler, objected to the central idea of structuralism—that we can best understand conscious experience by reducing it to its basic elements. **Gestalt psychology** emphasized that individuals perceive objects and patterns as whole units, and that the whole thus perceived is more than the sum of its parts. The German word *Gestalt* roughly means "whole, form, or pattern."

To support the Gestalt theory, Wertheimer, the leader of the Gestalt psychologists, presented his famous experiment demonstrating the phi phenomenon. In this experiment two light bulbs are placed a short distance apart in a dark room. The first light is flashed on and then turned off just as the second light is flashed on. As this pattern of flashing the lights on and off continues, an observer sees what looks like a single light moving back and forth from one position to another. Here, said the Gestaltists, is proof that people perceive wholes or patterns, not collections of separate and independent sensations.

When the Nazis came to power in Germany in the 1930s, the Gestalt school disbanded as its most prominent members emigrated to the United States. But even today Gestalt psychology continues to exert an influence, particularly in the fields of perception and learning.

Behaviorism: Never Mind the Mind

How did behaviorism differ from previous schools of psychology?

Psychologist John B. Watson (1878–1958) looked at the study of psychology as defined by the structuralists and functionalists and disliked virtually everything he saw. In Watson's view the study of mental processes, the concepts of mind and consciousness, and the primary investigative technique of introspection were not scientific. Watson pointed out that each person's introspection is strictly individual. He further maintained that self-reflection and internal ruminations cannot be observed, verified, understood, or communicated in objective, scientific terms. In his article "Psychology as the Behaviorist Views It" (1913), Watson argued that all the strictly subjective techniques and concepts in psychology must be thrown out. Out with introspection, the study of consciousness, and other fuzzy mentalistic concepts. Watson did not deny the existence of conscious thought or experience. He simply did not view them as appropriate subject matter for psychology.

Watson proposed a radically new approach to psychology. This new school of psychology, called **behaviorism,** redefined psychology as the "science of behavior." Behaviorism confined itself to the study of behavior because it was observable and measurable and, therefore, objective and scientific. Behaviorism also emphasized that behavior is determined primarily by factors in the environment.

B. F. Skinner: Continuing the Behaviorist Tradition Behaviorism soon became the most influential school of thought in American psychology and remained so until the 1960s. It is still a major force in modern psychology, in large part because of the profound influence of B. F. Skinner (1904–1990). Skinner agreed with Watson that concepts such as mind, consciousness, and feelings were neither objective nor measurable and, therefore, were not the appropriate subject matter of psychology. Furthermore, Skinner argued that these concepts are not needed in order to explain behavior. One can explain behavior, he claimed, by analyzing the conditions that were present before a behavior occurs and by analyzing the consequences that follow the behavior.

Gestalt psychology (geh-SHTALT): The school of psychology that emphasizes that individuals perceive objects and patterns as whole units and that the perceived whole is more than the sum of its parts.

behaviorism: The school of psychology founded by John B. Watson that views observable, measurable behavior as the appropriate subject matter for psychology and emphasizes the key role of environment as a determinant of behavior.

Skinner's research on operant conditioning emphasized the importance of reinforcement in learning and in shaping and maintaining behavior. Any behavior that is reinforced—followed by pleasant or rewarding consequences—is more likely to be performed again. Skinner's work has had a powerful influence on modern psychology.

Because the strict behaviorist position of Skinner and others ignores inner, mental processes like thoughts and feelings, behaviorism has been a continuing target of criticism. Today many behaviorists do not take as extreme a view of behavior as Skinner himself did. Although they still emphasize the central importance of the study of behavior, they are also willing to consider what mental processes contribute to behavior.

psychoanalysis (SY-ko-ah-NAL-ih-sis): The term Freud used for both his theory of personality and his therapy for the treatment of psychological disorders; the unconscious is the primary focus of psychoanalytic theory.

humanistic psychology: The school of psychology that focuses on the uniqueness of human beings and their capacity for choice, growth, and psychological health.

Psychoanalysis: It's What's Down Deep That Counts

What is the role of the unconscious in psychoanalysis, Freud's approach to psychology?

Whereas the behaviorists completely rejected unobservable mental forces in explaining behavior, this is precisely where Sigmund Freud looked in formulating his theory. Freud emphasized the importance of unseen, unconscious mental forces as the key to understanding human nature and behavior.

Sigmund Freud (1856–1939), whose life and work you will study in Chapter 14, developed a theory of human behavior based largely on case studies of his patients. Freud's theory, **psychoanalysis,** maintains that human mental life is like an iceberg. The smallest, visible part of the iceberg represents the conscious mental experience of the individual. But underwater, hidden from view, floats a vast store of unconscious impulses, thoughts, wishes, and desires. Freud insisted that individuals do not consciously control their thoughts, feelings, and behavior, which are instead determined by these unconscious forces.

In Good Will Hunting, *Robin Williams portrayed a psychiatrist who helps a young man (played by Matt Damon) "work through" a debilitating fear of rejection that resulted from a troubled childhood.*

Freud believed that the unconscious is the storehouse for material that threatens the conscious life of the individual—disturbing sexual and aggressive impulses as well as traumatic experiences that have been repressed or pushed down to the unconscious. Once there, rather than resting quietly (out of sight, out of mind), the unconscious material festers and seethes, like "the bubbling, boiling brew in a cauldron," Freud wrote.

The overriding importance that Freud placed on sexual and aggressive impulses caused much controversy both inside and outside the field of psychology. The most notable of Freud's famous students—Carl Jung, Alfred Adler, and Karen Horney—broke away from their mentor and developed their own theories of personality. These three are often collectively referred to as *neo-Freudians.*

When people think of Freud, many picture a psychiatrist using psychoanalysis with a patient on the familiar couch. The general public has heard of such concepts as the unconscious, repression, rationalization, and the Freudian slip. Such familiarity has made Sigmund Freud a larger-than-life figure rather than an obscure Austrian doctor resting within the dusty pages of history. Although Freud continues to influence popular culture, the volume of research on psychoanalysis has continued to diminish steadily (Robins et al., 1999).

Humanistic Psychology: Looking at Human Potential

What is the focus of humanistic psychology?

Humanistic psychology emerged in part as a reaction against behaviorism and psychoanalysis, the two major forces in psychology in the United States. In fact, its leading proponent, Abraham Maslow (1908–1970), called humanistic psychology the third force in psychology. **Humanistic psychology** focuses on the uniqueness of human beings and their capacity for choice, growth, and psychological health. The humanists reject the behaviorist notion that people have no free will and are shaped and controlled strictly by the environment. Humanists also reject Freud's theory that people are determined and driven from within, acting and marching to the dark drums of the unconscious.

Maslow objected to Freud's pessimistic view of human potential and pointed out that Freud had based his theory primarily on data from his disturbed patients. Maslow and other prominent humanistic psychologists, such as Carl Rogers (1902–1987), emphasized a much more positive view of human nature. They maintained that people are innately good and that they possess free will. The humanists believe that people are capable of making conscious, rational choices, which can lead to growth and psychological health.

Maslow proposed a theory of motivation that consists of a hierarchy of needs. He considered the need for self-actualization (developing to one's fullest potential) to be the highest need on the hierarchy. Carl Rogers developed his client-centered therapy and, with other humanists, popularized encounter groups and other techniques as part of the human potential movement.

Cognitive Psychology: Focusing on Mental Processes

What is the focus of cognitive psychology?

Cognitive psychology is a specialty that focuses on mental processes such as memory, problem solving, concept formation, reasoning and decision making, language, and perception. Just as behaviorism developed in part as a reaction against the focus on mental processes that was characteristic of structuralism and functionalism, so cognitive psychology grew and developed partly in response to strict behaviorism (Robins et al., 1999). Cognitive psychologists see humans not as passive recipients who are pushed and pulled by environmental forces, but as active participants who seek out experiences, who alter and shape them, and who use mental processes to transform information in the course of their own cognitive development. So how people perceive and explain an event, whether accurate or not, affects how they will respond to that event.

Beginning in the 1950s, a combination of forces—linguistics, computer science, neuroscience, and psychology—enabled researchers to undertake a more scientific approach to the study of mental structures and processes (Haberlandt, 1997). Cognitive psychology was influenced by the pioneering work of linguist Noam Chomsky, whose research laid important groundwork for investigating mental processes through the experimental study of language.

The advent of the computer provided cognitive psychologists with a new way to conceptualize mental structures and processes, known as the *information-processing approach.* According to this view, the brain processes information in sequential stages, or levels—in much the same way as a computer does serial processing. But as modern technology changed computers and computer programs, cognitive psychologists changed their cognitive models. "Increasingly, parallel processing models are developed in addition to stage models of processing" (Haberlandt, 1997, p. 22). Some cognitive psychologists have extended their study of problem solving, decision making, and other human mental processes to work on artificial intelligence. In this research, sophisticated computers are used to simulate the intellectual processes of the human brain.

Unlike the early behaviorists, researchers today *can* observe some mental processes directly. Thanks to modern brain-imaging techniques such as the PET scan, combined with sophisticated computer technology, researchers can observe the action of specific clusters of brain cells (neurons) involved in carrying out various mental processes (Raichle, 1994). Such mental activities as thinking, remembering, solving a problem, listening to a melody, speaking, viewing images and colors, and so on have all been "observed," providing a rich body of knowledge that cognitive psychologists use in their work. Today, cognitive psychology is recognized as the most prominent school of psychological thought (Robins et al., 1999).

cognitive psychology: A specialty that studies mental processes such as memory, problem solving, decision making, perception, language, and other forms of cognition; often uses the information-processing approach.

Evolutionary Psychology

Evolutionary psychology focuses on how humans have adapted the behaviors required for survival in the face of environmental pressures over the long course of evolution (Archer, 1996). Evolutionary psychologists study how genetically inherited tendencies and dispositions in humans influence a wide range of behaviors—from how we select mates to our level of intellectual performance and even why we tend to help others of our species. They consider how the common behavioral roots shared by all members of the human species are manifested today in the various cultures around the world. Their ultimate goal is to understand universal human behavior that is aimed at passing one's genes to future generations.

What is the focus of evolutionary psychology?

Evolutionary psychology has been called, simply, a combination of evolutionary biology and cognitive psychology (Evans & Zarate, 2000). Two widely recognized proponents of evolutionary psychology, Leda Cosmides and John Tooby, hold that this perspective combines the forces of evolutionary biology, anthropology, cognitive psychology, and neuroscience. These advocates explain that an evolutionary perspective can be applied to any topic within the field of psychology (Cosmides & Tooby, 2000).

Research in Evolutionary Psychology Among the more interesting research conducted by evolutionary psychologists is the work of David Buss (1999, 2000a, 2000b), whose cross-cultural studies of mate selection have investigated how we select a mate, the qualities we look for in a mate, and what makes us jealous. Before we look at Buss's research, complete the *Try It!* about jealous reactions.

Try It!

1. For each of the following situations, check the most accurate response.
   a. You are in a serious, committed, romantic relationship and you find your partner flirting with someone else. How jealous would you feel?

   ____ Not jealous at all ____ Slightly jealous __✓__ Moderately jealous ____ Quite jealous ____ Extremely jealous

   b. If you were flirting with someone else, how jealous would your partner be?

   ____ Not jealous at all __✓__ Slightly jealous ____ Moderately jealous __✓__ Quite jealous ____ Extremely jealous

2. Indicate which of the following two situations would make you angrier and/or hurt you more.
   a. You are in a serious, committed, romantic relationship, and you learn that your partner recently became involved in an emotional relationship with another person. There is no sex involved, not even kissing, but she/he spends a lot of time with the other person, seems quite attached, and talks about the person frequently.
   b. You are in a serious, committed, romantic relationship, and you learn that your partner recently had sex with another person, but there are no emotional ties at all and no commitment to the other person.

   Which situation would be more psychologically distressing to you?

   a. Emotional infidelity b. Sexual infidelity

3. Are you male or female? ____female____ Male.

   (The reason for this last question will become obvious as you continue reading the text.)

evolutionary psychology: The school of psychology that studies how humans' genetically inherited tendencies and dispositions influence a wide range of behaviors.

Buss (1999, 2000a) recently pointed out that dozens of studies prior to the 1990s had concluded that women and men are almost identical in their negative responses to the idea of their partners flirting with someone else. Even across many different cultures, it appeared that men and women were equally jealous and upset over various kinds of threats to their romantic relationships. But early in the 1990s, Buss and others (1992) had predicted the following: That men would be more distressed than women over sexual infidelity, whereas women would be more upset than men over emotional involvement with another person. And studies throughout the 1990s supported this prediction. In one study of more than 500 college students, 83% of the women but only 40% of the men were more upset over their partner's emotional infidelity. In contrast, 60% of the men and only 17% of the women found their partner's sexual infidelity more distressing (Buss, 1999; Buss et al., 1992). Buss (1999) stated that this difference of 43% in the responses from the two sexes is "huge . . . large by any standard in social sciences" (p. 326).

The Buss study, however, relied on statements made by the respondents, which are less convincing than more objective measures of psychological distress. So, Buss and his colleagues tested women and men in the laboratory and asked them to imagine the two types of infidelity while connected to instruments for measuring heart or pulse rate, electrodermal response (sweating), and tensing of the brow muscles (frowning). The men showed high physiological distress at the thought of sexual infidelity, but far less when considering emotional infidelity. The women tended to exhibit high physiological distress when imagining emotional infidelity by their partner, but much less when confronting sexual infidelity. Apparently, both women and men were feeling inside what they were reporting verbally. As far as can be determined, these and similar findings appear to be universal. This type of research has been conducted in 37 countries on six different continents (Buss et al., 1990). Results of a cross-cultural study in four of those countries (the United States, Germany, the Netherlands, and Korea) are shown in Figure 1.3.

The reason why evolutionary psychologists predict that men's jealousy will focus so heavily on sexual infidelity is that historically a man's certainty of his paternity was jeopardized if he learned that his mate had been sexually unfaithful. Of course, a man could pass on his genes to dozens (or even hundreds) of children. But a woman is infinitely more limited than a man in the possible number of children she can have. Consequently, the best chance a woman had to pass her genes on

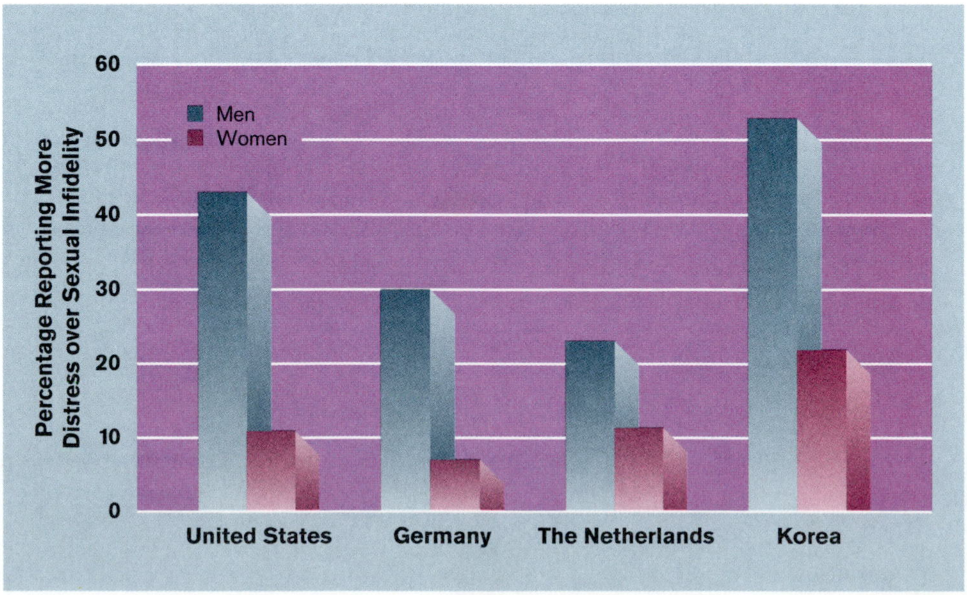

Figure 1.3

Gender Differences in Jealousy across Cultures

Across all cultures, men experience greater distress in response to sexual infidelity than women do, while women experience greater distress in response to emotional infidelity than men do. (From Buunk et al., 1996.)

to future generations was to have emotional commitment—the resources, the protection, and the support from a mate that would help her offspring survive and reach sexual maturity. The man's emotional commitment to her, then, was of paramount importance.

So, in the struggle for survival, individuals must compete with others to pass as many copies of their genes as possible on to future generations. Competition is an adaptive quality, and we must compete to survive. But cooperation is also an adaptive quality that enhances the chance of survival (Stewart, 2000). We all need other humans in our lives. Without some measure of cooperation, we could not have rewarding and satisfying relationships, or societies.

Review & Reflect 1.2 (on page 30) summarizes the major schools of thought in psychology.

According to evolutionary psychologists, actors Michael Douglas and Catherine Zeta-Jones have the qualities men and women seek in prospective mates, in order to be sure that their genes are passed on to future generations. He has attained success in his field, meaning that he can provide material support. Her youth and beauty are likely to secure his emotional commitment.

Women and Minorities: Pioneers in Psychology

From its beginning until the mid–20th century, psychology was shaped and dominated largely by White European and American males. The reason for this long-standing domination was the thinking of the times. For centuries conventional thought had held that higher education was the exclusive domain of White males, that women should rear the children and be the homemakers, and that minorities were best suited for manual labor. And, as Thomas Paine observed in his influential book *Common Sense*, "A long habit of not thinking a thing *wrong*, gives it a superficial appearance of being *right*." However, beginning in the late 19th century, women and minorities overcame these prejudices to make notable achievements in and contributions to the study of psychology.

Christine Ladd-Franklin (1847–1930) completed the requirements for a PhD at Johns Hopkins University in the mid-1880s but had to wait over 40 years before receiving her degree in 1926, when the university first agreed to grant it to women. Ladd-Franklin formulated a well-regarded, evolutionary theory of color vision.

In 1895, Mary Whiton Calkins (1863–1930) completed the requirements for a doctorate at Harvard. And even though William James described her as one of his most capable students, Harvard refused to grant the degree to a woman (Dewsbury, 2000). Undeterred, Calkins established a psychology laboratory at Wellesley College and developed the paired-associates test, an important research technique for the study of memory. She became the first female president of the American Psychological Association in 1905.

Margaret Floy Washburn (1871–1939) received her PhD in psychology from Cornell University and later taught at Vassar College (Dewsbury, 2000). She wrote several books, among them *The Animal Mind* (1908), an influential book on animal behavior, and *Movement and Mental Imagery* (1916).

Francis Cecil Sumner (1895–1954) was a self-taught scholar. Without benefit of a formal high school education, he became, in 1920, the first African American to earn a PhD in psychology, from Clark University. This feat was accomplished "in spite of innumerable social and physical factors mitigating against such achievements by black people in America" (Guthrie, 1998, p. 177). Sumner translated more than 3,000 articles from German, French, and Spanish. He chaired the psychology department at Howard University and is known as the "father" of African American psychology.

Albert Sidney Beckham (1897–1964), another African American psychologist, conducted some impressive early studies on intelligence and showed how it is related to success in numerous occupational fields. Beckham also established the first psychological laboratory at a Black institution of higher learning—Howard University.

A more recent African American pioneer, psychologist Kenneth Clark, achieved national recognition for his writings on the harmful effects of racial segregation. His work affected the Supreme Court ruling that declared racial segregation in the

Review & Reflect 1.2 Schools of Thought in Psychology

School	Description
Structuralism E. B. Titchener	The first formal school of psychology. Focused on analyzing the basic elements or structure of conscious mental experience through the use of introspection.
Functionalism William James	The first American school of psychology. Concerned with the study of mental processes and their role in facilitating adaptation to the environment. Broadened the scope of psychology to include the study of behavior as well as mental processes and the study of children, the mentally impaired, and animals.
Gestalt psychology Max Wertheimer Kurt Koffka Wolfgang Köhler	Emphasizes that individuals perceive objects and patterns as whole units. The perceived whole is more than the sum of its parts and is not best understood by analysis of its elemental parts (as suggested by the structuralists).
Behaviorism John Watson B. F. Skinner	Views observable, measurable behavior rather than internal mental processes as the appropriate subject matter of psychology. Stresses the key roles of learning and the environment in determining behavior.
Psychoanalysis Sigmund Freud	Emphasizes the roles of unconscious mental forces and conflicts in determining behavior.
Humanistic psychology Abraham Maslow Carl Rogers	Focuses on the uniqueness of human beings and their capacity for choice, growth, and psychological health. Called the third force in psychology (behaviorism and psychoanalysis being the other two forces).
Cognitive psychology	Focuses on mental processes such as memory, problem solving, reasoning, decision making, language, and perception. Uses the information-processing approach.
Evolutionary psychology	Concentrates on how people have adapted the behaviors needed for survival in the face of environmental demands throughout the course of human evolution.

schools to be unconstitutional. His wife, Mamie Phipps Clark, also achieved recognition when the couple published their works on racial identification and self-esteem, writings that have become classics in the field.

Hispanic American Jorge Sanchez conducted studies on bias in intelligence testing. He pointed out that both cultural differences and language differences work against Hispanic students when they take IQ tests.

These psychologists and others persevered to blaze the trail for the women and minorities who would follow.

Remember It!

1. Match the school of psychology with its major emphasis.

___ (1) the scientific study of behavior
___ (2) the perception of whole units or patterns
___ (3) the unconscious
___ (4) analysis of the basic elements of conscious mental experience
___ (5) the uniqueness of human beings and their capacity for conscious choice and growth
___ (6) the study of how human genetics influences behavior
___ (7) the function of conscious mental experience
___ (8) the study of mental processes

a. Gestalt psychology
b. structuralism
c. functionalism
d. evolutionary psychology
e. humanistic psychology
f. behaviorism
g. cognitive psychology
h. psychoanalysis

2. Match the major figure(s) with the appropriate school of psychology.

___ (1) James
___ (2) Freud
___ (3) Watson and Skinner
___ (4) Titchener
___ (5) Maslow and Rogers

a. humanistic psychology
b. structuralism
c. functionalism
d. psychoanalysis
e. behaviorism

Answers: 1. (1) f (2) a (3) h (4) b (5) e (6) d (7) c (8) g 2. (1) c (2) d (3) e (4) b (5) a

PSYCHOLOGY TODAY

Modern Perspectives in Psychology: Current Views on Behavior and Thinking

What are seven major perspectives in psychology today?

Modern psychologists are not easily categorized into specific schools of thought. There are no structuralists roaming the halls of psychology departments, and no professors calling themselves functionalists. Today, rather than discussing schools of psychology, it is more appropriate to refer to psychological perspectives—points of view used for explaining people's behavior and thinking, whether normal or abnormal. Psychologists need not limit themselves to only one perspective or approach. Many take an eclectic position, choosing a combination of approaches to explain a particular behavior or psychological problem.

Psychologists who adopt the **biological perspective** emphasize the role of biological processes and heredity as the key to understanding behavior and thinking. To explain thinking, emotion, and behavior, both normal and abnormal, biologically oriented psychologists study the structures of the brain and central nervous system, the functioning of the neurons, the delicate balance of neurotransmitters and hormones, and the impact of genes. For example, too much or too little of different neurotransmitters in the brain is related to various psychological disorders, such as schizophrenia and depression. Drugs already used in treating some of these disorders are designed to restore the brain's biochemical balance. Researchers and theorists who adopt the biological perspective are often referred to as physiological psychologists, psychobiologists, or neuropsychologists. And many of them are working under the umbrella of a new interdisciplinary field known as neuroscience. **Neuroscience** combines the work of psychologists, biologists, biochemists, medical researchers, and others in the study of the structure and function of the nervous system. The continuing development of medical technology in recent decades has spurred the research efforts of physiological psychologists, and many important findings in psychology have resulted from their work.

The psychoanalytic (psychodynamic) perspective in psychology is derived from the theory of Sigmund Freud. But the psychoanalytic approach has been modified considerably over the past several decades by psychologists known as neo-Freudians. The **psychoanalytic perspective** emphasizes the role of unconscious motivation and early childhood experiences in determining behavior and thought.

The biological approach looks inward to physical and biochemical processes to explain behavior, and the psychoanalytic approach looks deeply inward to the unconscious. But the **behavioral perspective** looks in exactly the opposite direction—outward—emphasizing learning and the role of environmental factors in shaping behavior. What factors in the environment reinforce and thus maintain certain behaviors? According to the behaviorists, it is primarily environmental factors that shape behavior. Psychologists must analyze these environmental factors in order to understand the causes of behavior and to establish programs of behavior modification to change problem behaviors.

The **cognitive perspective** considers the role of mental processes to be key. It is necessary to know more than what precedes a response and what follows it in order to understand behavior. The cognitive approach maintains that a given stimulus does not simply cause a given response. Rather, the individual consciously perceives, remembers, thinks, organizes, analyzes, decides, and then responds. To explain behavior more fully, according to cognitive psychologists, it is necessary to consider such cognitive processes as perception, thinking, memory, language, and others.

Humanistic psychologists reject with equal vigor (1) the pessimistic view of the psychoanalytic approach, that human behavior is determined primarily by unconscious forces, and (2) the behaviorist view that behavior is determined by factors in the environment. The **humanistic perspective** views humans as capable of making rational, conscious choices. It emphasizes the importance of people's own subjective experiences as the key to understanding their behavior. Less scientific and objective than many other approaches, the humanistic approach unashamedly admits the inherent subjective nature of its position.

The **evolutionary perspective** concentrates on how people have evolved and adapted the behaviors needed for continued existence in the face of a variety of environmental demands throughout evolution (Archer, 1996). But most evolutionary psychologists recognize that genes alone do not control an individual's ultimate destiny. Inherited tendencies are *not* set in concrete.

biological perspective: A perspective that emphasizes the role of biological processes and heredity as the key to understanding behavior.

neuroscience: A field that combines the work of psychologists, biologists, biochemists, medical researchers, and others in the study of the structure and function of the nervous system.

psychoanalytic perspective (SY-ko-AN-il-IT-ik): A perspective initially proposed by Freud that emphasizes the importance of the unconscious and of early childhood experiences as the keys to understanding behavior and thought.

behavioral perspective: A perspective that emphasizes the role of environment in shaping behavior.

cognitive perspective: A perspective that emphasizes the role of mental processes that underlie behavior.

humanistic perspective: A perspective that emphasizes the importance of an individual's subjective experience as a key to understanding behavior.

evolutionary perspective: A perspective that focuses on how humans have evolved and adapted behaviors required for survival against various environmental pressures over the long course of evolution.

Review & Reflect 1.3 Modern Perspectives in Psychology

Perspective	Emphasis
Biological	The role of biological processes and structures, as well as heredity, in explaining behavior
Psychoanalytic	The role of unconscious motivation and early childhood experiences in determining behavior and thought
Behavioral	The role of environment in shaping and controlling behavior
Cognitive	The role of mental processes–perception, thinking, and memory–that underlie behavior
Humanistic	The importance of an individual's subjective experience as a key to understanding his or her behavior
Evolutionary	The roles of inherited tendencies that have proven adaptive in humans
Sociocultural	The roles of social and cultural influences on behavior

The **sociocultural perspective** emphasizes social and cultural influences on human behavior and stresses the importance of understanding those influences when interpreting the behavior of others. Just as someone can be quoted out of context and thus misunderstood, the actions or gestures of a person from another culture can be misinterpreted because the observer does not understand the cultural context in which they occur. Gergen and others (1996) have claimed that there is a "desperate need" for culturally sensitive research about people's behavior in such areas as health, "birth control, child abuse, drug addiction, ethnic and religious conflict, and the effects of technology on society" (p. 502).

Review & Reflect 1.3 gives a brief summary of these seven perspectives in psychology today.

Psychologists at Work

What are some specialists in psychology, and in what settings are they employed?

Psychologists have many different orientations toward the practice of psychology. Some psychologists teach at colleges and universities; others have private clinical practices and counsel patients. Psychologists work in hospitals and other medical facilities, in elementary and secondary schools, and in business and industry. Wherever you find human activity, you are very like to encounter psychologists.

There are many specialties within the field of psychology. A few of them are briefly described here.

Clinical psychologists specialize in the diagnosis and treatment of mental and behavioral disorders. Some clinical psychologists also conduct research in these areas. Most clinical psychologists work in clinics, hospitals, and private practice, and many hold professorships at colleges and universities.

sociocultural perspective: A perspective that emphasizes social and cultural influences on human behavior and stresses the importance of understanding those influences when interpreting the behavior of others.

Psychologists work in a wide range of settings.

Counseling psychologists help people who have adjustment problems (marital, social, or behavioral) that are less severe than those generally handled by clinical psychologists. Counseling psychologists may also provide academic or vocational counseling. *Counselors* usually work in a nonmedical setting such as a school or university, or they may have a private practice. Some 55% of all psychologists in the United States may be classified as either clinical or counseling psychologists.

Physiological psychologists, also called neuropsychologists, study the relationship between physiological processes and behavior. They study the structure and function of the brain and central nervous system, the role of the neurotransmitters and hormones, and other aspects of body chemistry to determine how physical and chemical processes affect behavior in both people and animals.

Experimental psychologists specialize in the use of experimental research methods. They conduct experiments in most fields of specialization in psychology—learning, memory, sensation, perception, motivation, emotion, and other areas. Some experimental psychologists study the brain and nervous system and how they affect behavior; their work overlaps with that of physiological psychologists. Experimental psychologists usually work in a laboratory, where they can exert precise control over the humans or animals being studied. Many experimental psychologists are faculty members who teach and conduct their research in college or university laboratories. In most of these psychology laboratories, however, the array of laboratory fixtures of the past, such as specimen jars, "have been replaced largely by a single instrument, the computer" (Benjamin, 2000, p. 321).

Developmental psychologists study how people grow, develop, and change throughout the life span. Some developmental psychologists specialize in a particular age group, such as infancy, childhood (child psychologists), adolescence, or old age (gerontologists). Others may concentrate on a specific aspect of human development such as physical, language, cognitive, or moral development.

Educational psychologists specialize in the study of teaching and learning. They may help train teachers and other educational professionals or conduct research in teaching

Figure 1.4

What Psychologists Do

Clinical psychologists make up the largest percentage of members of the American Psychological Association who work in the field of psychology. (Data provided by the APA, 1995.)

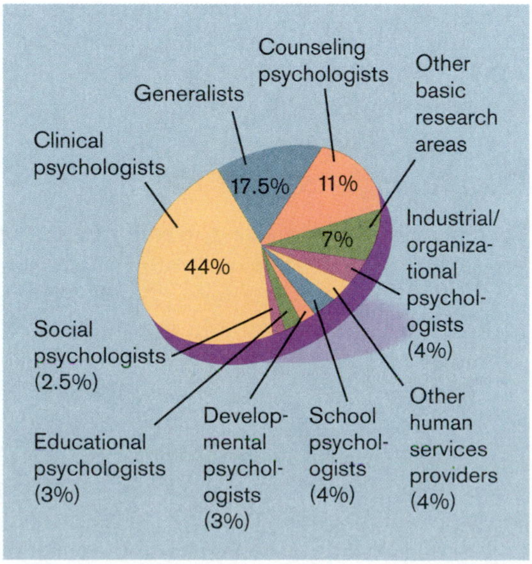

and classroom behavior. Some help prepare school curricula, develop achievement tests, or conduct evaluations of teaching and learning.

While most other psychologists are concerned with what makes the individual function, *social psychologists* investigate how the individual feels, thinks, and behaves in a social setting—in the presence of others.

Industry and business have found that expertise in psychology pays off in the workplace. *Industrial/organizational (I/O) psychologists* study the relationships between people and their work environments.

Figure 1.4 shows the percentages of psychologists who work in the specialties discussed in this section. As you can see, psychology is an enormously broad and diverse field of study.

Remember It!

Match the psychological perspective with its major emphasis.

___ (1) the role of biological processes and heredity
___ (2) the role of learning and environmental factors
___ (3) the role of mental processes
___ (4) the role of the unconscious and early childhood experiences
___ (5) the importance of the individual's own subjective experience
___ (6) the role of social and cultural influences
___ (7) the role of inherited tendencies that have proved adaptive in humans

a. psychoanalytic
b. biological
c. behavioral
d. cognitive
e. humanistic
f. evolutionary
g. sociocultural

Answers: (1) b (2) c (3) d (4) a (5) e (6) g (7) f

Apply It!

Study Skills and Critical Thinking

Studying–where, when, and how. Many years of research on memory have revealed a number of techniques you can use to help yourself study more efficiently and retain more of what you learn. More techniques will be presented in Chapter 6, but these will get you started.

- Establish a quiet place, free of distractions, where you do nothing else but study. You can condition yourself to associate this environment with studying, so that entering the room or area will be your cue to begin work. Moreover, you will be less tempted to do other things while you are there. Turn off the television, radio, or stereo, and let an answering machine take your calls.
- Schedule your study time. Research on memory has proven that spaced learning is more effective than massed practice (cramming). Instead of studying for 5 hours straight, try five study sessions of 1 hour each.
- Consider what your assignments are for the next several weeks. In order to be prepared for each class meeting, set yourself specific goals each week and for individual study sessions. Your goals should be challenging but not overwhelming. If the task for an individual study session is doable, it will be easier to sit down and face it. And completing the task that you have set for yourself will give you a sense of accomplishment.
- The more active a role you play in the learning process, the more you will

remember. Spend some of your study time *reciting* rather than *rereading* the material. One effective method is to use index cards as flash cards. Write a key term on the front of each card. On the back, list information from the text and lectures pertaining to that term. You should also have an index card for each study question, with the answer on the back of the card. Use these cards to help you prepare for tests. Test yourself before your professor does.

- *Overlearning* means studying beyond the point at which you can just barely recite the information you are trying to memorize. For best results, don't stop studying at this point. Review the information again and again until it is firmly locked in memory. If you are subject to test anxiety, overlearning will help. Overlearned information is more likely to survive an attack of nerves.
- Forgetting takes place most rapidly within the first 24 hours after you study. No matter how much you have studied for a test, *always* review shortly before you take it. Refreshing your memory will raise your grade.
- Sleeping immediately after you study will help you retain more of what you have learned. If you can't study before you go to sleep, at least review what you studied earlier in the day. This is a good time to go through your index cards. (When you read Chapter 6, you will learn why sleep facilitates memory and why following the other suggestions will help you remember more of what you study.)

Being a good consumer of psychological research. If you were thinking of buying a car, you probably wouldn't look in a junkyard or take the first car you saw. Similarly, when studying psychology, you must be a wise consumer in order to get accurate information–to become a critical thinker.

Some publications are more scientifically respectable than others–*Science News* and *Psychology Today* are more credible than *The National Enquirer* and *Cosmopolitan.* Science writers have more experience reading and understanding research and usually give more accurate reports of research results than general reporters do. Science writers tend to write more objectively than nonscience writers and are less likely to suggest that researchers' findings are the last word on the subject. General reporters, on the other hand, are more likely to make sweeping statements and extreme claims: "The most important study of our time," "Amazing new cure," "Dramatic results show . . . ."

James Bell (1991) suggests that to evaluate information you must be able to answer three key questions: "Who says so? What do they say? How do they know?" (p. 36). To critically evaluate research, you need to know who conducted the study and the methodology used. You need a description of the participants–their number, how they were selected, whether they were human or animal, and, if they were human, their age, gender, and other characteristics that are relevant to evaluating the researchers' conclusions.

Critical thinkers are those who determine whether the methodology used by the researchers would enable them to reach their conclusions, whether those conclusions are logical, whether they are supported by the data, and whether there are alternative explanations for the findings.

Critical thinkers carefully consider the biases of writers and researchers. Do they have "axes to grind"? Are they presenting information that can be confirmed as factual or merely expressing their own opinions?

Critical thinkers understand that testimonials and accounts of personal experience are no substitute for scientific evidence. Don't be convinced by testimonials ("I've used this headache remedy for years, and it has always worked for me") or anecdotal accounts ("My Uncle Joe lived to be 95, and he smoked three packs of cigarettes a day").

Finally, critical thinkers do not accept the results of one study as definitive evidence. They want to know whether the research has been replicated and what other studies have been published on the subject. As a critical thinker, you would not modify your life based on one study you read. "One study does not a finding make" (Weeks, quoted in Schmitz, 1991, p. 44).

THINKING CRITICALLY

Evaluation

Consider three major forces in psychology: behaviorism, psychoanalysis, and humanistic psychology. Which appeals to you most and which least, and why?

Point/Counterpoint

This chapter discussed deception in research and described a study that used deception to examine the effects of alcohol and expectations on aggression. Prepare convincing arguments to support each of these opinions:

a. Deception is justified in research studies.
b. Deception is not justified in research studies.

Psychology in Your Life

In this chapter you've learned something about experimental research and survey research. How can you use this new knowledge to evaluate research results you may read or hear about?

SUMMARY AND REVIEW

PSYCHOLOGY: AN INTRODUCTION

What is the scientific method?

The scientific method consists of the orderly, systematic procedures researchers follow as they identify a research problem, design a study to investigate the problem, collect and analyze data, draw conclusions, and communicate their findings.

What are the four goals of psychology?

The four goals of psychology are the description, explanation, prediction, and control of behavior and mental processes.

Key Terms
psychology (p. 5); scientific method (p. 5); theory (p. 5); basic research (p. 6); applied research (p. 6); critical thinking (p. 7)

DESCRIPTIVE RESEARCH METHODS

What are naturalistic and laboratory observation, and what are some of their advantages and limitations?

In naturalistic observation, researchers observe and record the behavior of subjects in a natural setting without attempting to influence or control it. Limitations include the researcher's lack of control over the observed situation, and the potential for observer bias. In laboratory observation, researchers exert more control.

What is the case study method, and for what purposes is it particularly well suited?

The case study is an in-depth study of one or several individuals through observation, interview, and sometimes psychological testing. It is particularly appropriate for studying people with rare psychological or physiological disorders.

What are the methods and purposes of survey research?

In survey research, investigators use interviews and/or questionnaires to gather information about the attitudes, beliefs, experiences, or behaviors of a group of people.

What is a representative sample, and why is it essential in a survey?

A representative sample is a sample of participants selected from the population of interest in such a way that important subgroups within the whole population are included in the same proportions in the sample. A sample must be representative for the findings to be applied to the larger population.

Key Terms
descriptive research methods (p. 7); naturalistic observation (p. 7); laboratory observation (p. 8); case study (p. 8); survey (p. 8); population (p. 9); sample (p. 9); representative sample (p. 9)

THE EXPERIMENTAL METHOD: SEARCHING FOR CAUSES

What is the main advantage of the experimental method?

The experimental method is the only research method that can be used to identify cause–effect relationships.

What is the difference between the independent variable and the dependent variable?

In an experiment an independent variable is a condition or factor manipulated by the researcher to determine its effect on the dependent variable. The dependent variable, measured at the end of the experiment, is presumed to vary as a result of the manipulations of the independent variable.

How do the experimental and control groups differ?

The experimental group is exposed to the independent variable. The control group is similar to the experimental group and is exposed to the same experimental environment but is not exposed to the independent variable.

What is selection bias, and what technique do researchers use to control for it?

Selection bias occurs when there are systematic differences among the groups before the experiment begins. Random assignment maximizes the probability that groups are similar at the beginning of the experiment.

What is the placebo effect, and how do researchers control for it?

The placebo effect occurs when a person's expectations influence the outcome of a treatment or experiment. To control for the placebo effect, the researcher must ensure that participants do not know if they are members of the experimental group (receiving the treatment) or of the control group (receiving the placebo).

What is experimenter bias, and how is it controlled?

Experimenter bias occurs when the researcher's expectations affect the outcome of the experiment. It is controlled by using the double-blind technique, in which neither the experimenter nor the participants know who is in the experimental group and who is in the control group.

Key Terms
experimental method (p. 11); hypothesis (p. 11); independent variable (p. 12); dependent variable (p. 12); experimental group (p. 12); control group (p. 13); confounding variables (p. 13); selection bias (p. 13); random assignment (p. 13); placebo effect (p. 14); placebo (p. 14); experimenter bias (p. 14); double-blind technique (p. 15)

OTHER RESEARCH METHODS

What is the correlational method, and when is it used?

The correlational method is a research method that determines the correlation, or degree of relationship, between two variables. It is often used when it is either impossible or unethical to conduct an experimental study.

What is a correlation coefficient?

A correlation coefficient is a numerical value that indicates the strength and direction of the relationship between two variables.

What is meta-analysis?

Meta-analysis is a complex statistical procedure researchers use to combine the results from many research studies on a particular topic in order to determine the degree to which a specific hypothesis can be supported.

Key Terms
correlational method (p. 16); correlation coefficient (p. 16); replication (p. 17); meta-analysis (p. 17)

HUMAN PARTICIPANTS IN PSYCHOLOGICAL RESEARCH: THE CHALLENGE OF DIVERSITY

What are some ethical guidelines governing the use of human participants in research?

Participation must be strictly voluntary. Participants must give informed consent, must be free to withdraw from the study at any time, and must be debriefed as soon as possible after they participate.

Why are animals used in research?

Animals provide a simpler model for studying similar processes in humans, researchers can exercise more control over animals and use a wider range of medical and other manipulations, it is easier to study the entire life span and even several generations in some species, and animals are readily available and more economical to study.

EXPLORING PSYCHOLOGY'S ROOTS

What was Wundt's contribution to psychology?

Wundt, considered the father of psychology, established the first psychological laboratory in 1879 and launched the study of psychology as a formal academic discipline.

What were the goals and method of structuralism, the first school of psychology?

Structuralism's main goal was to analyze the basic elements or structure of conscious mental experience through the use of introspection.

What was the goal of the early school of psychology known as functionalism?

Functionalism was concerned with how mental processes help humans and animals adapt to their environment.

What is the emphasis of Gestalt psychology?

Gestalt psychology emphasizes that individuals perceive objects and patterns as whole units and that the perceived whole is more than the sum of its parts.

How did behaviorism differ from previous schools of psychology?

Behaviorism, the school of psychology founded by John B. Watson, views observable, measurable behavior as the only appropriate subject matter for psychology. Behaviorism also emphasizes the environment as the key determinant of behavior.

What is the role of the unconscious in psychoanalysis, Freud's approach to psychology?

According to Freud's theory of psychoanalysis, an individual's thoughts, feelings, and behavior are determined primarily by the unconscious—the part of the mind that one cannot see and cannot control.

What is the focus of humanistic psychology?

Humanistic psychology focuses on the uniqueness of human beings and their capacity for choice, growth, and psychological health.

What is the focus of cognitive psychology?

Cognitive psychology is a specialty that focuses on mental processes such as memory, problem solving, concept formation, reasoning and decision making, language, and perception.

What is the focus of evolutionary psychology?

Evolutionary psychology focuses on how humans have adapted the behaviors necessary for survival in the face of environmental pressures over the course of evolution. This perspective looks at inherited human tendencies and dispositions.

Key Terms
structuralism (p. 23); functionalism (p. 23); Gestalt psychology (p. 24); behaviorism (p. 24); psychoanalysis (p. 25); humanistic psychology (p. 25); cognitive psychology (p. 26); evolutionary psychology (p. 27)

PSYCHOLOGY TODAY

What are seven major perspectives in psychology today?

Seven major perspectives in psychology today are (1) the biological perspective, which emphasizes the role of biological processes and heredity as the keys to understanding behavior and thought; (2) the psychoanalytic perspective, which focuses on the role of the unconscious and early childhood experiences; (3) the behavioral perspective, which emphasizes learning and the role of environmental factors in shaping behavior; (4) the cognitive perspective, which stresses the role of the mental processes (perceiving, thinking, remembering, etc.); (5) the humanistic perspective, which emphasizes the importance of an individual's subjective experience; (6) the evolutionary perspective, which looks at the inherited tendencies that have proved adaptive in humans; and (7) the sociocultural perspective, which emphasizes the role of social and cultural influences on behavior.

What are some specialists in psychology, and in what settings are they employed?

There are clinical and counseling psychologists, physiological psychologists, experimental psychologists, developmental psychologists, educational and school psychologists, social psychologists, and industrial/organizational psychologists. Psychologists are found in many different settings—colleges and universities, elementary and secondary schools, medical settings, business and industry, and private practice.

Key Terms
biological perspective (p. 32); neuroscience (p. 32); psychoanalytic perspective (p. 32); behavioral perspective (p. 32); cognitive perspective (p. 32); humanistic perspective (p. 32); evolutionary perspective (p. 32); sociocultural perspective (p. 33)

Surf It!

Want to be sure you've absorbed the material in Chapter 1, "Introduction to Psychology," before the big test? Visiting *www.abacon.com/wood* can put a top grade within your reach. The site is loaded with free practice tests, flashcards, activities, and links to help you review your way to an A. To enliven that inevitable study break, the site also offers personality assessment quizzes and a psychology career corner.

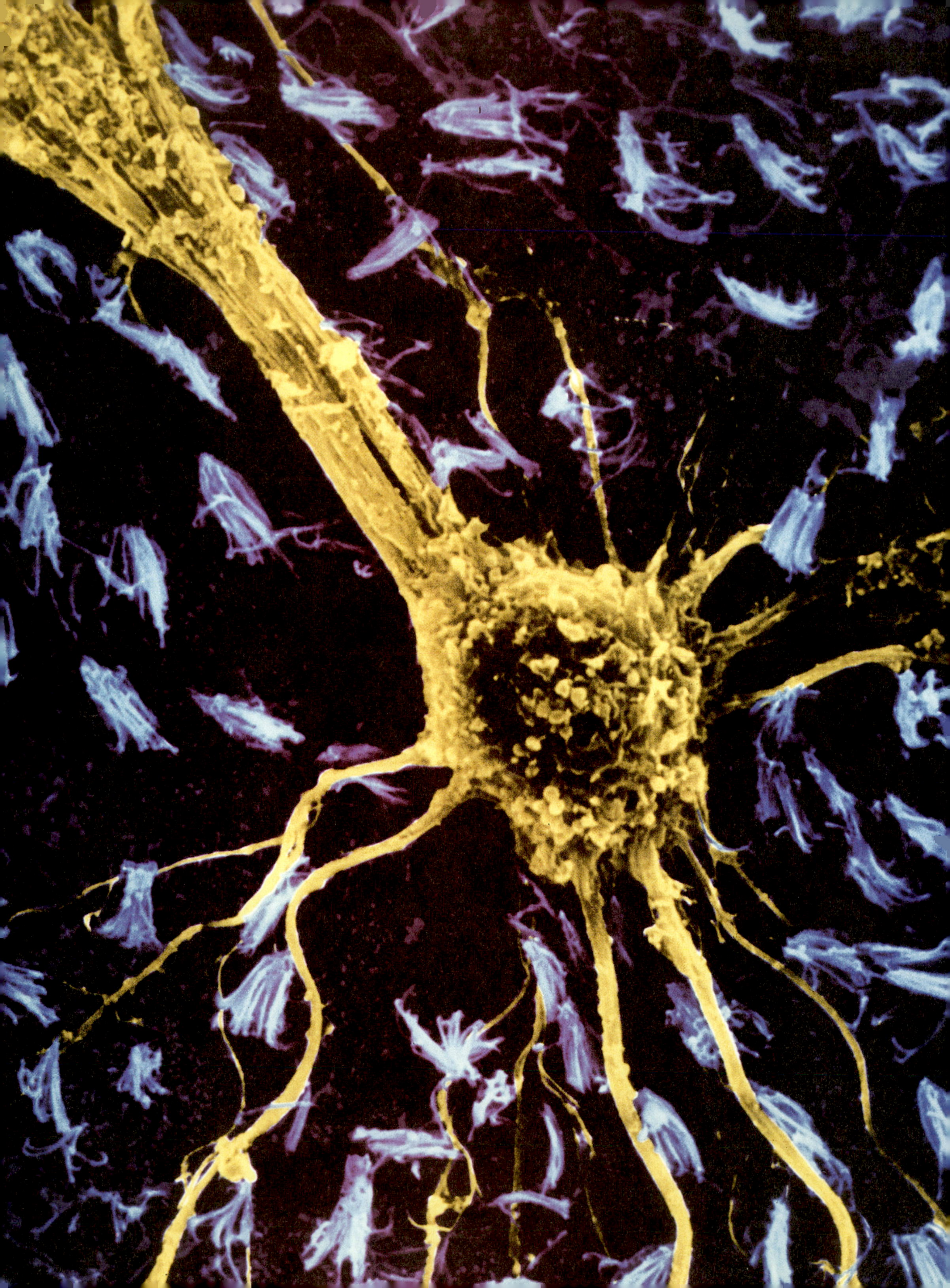

2 Biology and Behavior

On September 13, 1848, Phineas Gage, a 25-year-old foreman on a railroad construction crew, was using dynamite to blast away rock and dirt. Suddenly an unplanned explosion almost took Gage's head off, sending a 3½-foot-long, 13-pound metal rod under his left cheekbone and out through the top of his skull.

Much of the brain tissue in Gage's frontal lobe was torn away, along with flesh, pieces of his skull, and other bone fragments. This should have been the end of Phineas Gage, but it wasn't. He regained consciousness within a few minutes and was loaded onto a cart and wheeled to his hotel nearly a mile away. He got out with a little help, walked up the stairs, entered his room, and walked to his bed. He was still conscious when the doctor arrived nearly 2 hours later.

Gage recovered in about 5 weeks, but he was not the same man. Before the accident, he was described as a hard worker who was polite, dependable, and well liked. But the new Phineas Gage, without part of his frontal lobe, was found to be loud-mouthed and profane, rude and impulsive, and contemptuous toward others. He no longer planned realistically for the future and was no longer motivated and industrious, as he once had been. Gage lost his job as foreman and joined P. T. Barnum's circus as a sideshow exhibit at carnivals and county fairs. (Adapted from Harlow, 1848.)

Well over a century and a half has passed since the heavy metal rod tore through Phineas Gage's brain. During that time, much has been learned about the human brain—some of it puzzling and mysterious, all of it fascinating. How can the brain sustain such massive damage as in the case of Gage, who survived, while a small bullet fired through the brain in any one of a number of different places can result in instant death? In this chapter, you will learn how this remarkable 3-pound organ can be so tough and resilient and, at the same time, so fragile and vulnerable.

Chapter 1, the introduction to *The World of Psychology,* defined *psychology* as the scientific study of behavior and mental processes. Before you can gain an understanding and an appreciation of human behavior and mental processes, we must first explore the all-important biological connection. Every thought you think, every emotion you feel, every sensation you experience, every decision you reach, every move you make—in short, all of human behavior—is rooted in a biological event. Therefore, in this chapter, we study biology and behavior. The story begins where the action begins, in the smallest functional unit of the brain—the nerve cell, or neuron.

THE NEURONS AND THE NEUROTRANSMITTERS

The Neurons: The Nervous System's Messenger Cells

What is a neuron, and what are its three parts?

All our thoughts, feelings, and behavior can ultimately be traced to the activity of **neurons**—the specialized cells that conduct impulses through the nervous system. Most experts estimate that there may be as many as 100 billion neurons in the brain (Swanson, 1995). This would mean that you have about 17 times as many neurons as there are people living on the earth right now.

Neurons perform several important tasks: (1) Afferent (sensory) neurons relay messages from the sense organs and receptors—eyes, ears, nose, mouth, and skin—to the brain or spinal cord. (2) Efferent (motor) neurons convey signals from the brain and spinal cord to the glands and the muscles, enabling the body to move. (3) Interneurons, thousands of times more numerous than motor or sensory neurons, carry information between neurons in the brain and between neurons in the spinal cord.

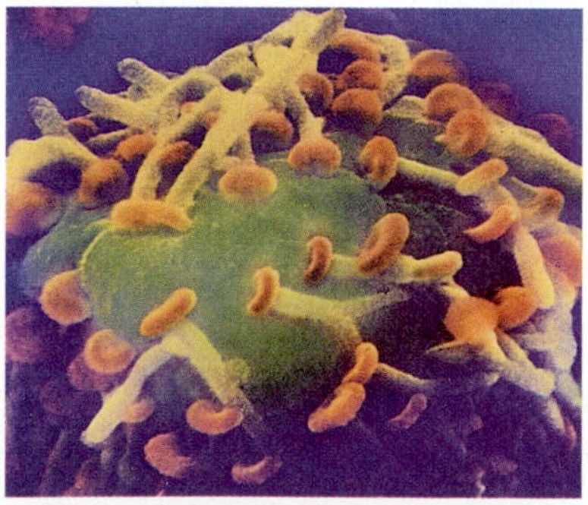

This scanning electron micrograph shows numerous axon terminals (the orange, button-shaped structures) that could synapse with the cell body of the neuron (shown in green).

Anatomy of a Neuron: Looking at Its Parts Although no two neurons are exactly alike, nearly all are made up of three important parts: the cell body (soma), dendrites, and the axon. The **cell body** contains the nucleus and carries out the metabolic, or life-sustaining, functions of the neuron. Branching out from the cell body are the **dendrites,** which look much like the leafless branches of a tree (*dendrite* comes from the Greek word for "tree"). The dendrites are the primary receivers of signals from other neurons, but the cell body can also receive signals directly. And dendrites do not merely receive signals from other neurons and relay them to the cell body. Scientists now know that dendrites relay messages backward—from the cell body to their own branches (a process called *back propagating*). These backward messages may shape the dendrites' responses to future signals they receive (Magee & Johnston, 1997; Sejnowski, 1997).

The **axon** is the slender, tail-like extension of the neuron that sprouts into many branches, each ending in a bulbous axon terminal. The axon terminals transmit signals to the dendrites or cell bodies of other neurons, and to muscles, glands, and other parts of the body. In humans, some axons are short—only thousandths of an inch. Others can be up to a meter long—39.37 inches—long enough to reach from the brain to the tip of the spinal cord, or from the spinal cord to remote parts of the body. Figure 2.1 shows a neuron's structure.

What is a synapse?

The Synapse Remarkably, the billions of neurons that send and receive signals are not physically connected. The axon terminals are separated from the receiving

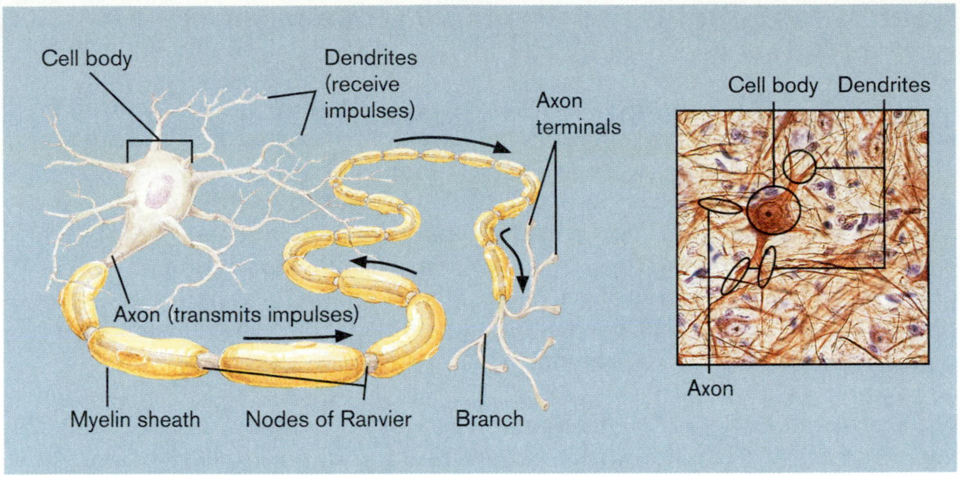

Figure 2.1

The Structure of a Typical Neuron

A typical neuron has three important parts: (1) a cell body, which carries out the metabolic functions of the neuron; (2) branched fibers called dendrites, which are the primary receivers of the impulses from other neurons; and (3) a slender, tail-like extension called an axon, the transmitting end of the neuron, which sprouts into many branches, each ending in an axon terminal. The photograph shows human neurons greatly magnified.

neurons by tiny, fluid-filled gaps called *synaptic clefts*. The **synapse** is the junction where the axon terminal of a sending (presynaptic) neuron communicates with a receiving (postsynaptic) neuron across the synaptic cleft. There may be as many as 100 trillion synapses in the human nervous system (Swanson, 1995). And a single neuron may synapse with thousands of other neurons (Kelner, 1997). A technique that has recently been developed to monitor the action at the synapses may soon enable researchers to visualize the activity of all the synapses of a single neuron.

If neurons are not physically connected, how do they communicate? How do they send and receive their messages?

The Neural Impulse: The Beginning of Thought and Action Researchers have known for some 200 years that cells in the brain, the spinal cord, and the muscles generate electrical potentials. These tiny electric charges play a part in all bodily functions. Every time you move a muscle, experience a sensation, or have a thought or a feeling, a small but measurable electrical impulse is present.

How does this biological electricity work? Even though the impulse that travels down the axon is electrical, the axon does not transmit it the way a wire conducts an electrical current. What actually moves through the axon is a change in the **permeability** of the cell membrane. This process allows ions (electrically charged atoms or molecules) to move into and out of the axon through ion channels in the membrane.

Body fluids contain ions, some with positive electrical charges and others with negative charges. Inside the axon, there are normally more negative than positive ions. When at rest (not firing), the axon membrane carries a negative electrical potential of about −70 millivolts (70 thousandths of a volt) relative to the fluid outside the cell. This slight negative charge is referred to as the neuron's **resting potential.**

When the excitatory effects on a neuron reach a certain threshold, ion channels begin to open in the cell membrane of the axon at the point closest to the cell body, allowing positive ions to flow into the axon. This inflow of positive ions causes the membrane potential to change abruptly, to a positive value of about +50 millivolts (Pinel, 2000). This sudden reversal of the resting potential, which lasts for about 1 millisecond (1 thousandth of a second), is the **action potential.** Then the ion channels admitting positive ions close, and other ion channels open, forcing some positive ions out of the axon. As a result, the original negative charge, or resting potential, is restored. The opening and closing of ion channels continues segment by segment down the length of the axon, causing the action potential to move along the axon (Cardoso & Sabbatini, 2000).

The action potential operates according to the "all or none" law—a neuron either fires completely or does not fire at all. Immediately after a neuron fires, it enters a *refractory period,* during which it cannot fire again for 1 to 2 milliseconds. But this rest period is often very short: When stimulated, neurons can fire up to 1,000 times per second.

What is the action potential?

neuron (NEW-ron): A specialized cell that conducts impulses through the nervous system and contains three major parts—a cell body, dendrites, and an axon.

cell body: The part of the neuron that contains the nucleus and carries out the neuron's metabolic functions.

dendrites (DEN-drytes): The branch-like extensions of a neuron that receive signals from other neurons.

axon (AK-sahn): The slender, tail-like extension of the neuron that transmits signals to the dendrites or cell body of other neurons or to muscles or glands.

synapse (SIN-aps): The junction where the axon of a sending neuron communicates with a receiving neuron across the synaptic cleft.

permeability (perm-ee-uh-BIL-uh-tee): The capability of being penetrated or passed through.

resting potential: The membrane potential of a neuron at rest, about −70 millivolts.

action potential: The sudden reversal of the resting potential, which initiates the firing of a neuron.

Neurotransmitters: The Chemical Messengers of the Brain

What are neurotransmitters, and what role do they play in the transmission of signals from one neuron to another?

Once a neuron fires, how does it get its message across the synaptic cleft and on to other neurons? Messages are transmitted between neurons by one or more of a large group of chemical substances known as **neurotransmitters.**

Where are the neurotransmitters located? Inside the axon terminal are many small, sphere-shaped containers with thin membranes called *synaptic vesicles*, which hold the neurotransmitters. (*Vesicle* comes from a Latin word meaning "little bladder.") When an action potential arrives at the axon terminal, synaptic vesicles move toward the cell membrane, fuse with it, and release their neurotransmitter molecules. This process is shown in Figure 2.2.

The Receptor: Locks for Neurotransmitter Keys Once released, neurotransmitters do not simply flow into the synaptic cleft and stimulate all the adjacent neurons. Each neurotransmitter has a distinctive molecular shape, and **receptors** on the surfaces of dendrites and cell bodies also have distinctive shapes. Neurotransmitters can affect only those neurons that have receptors designed to receive molecules of their particular shape. In other words, each receptor is somewhat like a locked door that only certain neurotransmitter keys can unlock (Cardoso & Sabbatini, 2000; Restak, 1993).

However, the binding of neurotransmitters with receptors is not as fixed and rigid a process as keys fitting locks or jigsaw puzzle pieces interlocking. Receptors in the brain are living matter; they can expand and contract their enclosed volumes.

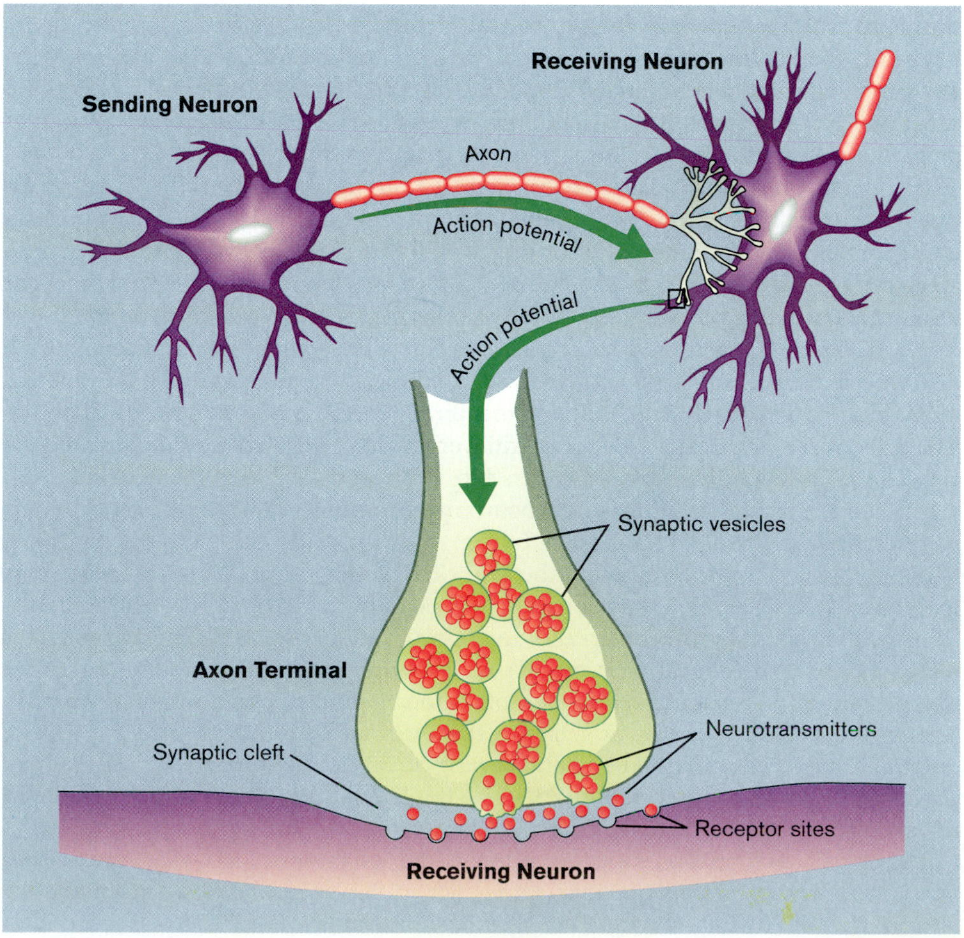

Figure 2.2
Synaptic Transmission

Sending neurons transmit their messages to receiving neurons by electrochemical action. When a neuron fires, the action potential arrives at the axon terminal and triggers the release of neurotransmitters from the synaptic vesicles. Neurotransmitters flow into the synaptic cleft and move toward the receiving neuron, which has numerous receptors. The receptors will bind only with neurotransmitters having distinctive molecular shapes that match their enclosed volumes. Neurotransmitters influence the receiving neuron only to fire or not to fire.

Consequently, the interaction where the neurotransmitter and the receptor meet is controlled not by the direct influence of one on the other, but by their *mutual* influence on each other. In such a dynamic interplay, a certain neurotransmitter may be competing for the same receptor with another neurotransmitter of a slightly different shape. The receptor will admit only one of the competing neurotransmitters—the one that fits it most perfectly. Thus, a receptor may receive a neurotransmitter at one time, but not at other times if another neurotransmitter molecule is present whose "affinity with the receptor is even stronger. As in dating and mating, what is finally settled for is always a function of what is available" (Restak, 1993, p. 28).

neurotransmitter (NEW-ro-TRANS-mit-er): A chemical that is released into the synaptic cleft from the axon terminal of a sending neuron, crosses a synapse, and binds to appropriate receptor sites on the dendrites or cell body of a receiving neuron, influencing the cell either to fire or not to fire.

receptors: Protein molecules on the dendrite or cell body of a neuron that will interact only with specific neurotransmitters.

reuptake: The process by which neurotransmitter molecules are taken from the synaptic cleft back into the axon terminal for later use, thus terminating their excitatory or inhibitory effect on the receiving neuron.

The Action of Neurotransmitters When neurotransmitters bind with receptors on the dendrites or cell bodies of receiving neurons, their action is either excitatory (influencing the neurons to fire) or inhibitory (influencing them not to fire). Because a single neuron may synapse with thousands of other neurons at the same time, there will always be both excitatory and inhibitory influences on receiving neurons. For the neuron to fire, the excitatory influences must exceed the inhibitory influences of neurotransmitter substances by a sufficient amount (the threshold).

For many years researchers believed that each individual neuron responded to only one neurotransmitter. But it is now known that individual neurons may respond to several different neurotransmitters, suggesting a greater flexibility of response, even at the level of a single neuron (Pinel, 2000).

You may wonder how the synaptic vesicles can continue to pour out neurotransmitters, yet have a ready supply so that the neuron can respond to continuing stimulation. First, the cell body of the neuron is always working to manufacture more of the neurotransmitter substance. Second, unused neurotransmitters in the synaptic cleft may be broken down into their component molecules and reclaimed by the axon terminal to be recycled and used again. Third, by an important process called **reuptake,** the neurotransmitter substance is taken back into the axon terminal, intact and ready for immediate use. This terminates the neurotransmitter's excitatory or inhibitory effect on the receiving neuron. Figure 2.3 illustrates the reuptake process.

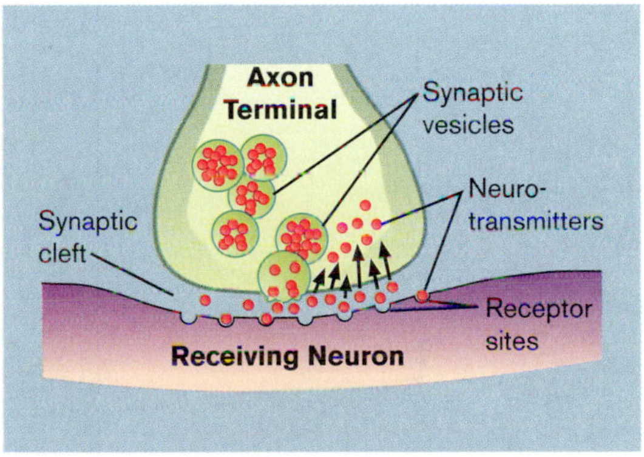

Figure 2.3

The Process of Reuptake

Through the process of reuptake, neurotransmitter molecules are taken back into the axon terminal, intact and ready for immediate use.

The nature of synaptic transmission—whether it is primarily chemical or electrical—was a subject of controversy during the first half of the 20th century. By the 1950s, it seemed clear that the means of communication between neurons was chemical. Yet, at some synapses, what was termed "gap junction," or electrical transmission, occurred between the neurons. Recent research has shown that this electrical transmission may be more frequent than neuroscientists once believed (Bennett, 2000). Even though synaptic transmission of information between neurons is primarily chemical, some electrical transmission is known to occur at synapses in the retina, the olfactory bulb (sense of smell), and the cerebral cortex, which we will discuss later in the chapter (Bennett, 2000).

The Effects of Drugs on Neural Transmission

In order for any drug to work, it must influence activity at the level of the cell. Like neurotransmitters, drugs are chemicals, and some of them fit specific receptors on the cell and mimic some of the effects of the neurotransmitter that would normally occupy those receptors. These chemicals are called *agonists.* Other drugs occupy receptors but do not mimic the effects of a neurotransmitter. Instead, they simply block the receptors so that the natural neurotransmitter is prevented from having its normal effect. These chemicals are called *antagonists.* Other drugs increase the effectiveness of neurotransmitters in the synapse by interfering with their reuptake or by slowing their breakdown in the synaptic cleft and reabsorption into the axon terminal.

The Variety of Neurotransmitters

What are some of the ways in which neurotransmitters affect behavior, and what are some of the major neurotransmitters?

Substances that act as neurotransmitters are manufactured in the brain, the spinal cord, the glands, and a few other parts of the body. Each kind of neurotransmitter affects the activity of the brain in a different way. Some neurotransmitters regulate the actions of glands and muscles; others affect learning and memory; still others promote sleep or stimulate mental and physical alertness. Some neurotransmitters orchestrate feelings and emotions, ranging from depression to euphoria, and others (endorphins) provide relief from pain.

Researchers have identified 75 or more chemical substances manufactured by the body that may act as neurotransmitters (Greden, 1994). Some neurotransmitters are always excitatory, and others are always inhibitory; however, some neurotransmitters can be either excitatory or inhibitory depending on the receptor with which they bind. Researchers long believed that an individual neuron could secrete only one neurotransmitter. But then it was demonstrated that some neurons secrete several different neurotransmitters (Changeux, 1993). Some neurons also release *neuromodulators*—chemical substances that can increase or decrease the effectiveness of the neurotransmitters' excitatory or inhibitory influences on the neurons.

Acetylcholine The neurotransmitter **acetylcholine** (ACh) exerts excitatory effects on the skeletal muscle fibers, causing them to contract so that the body can move. But it has an inhibitory effect on the muscle fibers in the heart. How can the same neurotransmitter excite some postsynaptic membranes and inhibit others? In such cases it is not the neurotransmitter itself that produces the effect, but the differing nature of the receptors on the postsynaptic (receiving) neuron that determines the effect.

Acetylcholine is involved in a variety of functions, including learning and memory, and in rapid eye movement (REM) sleep, during which dreaming occurs. Studies of acetylcholine and memory indicate that acetylcholine plays an excitatory role in stimulating the neurons involved in learning new information. At the same time, acetylcholine performs an inhibitory function in preventing "previously learned memories from interfering with the learning of new memories" (Hasselmo & Bower, 1993, p. 218). The severe memory loss of people suffering from Alzheimer's disease is associated with significantly reduced levels of acetylcholine in the brain.

The Monoamines An important class of neurotransmitters called *monoamines* includes four neurotransmitters—dopamine, norepinephrine (noradrenalin), epinephrine (adrenalin), and serotonin (Pinel, 2000).

Like acetylcholine, **dopamine** (DA) produces both excitatory and inhibitory effects and is involved in several functions, including learning, attention, movement, and reinforcement. A deficiency in dopamine is related to Parkinson's disease, a condition characterized by tremors and rigidity in the limbs. An oversensitivity to dopamine is thought to be related to some cases of schizophrenia, a severe psychotic disorder you will learn more about in Chapter 15. Some people with schizophrenia are helped by antipsychotic drugs, some of which are dopamine antagonists that reduce the effects of dopamine in the brain.

Norepinephrine (NE) has an effect on eating habits (it stimulates the intake of carbohydrates) and plays a major role in alertness and wakefulness.

Epinephrine affects the metabolism of glucose and causes the nutrient energy stored in muscles to be released during strenuous exercise. Epinephrine also acts as a neurotransmitter in the brain but plays a more minor role there than norepinephrine does.

Serotonin produces inhibitory effects at most of the receptors with which it interacts. It plays an important role in regulating mood, sleep, impulsivity, aggression, and appetite (Greden, 1994). A deficiency in serotonin has been associated with

acetylcholine (ah-SEET-ul-KOH-leen): A neurotransmitter that plays a role in learning, memory, and rapid eye movement (REM) sleep and causes the skeletal muscle fibers to contract.

dopamine (DOE-pah-meen): A neurotransmitter that plays a role in learning, attention, and movement; a deficiency of dopamine is associated with Parkinson's disease, and an oversensitivity to it is associated with some cases of schizophrenia.

norepinephrine (nor-EP-ih-NEF-rin): A neurotransmitter affecting eating and sleep; a deficiency of norepinephrine is associated with depression.

serotonin (ser-oh-TOE-nin): A neurotransmitter that plays an important role in regulating mood, sleep, aggression, and appetite; a serotonin deficiency is associated with anxiety, depression, and suicide.

such behaviors as suicide (Nordström et al., 1994) and impulsive violence (Sandou et al., 1994). Both serotonin and norepinephrine are related to positive moods, and a deficiency in them has been linked to depression. Some antidepressant drugs relieve the symptoms of depression by blocking the reuptake of serotonin or norepinephrine, thus increasing the neurotransmitter's availability in the synapses.

glil cell natural garbage disposal

Amino Acids Researchers believe that eight or more amino acids also serve as neurotransmitters. Two of particular importance are found more commonly than any other transmitter substances in the central nervous system. They are glutamate (glutamic acid) and GABA (gamma-aminobutyric acid). *Glutamate* is the primary excitatory neurotransmitter in the brain (Riedel, 1996). It may be released by about 40% of neurons and is active in areas of the brain involved in learning, thought, and emotions (Coyle & Draper, 1996).

GABA is the main inhibitory neurotransmitter in the brain (Miles, 1999). It is thought to facilitate the control of anxiety in humans. Tranquilizers, barbiturates, and alcohol appear to have a calming and relaxing effect because they bind with and stimulate one type of GABA receptor and thus increase GABA's anxiety-controlling effect. An abnormality in the neurons that secrete GABA is believed to be one of the causes of epilepsy, a serious neurological disorder in which neural activity can become so heightened that seizures result.

Because of the release of endorphins in their bodies, marathon runners often experience euphoric feelings known as runner's high.

Endorphins More than 25 years ago, Candace Pert and her fellow researchers (1974) demonstrated that a localized region of the brain contains neurons with receptors that respond to the opiates—drugs such as opium, morphine, and heroin. Later it was learned that the brain itself produces its own opiatelike substances, known as **endorphins.** Endorphins provide relief from pain or the stress of vigorous exercise and produce feelings of pleasure and well-being. "Runner's high" is attributed to the release of endorphins. (See Chapter 3 for more information on endorphins.)

When different types of opiate receptors are stimulated, different effects are produced. One effect is relief from pain. Another is stimulation of certain "pleasure centers" whose neurons are involved in reinforcement, or reward; this effect is important for learning, and it helps explain the addictive properties of opiates.

Review & Reflect 2.1 (on page 48) summarizes the major neurotransmitters and their functions.

The Rate of Neural Firing and the Speed of the Impulse

How can the brain tell the difference between a very strong and a very weak stimulus?

Consider this important question: If a neuron only fires or does not fire, how can we tell the difference between a very strong and a very weak stimulus? A jarring blow and a soft touch? A blinding light and a dim one? A shout and a whisper? The answer lies in the number of neurons firing at the same time and their rate of firing. A weak stimulus may cause relatively few neurons to fire, while a strong stimulus may trigger thousands of neurons to fire at the same time. Also, a weak stimulus may be signaled by neurons firing very slowly; a stronger stimulus may incite neurons to fire hundreds of times per second.

Once a neuron fires, how fast do you suppose impulses travel down the length of the axon? Impulses travel at speeds from about 1 meter per second to approximately 100 meters per second (about 224 miles per hour). The larger, longer axons—those that reach from the brain through the spinal cord, and from the spinal cord to remote parts of the body—send impulses at a faster speed than do neurons with smaller, shorter axons.

endorphins (en-DOOR-fins): Chemicals produced naturally by the brain that reduce pain and positively affect mood.

Review & Reflect 2.1 Major Neurotransmitters and Their Functions

Neurotransmitter	Functions
Acetylcholine (ACh)	Affects movement, learning, memory, REM sleep
Dopamine (DA)	Affects movement, attention, learning, reinforcement
Norepinephrine (NE)	Affects eating, alertness, wakefulness
Epinephrine	Affects metabolism of glucose, energy release during exercise
Serotonin	Affects mood, sleep, appetite, impulsivity, aggression
Glutamate	Neural excitation in the central nervous system
GABA	Neural inhibition in the central nervous system
Endorphins	Relief from pain, feelings of pleasure and well-being

The most important factor in speeding the impulse on its way is the **myelin sheath**—a white, fatty coating wrapped around some axons that acts as insulation. If you look again at Figure 2.1, you will see that the coating has numerous gaps, called *nodes of Ranvier.* These nodes cause the myelin sheath to look like links of sausage strung together. The electrical impulse is retriggered or regenerated at each node (or naked gap) on the axon. This regeneration speeds the impulse up to 100 times faster than impulses in axons without myelin sheaths.

Damage to the myelin sheath causes interruptions in the transmission of neural messages. In fact, the disease *multiple sclerosis* (MS) involves deterioration of the myelin sheath, resulting in loss of coordination, jerky movements, muscular weakness, and disturbances in speech.

myelin sheath (MY-uh-lin): The white, fatty coating wrapped around some axons that acts as insulation and enables impulses to travel much faster.

glial cells (GLEE-ul): Cells that help to make the brain more efficient by holding the neurons together, removing waste products such as dead neurons, making the myelin coating for the axons, and performing other manufacturing, nourishing, and cleanup tasks.

central nervous system (CNS): The brain and the spinal cord.

spinal cord: An extension of the brain, reaching from the base of the brain through the neck and spinal column, that transmits messages between the brain and the peripheral nervous system.

Glial Cells: The Neurons' Helper Cells

Glial cells are specialized cells in the brain and spinal cord that form the myelin sheath and perform many other important functions. *Glia* means "glue," and these cells hold the neurons together. Glial cells remove waste products such as dead neurons from the brain by engulfing and digesting them, and they handle other manufacturing, nourishing, and cleanup tasks. Glial cells serve another function when the brain is being formed and as it grows and develops. During this period of development, glial cells act as guides, taking the specialized neurons from where they are formed to where they will finally function (Zheng et al., 1996).

Glial cells are smaller than neurons but outnumber them about nine to one. And, remarkably, glial cells make up more than one-half the volume of the human brain. It is now known that glial cells interact with neurons in complex ways, and that they play a part in creating a more efficient brain (Abbott & Raff, 1991).

Remember It!

1. The branchlike extensions of neurons that act as the *primary* receivers of signals from other neurons are the
   a. dendrites. c. glia.
   b. axons. d. cell bodies.
2. The junction where the axon of a sending neuron communicates with a receiving neuron is called the
   a. reuptake site. c. synapse.
   b. receptor site. d. axon terminal.
3. When a neuron fires, neurotransmitters are released from the synaptic vesicles in the ______________ terminal into the synaptic cleft.
   a. dendrite c. receptor
   b. cell body's d. axon
4. The (resting, action) potential is the firing of a neuron that results when the charge within the neuron becomes more positive than the charge outside the cell membrane.
5. Receptor sites on the receiving neuron
   a. receive any available neurotransmitter molecules.
   b. receive only neurotransmitter molecules of specific shapes.
   c. can only be influenced by neurotransmitters from a single neuron.
   d. are located only on the dendrites.
6. Which of the following substances cross the synaptic cleft and enter receptor sites on the dendrites and cell bodies of receiving neurons?
   a. sodium ions c. neurotransmitters
   b. potassium ions d. synapse modulators
7. Endorphins, norepinephrine, dopamine, and serotonin are all examples of
   a. hormones. c. neuropeptides.
   b. neurotransmitters. d. neuromodulators.

Answers: 1. a 2. c 3. d 4. action 5. b 6. c 7. b

THE CENTRAL NERVOUS SYSTEM

We have discussed how neurons function individually and in groups through electrochemical action. But human functioning involves much more than the action of individual neurons. Collections of neurons, brain structures, and organ systems also play essential roles in the body. The nervous system is divided into two parts: (1) the **central nervous system (CNS),** which is composed of the brain and the spinal cord, and (2) the peripheral nervous system, which connects the central nervous system to all other parts of the body (see Figure 2.4 on page 50).

Now we will follow the spinal cord up through the brainstem and the other brain structures to the most distinctly human part of the brain—the cerebrum, with its incredible cortex. We will discuss the peripheral nervous system later in this chapter.

The Spinal Cord: An Extension of the Brain

Why is an intact spinal cord important to normal functioning?

The **spinal cord** can best be thought of as an extension of the brain. Like the brain, it has gray matter as well as white matter and is loaded with glial cells. A cylinder of neural tissue about the diameter of your little finger, the spinal cord reaches from the base of the brain, through the neck, and down the hollow center of the spinal column. The spinal cord is protected by bone and also by spinal fluid, which serves as a shock absorber. The spinal cord literally links the body with the brain. It transmits messages between the brain and the peripheral nervous system. Thus, sensory

Figure 2.4

Divisions of the Human Nervous System

The human nervous system is divided into two parts: (1) the central nervous system, consisting of the brain and the spinal cord, and (2) the peripheral nervous system.

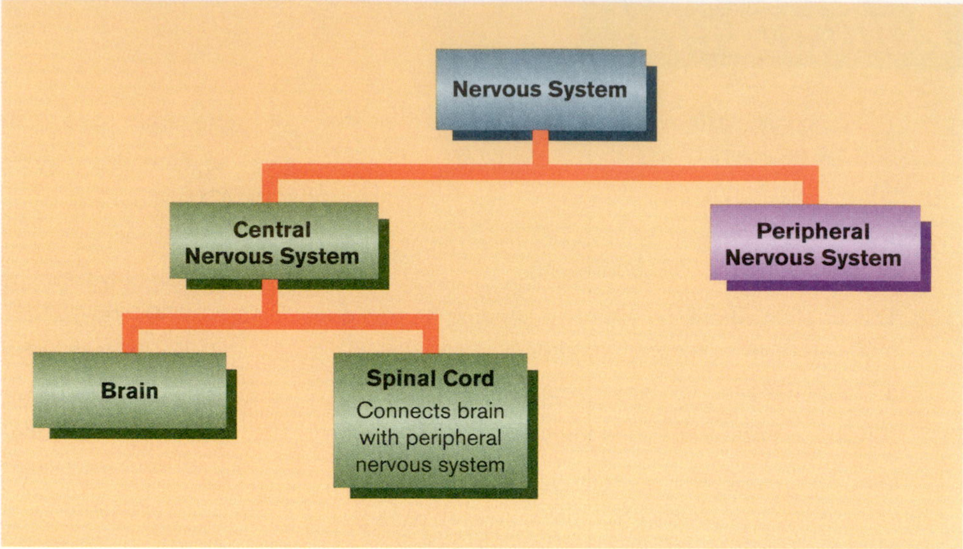

information can reach the brain, and messages from the brain can be sent to the muscles, the glands, and other parts of the body.

Although the spinal cord and the brain usually function together, the spinal cord can act without help from the brain to protect the body from injury. A simple withdrawal reflex triggered by a painful stimulus—from touching a hot stove burner, for example—involves three types of neurons. Sensory neurons in your fingers detect the painful stimulus and relay this information to interneurons in the spinal cord. These interneurons activate motor neurons that control the muscles in your arm, and you jerk your hand away. All this happens within a fraction of a second, without any involvement of the brain. The brain, however, quickly becomes aware and involved when the pain signal reaches it. At that point you might plunge your hand into cold water to relieve the pain.

The Brainstem: The Most Primitive Part of the Brain

What are the crucial functions handled by the brainstem?

The **brainstem** begins at the site where the spinal cord enlarges as it enters the skull. The brainstem includes the medulla, the pons, and the reticular formation, as shown in Figure 2.5. The brainstem handles functions that are so critical to physical survival that damage to it is life-threatening. The **medulla** is the part of the brainstem that controls heartbeat, breathing, blood pressure, coughing, and swallowing. Fortunately, the medulla handles these functions automatically, so you do not have to decide consciously to breathe or remember to keep your heart beating.

Extending through the central core of the brainstem into the pons is another important structure, the **reticular formation,** sometimes called the *reticular activating system* (RAS). Find it in Figure 2.5. The reticular formation plays a crucial role in arousal and attention (Kinomura et al., 1996; Steriade, 1996). Every day our sense organs are bombarded with stimuli, but we cannot possibly pay attention to everything we see or hear. The reticular formation screens messages entering the brain. It blocks some messages and sends others on to higher brain centers for processing.

The reticular formation also determines how alert we are. When it slows down, we doze off or go to sleep. But like an alarm clock, it also can jolt us into consciousness. Thanks to the reticular formation, important messages get through even when we are asleep. That is why parents may be able to sleep through a thunderstorm but will awaken to the slightest cry of their baby. (The next time you sleep through your alarm and are late for class, blame it on your reticular formation.)

brainstem: The structure that begins at the point where the spinal cord enlarges as it enters the brain and that includes the medulla, the pons, and the reticular formation.

medulla (muh-DUL-uh): The part of the brainstem that controls heartbeat, blood pressure, breathing, coughing, and swallowing.

reticular formation: A structure in the brainstem that plays a crucial role in arousal and attention and that screens sensory messages entering the brain.

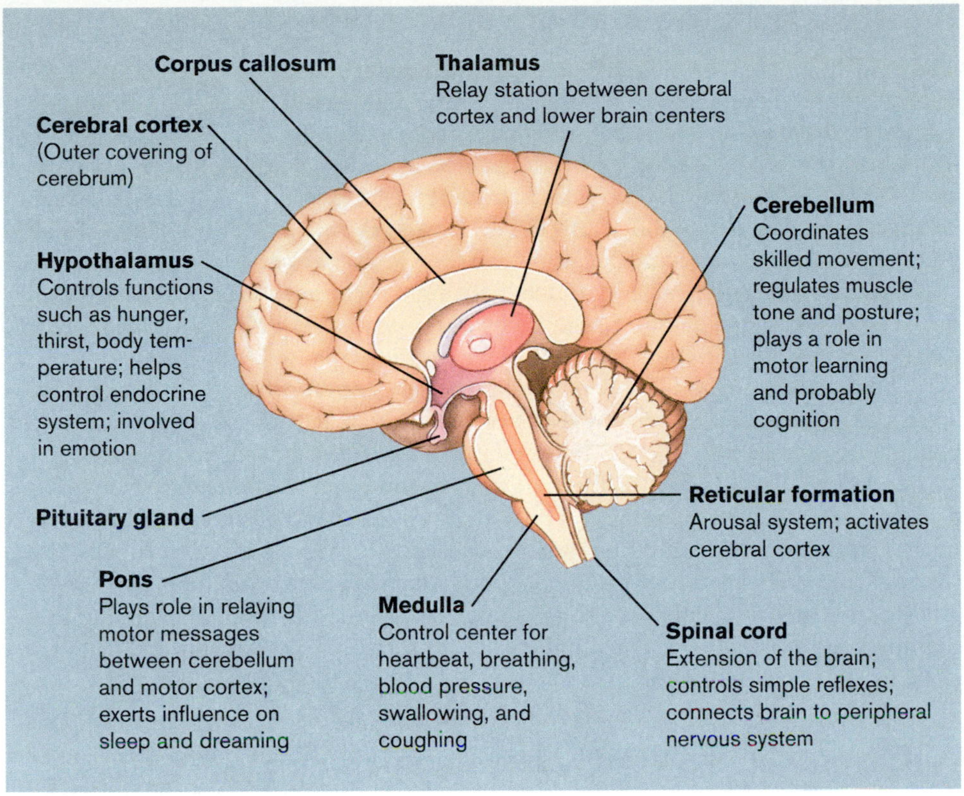

Figure 2.5

Major Structures of the Human Brain

Some of the major structures of the brain are shown in the drawing, and a brief description of the function of each is provided. The brain stem contains the medulla, the reticular formation, and the pons.

brain - 4 lobes
how ones memory is formed

Above the medulla and at the top of the brainstem is a bridgelike structure called the *pons* that extends across the top front of the brainstem and connects to both halves of the cerebellum. The pons plays a role in body movement and even exerts an influence on sleep and dreaming.

The Cerebellum: A Must for Graceful Movement

What are the primary functions of the cerebellum?

The **cerebellum** makes up about 10% of the brain's volume and, with its two hemispheres, resembles the larger cerebrum that lies above it (Swanson, 1995). Look again at Figure 2.5. The cerebellum is critically important to the body's ability to execute smooth, skilled movements; it also regulates muscle tone and posture. Furthermore, it has been found to play a role in motor learning and in retaining memories of motor activities (Lalonde & Botez, 1990). The cerebellum guides the graceful movements of the ballet dancer and the split-second timing of the skilled athlete. But more typically, it coordinates and orchestrates the series of movements necessary to perform many simple activities—such as walking in a straight line or touching your finger to the tip of your nose—without studied, conscious effort. For people who have damage to their cerebellum or who are temporarily impaired by too much alcohol, such simple acts may be difficult or impossible to perform.

Although some researchers remain skeptical, recent studies suggest that the cerebellum is involved in cognitive and social functions as well as motor functions (Fiez, 1996; Kim et al., 1994; Riva & Giorgi, 2000). The cerebellum may help to heighten our ability to focus attention on incoming sensory stimuli and to shift attention efficiently when conditions require (Allen et al., 1997). In addition, the cerebellum may increase our efficiency in acquiring sensory information and discriminating between sensory stimuli (Gao et al., 1996).

cerebellum (sehr-uh-BELL-um): The brain structure that executes smooth, skilled body movements and regulates muscle tone and posture.

The Thalamus: The Brain's Relay Station

What is the primary role of the thalamus?

Above the brainstem lie two extremely important structures—the thalamus and the hypothalamus (refer again to Figure 2.5). The **thalamus,** which consists of two egg-shaped structures, serves as the relay station for virtually all the information that flows into and out of the higher brain centers, including sensory information from all the senses except smell. (You'll learn more about the sense of smell in Chapter 3.) Incoming sensory information from the eyes, ears, skin, or taste buds travels first to parts of the thalamus or hypothalamus and then to the proper area of the cortex that handles vision, hearing, taste, or touch. Pain signals connect directly with the thalamus, which sends the pain message to the appropriate sensory areas of the cerebral cortex (Roland, 1992; Talbot et al., 1991).

The thalamus, or at least one small part of it, apparently affects our ability to learn new information, especially if it is verbal. This structure also plays a role in the production of language (Metter, 1991). Another function of the thalamus is the regulation of sleep cycles, which is thought to be accomplished in cooperation with the pons and the reticular formation. The synchronized firing of networks of neurons in one part of the thalamus has been observed during slow-wave (deep) sleep (Krosigk, 1993). The majority of people who have had acute brain injury and remain in an unresponsive "vegetative state" have also suffered significant damage to the thalamus, to the neural tissue connecting it to the higher brain centers, or to both (Adams et al., 2000).

The Hypothalamus: A Master Regulator

What are some of the processes regulated by the hypothalamus?

Nestled directly below the thalamus and weighing only about 2 ounces, the **hypothalamus** is, ounce for ounce, the most influential structure in the brain. It regulates hunger, thirst, sexual behavior, and a wide variety of emotional behaviors. The hypothalamus also regulates internal body temperature, starting the process that causes you to perspire when you are too hot and to shiver to conserve body heat when you are too cold. It also houses the biological clock—the mechanism responsible for the timing of the sleep/wakefulness cycle and the daily fluctuation in more than 100 body functions (Ginty et al., 1993). As small as it is, the hypothalamus maintains nearly all bodily functions except blood pressure, heart rhythm, and breathing.

The physiological changes in the body that accompany strong emotion are initiated by neurons concentrated primarily in the hypothalamus. You have felt these physical changes—sweaty palms, a pounding heart, a hollow feeling in the pit of your stomach, or a lump in your throat.

The electrical stimulation of parts of the hypothalamus has elicited some unusual reactions in animals. Long ago, researcher José Delgado (1969) implanted an electrode in a particular spot in the hypothalamus of a bull specifically bred for bull fighting in Spain. Delgado stood calmly in the ring as the bull charged toward him. He then pressed a remote control box that stimulated an area of the bull's hypothalamus. The bull stopped abruptly in its tracks. (Fortunately for Delgado, the batteries in the remote were working.) Apparently, aggression in animals can be turned on or off by stimulating specific areas of the hypothalamus. Not only that, even the sensations of pleasure can be produced if the right place on the hypothalamus is stimulated (Olds, 1956).

The Limbic System: Primitive Emotion and Memory

What is the role of the limbic system?

The **limbic system** is a group of structures in the brain, including the amygdala and the hippocampus, that are collectively involved in emotional expression, memory, and motivation. The **amygdala** plays an important role in emotion, particularly in response to unpleasant or punishing stimuli (LeDoux, 1994, 2000). Heavily involved in the learning of fear responses, the amygdala helps form vivid memories of emotional events, which enable humans and other animals to avoid dangerous situa-

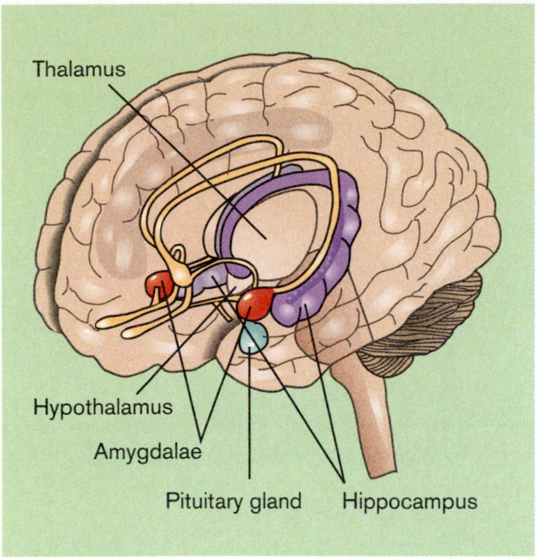

Figure 2.6

The Principal Structures in the Limbic System

The amygdala plays an important role in emotion; the hippocampus is essential in the formation of conscious memory.

how brain can be healed.

tions and unpleasant consequences (Cahill et al., 1995; LeDoux, 1995). The mere sight of frightened faces excites the firing of neurons in the amygdala (Morris et al., 1996). Damage to the amygdala can impair a person's ability to recognize facial expressions and tones of voice that are associated with fear and anger (LeDoux, 2000; Scott et al., 1997).

The **hippocampus** is an important brain structure of the limbic system located in the interior temporal lobes (see Figure 2.6). The hippocampus plays a central role in memory. If your hippocampal region—the hippocampus and the underlying cortical areas—were destroyed, you would not be able to store or recall any new personal or cognitive information, such as that day's baseball score or the phone number of the person you met at dinner (Eichenbaum, 1997; Gluck & Myers, 1997; Varga-Khadem et al., 1997). Yet memories already stored before destruction of the hippocampal region would remain intact. However, recent research indicates the possibility of cell regeneration in the hippocampus in human adults (Robertson & Murre, 1999). You will learn more about the central role of the hippocampal region in the formation of memories in Chapter 6.

Besides its critically important role in memory, researchers have discovered that the hippocampus is an essential part of a cortical network that detects and responds to unexpected or novel stimuli (Knight, 1996). The hippocampus also plays a role in the brain's internal representation of space in the form of neural "maps" that help us learn our way about in new environments and remember where we have been (Wilson & McNaughton, 1993). An interesting study of licensed taxi drivers in London revealed that their posterior (rear) hippocampus was significantly larger than that of participants in a control group who did not have extensive experience navigating the city's streets (Maguire et al., 2000). In fact, the more experience a taxi driver had, the larger that part of the hippocampus was. This study shows that the posterior hippocampus is important for navigational ability. More broadly, the study reveals a plastic capability in a structure of the adult human brain, an ability to respond to environmental demands (Maguire et al., 2000).

Autopsies performed on patients suffering from the severe memory impairment of Alzheimer's disease have revealed extensive damage to neurons in the hippocampus (West et al., 1994). An insidious brain disease that develops gradually, Alzheimer's disease continues to destroy neurons in brain areas that control memory. Former President Ronald Reagan announced in 1994 that neurological tests revealed he was in the early stages of Alzheimer's disease. You will learn more about Alzheimer's disease in Chapter 10.

thalamus (THAL-uh-mus): The structure, located above the brainstem, that acts as a relay station for information flowing into or out of the higher brain centers.

hypothalamus (HY-po-THAL-uh-mus): A small but influential brain structure that controls the pituitary gland and regulates hunger, thirst, sexual behavior, body temperature, and a wide variety of emotional behaviors.

limbic system: A group of structures in the brain, including the amygdala and hippocampus, that are collectively involved in emotion, memory, and motivation.

amygdala (ah-MIG-da-la): A structure in the limbic system that plays an important role in emotion, particularly in response to aversive stimuli.

hippocampus (hip-po-CAM-pus): A structure in the limbic system that plays a central role in the formation of long-term memories.

cerebrum (seh-REE-brum): The largest structure of the human brain, consisting of the two cerebral hemispheres connected by the corpus callosum and covered by the cerebral cortex.

cerebral hemispheres (seh-REE-brul): The right and left halves of the cerebrum, covered by the cerebral cortex and connected by the corpus callosum.

corpus callosum (KOR-pus kah-LO-sum): The thick band of nerve fibers that connects the two cerebral hemispheres and makes possible the transfer of information and the synchronization of activity between them.

cerebral cortex (seh-REE-brul KOR-tex): The gray, convoluted covering of the cerebral hemispheres that is responsible for higher mental processes such as language, memory, and thinking.

association areas: Areas of the cerebral cortex that house memories and are involved in thought, perception, learning, and language.

frontal lobes: The lobes that control voluntary body movements, speech production, and such functions as thinking, motivation, planning for the future, impulse control, and emotional responses.

Remember It!

1. The brain and the spinal cord make up the peripheral nervous system. (true/false)
2. The hypothalamus regulates all the following except
   a. internal body temperature.
   b. hunger and thirst.
   c. coordinated movement.
   d. sexual behavior.
3. The part of the limbic system primarily involved in the formation of memories is the (amygdala, hippocampus); the part involved in the responses to aversive stimuli is the (amygdala, hippocampus).
4. Match the brain structure with its description.

b (1)	connects the brain with the peripheral nervous system	a. medulla
a (2)	controls heart rate, breathing, and blood pressure	b. spinal cord
f (3)	consists of the medulla, the pons, and the reticular formation	c. reticular formation
c (4)	influences attention and arousal	d. thalamus
e (5)	coordinates complex body movements	e. cerebellum
d (6)	serves as a relay station for sensory information flowing into the brain	f. brainstem

Answers: 1. false 2. c 3. hippocampus; amygdala 4. (1) b (2) a (3) f (4) c (5) e (6) d

THE CEREBRAL HEMISPHERES

What are the cerebral hemispheres, the corpus callosum, and the cerebral cortex?

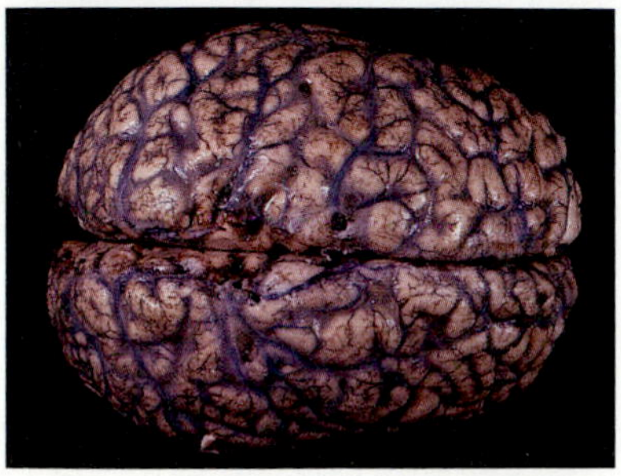

The two cerebral hemispheres show up clearly in this view looking down on an actual brain.

The most extraordinary and the most essentially human part of the magnificent 3-pound human brain is the cerebrum and its cortex. If you could peer into your skull and look down on your own brain, you would see a structure that resembles the inside of a huge walnut. Like a walnut, which has two matched halves connected to each other, the **cerebrum** is composed of two **cerebral hemispheres**—a left and a right hemisphere resting side by side (see Figure 2.7). The two hemispheres are physically connected at the bottom by a thick band of nerve fibers called the **corpus callosum.** This connection makes possible the transfer of information and the coordination of activity between the hemispheres. In general, the right cerebral hemisphere controls movement and feeling on the left side of the body. The left hemisphere controls the right side of the body. In over 95% of people, the left hemisphere also controls the language functions (Hellige, 1990).

The cerebral hemispheres have a thin outer covering about ⅛ inch thick called the **cerebral cortex,** which is primarily responsible for the higher mental processes of language, memory, and thinking. The presence of the cell bodies of billions of neurons in the cortex gives it a grayish appearance. Thus, the cortex is often referred to as *gray matter.* Immediately beneath the cortex are the white myelinated axons (referred to as *white matter*) that connect the neurons of the cortex with those of

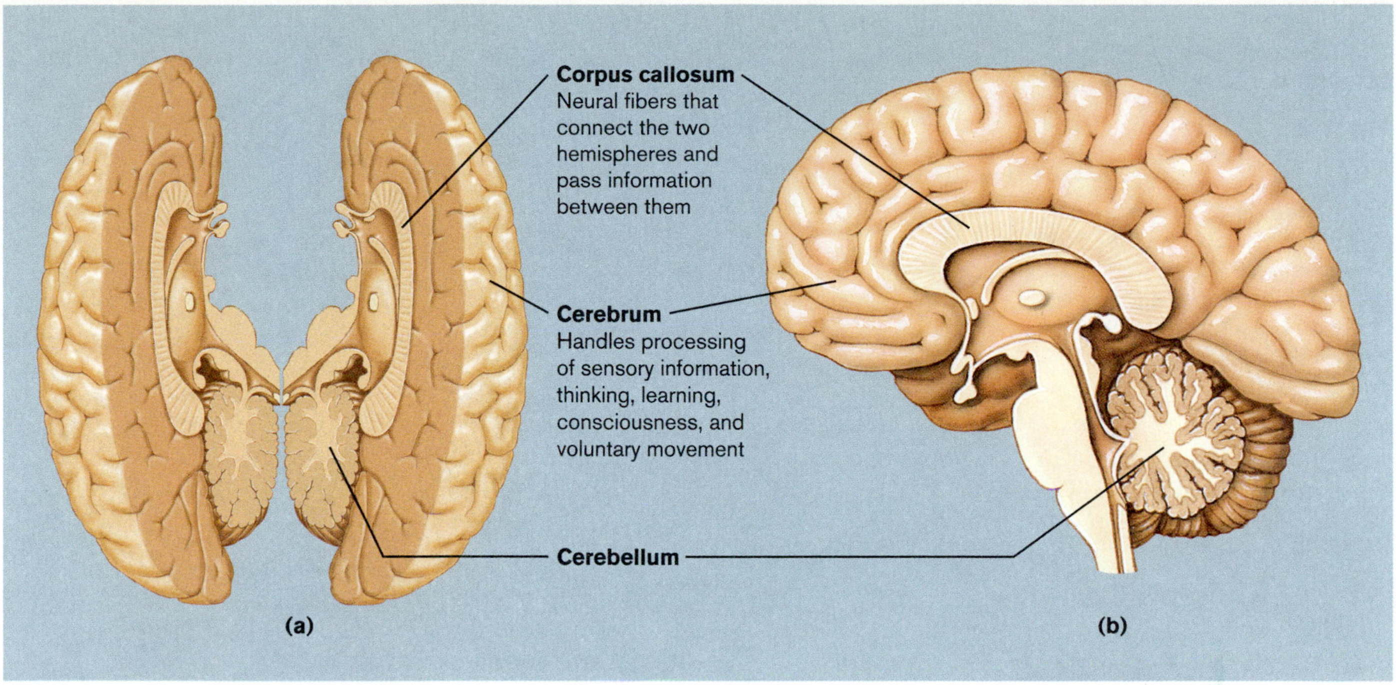

Figure 2.7

Two Views of the Cerebral Hemispheres

(a) The two hemispheres rest side by side like two matched halves, physically connected by the corpus callosum. (b) An inside view of the right hemisphere.

other brain regions. Research by Andreason and others (1993) indicated that the amount of gray matter is positively correlated with human intelligence. And a recent brain-imaging study showed that gray matter, but not white matter, is lost with normal aging in both hemispheres of the cerebellum (Sullivan et al., 2000). Age-related deficits due to this loss of gray matter are common. For example, the aged tend to experience problems with balance, they become less steady on their feet, and their gait is affected.

In humans the cortex is very large—if it were spread out flat, it would measure about 2 feet by 3 feet. Because the cortex is roughly three times the size of the cerebrum itself, it does not fit smoothly around the cerebrum. Rather, it is arranged in numerous folds or wrinkles called *convolutions.* About two-thirds of the cortex is hidden from view in the folds. The cortex of less intelligent animals is much smaller in proportion to total brain size and, therefore, is much less convoluted.

The cerebral cortex contains three types of areas: (1) sensory input areas, where vision, hearing, touch, pressure, and temperature register; (2) motor areas, which control voluntary movement; and (3) **association areas,** which house memories and are involved in thought, perception, and language.

The Lobes of the Brain

In each cerebral hemisphere there are four lobes—the frontal lobe, the parietal lobe, the occipital lobe, and the temporal lobe. Find them in Figure 2.8 (on page 56).

What are some of the main areas within the frontal lobes, and what are their functions?

The Frontal Lobes: For Moving, Speaking, and Thinking The frontal lobes are by far the largest of the brain's lobes. Beginning at the front of the brain, the **frontal lobes** extend to the top center of the skull. They contain the motor cortex, Broca's area, and the frontal association areas. A study recently provided the first evidence that neurons in the frontal cortex associate incoming visual and auditory stimuli and maintain those associations over time (Foster et al., 2000).

The Motor Cortex In 1870 two physicians, Fritsch and Hitzig, used a probe to apply a weak electrical current to the cortex of a dog. (The brain itself is insensitive to

Figure 2.8

The Cerebral Cortex of the Left Hemisphere

This illustration of the left cerebral hemisphere shows the four lobes: (1) the frontal lobe, including the motor cortex and Broca's area; (2) the parietal lobe, with the somatosensory cortex; (3) the occipital lobe, with the primary visual cortex; and (4) the temporal lobe, with the primary auditory cortex and Wernicke's area.

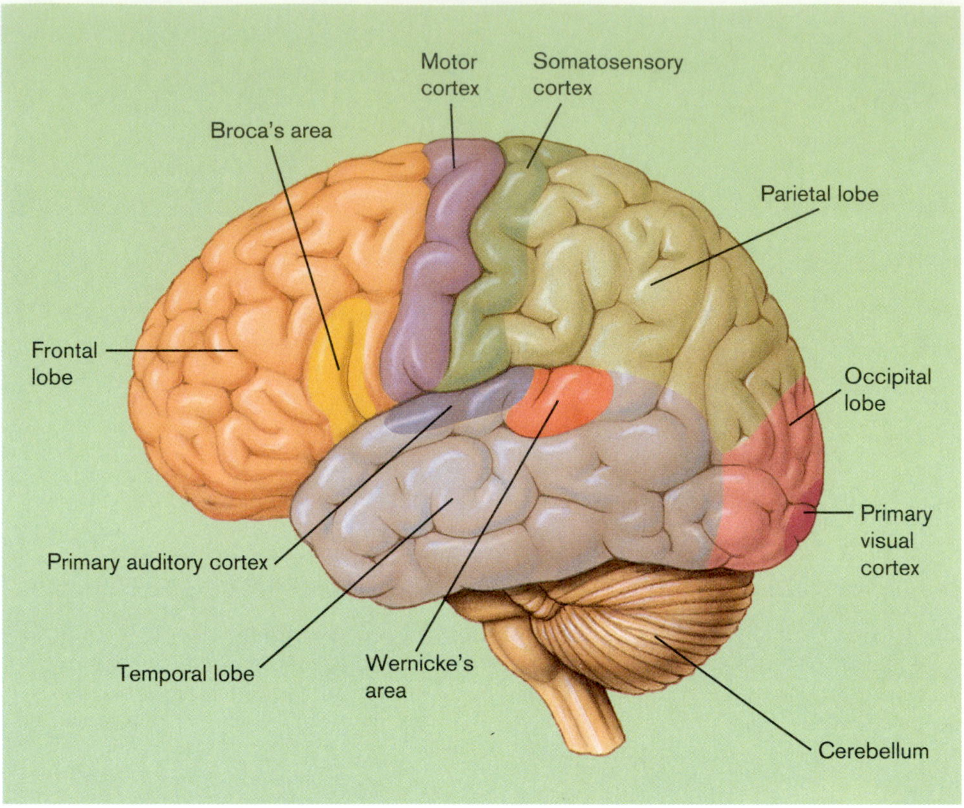

pain, so probing the brain causes no discomfort.) When they stimulated various points on the cortex along the rear of the frontal lobe, specific parts of the dog's body moved. Fritsch and Hitzig had discovered the **motor cortex**—the area that controls voluntary body movement (refer to Figure 2.8). The right motor cortex controls movement on the left side of the body, and the left motor cortex controls movement on the right side of the body.

In 1937 Canadian neurosurgeon Wilder Penfield applied electrical stimulation to the motor cortex of conscious human patients undergoing neurosurgery. He mapped the primary motor cortex in humans, as shown in Figure 2.9. Note the homunculus, or "little man," drawn next to the cross section of the motor cortex. The body parts are drawn in proportion to the amount of motor cortex involved in the movement of each body part. The parts of the body that are capable of the most finely coordinated movements, such as the fingers, lips, and tongue, have a larger share of the motor cortex. Movements in the lower parts of the body are controlled primarily by neurons at the top of the motor cortex, whereas movements in the upper body parts (face, lips, and tongue) are controlled mainly by neurons near the bottom of the motor cortex. For example, when you wiggle your right big toe, a cluster of brain cells firing at the top of the left motor cortex is chiefly responsible for producing the movement.

How accurately and completely does Penfield's homunculus map account for the control of body movement? Although it may be useful in a broad sense, more recent research has shown that there is not a precise one-to-one correspondence between specific points on the motor cortex and movement of particular body parts. Motor neurons that control the fingers, for example, play a role in the movement of more than a single finger. In fact, the control of movement of any single finger is handled by a network of neurons that are widely distributed over the entire hand area of the motor cortex (Sanes & Donoghue, 2000; Sanes et al., 1995; Schieber & Hibbard, 1993).

motor cortex: The strip of tissue at the rear of the frontal lobes that controls voluntary body movement.

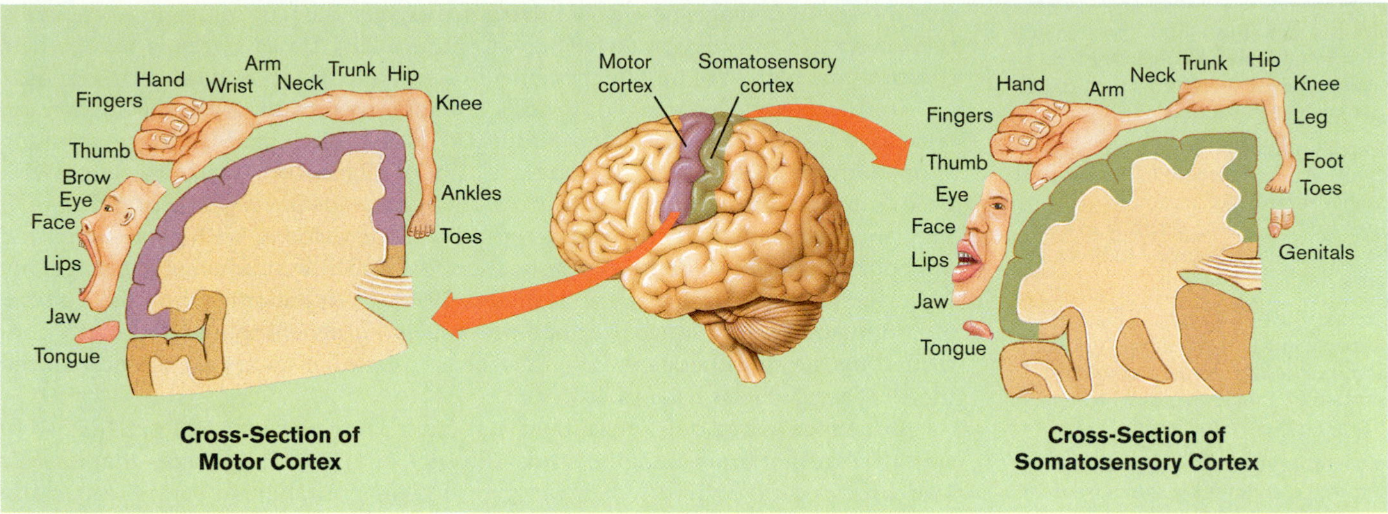

Figure 2.9

The Motor Cortex and the Somatosensory Cortex from the Left Hemisphere

The left motor cortex controls voluntary movement in the right side of the body. The left somatosensory cortex is the site where touch, pressure, temperature, and pain sensations from the right side of the body register. The more sensitive the body parts and the more capable they are of finely coordinated movements, the greater the areas of somatosensory cortex and motor cortex dedicated to those body parts.

What happens when part of the motor cortex is damaged? Depending on the severity of the damage, some degree of impairment of coordination can result. Sometimes damage in the motor cortex can cause the grand mal seizures of epilepsy. On the other hand, if an arm or leg is amputated, many of the neurons in the corresponding area of the motor cortex will eventually be dedicated to another function (Murray, 1995).

Evidence has come to light showing that the motor cortex does much more than control voluntary movement. It also participates in learning and cognitive events (Sanes & Donoghue, 2000). And the plasticity—the flexibility—of the motor cortex is maintained throughout life. This plasticity allows synapses to strengthen and reorganize their interconnections when stimulated by experience and practice. Even mental rehearsal, or imaging, can produce changes in the motor cortex (Sanes & Donoghue, 2000), but the changes are not as powerful as those generated by real rehearsal or performance. Thus, athletes often spend time before a game visualizing their upcoming performance on the field or court—but this "mental practicing" never replaces actual, physical practice. Moreover, the motor cortex in humans is responsive to both short-term and long-term experience (Liepert et al., 1999). Simply repeating a sequence of movements rapidly for as little as 5 to 10 minutes can alter the motor cortex very quickly (Classen et al., 1998). According to Sanes and Donoghue (2000), the motor cortex "must be considered as part of a larger cortical network that can be an active participant in making decisions to move on the basis of internally enacted cognitive effort" (p. 409).

Broca's Area In 1861 Paul Broca performed autopsies on two patients—one who had been totally without speech, and another who could say only four words (Jenkins et al., 1975). Broca found that both patients had damage in the left hemisphere, slightly in front of the part of the motor cortex that controls movement of the jaw, lips, and tongue. Broca was among the first scientists to demonstrate the existence of localized functions in the cerebral cortex (Schiller, 1993). He concluded

Broca's area (BRO-kuz): The area in the frontal lobe, usually in the left hemisphere, that controls the production of speech sounds.

Broca's aphasia (BRO-kuz uh-FAY-zyah): An impairment in the physical ability to produce speech sounds, or in extreme cases an inability to speak at all; caused by damage to Broca's area.

aphasia (uh-FAY-zyah): A loss or impairment of the ability to understand or communicate through the written or spoken word, which results from damage to the brain.

parietal lobes (puh-RY-uh-tul): The lobes that contain the somatosensory cortex (where touch, pressure, temperature, and pain register) and other areas that are responsible for body awareness and spatial orientation.

somatosensory cortex (so-MAT-oh-SENS-or-ee): The strip of tissue at the front of the parietal lobes where touch, pressure, temperature, and pain register in the cerebral cortex.

that the site of damage, now called **Broca's area,** was the part of the brain responsible for speech production (refer back to Figure 2.8). Broca's area is involved in directing the pattern of muscle movement required to produce the speech sounds.

If Broca's area is damaged, **Broca's aphasia** may result. **Aphasia** is a general term for a loss or impairment of the ability to use or understand language, resulting from damage to the brain (Goodglass, 1993). Characteristically, patients with Broca's aphasia know what they want to say but can speak very little or not at all. If they are able to speak, their words are produced very slowly, with great effort, and are poorly articulated. Broca's aphasia, then, is a deficit in producing language, not in understanding it (Maratsos & Matheny, 1994). Even patients who cannot speak are often able to sing songs they had previously known. Singing is normally controlled by the right hemisphere, and words to familiar songs are already stored there (Albert & Helm-Estabrooks, 1988).

But Broca's area does more than just controlling the physical production of speech. A recent brain-imaging study (Embick et al., 2000) indicates that Broca's area buzzes with activity when a person makes grammatical errors, especially errors in syntax (the aspect of grammar that specifies the rules for arranging and combining words to form phrases and sentences—see Chapter 7). This finding by Embick and others (2000) confirms the existence of distinct modules for language knowledge and provides direct evidence of a specialization for syntax in Broca's area.

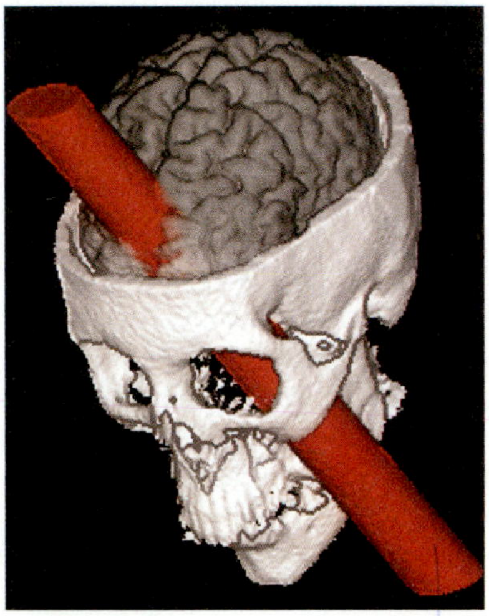

This computer-generated image shows the likely path of the bar that tore through Phineas Gage's skull.

Frontal Association Areas Much of the frontal lobes consists of association areas involved in thinking, motivation, planning for the future, impulse control, and emotional responses (Stuss et al., 1992). Damage to the frontal association areas produces deficiencies in the ability to plan and anticipate the consequences of actions. Sometimes pronounced changes in emotional responses occur when the frontal lobes are damaged. Phineas Gage, discussed in this chapter's opening, represents one case in which damage to the frontal lobes drastically altered impulse control and emotional responses.

What are the primary functions of the parietal lobes in general and the somatosensory cortex in particular?

The Parietal Lobes: Vital to the Sense of Touch The **parietal lobes** lie directly behind the frontal lobes, in the top middle portion of the brain. The parietal lobes are involved in the reception and processing of touch stimuli. The front strip of brain tissue in the parietal lobes is the **somatosensory cortex,** the site where touch, pressure, temperature, and pain register in the cortex (refer back to Figure 2.8) (Stea & Apkarian, 1992). The somatosensory cortex also makes you aware of movement in your body and the positions of your body parts at any given moment.

The two halves of the somatosensory cortex in the left and right parietal lobes are wired to opposite sides of the body. Also, cells at the top of the somatosensory cortex govern feeling in the lower extremities of the body. Drop a brick on your right foot, and the topmost brain cells of the left somatosensory cortex will fire and register the pain sensation. (Note, this is *not* a *Try It!* exercise.) Notice in Figure 2.9 the large somatosensory areas connected to sensitive body parts such as the tongue, lips, face, and hand, particularly the thumb and index finger. A person with damage to the somatosensory cortex of one hemisphere loses some sensitivity to touch on the opposite side of the body. If the damage is severe enough, the person might not

Because the left hand of a professional string player must rapidly and accurately execute fine movements and slight pressure variations, it is not surprising that these musicians have an unusually large area of the somatosensory cortex dedicated to the fingers of that hand.

be able to feel the difference between sandpaper and silk, or the affected part of the body might feel numb.

"Changes in sensory input produced by an event as traumatic as the loss of a limb or something as routine as daily violin practice" can cause long-term changes in the somatosensory cortex (Juliano, 1998, p. 1653). For example, compared to nonmusicians, professional musicians who play stringed instruments have a significantly larger area of the somatosensory cortex dedicated to the fingers of their left hand. And the earlier the age at which they began to play, the larger this dedicated cortical area is (Elbert et al., 1995).

Other parts of the parietal lobes are responsible for spatial orientation and sense of direction. The hippocampus cooperates with these parts of the parietal lobes in performing such functions, as the study of London taxi drivers discussed on page 53 indicates (Maguire et al., 2000). Other recent research reveals a gender-related difference in human navigational thinking. Female and male participants had to find their way out of a complex, three-dimensional, computer-simulated maze. Brain imaging showed that male participants relied heavily on the left hippocampus while navigating through the maze, and female participants consistently used both the right parietal cortex and the right frontal cortex (Gron et al., 2000).

There are association areas in the parietal lobes that house memories of how objects feel against the human skin, a fact that explains why we can identify objects by touch. People with damage to these areas could hold a computer mouse, a CD, or a baseball in their hand but not be able to identify the object by touch alone.

The Occipital Lobes: The Better to See You With Behind the parietal lobes at the rear of the brain lie the **occipital lobes,** which are involved in the reception and interpretation of visual information (refer back to Figure 2.8). At the very back of the occipital lobes is the **primary visual cortex,** the site where vision registers in the cortex.

Each eye is connected to the primary visual cortex in both the right and left occipital lobes. Look straight ahead and draw an imaginary line down the middle of what you see. Everything to the left of the line is referred to as the left visual field and registers in the right visual cortex. Everything to the right of the line is the right visual field and registers in the left visual cortex. A person who sustains damage to one primary visual cortex will still have partial vision in both eyes because each eye sends information to both the right and left occipital lobes.

The association areas in the occipital lobes are involved in the interpretation of visual stimuli. The association areas hold memories of past visual experiences and

What are the primary functions of the occipital lobes in general and the primary visual cortex in particular?

occipital lobes (ahk-SIP-uh-tul): The lobes that contain the primary visual cortex, where vision registers, and association areas involved in the interpretation of visual information.

primary visual cortex: The area at the rear of the occipital lobes where vision registers in the cerebral cortex.

enable us to recognize what is familiar among the things we see. When these areas are damaged, people can lose the ability to identify objects visually, although they are still able to identify the same objects by touch or through some other sense.

What are the major areas within the temporal lobes, and what are their functions?

The Temporal Lobes: Hearing's Here The **temporal lobes,** located slightly above the ears, are involved in the reception and interpretation of auditory stimuli. The site in the cortex where hearing registers is known as the **primary auditory cortex.** The primary auditory cortex in each temporal lobe receives sound inputs from both ears. Injury to one of these areas results in reduced hearing in both ears, and the destruction of both areas causes total deafness.

Wernicke's Area Adjacent to the primary auditory cortex in the left temporal lobe is **Wernicke's area,** which is the language area involved in comprehending the spoken word and in formulating coherent written and spoken language (refer back to Figure 2.8). In about 95% of people, Wernicke's area is in the left hemisphere. When you listen to someone speak, the sound registers first in the primary auditory cortex. The sound is then sent to Wernicke's area, where the speech sounds are unscrambled into meaningful patterns of words. The same areas that are active when you listen to someone speak are also active in deaf individuals when they watch a person using sign language (Söderfeldt et al., 1994). Wernicke's area is also involved when you select the words to use in speech and written expression (Nishimura et al., 1999).

Heather Whitestone, the first deaf person to become Miss America, uses the same areas in her brain while watching someone sign as a nondeaf person uses while listening to someone speak.

Wernicke's aphasia is a type of aphasia resulting from damage to Wernicke's area. Although speech is fluent and words are clearly articulated, the actual message does not make sense to others (Maratsos & Matheney, 1994). The content may be vague or bizarre and may contain inappropriate words, parts of words, or a gibberish of nonexistent words. One Wernicke's patient, when asked how he was feeling, replied, "I think that there's an awful lot of mung, but I think I've a lot of net and tunged in a little wheat duhvayden" (Buckingham & Kertesz, 1974). People with Wernicke's aphasia are not aware that anything is wrong with their speech.

Another kind of aphasia is *auditory aphasia,* or word deafness. It can occur if there is damage to the nerves connecting the primary auditory cortex with Wernicke's area. The person is able to hear normally but may not understand spoken language—just as when you hear a foreign language spoken, and perceive the sounds but have no idea what the speaker is saying.

The Temporal Association Areas The remainder of the temporal lobes consist of the association areas that house memories and are involved in the interpretation of auditory stimuli. For example, the association area where your memories of various sounds are stored enables you to recognize the sounds of your favorite band, a computer booting up, your roommate snoring, and so on. There is also a special association area where familiar melodies are stored.

temporal lobes: The lobes that contain the primary auditory cortex, Wernicke's area, and association areas for interpreting auditory information.

primary auditory cortex: The part of the temporal lobes where hearing registers in the cerebral cortex.

Wernicke's area: The language area in the temporal lobe involved in comprehension of the spoken word and in formulation of coherent speech and written language.

Wernicke's aphasia: Aphasia that results from damage to Wernicke's area and in which the person's spoken language is fluent, but the content is either vague or incomprehensible to the listener.

Remember It!

1. What is the thick band of fibers connecting the two cerebral hemispheres?
   a. cortex
   b. cerebrum
   c. corpus callosum
   d. motor cortex
2. The ⅛-inch outer covering of the cerebrum is the
   a. cerebral cortex.
   b. myelin sheath.
   c. cortex callosum.
   d. white matter.
3. Match the lobes with the brain areas they contain.

____ (1) primary auditory cortex, Wernicke's area	a. frontal lobes
____ (2) primary visual cortex	b. parietal lobes
____ (3) Broca's area, motor cortex	c. occipital lobes
____ (4) somatosensory cortex	d. temporal lobes

4. Match the specialized area with the appropriate description of function.

____ (1) site where hearing registers	a. primary visual cortex
____ (2) site where vision registers	b. motor cortex
____ (3) site where touch, pressure, and temperature register	c. frontal association area
____ (4) speech production	d. primary auditory cortex
____ (5) voluntary movement	e. somatosensory cortex
____ (6) formulation and understanding of the spoken and written word	f. Wernicke's area
____ (7) thinking, motivation, impulse control	g. Broca's area

Answers: 1. c 2. a 3. (1) d (2) c (3) a (4) b 4. (1) d (2) a (3) e (4) g (5) b (6) f (7) c

Specialized Functions of the Left Hemisphere: Language, First and Foremost

What are the specialized functions of the left hemisphere?

Although they may look very much alike, the two cerebral hemispheres make different but complementary contributions to our mental and emotional lives. Research has shown that some **lateralization** of the hemispheres exists; that is, each hemisphere is specialized, to some extent, to handle certain functions. Yet functions are usually not handled exclusively by one hemisphere; the two hemispheres always work together (Bradshaw, 1989; Efron, 1990). However, new evidence suggests that excessive prenatal exposure to the male hormone androgen can cause a shift in brain lateralization by which the right hemisphere becomes dominant (Kelso et al., 2000).

In 95% of right-handers and in about 62% of left-handers, the **left hemisphere** handles most of the language functions, including speaking, writing, reading, and understanding the spoken word (Hellige, 1990). But American sign language (ASL), used by deaf persons, is processed by both hemispheres (Neville et al., 1998). The left hemisphere is also specialized for mathematical abilities, particularly calculation, and it processes information in an analytical and sequential, or step-by-step, manner (Corballis, 1989). Logic is primarily a left hemisphere specialty.

The left hemisphere coordinates complex movements by directly controlling the right side of the body and by indirectly controlling the movements of the left side of the body. The left hemisphere accomplishes this by sending orders across the corpus

lateralization: The specialization of one of the cerebral hemispheres to handle a particular function.

left hemisphere: The hemisphere that controls the right side of the body, coordinates complex movements, and, in 95% of people, controls the production of speech and written language.

callosum to the right hemisphere so that the proper movements will be coordinated and executed smoothly. (Remember that the cerebellum also plays an important role in helping coordinate complex movements.)

Specialized Functions of the Right Hemisphere: The Leader in Visual-Spatial Tasks

What are the specialized functions of the right hemisphere?

The **right hemisphere** is generally considered to be the hemisphere more adept at visual-spatial relations. Artists, sculptors, architects, and do-it-yourselfers have strong visual-spatial skills. When you arrange your bedroom furniture, paint a friend's portrait, or learn Tae-Bo, you are calling primarily on your right hemisphere.

The right hemisphere processes information holistically rather than part by part or piece by piece, as the left hemisphere does. Auditory, visual, and tactile stimuli register in both hemispheres, but the right hemisphere appears to be more specialized than the left for complex perceptual tasks. Consequently, the right hemisphere is better at pattern recognition, whether of familiar voices, melodies, or visual patterns.

Although the left hemisphere is generally considered the language hemisphere, the right hemisphere also makes an important contribution to the understanding of language. The right hemisphere becomes actively involved when people generate the unusual verbal associations characteristic of creative thought and problem solving (Seger et al., 2000). For example, J. K. Rowling, author of the *Harry Potter* books, uses her right hemisphere when she creates the magical world depicted in her stories. According to Howard Gardner (1981), the right hemisphere is involved "in understanding the theme or moral of a story, in grasping metaphor . . . and even in supplying the punch line for a joke" (p. 74). Van Lancker (1987) points out that "although the left hemisphere knows best what is being said, the right hemisphere figures out how it is meant and who is saying it" (p. 13). It is the right hemisphere that is able to understand familiar idiomatic expressions such as "She let the cat out of the bag." A person whose right hemisphere is damaged may understand only the literal meaning of the statement.

To experience an effect of the specialization of the cerebral hemispheres, try your hand at the *Try It!*

Try It!

Get a meter stick or yardstick. Try balancing it vertically on the end of your left index finger, as shown in the drawing. Then try balancing it on your right index finger. Most people are better with their dominant hand—the right hand for right-handers, for example. Is this true for you?

Now try this: Begin reciting the ABCs out loud as fast as you can while balancing the stick with your *left* hand. Do you have less trouble this time? Why should that be? The right hemisphere controls the act of balancing with the left hand. However, your left hemisphere, though poor at controlling the left hand, still tries to coordinate your balancing efforts. When you distract the left hemisphere with a steady stream of talk, the right hemisphere can orchestrate more efficient balancing with your left hand without interference.

right hemisphere: The hemisphere that controls the left side of the body and that, in most people, is specialized for visual-spatial perception and for interpreting nonverbal behavior.

Creativity and intuition are typically considered right hemisphere specialties, but the left hemisphere shares these functions. The right hemisphere controls singing and seems to be more specialized for musical ability in untrained musicians (Kinsella et al., 1988). But in trained musicians, both hemispheres play important roles in musical ability. In fact, parts of the left auditory cortex are significantly larger in musicians with perfect pitch, indicating the involvement of the left hemisphere (Schlaug et al., 1995).

Patients with right hemisphere damage may have difficulty with spatial orientation, such as in finding their way around even in familiar surroundings. They may have attentional deficits and be unaware of objects in the left visual field, a condition called *unilateral neglect* (Deovell et al., 2000; Halligan & Marshall, 1994). Patients with this condition may eat only the food on the right side of the plate, read only the words on the right half of a page, and even groom only the right half of the body (Bisiach, 1996; Tham et al., 2000). And remarkably, some patients may even deny that the arm on the side opposite the brain damage belongs to them (Chen-Sea, 2000; Posner, 1996).

ways of imaging Brain catscan MRI

The Right Hemisphere's Role in Emotion: Recognizing and Expressing Emotion The right hemisphere is also more active in the recognition and expression of emotion (Borod, 1992). It even responds to the emotional message conveyed by another's tone of voice (LeDoux, 2000). For example, a professor sarcastically says to a student who enters the class late, "Well, I'm so glad you could come today." A student with right hemisphere damage might respond only to the actual meaning of the words rather than the sarcastic tone.

Reading and interpreting nonverbal behavior, such as gestures and facial expressions, is primarily a right hemisphere task (Hauser, 1993). Look at the two faces in the *Try It!*

Try It!

Pick out the happy face and the sad face (from Jaynes, 1976).

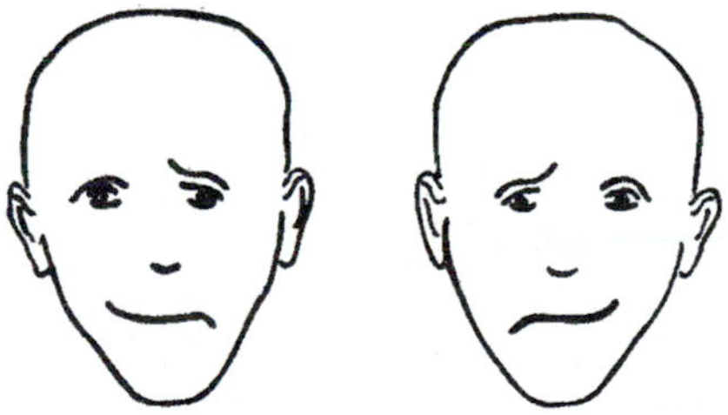

Even though the faces in the drawings are mirror images, right-handed people tend to see the face at the left as the happier face. If you are right-handed, you are likely to perceive the emotional tone revealed by the part of a face to your left as you view it (McGee & Skinner, 1987). The right hemisphere processes information from the left visual field, so right-handed people tend to be more emotionally affected by the left side of faces they view.

The right hemisphere is involved in our expression of emotion through tone of voice and particularly facial expressions. The left side of the face, controlled by the right hemisphere, usually conveys stronger emotion than the right side of the face. Lawrence Miller (1988) describes the facial expressions and the voice inflection of people with right hemisphere damage as "often strangely blank—almost robotic" (p. 39).

Evidence also continues to accumulate that brain mechanisms responsible for negative emotions reside in the right hemisphere, while those responsible for positive emotions are located in the left hemisphere (Hellige, 1993). Research shows that patients suffering from major depression experience decreased activity in the left prefrontal cortex, where positive emotions are produced (Drevets et al., 1997).

The Split Brain: Separate Halves or Two Separate Brains?

What is the significance of the split-brain operation?

The fact that parts of the human brain are specialized for some functions—the left hemisphere for speech and the right hemisphere for visual-spatial abilities—does not mean that some people are left-brained, while others are right-brained. Unless the hemispheres have been surgically separated, they do not operate in isolation and cannot be educated separately. The idea of the left- or right-brained person is more fiction than fact. It sprang from the tendency of journalists to oversimplify and embellish research findings (Coren, 1993). Such a notion is unscientific, yet it has served to heighten public interest in hemispheric specialization and neuroscience in general (Hellige, 1993). Even though each contributes its own important specialized functions, the cerebral hemispheres are always in intimate and immediate contact, thanks to the corpus callosum (shown in Figure 2.5). Not only does the corpus callosum preserve the brain's existing functions while allowing specialization of certain areas to occur (Gazzinaga, 2000), but it carries out a great deal of specialized functioning itself (Funnell et al., 2000).

There have been rare cases of people who have been born with no corpus callosum or who have had their corpus callosum severed in a drastic surgical procedure called the **split-brain operation.** Neurosurgeons Joseph Bogen and Philip Vogel (1963) found that patients with severe epilepsy, suffering frequent and uncontrollable grand mal seizures, could be helped by surgery that severed their corpus callosum. In this way, the pulsing waves of neural activity that occur during a seizure could be confined to one hemisphere rather than spreading across the corpus callosum and involving the entire brain.

The split-brain operation surgically separates the hemispheres, making the transfer of information between them impossible. The patient is then left with two independently functioning hemispheres. The operation has been quite successful, completely eliminating the seizures in some patients. And the surgery causes no major changes in personality, intelligence, or behavior.

Research with split-brain patients by Roger Sperry (1964) and colleagues Michael Gazzaniga (1970, 1989) and Jerre Levy (1985) has expanded knowledge of the unique capabilities of the individual hemispheres. Sperry (1968) found that when the brain was surgically separated, each hemisphere continued to have individual and private experiences, sensations, thoughts, and perceptions. However, most sensory experiences are shared almost simultaneously because each ear and eye has direct sensory connections to both hemispheres. For his work, Sperry won the Nobel Prize in Medicine in 1981.

Testing the Split-Brain Person Sperry's research revealed some fascinating findings. Look at Figure 2.10. In this illustration, a split-brain patient sits in front of a screen that separates the right and left fields of vision. If an orange is flashed to the right field of vision, it will register in the left (verbal) hemisphere. If asked what he saw, the patient will readily reply, "I saw an orange." Suppose that, instead, an apple is flashed to the left visual field and is relayed to the right (nonverbal) hemisphere. The patient will reply, "I saw nothing."

Why could the patient report that he saw the orange but not the apple? Sperry maintains that in split-brain patients, only the verbal left hemisphere can report what it sees. In these experiments, the left hemisphere does not see what is flashed to the right hemisphere, and the right hemisphere is unable to report verbally what it has viewed. But did the right hemisphere actually see the apple that was flashed in the left visual field? Yes, because with his left hand (which is controlled by the right hemisphere), the patient can pick out from behind a screen the apple or any other object shown to the right hemisphere. The right hemisphere knows and

split-brain operation: An operation, performed in severe cases of epilepsy, in which the corpus callosum is cut, separating the cerebral hemispheres and usually lessening the severity and frequency of grand mal seizures.

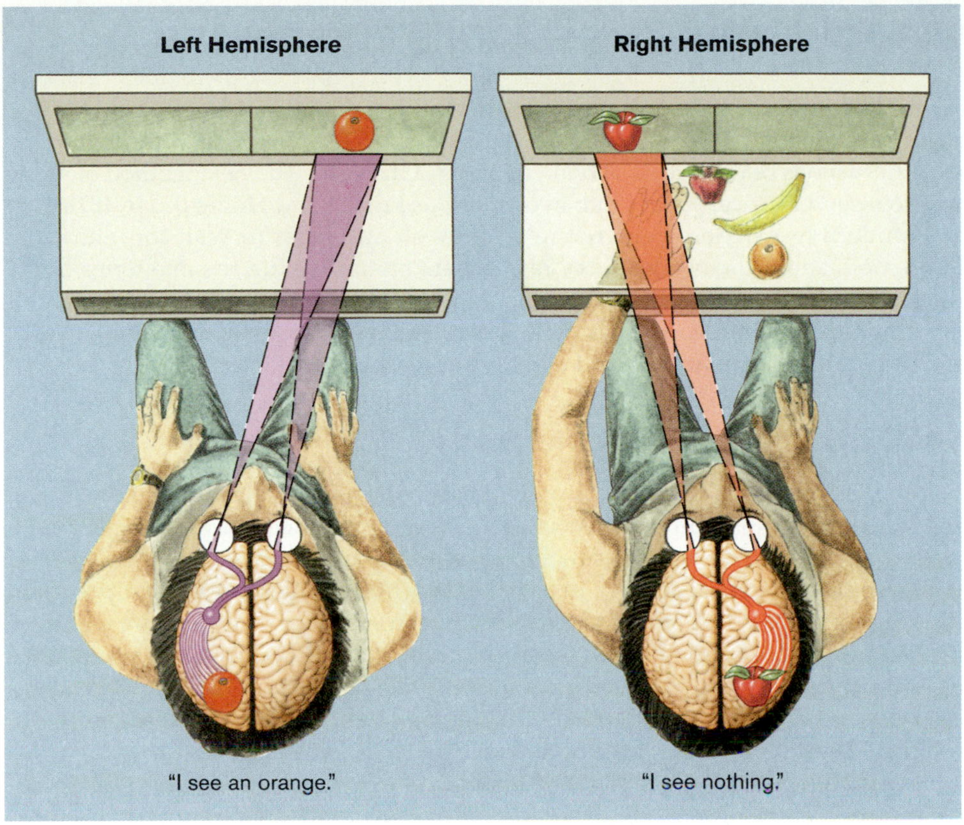

Figure 2.10

Testing a Split-Brain Person

Using special equipment, researchers are able to study the independent functioning of the hemispheres in split-brain persons. In this experiment, when a visual image (an orange) is flashed on the right side of the screen, it is transmitted to the left (talking) hemisphere. When asked what he sees, the split-brain patient replies, "I see an orange." When an image (an apple) is flashed on the left side of the screen, it is transmitted only to the right (nonverbal) hemisphere. Because the split-brain patient's left (language) hemisphere did not receive the image, he replies, "I see nothing." But he can pick out the apple by touch if he uses his left hand, proving that the right hemisphere "saw" the apple. (Based on Gazzaniga, 1983.)

remembers what it sees just as well as the left, but unlike the left hemisphere, the right cannot name what it has seen. (In these experiments, images must be flashed for no more than $\frac{1}{10}$ or $\frac{2}{10}$ of a second so that the subjects do not have time to refixate their eyes and send the information to the opposite hemisphere.)

Remember It!

1. Match the hemisphere with the specialized abilities usually associated with it.
   - ____ (1) visual-spatial skills
   - ____ (2) speech
   - ____ (3) recognition and expression of emotion
   - ____ (4) singing
   - ____ (5) mathematics

   a. right hemisphere
   b. left hemisphere

2. Which of these statements is *not* true of the split-brain operation?
   a. It is used for people suffering from severe epilepsy.
   b. It provides a means of studying the functions of the individual hemispheres.
   c. It causes major changes in intelligence, personality, and behavior.
   d. It makes transfer of information between the hemispheres impossible.

Answers: 1. (1) a (2) b (3) a (4) a (5) b 2. c

DISCOVERING THE BRAIN'S MYSTERIES

What are some methods that researchers have used to learn about brain function?

As we have seen, the first attempts to discover the mysteries of the human brain were through autopsies, such as those performed by Paul Broca, and through clinical observations of the effects of brain injury and diseases. The next method of study was to insert electrical probes into live brains, as Fritsch and Hitzig did in 1870.

Modern researchers need not rely solely on autopsies or wait for injuries to learn more about the brain. Today researchers are unlocking the mysteries of the human brain using the electroencephalograph (EEG), the microelectrode, and modern scanning techniques such as the CT scan, magnetic resonance imaging (MRI), the PET scan, functional MRI, and others (Andreasen et al., 1992).

The EEG and the Microelectrode

What is an electroencephalogram (EEG), and what are three of the brain-wave patterns it reveals?

Before 1924 there was no known way to measure the electrical activity in the brain. But in that year Austrian psychiatrist Hans Berger invented the electroencephalograph, a machine that amplifies a million times the electrical activity occurring in the brain. This electrical activity, detected by electrodes placed at various points on the scalp, provides the power to drive a pen across paper, producing a record of brain-wave activity called an **electroencephalogram (EEG).** The **beta wave** is the brain-wave pattern associated with mental or physical activity. The **alpha wave** is associated with deep relaxation, and the **delta wave** with slow-wave (deep) sleep. (You will learn more about these brain-wave patterns in Chapter 4.)

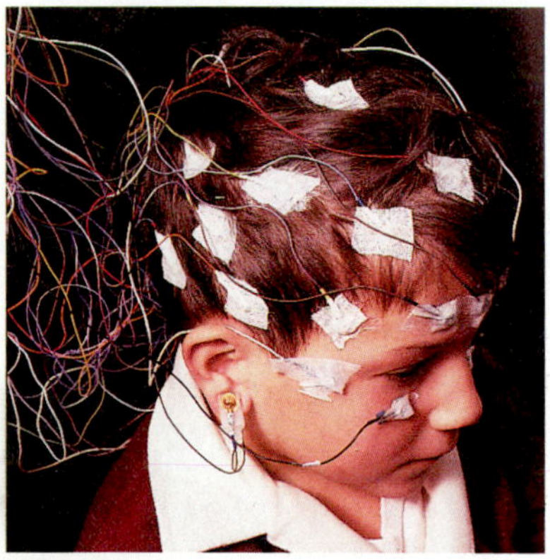

The electroencephalograph (EEG) uses electrodes placed on the scalp to amplify and record electrical activity in the brain.

An EEG computerized imaging technique shows the different levels of electrical activity occurring every millisecond on the surface of the brain (Gevins et al., 1995). It can show an epileptic seizure in progress and can be used to study neural activity in people with learning disabilities, schizophrenia, Alzheimer's disease, sleep disorders, and other neurological problems.

Although the EEG is able to detect electrical activity in different areas of the brain, it cannot reveal what is happening in individual neurons. The microelectrode can. A **microelectrode** is a wire so small that it can be inserted near or into a single neuron without damaging it. Microelectrodes can be used to monitor the electrical activity of a single neuron or to stimulate activity within it. Researchers have used microelectrodes to discover the exact functions of single cells within the primary visual cortex and the primary auditory cortex.

Since the 1970s, a number of brain-imaging techniques have been developed.

The CT Scan and Magnetic Resonance Imaging

The patient undergoing a **CT scan (computerized axial tomography)** is placed inside a large, doughnut-shaped structure where an X-ray tube encircles the entire head. The tube rotates in a complete circle and shoots X rays through the brain as it does so. A series of computerized, cross-sectional images reveal the structures within the brain (or other parts of the body) as well as abnormalities and injuries, including tumors and evidence of old or more recent strokes.

Another technique, **MRI (magnetic resonance imaging)**, produces clearer and more detailed images without exposing patients to the hazards of X-ray photography (Potts et al., 1993). MRI can be used to find abnormalities in the central nervous system and in other systems of the body. Although the CT scan and MRI do a remarkable job of showing what the brain looks like both inside and out, they cannot reveal what the brain is doing. But other technological marvels can.

electroencephalogram (EEG) (ee-lek-tro-en-SEFF-uh-lo-gram): A record of brain-wave activity made by the electroencephalograph.

beta wave (BAY-tuh): The brain wave associated with mental or physical activity.

alpha wave: The brain wave associated with deep relaxation.

delta wave: The brain wave associated with slow-wave (deep) sleep.

microelectrode: An electrical wire so small that it can be used either to monitor the electrical activity of a single neuron or to stimulate activity within it.

The PET Scan, fMRI, and Other Imaging Techniques

The **PET scan (positron-emission tomography)** is a powerful technique for identifying malfunctions that cause physical and psychological disorders and also for

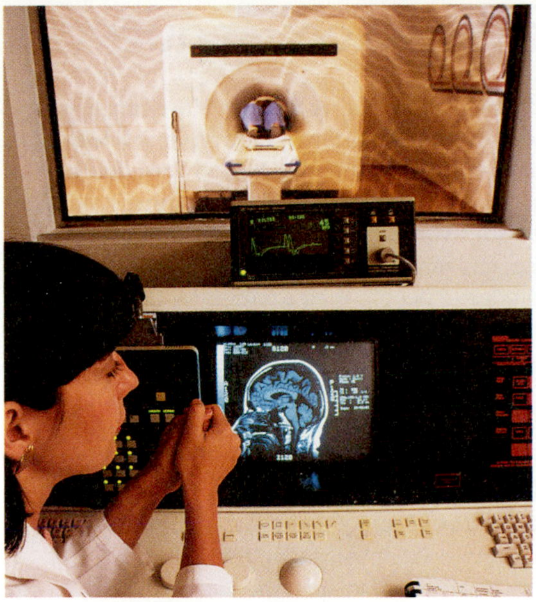

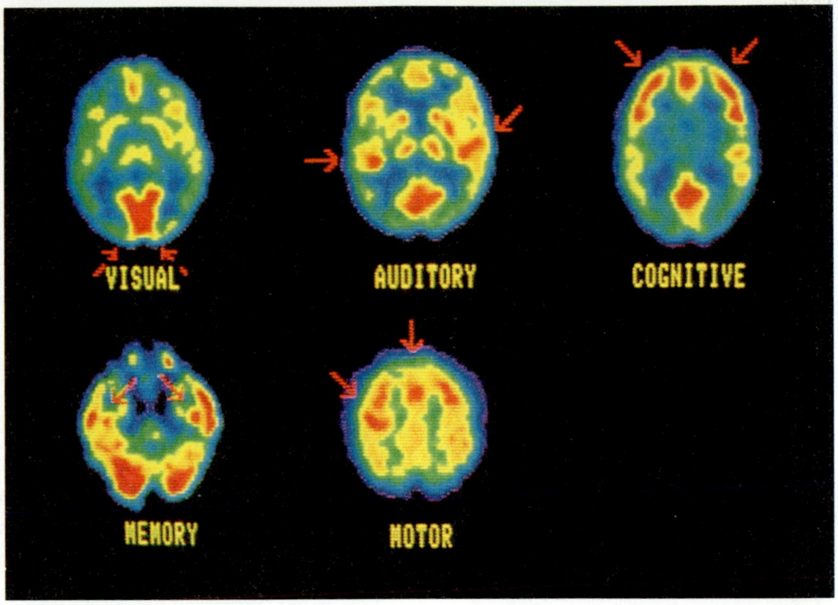

MRI (left) is a powerful tool for revealing what the brain looks like. Unlike PET, however, it cannot show what the brain is doing. PET scans (right) show activity in specific areas of the brain.

studying normal brain activity. The PET scan can map the patterns of blood flow, oxygen use, and glucose consumption (the food of the brain). It can also show the action of drugs and other biochemical substances in the brain and other bodily organs (Farde, 1996).

Still, the PET scan can detect only *changes* in blood flow and in oxygen and glucose consumption as they occur in the various brain areas. But many parts of the brain are always active, even when a person is doing nothing observable. How do researchers separate the activity of specific brain locations responsible for seeing, speaking, reading, and so on from the other unrelated brain areas that are active at the same time? Thanks to sophisticated computing techniques, researchers can subtract all other brain activity from the activity involved in the specific mental tasks subjects are performing (Raichle, 1994b).

A newer technique, **functional MRI (fMRI)** has several important advantages over PET: (1) It can image *both* brain structure and brain activity; (2) it requires no injections (of radioactive or other material); (3) it can image locations of activity more precisely than PET can; and (4) it can detect changes that take place in less than a second, compared with about a minute for PET ("Brain Imaging," 1997).

Still other imaging devices are now available. SQUID (superconducting quantum interference device) images brain activity by measuring magnetic changes produced by the electric current neurons discharge when they fire. Another imaging marvel, MEG (magnetoencephalography), also measures magnetic changes produced by the electrical activity from firing neurons. MEG can image neural activity within the brain as rapidly as it occurs, much faster than PET or fMRI.

Brain-imaging techniques have helped neuroscientists develop an impressive store of knowledge about how the normal brain performs a variety of cognitive tasks and what functions are disrupted by particular types of brain damage. These imaging techniques have also been used to show abnormal brain patterns peculiar to certain psychiatric disorders and to reveal where and how various drugs affect the brain (Tamminga & Conley, 1997). And some neuroscientists are experimenting with combining virtual reality with fMRI to study how the brain responds to situations and environments that would be impossible to observe using conventional imaging techniques (Travis, 1996).

CT scan (computerized axial tomography): A brain-scanning technique involving a rotating X-ray scanner and a high-speed computer analysis that produces slice-by-slice, cross-sectional images of the structure of the brain.

MRI (magnetic resonance imaging): A diagnostic scanning technique that produces high-resolution images of the structures of the brain.

PET scan (positron-emission tomography): A brain-imaging technique that reveals activity in various parts of the brain, based on the amount of oxygen and glucose consumed.

functional MRI (fMRI): A brain-imaging technique that reveals both brain structure and brain activity.

Squid is a relatively new brain-imaging tool that measures magnetic changes in the brain.

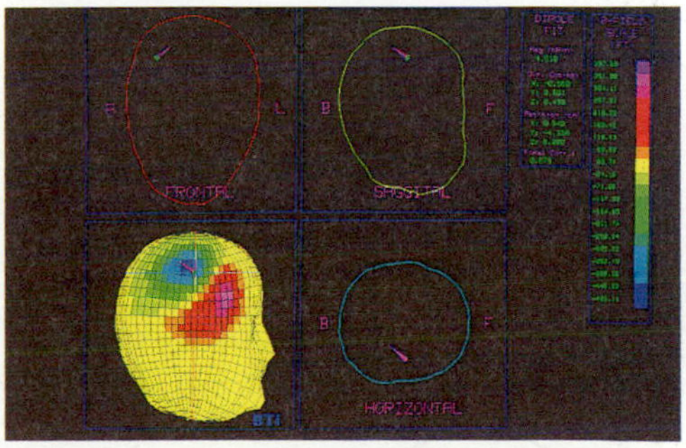

BRAIN DAMAGE: CAUSES AND CONSEQUENCES

Let's reconsider the question posed at the beginning of this chapter. How can someone like Phineas Gage, whose brain sustained such massive damage, survive, while a small bullet fired into a person's brain in a particular place can result in instant death? The precise location of a brain injury is the most important factor in determining whether a person lives or dies. Had the metal rod torn through Gage's brainstem, that would have been the end of him. Brain damage has many causes. Stroke, head injuries, diseases, tumors, and the abuse of drugs can leave people with a variety of disabilities.

Stroke

Why is a stroke so serious?

In the United States, a stroke is the most common cause of injury to the adult brain and the third most common cause of death. A **stroke** occurs when a blood clot or plug of fat blocks an artery and cuts off the blood supply to a particular area of the brain or when a blood vessel bursts, often as a result of high blood pressure. High doses of stimulants such as amphetamines and cocaine also increase the risk of stroke.

Of some 500,000 people who suffer strokes each year in the United States, about 150,000 die (Gorman, 1996). Another 100,000 to 150,000 are severely and permanently disabled (Zivin & Choi, 1991). Stroke patients may be left with impaired intellect, loss of coordination or sensation, or paralysis. A high percentage of stroke survivors suffer from depression (Angeleri et al., 1997), and about 25% have aphasia. But patients who receive TPA (a blood clot–dissolving drug used successfully in treating heart attacks) within 3 hours of the onset of a stroke are 30% more likely to have minimal or no disability (Gorman, 1996; National Institute of Neurological Disorders, 1995).

Many stroke victims are able to recover some of the lost functions. Former President Gerald Ford suffered a stroke in August 2000, but regained control of his left hand and much of his speech capability.

One striking gender difference among people recovering from strokes has puzzled researchers. After a stroke involving the left hemisphere, women are significantly less likely than men to be left with major deficits in their language skills. Using fMRI to investigate the reasons for this difference, Shaywitz (1996) found that the processing of certain language skills appears to occur only in the left hemisphere in men, but occurs in areas in both the left and right hemispheres in women. According to Shaywitz, these findings are the first to offer solid evidence of gender-based differences in brain organization for any cognitive function.

Head Injury

Each year more than 373,000 Americans survive injuries that leave them with significant brain damage (Ryan, 1997). Impaired motor coordination and language ability are often the most obvious results of head injury. Even more devastating is the loss of intellectual functioning—concentration, memory, reasoning, judgment, and problem-solving and decision-making abilities. Social behavior is frequently affected, as in the case of Phineas Gage, who became irritable, verbally abusive, and irresponsible. The precise disability depends largely on the area of the brain that is affected and the severity of the damage.

Many people who suffer injuries to the head develop epilepsy—a chronic brain disorder that results in recurring seizures and frequently a loss or impairment of consciousness. Grand mal seizures are marked by convulsions and loss of consciousness. Petit mal seizures involve sudden lapses of consciousness lasting several seconds, during which the victim neither falls nor has a convulsion.

Recovering from Brain Damage

What must occur in the brain for there to be some recovery from brain damage?

Some abilities lost through brain damage can be regained if areas near the damaged site take over the lost functions. In the case of aphasia, the undamaged hemisphere can sometimes be trained to handle the language function but can rarely restore it to normal. Yet, some individuals who have had an entire hemisphere removed early in life because of uncontrollable epilepsy have been able to lead nearly normal lives. One man who had only one hemisphere carried a double major in college and graduated with honors.

Damaged neurons can sprout new dendrites and reestablish connections with other neurons to restore some of the functions that were lost. Axons, too, are able to regenerate and grow (Fawcett, 1992). The ability of the brain to reorganize, to reshape itself in response to input from both internal (within the brain) and external (environmental) sources (Clifford, 2000), and to compensate for damage is termed **plasticity.** Plasticity is greatest in young children in whom the hemispheres are not yet completely lateralized. The importance of brain plasticity can hardly be overstated. If it were not for plasticity, every neuron in the brain, every synapse would be rigidly fixed at birth, coded for in the genome in such a way that no modification could result from experience. Neither learning nor the formation of memories would be possible. For everything we learn and every memory we retain require some lasting physical change in the brain (Clifford, 2000).

We have been taught that once neurons are destroyed, they are gone forever and will not be replaced. However, some exciting new research that questioned that assumption has indicated that the human hippocampus can regenerate neurons (Jones, 1999). Furthermore, in one of the most intriguing discoveries to be made in decades, researchers working with adult monkeys at Princeton University produced the first solid evidence that new neurons are generated in the lining of the ventricles (large fluid-filled areas) deep in the center of the brain and then migrate to the cerebral cortex. Given the similarities between the monkey brain and the human brain, this research opens the possibility that new neurons may be generated in the adult human brain (Gould et al., 1999).

stroke: The most common cause of damage to adult brains, arising when blockage of an artery cuts off the blood supply to a particular area of the brain or when a blood vessel bursts.

plasticity: The ability of the brain to reorganize and compensate for brain damage.

Remember It!

1. The CT scan and MRI are used to
   a. show the amount of activity in various parts of the brain.
   b. produce images of the structures within the brain.
   c. measure electrical activity in the brain.
   d. observe neural communication at synapses.
2. Which of the following reveals the electrical activity of the brain by producing a record of brain waves?
   a. electroencephalograph c. PET scan
   b. CT scan d. MRI
3. Which of the following reveals brain activity and function, rather than the structure of the brain?
   a. CT scan b. EEG c. PET scan d. MRI
4. Which of the following reveals both brain structure and brain activity?
   a. MRI b. PET scan c. fMRI d. CT scan
5. Match the brain-wave pattern with the state associated with it.
   b (1) slow-wave (deep) sleep a. beta wave
   c (2) deep relaxation while awake b. delta wave
   a (3) physical or mental activity c. alpha wave
6. Which of the following is *not* true of stroke?
   a. Stroke is the main cause of injury to the adult brain.
   b. Stroke can cause paralysis and total loss of language ability.
   c. Stroke is caused when the blood supply to part of the brain is cut off.
   d. Although stroke causes many disabilities, it is not life-threatening.
7. Plasticity of the brain increases with age. (true/false)

Answers: 1. b 2. a 3. c 4. c 5. (1) b (2) c (3) a 6. d 7. false

THE PERIPHERAL NERVOUS SYSTEM

What is the peripheral nervous system?

The **peripheral nervous system (PNS)** is made up of all the nerves that connect the central nervous system to the rest of the body. Without the peripheral nervous system, the brain and spinal cord, encased in their bone coverings, would be isolated and unable to send information to or receive information from other parts of the body. The peripheral nervous system has two subdivisions—the somatic nervous system and the autonomic nervous system. Figure 2.11 shows the subdivisions within the peripheral nervous system.

peripheral nervous system (PNS) (peh-RIF-er-ul): The nerves connecting the central nervous system to the rest of the body.

The *somatic nervous system* consists of (1) all the sensory nerves, which transmit information from the sense receptors—eyes, ears, nose, tongue, and skin—to the central nervous system; and (2) all the motor nerves, which relay messages from the central nervous system to all the skeletal muscles of the body. In short, the nerves of the somatic nervous system make it possible for us to sense our environment and to move, and they are primarily under conscious control.

The word *autonomic* is sometimes misread as "automatic," and that is not a bad synonym—because the *autonomic nervous system* operates quite well automatically, without any conscious control or awareness on your part. It transmits messages

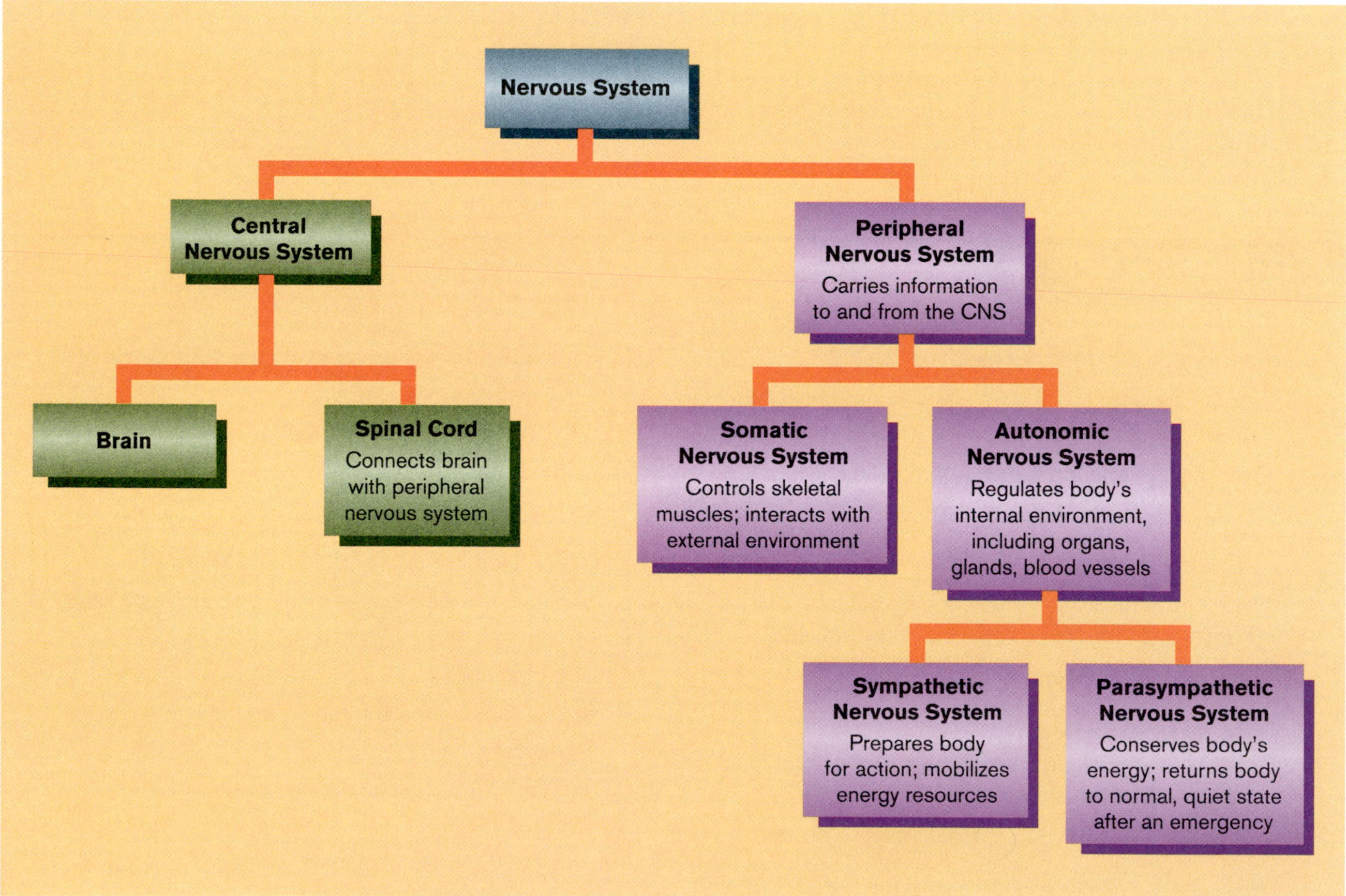

Figure 2.11

The Human Nervous System

The nervous system is divided into two parts: the central nervous system and the peripheral nervous system. The diagram shows the relationships among the parts of the nervous system and provides a brief description of the functions of those parts.

between the central nervous system and the glands, the cardiac (heart) muscle, and the smooth muscles, which are not normally under voluntary control (such as those in the large arteries and the gastrointestinal system).

The autonomic nervous system is further divided into two parts—the sympathetic and the parasympathetic nervous systems. Any time you are under stress or faced with an emergency, the **sympathetic nervous system** automatically mobilizes the body's resources, preparing you for action. This physiological arousal produced by the sympathetic nervous system was named the *fight-or-flight response* by Walter Cannon (1929, 1935). If an ominous-looking stranger started following you and quickened his pace as you turned down a dark, deserted street, your sympathetic nervous system would automatically set to work. Your heart would begin to pound, your pulse rate would increase rapidly, your breathing would quicken, and your digestive system would nearly shut down. The blood flow to your skeletal muscles would be enhanced, and all of your bodily resources would be made ready to handle the emergency—*run!*

But once the emergency is over, something must happen to bring these heightened bodily functions back to normal. The **parasympathetic nervous system** does just that. As a result of its action, your heart stops pounding and slows to normal, your pulse rate and breathing slow down, and your digestive system resumes its normal functioning. As shown in Figure 2.12, the sympathetic and parasympathetic branches act as opposing but complementary forces in the autonomic nervous system. Their balanced functioning is essential for health and survival.

What are the roles of the sympathetic and parasympathetic nervous systems?

sympathetic nervous system: The division of the autonomic nervous system that mobilizes the body's resources during stress, emergencies, or heavy exertion, preparing the body for action.

parasympathetic nervous system: The division of the autonomic nervous system that is associated with relaxation and the conservation of energy and that brings the heightened bodily responses back to normal following an emergency.

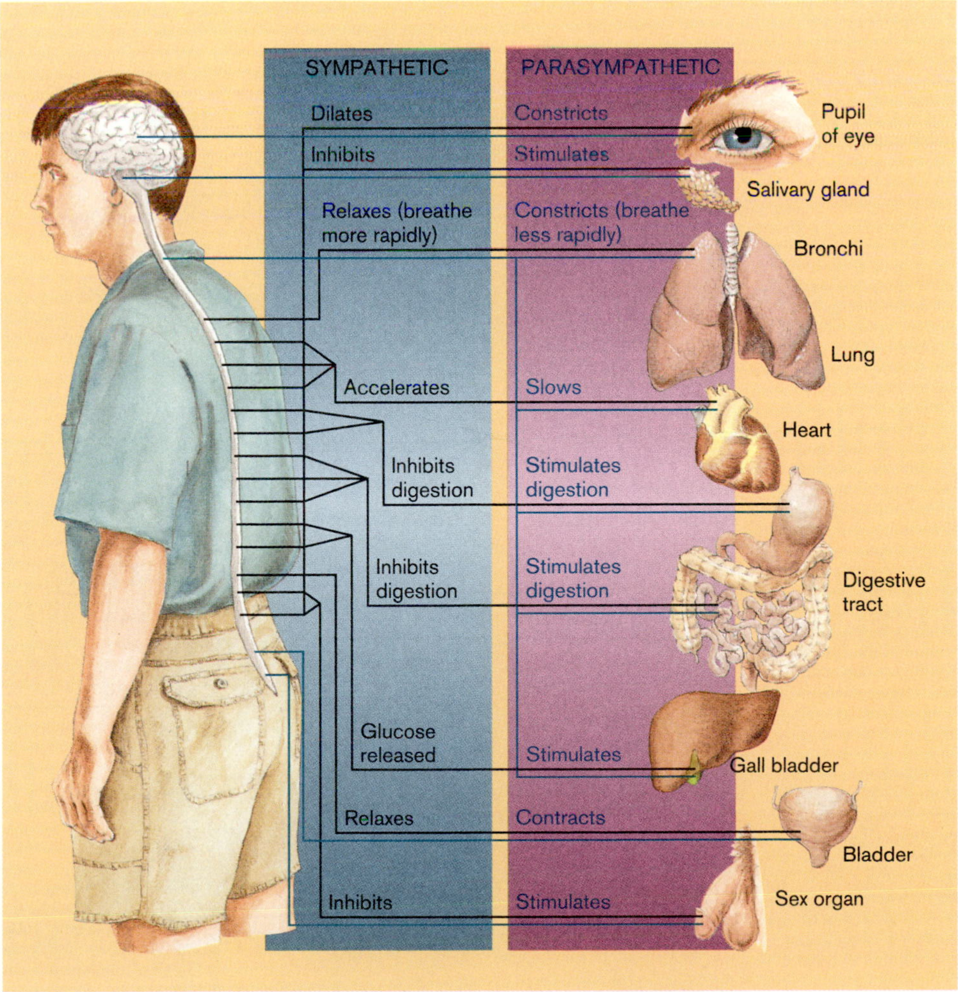

Figure 2.12

The Autonomic Nervous System

The autonomic nervous system consists of (1) the sympathetic nervous system, which mobilizes the body's resources during emergencies or during stress, and (2) the parasympathetic nervous system, which is associated with relaxation and which brings the heightened bodily responses back to normal after an emergency. This diagram shows the opposite effects of the sympathetic and parasympathetic nervous systems on various parts of the body.

THE ENDOCRINE SYSTEM

What is the endocrine system, and what are some of the glands within it?

We have seen how certain chemical substances, the neurotransmitters, exert their influence on the 100 billion or so neurons in the nervous system. There is another system in which chemical substances stimulate and regulate many other important functions in the body. The **endocrine system** is a series of ductless glands, located in various parts of the body, that manufacture and secrete chemical substances known as **hormones,** which are manufactured and released in one part of the body but have an effect on other parts of the body. Hormones are released into the bloodstream and travel throughout the circulatory system, but each hormone performs its assigned job only when it connects with the body cells that have receptors for it. Some of the same chemical substances that are neurotransmitters act as hormones as well—norepinephrine and vasopressin, to name two. Figure 2.13 shows the glands in the endocrine system and their locations in the body.

The **pituitary gland** rests in the brain just below the hypothalamus and is controlled by it (see Figure 2.13). The pituitary is considered to be the master gland of the body because it releases the hormones that "turn on," or activate, the other glands in the endocrine system—a big job for a tiny structure about the size of a pea. The pituitary also produces the hormone that is responsible for body growth (Howard et al., 1996). Too little of this powerful substance will make a person a dwarf; too much will produce a giant.

The *thyroid gland* rests in the front, lower part of the neck just below the voice box (larynx). The thyroid produces the important hormone thyroxin, which regulates the rate at which food is metabolized, or transformed into energy. The *pancreas* regulates the body's blood sugar levels by releasing the hormones insulin and

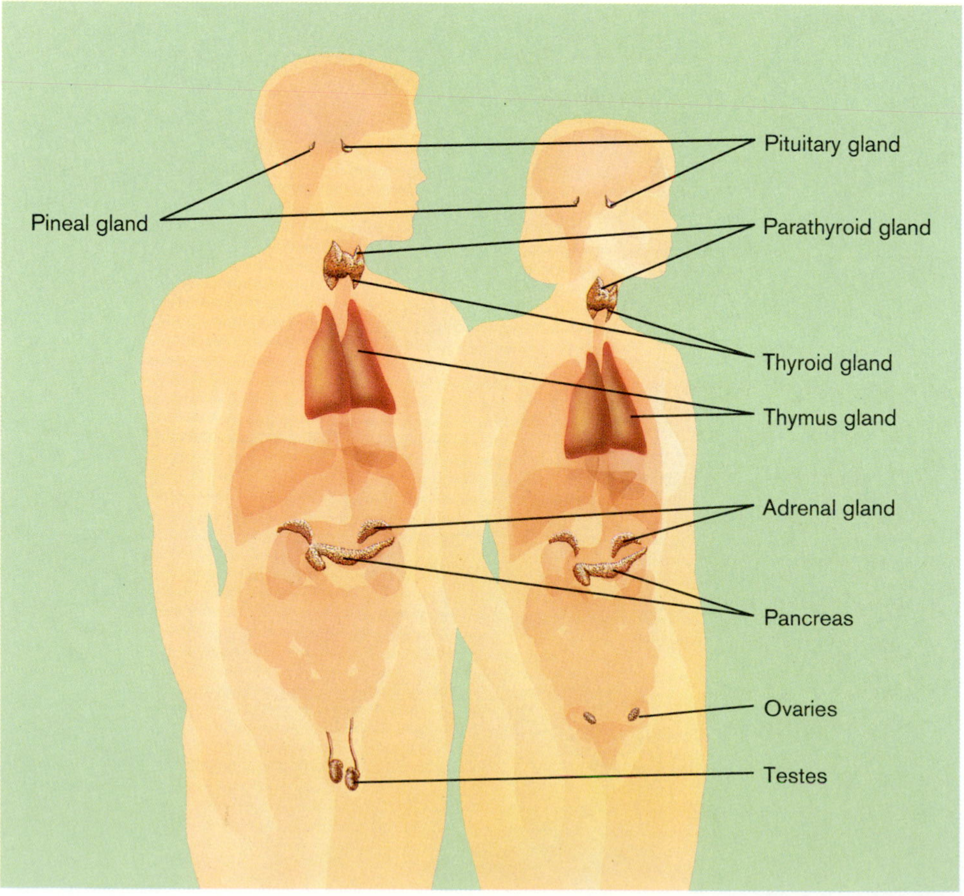

Figure 2.13
The Endocrine System
The endocrine system is a series of glands that manufacture and secrete hormones. The hormones travel through the circulatory system and have important effects on many bodily functions.

glucagon into the bloodstream. In people with diabetes, too little insulin is produced. Without insulin to break down the sugars in food, the blood-sugar levels can get dangerously high.

The two **adrenal glands,** which rest just above the kidneys (as shown in Figure 2.13), produce epinephrine and norepinephrine. By activating the sympathetic nervous system, these two hormones play an important role in the body's response to stress. The adrenal glands also release the corticoids, which control the important salt balance in the body, and small amounts of the sex hormones.

The *gonads* are the sex glands—the ovaries in females and the testes in males (see Figure 2.13). Activated by the pituitary gland, the gonads release the sex hormones that make reproduction possible and that are responsible for the secondary sex characteristics—pubic and underarm hair in both sexes, breasts in females, and facial hair and a deepened voice in males. Androgens, the male sex hormones, influence sexual motivation. Estrogen and progesterone, the female sex hormones, help regulate the menstrual cycle. Although both males and females have androgens and estrogens, males have considerably more androgens, and females have considerably more estrogens. (The sex hormones and their effects are discussed in more detail in Chapter 12.)

Biology and behavior are intimately related. However, there is much more to the scientific study of behavior and mental processes than can be revealed by studying the biological connection alone. Later chapters of this book will expand on other aspects of behavior and mental processes.

endocrine system (EN-duh-krin): A system of ductless glands in various parts of the body that manufacture and secrete hormones into the bloodstream or lymph fluids, thus affecting cells in other parts of the body.

hormone: A substance manufactured and released in one part of the body that affects other parts of the body.

pituitary gland: The endocrine gland located in the brain and often called the "master gland," which releases hormones that control other endocrine glands and also releases a growth hormone.

adrenal glands (ah-DREE-nal): A pair of endocrine glands that release hormones that prepare the body for emergencies and stressful situations and also release small amounts of the sex hormones.

Remember It!

1. The ______________ nervous system connects the brain and spinal cord to the rest of the body.
   a. central c. somatic
   b. peripheral d. autonomic

2. The ______________ nervous system mobilizes the body's resources during times of stress; the ______________ nervous system brings the heightened bodily responses back to normal when the emergency is over.
   a. somatic; autonomic
   b. autonomic; somatic
   c. sympathetic; parasympathetic
   d. parasympathetic; sympathetic

3. The endocrine glands secrete ______________ directly into the ______________ .
   a. hormones; bloodstream
   b. enzymes; digestive tract
   c. enzymes; bloodstream
   d. hormones; digestive tract

4. Match the endocrine gland with the appropriate description.

____ (1) keeps body's metabolism in balance	a. pituitary gland
____ (2) acts as a master gland that activates the other glands	b. adrenal glands
____ (3) regulates blood sugar	c. gonads
____ (4) makes reproduction possible	d. thyroid gland
____ (5) releases hormones that prepare the body for emergencies	e. pancreas

Answers: 1. b 2. c 3. a 4. (1) d (2) a (3) e (4) c (5) b

Apply It!

Handedness–Does It Make a Difference?

If you are left-handed, you are in good company. Alexander the Great, Michelangelo, Leonardo da Vinci, Benjamin Franklin, and Albert Einstein are among the better-known lefties from the past. Among left-handers in more recent times are Martina Navratilova, Whoopi Goldberg, Tom Cruise, and Bill Clinton.

The majority of people–about 90% of the world's population–are right-handed. Left-handedness occurs more often in males than in females. People who are left-handed are generally also left-footed, and to a lesser extent left-eyed and left-eared as well. There is a difference in the motor control provided by the two hemispheres of the brain. Thus, in a person whose left hand is dominant, the right hemisphere is providing superior motor control for that hand.

Is handedness inherited or learned? Scientists have long wondered why such a small percentage of humans are left-handed, and a number of possible explanations have been suggested. Some researchers propose a genetic cause (Annett, 1985; Levy & Nagylaki, 1972); others claim that handedness is for the most part environmentally influenced (Blau, 1946; Provins, 1997). No theory yet proposed is able to explain all the facts, although there is strong evidence of a genetic element in handedness. Hepper and others (1990) found that a hand preference is already apparent in the womb. Of the fetuses they observed, 94.6% were sucking their right thumb and only 5.4% were sucking their left thumb.

Over 20 years ago, Geschwind and Behan (1982) found evidence that a genetically based excess of testosterone or an increased sensitivity to testosterone slows the growth of the left hemisphere and thereby allows greater development of the right hemisphere, which may lead to left-handedness (see also Kelso et al., 2000).

Differences between lefties and righties. Investigators have identified a number of physiological differences between left-handed and right-handed people. On the average, the corpus callosum of left-handers is 11% larger and contains up to 2.5 million more nerve fibers than that of right-handers (Witelson, 1985). In about 60% of left-handers, language functions are controlled by the left hemisphere; in 25%, by the right hemisphere; and in about 15%, by both hemispheres. However, a recent study found right-hemisphere language dominance in 7.5% of 188 healthy male and female participants. These findings suggest that such dominance may be considerably more common than was once believed (Knecht et al., 2000).

In general, the two sides of the brain are less specialized in left-handers (Hellige et al., 1994). Because of this characteristic, left-handers tend to experience less language loss following an injury to either hemisphere. They are also more likely to recover, because the undamaged hemisphere can more easily take over the speech functions.

In many respects, left-handed people are at a disadvantage. Geschwind and Behan (1982) found that left-handers are 12 times more likely than right-handers to stutter and have learning disabilities such as dyslexia. Left-handers are also 2½ times more likely to have autoimmune diseases such as allergies, and they are more likely to suffer from migraine headaches, epilepsy, mental retardation, depression, and other mental disorders. A disproportionate number of premature and low-birth-weight infants are left-handed. It has even been suggested that, on the average, left-handers have a shorter life span than right-handers (Coren & Halpern, 1991). This hypothesis is somewhat controversial, and research on the subject continues (Halpern & Coren, 1993; L. J. Harris, 1993).

Left-handedness is also associated with a variety of positive traits. Benbow and Stanley (1983) found that over 20% of 12- and 13-year-olds with exceptionally high scores on the math portion of the SAT were left-handed. Left-handers are also overrepresented among musicians, artists, engineers, mathematicians, and major-league baseball players.

Left in a right-handed world. Although left-handers are five times more likely to suffer serious accidents than right-handers, and they are sometimes said to be clumsier than right-handers, this is probably because they must function in a world designed for right-handers (Coren, 1989). For example, the gear shift and pedal arrangement in a car are designed for right-handed (and right-footed) people.

Most left-handed people are able to adapt to these conditions. Some actually become ambidextrous as a result of using both hands for certain activities (working with tools, for example). Eating and writing, however, are rarely performed with the "other" hand. Fortunately some items–tools and sports equipment–are designed specifically for left-handers.

Most children show a consistent preference for one hand over the other by the age of 5; some, however, begin to rely on the use of one hand by 18 months. In the United States in the past and in some other parts of the world today, left-handed children have been trained to eat or write with their right hand. Most experts on child development agree that it is harmful to interfere with the hand preference of a young child. It can cause emotional distress and may lead to speech or reading problems (Herron, 1980).

THINKING CRITICALLY

Evaluation

Using your knowledge about how the human brain has been studied in the past and is studied today, point out the advantages and the disadvantages of the older investigative methods—the case study, the autopsy, and the study of people with brain injuries or who have had brain surgery (including the split-brain operation). Follow the same procedure to discuss the more modern techniques—EEG, CT scan, MRI, PET scan, and fMRI.

Point/Counterpoint

A continuing controversial issue is the ethical question of whether animals should be used in biological research. Review the chapter and find each instance of animals being used to advance scientific knowledge of the brain. Using what you have read in this chapter and any other information you have acquired, prepare arguments to support both of the following positions:

a. The use of animals in research projects is ethical and justifiable because of the possible benefits to humankind.

b. The use of animals in research projects is not ethical or justifiable on the grounds of possible benefits to humankind.

Psychology in Your Life

How would your life change if you had a massive stroke affecting your left hemisphere? How would it change if the stroke damaged your right hemisphere? Which stroke would be more tragic for you, and why?

SUMMARY AND REVIEW

THE NEURONS AND THE NEUROTRANSMITTERS

What is a neuron, and what are its three parts?

A neuron is a specialized cell that conducts messages through the nervous system. Its three main parts are the cell body, the dendrites, and the axon.

What is a synapse?

A synapse is the junction where the axon terminal of a sending neuron communicates with a receiving neuron across the synaptic cleft.

What is the action potential?

The action potential is the sudden reversal (from a negative to a positive value) of the resting potential on the cell membrane of a neuron, which initiates the firing of a neuron.

What are neurotransmitters, and what role do they play in the transmission of signals from one neuron to another?

Neurotransmitters are chemicals released into the synaptic cleft from the axon terminal of the sending neuron. They cross the synaptic cleft and bind to receptors on the receiving neuron, influencing the cell to fire or not to fire.

What are some of the ways in which neurotransmitters affect behavior, and what are some of the major neurotransmitters?

Neurotransmitters regulate the actions of glands and muscles, affect learning and memory, promote sleep, stimulate mental and physical alertness, and influence moods and emotions ranging from depression to euphoria. Some of the major neurotransmitters are acetylcholine, dopamine, norepinephrine, serotonin, glutamate, GABA, and endorphins.

How can the brain tell the difference between a very strong and a very weak stimulus?

A strong stimulus will cause many more neurons to fire and to fire much more rapidly than a weak stimulus will.

Key Terms

neuron (p. 42); cell body (p. 42); dendrites (p. 42); axon (p. 42); synapse (p. 43); permeability (p. 43); resting potential (p. 43); action potential (p. 43); neurotransmitter (p. 44); receptors (p. 44); reuptake (p. 45); acetylcholine (p. 46); dopamine (p. 46); norepinephrine (p. 46); serotonin (p. 46); endorphins (p. 47); myelin sheath (p. 48); glial cells (p. 48)

THE CENTRAL NERVOUS SYSTEM

Why is an intact spinal cord important to normal functioning?

The spinal cord is an extension of the brain connecting it to the peripheral nervous system. The spinal cord must be intact so that sensory information can reach the brain and messages from the brain can reach the muscles and glands.

What are the crucial functions handled by the brainstem?

The brainstem contains (1) the medulla, which controls heartbeat, breathing, blood pressure, coughing, and swallowing, and (2) the reticular formation, which plays a crucial role in arousal and attention.

What are the primary functions of the cerebellum?

The cerebellum allows the body to execute smooth, skilled movements and regulates muscle tone and posture.

What is the primary role of the thalamus?

The thalamus acts as a relay station for information flowing into and out of the higher brain centers.

What are some of the processes regulated by the hypothalamus?

The hypothalamus controls the pituitary gland and regulates hunger, thirst, sexual behavior, body temperature, and a variety of emotional behaviors.

What is the role of the limbic system?

The limbic system is a group of structures in the brain, including the amygdala and the hippocampus, which are collectively involved in emotion, memory, and motivation.

Key Terms

central nervous system (p. 49); spinal cord (p. 49); brainstem (p. 50); medulla (p. 50); reticular formation (p. 50); cerebellum (p. 51); thalamus (p. 52); hypothalamus (p. 52); limbic system (p. 52); amygdala (p. 52); hippocampus (p. 53)

THE CEREBRAL HEMISPHERES

What are the cerebral hemispheres, the corpus callosum, and the cerebral cortex?

The cerebral hemispheres are the two halves of the cerebrum, connected by the corpus callosum and covered by the cerebral cortex, which is responsible for higher mental processes such as language, memory, and thinking.

What are some of the main areas within the frontal lobes, and what are their functions?

The frontal lobes contain (1) the motor cortex, which controls voluntary motor activity; (2) Broca's area, which functions in speech production; and (3) the frontal association areas, which are involved in thinking, motivation, planning for the future, impulse control, and emotional responses.

What are the primary functions of the parietal lobes in general and the somatosensory cortex in particular?

The parietal lobes are involved in the reception and processing of touch stimuli. They contain the somatosensory cortex, where touch, pressure, temperature, and pain register.

What are the primary functions of the occipital lobes in general and the primary visual cortex in particular?

The occipital lobes are involved in the reception and interpretation of visual information. They contain the primary visual cortex, where vision registers in the cerebral cortex.

What are the major areas within the temporal lobes, and what are their functions?

The temporal lobes contain (1) the primary auditory cortex, where hearing registers in the cortex; (2) Wernicke's area, which is involved in comprehending the spoken word and in formulating coherent speech and written language; and (3) association areas, where memories are stored and auditory stimuli are interpreted.

What are the specialized functions of the left hemisphere?

The left hemisphere controls the right side of the body, coordinates complex movements, and handles most of the language functions, including speaking, writing, reading, and understanding the spoken word.

What are the specialized functions of the right hemisphere?

The right hemisphere controls the left side of the body; is specialized for visual-spatial perception, singing, and interpreting nonverbal behavior; and is more active in the recognition and expression of emotion.

What is the significance of the split-brain operation?

In the split-brain operation a surgeon cuts the corpus callosum, preventing the transfer of information between the cerebral hemispheres. Research on split-brain patients has extended scientific knowledge of the functions of the hemispheres.

Key Terms

cerebrum (p. 54); cerebral hemispheres (p. 54); corpus callosum (p. 54); cerebral cortex (p. 54); association areas (p. 55); frontal lobes (p. 55); motor cortex (p. 56); Broca's area (p. 58); Broca's aphasia (p. 58); aphasia (p. 58); parietal lobes (p. 58); somatosensory cortex (p. 58); occipital lobes (p. 59); primary visual cortex (p. 59); temporal lobes (p. 60); primary auditory cortex (p. 60); Wernicke's area (p. 60); Wernicke's aphasia (p. 60); lateralization (p. 61); left hemisphere (p. 61); right hemisphere (p. 62); split-brain operation (p. 64)

DISCOVERING THE BRAIN'S MYSTERIES

What are some methods that researchers have used to learn about brain function?

Researchers have learned about brain function from clinical studies of patients, through electrical stimulation of the brain, and from studies using the EEG, microelectrodes, CT scan, MRI, PET scan, and fMRI.

What is the electroencephalogram (EEG), and what are three of the brain-wave patterns it reveals?

The electroencephalogram (EEG) is a record of brain-wave activity. Three normal brain-wave patterns are the beta wave, the alpha wave, and the delta wave.

Key Terms

electroencephalogram (EEG) (p. 66); beta wave (p. 66); alpha wave (p. 66); delta wave (p. 66); microelectrode (p. 66); CT scan (p. 66); MRI (p. 66); PET scan (p. 66); fMRI (p. 67)

BRAIN DAMAGE: CAUSES AND CONSEQUENCES

Why is a stroke so serious?

In the United States, stroke is the most common cause of damage to the adult brain and the third leading cause of death. It leaves many of its victims with paralysis and/or aphasia.

What must occur in the brain for there to be some recovery from brain damage?

For some recovery from brain damage to occur, (1) damaged neurons must sprout new dendrites and reestablish connections with other neurons, (2) areas near the damaged site must take over the lost function, or (3) the undamaged hemisphere must assume the lost language function (as in aphasia).

Key Terms

stroke (p. 68); plasticity (p. 69)

THE PERIPHERAL NERVOUS SYSTEM

What is the peripheral nervous system?

The peripheral nervous system connects the central nervous system to the rest of the body. It has two subdivisions: (1) the somatic nervous system, which consists of the nerves that make it possible for the body to sense and move; and (2) the autonomic nervous system.

What are the roles of the sympathetic and parasympathetic nervous systems?

The autonomic nervous system has two parts: (1) the sympathetic nervous system, which mobilizes the body's resources during emergencies or during stress; and (2) the parasympathetic nervous system, which is associated with relaxation and brings the heightened bodily responses back to normal after an emergency.

Key Terms
peripheral nervous system (p. 70); sympathetic nervous system (p. 71); parasympathetic nervous system (p. 71)

THE ENDOCRINE SYSTEM

What is the endocrine system, and what are some of the glands within it?

The endocrine system is a system of glands in various parts of the body that manufacture hormones and secrete them into the bloodstream. The hormones then affect cells in other parts of the body. The pituitary gland releases hormones that control other glands in the endocrine system and also releases a growth hormone. The thyroid gland produces thyroxin, which regulates metabolism. The pancreas produces insulin and regulates blood sugar. The adrenal glands release epinephrine and norepinephrine, which prepare the body for emergencies and stressful situations; those glands also release small amounts of the sex hormones. The gonads are the sex glands, which produce the sex hormones and make reproduction possible.

Key Terms
endocrine system (p. 72); hormone (p. 72); pituitary gland (p. 72); adrenal glands (p. 73)

Surf It!

Want to be sure you've absorbed the material in Chapter 2, "Biology and Behavior," before the big test? Visiting *www.abacon.com/wood* can put a top grade within your reach. The site is loaded with free practice tests, flashcards, activities, and links to help you review your way to an A. To enliven that inevitable study break, the site also offers personality assessment quizzes and a psychology career corner.

3 Sensation and Perception

Sensation: The Sensory World

Vision

Hearing

Smell and Taste

The Other Senses

Perception: Ways of Perceiving

Additional Influences on Perception

Subliminal Persuasion and Extrasensory Perception

5 major senses.
sight - manometers.
theories about
why + how work
theory color vision
theory of hearing p.94 (2)

The man called S.B. had never seen a sunrise, a flower, a smile, or even his own face, for he had lost his sight in both eyes when he was only 10 months old. Despite his blindness, S.B. had managed to live a fairly full and happy life. He could get around on his own, cross streets, and even ride a bicycle with his friend's hand on his shoulder to guide him. He read Braille, and he loved to make things with tools in the small shed he used as a workshop.

All his life S.B. had wondered what it would be like to see. Then, when he was 50 years old, he learned that his useless, opaque corneas could be replaced through a cornea transplant. Finally, the miracle of sight he had dreamed about would be a reality.

When the surgeon first removed the bandages from S.B.'s eyes, people and objects were little more than large blurs to him. But the operation was successful, and after a few days S.B. could see quite well. He could walk up and down the hospital corridors without using a cane or holding onto the wall. Soon he was able to see and recognize objects by sight that he already knew well by touch. But all was not well.

S.B. had difficulty recognizing unfamiliar objects and things he had never touched. He never learned to read by sight, although he could recognize numbers and capital letters. S.B. had trouble perceiving distance. From the window of his hospital room he watched the cars and trucks pass in the street below. He thought his feet would touch the ground if he hung from the windowsill with his hands, yet his window was nearly 60 feet above the ground.

S.B.'s story did not have a happy ending. The world looked drab to him, and he was upset by the imperfections he saw. Objects he had once imagined to be perfect now had disappointing defects. He could no longer cross streets because seeing cars whizzing by terrified him. Often he would not even bother to turn on the lights at night, for he preferred to sit in his more comfortable world of darkness. As time passed, S.B. became more and more depressed and withdrawn. Within 3 years after the cornea transplant, he died. (Adapted from Gregory, 1978.)

Are you surprised that the miracle in S.B.'s life, the gift of sight, turned out to be hardly a gift at all? The surgeons were able to give him the sensation of sight but, sadly, not the 50 years of visual perceptual experience he had missed.

What is the difference between sensation and perception?

Sensation and perception are intimately related in everyday experience, but they are not the same. **Sensation** is the process through which the senses detect visual, auditory, and other sensory stimuli and transmit them to the brain. **Perception** is the process by which sensory information is actively organized and interpreted by the brain. Sensation furnishes the raw material of sensory experience, while perception provides the finished product.

To a large extent humans must learn to perceive, and people whose sight has been restored differ greatly in their ability to develop useful perception. S.B.'s life shows dramatically the great gap between sensation (the reception of sensory information) and perception (the process of giving it meaning). For many who regain their vision, it is truly a remarkable gift; but for others like S.B., gaining sight can be a major disappointment.

In this chapter we will explore the world of sensation, with a focus on the five primary senses—vision, hearing, touch, taste, and smell—along with such secondary senses as balance and pain. You will learn how the senses detect sensory information and how this sensory information is actively organized and interpreted by the brain. We begin with a closer look at sensation.

SENSATION: THE SENSORY WORLD

sensation: The process through which the senses pick up visual, auditory, and other sensory stimuli and transmit them to the brain; sensory information that has registered in the brain but has not been interpreted.

perception: The process by which sensory information is actively organized and interpreted by the brain.

Our senses serve as ports of entry for all information about the world. Virtually everything we experience is detected initially by our senses. Yet it is amazing how little of the sensory world we actually sense. For example, we can see only a thin slice of the vast spectrum of electromagnetic energy. We cannot perceive microwaves, X rays, or ultraviolet light. We are unable to hear the ultrasonic sound of a dog whistle and can detect a scant 20% of the sounds a dolphin or a bat can hear. Nor can we sense the outline of a warm-blooded animal from its infrared heat pattern at night, as rattlesnakes and other pit vipers can. Yet all these sensory stimuli exist in the real, physical world.

No matter which of the senses are compared, humans are not at the top of the list for quality or sensitivity. Some animals have a superior sense of hearing (bats and dolphins); others have sharper vision (hawks); still others have a superior sense of smell (bloodhounds); and so on. Nevertheless, humans have remarkable sensory abilities and superior abilities of perception.

Along the U.S.–Mexican border, infrared-sensitive cameras are used to allow police to "see" illegal entrants in the dark. Their body heat is what makes the two people show up in this infrared photo.

The Absolute Threshold: To Sense or Not to Sense

What is the difference between the absolute threshold and the difference threshold?

What is the softest sound you can hear, the dimmest light you can see, the most diluted substance you can taste? What is the lightest touch you can feel, the faintest odor you can smell? Researchers in sensory psychology and psychophysics have performed many experiments over the years to answer these questions. Their research has established measures for the senses known as *absolute thresholds.* Just as the threshold of a doorway is the dividing point between being outside a room and inside, the **absolute threshold** of a sense marks the difference between not being able to perceive a stimulus and being just barely able to perceive it. Psychologists have arbitrarily defined this absolute threshold as the minimum amount of sensory stimulation that can be detected 50% of the time. The absolute thresholds established for the five primary senses in humans are (1) for vision, a candle flame 30 miles away on a clear night; (2) for hearing, a watch ticking 20 feet away; (3) for taste, 1 teaspoon of sugar dissolved in 2 gallons of water; (4) for smell, a single drop of perfume in a three-room house; and (5) for touch, a bee's wing falling a distance of 1 centimeter onto the cheek.

Important as it is, the absolute threshold, once crossed, says nothing about the broad range of sensory experiences. To sense or not to sense—that is the only question the absolute threshold answers. But read on—there are other questions to be answered.

The Difference Threshold: Detecting Differences

If you are listening to music, the very fact that you can hear it means that the absolute threshold has been crossed. But how much must the volume be turned up or down for you to notice a difference? Or, if you are carrying a load of books, how much weight must be added or subtracted for you to be able to sense that your load is heavier or lighter? The **difference threshold** is a measure of the smallest increase or decrease in a physical stimulus that is required to produce the **just noticeable difference (JND).** The JND is the smallest change in sensation that a person is able to detect 50% of the time. If you were holding a 5-pound weight and 1 pound were added, you could easily notice the difference. But if you were holding 100 pounds and 1 additional pound were added, you could not sense the difference. Why not?

More than 150 years ago, researcher Ernst Weber (1795–1878) observed that the JND for all the senses depends on a proportion or percentage of change rather than a fixed amount of change. This observation became known as **Weber's law.** A weight you are holding must increase or decrease by a ratio of 1/50, or 2%, for you to notice the difference. According to Weber's law, the greater the original stimulus, the more it must be increased or decreased for the difference to be noticeable.

The difference threshold is not the same for all the senses. A very large (1/5, or 20%) difference is necessary for some changes in taste to be detected. In contrast, if you were listening to music, you would notice a difference if a tone became slightly higher or lower in pitch by only about 0.33%.

Aren't some people more sensitive to sensory changes than others? Yes, the difference thresholds for the various senses are not the same for all people. In fact, there are great individual differences. Expert wine tasters would know if a particular vintage was a little too sweet, even if its sweetness varied by only a fraction of the 20% necessary for changes in taste. Actually, Weber's law best fits people with average sensitivities, and sensory stimuli that are neither very strong (loud thunder) nor very weak (a faint whisper). Furthermore, people who have lost one sensory

absolute threshold: The minimum amount of sensory stimulation that can be detected 50% of the time.

difference threshold: The smallest increase or decrease in a physical stimulus required to produce a difference in sensation that is noticeable 50% of the time.

just noticeable difference (JND): The smallest change in sensation that a person is able to detect 50% of the time.

Weber's law: The law stating that the just noticeable difference (JND) for all the senses depends on a proportion or percentage of change in a stimulus rather than on a fixed amount of change.

signal detection theory: The view that detection of a sensory stimulus involves discriminating a stimulus from background "noise" and deciding whether the stimulus is actually present.

sensory receptors: Specialized cells in the sense organs that detect and respond to sensory stimuli—light, sound, odors, etc.—and transduce (convert) the stimuli into neural impulses.

transduction: The process by which sensory receptors convert sensory stimuli—light, sound, odors, etc.—into neural impulses.

sensory adaptation: The process of becoming less sensitive to an unchanging sensory stimulus over time.

ability often gain greater sensitivity in the others. For example, one study found that children with early-onset blindness were more capable of correctly labeling 25 common odors than were sighted children (Rosenbluth et al., 2000).

Signal Detection Theory

You may have realized that the classic methods in psychophysics for measuring sensory thresholds have a serious limitation. They focus exclusively on the physical stimulus—how strong or weak it is or how much the stimulus must change for the difference to be noticed. But even within the same individual, sensory capabilities are sharper and duller from time to time and under different conditions. Factors that affect a person's ability to detect a sensory signal are, in addition to the strength of the stimulus, the person's motivation to detect it, previous experience, expectation that it will occur, and alertness or level of fatigue.

Another approach takes these factors into account. **Signal detection theory** is the view that the detection of a sensory stimulus involves discriminating that stimulus from background "noise" and deciding whether the stimulus is actually present. Deciding that a stimulus is present depends partly on the probability that the stimulus will occur and partly on the potential gain or loss associated with deciding that it is present or absent.

Suppose you were given the description of a cousin you had never seen before and were asked to pick her up at the airport. Your task would be to scan a sea of faces for someone fitting the description and then to decide which of the several people who fit the description was actually your cousin. All the other faces and objects in your field of vision would be considered background noise. How sure you would have to be before you approached someone would depend on several factors—among them the embarrassment you might feel approaching the wrong person as opposed to the distress you would feel if you failed to find your cousin.

Signal detection theory has special relevance to people in many occupations—air traffic controllers, police officers, military personnel on guard duty, medical professionals, poultry inspectors, to name a few. Whether these professionals detect certain stimuli can have important consequences for the health and welfare of vast numbers of people (Swets, 1992).

Transduction: Transforming Sensory Stimuli into Neural Impulses

How are sensory stimuli in the environment experienced as sensations?

You may be surprised to learn that our eyes do not actually see; nor do our ears hear. The sense organs provide only the beginning point of sensation that must be completed by the brain. As you learned in Chapter 2, specific clusters of neurons in specialized parts of the brain must be stimulated for you to see, hear, taste, and so on. Yet the brain itself cannot respond directly to light, sound waves, odors, and tastes. How, then, does it get the message? The answer is through the sensory receptors.

The body's sense organs are equipped with specialized cells called **sensory receptors,** which detect and respond to one type of sensory stimuli—light, sound waves, odors, and so on. Then, through a process known as **transduction,** the receptors change or convert the sensory stimulation into neural impulses, the electrochemical language of the brain. The neural impulses are then transmitted to precise locations in the brain, such as the primary visual cortex for vision or the primary auditory cortex for hearing. You experience a sensation only when the appropriate part of the brain is stimulated. The sense receptors provide the essential link between the physical sensory world and the brain.

Sensory Adaptation

All of our senses are more receptive, more finely tuned, to changes in sensory stimuli than to sameness. After a time the sensory receptors grow accustomed to constant, unchanging levels of stimuli—sights, sounds, smells—so that we notice them less and less, or not at all. This process of becoming less sensitive to an unchanging sensory stimulus over time is known as **sensory adaptation.**

In going for a swim, when you first enter the water, the temperature receptors in your skin may vigorously signal "ice water." But gradually sensory adaptation occurs, and the water feels comfortable. Similarly, you have undoubtedly noticed the distinctive odor of your home when you first walk through the door, but after a few minutes you are not aware of it. A continuous odor will stimulate the smell receptors to respond only for a while. Then, if there is no change in the odors, the receptors will steadily diminish their firing rate, and smell adaptation will occur. However, sensory adaptation is not likely to occur in the presence of a very strong stimulus—such as the smell of ammonia, an ear-splitting sound, or the taste of rancid food.

When members of the Polar Bear Club go swimming in icy waters in midwinter, they experience sensory adaptation, which helps their bodies adjust to freezing temperatures.

Even though it reduces your sensory awareness, sensory adaptation enables you to shift your attention to what is most important at any given moment. You don't need to constantly sense the feel of the clothing on your body, background noises around you, or any persistent odors in your environment. Thanks to sensory adaptation, you can give full concentration to new incoming stimuli.

Remember It!

1. The process through which the senses detect sensory information and transmit it to the brain is called (sensation, perception).
2. The point at which you can barely sense a stimulus 50% of the time is called the (absolute, difference) threshold.
3. The difference threshold is the same for all individuals. (true/false)
4. Which of the following is *not* true of sensory receptors?
   a. They are specialized to detect certain sensory stimuli.
   b. They transduce sensory stimuli into neural impulses.
   c. They are located in the brain.
   d. They provide the link between the physical sensory world and the brain.
5. The process by which a sensory stimulus is converted into a neural impulse is called ________________.
6. Each day when Jessica goes to work at a coffee house, she smells the strong odor of fresh-brewed coffee. After she is there for a few minutes, she is no longer aware of it. What accounts for this?
   a. signal detection theory
   b. sensory adaptation
   c. transduction
   d. the just noticeable difference

Answers: 1. sensation 2. absolute 3. false 4. c 5. transduction 6. b

VISION

For most people, vision is the most valued sensory experience, and it is the sense that has been most investigated. But, before looking at *how* you see, let's consider *what* you see. You cannot see any object unless light is reflected from it or given off by it.

Figure 3.1

The Electromagnetic Spectrum

Human eyes can perceive only a very thin band of electromagnetic waves known as the visible spectrum.

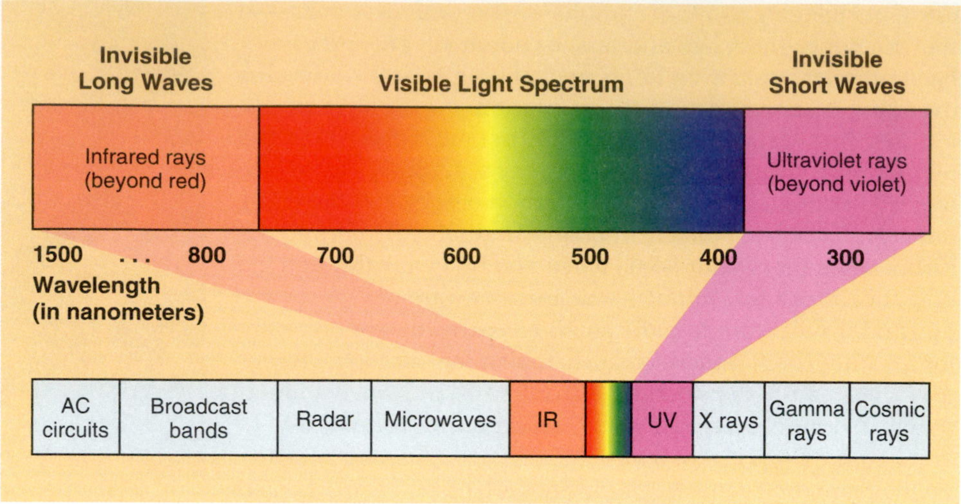

Light: What We See

Light is one form of electromagnetic rays made up of tiny particles called *photons,* which travel in waves. But light is only a small portion of the spectrum of electromagnetic waves (see Figure 3.1). Cosmic rays, gamma rays, X rays, and ultraviolet rays have wavelengths too short for human eyes to perceive. And the wavelengths of infrared rays, microwaves, radar waves, radio and TV waves, and AC circuits are too long. Our eyes can respond only to a very narrow band of electromagnetic waves, a band called the **visible spectrum.**

The length of a light wave primarily determines the color the human eye perceives. The shortest light waves we can see appear violet, while the longest visible waves appear red. *What* we see is confined to the visible spectrum, but *how* we see depends on the many parts of the eye and brain that bring us the world of sight.

The Eye: Window to the Visual Sensory World

For most of us, the eyes are the most important sensory connection to the world. Vision provides most of the information on which the brain feeds. Look at the parts of the eye shown in Figure 3.2 as you read about the role each structure plays in vision.

Figure 3.2

The Major Parts of the Human Eye

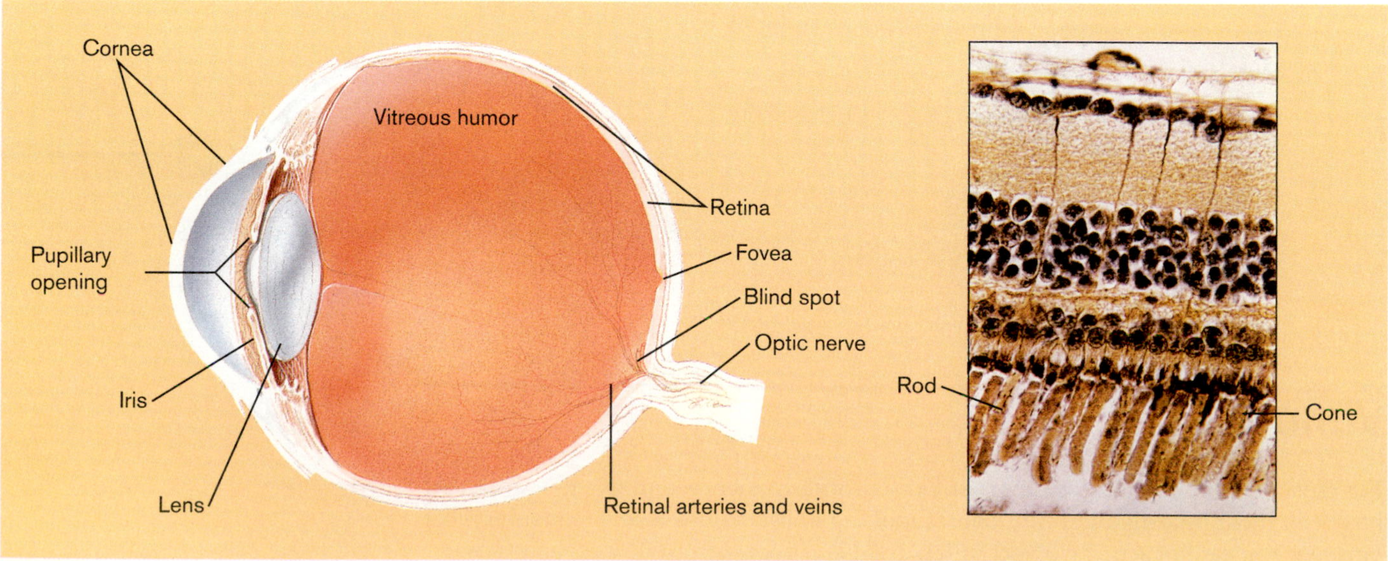

The Cornea, Iris, and Pupil: Up Front in the Eye The globe-shaped human eyeball measures about 1 inch in diameter. Bulging from its front surface is the **cornea**—the tough, transparent, protective layer covering the front of the eye. About the size of a dime, the cornea performs the first step in vision by bending the light rays inward. It herds the light rays through the pupil—the small, dark opening in the center of the iris.

How do the cornea, the iris, and the pupil function in vision?

The iris is the circular, colored part of the eye, which researchers have found to be even more unique to individuals than their fingerprints (Johnson, 1996). Two muscles in the iris dilate and contract the pupil and thus regulate the amount of light entering the eye. Although the pupil never closes completely, the iris can contract it to the size of the head of a pin in very bright light and can dilate it to the size of a pencil eraser in very dim light. You have no control over the dilation and contraction of your pupils; the motion is a reflex, completely automatic. The connective tissue of the iris consists largely of collagen, which is extremely durable, even though it goes through large and frequent changes in pupil size (Wyatt, 2000).

The pupils respond to emotions as well as to light. When a person looks at someone or something highly desirable, the pupils dilate as if to take in more of the pleasing view (Hess, 1965). The pupils also dilate when a person is frightened, telling a lie, or sexually aroused. Pupil size is also related to mental effort—the more intense the mental activity, the larger the pupils become.

From Lens to Retina: Focusing Images Suspended just behind the iris and the pupil, the **lens** is composed of many thin layers and looks like a transparent disc. The lens performs the task of focusing on objects closer than 20 feet. It flattens as it focuses on objects viewed at a distance, but it becomes more spherical, bulging in the center, as it focuses on close objects. This flattening and bulging action of the lens is known as **accommodation.** With age, the lens loses some elasticity and is subject to swelling and bloating. Hence, it loses the ability to change its shape to accommodate for near vision, a condition called *presbyopia* ("old eyes"). This is why many people over age 40 must hold a book or newspaper at arm's length or use reading glasses to magnify the print. This accommodation loss is the most rapid age-related physical change that humans experience (Weale, 2000). As a result of aging, disease, or injury, some people develop *cataracts*—a clouding of the lens that grows worse with time and can lead to blindness if not treated.

What are the lens and the retina?

The lens focuses the incoming image onto the **retina**—a layer of tissue about the size of a small postage stamp and as thin as onion skin, located on the inner surface of the eyeball and containing the sensory receptors for vision. The image projected onto the retina is upside down and reversed left to right. You can demonstrate this for yourself in the *Try It!*

Try It!

Take an ordinary teaspoon—one in which you can see your reflection. Looking at the bottom (the convex surface) of the spoon, you will see an image of your face that is right side up—the way the image enters the eye. Turn the spoon over and look at the inside (the concave surface), and you will see your face upside down and reversed left to right—the way the image appears on the retina. The brain, however, perceives images right side up.

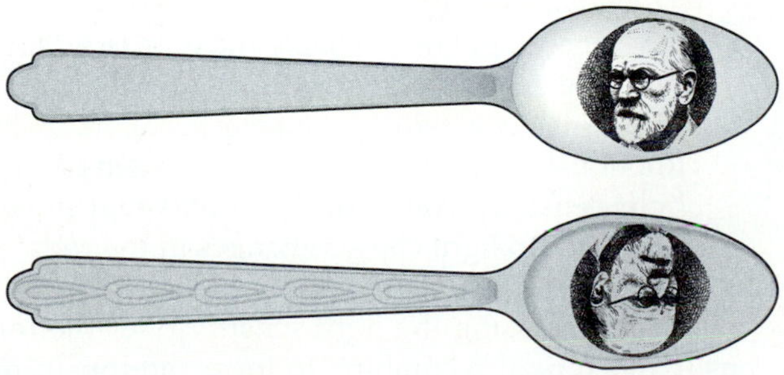

visible spectrum: The narrow band of electromagnetic waves, 380–760 nm in length, that are visible to the human eye.

cornea (KOR-nee-uh): The transparent covering on the front surface of the eyeball that bends light rays inward through the pupil.

lens: The transparent structure behind the iris that changes shape as it focuses images on the retina.

accommodation: The action of the lens in changing shape as it focuses objects on the retina, becoming more spherical for near objects and flatter for far objects.

retina: The layer of tissue at the back of the eye that contains the rods and the cones and onto which the incoming image is projected by the lens.

rods: The light-sensitive receptors in the retina that allow humans to see in black, white, and shades of gray in dim light.

cones: The receptor cells in the retina that enable humans to see color and fine detail in adequate light, but that do not function in dim light.

fovea (FO-vee-uh): A small area of the retina, 1/50 of an inch in diameter, that provides the clearest and sharpest vision because it has the largest concentration of cones.

What roles do the rods and cones play in vision?

In some people, the distance through the eyeball (from the lens to the retina) is either too short or too long for proper focusing. Nearsightedness (myopia) occurs when the lens focuses images of distant objects in front of, rather than on, the retina. A person with this condition will be able to see near objects clearly, but distant images will be blurred. Farsightedness (hyperopia) occurs when the focal image is longer than the eye can handle, as if the image should focus behind the retina (see Figure 3.3). The individual is able to see far objects clearly, but close objects are blurred. Both conditions are correctable with eyeglasses, contact lenses, or a surgical procedure known as *LASIK*.

The Rods and Cones: Receptors for Light and Color At the back of the retina is a layer of light-sensitive receptor cells—the **rods** and the **cones.** Named for their shapes, the rods look like slender cylinders, and the cones appear shorter and more rounded. There are about 120 million rods and 6 million cones in each retina.

The cones are the receptor cells that enable us to see color and fine detail in adequate light, but they do not function in very dim light. There are three types of cones, each particularly sensitive to one of three colors—red, green, or blue (Roorda & Williams, 1999). The bipolar cells and the ganglion cells in the retina begin the work that the brain completes in computing the perceived colors and analyzing the relative activity in the three types of cones (Masland, 1996; Nathans, 1989). You will read more about color vision later in this chapter.

If someone were to plot an imaginary line through the middle of your pupil, the line would strike the center of the retina in the **fovea,** a small pit-like area about the size of the period at the end of this sentence (refer to Figure 3.2). When you look directly at an object, the image of the object is focused on the center of your fovea. The clearest point of your vision, the fovea is the part of the retina that you use for fine detail work. A normal fovea precisely and accurately maps visual stimuli from the retina to the visual cortex (Levi et al., 2000).

Only 1/50 of an inch in diameter, the fovea contains no rods but has some 30,000 cones tightly packed together (Beatty, 1995). Anatomical evidence confirms that cones are most densely packed at the center of the fovea; their density decreases sharply just a few degrees beyond the fovea's center and levels off more gradually to the periphery of the retina (Abramov & Gordon, 1994). On this peripheral region of the retina, the cones—at least, the red (long-wavelength) and the green (medium-wavelength) ones—appear to be randomly spaced (Otake et al., 2000).

The rods respond to black and white light, and they encode all other visible wavelengths but encode them in shades of gray instead of in color. More sensitive to light than the cones, the rods enable us to see in very dim light and provide night vision. The rods in the human eye are extremely sensitive, allowing the eye to respond to as few as five photons of light (Hecht et al., 1942). Even though the rods are more sensitive to light and enable us to see in dim light, they do not provide the sharp, clear images that the cones make possible.

What happens to enable the eyes to adapt to very different lighting conditions, from extremely dim to brightly illuminated? The answer lies primarily in a reddish-purple pigment in the rods called *rhodopsin.* Rhodopsin is a large molecule composed of a protein (opsin) bonded to a light-sensitive compound (retinal) that is very similar to vitamin A. Exposure to light causes changes in the rods' rhodopsin molecules that eventually result in the release of retinal from opsin, thereby inactivating the rhodopsin and decreasing the light sensitivity of the rods. In dim light or in the dark, opsin and retinal recombine to form rhodopsin molecules and restore the rods' sensitivity to light.

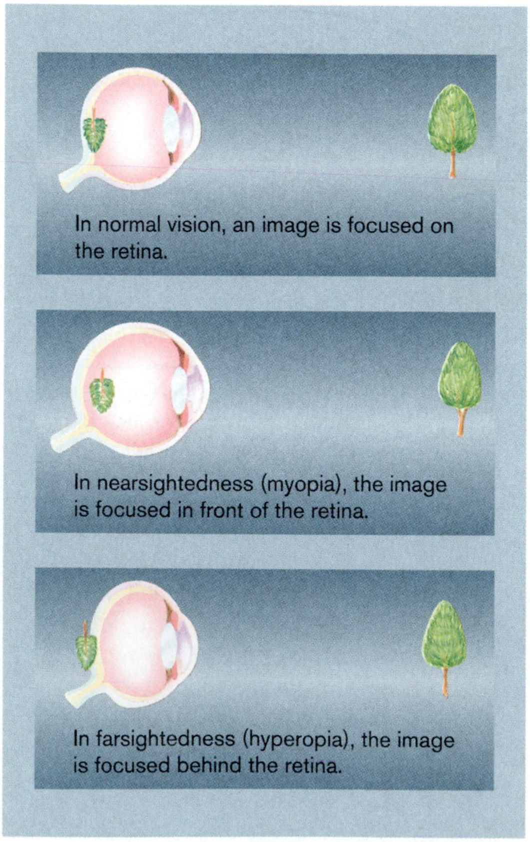

Figure 3.3
Normal Vision, Nearsightedness, and Farsightedness

Dark Adaptation Step from the bright sunlight into a darkened movie theater and at first you can hardly tell which seats are occupied and which are empty. After a few moments in the dark, your eyes begin to adapt and you can see dimly. Yet it takes about half an hour or more for your eyes to adapt completely. After complete **dark adaptation**, you can see light that is 100,000 times less bright than daylight. You may have thought that dark adaptation was a direct result of the dilation of your pupils, but this accounts for only a sixteenfold difference in your sensitivity to light. Dark adaptation cannot occur until the opsin and retinal in the rods recombine, restoring the rods' sensitivity to light.

dark adaptation: The eye's increasing ability to see in dim light, which results from regeneration of rhodopsin molecules from opsin and retinal in the rods and the dilation of the pupil.

optic nerve: The nerve that carries visual information from the retina to the brain.

When you leave a movie theater, your eyes are dark-adapted, and the return to the bright sunlight is a "blinding" experience. However, it takes only about 60 seconds, not half an hour, to become light-adapted again.

In light adaptation, a reflexive action occurs; the pupils immediately become smaller, permitting less light to enter the eyes. And soon after you move from the dark into the light, the rhodopsin molecules in the rods in your retinas break apart, resulting in a great reduction in the rods' sensitivity to light. But even though the rods are not functioning fully until they become light-adapted, the ample light is sufficient to stimulate the cones so that they become fully functional.

From the Retina to the Brain: From Visual Sensation to Visual Perception

What path does the neural impulse take from the retina to the primary visual cortex?

Although visual information is processed mostly in the brain, the initial stages of processing take place in the retina's sensory receptors—the rods and cones. They transduce, or change, light waves into neural impulses that are fed to the bipolar cells, which in turn pass the impulses along to the ganglion cells. The approximately 1 million axonlike extensions of the ganglion cells are bundled together in a pencil-sized cable that extends through the wall of the retina, leaving the eye and leading to the brain. Where the cable runs through the retinal wall, there can be no rods or cones, and so this point is a *blind spot* in each eye. You can find your own blind spot if you perform the *Try It!*

Try It!

To locate one of your blind spots, hold this book at arm's length. Close your right eye and look directly at the magician's eyes. Now slowly bring the book closer, keeping your eye fixed on the magician. When the rabbit disappears, you have found the blind spot in your left eye.

Beyond the retinal wall of the eye, the cable becomes the **optic nerve.** (See Figure 3.4 on p. 88) The two optic nerves come together at the *optic chiasm*, a point where some of the nerve fibers cross to the opposite side of the brain. The visual fibers from the right half of each retina go to the right hemisphere, and the visual fibers from the left half of each retina go to the left hemisphere. This switching is important because it allows visual information from a single eye to be represented in the primary visual cortex of both hemispheres of the brain. Moreover, it plays an

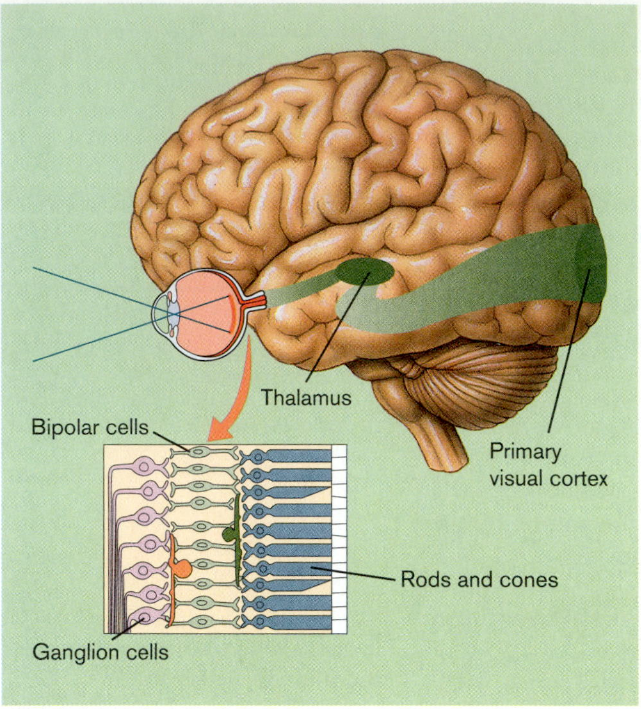

Figure 3.4
From the Retina to the Brain

important part in depth perception. But if one eye is covered and deprived of vision during a critical period of visual development early in life, the visual cortex almost completely stops responding to that eye (Fagiolini & Hensch, 2000; Hensch & Stryker, 1996).

From the optic chiasm, the optic nerve travels to the thalamus (specifically, to its lateral geniculate nucleus). There it synapses with neural fibers that transmit the impulses to the primary visual cortex. Approximately one-fourth of the primary visual cortex is dedicated exclusively to analyzing input from the fovea, which, as we have seen, is a very small but extremely important part of the retina.

Mapping the Primary Visual Cortex and Discovering the Feature Detectors During the last few decades, researchers have learned a great deal about how the primary visual cortex works to produce the sensation of vision. Much of the pioneering work in this field has been conducted by researchers David Hubel and Torsten Wiesel (1959, 1979; Hubel, 1963, 1995), who won a Nobel Prize for their work in 1981. Using cats as their subjects, Hubel and Wiesel placed a microelectrode in a single cell in the animal's visual cortex. They then flashed different patterns of lines on a screen in the cat's field of vision. They observed that the neurons appeared to be highly specialized, firing only in response to particular patterns of lines.

Hubel and Wiesel moved the tiny electrode carefully and precisely from cell to cell in order to map the visual responses over a sizable area of the cat's visual cortex. They found numbers of single neurons that respond only to lines and angles. One neuron, for example, would fire only when the cat saw a vertical line, while another neuron would respond only to a horizontal line. Some neurons were responsive to nothing but right angles; other neurons were sensitive only to lines of a certain length. All of these neurons are known as **feature detectors,** and they are already coded at birth to make their unique responses. These kinds of neurons respond not only to specific lines and angles but to several other features as well, including movement, texture, and color (Carlson, 1994) and even brightness (Rossi et al., 1996). The feature detectors are not randomly placed. They are grouped in columns according to their response orientations, and the columns extend into the deeper visual cortex (Maldonado et al., 1997).

Yet we see whole images, not collections of isolated features. Visual perceptions are complete only when the primary visual cortex transmits millions of pieces of visual information to other areas in the brain, where they are combined and assembled into whole visual images.

Color Vision: A Multicolored World

What are the three dimensions that combine to provide the colors people perceive?

Some light waves striking an object are absorbed by it, and others are reflected from it. We see only the wavelengths that are reflected, not those that are absorbed. Why does an apple look red? If you hold a red apple in bright light, light waves of all the different wavelengths are striking the apple, but more of the longer red wavelengths of light are reflected from the apple's skin. The shorter wavelengths are absorbed, so you see only the reflected red. Bite into the apple, and it looks white. Why? You see white because, rather than being absorbed, all the wavelengths of the visible spectrum are reflected from the inside part of the apple. The presence of all visible wavelengths gives the sensation of white.

Our everyday visual experience goes far beyond the colors in the rainbow. We can detect thousands of subtle color shadings. What produces these fine color distinctions? Researchers have identified three dimensions that combine to provide the rich world of color we experience: (1) The chief dimension is **hue,** which refers to the specific color perceived—red, green, and so forth. (2) **Saturation** refers to the purity of a color. A color becomes less saturated, or less pure, as other wavelengths of light are mixed with it. (3) **Brightness** refers to the intensity of the light energy that is perceived.

Theories of Color Vision: How the Eyes Sense Color Two major theories have been offered to explain color vision, and both were formulated before the development of laboratory technology capable of testing them. The **trichromatic theory,** first proposed by Thomas Young in 1802, was modified by Hermann von Helmholtz about 50 years later. This theory states that there are three kinds of cones in the retina and that each kind makes its maximum chemical response to one of three colors—blue, green, or red. Research in the 1950s and the 1960s by Nobel Prize winner George Wald (1964; Wald et al., 1954) supports the trichromatic theory. Wald discovered that even though all cones have basically the same structure, the retina does indeed contain three kinds of cones.

What two major theories attempt to explain color vision?

The trichromatic theory alone, however, cannot explain how we are able to perceive such a rich variety of colors. Researchers now know that there must be color-coding processes that combine color information in a more complex way than occurs in the cones.

The other major attempt to explain color vision is the **opponent-process theory,** which was first proposed by physiologist Ewald Hering in 1878 and revised in 1957 by researchers Leon Hurvich and Dorthea Jamison. According to the opponent-process theory, three classes of cells respond by increasing or decreasing their rate of firing when different colors are present. The red/green cells increase their firing rate when red is present and decrease it when green is present. The yellow/blue cells have an increased response to yellow and a decreased response to blue. Another type of cell increases its response rate for white light and decreases it in the absence of light. Think of the opponent-process theory as opposing pairs of cells on a seesaw. As one goes up, the other goes down, and vice versa. The relative firing positions of the three pairs of cells transmit color information to the brain.

Does the opponent process operate in the cones, or elsewhere? Researchers now believe that the cones pass on information about wavelengths of light to higher levels of visual processing. Researchers De Valois and De Valois (1975) proposed that the opponent processes might operate at the ganglion cells in the retina and in the higher brain centers rather than at the level of the receptors, the cones. Recent research evidence shows that color perception starts at the level of the retina and continues in the color detectors in the visual cortex (Sokolov, 2000).

If you look long enough at one color in the opponent-process pair and then look at a white surface, your brain will give you the sensation of the opposite color—a negative **afterimage.** After you have stared at one color in an opponent-process pair (red/green, yellow/blue, black/white), the cell responding to that color tires and the opponent cell begins to fire, producing the afterimage. Demonstrate this for yourself in the *Try It!* on page 90.

Color Blindness: Weakness for Sensing Some Colors Not everyone sees the world in the same colors. If normal genes for the three color pigments are not present, a person will experience some form of **color blindness**—the inability to distinguish some colors or, in rare cases, the total absence of color vision. Total color blindness affects only about 1 in 100,000 people (Nathans et al., 1989). Researchers discovered what the world looks like to a color-blind person by studying people

feature detectors: Neurons in the brain that respond to specific features of a sensory stimulus (for example, to lines or angles).

hue: The property of light commonly referred to as color (red, blue, green, etc.), determined primarily by the wavelength of light reflected from a surface.

saturation: The degree to which light waves producing a color are of the same wavelength; the purity of a color.

brightness: The dimension of visual sensation that is dependent on the intensity of light reflected from a surface and that corresponds to the amplitude of the light wave.

trichromatic theory: The theory of color vision suggesting that there are three types of cones, which are maximally sensitive to red, green, or blue, and that varying levels of activity in these receptors can produce all of the colors.

opponent-process theory: The theory that three classes of cells increase their firing rate to signal one color and decrease their firing rate to signal the opposing color (red/green, yellow/blue, white/black).

afterimage: The visual sensation that remains after a stimulus is withdrawn.

color blindness: The inability to distinguish some or all colors, resulting from a defect in the cones.

Try It!

Stare at the dot in the green, black, and yellow flag for approximately 1 minute. Then shift your gaze to the dot in the blank rectangle. You will see the American flag in its true colors—red, white, and blue, which are the opponent-process opposites of green, black, and yellow.

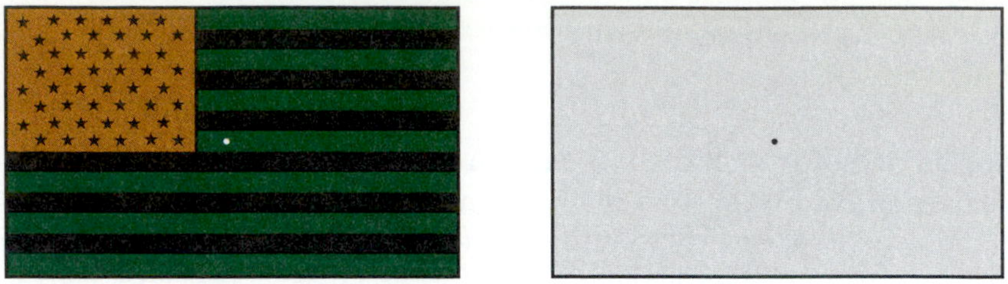

who have normal vision in one eye but some form of color blindness in the other. Most color vision defects are actually weaknesses—color confusion rather than color blindness. Many people who have some type of color defect are not even aware of it.

Until recently, scientists believed that in order to have normal color vision, a person must inherit three genes for color—one gene for blue on chromosome 7 and one gene each for red and green on the X chromosome. However, DNA evidence from a group of men with normal color vision revealed that the number of genes for red and green on the X chromosome ranged from two to nine (Neitz & Neitz, 1995). This study suggests that people's ability to perceive color actually ranges over a continuum from red-green color blindness in those missing one or both of the color genes on the X chromosome to exceptional red-green color vision in those with multiple color genes on that chromosome. Some form of red-green color blindness is found in about 5% of males, compared with less than 1% of females (Neitz et al., 1996). The large difference is due to the fact that males have only one X chromosome.

Before leaving the topic of vision, let us dispel the myth that some mammals, especially dogs, generally lack color vision. Research has confirmed that some form of color vision is present in virtually all species of mammals (Jacobs, 1993).

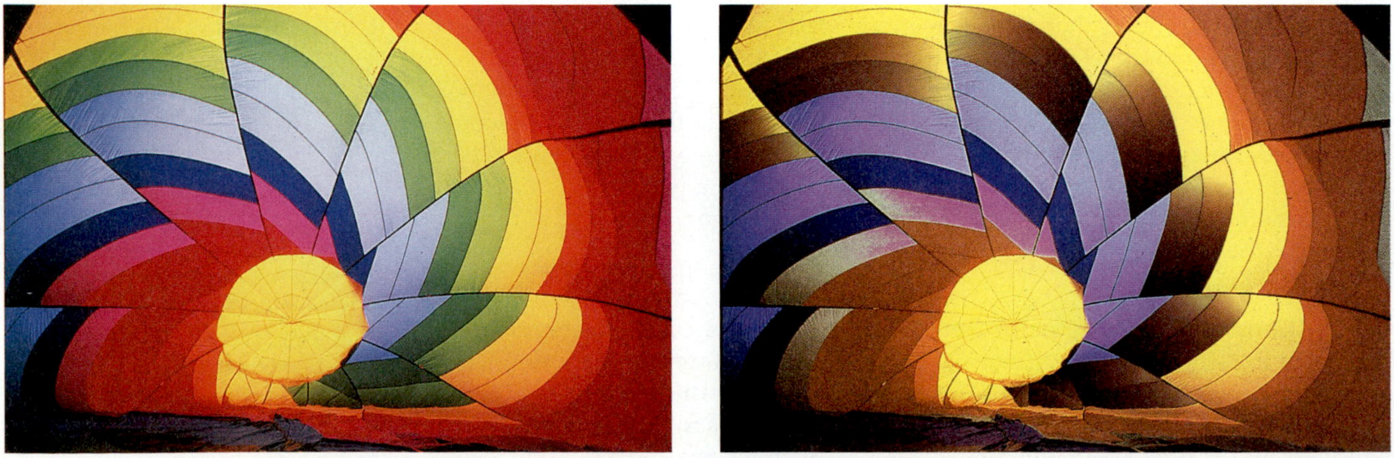

On the left a hot air balloon is shown as it would appear to a person with normal color vision; on the right is the same balloon as it would appear to a person with red-green color blindness.

Remember It!

1. Match the parts of the eye with its description.

   d (1) the colored part of the eye
   c (2) the opening in the iris that dilates and constricts
   b (3) the transparent covering of the iris
   e (4) the transparent structure that focuses an inverted image on the retina
   a (5) the thin, photosensitive membrane at the back of the eye on which the lens focuses an inverted image

   a. retina
   b. cornea
   c. pupil
   d. iris
   e. lens

2. The receptor cells in the retina that enable you to see in dim light are the (cones, rods); the cells that enable you to see color and sharp images are (cones, rods).

3. Neural impulses are carried from the retina to the thalamus by the ______________ and then relayed to their final destination, the ______________.

   a. optic chiasma; primary visual cortex
   b. rods and cones; optic nerve
   c. optic nerve; primary visual cortex
   d. optic nerve; optic chiasma

4. Most people who are color blind see no color at all. (true/false)

Answers: 1. (1) d (2) c (3) b (4) e (5) a 2. rods; cones 3. c 4. false

HEARING

Years ago, the frightening science fiction movie *Alien* was advertised this way: "In space no one can hear you scream!" Although the movie was fiction, the statement is true. Light can travel through the vast nothingness of space, a vacuum, but sound cannot. In this section, you will learn why.

Sound: What We Hear

What determines the pitch and the loudness of sound, and how is each quality measured?

Sound requires a medium through which to move, such as air, water, or a solid object. This fact was first demonstrated by Robert Boyle in 1660 when he suspended a ringing pocket watch by a thread inside a specially designed jar. When Boyle pumped all the air out of the jar, he could no longer hear the watch ring. But when he pumped the air back into the jar, he could again hear the watch ringing.

If you attend a very loud rock concert, you not only hear but actually feel the mechanical vibrations. The pulsating speakers may cause the floor, your seat, the walls, and the air around you to shake or vibrate. What you feel are the moving air molecules being pushed toward you in waves as the speakers blast their vibrations outward.

Frequency is an important characteristic of sound and is determined by the number of cycles completed by a sound wave in one second. The unit used to measure frequency, or the cycles per second, is known as the hertz (Hz). The pitch, how high or low the sound is, is chiefly determined by frequency—the higher the frequency (the more vibrations per second), the higher the sound (see Figure 3.5 on p. 92). The human ear can hear sound frequencies from low bass tones of around 20 Hz up to high-pitched sounds of about 20,000 Hz. The lowest tone on a piano sounds at a frequency of about 28 Hz and the highest tone at about 4,214 Hz. Many mammals—dogs, cats, bats, and rats—can hear tones much higher in frequency than 20,000 Hz. Amazingly, dolphins can respond to sounds up to 100,000 Hz.

The loudness of a sound is determined largely by a measure called **amplitude.** Amplitude depends on the energy of the sound wave (refer to Figure 3.5). The force

frequency: Measured in the unit called the hertz, the number of sound waves or cycles per second, determining the pitch of the sound.

amplitude: Measured in decibels, the magnitude or intensity of a sound wave, determining the loudness of the sound; the *amplitude* of a light wave affects the brightness of a visual stimulus.

Figure 3.5

The Frequency and Amplitude of a Sound Wave

The frequency of a sound wave—the number of cycles completed per second—determines the pitch of the sound. Loudness is determined by amplitude—the energy, or height, of the sound wave.

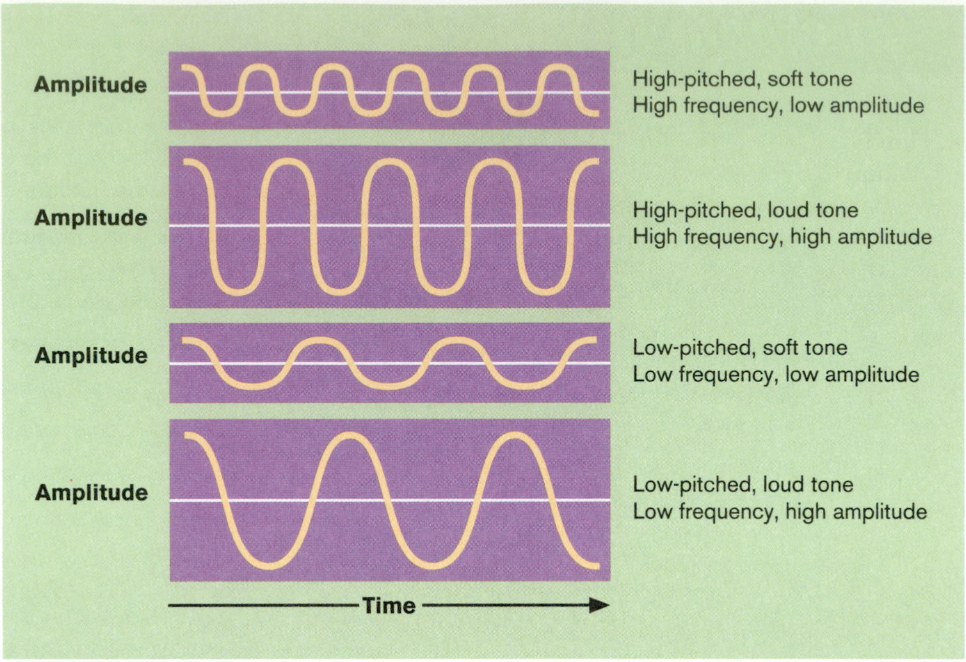

decibel (DES-ih-bel): A unit of measurement of the intensity or loudness of sound based on the amplitude of the sound wave.

or pressure with which air molecules move chiefly determines loudness. The sound pressure level (loudness) of sounds is measured using a unit called the *bel*, named for Alexander Graham Bell. Because the bel is a rather large unit, sound levels are expressed in tenths of a bel, or **decibels** (dB). The threshold of human hearing is set at 0 dB, which does not mean the absence of sound but the softest sound that can be heard in a very quiet setting. Each increase of 10 decibels makes a sound 10 times louder. A whisper is about 20 dB, but that is 100 times louder than 0 dB. A normal conversation, around 60 dB, is 10,000 times louder than a soft whisper at 20 dB. Figure 3.6 shows comparative decibel levels for a variety of sounds.

Figure 3.6

Decibel Levels of Various Sounds

The loudness of a sound (its amplitude) is measured in decibels. Each increase of 10 decibels makes a sound 10 times louder. A normal conversation at 3 feet measures about 60 decibels, which is 10,000 times louder than a soft whisper of 20 decibels. Any exposure to sounds of 130 dB or higher puts a person at immediate risk for hearing damage.

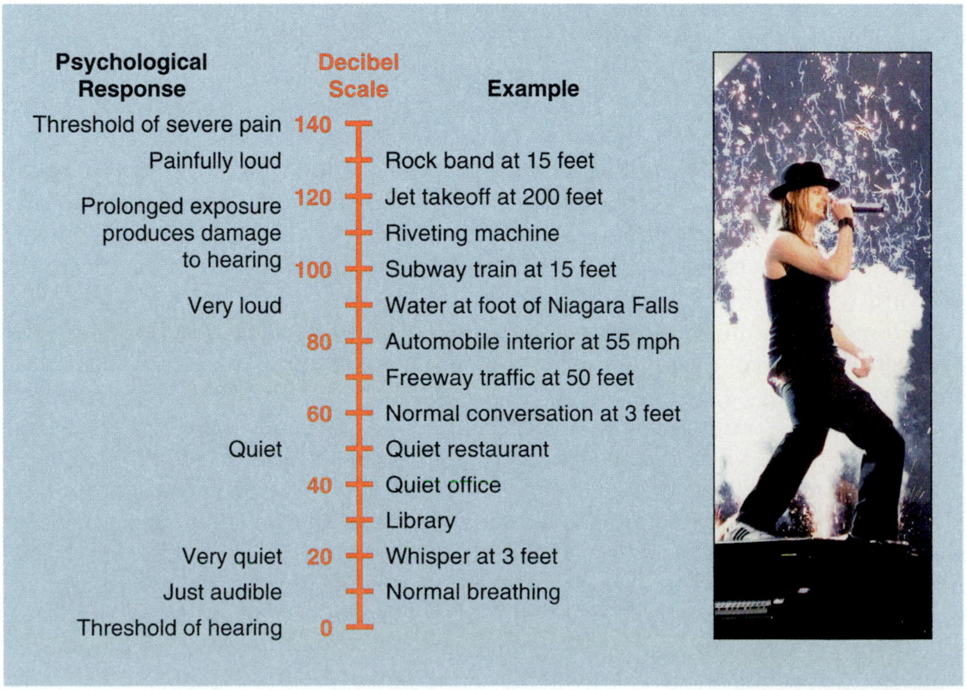

If pitch and loudness were the only perceptual dimensions of sound, we could not tell the difference between two instruments if both were playing exactly the same note at the same decibel level. A third characteristic of sound, **timbre,** refers to the distinct quality of a sound that distinguishes it from other sounds of the same pitch and loudness. Unlike the pure sound of a tuning fork, which has only one frequency, most sounds consist of several different frequencies. The frequencies that form the sound pattern above any tone a musical instrument produces are called *overtones,* or *harmonics.* Overtones are not actually heard as tones, but they give musical instruments their characteristic quality of sound, or timbre. The rich, full sound of a French horn, for example, is due to the large number of overtones it produces.

timbre (TAM-burr): The distinctive quality of a sound that distinguishes it from other sounds of the same pitch and loudness.

audition: The sensation of hearing; the process of hearing.

outer ear: The visible part of the ear, consisting of the pinna and the auditory canal.

middle ear: The portion of the ear containing the ossicles, which connect the eardrum to the oval window and amplify the vibrations as they travel to the inner ear.

inner ear: The innermost portion of the ear, containing the cochlea, the vestibular sacs, and the semicircular canals.

cochlea (KOK-lee-uh): The snail-shaped, fluid-filled chamber in the inner ear that contains the hair cells (the sound receptors).

The Ear: More to It Than Meets the Eye

The part of the body called the ear plays only a minor role in human **audition.** In fact, even if your visible outer ears were cut off, your hearing would suffer very little. Let's see how each part of the ear contributes to the ability to hear.

How do the outer, middle, and inner ears function in hearing?

The Structure of the Ear: The Outer, Middle, and Inner Ears The oddly shaped, curved flap of cartilage and skin called the *pinna* is the visible part of the **outer ear** (see Figure 3.7). Inside the ear, the *auditory canal* is about 1 inch long, and its entrance is lined with hairs. At the end of the auditory canal is the *eardrum* (or tympanic membrane), a thin, flexible membrane about ⅓ inch in diameter. The eardrum moves in response to the sound waves that strike it.

The **middle ear** is no larger than an aspirin tablet. Inside its chamber are the *ossicles,* the three smallest bones in your body, each "about the size of a grain of rice" (Strome & Vernick, 1989). Named for their shapes, the three connected ossicles—the hammer, the anvil, and the stirrup—link the eardrum to the oval window (see Figure 3.7). The ossicles amplify the sound some 22 times (Békésy, 1957).

The **inner ear** begins at the inner side of the oval window on the base of the **cochlea**—a fluid-filled, snail-shaped, bony chamber. When the stirrup pushes

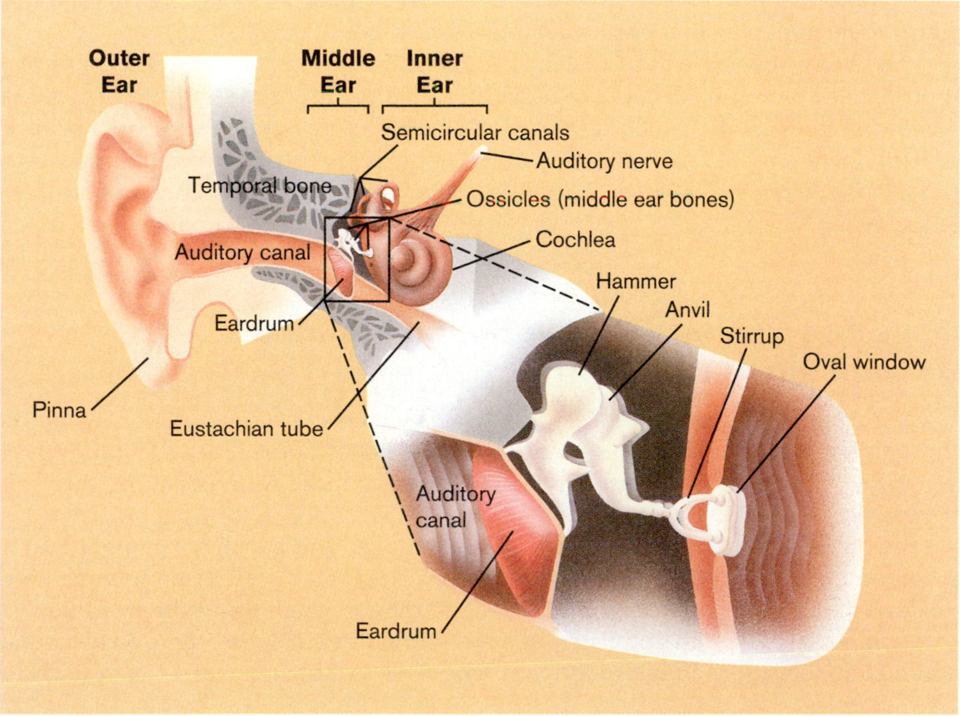

Figure 3.7

Anatomy of the Human Ear

Sound waves pass through the auditory canal to the eardrum, causing it to vibrate and set in motion the ossicles in the middle ear. When the stirrup pushes against the oval window, it sets up vibrations in the inner ear. This moves the fluid in the cochlea back and forth and sets in motion the hair cells, causing a message to be sent to the brain via the auditory nerve.

against the oval window, it sets up vibrations that move the fluid in the cochlea back and forth in waves. The movement of the fluid sets in motion the thin *basilar membrane* that runs through the cochlea. Attached to the basilar membrane are about 15,000 sensory receptors called **hair cells,** each with a bundle of tiny hairs protruding from it. The tiny hair bundles are pushed and pulled by the motion of the fluid inside the cochlea. If the tip of the hair bundle is moved only as much as the width of an atom, an electrical impulse is generated, which is transmitted to the brain by way of the auditory nerve (Hudspeth, 1983).

Having two ears, one on each side of the head, enables us to determine the direction from which sounds are coming (Konishi, 1993). Unless a sound is directly above, below, in front of, or behind you, it reaches one ear slightly before it reaches the other (Spitzer & Semple, 1991). The brain detects differences as small as 0.0001 second and interprets them, revealing the direction of the sound (Rosenzweig, 1961). The source of a sound may also be determined by the difference in intensity of the sound reaching each ear (Middlebrooks & Green, 1991). Bats are especially adept at determining the direction and the precise distance to the source of a sound; they use echolocation to find their prey (Covey, 2000).

Theories of Hearing: How Hearing Works

What two major theories attempt to explain hearing?

In the 1860s Hermann von Helmholtz helped develop **place theory,** one of the two major theories of hearing. This theory holds that each individual pitch a person hears is determined by the particular spot or place along the basilar membrane of the cochlea that vibrates the most. Observing the living basilar membrane, researchers have verified that different locations do indeed vibrate in response to differently pitched sounds (Ruggero, 1992). Even so, place theory cannot explain how humans perceive the low frequencies below 150 Hz.

Another attempt to explain hearing is **frequency theory.** According to this theory, the hair cell receptors vibrate the same number of times per second as the sounds that reach them. Thus, a tone of 500 Hz would stimulate the hair cells to vibrate 500 times per second as well. Frequency theory seems valid for low-pitched tones, but it cannot account for frequencies higher than 1,000 Hz. Individual neurons cannot fire more than about 1,000 times per second. Therefore, they could not signal to the brain the higher-pitched tones exceeding 1,000 Hz.

The *volley principle* was put forth to suggest that groups, or volleys, of neurons, if properly synchronized, could together produce the firing rate required for tones somewhat higher than 1,000 Hz (Wever, 1949). Today, however, researchers believe that frequency theory best explains how we perceive low frequencies and place theory best accounts for how we perceive the remaining frequencies (Matlin & Foley, 1997).

Bone Conduction: Hearing Sound Vibrations through the Bones

The eardrum is not required for all the sounds we hear. We can hear some sounds through **bone conduction**—the vibrations of the bones in the face and skull. When you click your teeth or eat crunchy food, you hear these sounds mainly through bone conduction.

If you have heard a recording of your own voice, you may have thought that it sounded quite unlike your normal speaking voice. When you listen to your own voice as you speak, you hear sound waves coming through the auditory canal *and* through bone. But when you listen to a recording of your voice, there are no bone conduction vibrations in the sound you hear. This is the way your voice sounds to other people.

hair cells: Sensory receptors for hearing, found in the cochlea.

place theory: The theory that sounds of different frequency or pitch cause maximum activation of hair cells at certain locations along the basilar membrane.

frequency theory: The theory that hair cell receptors vibrate the same number of times as the sounds that reach them, thereby accounting for how variations in pitch are transmitted to the brain.

bone conduction: The transmission of vibrations along the bones of the skull or face directly to the cochlea.

Hearing Loss: Kinds and Causes

What are some major causes of hearing loss?

About 28 million people in the United States suffer from hearing loss (Kalb, 1997), which is the most common sensory defect in humans. Almost 15% of American children have low- or high-frequency hearing loss (Niskan et al., 1998). Hearing loss and deafness can be caused by disease, birth defects, injury, excessive noise, and old age. Hearing loss affects normal communication in 10% of people who are 65 or older (Willems, 2000). Conductive hearing loss, or *conduction deafness,* is usually caused by disease or injury to the eardrum or the bones of the middle ear, which prevents sound waves from being conducted to the cochlea. Almost all conductive hearing loss can be repaired medically or surgically. And in rare cases, a person can be fitted with a hearing aid that bypasses the middle ear, using bone conduction to send sound vibrations to the cochlea.

Most adults with hearing loss suffer from *sensorineural hearing loss,* which involves damage to either the cochlea or the auditory nerve. Large numbers of the cochlea's delicate hair cells, which transduce sound waves into neural impulses, may be damaged or destroyed. If the damage is not too severe, a conventional hearing aid may reduce the effects of this type of hearing loss (Bramblett, 1997). But hearing aids are useless if the damage is to the auditory nerve, which connects the cochlea to the brain; in such cases the hearing loss is usually total. Although hearing loss occurs most often in older people, about 75% of the cases of hearing loss appear to be caused by lifelong exposure to excessive noise rather than by aging (Kalb, 1997).

Older persons in one culture, the Mabaan tribe in the Sudan in Africa, don't appear to suffer much hearing loss as they age. In fact, when hearing tests were conducted on Mabaan tribe members, some 80-year-olds could hear as well as 20-year-old people in industrialized countries. The Mabaan pride themselves on their sensitive hearing, and an important tribal custom is never to raise their voices. Even their festivals and celebrations are quiet affairs, featuring dancing and soft singing accompanied by stringed instruments rather than drums. (Bennett, 1990).

Members of some Sudanese tribes play stringed instruments rather quietly during celebrations. Perhaps because they are not exposed to much noise, these people generally have very sharp hearing.

Remember It!

1. Pitch is chiefly determined by ________; loudness is chiefly determined by ________.
   a. amplitude; frequency
   b. wavelength; frequency
   c. intensity; amplitude
   d. frequency; amplitude
2. Pitch is measured in (hertz, decibels); loudness is measured in (decibels, hertz).
3. Match the part of the ear with the structures it contains.
   __b__ (1) ossicles — a. outer ear
   __a__ (2) pinna, auditory canal — b. middle ear
   __c__ (3) cochlea, hair cells — c. inner ear
4. The receptors for hearing are found in the
   a. ossicles.
   b. auditory canal.
   c. auditory membrane.
   d. cochlea.
5. The two major theories that attempt to explain hearing are
   a. conduction theory and place theory.
   b. hair cell theory and frequency theory.
   c. place theory and frequency theory.
   d. conduction theory and hair cell theory.
6. According to the text, lifelong exposure to excessive noise may be more of a factor in hearing loss than aging. (true/false)

Answers: 1. d 2. hertz; decibels 3. (1) b (2) a (3) c 4. d 5. c 6. true

olfaction (ol-FAK-shun): The sensation of smell; the process of smelling.

olfactory epithelium: Two 1-square-inch patches of tissue, one at the top of each nasal cavity, which together contain about 10 million olfactory neurons, the receptors for smell.

olfactory bulbs: Two matchstick-sized structures above the nasal cavities, where smell sensations first register in the brain.

pheromones: Chemicals excreted by humans and other animals that act as signals to and elicit certain patterns of behavior from members of the same species.

Odors have a powerful ability to evoke memories and stir up emotions.

What path does a smell message take from the nose to the brain?

SMELL AND TASTE

You have been reading about the importance of the abilities to sense light and sound. Now let's explore the chemical senses, smell and taste.

Smell: Sensing Scents

Consider what it would be like to live in a world without smell. "Not really so bad," you might say. "Although I could not smell flowers, perfume, or my favorite foods, I would never again have to endure the foul odors of life. It's a trade-off, so what's the difference?"

The difference is large indeed. Your ability to detect odors close at hand and at a distance is an aid to survival. You smell smoke and can escape before the flames of a fire envelop you. Your nose broadcasts an odor alarm to the brain when certain poisonous gases or noxious fumes are present. But the survival value of odor detection in humans does not stop there. Smell, aided by taste, is the last line of defense—your final chance to avoid putting spoiled food or drink into your body.

Odors have a powerful ability to call forth old memories and rekindle strong feelings, even decades after the experiences originally occurred. In his novel *Remembrance of Things Past,* the French novelist Marcel Proust described how the smell of a "petite Madeline" (a small cake or cookie) dipped in a cup of tea brought a flood of freshened childhood memories from his aunt's old home. Recent research on the connection between odors and memories suggests that the intensity of odor-cued memories peaks between the ages of 6 and 10 and then decreases slowly but steadily (Chu & Downes, 2000). The association of memories with odors is thought to occur because the olfactory system first sends information to the limbic system, an area in the brain that plays an important role in emotions and memories as well (Horwitz, 1997). Brain imaging-studies of human olfactory functioning have recently established key connections among the sense of smell, emotion, and memory (Pause & Krauel, 2000; Zald & Pardo, 2000).

The human olfactory system is capable of sensing and distinguishing 10,000 different odors. And, believe it or not, every single individual gives off a unique scent, which is genetically determined (Axel, 1995). But there are large individual differences in sensitivity to smells. For example, perfumers and whiskey blenders can distinguish subtle variations in odors that are indistinguishable to the average person. Women are generally more sensitive to odors than men are and more sensitive still during ovulation. Young people are more sensitive to odors than older people, and nonsmokers are more sensitive than smokers (Matlin & Foley, 1997).

The Mechanics of Smell: How the Nose Knows **Olfaction**—the sense of smell—is a chemical sense. You cannot smell a substance unless some of its molecules vaporize—pass from a solid or liquid into a gaseous state. Heat speeds up the evaporation of molecules, which is why food that is cooking has a stronger and more distinct odor than uncooked food. When odor molecules vaporize, they become airborne and make their way up each nostril to the olfactory epithelium. The **olfactory epithelium** consists of two 1-square-inch patches of tissue, one at the top of each nasal cavity, which together contain about 10 million olfactory neurons—the receptor cells for smell. Each of these neurons contains only one of the 1,000 different types of odor receptors (Bargmann, 1996). Because humans are able to detect some 10,000 odors, each of the 1,000 types of odor receptors must be able to respond to more than one kind of odor molecule. Moreover, some odor molecules trigger more than one type of odor receptor (Axel, 1995). The intensity of a smell stimulus—how strong or weak it is—is apparently determined by the number of olfactory neurons firing at the same time (Freeman, 1991). Figure 3.8 shows a diagram of the human olfactory system.

Have you ever wondered why dogs have a keener sense of smell than humans? Not only do many dogs have a long snout, but in some breeds the olfactory epithelium can be as large as the area of a handkerchief and can contain up to 20 times as many olfactory neurons as the human nose does (Engen, 1982). It is well known that dogs use scent to recognize not only other members of their species, but also the humans they live with. And humans also have this ability. The mothers of newborns can recognize their own babies by smell within hours after birth. But can humans recognize the scents of other species, their own pets, for example? Yes, to a remarkable degree. When presented with blankets permeated with the scent of their dogs, some 89% of the dog owners easily identified their own dog by smell (Wells & Hepper, 2000).

Olfactory neurons are different from all other sensory receptors. They are special types of neurons that both come into direct contact with sensory stimuli and reach directly into the brain. And these neurons have a short lifespan; after functioning for only about 60 days, they die and are replaced by new cells (Buck, 1996). Layers of stem cells below the olfactory epithelium generate new olfactory neurons continuously. Researchers have found that our memories of smells continue because the axons of neurons that express the same olfactory receptor always migrate to the same place (Buck, 1996).

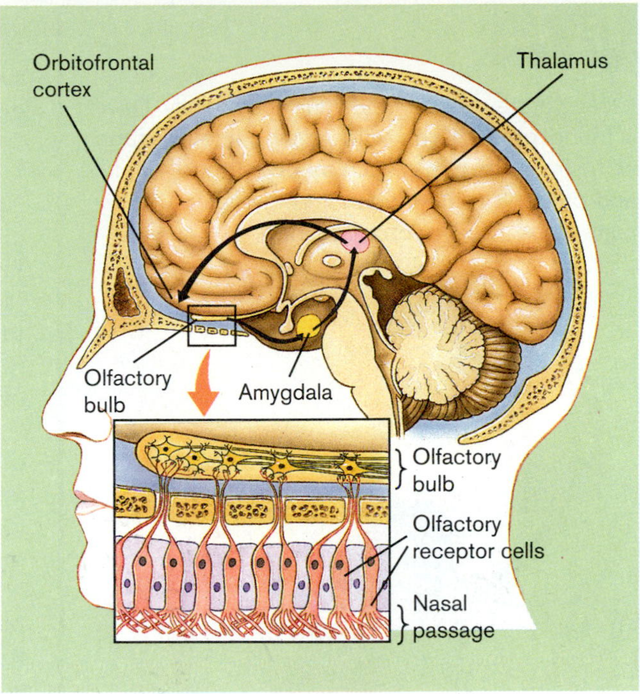

Figure 3.8

The Olfactory System

Odor molecules travel up the nostrils to the olfactory epithelium, which contains the receptor cells for smell. Olfactory receptors are special neurons whose axons form the olfactory nerve. The olfactory nerve relays smell messages to the olfactory bulbs, which pass them on to the thalamus, the orbitofrontal cortex, and other parts of the brain.

The axons of the olfactory neurons relay a smell message directly to the **olfactory bulbs**—two brain structures the size of matchsticks that rest above the nasal cavities (refer to Figure 3.8). From the olfactory bulbs, the message is relayed to the thalamus and orbitofrontal cortex, which distinguish the odor and relay that information to other parts of the brain.

Pheromones Many animals excrete chemicals called **pheromones,** which can have a powerful effect on the behavior of other members of the same species. Animals use pheromones to mark off territories and to signal sexual receptivity. A female mouse in heat will find the pheromone secreted from a gland on the penis of a male mouse irresistible; the same pheromone will enrage another male mouse. "When in heat, dogs, wolves, coyotes, foxes, and a host of others discharge a scent that is virtually irresistible to able-bodied males" (Dobb, 1989, p. 51). Higher mammals such as monkeys also make use of pheromones in their sexual behavior. And Stern and McClintock have recently found clear evidence of at least two human pheromones.

Studies conducted by Viennese researcher Karl Grammer (cited in Holden, 1996) suggest that humans, although not consciously aware of it, respond to pheromones when it comes to mating. In his research, Grammer analyzed the saliva of 66 young men who had used an inhalant to sniff copulines—pheromones found in female vaginal secretions. The secretions were taken during three different times in the menstrual cycle. The ovulatory secretions were the only ones to cause a rise in testosterone levels in the men's saliva. The men apparently recognized, though not consciously, which of the women were most likely to be fertile.

Taste: What the Tongue Can Tell

What are the primary taste sensations, and how are they detected?

Fresh-baked bread, fried chicken, chocolate ice cream—does the sense of taste alone tell us what these foods taste like? Surprisingly, no. As you taste, you feel the texture and temperature of foods you put in the mouth. But most of the pleasure you attribute to the sense of taste actually arises from smells, which are due to odor molecules forced up the nasal cavity by the action of the tongue, cheeks, and throat when you chew and swallow.

Try It!

Close your eyes and hold your nose tightly. Have a friend present you with small pieces of food with similar textures, such as raw potato, apple, and onion. See if you can identify each food by taste alone. Most people cannot.

Psychology textbooks have long maintained that **gustation,** the sense of taste, produces four distinct kinds of taste sensations: sweet, sour, salty, and bitter. This is true. But recent research suggests that there is also a fifth taste sensation in humans (Herness, 2000). This fifth taste sensation is for monosodium glutamate, which is widely used as a flavoring in Asian foods (Matsunami et al., 2000). Many protein-rich foods, such as meat, milk, aged cheese, and seafood, contain glutamate. The fifth taste sensation, also known as "umami," was first identified nearly 100 years ago by a Japanese researcher, Kikunae Ikeda (Lindermann, 2000). This distinct sensation cannot be produced by any combination of the other four tastes, and it can be recognized by humans, rats, and various other species (Chaudhari et al., 2000).

Although aging typically is accompanied by a decline in the other senses, people lose very little of their ability to detect the primary taste sensations as they age. When older people complain that food doesn't taste as good as it once did, the reason is usually a loss of smell rather than a failing sense of taste (Bartoshuk, 1989).

Even color can contribute to the sense of taste. Many participants in one study could not even recognize the taste of root beer when it was colored red (Hyman, 1983). And many common foods with similar textures cannot be identified by taste alone. Prove this for yourself by doing the *Try It!*

The Taste Receptors: Taste Detectors If you look at your tongue in a mirror, you will see many small bumps called *papillae.* There are four different types of papillae, and three of them contain **taste buds,** which cluster around the cracks and crevices between the papillae (see Figure 3.9). Each taste bud is composed of from 60 to 100 receptor cells, which resemble the petals of a flower (Kinnamon, 1988). But even a person with no tongue could still taste to some extent, thanks to the taste receptors found in the palate, in the mucus lining of the cheeks and lips, and in parts of the throat, including the tonsils. The life span of the receptor cells for taste is very short, only about 10 days, and they are continually replaced.

Taste buds are most densely packed on the tip of the tongue, less densely packed on the rear edges, and absent from the center of the tongue (Bartoshuk, 1989). But taste is poorly localized, and taste sensations appear to come from all over the mouth. Even people with damage over large areas of the mouth are usually

Figure 3.9

The Tongue's Papillae and Taste Buds

(a) A photomicrograph of the surface of the tongue shows several papillae. (b) This vertical cross section through a papillae reveals the location of the taste buds and taste receptors.

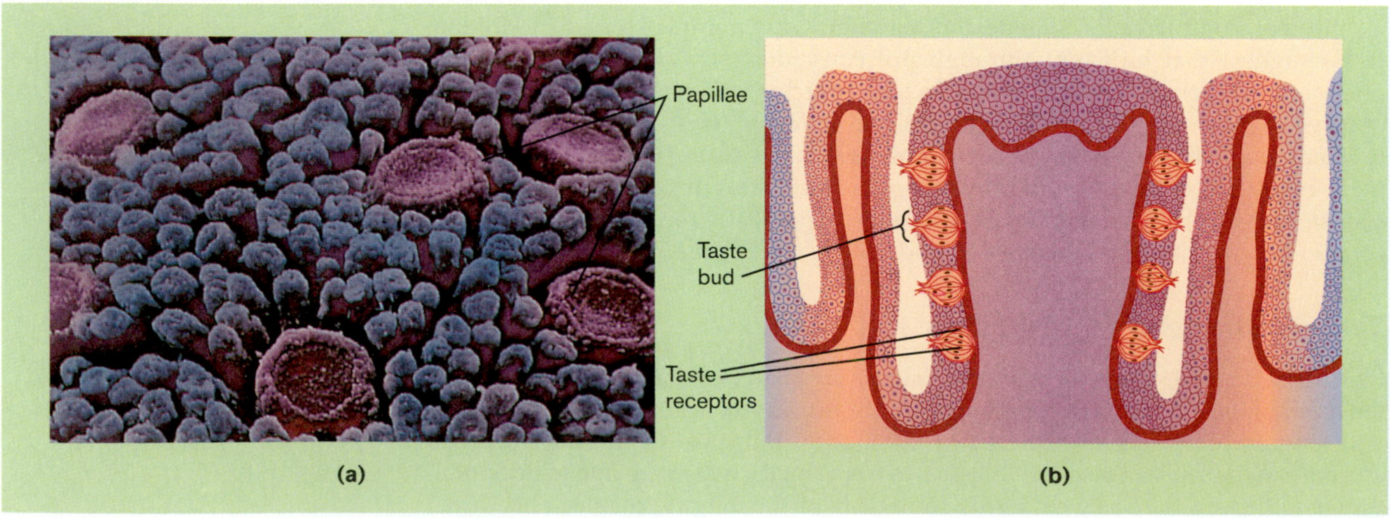

unaware of the loss of taste buds, because very intense sensations can be produced by rather small areas of normal tissue (Bartoshuk et al., 1987).

For many years textbooks included a "tongue map" showing the four basic tastes spatially distributed over different areas of the tongue. But the tongue map is an error that resulted from a mistranslation of a 1901 article written in German. Researchers who have performed extensive spatial testing for the original four taste sensations report that all four can be detected by taste buds on all locations of the tongue (Bartoshuk & Beauchamp, 1994).

Taste Sensitivities: Nontasters to Supertasters There are large differences among individuals in taste sensitivity, and specific taste abilities appear to be genetically determined. Research indicates that humans can be divided into three groups according to taste sensitivity for certain sweet and bitter substances—nontasters, medium tasters, and supertasters (Bartoshuk et al., 1992). Nontasters are unable to taste some sweet and bitter compounds, but they do taste most other substances, although with less sensitivity. Supertasters taste certain sweet and bitter compounds with far stronger intensity than other people. For example, supertasters tend to take only half as much sugar or saccharin as other people to sweeten their coffee or tea, yet such sweeteners as aspartame are perceived as having the same level of sweetness by supertasters and other tasters alike. Supertasters also suffer more from oral burn when they eat chili peppers, being supersensitive to the active ingredient, capsaicin (Karrer & Bartoshuk, 1991).

Researchers, using videomicroscopy, have actually counted the number of taste buds on the tongues of various individuals (Miller & Reedy, 1990). Not surprisingly, nontasters had the smallest number of taste buds per square centimeter, with an average of 96. Medium tasters averaged nearly twice as many taste buds at 184, and supertasters had more than four times as many taste buds, an average of 425. But the fact that supertasters do not taste all substances with greater intensity suggests that number of taste buds alone does not fully explain taste sensitivity.

Researchers Cruz and Green (2000) have shown for the first time that temperature changes affecting small areas of the tongue can create taste sensations in humans. Warming the tip of the tongue elicited a weak but unmistakably sweet sensation for some of the tasters in the study, whereas cooling the tip of the tongue caused a sour and/or salty sensation. You can test yourself for these sensations in the *Try It!*

Try It!

The following experiment worked for many tasters in the Cruz and Green (2000) study. Does it work for you?

Dip the tip of your tongue in a cup of warm water. (Make sure it's just warm, not scalding, or you won't be able to taste anything for a while!) Can you discern a slight sweet taste? Now place an ice cube on the tip of your tongue. You may be able to sense a fairly salty and/or sour sensation.

Cruz and Green (2000) found that approximately one-half of human taste receptors probably code for temperature changes as well. This research confirms what one famous researcher suggested about taste and temperature sensations some 40 years ago (Frank, 2000): Georg von Békésy first suggested this possibility in his classic work "Duplicity Theory in Taste" in 1964.

gustation: The sensation of taste.

taste buds: Structures composed of 60 to 100 sensory receptors for taste.

Remember It!

1. The technical name for the process or sensation of smell is (gustation, olfaction).
2. The olfactory, or smell, receptors are located in the
   a. olfactory tract.
   b. olfactory nerve.
   c. olfactory epithelium.
   d. olfactory bulbs.
3. The primary taste sensations are ______, ______, ______, ______, and ______.
4. A person's ability to identify foods with similar textures is most influenced by the sense of (taste, smell).
5. Each (papilla, taste bud) contains from 60 to 100 receptor cells.
6. Taste receptor cells have a very short life span and are continually replaced. (true/false)
7. Supertasters have the same number of taste buds as medium tasters and nontasters. (true/false)

Answers: 1. olfaction 2. c 3. sweet, salty, sour, bitter, and glutamate 4. smell 5. taste bud 6. true 7. false

THE OTHER SENSES

Our other senses are the sense of touch (the tactile sense), the kinesthetic sense, and the sense of balance (the vestibular sense).

The Skin Senses: Information from the Natural Clothing

How does the skin provide sensory information?

Your natural clothing, the skin, is the largest organ of your body. It performs many important biological functions while also providing much of what is known as sensual pleasure. Your skin can detect heat, cold, pressure, pain, and a vast range of touch sensations—caresses, pinches, punches, pats, rubs, scratches, and the feel of many different textures, from cotton to a cactus.

The Mechanism of Touch: How Touch Works **Tactile** information is conveyed to the brain when an object touches and depresses the skin, stimulating one or more of the several distinct types of receptors found in the nerve endings. These sensitive nerve endings in the skin send the touch message through nerve connections to the spinal cord. The message travels up the spinal cord and through the brainstem and the lower brain centers, finally reaching the brain's somatosensory cortex. (Remember from Chapter 2 that the somatosensory cortex is the strip of tissue at the front of the parietal lobes where touch, pressure, temperature, and pain register.) Once the somatosensory cortex has been activated, you become aware of where and how hard you have been touched. Figure 3.10 presents a brain scan showing how stimulation of the right hand activates areas in the left somatosensory cortex.

If you could examine the skin from the outermost to the deepest layer, you would find a variety of nerve endings that differ markedly in appearance. Most or all of these nerve endings appear to respond in some degree to all different types of tactile stimulation. The more densely packed a part of the body's surface with such sensory receptors, the more sensitive it is to tactile stimulation.

In the 1890s one of the most prominent researchers of the tactile sense, Max von Frey, discovered the two-point threshold that measures how far apart two points

tactile: Pertaining to the sense of touch.

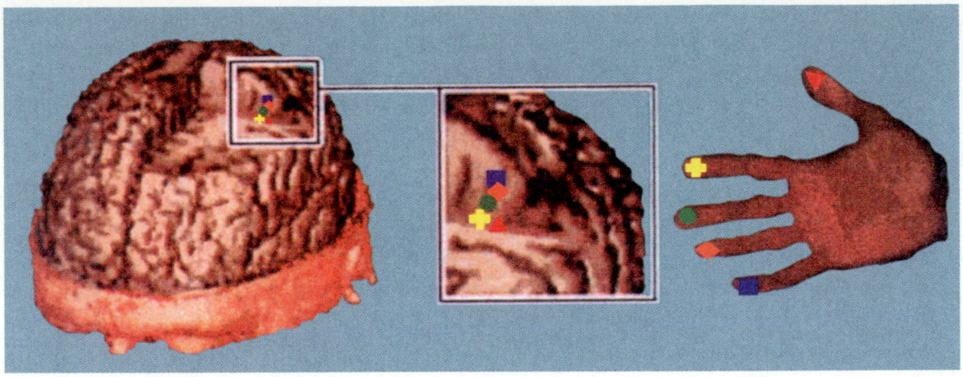

Figure 3.10

The Sense of Touch and the Brain

The color coding in this combined MRI/MEG image shows that the thumb and fingers of the right hand are connected in maplike fashion with areas of the left somatosensory cortex. (From Rodolfo Llinás, © NAS.)

3 minor senses.

must be before they are felt as two separate touches. Demonstrate the two-point threshold for yourself with the *Try It!*

Try It!

Have someone touch the palm of your hand with two toothpicks held about 1½ inches apart. Do you feel one point or two? How far apart do the toothpicks have to be before you perceive them as two separate touch sensations? How far apart do they have to be on your face? On your forearm? On your fingers? On your toes? Which of these body parts are the most sensitive? Which are the least sensitive?

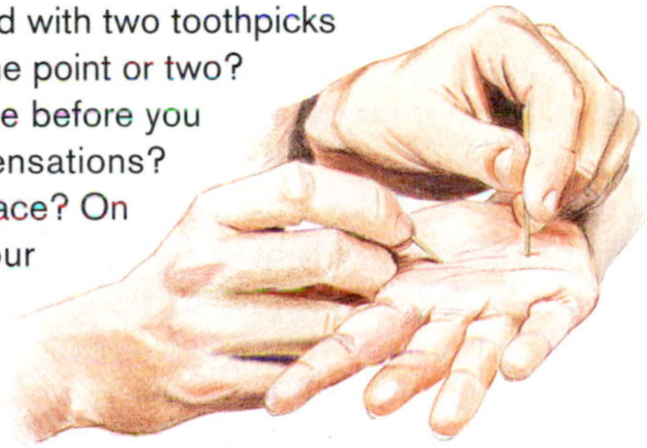

Touch: The Most Intimate Sense Touch is the sense we use to express our most intimate feelings. Lovers kiss, embrace, cuddle. Touch has the power to comfort and reassure. A pat on the back may motivate someone. Even social greetings and partings are punctuated by touching—the handshake and the more intimate embrace. But touch is not simply a means of communicating emotion—it is vitally important to human growth and development.

Research in the mid-1980s established the importance of touch in human development. Premature infants who were massaged for 15 minutes three times a day gained weight 47% faster than other premature infants who received only regular intensive care treatment (Field et al., 1986). The massaged infants were more responsive and were able to leave the hospital about 6 days earlier on average than those who were not massaged. And 8 months later they scored higher on tests of motor and mental ability.

Pain: Physical Hurts

What beneficial purpose does pain serve?

Although the tactile sense delivers a great deal of pleasure, it brings us pain as well. Pain is definitely not pleasant, but what if we couldn't feel any pain? Would we be better off? Decide for yourself as you read the following description:

> [This young boy] has never had a headache or a toothache, never felt the pain of a cut, a bruise, or a burn. If you are thinking, "How lucky!" you are completely

wrong. His arms and legs are twisted and bent. Some of his fingers are missing. A large, bloody wound covers one of his knees, and his lips are chewed raw.

A battered child? No. Born with a very rare genetic defect, he is totally insensitive to pain. He does not even notice a deep cut, a burn, or a broken bone when it happens, so he continues whatever he is doing and injures himself severely. (Adapted from Wallis, 1984.)

This story shows that pain functions as a valuable warning and protective mechanism. It motivates us to tend to injuries, to restrict activity, and to seek medical help. Pain also teaches us to avoid pain-producing circumstances in the future. Chronic pain, however, persists long after it serves any useful function and is itself a serious medical problem for some 34 million Americans (Brownlee & Schrof, 1997). The three major types of chronic pain are low-back pain, headache, and arthritis pain. For its victims, chronic pain is like a fire alarm that no one can turn off. Yet a course in pain management is required in only a fraction of medical residency programs (Brownlee & Schrof, 1997).

What is the gate-control theory of pain?

The Gate-Control Theory: Conducting Pains Great and Small Pain is probably the least understood of all the sensations. Scientists are not certain how pain works, but one major theory seeks to explain it—the **gate-control theory** of Melzack and Wall (1965, 1983). They contend that there is an area in the spinal cord that can act like a "gate" and either inhibit pain messages or transmit them to the brain. Only so many messages can go through the gate at any one time. You feel pain when pain messages carried by the small, slow-conducting nerve fibers reach the gate and cause it to open. Large, fast-conducting nerve fibers carry other sensory messages from the body, and these can effectively tie up traffic at the gate so that it will close and keep many of the pain messages from getting through. What is the first thing you do when you stub your toe or pound your finger with a hammer? If you rub or apply gentle pressure to the injury, you are stimulating the large, fast-conducting nerve fibers, which get their message to the spinal gate first and block some of the pain messages from the slower nerve fibers. Applying ice, heat, or electrical stimulation to the painful area also stimulates the large nerve fibers and closes the spinal gate.

The gate-control theory also accounts for the fact that psychological factors, both cognitive and emotional, can influence the perception of pain. Melzack and Wall contend that messages from the brain to the spinal cord can inhibit the transmission of pain messages at the spinal gate and thereby affect the perception of pain. This explains why some people can undergo surgery under hypnosis and feel little or no pain. It also explains why soldiers injured in battle or athletes injured during games can be so distracted that they do not experience pain until some time after the injury.

The experience of pain is affected by cultural background, and even the pain of childbirth is endured more stoically in some cultures.

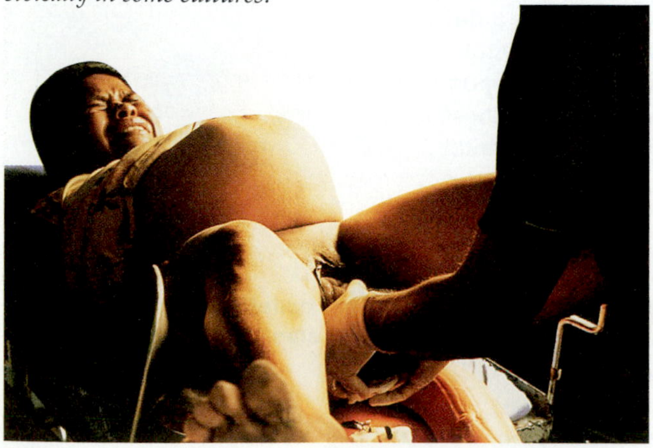

Psychological and Cultural Influences on the Experience of Pain The experience of pain has both a physical and an emotional component, and both vary from person to person. Pain experts distinguish between pain and suffering, suffering being the affective, or emotional, response to pain.

Sullivan and others (1995) found that people suffered most from pain when they harbored negative thoughts about it, feared its potential threat to their well-being, and expressed feelings of helplessness.

Culture also influences the way pain is experienced and expressed. The most often cited work on pain and culture is that of Zborowski (1952), who compared the responses to pain of Italian, Jewish, Irish, and native-born Anglo-Saxon patients in a large hospital in New York. Among the four groups,

Jewish and Italian patients responded more emotionally and showed heightened expressions of pain.

Culture even influences the experience and expression of pain during childbirth. The Chinese value silence, and Chinese women enduring the pain of childbirth typically do not engage in loud and highly emotional responses for fear they will dishonor themselves and their families (Weber, 1996). In stark contrast are some Pakistani women who believe that the greater their suffering and the louder their response to the pain, the more caring their husbands will be during the following weeks (Ahmed, 1994).

Endorphins: Natural Pain Relievers Americans spend more money trying to get rid of pain than for any other medical purpose. Over $40 billion is spent each year on treatments for chronic pain ranging from over-the-counter medications to surgery and psychotherapy (Brownlee & Schrof, 1997). The body produces its own natural painkillers, the **endorphins,** which block pain and produce a feeling of well-being. Endorphins are released when you are injured, when you experience stress or extreme pain, and when you laugh, cry, or exercise.

What are endorphins?

Some people release endorphins even when they only *think* they are receiving pain medication but are given, instead, a placebo in the form of a sugar pill or an injection of saline solution. Asthma, high blood pressure, and even heart disease can respond to placebo "treatment" (Brown, 1998). About 35% of the patients who receive placebos report relief from pain (Melzack & Wall, 1983). Why? Apparently, when patients believe that they have received a drug for pain, that belief stimulates the release of their own natural pain relievers, the endorphins.

When injected into patients, the drug **naloxone** blocks the action of endorphins by binding to their receptor sites, thereby preventing the endorphins from having the pain-relieving effect. Joggers who normally experience runner's high will not experience it if they are injected with naloxone before they run, an indication that jogging stimulates the release of endorphins.

Acupuncture, the ancient Chinese technique for relieving pain, appears to work because the fine needles that are inserted at specific points on the body seem to stimulate the release of endorphins, thereby relieving pain. But endorphins do not account for other methods of pain relief, such as meditation, relaxation, distraction, and hypnosis, which we will discuss in Chapter 4. The next time you experience pain, you may want to try the techniques in the *Try It!*

gate-control theory: The theory that the pain signals transmitted by slow-firing nerve fibers can be blocked at the spinal gate if fast-firing fibers get their messages to the gate first, or if the brain itself inhibits transmission of the pain messages.

endorphins (en-DOR-fins): Chemicals, produced naturally by the pituitary gland, that reduce pain and positively affect mood.

naloxone: A drug that blocks the action of endorphins.

Try It!

If you experience pain, you can try any of the following techniques for controlling it:

- Distraction can be particularly effective for controlling brief or mild pain. Generally, activities or thoughts that require a great deal of attention will provide more relief than passive distractions.
- Counterirritation–stimulating or irritating one area of the body in order to mask or diminish pain in another area–can be accomplished with ice packs, heat, massage, mustard packs, or electrical stimulation.
- Relaxation techniques such as the one described on page 143 are useful for reducing the stress and muscular tension that usually accompany pain.
- Positive statements can help you cope, whereas negative thoughts tend to increase your anxiety. For example, replace "I can't stand this anymore" with "I have had worse pain than this before, and I lived through it."
- Attention and sympathy from family members and friends should be kept at a moderate level; too much attention may prove to be so reinforcing that it serves to prolong pain.

The other two senses we will explore may seem minor, but they too make important contributions to your sensory world.

The Kinesthetic Sense: Keeping Track of the Body's Parts

What kind of information does the kinesthetic sense provide, and how is this sensory information detected?

The **kinesthetic sense** provides information about (1) the position of body parts in relation to each other and (2) the movement of various body parts. This information is detected by receptors in the joints, ligaments, and muscles. The other senses, especially vision, provide additional information about body position and movement, but the kinesthetic sense works well on its own. Thanks to the kinesthetic sense, we are able to perform smooth and skilled body movements without visual feedback or a studied, conscious effort. A companion sense, the vestibular sense, involves equilibrium, or the sense of balance.

The Vestibular Sense: Sensing Up and Down and Changes in Speed

What is the vestibular sense, and where are its sensory receptors located?

The **vestibular sense** detects movement and provides information about the body's orientation in space. The vestibular sense organs are located in the semicircular canals and the *vestibular sacs* in the inner ear. The **semicircular canals** sense the rotation of your head, such as when you are turning your head from side to side or when you are spinning around (see Figure 3.11). Because the canals are filled with fluid, rotating movements of the head in any direction send the fluid coursing through the tubelike semicircular canals. In the canals the moving fluid bends the hair cells, which act as receptors and send neural impulses to the brain. Because there are three canals, each positioned on a different plane, the hair cells in one canal will bend more than the hair cells in the other canals, depending on the direction of rotation.

The semicircular canals and the vestibular sacs signal only *changes* in motion or orientation. If you were blindfolded and had no visual or other external cues, you would not be able to sense motion once your speed reached a constant rate. For example, in an airplane you feel the takeoff and the landing as well as any sudden changes in speed. But once the plane levels off and maintains a fairly constant cruising speed, your vestibular organs do not signal the brain that you are moving, even if you are traveling at a rate of hundreds of miles per hour.

kinesthetic sense: The sense providing information about relative position and movement of body parts.

vestibular sense (ves-TIB-yu-ler): Sense that provides information about the body's movement and orientation in space through sensory receptors in the semicircular canals and the vestibular sacs, which detect changes in the movement and orientation of the head.

semicircular canals: Three fluid-filled tubular canals in the inner ear that provide information about rotating head movements.

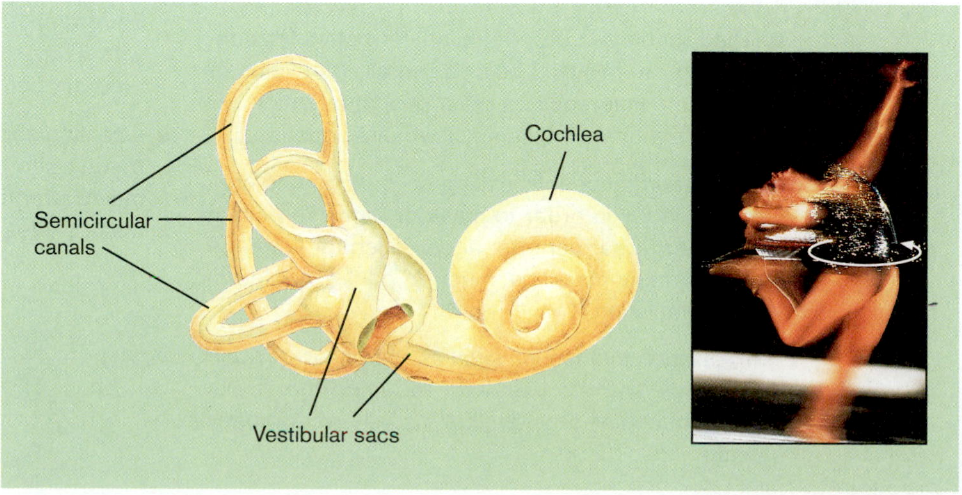

Figure 3.11

Sensing Balance and Movement

You sense the rotation of your head in any direction because the movement sends fluid coursing through the tubelike semicircular canals in the inner ear. The moving fluid bends the hair cell receptors–which, in turn, send the message to the brain.

Remember It!

1. Each skin receptor responds only to touch, pressure, warmth, or cold. (true/false)
2. People would be better off if they could not feel pain. (true/false)
3. Match the substance with the appropriate description.
   ____ (1) a sugar pill or saline injection that a person believes to be a drug
   ____ (2) pain-relieving substances produced by the body and thought to cause "runner's high"
   ____ (3) a drug that blocks the action of endorphins

   a. naloxone
   b. endorphins
   c. placebo
4. The (kinesthetic, vestibular) sense provides information about the position of body parts in relation to each other and about movement in those body parts.
5. The receptors for the (kinesthetic, vestibular) sense are located in the semicircular canals and vestibular sacs in the (middle ear, inner ear).

Answers: 1. false 2. false 3. (1) c (2) b (3) a 4. kinesthetic 5. vestibular, inner ear

PERCEPTION: WAYS OF PERCEIVING

In the first part of this chapter, you learned how the senses detect visual, auditory, and other sensory information and transmit it to the brain. Now we will explore **perception**—the process by which this sensory information is actively organized and interpreted by the brain. Humans *sense* sounds in hertz and decibels, but *perceive* melodies. They *sense* light of certain wavelengths and intensities, but *perceive* a multicolored world of objects and people. Sensations are the raw materials of human experiences; perceptions are the finished products.

Scientists can analyze physical objects down to their smallest parts. But can perception be analyzed and understood in the same way—broken down into its smallest sensory elements? The answer is no, according to Gestalt psychology, a school of thought that began in Germany early in the 20th century.

The Gestalt Principles of Perceptual Organization

What are the Gestalt principles of perceptual organization?

The Gestalt psychologists maintained that people cannot understand the perceptual world by breaking down experiences into tiny parts and analyzing them separately. When sensory elements are brought together, something new is formed. The whole is more than just the sum of its parts, insisted the Gestalt psychologists. The German word **Gestalt** has no exact English equivalent, but it roughly refers to the whole form, pattern, or configuration that a person perceives.

How do human beings organize the world of sights, sounds, and other sensory stimuli in order to perceive the way they do? The Gestalt psychologists claimed that sensory experience is organized according to certain basic principles of perceptual organization. The principles include the figure-ground relationship and other principles of perceptual grouping.

perception: The process by which sensory information is actively organized and interpreted by the brain.

Gestalt (geh-SHTALT): A German word roughly meaning "form" or "pattern."

Figure 3.12

Reversing Figure and Ground

In this illustration, you can see a white vase as figure against a black background, or two black faces in profile on a white background. Exactly the same visual stimulus produces two opposite figure-ground perceptions.

Figure and Ground: One Stands Out The **figure-ground** relationship is the most fundamental principle of perceptual organization and is, therefore, the best place to start analyzing how we perceive. As you view your world, some object (the figure) seems to stand out from the background (the ground).

Many psychologists believe that the figure-ground perceptual ability is **innate,** that is, does not have to be learned. Figure-ground perception is present very early in life. It is also the first ability to appear in patients blind from birth who have received their sight as adults, like S.B., whose case study opened this chapter. Figure-ground perception is not limited to vision. If you listen to a symphony orchestra or a rock band, the melody line tends to stand out as figure, while the chords and the rest of the accompaniment are heard as background. An itch or a pain immediately gets your attention, while the remaining tactile stimuli you feel fade to ground. But is figure-ground perception really achieved by the perceptual system, or is it partly due to the nature of the sensory stimulus itself? Recent research has confirmed that neural mechanisms in the primary visual cortex are responsible for figure-ground perception (Skiera et al., 2000).

In the reversible figure in Figure 3.12, figure and ground seem to shift back and forth between two distinct possibilities. Sometimes a figure or an object blends so well with its background that it can barely be seen. When there are no sharp lines of contrast between a figure and its background, a figure is *camouflaged.* For many animals, camouflage provides protection from predators.

Gestalt Principles of Grouping: Perceptual Arrangements The Gestalt psychologists believed that when people see figures or hear sounds, they organize or integrate them according to the simplest, most basic arrangement possible. The following are the Gestalt principles of grouping: similarity, proximity, continuity, and closure. These principles, discovered by Max Wertheimer (1912, 1958), launched the Gestalt movement in psychology (Steinman et al., 2000).

Similarity We tend to group visual, auditory, or other stimuli according to the principle of similarity. Objects that have similar characteristics are perceived as a unit. In Figure 3.13(a), dots of a similar color are perceived as belonging together to form horizontal rows on the left and vertical columns on the right. When you listen to music, you group the instruments and perceive them as units—the violins, trumpets, and so on—on the basis of similarity in sound.

Proximity Objects that are close together in space or time are usually perceived as belonging together, because of a principle of grouping called *proximity.* Because of their spacing, the lines in Figure 3.13(b) are perceived as four pairs of lines rather than as eight separate lines. Musical notes sounded close together in time are perceived as belonging together in musical phrases.

Figure 3.13

Gestalt Principles of Grouping

Gestalt psychologists proposed four principles of perceptual grouping: similarity, proximity, continuity, and closure.

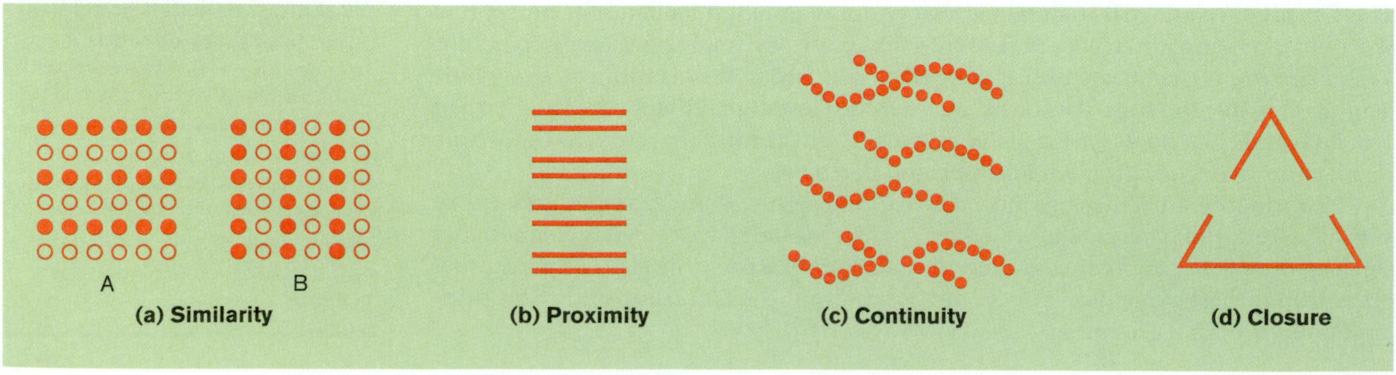

Continuity The principle of continuity means that we tend to perceive figures or objects as belonging together if they appear to form a continuous pattern, as in Figure 3.13(c). When two singers sing or two instruments play in harmony, you perceive the notes in the melody line as belonging together, and the notes in the harmony line as belonging together, even if they converge on the same note and then cross over.

Closure The principle of closure attempts to explain the tendency to complete figures with gaps in them. Even though parts of the figure in Figure 3.13(d) are missing, you use closure and perceive it as a triangle. If you were listening to your favorite song on the radio and interference periodically interrupted it, you would fill in the gaps to perceive the whole song.

Perceptual Constancy

What is perceptual constancy, and what are the four types?

Even though we view objects or other people from different angles and distances and under different lighting conditions, we tend to see them as maintaining the same size, shape, brightness, and color. Scientists call this phenomenon **perceptual constancy.**

Size Constancy: When Smaller Means Farther Away When you say goodbye to friends and watch them walk away, the image they cast on your retina grows smaller and smaller until they finally disappear in the distance. But the shrinking-size information that the retina sends to the brain (the sensation) does not fool the perceptual system. As objects or people move farther away, you continue to perceive them as being about the same size.

This perceptual phenomenon is known as **size constancy.** We do not make a literal interpretation about the size of objects from the **retinal image**—the image projected onto the retina of objects in the visual field. If we did, we would believe that objects become larger as they approach and smaller as they move away. Some evidence suggests that size constancy is learned. Recall that S.B. had trouble perceiving visual sensations he had never experienced. He so grossly misjudged distances that he perceived the automobiles 60 feet below his hospital window as toy cars nearby.

Shape Constancy: Seeing Round as Round from Any Angle The shape or image of an object projected onto the retina changes according to the angle from which it is viewed. But our perceptual ability includes **shape constancy**—the tendency to perceive objects as having a stable or unchanging shape regardless of changes in the retinal image resulting from differences in viewing angle. In other words, you perceive a door as rectangular and a plate as round from whatever angle you view them (see Figure 3.14 on p. 108).

Brightness Constancy: Perceiving Brightness in Sunlight and Shadow People normally see objects as maintaining a constant level of brightness regardless of differences in lighting conditions—a phenomenon known as **brightness constancy.** Nearly all objects reflect some part of the light that falls on them, and white objects reflect more light than black objects. However, a black asphalt driveway at noon in bright sunlight actually reflects more light than a white shirt does indoors at night in dim lighting. Nevertheless, the driveway still looks black and the shirt still looks white. Why? We learn to infer the brightness of objects by comparing them with the brightness of all other objects viewed at the same time.

Color Constancy: When Colors Stay the Same in Sunlight or Shadow Colors can change considerably under different lighting conditions. But when objects are familiar, they appear to look about the same color under different conditions of illumination. This is called **color constancy.** Like brightness constancy, color constancy depends on the comparisons we make between differently colored objects viewed at the same time (Brou et al., 1986). Color constancy is apparently

figure-ground: A principle of perceptual organization whereby the visual field is perceived in terms of an object (figure) standing out against a background (ground).

innate: Inborn, unlearned.

perceptual constancy: The tendency to perceive objects as maintaining stable properties, such as size, shape, brightness, and color, despite differences in distance, viewing angle, and lighting.

size constancy: The tendency to perceive an object as the same size regardless of changes in the retinal image.

retinal image: The image of objects in the visual field projected onto the retina.

shape constancy: The tendency to perceive an object as having a stable or unchanging shape regardless of differences in viewing angle.

brightness constancy: The tendency to see an object as maintaining the same brightness regardless of differences in lighting conditions.

color constancy: The tendency to see an object as about the same color regardless of differences in lighting conditions.

Figure 3.14

Shape Constancy

The door projects very different images on the retina when viewed from different angles. But because of shape constancy, you continue to perceive the door as rectangular.

determined by neural processing farther up in the cerebral cortex than the visual cortex (Rinner & Gegenfurtner, 2000).

Imagine what a strange world we would live in if it were not for the perceptual constancies. If the brain interpreted all retinal images literally, familiar sizes, shapes, and colors would appear to change back and forth before our eyes. Fortunately, the perceptual constancies, so natural and commonplace, provide a stable perceptual world.

Remember It!

1. Camouflage blurs the distinction between
   a. sensation and perception.
   b. figure and ground.
   c. continuation and closure.
   d. proximity and similarity.
2. The Gestalt principle of (continuity, closure) refers to the tendency to complete figures with gaps in them.
3. Which of the perceptual constancies cause people to perceive objects as being different from the retinal image they project?
   a. brightness constancy and color constancy
   b. color constancy and shape constancy
   c. shape constancy and size constancy
   d. color constancy and size constancy
4. Which of the perceptual constancies depend on a comparison of one object with other objects viewed under the same lighting conditions?
   a. brightness constancy and color constancy
   b. color constancy and shape constancy
   c. shape constancy and size constancy
   d. color constancy and size constancy

Answers: 1. b 2. closure 3. c 4. a

Depth Perception: Perceiving What's Up Close and Far Away

Depth perception is the ability to perceive the visual world in three dimensions and to judge distances accurately. We judge how far away objects and other people are. We climb and descend stairs without stumbling and perform other visual tasks too numerous to list, all requiring depth perception.

Depth perception is three-dimensional. Yet each eye is able to provide only a two-dimensional view. The images cast on the retina do not contain depth; they are flat, just like a photograph. How, then, do we perceive depth so vividly?

Binocular Depth Cues: The Cues Only Two Eyes Reveal Some cues to depth perception depend on both eyes working together. These are called **binocular depth cues,** and they include convergence and binocular disparity. **Convergence** occurs when the eyes turn inward to focus on nearby objects—the closer the object, the greater the convergence. Hold the tip of your finger about 12 inches in front of your nose and focus on it. Now slowly begin moving your finger toward your nose. Your eyes will turn inward so much that they virtually cross when the tip of your finger meets the tip of your nose. Many psychologists believe that the tension of the eye muscles as they converge conveys information to the brain that serves as a cue for distance and depth perception.

Fortunately, the eyes are just far enough apart, about 2½ inches or so, to give each eye a slightly different view of the objects focused on and, consequently, a slightly different retinal image. The difference between the two retinal images, known as **binocular disparity** (or *retinal disparity*), provides an important cue for depth and distance (see Figure 3.15). The farther away from the eyes the objects being looked at are (up to 20 feet or so), the less the disparity, or difference, between the two retinal images. The brain integrates the two slightly different retinal images and gives the perception of three dimensions (Wallach, 1985a). Ohzawa and others (1990) suggest that there are specific neurons in the visual cortex particularly suited to detecting disparity.

depth perception: The ability to see in three dimensions and to estimate distance.

binocular depth cues: Depth cues that depend on two eyes working together; convergence and binocular disparity.

convergence: A binocular depth cue in which the eyes turn inward as they focus on nearby objects—the closer an object, the greater the convergence.

binocular disparity: A binocular depth cue resulting from differences between the two retinal images formed of an object viewed at distances up to about 20 feet.

What are the binocular depth cues?

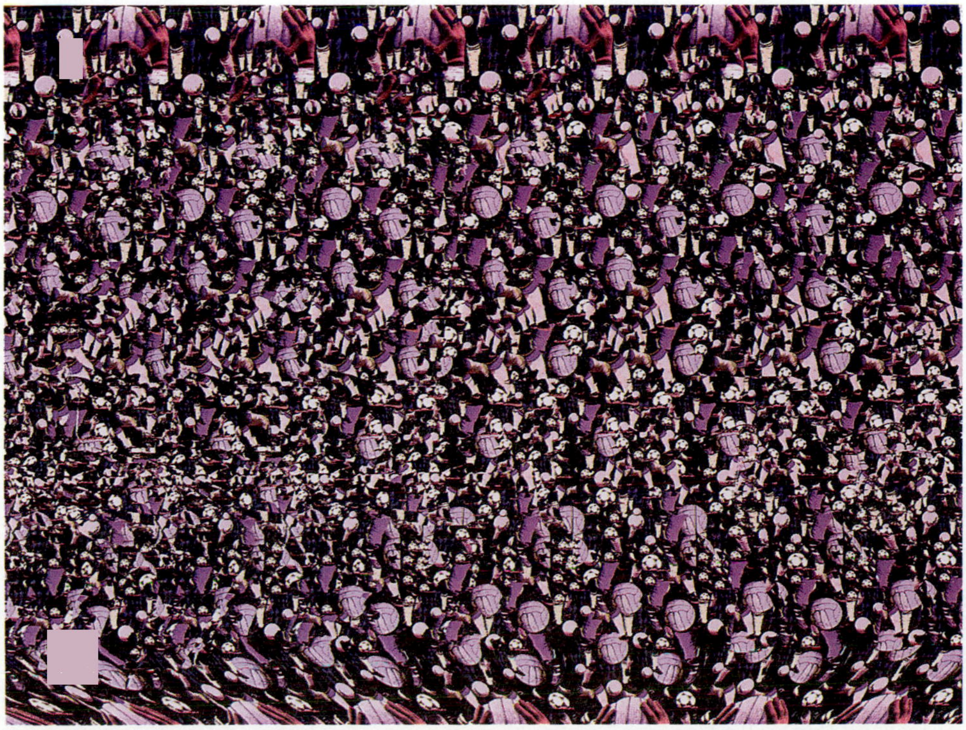

Figure 3.15

Retinal Disparity and Viewing a Stereogram

Retinal disparity enables most of us to perceive 3-D images in stereograms. Place this picture against the tip of your nose and then very, very slowly move the book straight back from your face. Look at the image without blinking. A 3-D picture of soccer players and their fans will suddenly appear.

Ordinarily you are not aware that each eye provides a slightly different view of the objects you see, but you can prove this for yourself in the *Try It!*

Try It!

Hold your forefinger or a pencil at arm's length straight in front of you. Close your right eye and focus on the pencil. Now quickly close your left eye at the same time that you open your right eye. Repeat this procedure, closing one eye just as you open the other one. The pencil will appear to move from side to side in front of your face.

Now slowly bring the pencil closer and closer until it almost reaches your nose. The closer you bring the pencil, the more it appears to move from side to side. This is because there is progressively more disparity between the two retinal images as a viewed object gets closer and closer to your eyes.

Convergence and binocular disparity provide depth or distance cues only for nearby objects. Fortunately, each eye by itself provides cues for objects at greater distances.

What are seven monocular depth cues?

Monocular Depth Cues: The Cues One Eye Can Detect Close one eye and you will see that you can still perceive depth. The visual depth cues perceived by one eye alone are called **monocular depth cues.** The following is a description of seven monocular depth cues, many of which have been used by artists in Western cultures to give the illusion of depth to their paintings.

Because of texture gradient, the wheat stalks in the foreground appear sharply defined, while those farther back are less well defined, almost fuzzy. Also, the snow-capped mountain in the background is relatively small and thus accurately perceived as being far way.

- *Interposition.* Some psychologists consider interposition, or overlapping, to be the most powerful depth cue of all. When one object partly blocks your view of another, you perceive the partially blocked object as farther away.
- *Linear perspective.* Linear perspective is a depth cue in which parallel lines that are known to be the same distance apart appear to grow closer together, or converge, as they recede into the distance. Linear perspective was used extensively by Renaissance artists in the 15th century.
- *Relative size.* Larger objects are perceived as being closer to the viewer, and smaller objects as being farther away. We know that most adults are between 5 and 6 feet tall, so when images of the people we view are two, three, or many times smaller than their normal size, we perceive them as being two, three, or as many times farther away.
- *Texture gradient.* Texture gradient is a depth cue in which near objects appear to have sharply defined textures, while similar objects appear progressively smoother and fuzzier as they recede into the distance.
- *Atmospheric perspective.* Atmospheric perspective, sometimes called *aerial perspective,* is a depth cue in which objects in the distance have a bluish tint and appear more blurred than objects close at hand.
- *Shadow or shading.* When light falls on objects, they cast shadows. You can distinguish bulges from indentions by the shadows they cast. This ability appears to be learned (Hess, 1961).

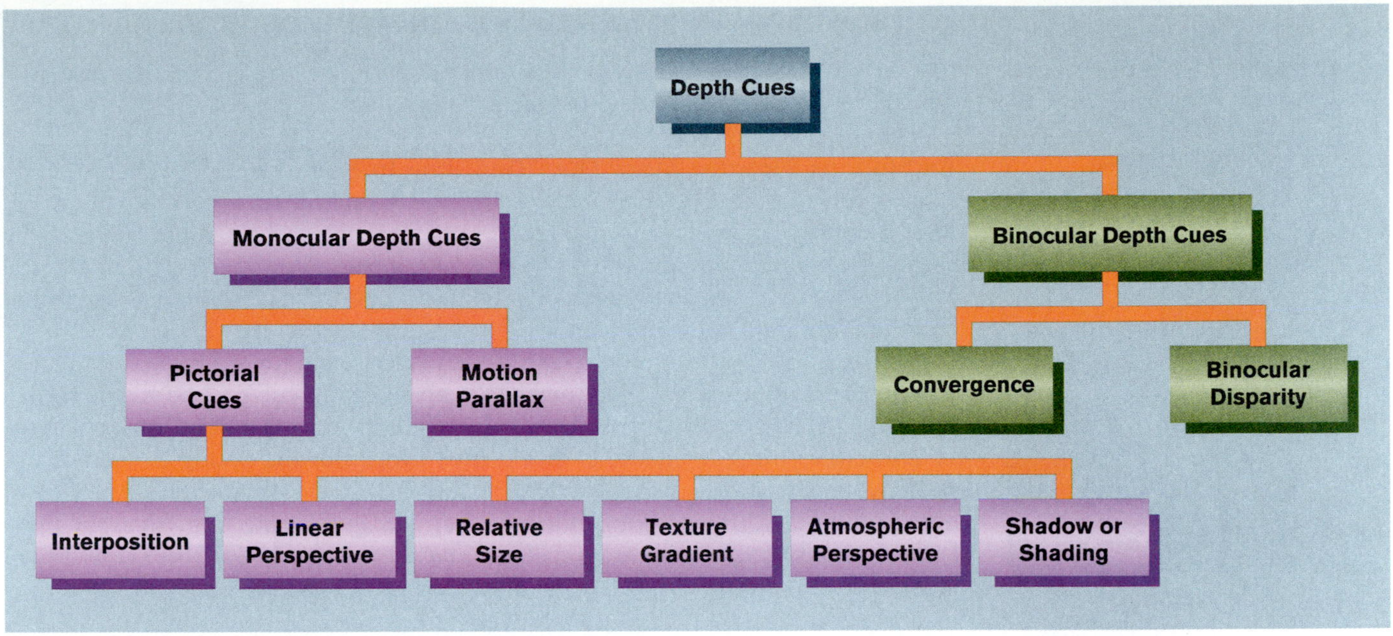

Figure 3.16

Binocular and Monocular Depth Cues

Depth cues that require two eyes working together are binocular; those that require only one eye are monocular.

- *Motion parallax.* When you ride in a moving vehicle and look out the side window, the objects you see outside appear to be moving in the opposite direction. The objects also seem to be moving at different speeds—those closest to you appear to be moving faster than those in the distance. This phenomenon, called *motion parallax,* provides another monocular cue to depth perception. Objects very far away, such as the moon and the sun, appear to move in the same direction as the viewer.

Figure 3.16 summarizes the binocular and monocular depth cues.

Perception of Motion

When we focus and concentrate on visual and other sensory information, we must disregard a great deal. We fix our attention on the information that is important to us and ignore the rest. There is, however, one universal visual attention-getter: Movement catches the attention of humans, and of practically every other animal. We notice motion, usually regardless of where in the visual field it occurs. When objects do move in the field of vision, they project images that move across the retina, but this alone does not explain our perception of movement, known as *motion detection.* Recent research indicates that motion detection is due to brain mechanisms linked to the retina (Bach & Hoffman, 2000). We can perceive movement, that is, **apparent motion,** even when objects do not move at all.

If several stationary lights are flashed on and off in sequence, the light will actually appear to move from one spot to the next. This type of apparent motion, called the **phi phenomenon,** was first discussed by Max Wertheimer (1912), one of the founders of Gestalt psychology. How many neon signs have you seen that caused you to perceive motion? The neon lights don't move; they simply flash on and off in a particular sequence.

When you watch a motion picture, you are seeing apparent motion. People and objects appear to be moving, but in reality you are seeing *stroboscopic motion,* a series of still pictures of successive phases of movement. The pictures are flashed in rapid succession to give the illusion of movement. Changes in a scene, even extensive ones, are sometimes difficult to notice if we momentarily shift our gaze or if the image is "flickering." But we usually detect such changes even though we are not consciously aware of having done so (Rensink, 2000).

monocular depth cues (mah-NOK-yu-ler): Depth cues that can be perceived by only one eye.

apparent motion: The perception of motion when none is occurring (as in the phi phenomenon or in stroboscopic movement).

phi phenomenon: An illusion of movement occurring when two or more stationary lights are flashed on and off in sequence, giving the impression that one light is actually moving from one spot to the next.

Extraordinary Perceptions: Puzzling Perceptions

What are three types of puzzling perceptions?

Not only can we perceive motion that does not exist, we can also perceive ambiguous figures, impossible figures, and illusions.

Figure 3.17

"Old Woman/Young Woman" by E. G. Boring

The most famous ambiguous figure can be seen alternately as a young woman or an old woman, depending on where your eyes fixate.

Ambiguous Figures: More Than One Way to See Them When you are faced for the first time with an *ambiguous figure,* you have no experience to call on. Your perceptual system is puzzled and tries to work its way out of the quandary by seeing the ambiguous figure first one way and then another, but not both at once. You never get a lasting impression of ambiguous figures because they seem to jump back and forth beyond your control.

In some ambiguous figures, two different objects or figures are seen alternately. The best known of these, "Old Woman/Young Woman," by E. G. Boring, is shown in Figure 3.17. If you direct your gaze to the left of the drawing, you are likely to see an attractive young woman, her face turned away. But the young woman disappears when you suddenly perceive the image of the old woman. Such examples of object ambiguity offer striking evidence that perceptions are more than the mere sum of sensory parts. It is hard to believe that the same drawing (the same sum of sensory parts) can convey such dramatically different perceptions.

Impossible Figures: This Can't Be At first glance, many impossible figures do not seem so unusual—not until you examine them more closely. Would you invest your money in a company that manufactured three-pronged tridents as shown in Figure 3.18? Such an object could not be made as pictured because the middle prong appears to be in two different places at the same time. However, this type of impossible figure is more likely to fool the depth-perception sensibilities of people from Western cultures. People in some African cultures do not represent three-dimensional visual space in their art, and they do not perceive depth in drawings that contain pictorial depth cues. These people see no ambiguity in drawings similar to the three-pronged trident, and they can draw the figure accurately from memory much more easily than people from Western cultures can (Bloomer, 1976).

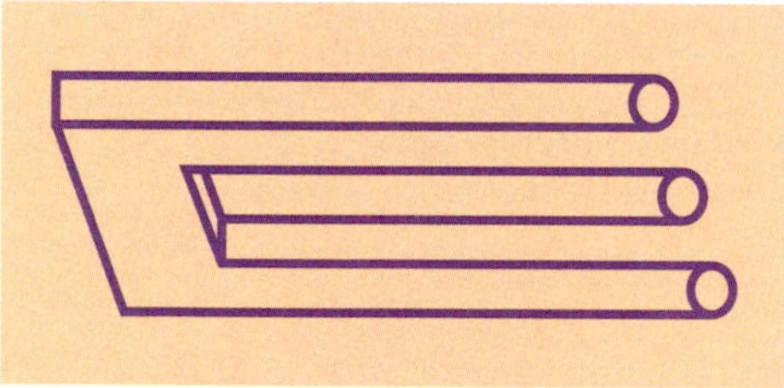

Figure 3.18

The Three-Pronged Trident

This is an impossible figure because the middle prong appears to be in two places at the same time.

Illusions: False Perceptions An **illusion** is a false perception or a misperception of an actual stimulus in the environment. We can misperceive size, shape, or the relationship of one element to another. We need not pay to see illusions performed by magicians. Illusions occur naturally, and we see them all the time. An oar in the water appears to be bent where it meets the water. The moon looks much larger at the horizon than it does overhead. Why? One explanation of the moon illusion involves relative size. This idea suggests that the moon looks very large on the horizon because it is viewed in comparison to trees, buildings, and other objects. When viewed overhead, the moon cannot be compared with other objects, and it appears smaller. People have been speculating about the moon illusion for 22 centuries and experimenting for 50 years to determine its cause, but there is still no agreement (Hershenson, 1989).

The Müller-Lyer Illusion In Figure 3.19(a), which horizontal line is longer, the upper or the lower one? Although the two lines are the same length, the diagonals extending outward from both ends of the upper line make it look longer than the lower line, which has diagonals pointing inward. British psychologist R. L. Gregory (1978) has suggested that the Müller-Lyer illusion is actually a misapplication of size constancy. In Figure 3.19(b), the corner on the left projects forward, toward the viewer, and is therefore perceived to be closer. The corner on the right appears to be more distant because it seems to recede from the viewer. When two lines are the same length, the line we perceive to be farther away will look longer.

illusion: A false perception of actual stimuli involving a misperception of size, shape, or the relationship of one element to another.

The Ponzo Illusion The Ponzo illusion also plays an interesting trick on our estimation of size. Look at Figure 3.20. Which obstruction on the railroad tracks looks

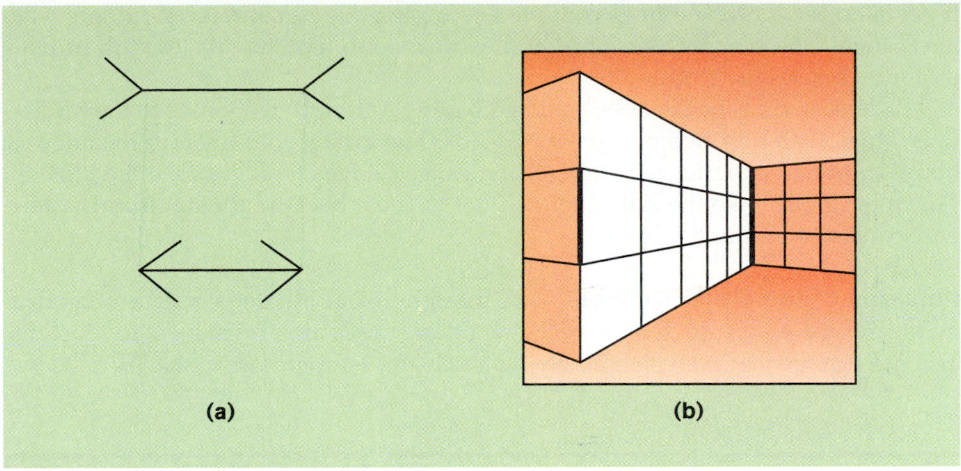

Figure 3.19

The Müller-Lyer Illusion

The two horizontal lines in (a) are identical in length. Look at the two dark vertical lines in (b). Which looks longer? They are actually the same length, although the line in the back looks much longer. The illusion occurs because your brain thinks it is seeing the effects of perspective. (Based on Gregory, 1978.)

larger? You have undoubtedly guessed by now that, contrary to your perceptions, A and B are the same size. Again, perceptions of size and distance, which we trust and which are normally accurate in informing us about the real world, can be wrong. If you saw two obstructions like the ones in the illusion on real railroad tracks, the one that looks larger would indeed be larger. So the Ponzo illusion is not a natural illusion but rather a contrived one. In fact, all these illusions are really misapplications of principles that nearly always work properly in normal everyday experience.

False Perception of Color When under hypnosis, highly hypnotizable individuals perceive color when the hypnotist suggests it, even though they are viewing a colorless, gray background. Brain-imaging studies indicated that the brain areas responsible for color perception were highly activated when these participants were told that they were viewing color (Kosslyn et al., 2000).

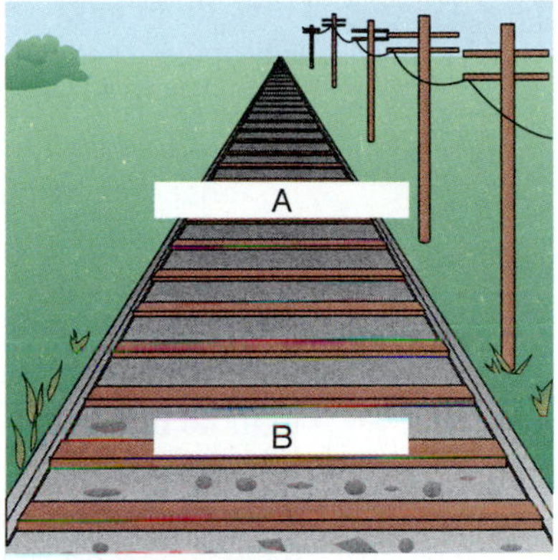

Figure 3.20

The Ponzo Illusion

The two white bars superimposed on the railroad track are actually identical in length. Because A appears farther away than B, you perceive it as longer.

Cultural Differences in the Perception of Visual Illusions British psychologist R. L. Gregory believed that susceptibility to the Müller-Lyer and other such illusions is not inborn. Rather, the culture in which people live is responsible to some extent for the illusions they perceive.

To test whether susceptibility to the Müller-Lyer and similar illusions is due to experience, Segall and others (1966) tested 1,848 adults and children from 15 different cultures in Africa, the Philippines, and the United States. Included were a group of Zulus from South Africa and a group of Illinois residents. The study revealed that "there were marked differences in illusion susceptibility across the cultural groups included in this study" (Segall, 1994, p. 137). People in all the cultures showed some tendency to see the illusion, indicating a biological component, but experience was clearly a factor. Zulus, who have round houses and see few corners of any kind, are not fooled by the Müller-Lyer illusion. Illinois residents saw the illusion readily, while the Zulu tribespeople tended not to see it.

Some researchers suggested that race might offer an explanation for the cultural differences observed (Pollack, 1970). But a study by Stewart (1973) provides evidence to indicate that it is fundamentally culture, not race, that drives perceptions of illusions. When two groups of schoolchildren from Illinois (60 African Americans and 60 Whites) were tested with the Müller-Lyer and other illusions, no significant differences were found in susceptibility to the illusions. And in Zambia, researchers tested five different groups of Black African schoolchildren using the same illusions. Children's tendency to see the illusions had nothing to do with race but was strongly influenced by culture. Those children who

Some visual illusions seem to be culture-dependent. For example, Zulus and people from other cultures in which the houses lack straight sides and corners do not perceive the Müller-Lyer illusion.

lived in areas where buildings consisted of angles, edges, corners, and doors were likely to be fooled by the illusions; those who lived in remote villages with primarily round houses were not.

Pedersen and Wheeler (1983) studied Native American responses to the Müller-Lyer illusion among two groups of Navajos. The group who lived in rectangular houses and had experienced corners, angles, and edges tended to see the illusion. The other group, like the Zulus, tended not to see it because their cultural experience consisted of round houses.

Illusions of the Other Senses Although visual illusions are the most dramatic and the easiest to demonstrate, the other senses are also subject to illusions. You can experience an illusion involving touch and temperature in the *Try It!*

Try It!

Take three large cereal bowls or small mixing bowls. Fill one with very cold water, another with hot water (*not* boiling or scalding), and the third with lukewarm water. Hold your left hand in the cold water and your right hand in the hot water for at least 1 minute. Then quickly plunge both hands into the lukewarm water at the same time.

Why do you experience the illusion that the lukewarm water feels simultaneously warmer and colder than its actual temperature? The answer is adaptation. You perceive the lukewarm water as warm on your cold-adapted left hand and as cold on your warm-adapted right hand. This illustrates that our perceptions of sensory stimuli are relative and are affected by differences between stimuli we are already adapted to and new stimuli.

Remember It!

1. Retinal disparity and convergence are two (monocular, binocular) depth cues.
2. Match the appropriate monocular depth cue with each example.

____ (1) one building partly blocking another
____ (2) railroad tracks converging in the distance
____ (3) closer objects appearing to move faster than objects farther away
____ (4) objects farther away looking smaller than near objects

a. motion parallax
b. linear perspective
c. interposition
d. relative size

3. The type of apparent motion produced by motion pictures is (motion parallax, stroboscopic motion).
4. An illusion is
   a. an imaginary sensation.
   b. an impossible figure.
   c. a misperception of a real stimulus.
   d. a figure-ground reversal.

Answers: 1. binocular 2. (1) c (2) b (3) a (4) d 3. stroboscopic motion 4. c

ADDITIONAL INFLUENCES ON PERCEPTION

Why don't we all perceive sights, sounds, odors, and events in the same way? The reason is that our perceptions involve more than just the sensory stimuli themselves.

Bottom-Up and Top-Down Processing

In what types of situations do people rely more on bottom-up processing or top-down processing?

Psychologists distinguish between two distinct information-processing techniques that people use in recognizing patterns: bottom-up processing and top-down processing.

Bottom-up processing begins with the individual components of a stimulus that are detected by the sensory receptors. The information is then transmitted to areas in the brain where it is combined and assembled into the whole patterns that a person perceives.

In **top-down processing,** on the other hand, past experience and knowledge of the context play a role in forming a perception. In other words, what we perceive is more than the sum of the individual elements taken in by our sensory receptors. If you have ever tried to decipher a prescription written by your doctor (bottom-up processing), you may have been amazed that your pharmacist could fill it. But prior knowledge and experience enabled the pharmacist to use top-down processing.

Of course, we use both bottom-up and top-down processing to form perceptions. In unfamiliar situations, we are likely to use bottom-up processing. In familiar situations, where we have some prior knowledge and experience, we tend to use top-down processing.

The Role of Psychological Factors in Perception

What are some psychological factors that affect perceptions?

We make perceptual judgments from our own individual points of reference. Other people are perceived as tall or short, young or old, depending on one's own height or age. Words such as *intelligent, attractive, expensive, thin, successful, sensible, talented, rich, exciting, loud,* and so on are all measured from one's own perceptual point of view. Perceptions are also affected by values, needs, interests, and emotions.

The **perceptual set**—what people expect to perceive—determines, to a large extent, what you actually see, hear, feel, taste, and smell. If you ordered raspberry sherbet and it was colored green, would it still taste like raspberry, or might it taste more like lime? Once their expectations are set, people often bend reality to make it fit them. Psychologist David Rosenhan (1973) and some of his colleagues were admitted as patients to various mental hospitals with "diagnoses" of schizophrenia. Once admitted, they acted normal in every way. The purpose? They wondered how long it would take the doctors and the hospital staff to realize that they were not mentally ill. But the doctors and the staff members saw only what they expected to see and not what actually occurred. They perceived everything the pseudo-patients said and did, such as notetaking, to be symptoms of their illness. But the real patients were not fooled. They were the first to realize that the psychologists were not really mentally ill.

bottom-up processing: Information processing in which individual components or bits of data are combined until a complete perception is formed.

top-down processing: Application of previous experience and conceptual knowledge to recognize the whole of a perception and thus easily identify the simpler elements of that whole.

perceptual set: An expectation of what will be perceived, which can affect what actually is perceived.

SUBLIMINAL PERSUASION AND EXTRASENSORY PERCEPTION

So far we have considered perceptions that are formed above the threshold of awareness and perceptions that arise from known sensory abilities. Can people be influenced by persuasive messages below the level of awareness, through subliminal persuasion? And are people able to gain information by some means other than known sensory channels, through extrasensory perception?

Subliminal Persuasion: Does It Work?

Is subliminal persuasion effective in influencing behavior?

Decades ago, it was reported that moviegoers in a New Jersey theater were exposed to advertising messages flashed on the screen so briefly that they were not aware of them. An advertising executive claimed that the words "Eat popcorn" and "Drink Coca-Cola" were projected on the screen for only 1/3000 of a second every 5 seconds during the movie. The purpose of the messages was to influence audience members to buy popcorn and Coca-Cola, not by getting their conscious attention, but by sending persuasive messages below their level of awareness, a technique called **subliminal persuasion.** During the 6-week period the messages ran, popcorn sales supposedly went up by 57.5%, and Coca-Cola sales rose by more than 18% (McConnell et al., 1958). But the advertising executive who released the story later admitted that it was a hoax—no subliminal messages had actually been flashed. You might remember a similar incident— the infamous "rats" commercial that the Republican party ran during the 2000 presidential campaign and in which the word *bureaucrats* was reduced to *rats* for 1/30 second. Democrats accused Republicans of attempting to subliminally influence voters against Al Gore, the Democratic presidential candidate. Republican candidate George W. Bush dismissed the occurrence as an accident, but the question remained: Was a subliminal message sent?

Technically, **subliminal perception** would be defined as the perception of sensory stimuli that are below the absolute threshold. But subliminal persuasion experiments are limited to messages flashed so quickly that they could *never* be perceived normally at all. Can people actually perceive information that is completely below their level of awareness? There are audiotapes that claim to help people remedy virtually every ill (relieve depression, cure migraine headaches), solve every problem (reduce stress, quit smoking), and meet every need (increase confidence, gain peace of mind). Embedded in the recordings of soothing music or ocean waves lapping the shore are subliminal messages for those who want to lose weight ("I eat less"), reduce stress ("I am calm"), or improve their self-image ("I am capable").

Researchers conducting double-blind studies found that audiotapes that claimed to influence behavior with subliminal messages were no more effective in doing so than tapes containing unrelated subliminal messages or no subliminal messages whatsoever (Greenwald, 1992; Greenwald et al., 1991; Russell et al., 1991). But if subliminal persuasion does not influence behavior, why do some users insist that the tapes have helped them to quit smoking, lose weight, and so on? Evidently the change is due to the power of suggestion or the placebo effect, and not to the messages on the tapes (Pratkanis et al., 1994; Smith & Rogers, 1994). Claims have been made that backmasking—the embedding of backward messages in recordings of rock music—was done to convey evil, or even satanic, messages subliminally to young listeners. Canadian researchers Begg and others (1993) have conducted extensive studies but have found no evidence that backmasking has any influence on the listener.

Extrasensory Perception: Does It Exist?

What is extrasensory perception, and have the claims of psychics been verified scientifically?

Is it possible to perceive information that does not come through the senses? Is there such a thing as **extrasensory perception (ESP)**—gaining information about objects, events, or another's thoughts through some means other than the known sensory channels? Can some people read minds or foretell the future? Almost 50% of Americans believe in ESP (Gallup & Newport, 1990b). Extrasensory perception is part of a larger area of interest known as **parapsychology,** the study of psychic phenomena. Reported cases of ESP roughly fall into three categories—telepathy, clairvoyance, and precognition.

Telepathy means gaining awareness of the thoughts, the feelings, or the activities of another without the use of the senses—in other words, reading a person's mind.

Clairvoyance means gaining information about objects or events without use of the senses, such as knowing the contents of a letter before opening it. *Precognition* refers to an awareness of an event before it occurs. Most of the reported cases of precognition in everyday life have occurred while people were dreaming.

One researcher revealed the poor record of well-known psychics who made New Year's predictions for the *National Enquirer* between 1978 and 1985. Only two of their 425 predictions proved to be accurate (Strentz, 1986). Many psychics also made predictions about the millennium in the late 1990s. For example, some predicted that a cure for both cancer and AIDS would be found before the year 2000. Because psychic phenomena violate what they know about the real, measurable, physical world, scientists and skeptics naturally demand proof of their existence (Hansel, 1966, 1980; Randi, 1980). Time after time, investigators have discovered trickery when examining the claims of psychics who assert that they can read minds or contact and communicate with the dead. Uri Geller, well known for his ability to bend spoons and keys, to "read" the contents of sealed envelopes, and to perform other feats supposedly using his mind alone, was found to use magic tricks and fraud to deceive the public.

One professional magician, the Amazing Randi (1980), gained popularity in exposing the fraudulent techniques used by Uri Geller and others who claim great powers or abilities (Yam, 1995b). In 1980 Randi offered to pay $10,000 "to any person or group that can perform *one* paranormal feat of *any* kind under the proper observing conditions" (p. 3). Although the offer has been raised to over $1 million, he has not found a single person able to demonstrate psychic ability under controlled conditions.

Earlier we noted that sensation and perception are so closely linked in everyday experience that it is hard to see clearly where one ends and the other begins. But in this chapter, you have seen many examples of what is sensed and what is perceived. Our perceptual system is continuously trying to complete what we merely sense. We are always busy filling in, organizing, and making more complete perceptual sense out of the sensory parts that we are able to see, hear, touch, taste, and smell.

subliminal persuasion: Sending persuasive messages below the recipient's level of awareness.

subliminal perception: Perceiving sensory stimulation that is below the absolute threshold.

extrasensory perception (ESP): Gaining awareness of or information about objects, events, or another's thoughts through some means other than the known sensory channels.

parapsychology: The study of psychic phenomena, including extrasensory perception (ESP).

Remember It!

1. In situations where you have some prior knowledge and experience, you are likely to rely more on (bottom-up, top-down) processing.
2. Perceptual set is most directly related to a person's
   a. needs.
   b. interests.
   c. expectations.
   d. emotions.
3. Subliminal advertising has been proven effective in influencing consumers to buy products. (true/false)
4. Match the type of psychic phenomenon with the description:
   c (1) reading someone's mind
   b (2) gaining awareness of events before they occur
   a (3) gaining information about objects or events without the use of the senses

   a. clairvoyance
   b. precognition
   c. telepathy
5. Carefully controlled and repeatable laboratory experiments have proved the existence of extrasensory perception. (true/false)

Answers: 1. top-down 2. c 3. false 4. (1) c (2) b (3) a 5. false

Apply It!

Noise and Hearing Loss: Bad Vibrations

Hearing loss is increasing rapidly in the industrialized world, and the main reason for the increase is NOISE. Jet engines, power mowers, radios, firecrackers, motorcycles, chain saws, and other power tools are well-known sources of noise that can injure the ear.

Currently, U.S. government regulations protect employees from exposure to sound levels of more than 85 dB in the workplace during an 8-hour day (Martin, 1994). But, there are no laws to protect people outside of the workplace from hearing loss. And people are in more danger of losing their hearing off the job than at the worksite. Without proper protection, a person's hearing can be more damaged by recreational hunting, rock concerts, and some sports events than by industrial noise. People would probably be more willing to wear protective devices if they were aware of their benefits (Lusk et al., 1995).

Noisy toys and other hazards. Exposure to hazardous noise can begin long before a person is old enough to listen to a CD player. Researchers Axelsson and Jerson (1985) tested seven squeaking toys that, at a distance of 10 centimeters, emitted sound levels loud enough to put toddlers at risk for hearing loss at only 2 minutes of daily exposure.

And if older children play with toy weapons, noise-induced hearing loss can occur with only seconds of exposure. Researchers tested several toy weapons and found that, at a distance of 50 centimeters, the guns produced explosive sound levels ranging from 144 to 152 dB (Axelsson & Jerson, 1985). All exceeded the 130-dB peak level that is considered the upper limit for exposure to short-lived explosive sounds if hearing loss is to be avoided.

Firecrackers pose a particular hazard if they explode close to the ear. In one study a number of firecrackers were tested at 3 meters, and sound levels were found to range from 130 dB to an unbelievable and highly dangerous 190 dB (Gupta & Vishwakarma, 1989).

The destructive effects of noise. Explosions, gun blasts, and other extremely loud noises may burst the eardrum or may fracture or dislocate the tiny ossicles in the middle ear. Often these injuries can be repaired surgically, but noise injuries to the inner ear cannot. "Extremely intense sounds can rip the delicate sensory [hair] cells completely off the basilar membrane on which they normally sit, kill the cells, or merely injure them permanently" (Bennett, 1990, p. 3). Rock musician Kathy Peck lost 40% of her hearing in one evening after her band opened a stadium concert.

How much noise is too much? How can you tell when noise levels are high enough to jeopardize your hearing? You are putting yourself at risk if you have difficulty talking over the noise level, or if the noise exposure leaves you with a ringing in your ears or a temporary hearing loss (Dobie, 1987).

Experts claim that exposure to noise of 90 dB (a lawn mower, for example) for more than 8 hours in a 24-hour period can damage hearing. For every increase of 5 dB, maximum exposure time should be cut in half–4 hours for 95 dB, 2 hours for 100 dB, and 1 hour for 105 dB. The Department of Labor considers 115 dB to be the maximum allowable level of exposure to steady sound levels (Catlin, 1986). And 120 decibels, what you would hear directly in front of the speakers at a rock concert, would immediately destroy some of the hair cells.

In 1986 the rock group The Who entered the *Guiness Book of World Records* as the loudest rock band on record, blasting out deafening sound intensities that measured 120 decibels at a distance of 164 feet from the speakers. Unless their ears were protected, audience members within that 164-foot radius probably suffered some irreversible hearing loss. And the band members? Pete Townshend of The Who has severely damaged hearing and, in addition, is plagued by tinnitus, an annoying condition that causes him to experience a continuous ringing in the ears.

In an article in *Rolling Stone,* Ted Nugent admitted his hearing problem. "My left ear is there just to balance my face, because it doesn't work at all" (Murphy, 1989, p. 101). In the early 1990s a rash of lawsuits were filed against rock musicians and promoters by fans complaining of tinnitus and hearing loss suffered after attending their concerts.

Protecting yourself from hearing loss. What can you do to protect yourself from the effects of noise?

- If you must be exposed to loud noise, use earplugs (not the kind used for swimming) or earmuffs to reduce noise by as much as 15–30 dB (Dobie, 1987).
- If you must engage in an extremely noisy activity, such as cutting wood with a chain saw, limit periods of exposure so that stunned hair cells can recover.
- Keep the volume down on your Walkman-type radio or CD player. If the volume control is numbered 1 to 10, a volume above 4 probably exceeds the federal standards for noise. If you have a ringing in your ears, if sounds seem muffled, or if you have a tickling sensation in your ears after you remove your headset, you could have sustained some hearing loss.
- Begin humming before you are exposed to loud noise. Humming will set in motion the very tiny muscles in the middle ear that dampen the sound and provide some measure of protection (Borg & Counter, 1989).
- Put your fingers in your ears or leave the scene.

THINKING CRITICALLY

Evaluation

Using what you have learned about the factors that contribute to hearing loss, prepare a statement indicating what you think the government should do to control noise pollution, even to the extent of banning certain noise hazards. Consider the workplace, the home, automobiles and other vehicles, toys, machinery, rock concerts, and so on.

Point/Counterpoint

Polls indicate that about half of Americans believe in ESP. Prepare a sound, logical argument supporting one of the following positions:

a. There is evidence to suggest that ESP exists.
b. There is no evidence to suggest that ESP exists.

Psychology in Your Life

Vision and hearing are generally believed to be the two most highly prized senses. How would your life change if you lost your sight? How would your life change if you lost your hearing? Which sense would you find more traumatic to lose? Why?

SUMMARY AND REVIEW

SENSATION: THE SENSORY WORLD

What is the difference between sensation and perception?

Sensation is the process through which the senses pick up sensory stimuli and transmit them to the brain. Perception is the process by which this sensory information is actively organized and interpreted by the brain.

What is the difference between the absolute threshold and the difference threshold?

The absolute threshold is the minimum amount of sensory stimulation that can be detected 50% of the time. The difference threshold is a measure of the smallest increase or decrease in a physical stimulus that can be detected 50% of the time.

How are sensory stimuli in the environment experienced as sensations?

For each of the senses, the body has sensory receptors that detect and respond to sensory stimuli. Through a process known as transduction, the receptors convert sensory stimuli into neural impulses, which are then transmitted to special locations in the brain.

Key Terms
sensation (p. 80); perception (p. 80); absolute threshold (p. 81); difference threshold (p. 81); just noticeable difference (p. 81); Weber's law (p. 81); signal detection theory (p. 82); sensory receptors (p. 82); transduction (p. 82); sensory adaptation (p. 83)

VISION

How do the cornea, the iris, and the pupil function in vision?

The cornea bends light rays inward through the pupil—the small, dark opening in the eye. The iris dilates and contracts the pupil to regulate the amount of light entering the eye.

What are the lens and the retina?

The lens changes its shape as it focuses images of objects from varying distances on the retina, a thin tissue containing the sensory receptors for vision.

What roles do the rods and cones play in vision?

The cones detect color, provide the sharpest vision, and function best in high illumination. The rods enable vision in dim light. Rods respond to black and white light, and they encode all other visible wavelengths in shades of gray.

What path does the neural impulse take from the retina to the primary visual cortex?

The rods and the cones transduce light waves into neural impulses that pass from the bipolar cells to the ganglion cells, whose axons form the optic nerve. At the optic chiasma, some of the fibers of the optic nerve cross to the opposite side of the brain, before reaching the thalamus. From the thalamus, the neural impulses travel to the primary visual cortex.

What are the three dimensions that combine to provide the colors people perceive?

The three dimensions of color are hue, saturation, and brightness.

What two major theories attempt to explain color vision?

Two major theories that attempt to explain color vision are the trichromatic theory and the opponent-process theory.

Key Terms
visible spectrum (p. 84); cornea (p. 85); lens (p. 85); accommodation (p. 85); retina (p. 85); rods (p. 86); cones (p. 86); fovea (p. 86); dark adaptation (p. 87); optic nerve (p. 87); feature detectors (p. 88); hue (p. 89); saturation (p. 89); brightness (p. 89); trichromatic theory (p. 89); opponent-process theory (p. 89); afterimage (p. 89); color blindness (p. 89)

HEARING

What determines the pitch and loudness of a sound, and how is each quality measured?

The pitch of a sound is determined by the frequency of the sound waves, which is measured in hertz. The loudness of a sound is determined largely by the amplitude of the sound waves and is measured in decibels.

How do the outer, middle, and inner ears function in hearing?

Sound waves enter the pinna, the visible part of the outer ear, and travel to the end of the auditory canal, causing the eardrum to vibrate. This sets in motion the ossicles in the middle ear, which amplify the sound waves. The vibration of the oval window causes activity in the inner ear, setting in motion the fluid in the cochlea and moving the hair cells, which transduce the vibrations into neural impulses. The auditory nerve carries the neural impulses to the brain.

What two major theories attempt to explain hearing?

Two major theories that attempt to explain hearing are place theory and frequency theory.

What are some major causes of hearing loss?

Some major causes of hearing loss are noise, disease, birth defects, injury, and aging.

Key Terms
frequency (p. 91); amplitude (p. 91); decibel (p. 92); timbre (p. 93); audition (p. 93); outer ear (p. 93); middle ear (p. 93); inner ear (p. 93); cochlea (p. 93); hair cells (p. 94); place theory (p. 94); frequency theory (p. 94); bone conduction (p. 94)

SMELL AND TASTE

What path does a smell message take from the nose to the brain?

The act of smelling begins when odor molecules reach the smell receptors in the olfactory epithelium at the top of the nasal cavity. The axons of these receptors form the olfactory nerve, which relays the smell message to the olfactory bulbs. From there the smell message travels to the olfactory cortex and on to other parts of the brain.

What are the primary taste sensations, and how are they detected?

The primary taste sensations are sweet, salty, sour, and bitter, along with a newly discovered one for monosodium glutamate. The receptor cells for taste are found in the taste buds on the tongue and in other parts of the mouth and throat.

Key Terms
olfaction (p. 96); olfactory epithelium (p. 96); olfactory bulbs (p. 97); pheromones (p. 97); gustation (p. 98); taste buds (p. 98)

THE OTHER SENSES

How does the skin provide sensory information?

Nerve endings in the skin (the sensory receptors) respond to different kinds of stimulation, including heat and cold, pressure, pain, and a vast range of touch sensations. The neural impulses ultimately register in the somatosensory cortex.

What beneficial purpose does pain serve?

Pain can be a valuable warning and a protective mechanism, motivating people to tend to an injury, to restrict activity, and to seek medical help if needed.

What is the gate-control theory of pain?

Melzack and Wall's gate-control theory of pain holds that pain signals transmitted by slow-conducting fibers can be blocked at the spinal gate (1) if fast-conducting fibers get their message to the gate first, or (2) if the brain itself inhibits their transmission.

What are endorphins?

Endorphins are the body's natural painkillers. Released when a person is stressed or injured or exercises vigorously, they block pain and produce a feeling of well-being.

What kind of information does the kinesthetic sense provide, and how is this sensory information detected?

The kinesthetic sense provides information about the relative position of body parts and movement of those parts. The position or motion is detected by sensory receptors in the joints, ligaments, and muscles.

What is the vestibular sense, and where are its sensory receptors located?

The vestibular sense provides information about movement and the body's orientation in space. Sensory receptors in the semicircular canals and in the vestibular sacs detect changes in the movement and orientation of the head.

Key Terms
tactile (p. 100); gate-control theory (p. 102); endorphins (p. 103); naloxone (p. 103); kinesthetic sense (p. 104); vestibular sense (p. 104); semicircular canals (p. 104)

PERCEPTION: WAYS OF PERCEIVING

What are the Gestalt principles of perceptual organization?

The Gestalt principles of perceptual organization include the figure-ground relationship and four principles of perceptual grouping—similarity, proximity, continuity, and closure.

What is perceptual constancy, and what are the four types?

Perceptual constancy is the tendency to perceive objects as maintaining the same size, shape, brightness, and color despite changes in lighting conditions or changes in the retinal image that result when objects are viewed from different angles and distances.

What are the binocular depth cues?

The binocular depth cues are convergence and binocular disparity, and they depend on both eyes working together for depth perception.

What are seven monocular depth cues?

The monocular depth cues, those that can be perceived by one eye, include interposition, linear perspective, relative size, texture gradient, atmospheric perspective, shadow or shading, and motion parallax.

What are three types of puzzling perceptions?

Three types of puzzling perceptions are ambiguous figures, impossible figures, and illusions.

Key Terms
perception (p. 105); Gestalt (p. 105); figure-ground (p. 106); innate (p. 106); perceptual constancy (p. 107); size constancy (p. 107); retinal image (p. 107); shape constancy (p. 107); brightness constancy (p. 107); color constancy (p. 107); depth perception (p. 109); binocular depth cues (p. 109); convergence (p. 109); binocular disparity

(p. 109); monocular depth cues (p. 110); apparent motion (p. 111); phi phenomenon (p. 111); illusion (p. 112)

ADDITIONAL INFLUENCES ON PERCEPTION

In what types of situations do people rely more on bottom-up processing or top-down processing?

People use bottom-up processing more in unfamiliar situations and top-down processing more in situations about which they have some prior knowledge and experience.

What are some psychological factors that affect perceptions?

People's perceptions are affected by their point of reference, by the value they attach to a stimulus, and by their perceptual set—what they expect to perceive.

Key Terms
bottom-up processing (p. 115); top-down processing (p. 115); perceptual set (p. 115)

SUBLIMINAL PERSUASION AND EXTRASENSORY PERCEPTION

Is subliminal persuasion effective in influencing behavior?

In experimental studies, subliminal persuasion has not been found to influence behavior.

What is extrasensory perception, and have the claims of psychics been verified scientifically?

Extrasensory perception refers to gaining awareness of information about objects, events, or another's thoughts through some means other than known sensory channels. Experiments claiming to prove psychic phenomena have not been repeatable under carefully controlled conditions.

Key Terms
subliminal persuasion (p. 116); subliminal perception (p. 116); extrasensory perception (ESP) (p. 116); parapsychology (p. 116)

Surf It!

Want to be sure you've absorbed the material in Chapter 3, "Sensation and Perception," before the big test? Visiting *www.abacon.com/wood* can put a top grade within your reach. The site is loaded with free practice tests, flashcards, activities, and links to help you review your way to an A. To enliven that inevitable study break, the site also offers personality assessment quizzes and a psychology career corner.

4 States of Consciousness

- What Is Consciousness?
- Circadian Rhythms: 24-Hour Highs and Lows
- Sleep: That Mysterious One-Third of Life
- Sleep Disorders
- Altering Consciousness through Concentration and Suggestion
- Altered States of Consciousness and Psychoactive Drugs

For the most part, British imports have had an extremely positive influence on life in the United States. But this is not so for rave dances. Long popular in Britain, these dances gained quite a following in the 1990s among American adolescents and young adults, a popularity that continues to grow in the 21st century. Typically, rave dances are held in large facilities, where as many as 2,000 party-goers tightly packed together dance all night to heavily mixed, electronically generated music accompanied by stunning laser light shows. This may sound like fun, but officials at the National Institute on Drug Abuse and others have become alarmed—not because of the dancing, but because of an illegal drug called MDMA, or "Ecstasy," which has become so closely identified with raves that it is virtually synonymous with them.

Users of MDMA describe a wonderfully pleasant state of consciousness, in which even the most backward, bashful, self-conscious people shed their inhibitions. Pretenses melt away, and the users become "emotionally synthesized" with other ravers and with the music and the lighting effects. Users feel that the drug allows them to be who they "really are." They report an immediate and deep acceptance and understanding of others; interpersonal barriers disappear, along with emotional and sexual inhibitions. And it is said that the frequent, spontaneous outbursts of mass hugging and kissing make MDMA users feel that they are accepted, even loved. But there is a price to be paid for entering this "joyous" state.

Research evidence suggests that chronic, moderate to heavy use of MDMA can cause brain damage, impair memory and verbal reasoning (Morgan, 1999; Reneman et al., 2000), and lower performance on tasks that require sustained attention (McCann et al., 1999). The neurotransmitter serotonin has been implicated in the cognitive impairments related to MDMA abuse. Serotonin is known to influence cognitive functions, including memory, as well as moods, sleep cycles, and the ability to control impulses (Reneman et al., 2000).

The available evidence is compelling enough to conclude that use of MDMA is a highly risky way to alter consciousness. But before we look more closely at altered states of consciousness, let's first ask, what is consciousness?

WHAT IS CONSCIOUSNESS?

What are some different states of consciousness?

Consciousness is one of the most basic concepts in the study of psychology, and yet it remains rather elusive. You may think of **consciousness** as an awareness of one's own perceptions, thoughts, feelings, sensations, and external environment.

The American psychologist William James likened consciousness to a flowing stream. This "stream of consciousness," he believed, wanders, meanders, and flows, sometimes where the person wills and sometimes not. You control the flow of consciousness when you concentrate and focus the attention. At other times, we do not control it, as images, thoughts, and feelings, like uninvited guests, slip into the stream of consciousness and capture it temporarily.

Sigmund Freud looked beneath the stream of consciousness as envisioned by James. There he identified what he termed the *unconscious*, which holds wishes, ideas, and impulses, primarily sexual and aggressive in nature, of which a person is unaware. Freud advanced the notion of various levels of awareness in consciousness.

When you are at the highest level of consciousness, your thoughts are fixed on the object of your concentration, such as studying, taking an exam, learning a new skill, and so on. At such times you are less conscious of other potentially competing stimuli, both external (the noise around you) and internal (whether you are hungry). Athletes at full concentration during a game may be oblivious to pains, even those that signal potentially serious injuries.

A lower level of awareness involves such mental activities as daydreaming. Daydreaming may involve fantasies and wishful thoughts, but much more often it is simply a form of mental drifting—planning for some future event, thinking about what you *should* have said or rehearsing what you are going to say to someone. Daydreams typically appear when a person is bored, lying in bed waiting to

consciousness: An awareness of one's own perceptions, thoughts, feelings, sensations, and external environment.

fall asleep, or engaged in activities that do not require full conscious awareness, such as driving to school or work. Sexual fantasies, too, are frequent topics of daydreaming and are far more frequent in males than in females (Leitenberg & Henning, 1995).

Is daydreaming merely a waste of time? Not according to some experts, who suggest that daydreaming may serve a variety of useful functions (Klinger, 1987). Daydreaming is a highly effective way to rehearse for some future action, to explore a variety of solutions for everyday problems, or even to provide motivation to achieve a goal (Singer, 1975).

A still lower level of awareness is the state of consciousness to which we descend when we sleep. But asleep or awake, a great deal of nonconscious (below the level of awareness) information processing is going on constantly. The decisions we reach, the values we embrace, the ideas we conceive, the plans we make, even the friends we choose are all heavily influenced by nonconscious information processing. Furthermore, many of the actions we perform—driving a car, riding a bicycle, walking to class—are accomplished by means of automatic processing, thus freeing conscious awareness to focus on other things.

We will now explore the various states of consciousness and examine the many ways in which consciousness may be altered. Ordinary waking consciousness can be altered by substances such as alcohol or drugs and by focused concentration as in meditation and hypnosis. This chapter will explore these **altered states of consciousness.**

The most fundamental altered state is one in which people spend about one-third of their lives, the one they visit for several hours nearly every night—sleep.

CIRCADIAN RHYTHMS: 24-HOUR HIGHS AND LOWS

What is a circadian rhythm, and which rhythms are most relevant to the study of sleep?

Do you notice changes in the way you feel throughout the day—fluctuations in your energy level, moods, or efficiency? Over 100 bodily functions and behaviors follow **circadian rhythms**—that is, they fluctuate regularly from a high to a low point over a 24-hour period (Dement, 1974). Circadian rhythms play a critical role in the timing of life-sustaining processes in virtually all organisms, from the most complex—humans and other vertebrates—to plants and even single-cell life forms (Kay, 1997). Blood pressure, heart rate, appetite, secretion of hormones and digestive enzymes, sensory acuity, elimination, and even the body's response to medication all follow circadian rhythms (Hrushesky, 1994). Learning efficiency, ability to perform a wide range of tasks, and even moods ebb and flow according to these daily rhythms (Boivin et al., 1997; Johnson et al., 1992). In fact, the importance of the circadian timing system can hardly be overstated: It is involved in the 24-hour variation of virtually every physiological and psychological variable researchers have studied (Kunz & Hermann, 2000).

Two circadian rhythms of particular importance to the study of sleep are the sleep/wakefulness cycle and body temperature. Normal human body temperature can range from a low of about 97 or 97.5 degrees between 3:00 and 4:00 A.M. to a high of about 98.6 degrees between 5:00 and 8:00 P.M. People sleep best when their body temperature is lowest, and they are most alert when their body temperature is at its daily high point. Alertness also follows a circadian rhythm, one that is quite separate from the sleep/wakefulness rhythm (Monk, 1989). For most people, alertness decreases between 2:00 and 5:00 P.M. and between 2:00 and 7:00 A.M. (Webb, 1995).

What are the mechanisms that control or disrupt our circadian rhythms?

altered state of consciousness: A mental state other than ordinary waking consciousness, such as sleep, meditation, hypnosis, or a drug-induced state.

circadian rhythm (sur-KAY-dee-un): Within each 24-hour period, the regular fluctuation from high to low points of certain bodily functions.

The Suprachiasmatic Nucleus: The Body's Timekeeper

What is the suprachiasmatic nucleus?

In their studies of circadian rhythms in mammals, researchers have found that the biological clock is the **suprachiasmatic nucleus (SCN),** located in the brain's hypothalamus (Ginty et al., 1993; Ralph, 1989). The SCN, a pair of tiny brain structures, each about the size of a pinhead, controls the timing of circadian rhythms (Moore-Ede, 1993).

But the ebb and flow of circadian rhythms is not strictly biological. Environmental cues also play a part. The most significant environmental cue is bright light, particularly sunlight. Specialized cells (photoreceptors) in the retina at the back of each eye respond to the amount of light reaching the eye and relay this information via the optic nerve to the SCN. The SCN acts on this information by signaling the pineal gland, located in the center of the brain. In response, the pineal gland secretes the hormone **melatonin** from dusk to shortly before dawn and suppresses secretion of melatonin during daylight. Melatonin acts to induce sleep, which may be a function of its ability to lower the activity of neurons in the SCN (Barinaga, 1997).

Other types of cells may also respond to daily light-dark cycles. Researchers studying vertebrates less complex than humans have found that exposing some bodily organs to light sets the "circadian clock" and maintains circadian rhythms. Even certain single cells from these vertebrates, when placed in cultures in the laboratory, responded directly to the light-dark cycles they were exposed to (Whitmore et al., 2000).

Circadian rhythms are slightly disrupted each year when daylight saving time begins and ends. An even greater disruption occurs when people fly across a number of time zones or work rotating shifts.

Jet Lag: Where Am I and What Time Is It?

Suppose you fly from Chicago to London, and the plane lands at 12:00 midnight Chicago time, about the time you usually go to sleep. At the same time that it is midnight in Chicago, it is 6:00 A.M. in London, almost time to get up. The clocks, the sun, and everything else in London tell you it is early morning, but you still feel like it is 12:00 midnight. You are experiencing jet lag.

The problem is not simply the result of losing a night's sleep. You are fighting your own biological clock, which is synchronized with your usual time zone and not the time zone you are visiting. It is difficult to try to sleep when your biological clock is telling you to wake up and feel alert. It is even harder to remain awake and alert when your internal clock is telling you to sleep.

Some people experience a problem similar to jet lag without the benefit of a trip to Europe or Asia. These people are shift workers.

Shift Work: Working Day and Night

What are some problems experienced by people who work rotating shifts?

The United States is increasingly become a 24-hour society (Moore-Ede, 1993). About 20% of Americans work at night and sleep during the day (Slon, 1997). The health care, data-processing, and transportation industries are the largest employers of shift workers.

Not surprisingly, shift workers complain of sleepiness and sleeping difficulties. Shift workers average 2 to 4 hours less sleep than nonshift workers of the same age (Campbell, 1995). From 75% to 90% of workers complain of sleepiness during the night shift, and many actually fall asleep during their shift (Leger, 1994). And, in one study of commercial long-haul truck drivers, more than 17% of the drivers studied admitted to having experienced "near misses" while dozing off behind the wheel (Häkkänen & Summala, 1999).

What about performance on the job? Alertness and performance deteriorate if people work during **subjective night,** when their biological clock is telling them to go to sleep (Åkerstedt, 1990; Folkard, 1990). During subjective night, energy and efficiency are at their lowest point, reaction time is slowest, productivity is diminished, and industrial accidents are significantly higher.

Many air, rail, marine, and highway accidents have occurred when the shift workers in charge suffered sleep loss and fatigue because of the disruption of their circadian rhythms (Lauber & Kayten, 1988). More errors in judgment and most accidents occur during the night shift. The failure of the nuclear reactor at Three Mile Island and the Russian nuclear disaster at Chernobyl both occurred in the middle of the night when those directly responsible were dangerously fatigued (Moore-Ede, 1993). Even the slight circadian disruption due to the 1-hour sleep loss when people move their clocks forward in spring for daylight saving time is associated with an increase in traffic accidents and a short-term but significant 6.5% increase in accidental deaths (Coren, 1996a, 1996b).

What are the physical and psychological effects of disturbing the normal sleep/wakefulness cycle when a person works the night shift, as this printing press operator does?

When people must work at night, the rhythms of many of their bodily functions normally synchronized for efficient daytime functioning are disrupted. These rhythm disruptions can cause a variety of physical and psychological problems. Shift workers have more gastrointestinal and cardiovascular problems, use more prescription drugs, experience higher levels of personal and family stress and more mood problems, and have higher divorce rates (Campbell, 1995; Moore-Ede, 1993).

What can be done to make shift rotation less disruptive? Rotating work schedules forward from days to evenings to nights makes adjustment easier because people find it easier to go to bed later and wake up later than the reverse. And rotating shifts every three weeks instead of every week lesson the effect on sleep even more (Pilcher et al., 2000). Some researchers have even suggested scheduling brief nap periods during their shifts for sleepy workers to help them adjust to rotating shifts (Goh et al., 2000).

In simulated night-shift schedules, exposure to appropriately timed bright light or even light of medium intensity has been found to reset young adults' biological clocks and improve their performance (Martin & Eastman, 1998). Even light focused on the back of a person's knees can reset the biological clock (Campbell & Murphy, 1998). And some researchers have helped shift workers reset their biological clocks by having them take melatonin supplements at specifically determined times. Industries, police departments, and hospitals should seriously consider the research in this field to help workers adjust to shift changes.

Taking Melatonin as a Sleep Aid

Melatonin is a hormone that has a significant effect on our circadian rhythms and sleep. It has not been approved by the FDA as a drug, but it is sold over the counter as a sleep aid or dietary supplement. Taking melatonin helps reset the biological clock in night-shift workers and in those suffering from jet lag. Low doses (0.3–1.0 milligram) taken several hours before bedtime have been found to promote sleep in healthy young males, without significantly altering the structure of sleep and without creating negative aftereffects the following morning (Zhdanova et al., 1996). Some researchers suggest that melatonin may facilitate sleep by lowering the core body temperature (Dawson et al., 1995; Hughes & Badia, 1997).

Although these sound like good reasons to take a melatonin supplement, there are even better reasons not to take it. First, a second biological clock that secretes melatonin has been found in the retinas of hamsters (Tosini & Menaker, 1996). This suggests that another biological clock might be found in the human retina as well. According to expert Alfred Lewy, if melatonin has a significant impact on the human eye, it should be studied further before becoming widely available (Raloff, 1996). Lewy's reasoning may be based on the fact that the eye is such a sensitive and important organ. Also, since melatonin reduces neuron activity in the SCN, too

suprachiasmatic nucleus (SCN): A tiny structure in the brain's hypothalamus that controls the timing of circadian rhythms; the biological clock.

melatonin: A hormone secreted by the pineal gland that acts to reduce activity and induce sleep.

subjective night: The time during a 24-hour period when body temperature is lowest and when the biological clock is telling a person to go to sleep.

much of it could actually shut down the biological clock (Barinaga, 1997). Some supplements contain 2.5 or 3 milligrams of melatonin, 10 times more than is needed to promote normal sleep and enough to raise blood melatonin levels to 30 times their normal nighttime level (Zhdanova & Wurtman, 1996). The safety and long-term effects of such dosage levels are not yet known (Caldwell, 2000; Haimov & Lavie, 1996; Kayumov et al., 2000).

Remember It!

1. Which of the following best defines consciousness?
   a. awareness c. receptiveness
   b. wakefulness d. rationality
2. The two circadian rhythms most relevant to the study of sleep are the sleep/wakefulness cycle and
   a. blood pressure. c. body temperature.
   b. secretion of hormones. d. heart rate.
3. People sleep best when their body temperature is at its low point in the 24-hour cycle. (true/false)
4. The structure that serves as the body's biological clock is the ______________.
5. The long-term use of melatonin to induce sleep is known to be safe. (true/false)
6. People who are suffering from jet lag or the effects of working rotating shifts or night shifts are experiencing
   a. a deficiency in melatonin production.
   b. an excess of melatonin production.
   c. a defect in their suprachiasmatic nucleus.
   d. a disturbance in their circadian rhythms.
7. The performance of shift workers is enhanced during their subjective night. (true/false)

Answers: 1. a 2. c 3. true 4. suprachiasmatic nucleus 5. false 6. d 7. false

SLEEP: THAT MYSTERIOUS ONE-THIRD OF LIFE

Over a lifetime, a person spends about 25 years sleeping. Before the 1950s, there was little understanding of what goes on during the state of consciousness known as sleep. Then, in the 1950s, several universities set up sleep laboratories where people's brain waves, eye movements, chin-muscle tension, heart rate, and respiration rate were monitored through a night of sleep. From analyses of sleep recordings, known as *polysomnograms,* researchers discovered the characteristics of two major categories of sleep.

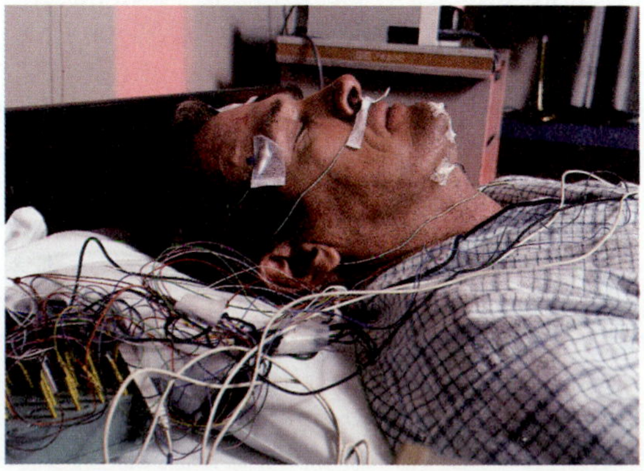

In a sleep laboratory or sleep clinic, researchers attach electrodes to a person's head to monitor brain-wave activity, eye movements, and muscle tension.

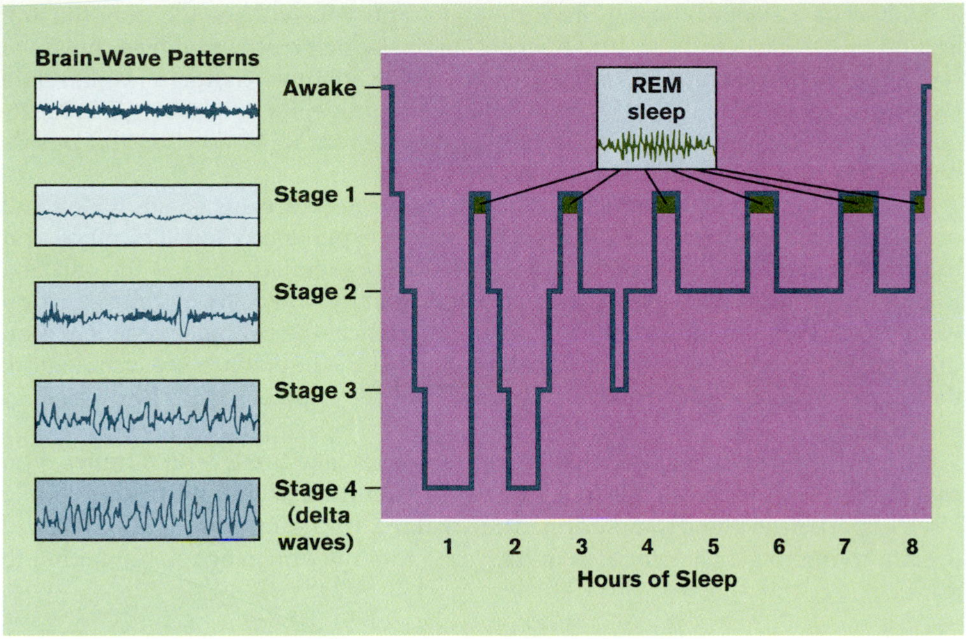

Figure 4.1

Brain-Wave Patterns Associated with Different Stages of Sleep

By monitoring brain-wave activity with the EEG throughout a night's sleep, researchers have identified the brain-wave patterns associated with different stages of sleep. As sleepers progress through the four NREM stages, the brain-wave pattern changes from faster, low-voltage waves in Stages 1 and 2 to the slower, larger delta waves in Stages 3 and 4. Notice that the brain-wave activity during REM sleep is similar to that of the subject when awake.

NREM and REM Sleep: Watching the Eyes

The two categories of sleep are NREM (non–rapid eye movement) sleep and REM (rapid eye movement) sleep.

How does a sleeper react physically during NREM sleep?

NREM Sleep: From Light to Deep Sleep in Stages **NREM** (pronounced NON-rem) **sleep** is sleep in which there are no rapid eye movements. It is often called "quiet sleep," because heart rate and respiration are slow and regular, there is little body movement, and blood pressure and brain activity are at their lowest points of the 24-hour period. There are four stages of NREM sleep—Stages 1, 2, 3, and 4—with Stage 1 being the lightest sleep and Stage 4 being the deepest. Sleepers pass gradually rather than abruptly from one stage to the next. Each stage can be identified by its brain-wave pattern, as shown in Figure 4.1. Growth hormone is secreted primarily in Stage 3 and Stage 4 sleep (Gronfier et al., 1996; Van Cauter, 2000); this timing is significant because older people get little of this slow-wave sleep.

How does the body respond physically during REM sleep?

REM Sleep: Rapid Eye Movements and Dreams Most of us envision sleep as a time of deep relaxation and calm. But **REM sleep,** sometimes called "active sleep," is anything but calm, and it constitutes 20–25% of a normal night's sleep in adults. During the REM state, there is intense brain activity. In fact, within 1 to 2 minutes after REM sleep begins, brain metabolism increases and brain temperature rises rapidly (Krueger & Takahashi, 1997). The body reacts as if to a daytime emergency. Epinephrine (adrenaline) shoots into the system, blood pressure rises, and heart rate and respiration become faster and irregular. Ulcer patients may secrete 3 to 20 times as much stomach acid as during the day and may awaken with stomach pains (Webb, 1975). In contrast to this storm of internal activity, there is an external calm during REM sleep. The large muscles of the body—arms, legs, trunk—become paralyzed (Chase & Morales, 1990). Some researchers suggest that this paralysis prevents people from acting out their dreams. But there is a rare condition known as *REM sleep behavior disorder,* in which individuals are not paralyzed during REM sleep. Consequently, while dreaming, they may become violent, causing injury to themselves and their bed partners and damage to their homes (Broughton & Shimizu, 1995; Moldofsky et al., 1995).

NREM sleep: Non–rapid eye movement sleep, consisting of the four sleep stages and characterized by slow, regular respiration and heart rate, an absence of rapid eye movements, and blood pressure and brain activity that are at a 24-hour low point.

REM sleep: Sleep characterized by rapid eye movements, paralysis of large muscles, fast and irregular heart rate and respiration rate, increased brain-wave activity, and vivid dreams.

Observe a sleeper during the REM state, and you will see the eyes darting around under the eyelids. In 1952 Eugene Azerinsky first discovered these bursts of rapid eye movements, and William Dement and Nathaniel Kleitman (1957) made the connection between rapid eye movements and dreaming. It is during REM periods that most vivid dreams occur. When awakened from REM sleep, 80% of people report dreaming (Carskadon & Dement, 1989).

Almost from birth, regardless of the content of their dreams, males have a full or partial erection during REM sleep, and females experience vaginal swelling and lubrication. Because sleepers are more likely to awaken naturally at the end of a REM period than during NREM sleep, men usually wake up with an erection (Campbell, 1985). In males suffering from impotence, the presence of an erection during REM sleep, even occasionally, indicates that the impotence is psychological; the consistent absence of an erection indicates that the impotence may be physiological in origin.

If you awaken during REM sleep and remain awake for several minutes, you may not go back into REM sleep for at least 30 minutes. This is why most people have experienced the disappointment of waking in the middle of a wonderful dream, trying to get back to sleep quickly and into the dream again, but failing to do so.

Sleep Cycles: The Nightly Pattern of Sleep

What is the progression of NREM stages and REM sleep that a person follows in a typical night?

You may be surprised to learn that sleep follows a fairly predictable pattern each night. We all sleep in cycles. During each **sleep cycle,** which lasts about 90 minutes, a person has one or more stages of NREM sleep followed by a period of REM sleep. Let's look closely at a typical night of sleep for a young adult.

The first sleep cycle begins with a few minutes in Stage 1 sleep, sometimes called "light sleep." Stage 1 is actually a transition stage between waking and sleeping. Then sleepers descend into Stage 2 sleep, in which they are somewhat more deeply asleep and harder to awaken. (About 50% of a total night's sleep is spent in Stage 2 sleep.) As sleep gradually becomes deeper, brain activity slows, and more **delta waves** (slow waves) appear in the EEG. When the EEG registers 20% delta waves, sleepers enter Stage 3 sleep, the beginning of **slow-wave sleep** (or deep sleep). Delta waves continue to increase, and when they reach more than 50%, people enter **Stage 4 sleep**—the deepest sleep, from which they are hardest to awaken (Carskadon & Rechtschaffen, 1989; Cooper, 1994). Perhaps you have taken an afternoon nap and awakened confused, not knowing whether it was morning or night, a weekday or a weekend. If so, you probably awakened during Stage 4 sleep.

In Stage 4 sleep, delta waves may reach nearly 100% on the EEG, but after about 40 minutes in this stage, brain activity increases and the delta waves begin to disappear. Sleepers ascend back through Stage 3 and Stage 2 sleep, then enter their first REM period, which lasts 10 or 15 minutes. At the end of this REM period, the first sleep cycle is complete, and the second sleep cycle begins. Unless people awaken after the first sleep cycle, they go directly from REM into Stage 2 sleep. They then follow the same progression as in the first sleep cycle, through Stages 3 and 4 and back again into REM sleep.

After the first two sleep cycles of about 90 minutes each (3 hours total), the sleep pattern changes and sleepers usually get no more Stage 4 sleep. From this point on, during each 90-minute sleep cycle, people alternate mainly between Stage 2 and REM sleep for the remainder of the night. With each sleep cycle, the REM periods (and therefore dreaming time) get progressively longer. At the end of the night, REM periods may last 30 to 40 minutes. Most people have about five sleep cycles (7½ to 8 hours) and average about 1½ hours of slow-wave sleep and 1½ hours of REM sleep. Figure 4.1 shows the progression through NREM and REM sleep during a typical night.

sleep cycle: A cycle of sleep lasting about 90 minutes and including one or more stages of NREM sleep followed by a period of REM sleep.

delta wave: The slowest brain-wave pattern, associated with Stage 3 sleep and Stage 4 sleep.

slow-wave sleep: Stage 3 and Stage 4 sleep; deep sleep.

Stage 4 sleep: The deepest stage of NREM sleep, characterized by an EEG pattern of more than 50% delta waves.

Variations in Sleep: How People Differ

There are great individual variations in patterns of sleep; the major factor contributing to this variation is age.

Sleep Changes over the Life Span: The Older We Get, the Less We Sleep

How do sleep patterns change over the life span?

Infants and young children have the longest sleep time and the highest percentage of REM and slow-wave sleep, but they get even more REM sleep before birth. A fetus spends up to 80% of the time in REM sleep (Hobson, 1989). Children from age 6 to puberty are the champion sleepers and wakers. They fall asleep easily, sleep soundly for 8½ to 9 hours at night, and feel awake and alert during the day. Teenagers average 7.2 hours of sleep but need about 2 more hours more than that to do well in school (Carskadon & Wolfson, 1997).

As people age, the quality and quantity of sleep usually decrease (Reyner & Horne, 1995). In one large study of 9,000 participants aged 65 and over, only 12% reported no sleep problems (Foley et al., 1995). Older adults have more difficulty falling asleep than younger people do and typically sleep more lightly. Moreover, they spend more time in bed but less time asleep, averaging about 6½ hours of sleep a night (Prinz et al., 1990). Slow-wave sleep decreases substantially from age 30 to age 50 (Mourtazaev et al., 1995; Van Cauter, 2000). The percentage of REM sleep stays about the same (Moran & Stoudemire, 1992).

How much sleep does the average person need? More than he or she gets, according to sleep researcher William Dement. And a temporary increase in mental activity can increase the need for sleep.

Larks and Owls: Early to Rise and Late to Bed Some people awaken early every morning and leap out of bed with enthusiasm, eager to start the day. Others fumble for the alarm clock and push a snooze button to get a few more precious minutes of sleep. Early risers find it hard to keep from yawning after 10:00 P.M. and have an overwhelming urge to get to bed. But this is precisely the time when the night people come to life. Sleep researchers have names for these two types—larks and owls—and there is a physical explanation for the difference in the way they feel. About 25% of people are larks, people whose body temperature rises rapidly after they awaken and stays high until about 7:30 P.M. Larks turn in early and have the fewest sleep problems. Then there are the 25% of people who are owls and the 50% who are somewhere in between. The body temperature of an owl gradually rises throughout the day, peaking in the afternoon and not dropping until later in the evening.

Guthrie and others (1995) compared the performance of several hundred college students classified as larks or owls. They found that the larks made better grades in early morning classes, while the owls made higher grades in classes they took later in the day. One of the genes that run the biological clock is responsible, in part, for the differences between larks and owls (Katzenberg et al., 1998). Are you a lark or an owl? To find out, complete the *Try It!* on page 132.

What factors influence sleep needs?

How Much Sleep Do You Need? More Than You Probably Get Maybe you have wondered how much sleep you need in order to feel good, and perhaps you are hoping to find the answer in this chapter. When it comes to sleep, the expression "one size fits all" does *not* apply. Although adults average about 7½ hours of sleep daily with an extra hour on weekends, this is too much for some people and too little for others. Short sleepers are the 20% who require less than 6 hours of sleep; long sleepers are the 10% who require more than 9 hours. There seems to be a limit below which most people cannot go. In one study, not a single participant could get by with less than 4½ hours of sleep, and 6½ hours appears to be the minimum most people require.

What accounts for the large variation in the need for sleep? Genetics appears to play a part. Identical twins, for example, have strikingly similar sleep patterns compared to fraternal twins (Webb & Campbell, 1983). Laboratory animals have even

Try It!

Answer the following questions and score each choice as 1 point, 3 points, or 5 points, as indicated in parentheses.

1. On days when I can get up when I choose, I am usually up:

    ____ Before 7 A.M. (1) ____ Between 7 and 9 A.M. (3) ____ After 9 A.M. (5)

2. For me, getting out of bed on school or work days is:

    ____ Fairly easy (1) ____ Sometimes difficult (3) ____ Very difficult (5)

3. When I get up in the morning, I usually feel:

    ____ Alert/fresh (1) ____ It varies (3) ____ Sleepy/tired (5)

4. If I could go to bed whenever I chose, it would probably be:

    ____ By 10:30 P.M. (1) ____ Between 10:30 P.M. and midnight (3) ____ After midnight (5)

5. About an hour or two before going to bed on school days, I usually feel:

    ____ Very tired/sleepy (1) ____ Moderately tired (3) ____ Not very tired (5)

Add all your points together: ______________

Total score	
5–10	Chirp! You are a lark. Be sure to take some photos of those beautiful sunrises for the rest of us—just don't wake us up to see them.
11–19	Ahh, mediocrity. You are neither a lark nor an owl, but don't worry . . . 50% of the population is right there with you.
20–25	Congratulations—you and your fellow owls keep the late-night talk shows on the air.

The amount of physical activity an occupation requires does not affect the amount of sleep a person needs. On average, the fans in the stadium need as much sleep as St. Louis Rams quarterback Kurt Warner and his teammates.

been bred to be short or long sleepers. But genetics aside, people need more sleep when they are depressed, under stress, or experiencing significant life changes such as changing jobs or schools. Temporary increases in mental, physical, or emotional effort also increase the need for sleep (Hartmann, 1973). Contrary to popular opinion, the amount of activity required in an occupation does not affect the amount of sleep a person needs. But, if excessive daytime sleepiness can't be attributed to lifestyle or work schedule, it is often symptomatic of a sleep disorder (Mahowald, 2000).

Do you feel like you get all the sleep you need? Data from a number of studies indicate that more than 36% of the U.S. population is chronically sleep-deprived (Bonnet & Arand, 1995). Long-haul truck drivers, for example, average only 5 hours of sleep per day (Mitler et al., 1997).

The Functions of Sleep: The Restorative and Circadian Theories

What are the two main theories that attempt to explain the function of sleep?

The very fact that people spend about one-third of their lives sleeping indicates that sleep must serve important functions (Rechtschaffen, 1998). But what functions? Why do we need to sleep at all?

Two general theories have been advanced to explain the function of sleep. One, the **restorative theory,** holds that being awake produces wear and tear on the body and the brain, and sleep serves the function of restoring body and mind (Gökcebay et al., 1994). There is now convincing evidence for this theory: The functions of sleep do include the restoration of brain energy and the consolidation of memory (Kunz & Herrmann, 2000).

Yet there are many known aspects of sleep that a restorative theory alone cannot explain. For example, if you intentionally stay awake for a night, why do you find it so difficult to keep your eyes open during the middle of the night and yet are much less sleepy and more alert in the morning, without having had any restorative sleep?

A second explanation, the **circadian theory,** argues that sleepiness and alertness ebb and flow according to circadian rhythms. The circadian theory of sleep is based on the premise that sleep evolved to keep humans out of harm's way during the dark of night and possibly from becoming prey for some nocturnal predator.

Alexander Borbely (1984; Borbely et al., 1989) makes an argument that blends the circadian and restorative theories. That people feel sleepy at certain times of day is consistent with the circadian theory. And that sleepiness increases the longer a person is awake is consistent with the restorative theory. In other words, the urge to sleep is partly a function of how long a person has been awake and partly a function of the time of day (Webb, 1995).

What happens when you are sleep-deprived and miss the restorative interval of sleep?

Sleep Deprivation: What Are Its Effects?

What is the longest you have ever stayed awake—two days, three days? According to the *Guinness Book of World Records,* Robert McDonald stayed awake 453 hours and 40 minutes (almost 19 days) in a 1986 rocking-chair marathon. Unlike McDonald, most people have missed no more than a few consecutive nights of sleep, perhaps studying for final exams. If you have ever missed two or three nights of sleep, you may remember having had difficulty concentrating, lapses in attention, and general irritability. Figure 4.2 shows the dramatic decrease in cognitive performance produced by 48 hours of sleep deprivation. After 60 hours without sleep, some people even have minor hallucinations. Most people who try to stay awake for long periods of time will have **microsleeps,** 2- to 3-second lapses from wakefulness into

restorative theory: The theory that the function of sleep is to restore body and mind.

circadian theory: The theory that sleep evolved to keep humans out of harm's way during the night and that sleepiness ebbs and flows according to a circadian rhythm.

microsleep: A momentary lapse from wakefulness into sleep, usually occurring when a person has been sleep-deprived.

Figure 4.2

Effect of Sleep Deprivation on Cognitive Performance

Sleep deprivation lasting for 48 hours had a negative effect on performance of a cognitive task (serial addition and subtraction exercises). The initial upward slope of the performance curve is a learning curve for the task. (Department of Behavior Biology, Walter Reed Army Institute of Research, 1997.)

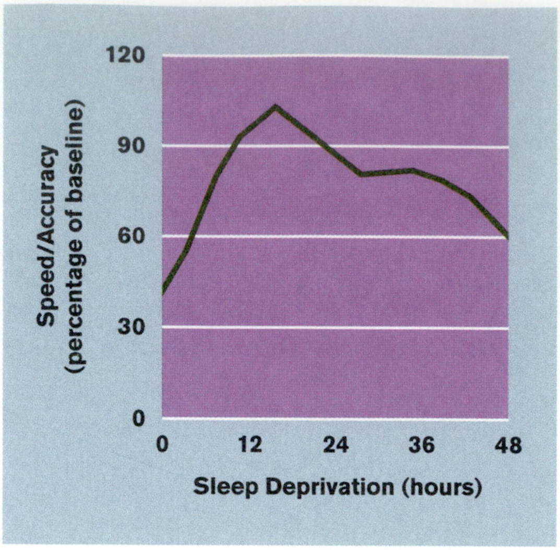

sleep. You may have experienced a microsleep if you have ever caught yourself nodding off for a few seconds in class or on a long automobile trip. Note that if you do become sleepy while driving, you should not rely on a blast of cold air or higher volume on your radio to keep you awake for more than about 30 minutes (Reyner & Horne, 1998).

What suffers most from prolonged sleep loss is the motivation to sustain performance. A meta-analysis using data from more than 1,900 subjects indicated that sleep deprivation seriously impairs human functioning (Pilcher & Huffcutt, 1996). It negatively impacts mood, alertness, and performance and reduces the body's ability to warm itself, even at relatively comfortable temperatures (Bonnet & Arand, 1995; Landis et al., 1998). And partial sleep loss, even for one night, can significantly reduce the effectiveness of the human immune system. After one full night of sleep, however, the immune function appears to return to normal (Irwin et al., 1994).

If you know you will miss a night's sleep, a long nap beforehand will improve alertness, performance, and mood during the next 24 hours (Bonnet et al., 1995). And a short nap the day after a restricted night's sleep (4 hours or less) can improve alertness the following day (Gillberg et al., 1996). But what if you cannot sleep more hours each night? Going to sleep and waking up on a regular schedule seems to increase alertness, reduce sleepiness, and improve sleep efficiency.

Sleep Deprivation and the Brain How does a lack of sleep affect the brain? Researchers have known for some time that sleep deprivation impairs a variety of cognitive functions, such as the retrieval of recently learned information from memory (Harrison & Horne, 2000). But the specific brain areas that are most (and least) active when sleep-deprived and non–sleep-deprived individuals perform cognitive tasks remained unidentified.

Recently, Drummond and others (2000) used sophisticated brain-imaging techniques to map the patterns of brain activity during a verbal learning task in two groups of participants: Those in an experimental group were deprived of sleep for about 35 hours, while those in a control group had slept normally. In the control group, the prefrontal cortex was highly active, as were the temporal lobes. As expected, on average, these rested participants scored significantly higher on the learning task than did their sleep-deprived counterparts. Surprisingly, however, areas of the prefrontal cortex were even more active in the sleep-deprived participants than in those who slept normally. Moreover, the temporal lobes that were so active in the rested group were almost totally inactive in the sleep-deprived group. The parietal lobes of the latter group became highly active, however, as if to compensate for their sleep-deprived condition. And, the more active the parietal lobes, the higher a sleep-deprived participant scored on the learning task.

Therefore, this study, the first to examine the effects of sleep deprivation on verbal learning using brain-imaging techniques, indicates that the cognitive functions used in such learning are significantly impaired by sleep deprivation. It also shows that there are compensatory mechanisms in the parietal lobes that can reduce this impairment to some degree (Drummond et al., 2000).

Remember It!

1. State the type of sleep–NREM or REM–that corresponds to each characteristic:

   a (1) paralysis of large muscles
   b (2) slow, regular respiration and heart rate
   a (3) rapid eye movements
   a (4) penile erection and vaginal swelling
   a (5) vivid dreams

   a. REM
   b. NREM

2. The average length of a sleep cycle in adults is
   a. 30 minutes.
   b. 60 minutes.
   c. 90 minutes.
   d. 120 minutes.

3. After the first two sleep cycles, most people get equal amounts of deep sleep and REM sleep. (true/false)

4. Match the age group with the appropriate description of sleep.

   d (1) have most difficulty sleeping, most awakenings
   b (2) sleep best at night; feel best during day
   a (3) have highest percentage of REM and deep sleep
   c (4) are usually sleepy during the day regardless of the amount of sleep at night

   a. infants
   b. children aged 6 to puberty
   c. adolescents
   d. adults over 65

5. Which factor *least* affects the amount of sleep people need?
   a. their genetic makeup
   b. their emotional state
   c. the amount of stress in their life
   d. the amount of physical activity required by their occupation

6. The two main theories that attempt to explain the function of sleep are the restorative theory and the carcadicin theory.

7. Cognitive functions important for verbal learning are significantly impaired by sleep deprivation. (true/false)

Answers: 1. (1) a (2) b (3) a (4) a (5) a 2. c 3. false 4. (1) d (2) b (3) a (4) c 5. d 6. restorative theory, circadian theory 7. true

REM dream: A type of dream having a dreamlike and storylike quality and occuring almost continuously during each REM period; more vivid, visual, and emotional than NREM dreams.

NREM dream: Mental activity occurring during NREM sleep that is more thoughtlike in quality than REM dreams are.

Dreaming: Mysterious Mental Activity during Sleep

How do REM and NREM dreams differ?

Humans have always been fascinated by dreams. The vivid dreams people remember and talk about are **REM dreams**—the type that occur almost continuously during each REM period. But people also have **NREM dreams,** dreams that occur during NREM sleep, although they are typically less frequent and less memorable than REM dreams (Foulkes, 1996). REM dreams have a storylike or dreamlike quality and are more visual, vivid, and emotional than NREM dreams (Hobson, 1989).

Blind people who lose their sight before age 5 usually do not have visual dreams. Nevertheless, they have vivid dreams involving the other senses.

You may have heard that an entire dream takes place in an instant. Do you find that hard to believe? In fact, it is not true. Sleep researchers have discovered that it takes about as long to dream a dream as it would to experience the same thing in real life (Kleitman, 1960). Let's take a closer look at the dream state.

Dream Memories: We Remember Only a Few Although some people insist that they do not dream at all, sleep researchers say that all people dream unless they are drinking heavily or taking drugs that suppress REM sleep. Sleepers have the best recall of a dream if they are awakened during the dream; the more time that passes after the dream ends, the poorer the recall. If you awaken 10 minutes or more after a dream is over, you probably will not remember it. Even the dreams you remember on awakening will quickly fade from memory unless you mentally rehearse them or write them down. Very few dreams are memorable enough to be retained very long. Some researchers suggest that human brain chemistry during sleep differs from that in the waking state and does not facilitate the storing of memories (Hobson, 1996; Hobson & Stickgold, 1995). Do you remember your own dreams? What do you dream about?

In general, what have researchers found regarding the content of dreams?

The Content of Dreams: Bizarre or Commonplace? What do people dream about? You may be surprised to learn that dreams are less bizarre and less filled with emotion than is generally believed (Cipolli et al., 1993; Hall & Van de Castle, 1966; Snyder, 1971). Because dreams are notoriously hard to remember, the features that stand out tend to be those that are bizarre or emotional.

Sleep researchers generally agree that dreams reflect a person's preoccupations in waking life—hopes and plans, worries and fears. Most dreams have rather commonplace settings with real people, half of whom are known to the dreamer. In general, dreams are more unpleasant than pleasant, and they contain more aggression than friendly interactions and more misfortune than good fortune. Fear and anxiety, often quite intense, are common in REM dreams (Hobson, 1996). Some dreams are in "living color," while others are in black and white.

Griffith and others (1958) asked 250 college students about the themes of their dreams. The percentage of students in the study reporting each of the 20 most common dream themes is shown in parentheses in the *Try It!*

Try It!

On this list of 20 common dream themes (Griffith et al., 1958), place a check mark next to each one you have dreamed about.

___ Falling (83%)
___ Being attacked or pursued (77%)
___ Trying repeatedly to do something (71%)
___ School, teachers, studying (71%)
___ Sexual experiences (66%)
___ Arriving too late (64%)
___ Eating (62%)
___ Being frozen with fright (58%)
___ Death of a loved person (57%)
___ Being locked up (56%)
___ Finding money (56%)
___ Swimming (52%)
___ Snakes (49%)
___ Being dressed inappropriately (46%)
___ Being smothered (44%)
___ Being nude in public (43%)
___ Fire (41%)
___ Failing an examination (39%)
___ Flying (34%)
___ Seeing self as dead (33%)

Some people are troubled by unpleasant recurring dreams. The two most common themes are falling and being chased (Stark, 1984). People who have recurring dreams seem to have a greater number of minor physical complaints, greater stress, and more anxiety and depression than other people (Brown & Donderi, 1986). Is there anything that can be done to stop recurring dreams? Some people have been taught to use **lucid dreams** (dreams in which people are aware that they are dreaming) to bring about satisfactory resolutions to their unpleasant recurring dreams. Many lucid dreamers are able to change a dream while it is in progress, and a few virtuosos claim to be able to dream about any subject at will (Gackenbach & Bosveld, 1989; La Berge, 1981).

Most of our dreams reflect our daily routines and preoccupations and involve people we know. Some dreams, however, can be as bizarre as Dorothy's in The Wizard of Oz.

Interpreting Dreams: Are There Hidden Meanings in Dreams? Sigmund Freud believed that dreams function to satisfy unconscious sexual and aggressive wishes. Because such wishes are unacceptable to the dreamer, they have to be disguised and therefore appear in a dream in symbolic form. Freud (1900/1953a) claimed that objects like sticks, umbrellas, tree trunks, and guns symbolize the male sex organ; objects such as chests, cupboards, and boxes represent the female sex organ. Freud differentiated between the *manifest content* of the dream—the dream as recalled by the dreamer—and the underlying meaning of the dream, called the *latent content*, which he considered more significant.

In recent years there has been a major shift away from the Freudian interpretation of dreams. Now there is a greater focus on the manifest content, the actual dream itself—which is seen more as an expression of a broad range of the dreamer's concerns than as primarily an expression of sexual impulses (Webb, 1975). And from an evolutionary viewpoint, dreams are viewed as a mechanism for simulating threatening and dangerous life events so that the dreamer can "rehearse" and thus enhance the chances for survival (Revensuo, 2000).

Well-known sleep researcher J. Allan Hobson (1988) rejects the notion that nature would equip humans with a capability and a need to dream dreams that would require a specialist to interpret. Hobson and McCarley (1977) advanced the *activation-synthesis hypothesis* of dreaming. This hypothesis suggests that dreams are simply the brain's attempt to make sense of the random firing of brain cells during REM sleep. Just as people try to make sense of input from the environment during their waking hours, they try to find meaning in the conglomeration of sensations and memories that are generated internally by this random firing of brain cells. Hobson (1989) believes that dreams also have psychological significance, because the meaning a person imposes reflects that person's experiences, remote memories, associations, drives, and fears. (As we'll see shortly, some recent research has questioned Hobson's position.)

REM Sleep, Dreaming, and the Brain During periods of REM sleep, the cerebral cortex is activated much as it is during wakefulness. But different neurotransmitters are dominant in the cortex during wakefulness and during REM sleep (Gottesmann, 2000). When we are awake, powerful inhibiting influences exert control over the functioning of the cortex, keeping us anchored to reality, less subject to impulsive thoughts and acts, and more or less "sane." These inhibiting influences are maintained principally by cortical neurons that are responding to serotonin and noradrenalin (norepinephrine). These inhibiting neurotransmitters are far less plentiful during REM dreaming, when a higher level of dopamine causes other cortical neurons to show intense activity. This uninhibited and dopamine-stimulated activity of the dreaming brain has been likened to a psychotic mental state (Gottesmann, 2000).

Hobson (2000, Hobson et al., 1998) has recently pointed out that dreaming in REM sleep is marked by sensory and motor hallucinations, an intense rise in

lucid dream: A dream during which the dreamer is aware of dreaming and is often able to influence the content of the dream while it is in progress.

emotional and instinctive behavior, weird or bizarre images, a reduction in reality, and other phenomena often observed in schizophrenics. According to this research, there are striking similarities between the schizophrenic brain and the dreaming brain. Other research has shown that an excess of dopamine is associated with psychotic disorders (Buffenstein et al., 1999). Most drugs used to treat schizophrenia reduce the influence of dopamine in the brain's cortex and limbic system (Kinon & Lieberman, 1996). And some newer drugs also increase the inhibitory control of the cortical neurons by stimulating the release of the inhibiting neurotransmitters such as noradrenalin (Nutt et al., 1997).

REM Sleep and Dreaming: Are They the Same? Are dreaming and REM sleep essentially one and the same? Some researchers (Solms, 2000) have questioned an assumption long held by Hobson and other sleep experts that dreaming is simply the brain's effort to make sense of the random firing of neurons that occurs during REM sleep. Are the brain mechanisms responsible for REM sleep the same ones that create the rich dream world we experience? The answer may be no. It is known that dreams do occur outside of REM sleep. Moreover, the REM state can exist without dreams. These two facts suggest that different but complementary brain mechanisms are responsible for REM sleep and the dreaming that normally occurs within it. There is mounting evidence, says British researcher Mark Solms (2000), that dreaming and REM sleep, while normally occuring together, are not one and the same. Rather, the REM state is controlled by neural mechanisms in the brain stem, while areas farther up in the forebrain provide the common pathway that gives us the complex and often vivid mental experiences we call dreams.

The Function of REM Sleep: Necessary, but Why? Other researchers suggest that REM sleep aids in information processing, helping people sift through daily experience, to organize and store in memory information that is relevant to them.

What function does REM sleep appear to serve, and what happens when people are deprived of REM sleep?

Animal studies provide strong evidence for a relationship between REM sleep and learning (Hennevin et al., 1995; Smith, 1995; Winson, 1990). Some studies have revealed that animals increase their REM sleep following learning sessions. Other studies have indicated that when animals are deprived of REM sleep after new learning, their performance on the learned task is impaired the following day. But depriving subjects of NREM sleep had no such effect in the studies.

Research has shown that REM sleep serves an information-processing function in humans and is involved in the consolidation of memories after human learning. Karni and others (1994) found that research participants learning a new perceptual skill showed an improvement in performance, with no additional practice, 8 to 10 hours later if they had a normal night's sleep or if the researchers disturbed only their NREM sleep. Performance did not improve, however, in those who were deprived of REM sleep.

An opposite view is proposed by Francis Crick and Graeme Mitchison (1983, 1995). They suggest that REM sleep functions as mental housecleaning, erasing trivial and unnecessary memories and clearing overloaded neural circuits that might interfere with memory and rational thinking. In other words, they say, people dream in order to forget.

There is no doubt that REM sleep serves an important function, even if psychologists do not know precisely what that function is. The fact that newborns have such a high percentage of REM sleep has led to the conclusion that REM sleep is necessary for maturation of the brain in infants (Marks et al., 1995). Furthermore, when people are deprived of REM sleep as a result of general sleep loss or illness, they will make up for the loss by getting an increased amount of REM sleep after the deprivation. This increase in the percentage of REM sleep to make up for REM deprivation is called a **REM rebound.** Because the intensity of REM sleep is increased during a REM rebound, nightmares often occur. Alcohol, amphetamines, cocaine, and LSD suppress REM sleep, and withdrawal from these drugs results in a REM rebound (Porte & Hobson, 1996).

REM rebound: The increased amount of REM sleep that occurs after REM deprivation; often associated with unpleasant dreams or nightmares.

Remember It!

1. Compared with REM dreams, NREM dreams are
   a. more emotional.
   b. more visual.
   c. more thoughtlike.
   d. more vivid.
2. Dream memories usually do not persist for more than 10 minutes after a dream has ended. (true/false)
3. According to researchers, each of the following statements about the content of dreams is correct *except*
   a. dreams are generally bizarre and filled with emotion.
   b. dreams generally reflect our waking preoccupations.
   c. dreams are generally more unpleasant than pleasant.
   d. dreams contain more aggression than friendly interactions.
4. Experts tend to agree on how dreams should be interpreted. (true/false)
5. Following REM deprivation, there is usually
   a. an absence of REM sleep.
   b. an increase in REM sleep.
   c. a decrease in REM sleep.
   d. no change in the amount of REM sleep.
6. Which type of sleep seems to aid learning and memory in humans and other animals?
   a. Stage 1
   b. Stage 2
   c. Stages 3 and 4
   d. REM sleep

Answers: 1. c 2. true 3. a 4. false 5. b 6. d

SLEEP DISORDERS

What are the characteristics common to sleepwalking and sleep terrors?

So far our discussion has centered on a typical night for a typical sleeper. But a significant number of American adults report sleep problems (Rosekind, 1992), and many children also experience sleep disturbances. Sleep problems range from mild to severe and from problems that affect only sleep to those that affect a person's entire life. Yet medical schools, on average, provide less than 2 hours of instruction on sleep and sleep disorders (Rosen et al., 1993).

Parasomnias: Unusual Behaviors during Sleep

Parasomnias are sleep disturbances in which behaviors and physiological states that normally occur only in the waking state take place during sleep or the transition from sleep to wakefulness (Schenck & Mahowald, 2000).

Sleepwalking and Sleep Terrors: Stage 4 Sleep Disturbances Sleepwalking **(somnambulism)** and sleep terrors are parasomnias that often run in families. They occur during a partial arousal from Stage 4 sleep in which the sleeper does not come to full consciousness. Typically, there is no memory of the episode the following day (Moldofsky et al., 1995). Most cases begin in childhood and are attributed primarily to a delayed development of the nervous system (Masand et al., 1995). The child usually outgrows the disturbance by adolescence.

Sleepwalking: Walking Around but Sound Asleep Cartoonists often depict sleepwalkers groping about with their eyes closed and their arms extended forward. But sleepwalkers actually have their eyes open with a blank stare, and rather than walking normally, they shuffle about. Their coordination is poor, and if they talk, their speech is usually unintelligible.

somnambulism (som-NAM-bue-lism): Sleepwalking that occurs during a partial arousal from Stage 4 sleep.

If an EEG recording were made during a sleepwalking episode, it would show a combination of delta waves, indicating deep sleep, and alpha and beta waves, signaling the waking state. Sleepwalkers are awake enough to carry out activities that do not require their full attention, but asleep enough not to remember having done so the following day. Sleepwalkers may get up and roam through the house, or simply stand for a short time and then go back to bed. Occasionally they get dressed, eat a snack, or go to the bathroom. Some sleepwalkers have even been known to drive during an episode (Schenck & Mahowald, 1995).

The most important concern in sleepwalking is safety. Because their alertness and coordination are reduced, sleepwalkers are at risk of hurting themselves. They have been known to walk out windows, fall down stairs, and more.

Episodes of sleepwalking in adults often occur during periods of stress or major life events and are more likely to be associated with a psychiatric disorder (Masand et al., 1995). Although it is not dangerous to awaken a sleepwalker, experts suggest that it is better to simply guide the individual back to bed (Masand et al., 1995). Rare, but not unheard of, are individuals who commit violent acts while sleepwalking (Broughton & Shimizu, 1995; Moldofsky et al., 1995; Schenck & Mahowald, 1995).

What is a sleep terror?

Sleep Terrors: Screams in the Night **Sleep terrors** usually begin with a piercing scream. The sleeper springs up in a state of panic—eyes open, perspiring, breathing rapidly, with the heart pounding at two or more times the normal rate (Karacan, 1988). Episodes usually last from 5 to 15 minutes, and then the person falls back to sleep. If not awakened during a night terror, children usually have no memory of the episode the next morning. If awakened, however, they may recall a single frightening image.

Parents should not be unduly alarmed by sleep terrors in young children, but episodes that continue through adolescence into adulthood are more serious (Horne, 1992). Sleep terrors in adults often indicate extreme anxiety or other psychological problems. Up to 5% of children have sleep terrors (Keefauver & Guilleminault, 1994), but only about 1% of adults experience them (Partinen, 1994).

How do nightmares differ from sleep terrors?

Nightmares: The Worst of Dreams Unlike sleep terrors, **nightmares** are very frightening dreams that occur during REM sleep and are likely to be remembered in vivid detail. The most common themes are falling and being chased, threatened, or attacked. Nightmares can be a reaction to traumatic life experiences, and they are more frequent at times of high fevers, anxiety, and emotional upheaval. REM rebound during drug withdrawal or following long periods without sleep can also produce nightmares. Sleep terrors occur early in the night during Stage 4 sleep, while anxiety nightmares occur toward morning, when the REM periods are longest.

According to the American Psychiatric Association (1994), from 10% to 50% of children between ages 3 and 5 have nightmares severe enough to worry their parents. And about 50% of adults have occasional nightmares, which are nothing to be alarmed about. But frequent nightmares may be associated with psychological maladjustment (Berquier & Aston, 1992).

Sleeptalking (Somniloquy): Might You Reveal Secrets? Do you sometimes talk in your sleep? Are you afraid that you might confess to something embarrassing or reveal some deep, dark secret? Relax. Sleeptalkers rarely reply to questions, and they usually mumble words or phrases that make no sense to the listener. Sleeptalking can occur during any sleep stage and is more frequent in children than in adults. There is no evidence at all that sleeptalking is related to a physical or psychological disturbance—not even to a guilty conscience.

sleep terror: A sleep disturbance in which a person partially awakens from Stage 4 sleep with a scream, dazed and groggy, in a panic state, and with a racing heart.

nightmare: A very frightening dream occurring during REM sleep.

Major Sleep Disorders

Some sleep disorders can be so debilitating that they affect a person's entire life. These disorders are narcolepsy, sleep apnea, and insomnia.

Narcolepsy: Sudden Attacks of REM Sleep Many people complain about having difficulty falling asleep, but a more serious problem is not being able to stay awake during the day. **Narcolepsy** is an incurable sleep disorder characterized by excessive daytime sleepiness and uncontrollable attacks of REM sleep, usually lasting 10 to 20 minutes (American Psychiatric Association, 1994). People with narcolepsy—who number from 250,000 to 350,000 in the United States—suffer the effects of a drastically lowered quality of life (Broughton & Broughton, 1994). They are subject to more accidents virtually everywhere—driving automobiles, at work, and at home. There is an emotional price to pay as well. They are often stigmatized as lazy, depressed, and disinterested in their work.

Anything that causes an ordinary person to be tired can trigger a sleep attack in a person with narcolepsy—a heavy meal, sunbathing at the beach, or a boring lecture. A sleep attack can also be brought on by laughter or by any situation that is exciting (such as lovemaking) or that causes a strong emotion (such as anger or elation).

Narcolepsy is a physiological disorder caused by an abnormality in the part of the brain that regulates sleep, and it appears to have a strong genetic component (Billiard et al., 1994; Partinen et al., 1994). Some dogs are subject to narcolepsy, and much has been learned about the genetics of this disorder from research on canine subjects (Lamberg, 1996). Although there is no cure for narcolepsy, stimulant medications improve daytime alertness in most patients (Guilleminault, 1993; Mitler et al., 1994). Experts also recommend scheduled naps to relieve sleepiness (Garma & Marchand, 1994).

What are the major symptoms of narcolepsy?

Sleep researcher William Dement holds a dog that is experiencing a narcoleptic sleep attack. Much has been learned about narcolepsy through research with dogs. For example, Dement has found that certain breeds of dogs are more likely than others to have narcolepsy.

Sleep Apnea: When Breathing Stops during Sleep Over 1 million Americans—mostly obese men—suffer from another dangerous sleep disorder, sleep apnea. **Sleep apnea** consists of periods during sleep when breathing stops, and the individual must awaken briefly in order to breathe (White, 1989). The major symptoms of sleep apnea are excessive daytime sleepiness and extremely loud snoring (as loud as a jackhammer), often accompanied by snorts, gasps, and choking noises.

What is sleep apnea?

A person with sleep apnea will drop off to sleep, stop breathing altogether, and then awaken struggling for breath. After gasping several breaths in a semiawakened state, the person falls back to sleep and stops breathing again. People with severe sleep apnea may partially awaken as many as 800 times a night to gasp for air. Alcohol and sedatives aggravate the condition (Langevin et al., 1992).

Severe sleep apnea can lead to chronic high blood pressure, heart problems, and even death (Lavie et al., 1995). Treatments for sleep apnea include greatly reducing body weight (Strobel & Rosen, 1996) and surgically modifying the upper airway (Sher et al., 1996). The favored treatment, however, is the use of a continuous positive airway pressure (CPAP) device, which delivers air through a mask worn over the nose at night (Lévy & Robert, 1996; Randerath et al., 2000; Rapoport, 1996).

Insomnia: The Most Common Sleep Disorder Approximately one-third of adults in the United States suffer from **insomnia**—a sleep disorder characterized by difficulty falling or staying asleep, by waking too early, or by sleep that is light, restless, or of poor quality. Any of these symptoms can lead to distress and impairment in daytime functioning (Costa E Silva et al., 1996; Roth, 1996b; Sateia et al., 2000). Transient (temporary) insomnia, lasting 3 weeks or less, can result from jet lag, emotional highs (an upcoming wedding) or lows (losing a loved one or a job), or a brief illness or injury that interferes with sleep (Reite et al., 1995). Much more serious is chronic insomnia, which lasts for months or even years and plagues about 10% of the adult population (Roth, 1996b). The percentages are even higher for women, the elderly, and people suffering from psychiatric and medical disorders (Costa E Silva et al., 1996). Chronic insomnia may begin as a reaction to a psychological or medical problem but persist long after the problem is resolved. Individuals with chronic insomnia experience "higher psychological distress [and] greater impairments of daytime functioning, are involved in more fatigue-related accidents, take more sick leave, and utilize health care resources more often than good sleepers" (Morin & Wooten, 1996, p. 522).

What is insomnia?

narcolepsy (NAR-co-lep-see): A serious sleep disorder characterized by excessive daytime sleepiness and sudden, uncontrollable attacks of REM sleep.

sleep apnea: A sleep disorder involving periods during sleep when breathing stops and the person must awaken briefly in order to breathe; major symptoms are excessive daytime sleepiness and loud snoring.

insomnia: A sleep disorder characterized by difficulty falling or staying asleep, by waking too early, or by light, restless, or poor sleep.

Remember It!

1. Sleepwalking and sleep terrors occur during a partial arousal from
   a. Stage 1 sleep. c. Stage 4 sleep.
   b. Stage 2 sleep. d. REM sleep.
2. Sleepwalking episodes and sleep terrors are rarely recalled. (true/false)
3. Match each sleep problem with the description or associated symptom.

____ (1) uncontrollable sleep attacks during the day	a. narcolepsy
____ (2) cessation of breathing during sleep	b. sleep apnea
____ (3) difficulty falling or staying asleep	c. insomnia
____ (4) very frightening REM dream	d. nightmare

Answers: 1. c 2. true 3. (1) a (2) b (3) c (4) d

ALTERING CONSCIOUSNESS THROUGH CONCENTRATION AND SUGGESTION

Sleep is an altered state of consciousness and a necessary one. We all have to sleep. But there are other forms of altered consciousness that we may experience only if we choose to do so. Meditation and hypnosis are two of these.

Meditation: Expanded Consciousness or Relaxation?

For what purposes is meditation used?

Meditation (the concentrative form) is a group of techniques that involve focusing attention on an object, a word, one's breathing, or body movement in order to block out all distractions, to enhance well-being, and to achieve an altered state of consciousness. Some forms of concentrative meditation—yoga, Zen, and transcendental meditation (TM)—have their roots in Eastern religions and are practiced by followers of those religions to attain a higher spiritual state. In the United States these approaches are often used to increase relaxation, reduce arousal, or expand consciousness.

Many people engage in some form of meditation to achieve an enhanced state of well-being. Here "material girl" Madonna is practicing yoga, perhaps seeking a more spiritual state.

In practicing yoga, a meditator typically assumes a cross-legged position known as the lotus and gazes at a visual stimulus—a mandala (a symbolic circular pattern) or an object such as a vase or a flower. During Zen meditation, the individual counts breaths or concentrates on the breathing process. In transcendental meditation, the meditator is given a *mantra,* a secret word assigned by a teacher. The meditator sits quietly with closed eyes and silently repeats the mantra over and over during meditation. With all three approaches, the meditator's goal is to block out unwanted thoughts and facilitate the meditative state. Herbert Benson (1975) suggests that any word or sound can be used for transcendental meditation, although some would disagree with him. Moreover, he claims that the beneficial effects of meditation can be achieved through simple relaxation techniques. Do the *Try It!* to experience Benson's relaxation response.

Try It!

Find a quiet place and sit in a comfortable position.

1. Close your eyes.
2. Relax all your muscles deeply. Begin with your feet and move slowly upward, relaxing the muscles in your legs, buttocks, abdomen, chest, shoulders, neck, and finally your face. Allow your whole body to remain in this deeply relaxed state.
3. Now concentrate on your breathing, and breathe in and out through your nose. Each time you breathe out, silently say the word *one* to yourself.
4. Repeat this process for 20 minutes. (You can open your eyes to look at your watch periodically but don't use an alarm.) When you are finished, remain seated for a few minutes–first with your eyes closed, then with them open.

Benson recommends that you maintain a passive attitude. Don't try to force yourself to relax. Just let it happen. If a distracting thought comes to mind, ignore it and just repeat *one* each time you exhale. It is best to practice this exercise one or two times each day, but not within two hours of your last meal. Digestion interferes with the relaxation response.

Hypnosis: The Power of Suggestion

What is hypnosis, and when is it most useful?

Have you ever been hypnotized? Many people are fascinated by this unusual, somewhat mysterious phenomenon. **Hypnosis** may be defined as a procedure through which one person, the hypnotist, uses the power of suggestion to induce changes in thoughts, feelings, sensations, perceptions, or behavior in another person, the subject. Under hypnosis, people suspend their usual rational and logical ways of thinking and perceiving and allow themselves to experience distortions in perceptions, memories, and thinking. They may experience positive hallucinations, in which they see, hear, touch, smell, or taste things that are not present in the environment. Or they may have negative hallucinations in which they fail to perceive things that are actually present.

About 80–95% of people are hypnotizable to some degree, but only 5% can reach the deepest levels of the hypnotic state (Nash & Baker, 1984). The ability to become completely absorbed in imaginative activities is characteristic of highly hypnotizable people (Nadon et al., 1991). Silva and Kirsch (1992) found that individuals' fantasy-proneness and their expectation of responding to hypnotic suggestions were predictors of hypnotizability.

Myths about Hypnosis: Separating Fact from Fiction There are many misconceptions about hypnosis, some of which probably stem from its long and unfortunate association with stage entertainers. Have you ever believed one of these myths?

- *Hypnotized people are under the complete control of the hypnotist and will violate their moral values if told to do so.* Hypnosis is not something that is done to people. Subjects retain the ability to refuse to comply with the hypnotist's suggestions, and they will not do anything that is contrary to their true moral beliefs.
- *People can demonstrate superhuman strength and perform amazing feats under hypnosis.* Subjects are not stronger or more powerful under hypnosis (Druckman & Bjork, 1994).

meditation (concentrative): A group of techniques that involve focusing attention on an object, a word, one's breathing, or body movement in order to block out all distractions, to enhance well-being, and to achieve an altered state of consciousness.

hypnosis: A procedure through which one person, the hypnotist, uses the power of suggestion to induce changes in thoughts, feelings, sensations, perceptions, or behavior in another person, the subject.

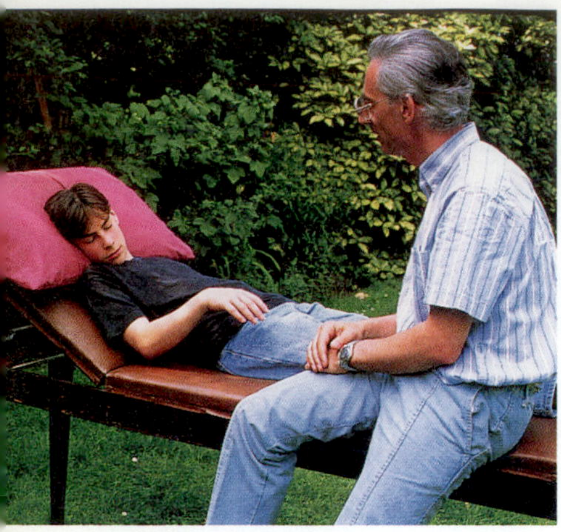

A hypnotized person is in a state of heightened suggestibility. This hypnotherapist suggested to the subject that a balloon was tied to his right hand and his arm raised accordingly.

- *Memory is more accurate under hypnosis.* Although it is true that hypnotized subjects supply more information and are more confident of their recollections, the information is often inaccurate (Dywan & Bowers, 1983; Kihlstrom & Barnhardt, 1993; Nogrady et al., 1985; Weekes et al., 1992). And in the process of trying to help people recall certain events, hypnotists may instead create in them false memories, or *pseudomemories* (Lynn & Nash, 1994; Yapko, 1994).
- *People under hypnosis will reveal embarrassing secrets.* Hypnosis is not like a truth serum. Subjects can keep secrets or lie under hypnosis.
- *People under hypnosis can relive an event as it occurred when they were children and can function mentally as if they were that age.* Careful reviews of studies on hypnotic age regression have found no evidence to support this claim. "Although hypnotically regressed subjects may undergo dramatic changes in demeanor and subjective experience, their performance is not accurately childlike" (Nash, 1987, p. 50).

Medical Uses of Hypnosis: It's Not Just Entertainment Hypnosis has come a long way from the days when it was used mainly by stage entertainers. It is now recognized as a viable technique to be used in medicine, dentistry, and psychotherapy (Lynn et al., 2000). Hypnosis is accepted by the American Medical Association, the American Psychological Association, and the American Psychiatric Association. Hypnosis has been particularly helpful in the control of pain (Hilgard, 1975; Kihlstrom, 1985; Montgomery et al., 2000). It has also been used successfully to treat a wide range of disorders, including high blood pressure, bleeding, psoriasis, severe morning sickness, and the side effects of chemotherapy. Other problems that have responded well to hypnosis are asthma, severe insomnia, some phobias (Orne, 1983), dissociative identity disorder (Kluft, 1992), and posttraumatic stress disorder (Cardena, 2000). Furthermore, there are studies suggesting that hypnosis can be useful in treating warts (Ewin, 1992), pain due to severe burns (Patterson & Ptacek, 1997), repetitive nightmares (Kingsbury, 1993), and sexual dysfunctions such as inhibited sexual desire and impotence (Crasilneck, 1992; Hammond, 1992). Suppose you are overweight, or you smoke or drink heavily. Would a quick trip to a hypnotist rid you of overeating or other bad habits? Hypnosis has been only moderately effective in weight control and virtually useless in overcoming drug and alcohol abuse or nicotine addiction (Abbot et al., 2000; Green & Lynn, 2000; Orne, 1983).

For the most hypnotizable people, hypnosis can be used instead of a general anesthetic in surgery. In one remarkable case, a young Canadian dentist had gall bladder surgery, using only hypnosis. From the time of the first incision until the operation was over, the patient maintained a steady pulse rate and blood pressure. Unbelievably, he claimed that he felt nothing that could be described as pain, only a tugging sensation (Callahan, 1997). Did the dentist have the world's greatest hypnotist? No, most experts in hypnosis believe that "hypnotic responsiveness depends more on the efforts and abilities of the person hypnotized than on the skill of the hypnotist" (Kirsch & Lynn, 1995, p. 846).

What are the three main theories that have been proposed to explain hypnosis?

What Is Hypnosis? Is hypnosis a trancelike, altered state of consciousness? Today, most hypnosis researchers reject the notion that hypnosis is a genuinely altered state of consciousness (Kirsch & Lynn, 1995). Rather, most believe that the impressive, sometimes stunning, effects of hypnosis can be accounted for by the demands of the situation—the same social and cognitive influences that explain ordinary, nonhypnotic behavior.

The Sociocognitive Theory According to the **sociocognitive theory of hypnosis,** the behavior of a hypnotized person is a function of that person's expectations about how subjects behave under hypnosis. People are motivated to be good subjects, to follow the suggestions of the hypnotist, and to fulfill the social role of the hypnotized person as they perceive it (Spanos, 1986, 1991, 1994). But does this mean that hypnotized people are merely acting or faking it? No, "most hypnotized persons are neither faking nor merely complying with suggestions" (Kirsch & Lynn, 1995, p. 847). In fact, using the single most effective and reliable indicator of deception in the laboratory, skin conductance, which indicates emotional response by measuring perspiration, Kinnunen and others (1994) found that 89% of supposedly hypnotized people had been truly hypnotized.

Three decades ago, Barber (1970) claimed that behavior of subjects under hypnosis is not different from behavior of other highly motivated people. He reported that "both hypnotic and waking control subjects are responsive to suggestions for analgesia [pain relief], age regression, hallucinations and amnesia if they have positive attitudes toward the situation and are motivated to respond" (p. 27). But does this include *all* behavior under hypnosis? Apparently not. Some researchers have found that although social suggestibility alone can explain the performance of less difficult actions under hypnosis, it becomes less of a factor as the difficulty of the action increases (Woody et al., 1997). It is hard to imagine how the Canadian dentist could tolerate the pain of major surgery armed with nothing more than social suggestibility and strong motivation.

The Neodissociation Theory Ernest Hilgard (1986, 1992) has proposed a theory to explain the accomplishment of very difficult acts under hypnosis, even undergoing surgery without anesthesia. According to his **neodissociation theory of hypnosis,** hypnosis induces a split, or dissociation, between two aspects of the control of consciousness that are ordinarily linked—the planning and the monitoring functions. During hypnosis, it is the planning function that carries out the suggestions of the hypnotist and remains a part of the subject's conscious awareness. The monitoring function monitors or observes everything that happens to the subject, but without his or her conscious awareness. Hilgard called the monitoring function, when separated from conscious awareness, "the hidden observer."

Hilgard demonstrated the presence of the hidden observer many times. In one series of experiments (Hilgard, 1979), he hypnotized a participant, had the person place one hand in ice water, and suggested that he or she would feel no discomfort. And, indeed, subjects did not report any discomfort. But, according to Hilgard, through automatic writing or talking, a subject's hidden observer was able to describe how the water felt, even though the subject was not consciously aware of having experienced the extreme cold. This type of experiment has been replicated by other researchers (Kihlstrom, 1985; Zamansky & Bartis, 1985).

Theory of Dissociated Control Bowers and his colleagues (Bowers, 1992; Woody & Bowers, 1994) have proposed a view of hypnosis as an authentic altered state of consciousness. Their **theory of dissociated control** maintains that hypnosis does not induce a splitting of different aspects of consciousness, as Hilgard's model suggests. Rather, they believe that hypnosis weakens the control of the executive function over other parts (subsystems) of consciousness. In their view, the hypnotist's suggestions not only weaken the executive control, but contact and influence the other subsystems directly. Bowers further believes that the hypnotized person's responses are automatic and involuntary, not mediated by normal cognitive functions (Kirsch & Lynn, 1995). And, indeed, some research supports this belief (Bowers & Woody, 1996; Hargadon et al., 1995).

How can the various theories of hypnosis be reconciled? Or can they be? Considering the evidence presented here, which theory seems most logical to you? Although the majority of hypnosis researchers seem to support the sociocognitive theory of hypnosis, most clinicians apparently believe that hypnosis is a unique altered state of consciousness (Kirsch & Lynn, 1995). And so do some influential researchers in the field (Nash, 1991; Woody & Bowers, 1994). Kihlstrom (1986) has suggested that a more complete picture of hypnosis would emerge from some combination of the sociocognitive approach of Spanos and the neodissociation position of Hilgard. But even though researchers have some serious theoretical differences, hypnosis is increasingly used in clinical practice and in selected areas of medicine and dentistry.

sociocognitive theory of hypnosis: A theory suggesting that the behavior of hypnotized people is a function of their expectations about how a person behaves under hypnosis and their motivation to be good subjects.

neodissociation theory of hypnosis: A theory proposing that hypnosis works by causing a split, or dissociation, between two aspects of consciousness that are ordinarily linked: the planning and the monitoring functions.

theory of dissociated control: The theory that hypnosis is an authentic altered state of consciousness in which the control the executive function exerts over other subsystems of consciousness is weakened.

Culture and Altered States of Consciousness

In every culture around the world, and throughout recorded history, human beings have found ways to induce altered states of consciousness. Some means of inducing altered states in other cultures may seem strange and exotic to most Westerners. Entering ritual trances and experiencing spirit possession are forms of altered states of consciousness used in many cultures in the course of religious rites and tribal ceremonies. Typically, people induce ritual trance by flooding the senses with repetitive chanting, clapping, or singing; by whirling in circles until they achieve a dizzying speed; or by burning strong, pungent incense.

The ritualized spinning dance of the whirling dervishes produces an altered state of consciousness that is recognized as part of their religious practice.

The fact that so many different means of altering consciousness are practiced by members of so many varied cultures around the world has led some experts to ask whether "there may be a universal human need to produce and maintain varieties of conscious experiences" (Ward, 1994, p. 60). Whatever the method used to induce it, the experience of an altered state of consciousness can vary greatly from one culture to another.

Remember It!

1. Which is *not* a proposed use of meditation?
   a. To promote relaxation
   b. To substitute for anesthesia during surgery
   c. To bring a person to a higher level of spirituality
   d. To alter consciousness
2. A mantra is used in transcendental meditation. (true/false)
3. According to Herbert Benson, the beneficial effects of meditation cannot be duplicated with simple relaxation techniques. (true/false)
4. Which of the following statements is true of people under hypnosis?
   a. They will often violate their moral code.
   b. They are much stronger than they are in the normal waking state.
   c. They can be made to experience distortions in their perceptions.
   d. Their memory is more accurate than it is during the normal waking state.
5. For a moderately hypnotizable person, which use of hypnosis would probably be most successful?
   a. for relief from pain
   b. instead of a general anesthetic during surgery
   c. for treating drug addiction
   d. for improving memory
6. The three main theories proposed to explain hypnosis are the ______________, ______________, and ______________ theories.

Answers: 1. b 2. true 3. false 4. c 5. a 6. sociocognitive, neodissociation, dissociated control

ALTERED STATES OF CONSCIOUSNESS AND PSYCHOACTIVE DRUGS

The altered states of consciousness we have examined thus far are natural ones. We will now explore psychoactive drugs, a wide range of substances that are used to modify natural consciousness. A **psychoactive drug** is any substance that alters mood, perception, or thought. Some of these drugs are legal, but most are **illicit** (illegal). When psychoactive drugs are approved for medical use, they are called *controlled substances.*

Of all the industrial nations in the world, the United States has the highest rate of illicit drug use. Some 70% of Americans have tried illicit drugs, and close to 20% have used them during the past year (Gazzaniga, 1997). About 5.5 million Americans are addicted to illicit drugs (Holloway, 1991). But in terms of sheer numbers of those addicted, damage to users, and harm to society, the most serious problems for U.S. society are the legal drugs tobacco and alcohol (Goldstein & Kalant, 1990).

Why do so many Americans use psychoactive drugs? There are many reasons for taking drugs, and users often do not recognize their real motivation. Stress-related variables are reliable predictors of substance abuse (Sussman & Dent, 2000). For example, recent research indicates that family violence strongly predicts drug use (Easton et al., 2000). One study found that females are much more likely than males to use drugs to cope with family dysfunction and the symptoms that arise from internalizing various forms of abuse (Dakof, 2000). Additionally, a large number of women who report sexual abuse turn to substance use (Knisely et al., 2000). However, some people who are not experiencing stressful life situations, dysfunctional families, violence, or any form of abuse still use drugs—out of boredom, just to feel good, for perceived social rewards, or to conform to social pressures (MacLean & Lecci, 2000). Others use psychoactive drugs for their medical benefits.

Every year since 1975, the University of Michigan's Institute for Social Research has conducted surveys on drug use, and on attitudes and beliefs about drug use, among high school students and young adults. These surveys show that drug use among high school seniors had been falling continuously from 1980 to 1992. But in 1992 it began to increase dramatically, as shown in Figure 4.3 (on p. 148). Then, from 1997 to 1998, drug use decreased slightly but was beginning to edge upward again in 1999 (Johnston et al., 2001). Researchers Johnston and colleagues (1997) believe one reason for the increases may be that from 1992 until recently there has been a decline in the perception of the harmfulness of certain drugs and less disapproval associated with their use.

Several protective factors tend to lower the risk of drug use by young people. These include parental support, behavioral coping skills, academic and social competence (Newcomb, 1997; Wills & Cleary, 1996; Wills et al., 1996), and traditional religious beliefs (Kendler et al., 1997). Asian-American adolescents are less likely than other young Americans to use alcohol, cigarettes, or illicit drugs. Researchers attribute this fact to healthy social influences, such as an abstinence-promoting environment and a greater likelihood of having an intact family. Also, young Asian-Americans spend more time with their families and less time with friends and other peers thus minimizing potentially bad influences and peer group pressures (Au & Donaldson, 2000).

The earlier adolescents start using drugs, the more likely they are to progress into "the most severe forms of drug use" (Kandel & Davies, 1996). Those who began early and escalated rapidly were found to have "greater life stress, lower parental support, more parental substance use, more deviant attitudes and maladaptive coping, lower self-control ability, and greater affiliation with peers who use substances (particularly marijuana)" (Wills et al., 1996, p. 177), as well as more family violence (Easton et al., 2000). Adolescents who use drugs seek out peers who also use and, in

psychoactive drug: A drug that alters normal mental functioning—mood, perception, or thought; called a controlled substance if used medically.

illicit drug: An illegal drug.

Figure 4.3

Results of a Survey of 8th, 10th, and 12th Graders about Their Use of Any (Illicit) Illegal Drug during the Previous 12 Months

The graph shows the percentage of high school seniors for 1976 through 2000 and the percentages of 8th and 10th graders for 1991 through 2000 who reported using any illicit (illegal) drug during the previous 12 months. After declining steeply from 1982 to 1992, the use of illicit drugs began to increase dramatically in 1992 and continued to climb until 1997. Then drug use decreased slightly in 1997 and 1998 but was beginning to creep upward again in 1999. (Data from Johnston et al., 2001.)

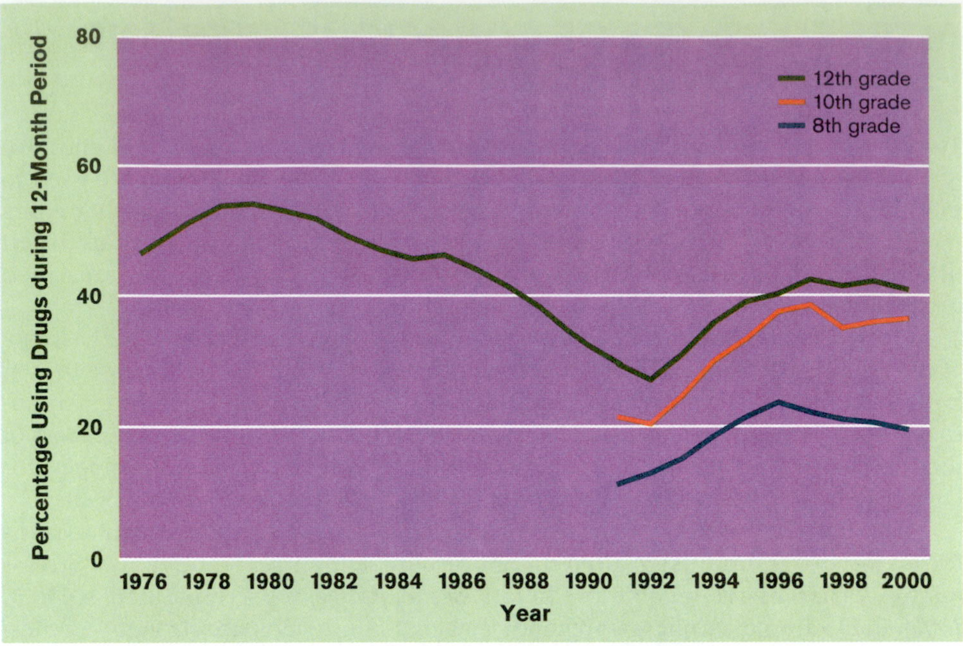

physical drug dependence: A compulsive pattern of drug use in which the user develops a drug tolerance coupled with unpleasant withdrawal symptoms when the drug use is discontinued.

drug tolerance: A condition in which the user becomes progressively less affected by the drug so that larger and larger doses are necessary to maintain the same effect.

turn, are influenced by those peers (Curran et al., 1997). In a 16-year longitudinal study that followed 552 7th, 8th, and 9th graders into adulthood, Newcomb (1997) found that drug use and abuse in adolescents was associated with a number of problem behaviors, including "cigarette use, alcohol abuse, . . . precocious sexual involvement, academic problems, frequency of various sexual activities, deviant attitudes, and delinquent behavior" (Newcomb, 1997, p. 65). Substance abuse among adolescents is also related to the propensity to take risks, and a significant percentage of risk-taking drug users (15%) reported suffering injuries while engaging in substance use (Spirito et al., 2000).

Variables Influencing Individual Responses to Drugs

The effects of drugs are not always predictable. There are individual differences in the way people respond to drugs. Some differences result from the physical characteristics of the user, such as weight, gender, metabolism, and, of course, individual genetic makeup. Psychological factors also strongly influence a person's response to a drug. These factors include expectations about the effect of a drug, mood, mental or psychological health, and past experiences with the drug. Finally, the environment in which a drug is taken (the people present and the setting) and whether it is taken in combination with any other drug can profoundly influence its effect on the user.

Drug Addiction: Slavery to a Substance

What is the difference between physical and psychological drug dependence?

The trip from first use to abuse of a drug may be a long one or a very short one. *Substance abuse* may be defined as continuing drug use that interferes with a person's major life roles at home, in school, at work, or elsewhere and contributes to legal difficulties or any psychological problems (American Psychiatric Association, 1994). Some drugs create a physical or chemical dependence; others create a psychological dependence. **Physical drug dependence** comes about as a result of the body's natural ability to protect itself against harmful substances by developing a **drug tolerance.** This means that the user becomes progressively less affected by the drug and must take larger and larger doses to get the same effect or high (Ramsay & Woods, 1997). Tolerance occurs because the brain adapts to the presence of the drug by responding less intensely to it. In addition, the liver produces more enzymes to break down the drug. The various bodily processes adjust in order to continue to function with the drug in the system.

Once drug tolerance is established, a person cannot function normally without the drug. If the drug is taken away, the user begins to suffer withdrawal symptoms. The **withdrawal symptoms,** both physical and psychological, are usually the exact opposite of the effects produced by the drug. For example, withdrawal from stimulants leaves a person exhausted and depressed; withdrawal from tranquilizers leaves a person nervous and agitated.

Shown here in happier times, comedian/actor Chris Farley was found dead in his Chicago apartment in 1997. Only 33 years old, he overdosed on cocaine and opiates.

withdrawal symptoms: The physical and psychological symptoms (usually the opposite of those produced by the drug) that occur when a regularly used drug is discontinued and that terminate when the drug is taken again.

psychological drug dependence: A craving or irresistible urge for a drug's pleasurable effects.

stimulants: A category of drugs that speed up activity in the central nervous system, suppress appetite, and cause a person to feel more awake, alert, and energetic; also called "uppers."

If physical dependence alone explained drug addiction, now termed *substance dependence,* there would be no problem with drugs long thought to be physically nonaddictive. Also, once the period of physical withdrawal was over, the desire for the drug would end along with the withdrawal symptoms. But this is not the case. There is more to drug addiction than physical dependence. **Psychological drug dependence** is a craving or irresistible urge for the drug's pleasurable effects, and it is more difficult to combat than physical dependence (O'Brien, 1996).

Four factors influence the addictive potential of a drug: (1) how fast the effects of the drug are felt, (2) how pleasurable the drug's effects are in producing euphoria or in extinguishing pain, (3) how long the pleasurable effects last, and (4) how much discomfort is experienced when the drug is discontinued (Medzerian, 1991). The pleasurable effects of the most addictive drugs are felt almost immediately, and they are short-lived. For example, the intense, pleasurable effects of crack are felt in 7 seconds, and last only about 5 minutes. The discomfort after the pleasurable effects wear off is intense, so a user is highly motivated to take more of the drug. The addictive potential of an addictive drug is higher if it is injected rather than taken orally, and slightly higher still if it is smoked rather than injected.

Psychoactive drugs alter consciousness in a variety of ways. Let's consider the various alterations produced by the major categories of drugs: stimulants, depressants, and hallucinogens (or psychedelics).

Stimulants: Speeding Up the Nervous System

How do stimulants affect the user?

Stimulants, often called "uppers," speed up the central nervous system, suppress appetite, and can make a person feel more awake, alert, and energetic. Stimulants increase pulse rate, blood pressure, and respiration rate, and they reduce cerebral blood flow (Mathew & Wilson, 1991). In higher doses, stimulants make people feel nervous, jittery, and restless, and they can cause shaking or trembling and interfere with sleep.

No stimulant actually delivers energy to the body. Instead, a stimulant forces the body to use some of its own stored-up energy sooner and in greater amounts than it would naturally. When the stimulant's effect wears off, the body's natural energy is depleted, leaving the person feeling exhausted and depressed.

There are legal stimulants, such as caffeine and nicotine; controlled stimulants, such as amphetamines; and illegal stimulants, such as cocaine.

Caffeine: The Most Widely Used Drug Caffeine is the world's most widely used drug, and more than 85% of Americans ingest it daily in one form or another (Levinthal, 1996). If you cannot start your day without a cup of coffee (or two, or more), you may be addicted to the stimulant caffeine. Coffee, tea, cola drinks, chocolate, and more than 100 prescription and over-the-counter drugs contain caffeine. They provide a mild jolt to the nervous system that perks up the user, at least temporarily. Caffeine makes people more mentally alert and can help them stay awake. Many people use caffeine to lift their mood; but laboratory studies reveal that 1 hour after consuming medium or high doses of caffeine, participants show significantly higher levels of anxiety, depression, and hostility (Veleber & Templer, 1984).

When moderate to heavy caffeine users abstain, they suffer withdrawal symptoms such as nervousness, instability, headaches, drowsiness, and decreased alertness. Using EEGs and sonograms, researchers looked at the effects of these withdrawal symptoms on the brain and were able to correlate the caffeine withdrawal symptoms with significant increases in blood pressure and in the velocity of blood flow in all four of the cerebral arteries. The EEGs also showed an increase in slower (theta) brain waves, which correlates with decreased alertness and drowsiness (Jones et al., 2000).

Nicotine A growing body of scientific evidence indicates that nicotine's addictive power is not unlike that of major abused drugs, such as amphetamines, morphine, and cocaine (Iversen, 1996). And nicotine addiction may be genetically influenced. A recent study of 493 families (whose members were mostly smokers) indicated that a dominant gene plays a major role in the prevalence of smoking over the three generations studied (Cheng et al., 2000).

It is estimated that 45 million Americans smoke cigarettes, cigars, or pipes, and several million more use snuff or chewing tobacco ("Nicotine Dependence—Part I," 1997). Teen smoking has been steadily increasing, and in 1996 34% of high school seniors smoked, compared with 25% of adults (Johnston et al., 1997). White adolescents smoke more than their African American and Hispanic counterparts. Among 12th graders, 38.1% of Whites smoke, compared with 14.2% of African Americans and 25.4% of Hispanics. Tobacco kills 434,000 Americans every year (Raloff, 1994), and "cigarette smoking results in the premature death of approximately 50% of smokers" (Henningfield et al., 1996, p. 1857). Yet, a recent study suggests that university students dramatically underestimate the number of smoking-related deaths and overestimate deaths related to such drugs as cocaine. Thus, the study says, they lack an accurate view of the dangers of tobacco use (Giacopassi & Vandiver, 1999).

Few people who have tried to quit smoking doubt the addictive power of nicotine. Yet, most treatment methods advertised as being helpful to smokers trying to quit have been largely unsuccessful. What about hypnosis? Hypnotherapy, along with a variety of other stop-smoking treatments, had no greater 6-month quit rate than was produced by no treatment at all (Abbot et al., 2000). Other researchers (Green & Lynn, 2000) reviewed the results of 59 studies of hypnosis and smoking and concluded that hypnosis cannot be considered effective at helping smokers break the habit. However, one study did find that a single dose of glucose had a fairly rapid and measurable effect, making smokers who were trying to abstain less frantic to have another cigarette for a period of up to 10 minutes (West et al., 1999).

The many serious health problems associated with smoking are discussed in Chapter 13.

What effects do amphetamines have on the user?

Amphetamines: Energy to Burn, but at a Price **Amphetamines** are a class of stimulants that increase arousal, relieve fatigue, improve alertness, suppress the appetite, and give a rush of energy. In low to moderate doses, they may temporarily boost athletic and intellectual performance. A person who takes amphetamines becomes more alert and energetic, mildly euphoric, and usually more talkative, animated, and restless.

In high doses (100 milligrams or more) amphetamines can cause confused and disorganized behavior, extreme fear and suspiciousness, delusions and hallucinations, aggressiveness and antisocial behavior, even manic behavior and paranoia. The powerful amphetamine methamphetamine (known as "crank" or "speed") comes in smokable form—"ice," which is highly addictive and can be fatal.

Withdrawal from amphetamines leaves a person physically exhausted, sleeping for 10 to 15 hours or more, only to awaken in a stupor, extremely depressed and intensely hungry. Stimulants constrict the tiny capillaries and the small arteries. Over time, high doses can stop blood flow, causing hemorrhaging and leaving parts of the brain deprived of oxygen. In fact, victims of fatal overdoses of stimulants usually have multiple hemorrhages in the brain.

Yet some amphetamines have therapeutic value in the treatment of narcolepsy and attention-deficit/hyperactivity disorder (ADHD). Recent research suggests that amphetamines can work to stimulate brain activity in whatever brain regions are most essential in performing a specific mental task, while decreasing activity in other brain areas not required for the task (Mattay et al., 1996). This may explain why the stimulants Ritalin and Cylert are useful in treating ADHD.

How does cocaine affect the user?

Cocaine: Snorting White Powder, Smoking Crack "Cocaine can make you feel brilliant, masterful, invulnerable. It can also kill you" (Gold, 1986).

Cocaine, a stimulant derived from coca leaves, can be sniffed as a white powder, injected intravenously, or smoked in the form of crack. The rush of well-being is dramatically intense and powerful, but it is just as dramatically short-lived. The effects of snorting cocaine are felt within 2 to 3 minutes, and the high lasts 30 to 45 minutes. With crack, however, the effects are felt in 8 to 10 seconds but last no more than 5 to 10 minutes (Julien, 1995). The euphoria from cocaine is followed by an equally intense **crash,** marked by depression, anxiety, agitation, and a powerful craving for more of the drug.

Cocaine stimulates the reward or "pleasure" pathways in the brain, which use the neurotransmitter dopamine (Landry, 1997). With continued use, the reward systems fail to function normally, and the user becomes incapable of feeling any pleasure except from the drug. The main withdrawal symptoms are psychological—the inability to feel pleasure and the craving for more cocaine.

Cocaine constricts the blood vessels, raises blood pressure, speeds up the heart, quickens respiration, and can even cause epileptic seizures in people who have no history of epilepsy (Pascual-Leone et al., 1990). Over time, or even quickly in high doses, cocaine can cause heart palpitations, an irregular heartbeat, and heart attacks, and high doses can cause strokes in healthy young individuals.

Animals become addicted more readily to cocaine than to any other drug. Given unlimited access to cocaine, animals will lose interest in everything else—food, water, and sex—and will rapidly and continually self-administer cocaine. They die within 14 days, usually from cardiopulmonary collapse (Gawin, 1991). Cocaine-addicted monkeys will press a lever as many as 12,800 times to get one cocaine injection (Yanagita, 1973).

Crack, or "rock," the most dangerous form of cocaine, can produce a powerful dependency in several weeks. Dr. Jeffrey Rosecan, a drug abuse consultant to the National Football League, called cocaine "the most addicting substance known to man"; and crack, he said, is "the most addicting form of the most addicting drug" (Lundgren, 1986, p. 7). Research supports this claim that crack is the most addictive form of cocaine. Users who begin with cocaine in powder form are likely to progress to crack, while users who start on crack are more likely to continue using it exclusively. When both powder and crack are used interchangeably, a mutual reinforcement seems to occur, and the user develops a dependence on both forms of cocaine (Shaw et al., 1999).

amphetamines: A class of stimulants that increase arousal, relieve fatigue, improve alertness, and suppress the appetite.

cocaine: A type of stimulant that produces a feeling of euphoria.

crash: The feelings of depression, exhaustion, irritability, and anxiety that occur following an amphetamine, cocaine, or crack high.

crack: A form of cocaine that is smoked; the most potent and addictive form of cocaine.

Remember It!

1. Drug use among adolescents has been declining since the early 1990s. (true/false)
2. Which of the following does not necessarily occur with drug tolerance?
   a. The body adjusts to functioning with the drug in the system.
   b. The user needs larger and larger doses of the drug to get the desired effect.
   c. The user becomes progressively less affected by the drug.
   d. The user develops a craving for the pleasurable effects of the drug.
3. During withdrawal from a drug, the user experiences symptoms that are the opposite of the effects produced by the drug. (true/false)
4. Psychological dependence on a drug is more difficult to combat than physical dependence. (true/false)
5. Match the stimulant with the appropriate description.

____ (1) responsible for the most deaths		a. caffeine
____ (2) used to increase arousal, relieve fatigue, and suppress appetite		b. cigarettes
____ (3) found in coffee, tea, chocolate, and colas		c. amphetamines
____ (4) snorted or injected		d. crack
____ (5) most dangerous, potent, and addictive form of cocaine		e. cocaine

Answers: 1. false 2. d 3. true 4. true 5. (1) b (2) c (3) a (4) e (5) d

Depressants: Slowing Down the Nervous System

What are some of the effects of depressants, and what drugs make up this category?

Another class of drugs, the **depressants** (sometimes called "downers") decrease activity in the central nervous system, slow down body functions, and reduce sensitivity to outside stimulation. Within this category are the sedative-hypnotics (alcohol, barbiturates, and minor tranquilizers) and the narcotics, or opiates. When different depressants are taken together, their sedative effects are additive, and thus potentially dangerous.

Alcohol: The Nation's Number One Drug Problem Even though **alcohol** is a depressant, the first few drinks seem to relax and enliven a person at the same time. But the more alcohol a person consumes, the more the central nervous system is depressed. As drinking increases, the symptoms of drunkenness mount—slurred speech, poor coordination, staggering. Men tend to become more aggressive (Pihl et al., 1997) and more sexually aroused (Roehrich & Kinder, 1991) but less able to perform sexually (Crowe & George, 1989). Binge drinking is becoming widespread on college and university campuses, and fraternity parties are notorious for making a game of rapid, excessive drinking (Cohen, 1997). But excessive alcohol can cause a person to lose consciousness, and extremely large amounts can kill. Sadly, several student deaths have resulted from binge drinking parties.

One study on binge drinking among college students suggests that drinking with others at events where food is available seems to lessen the chances that binge drinking will occur. But drinking where illegal drugs are available increases the risk of problem drinking (Clapp et al., 2000). A study by Bennett and others (1999) found similar results—that combining use of other drugs with drinking was associated with more problem drinking and more negative consequences. This study of more than 2,700 college students spanned a 3-year period and revealed that more than one-third of the students admitted to binge drinking at some time during that period.

Alcohol is a problem substance responsible for much misery in the United States. We will discuss the health consequences of alcohol abuse in detail in Chapter 13.

depressants: A category of drugs that decrease activity in the central nervous system, slow down bodily functions, and reduce sensitivity to outside stimulation; also called "downers."

alcohol: A central nervous system depressant.

Cultural Variations in the Use and Abuse of Alcohol There is great cultural variation in drinking habits and styles, and in attitudes toward alcohol. Moderate drinking is prevalent in some American ethnic groups, most notably Jewish, Greek, Chinese, and Italian (Colón & Wuollet, 1994; Peele, 1984). In these cultures alcohol is used primarily in the family or larger social settings where young people are gradually included. Alcohol is rarely used excessively and is controlled by cultural norms and social customs. Alcohol use is rare or nonexistent among some religious groups in the United States, especially the Amish, Mennonites, and Mormons. The use of alcohol is forbidden for members of these three religions, as is the use of other psychoactive drugs (Trimble, 1994).

The use of alcohol in religious rites and social celebrations is more common among some cultural, religious, and ethnic groups within the United States than others.

Culture, more than genes, seems to drive the patterns of use and abuse of alcohol. Certain genetic similarities have been found among Native Americans and Chinese Americans. Yet Native Americans have a high rate of alcoholism, while Chinese Americans have an unusually low rate.

About 36% of Americans are total abstainers, and 64% define themselves as drinkers (McAneny, 1992). More men (72%) drink than women (57%), considerably more Whites (66%) drink than nonwhites (50%), and more college graduates (78%) drink than high school graduates (65%).

Barbiturates: Sedatives That Can Kill in Overdose **Barbiturates** depress the central nervous system, and, depending on the dose, a barbiturate can act as a sedative or a sleeping pill. People who abuse barbiturates become drowsy and confused, their thinking and judgment suffer, and their coordination and reflexes are affected (Henningfield & Ator, 1986). Barbiturates can kill if taken in overdose, and a lethal dose can be as little as only three times the prescribed dose. Alcohol and barbiturates, when taken together, are a potentially fatal combination.

The Minor Tranquilizers: Prescribed by the Millions The popular **minor tranquilizers,** the benzodiazepines, came on the scene in the early 1960s and are sold under the brand names Valium, Librium, Dalmane, and, more recently, Xanax (also used as an antidepressant). About 90 million prescriptions for minor tranquilizers are filled each year. Benzodiazepines are prescribed for several medical and psychological disorders. A more detailed discussion of tranquilizers can be found in Chapter 16.

What are the general effects of narcotics, and what are several drugs in this category?

Narcotics: Drugs from the Opium Poppy **Narcotics** are derived from the opium poppy and produce both a pain-relieving and a calming effect. Opium affects mainly the brain and the bowel. It paralyzes the intestinal muscles, which is why it is used medically to treat diarrhea. If you have ever taken paregoric, you have had a little tincture of opium. Because opium suppresses the cough center, it is used in some cough medicines. Both morphine and codeine, two drugs prescribed for pain, are natural constituents of opium.

A highly addictive narcotic derived from morphine is **heroin.** It has become popular in Hollywood, on college campuses, and at all levels of society, and its use doubled from the mid-1980s to the mid-1990s (Leland, 1996). Heroin addicts describe a sudden "rush" of euphoria, followed by drowsiness, inactivity, and impaired concentration. Withdrawal symptoms begin about 6 to 24 hours after use, and the addict becomes physically sick. Nausea, diarrhea, depression, stomach cramps, insomnia, and pain grow worse and worse until they become intolerable—unless the person gets another fix.

Heroin addicts are typically both physically and psychologically addicted. And, as with other addictions, drug-taking cues—the people, places, and things associated with using—can produce a strong craving for the substance (Hillebrand, 2000). Some researchers have found that people addicted to opiates selectively pay attention to drug-related cues, ignoring virtually all non-drug cues any time the drug

barbiturates: A class of addictive depressants used as sedatives, sleeping pills, and anesthetics; overdoses can cause coma or death.

minor tranquilizer: A central nervous system depressant that calms the user.

narcotics: A class of depressant drugs derived from the opium poppy and producing pain-relieving and calming effects.

heroin: A highly addictive, partly synthetic narcotic derived from morphine.

cues are present (Lubman et al., 2000). However, "selective attention" probably isn't the most descriptive term for what is happening in a drug addict's brain. The addict doesn't consciously choose to pay attention to drug-related cues; it's almost as if his or her entire state of consciousness is hijacked, and the attention is fixed like a magnet toward any cue related to use of the drug.

Inhalants Not all substances that are abused are purchased illegally. Some everyday household products, if sniffed or inhaled, are capable of delivering intoxicating and euphoric highs, as dramatic and perhaps as deadly as the effects of the most dangerous street drugs. Many inhalants can be found in any household—under the kitchen sink or in kitchen cabinets, in the bathroom, or in the garage (Levinthal, 1996). Those most often used by a sample of juvenile offenders were gasoline (57.4%), Freon (40.45%), butane lighter fluid (38.3%), glue (29.8%) and nitrous oxide (23.4%) (McGarvey et al., 1999). Such inhalants produce a quick intoxication and a feeling of euphoria. And not only does psychological dependence often develop, but the toxic effect on body organs—heart, lungs, kidneys, and/or liver—may present major problems. The behavioral effects of inhalants can be as deadly as the physical effects. Some young abusers of inhalants, feeling indestructible, leap off rooftops attempting to fly, dash into oncoming traffic, lie down on railroad tracks, and engage in other dangerous behaviors (Levinthal, 1996).

Most users of inhalants are in junior high school and have friends who also use inhalants (Yarnold, 1996). But some users are much younger. According to one study, the mean age of initial inhalant use was 9.7 years, which puts these first-time inhalant users in 4th or 5th grade (Young et al., 1999).

Hallucinogens: Seeing, Hearing, and Feeling What Is Not There

What are the main effects of hallucinogens, and what are three psychoactive drugs classified as hallucinogens?

The **hallucinogens,** or psychedelics, are drugs that can alter and distort perceptions of time and space, alter mood, and produce feelings of unreality. As the name implies, hallucinogens also cause hallucinations, sensations that have no basis in external reality (Andreasen & Black, 1991; Miller & Gold, 1994). Hallucinogens have been used in religious and recreational rituals and ceremonies in diverse cultures since ancient times (Millman & Beeder, 1994).

Mescaline, the psychedelic derivative from the mescal cactus, has long been used by some groups of Native Americans to produce hallucinations in their religious ceremonies. Other people have also used peyote, another mescal derivative, but typically only to get high. Is the altered state of consciousness induced by either mescaline or peyote the same for Native Americans and for nonreligious recreational users? No, the descriptions of the hallucinatory experiences of these two cultural groups tend to be so different that they do not even seem to be taking the same substance (Ward, 1994). So in these two groups, at least, the culture and the motives, more than the substance itself, seem to define the quality of the altered state.

Rather than producing a relatively predictable effect like most other drugs, hallucinogens usually magnify the mood of the user at the time the drug is taken. The hallucinogens we will discuss are marijuana, LSD, and MDMA.

Marijuana, the most widely used illicit drug in the United States, has been associated with loss of motivation, general apathy, decline in school performance, small brain volume, and stunted growth.

Marijuana: More Harmful Than Once Believed About 20 million people in the United States use marijuana regularly, making it the most widely used illicit drug (Andreasen & Black, 1991). In general, **marijuana** tends to produce a feeling of well-being, promote relaxation, lower inhibitions, and relieve anxiety. The user may experience an increased sensitivity to sights, sounds, and touch, as well as perceptual distortions and a perceived slowing of time.

THC (tetrahydrocannabinol), the ingredient in marijuana that produces the high, remains in the body "for days or even weeks" (Julien, 1995). Marijuana impairs attention and coordination and slows reaction time, and these effects make operating complex machinery such as an automobile dangerous, even after the feeling of intoxication has passed. Marijuana can interfere with concentration, logical thinking, and the ability to form new memories. It can produce fragmentation in thought and confusion in remembering recent occurrences (Herkenham, 1992). A 17-year longitudinal study of Costa Rican men supports the claim that long-term use has a negative impact on short-term memory and the ability to focus sustained attention (Fletcher et al., 1996). Many of the receptors for marijuana are in the hippocampus, which explains why it affects memory (Matsuda et al., 1990). Chronic use of marijuana has been associated with loss of motivation, general apathy, and decline in school performance—referred to as *amotivational syndrome* (Andreasen & Black, 1991). Studies comparing marijuana users who began before age 17 with those who started later show that early marijuana use is associated with a somewhat smaller brain volume and a lower percentage of the all-important gray matter in the brain's cortex. Marijuana users who started younger were also shorter and weighed less than users who started when older (Wilson et al., 2000).

What are some harmful effects of heavy marijuana use?

However, an advisory panel of the National Institute of Drug Abuse, after reviewing the scientific evidence, concluded that marijuana shows promise as a treatment for certain medical conditions. It has been found effective for treating the eye disease glaucoma, for controlling nausea and vomiting in cancer patients receiving chemotherapy, and for improving appetite and curtailing weight loss in some AIDS patients (Fackelmann, 1997). But there is a continuing controversy over whether marijuana should be legalized for medical purposes.

LSD (Lysergic Acid Diethylamide): Mind Altering, Not Mind Expanding

LSD is lysergic acid diethylamide, sometimes referred to simply as "acid." The average LSD "trip" lasts for 10 to 12 hours and usually produces extreme perceptual changes—visual hallucinations and distortions. Emotions can become very intense and unstable, ranging from euphoria to anxiety, panic, depression, or even suicidal thoughts and actions (Miller & Gold, 1994). LSD can cause bad trips that can be terrifying and leave the user in a state of panic. On occasion, bad LSD trips have ended tragically in accidents, death, or suicide. Sometimes a person who has, in the past, taken LSD experiences a **flashback**, a brief recurrence of a previous trip that occurs suddenly and without warning. Flashbacks reportedly can occur for months after LSD use. The use of marijuana and some other drugs may trigger these LSD flashbacks (Gold, 1994).

The number of 12th graders who had used LSD in the previous year doubled from 1985 to 1996, going from 4.4% to 8.8% (Johnston et al., 1997).

MDMA (Ecstasy) **MDMA** (methylene-dioxy-methamphetamine), or Ecstasy, is not a new drug. The patent for the drug was granted to the Merck pharmaceutical company in 1914. An amphetamine derivative with both stimulant and psychedelic effects (similar to those from mescaline), MDMA produces a distinctive form of altered consciousness. It is a popular drug of abuse with teenagers, especially at "raves" (Schwartz & Miller, 1997). The drug's main appeal is its psychological effect—a feeling of relatedness and connectedness with others (Taylor, 1996). But animal experiments with MDMA have revealed some disturbing findings—irreversible destruction of serotonin-releasing neurons (Green & Goodwin, 1996). MDMA is also more toxic than most other hallucinogens, and it should be considered a dangerous drug.

Brain damage—resulting in impairments in memory and verbal reasoning (Morgan, 1999; Reneman et al., 2000) and in tasks that require sustained attention (McCann et al., 1999)—has been linked to chronic, moderate to heavy use of MDMA. The neurotransmitter serotonin has been implicated in the cognitive impairments related to MDMA abuse. Serotonin, as you learned in Chapter 2, influences cognitive

hallucinogens (hal-LU-sin-o-jenz): A category of drugs, sometimes called psychedelics, that alter perception and mood and can cause hallucinations.

marijuana: A hallucinogen with effects ranging from relaxation and giddiness to perceptual distortions and hallucinations.

THC (tetrahydrocannabinol): The principal psychoactive ingredient in marijuana and hashish.

LSD (lysergic acid diethylamide): A powerful hallucinogen with unpredictable effects ranging from perceptual changes and vivid hallucinations to states of panic and terror.

flashback: The brief recurrence, occurring suddenly and without warning at a later time, of effects a person has experienced while taking LSD.

MDMA (Ecstasy): An amphetamine derivative that produces both stimulant and psychedelic effects and can cause permanent damage to the serotonin-releasing neurons.

performance (including memory), as well as moods, sleep cycles, and the ability to control impulses (Reneman et al., 2000; Volkow & Fowler, 2000).

Review & Reflect 4.1 provides a summary of the effects and withdrawal symptoms of the major psychoactive drugs.

Review & Reflect 4.1 The Effects and Withdrawal Symptoms of Some Psychoactive Drugs

Psychoactive Drug	Effects	Withdrawal Symptoms
Stimulants		
Caffeine	Produces wakefulness and alertness; increases metabolism but slows reaction time	Headache, depression, fatigue
Tobacco (nicotine)	Effects range from alertness to calmness; lowers appetite for carbohydrates; increases pulse rate and other metabolic processes	Irritability, anxiety, restlessness, increased appetite
Amphetamines	Increase metabolism and alertness; elevate mood, cause wakefulness, suppress appetite	Fatigue, increased appetite, depression, long periods of sleep, irritability, anxiety
Cocaine	Brings on euphoric mood, energy boost, feeling of excitement; suppresses appetite	Depression, fatigue, increased appetite, long periods of sleep, irritability
Depressants		
Alcohol	First few drinks stimulate and enliven while lowering anxiety and inhibitions; higher doses have a sedative effect, slowing reaction time, impairing motor control and perceptual ability	Tremors, nausea, sweating, depression, weakness, irritability, and in some cases hallucinations
Barbiturates (e.g., phenobarbital)	Promote sleep, have calming and sedative effect, decrease muscular tension, impair coordination and reflexes	Sleeplessness, anxiety; sudden withdrawal can cause seizures, cardiovascular collapse, and death
Tranquilizers (e.g., Valium, Xanax)	Lower anxiety, have calming and sedative effect, decrease muscular tension	Restlessness, anxiety, irritability, muscle tension, difficulty sleeping
Hallucinogens		
Marijuana	Generally produces euphoria, relaxation; affects ability to store new memories	Anxiety, difficulty sleeping, decreased appetite, hyperactivity
LSD	Produces excited exhilaration, hallucinations, experiences perceived as insightful and profound	
MDMA (Ecstasy)	Typically produces euphoria and feelings of understanding others and accepting them; lowers inhibitions; often causes overheating, dehydration, nausea; can cause jaw clenching, eye twitching, and dizziness	Depression, fatigue, and in some cases a "crash," during which the person may be sad, scared, or annoyed

How Drugs Affect the Brain

What effect on the brain do all addictive drugs have in common?

Eating, drinking, and sexual activity—in fact, all natural reinforcers—have one thing in common with all addictive drugs. They increase the availability of the neurotransmitter dopamine in a part of the brain's limbic system known as the *nucleus accumbens.* The stimulation of the nucleus accumbens by dopamine plays an important role in reinforcement and reward (Di Chiara, 1997). Although the nucleus accumbens (Cornish & Kalivas, 2000) and the amygdala are known to play a central role in drug addiction, recent brain-imaging studies have shown that other brain structures are also involved in sustaining addictive behavior (Porrino & Lyons, 2000; Volkow & Fowler, 2000). It is now known that the irrational behavior of substance abuse is associated with dynamic changes in the orbitofrontal cortex and other brain structures to which it is connected. Impaired decision making, irrestible craving for the abused substance, and the willingness to do anything to get it are all sustained in part by this drug-disabled brain area (London et al., 2000).

Where is the orbitofrontal cortex? Point your index finger between your eyes where your nose meets your skull. You are pointing directly toward your orbitofrontal cortex, which lies at the very front of the cortex at its lowermost point, just behind the eye sockets. This brain structure is anatomically connected to the association areas for all five of your senses, to structures in the limbic system (such as the amygdala, which has so much to do with emotions), and to other regions in the frontal cortex that handle decision making (Bechara et al., 2000). Thus, the orbitofrontal cortex is intimately involved in everything you see, hear, touch, taste, and smell, in the emotions you feel, and even in the decisions you make. Now, imagine what happens when it is abnormally activated by illicit drugs! It is no wonder that addictive behavior is so irrational.

Researchers Norma Volkow and others (1999) were the first to pinpoint the part of the orbitofrontal cortex associated with craving in cocaine addicts. The right side of this brain area (but not the left) produced this craving in the addicts when it was activated. Interestingly, this same area was found to be abnormal in people diagnosed with obsessive-compulsive disorder (Volkow & Fowler, 2000).

There is ample evidence that a surge of dopamine is involved in the rewarding and motivational effects produced by a long list of psychoactive drugs, including alcohol, amphetamines, cocaine (Carlson, 1998), marijuana, heroin (Tanda et al., 1997), and nicotine (Pich et al., 1997; Pontieri et al., 1996). Amphetamines affect dopamine transmission directly by stimulating its release and, to some extent, by blocking its reuptake. Cocaine is highly efficient at blocking the reuptake of dopamine at the synapses, thus increasing and prolonging its reinforcing effects (Landry, 1997; Volkow et al., 1997, 1998).

Beyond affecting the dopamine system, opiates such as morphine and heroin mimic the effects of the brain's own *endorphins,* chemicals that have pain-relieving properties and produce a feeling of well-being. Opiate molecules and endorphin molecules have similar shapes, and opiates bind with the same receptors in the brain as endorphins do, producing virtually the same physiological and psychological effects.

Research has shown that alcohol, barbiturates, and benzodiazepines (such as Valium and Librium) act on GABA receptors (Harris et al., 1992). GABA, an inhibitory neurotransmitter, slows down the central nervous system. Thus, stimulating the release of GABA with alcohol or tranquilizers has a calming, sedating effect. If enough GABA is released, it can shut down the brain. This is why alcohol and tranquilizers together are such a potentially deadly duo.

Research on the neurobiology of drug and alcohol addiction continues to shed new light on the problem, and the work in progress may well point the way toward more effective means for dealing with this societal problem.

Remember It!

1. Decreased activity in the central nervous system is the chief effect of
   a. stimulants.
   b. depressants.
   c. hallucinogens.
   d. narcotics.
2. Which of the following is a narcotic?
   a. cocaine c. LSD
   b. heroin d. Valium
3. Narcotics have
   a. pain-relieving effects.
   b. stimulating effects.
   c. energizing effects.
   d. perception-altering effects.
4. Which category of drugs alters perception and mood and can cause hallucinations?
   a. stimulants c. hallucinogens
   b. depressants d. narcotics
5. Which of the following is *not* associated with long-term use of marijuana?
   a. impaired short-term memory
   b. loss of motivation
   c. inability to focus sustained attention
   d. increased risk of heart attack and stroke
6. All addictive drugs increase the effect of the neurotransmitter _______________ in the nucleus accumbens.
   a. acetylcholine c. dopamine
   b. GABA d. serotonin

Answers: 1. b 2. b 3. a 4. c 5. d 6. c

Apply It!

Should You Kick Your Caffeine Habit?

What would mornings be like without a cup of fresh-brewed coffee or hot tea? But could the caffeine these beverages contain be bad for you?

People have been drinking beverages containing caffeine for thousands of years. Records of tea being consumed in China date back to as early as 2737 B.C., and coffee originated in Africa around 575 A.D. The first caffeinated soft drinks were created in the United States in the 1880s. Today, people throughout the world enjoy these beverages and drink them daily. Yet there are numerous misconceptions about caffeine as well as controversy about its possible addicting effects.

The most popular caffeine-containing beverage in the United States is coffee. Americans drink more than half a billion cups of coffee daily, with most coffee drinkers consuming at least two cups. In addition to appreciating coffee's flavor and aroma, coffee drinkers say that it makes them feel more energetic and alert. The caffeine in coffee improves muscular coordination, thus facilitating work activities such as typing, and it may improve memory and reasoning. For people with tight airways, it opens breathing passages. It is also a mild diuretic. Caffeine, in short, is a natural stimulant.

Does caffeine cause health problems? Caffeine has long been suspected of contributing to health problems such as cancer, cardiovascular disease, and osteoporosis. During the past two decades, extensive research has been conducted on possible links between caffeine use and these conditions. The results have been mixed: For every study that implicates caffeine as a possible health risk, another finds no connection. For example, coffee consumption had been linked to increased risk of coronary artery disease and heart attack, but a 1996 study found that when researchers adjusted for cigarette smoking among coffee drinkers, the link disappeared (Mayo Clinic, 1997).

This is not to say that caffeine is entirely harmless. Even a couple of cups of coffee can make you nervous, anxious, and irritable. It can produce heartburn and irritate existing ulcers, and it causes bladder irritation in some people. It can also cause a temporary rise in blood pressure.

Who is most likely to be affected by caffeine? Any health problems related to caffeine consumption are usually found only in people who drink large quantities of coffee—eight or more cups a day (Mayo Clinic, 1997). Most experts agree that moderate consumption of foods and beverages containing caffeine poses no health risk. The U.S.

Food and Drug Administration has classified caffeine as "Generally Recognized As Safe," and the American Medical Association has stated, "Moderate tea or coffee drinkers probably need have no concern for their health relative to their caffeine consumption provided other lifestyle habits (diet, alcohol consumption) are moderate, as well" (quoted in International Food Information Council Foundation [IFIC], 1998).

People differ greatly in their sensitivity to caffeine, however. Some can drink several cups of coffee, tea, or caffeinated soft drink in an hour and feel no effects; others may feel stimulated after drinking a single cup. Thus, the effects of caffeine on an individual depend on the amount consumed, the frequency of consumption, the individual's metabolism, and the individual's sensitivity to caffeine.

Is caffeine addictive? Caffeine may not adversely affect health, but is it addictive? Some people say that they are "addicted" to coffee because they feel unable to start the day without it. What they really mean is that they depend on caffeine's stimulant effects to get them going.

It has been suggested that dependence on caffeine is similar to dependence on alcohol or tobacco. The major evidence for this is that halting caffeine consumption abruptly can cause withdrawal symptoms such as headaches, fatigue, and depression. It is also true that regular consumption leads to a tolerance for many of the effects of caffeine. However, caffeine consumption patterns differ from those associated with serious drug dependence: Caffeine use does not result in a craving for ever-higher doses, and it is not very difficult to stop consuming it. And most consumers of caffeine do not exhibit the compulsive behavior characteristics of those dependent on illicit drugs. As one expert points out, "Addiction means a dysfunctional use of a drug . . . that a drug has taken control of a person's life" (O'Brien, quoted in IFIC, 2000). This is certainly not true in the case of caffeine. According to the World Health Organization, "There is no evidence whatsoever that caffeine use has even remotely comparable physical and social consequences which are associated with serious drugs of abuse" (quoted in IFIC, 1998).

Should you try to kick your caffeine habit? If you are particularly sensitive to caffeine or have been consuming it in large quantities, you may be experiencing side effects such as excessive nervousness—"coffee nerves"—and insomnia. If so, you may wish to cut back on or eliminate caffeine. This does not mean that you have to suffer withdrawal symptoms. Experts agree that these can be avoided by tapering off your consumption gradually—the slower the tapering, the easier the withdrawal. While you're cutting back, decaffeinated coffee, tea, or soft drinks can provide the flavor you're use to without the stimulant effects.

If you do develop withdrawal symptoms such as headaches or nausea, they are likely to last only a day or two and can be alleviated by taking pain-relieving medication. One expert (Haas, 1992) suggests that an alkaline diet may be helpful during the tapering-off period: Increase your consumption of fruits, salads, and soups; avoid meats and baked goods; and drink six to eight glasses of water a day. Finally, if you're not trying to eliminate caffeine altogether, consider avoiding it for three days every two or three weeks to give your body a rest from the continual stimulation.

THINKING CRITICALLY

Evaluation

Suppose you have been hired by a sleep clinic to formulate a questionnaire for evaluating patients' sleep habits. List 10 questions you would include in your questionnaire.

Point/Counterpoint

You hear much debate about the pros and cons of legalizing drugs. Present the most convincing argument possible to support each of these positions:

a. Illicit drugs should be legalized.
b. Illicit drugs should not be legalized.

Psychology in Your Life

You have been asked to make a presentation to 7th and 8th graders about the dangers of drugs. What are the most persuasive general arguments you can give to convince them not to start using drugs? What are some convincing, specific arguments against using each of these drugs: alcohol, marijuana, cigarettes, cocaine, and MDMA (Ecstasy)?

SUMMARY AND REVIEW

WHAT IS CONSCIOUSNESS?

What are some different states of consciousness?

Various states of consciousness include ordinary waking consciousness, daydreaming, sleep, and altered states brought about through meditation, hypnosis, or the use of psychoactive drugs.

Key Terms
consciousness (p. 124); altered state of consciousness (p. 125)

CIRCADIAN RHYTHMS: 24-HOUR HIGHS AND LOWS

What is a circadian rhythm, and which rhythms are most relevant to the study of sleep?

A circadian rhythm is the regular fluctuation in certain body functions from a high point to a low point within a 24-hour period. Two rhythms most relevant to sleep are the sleep/wakefulness cycle and body temperature.

What is the suprachiasmatic nucleus?

The suprachiasmatic nucleus is the body's biological clock, which regulates circadian rhythms and signals the pineal gland to secrete or suppress secretion of melatonin.

What are some problems experienced by people who work rotating shifts?

People working rotating shifts experience a disruption in their circadian rhythms that can cause sleep difficulties; lowered alertness, efficiency, productivity, and safety during subjective night; and a variety of psychological and physical problems.

Key Terms
circadian rhythm (p. 125); suprachiasmatic nucleus (SCN) (p. 126); melatonin (p. 126); subjective night (p. 126)

SLEEP: THAT MYSTERIOUS ONE-THIRD OF LIFE

How does a sleeper react physically during NREM sleep?

During NREM sleep, heart rate and respiration are slow and regular, blood pressure and brain activity are at a 24-hour low point, and there is little body movement and no rapid eye movements.

How does the body respond physically during REM sleep?

During REM sleep, the large muscles of the body are paralyzed, respiration and heart rate are fast and irregular, brain activity increases, and rapid eye movements and vivid dreams occur.

What is the progression of NREM stages and REM sleep that a person follows in a typical night of sleep?

During a typical night, a person sleeps in sleep cycles, each lasting about 90 minutes. The first sleep cycle contains Stages 1, 2, 3, and 4 and REM sleep; the second contains Stages 2, 3, and 4 and REM sleep. In the remaining sleep cycles, the sleeper alternates mainly between Stage 2 and REM sleep, with each sleep cycle having progressively longer REM periods.

How do sleep patterns change over the life span?

Infants and young children have the longest sleep time and largest percentage of REM and slow-wave sleep. Children from age 6 to puberty sleep best. The elderly typically have shorter total sleep time, more awakenings, and substantially less slow-wave sleep.

What factors influence sleep needs?

Factors that influence sleep needs are heredity, the amount of stress in a person's life, and the person's emotional state.

What are the two main theories that attempt to explain the function of sleep?

The two main theories about the function of sleep are the restorative theory and the circadian theory.

How do REM and NREM dreams differ?

REM dreams have a dreamlike, storylike quality and are more vivid, visual, and emotional than the more thoughtlike NREM dreams.

In general, what have researchers found regarding the content of dreams?

Dreams usually reflect the dreamer's preoccupations in waking life. They tend to have commonplace settings, to be more unpleasant than pleasant, and to be less emotional and bizarre than people remember them.

What function does REM sleep appear to serve, and what happens when people are deprived of REM sleep?

REM sleep appears to aid in learning and memory. Following REM deprivation, people experience a REM rebound—an increase in the percentage of REM sleep.

Key Terms
NREM sleep (p. 129); REM sleep (p. 129); sleep cycle (p. 130); delta wave (p. 130); slow-wave sleep (p. 130); Stage 4 sleep (p. 130); restorative theory (p. 133); circadian theory (p. 133); microsleep (p. 133); REM dreams (p. 135); NREM dreams (p. 135); lucid dream (p. 137); REM rebound (p. 138)

SLEEP DISORDERS

What are the characteristics common to sleepwalking and sleep terrors?

Sleepwalking and sleep terrors occur during a partial arousal from Stage 4 sleep, and the person does not come to full consciousness. Episodes are rarely recalled. These disorders are typically found in children, who outgrow them by adolescence, and they tend to run in families.

What is a sleep terror?

A sleep terror is a parasomnia in which the sleeper awakens from Stage 4 sleep with a scream, dazed and groggy, in a panic state, and with a racing heart.

How do nightmares differ from sleep terrors?

Nightmares are frightening dreams that occur during REM sleep and are remembered in vivid detail. Sleep terrors occur during Stage 4 sleep and are rarely remembered, but often involve a single, frightening image.

What are the major symptoms of narcolepsy?

The symptoms of narcolepsy include excessive daytime sleepiness and sudden attacks of REM sleep.

What is sleep apnea?

Sleep apnea is a serious sleep disorder in which a sleeper's breathing stops and the person must awaken briefly to breathe. Its major symptoms are excessive daytime sleepiness and loud snoring.

What is insomnia?

Insomnia is a sleep disorder that involves difficulty in falling or staying asleep, waking too early, or sleep that is light, restless, or of poor quality.

Key Terms

somnambulism (p. 139); sleep terror (p. 140); nightmare (p. 140); narcolepsy (p. 141); sleep apnea (p. 141); insomnia (p. 141)

ALTERING CONSCIOUSNESS THROUGH CONCENTRATION AND SUGGESTION

For what purposes is meditation used?

Meditation is used by some to promote relaxation and reduce arousal, and by others to expand consciousness or attain a higher spiritual level.

What is hypnosis, and when is it most useful?

Hypnosis is a procedure through which a hypnotist uses the power of suggestion to induce changes in thoughts, feelings, sensations, perceptions, or behavior of a subject. It has been used most successfully for the control of pain.

What are the three main theories that have been proposed to explain hypnosis?

The three main theories proposed to explain hypnosis are the sociocognitive theory, the neodissociation theory, and the theory of dissociated control.

Key Terms

meditation (concentrative) (p. 142); hypnosis (p. 143); sociocognitive theory of hypnosis (p. 144); neodissociation theory of hypnosis (p. 145); theory of dissociated control (p. 145)

ALTERED STATES OF CONSCIOUSNESS AND PSYCHOACTIVE DRUGS

What is the difference between physical and psychological drug dependence?

With physical drug dependence, the user develops a drug tolerance so that larger and larger doses are needed to get the same effect. Withdrawal symptoms appear when the drug is discontinued and disappear when the drug is taken again. Psychological drug dependence involves an intense craving for the drug.

How do stimulants affect the user?

Stimulants speed up activity in the central nervous system, suppress appetite, and make a person feel more awake, alert, and energetic.

What effects do amphetamines have on the user?

Use of amphetamines energizes, increases arousal, and suppresses the appetite, but continued use results in exhaustion, depression, and agitation.

How does cocaine affect the user?

Cocaine energizes, causes a feeling of euphoria, and is highly addictive. Heavy use can cause heart damage, seizures, and even heart attacks.

What are some of the effects of depressants, and what drugs make up this category?

Depressants decrease activity in the central nervous system, slow down body functions, and reduce sensitivity to outside stimulation. Depressants include sedative-hypnotics (alcohol, barbiturates, and minor tranquilizers) and narcotics (opiates).

What are the general effects of narcotics, and what are several drugs in this category?

Narcotics, which include opium, codeine, morphine, and heroin, have both pain-relieving and calming effects.

What are the main effects of hallucinogens, and what are three psychoactive drugs classified as hallucinogens?

Hallucinogens—including marijuana, LSD, and MDMA—can alter perception and mood and cause hallucinations.

What are some harmful effects of heavy marijuana use?

There is some evidence that heavy marijuana use can cause memory problems, respiratory damage, loss of motivation, impotence, lowered testosterone level and sperm count, and irregular menstrual cycles.

What effect on the brain do all addictive drugs have in common?

All addictive drugs increase the availability of dopamine in the nucleus accumbens.

Key Terms

psychoactive drug (p. 147); illicit drug (p. 147); physical drug dependence (p. 148); drug tolerance (p. 148); withdrawal symptoms (p. 149); psychological drug dependence (p. 149); stimulants (p. 149); amphetamines (p. 150); cocaine (p. 151); crash (p. 151); crack (p. 151); depressants (p. 152); alcohol (p. 152); barbiturates (p. 153); minor tranquilizers (p. 153); narcotics (p. 153); heroin (p. 153); hallucinogens (p. 154); marijuana (p. 154); THC (p. 155); LSD (p. 155); flashback (p. 155); MDMA (p. 155)

Surf It!

Want to be sure you've absorbed the material in Chapter 4, "States of Consciousness," before the big test? Visiting *www.abacon.com/wood* can put a top grade within your reach. The site is loaded with free practice tests, flashcards, activities, and links to help you review your way to an A. To enliven that inevitable study break, the site also offers personality assessment quizzes and a psychology career corner.

5 Learning

- Classical Conditioning: The Original View
- Classical Conditioning: The Contemporary View
- Operant Conditioning
- Cognitive Learning

Our cat Missy's favorite food is tuna, and she always comes running when that special treat appears. Some time ago, Missy developed the habit of wanting to be put outdoors at about 3:00 A.M. She got her way by hiding somewhere in the house before we went to bed at night. Then, when the spirit moved her, she would leap on the bed or scratch at the bedroom door to awaken us. Obviously, we were motivated to put her outside for the rest of the night so that we could get back to sleep.

Wanting to avoid these unwelcome interruptions, we began a nightly ritual—going through the house looking for Missy in closets and under the beds and calling her name. But she never came when we called her at bedtime, and we were rarely able to find her then. Missy had associated our calling her at that time with being put outside before she was ready.

After many nights of interrupted sleep, we were desperate for a solution to the problem. Then one night, when we were opening a can of soup, Missy raced through the house and slid to a stop in front of her bowl, no doubt expecting delicious chunks of tuna to materialize. She had learned to associate the sound of the can opener with her favorite food.

By applying simple principles of learning, we solved our problem. Now, instead of calling Missy before bedtime, we simply turn the can opener a few times, and she comes rushing to her bowl. We must admit, though, that we feel a little guilty each time we trick her, and we know it's only a matter of time before she catches on.

Our experience with Missy provides examples of two basic types of learning psychologists study: classical conditioning and operant conditioning. In *classical conditioning,* an association is formed between one stimulus and another. A **stimulus** (plural, *stimuli*) is any event or object in the environment to which an organism responds. In Missy's case, the sound of a can opener became associated with food. In *operant conditioning,* an association is formed between a behavior and its consequences. Missy learned to associate coming when her name was called late at night with being put outdoors.

Psychologists also study another form of learning, observational learning. In *observational learning,* individuals learn by observing the behavior of others and then may imitate that behavior. These three kinds of learning are powerful forces that influence human thought and behavior for good and for ill. But let's look at learning more broadly.

Learning may be defined as a relatively permanent change in behavior, knowledge, capability, or attitude that is acquired through experience and cannot be attributed to illness, injury, or maturation. Several parts of this definition warrant further explanation. First, defining learning as a "relatively permanent change" excludes temporary changes that could result from illness, fatigue, or fluctuations in mood. Second, referring to changes that are "acquired through experience" excludes some readily observable changes in behavior that occur as a result of brain injuries or certain diseases. Also, certain observable changes that occur as individuals grow and mature have nothing to do with learning. For example, a young male at puberty does not *learn* to speak in a deeper voice—his voice changes to a lower pitch because of maturation.

Psychologists cannot observe learning directly but must infer that it has occurred. They draw inferences from changes in observable behavior or in measurable capabilities and attitudes. Certainly much learning occurs that psychologists are not able to observe or measure. As a student, you might have experienced occasions when you had learned more than your test scores reflected. But learning does not always result in a change in behavior. Often we learn or acquire a capability that we may not demonstrate until we are motivated to do so.

Learning is one of the most important topics in the field of psychology, and available evidence suggests that we learn through many different avenues. This chapter explores the three basic forms of learning—classical conditioning, operant conditioning, and observational learning (a type of cognitive learning).

stimulus (STIM-yu-lus): Any event or object in the environment to which an organism responds; plural is *stimuli.*

learning: A relatively permanent change in behavior, knowledge, capability, or attitude that is acquired through experience and cannot be attributed to illness, injury, or maturation.

classical conditioning: A learning process through which one stimulus comes to predict the occurrence of another stimulus and to elicit a response similar to or related to the response evoked by that stimulus.

CLASSICAL CONDITIONING: THE ORIGINAL VIEW

Classical conditioning is a form of learning that has a powerful effect on attitudes, likes and dislikes, and emotional responses. It is said to be the simplest form of learning by association (Büchel & Dolan, 2000): We learn to respond in specific ways to a variety of words and symbols. Adolf Hitler, the IRS, Santa Claus, and the

American flag are just sounds and symbols, but they tend to evoke strong emotional responses because of their associations.

When you meet someone who has the same name as another person you like very much, the name may carry such a positive association that you like the new person from the start. The explanation for these feelings seems clear—learning by association. You associate one thing with another—a positive or a negative attitude with a name, a particular gesture, a style of dress, or a manner of speaking. When you hear the name or observe the gesture, that single stimulus calls to mind the positive or negative association. People's lives are profoundly influenced by the associations learned through classical conditioning, sometimes referred to as *respondent conditioning,* or *Pavlovian conditioning.*

Pavlov and Classical Conditioning

What was Pavlov's major contribution to psychology?

3 ways
- classical conditioning learning by associa
- operant conditioning behavior of person. primary or secondary
- observational learning "Modeling" learn by observing others.

Ivan Pavlov (1849–1936) organized and directed research in physiology at the Institute of Experimental Medicine in St. Petersburg, Russia, from 1891 until his death 45 years later. There he conducted his classic experiments on the physiology of digestion, which won him a Nobel Prize in 1904—the first time this honor went to a Russian.

Like so many other important scientific discoveries, Pavlov's contribution to psychology came about quite by accident. To conduct his study of the salivary response in dogs, Pavlov made a small incision in the side of each dog's mouth. Then he attached a tube so that the flow of saliva could be diverted from inside the animal's mouth, through the tube, and into a container, where the saliva was collected and measured.

Pavlov's purpose was to collect the saliva that the dogs would secrete naturally in response to food placed inside the mouth. But he noticed that, in many cases, the dogs would begin to salivate even before the food was presented. Pavlov observed drops of saliva collecting in the containers when the dogs heard the footsteps of the laboratory assistants coming to feed them. He observed saliva collecting when the dogs heard their food dishes rattling, or saw the attendant who fed them, or merely sighted their food. How could an involuntary response such as salivation come to be associated with the sights and sounds involved in feeding? Pavlov spent the rest of his life studying this question. The type of learning he studied is known today as classical conditioning.

Pavlov's Laboratory: Leaving Nothing to Chance Just how meticulous Pavlov was as a researcher is reflected in this description of the laboratory he planned and built in St. Petersburg, Russia, more than a century ago:

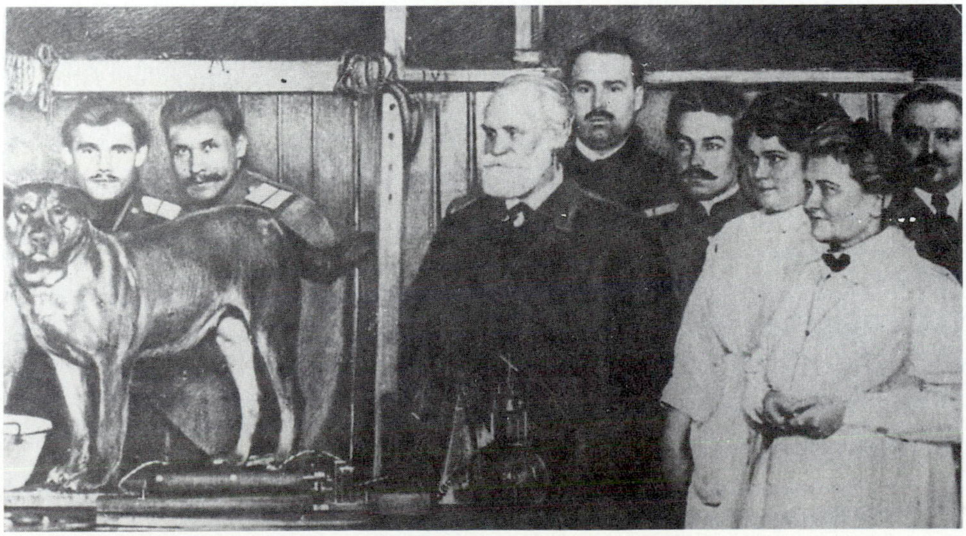

Ivan Pavlov (1849–1936) earned fame by studying the conditioned reflex in dogs.

Figure 5.1

The Experimental Apparatus Used in Pavlov's Classical Conditioning Studies

In Pavlov's classical conditioning studies, the dog was restrained in a harness in the cubicle and isolated from all distractions. An experimenter observed the dog through a one-way mirror and, by remote control, presented the dog with food and other conditioning stimuli. A tube carried the saliva from the dog's mouth to a container where it was measured.

> The windows were covered with extra thick sheets of glass; each room had double steel doors which sealed hermetically when closed; and the steel girders which supported the floors were embedded in sand. A deep moat filled with straw encircled the building. Thus, vibration, noise, temperature extremes, odors, even drafts were eliminated. Nothing could influence the animals except the conditioning stimuli to which they were exposed. (Schultz, 1975, pp. 187–188)

In Pavlov's studies, the dogs were isolated inside soundproof cubicles and placed in harnesses to restrain their movements. From an adjoining cubicle, the experimenter observed the dogs through a one-way mirror. Food and other stimuli were presented and the flow of saliva measured by remote control (see Figure 5.1). What did Pavlov and his colleagues learn?

The Elements and Processes of Classical Conditioning

The Reflex: It Can't Be Helped A **reflex** is an involuntary response to a particular stimulus. Two examples are salivation in response to food placed in the mouth and the eyeblink response to a puff of air (Green & Woodruff-Pak, 2000). There are two kinds of reflexes—conditioned and unconditioned. Think of the term *conditioned* as meaning "learned" and the term *unconditioned* as meaning "unlearned." Salivation in response to food is an unconditioned reflex because it is an inborn, automatic, unlearned response to a particular stimulus. Unconditioned reflexes are built into the nervous system.

When Pavlov observed that his dogs would salivate at the sight of food or the sound of rattling dishes, he realized that this salivation reflex was the result of learning. He called these learned involuntary responses **conditioned reflexes.**

How was classical conditioning accomplished in Pavlov's experiments?

The Conditioned and Unconditioned Stimulus and Response Pavlov (1927/1960) continued to investigate the circumstances under which a conditioned reflex is formed. He used tones, bells, buzzers, lights, geometric shapes, electric shocks, and metronomes in his conditioning experiments. In a typical experiment, food powder was placed in the dog's mouth, causing salivation. Because dogs do not need to be conditioned to salivate to food, salivation to food is an unlearned response, or **unconditioned response (UR).** Any stimulus, such as food, that without learning will automatically elicit, or bring forth, an unconditioned response is called an **unconditioned stimulus (US).**

Remember, a reflex is made up of both a stimulus and a response. Following is a list of some common unconditioned reflexes, showing their two components—the unconditioned stimulus and the unconditioned response.

Unconditioned Reflexes

Unconditioned Stimulus (US)		*Unconditioned Response (UR)*
food	→	salivation
loud noise	→	startle
light in eye	→	contraction of pupil
puff of air in eye	→	eyeblink response

Pavlov demonstrated that dogs could be conditioned to salivate to a variety of stimuli never before associated with food. During the conditioning or acquisition process, the researcher would present a neutral stimulus such as a musical tone shortly before placing food powder in the dog's mouth. The food powder would cause the dog to salivate. Pavlov found that after the tone and food were paired many times, usually 20 or more, the tone alone would elicit salivation (Pavlov, 1927/1960, p. 385). Because dogs do not naturally salivate in response to musical tones, he concluded that this salivation was a learned response. Pavlov called the tone the learned stimulus, or **conditioned stimulus (CS),** and salivation to the tone the learned response, or **conditioned response (CR).** (See Figure 5.2.)

reflex: An involuntary response to a particular stimulus, such as the eyeblink response to a puff of air or salivation when food is placed in the mouth.

conditioned reflex: A learned reflex rather than a naturally occurring one.

unconditioned response (UR): A response that is invariably elicited by the unconditioned stimulus without prior learning.

unconditioned stimulus (US): A stimulus that elicits a specific response without prior learning.

conditioned stimulus (CS): A neutral stimulus that, after repeated pairing with an unconditioned stimulus, becomes associated with it and elicits a conditioned response.

conditioned response (CR): That response that comes to be elicited by a conditioned stimulus as a result of its repeated pairing with an unconditioned stimulus.

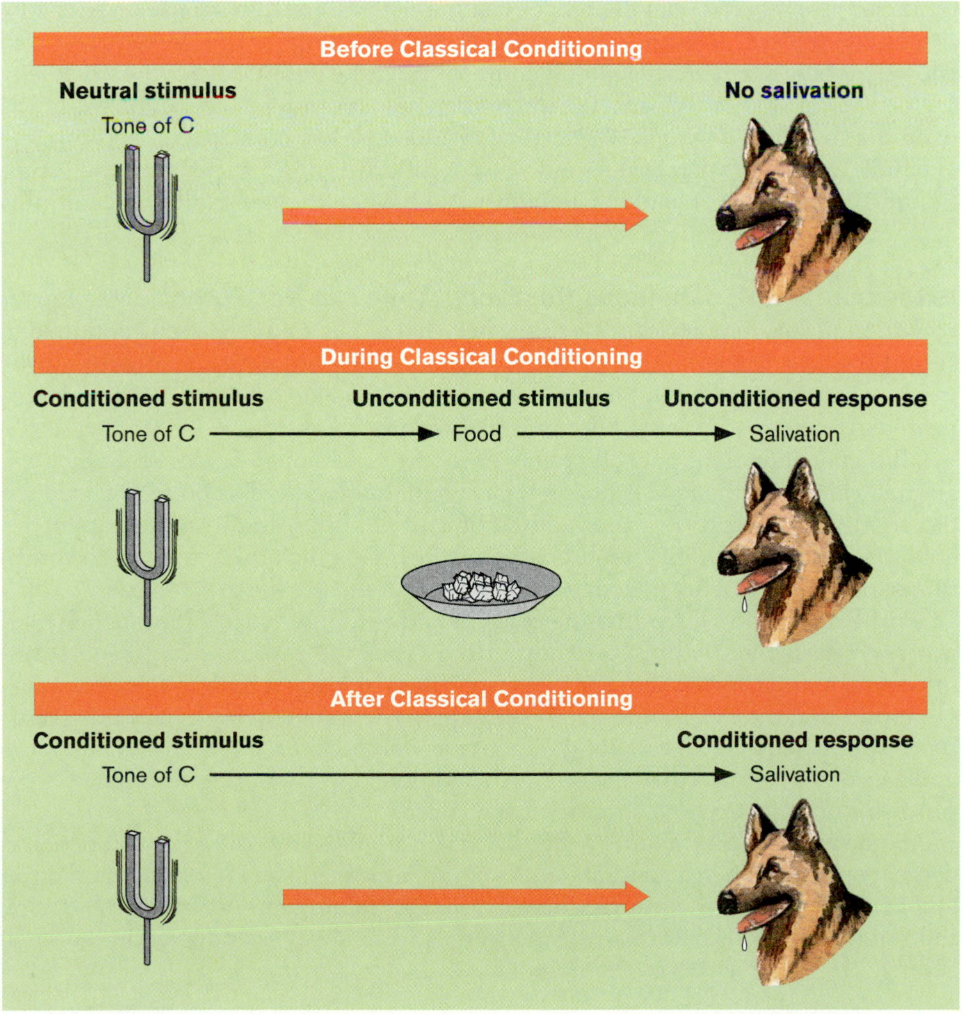

Figure 5.2

Classically Conditioning a Salivation Response

A neutral stimulus (a tone) elicits no salivation until it is repeatedly paired with the unconditioned stimulus (food). After many pairings, the neutral stimulus (now called conditioned stimulus) alone produces salivation. Classical conditioning has occurred.

Figure 5.3

Extinction of a Classically Conditioned Response

When a classically conditioned stimulus (the tone) was presented in a series of trials without the unconditioned stimulus (the food), Pavlov's dogs salivated less and less until there was virtually no salivation. But after a 20-minute rest, one sound of the tone caused the conditioned response to reappear in a weakened form (producing only a small amount of salivation), a phenomenon Pavlov called *spontaneous recovery.* (Data from Pavlov, 1927/1960, p. 58.)

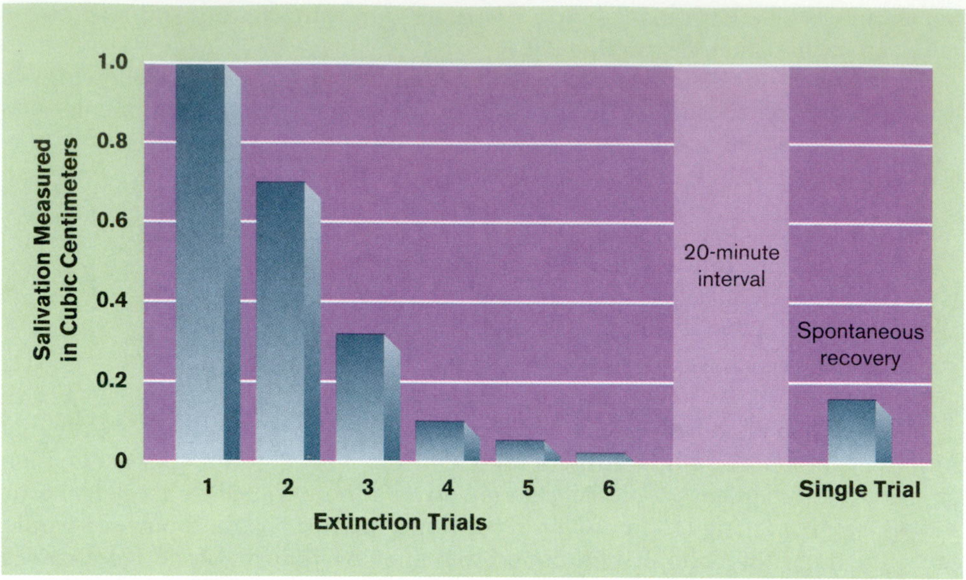

In a modern view of classical conditioning, the conditioned stimulus can be thought of as a signal that the unconditioned stimulus will follow (Schreurs, 1989). In Pavlov's experiment the tone became a signal that food would follow shortly. So, the signal (conditioned stimulus) gives advance warning, and the organism (animal or person) is prepared with the proper response (conditioned response) even before the unconditioned stimulus arrives (Gallistel & Gibbon, 2000). Recent research shows that the cerebellum is involved in forming the simple association between the conditioned stimulus and the unconditioned stimulus in conditioning of the eyeblink response (Green & Woodruff-Pak, 2000). Also, researchers studying the eyeblink response found that it could be conditioned more efficiently if the conditioned stimulus was extended beyond the time when the unconditioned stimulus appeared (Kehoe, 2000).

How does extinction occur in classical conditioning?

Extinction and Spontaneous Recovery: Gone but Not Forgotten After conditioning an animal to salivate to a tone, what would happen if you continued to sound the tone but no longer paired it with food? Pavlov found that without the food, salivation to the tone became weaker and weaker and then finally disappeared altogether—a process known as **extinction.**

But extinction does not completely erase the conditioned response. Rather, the animal learns that the tone is no longer a signal that food will soon follow, and the old conditioned response is gradually inhibited or suppressed. Animals are better able to adapt to a changing environment if they have the ability to discard conditioned responses that are no longer useful or needed.

How did Pavlov learn that the conditioned response, once extinguished, had not been permanently erased or forgotten? After the response had been extinguished, Pavlov allowed the dog to rest and then brought it back to the laboratory. He found that the dog would again salivate to the tone. Pavlov called this recurrence **spontaneous recovery.** But the spontaneously recovered response was weaker and shorter in duration than the original conditioned response. Figure 5.3 shows the processes of extinction and spontaneous recovery.

Some research (Bouton, 1993; Bouton & Ricker, 1994) indicates that extinction is context-specific. When a conditioned response is extinguished in one setting, it can still be elicited in other settings where extinction training has not occurred. Pavlov did not discover this because his experiments were always conducted in the same setting.

extinction: The weakening and often eventual disappearance of a learned response (in classical conditioning, the conditioned response is weakened by repeated presentation of the conditioned stimulus without the unconditioned stimulus).

spontaneous recovery: The reappearance of an extinguished response (in a weaker form) when an organism is exposed to the original conditioned stimulus following a rest period.

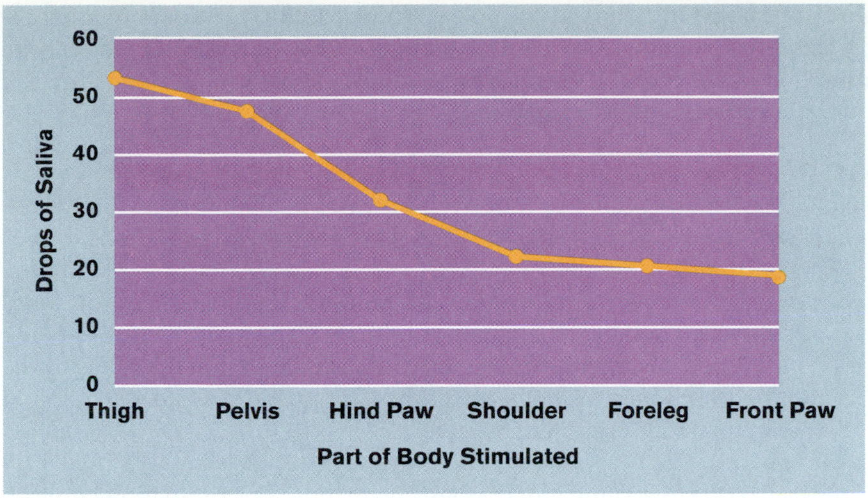

Figure 5.4

Generalization of a Conditioned Response

Pavlov attached small vibrators to different parts of a dog's body. After conditioning salivation to stimulation of the dog's thigh, he stimulated other parts of the dog's body. Due to generalization, the salivation also occurred when other body parts were stimulated. But the farther away from the thigh the stimulus was applied, the weaker the salivation response. (From Pavlov, 1927.)

What is generalization?

Generalization: Responding to Similarities Assume that you have conditioned a dog to salivate when it hears the tone middle C played on the piano. Would it also salivate if you played a slightly different tone, say B or D? Pavlov found that a tone similar to the original conditioned stimulus would produce the conditioned response (salivation), a phenomenon called **generalization.** But the salivation decreased the farther the tone was from the original conditioned stimulus, until the tone became so different that the dog would not salivate at all.

Pavlov was able to demonstrate generalization using other senses, such as touch. He attached a small vibrator to a dog's thigh and conditioned the dog to salivate when the thigh was stimulated. Once generalization was established, salivation also occured when other parts of the dog's body were stimulated. But the farther away the point of stimulation was from the thigh, the weaker the salivation response became (see Figure 5.4).

A child who has been attacked by a dog can develop a long-lasting fear of all dogs through the process of generalization.

It is easy to see the value of generalization in daily life. Suppose that as a child you had been bitten by a large, gray dog. To experience fear in the future, you probably would not need to see exactly the same dog—or even one of the same breed or color—coming toward you. Your original fear would probably generalize to all large dogs of any description.

Because of generalization, we do not need to learn a conditioned response to every stimulus that may differ only slightly from an original one. Rather, we learn to approach or avoid a range of stimuli similar to the one that produced the original conditioned response.

generalization: In classical conditioning, the tendency to make a conditioned response to a stimulus similar to the original conditioned stimulus.

What is discrimination in classical conditioning?

Discrimination: Learning That Stimuli Are Not All Alike Not only must we be able to generalize, we must also learn to distinguish between stimuli that may be very similar. Let's return to the example of a dog being conditioned to a musical tone to trace the process of **discrimination.**

Step 1: The dog is conditioned to salivate in response to the tone C.

Step 2: Generalization occurs, and the dog salivates to a range of musical tones above and below C. The dog salivates less and less as the tone moves away from C.

Step 3: The original tone C is repeatedly paired with food. Neighboring tones are also sounded, but they are not followed by food. The dog is being conditioned to discriminate. Gradually, the salivation response to the neighboring tones (A, B, D, and E) is extinguished, while salivation to the original tone C is strengthened.

Like generalization, discrimination has survival value. Discriminating between the odors of fresh and spoiled milk will spare you an upset stomach. Discriminating between a rattlesnake and a garter snake could save your life.

Higher-Order Conditioning Classical conditioning would be somewhat limited in its effect on behavior if a conditioned response could be produced in only two ways: (1) by the pairing of a conditioned stimulus with an unconditioned stimulus, or (2) through generalization. Fortunately, classical conditioning can occur in another way—through higher-order conditioning. **Higher-order conditioning** takes place when a neutral stimulus is paired with an existing conditioned stimulus, becomes associated with it, and gains the power to elicit the same conditioned response. Suppose that after Pavlov conditioned the dogs to salivate to a tone, he presented a light (a neutral stimulus) immediately before the tone a number of times. Then the light would become associated with the tone, and the dogs would learn to give the salivation response to the light alone.

Higher-order conditioning can account for many of the positive and negative feelings toward stimuli that people associate with certain other people or situations. A student may develop an intense dislike of an algebra professor who has given him his first and only F in college. From then on, he may get angry not only when he sees the professor but when he walks by her classroom or office, when he sees her car in the parking lot, or even when he hears the word *algebra.*

John Watson, Little Albert, and Peter

How did Watson demonstrate that fear could be classically conditioned?

Little Albert and the Conditioned Fear Response: Learning to Fear John Watson (1878–1958) believed that in humans all fears except those of loud noises and loss of support are classically conditioned. In 1919 Watson and his assistant, Rosalie Rayner, conducted a now-famous study to prove that fear could be classically conditioned. The subject of the study, known as Little Albert, was a healthy and emotionally stable 11-month-old infant. When tested, he showed no fear except of the loud noise Watson made by striking a hammer against a steel bar near Albert's head. In this classic study, Watson tested whether he could condition Albert to fear a white rat by causing him to associate the rat with a loud noise.

In the laboratory, Rayner presented Little Albert with a white rat. As Albert reached for the rat, Watson struck the steel bar with a hammer just behind Albert's head. This procedure was repeated, and Albert "jumped violently, fell forward and began to whimper" (Watson & Rayner, 1920, p. 4). A week later, Watson continued the experiment, pairing the rat with the loud noise five more times. Then at the sight of the white rat alone, Albert began to cry.

When Albert returned to the laboratory 5 days later, the fear had generalized to a rabbit and, somewhat less, to a dog, a seal coat, Watson's hair, and a Santa Claus

discrimination: The learned ability to distinguish between similar stimuli so that the conditioned response occurs only to the original conditioned stimulus but not to similar stimuli.

higher-order conditioning: Conditioning that occurs when a neutral stimulus is paired with an existing conditioned stimulus, becomes associated with it, and gains the power to elicit the same conditioned response.

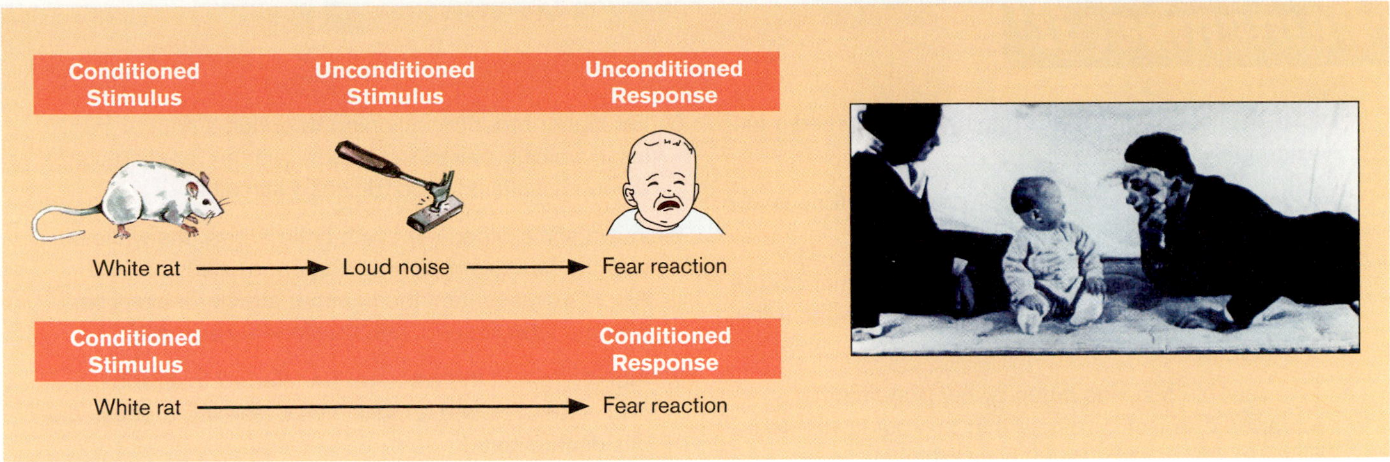

Figure 5.5

The Conditioned Fear Response

Little Albert's fear of a white rat was a conditioned response that was generalized to other stimuli, including a rabbit and, to a lesser extent, a Santa Claus mask.

mask (see Figure 5.5). After 30 days Albert made his final visit to the laboratory. His fears were still evident, although they were somewhat less intense. Watson concluded that conditioned fears "persist and modify personality throughout life" (Watson & Rayner, 1920, p. 12).

Although Watson had formulated techniques for removing conditioned fears, Albert moved out of the city before they could be tried on him. Some of Watson's ideas for removing fears were excellent and laid the groundwork for some behavior therapies used today. One method consisted of pairing the feared object with a positive stimulus and conditioning a new association. In Albert's case, candy or other food could have been given just as the white rat was presented. Another procedure was a modeling technique in which Albert could have observed other children playing happily with the white rat. Since Watson apparently knew that Albert would be moving away before these fear-removal techniques could be applied, he clearly showed a disregard for the child's welfare. Fortunately, the American Psychological Association now has strict ethical standards for the use of human and animal participants in research experiments and would not sanction an experiment such as Watson's.

Removing Peter's Fears: The Triumph of Candy and Patience Some 3 years after his experiment with Little Albert, Watson and a colleague, Mary Cover Jones (1924), found 3-year-old Peter, who, like Albert, was afraid of white rats. He was also afraid of rabbits, a fur coat, feathers, cotton, and a fur rug. Peter's fear of the rabbit was his strongest fear, and this became the target of Watson's fear-removal techniques.

Peter was brought into the laboratory, seated in a high chair, and given candy to eat. A white rabbit in a wire cage was brought into the room but kept far enough away from Peter that it would not upset him. Over the course of 38 therapy sessions, the rabbit was brought closer and closer to Peter, who continued to enjoy his candy. Occasionally some of Peter's friends were brought in to play with the rabbit at a safe distance from Peter so that he could see firsthand that the rabbit did no harm. Toward the end of Peter's therapy, the rabbit was taken out of the cage and eventually put in Peter's lap. By the final session, Peter had grown fond of the rabbit. What is more, he had lost all fear of the fur coat, cotton, and feathers, and he could tolerate the white rats and the fur rug.

Remember It!

1. Classical conditioning was originally researched most extensively by ______________.
2. A dog's salivation in response to a musical tone is a(n) (conditioned, unconditioned) response.
3. The weakening of a conditioned response that occurs when a conditioned stimulus is presented without the unconditioned stimulus is called ______________.
4. Five-year-old Mia was bitten by her grandmother's labrador. She won't go near that dog but seems to have no fear of other dogs, even other labradors. Which learning process accounts for her behavior?

   a. generalization c. extinction

   b. discrimination d. spontaneous recovery

5. For higher-order conditioning to occur, a neutral stimulus is typically paired repeatedly with an (existing conditioned stimulus; unconditioned stimulus).
6. In Watson's experiment with Little Albert, the white rat was the (conditioned, unconditioned) stimulus, and Albert's crying when the hammer struck the steel bar was the (conditioned, unconditioned) response.
7. Albert's fear of the white rat transferred to a rabbit, a dog, a fur coat, and a mask. What learning process did this demonstrate?

   a. generalization c. extinction

   b. discrimination d. spontaneous recovery

Answers: 1. Ivan Pavlov 2. conditioned 3. extinction 4. b 5. existing conditioned stimulus 6. conditioned, unconditioned 7. a

So far we have considered classical conditioning primarily in relation to Pavlov's dogs and Watson's human subjects. How is classical conditioning viewed today?

CLASSICAL CONDITIONING: THE CONTEMPORARY VIEW

Pavlov viewed classical conditioning as a mechanical process that resulted in a conditioned reflex more or less automatically if certain conditions were met. He believed that the critical element in classical conditioning was the repeated pairing of the conditioned stimulus and the unconditioned stimulus, with only a brief interval between the two. The most effective arrangement, according to Pavlov, was to present the conditioned stimulus slightly before the unconditioned stimulus. He thought that if these criteria were met, almost anything could act as a conditioned stimulus.

Beginning in the late 1960s, researchers began to discover exceptions to some of the general principles Pavlov identified. Today, many researchers acknowledge that classical conditioning is a much more complex phenomenon than originally thought.

The Cognitive Perspective: Prediction Is the Critical Element

According to Rescorla, what is the critical element in classical conditioning?

More than any other single researcher, Robert Rescorla (1967, 1968, 1988; Rescorla & Wagner, 1972) is responsible for changing how psychologists view classical conditioning. Rescorla was able to demonstrate that the critical element in classical conditioning is not the repeated pairing of the conditioned stimulus and unconditioned stimulus. Rather, the important factor is whether the conditioned stimulus provides information that enables the organism to reliably predict the occurrence of the unconditioned stimulus. How was Rescorla able to prove that prediction is the critical element?

Using rats as his subjects, Rescorla used a tone as the conditioned stimulus and a shock as the unconditioned stimulus. For one group of rats the tone and shock were paired 20 times—the shock always occurred during the tone. The other group of rats also received a shock 20 times while the tone was sounding, but this group also received 20 shocks that were not paired with the tone. If the only critical element in classical conditioning was the number of pairings of the conditioned stimulus and the unconditioned stimulus, both groups of rats should have developed a conditioned fear response to the tone, because both groups experienced exactly the same number of pairings of tone and shock. But this was not the case. Only the first group, for which the tone was a reliable predictor of the shock, developed the conditioned fear response to the tone. The second group showed little evidence of conditioning, because the shock was just as likely to occur without the tone as with it. In other words, for this group the tone provided no additional information about the shock.

More evidence that a classically conditioned response depends on information provided by the conditioned stimulus about the unconditioned stimulus comes from research by Leon Kamin (1968) on a phenomenon known as *blocking.* Blocking occurs when previous conditioning to one stimulus prevents conditioning to a second stimulus with which it has been paired.

Using rats as subjects, Kamin repeatedly sounded a tone slightly before a shock was delivered. As expected, the rats developed a conditioned fear response to the tone. Then Kamin repeatedly presented a light along with the tone just before the shock was administered. Again, the rats exhibited the conditioned fear response to the tone/light combination. Next, Kamin wondered if the rats would exhibit a conditioned fear response to the light alone, but he found little evidence of such conditioning. What was Kamin's explanation? Because the tone already signaled the occurrence of the shock, the light provided no useful additional information that added to the predictability of the shock. Previous conditioning to the tone *blocked* conditioning to the light.

Both Rescorla's and Kamin's research demonstrates that the mere pairing of a second stimulus with an unconditioned stimulus will not result in a conditioned response. But if the second stimulus provides information that helps predict the occurrence of the unconditioned stimulus, a conditioned response will occur.

Rescorla (1988) takes a broader view of classical conditioning than Pavlov did. He does not see it as "a stupid process by which the organism willy-nilly forms associations between any two stimuli that happen to co-occur" (p. 154). Rather, for Rescorla, classical conditioning is the learning of relations between stimuli that results when one stimulus gives information about another. And this learning goes beyond simply forming an association between the conditioned stimulus and the unconditioned stimulus. Also learned are relations between and among other stimuli in the context. In this way, humans and other animals are able construct a more complete representation of their world.

Some recent research provides support for Rescorla's model of learning (Fox et al., 2000a), but other recent research does not. A study by Lachnit and Kimmel (2000) used human participants and concluded that humans' responses are probably also affected by abstract features in addition to concrete stimuli, such as those used by Rescorla in his studies with animals. For example, if an animal and a human both received an electric shock, the animal would dislike the shock itself, which is the concrete stimulus. However, the human might take the dislike a step further by attempting to figure out why he or she received the shock in the first place and what might be done to avoid future shocks.

But what about Pavlov's belief that almost any neutral stimulus could serve as a conditioned stimulus? Later research revealed that organisms' biological predispositions can limit the associations they can form through classical conditioning.

taste aversion: The dislike and/or avoidance of a particular food that has been associated with nausea or discomfort.

Biological Predispositions: Their Role in Classical Conditioning

Remember that Watson conditioned Little Albert to fear the white rat by pairing the presence of the rat with the loud noise of a hammer striking against a steel bar. Do you think Watson could just as easily have conditioned a fear response to a flower or a piece of ribbon?

Why do most fears and phobias people have center around a fairly limited number of stimuli—especially snakes, insects, the dark, storms, and heights? According to Martin Seligman (1972), most common fears "are related to the survival of the human species through the long course of evolution" (p. 455). Seligman (1970) has suggested that humans and other animals are *prepared* to associate only certain stimuli with particular consequences. One example of this preparedness is the tendency to develop **taste aversions**—the intense dislike and/or avoidance of particular foods that have been associated with nausea or discomfort.

Experiencing nausea and vomiting after eating a certain food is often enough to condition a long-lasting taste aversion. Taste aversions can be classically conditioned when the delay between the conditioned stimulus (food or drink) and the unconditioned stimulus (nausea) is as long as 12 hours. Researchers believe that many taste aversions begin when children are between 2 and 3 years old, so adults may not remember how they originated (Rozin & Zellner, 1985).

What two exceptions to traditional ideas about classical conditioning did Garcia and Koelling find?

In a classic study on taste aversion, Garcia and Koelling (1966) exposed rats to a three-way conditioned stimulus: a bright light, a clicking noise, and flavored water. For one group of rats, the unconditioned stimulus was being exposed to either X rays or lithium chloride, either of which produces nausea and vomiting several hours after exposure; for the other group, the unconditioned stimulus was an electric shock to the feet. The rats that were made ill associated the flavored water with the nausea and avoided it at all times, but they would still drink unflavored water when the bright light and the clicking sound were present. The rats receiving the electric shock continued to prefer the flavored water over unflavored water, but they would not drink at all in the presence of the bright light or the clicking sound. The rats in one group associated nausea only with the flavored water; those in the other group associated electric shock only with the light and the sound.

Garcia and Koelling's research established two exceptions to traditional ideas of classical conditioning. First, the finding that rats formed an association between nausea and flavored water ingested several hours earlier contradicted the principle that the conditioned stimulus must be presented shortly before the unconditioned stimulus. The finding that rats associated electric shock *only* with noise and light, and nausea *only* with flavored water revealed that animals are apparently biologically predisposed to make certain associations and that associations between *any* two stimuli cannot be readily conditioned.

Chemotherapy treatments can result in conditioned taste aversions, but providing patients with a "scapegoat" target for the taste aversion can help them maintain a proper diet.

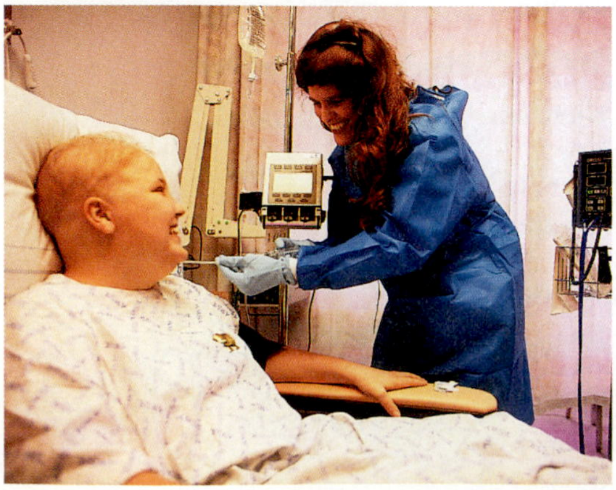

Other research on conditioned taste aversions has led to the solution of practical problems such as controlling predators and helping cancer patients. Plagued by wild coyotes attacking and killing their sheep, ranchers in the western United States tried to solve their problem simply by killing the coyotes. But Gustavson and others (1974) applied research on conditioned taste aversion in animals to spare the lambs and save the coyotes. They set out lamb flesh laced with lithium chloride, a poison that made the coyotes extremely ill but was not fatal. The plan was so successful that after one or two experiences, the coyotes would get sick even at the sight of a lamb.

Knowledge about conditioned taste aversion is useful in solving other problems as well. One unfortunate side effect of chemotherapy treatment is that cancer patients often associate nausea with the foods they have eaten in the several hours before the treatment (Jacobsen et al., 1993). As a result, patients often develop taste aversions to foods they normally eat. This response can lead to a loss of appetite and weight at a time when good nutrition is particularly important.

Bernstein and others (1982; Bernstein, 1985) devised a technique to help patients avoid aversions to desirable foods. A group of cancer patients were given a novel-tasting, maple-flavored ice cream before chemotherapy. The nausea caused by the treatment resulted in a taste aversion to the ice cream. The researchers found that when an unusual or unfamiliar food becomes the "scapegoat," or target for taste aversion, other foods in the patient's diet may be protected, and the patient will continue to eat them regularly. So cancer patients should refrain from eating preferred or nutritious foods prior to chemotherapy. Instead, they should be given an unusual-tasting food shortly before treatment.

Classical Conditioning in Everyday Life

What types of responses can be acquired through classical conditioning?

Do certain songs have special meaning because they remind you of a current or past love? Do you find the scent of a particular perfume or after-shave pleasant or unpleasant because it reminds you of a certain person? Many of our emotional responses, whether positive or negative, result from classical conditioning (often higher-order conditioning). Neutral cues become associated with particular people, objects, locations, situations, or even words and develop the power to elicit the same feeling as the original stimulus.

Fears and phobias often result from classical conditioning. For example, many people who have had painful dental work develop a dental phobia. Not only do they come to fear the dentist's drill, but they develop anxiety in response to a wide range of stimuli associated with it—the dental chair, the waiting room, or even the building where the dentist's office is located. In conditioning of fear, a conditioned stimulus (CS), such as a tone, is paired with an aversive stimulus (US), such as a foot shock, in a new or unfamiliar environment (context). After just one pairing, an animal exhibits a long-lasting fear of the CS *and* of the context. An intact amygdala is required for conditioning of fear to both the context and the tone (CS), and context fear conditioning further depends on the hippocampus (Anagnostaras et al., 2000). Other experiments have confirmed that animals that receive a foot shock in an unfamiliar environment (context) show far stronger fear conditioning to that context than do animals that receive a foot shock in a familiar context (Antoniadis & McDonald, 2000; Hall et al., 2000).

Through classical conditioning, environmental cues associated with drug use can become conditioned stimuli and later produce the conditioned responses of drug craving (London et al., 2000). As you learned in Chapter 4, the brain's reward circuits are highly responsive to all forms of conditioning (Volkow & Fowler, 2000). And the conditioned stimuli associated with drugs become powerful, often irresistible, forces that lead individuals to seek out and use those substances (Porrino & Lyons, 2000). Consequently, drug counselors strongly urge recovering addicts to avoid any cues (people, places, and things) associated with their past drug use. Relapse is far more common in those who do not avoid such associated environmental cues. This observation helps explain why the American soldiers who used heroin heavily in Vietnam had only a 7% addiction rate when they returned to the United States, where they no longer encountered many of the environmental cues associated with use of the drug (Basic Behavioral Science Task Force, 1996).

Businesspeople wine and dine customers, hoping that they and their product or service will elicit the same positive response as the pleasant setting and fine food. Advertisers seek to classically condition consumers when they show products along with great-looking models or celebrities or in situations where people are enjoying themselves. Advertisers reason that if the "neutral" product is associated with people, objects, or situations consumers particularly like, then in time the product will elicit a similarly positive response. Pavlov found that presenting the tone just before the food was the most efficient way to condition salivation in dogs. Television

Classical conditioning has proved to be a highly effective tool for advertisers. Here a neutral product (clothing) is paired with images of very attractive people.

advertisements, too, are most effective when the products are presented *before* the beautiful people or situations are shown (van den Hout & Merckelbach, 1991).

You might want to get an idea of just how the principles of classical conditioning are applied in TV advertising with the *Try It!*

Research indicates that even the immune system is subject to classical conditioning (Ader, 1985; Ader & Cohen, 1982, 1993; Exton et al., 2000). In the mid-1970s Robert Ader was conducting an experiment with rats, conditioning them to avoid saccharin-sweetened water. Immediately after drinking the sweet water (which rats consider a treat), the rats were injected with a tasteless drug (cyclophosphamide) that causes severe nausea. The conditioning worked, and from that time on, the rats would not drink the sweet water, with or without the drug. Attempting to reverse the conditioned response, Ader had to force-feed the sweet water to the rats for many days; but later, unexpectedly, many of them died. Ader was puzzled, because the saccharin water was in no way lethal. Checking further into the properties of the tasteless drug, Ader learned that it suppresses the immune system. A few doses of an immune-suppressing drug paired with sweetened water had produced a conditioned response. As a result, the sweet water alone continued to suppress the immune system, causing the rats to die. Ader and Cohen successfully repeated the experiment with strict controls to rule out other explanations. How far-reaching the power of classical conditioning must be if a neutral stimulus such as sweetened water can produce effects similar to those of a powerful drug!

Try It!

Some commercials simply give information about a product or place of business. Others attempt to classically condition the viewer to form a positive association. One night while you are watching TV, keep a record of the commercials you see. What proportion rely on classical conditioning? What are the kinds of cues (people, objects, or situations) with which the products are to be associated? Are the products introduced slightly before, during, or after these cues?

Bovbjerg and others (1990) found that in some cancer patients undergoing chemotherapy, environmental cues in the treatment setting (context) eventually came to elicit nausea and immune suppression. These were the same conditioned responses that the treatment alone had caused earlier. Other researchers showed that classical conditioning could be used to suppress the immune system in order to prolong the survival of mice heart tissue transplants (Grochowicz et al., 1991). And not only can classically conditioned stimuli suppress the immune system, they can be used to boost it as well (Exton et al., 2000; Markovic et al., 1993).

Recent research (Stanton, 2000) suggests that there are three basic components of learning involved in classical conditioning: the sensorimotor, the affective (emotional), and the cognitive. Even the simplest of conditioned responses, such as the eyeblink reflex, involves all three of these learning components. Sensorimotor learning results in the eyeblink itself and is handled by neural circuits in the cerebellum. The affective component of learning encodes the conditioned "fear" and depends on the neural circuitry of the amygdala. The cognitive component of learning consists of all higher-order learning and memory processes. It forms a representation of the entire conditioning episode, including the relations between the conditioned stimulus (CS) and the unconditioned stimulus (US) and the context (environment) in which conditioning occurs. The neural circuitry handling the cognitive component of conditioning is in the brain's hippocampus (Stanton, 2000; Green & Woodruff-Pak, 2000). Figure 5.6 is a diagram showing the three components of eyeblink conditioning and the brain structures associated with them.

Research clearly indicates that the cerebellum is the essential brain structure for motor (movement) conditioning and also the storage site for the memory traces formed during such conditioning (Steinmetz, 2000; Thompson et al., 2000). Moreover, new research shows that the cerebellum plays a more extensive role than was once believed in cognition, including language learning and memory (Silveri & Misciagna, 2000). Damage to the cerebellum causes some impairments in information-processing speed, learning through conditioning, and certain aspects of mem-

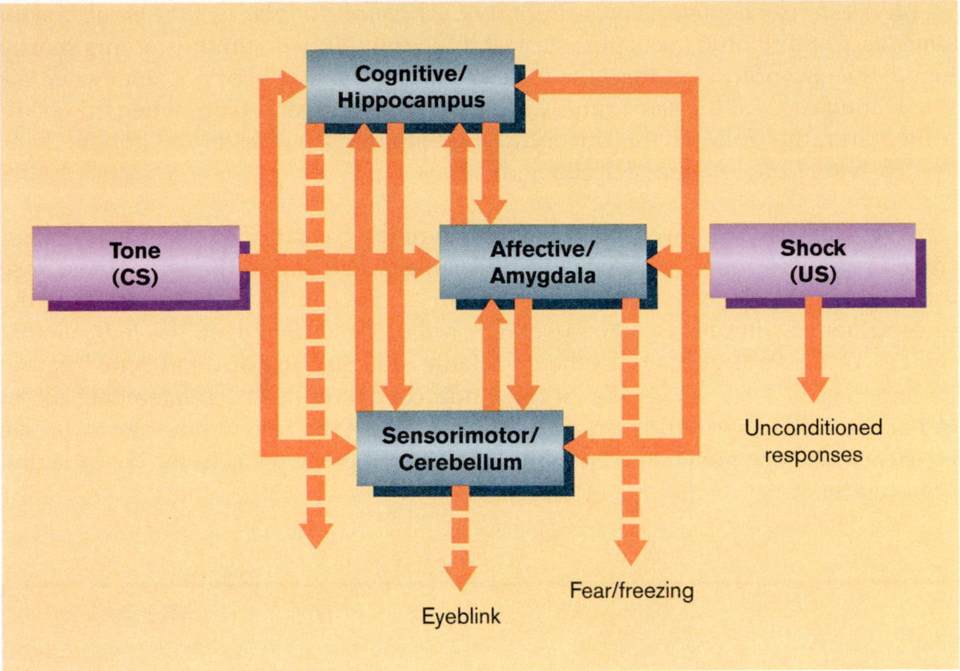

Figure 5.6

Three Components of Eyeblink Conditioning and the Brain Structures Associated with Them

The cognitive component (the higher-order processes of learning and memory) is handled by the hippocampus. The affective (emotional) component of conditioning is processed by the amygdala, and the sensorimotor (movement) component is based in the cerebellum.

ory (Lalonde & Botez-Marquard, 2000). Does the amygdala also store memories of conditioning episodes? Apparently not. Although neural circuits in the amygdala produce the intense emotion that is part of fear conditioning, enduring memories of such conditioning are apparently stored elsewhere in the brain (Lehmann et al., 2000; Vazdarjanova, 2000).

Factors Influencing Classical Conditioning

What are four factors that influence classical conditioning?

In summary, there are four major factors that facilitate the acquisition of a classically conditioned response:

1. *How reliably the conditioned stimulus predicts the unconditioned stimulus.* Rescorla (1967, 1988) has shown that classical conditioning does not occur automatically just because a neutral stimulus is repeatedly paired with an unconditioned stimulus. The neutral stimulus must also reliably predict the occurrence of the unconditioned stimulus. A smoke alarm that never goes off except in response to a fire will elicit more fear when it sounds than one that occasionally gives false alarms. A tone that is *always* followed by food will elicit more salivation than one that is followed by food only some of the time.

2. *The number of pairings of the conditioned stimulus and the unconditioned stimulus.* The number of pairings required to acquire a conditioned response varies considerably, depending on the individual characteristics of the person or animal being conditioned. But in general, the greater the number of pairings, the stronger the conditioned response. But one pairing is all that is needed to classically condition a taste aversion or a strong emotional response to cues associated with some traumatic event, such as an earthquake or rape.

3. *The intensity of the unconditioned stimulus.* If a conditioned stimulus is paired with a very strong unconditioned stimulus, the conditioned response will be stronger and will be acquired more rapidly than if it is paired with a weaker unconditioned stimulus (Gormezano, 1984). Striking the steel bar with the hammer produced stronger and faster conditioning in Little Albert than if Watson had merely clapped his hands behind Albert's head.

4. *The temporal relationship between the conditioned stimulus and the unconditioned stimulus.* Conditioning takes place fastest if the conditioned stimulus occurs shortly before the unconditioned stimulus. It takes place more slowly or not at all when the two stimuli occur at the same time. Conditioning rarely takes place when the conditioned stimulus follows the unconditioned stimulus (Gallistel & Gibbon, 2000; Spetch et al., 1981; Spooner & Kellogg, 1947).

The ideal time between the presentation of the conditioned and the unconditioned stimuli is about ½ second, but this varies according to the type of response being conditioned and the nature and intensity of the conditioned stimulus and the unconditioned stimulus (see Wasserman & Miller, 1997). Some studies indicate that the age of the subject may also be a variable affecting the optimal time interval (Solomon et al., 1991). In general, if the conditioned stimulus occurs too long before the unconditioned stimulus, an association between the two will not form. As we have seen, the one notable exception to this general principle is in the conditioning of taste aversions.

Remember It!

1. According to Rescorla, which is the most critical element in classical conditioning?
   a. how often the conditioned and unconditioned stimuli are paired
   b. presenting the conditioned stimulus slightly before the unconditioned stimulus
   c. using a very intense unconditioned stimulus
   d. always following the conditioned stimulus with the unconditioned stimulus
2. Garcia and Koelling's research supports Pavlov's contention that almost any neutral stimulus can serve as a conditioned stimulus. (true/false)
3. Which of the following responses contradicts the general principle of classical conditioning that the unconditioned stimulus should occur immediately after the conditioned stimulus and the two should be paired repeatedly?
   a. salivation response
   b. immune response
   c. taste aversion
   d. conditioned drug cravings
4. In everyday life, which of the following are *not* acquired through classical conditioning?
   a. positive feelings
   b. negative feelings
   c. skills
   d. fears and phobias
5. Classical conditioning can be used to suppress or to boost the immune system. (true/false)

Answers: 1. d 2. false 3. c 4. c 5. true

OPERANT CONDITIONING

Thorndike and the Law of Effect

What was Thorndike's major contribution to psychology?

Before Pavlov began his experiments with dogs, American psychologist Edward Thorndike (1874–1949) was designing and conducting experiments to study animal intelligence. Profoundly influenced by Darwin's theory of evolution, Thorndike attempted to answer questions about the nature of learning across animal species. He investigated **trial-and-error learning** in cats, dogs, chicks, and monkeys.

In his best-known experiments, Thorndike would place a hungry cat in a wooden box with slats, which was called a *puzzle box.* It was designed so that the animal had to manipulate a simple mechanism—pressing a pedal or pulling down a loop—to escape and claim a food reward just outside the box. The cat would first try to squeeze through the slats; when these attempts failed, it would scratch, bite, and claw inside the box. In time, the cat would accidentally trip the mechanism, which would open the door and release it. Each time, after winning freedom and claiming the food reward, the cat was returned to the box. After many trials, the cat learned through trial and error to open the door almost immediately after being placed in the box.

Based on the puzzle-box experiments, Thorndike (1911/1970) formulated several laws of learning, the most important being the law of effect. The **law of effect** states that the consequence, or effect, of a response will determine whether the tendency to respond in the same way in the future will be strengthened or weakened. Responses closely followed by satisfying consequences are more likely to be repeated. Thorndike (1898) insisted that it was "unnecessary to invoke reasoning" to explain how the learning took place. Thorndike's law of effect formed the conceptual starting point for B. F. Skinner's work in operant conditioning.

trial-and-error learning: Learning that occurs when a response is associated with a successful solution to a problem after a number of unsuccessful responses.

law of effect: Thorndike's law of learning, which states that connections between a stimulus and a response will be strengthened if the response is followed by a satisfying consequence and weakened if the response is followed by discomfort.

operant conditioning: A type of learning in which the consequences of behavior are manipulated in order to increase or decrease that behavior in the future.

B. F. Skinner: A Pioneer in Operant Conditioning

What was Skinner's major contribution to psychology?

Burrhus Frederic Skinner (1904–1990) became fascinated at an early age by the complex tricks he saw trained pigeons perform at country fairs. He was also interested in constructing mechanical devices and in collecting an assortment of animals, which he kept as pets. These interests were destined to play a major role in his later scientific achievements (Bjork, 1993).

After a failed attempt at becoming a writer after graduating from college, Skinner began reading the books of Pavlov and Watson. He became so intrigued that he entered graduate school at Harvard and completed his PhD in psychology in 1931.

Like Watson before him, Skinner believed that the causes of behavior are in the environment and do not result from inner mental events such as thoughts, feelings, or perceptions. Rather, Skinner claimed that these inner mental events are themselves behaviors, and like any other behaviors, are shaped and determined by environmental forces.

Skinner conducted much of his research in operant conditioning at the University of Minnesota in the 1930s and wrote *The Behavior of Organisms* (1938), now a classic. Gaining more attention was his first novel, *Walden Two* (1948b), set in a fictional utopian community where reinforcement principles are used to produce happy, productive, and cooperative citizens. In 1948 Skinner returned to Harvard and continued his research and writing. There he wrote *Science and Human Behavior* (1953), which provides a description of the process of operant conditioning.

In a later and highly controversial book, *Beyond Freedom and Dignity* (1971), Skinner was critical of society's preoccupation with the notion of freedom. He maintained that free will is a myth and that a person's behavior is always shaped and controlled by others—parents, teachers, peers, advertising, television. He argued that rather than leaving the control of human behavior to chance, societies should systematically shape the behavior of their members for the larger good.

Although Skinner's social theories generated controversy, little controversy exists about the significance of his research in operant conditioning.

The Elements and Processes of Operant Conditioning

How are responses acquired through operant conditioning?

Recall that in classical conditioning, the organism does not learn a new response. Rather, it learns to make an old or existing response to a new stimulus. Classically conditioned responses are involuntary or reflexive, and in most cases the person or animal cannot help but respond in expected ways. In contrast, **operant conditioning** is a method for conditioning *voluntary* responses.

Operant conditioning does not begin, as does classical conditioning, with the presentation of a stimulus to elicit a response. Rather, the response comes first, and then the consequence that follows tends to modify this response in the future. In

B. F. Skinner shapes a rat's bar-pressing behavior in a Skinner box.

How is shaping used to condition a response?

operant conditioning, the consequences of behavior are manipulated in order to increase or decrease the frequency of a response or to shape an entirely new response. Behavior that is reinforced—followed by rewarding consequences—tends to be repeated. A **reinforcer** is anything that strengthens or increases the probability of the response it follows. Behavior that is ignored or punished is less likely to be repeated.

Operant conditioning permits the learning of a broad range of new responses. A simple response can be operantly conditioned if a researcher simply waits for it to appear and then reinforces it. But this can be time-consuming. The process can be speeded up with a technique called *shaping*. Shaping also can be used to condition responses that would never occur naturally. Humans can learn to modify their brain-wave patterns through operant conditioning if they are given immediate positive reinforcement for the brain-wave changes that show the desired direction. Such operantly conditioned changes can result in better performance on motor tasks and faster responses on a variety of cognitive tasks (Pulvermüller et al., 2000).

Shaping Behavior: Just a Bit at a Time **Shaping,** a technique B. F. Skinner used, is particularly effective in conditioning complex behaviors. With shaping, rather than waiting for the desired response to occur and then reinforcing it, a researcher (or parent or animal trainer) reinforces any movement in the direction of the desired response, gradually guiding the responses closer and closer to the ultimate goal.

Skinner designed a soundproof apparatus, commonly called a **Skinner box,** with which he conducted his experiments in operant conditioning. One type of box is equipped with a lever, or bar, that a rat presses to gain a reward of food pellets or water from a dispenser. A record of the animal's bar pressing is registered on a device called a *cumulative recorder,* also invented by Skinner. Through the use of shaping, a rat in a Skinner box is conditioned to press a bar for rewards. It may be rewarded first for simply turning toward the bar. The next reward comes only when the rat moves closer to the bar. Each step closer to the bar is rewarded. Next the rat must touch the bar to receive a reward; finally, it is rewarded only when it presses the bar.

Shaping—rewarding **successive approximations** of the desired response—has been used effectively to condition complex behaviors in people as well as other animals. Parents may use shaping to help their children develop good table manners, praising them each time they show an improvement. Teachers often use shaping with disruptive children, reinforcing them at first for very short periods of good behavior and then gradually expecting them to work productively for longer and longer periods. Through shaping, circus animals have learned to perform a wide range of amazing feats, and pigeons have learned to bowl and play Ping-Pong.

Of course, the motive of the shaper is very different from that of the person or animal whose behavior is being shaped. The shaper seeks to change another's behavior by controlling its consequences. The person or animal's motive is to gain rewards or avoid unwanted consequences. You might want to try shaping your own behavior using the next *Try It!*

When athletes such as these New York Mets are on a winning streak, they may engage in superstitious behaviors because they believe these behaviors will maintain their good luck. One example of a superstitious behavior is wearing a particular item of clothing, such as socks, for every game.

Superstitious Behavior: Mistaking a Coincidence for a Cause Sometimes a reward follows a response but the two are not related. Superstitious behavior occurs if an individual falsely believes that a connection exists between an act and its consequences. A gambler in Las Vegas blows on the dice just before he rolls them and wins $1,000. On the next roll, he follows the same ritual and wins again. Although a rewarding event follows the ritual of blowing on the dice, there is no connection between the two.

Superstitious behavior is not confined to humans. Skinner (1948a) developed superstitious behavior in pigeons by giving food rewards every 15 seconds regardless of the pigeons' behavior. Whatever response the pigeons happened to be mak-

Try It!

Use conditioning to modify your own behavior.

1. *Identify the target behavior.* It must be both observable and measurable. You might choose, for example, to increase the amount of time you spend studying.

2. *Gather and record baseline data.* Keep a daily record of how much time you spend on the target behavior for about a week. Also note where the behavior takes place and what cues (or temptations) in the environment precede any slacking off from the target behavior.

3. *Plan your behavior modification program.* Formulate a plan and set goals to either decrease or increase the target behavior.

4. *Choose your reinforcers.* Any activity you enjoy more can be used to reinforce any activity you enjoy less. For example, you could reward yourself with a movie after a specified period of studying.

5. *Set the reinforcement conditions and begin recording and reinforcing your progress.* Be careful not to set your reinforcement goals so high that it becomes nearly impossible to earn a reward. Keep in mind Skinner's concept of shaping–rewarding small steps toward the desired outcome. Be perfectly honest with yourself and claim a reward only when you meet the goals. Chart your progress as you work toward gaining more control over the target behavior.

ing was reinforced, and before long each pigeon developed its own ritual, such as turning counterclockwise in the cage several times or making pendulum movements with its head.

How does extinction occur in operant conditioning?

Extinction: Withholding Reinforcers We have seen that responses followed by reinforcers tend to be repeated and that responses no longer followed by reinforcers will occur less and less frequently and eventually die out. In operant conditioning, **extinction** occurs when reinforcers are withheld. A rat in a Skinner box will eventually stop pressing a bar when it is no longer rewarded with food pellets.

In humans and other animals, the withholding of reinforcement can lead to frustration or even rage. Consider a child having a temper tantrum. If whining and loud demands do not bring the reinforcer, the child may progress to kicking and screaming. If a vending machine takes your coins but fails to deliver candy or soda, you might shake the machine or even kick it before giving up. What we expect but don't get is what makes us angry.

The process of spontaneous recovery, which we discussed in relation to classical conditioning, also occurs in operant conditioning. A rat whose bar pressing has been extinguished may again press the bar a few times when it is returned to the Skinner box after a period of rest.

Generalization and Discrimination Skinner conducted many of his experiments with pigeons placed in a specially designed Skinner box. The box contained small illuminated disks that the pigeons could peck to receive bits of grain from a food tray. Skinner found that **generalization** occurs in operant conditioning. A pigeon reinforced for pecking at a yellow disk is likely to peck at another disk similar in color. The less similar a disk is to the original color, the lower the rate of pecking will be.

Discrimination in operant conditioning involves learning to distinguish between a stimulus that has been reinforced and other stimuli that may be very similar. Discrimination is learned when the response to the original stimulus is reinforced but responses to similar stimuli are not reinforced. For example, to encourage discrimination, a researcher would reinforce the pigeon for pecking at the yellow disk but not for pecking at the orange or red disk. Pigeons have even been conditioned to discriminate between a cubist-style Picasso painting and a Monet with 90% accuracy. However, they weren't able to tell a Renoir from a Cezanne ("Psychologists' pigeons . . . ," 1995).

reinforcer: Anything that strengthens a response or increases the probability that it will occur.

shaping: An operant conditioning technique that consists of gradually molding a desired behavior (response) by reinforcing responses that become progressively closer to it.

Skinner box: A soundproof chamber with a device for delivering food and either a bar for rats to press or a disk for pigeons to peck; used in operant conditioning experiments.

successive approximations: A series of gradual steps, each of which is more like the final desired response.

extinction: The weakening and often eventual disappearance of a learned response (in operant conditioning, the conditioned response is weakened by withholding reinforcement).

generalization: In operant conditioning, the tendency to make the learned response to a stimulus similar to the one for which it was originally reinforced.

discriminative stimulus: A stimulus that signals whether a certain response or behavior is likely to be followed by reward or punishment.

Certain cues come to be associated with reinforcement or punishment. For example, children are more likely to ask their parents for a treat when the parents are smiling than when they are frowning. A stimulus that signals whether a certain response or behavior is likely to be rewarded, ignored, or punished is called a **discriminative stimulus.** If a pigeon's peck at a lighted disk results in a reward but a peck at an unlighted disk does not, the pigeon will soon be pecking at the lighted disk but not at the unlighted one. The presence or absence of the discriminative stimulus, in this case the lighted disk, will control whether the pecking takes place.

Why do children sometimes misbehave with a grandparent but not with a parent, or make one teacher's life miserable yet be model students for another? The children may have learned that in the presence of some people (the discriminative stimuli), their misbehavior will almost certainly lead to punishment, but in the presence of certain other people, it may even be rewarded.

Remember It!

1. Who researched trial-and-error learning using cats in puzzle boxes and formulated the law of effect?

   a. Watson b. Thorndike c. Skinner d. Pavlov

2. Operant conditioning has been researched most extensively by

   a. Watson. b. Thorndike. c. Skinner. d. Pavlov.

3. Operant conditioning can be used effectively for all of the following except

   a. learning new responses.
   b. learning to make an existing response to a new stimulus.
   c. increasing the frequency of an existing response.
   d. decreasing the frequency of an existing response.

4. Even though the B that Sarah wrote looked more like a D, her teacher, Mr. Ramirez, praised her because it was better than her previous attempts. Mr. Ramirez is using a procedure called ______________.

5. Which of the following processes occurs in operant conditioning when reinforcers are withheld?

   a. generalization c. spontaneous recovery
   b. discrimination d. extinction

Answers: 1. b 2. c 3. b 4. shaping 5. d

Reinforcement: What's the Payoff?

What is the goal of both positive reinforcement and negative reinforcement, and how is the goal accomplished with each?

Positive and Negative Reinforcement: Adding the Good, Taking Away the Bad **Reinforcement** is a key concept in operant conditioning and may be defined as any event that strengthens or increases the probability of the response that it follows. There are two types of reinforcement, positive and negative. **Positive reinforcement,** roughly the same thing as a reward, refers to any *positive* consequence that, if applied after a response, increases the probability of that response. Many employees will work hard for a raise or a promotion, salespeople will increase their efforts to get awards and bonuses, students will study to get good grades, and children will throw temper tantrums to get candy or ice cream. In these examples, the raises, promotions, awards, bonuses, good grades, candy, and ice cream are positive reinforcers.

Just as people engage in behaviors to get positive reinforcers, they also engage in behaviors to avoid or escape aversive, or unpleasant, conditions. With **negative reinforcement,** a person's or animal's behavior is reinforced by the termination or avoidance of an aversive condition. If you find that a response successfully ends an aversive condition, you are likely to repeat it. You will turn on the air conditioner to terminate the heat and will get out of bed to turn off a faucet and end the annoying "drip, drip, drip." Heroin addicts will do almost anything to obtain heroin to terminate their painful withdrawal symptoms. In these instances, negative reinforcement involves putting an end to the heat, the dripping faucet, and the withdrawal symptoms.

Responses that end discomfort and those that are followed by rewards are likely to be strengthened or repeated because *both* lead to a more desirable outcome. Some behaviors are influenced by a combination of positive and negative reinforcement. If you eat a plateful of rather disgusting leftovers to relieve intense hunger, then you are eating solely to remove hunger, a negative reinforcer. But if your hunger is relieved by a delicious dinner at a fine restaurant, both positive and negative reinforcement will have played a role. Your hunger has been removed, and the dinner has been a reward in itself.

How do positive and negative reinforcement affect your behavior? Complete the *Try It!* to find out.

reinforcement: An event that follows a response and increases the strength of the response and/or the likelihood that it will be repeated.

positive reinforcement: A reward or pleasant consequence that follows a response and increases the probability that the response will be repeated.

negative reinforcement: The termination of an unpleasant stimulus after a response in order to increase the probability that the response will be repeated.

primary reinforcer: A reinforcer that fulfills a basic physical need for survival and does not depend on learning.

secondary reinforcer: A neutral stimulus that becomes reinforcing after repeated pairings with other reinforcers.

Try It!

Make a chart like the one shown below, and list all your behaviors during the course of a day that were influenced by either positive or negative reinforcement. Also list the behaviors that were influenced by a combination of the two. During that day, were more behaviors positively or negatively reinforced?

Behavior	Positive Reinforcement	Negative Reinforcement	Combination
Ate breakfast *Attended class*			
Totals:			

Primary and Secondary Reinforcers: The Unlearned and the Learned A **primary reinforcer** is one that fulfills a basic physical need for survival and does not depend on learning. Food, water, sleep, and termination of pain are examples of primary reinforcers. And sex is a powerful reinforcer that fulfills a basic physical need for survival of the species. Fortunately, learning does not depend solely on primary reinforcers. If that were the case, people would need to be hungry, thirsty, or sex starved before they would respond at all. Much observed human behavior occurs in response to secondary reinforcers. A **secondary reinforcer** is acquired or learned by association with other reinforcers. Some secondary reinforcers (money, for example) can be exchanged at a later time for other reinforcers. Praise, good grades, awards, applause, attention, and signals of approval such as a smile or a kind word are all examples of secondary reinforcers.

What are the four types of schedules of reinforcement, and which schedule yields the highest response rate and the greatest resistance to extinction?

Schedules of Reinforcement: When Will I Get My Reinforcers? Initially, Skinner conditioned rats by reinforcing each bar-pressing response with a food pellet. Reinforcing every correct response, known as **continuous reinforcement,** is the most efficient way to condition a new response. However, after a response has been conditioned, partial or intermittent reinforcement is more effective in maintaining or increasing the rate of response. **Partial reinforcement** is operating when some but not all responses are reinforced. In real life, reinforcement is almost never continuous. Partial reinforcement is the rule.

Migrant farm workers are paid according to a fixed-ratio schedule. Since their earnings depend on the number of bushels of tomatoes they pick, they are motivated to work quickly.

Partial reinforcement may be administered according to different **schedules of reinforcement.** Different schedules produce distinct rates and patterns of responses, as well as varying degrees of resistance to extinction when reinforcement is discontinued. The effects of reinforcement schedules can vary somewhat with humans depending on any instructions given to participants that could change their expectations (Lattal & Neef, 1996).

The two basic types of schedules are ratio and interval schedules. Ratio schedules require that a certain *number of responses* be made before one of the responses is reinforced. With interval schedules, a given *amount of time* must pass before a reinforcer is administered. These types of schedules are further subdivided into fixed and variable categories. (See Figure 5.7.)

The Fixed-Ratio Schedule On a **fixed-ratio schedule,** a reinforcer is given after a fixed number of nonreinforced responses. If the fixed ratio is set at 30 responses (FR-30), a reinforcer is given after 30 correct responses. Examples are payments to factory workers according to the number of units produced and to migrant farm workers for each bushel of fruit they pick.

The fixed-ratio schedule is a very effective way to maintain a high response rate, because the number of reinforcers received depends directly on the response rate. The faster people or animals respond, the more reinforcers they earn and the sooner they earn them. When large ratios are used, people and animals tend to

Figure 5.7

Four Types of Reinforcement Schedules

Skinner's research revealed distinctive response patterns for four partial reinforcement schedules (the reinforcers are indicated by the diagonal marks). The ratio schedules, based on the number of responses, yielded a higher response rate than the interval schedules, which are based on the amount of time elapsed between reinforcers.

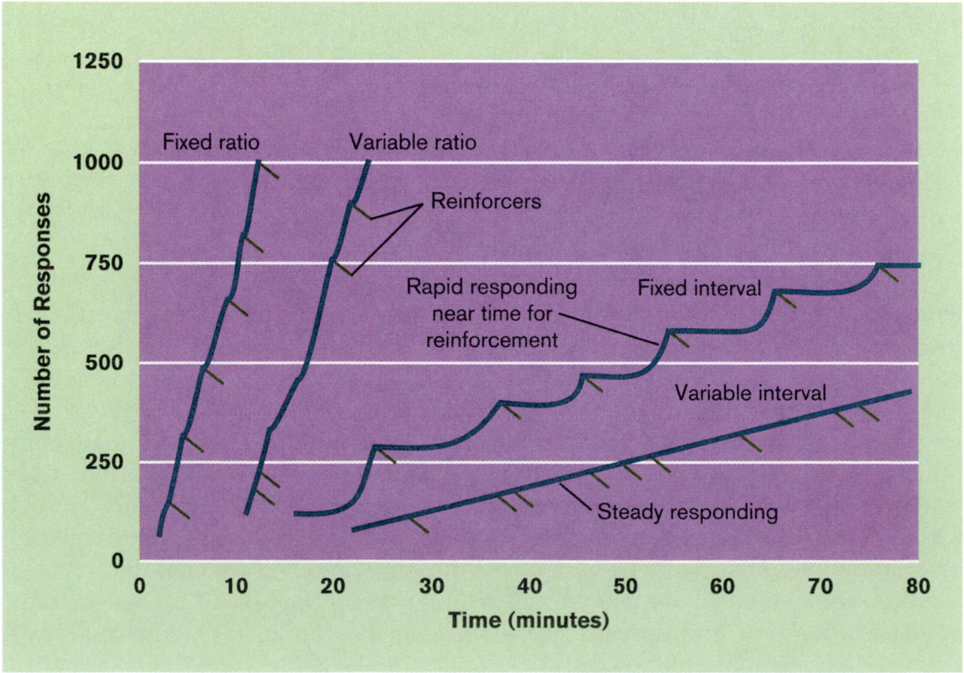

pause after each reinforcement but then return to the characteristic high rate of responding.

The Variable-Ratio Schedule Pauses after reinforcement with a high fixed-ratio schedule normally do not occur with the variable-ratio schedule. On a **variable-ratio schedule,** a reinforcer is given after a varying number of nonreinforced responses based on an average ratio. With a variable ratio of 30 responses (VR-30), people might be reinforced one time after 10 responses, another after 50, another after 30 responses, and so on. They cannot predict exactly which responses will be reinforced, but in this example, reinforcement would average 1 in 30.

Variable-ratio schedules result in higher, more stable rates of responding than fixed-ratio schedules. Skinner (1953) reports that on this schedule "a pigeon may respond as rapidly as five times per second and maintain this rate for many hours" (p. 104). According to Skinner (1988), the variable-ratio schedule is useful because "it maintains behavior against extinction when reinforcers occur only infrequently. The behavior of the dedicated artist, writer, businessman, or scientist is sustained by an occasional, unpredictable reinforcement" (p. 174).

An insurance agent, working on a variable-ratio schedule, may sell policies to 2 clients in a row but have to contact 20 more prospects before making another sale. The best example of the seemingly addictive power of the variable-ratio schedule is found in the gambling casino. Slot machines, roulette wheels, and most other games of chance pay on this type of schedule. In general, the variable-ratio schedule produces the highest response rate and the most resistance to extinction.

The Fixed-Interval Schedule On a **fixed-interval schedule,** a specific time interval must pass before a response is reinforced. For example, on a 60-second fixed-interval schedule (FI-60), a reinforcer is given for the first correct response that occurs 60 seconds after the last reinforced response. People working on salary are reinforced on the fixed-interval schedule.

Unlike ratio schedules, reinforcement on interval schedules does not depend on the number of responses made, only on the one correct response made after the time interval has passed. Characteristic of the fixed-interval schedule is a pause or a sharp decline in responding immediately after each reinforcement and a rapid acceleration in responding just before the next reinforcer is due.

As an example of this schedule, think of a psychology test as a reinforcer (what a joke!) and studying for the test as the desired response. Suppose you have four tests scheduled during the semester. Your study responses will probably drop to zero immediately after the first test, gradually accelerate and perhaps reach a frenzied peak just before the next scheduled exam, then immediately drop to zero again.

The Variable-Interval Schedule Variable-interval schedules eliminate the pause after reinforcement typical of the fixed-interval schedule. On a **variable-interval schedule,** a reinforcer is given after the first correct response following a varying time of nonreinforced responses based on an average time. Rather than being given every 60 seconds, for example, a reinforcer might be given after a 30-second interval, with others following after 90-, 45-, and 75-second intervals. But the average time elapsing between reinforcers would be 60 seconds (VI-60). This schedule maintains remarkably stable and uniform rates of responding, but the response rate is typically lower than that of the ratio schedules, because reinforcement is not tied directly to the *number* of responses made.

Again, a psychology test could be thought of as the reinforcer and studying for the test as the response. Rather than a regularly scheduled exam, however, pop quizzes illustrate the variable-interval schedule. Because you cannot predict when a

continuous reinforcement: Reinforcement that is administered after every desired or correct response; the most effective method of conditioning a new response.

partial reinforcement: A pattern of reinforcement in which some portion, rather than 100%, of the correct responses are reinforced.

schedule of reinforcement: A systematic program for administering reinforcements that has a predictable effect on behavior.

fixed-ratio schedule: A schedule in which a reinforcer is given after a fixed number of correct responses.

variable-ratio schedule: A schedule in which a reinforcer is given after a varying number of nonreinforced responses based on an average ratio.

fixed-interval schedule: A schedule in which a reinforcer is given following the first correct response after a fixed period of time has elapsed.

variable-interval schedule: A schedule in which a reinforcer is given after the first correct response following a varying time of nonreinforcement based on an average time.

Gamblers receive payoffs according to a variable-ratio schedule. They cannot predict when they will be reinforced, so they are highly motivated to keep playing.

Review & Reflect 5.1 Reinforcement Schedules Compared

Schedule of Reinforcement	Response Rate	Pattern of Responses	Resistance to Extinction
Fixed-ratio schedule	Very high	Steady response with low ratio. Brief pause after each reinforcement with very high ratio.	The higher the ratio, the more resistance to extinction.
Variable-ratio schedule	Highest response rate	Constant response pattern, no pauses.	Most resistance to extinction.
Fixed-interval schedule	Lowest response rate	Long pause after reinforcement, followed by gradual acceleration.	The longer the interval, the more resistance to extinction.
Variable-interval schedule	Moderate	Stable, uniform response.	More resistance to extinction than fixed-interval schedule with same average interval.

pop quiz will be given, your study responses will be more uniform and stable. Also, the response rate tends to be higher with shorter intervals and lower with longer ones. If your professor gives a pop quiz once a week on the average, your study response will be higher than if you average only one quiz per month. Random drug testing in the workplace is an excellent example of application of the variable-interval schedule and appears to be quite effective.

Review & Reflect 5.1 summarizes the characteristics of the four schedules of reinforcement.

What is the partial-reinforcement effect?

The Effect of Continuous and Partial Reinforcement on Extinction One way to understand extinction in operant conditioning is to consider how consistently a response is followed by reinforcement. On a continuous schedule, a reinforcer is expected without fail after each correct response. When a reinforcer is withheld, it is noticed immediately. But on a partial-reinforcement schedule, a reinforcer is not expected after every response. Thus, no immediate difference is apparent between the partial-reinforcement schedule and the onset of extinction.

When you put money in a vending machine and pull the lever but no candy or soda appears, you know immediately that something is wrong with the machine. But if you were playing a broken slot machine, you could have many nonreinforced responses before you would suspect the machine of malfunctioning.

Partial reinforcement results in a greater resistance to extinction than does continuous reinforcement (Lerman et al., 1996). This result is known as the **partial-reinforcement effect.** There is an inverse relationship between the percentage of responses that have been reinforced and resistance to extinction. That is, the lower the percentage of responses that are reinforced, the longer extinction will take when reinforcement is withheld. The strongest resistance to extinction ever observed occurred in one experiment in which pigeons were conditioned to peck at a disk. Holland and Skinner (1961) report that "after the response had been maintained on a fixed ratio of 900 and reinforcement was then discontinued, the pigeon emitted 73,000 responses during the first 4½ hours of extinction" (p. 124).

partial-reinforcement effect: The greater resistance to extinction that occurs when a portion, rather than all, of the correct responses are reinforced.

Parents often wonder why their children continue to nag in order to get what they want, even though the parents *usually* do not give in to the nagging. Unwittingly, parents are reinforcing nagging on a variable-ratio schedule, which results in the most persistent behavior. This is why experts always caution parents to be consistent. If parents *never* reward nagging, the behavior will extinguish; if they give in occasionally, it will persist and be extremely hard to extinguish. Reward seeking is indeed a powerful motivating force for both humans and animals. There is little doubt that rewards are among the most important of the influences that shape behavior (Elliott et al., 2000b). However, the results of more than 100 studies suggest that the overuse of tangible rewards may have certain long-term negative effects, such as undermining people's intrinsic motivation to regulate their own behavior (Deci et al., 1999).

Factors Influencing Operant Conditioning

What three factors, in addition to the schedule of reinforcement, influence operant conditioning?

We have seen that responses are acquired more quickly with continuous rather than partial reinforcement and that the schedule of reinforcement influences both response rate and resistance to extinction. Three other factors affect response rate, resistance to extinction, and how quickly a response is acquired:

1. *The magnitude of reinforcement.* In general, as the magnitude of reinforcement increases, acquisition of a response is faster, the rate of responding is higher, and resistance to extinction is greater (Clayton, 1964). Yard crews would be motivated to work harder and faster if they were paid $30 for each yard mowed rather than only $10. Other research indicates that level of performance is also influenced by the relationship between the amount of reinforcement expected and what is actually received (Crespi, 1942). For example, your performance on the job would undoubtedly be affected if your salary were suddenly cut in half. Also, it might improve dramatically, at least temporarily, if your employer doubled your pay.

2. *The immediacy of reinforcement.* In general, responses are conditioned more effectively when reinforcement is immediate. As a rule, the longer the delay in reinforcement, the more slowly a response is acquired (Church, 1989; Mazur, 1993). (See Figure 5.8.) In animals, little learning occurs when there is any delay at all in reinforcement, because even a short delay obscures the relationship between the behavior and the reinforcer. In humans, a reinforcer sometime in the future is usually no match for immediate reinforcement in controlling behavior. Overweight people have difficulty changing their eating habits partly because of the long delay between their behavior change and the rewarding consequences of weight loss.

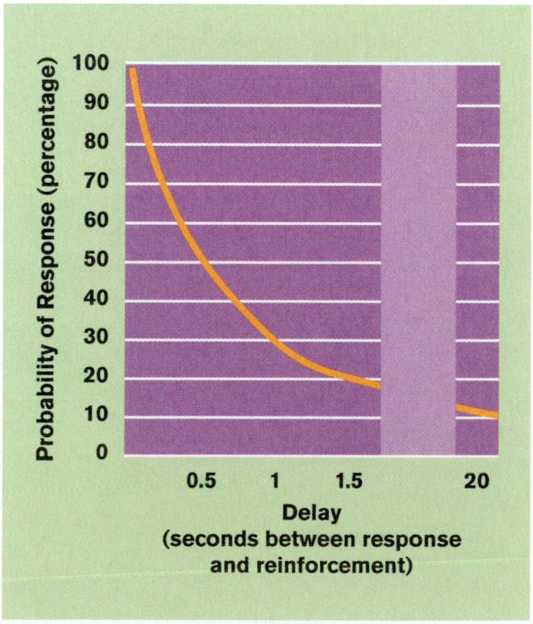

Figure 5.8

The Effect of a Delay in Reinforcement on the Conditioning of a Response

In general, responses are conditioned more effectively when reinforcement is immediate. The longer the delay in reinforcement, the lower the probability that a response will be acquired.

3. *The level of motivation of the learner.* If you are highly motivated to learn to play tennis, you will learn faster and practice more than if you have no interest in the game. Skinner found that when food is the reinforcer, a hungry animal will learn faster than a full animal.

To maximize motivation, he used rats that had been deprived of food for 24 hours and pigeons that were maintained at 75–80% of their normal body weight.

Comparing Classical and Operant Conditioning: What's the Difference?

In summary, the processes of generalization, discrimination, extinction, and spontaneous recovery occur in both classical and operant conditioning. Both types of conditioning depend on associative learning. In classical conditioning, an association is formed between two stimuli—for example, a tone and food, a white rat and a loud noise, a product and a celebrity. In operant conditioning, the association is established between a response and its consequences—studying hard and a high test grade, or, in the world of rats, bar pressing and food.

In classical conditioning, the focus is on what precedes the response. Pavlov focused on what led up to the salivation in his dogs, not on what happened after they salivated. In operant conditioning, the focus is on what follows the response. If a rat's bar pressing or your studying is followed by a reinforcer, that response is more likely to occur in the future.

Generally, in classical conditioning, the subject is passive and responds to the environment rather than acting on it. In operant conditioning, the subject is active and *operates* on the environment. Children *do* something to get their parents' attention or their praise.

In fact, although the differences between operant and classical conditioning are fairly easy to understand, the two types can actually occur together. Recent research shows clearly that during operant conditioning, classically conditioned associations can be formed as well (Brembs & Heisenberg, 2000).

Review & Reflect 5.2 highlights the major differences between classical and operant conditioning.

Review & Reflect 5.2 Classical and Operant Conditioning Compared

Characteristics	Classical Conditioning	Operant Conditioning
Type of association	Between two stimuli	Between a response and its consequence
State of subject	Passive	Active
Focus of attention	On what precedes response	On what follows response
Type of response typically involved	Involuntary or reflexive response	Voluntary response
Bodily response typically involved	Internal responses: emotional and glandular reactions	External responses: muscular and skeletal movement and verbal responses
Range of responses	Relatively simple	Simple to highly complex
Responses learned	Emotional reactions: fears, likes, dislikes	Goal-oriented responses

Remember It!

1. Many people take aspirin to relieve painful headaches. Taking aspirin is a behavior that is likely to continue because of the effect of (positive, negative) reinforcement.
2. (Partial, Continuous) reinforcement is most effective in conditioning a new response; once a response is acquired, (partial, continuous) reinforcement results in greater resistance to extinction.
3. Glen and Megan are both employed raking leaves. Glen is paid $1 for each bag of leaves he rakes; Megan is paid $4 per hour. Glen is paid according to the ______________ schedule; Megan is paid according to the ______________ schedule.
   a. fixed-interval; fixed-ratio
   b. variable-ratio; fixed-interval
   c. variable-ratio; variable-interval
   d. fixed-ratio; fixed-interval
4. Which schedule of reinforcement yields the highest response rate and the greatest resistance to extinction?
   a. variable-ratio schedule
   b. fixed-ratio schedule
   c. variable-interval schedule
   d. fixed-interval schedule
5. Logan's parents have noticed that he has been making his bed every day, and they would like this to continue. Because they understand the partial-reinforcement effect, they will want to reward him *every* time he makes the bed. (true/false)
6. People often engage in behavior that is reinforcing in the short term but is not in their long-term interest. This reflects the influence of
   a. the magnitude of reinforcement.
   b. their level of motivation.
   c. the immediacy of reinforcement.
   d. the schedule of reinforcement.
7. Recall what you have learned about classical and operant conditioning. Which of the following is descriptive of operant conditioning?
   a. An association is formed between a response and its consequence.
   b. The responses acquired are usually emotional reactions.
   c. The subject is usually passive.
   d. The response acquired is usually an involuntary or reflexive response.

Answers: 1. negative 2. Continuous, partial 3. d 4. a 5. false 6. c 7. a

Punishment: That Hurts!

How does punishment differ from negative reinforcement?

In many ways **punishment** is the opposite of reinforcement. Punishment tends to lower the probability of a response by following it with an aversive or unpleasant consequence. And punishment can be accomplished by either adding an unpleasant stimulus or removing a pleasant stimulus. The added unpleasant stimulus might take the form of criticism, a scolding, a disapproving look, a fine, or a prison sentence. The removal of a pleasant stimulus might consist of withholding affection and attention, suspending a driver's license, or taking away a privilege such as watching television.

It is common to confuse punishment and negative reinforcement because both involve an unpleasant condition, but there is a big difference between the two. Punishment may involve adding a negative condition, but with negative reinforcement, a negative condition is terminated or avoided. Moreover, the two are designed to have opposite effects: Punishment is applied to discourage a behavior; negative reinforcement is used to encourage or strengthen a behavior. Unlike punishment, negative reinforcement *increases* the probability of a desired response by removing an unpleasant stimulus when the correct response is made. "Grounding" can be

punishment: The removal of a pleasant stimulus or the application of an unpleasant stimulus, which tends to suppress a response.

used as either punishment or negative reinforcement. If a teenager fails to clean her room after many requests to do so, her parents could ground her for the weekend—a punishment. An alternative approach would be to use negative reinforcement—to tell her she is grounded *until* the room is clean. Which approach is more likely to be effective?

What are some disadvantages of punishment?

The Disadvantages of Punishment: Its Downside A number of potential problems are associated with the use of punishment:

1. According to Skinner, *punishment does not extinguish an undesirable behavior; rather, it suppresses that behavior when the punishing agent is present.* But the behavior is apt to continue when the threat of punishment is removed and in settings where punishment is unlikely. If punishment (imprisonment, fines, and so on) reliably extinguished unlawful behavior, there would be fewer repeat offenders in the criminal justice system.

2. *Punishment indicates that a behavior is unacceptable but does not help people develop more appropriate behaviors.* If punishment is used, it should be administered in conjunction with reinforcement or rewards for appropriate behavior.

3. *The person who is severely punished often becomes fearful and feels angry and hostile toward the punisher.* These reactions may be accompanied by a desire to retaliate or to avoid or escape from the punisher and the punishing situation. Many runaway teenagers leave home to escape physical abuse. Punishment that involves a loss of privileges is more effective than physical punishment and engenders less fear and hostility (Walters & Grusec, 1977).

4. *Punishment frequently leads to aggression.* Those who administer physical punishment may become models of aggressive behavior—people who demonstrate aggression as a way of solving problems and discharging anger. Children of abusive, punishing parents are at greater risk than other children of becoming aggressive and abusive themselves (Widom, 1989b).

If punishment can cause these problems, what can be done to discourage undesirable behavior?

Alternatives to Punishment: Better Ways to Change Behavior Many psychologists believe that removing the rewarding consequences of undesirable behavior is the best way to extinguish a problem behavior. According to this view, parents should extinguish a child's temper tantrums not by punishment but by *never* giving in to the child's demands during a tantrum. A parent might best extinguish problem behavior performed merely to get attention by ignoring it and giving attention to more appropriate behavior. Sometimes, simply explaining why certain behaviors are not appropriate is all that is required to extinguish the behavior.

Using positive reinforcement such as praise will make good behavior more rewarding for children. This approach brings with it the attention that children want and need—attention that often only comes when they misbehave.

It is probably unrealistic to believe that punishment can be dispensed with entirely. If a young child runs into the street, puts a finger near an electrical outlet, or reaches for a hot pan on the stove, a swift punishment may save the child from a potentially disastrous situation.

Review & Reflect 5.3 summarizes the differences between reinforcement and punishment.

What three factors increase the effectiveness of punishment?

Making Punishment More Effective: Some Suggestions Research has revealed several factors that influence the effectiveness of punishment: its *timing*, its *intensity*, and the *consistency* of its application (Parke, 1977).

Review & Reflect 5.3 The Effects of Reinforcement and Punishment

Reinforcement (increases or strengthens a behavior)	Punishment (decreases or suppresses a behavior)
Adding a Positive (positive reinforcement) Presenting food, money, praise, attention, or other rewards.	**Adding a Negative** Delivering a pain-producing or otherwise aversive stimulus, such as a spanking or an electric shock.
Subtracting a Negative (negative reinforcement) Removing or terminating some pain-producing or otherwise aversive stimulus, such as an electric shock.	**Subtracting a Positive** Removing some pleasant stimulus or taking away privileges, such as TV watching, use of automobile.

1. *Punishment is most effective when it is applied during the misbehavior or as soon afterward as possible.* Interrupting the problem behavior is most effective because doing so abruptly halts its rewarding aspects. The longer the delay between the response and the punishment, the less effective the punishment is in suppressing the response (Camp et al., 1967). When there is a delay, most animals do not make the connection between the misbehavior and the punishment. With humans, however, if the punishment must be delayed, the punisher should remind the perpetrator of the incident and explain why the behavior was inappropriate.

2. *Ideally, punishment should be of the minimum severity necessary to suppress the problem behavior.* Animal studies reveal that the more intense the punishment, the greater the suppression of the undesirable behavior (Church, 1963). But the intensity of the punishment should match the seriousness of the misdeed. Unnecessarily severe punishment is likely to produce the negative side effects mentioned earlier. Yet, if the initial punishment is too mild, it will have no effect. Similarly, gradually increasing the intensity of the punishment is not effective because the perpetrator will gradually adapt to it, and the unwanted behavior will persist (Azrin & Holz, 1966). At a minimum, if a behavior is to be suppressed, the punishment must be more punishing than the misbehavior is rewarding. In human terms, a $200 ticket is more likely to suppress the urge to speed than a $2 ticket.

A person who wishes to apply punishment must understand that the purpose of punishment is not to vent anger but rather to modify behavior. Punishment meted out in anger is likely to be more intense than necessary to bring about the desired result.

3. *To be effective, punishment must be applied consistently.* A parent cannot ignore misbehavior one day and punish the same act the next. And both parents should react to the same misbehavior in the same way. An undesired response will be suppressed more effectively when the probability of punishment is high. Would you be tempted to speed if you saw a police car in your rear-view mirror?

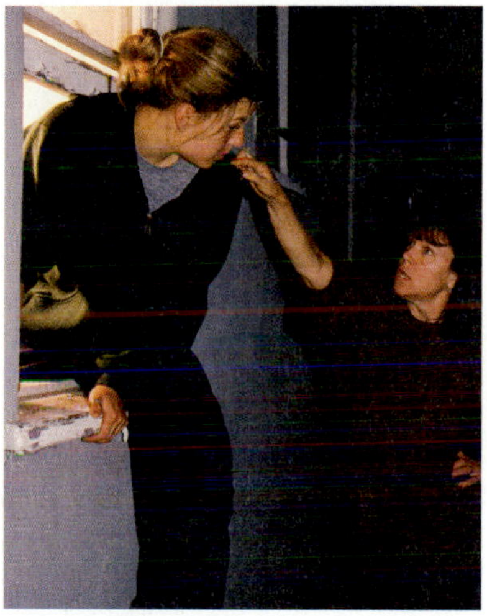

Since punishment works most effectively when applied during or shortly after the misbehavior, this teenager's parent should ground her immediately for trying to sneak out at night.

Culture and Punishment Punishment has been used throughout recorded history to control and suppress people's behavior. It is administered when important values, rules, regulations, and laws are violated. But not all cultures share the same values or have the same laws regulating behavior. U.S. citizens traveling in other countries need to be aware of how different cultures view and administer punishment. A widely publicized incident revealed sharp differences in concepts of crime and punishment between the United States and Singapore.

Michael Fay, an 18-year-old American living in Singapore, was arrested and charged with 53 counts of vandalism, including the spray painting of dozens of cars. He was fined approximately $2,000, sentenced to 4 months in jail, and received four lashes with a rattan cane, an agonizingly painful experience. In justifying their system of punishment, the officials in Singapore were quick to point out that their city, about the same size as Los Angeles, is virtually crime-free—few murders, rapes, beatings, or robberies. Among Americans, sentiment about the caning was mixed. Some, including Michael's parents, viewed it as barbarous and cruel. But many Americans (51% in a CNN poll) expressed the view that caning might be an effective punishment under certain circumstances.

Escape and Avoidance Learning

Learning to perform a behavior because it terminates an aversive event is called *escape learning,* and it reflects the power of negative reinforcement. Running away from a punishing situation and taking aspirin to relieve a pounding headache are examples of escape behavior. In these situations the aversive event has begun and an attempt is being made to escape it.

Avoidance learning, in contrast, depends on two types of conditioning. First, through classical conditioning, an event or condition comes to signal an aversive state. Drinking and driving may be associated with automobile accidents and death. Because of such associations, people may engage in behaviors to avoid the anticipated aversive consequences. Making it a practice to avoid riding in a car with a driver who has been drinking is sensible avoidance behavior.

Many avoidance behaviors are maladaptive, however, and occur in response to phobias. Students who have had a bad experience speaking in front of a class may begin to fear any situation that involves speaking before a group. Such students may avoid taking courses that require class presentations or taking leadership roles that necessitate public speaking. Avoiding such situations prevents them from suffering the perceived dreaded consequences. But the avoidance behavior is negatively reinforced and thus strengthened through operant conditioning. Maladaptive avoidance behaviors are very difficult to extinguish, because people never give themselves a chance to learn that the dreaded consequences probably will not occur, or that they are greatly exaggerated.

Learned Helplessness

There is an important exception to the ability of humans and other animals to learn to escape and avoid aversive situations. Research on learned helplessness suggests that if people or animals are exposed to repeated aversive events that they cannot escape or avoid, they may learn to do nothing—simply to sit or stand helplessly and suffer the punishment. **Learned helplessness** is a passive resignation to aversive conditions learned by repeated exposure to aversive events that are inescapable and unavoidable.

The initial experiment on learned helplessness was conducted by Overmeier and Seligman (1967), who used dogs as their subjects. Dogs in the experimental group were strapped, one at a time, into a harness from which they could not escape and were exposed to electric shocks. Later, these same dogs were placed in a shuttle box with two experimental compartments separated by a low barrier. The dogs then experienced a series of trials in which a warning signal was followed by an electric shock. The floor on one side was electrified, and the dogs should have learned quickly to escape the electric shocks simply by jumping the barrier. Surprisingly, the dogs did not do so; they simply suffered as many shocks as the experimenter chose to deliver *as if* escape were impossible. Another group of dogs, the control group, had not previously experienced the inescapable shock and behaved in an entirely different manner. These dogs quickly learned to jump the barrier when the warning signal sounded and thus to escape the shock. Seligman reported that the dogs expe-

avoidance learning: Learning to avoid events or conditions associated with dreaded or aversive outcomes.

learned helplessness: The learned response of resigning oneself passively to aversive conditions, rather than taking action to change, escape, or avoid them; learned through repeated exposure to inescapable or unavoidable aversive events.

riencing the inescapable shock were less active than normal, suffered loss of appetite, and showed other symptoms resembling those of depression.

Seligman (1975) later reasoned that humans who have suffered painful experiences they could neither avoid nor escape may also experience learned helplessness. Then, having experienced helplessness, they may simply give up and react to disappointment in life by becoming inactive, withdrawn, and depressed (Seligman, 1991).

Applications of Operant Conditioning

What are some applications of operant conditioning?

Operant conditioning has numerous applications, from training animals, to biofeedback, to behavior modification.

Shaping the Behavior of Animals The principles of operant conditioning are used effectively to train animals that help physically challenged people lead more independent lives. Dogs and monkeys have been trained to help people who are paralyzed or confined to wheelchairs, and of course, for years, seeing-eye dogs have been trained to assist the blind.

Through the use of shaping, animals at zoos, circuses, and marine parks have been conditioned to perform a wide range of amazing feats. After conditioning thousands of animals from over 38 different species to perform numerous feats for advertising and entertainment purposes, Breland and Breland (1967) concluded that biological predispositions in various species can affect how easily responses can be learned. When an animal's instinctual behavior runs counter to the behavior being conditioned, the animal will eventually resume its instinctual behavior, a phenomenon known as *instinctual drift*. For example, picking up coins and depositing them in a bank is a task that runs counter to the natural tendencies of raccoons and pigs. In time, a raccoon will hold the coins and rub them together instead of dropping them in the bank, and the pigs will drop them on the ground and push them with their snouts.

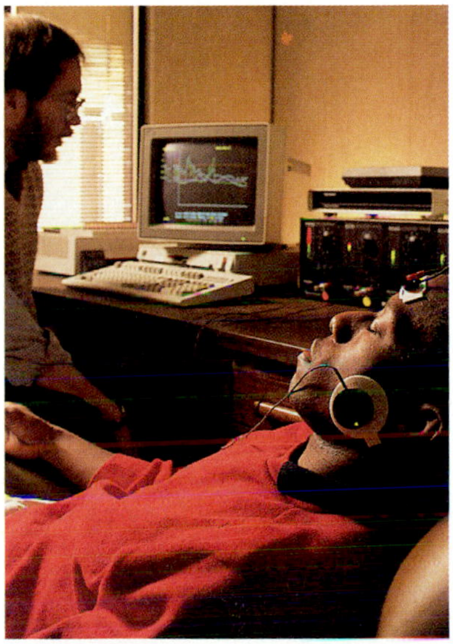

With biofeedback devices, people can see or hear evidence of internal physiological states and learn how to control them through various mental strategies.

Biofeedback: Observable Evidence of Internal Processes For years scientists believed that internal responses such as heart rate, brain-wave patterns, and blood flow were not subject to operant conditioning. It is now known that when people are given very precise feedback about these internal processes, they can learn, with practice, to exercise control over them. **Biofeedback** is a way of getting information about internal biological states. Biofeedback devices have sensors that monitor slight changes in these internal responses and then amplify and convert them into visual or auditory signals. Thus, people can *see* or *hear* evidence of internal physiological processes, and by trying out various strategies (thoughts, feelings, or images), they can learn which ones routinely increase, decrease, or maintain a particular level of activity.

Biofeedback has been used to regulate heart rate and to control migraine and tension headaches, gastrointestinal disorders, asthma, anxiety tension states, epilepsy, sexual dysfunctions, and neuromuscular disorders such as cerebral palsy, spinal-cord injuries, and stroke (Kalish, 1981; L. Miller, 1989; N. E. Miller, 1985).

biofeedback: The use of sensitive equipment to give people precise feedback about internal physiological processes so that they can learn, with practice, to exercise control over them.

behavior modification: The systematic application of the learning principles of operant conditioning, classical conditioning, or observational learning to individuals or groups in order to eliminate undesirable behavior and/or encourage desirable behavior.

token economy: A program that motivates and reinforces socially acceptable behaviors with tokens that can be exchanged for desired items or privileges.

Behavior Modification: Changing One's Act **Behavior modification** is a method of changing behavior through a systematic program based on the principles of learning—classical conditioning, operant conditioning, or observational learning (which we will discuss soon). Most behavior modification programs use the principles of operant conditioning.

Many institutions—schools, mental hospitals, homes for youthful offenders, prisons—have used behavior modification programs with varying degrees of success. Institutions are well suited to such techniques because they provide a restricted environment where the consequences of behavior can be more strictly controlled. Some institutions such as prisons or mental hospitals use a **token economy**—a program that motivates socially desirable behavior by reinforcing it with tokens. The tokens (poker chips or coupons) may later be exchanged for desired goods like candy or cigarettes and privileges such as weekend passes, free time, or participation in desired activities. People in the program know in advance exactly what behaviors will be reinforced and how they will be reinforced. Token economies have been used effectively in mental hospitals to encourage patients to attend to grooming, to interact with other patients, and to carry out housekeeping tasks (Ayllon & Azrin, 1965, 1968). Although the positive behaviors generally stop when the tokens are discontinued, this does not mean that the programs are not worthwhile. After all, most people who are employed would probably quit their jobs if they were no longer paid.

Many classroom teachers and parents use *time out*—a behavior modification technique in which a child who is misbehaving is removed for a short time from sources of positive reinforcement. (Remember, according to operant conditioning, a behavior that is no longer reinforced will extinguish.)

Behavior modification is also used successfully in business and industry to increase profits and to modify employee behavior related to health, safety, and learning. In order to keep their premiums down, some companies give annual rebates to employees who do not use up the deductibles in their health insurance plan. To reduce costs associated with automobile accidents and auto theft, insurance companies offer incentives in the form of reduced premiums for installing airbags and burglar alarm systems. To encourage employees to take company-approved college courses, some companies offer tuition reimbursement to employees who complete such courses with acceptable grades. Many companies promote sales by giving salespeople bonuses, trips, and other prizes for increasing sales.

One of the most successful applications of behavior modification has been in the treatment of psychological problems ranging from phobias to addictive behaviors. In this context, behavior modification is called *behavior therapy,* which is discussed in Chapter 16.

Remember It!

1. Punishment is roughly the same as negative reinforcement. (true/false)
2. Which of the following is *not* presented in the text as one of the major factors influencing the effectiveness of punishment?

   a. timing b. consistency c. intensity d. frequency
3. Punishment usually does *not* extinguish undesirable behavior. (true/false)
4. Depending on the circumstances, avoidance learning can be either adaptive or maladaptive. (true/false)
5. Victims of spousal abuse who have repeatedly failed to escape or avoid the abuse may eventually passively resign themselves to it, a condition known as ______________.
6. Using sensitive electronic equipment to monitor physiological processes in order to bring them under conscious control is called ______________.
7. Applying learning principles to eliminate undesirable behavior and/or encourage desirable behavior is called ______________.

Answers: 1. false 2. d 3. true 4. true 5. learned helplessness 6. biofeedback 7. behavior modification

COGNITIVE LEARNING

Behaviorists such as Skinner and Watson believed that learning through operant and classical conditioning could be explained without reference to internal mental processes. Today, however, a growing number of psychologists stress the role of mental processes. They choose to broaden the study of learning to include such **cognitive processes** as thinking, knowing, problem solving, remembering, and forming mental representations. According to cognitive theorists, these processes are critically important in a more complete, more comprehensive view of learning.

We will consider the work of three important researchers in the field of cognitive learning: Wolfgang Köhler, Edward Tolman, and Albert Bandura.

Learning by Insight: Aha! Now I Get It

What is insight, and how does it affect learning?

Wolfgang Köhler (1887–1967), a German psychologist, studied anthropoid apes and became convinced that they behaved intelligently and were capable of problem solving. In his book *The Mentality of Apes* (1925), Köhler describes experiments he conducted on chimpanzees confined in caged areas.

In one experiment, Köhler hung a bunch of bananas inside the caged area but overhead, out of reach of the apes; boxes and sticks were left around the cage. Köhler observed the chimps' unsuccessful attempts to reach the bananas by jumping up or swinging sticks at them. Eventually the chimps solved the problem by piling the boxes one on top of the other until they could reach the bananas.

In another experiment, Sultan, the brightest of the chimps, was given one short stick; beyond reach outside the cage was a longer stick and a bunch of bananas. After failing to reach the bananas with the short stick, Sultan used it to drag the long stick within reach. Then, finding that the long stick did not reach the bananas, Sultan finally solved the problem by fitting the two sticks together to form one long stick. With this stick, he successfully retrieved the bananas.

Köhler observed that the chimps sometimes appeared to give up in their attempts to get the bananas. However, after an interval, they returned and came up with the solution to the problem as if it had come to them in a flash of **insight.** They seemed to have suddenly discovered the relationship between the sticks or boxes and the bananas. Köhler insisted that insight, rather than trial-and-error learning, accounted for the chimps' successes, because they could easily repeat the solution and transfer this learning to similar problems. In human terms, a solution gained through insight is more easily learned, less likely to be forgotten, and more readily transferred to new problems than solutions learned through rote memorization (Rock & Palmer, 1990).

Latent Learning and Cognitive Maps: I Might Use That Later

What is latent learning?

Like Köhler, Edward Tolman (1886–1959) held views that differed from the prevailing ideas on learning. First, Tolman (1932) believed that learning could take place without reinforcement. Second, he differentiated between learning and performance. He maintained that **latent learning** could occur—that is, learning could occur without apparent reinforcement but not be demonstrated until the organism was motivated to do so. A classic experimental study by Tolman and Honzik (1930) supports this position.

Three groups of rats were placed in a maze daily for 17 days. The first group always received a food reward at the end of the maze. The second group never received a reward, and the third group did not receive a food reward until the 11th day. The first group showed a steady improvement in performance over the 17-day period. The second group showed slight, gradual improvement. The third group, after being rewarded on the 11th day, showed a marked improvement the next day and from then on, outperforming the rats that had been rewarded daily (see Figure 5.9 on p. 196). The rapid improvement of the third group indicated to Tolman that latent learning had occurred—that the rats had actually learned the maze during the first 11 days.

Skinner was still in graduate school in 1930, when Tolman provided this exception to a basic principle of operant conditioning—that reinforcement is required for learning new behavior. The rats in the learning group *did* learn something before reinforcement and without exhibiting any evidence of learning by overt, observable behavior. But what did they learn? Tolman concluded that the rats had learned to

cognitive processes (COG-nuh-tiv): Mental processes such as thinking, knowing, problem solving, and remembering.

insight: The sudden realization of the relationship between elements in a problem situation, which makes the solution apparent.

latent learning: Learning that occurs without apparent reinforcement but that is not demonstrated until sufficient reinforcement is provided.

Figure 5.9

Latent Learning

Rats in Group 1 were rewarded for running the maze correctly, while rats in Group 2 were never rewarded. Group 3 rats were rewarded only on the 11th day, and thereafter outperformed the rats in Group 1. The rats had "learned" the maze but were not motivated to perform until rewarded, demonstrating that latent learning had occurred. (From Tolman & Honzik, 1930.)

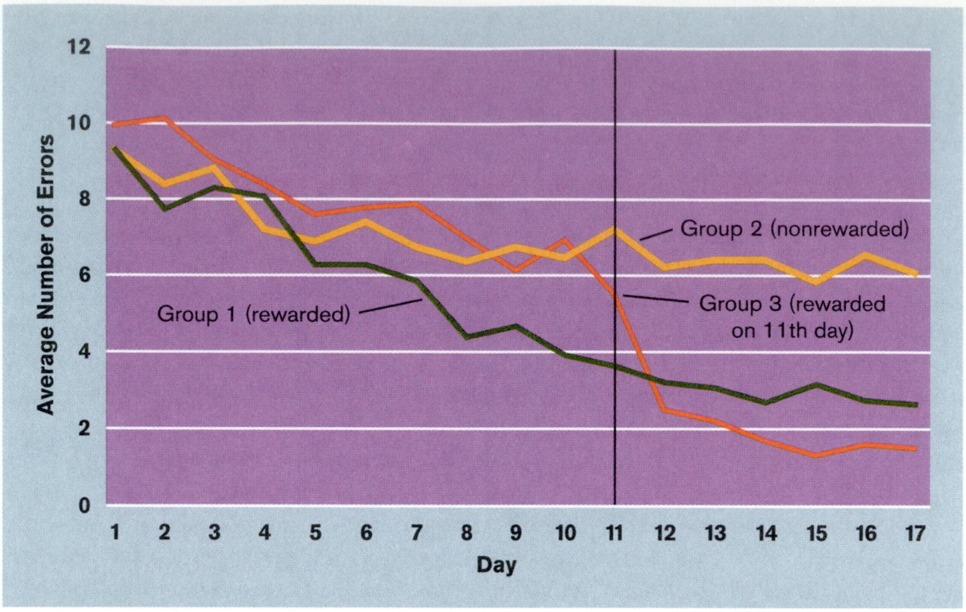

form a **cognitive map,** a mental representation or picture, of the maze but had not demonstrated their learning until they were reinforced. In later studies, Tolman showed how rats quickly learn to rearrange learned cognitive maps and find their way through increasingly complex mazes with ease.

The very notion of explaining the rats' behavior with the concept of cognitive maps is counter to Skinner's most deeply held belief—that mental processes do not explain the causes of behavior. But the concepts of cognitive maps and latent learning have a far more important place in psychology today than was true in Tolman's lifetime. They provide a cognitive perspective on operant conditioning.

Observational Learning: Watching and Learning

What is observational learning?

In the earlier discussion of operant conditioning, we saw how people and other animals learn by directly experiencing the consequences, positive or negative, of their behavior. But must people experience rewards and punishment firsthand in order to learn? Not according to Albert Bandura (1986), who contends that many behaviors or responses are acquired through observational learning. **Observational learning,** sometimes called **modeling,** results when people observe the behavior of others and note the consequences of that behavior.

The person who demonstrates a behavior or whose behavior is imitated is called the **model.** Parents, movie stars, and sports personalities are often powerful models. The effectiveness of a model is related to his or her status, competence, and power. Other important factors are the age, sex, attractiveness, and ethnicity of the model. Whether learned behavior is actually performed depends largely on whether the observed models are rewarded or punished for their behavior and whether the observer expects to be rewarded for the behavior (Bandura, 1969a, 1977a). Recent research has also shown that observational learning is improved when several sessions of observation (watching the behavior) precede attempts to perform the behavior and are also repeated in the early stages of practicing it (Weeks & Anderson, 2000).

People use observational learning to acquire new responses or to strengthen or weaken existing responses. Consider your attitudes, gestures, personality traits, habits, moral values, and food preferences. Do you share any of these with your parents? While you were growing up, their example probably influenced your behavior for better or worse. Look around the classroom, and observe the clothes, hairstyles, and verbal patterns of the other students. Most people have been greatly influenced by observing others.

cognitive map: A mental representation of a spatial arrangement such as a maze.

observational learning: Learning by observing the behavior of others and the consequences of that behavior; learning by imitation.

modeling: Another name for observational learning.

model: The individual who demonstrates a behavior or serves as an example in observational learning.

Observational learning is particularly useful in unusual situations. Picture yourself as a guest at an elaborate state dinner at the White House. More pieces of silverware extend from the plate than you have ever seen before. Which fork should be used for what? How should you proceed? You might decide to take your cue from the First Lady—observational learning.

People may find their inhibitions decreasing or disappearing entirely as a result of observing the behavior of others. Adolescents can lose whatever resistance they may have to drinking, drug use, or sexual activity by seeing or hearing about peers engaging in these behaviors. There is often an overwhelming tendency to conform to the behavior and accept the values of the peer group. But inhibitions can also be strengthened through observational learning. A person does not need to experience the unfortunate consequences of dangerous behavior to avoid it.

Fears, too, can be acquired through observational learning. Muris and others (1996) found that children whose mothers expressed fears of animals, injuries, or medical problems or procedures had significantly higher levels of fear than children whose mothers did not express such fears. Conversely, children who see "a parent or peer behaving nonfearfully in a potentially fear-producing situation may be 'immunized'" to feeling fear when confronting a similar frightening situation later (Basic Behavioral Science Task Force, 1996, p. 139). And observational learning is not restricted to humans. Monkeys, for example, learn specific fears by observing other monkeys (Cook et al., 1985). And the octopus can learn some responses by observing others of its species (Fiorito & Scotto, 1992), and so can pigeons (Zeutall et al., 1996).

Apply what you know about the three basic types of learning to do the *Try It!*

Children can learn effectively by observing and imitating the behavior of others.

Try It!

Think about everything you did yesterday from the time you woke up until the time you went to sleep. List ten behaviors and indicate whether observational learning (OL), operant conditioning (OC), and/or classical conditioning (CC) played some role in the acquisition and maintenance of each behavior. Remember, a behavior might originally have been learned by some combination of the three types of learning and then maintained by one or more of the types.

You probably learned to brush your teeth through a combination of observational learning (watching a parent demonstrate how to brush) and operant conditioning (being praised as your technique improved–shaping). That behavior is maintained through operant conditioning, namely, negative reinforcement (getting rid of the terrible taste in your mouth). Avoiding cavities and the scorn of those around you is a bonus.

	Acquired through:			Maintained through:		
Behavior	**OL**	**OC**	**CC**	**OL**	**OC**	**CC**
Brushing teeth	X	X			X	

Which kind of learning had the most checks on your chart?

Violence portrayed on television as an acceptable way to solve problems tends to encourage aggressive behavior in children.

Learning Aggression: Copying What We See Albert Bandura suspected that aggressive behavior is particularly subject to observational learning and that aggression and violence on television programs, including cartoons, tend to increase aggression in children. His pioneering work has greatly influenced current thinking on these issues. In several classic experiments, Bandura demonstrated how children are influenced by exposure to aggressive models.

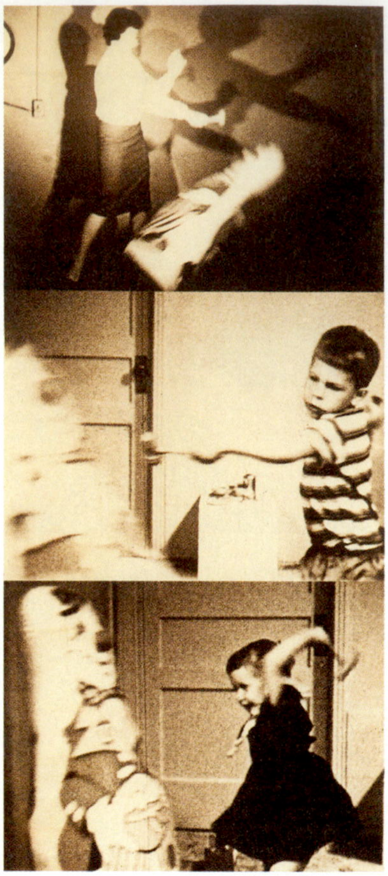

In Bandura's observational learning research, children learned to copy aggression by observing adult models act aggressively toward a Bobo doll.

One study involved three groups of preschool children. Children in one group individually observed an adult model punching, kicking, and hitting a 5-foot, inflated plastic "Bobo Doll" with a mallet, while uttering aggressive phrases (Bandura et al., 1961, p. 576). Children in the second group observed a nonaggressive model who ignored the Bobo Doll and sat quietly assembling Tinker Toys. The control group was placed in the same setting with no adult present. Later, each child was observed through a one-way mirror. Children exposed to the aggressive model imitated much of the aggression and also engaged in significantly more nonimitative aggression than either of the other groups. Children who had observed the nonaggressive model showed less aggressive behavior than the control group.

A further study compared the degree of aggression in children following exposure to (1) a live aggressive model, (2) a filmed version of the episode, and (3) a film depicting an aggressive cartoon character using the same aggressive behaviors in a fantasylike setting (Bandura et al., 1963). A control group was not exposed to any of the three situations of aggression. The groups exposed to aggressive models used significantly more aggression than the control group. The researchers concluded that "of the three experimental conditions, exposure to humans on film portraying aggression was the most influential in eliciting and shaping aggressive behavior" (p. 7).

Bandura's research provided the impetus for studying the effects of televised violence and aggression in both cartoons and regular programming. Although there has been some consciousness raising about the negative impact of media violence, the amount of television violence is still excessive. The problem is compounded by the fact that the average family watches more than 7 hours of television each day. Watching excessive violence gives people an exaggerated view of the pervasiveness of violence in society, while making them less sensitive to the victims of violence. Media violence also encourages aggressive behavior in children by portraying aggression as an acceptable and effective way to solve problems and by teaching new forms of aggression (Wood et al., 1991). But just as children imitate the aggressive behavior they observe on television, they also imitate the prosocial, or helping, behavior they observe. Programs like *Mister Rogers' Neighborhood* and *Sesame Street* have been found to have a positive influence on children.

Remember It!

1. The sudden realization of the relationship between the elements in a problem situation that results in the solution to the problem is called (latent learning, insight).
2. Learning not demonstrated until one is motivated to perform the behavior is called
   a. learning by insight. c. classical conditioning.
   b. observational learning. d. latent learning.
3. Grant has been afraid of mice for as long as he can remember, and his mother has the same paralyzing fear. Grant most likely acquired his fear through
   a. learning by insight. c. classical conditioning.
   b. observational learning. d. latent learning.
4. Match the researcher with the subject(s) researched.
   ____ (1) Edward Tolman a. observational learning
   ____ (2) Albert Bandura b. cognitive maps
   ____ (3) Wolfgang Köhler c. learning by insight
   d. latent learning

Answers: 1. insight 2. d 3. b 4. (1) b, d (2) a (3) c

Apparently many avenues of learning are available to humans and other animals. Luckily, people's capacity to learn seems practically unlimited. Certainly, advances in civilization could not have been achieved without the ability to learn.

Apply It!

How to Win the Battle against Procrastination

"So much to do and so little time to do it in." How often have you thought that you could accomplish a great deal more if only you had more time? Such a thought is as appealing as it is irrational. Instead of wishing for the impossible, it makes more sense to use the time you *do* have wisely. And your only hope for using your time more wisely is to learn how to overcome the greatest time waster of all—procrastination.

You can use behavior modification techniques such as those in the *Try It!* on page 181 to systematically apply the following suggestions for keeping procrastination from interfering with your studying.

- *Identify the environmental cues that habitually interfere with your studying.* What competing interests are most likely to cause you to put off or interrupt your studying? Television, sleeping, snacking, talking on the telephone, visiting friends or family members?
- *Select your work environment.* Select a place to study that you associate only with studying, preferably away from the distracting environmental cues you have identified. The library might be such a place.
- *Schedule your study time.* Schedule your study time in advance, maybe even the previous day, so your decisions about when to start work will not be ruled by the whim of the moment.
- *Get started.* The most difficult part is getting started. Give yourself an extra reward for starting on time and, perhaps, a penalty for not starting on time. Let the clock rather than your mood be the signal to begin studying. Once you begin, you will probably find that the work is not as distasteful as you had imagined.
- *Use visualization.* Much procrastination results from the failure to consider its negative consequences. Visualizing the consequences of *not* studying can be an effective tool for combating procrastination. Suppose you are considering going out of town with friends for the weekend instead of studying for a midterm test on Monday. Picture this! You walk into the classroom Monday morning unprepared; you know the answers to very few questions; you flunk the test. Now visualize the outcome if you stay home for the weekend and study. Picture how much better you will feel as you breeze through the test on Monday and get a good grade.
- *Become better at estimating how long it takes to complete an assignment.* Estimate how long it will take to complete an assignment, and then keep track of how long it actually takes. If you habitually underestimate the time involved, begin scheduling longer periods of time to accomplish your work.
- *Beware of jumping to another task when you reach a difficult part of an assignment.* This is a procrastination tactic designed to give you the feeling that you are busy and accomplishing something, but it is, nevertheless, an avoidance tactic.
- *Beware of preparation overkill.* Procrastinators may actually spend hours preparing for the task rather than working on the task itself. They may gather enough materials in the library to write a book rather than a five-page term paper. This enables them to postpone writing the paper.
- *Keep a record of the reasons you give yourself for postponing studying or completing important assignments.* If a favorite rationalization is "I'll wait until I'm in the mood to do this," count the number of times in a week you are seized with the desire to study. The mood to study typically arrives after you begin, not before.
- *Stop believing your own promises.* All too often procrastinators break their own promises to themselves. How much confidence would you have in a friend who made promises to you but never followed through? Can you relate to any of these self-promises?

  "I'll do this tomorrow." Why is tomorrow going to be a better day? You told yourself this yesterday, and now you are not following through.

  "I'll go out with my friends, but only for a few hours." As a rule, does your time with friends turn out to be a few hours or a whole day or night?

  "I'll get some sleep and set my alarm for 3:00 A.M. and then study." Are you usually able to get up at 3:00 A.M.? Is that really the ideal time for you to study? Research on sleep indicates that the middle of your subjective night is the worst time.

  "I'll watch TV for a few minutes and then get back to studying." Does a few minutes often turn into several hours?

  "I'll rest for a few minutes and clear my mind so I can think better." Does your ability to think really improve, or do you find that you are more tired than you realized and that you need to rest longer?

Don't procrastinate! Begin now! Apply the steps outlined here to gain more control over your behavior and win the battle against procrastination.

THINKING CRITICALLY

Evaluation

In this chapter you learned about three major types of learning: classical conditioning, operant conditioning, and observational learning. Outline the strengths and limitations of each of these three forms of learning in explaining how behaviors are acquired and maintained.

Point/Counterpoint

The use of behavior modification has been highly controversial in our society. Prepare arguments supporting each position:

a. Behavior modification should be used to shape the behavior of others.
b. Behavior modification should not be used to shape the behavior of others.

Psychology in Your Life

Think of a behavior of a friend, family member, or professor that you would like to change. Using what you know about classical conditioning, operant conditioning, and observational learning, formulate a detailed plan for changing the behavior of the target person.

SUMMARY AND REVIEW

CLASSICAL CONDITIONING: THE ORIGINAL VIEW

What was Pavlov's major contribution to psychology?

Pavlov's study of the conditioned reflex provided a model of learning called classical conditioning.

How was classical conditioning accomplished in Pavlov's experiments?

In Pavlov's experiments, a neutral stimulus (a tone) was presented shortly before the unconditioned stimulus (food), which naturally elicited, or brought forth, an unconditioned response (salivation). After repeated pairings, the conditioned stimulus (the tone) alone came to elicit the conditioned response (salivation).

How does extinction occur in classical conditioning?

If the conditioned stimulus (tone) is presented repeatedly without the unconditioned stimulus (food), the conditioned response (salivation) becomes progressively weaker and eventually disappears.

What is generalization?

Generalization occurs when an organism makes a conditioned response to a stimulus similar to the original conditioned stimulus.

What is discrimination in classical conditioning?

Discrimination is the ability to distinguish between similar stimuli, so that the organism makes the conditioned response only to the original conditioned stimulus.

How did Watson demonstrate that fear could be classically conditioned?

Watson showed that fear could be classically conditioned by presenting a white rat along with a loud, frightening noise, thereby conditioning Little Albert to fear the white rat.

Key Terms
stimulus (p. 164); learning (p. 164); classical conditioning (p. 164); reflex (p. 166); conditioned reflex (p. 166); unconditioned response (p. 166); unconditioned stimulus (p. 167); conditioned stimulus (p. 167); conditioned response (p. 167); extinction (p. 168); spontaneous recovery (p. 168); generalization (p. 169); discrimination (p. 170); higher-order conditioning (p. 170)

CLASSICAL CONDITIONING: THE CONTEMPORARY VIEW

According to Rescorla, what is the critical element in classical conditioning?

The critical element in classical conditioning is whether the conditioned stimulus provides information that enables the organism to reliably predict the occurrence of the unconditioned stimulus.

What two exceptions to traditional ideas about classical conditioning did Garcia and Koelling find?

The fact that rats formed an association between nausea and the flavored water ingested several hours earlier was an exception to the principle that the conditioned stimulus must be presented shortly before the unconditioned stimulus. The finding that rats associated electric shock *only* with noise and light and nausea *only* with flavored water proved that associations cannot be readily conditioned between *any* two stimuli.

What types of responses can be acquired through classical conditioning?

Types of responses acquired through classical conditioning include positive and negative emotional responses (including likes, dislikes, fears, and phobias), drug cravings in former drug users, and conditioned immune responses.

What are four factors that influence classical conditioning?

Four factors influencing classical conditioning are (1) the number of pairings of conditioned stimulus and unconditioned stimulus, (2) the intensity of the unconditioned stimulus, (3) how reliably the conditioned stimulus predicts the unconditioned stimulus, and (4) the temporal relationship between the conditioned and the unconditioned stimulus.

Key Term
taste aversion (p. 174)

OPERANT CONDITIONING

What was Thorndike's major contribution to psychology?

Thorndike formulated the law of effect, which was the conceptual starting point for Skinner's work on operant conditioning.

What was Skinner's major contribution to psychology?

Skinner's major contribution to psychology was his extensive and significant research on operant conditioning.

How are responses acquired through operant conditioning?

Operant conditioning is a method for conditioning voluntary responses. The consequences of behavior are manipulated to shape a new response or to increase or decrease the frequency of an existing response.

How is shaping used to condition a response?

In shaping, rather than waiting for the desired response to be emitted, a researcher selectively reinforces successive approximations toward the desired response until that response is achieved.

How does extinction occur in operant conditioning?

In operant conditioning, extinction occurs when reinforcement is withheld.

What is the goal of both positive reinforcement and negative reinforcement, and how is the goal accomplished with each?

Both positive reinforcement and negative reinforcement are used to strengthen or increase the probability of a response. With positive reinforcement, the desired response is followed by a reward; with negative reinforcement, it is followed by the termination of an aversive stimulus.

What are the four types of schedules of reinforcement, and which schedule yields the highest response rate and the greatest resistance to extinction?

The four types of schedules of reinforcement are the fixed-ratio, variable-ratio, fixed-interval, and variable-interval schedules. The variable-ratio schedule provides the highest response rate and the most resistance to extinction.

What is the partial-reinforcement effect?

The partial-reinforcement effect is the greater resistance to extinction that occurs when responses are maintained under partial reinforcement rather than under continuous reinforcement.

What three factors, in addition to the schedule of reinforcement, influence operant conditioning?

In operant conditioning, acquisition of a response, response rate, and resistance to extinction are influenced by the magnitude of reinforcement, the immediacy of reinforcement, and the motivation of the organism.

How does punishment differ from negative reinforcement?

Punishment is used to decrease the frequency of a response; negative reinforcement is used to increase the frequency of a response.

What are some disadvantages of punishment?

Punishment generally suppresses rather than extinguishes behavior; it does not help people develop more appropriate behaviors. And it can cause fear, anger, hostility, and aggression in the punished person.

What three factors increase the effectiveness of punishment?

Punishment is most effective when it is given immediately after undesirable behavior, when it is consistently applied, and when it is just intense enough to suppress the behavior.

What are some applications of operant conditioning?

Applications of operant conditioning include training animals to provide entertainment or to help physically challenged people, the use of biofeedback to gain control over internal physiological processes, and the use of behavior modification techniques to eliminate undesirable behavior and/or encourage desirable behavior in individuals or groups.

Key Terms
trial-and-error learning (p. 178); law of effect (p. 179); operant conditioning (p. 179); reinforcer (p. 180); shaping (p. 180); Skinner box (p. 180); successive approximations (p. 180); extinction (p. 181); generalization (p. 181); discriminative stimulus (p. 182); reinforcement (p. 182); positive reinforcement (p. 182); negative reinforcement (p. 183); primary reinforcer (p. 183); secondary reinforcer (p. 183); continuous reinforcement (p. 184); partial reinforcement (p. 184); schedule of reinforcement (p. 184); fixed-ratio schedule (p. 184); variable-ratio schedule (p. 185); fixed-interval schedule (p. 185); variable-interval schedule (p. 185); partial-reinforcement effect (p. 186); punishment (p. 189); avoidance learning (p. 192); learned helplessness (p. 192); biofeedback (p. 193); behavior modification (p. 193); token economy (p. 193)

COGNITIVE LEARNING

What is insight, and how does it affect learning?

Insight is the sudden realization of the relationship of the elements in a problem situation that makes the solution apparent; this solution is easily learned and transferred to new problems.

What is latent learning?

Latent learning occurs without apparent reinforcement, but it is not demonstrated in the organism's performance until the organism is motivated to do so.

What is observational learning?

Observational learning is learning by observing the behavior of others (called models) and the consequences of that behavior.

Key Terms
cognitive processes (p. 194); insight (p. 195); latent learning (p. 195); cognitive map (p. 196); observational learning (p. 196); modeling (p. 196); model (p. 196)

Surf It!

Want to be sure you've absorbed the material in Chapter 5, "Learning," before the big test? Visiting *www.abacon.com/wood* can put a top grade within your reach. The site is loaded with free practice tests, flashcards, activities, and links to help you review your way to an A. To enliven that inevitable study break, the site also offers personality assessment quizzes and a psychology career corner.

6 Memory

"Shut up, or I'll cut you," Jennifer's attacker warned her as he held the knife against her throat.

Just moments before, Jennifer had screamed as the man grabbed her, threw her down on the bed, and pinned her hands behind her. Now, feeling the pain of the knife's sharp point on her throat, she knew he meant what he said.

Twenty-two-year-old Jennifer Thompson's world was shattered that day when she was brutally raped. But even though she was overpowered at the time, she decided she could do one thing: If she survived, she would remember this man well enough to send him to prison.

She steeled herself to study the rapist—his facial features, scars, tattoos, voice, mannerisms. She would be the "perfect witness."

Hours after her ordeal, Jennifer was swabbed for semen samples at a hospital. At the police station later, she viewed photos showing various facial features, searching for those of her rapist—his pencil-thin moustache, eyebrows, nose, and other features. She then selected a composite photo that looked like the rapist.

A week later, she viewed six suspects who resembled the description. The suspects sat holding cards numbered 1 to 6. Jennifer looked at suspect number 5 and announced with total confidence, "That's the man who raped me."

The man was Ronald Cotton. The same age as Jennifer, he had already served a year and a half in prison for attempted sexual assault.

In court, Jennifer was indeed the perfect witness, unshakably confident, so sure that this man had raped her. Cotton was not so impressive. Of course, his record didn't help. But he was nervous, frightened. His alibis didn't check out, he got his dates mixed up, and a piece missing from one of his shoes resembled a piece found at the crime scene. But it wasn't the circumstantial evidence that convicted Ronald Cotton. It was the confident, unwavering testimony of the only eyewitness, Jennifer Thompson. The jury found him guilty and sentenced him to life in prison, just as Jennifer had hoped. She celebrated her victory with champagne.

"God knows I'm innocent," said Cotton, and he vowed to prove that somehow. He wrote lawyers, newspapers, and anyone he thought would listen.

Then, remarkably, after Cotton had been in prison for more than a year, a new inmate, Bobby Poole, convicted of a series of brutal rapes, joined him at his work assignment in the kitchen. When Cotton told Poole that he had been convicted of raping Jennifer Thompson, Poole laughed and bragged that Cotton was doing some of his time.

Finally, after Cotton had served 11 years, law professor Richard Rosen heard his story and agreed to help him. Rosen was critical of the heavy reliance on eyewitness testimony, which he knew is far from infallible. He also knew that DNA tests could be performed that were far more sophisticated than those that had been available 11 years earlier. It was Cotton's DNA samples that cleared him of the crime. Bobby Poole's DNA samples, however, proved that he had raped Jennifer Thompson.

A new nightmare now plagued Jennifer: She had sent an innocent man to prison. But she met with Ronald Cotton and, in tears, expressed her sorrow for his ordeal. Cotton responded softly, "I'm not mad at you. I've never been mad at you. I just want you to have a good life." Jennifer tearfully thanked him for his forgiveness.

Ronald Cotton is now married with a beautiful daughter, Raven. With Jennifer Thompson's help, he got a six-figure settlement from the state government. (Adapted from O'Neil, 2000.)

After being proved innocent and released from prison, Ronald Cotton talked with and forgave Jennifer Thompson, who had falsely accused him of rape.

Does this case simply reflect the rare and unusual in human memory, or are memory errors common occurrences? This and many other questions you may have about memory will be answered in this chapter. We will look closely at three memory systems: sensory, short-term, and long-term. You will learn how much information each system holds, for how long, and in what form. You will discover why virtually everyone finds it harder to remember names than faces. Is memory like a video cassette recorder, in which the sights and sounds we experience are captured intact and simply played back in exact detail? Or do we "reconstruct" the past when we remember, leaving out certain bits and pieces of events that actually happened and adding others that did not?

Would you like to improve your memory? You will learn some techniques that can help you study more effectively, and some mnemonic devices (memory strategies) that can be used in practical ways every day as memory aids.

like a computer way to get in brain, store it retrieve it

REMEMBERING

Memory, the vast mental storehouse containing everything we know, enables us to recognize who and (usually) where we are when we awaken each morning. Memory provides the continuity of life—the long thread to which are tied our joys and sorrows, knowledge and skills, triumphs and failures, and the people and places of our lives.

Most current efforts to understand human memory have been conducted within a framework known as the *information-processing approach* (Klatzky, 1984). This approach makes use of modern computer science and related fields to provide models that help psychologists understand the processes involved in memory (Kon & Plaskota, 2000).

The Three Processes in Memory: Encoding, Storage, and Retrieval

What three processes are involved in the act of remembering?

What must occur to enable you to remember a friend's name, a fact from history, or an incident from your past? The act of remembering requires the successful completion of three processes: encoding, storage, and retrieval. The first process, **encoding,** involves transforming information into a form that can be stored in memory. Sometimes you encode information automatically, without any effort, but often you must do something with the information in order to remember it. For example, if you met someone named Will at a party, you might associate his name with Will Smith or Will Truman, the character played by Eric McCormack on NBC's *Will & Grace.* Such simple associations can markedly improve your ability to recall names and other information. The careful encoding of information greatly increases the chance that you will remember it.

The second memory process, **storage,** involves keeping or maintaining information in memory. For encoded information to be stored, some physiological change in the brain must take place—a process called **consolidation.** If a person loses consciousness for any reason, the consolidation process can be disrupted and a permanent memory may not form. That is why someone who has been in a serious car accident may awaken in a hospital and not remember what has happened.

The final process, **retrieval,** occurs when information stored in memory is brought to mind. Calling Will by name the next time you meet him shows that you have retrieved his name from memory. To remember, you must perform all three processes—encode the information, store it, and then retrieve it. Memory failure can result from the failure of any one of the three (see Figure 6.1 on p. 206).

Similar steps are required in the processing of information by computers. Information is encoded (entered in some form the computer is able to use), then stored on disk, and later retrieved on the screen. You would not be able to retrieve

encoding: Transforming information into a form that can be stored in short-term or long-term memory.

storage: The act of maintaining information in memory.

consolidation: A physiological change in the brain that must take place for encoded information to be stored in memory.

retrieval: The act of bringing to mind material that has been stored in memory.

Figure 6.1

The Processes Required in Remembering

The act of remembering requires successful completion of all three of these processes: encoding, storage, and retrieval.

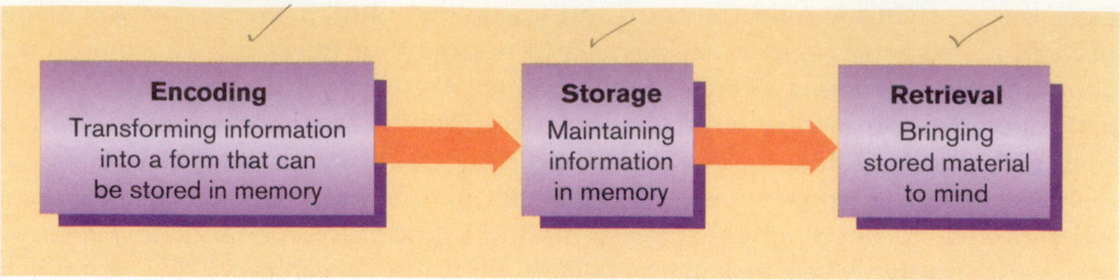

the material if you had failed to enter it, if a power failure occurred before you could save what you had entered, or if you forgot which disk or file contained the needed information.

As mentioned above, physiological changes must occur during the process called consolidation, which allows new information to be stored in memory for later retrieval. These physiological changes require the synthesis of new protein molecules (Lopez, 2000). Once the consolidation process is completed, a memory can last indefinitely, even as long as a lifetime. Current research suggests that our genes assist in the process of memory consolidation. Specific genes initiate the chain of events that causes changes at the activated synapses, enabling them to form a memory that will endure (Dudai, 2000).

Until recently, conventional wisdom held that the process of consolidation had to occur only once for each item memorized. But as we will see later in the chapter in the section on the causes of forgetting, some seemingly safely consolidated memories can be induced to disappear (Nader et al., 2000).

The Three Memory Systems: The Long and the Short of It

How are memories stored? According to one widely accepted view, the Atkinson–Shiffrin model, there are three different, interacting memory systems known as sensory, short-term, and long-term memory (Atkinson & Shiffrin, 1968; Broadbent, 1958). Considerable research in the biology of memory lends support to the model (Squire et al., 1993). We will examine each of these three memory systems, which are shown in Figure 6.2.

What is sensory memory?

Sensory Memory: Images and Echoes As information comes in through the senses, virtually everything we see, hear, or otherwise sense is held in **sensory memory,** but only for the briefest period of time. Sensory memory normally holds

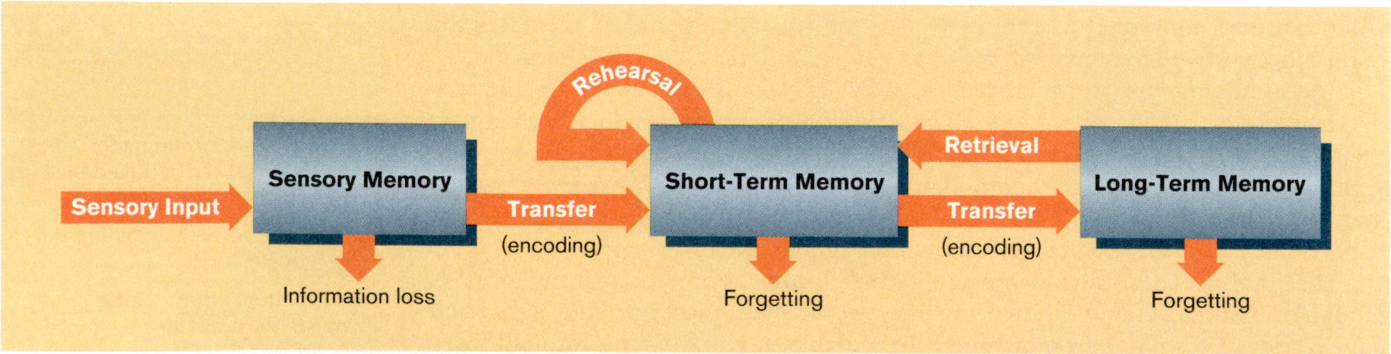

Figure 6.2

The Three Memory Systems

According to the Atkinson-Shiffrin model, there are three separate memory systems: sensory memory, short-term memory, and long-term memory.

visual images for a fraction of a second and sounds for about 2 seconds (Crowder, 1992). Visual sensory memory lasts just long enough to keep whatever you are viewing from disappearing when you blink your eyes.

When we view a motion picture, the "motion" we see is an illusion. A motion picture is in reality a series of "still" pictures, basically photographs, that are presented in sequence at the proper speed to create the illusion of movement. Your visual sensory memory retains one frame until the next one arrives, enabling you to see a flow of movement rather than discrete, still pictures. You can demonstrate visual sensory memory for yourself by doing the *Try It!*

sensory memory: The memory system that holds information coming in through the senses for a period ranging from a fraction of a second to several seconds.

learning theory Herman curve

Try It!

To prove the existence of visual sensory memory, move your forefinger back and forth rapidly in front of your face. You will see what appears to be the blurred images of many fingers. This occurs because your sensory memory briefly holds a trace of the various positions that your finger occupies as it moves.

Exactly how long does visual sensory memory last? In 1740, Senger, a Swedish investigator, tried to answer this question. He attached a glowing ember to a rotating wheel and found that when he rotated the wheel rapidly, he could see a complete circle. When he rotated the wheel more slowly, he could see only a part of the circle. Senger then rotated the wheel at the exact speed that just allowed a complete circle to be perceived. He calculated the time of one revolution to be approximately $\frac{1}{10}$ of a second (Baddeley, 1982).

Sensory memory holds a visual image, such as a lightning bolt, for a fraction of a second—just long enough for you to perceive a flow of movement.

For a fraction of a second, glance at the three rows of letters shown below and then close your eyes. How many of the items can you recall?

X B D F
M P Z G
L C N H

Most people can recall correctly only four or five of the items when they are briefly presented. Does this indicate that visual sensory memory can hold only four or five items at a time? No. Researcher George Sperling (1960) knew that the human visual sensory capacity should enable a person to take in most or all of the 12 items at a single glance. Could it be that sensory memory is so short-lived that while a person is reporting some items, others have already faded from sensory memory? Sperling thought of an ingenious method to test this notion. He briefly flashed 12 items as shown above to participants. Immediately upon turning off the display, he sounded a high, medium, or low tone that signaled the participants to report *only* the top, middle, or bottom row of items. Before they heard the tone, the participants had no way of knowing which row they would have to report. Yet Sperling found that, when the participants could view the letters for $\frac{15}{1000}$ to $\frac{1}{2}$ second, they could report correctly all the items in any row nearly 100% of the time. But the items fade from sensory memory so quickly that during the time it takes to report three or four of the items, the other eight or nine have already disappeared.

Sensory memory for sound is similar to that for vision. You experience auditory sensory memory when the last few words someone has spoken seem to echo briefly in your head. Auditory sensory memory lasts about 2 seconds, compared with a fraction of a second for visual sensory memory (Klatzky, 1980).

It is clear that an abundance of information in raw, natural form can be stored briefly in sensory memory. This brief period is just long enough for a person to begin to process the sensory stimuli and to select the most important information for further processing in the second memory system—short-term memory.

What are the characteristics of short-term memory?

Short-Term Memory: Short Life, Small Capacity

Whatever you are thinking about right now is in your **short-term memory** (STM). You use short-term memory when you carry on a conversation, solve a problem, or look up a telephone number and remember it just long enough to dial it.

Unlike sensory memory, which holds virtually the exact sensory stimulus, short-term memory usually codes information according to sound, that is, in acoustic form (Conrad, 1964). The letter *T* is coded as the sound "tee," not as the shape T. Short-term memory can also hold visual images and store information in semantic form (according to meaning) as well (Shulman, 1972).

The Capacity of Short-Term Memory Compared with sensory memory, which can hold vast amounts of information briefly, short-term memory has a very limited capacity—about seven (plus or minus two) different items or bits of information at one time. Test the capacity of your short-term memory in the *Try It!*

Try It!

Read aloud the digits in row (a) at a steady rate of about two per second. Then, from memory, write them down on a sheet of paper, being sure to cover up this page while you write.

Repeat the process, row by row.

a. 3 8 7 1
b. 9 6 4 7 3
c. 1 8 3 0 5 2
d. 8 0 6 5 9 1 7
e. 5 2 9 7 3 1 2 5
f. 2 7 4 0 1 9 6 8 3
g. 3 9 1 6 5 8 4 5 1 7

How well did you do in the *Try It?* Most people recall about seven items. This is just enough for phone numbers and ordinary zip codes. (Nine-digit zip codes strain the capacity of most people.) When short-term memory is filled to capacity, **displacement** can occur. In displacement, each new, incoming item pushes out an existing item, which is then forgotten.

One way to overcome the limitation of seven or so bits of information is to use a technique that George A. Miller (1956), a pioneer in memory research, calls *chunking*—organizing or grouping separate bits of information into larger units, or chunks. A *chunk* is an easily identifiable unit such as a syllable, a word, an acronym, or a number (Cowan, 1988). For example, the numbers 5 2 9 7 3 1 2 5 can be chunked as 52 97 31 25, leaving the short-term memory with the easier task of dealing with four chunks of information rather than eight separate bits. Complete the next *Try It!* and see if chunking works for you.

Chunking is a very useful technique for increasing the capacity of short-term memory, but there are limits. Simon (1974) suggests that the larger the chunks, the fewer chunks people can remember. Yet the limited capacity of short-term memory maximizes the likelihood of early detection of useful relations and correlations among incoming stimuli. This occurs because short-term memory requires concentration, a narrowing of attention in order to focus closely on those stimuli that are to be remembered (Kareev, 2000).

The Duration of Short-Term Memory Items in short-term memory are lost very quickly, in less than 30 seconds, unless you repeat them over and over to yourself, silently or out loud, to retain them. This process is known as **rehearsal.** People rehearse a telephone number they have looked up to keep it in short-term memory long enough to dial the number. But short-term memory is easily disrupted. It is so

short-term memory: The second stage of memory, which holds about seven (a range of five to nine) items for less than 30 seconds without rehearsal; working memory; the mental workspace a person uses to keep in mind tasks being thought about at any given moment.

displacement: The event that occurs when short-term memory is holding its maximum and each new item entering short-term memory pushes out an existing item.

rehearsal: The act of purposely repeating information to maintain it in short-term memory or to transfer it to long-term memory.

Try It!

Read the following letters individually at the rate of about one per second and then see if you can repeat them.

N-F L-C-B S-U-S A-V-C R-F-B I

Did you have difficulty? Probably so, because there are 15 different letters.

Now try this:

NFL CBS USA VCR FBI

Did you find that five chunks are easier to remember than 15 separate items?

fragile, in fact, that an interruption or a distraction can cause information to be lost in just a few seconds. Distractions that are stressful are especially likely to disrupt short-term memory. And a threat to survival certainly does, as researchers showed when they pumped the odor of a feared predator, a fox, into a laboratory where rats were performing a task requiring short-term memory (Morrow et al., 2000).

How long does short-term memory last if rehearsal is prevented? In a series of early studies, participants were briefly shown three consonants, such as H, G, and L, and then asked to count backward by threes from a given number (738, 735, 732, and so on) (Peterson & Peterson, 1959). After intervals lasting from 3 to 18 seconds, participants were instructed to stop counting backward and recall the three letters. Following a delay of 9 seconds, the participants could recall an average of only one of the three letters. After 18 seconds, there was practically no recall whatsoever. An 18-second distraction had completely erased the three letters from short-term memory.

Short-Term Memory as Working Memory Allan Baddeley (1990, 1992, 1995) has suggested that "working memory" is a more fitting term than short-term memory. More than just a temporary way station between sensory memory and long-term memory, working memory is a kind of mental workspace that temporarily holds incoming information from sensory memory or information retrieved from long-term memory for performing some conscious cognitive task.

> Without it you couldn't understand this sentence, add up a restaurant tab in your head, or find your way home. . . . Working memory is . . . an erasable mental blackboard that allows you to hold briefly in your mind and manipulate the information—whether it be words, menu prices, or a map of your surroundings—essential for comprehension, reasoning, and planning. (Wickelgren, 1997, p. 1580)

Research shows that the prefrontal cortex is the primary area responsible for working memory (Courtney et al., 1997; Rao et al., 1997).

What is long-term memory, and what are its subsystems?

Long-Term Memory: As Long as a Lifetime Some information from short-term memory makes its way into long-term memory. **Long-term memory** (LTM) is a person's vast storehouse of permanent or relatively permanent memories. There are no known limits to the storage capacity of long-term memory, and long-term memories can last for years, some of them for a lifetime.

When people talk about memory in everyday conversation, they are usually referring to long-term memory. Long-term memory holds all the knowledge you have accumulated, the skills you have acquired, and the memories of your past experiences. Information in long-term memory is usually stored in semantic form, although visual images, sounds, and odors can be stored there, as well.

long-term memory: The relatively permanent memory system with a virtually unlimited capacity.

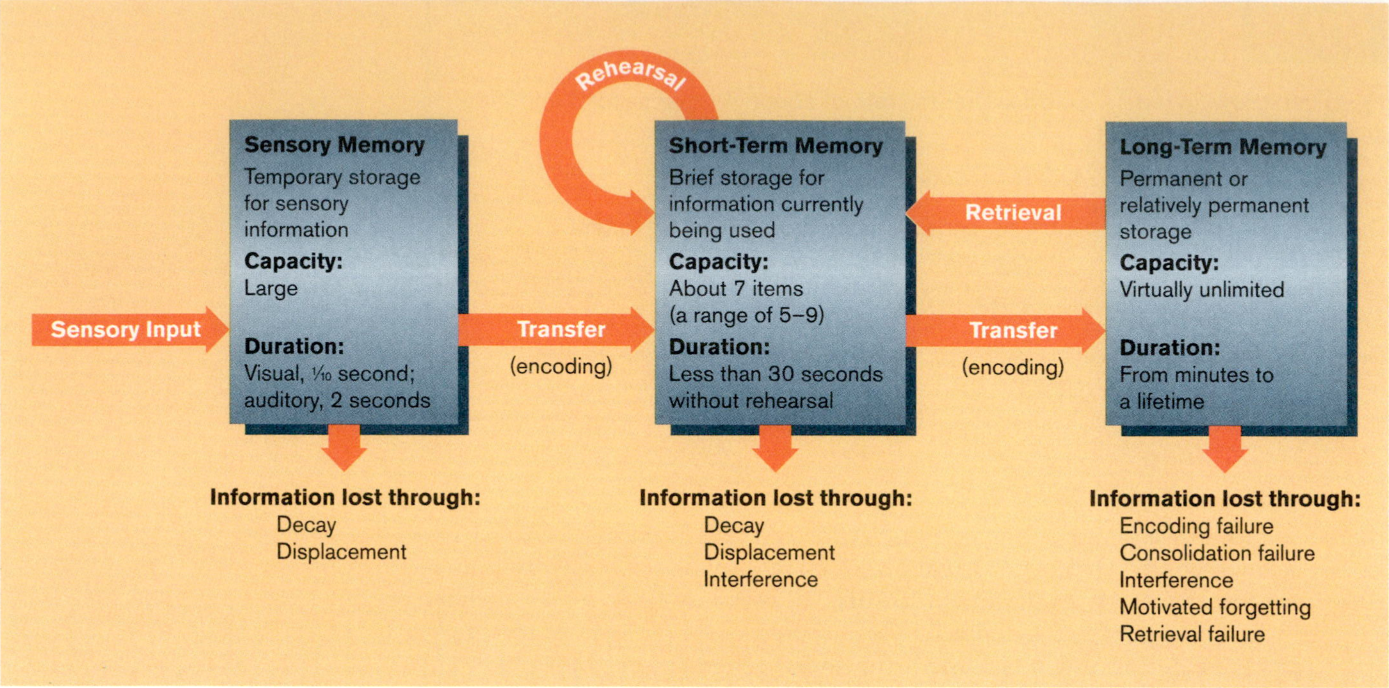

Figure 6.3

Characteristics of and Processes Involved in the Three Memory Systems

The three memory systems differ in what and how much they hold and for how long they store it. (From Peterson & Peterson, 1959.)

But how does this vast store of information make its way from short-term memory into long-term memory? People seem to remember some information with ease, almost automatically, but other kinds of material require great effort. Sometimes, through mere repetition or rehearsal, a person is able to transfer information into long-term memory. Your teachers may have used drill to try to cement the multiplication tables and other material in your long-term memory. This rote rehearsal, however, is not usually the best way to transfer information to long-term memory (Craik & Watkins, 1973). For better results, try **elaborative rehearsal.** Consider the meaning of new information and relate it to information already in your long-term memory, information about yourself whenever possible (Symons & Johnson, 1997). Forming multiple associations will increase your chance of retrieving the new information later.

Figure 6.3 summarizes the three memory systems.

Some experts believe that there are two main subsystems within long-term memory—declarative memory and nondeclarative memory.

Declarative Memory **Declarative memory** (also called *explicit memory*) stores facts, information, and personal life events that can be brought to mind verbally or in the form of images and then declared or stated. It holds information that we intentionally and consciously recollect. There are two types of declarative memory—episodic memory and semantic memory.

Episodic memory is the subpart of declarative memory that contains the memory of events as they have been subjectively experienced (Wheeler et al., 1997). It is somewhat like a mental diary, recording the episodes of your life—the people you have known, the places you have seen, and the personal experiences you have had. According to Canadian psychologist Endel Tulving (1989), "episodic memory enables people to travel back in time, as it were, into their personal past, and to become consciously aware of having witnessed or participated in events and hap-

elaborative rehearsal: A technique used to encode information into long-term memory by considering its meaning and associating it with other information already stored in long-term memory.

declarative memory: The subsystem within long-term memory that stores facts, information, and personal life experiences; also called *explicit memory.*

episodic memory (ep-ih-SOD-ik): The subpart of declarative memory that contains memories of personally experienced events.

Declarative memory stores facts, information, and personal life events, such as a trip to a foreign country. Nondeclarative memory encompasses motor skills, such as the expert swing of professional golfer Tiger Woods. Once learned, such movements can be carried out with little or no conscious effort.

Eyewittness testemony difference between flashbulb + idatictic memories

penings at earlier times" (p. 362). A person would be using episodic memory to make this statement: "I remember being in Florida on my vacation last spring, lying on the sand, soaking up some rays, and listening to the sound of the waves rushing to the shore."

Semantic memory, the second subpart of declarative memory, is memory for general knowledge, or objective facts and information. In other words, semantic memory is a mental dictionary or encyclopedia of stored knowledge:

Dictionary is spelled d-i-c-t-i-o-n-a-r-y.
10 times 10 equals 100.
The three memory systems are sensory, short-term, and long-term.

If you have ever played along when watching *Who Wants to Be a Millionaire,* you called on semantic memory almost exclusively to answer the questions. As a rule, the facts stored in semantic memory are not personally referenced to time and place as episodic memories are. You probably do not remember exactly where and when you learned to spell *dictionary* or that 10 times 10 equals 100.

Brain-imaging studies show that the range of activity for semantic memory is larger in the left than in the right hemisphere (Koivisto & Revensuo, 2000). Does this imply that the two types of declarative memory work independently? Could major damage be done to semantic memory without affecting episodic memory? Not according to Tulving, who hypothesizes that episodic memory is dependent on an intact semantic memory and must be mediated through it (Tulving, 1995). See Figure 6.4 (a) on page 212 for a diagram representing Tulving's model. However, researchers have recently demonstrated that some people who have suffered selective damage to their long-term semantic memory can still learn and remember using episodic memory (Graham et al., 2000). Patients with "semantic dementia" perform poorly on any semantic task, such as picture naming, giving examples of general categories (e.g., household items), or sorting words or pictures into specified categories (e.g., living versus nonliving things). Yet their episodic memory is mainly unaffected (Hodges et al., 1995; Snowden et al., 1996). The diagram in Figure 6.4 (b) shows that although episodic and semantic memory are connected, episodic memory can store perceptual information without direct aid from or dependence on semantic memory (Graham et al., 2000).

semantic memory: The subpart of declarative memory that stores general knowledge; a mental encyclopedia or dictionary.

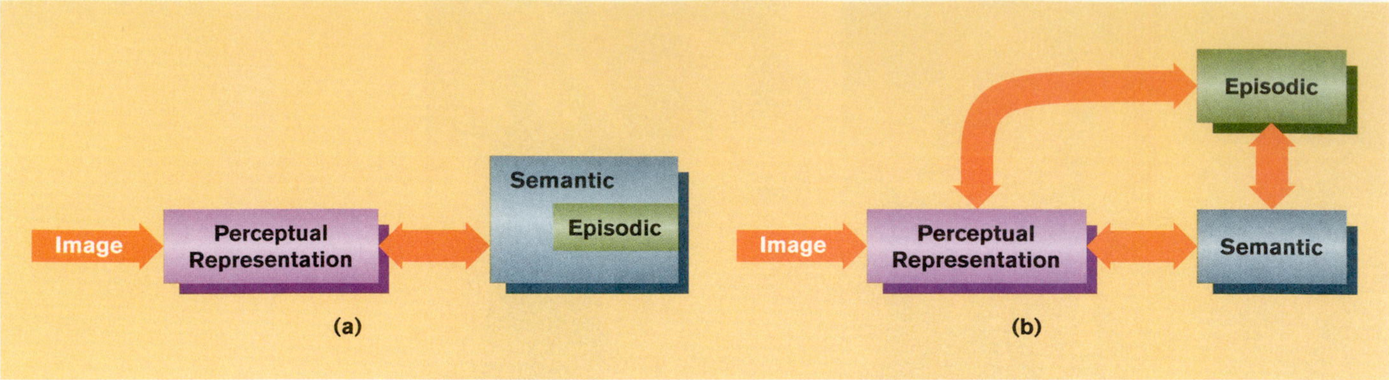

Figure 6.4

Two Models of the Relationship of Episodic and Semantic Memory

(a) Tulving's model shows the dependence of episodic memory on semantic memory.
(b) The model of Graham and others (2000) shows the reliance of episodic memory on perceptual input and semantic memory.

Nondeclarative Memory **Nondeclarative memory** (also called *implicit memory*) consists of motor skills, habits, and simple classically conditioned responses (Squire et al., 1993). Motor skills are acquired through repetitive practice and include such things as eating with a fork, riding a bicycle, or driving a car. Although acquired slowly, once learned, these skills become habit, are quite reliable, and can be carried out with little or no conscious effort. For example, you probably use the keyboard on a computer without consciously being able to name the keys in each row from left to right.

Associated with nondeclarative, or implicit, memory is a phenomenon known as **priming,** by which an earlier encounter with a stimulus (such as a word or a picture) increases the speed or accuracy of naming that stimulus or a related stimulus at a later time. Such improvement occurs without the person's conscious awareness of having seen or heard the stimulus. For example, a researcher might flash the word *elephant* on a computer screen so briefly that it is not consciously perceived. But if asked later to name as many animals as come to mind, the person is quite likely to include *elephant* on the list (Challis, 1996).

Priming can influence not only performance, but preferences and behavior as well. People exposed briefly (even subliminally) to pictures of abstract art showed greater preferences for that type of art than others not exposed. And in one study, participants subliminally exposed to faces of real people later interacted with those people more than individuals not exposed to the photos (Basic Behavioral Science Task Force, 1996).

Figure 6.5 shows the subsystems of long-term memory.

nondeclarative memory: The subsystem within long-term memory that consists of skills acquired through repetitive practice, habits, and simple classically conditioned responses; also called *implicit memory.*

priming: The phenomenon by which an earlier encounter with a stimulus (such as a word or a picture) increases the speed or accuracy with which that stimulus or a related stimulus can be named at a later time.

levels-of-processing model: A model of memory as a single system in which retention depends on how deeply information is processed.

The Levels-of-Processing Model: Another View of Memory

Not all psychologists support the notion of three memory systems. Craik and Lockhart (1972) propose instead a **levels-of-processing model.** They suggest that whether people remember an item for a few seconds or a lifetime depends on how deeply they process the information. With the shallowest levels of processing, a person is merely aware of the incoming sensory information. Deeper processing takes place only when the person does something more with the information, such as forming relationships, making associations, attaching meaning to a sensory impression, or engaging in active elaborations on new material. However, the deeper levels of processing that establish a memory also require background knowledge, so that lasting connections can be formed between the person's existing store of knowledge and the new information (Willoughby et al., 2000).

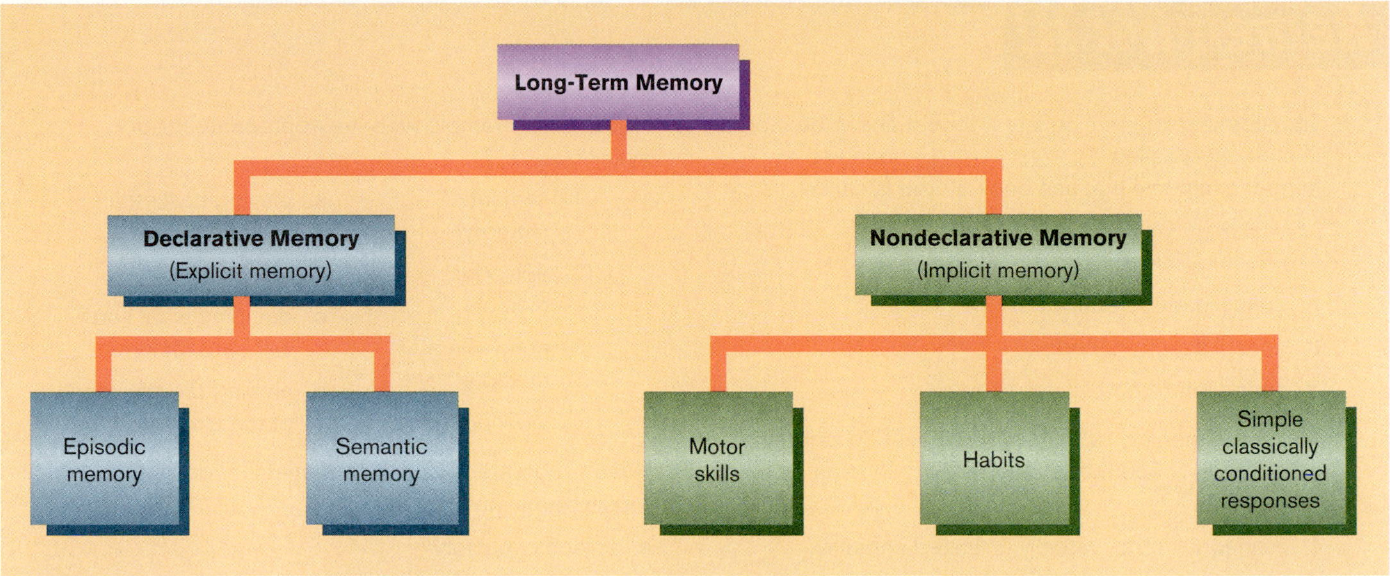

Figure 6.5

Subsystems of Long-Term Memory

Declarative memory can be divided into two subparts—episodic memory, which stores memories of personally experienced events, and semantic memory, which stores facts and information. Nondeclarative memory consists of motor skills acquired through repetitive practice, habits, and simple classically conditioned responses.

Craik and Tulving (1975) tested the levels-of-processing model. They had participants answer *yes* or *no* to questions asked about words just before the words were flashed to them for ⅕ of a second. The participants had to process the words in three ways: (1) visually (is the word in capital letters?); (2) acoustically (does the word rhyme with another particular word?); and (3) semantically (does the word make sense when used in a particular sentence?). Test yourself in the *Try It!*

Try It!

1. Is the word *LARK* in capital letters? ____ Yes ____ No
2. Does the word *speech* rhyme with *sleet*? ____ Yes ____ No
3. Would the word *park* make sense in this sentence?

   The woman passed a ______________ on her way to work.
   ____Yes ____ No

Wait a few minutes and see which words you can recall.

The test required shallow processing for the first question, deeper processing for the second question, and still deeper processing for the third question. Later retention tests showed that the deeper the level of processing, the higher the accuracy rate of memory. But this conclusion is equally valid for the three-system model. Some brain-imaging studies with fMRI revealed that semantic (deeper) encoding causes greater activity in the left prefrontal cortex (Gabrieli et al., 1996). Other studies of how brain activity is related to depth of processing (semantic processing) reveal two kinds of memory-related brain activity: information search operations and information retrieval (Rugg et al., 2000).

Remember It!

1. Transforming information into a form that can be stored in memory is called ______________; bringing to mind the material that has been stored is called ______________.
   a. encoding; decoding
   b. consolidation; retrieval
   c. consolidation; decoding
   d. encoding; retrieval
2. Match the memory system with the best description of its capacity and the duration of time it holds information:

(1) sensory memory	a. virtually unlimited capacity; long duration
(2) short-term memory	b. large capacity; short duration
(3) long-term memory	c. very limited capacity; short duration

3. Match each example with the appropriate memory system:

____ (1) semantic memory	a. playing basketball
____ (2) episodic memory	b. remembering your first date
____ (3) nondeclarative memory	c. deciding what you will have for lunch
____ (4) working memory	d. naming the presidents of the United States

4. Which subsystem of long-term memory does not require conscious awareness?
   a. episodic memory
   b. semantic memory
   c. nondeclarative memory
   d. declarative memory

Answers: 1. d 2. (1) b (2) c (3) a 3. (1) d (2) b (3) a (4) c 4. c

MEASURING MEMORY

Three Methods of Measuring Memory

What are three methods of measuring retention?

Psychologists have used three main methods to measure memory: recall, recognition, and the relearning method.

Recall: Memory at Its Best In **recall** a person must produce required information by searching memory without the help of **retrieval cues.** Trying to remember someone's name, recalling items on a shopping list, memorizing a speech or a poem word for word, and remembering appointments are all recall tasks. Test items such as essay and fill-in-the-blank questions require recall. Try to answer the following question:

> The three processes involved in memory are ______________, ______________, and ______________.

To recall, you must remember information "cold." A recall task may be made a little easier if cues are provided to jog memory. Such a cue might consist of providing the first letters of the required words for fill-in-the-blank questions. If you could not recall the three terms to respond to the question above, try again with cued recall:

> The three processes involved in memory are e______________, s______________, and r______________.

recall: A measure of retention that requires a person to remember material with few or no retrieval cues, as in an essay test.

retrieval cue: Any stimulus or bit of information that aids in the retrieval of particular information from long-term memory.

Sometimes serial recall is required; that is, information must be recalled in a specific order. This is the way you learned your ABCs, memorized poems, and learned any sequences that had to be carried out in a certain order. Often serial recall is easier than free recall—recalling the items in any order—because in serial recall, each letter, word, or task may serve as a cue for the one that follows.

You may fail to recall information in a memory task even if you are given many different retrieval cues, but this does not necessarily mean that the information is not in long-term memory. You still might be able to remember if a recognition test were used to measure memory.

These drama students must use serial recall to remember in precise order their lines, gestures, movements, and stage directions.

Recognition: I've Seen That Before **Recognition** is exactly what the name implies. A person simply recognizes something as familiar—a face, a name, a taste, a melody. Multiple-choice, matching, and true/false questions are examples of recognition test items. Answer the following question:

Which of the following is *not* one of the processes involved in memory?
a. encoding b. assimilation c. storage d. retrieval

Was this recognition question easier than the recall version? The main difference between recall and recognition is that a recognition task does not require you to supply the information but only to recognize it when you see it. The correct answer is included along with other items in a recognition question.

Are you better at remembering faces than names? Have you ever wondered why? Actually the task involves recognition as opposed to recall. You must recall the name but merely recognize the face; and, as you have seen, recognition is easier than recall. Remembering faces would be considerably more difficult if you had to recall each feature of a face rather than simply recognizing it. But are you better at recognizing faces than names? No. When recognition is the memory task, there is no difference in people's ability to recognize faces and names (Faw, 1990).

Recent brain-imaging studies have discovered that the hippocampus plays an extensive role in memory tasks involving recognition, and the degree of hippocampal activity varies with the exact nature of the task. When the task is recognizing famous faces, widespread brain activity takes place in both hemispheres, involving the prefrontal and temporal lobes and including the hippocampus and surrounding hippocampal region. Less widespread brain activity is observed during the recognition of recently encoded faces or the encoding of faces seen for the first time. Studies with monkeys having brain damage limited to the hippocampal region show conclusively that this region is absolutely essential for normal recognition tasks (Teng et al., 2000; Zola et al., 2000). Other recent studies show that the hippocampal region also plays an important role in the recollection of recently stored facts and events (Stark and Squire, 2000).

The Relearning Method: Learning Is Faster the Second Time Around There is yet another way to measure memory that is even more sensitive than recognition. With the **relearning method** (the savings method), retention is expressed as the percentage of time saved when material is relearned compared with the time required to learn the material originally. Suppose it took you 40 minutes to memorize a list of words, and 1 month later you were tested, using recall or recognition. If you could not recall or recognize a single word, would this mean that you had absolutely no memory of anything on the test? Or could it mean that the recall and the recognition methods of testing were not sensitive enough to pick up what little information you may have stored? How could a researcher measure a remnant of this former

recognition: A measure of retention that requires a person to identify material as familiar, or as having been encountered before.

relearning method: Measuring retention in terms of the percentage of time or learning trials saved in relearning material compared with the time required to learn it originally; also called the savings method.

learning? Using the relearning method, a researcher could time how long it would take you to relearn the list of words. If it took 20 minutes to relearn the list, this would represent a 50% savings over the original learning time of 40 minutes. The percentage of time saved—the **savings score**—reflects how much material remains in long-term memory.

savings score: The percentage of time or learning trials saved in relearning material over the amount of time or number of learning trials required for the original learning.

nonsense syllable: A consonant-vowel-consonant combination that does not spell a word; used to control for the meaningfulness of the material.

College students demonstrate the relearning method each semester when they study for comprehensive final exams. Relearning material for the final exams takes less time than it took to learn the material originally.

Ebbinghaus and the First Experimental Studies on Learning and Memory

What was Ebbinghaus's major contribution to psychology?

Hermann Ebbinghaus (1850–1909) conducted the first experimental studies on learning and memory. Realizing that some materials are easier than others to understand and remember, Ebbinghaus was faced with the task of finding materials that would all be equally difficult to memorize. So he invented the **nonsense syllable**—a consonant-vowel-consonant combination that is not an actual word. Examples are LEJ, XIZ, LUK, and ZOH. The use of nonsense syllables largely accomplished Ebbinghaus's goal. But did you notice that some of the syllables sound more like actual words than others and would, therefore, still be easier to remember?

Ebbinghaus (1885/1964) conducted his studies on memory using 2,300 nonsense syllables as his material and himself as the only participant. He carried out all his experiments at about the same time of day in the same surroundings, eliminating all possible distractions. Ebbinghaus memorized lists of nonsense syllables by repeating them over and over at a constant rate of 2.5 syllables per second, marking time with a metronome or a ticking watch. He repeated a list until he could recall it twice without error, a point that he called *mastery.*

Ebbinghaus recorded the amount of time or the number of trials it took to memorize his lists to mastery. Then, after different periods of time had passed and forgetting had occurred, he recorded the amount of time or number of trials needed to relearn the same list to mastery. Ebbinghaus compared the time or trials required for relearning with those of the original learning and then computed the percentage of time saved—the *savings score.* The percentage of savings represented the percentage of the original learning that remained in memory.

Ebbinghaus learned and relearned more than 1,200 lists of nonsense syllables to discover how rapidly forgetting occurs. Figure 6.6 shows his famous curve of for-

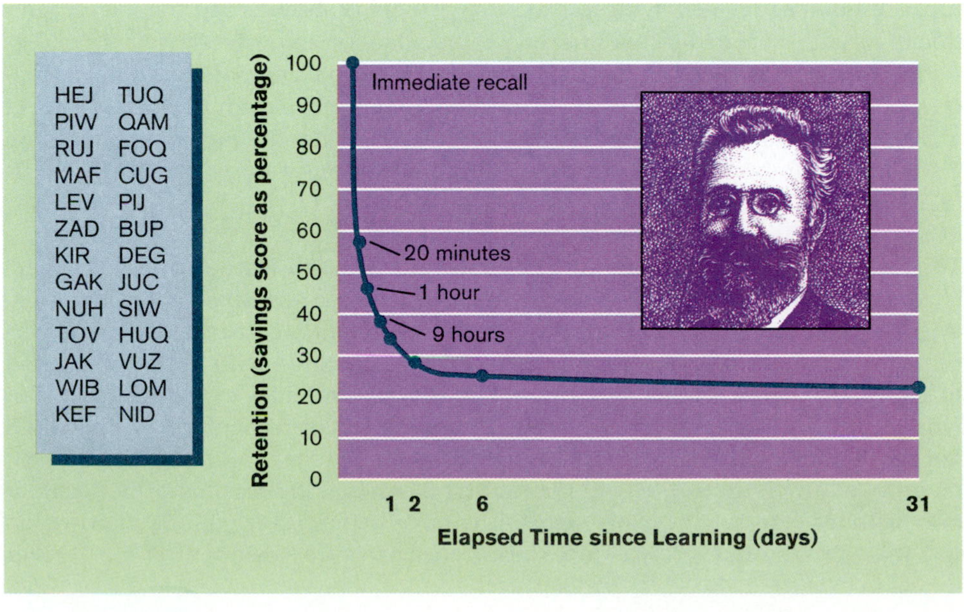

Figure 6.6

Ebbinghaus's Curve of Forgetting

After memorizing lists of nonsense syllables similar to those at left, Ebbinghaus measured his retention after varying intervals of time using the relearning method. Forgetting was most rapid at first, as shown by his retention of only 58% after 20 minutes and 44% after 1 hour. Then the rate of forgetting tapered off, with a retention of 34% after 1 day, 25% after 6 days, and 21% after 31 days. (Data from Ebbinghaus, 1913.)

getting, which consists of savings scores at various time intervals after the original learning. The curve of forgetting shows that the largest amount of forgetting occurs very quickly and then forgetting tapers off. If Ebbinghaus retained information as long as a day or two, very little more would be forgotten even a month later. But remember, this curve of forgetting applies to nonsense syllables. Meaningful material is usually forgotten more slowly, as is material that was carefully encoded, deeply processed, and frequently rehearsed.

What Ebbinghaus learned about the rate of forgetting is relevant for everyone. Do you, like most students, cram before a big exam? If so, don't assume that everything you memorize on Monday can be held intact until Tuesday. So much forgetting occurs within the first 24 hours that it is wise to spend at least some time reviewing the material on the day of the test. The less meaningful the material is to you, the more you will forget and the more necessary a review will be.

When researchers measured psychology students' retention of names and concepts, they found that the pattern of forgetting was similar to Ebbinghaus's curve. Forgetting of names and concepts was rapid over the first several months, leveled off in approximately 36 months, and remained about the same for the next 7 years (Conway et al., 1991).

Remember It!

1. Which of the following methods is the most sensitive way of measuring retention and can detect learning when other methods cannot?
   a. recall c. relearning
   b. recognition d. retrieval

2. Who invented the nonsense syllable, conceived the relearning method for testing retention, and plotted the curve of forgetting?
   a. George Sperling c. Frederick Bartlett
   b. H. E. Burtt d. Hermann Ebbinghaus

3. The curve of forgetting shows that memory loss
   a. occurs most rapidly at first and then levels off to a slow decline.
   b. begins to occur about 3 to 4 hours after learning.
   c. occurs at a fairly steady rate over a month's time.
   d. occurs slowly at first and increases steadily over a month's time.

4. Match each example with the corresponding method of measuring retention:

____ (1) identifying a suspect in a lineup
____ (2) answering a fill-in-the-blank question on a test
____ (3) having to study less for a comprehensive final exam than for all of the previous exams put together
____ (4) answering questions on this *Remember It!*
____ (5) reciting one's lines in a play

a. recognition
b. relearning
c. recall

Answers: 1. c 2. d 3. a 4. (1) a (2) c (3) b (4) a (5) c

FORGETTING

Most people think of forgetting as a problem to be overcome, but forgetting is not all bad. Wouldn't it be depressing if you were condemned to remember in stark detail all the bad things that ever happened to you?

The Causes of Forgetting

What are six causes of forgetting?

There are many reasons why people fail to remember. Among them are encoding failure, decay, interference, consolidation failure, motivated forgetting, and retrieval failure.

Encoding Failure: Never Entering Long-Term Memory There is a distinction between forgetting and not being able to remember. Forgetting is the inability to recall something that you could recall previously. But often when people say they cannot remember, they have not actually forgotten. The inability to remember may be a result of **encoding failure**—the information never entered long-term memory in the first place.

Of the many things we encounter every day, it is surprising how little we actually encode. Can you recall accurately, or even recognize, something you have seen thousands of times before? Read the *Try It!* to find out.

Try It!

On a sheet of paper, draw a sketch of a U.S. penny from memory using recall. In your drawing, show the direction in which President Lincoln's image is facing and the location of the date, and include all the words on the "heads" side of the penny. Or try the easier recognition task and see if you can recognize the real penny in the drawings below. (From Nickersen & Adams, 1979.)

In your lifetime you have seen thousands of pennies, but unless you are a coin collector, you probably have not encoded the details of a penny. If you did poorly on the *Try It!*, you have plenty of company. After studying a large group of participants, Nickerson and Adams (1979) reported that few people could reproduce a penny from recall. In fact, only a handful of participants could even recognize a drawing of a real penny when it was presented along with incorrect drawings. (The correct penny is the one labeled A in the *Try It!*)

When preparing for tests, do you usually take on a passive role? Do you merely read and reread your textbook and your notes and assume that this process will eventually result in learning? If you don't test yourself by reciting the material, you may find that you have been the unwilling victim of encoding failure.

Decay: Fading Away with Time **Decay theory,** probably the oldest theory of forgetting, assumes that memories, if not used, fade with time and ultimately disappear entirely. The term *decay* implies a physiological change in the neural trace that recorded the experience. According to this theory, the neural trace may decay or fade within seconds, days, or much longer periods of time.

Most psychologists now accept the notion of decay, or fading of the memory trace, as a cause of forgetting in sensory and short-term memory but not in long-term memory. There does not appear to be a gradual, inevitable decay of the long-term memory trace. In one study, Harry Bahrick and others (1975) found that after 35 years, participants could recognize 90% of their high school classmates' names and photographs—the same percentage as for recent graduates.

What is interference, and how can it be minimized?

Interference: The Greatest Enemy of Forgetting A major cause of forgetting that affects people every day is **interference.** Whenever you try to recall any given memory, two types of interference can hinder the effort. Information or associations stored either before or after an item can interfere with the ability to remember it (see Figure 6.7). Interference can reach either forward or backward in time to affect memory. It gets us coming and going. Also, the more similar the interfering associa-

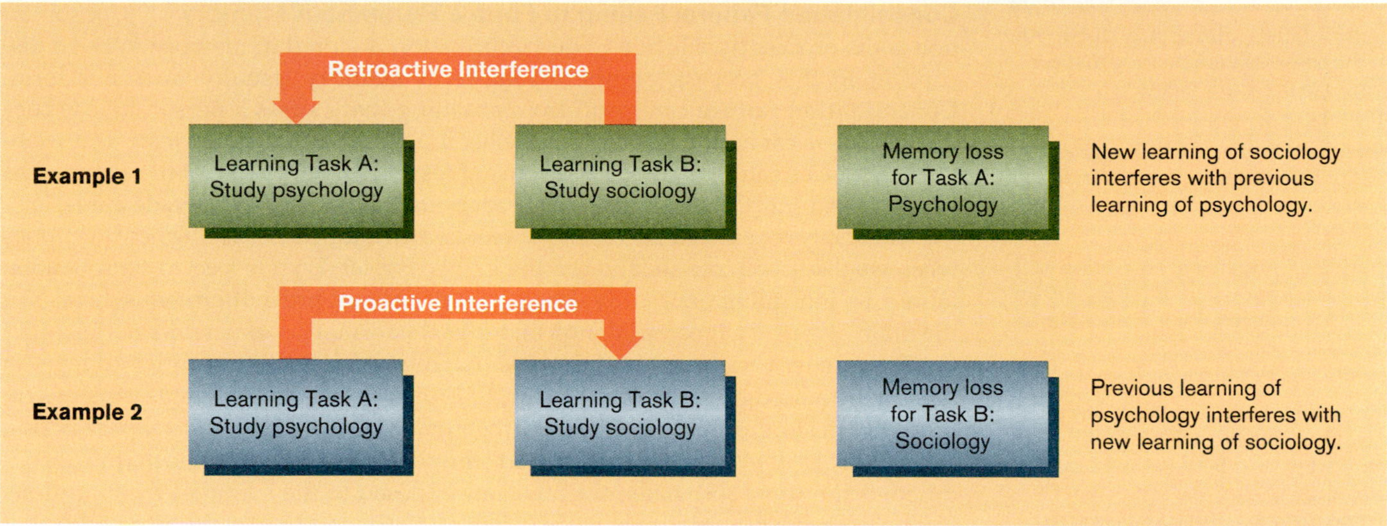

Figure 6.7

Retroactive and Proactive Interference

As shown in Example 1, retroactive interference occurs when new learning hinders the ability to recall information learned previously. As shown in Example 2, proactive interference occurs when prior learning hinders new learning.

tions are to information a person is trying to recall, the more difficult it is to recall the information (Underwood, 1964).

Proactive Interference Laura's romance with her new boyfriend, Todd, got off to a bad start when she accidentally called him Dave, her former boyfriend's name. How many checks written in early January do you suppose have the wrong year? These are two examples of mistakes that result from proactive interference. *Proactive interference* occurs when information or experiences already stored in long-term memory hinder the ability to remember newer information (Underwood, 1957). For example, when you drive a new car, it may take a while to feel comfortable with the arrangement of the dashboard. Your earlier habits of responding to your old car's dashboard may interfere with your driving at first. This type of proactive interference is called *negative transfer.* One explanation for interference is the competition between old and new responses (Bower et al., 1994).

Retroactive Interference New learning or experience that interferes with the ability to remember information previously stored is called *retroactive interference.* The more similar the new learning or experience is to the previous learning, the more interference there is. Is there any way to minimize interference? You may be surprised to learn that of all human activities, sleep interferes with previous learning the least.

What can you do to lessen the effects of retroactive interference on memory?

- When possible, study before going to sleep.
- If you can't study before going to sleep, at least review at that time the material you need to remember.
- Try not to study similar subjects back-to-back. Better yet, after studying one subject, take a short break before beginning the next subject.
- Schedule your classes so that courses with similar subject matter do not follow each other.

encoding failure: A cause of forgetting resulting from material never having been put into long-term memory.

decay theory: A theory of forgetting that holds that the memory trace, if not used, disappears with the passage of time.

interference: Memory loss that occurs because information or associations stored either before or after a given memory hinder the ability to remember it.

consolidation failure: Any disruption in the consolidation process that prevents a permanent memory from forming.

retrograde amnesia (RET-ro-grade): A loss of memory affecting experiences that occurred shortly before a loss of consciousness.

motivated forgetting: Forgetting through suppression or repression in order to protect oneself from material that is too painful, anxiety- or guilt-producing, or otherwise unpleasant.

repression: Removing from one's consciousness disturbing, guilt-provoking, or otherwise unpleasant memories so that one is no longer aware that a painful event occurred.

amnesia: A partial or complete loss of memory resulting from brain trauma or psychological trauma.

Consolidation Failure: Failing to Form a Permanent Memory Consolidation is the process by which encoded information is stored in memory. When a disruption in this process occurs, a long-term memory usually does not form. **Consolidation failure** can result from anything that causes a person to lose consciousness—a car accident, a blow to the head, a grand mal seizure, or an electroconvulsive shock treatment given for severe depression. Memory loss of the experiences that occurred shortly before the loss of consciousness is called **retrograde amnesia.**

We briefly considered the biological requirements for consolidating new memories when we discussed consolidation earlier in this chapter. With respect to consolidation failure, an intriguing new study shows how drugs that prevent protein synthesis in the brain also prevent consolidation and thus the formation of new memories.

Researchers Nader and others (2000) demonstrated that conditioned fears in rats can be erased by infusing into the rats' brains a drug that prevents protein synthesis (such synthesis is necessary for memory consolidation). Rats experienced a single pairing of a tone (the conditioned stimulus, CS) and a foot shock (the unconditioned stimulus, US). Later, the rats were exposed to the sound of the tone alone (CS) and showed a fear response of "freezing" (becoming totally immobile as if frozen with fright). Clearly, the rats remembered the feared stimulus. Twenty-four hours later, the rats were again exposed to the tone alone, and it elicited fear, causing them to freeze. Immediately, the drug anisomycin, which prevents protein synthesis in the brain, was infused into the rats' amygdalae (the part of the brain that processes "fear" stimuli). After the drug was infused, the rats were shocked again, but they showed no fear response (freezing). The rats in the study had already consolidated the memory of the fear, but it was completely wiped out after the drug prevented protein synthesis from occurring. This means that fear memories, once activated, must be "reconsolidated," or they may disappear.

This finding has positive implications. If fear memories can be activated and then wiped out with drugs that prevent protein synthesis, a new therapy may be on the horizon for people who suffer from debilitating fears (Nader et al., 2000).

We have discussed ways to avoid forgetting, but there are occasions when people may need to avoid remembering—times when they want to forget.

Motivated Forgetting: Don't Remind Me Victims of rape or physical abuse, war veterans, and survivors of airplane crashes or earthquakes all have had terrifying experiences that may haunt them for years. These victims are certainly motivated to forget their traumatic experiences, but even people who have not suffered any trauma use **motivated forgetting** to protect themselves from experiences that are painful, frightening, or otherwise unpleasant.

With one form of motivated forgetting, *suppression,* a person makes a conscious, active attempt to put a painful, disturbing, anxiety- or guilt-provoking memory out of mind, but the person is still aware that the painful event occurred. With another type of motivated forgetting, **repression,** unpleasant memories are literally removed from consciousness, and the person is no longer aware that the unpleasant event ever occurred (Freud, 1922). People who have **amnesia** (memory loss) that is not due to loss of consciousness or brain damage have actually repressed the events they no longer remember. Motivated forgetting is probably used by more people than any other method to deal with unpleasant memories. It seems to be a natural human tendency to forget the unpleasant circumstances of life and to remember the pleasant ones (Linton, 1979; Meltzer, 1930).

Retrieval Failure: Misplaced Memories How many times have these experiences happened to you? You are with a friend when you meet an acquaintance, but you can't introduce the two because you cannot recall the name of your acquaintance. Or, while taking a test, you can't remember the answer to a question that you are sure you know. Often people are certain that they know something, but they are not able to retrieve the information when they need it. This type of forgetting is called *retrieval failure.*

Endel Tulving (1974) claims that much of what people call forgetting is really an inability to locate the needed information. The information is in long-term memory, but the person cannot retrieve it. In his experiments, Tulving found that participants could recall a large number of items they seemed to have forgotten if he provided retrieval cues to jog their memory. For example, odors often provide potent reminders of experiences from the past, and certain odors can serve as retrieval cues for information that was learned when those odors were present (Schab, 1990).

A common retrieval failure experience is known as the *tip-of-the-tongue (TOT) phenomenon* (Brown & McNeil, 1966). Surely you have experienced trying to recall a name, a word, or some other bit of information, knowing what you were searching for almost as well as your own name. You were on the verge of recalling the word or name, perhaps aware of the number of syllables and the beginning or ending letter of the word. It was on the tip of your tongue, but it just wouldn't quite come out.

prospective forgetting: Forgetting to carry out some action, such as mailing a letter.

Prospective Forgetting: Forgetting to Remember

Do you have trouble remembering appointments? Do you forget to mail birthday cards on time, pick up your clothes at the dry cleaner, pay your bills, or water your plants? If you do, you are not alone. In a study of everyday forgetting, Terry (1988) had 50 participants keep a diary of the instances of forgetting that occurred each day. Of the 751 recorded instances of forgetting, most did not involve forgetting names, facts, or other information already known. Most instances involved **prospective forgetting**—forgetting to carry out some intended action. For many older adults, prospective forgetting can be more than just an irritating inconvenience. An everyday memory problem for these individuals is forgetting to take their medicine as prescribed, and such prospective forgetting can have serious health consequences (Hertzog et al., 2000).

Prospective forgetting is largely influenced by motivation. People are most likely to forget to do the things they view as unimportant, unpleasant, or burdensome. They are less likely to forget things that are pleasurable or important to them (Winograd, 1988).

Remember It!

1. Match the example with the appropriate cause of forgetting:

   ____ (1) encoding failure
   ____ (2) consolidation failure
   ____ (3) retrieval failure
   ____ (4) repression
   ____ (5) interference

   a. failing to remember the answer on a test until after you turn the test in
   b. forgetting a humiliating childhood experience
   c. not being able to describe the back of a dollar bill
   d. calling a friend by someone else's name
   e. waking up in the hospital and not remembering you had an automobile accident

2. To minimize interference, it is best to follow learning with

   a. rest. c. sleep.
   b. recreation. d. unrelated study.

3. In older people, decay is the main cause of forgetting in long-term memory. (true/false)

4. According to the text, the major cause of forgetting is interference. (true/false)

Answers: 1. (1) c (2) e (3) a (4) b (5) d 2. c 3. false 4. true

THE NATURE OF REMEMBERING AND FORGETTING

Memory as a Permanent Record: The Video Cassette Recorder Analogy

For hundreds of years people have speculated about the nature of memory. Aristotle suggested that the senses imprint memories in the brain like signet rings stamping impressions in wax. Sigmund Freud believed that all memories are permanently preserved, with some lying deep in the unconscious. Wilder Penfield (1969), a Canadian neurosurgeon, claimed that experiences leave a "permanent imprint on the brain . . . as though a tape recorder had been receiving it all" (p. 165). What would lead him to such a conclusion?

Beginning in 1993, Penfield (1975) performed over 1,100 operations on patients with epilepsy. He found that when parts of the temporal lobes were stimulated with an electrical probe, 3.5% of patients reported flashback experiences, as though they were actually reliving parts of their past. After reviewing Penfield's findings, other researchers offered different explanations for his patients' responses. Neisser (1967) suggested that the experiences patients reported were "comparable to the content of dreams," rather than the recall of actual experiences (p. 169).

Memory as a Reconstruction: Partly Fact and Partly Fiction

What is meant by the statement "Memory is reconstructive in nature"?

Other than Penfield's work, there is no research to suggest that memory works like a video cassette recorder, capturing every part of an experience exactly as it happens. Normally what a person recalls is not an exact replica of an event, according to Elizabeth Loftus, a leading memory researcher. Rather a memory is a **reconstruction**—an account pieced together from a few highlights, using information that may or may not be accurate (Loftus & Loftus, 1980). Put another way, "memory is not so much like reading a book as it is like writing one from fragmentary notes" (Kihlstrom, 1995, p. 341). There is ample evidence indicating that memory is quite often inaccurate. "Critical details of an experience can be forgotten or become distorted, their source and order may be misremembered, and under certain circumstances completely new details may be incorporated into a memory" (Conway et al., 1996, p. 69). Recall is, even for people with the most accurate memories, partly truth and partly fiction. This was the finding of another pioneer in memory research, Englishman Sir Frederick Bartlett.

When people recall an event, such as a car accident, they are actually reconstructing it from memory by piecing together bits of information that may or may not be totally accurate.

Sir Frederick Bartlett (1886–1969) Ebbinghaus explored memory by memorizing nonsense syllables under rigidly controlled experimental conditions. In contrast, Sir Frederick Bartlett studied memory using rich and meaningful material learned and remembered under more lifelike conditions. Bartlett (1932) gave participants stories to read and drawings to study, and at varying time intervals he had them reproduce the original material. Accurate reports were rare. The participants seemed to reconstruct the material they had learned, rather than actually remember it. They recreated the stories, making them shorter and more consistent with their own individual viewpoints. They rationalized puzzling features of the stories to fit their own expectations and often changed details, substituting more familiar objects or events instead. Errors in memory increased with time, and Bartlett's participants were not aware that they had partly remembered and partly invented. Ironically, the parts his participants had created were often the very parts that they most adamantly claimed to have remembered.

What is Bartlett's contribution to scientists' understanding of memory?

Bartlett concluded that people systematically distort the facts and the circumstances of experiences. Information already stored in long-term memory exerts a strong influence on how people remember new information and experiences. As Bartlett (1932) put it, "The past is being continually remade, reconstructed in the interest of the present" (p. 309).

Schemas and Memory Bartlett suggested that his participants' inaccuracies in memory reflected their **schemas**—the integrated frameworks of knowledge and assumptions they had about people, objects, and events. Schemas aid in processing large amounts of material, because they provide frameworks into which people can incorporate new information and experience. Schemas also provide association cues that can help in retrieval.

What are schemas, and how do they affect memory?

Once formed, schemas influence what people notice and how they encode and recall information. When we encounter new information or have a new experience related to an existing schema, we try to make it fit or be consistent with that schema. To accomplish this, we may have to distort some aspects of the information and ignore or forget other aspects. Some of the distorting and ignoring occurs as the material is being encoded; more can occur when we try to remember or reconstruct the original experience.

Distortion in Memory When people reconstruct memories, they do not purposely try to distort the actual experience—unless, of course, they are lying. But people tend to omit some facts that actually occurred and to supply other details from their own imaginations. Distortion occurs when people alter the memory of an event or an experience in order to fit their beliefs, expectations, logic, or prejudices.

The tendency toward systematic distortion of actual events has been proven many times. The *Try It!* demonstrates distortion in memory.

Try It!

Read this list of words aloud at a rate of about one word per second. Then close your book, and write down all the words you can remember.

bed	awake	dream	snooze	nap	snore
rest	tired	wake	doze	yawn	slumber

Now check your list. Did you "remember" the word *sleep*? Many people do, even though it is not one of the words on the list (Deese, 1959).

reconstruction: A memory that is not an exact replica of an event but has been pieced together from a few highlights, using information that may or may not be accurate.

schemas: The integrated frameworks of knowledge and assumptions a person has about people, objects, and events, which affect how the person encodes and recalls information.

The *Try It!* shows that we are very likely to alter or distort what we see or hear to make it fit with what we believe *should* be true. All the words on the list are related to sleep, so it seems logical that *sleep* should be one of the words. In experiments using word lists similar to the one in the *Try It!* between 40% and 55% of the participants "remembered" the key related word that was not on the list (Roediger & McDermott, 1995). If you "remembered" the word *sleep* in doing the *Try It!*, you created a false memory, which probably seemed as real to you as a true memory (Dodson et al., 2000).

The tendency to distort makes the world more understandable and enables people to organize their experiences into their existing systems of beliefs and expectations. But this tendency often causes gross inaccuracies in what people remember. People distort memories of their own lives in the positive direction. Bahrick and others (1996) found that 89% of college students accurately remembered the A's they earned in high school, but only 29% accurately recalled the D's. The most dramatic examples of systematic distortion often occur in eyewitness testimony.

Eyewitness Testimony: Is It Accurate?

What conditions reduce the reliability of eyewitness testimony?

When someone says, "I ought to know—I saw it with my own eyes," you might accept their statement almost without question. After all, seeing is believing. Or is it?

Traditionally, eyewitness testimony has been viewed as reliable by the legal system in the United States and elsewhere (Brigham & Wolfskeil, 1983). Recall from the opening story Ronald Cotton, who was a victim of faulty eyewitness identification. Is his case merely an isolated incident? According to Elizabeth Loftus (1993a), a staggering number of wrongful convictions in the United States each year are based on eyewitness testimony. According to Huff and others (1995), the number is probably at least 10,000. Yet it was not until October 1999 that the U.S. Department of Justice prepared the first national guidelines for the collection of eyewitness evidence (Wells et al., 2000).

Studies on the accuracy of human memory suggest that eyewitness testimony is highly subject to error, and that it should always be viewed with caution (Loftus, 1979). Nevertheless, it does play a vital role in the U.S. justice system. Says Loftus (1984), "We can't afford to exclude it legally or ignore it as jurors. Sometimes, as in cases of rape, it is the only evidence available, and it is often correct" (p. 24).

Fortunately, eyewitness mistakes can be minimized. Eyewitnesses to crimes typically identify suspects from a lineup. If shown photographs of a suspect before viewing the lineup, eyewitnesses may mistakenly identify that suspect in the lineup because the person looks familiar. The familiarity may result from seeing the mug shot, not from seeing the suspect at the scene of the crime. The procedure followed when using mug shots affects the accuracy of eyewitnesses' recognition and identification. Research suggests that it is better to have an eyewitness first describe the perpetrator and then search for photos matching that description than to have the eyewitness start by looking through photos and making judgments as to their similarity to the perpetrator (Pryke et al., 2000).

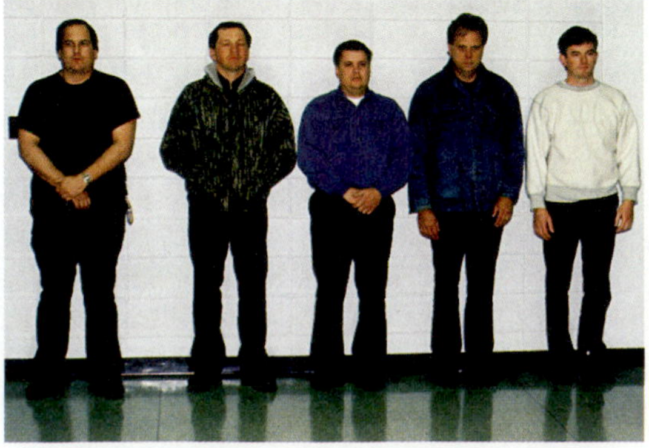

The composition of this police lineup is consistent with research findings that suggest that all individuals in a lineup should be similar to the suspect with respect to age, race, body build, and other physical characteristics.

The composition of the lineup is also important. Other subjects in a lineup must resemble the suspect in age, body build, and certainly in race. Even then, if the lineup does not contain the guilty party, eyewitnesses may identify the person who most resembles the perpetrator (Gonzalez et al., 1993). Eyewitnesses are less likely to make errors if a sequential lineup is used, that is, if the members of the lineup are viewed one after the other, rather than simultaneously (Loftus, 1993a). Some police officers and researchers prefer a "showup"—presenting only one suspect and having the witness indicate whether that person is the perpetrator. There are fewer misidentifications with a showup, but also more failures in making positive identifications (Wells, 1993).

Eyewitnesses are more likely to identify the wrong person if the person's race is different from their own. According to Egeth (1993), misidentifications are approximately 15% higher in cross-race than in same-race identifications. Misidentification is also somewhat more likely to occur when a weapon is used in a crime. The witnesses may pay more attention to the weapon than to the physical characteristics of the criminal (Steblay, 1992).

Even questioning witnesses after a crime can influence what they later remember. Because leading questions can substantially change a witness's memory of an event, it is critical that the interviewers ask neutral questions (Leichtman & Ceci, 1995). Misleading information supplied after the event can result in erroneous recollections of the actual event, a phenomenon known as the *misinformation effect* (Kroll et al., 1988; Loftus & Hoffman, 1989). Loftus (1997) and her students have conducted "more than 20 experiments involving over 20,000 participants that document how exposure to misinformation induces memory distortion" (p. 71). Furthermore, after eyewitnesses have repeatedly recalled information, whether accurate or inaccurate, they become even more confident when they testify in court because the information is so easily retrieved (Shaw, 1996).

Witnessing a crime is highly stressful. How does stress affect eyewitness accuracy? Research suggests that eyewitnesses do tend to remember the central, critical details of the event even though their arousal is high, but the memory of peripheral details suffers (Burke et al., 1992; Christianson, 1992).

Eyewitness identification poses another problem. As was demonstrated in the case of Jennifer Thompson in this chapter's opening story, the confidence eyewitnesses have in their testimony is not necessarily an indication of its accuracy (Loftus, 1993a; Sporer et al., 1995). In fact, eyewitnesses who perceive themselves to be more objective have more confidence in their testimony, regardless of its accuracy, and are more likely to include incorrect information in their verbal descriptions (Geiselman et al., 2000). When witnesses make incorrect identifications with great certainty, they can be highly persuasive to judges and jurors alike. "A false eyewitness identification can create a real-life nightmare for the identified person, friends, and family members. . . . False identifications also mean that the actual culprit remains at large—a double injustice" (Wells, 1993, p. 568).

Does hypnosis improve the memory of eyewitnesses?

Hypnosis for Eyewitnesses You have probably heard accounts of how eyewitnesses, when hypnotized, recalled important information about a crime. But research suggests that under controlled laboratory conditions, people do not show improved memory under hypnosis (Buckhout et al., 1981). Hypnotized subjects supply more information and are more confident of their recollections, but they supply more inaccurate information as well (Dywan & Bowers, 1983; Nogrady et al., 1985). Because people are much more confident of their memories after hypnosis, they are very convincing witnesses. Some critics of hypnosis oppose using it in court to aid eyewitness testimony, but believe that it can be a valuable investigative tool during the course of criminal investigations.

Recovering Repressed Memories: A Controversy

What is the controversy regarding the therapy used to recover repressed memories of childhood sexual abuse?

Nearly a century ago, Sigmund Freud ignited a controversy about alleged recollections of childhood sexual abuse, and it has been renewed during the last decade (Del Monte, 2000). Thousands of people, the majority of them adult women under the age of 50, have claimed that they were sexually abused as children but repressed all memory of the abuse until they underwent therapy or read a "self-help" book for survivors of childhood sexual abuse. Can people endure repeated episodes of childhood sexual abuse for years, selectively repress all memory of the abuse, and then

As the debate over the existence of repressed memories continues, some—such as Gary Ramona (left)—have fought back. Ramona went to court to accuse his daughter's therapist of using improper suggestions and drugs to implant false memories of molestation.

recover the repressed memories as adults? A growing number of therapists specialize in helping people recover such repressed memories. However, many psychologists are skeptical, claiming that the"recovered" memories are being created or implanted by these therapists while they are trying to treat what the skeptics call "false memory syndrome" (Sher, 2000).

In 1988, Ellen Bass and Laura Davis published *The Courage to Heal*, a self-help book for survivors of childhood sexual abuse. This best-selling book became the "bible" for sex abuse victims and the leading "textbook" for some therapists who specialize in treating them. Bass and Davis not only seek to help survivors who remember having suffered sexual abuse; they reach out as well to other people who have no memory of any sexual abuse and try to help them determine whether they might have been abused. They suggest that "if you are unable to remember any specific instances . . . but still have a feeling that something abusive happened to you, it probably did" (p. 21). They offer a definite conclusion: "If you think you were abused and your life shows the symptoms, then you were" (p. 22). And they free potential victims of sexual abuse from the responsibility of establishing any proof: "You are not responsible for proving that you were abused" (p. 37).

Critics "argue that repression of truly traumatic memories is rare" (Bowers & Farvolden, 1996, p. 355). Moreover, they maintain that "when it comes to a serious trauma, intrusive thoughts and memories of it are the most characteristic reaction" (p. 359). According to Loftus (1993b), "The therapist convinces the patient with no memories that abuse is likely, and the patient obligingly uses reconstructive strategies to generate memories that would support that conviction" (p. 528). Repressed-memory therapists believe, however, that healing hinges on their patient's being able to recover the repressed memories.

Critics charge that recovered memories of sexual abuse are suspect because of the techniques therapists usually use to uncover them—namely, hypnosis and guided imagery. As you have learned, hypnosis does *not* improve the accuracy of memory, only the confidence that what one remembers is accurate. And a therapist using guided imagery might tell a patient something similar to what Wendy Maltz (1991) advocates in her book:

> Spend time imagining that you were sexually abused, without worrying about accuracy, proving anything, or having your ideas make sense. . . . Ask yourself . . . these questions: What time of day is it? Where are you? Indoors or outdoors? What kind of things are happening? (p. 50)

Can merely imagining experiences lead people to believe that those experiences had actually happened to them? Yes, according to some studies. About 25% of participants who had imagined that a fictitious event had happened, did in fact develop a false memory of the imagined event after they had been interviewed about it several times (Hyman et al., 1995; Hyman & Pentland, 1996; Loftus & Pickrell, 1995). Garry and Loftus (1994) were able to implant a false memory of being lost in a shopping mall at 5 years of age in 25% of participants aged 18 to 53, after verification of the fictitious experience by a relative. Repeated exposure to suggestions of false memories can create those memories (Zaragoza & Mitchell, 1996).

Critics are especially skeptical of recovered memories of events that occurred in the first few years of life; in part because the hippocampus, vital in the formation of episodic memories, is not fully developed then. And neither are the areas of the cortex where memories are stored (Squire et al., 1993). Furthermore, young children, who are still limited in language ability, do not store memories in the categories that would be accessible to them later in life. The relative inability of older children and adults to recall events from the first few years of life is referred to as **infantile amnesia.**

False accusations of childhood sexual abuse are apparently widespread, and a group of parents who deny the accusations against them have formed an organization known as the False Memory Syndrome (FMS) Foundation. The foundation has received more than 1,000 reports about individuals who recovered what they believed to be repressed memories of sexual abuse during therapy but later denied that any abuse had occurred (Merskey, 1996).

Is it possible *not* to recall incidents of childhood sexual abuse? Widom and Morris (1997) found that 64% of a group of women who had been sexually abused as children reported no memory of the abuse in a 2-hour interview 20 years later. Following up on women who had documented histories of sexual victimization, Williams (1994) found that 38% of them did not report remembering the sexual abuse some 17 years later. Memories of abuse were better when the victimization took place between the ages of 7 and 17 than when it occurred in the first 6 years of life. You should keep in mind, however, that it is possible that some of the women may have remembered the abuse but, for whatever reason, chose not to admit it.

The American Psychological Association (1994), the American Psychiatric Association (1993), and the American Medical Association (1994) have issued status reports on memories of childhood abuse. The position of all three groups is that current evidence supports the possibility that repressed memories exist as well as that false memories can be constructed in response to suggestions of abuse. This position suggests that recovered memories of abuse should be verified independently before they are accepted as facts. Taking such a position is critically important. As we saw in the *Try It!* on page 223, false memories are easily formed. And, once formed, they are often relied on with great confidence (Dodson et al., 2000; Henkel et al., 2000).

infantile amnesia: The relative inability of older children and adults to recall events from the first few years of life.

flashbulb memory: An extremely vivid memory of the conditions surrounding one's first hearing the news of a surprising, shocking, or highly emotional event.

Unusual Memory Phenomena

Flashbulb Memories: Extremely Vivid Memories Most people over age 50 remember the assassination of President John F. Kennedy, and many claim to have unusually vivid memories of exactly when and where they received the news of the assassination. And many people around the world remember with great clarity when and where they learned of Princess Diana's tragic death. This type of extremely vivid memory is called a **flashbulb memory** (Bohannon, 1988). Brown and Kulik (1977) suggest that a flashbulb memory is formed when a person learns of an event that is very surprising, shocking, and highly emotional. You might have a flashbulb memory of when you received the news of the death or the serious injury of a close family member or a friend.

Pillemer (1990) argues that flashbulb memories do not constitute a different type of memory altogether. Rather, he suggests, all memories can vary on the dimensions of emotion, consequentiality (the importance of the consequences of the event), and rehearsal (how often people think or talk about the event afterwards). Flashbulb memories rank high in all three dimensions and thus are extremely memorable. Therefore, flashbulb memories should be the most accurate of any memories. But are they infallible? Hardly.

Several studies suggest that flashbulb memories are not as accurate as people believe them to be. Neisser and Harsch (1992) questioned university freshmen about the Challenger disaster the following morning. When the same students were questioned again 3 years later, one-third gave accounts that differed markedly from those given initially, even though they were extremely confident of their recollections. Weaver (1993)

A flashbulb memory can be formed when a person learns of a shocking and highly emotional event, such as the death of Princess Diana in a car crash in Paris. Do you remember where you were when you first heard of her death?

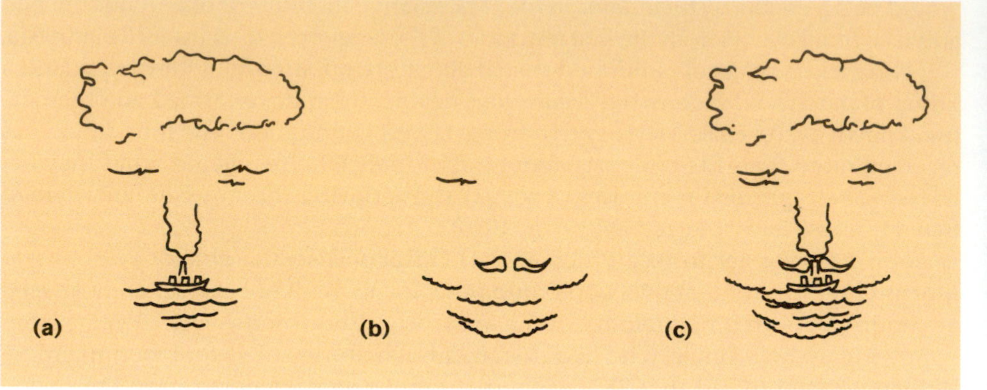

Figure 6.8

Test for Eidetic Imagery

Researchers test children for eidetic imagery by having them stare for 30 seconds at a picture like the one in (a). A few minutes later, the drawing in (b) is shown to the children, who are asked to report what they see. Those with eidetic imagery usually claim that they see a face and describe the composite sketch in (c). The face can be perceived only if the child retains the image of the first picture and fuses it with the middle drawing. (From Haber, 1980.)

questioned students following the bombing of Iraq that signaled the beginning of the Gulf War and again 1 year later. He found that the accuracy of the students' accounts decreased, although confidence in their recollections had not.

Eidetic Imagery: Almost Like "Photographic Memory" Have you ever wished that you had a photographic memory? Perhaps you have heard of someone who is able to read a page in a book and recall it word for word. More than likely, that person has developed an enviable memory by learning and applying principles of memory improvement. Psychologists doubt that there are more than a few rare cases of a truly photographic memory that captures all the details of an experience and retains them perfectly. But some studies do show that about 5% of children apparently have something akin to photographic memory that psychologists call **eidetic imagery** (Haber, 1980). This is the ability to retain the image of a visual stimulus, such as a picture, for several minutes after it has been removed from view and to use this retained image to answer questions about the visual stimulus (see Figure 6.8).

Children with eidetic imagery generally have no better long-term memory than others their age. And virtually all children with eidetic imagery lose it before adulthood. One exceptional case, however, is Elizabeth, a teacher and a skilled artist. She can create on canvas an exact duplicate of a remembered scene in all its rich detail. Just as remarkable is her ability to retain visual images of words. "Years after having read a poem in a foreign language, she can fetch back an image of the printed page and copy the poem from the bottom line to the top line as fast as she can write" (Stromeyer, 1970, p. 77).

Memory and Culture

Sir Frederick Bartlett (1932) believed that some impressive memory abilities operate within a social or cultural context and cannot be understood as a pure process. He stated that "both the manner and matter of recall are often predominantly determined by social influences" (p. 244). Studying memory in a cultural context, Bartlett (1932) described the amazing ability of the Swazi people of Africa to remember the slight differences in individual characteristics of their cows. One Swazi herdsman, Bartlett claimed, could remember details of every cow he had tended the year before. Such a feat is less surprising when you consider that the key component of

eidetic imagery (eye-DET-ik): The ability to retain the image of a visual stimulus several minutes after it has been removed from view.

traditional Swazi culture is the herds of cattle the people tend and depend on for their living. Do the Swazi people have super powers of memory? Bartlett asked young Swazi men and young European men to recall a message consisting of 25 words. The Swazi had no better recall ability than the Europeans.

Among many of the tribal peoples in Africa, the history of the tribe is preserved orally. Thus an oracle, or specialist, must be able to encode, store, and retrieve huge volumes of historical data (D'Azevedo, 1982). Elders of the Iatmul people of New Guinea are also said to have committed to memory the lines of descent for the various clans of their people stretching back generation upon generation (Bateson, 1982). The unerring memory of the elders for the kinship patterns of their people are used to resolve disputed property claims (Mistry & Rogoff, 1994).

In many traditional cultures, elders may be oral historians—remembering and passing on the details of tribal traditions and myths as well as genealogical data.

Barbara Rogoff, an expert in cultural psychology, maintains that such phenomenal, prodigious memory feats are best explained and understood in their cultural context (Rogoff & Mistry, 1985). The tribal elders perform their impressive memory feats because it is an integral and critically important part of the culture in which they live. Most likely, their ability to remember lists of nonsense syllables would be no better than your own.

Remember It!

1. What early memory researcher found that, rather than accurately recalling information detail by detail, people often reconstruct and systematically distort facts to make them more consistent with past experiences?
   a. Hermann Ebbinghaus
   b. Frederick Bartlett
   c. Wilder Penfield
   d. William James
2. Which of the following is *not* true of schemas?
   a. Schemas are the integrated frameworks of knowledge and assumptions a person has about people, objects, and events.
   b. Schemas affect the way a person encodes information.
   c. Schemas affect the way a person retrieves information.
   d. When a person uses schemas, memories are accurate.
3. There are fewer errors in eyewitness testimony if
   a. eyewitnesses are identifying a person of their own race.
   b. eyewitnesses view suspects' photos prior to a lineup.
   c. a weapon has been used in the crime.
   d. questions are phrased to provide retrieval cues for the eyewitness.
4. As a rule, people's memories are more accurate under hypnosis. (true/false)
5. The ability to retain a visual image several minutes after it has been removed is called
   a. photographic memory.
   b. flashbulb memory.
   c. eidetic imagery.
   d. sensory memory.

Answers: 1. b 2. d 3. a 4. false 5. c

FACTORS INFLUENCING RETRIEVAL

Researchers in psychology have identified several factors that influence memory. A person can control some of these factors, but not all of them.

The Serial Position Effect: To Be Remembered, Be First or Last But Not in the Middle

What is the serial position effect?

If you were introduced to a dozen people at a party, you would most likely recall the names of the first few people you met and the last one or two, but forget more of the names in the middle. The reason is the **serial position effect**—the finding that for information learned in sequence, recall is better for items at the beginning and the end than for items in the middle of the sequence.

Information at the beginning of a sequence is subject to the **primacy effect** and is likely to be recalled because it already has been placed in long-term memory. Information at the end of a sequence is subject to the **recency effect** and has an even higher probability of being recalled because it is still in short-term memory. The poorer recall of information in the middle of a sequence occurs because that information is no longer in short-term memory and has not yet been placed in long-term memory. The serial position effect lends strong support to the notion of separate systems for short-term and long-term memory (Postman & Phillips, 1965).

Primacy and recency effects can also have an impact on information stored for longer periods of time (Roediger, 1991). For example, children learning their ABCs are likely to remember the first and last several letters of the alphabet better than many of the letters in the middle.

Environmental Context and Memory

How does environmental context affect memory?

Have you ever stood in your living room and thought of something you needed from your bedroom, only to forget what it was when you got there? Did the item come to mind when you returned to the living room? Some research reveals that people recall information better when they are in the same location—the same environmental context—as when the information was originally encoded.

Tulving and Thompson (1973) suggest that many elements of the physical setting in which a person learns information are encoded along with the information and become part of the memory trace. If part or all of the original context is reinstated, it may serve as a retrieval cue. Then the information learned in that context may come to mind. This is why criminal investigators often bring eyewitnesses back to the crime scene or ask them to visualize it to help them recall more details of the crime.

Godden and Baddeley (1975) conducted one of the early studies of context and memory with members of a university diving club. Participants memorized a list of words when they were either 10 feet underwater or on land. They were later tested for recall of the words in the same or in a different environment. The results of the study suggest that recall of information is strongly influenced by environmental context (see Figure 6.9). Words learned underwater were best recalled underwater, and words learned on land were best recalled on land. In fact, when the scuba divers learned and recalled the words in the same context, their scores were 47% higher than when the two contexts were different.

Godden and Baddeley (1980) found that changes in context had no effect, however, when they measured memory using recognition rather than recall. Why? The original context provides retrieval cues that make recall easier. But in a recognition task, people have only to recognize the information as familiar, so there is less need for the extra retrieval cues that the original context provides.

Going from 10 feet underwater to dry land is a rather drastic change in context, yet some researchers find the same effects even with more subtle context changes, such as going from one room to another. Steven Smith and others (1978) had stu-

serial position effect: The tendency to remember the beginning and ending items of a sequence or list better than the middle items.

primacy effect: The tendency to recall the first items on a list more readily than the middle items.

recency effect: The tendency to recall the last items on a list more readily than those in the middle of the list.

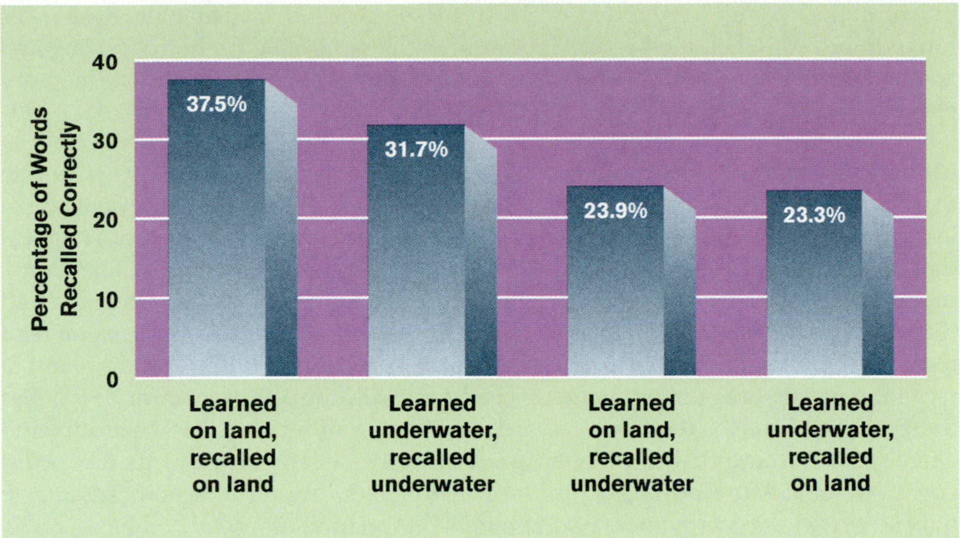

Figure 6.9
Context-Dependent Memory

Godden and Baddeley showed the strong influence of environmental context on recall. Scuba divers who memorized a list of words, either on land or underwater, had significantly better recall in the same physical context in which the learning had taken place. (Data from Godden & Baddeley, 1975.)

dents memorize lists of words in one room. The following day, students tested in the same room recalled 50% more words than those tested in another room. Again, there were no significant differences on recognition tests. Smith (1979) also found that students who simply visualized the room in which they had learned the words could remember almost as much when tested in a different room as students who learned and were tested in the same room. When both learning and remembering take place in the same context, the context itself can be a powerful memory aid. In fact, the context in which the remembering occurs has such a powerful effect that changing even one aspect or component of the context affects memory. In one study, participants viewed videotapes and then were tested on their memory of the videos in two separate interviews conducted two days apart. The memory context was the same for all the participants, with one exception. Half the participants were questioned by different interviewers, whereas the other half were questioned by the same interviewer in both sessions. As you might expect, participants who were questioned twice by the same interviewer (same context) performed better than the other participants on the memory task (Bjorkland et al., 2000).

Odors can also supply powerful and enduring retrieval cues for memory. In a study by Morgan (1996), participants were placed in isolated cubicles and exposed to a list of 40 words. They were instructed to perform a cognitive task using the words but were not asked to remember them. But back in the cubicle 5 days later, participants were unexpectedly tested for recall of the 40 words. Experimental participants who experienced a pleasant odor during learning and again when tested 5 days later had significantly higher recall than control participants who did not experience the odor during both learning and recall.

The more completely and carefully people encode material to be remembered, the less dependent they are on reinstating the original context.

The State-Dependent Memory Effect

What is the state-dependent memory effect?

If, as we have seen, the external environment can affect memory, might a person's internal state (happy or sad, intoxicated or sober) also influence memory performance? The answer is yes. People tend to recall information better if they are in the same internal state as when the information was encoded. Psychologists call this the **state-dependent memory effect.**

state-dependent memory effect: The tendency to recall information better if one is in the same pharmacological or psychological (mood) state as when the information was encoded.

Alcohol, Other Drugs, and Memory Some studies have shown a state-dependent memory effect for alcohol and drugs such as marijuana, amphetamines, and barbiturates (Eich, 1980). Participants learned (encoded) material while sober or intoxicated, and later were tested in either the sober or intoxicated state. Recall was found to be best when the participants were in the same state for both learning and testing (Weingartner et al., 1976). As in other studies, the state-dependent memory effect was evident for recall but not for recognition.

Mood and Memory Researchers have not been able to demonstrate reliably that recall is best if participants are in the same mood (happy or sad) when they encode or learn material as when they try to recall it. However, some evidence does suggest that pleasant experiences are more likely to be recalled when people are in a happy mood, and negative experiences when people are experiencing a negative mood (Eich et al., 1994; Teasdale & Fogarty, 1979). Adults who are clinically depressed tend to recall more negative life experiences (Clark & Teasdale, 1982) and are likely to recall their parents as unloving and rejecting (Lewinsohn & Rosenbaum, 1987). But as depression lifts, the tendency toward negative recall reverses itself. Seidlitz and Diener (1993) found that recall of either positive or negative life events was influenced by subjective well-being (life satisfaction and long-term happiness), rather than by current mood (momentary happiness or unhappiness).

Stress can affect memory. Would your memory for facts work normally if you were under the scrutiny of TV cameras and lights, a live studio audience, and millions of viewers at home as Regis Philbin asked you, "Is that your final answer?"

Stress, Anxiety, Depression, and Memory

Have you ever watched a TV quiz show and thought you could have easily won the prize? Would your memory work as well under the stress of cameras, lights, and millions of people watching as it does in the privacy and comfort of your own home? Psychologists who study stress and memory say that either too much or too little stress and emotional arousal can hinder memory performance.

People with high levels of general anxiety perform less well on memory tests than those with lower levels of anxiety (Loftus, 1980). Moreover, people going through great life stress—death of a loved one, loss of a job, divorce—do more poorly on tests of recent memories. A meta-analysis of 48 studies revealed a significant relationship between depression and memory impairment. And recognition and recall were more impaired in younger depressed patients than in older ones (Burt et al., 1995).

Remember It!

1. When children learn the alphabet, they often can recite "A, B, C, D . . ." and ". . . W, X, Y, Z" before they can recite the letters in between. This is because of the
   a. primacy effect.
   b. recency effect.
   c. serial position effect.
   d. state-dependent memory effect.
2. Recall is about as good when people visualize the context in which learning occurred as it is when recall and learning occur in the same context. (true/false)
3. Scores on recognition tests (either multiple-choice or true/false) will be higher if testing and learning take place in the same physical environment. (true/false)
4. Which best explains why drugs such as alcohol and marijuana can interfere with recall if the drugs are taken during learning but not during retrieval?
   a. the consistency effect
   b. the state-dependent memory effect
   c. context-dependent memory
   d. consolidation failure
5. Compared with nondepressed people, depressed people tend to have more sad memories. (true/false)

Answers: 1. c 2. true 3. false 4. b 5. true

BIOLOGY AND MEMORY

Obviously a person's vast store of memories must exist physically somewhere in the brain. But where?

Brain Damage: A Clue to Memory Formation

What role do the hippocampus and the rest of the hippocampal region play in episodic and semantic memory?

Researchers are finding specific locations in the brain that house and mediate functions and processes in memory. One important source of information comes from people who have suffered memory loss resulting from damage to specific brain areas. One such person is H.M., a man who has had a major influence on scientists' knowledge of human memory, not as a researcher but as a subject.

The Case of H.M. H.M. suffered from such severe epilepsy that, out of desperation, he agreed to a radical surgical procedure. The surgeon removed the part of the brain believed to be causing H.M.'s seizures, the medial portions of both temporal lobes—the amygdala and the **hippocampal region,** which includes the hippocampus itself and the underlying cortical areas. It was 1953, and H.M. was 27 years old.

> After his surgery, H.M. remained intelligent and psychologically stable, and his seizures were drastically reduced. But unfortunately, the tissue cut from H.M.'s brain housed more than the site of his seizures. It also contained his ability to form new, conscious long-term memories. Though his short-term memory is still as good as ever and he easily remembers the events of his life stored well before the operation, H.M. suffers from **anterograde amnesia.** He has not been able to remember a single event that has occurred since the surgery. And though H.M. turned 75 in 2001, as far as his conscious long-term memory is concerned, it is still 1953 and he is still 27 years old.
>
> Surgery affected only H.M.'s declarative, long-term memory—his ability to store facts, personal experiences, names, faces, telephone numbers, and the like. But researchers were surprised to discover that he could still form nondeclarative memories; that is, he could still acquire skills through repetitive practice although he could not remember having done so. For example, since the surgery, H.M. has learned to play tennis and improve his game, but he has no memory of ever having played. (Adapted from Milner, 1966, 1970; Milner et al., 1968.)

H.M.'s case was one of the first indications that the hippocampal region is involved in forming long-term memories. Other patients who have suffered similar brain damage show the same types of memory loss (Squire, 1992). The most recent research indicates that the hippocampus is critically important in forming episodic memories (Eichenbaum, 1997; Gluck & Myers, 1997). Semantic memory, however, depends not only on the hippocampus, but also on the other parts of the hippocampal region underlying it (Vargha-Khadem et al., 1997). The hippocampal region is needed for only a limited time after learning (Kim & Fanselow, 1992). It plays a continuing role during the process of reorganization and consolidation through which memories are finally stored in other areas of the cortex (Ungerleider, 1995). Once stored, however, memories can be retrieved without the involvement of the hippocampus (Gluck & Myers, 1997; McClelland et al., 1995).

An interesting recent study (Maguire et al., 2000) that was described briefly in Chapter 2 suggests that the hippocampus may serve special functions in addition to those already known. A part of the hippocampus evidently specializes in navigational skills by helping to create intricate neural spatial maps. Magnetic resonance imaging (MRI) scans revealed that the rear (posterior) region of the hippocampus of London taxi drivers was significantly larger than that of participants in a matched control group whose living did not depend on navigational skills (see Figure 6.10 on p. 234). In addition, the more time spent as a taxi driver, the greater the volume of the posterior hippocampus. Further, in many small mammals and birds, the volume

hippocampal region: A part of the limbic system, which includes the hippocampus itself (primarily involved in the formation of episodic memories) and its underlying cortical areas (involved in the formation of semantic memories).

anterograde amnesia: The inability to form long-term memories of events occurring after a brain injury or brain surgery, although memories formed before the trauma are usually intact.

Figure 6.10

MRI Scans Showing the Larger Size of the Posterior Hippocampus in the Brain of an Experienced Taxi Driver

The posterior (rear) hippocampus of an experienced London taxi driver, shown in red in MRI scan (a), is significantly larger than the posterior hippocampus of a research participant who was not a taxi driver, shown in red in scan (b). (Adapted from Maguire et al., 2000.)

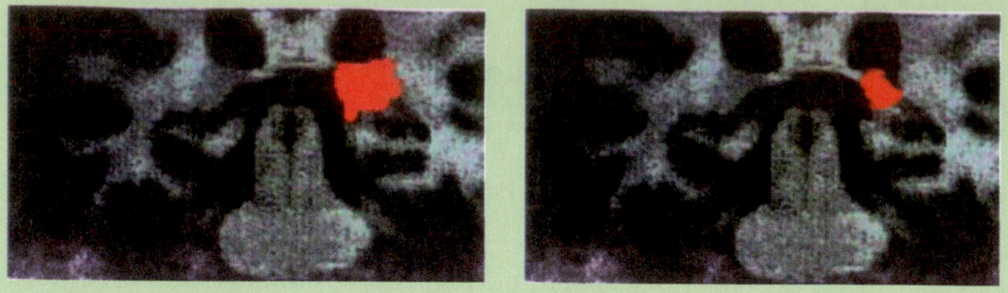

of the hippocampus increases seasonally, as navigational skills and spatial maps showing where food is hidden become critical for survival (Clayton, 1998; Colombo & Broadbent, 2000).

Thus, research has established that the hippocampus is critically important for storing and using mental maps to navigate in the environment. And the observed reorganization of neural circuits in the hippocampus of the London taxi drivers confirms that brain plasticity in response to environmental demands can continue into adulthood. These findings also raise the possibility of neurogenesis, the generation of new neurons in the adult hippocampus.

We have considered how researchers have identified and located some of the brain structures that play a role in memory. But what happens within these brain structures as they change, reshape, and rearrange to make new memories?

Neuronal Changes in Memory: Brain Work

Some researchers are exploring memory more minutely, by studying the actions of single neurons. Others are studying collections of neurons and their synapses, and the neurotransmitters whose chemical action begins the process of recording and storing a memory. The first close look at the nature of memory in single neurons was provided by Eric Kandel and his colleagues, who traced the effects of learning and memory in the sea snail *Aplysia* (Dale & Kandel, 1990). Using tiny electrodes implanted in several single neurons in the sea snail, the researchers mapped the neural circuits that are formed and maintained as the animal learns and remembers. They also discovered the different types of protein synthesis that facilitate short-term and long-term memory (Sweatt & Kandel, 1989). Kandel won a Nobel Prize in 2000 for his work.

But the studies of learning and memory in *Aplysia* reflect only simple classical conditioning, which is a type of nondeclarative memory. Other researchers studying mammals report that physical changes occur in the neurons and synapses in brain regions involved in declarative memory.

What is long-term potentiation, and why is it important?

Long-Term Potentiation: Prolonged Action at the Synapses As far back as the 1940s, Canadian psychologist Donald O. Hebb (1949) argued that the necessary neural ingredients for learning and memory must involve the enhancement of transmission at the synapses.

The most widely studied model for learning and memory at the level of the neurons meets the requirements of the mechanism Hebb described (Fischbach, 1992). **Long-term potentiation (LTP)** is an increase in the efficiency of neural transmission at the synapses that lasts for hours or longer (Bliss & Lomo, 2000; Martinez & Derrick, 1996; Nguyen et al., 1994). (To *potentiate* means "to make potent or to

long-term potentiation: A long-lasting increase in the efficiency of neural transmission at the synapses.

strengthen.") LTP is important because it appears to be the basis for learning and memory at the level of the neurons.

Long-term potentiation does not take place unless *both* the sending and receiving neurons are activated at the same time by intense high-frequency stimulation. Also, the receiving neuron must be depolarized (ready to fire) when stimulation arrives, or LTP will not occur. LTP is a common occurrence in the hippocampal region, which, as you have learned, is essential in the formation of declarative memories (Eichenbaum & Otto, 1993).

If the changes in synapses produced by LTP are the same changes that take place in learning, then blocking or interfering with LTP should likewise interfere with learning. And it does. When Davis and others (1992) gave rats a drug that blocks certain receptors in sufficient doses to interfere with a maze-running task, they discovered that LTP in the hippocampus was also disrupted. In contrast, Riedel (1996) found that LTP is enhanced and memory is improved when a drug that excites those same receptors is administered shortly after maze training.

Researchers now believe that LTP has the required characteristics to be a process involved in consolidating new memories (Cotman & Lynch, 1989). However, controversy continues as to whether LTP's observed increase in synaptic efficiency over periods of hours or longer is the result of an increase in amount of neurotransmitter released, an increase in the number of receptors at the synapses, or both (Bennett, 2000).

Hormones and Memory

How do memories of threatening situations that elicit the "fight or flight response" compare with ordinary memories?

The strongest and most lasting memories are usually those fueled by emotion. Research by McGaugh and Cahill (1995) suggests that there may be two pathways for forming memories—one for ordinary information and another for memories that are fired by emotion. When a person is emotionally aroused, the adrenal glands release the hormones adrenalin (epinephrine) and noradrenaline (norepinephrine) into the bloodstream. Long known to be involved in the "fight or flight response," these hormones enable humans to survive, and they also imprint powerful and enduring memories of the circumstances surrounding threatening situations.

Such emotionally laden memories activate the amygdala (known to play a central role in emotion) and other parts of the memory system. Emotional memories are lasting memories, and this may be the most important factor in explaining the intensity and durability of flashbulb memories.

Other hormones may have important effects on memory. Estrogen, the female sex hormone, appears to improve learning and memory, not only in healthy women but in patients with Alzheimer's disease as well. Estrogen appears to exert this effect by helping to build and maintain synapses between neurons in brain areas known to be involved in memory, such as the hippocampal region (Woolley et al., 1997).

The strongest and most lasting memories are usually fueled by emotion. Here a mourner adds a tribute outside the home of John F. Kennedy, Jr. after his untimely death.

IMPROVING MEMORY: SOME HELPFUL STUDY HABITS

What are four study habits that can aid memory?

There are no magic formulas for improving your memory. Remembering is a skill and, like any other skill, requires knowledge and practice. In this section we will consider several study habits and techniques that can improve your memory.

Organization: Everything in Its Place

People tend to retrieve information from long-term memory according to the way they have organized it for storage. Almost anyone can name the months of the year in about 10 seconds, but how long would it take to recall them in alphabetical order? The same 12 items, all well-known, are much harder to retrieve in alphabetical order, because they are not organized that way in memory. A telephone directory would be of little use to you if the names and phone numbers were listed in random order. Similarly, you are giving your memory a task it probably will not accept if you try to remember large amounts of information in a haphazard fashion. Try to organize items you want to remember in alphabetical order, or according to categories, historical sequence, size, shape, or any other way that will make retrieval easier.

Organizing material to be learned is a tremendous aid to memory. You can prove this for yourself by completing the *Try It!*

Try It!

Have a pencil and a sheet of paper handy. Read the following list of items out loud and then write down as many as you can remember.

peas	shaving cream	cookies
toilet paper	fish	grapes
carrots	apples	bananas
ice cream	pie	ham
onions	perfume	chicken

If you organize this list, the items are much easier to remember. Now read each category heading and the items listed beneath it. Write down as many items as you can remember.

Desserts	Fruits	Vegetables	Meat	Toilet Articles
pie	bananas	carrots	chicken	perfume
ice cream	apples	onions	fish	shaving cream
cookies	grapes	peas	ham	toilet paper

Overlearning: Reviewing Again, and Again, and Again

What is overlearning, and why is it important?

Do you still remember the words to songs that were popular when you were in high school? Can you recite many of the nursery rhymes you learned as a child even though you haven't heard them in years? You probably can because of **overlearning.**

Suppose that you wanted to memorize a list of words, and you studied until you could recite them once without error. Would this amount of study or practice be sufficient? Research suggests that people remember material better and longer if they overlearn it, that is, if they practice or study beyond the minimum needed to barely learn it (Ebbinghaus, 1885/1964). A pioneering study in overlearning by Krueger (1929) showed very substantial long-term gains for participants who engaged in 50% and 100% overlearning (see Figure 6.11). Furthermore, overlearning makes material more resistant to interference and is perhaps the best insurance against stress-related forgetting.

overlearning: Practicing or studying material beyond the point where it can be repeated once without error.

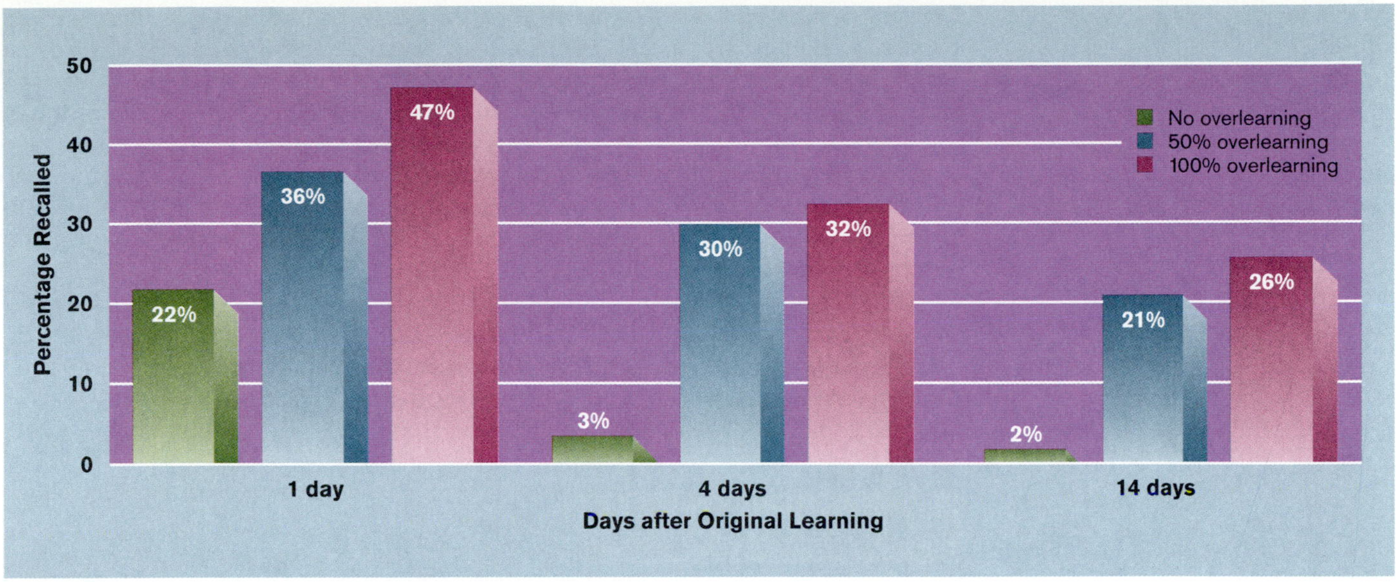

Figure 6.11

Overlearning

When a person learns material only to the point of one correct repetition, forgetting is very rapid. Just 22% is retained after 1 day, 3% after 4 days, and 2% after 14 days. When participants spend 50% more time going over the material, the retention increases to 36% after 1 day, 30% after 4 days, and 21% after 14 days. (Data from Krueger, 1929.)

The next time you study for a test, don't stop studying as soon as you think you know the material. Spend another hour or so going over it, and you will be surprised at how much more you will remember.

Spaced Practice versus Massed Practice: A Little at a Time Beats All at Once

Most students have tried cramming for examinations, but spacing study over several different sessions generally is more effective than **massed practice**—learning in one long practice session without rest periods (Glover & Corkill, 1987).

You will remember more with less total study time if you space your study over several sessions. Long periods of memorizing make material particularly subject to interference and often result in fatigue and lowered concentration. Also, when you space your practice, you probably create a new memory that may be stored in a different place, thus increasing your chance for recall.

Finally, recent research suggests that significant improvement in learning results when spaced study sessions are accompanied by short, frequent tests of the material being studied (Cull, 2000). Thus, you should be doing well in this course if you are completing all of the *Remember Its!*

The spacing effect applies to learning motor skills as well as to learning facts and information. Music students can tell you that it is better to practice for half an hour each day, every day, than to practice many hours in a row once a week.

massed practice: Learning in one long practice session as opposed to spacing the learning in shorter practice sessions over an extended period.

Recitation versus Rereading: Recitation Wins

Many students simply read and reread their textbook and notes when they study for an exam. Research over many years shows that you will recall more if you increase the amount of recitation in your study. For example, it is better to read a page or a few paragraphs and then recite or practice recalling what you have just read. Then continue reading, stop and practice reciting again, and so on. When you study for a psychology test and review the assigned chapter, try to answer each of the questions in the Summary and Review Section at the end of the chapter. Then read the material that follows each question and check to see if you answered the question correctly. This will be your safeguard against encoding failure. Don't simply read each section and assume that you can answer the question. Test yourself before your professor does.

A. I. Gates (1917) tested groups of students who spent the same amount of time in study, but who spent different percentages of that time in recitation and rereading. Participants recalled two to three times more if they increased their recitation time up to 80% and spent only 20% of their study time rereading.

Remember It!

1. The hippocampus itself is involved primarily in the formation of _______________ memories; the rest of the hippocampal region is involved primarily in the formation of _______________ memories.
2. H.M. retained his ability to add to his nondeclarative memory. (true/false)
3. What is the term for the long-lasting increase in the efficiency of neural transmission at the synapses that may be the basis for learning and memory at the level of the neurons?
   a. long-term potentiation
   b. synaptic facilitation
   c. synaptic potentiation
   d. presynaptic potentiation
4. Memories of circumstances surrounding threatening situations that elicit the "fight or flight response" tend to be more powerful and enduring than ordinary memories. (true/false)
5. When studying for an exam, it is best to spend
   a. more time reciting than rereading.
   b. more time rereading than reciting.
   c. equal time rereading and reciting.
   d. all of the time reciting rather than rereading.
6. The ability to recite a number of nursery rhymes from childhood is probably due mainly to
   a. spaced practice.
   b. organization.
   c. mnemonics.
   d. overlearning.

Answers: 1. episodic; semantic 2. true 3. a 4. true 5. a 6. d

Apply It!

Improving Memory with Mnemonic Devices

Most people use external aids to help them remember. Writing notes, making lists, writing on a calendar, or keeping an appointment book is often more reliable and accurate than trusting to memory (Intons-Peterson & Fournier, 1986). But there are times, such as when you are taking a test, when you cannot rely on external prompts. What if you need information at some unpredictable time, when you do not have external aids handy?

Several *mnemonics,* or memory devices, have been developed over the years to aid memory (Bower, 1973; Higbee, 1977; Roediger, 1980). We will explore rhyme, the method of loci, the first-letter technique, and the peg-word system.

Rhyme. Rhymes are a common aid to remembering material that otherwise might be difficult to recall. Perhaps as a child you learned your ABCs by using a rhyming song: "A-B-C-D-E-F-G-H-I-J-K-L-M-N-O-P. . ." You may repeat the verse "Thirty days hath September" when you try to recall the number of days in each month, or the saying "*i* before *e* except after *c*" when you are trying to spell a word. Rhymes are useful because they ensure that information is recalled in the proper sequence.

The method of loci: "In the first place." The *method of loci* is a mnemonic device that can be used when you want to remember a list of items such as a grocery list, or when you give a speech or a class report and need to make your points in order without using notes. The word *loci* (pronounced loh'-sye) is the plural form of *locus,* which means "location" or "place."

Figure 6.12 shows how to use the method of loci. Select any familiar location—your home, for example—and simply associate the items to be remembered with places there. Begin by picturing the first locus, for example, your driveway; the second locus, your garage; the third locus, the walk leading to your front door; and the fourth locus, perhaps the front hall closet. Progress through your house from room to room in an orderly fashion. Visualize the first item or idea you want to remember in its place on the driveway, the second item in your garage, the third at your front door, and so on until you

Figure 6.12

The Method of Loci

Begin by thinking of locations, perhaps in your home, that are in a sequence. Then visualize one of the items to be remembered in each location.

have associated each item you want to remember with a specific place. You may find it helpful to conjure up oversized images of the items that you place at each location (see Figure 6.12).

When you want to recall the items, take an imaginary walk starting at the first place—the first item will pop into your mind. When you think of the second place, the second item will come to mind, and so on.

Research suggests that the method of loci is very effective. In one study, college students memorized a different list of 40 nouns on each of four consecutive days. They visualized each word at specific locations on campus (Ross & Lawrence, 1968). When tested immediately after memorizing each list, the average recall was 37 out of 40 words in the exact order in which they were memorized. Average recall one day later was 34 words, and average recall at the end of all four lists was 29 words per 40-word list.

The first-letter technique. Another useful technique is to take the first letter of each item to be remembered and form a word, a phrase, or a sentence with those letters (Matlin, 1989). For example, suppose you had to memorize the seven colors of the visible spectrum in their proper order:

Red
Orange
Yellow
Green
Blue
Indigo
Violet

You could make your task easier by using the first letter of each color to form the name Roy G. Biv. Three chunks are easier to remember than seven different items.

As a child taking music lessons, you may have learned the saying "*E*very *g*ood *b*oy *d*oes *f*ine" to remind you of the lines of the treble clef, and *FACE* as a reminder of the spaces. To remember their license plate more easily, the authors think of the letters PCS as "poor civil servant."

The pegword system. Another mnemonic that has been proven effective is the *pegword system* (Harris & Blaiser, 1997). Developed in England around 1879, it uses rhyming words: one = bun; two = shoe; three = tree; four = door; five = hive; six = sticks; seven = heaven; eight = gate; nine = wine; ten = hen. Many children in English-speaking countries have learned these rhyming associations from the nursery rhyme "One, two, buckle my shoe—three, four, close the door." The rhyming words are memorized in sequence and then linked through vivid associations with any items you wish to remember in order, as shown in Figure 6.13.

For example, suppose you want to remember to buy five items at the store: milk, bread, grapefruit, laundry detergent, and eggs. Begin by associating the milk with the bun (your first pegword) by picturing milk pouring over a bun. Next picture the shoe, the second pegword, kicking a loaf of bread. Then continue by associating each item on your list with a pegword. To recall the items, simply go through your list of pegwords and the associated word will immediately come to mind.

Figure 6.13

The Pegword System

Items to be recalled are each associated with a pegword using a mental image. (Adapted from Bower, 1973.)

THINKING CRITICALLY

Evaluation

Some of the research studies cited in this chapter involved only one or just a few participants.

a. Select two of these studies and discuss the possible problems in drawing conclusions on the basis of studies using so few participants.
b. Suggest several possible alternative explanations for the studies' findings, other than those proposed by the researchers.
c. In your view, should such limited studies even be mentioned in a textbook? Why or why not?

Point/Counterpoint

Prepare an argument in favor of each of the following statements regarding therapeutic approaches for treating depression and eating disorders in patients who at the outset have no memory of childhood sexual abuse:

a. Attempting to recover repressed memories of childhood sexual abuse through hypnosis is useful.
b. Attempting to recover repressed memories of childhood sexual abuse through hypnosis can cause more harm than good.

Psychology in Your Life

Drawing on your knowledge, formulate a plan that you can put into operation to help improve your memory and avoid the pitfalls that cause forgetting.

SUMMARY AND REVIEW

REMEMBERING

What three processes are involved in the act of remembering?

Three processes involved in remembering are (1) encoding—transforming information into a form that can be stored in memory; (2) storage—maintaining information in memory; and (3) retrieval—bringing stored material to mind.

What is sensory memory?

Sensory memory holds information coming in through the senses for up to several seconds. This is just long enough for the nervous system to begin to process the information and send some of it on to short-term memory.

What are the characteristics of short-term memory?

Short-term (working) memory holds about seven unrelated items of information for less than 30 seconds without rehearsal. Short-term memory also acts as a mental workspace while the person carries out any mental activity.

What is long-term memory, and what are its subsystems?

Long-term memory is the permanent or relatively permanent memory system with a virtually unlimited capacity. Its subsystems are (1) declarative memory, which holds facts and information (semantic memory) along with personal life experiences (episodic memory); and (2) nondeclarative memory, which consists of motor skills acquired through repetitive practice, habits, and simple classically conditioned responses.

Key Terms
encoding (p. 205); storage (p. 205); consolidation (p. 205); retrieval (p. 205); sensory memory (p. 206); short-term memory (p. 208); displacement (p. 208); rehearsal (p. 209); long-term memory (p. 209); elaborative rehearsal (p. 210); declarative memory (p. 210); episodic memory (p. 210); semantic memory (p. 211); nondeclarative memory (p. 212); priming (p. 212); levels-of-processing model (p. 212)

MEASURING MEMORY

What are three methods of measuring retention?

Three methods of measuring retention are (1) recall, where information must be supplied with few or no retrieval cues; (2) recognition, where information must simply be recognized as having been encountered before; and (3) the relearning method, which measures retention in terms of time saved in relearning material compared with the time required to learn it originally.

What was Ebbinghaus's major contribution to psychology?

Hermann Ebbinghaus conducted the first experimental studies of learning and memory. He invented the nonsense syllable, conceived the relearning method as a test of memory, and plotted the curve of forgetting.

Key Terms
recall (p. 214); retrieval cue (p. 214); recognition (p. 215); relearning method (p. 215); savings score (p. 216); nonsense syllable (p. 216)

FORGETTING

What are six causes of forgetting?

Six causes of forgetting are encoding failure, consolidation failure, decay, interference, motivated forgetting, and retrieval failure.

What is interference, and how can it be minimized?

Interference occurs when information or associations stored either before or after a given memory hinder the ability to remember it. To minimize interference, follow a learning activity with sleep, and arrange learning so that you do not study similar subjects back to back.

Key Terms
encoding failure (p. 218); decay theory (p. 218); interference (p. 218); consolidation failure (p. 220); retrograde amnesia (p. 220); motivated forgetting (p. 220); repression (p. 220); amnesia (p. 220); prospective forgetting (p. 221)

THE NATURE OF REMEMBERING AND FORGETTING

What is meant by the statement "Memory is reconstructive in nature"?

Memory does not work like a video cassette recorder. People reconstruct memories, piecing them together from a few highlights and using information that may or may not be accurate.

What is Bartlett's contribution to scientists' understanding of memory?

Sir Frederick Bartlett found that people do not recall facts and experiences detail by detail. Rather, they systematically reconstruct and distort them to fit information already stored in memory.

What are schemas, and how do they affect memory?

Schemas are the integrated frameworks of knowledge and assumptions that people have about other people, objects, and events; schemas affect how people encode and recall information.

What conditions reduce the reliability of eyewitness testimony?

The reliability of eyewitness testimony is reduced when witnesses view a photograph of the suspect before viewing the lineup, when members of a lineup are viewed at the same time rather than one by one, when the perpetrator's race is different from that of the eyewitness, when a weapon has been used in the crime, and when leading questions are asked to elicit information.

Does hypnosis improve the memory of eyewitnesses?

Hypnotized subjects supply more information and are more confident of their recollections, but they supply more inaccurate information as well.

What is the controversy regarding the therapy used to recover repressed memories of childhood sexual abuse?

Critics argue that therapists using hypnosis and guided imagery to help their patients recover repressed memories of childhood sexual abuse are actually implanting false memories in those patients. Therapists who use these techniques believe that a number of psychological problems can be treated successfully by helping patients recover repressed memories of sexual abuse.

Key Terms
reconstruction (p. 222); schemas (p. 223); infantile amnesia (p. 227); flashbulb memory (p. 227); eidetic imagery (p. 228)

FACTORS INFLUENCING RETRIEVAL

What is the serial position effect?

The serial position effect is the tendency, when recalling a list of items, to remember the items at the beginning of the list (primacy effect) and the items at the end of the list (recency effect) better than items in the middle.

How does environmental context affect memory?

People tend to recall material more easily if they are in the same physical location during recall as during the original learning.

What is the state-dependent memory effect?

The state-dependent memory effect is the tendency to recall information better if one is in the same pharmacological or psychological state as when the information was learned.

Key Terms
serial position effect (p. 230); primacy effect (p. 230); recency effect (p. 230); state-dependent memory effect (p. 231)

BIOLOGY AND MEMORY

What role do the hippocampus and the rest of the hippocampal region play in episodic and semantic memory?

The hippocampus itself is involved primarily in the formation of episodic memories; the rest of the hippocampal region is involved primarily in forming semantic memories.

What is long-term potentiation, and why is it important?

Long-term potentiation is a long-lasting increase in the efficiency of neural transmission at the synapses. LTP is important because it may be the basis for learning and memory at the level of the neurons.

How do memories of threatening situations that elicit the "fight or flight response" compare with ordinary memories?

Memories of threatening situations tend to be more powerful and enduring than ordinary memories.

Key Terms
hippocampal region (p. 233); anterograde amnesia (p. 233); long-term potentiation (p. 234)

IMPROVING MEMORY: SOME HELPFUL STUDY HABITS

What are four study habits that can aid memory?

Four study habits that can aid memory are organization, overlearning, the use of spaced rather than massed practice, and spending a higher percentage of time reciting than rereading material.

What is overlearning, and why is it important?

Overlearning means practicing or studying material beyond the point where it can be repeated once without error. You remember overlearned material better and longer, and it is more resistant to interference and stress-related forgetting.

Key Terms
overlearning (p. 236); massed practice (p. 237)

Surf It!

Want to be sure you've absorbed the material in Chapter 6, "Memory," before the big test? Visiting *www.abacon.com/wood* can put a top grade within your reach. The site is loaded with free practice tests, flashcards, activities, and links to help you review your way to an A. To enliven that inevitable study break, the site also offers personality assessment quizzes and a psychology career corner.

7 Cognition and Language

Seeing Eye dogs may soon be replaced by an almost unbelievable application of human cognition. In January 2000, a biomedical engineering research team at the Dobelle Institute announced that it had developed an artificial vision system that could make possible unassisted, independent mobility for the blind. William Dobelle, who leads the team, stated that the artificial vision system gives a totally blind person a visual acuity of about 20/400 in a narrow field.

The system consists of a subminiature TV camera and an ultrasonic distance sensor, both mounted on a pair of eyeglasses. The camera and distance sensor are connected through a cable to a microcomputer carried in a pack worn on the person's belt. Once the video and distance signals are processed, this computer simplifies the images using the latest imaging technology, including edge-detection devices. Then the computer activates a second microcomputer, which transmits pulses to an array of 68 platinum electrodes that are implanted on the person's visual cortex. When stimulated, each of these 68 electrodes produces from one to four closely spaced *phosphenes,* which are said to resemble "stars in the sky." These white phosphenes are "seen" by the blind person against a black background map.

The participant in this research effort is a 62-year-old male who was totally blinded by a traumatic injury when he was 36. But now he can see well enough to read enlarged letters at a distance of about 5 feet. What's more, he is able to get around quite well in unfamiliar environments. In fact, he can navigate the New York subway system! Then, when he returns home, he replaces the subminiature TV camera with an electronic interface and "watches" television. He is also learning to use a computer to access the Internet.

What is meant by cognition, and what specific processes does it include?

Until recently, could anyone have envisioned the development of technology capable of giving artificial sight to the blind? Surprisingly, the ancient Greek thinker Aristotle (382–322 B.C.), who furthered the study of human cognition by inventing laws for reasoning and who stressed the importance of mental imagery, foresaw something similar:

> If every instrument could accomplish its own work, obeying or anticipating the will of others. . . . If the shuttle could weave, and the pick touch the lyre, without a hand to guide them, chief workmen would not need servant, nor masters slaves.

What Aristotle envisioned when he wrote these words over 2,300 years ago—shuttles that could weave without a weaver, lyres that could play music without a musician—were high-tech machines much like the robots that guide manufacturing processes and the computerized sound systems that assist rock bands. What Aristotle foresaw now exists, thanks to the science of artificial intelligence. But even Aristotle would be amazed by artificial vision for the blind and other achievements in artificial intelligence and modern robotics, all accomplished by the power of human cognition. Just what is cognition?

Cognition refers collectively to the mental processes involved in acquiring, storing, retrieving, and using knowledge (Matlin, 1989). In earlier chapters we looked at the cognitive processes of sensation, perception, and memory. In this chapter we first consider several other cognitive processes: imagery, concept formation, reasoning, decision making, and problem solving. Then we will explore recent developments in artificial intelligence and robotics—two high-tech applications of cognition. Finally, we will look at language, which plays a vital role in both cognition and communication.

IMAGERY AND CONCEPTS: TOOLS OF THINKING

cognition: The mental processes that are involved in acquiring, storing, retrieving, and using information and that include sensation, perception, imagery, concept formation, reasoning, decision making, problem solving, and language.

In trying to prove his existence, the great French philosopher René Descartes (1596–1650) said, "I think, therefore I am." Unfortunately, he did not proceed to describe the act of thinking itself. All of us have an intuitive notion of what thinking is. We say, "I think it's going to rain" (a prediction); "I think this is the right answer" (a choice); "I think I will resign" (a decision). But our everyday use of the word *think* does not suggest the processes we use to perform the act itself. Sometimes thinking is free-flowing rather than goal-oriented. At other times it is directed and aimed at a goal such as solving a problem or making a decision. Just how is the act of thinking accomplished? There is general agreement that it makes use of at least two tools—images and concepts.

Imagery: Picture This

What is imagery?

Can you imagine hearing a recording of your favorite song or someone calling your name? Can you picture yourself jogging, walking, or kissing someone you love? In your imagination, can you smell ammonia or taste your favorite ice cream? In doing these things, you take advantage of your own ability to use mental **imagery**—that is, to represent or picture a sensory experience mentally. Albert Einstein is said to have done much of his thinking in images.

In a survey of 500 adults conducted by McKellar (1972), 97% said they had visual images; 93% reported auditory images (imagine your psychology professor's voice); 74% claimed to have motor imagery (imagine raising your hand); 70%, tactile or touch images (imagine rubbing sandpaper); 67%, gustatory images (imagine the taste of a dill pickle); and 66%, olfactory images (imagine smelling a rose). Visual imagery is certainly the most common, although auditory imagery is not far behind.

Our mental images may be dimmer and less vivid than actual experiences, but the images are not limited to time and space, size, or other physical realities. You can imagine yourself flying though the air like an eagle, singing to the thundering applause of adoring fans, or performing all sorts of amazing feats. But normally our imaging is quite similar to the real world we are thinking about. In a recent study, memory researcher Alan Baddeley reported that the vividness of mental images, at least the visual and auditory ones he studied, are clearly influenced by both short-term (working) memory and long-term memory (Baddeley & Andrade, 2000).

Many people believe that visual mental images are formed all at once. But according to Stephen Kosslyn (1988), they are not. Rather, we mentally construct the objects we image, one part at a time. Studies with split-brain patients (discussed in Chapter 2) and normal people suggest that two types of processes are used in the formation of visual images. First, stored memories of how parts of an object look are retrieved, and then mental processes are used to arrange or assemble those parts into the proper whole. Both the left and right hemispheres participate in the processes of forming visual images. Try forming visual images as you do the *Try It!*

Try It!

a. Picture an ant crawling on a newspaper about 3 feet away. How many legs does the ant have?

b. Picture an ant perched on the end of a toothpick right in front of your eyes. Does the ant have eyelashes?

In which mental picture is the ant larger, a or b? Which mental picture provides more detail of the ant? (After Finke, 1985.)

Kosslyn (1975, 1983) asked research participants many questions like those in the *Try It!* and found that they answered questions concerning larger images about ⅕ second faster than questions about small images. It takes us slightly longer to zoom in on smaller images than on larger ones, just as it does when we visually scan real objects (Ochsner & Kosslyn, 1994).

But what if we are forming new images rather than answering questions about large and small images already formed? Picture an elephant standing 2 feet away.

imagery: The representation in the mind of a sensory experience—visual, auditory, gustatory, motor, olfactory, or tactile.

Now picture a rabbit standing at the same distance. Which image took longer to form? Kosslyn (1975) discovered that it takes people longer to form large mental images than to conjure up small ones. It takes longer to view the elephant because there is more of it to view, and likewise more of it to image.

This congruence between images and reality is not limited to visual imaging alone. You can form a realistic image of an action involving motion and tactile sensations, such as carrying a heavy load or a light load. Prove this for yourself in the *Try It!*

Try It!

Imagine yourself walking across your living room or bedroom, carrying a bowling ball. Now repeat the same walk in your imagination, but this time holding a balloon. Which imaginary walk took longer?

Did you imagine yourself walking faster when holding the balloon? This was the experience of participants in a similar imaging experiment (Intons-Peterson & Roskos-Ewoldsen, 1989). Why should this be true? This study suggested that imaging involves more than simply calling up visual images. Imaging reflects, as well, knowing how different objects behave under different circumstances in the real world. If you had not factored in the realization that you tend to walk faster when holding light objects than when lugging heavy objects, your imaginary walk across the room would have been equally fast with either the balloon or the bowling ball.

Not only can we form a mental image of an object, but we can manipulate and move it around mentally much as we would if we were actually holding and looking at the object (Cooper & Shepard, 1984; Farah, 1995; Kosslyn & Sussman, 1995). In an early study, Shepard & Metzler (1971) asked eight research participants to judge some 1,600 pairs of drawings like the ones in Figure 7.1. Participants had to rotate the objects mentally to see if they matched. Try doing this before reading further. As you may have discovered, the objects in Figure 7.1 (a) and (b) match; those in Figure 7.1 (c) do not. The more the objects had to be rotated mentally, the longer it took participants to decide whether they matched. This is precisely what would happen if the participants had rotated real objects—the more the objects needed to be rotated, the longer it would take to make the decision. In fact, recent brain-imaging studies indicate that the same regions in the motor cortex and related areas that are involved in the physical movements required for rotation of objects are also very active during mental imaging (Richter et al., 2000). But apparently age takes its toll on performance of mental rotation tasks. The performance of younger (aged 18–28) and older (aged 60–76) participants on a mental rotation task were compared. Older participants made more errors and had a much larger reduction in speed following an error than did their younger counterparts (Band & Kok, 2000).

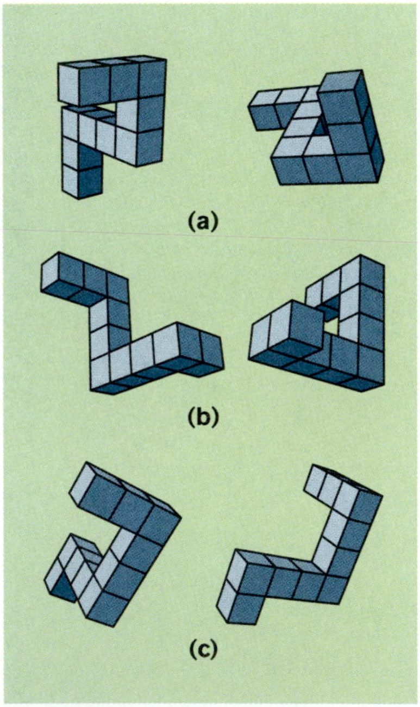

Figure 7.1

Samples of Geometric Patterns in Shepard and Metzler's Mental Rotation Study

Mentally rotate one of the patterns in each pair–(a), (b), and (c)–and decide whether the two patterns match. Do you find that the more you have to rotate the objects mentally, the longer it takes to decide if they match? (From Shepard & Metzler, 1971.)

Are the images we form subject to interference, just like our actual perceptions? Close your eyes, and form a mental image of your psychology professor. Now keep the visual image, and open your eyes. Doesn't the mental image fade or disappear as soon as you see a real object? If viewing an actual object interferes with a visual image, is the reverse also true? Will a vivid visual image interfere with a real object?

Yes, according to Craver-Lemley and Reeves (1992). In an earlier study, Segal and Fusella (1970) asked student participants to form either a visual image of a tree or an auditory image of the sound of a typewriter. The researchers then made a faint sound on a harmonica or flashed a small, dimly lighted blue arrow, or did nothing at all. Participants who were holding the visual image of a tree were more likely to miss seeing the blue arrow but more likely to hear the harmonica. But participants imaging the sound of a typewriter had the opposite experience. They saw the arrow but missed the sound of the harmonica. This study suggests that similar mental processes are used in both perceiving and imaging. Furthermore, using the same processes *simultaneously* on two different tasks causes interference.

There is general agreement that certain higher-order visual areas in the temporal and parietal lobes are involved both in imagery and in perception (Moscovitch et al., 1994). But not all researchers who study imagery and perception agree that similar mental processes are at work in both (Roland & Gulyás, 1994). And some researchers claim that even though the same neural pathways are used for both imaging and perceiving objects, those for imaging are activated in reverse order from those for perceiving (Kosslyn, 1994; Kosslyn & Ochsner, 1994; Miyashita, 1995).

concept: A mental category used to represent a class or group of objects, people, organizations, events, situations, or relations that share common characteristics or attributes.

Professionals in many fields—mathematicians, scientists, writers, artists, and musicians—use imaging effectively. A professional pianist, Liu Chi Kung, was imprisoned for 7 years during China's cultural revolution. Soon after being released, he was back on the tour circuit playing better than ever, according to critics who judged his performances. How did he do it without practicing for 7 long years? Using mental imagery, he rehearsed every day, playing every piece he knew in his imagination (Garfield, 1986). And sports psychologists have found that athletes skilled in visualization can actually improve their performance by practicing mentally (Ungerleider, 1992). When athletes are engaged in such mental practice, they primarily use "physical imagery," in which they imagine an object (i.e., a baseball bat) causing a change to a second object (i.e., a baseball) (Schwartz, 2000). It is said that Mark McGuire of the St. Louis Cardinals used imaging in this way in becoming the new home run king in the summer of 1999.

Baseball's home run king, Mark McGwire of the St. Louis Cardinals, uses imagery to form a mental picture of his bat connecting with the ball and powering it out of the stadium.

How can visualization be so effective in improving performance? Brain-imaging studies show that generally the same brain areas are activated whether a person is performing a given task or mentally rehearsing the task using imagery (Stephan et al., 1995). In other words, similar brain mechanisms are active when a person actually moves his or her hand and when the person merely imagines moving the hand. Recently, researchers found that the frontal and parietal lobes showed similar levels of activity during actual performance of a movement and during imaging of the movement. But the cerebellum, which coordinates well-timed and graceful movement, was more active during the actual performance of the movement; when the subjects were using mental imagery, the cerebellum exerted an inhibiting influence on physical movement (Lotze et al., 1999).

There is both direct and indirect evidence that the brain's visual system is active during visualization. PET scans reveal that the mental operations performed are similar whether a person is constructing a visual image or perceiving a stimulus that is physically present (Kosslyn et al., 1993; Posner & Raichle, 1995). People who have brain damage in the primary visual cortex lose some ability to form visual images (Farah, 1988). And Cohen and colleagues (1996) used functional MRI to discover that participants carrying out mental rotation tasks showed heightened activation in the cortical areas used to track moving objects and to encode spatial relations, as well as in the brain areas involved in visual perception. Another study, which measured participants' regional cerebral blood flow (rCBF), revealed that engaging in imaging based on verbal descriptions alone activated regions of the brain known to be involved in higher-level visual processing (Mellet et al., 2000).

Concepts: A Mental Classification System (Is a Penguin a Bird?)

What is a concept?

Fortunately, thinking is not limited to conjuring up images of sights, sounds, touches, tastes, and smells. We humans are capable of conceptualizing as well. A **concept** is a mental category used to represent a class or group of objects, people, organizations, events, situations, or relations that share common characteristics or attributes. *Furniture, tree, student, college, wedding* are all examples of concepts. As fundamental units of thought, concepts are useful tools that help us to order our world and to think and communicate with speed and efficiency.

Thanks to our ability to use concepts, we are not forced to consider and describe everything in great detail before we make an identification. We do not need a different name to identify and describe every single rock, tree, animal, or situation. If you see a hairy, brown and white, four-legged animal with its mouth open, tongue hanging out, and tail wagging, you recognize it immediately as a representative of the concept *dog*. *Dog* is a concept that stands for a class of animals that share similar characteristics or attributes, even though they may differ in significant ways. Great Danes, dachshunds, collies, Chihuahuas, and other breeds—you recognize all these varied creatures according to the concept *dog*.

Household pet is a broader concept, which might include dogs, cats, birds, and so on. Although other creatures—cockroaches, mice, or houseflies—may take up residence in the house, they are not likely to fit the concept *household pet*.

We have concepts of abstractions as well as of tangible objects and organisms. *Love, beauty,* and *justice* are abstract concepts. We can identify and consider aspects of beauty and justice because we have formed concepts of them. We also use relational concepts in our thinking—*larger than, smaller than, older than, younger than,* and so on—to compare individuals, objects, and ideas.

Other species of animals are capable of recognizing individual examples of concepts. Chimpanzees, in particular, show evidence of forming concepts, as you will learn when we discuss animal language later in this chapter. Even pigeons have learned to categorize pictures of cats, people, flowers, cars, and chairs as instances of those concepts (Wasserman, 1995).

What is the difference between a formal concept and a natural concept?

Formal and Natural Concepts Psychologists identify two basic types of concepts: formal (also known as artificial) concepts and natural (also known as fuzzy) concepts.

Some concepts are learned in an orderly, systematic way, rather than in a random, informal fashion. For example, elementary school students learn that, by definition, a triangle has three sides. Such a concept is generally a **formal concept,** one that is clearly defined by a set of rules, a formal definition, or a classification system. Formal concepts are common in the sciences and other academic disciplines.

Eleanor Rosch (1973, 1978) argues that formal concepts tend to be rather artificial and not related to actual experience. Most of the concepts we form and use are **natural concepts,** acquired not from definitions but through everyday perceptions and experiences. Rosch and her colleagues studied concept formation in its natural setting and concluded that in real life, natural concepts (such as *fruit, vegetable,* and *bird*) are somewhat fuzzy, rather than clear-cut and systematic.

We acquire many natural concepts through experiences with examples, or positive instances of the concept. When children are young, parents may point out examples of a car—the family car, the neighbor's car, cars on the street, and pictures of cars in books. But if a child points to some other type of moving vehicle and says "car," the parent will say, "No, that is a truck," or "This is a bus." *Truck* and *bus* are negative instances, or nonexamples, of the concept *car*. After experience with positive and negative instances of the concept, a child begins to grasp some of the properties of a car that distinguish it from other wheeled vehicles.

It is often said that the best examples of a given category are the average members, those that are most like the majority of members in the category. But is it always the case that the average, common, or typical features of a concept are selected in goodness-of-example ratings? Researchers Lynch and others (2000) asked participants who were experts on trees and those who were novices and knew little about trees to rate 48 trees according to how well the trees represented the concept of *tree*. The researchers found that the concept *tree* differed between the experts and the nonexperts, but neither group selected typical "average" trees as

formal concept: A concept that is clearly defined by a set of rules, a formal definition, or a classification system; an artificial concept.

natural concept: A concept acquired not from a definition but through everyday perceptions and experiences; a fuzzy concept.

prototype: The example that embodies the most common and typical features of a concept.

exemplars: The individual instances of a concept that are stored in memory from personal experience.

their top-rated examples. For the novices, familiarity determined the goodness-of-example selections. The tree experts, in contrast, often selected the "ideal" tree, the best of the best, as the best example; for instance, experts selected trees that were extremely tall, not those of average height. Thus, goodness-of-example ratings may depend more on the goal-related experience of the rater than on the attributes or qualities of the selections being rated (Lynch et al., 2000).

In using natural concepts, we are likely to picture a **prototype** of the concept—an example that embodies its most common and typical features. What is your prototype for the concept *bird*? Chances are it is not a penguin, an ostrich, or a kiwi. All three are birds that cannot fly. A more likely bird prototype is a robin or perhaps a sparrow. Most birds can fly, but not all; most mammals cannot fly, but bats are mammals, have wings, and can fly. So not all examples of a natural concept fit it equally well. This is why natural concepts often seem less clear-cut than formal ones. Nevertheless, the prototype most closely fits a given natural concept, and other examples of the concept most often share more attributes with that prototype than with the prototype of any other concept.

One theory of concept formation suggests that concepts are represented by their **exemplars**—individual instances, or examples, of a concept that are stored in memory from personal experience (Estes, 1994). To decide whether an unfamiliar item belongs to a concept, we compare it with exemplars (other examples) of that concept.

The concepts we form do not exist in isolation, but rather in hierarchies. For example, the canary and the cardinal are subsets of the concept *bird;* at a higher level, birds are subsets of the concept *animal;* and at a still higher level, animals are a subset of the concept *living things.* Thus, concept formation has a certain logic to it, an aspect it shares with the type of logical thinking called reasoning, which we consider next.

A prototype is an example that embodies the most typical features of a concept. Which of the animals shown here best fits your prototype for the concept bird?

Remember It!

1. Cognition includes the processes of sensation and perception. (true/false)
2. The two most common forms of imagery are
   a. visual and motor. c. visual and auditory.
   b. auditory and tactile. d. visual and gustatory.
3. The images people form typically reflect their knowledge and experience in the real world. (true/false)
4. A mental category that represents a class or group of items that share common characteristics or attributes is called a(n)
   a. image. c. positive instance.
   b. concept. d. prototype.
5. Natural concepts are likely to be more accurate than formal concepts. (true/false)
6. A prototype is the most ______________ example of a concept.
   a. abstract b. unusual c. recent d. typical
7. A stork is an exemplar of the concept bird. (true/false)

Answers: 1. true 2. c 3. true 4. b 5. false 6. d 7. true

DEDUCTIVE AND INDUCTIVE REASONING: LOGICAL THINKING

What is the difference between deductive and inductive reasoning?

Reasoning is a form of thinking in which conclusions are drawn from a set of facts. The two basic forms of reasoning are deductive reasoning and inductive reasoning. In Aristotle's time, the use of formal logic was considered to be the surest path to sound conclusions. And deductive reasoning was considered the foundation of logic (Haberlandt, 1997).

Deductive reasoning is reasoning from the general to the specific, or drawing particular conclusions from general principles. Aristotle introduced a formal method for deductive reasoning—the syllogism. A **syllogism** is a scheme for logical reasoning in which two statements known as *premises* (the major premise and the minor premise) are followed by a valid conclusion. The power of the syllogism is not in its content but in its form. It is organized in such a way that the conclusion must be true if both premises are true *and* if the premises follow the rules of formal logic.

Consider this syllogism:

Major premise: All standard cars have four wheels.
Minor premise: Maria's vehicle is a standard car.
Conclusion: Therefore, Maria's vehicle has four wheels.

Clearly, the conclusion is valid because the entire class of standard cars fits within the larger concept of four-wheeled vehicles. Maria's vehicle is within *standard cars,* and thus within the larger concept *four-wheeled vehicles.*

Now consider this syllogism, which does not adhere to the rules of formal logic:

Major premise: All standard cars have four wheels.
Minor premise: Maria's vehicle has four wheels.
Conclusion: Therefore, Maria's vehicle is a standard car.

The conclusion is invalid. Even though the major and minor premises are both true, a valid conclusion does not follow from them. The minor premise is too general to be used deductively: Some trucks and other vehicles, such as tractors, also have four wheels. Therefore, logically we cannot conclude that Maria's vehicle is a standard car.

Inductive reasoning is a form of reasoning in which general conclusions are drawn from particular facts or individual cases. Psychologists frequently use inductive reasoning in their research. First, they formulate a hypothesis, or tentative explanation, based on particular instances or limited evidence. Then, they test the hypothesis against a larger body of related evidence to reach a general conclusion. Inductive reasoning is also used when researchers try to select samples that are representative of a larger population of interest in order to draw general conclusions about that population, as is often done in polls and surveys. Although psychologists and other scientists rely heavily on inductive reasoning, conclusions drawn from such reasoning can be wrong. Consequently, the conclusions usually are not widely accepted until replications of the research can supply supporting evidence.

Many people, especially those who don't listen carefully to instructions or follow them well, have difficulty with formal reasoning problems. In one study, researchers presented several premises to participants, told them that only one of the set was true, and asked them to select that premise. After the participants had selected the premise they believed to be true, they were not convinced that all the others were false. Even when researchers used only two premises and stated that one of them was true and one was false, some of the participants were still not totally convinced that one of the premises had to be false. Only when the researchers told the participants to check their conclusions again, but to remember that only one premise was true, were the participants totally convinced none of the others could be true (Goldvarg & Johnson-Laird, 2000).

reasoning: A form of thinking in which conclusions are drawn from a set of facts.

deductive reasoning: Reasoning from the general to the specific, or drawing particular conclusions from general principles.

syllogism: A scheme for logical reasoning in which two statements known as premises are followed by a valid conclusion.

inductive reasoning: A form of reasoning in which general conclusions are drawn from particular facts or individual cases.

Remember It!

1. A person using (deductive, inductive) reasoning draws general conclusions from particular facts or individual cases.
2. A scheme for logical reasoning that includes two premise statements followed by a conclusion is called a(n)

   a. concept. b. syllogism. c. deduction. d. induction.
3. Syllogisms involve (deductive, inductive) reasoning.

Answers: 1. inductive 2. b 3. deductive

DECISION MAKING: MAKING CHOICES IN LIFE

Reasoning, both deductive and inductive, is a vital component of decision making. And the quality of our lives is strongly influenced by the decisions we make. Many decisions are simple and mundane—what to have for dinner or what clothes to put on in the morning. But other decisions are more far-reaching—what career to pursue or whether to remain in a relationship. **Decision making** is the process of considering alternatives and choosing among them. Decisions are influenced by many factors, including values, interests, life goals, experiences, and knowledge.

Psychologists have identified various approaches to decision making. Let's examine some of these approaches.

The Additive Strategy

How is the additive strategy used in decision making?

Suppose you wanted to rent an apartment starting next semester. How would you go about deciding among different apartments? You could use the **additive strategy**—a decision-making approach in which each alternative is rated on each of the important factors affecting the decision and the alternative with the highest overall rating is chosen.

Suppose you decided that the important factors in choosing an apartment were those listed in Table 7.1. Having identified the factors, you would arbitrarily select a

Table 7.1 Selecting an Apartment Using the Additive Strategy

Factors to Be Considered	Apartment A		Apartment B		Apartment C	
Convenience of location	+2	(+4)	+3	(+6)	+2	(+4)
Safety of neighborhood	+3	(+6)	−1	(−2)	+1	(+2)
Rent	−3	−3	+3	+3	0	0
Attractiveness	+3	+3	0	0	0	0
Availability of parking	+2	+2	+3	+3	+2	+2
	7	(12)	8	(10)	5	(8)

Note: Numbers in parentheses are ratings that reflect a weighting of the factors.

decision making: The process of considering alternatives and choosing among them.

additive strategy: A decision-making approach in which each alternative is rated on each important factor affecting the decision and the alternative rated highest overall is chosen.

heuristic (yur-RIS-tik): A rule of thumb that is derived from experience and used in decision making and problem solving, even though there is no guarantee of its accuracy or usefulness.

availability heuristic: A cognitive rule of thumb that says that the probability of an event or the importance assigned to it is based on its availability in memory.

rating scale, such as −3 to +3, and rate each of the apartments on each factor (see the number in the first column for each apartment in Table 7.1). Then, you would add the ratings and select the apartment with the highest total, which in this example is apartment B.

But if you are like most people, some factors are more important than others when selecting a suitable place to live. To take the difference into account, you can weight, or give more emphasis to, the factors that are most important. In Table 7.1, a convenient location and safety are weighted as being most important, and their ratings are multiplied by 2 (see the numbers in the second column for each apartment). With this weighted additive strategy, apartment A is the best choice.

Elimination by Aspects

When is the elimination-by-aspects strategy most useful?

With the additive strategy, one or more desirable aspects of an alternative are considered sufficient compensation for other less desirable aspects. In the example we just considered, the convenience of the location and the safety of the neighborhood compensated for the higher rent of apartment A.

Another decision-making strategy is called *elimination by aspects* (Tversky, 1972). With this approach, the factors on which the alternatives are to be evaluated are ordered from most important to least important. Any alternative that does not satisfy the most important factor is automatically eliminated. The process of elimination continues as each factor is considered in order. The alternative that survives is the one chosen. For example, if the most important factor for your apartment search was that the maximum rent you could afford was $800 per month, then you would automatically eliminate all the apartments that rented for more than that. Then, if the second most important factor was availability of parking, you would take the lists of apartments that cost $800 or less per month and weed out those without appropriate parking. You would then continue with your third most important factor and so on, until you had whittled the list down.

The elimination-by-aspects strategy is an example of a *noncompensatory decision strategy*—one that does not allow a high ranking on one factor to compensate for a low ranking on another. This type of approach is most useful when there are many alternatives and multiple factors to be considered. It is usually best to use the elimination-by-aspects strategy first to quickly and efficiently reduce the number of alternatives. Then the additive strategy can be used to make the best choice among the surviving alternatives.

Heuristics and Decision Making

Sometimes we make decisions based on a belief that an event or a set of circumstances carries a certain probability. Such probability assumptions are often based on **heuristics**—rules of thumb that are derived from experience and used in decision making and problem solving, although there is no guarantee of their accuracy or usefulness.

What is the availability heuristic?

The Availability Heuristic Decision making is quite likely to be influenced by how quickly and easily information bearing on the decision comes to mind—that is, how readily available that information is in memory. The cognitive rule of thumb that the probability of an event or the importance assigned to it is based on its availability in memory is known as the **availability heuristic.**

Any information affecting a decision, whether it is accurate or not, is more likely to be considered if it is readily available. Are travelers more likely to die in a plane or an automobile accident? Although it is common knowledge that many more people die in automobile accidents, some people have an inordinate fear of flying. This arises because every fatal plane crash is publicized—some, like the crash of TWA flight 800, dramatically and persistently. Thus, images of plane crashes are typically more readily available in memory.

The high level of media attention given to plane crashes such as that of the Concorde in 2000 makes images like this one readily available in most people's memories. This leads many to use the availability heuristic and thus exaggerate the dangers of flying, which is actually far safer than driving or riding in a car.

In 1998, Oprah Winfrey was sued by the cattle industry for comments made on her show about "mad cow disease" and the possibility that it made eating hamburgers too risky. In other words, the cattle industry was blaming Oprah for establishing an availability heuristic that led viewers to decide *not* to eat its product.

Complete the *Try It!* and see how subject you are to the availability heuristic.

Try It!

Read the names in this list quickly:

Louisa May Alcott	Henry Vaughn	Allan Nevins
John Dickson Carr	Peter Wright	Jane Austen
Emily Dickinson	Judy Blume	Henry Crabb Robinson
Thomas Hughes	Richard Watson Gilder	Joseph Lincoln
Laura Ingalls Wilder	Harriet Beecher Stowe	Emily Brontë
Jack Lindsay	Pearl Buck	Arthur Hutchinson
Edward George Lytton	Amy Lowell	James Hunt
Margaret Mitchell	Robert Lovett	Erica Jong
Michael Drayton	Judith Krantz	Brian Hooker
Edith Wharton	George Nathan	Agatha Christie

Without looking back at the list, do you recall whether it includes more males or females? Even though there were 15 male names and 14 female names, you probably guessed that there were more females. The explanation for this is the availability heuristic. The female names are those of well-known authors, whereas the male names are those of lesser-known authors. Being more familiar, the female names are more readily available in memory. About 80% of research participants concluded that there were more female names on a similar list that actually contained more male names (Tversky & Kahneman, 1973).

What is the representativeness heuristic?

The Representativeness Heuristic Another common heuristic used in decision making, in judging people, or in predicting the probability of certain events is the representativeness heuristic. The **representativeness heuristic** is a thinking strategy based on how closely a new object or situation is judged to resemble or match an existing prototype of that object or situation (Pitz & Sachs, 1984). The representativeness heuristic is an effective decision-making strategy that can lead to good decisions *if* the instance selected truly matches the appropriate prototype.

Suppose you were playing a coin-tossing game in which you had to predict whether the outcome of each toss would be heads or tails. Let's say the first five coin tosses came up heads. What would you predict the next toss to be? Many people would predict tails to be more likely on the next toss, because a sample of coin tosses should be approximately 50% heads. Thus, a tail is long overdue, they reason. Nevertheless, the next toss is just as likely to be a head as a tail. After 100 coin tosses, the proportions of heads and tails should be about equal, but for each *individual* coin toss, the probability still remains 50–50. This example illustrates how people tend to estimate the probability of something turning out a certain way based not on the actual likelihood of it being that way, but rather on their own mental representation of the likelihood.

Another example of the use of the representativeness heuristic occurs when people judge others based on stereotypes. A person may expect someone from California to be either a surfer or an actor because that fits the person's mental representation of a Californian. In reality, however, most Californians are neither surfers nor actors; only a small fraction fit this stereotype.

Framing and Decision Making

What is framing?

Words matter! The way information is "framed" tends to influence decision making. **Framing** refers to the way information is presented so as to emphasize either a potential gain or a potential loss as the outcome.

To study the effects of framing on decision making, Kahneman and Tversky (1984) presented the following options to a group of participants. Which program would you choose?

> The United States is preparing for the outbreak of a dangerous disease, which is expected to kill 600 people. There have been designed two alternative programs to combat the disease. If program A is adopted, 200 people will be saved. If program B is adopted, there is a one-third probability that all 600 will be saved and a two-thirds probability that no people will be saved.

The researchers found that 72% of the participants selected the "sure thing" of program A over the "risky gamble" of program B. Now consider the options as they were reframed:

> If program C is adopted, 400 people will die. If program D is adopted, there is a one-third probability that nobody will die and a two-thirds probability that all 600 people will die.

Which program did you choose? Of research participants given this version of the problem, 78% chose program D. A careful reading will reveal that program D has the exact same consequences as program B in the earlier version. How can this result be explained?

The first version of the problem was framed to focus attention on the number of lives that could be saved. And when people are primarily motivated to achieve gains (save lives), they are more likely to choose a safe option over a risky one, as

representativeness heuristic: A thinking strategy based on how closely a new object or situation is judged to resemble or match an existing prototype of that object or situation.

framing: The way information is presented so as to emphasize either a potential gain or a potential loss as the outcome.

72% of the participants did. The second version was framed to focus attention on the 400 lives that would be lost. When trying to avoid losses, people appear much more willing to choose a risky option, as 78% of the participants were.

There are numerous practical applications of framing to decision making. Customers are more readily motivated to buy products if they are on sale than if they are simply priced lower than similar products to begin with. As a result, customers focus on what they save—a gain—rather than on what they spend—a loss. People seem more willing to purchase an $18,000 car and receive a $1,000 rebate (a gain) than to simply pay $17,000 for the same car.

Which of these two phrases sounds more appealing to you: "cash discount" or "credit card surcharge"? Companies have learned that customers prefer a cash discount over a credit card surcharge by a wide margin, even when the final cost of an item is the same in either case (Thaler, 1980). Apparently people find it less painful to forgo a gain than to absorb a loss.

Heuristics can certainly be effective and efficient cognitive techniques. But the downside is that they can also lead to errors in perceptions and decisions. The *Apply It!* at the end of this chapter will let you look more closely at errors in decision making and how to avoid them.

Remember It!

1. The (additive strategy, elimination-by-aspects strategy) allows the more desirable aspects of a situation to compensate for other less desirable aspects.
2. Heuristics can be useful shortcuts for decision making, but they sometimes lead to inaccurate perceptions or bad decisions. (true/false)
3. When sales of flood insurance rise dramatically after major flooding, the purchasers' decisions are most likely influenced by the (availability, representativeness) heuristic.
4. ______________ refers to the way information is presented so as to focus on a potential gain or loss.

Answers: 1. additive strategy 2. true 3. availability 4. Framing

PROBLEM SOLVING: BEYOND DECISION MAKING

Approaches to Problem Solving: Helpful Basic Techniques

What are three basic approaches to problem solving?

We all face problems that must be solved—problems both great and small. We solve many everyday problems with little difficulty and a minimum of mental effort. Some problems can be solved by insight, as described in Chapter 5. But some problems are more challenging. **Problem solving** refers to thoughts and actions required to achieve a desired goal that is not readily attainable. Three basic approaches to problem solving are trial and error, algorithms, and heuristics.

problem solving: Thoughts and actions required to achieve a desired goal that is not readily attainable.

How would you go about solving the problem described in the *Try It!* on page 258?

Try It!

Insert the numbers 1 through 7 in the seven boxes, one digit to a box, in such a way that no consecutive numbers are next to each other horizontally, vertically, or diagonally. Several solutions are possible.

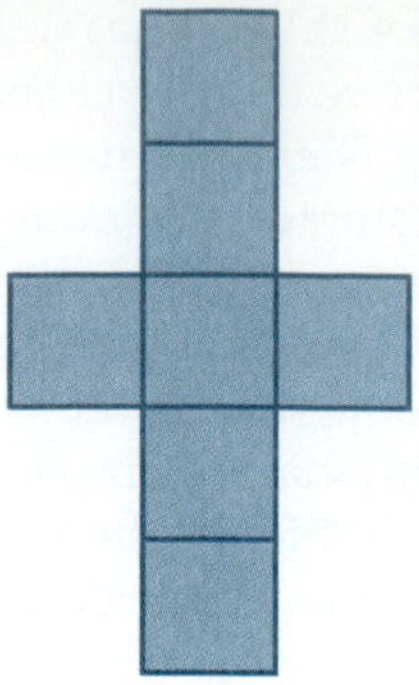

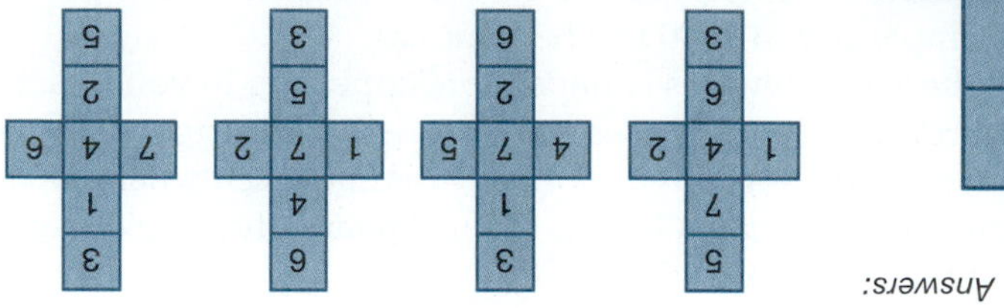

Trial and Error: If at First You Don't Succeed . . . How did you choose to solve the *Try It!* problem? Some people examine the problem carefully and devise a strategy—such as placing the 1 or the 7 in the middle box because each has only *one* forbidden consecutive number (2 or 6) to avoid. Many people, however, simply start placing the numbers in the boxes and then change them around when a combination doesn't work. This approach, called **trial and error,** involves trying one solution after another, in no particular order, until hitting upon the answer by chance. Even nonhuman animals use trial and error, as you have learned in Chapter 6.

Trial and error can be very time-consuming and perhaps even dangerous. Would you feel comfortable with a surgeon who operated on you using trial and error? You might not survive the errors to enjoy the solution. Of course, most of our problems are not life-or-death situations, and if all else fails in our efforts to solve a problem, we may be reduced to trial and error. But other techniques are far more effective and less time-consuming.

Applying Prior Knowledge: Don't Start from Scratch Rather than beginning with a haphazard, trial-and-error approach, it is best to reflect on a problem and see if you already have any knowledge that might help you find a solution. Some problems can be solved with only a little ready knowledge. The problem in the next *Try It!* is a good example.

Try It!

Order the four colors shown below from least to greatest in numerical value.

Green + Green = Yellow

Orange + Brown = Yellow

Orange + Green = Brown

Orange + Orange = Green

Least ______ ______ ______ ______ Greatest

From the *Try It!* you can see that yellow is twice the value of green, and green is twice the value of orange. So yellow is four times the value of orange. Then you can see that brown is numerically greater than either orange or green, but less than yellow. Also, you should realize that both yellow and green must be even numbers, because any two odd numbers or any two even numbers will always equal an even number. Thus, from least value to greatest value, the colors are as follows: orange, green, brown, and yellow.

What is an algorithm?

Algorithms: Formulas That Can't Miss Another major problem-solving method is the algorithm (Newell & Simon, 1972). An **algorithm** is a systematic, step-by-step procedure that guarantees a solution to a problem of a certain type if the algorithm is appropriate and is executed properly. Scientific and mathematical formulas, such as Einstein's famous $E = mc^2$, are algorithms. Another type of algorithm is a systematic strategy for exploring every possible solution to a problem until the correct one is reached. In some cases millions or even billions or more possibilities may have to be considered before the solution is found. Often computers are programmed to solve problems using such algorithms, because with a computer an accurate solution is guaranteed and millions of possible solutions can be tried in a few seconds.

Many problems do not lend themselves to solution by algorithms, however. Suppose you were a contestant on "Wheel of Fortune," trying to solve this missing-letter puzzle: P_Y_ _ _L_ _ Y. An exhaustive search algorithm would be out of the question—even Vanna White's smile would fade long before the nearly 9 billion possibilities could be considered. An easier way to solve such problems is by using a heuristic strategy.

What are three heuristics used in problem solving?

Heuristics and Problem Solving: Fast But Not Infallible As we have seen, using a heuristic does not guarantee success but offers a promising way to attack a problem and arrive at a solution. Chess players must use heuristics because there is not enough time in a lifetime to consider all of the moves and countermoves that would be possible in a single game of chess.

People use heuristic techniques to eliminate useless steps and to take the shortest probable path toward a solution. The missing-letter puzzle presented earlier is easily solved through a simple heuristic approach that makes use of your existing knowledge of words (prefixes, roots, suffixes). You can supply the missing letters and spell out PSYCHOLOGY.

Working Backwards One heuristic that is effective for solving some problems is **working backwards,** sometimes called the *backward search.* This approach starts with the solution, a known condition, and works back through the problem. Once the backward search has revealed the steps to be taken and their order, the problem can be solved. Try working backwards to solve the water lily problem in the *Try It!* on page 260.

Means–End Analysis A popular heuristic strategy is **means–end analysis,** in which the current position is compared with a desired goal, and a series of steps is formulated and then taken to close the gap between the two (Sweller & Levine, 1982). Many problems are large and complex and must be broken down into smaller steps or subproblems before a solution can be reached. If your professor assigns a term paper, for example, you probably do not simply sit down and write it. You must first determine how you will deal with your topic, research the topic, make an outline, and then write the sections over a period of time. At last you are ready to assemble the complete term paper, write several drafts, and put the finished product in final form before handing it in and receiving your A.

The Analogy Heuristic Another problem-solving strategy is the **analogy heuristic**—applying a solution used for a past problem to a current problem that shares many similar features. Situations with many features in common are said to be analogous.

trial and error: An approach to problem solving in which one solution after another is tried in no particular order until an answer is found.

algorithm: A systematic, step-by-step procedure, such as a mathematical formula, that guarantees a solution to a problem of a certain type if the algorithm is appropriate and is executed properly.

working backwards: A heuristic strategy in which a person discovers the steps needed to solve a problem by defining the desired goal and working backwards to the current condition.

means–end analysis: A heuristic strategy in which the current position is compared with the desired goal, and a series of steps are formulated and taken to close the gap between them.

analogy heuristic: A rule of thumb that applies a solution that solved a problem in the past to a current problem that shares many similar features.

Try It!

Water lilies double the area they cover every 24 hours. At the beginning of the summer there is one water lily on a pond. It takes 60 days for the pond to become covered with water lilies. On what day is the pond half covered? (From Fixx, 1978.)

Answer: The most important fact is that the lilies double in number every 24 hours. If the pond is to be completely covered on the 60th day, it has to be half covered on the 59th day.

When faced with a new problem to solve, you can look for commonalities between the new problem and other problems you have solved before and apply a strategy similar to one that has worked in the past. For example, if your car is making strange sounds and you take it to an auto mechanic, the mechanic may be able to diagnose the problem by analogy—the sounds your car is making are comparable to sounds heard before and associated with a particular problem.

Some evidence suggests that people regularly solve problems by analogy but may not be aware that they are doing so (Burns, 1996; Schunn & Dunbar, 1996). If you use the analogy heuristic, you must be certain that the new problem and the ones you are comparing it with are sufficiently similar.

Laboratory studies on reasoning by analogy have found that many participants tend to consider only shallow, superficial similarities. But people typically generate better analogies when reasoning about real-world situations because they consider deeper, underlying similarities. Blanchette and Dunbar (2000) found that when laboratory conditions were made more favorable in studies on reasoning and analogies, participants tended to use deeper structural features in making comparisons, much as they would in real-life settings. The researchers concluded that the ability to reason by analogy has been underestimated in much of the research on this form of reasoning.

Impediments to Problem Solving: Mental Stumbling Blocks

How do functional fixedness and mental set impede problem solving?

Sometimes we face problems that seem to defy solution despite our best efforts. We may lack the relevant knowledge or experience to solve some problems or sufficient material resources to solve others. Do you have any problems that could be solved if money were no object? There are other impediments to problem solving that serve as stumbling blocks for many. Two of these are functional fixedness and mental set.

functional fixedness: The failure to use familiar objects in novel ways to solve problems because of a tendency to view objects only in terms of their customary functions.

Functional Fixedness: Every Tool Has Only One Function Many of us are hampered in our efforts to solve problems in daily life because of **functional fixedness**—the failure to use familiar objects in novel ways to solve problems. We tend to see objects only in terms of their customary functions. Just think of all the items you use daily—tools, utensils, and other equipment—that help you perform certain functions. Often the normal functions of objects become fixed in your thinking so that you do not consider using them in new and creative ways.

Suppose you injured your leg and knew that you should apply ice to prevent swelling, but you had no ice cubes or ice bag in your refrigerator. Or what if you wanted a cup of coffee, but the decanter for your coffeemaker was broken? If you suffered from functional fixedness, you might come to the conclusion that there was nothing you could do to solve your problem at that moment. But, rather than thinking about the object or utensil that you *don't* have, think about the function that will solve your problem. In the first instance, what you need is something very cold, not necessarily an ice bag or ice per se. A cold can of soda or perhaps a bag of frozen peas might be a solution. In the second case, what you need is something to catch the coffee, rather than the specific glass decanter that came with the coffeemaker. Could you catch the coffee in some bowl or cooking utensil, or even in a coffee mug?

Mental Set: But I've Always Done It This Way Another impediment to problem solving, similar to functional fixedness but much broader, is mental set. **Mental set** is a mental rut in one's approach to solving problems, the tendency to continue to use the same old method even though another approach might be better. Perhaps you hit on a way to solve a problem once in the past and continue to use the same technique in similar situations, even though it is not highly effective or efficient. People are much more susceptible to mental set when they fail to consider the special requirements of a problem. Not surprisingly, the same people who are subject to mental set are also more likely to have trouble with functional fixedness when they attempt to solve problems (McKelvie, 1984).

Recent research indicates that our problem-solving abilities may remain relatively undiminished over our lifetimes, even though our pace may slow down a little with age. Haught and others (2000) reported that older problem solvers performed as well as younger ones on practical, everyday problems. And even though the older problem solvers needed more time than the younger ones to finish an identification task, the numbers of errors were similar for the two groups.

Humans are not unique as problem solvers. As we have seen, many animals can also solve problems. How about machines?

HIGH-TECH APPLICATIONS OF COGNITION: ARTIFICIAL INTELLIGENCE AND ROBOTICS

Artificial Intelligence

What is artificial intelligence?

Amazing progress has been made in the field of artificial intelligence since the term was first used by researcher John McCarthy in 1956. **Artificial intelligence,** or AI, refers to the programming of computer systems to simulate human thinking in solving problems and in making judgments and decisions. The first successful effort to program computers to mimic human thinking was made by Allen Newell and Herbert A. Simon. They developed programs that could play chess as well as a human expert could, although not as well as master players. Eventually, AI experts at IBM created a computer called Deep Blue, which defeated long-time world chess champion Garry Kasparov in 1997.

Some experts stated that Deep Blue could not really think on its own. They insisted that even the most sophisticated "thinking" of computers is not really analogous to human cognition, because, unlike humans, these machines are merely following a set of rules, no matter how complex those rules may be.

Stunned by his defeat, Kasparov disagreed with Deep Blue's critics. As the match proceeded, he felt that the computer was showing signs of human-like

mental set: The tendency to apply a familiar strategy to the solution of a problem without carefully considering the special requirements of that problem.

artificial intelligence: Programming computer systems to simulate human thinking in solving problems and in making judgments and decisions.

World champion Garry Kasparov contemplates a move against Deep Blue, an IBM computer that exhibits artificial intelligence in the area of top-level chess play.

cognitive ability in the form of strategic understanding. Somewhere along the way, the tactics (specific rules for playing chess) that had been programmed into Deep Blue had apparently been transformed into strategy—the formulation of an overall game plan. Decades before Deep Blue's stunning defeat of the reigning world chess champion, Newell and Simon opened the door for computer systems able to do far more than play chess like an expert.

Today's expert systems "perform a substantial number of human tasks at a professional level" (Simon, 1995, p. 507). Some expert systems use the collective knowledge and problem-solving strategies of the top experts in a field. The first of this breed of expert systems was MYCIN, a computerized diagnostician in the area of blood diseases and meningitis. Other expert systems perform a range of functions in medicine, psychotherapy, space technology, military defense, weather prediction, and a variety of other fields.

Expert systems operate in well-defined domains; that is, such a system's knowledge base, or store of information, is not inordinately large and is limited to a specific area of expertise (Hendler, 1994). Outside its area of expertise, an expert system cannot function. Expert systems, then, are useful only as assistants to humans; they cannot stand alone. Yet, these systems far surpass the human brain in their ability to retrieve massive amounts of stored data and use it to make decisions based on specific facts and rules that have been preprogrammed into their software. In addition, because they run on computers, expert systems are vastly superior to humans in carrying out complex mathematical operations, all at lightning speed.

Computer Neural Networks Most computers have a single central processing unit that solves problems one step at a time. In contrast, supercomputers contain a number of processors that work in parallel. A problem can be divided into parts and handled simultaneously by more than one processor; this division of labor not only enables the job to be completed much more quickly, but also allows more complex problems to be tackled.

A parallel-processing supercomputer resembles the human brain in that it can carry out many functions at the same time. And scientists are devising ever more sophisticated computer systems based on their understanding of how neurons in certain parts of the brain are connected and how the connections develop (Buonomano & Merzenich, 1995; Hinton et al., 1995). Computer systems that are intended to mimic the human brain are called **neural networks.** Like synaptic connections in the brain, the connections in a computer neural network can be strengthened or weakened as a result of experience. Using neural networks, psychologists can test theories about how the brain works, and computer scientists can use the knowledge gained to develop even better simulations of brain function.

neural networks: Computer systems that are intended to mimic the human brain.

Computer scientist Alex Waibel and colleagues used a neural network in their research on speech recognition. They developed a system "programmed to modify itself according to whatever signals come into the system . . . the speech recognizer actually learns how to identify sounds and words" (Peterson, 1993, p. 254). Voice recognition systems are already used by banks and credit card companies and in other commercial settings. But, unlike humans, such computer systems cannot understand the subtleties of language—tone of voice, accompanying nonverbal behavior, or even level of politeness (Peterson, 1993).

In fact, no computer system can yet approach the complexity and capability of the human brain. Even so, some new applications in artificial intelligence may be edging closer.

Robotics

One area in which human cognition has been applied to develop technological marvels is *robotics*—the science of automating human functions. The impressive achievements in this field include the following:

- Robots help stroke patients toward recovery by assisting them in exercise movement.
- Robotic surgical assistants help surgeons make remarkable gains in precision for some difficult surgeries.
- Robotic filling stations will keep spy satellites aloft.
- Miniature robots will assist tomorrow's soldiers.
- Robots can perform many duties too dangerous for humans (cleaning up toxic spills, finding and destroying land mines, cleaning up nuclear waste sites, etc.).

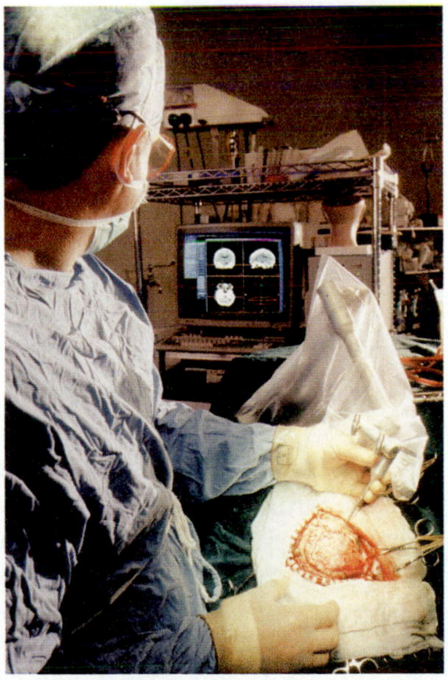

High-tech robotics has enhanced many human skills, including those involved in brain surgery. Here the exact position of a tumor is located and displayed to a surgeon on a monitor; the surgeon guides the computer-controlled robotic arm, called a "magic wand," to remove the tumor with pinpoint accuracy.

But perhaps the most impressive development in this field—controlling robots with brain power—sounds more like science fiction than reality. Imagine what it would be like to control a robot by your brain activity alone—merely by thinking. Amazingly, such an application of robotics has been achieved. Dr. John Chapin of MCP Hahnemann University School of Medicine in Philadelphia has demonstrated for the first time that brain cell activity alone can control a robotic arm.

Chapin and other researchers trained rats to press a small lever to obtain drinking water from a robotic arm. Each of the rats had electrodes implanted in its brain that recorded the activity of specific groups of neurons. The researchers analyzed the patterns of brain activity occurring while the rats were pressing the lever and identified the exact locations of activity associated with the movements of the rats' paws. After developing a new mathematical technique for analyzing the brain signals, the researchers connected the robotic arm to the electrodes that had been implanted in the rats' brains. Now the rats had control of the robotic arm directly through those electrodes. At first, the rats continued to press the lever, even though it was no longer necessary to do so. Soon, however, many of the rats discovered that they could produce water from the robotic arm by brain activity alone, and they stopped pressing the lever.

The implications of this research for the physically handicapped are astounding: For example, paralyzed patients could be fitted with artificial limbs that can be controlled at will simply by thought, just as normal limbs are controlled (Whitehouse, 2000).

Some of the applications of robotics and artificial intelligence are so remarkable that it is easy to lose sight of how they came to be. Keep in mind that the real power lies not in the machines, but in their creator—human cognition.

Remember It!

1. Which of the following is guaranteed, if properly applied, to result in the correct answer to a problem?
   a. an algorithm c. trial and error
   b. a heuristic d. applying prior knowledge
2. Working backwards and means–end analysis are examples of
   a. algorithms. c. mental sets.
   b. heuristics. d. functional fixedness.
3. The ______________ heuristic involves applying a solution that worked for a past problem to a current problem that shares many similar features.
4. Rich uses a wastebasket to keep a door from closing. According to the text, in solving his problem, he was not hindered by
   a. a heuristic. c. functional fixedness.
   b. an algorithm. d. mental set.
5. One characteristic of good problem solvers is mental set. (true/false)
6. Computer-based expert systems surpass the problem-solving ability of human experts in a number of fields. (true/false)
7. Computer systems intended to mimic the functioning of the human brain are called ______________ ______________.

Answers: 1. a 2. b 3. analogy 4. c 5. false 6. false 7. neural networks

LANGUAGE

It is true that we can think without language. We can use imagery, picture steps in a process, think kinesthetically in terms of body movements, and so on. Yet language remains a critically important tool of thought. Language increases the ability to think abstractly, to grasp and formulate concepts, to reason by analogy, to solve problems, and to express ideas. Without language, there would be no books to read, no papers to write, no lectures to endure. Not bad so far, you may be thinking. But consider: Without language, each of us would each live in a largely solitary and isolated world, unable to communicate or receive any information.

Language is a means of communicating thoughts and feelings, using a system of socially shared but arbitrary symbols (sounds, signs, or written symbols) arranged according to rules of grammar. Fortunately, language is creative and generative. Language allows us to form and comprehend a virtually infinite number of meaningful sentences. If this were not the case, we would be limited to merely repeating statements we had heard or read. Moreover, language is not bound by space or time. Language enables us to communicate about things that are abstract or concrete, present or not present, and about what has been, is now, or conceivably

language: A means of communicating thoughts and feelings, using a system of socially shared but arbitrary symbols (sounds, signs, or written symbols) arranged according to rules of grammar.

might be. Thanks to language, we can profit from the experience, the knowledge, and the wisdom of others and can benefit others with our own. Language makes available the wisdom of the ages from every corner of the world.

Truly, language is one of the most important capabilities of the human species. Whether spoken, written, or signed, it is the most important cognitive tool. In Chapter 10, we will discuss how language is acquired by infants. Here we explore the components and the structure of this amazing form of human communication.

The Structure of Language

What are the four important components of language?

Psycholinguistics is the study of how language is acquired, produced, and used and how the sounds and symbols of language are translated into meaning. Psycholinguists devote much effort to the study of the structure of language and the rules governing its use. The structure and rules governing language involve four different components—phonemes, morphemes, syntax, and semantics.

Phonemes The smallest units of sound in a spoken language are known as **phonemes.** Phonemes form the basic building blocks of a spoken language. Three phonemes together form the sound of the word *cat*—the *c* (which sounds like *k*), *a*, and *t*. Phonemes do not sound like the single letters of the alphabet as you recite them, *a-b-c-d-e-f-g*, but like the sounds of the letters as they are used in words, like the *b* in *boy*, the *p* in *pan*, and so on. The sound of the phoneme *c* in the word *cat* is different from the sound of the phoneme *c* in the word *city.*

Letters combined to form sounds are also phonemes, such as the *th* in *the* and the *ch* in *child.* The same sound (phoneme) may be represented by different letters in different words, as the *a* in *stay* and the *ei* in *sleigh.* And, as you saw with *c*, the same letter can serve as different phonemes. The letter *a*, for example, is sounded as four different phonemes in *day, cap, watch,* and *law.*

How many phonemes are there? About 100 or so different sounds could serve as phonemes, but most languages have far fewer. English uses about 45 phonemes, while some languages may have as few as 15 and others as many as 85 (Solso, 1991). Though phonemes are the basic building blocks of language, they alone, with a few exceptions, do not provide language with meaning. Meaning is based on the next component of language, the morphemes.

Morphemes **Morphemes** are the smallest units of meaning in a language. In almost all cases in the English language, a morpheme is made of two or more phonemes. But a few phonemes also serve as morphemes, such as the article *a* and the personal pronoun *I.* Many words in English are single morphemes—*book, word, learn, reason,* and so on. In addition to root words, morphemes may also be prefixes (such as *re* in *relearn*) or suffixes (such as *ed* to show past tense, as in *learned*). The single morpheme *reason* becomes the dual morpheme *reasonable.* Another morpheme—the prefix *un*—added to *reasonable* will reverse its meaning—*unreasonable.* The letter *s* gives a plural meaning to a word and is thus a morpheme. The morpheme *book* (singular) becomes two morphemes, *books* (plural).

So morphemes, singly and in combination, form the words in a language and provide meaning. But sounds and single words alone are not enough. A language also requires rules for structuring or putting together words in orderly and meaningful fashion. This is where syntax enters the picture.

Syntax **Syntax** is the aspect of grammar that specifies the rules for arranging and combining words to form phrases and sentences. For example, an important rule of syntax in English is that adjectives usually come before nouns. So we refer to the residence of the U.S. President as the White House. But in Spanish the noun usually comes before the adjective, and speakers would say, "la Casa Blanca," or "the House White." So the rules of word order, or syntax, differ from one language to

psycholinguistics: The study of how language is acquired, produced, and used, and how the sounds and symbols of language are translated into meaning.

phonemes: The smallest units of sound in a spoken language.

morphemes: The smallest units of meaning in a language.

syntax: The aspect of grammar that specifies the rules for arranging and combining words to form phrases and sentences.

another. In English, we ask, "Do you speak German?" But speakers of German would ask, "Sprechen sie Deutsch?" or "Speak you German?"

Semantics **Semantics** refers to the meaning derived from morphemes, words, and sentences. The same word can have different meanings depending on how it is used in sentences: "I don't mind." "Mind your manners." "He has lost his mind." Or consider another example: "Loving to read, the young girl read three books last week." Here the word *read* is pronounced two different ways and in one case is in the past tense.

Surface and Deep Structure The noted linguist and creative theorist Noam Chomsky (1986, 1990) maintained that the ability to glean a meaningful message from a sentence is stored in a different area of the brain than are the words used to compose the sentence. Moreover, he distinguished between the surface structure and the deep structure of a sentence. The **surface structure** of a sentence refers to the literal words that are spoken or written (or signed). The **deep structure** is the underlying meaning of the sentence.

In some sentences, the surface structure and the deep structure are the same. This is true of the sentence "Lauren read the book." But if this sentence is rewritten in the passive voice—"The book was read by Lauren"—the surface structure changes, yet the deep structure remains the same. Alternatively, a single sentence may have one or more different deep structures. For example, in the sentence "John enjoys charming people," two competing deep structures produce ambiguity. Does John enjoy people who are charming, or does he enjoy exercising his charm on other people?

Brain Activity and Aspects of Language Use How would you pronounce the nonword *zat*? Most English speakers would probably pronounce it to rhyme with *bat.* But other nonwords are not as easy to pronounce. For instance, how should *mough* be pronounced—to rhyme with *rough, bough, dough,* or *cough*? This is just one example of the many confusing inconsistencies in the way English words are spelled and pronounced. However, some languages, such as Italian, have very few inconsistencies in the way words are spelled and pronounced. Thus, speakers of Italian should be able to pronounce written words more easily and more quickly than those who speak English—and they do, according to new research by Paulesu and others (2000).

These researchers used PET (positron emission tomography) scans to view activity in areas of the brains of Italian and English speakers while they read aloud a list of words and nonwords. The English speakers took longer than the Italian speakers to begin reading the words and even longer to begin reading the nonwords. As a control measure to find out if the English speakers were just slower than the Italians, both groups were compared on another test—in which they had to produce the words for pictured objects. In this test, no difference in performance time was found between Italian and English participants, most likely because naming pictured objects does not require a translation from spelling to pronunciation.

The PET scans of all participants in this study revealed heightened activity in a widespread area of the brain known to be associated with reading, as was expected. But the new information that Paulesu and colleagues (2000) uncovered is that the brain activity in three regions varied according to the speaker's native language. Compared with the English speakers, the Italian speakers showed greater brain activity in an upper area of the left temporal lobe when reading words and nonwords. English speakers showed increased brain activity in the left frontal lobe and in an upper region of the left temporal lobe when reading nonwords.

This study assumed that the more proficient and the more expert a person is at a given task, the greater the blood flow, which, in turn, increases the neural activity in the brain structure that handles that task. Some other studies support this assumption. For example, compared with nonmusicians, piano players show greater activity in the motor-related regions of the brain while performing a finger-

semantics: The meaning or the study of meaning derived from morphemes, words, and sentences.

surface structure: The literal words of a sentence that are spoken or written (or signed).

deep structure: The underlying meaning of a sentence.

moving task (Hund-Georgiadis & von Cramon, 1999). Other brain-imaging research, however, challenges the notion that the more expert a person is at a task, the greater the brain activity during that task. Several years ago, researchers Raichle and others (1994) found what appears to be convincing evidence that greater expertise at a task is associated with comparatively lower levels of blood flow in brain areas that are active during performance of that task. The reasoning was that the more a specific brain area is used, the more efficient it becomes and the less effort it has to exert to accomplish the task. It seems logical that in a person who is first learning to do something, the brain area responsible for the task would be literally sparkling with activity, while the brain of a more proficient person would need to work less hard.

There is another valuable way of viewing the findings of the study by Paulesu and others (2000). The smaller increases in activity in the left frontal and lower posterior temporal regions of the Italian speakers could represent their greater skill in pronouncing nonwords compared with their English-speaking counterparts. Another interesting sidelight on this study is that the area of the upper left temporal lobe that showed greater activity in the Italian speakers showed lower than the normal activity levels when dyslexic subjects attempted to read words (Rumsey et al., 1997).

Research indicates that motor-related areas of the brains of musicians such as these pianists have a more complex organization and show higher levels of activity than the same areas in the brains of nonmusicians.

The work by Paulesu and colleagues shows how brain imaging can be used in answering basic research questions about brain-behavior relationships and suggests how the results can be applied in both clinical and educational settings (Fiez, 2000).

What parts of the brain are key in processing syntactical and semantic aspects of language? Of course, the brain's language centers are widespread, but recent brain-imaging studies have identified one area in the lower rear section of the left temporal lobe that plays a major role in processing information about both syntax and semantics. Moreover this same area seems to be especially involved in constructing a higher level of meaning in sentences (Kuperberg et al., 2000).

Two brain areas that are important for processing language are Broca's area and Wernicke's area (as you learned in Chapter 2). The role of Broca's area was long believed to be largely restricted to the physical production of speech. But a recent brain-imaging study (Ni et al., 2000) revealed that Broca's area was highly activated when participants were processing errors in syntax, such as the wrong usage in the sentence "Trees can grew." This brain-imaging study by Ni and others also showed that Wernicke's area plays a key role in processing semantic errors, such as the illogical sentence "Trees can eat."

Language is a universal human phenomenon, yet there is great diversity in the way language is used around the world—there are some 6,000 spoken languages (Berreby, 1994). But however it is spoken, written, signed, and otherwise used, language is one of the most complex human capabilities. Is language confined to the human species?

Animal Language

How does language in trained chimpanzees differ from human language?

Ask people what capability most reliably sets humans apart from all other animal species, and most will answer language. And for good reason. As far as scientists know, humans are the only species to have developed this rich, varied, and complex system of communication. But even though they have never developed language, could our nearest cousins, the chimpanzees, learn to master its rudiments and complexities if humans taught them? The earliest attempts to answer this question date back 70 years, to the early 1930s, and they met with little success.

Teaching Chimps Sign Language Psychologists Allen and Beatrix Gardner (1969) took in a 1-year-old chimp named Washoe and taught her sign language. Washoe learned signs for objects, and certain commands and concepts such as "flower," "give me," "come," "open," and "more." By the end of her fifth year she had mastered about 160 signs (Fleming, 1974).

Figure 7.2

Sarah's Symbols

A chimpanzee named Sarah learned to communicate using plastic chips of various shapes, sizes, and colors to represent words in an artificial language developed by her trainer, David Premack. (From Premack, 1971.)

Symbol Boards: The Next Step Psychologist David Premack taught another chimp, Sarah, to use an artificial language he developed. Its symbols consisted of magnetized chips of various shapes, sizes, and colors, as shown in Figure 7.2. Premack used operant conditioning techniques to teach Sarah to select the magnetic chip representing a fruit and place it on a magnetic language board. The trainer would then reward Sarah with the fruit she had requested. Sarah mastered the concepts of similarities and differences, and eventually she could signal whether two objects were the same or different with nearly perfect accuracy (Premack & Premack, 1983). She even performed well on part–whole relationships and could match such things as half an apple and a glass half filled with water. Despite Sarah's accomplishments, Premack firmly maintained that it is unlikely that animals are capable of language (Premack & Premack, 1983).

At the Yerkes Primate Research Center at Emory University, a chimp named Lana participated in a computer-controlled language-training program. She learned to press keys imprinted with geometric symbols that represented words in an artificial language called Yerkish. One day her trainer Tim had an orange that she wanted. Lana had available symbols for many fruits—apple, banana, and so on—but none for an orange. Yet there was a colored symbol for the color orange. So Lana improvised and signaled, "Tim give apple which is orange." (Savage-Rumbaugh, 1986).

Was human-like language being displayed in these studies with primates? Not according to Herbert Terrace (1981), who examined the research of others and conducted his own.

Nim Chimpsky Terrace and coworkers taught sign language to a chimp they called Nim Chimpsky (after the famed linguist Noam Chomsky) and reported [illegible] the age of 2 weeks to 4 years. Nim learned 125 symbols, which [illegible] ply imitating their trainers and [illegible] laws of operant conditioning, not the laws of language (Terrace, 1985, 1986).

Kanzi: The Exceptional Chimp The most impressive performance to date is that of a pygmy chimpanzee, Kanzi, who developed an amazing ability to

From their studies of communication among chimps and other animals, researchers have gained useful insights into the nature of language. The pygmy chimp Kanzi became skilled at using a special symbol board to communicate.

communicate with his trainers. Kanzi eventually demonstrated an advanced understanding (for chimps) of spoken English and could respond correctly even to new commands, such as "Go to the refrigerator and get out a tomato" (Savage-Rumbaugh, 1990; Savage-Rumbaugh et al., 1992). By the time Kanzi was 6 years old, a team of researchers who worked with him had recorded more than 13,000 "utterances" and reported that the chimp could communicate using some 200 different geometric symbols (Gibbons, 1991). And reportedly, Kanzi could respond just as well when requests were made over earphones so that no one else in the room could signal to him purposely or inadvertently.

Communication in Other Animals Most animal species studied by language researchers are limited to motor responses, such as sign language, gestures, using magnetic symbols, or pressing keys on symbol boards. But these limitations do not extend to some bird species, such as parrots, which *are* capable of making humanlike speech sounds. One remarkable case is Alex, an African grey parrot who not only mimics human speech, but seems to do so intelligently. Able to recognize and name various colors, objects, and shapes, Alex answers questions about them in English (Pepperberg, 1991, 1994b). And he can count as well. When asked such questions as "How many red blocks?" Alex answers correctly about 80% of the time (Pepperberg, 1994a).

Research with sea mammals such as whales and dolphins has established that they apparently use complicated systems of grunts, whistles, clicks, and other sounds to communicate within their species (Herman, 1981; Savage-Rumbaugh, 1993). Dolphins can learn to pick out an object and put it on the right or left of a basket, for example, and comprehend such commands as "in the basket" and "under the basket" (Chollar, 1989).

Many of the remarkable communication feats reported for animal species are impressive, especially those of chimpanzees. Clearly chimpanzees can learn to string together requests. But these are constructions, not sentences. The difference between a construction—such as Lana's "Tim give apple which is orange"—and a sentence (a fundamental element of human language) was captured by the philosopher Bertrand Russell. Someone once asked Russell if apes might ever learn to speak. He is said to have answered that he would be persuaded if an ape could demonstrate understanding of a sentence such as "My father was poor but honest" (quoted in Restak, 1988, p. 202).

Language and Thinking

In general, does thought influence language more, or does language influence thought more?

If language is unique to humans, then does language drive human thinking? Does the fact that you speak English mean that you reason, think, and perceive your world differently than does someone who speaks Spanish, or Chinese, or Swahili? According to one hypothesis presented more than 45 years ago, it does.

Benjamin Whorf (1956) put forth his **linguistic relativity hypothesis** suggesting that the language a person speaks largely determines the nature of that person's thoughts. According to this hypothesis, people's worldview would be constructed primarily by the words in their language. As proof, Whorf offered his classic example: The languages used by the Eskimo people have a number of different words for snow, "*apikak,* first snow falling; *aniv,* snow spread out; *pukak,* snow for drinking water," while the English-speaking world has but one word, *snow* (Restak, 1988, p. 222). Whorf claimed that such a rich and varied selection of words for snow enabled Eskimos to think differently about it than do people whose languages lack specific words for various snow conditions. No matter what language you speak, however, you can perceive and think about snow according to whether it is falling or on the ground, powdery or slushy, fluffy or packed, without having specific words for snow in those conditions.

linguistic relativity hypothesis: The notion that the language a person speaks largely determines the nature of that person's thoughts.

Eleanor Rosch (1973) tested whether people whose language contains many names for colors are better at thinking about and discriminating among colors than people whose language has only a few color names. Her subjects were English-speaking Americans and members of the Dani, a remote tribe in New Guinea whose language has only two names for colors—*mili* for dark, cool colors and *mola* for bright, warm colors.

Rosch showed members of both groups single-color chips of 11 colors—black, white, red, yellow, green, blue, brown, purple, pink, orange, and gray—for 5 seconds each. Then, after 30 seconds, she had the participants select the 11 colors they had viewed from an assortment of 40 color chips. Rosch found no significant differences between the Dani and the Americans in discriminating, remembering, or thinking about the 11 basic colors.

Rosch's study did not support the linguistic relativity hypothesis. And neither did an earlier and larger study of 98 different languages by Berlin and Kay (1969). These researchers found a consistent pattern in establishing names for colors in all the cultures they studied. They concluded that people in cultures throughout the world think about colors in much the same way, regardless of the language they speak. Thought both influences and is influenced by language, and language appears to *reflect* cultural differences more than it determines them (Pinker, 1994; Rosch, 1987).

Consider the vast number of words that have been added to the English language within the last few decades—*CD, fax, e-mail, the Internet, web site, virtual reality,* and a host of other new words from medicine, science, engineering, and so on. New ideas preceded the introduction of these and other new words. But once new words appear, they are useful in giving rise to still newer ideas. Humans think both with and without language (as in imagery). A large and rich vocabulary is one of our most important tools for thinking. And there is a strong, consistent correlation between one's vocabulary and one's performance on most of the widely accepted tests for measuring intelligence.

Sexism in Language The words people use matter a great deal. Consider the generic use of the pronoun *he* to refer to people in general. If your professor says, "I expect each student in this class to do the best he can," does this announcement mean the same to males and females? Not according to research conducted by Gastil (1990) in which participants read sentences worded in three different forms. Perform Gastil's experiment yourself by completing the *Try It!*

Try It!

After reading each of these three sentences, pause and jot down any image that comes to mind.

1. The average American believes he watches too much television.
2. The average American believes he/she watches too much television.
3. Average Americans believe they watch too much television.

Whether you are male or female, the odds are high that you imaged a male after reading the first sentence in the *Try It!* Other studies confirm that the generic *he* is not interpreted very generically. It is interpreted heavily in favor of males (Hamilton, 1988; Henley, 1989; Ng, 1990). If this were not the case, then this sentence would not seem unusual at all: "Like other mammals, man bears his offspring live."

Bilingualism

What is the best time of life to learn a second language, and why?

Most native-born Americans speak only their native tongue, English. But in many other countries around the world, the majority of citizens speak two or even more languages (Snow, 1993). In European countries, most students learn English in addition to the languages of the countries bordering their own. Dutch is the native language of the Netherlands, but all Dutch schoolchildren learn German, French, and English. You would have to look long and hard for a native of the Netherlands who does not speak English.

In the United States today, there are between 30 and 35 million people aged 5 and older for whom English is a second language. Among the languages spoken at home by these people, Spanish is by far the leader (used by 17–18 million people). Following Spanish, other languages spoken in many U.S. homes are French (by under 2 million people), German (a little over 1.5 million), Italian (1.4 million), and Chinese (1.3 million).

Most linguists are convinced that being bilingual has many advantages (Genesee, 1994). For example, in Canada, where most students study both French and English, bilingual students are said to score higher on aptitude and math tests than their counterparts who speak only one language (Lambert et al., 1993).

People who are older when they learn a new language are far more likely to have an obvious accent and to make more grammatical errors than those who learn a new language as young children (McDonald, 1997). Apparently, for learning to speak a second language like a native, with great fluency and no accent, the younger the better is the rule. One reason for this difference between early and late language learners may have to do with slight variations in neural processing in Broca's area, the area of the brain that controls speech production. Research by Kim and others (1997) suggests that bilinguals who learned a second language early (younger than age 10 or 11) rely on the same patch of tissue in Broca's area for both of the languages they speak. But in those who were older when they learned a second language, two different sections of Broca's area are active while they are performing language tasks—one section for the native language and another for the second language. Yet the two sections are very close, only ⅓ inch apart. An earlier study by Klein and others (1995) also found that the same patch of tissue in Broca's area was activated by both the native and the second languages in research participants whose mean age was 7.3 years when they learned their second language.

Americans, as noted earlier, lag far behind citizens of most other technologically advanced nations in their knowledge of languages other than their native tongue and have much catching up to do. The ability to communicate in more than one language will surely become increasingly important as we move further into the new millennium.

In Quebec City and other places in Canada, bilingualism is common, and businesses must be prepared to communicate with customers in either French or English.

Remember It!

1. Match the component of language with the appropriate description.

   ____ (1) the smallest units of meaning

   ____ (2) the meaning derived from phonemes, morphemes, and sentences

   ____ (3) grammatical rules for arranging and combining words to form phrases and sentences

   ____ (4) the smallest units of sound in a spoken language

   a. syntax

   b. morphemes

   c. semantics

   d. phonemes

2. Sentences are more likely to be ambiguous if they have two or more (surface, deep) structures.
3. Communication in trained chimpanzees approaches human language in form and complexity. (true/false)
4. The linguistic relativity hypothesis is not supported by research. (true/false)
5. In general, thought influences language more than language influences thought. (true/false)
6. The best time to learn a second language is during (childhood, adolescence, adulthood).

Answers: 1. (1) b (2) c (3) a (4) d 2. deep 3. false 4. true 5. true 6. childhood

Apply It!

Avoiding Bad Decisions

What should I wear today–slacks and a sweater, or jeans and a shirt? Should I have a muffin for breakfast or some scrambled eggs? Orange juice or apple juice? . . . Every day you make a large number of decisions. Fortunately, most of them are minor and inconsequential. If you tune in to a nature program and later find out that you missed an episode of "Whose Line Is It, Anyway?," it doesn't matter much. You can always catch the rerun.

But occasionally you must make a decision that has serious or long-term implications: What job should I take? Which car will give the best value for my money? What kind of care can I arrange for my aging and ailing parents? Here mistakes can carry heavier consequences in terms of problems with your career, finances, relationships, or general well-being. Why do we often make bad decisions?

Factors leading to bad decisions. Psychologists have identified several erroneous ways of thinking that contribute to bad decisions. A major one is the *belief bias*–the tendency to allow personal beliefs to interfere with careful consideration of the facts. If, for example, you believe that only imported cars are safe, you will exclude American cars from consideration when buying a new one. Failure to consider the safety features and records of all the available cars could lead to purchasing one that is not as safe as you would like.

Related to belief bias is *confirmation bias*–the tendency to seek out and attend to information that confirms one's existing beliefs or positions while ignoring or not considering information that contradicts them. This tendency might lead you, for example, to read only newspaper and magazine articles by writers whose views you agree with, and avoiding those by writers whose opinions you don't share. And confirmation bias can have more serious consequences. For example, a therapist who is convinced that women who suffer from depression and eating disorders do so because they have been sexually abused may fail to consider other possible causes and thus be unable to help certain clients.

Various logical fallacies also interfere with sound decision making. One of these is the *gambler's fallacy*—the belief that the odds in favor of a given chance event (such as a tossed coin turning up heads) increase if the event hasn't occurred recently. In reality, the odds of such an event are the same in every instance.

Another common fallacy is the *fallacy of positive instances*—the tendency to remember uncommon events that seem to confirm one's beliefs or opinions while forgetting more common events that do not confirm them. A classic example illustrating this fallacy is the accusation "You always call when I'm in the shower!"

Still another pitfall to avoid is the *fallacy of small numbers*—the mistaken belief that a small sample is representative of a larger group. For example, suppose one person in a large office is planning the company's annual holiday party and must let the caterer know whether to serve the traditional turkey with all the trimmings or prime rib. Being in a rush, she asks five employees who work near her for their preferences. Three of the five, or 60%, say that prime rib would be a nice change. Thinking that this is a sound majority, the party planner goes with the prime rib. To her chagrin, she discovers later that most of the dozens of people at the party were disappointed with the nontraditional meal. It is easy to come up with a bad estimate of reality from a small sample.

Guidelines for making better decisions. Much unhappiness in life can be traced to bad decisions. Simply being aware of the biases and fallacies that interfere with sound thinking can help you improve your decision-making skills. But there are some more positive steps you can take as well:

- *Focus on the facts.* Gather as much information as possible before making a decision. Think about whether your personal beliefs or opinions are causing you to ignore relevant facts.
- *Consider alternative views.* When you have gathered all the information you need, consider various ways of interpreting that information. Don't jump to conclusions.
- *Evaluate all options.* There may be several ways of accomplishing the same goal, and one of them may be less expensive, stressful, or time-consuming than the others. Try to determine which option will be best overall.
- *Remain flexible.* Having made a decision, you may tend to consider the case closed and to want to move on to other things. But there are times when you need to reevaluate a decision, especially one with major consequences. Even though you may dread going through the decision-making process again or find it difficult to admit that you made a mistake, it's far worse to continue with an ill-advised course of action.
- *Avoid being trapped by emotions.* Sometimes you may have feelings—inhibitions or fears or even desires—that can get in the way of good decisions. Try to put such emotions aside and look at the facts as objectively as possible.
- *Consider the consequences of your decisions.* Especially guard against making choices hastily, on impulse.

THINKING CRITICALLY

Evaluation

Review the three basic approaches to problem solving discussed in this chapter. Which approach do you think is most practical and efficient for solving everyday problems?

Point/Counterpoint

Prepare an argument supporting each of the following positions:

a. English is the only language that should be taught in U.S. public schools.
b. Bilingual education should be provided for all U.S. students for whom English is a second language.
c. All students in U.S. public schools should be required to learn a language other than their native ones.

Psychology in Your Life

Give several examples of how tools of thinking (imagery and concepts) and decision-making strategies (the additive strategy, the elimination-by-aspects strategy, and heuristics) can be applied in your school and personal life.

SUMMARY AND REVIEW

What is meant by cognition, and what specific processes does it include?

Cognition refers collectively to the mental processes involved in acquiring, storing, retrieving, and using knowledge. These mental processes include sensation, perception, imagery, concept formation, reasoning, decision making, problem solving, and language.

Key Term
cognition (p. 246)

IMAGERY AND CONCEPTS: TOOLS OF THINKING

What is imagery?

Imagery is the mental representation of a sensory experience—visual, auditory, gustatory, motor, olfactory, or tactile.

What is a concept?

A concept is a mental category that represents a class or group of objects, people, organizations, events, or relations that share common characteristics or attributes.

What is the difference between a formal concept and a natural concept?

A formal concept is one that is clearly defined by a set of rules, a formal definition or a characteristic. A natural concept is formed on the basis of everyday perceptions and experiences and is somewhat fuzzy. In using a natural concept, a person is likely to picture a prototype of the concept—an example that embodies its most common and typical features.

Key Terms
imagery (p. 247); concept (p. 249); formal concept (p. 250); natural concept (p. 250); prototype (p. 251); exemplars (p. 251)

DEDUCTIVE AND INDUCTIVE REASONING: LOGICAL THINKING

What is the difference between deductive and inductive reasoning?

Deductive reasoning involves reasoning from the general to the specific, or drawing particular conclusions from general principles. Inductive reasoning is a form of reasoning in which general conclusions are drawn from particular facts or individual cases.

Key Terms
reasoning (p. 252); deductive reasoning (p. 252); syllogism (p. 252); inductive reasoning (p. 252)

DECISION MAKING: MAKING CHOICES IN LIFE

How is the additive strategy used in decision making?

The additive strategy is a decision-making approach in which each alternative is rated on each important factor affecting the decision and the alternative with the highest overall rating is chosen.

When is the elimination-by-aspects strategy most useful?

The elimination-by-aspects strategy is most useful when a decision involves many alternatives and multiple factors. With this approach, some alternatives are eliminated because they do not satisfy the most important factors. Then the additive strategy is typically used to make the best choice among the surviving alternatives.

What is the availability heuristic?

The availability heuristic is a rule of thumb that says that the probability of an event or the importance assigned to it is based on its availability in memory, that is, the ease with which the information comes to mind.

What is the representativeness heuristic?

The representativeness heuristic is a thinking strategy that is used in decision making and that assesses how closely a new object or situation matches an existing prototype of that object or situation.

What is framing?

Framing is the way information is presented so as to focus on either a potential gain or a potential loss.

Key Terms
decision making (p. 253); additive strategy (p. 253); heuristic (p. 254); availability heuristic (p. 254); representativeness heuristic (p. 256); framing (p. 256)

PROBLEM SOLVING: BEYOND DECISION MAKING

What are three basic approaches to problem solving?

Three basic approaches to problem solving are trial and error, algorithms, and heuristics.

What is an algorithm?

An algorithm is a systematic, step-by-step procedure or formula that guarantees a solution to a certain type of problem if the algorithm is appropriate and is executed properly.

What are three heuristics used in problem solving?

Three heuristics used in problem solving are working backwards, means–end analysis, and the analogy heuristic.

How do functional fixedness and mental set impede problem solving?

Functional fixedness, or the tendency to view objects only in terms of their customary functions, results in a failure to use the objects in novel ways to solve problems. Mental set is the tendency to apply a strategy that was successful in the past to solve new problems, even though it may not be appropriate for their requirements.

Key Terms
problem solving (p. 257); trial and error (p. 258); algorithm (p. 259); working backwards (p. 259); means–end analysis (p. 259); analogy heuristic (p. 259); functional fixedness (p. 260); mental set (p. 261)

HIGH-TECH APPLICATIONS OF COGNITION: ARTIFICIAL INTELLIGENCE AND ROBOTICS

What is artificial intelligence?

Artificial intelligence refers to the programming of computer systems to simulate human thinking in solving problems and in making judgments and decisions.

Key Terms
artificial intelligence (p. 261); neural networks (p. 262)

LANGUAGE

What are the four important components of language?

The four important components of language are (1) phonemes, the smallest units of sound in a spoken language; (2) morphemes, the smallest units of meaning; (3) syntax, the grammatical rules for arranging and combining words to form phrases and sentences; and (4) semantics, the meaning derived from phonemes, morphemes, and sentences.

How does language in trained chimpanzees differ from human language?

Chimpanzees' communication using sign language or symbols consists of constructions strung together rather than actual sentences.

In general, does thought influence language more, or does language influence thought more?

In general, thought has a greater influence on language than vice versa. Whorf's linguistic relativity hypothesis has not been supported by research.

What is the best time of life to learn a second language, and why?

People who learn a second language when they are younger than 10 or 11 usually speak without an accent, are more fluent, and make fewer grammatical errors than do those who are older when they learn another language.

Key Terms
language (p. 264); psycholinguistics (p. 265); phonemes (p. 265); morphemes (p. 265); syntax (p. 265); semantics (p. 266); surface structure (p. 266); deep structure (p. 266); linguistic relativity hypothesis (p. 269)

Surf It!

Want to be sure you've absorbed the material in Chapter 7, "Cognition and Language," before the big test? Visiting *www.abacon.com/wood* can put a top grade within your reach. The site is loaded with free practice tests, flashcards, activities, and links to help you review your way to an A. To enliven that inevitable study break, the site also offers personality assessment quizzes and a psychology career corner.

8 Intelligence and Creativity

How IQ is determined
David Veschler -

Who has the highest IQ score ever recorded on an intelligence test? The name of Albert Einstein quickly comes to mind and perhaps a host of other great thinkers of the past—mostly men. But the person with the highest IQ score ever recorded happens to be a woman.

Marilyn Mach, born in St. Louis, in 1946, scored an amazing 230 on the Stanford–Binet IQ test when she was a 10-year-old elementary school student. How high is a 230 IQ? The average Stanford–Binet IQ score is set at 100, and a score of 116—only about half as high as Marilyn Mach's lofty score—places a person in the top 16 percent of the population. Not only does Marilyn Mach have no peer when it comes to measured intelligence, she doesn't even have a competitor. Her score is nearly 30 points higher than that of her nearest rival.

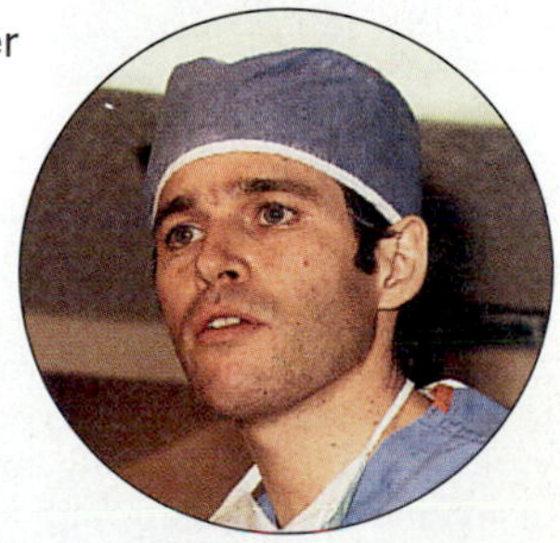

Descended from the Austrian philosopher and physicist Ernst Mach, who did pioneering work in the physics of sound (Mach 1, Mach 2), Marilyn added her mother's birth name as an adult and became known as Marilyn Mach vos Savant. She completed about 2 years of college courses but has no college degree. Her primary intellectual interest is creative writing, and she has written 12 books and 3 plays. Her first published work was the Omni IQ Quiz Contest. Marilyn lives with her husband in New York, where she writes the "Ask Marilyn" column for *Parade* magazine, lectures on intelligence, and pursues various other interests.

Now consider another person, Dr. Robert Jarvik, the world-famous inventor of the Jarvik artificial heart. Dr. Jarvik combined his medical knowledge and his mechanical genius to produce the world's first workable artificial heart. But his path wasn't easy. Unlike Marilyn Mach vos Savant, Jarvik was a poor test taker. In fact, he scored too low on intelligence and admissions tests to be admitted to any medical school in the United States. Eventually, despite his low test scores, he was accepted by a medical school in Italy, where he completed his studies and received his M.D. degree. Then he returned to practice in the United States and made his contribution to medical science–a contribution that kept alive many gravely ill heart patients until a suitable heart transplant could be performed.

Perhaps, if Dr. Jarvik wishes, he can learn to score higher on IQ tests. His wife, Marilyn Mach vos Savant–Jarvik, might be willing to teach him.

Like Dr. Jarvik, many highly creative individuals have tested poorly in school. Some of the most prominent are the famous American inventor Thomas A. Edison; Winston Churchill, whose teachers thought he was mentally limited; and even the great Albert Einstein, who was labeled a dunce in math.

In this chapter we will explore cognitive and emotional intelligence and creativity. You will learn about the nature of intelligence and how it is measured. Where does human intelligence come from—genes, experiences provided by the environment, or both? We will look at the extremes in intelligence—the mentally gifted and the mentally retarded. We will also consider how creative people think.

First, let's ask the most obvious question: What is intelligence? A task force of experts from the American Psychological Association (APA) defined **intelligence** as an individual's "ability to understand complex ideas, to adapt effectively to the environment, to learn from experience, to engage in various forms of reasoning, and to overcome obstacles by taking thought" (Neisser et al., 1996, p. 77).

intelligence: An individual's ability to understand complex ideas, to adapt effectively to the environment, to learn from experience, to engage in various forms of reasoning, and to overcome obstacles through mental effort.

No concept in psychology has been at the center of more public policy debates and more scientific disagreement than intelligence (Moffitt et al., 1993). Is intelligence a single, general capability, or are there multiple types of intelligence? Is intelligence influenced more by heredity or by environment? Is it fixed or changeable, culture-free or culture-bound? The nature of intelligence continues to be hotly debated.

THE NATURE OF INTELLIGENCE

The Search for Factors Underlying Intelligence

Is intelligence a single trait or capability? Is it many capabilities unrelated to each other? Are there certain common factors that underlie intelligence?

What factors underlie intelligence, according to Spearman and Thurstone?

Spearman and General Intelligence: The *g* Factor Traditionally, intelligence has been considered as more or less a single entity. This notion was first suggested by English psychologist Charles Spearman (1863–1945), who observed that people who are good at one type of thinking or cognition tend to do well in other types as well. In other words, they tend to be generally intelligent. Spearman (1927) came to believe that intelligence is composed of a general ability, or ***g* factor,** which underlies all intellectual functions.

Spearman arrived at his "*g* theory" when he found positive relationships among scores on the subtests of intelligence tests. Spearman theorized that this positive relationship meant that the tests were measuring something in common—that general ability was expressed to some degree in all of them. This, said Spearman, was evidence of the *g* factor—general intelligence.

But some of the correlations between subtests are much higher than others. Therefore, some other abilities in addition to the *g* factor must be present. These other abilities Spearman named "*s* factors" for specific abilities.

Spearman concluded that intelligence tests tap a person's *g* factor, or general intelligence, and a number of *s* factors, or specific intellectual abilities. Spearman's influence can be seen in those intelligence tests, such as the Stanford–Binet, that yield one IQ score to indicate the level of general intelligence.

Spearman's theory continues to be influential, according to some leading researchers in the field of intelligence. For example, Robert Plomin (1999) asserts that the *g* factor is among the most valid and reliable measures of intelligence, better than other measures in predicting success in social, educational, and occupational endeavors.

Where might processing related to high general intelligence be located in the brain? It was expected that tasks related to general intelligence would show a broad, diffuse pattern of brain function. But, instead, brain-imaging studies show that general intelligence tasks, whether they involve verbal or perceptual skills or geometry, are associated with specific areas of the lateral frontal cortex in one or both hemispheres (Duncan et al., 2000).

Thurstone's Primary Mental Abilities: Primarily Seven Another early researcher, Louis L. Thurstone (1938), rejected Spearman's notion of a general intellectual ability, or *g* factor. After analyzing the scores of many research participants on 56 separate tests, Thurstone identified seven **primary mental abilities:** verbal comprehension, numerical ability, spatial relations, perceptual speed, word fluency, memory, and reasoning. He maintained that all intellectual activities involve one or more of these primary mental abilities. Thurstone and his wife, Thelma G. Thurstone, developed their Primary Mental Abilities Tests to measure these seven abilities.

Thurstone believed a single IQ score obscured more than it revealed. He suggested that a profile showing relative strengths and weaknesses on the seven primary abilities would provide a more accurate picture of a person's mental ability.

What types of intelligence did Gardner and Sternberg identify?

***g* factor:** Spearman's term for a general intellectual ability that underlies all mental operations to some degree.

primary mental abilities: According to Thurstone, seven relatively distinct abilities that singly or in combination are involved in all intellectual activities.

Intelligence: More Than One Type?

Some theorists, instead of searching for the factors that underlie intelligence, propose that there are different types of intelligence. Two such modern theorists are Howard Gardner and Robert Sternberg.

Gardner's Theory of Multiple Intelligences: Eight Frames of Mind Harvard psychologist Howard Gardner (1983; Garner & Hatch, 1989) also denies the existence of a *g* factor. Instead he proposes eight independent forms of intelligence:

1. *Linguistic* (language skills)
2. *Logical/mathematical* (math and quantitative skills)
3. *Musical*
4. *Spatial* (skills used by painters, sculptors, and architects to manipulate and create forms)
5. *Bodily/kinesthetic* (body control and manual dexterity as exemplified by athletes, dancers, and carpenters)
6. *Interpersonal* (the ability to understand the behavior and read the moods, desires, and intentions of others)
7. *Intrapersonal* (the ability to understand one's own feelings and behavior)
8. *Naturalistic* (knowledge of and ability to survive in the natural environment)

Kelly Wigglesworth, shown here on the left, became one of the two finalists on the first Survivor *series. She probably has a high level of Gardner's naturalistic component of intelligence.*

A recent example of the use of this eighth type of intelligence would be the winning strategy employed by Richard Hatch, who won the million-dollar prize on the popular TV program *Survivor.* In fact, all four of the finalists (Rich, Kelly, Sue, and Rudy) on that program would probably score high in Gardner's naturalistic intelligence.

Gardner (1983) first developed his theory by studying patients with different types of brain damage that affect some forms of intelligence but leave others intact. He also studied reports of people with *savant syndrome*—who possess a strange combination of mental retardation and unusual talent or ability. Finally, Gardner considered how various abilities and skills have been valued differently in other cultures and periods of history.

Perhaps the most controversial aspect of Gardner's theory is his view that all forms of intelligence are of equal importance. In fact, different cultures assign varying importance to the types of intelligence. For example, linguistic and logical/mathematical intelligences are valued most in the United States and other Western cultures; bodily/kinesthetic intelligence is more highly prized in cultures that depend on hunting for survival.

Gardner's theory "has enjoyed wide popularity, especially among educators, but [his] ideas are based more on reasoning and intuition than on the results of empirical research studies" (Aiken, 1997, p. 196). Gardner's critics doubt that all the forms of intelligence he proposes are of equal value in education and in life. Robert Sternberg (1985b) claims that "the multiple intelligences might better be referred to as multiple talents" (p. 1114). He asks whether an adult who is tone-deaf and has no sense of rhythm can be considered mentally limited in the same way as one who has never developed any verbal skills. In addition to differing with Gardner, Sternberg (2000) is also critical of heavy reliance on Spearman's *g* factor for measuring intelligence. But Sternberg is not merely a critic; he has developed his own theory of intelligence.

Sternberg's Triarchic Theory of Intelligence: The Big Three Robert Sternberg uses the information-processing approach to understand intelligence. This approach involves a step-by-step analysis of the cognitive processes people use as they acquire knowledge and use it to solve problems.

triarchic theory of intelligence: Sternberg's theory that there are three types of intelligence—componential (analytical), experiential (creative), and contextual (practical).

Sternberg (1985a; 1986a) has formulated a **triarchic theory of intelligence,** which, as the term *triarchic* implies, proposes that there are three types of intelligence—componential (analytical), experiential (creative), and contextual (practical) (see Figure 8.1). The first type, *componential intelligence,* refers to the mental abilities most closely

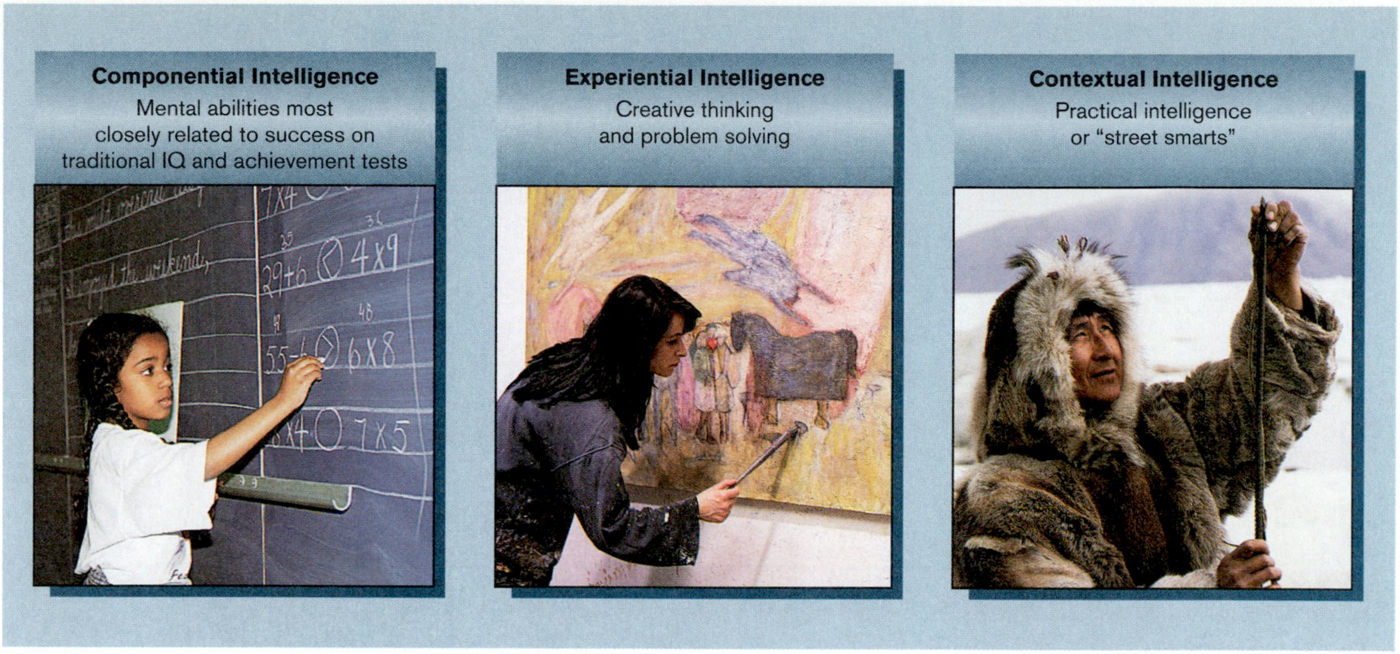

Figure 8.1

Sternberg's Triarchic Theory of Intelligence

According to Sternberg, there are three types of intelligence: componential, experiential, and contextual.

related to success on conventional IQ and achievement tests. Sternberg claims that traditional IQ tests measure only componential, or analytical, intelligence.

The second type, *experiential intelligence,* is reflected in creative thinking and problem solving. People with high experiential intelligence are able to solve novel problems and deal with unusual and unexpected challenges. Another aspect of experiential intelligence is finding creative ways to perform common daily tasks more efficiently and effectively, almost automatically.

The third type, *contextual intelligence,* or practical intelligence, might be equated with common sense or "street smarts." People with high contextual intelligence are survivors who capitalize on their strengths and compensate for their weaknesses. They either adapt well to their environment, change the environment so that they can succeed, or if necessary, find a new environment. People who have succeeded in spite of hardships and adverse circumstances probably have a great deal of contextual intelligence.

Sternberg and others (1995; 2000) argue that intelligence test scores fail to account for more than 25% of the variance in people's abilities as measured by real-world criteria such as job performance. What is the distinction between academic performance and practical, real-world functioning? Sternberg maintains that the distinction is based on two different types of knowledge: *formal academic knowledge,* or the knowledge that intelligence tests and various aptitude tests measure, and *tacit knowledge,* or the primary type of knowledge that makes up practical intelligence. Unlike formal academic knowledge, tacit knowledge is action-oriented and is acquired without direct help from others. And it allows people to pursue goals they value personally. An abundant store of tacit knowledge and expertise in its use are apparently important ingredients in successful real-world performance. Acquired during the course of real life, tacit knowledge "takes the form of 'knowing how' rather than 'knowing that'" (Sternberg et al., 1995, p. 916).

Accumulating evidence suggests that performance on practical intelligence measures (tacit knowledge) is related to various aspects of real-world performance but is more or less unrelated to conventional academic measures of intelligence. Sternberg and others (1995) maintain that testing both academic and practical intelligence yields more accurate predictions about real-world performance than does testing either kind alone.

Remember It!

Match the theorist with the theory of intelligence.

____ (1) triarchic theory of intelligence	a. Spearman
____ (2) seven primary mental abilities	b. Thurstone
____ (3) multiple intelligences	c. Sternberg
____ (4) the *g* factor	d. Gardner

Answers: (1) c (2) b (3) d (4) a

MEASURING INTELLIGENCE

Binet and the First Successful Intelligence Test

What is Binet's major contribution to psychology?

The first successful effort to measure intelligence resulted not from a theoretical approach, but as a practical means of solving a problem in the schools of France. At the very beginning of the 20th century, the Ministry of Public Instruction in Paris was struggling with a problem—trying to find some objective means of sorting out children whose intelligence was too low for them to profit from regular classroom instruction. The ministry wanted to ensure that average or brighter children would not be wrongly assigned to special classes and that children of limited ability would not be subjected to the regular program of instruction. In 1903 a commission was formed to study the problem, and one of its members was French psychologist Alfred Binet (1857–1911).

Working with psychiatrist Theodore Simon to develop a test for evaluating children's intelligence, Alfred Binet (shown here) began testing Parisian students in 1904.

With the help of his colleague, psychiatrist Theodore Simon, Binet began testing the schoolchildren of Paris in 1904. The two men used a wide variety of tests, and they kept only those items that discriminated well between older and younger children. Binet and Simon published their intelligence scale in 1905 and revised it in 1908 and again in 1911. The Binet–Simon Intelligence Scale was an immediate success.

Test items on the scale were structured according to increasing difficulty—with the easiest item first and each succeeding item becoming more difficult. Children went as far as they could, and then their progress was compared with that of other children of the same age. A child with the mental ability of a normal 5-year-old could be said to have a mental level of 5. Binet established the concept that mental retardation and mental superiority are a function of the difference between chronological age (actual age in years) and mental age. An 8-year-old with a mental age of 8 is normal or average. An 8-year-old with a mental age of 5 is seriously deficient; an 8-year-old with a mental age of 11 is mentally superior.

Binet believed that children with a mental age 2 years below their chronological age were retarded and should be placed in special education classes. But there was a flaw in his thinking. A 4-year-old with a mental age of 2 is far more retarded than a 12-year-old with a mental age of 10. How could a similar degree of retardation at different ages be expressed?

German psychologist William Stern (1914) provided an answer. In 1912 he devised a simple formula for calculating an index of intelligence—the *intelligence quotient.* He divided a child's mental age by his or her chronological age.

Intelligence Testing in the United States

The Stanford–Binet Intelligence Scale: A Famous IQ Test Lewis M. Terman, a psychology professor at Stanford University, published a thorough revision of the Binet–Simon scale in 1916. Terman revised and adapted the items for American children, added new items, and established new **norms**—standards based on the scores of a large number of people and used as bases for comparison. Within 2½ years, 4 million children had taken Terman's revision, known as the **Stanford–Binet Intelligence Scale.** It was the first test to make use of Stern's formula for the **intelligence quotient (IQ)**, but Terman improved the formula by multiplying the result by 100 to eliminate the decimal. He also introduced the abbreviation IQ.

What is the Stanford–Binet Intelligence Scale?

What does IQ mean, and how has the method for calculating it changed over time?

$$\frac{\text{Mental age}}{\text{Chronological age}} \times 100 = \text{IQ}$$

Here is how some IQs for 10-year-olds would be calculated:

$$\frac{14}{10} \times 100 = 1.40 \times 100 = \text{IQ } 140 \text{ (superior IQ)}$$

$$\frac{10}{10} \times 100 = 1.00 \times 100 = \text{IQ } 100 \text{ (normal IQ)}$$

$$\frac{6}{10} \times 100 = 0.60 \times 100 = \text{IQ } 60 \text{ (below normal IQ)}$$

nature vs. nurture

The highly regarded Stanford–Binet is an individually administered IQ test for those aged 2 to 23. It contains four subscales: verbal reasoning, quantitative reasoning, abstract visual reasoning, and short-term memory. An overall IQ score is derived from scores on the four subscales, and the test scores correlate well with achievement test scores (Laurent et al., 1992).

What did Wechsler's tests provide that the Stanford–Binet did not?

Intelligence Testing for Adults: A Scale for All Ages Intelligence testing became increasingly popular in the United States in the 1920s and 1930s, but it quickly became obvious that the Stanford–Binet Intelligence Scale was not useful for testing adults. The original IQ formula could not be applied to adults, because at a certain age people achieve maturity in intelligence. According to the original IQ formula, a 40-year-old with the same IQ test score as the average 20-year-old would be considered mentally retarded, with an IQ of only 50. Obviously, something was wrong with the formula when applied to populations of all ages.

Today psychologists still use the term *IQ*, but for adults, IQ is a **deviation score** derived by comparing an individual's score with scores of others the *same age* on whom the test was normed. The deviation score is a contribution of David Wechsler, another pioneer in mental testing.

The Wechsler Intelligence Tests: Among the Best In 1939 psychologist David Wechsler developed the first successful individual intelligence test for adults, designed for those age 16 and older. The original test has been revised, restandardized, and renamed the **Wechsler Adult Intelligence Scale (WAIS-III)** and is one of the most widely used psychological tests. The test contains both verbal and performance (nonverbal) subtests, which yield separate verbal and performance IQ scores as well as an overall IQ score. This test is a departure from the Stanford–Binet scale, which yields a single IQ score.

Wechsler also published the Wechsler Intelligence Scale for Children (WISC-III) and the Wechsler Preschool and Primary Scale of Intelligence (WPPSI), which is normed for children aged 4 to 6½. Table 8.1 (on p. 284) describes the types of tasks found on the Wechsler Intelligence Scale for Children.

norms: Standards based on the range of test scores of a large group of people who are selected to provide the bases of comparison for those who take the test later.

Stanford–Binet Intelligence Scale: An individually administered IQ test for those aged 2 to 23; Terman's adaptation of the Binet–Simon Scale.

intelligence quotient (IQ): An index of intelligence originally derived by dividing mental age by chronological age and then multiplying by 100; now derived by comparing an individual's score with the scores of others of the same age.

deviation score: A test score calculated by comparing an individual's score with the scores of others of the same age.

Wechsler Adult Intelligence Scale (WAIS-III): An individual intelligence test for adults that yields separate verbal and performance (nonverbal) IQ scores as well as an overall IQ score.

verbal + non-verbal different test scores for each area

Table 8.1 Typical Subtests on the Wechsler Intelligence Scale for Children (WISC)

Verbal Subtests		Performance Subtests	
Subtest	**Sample Items**	**Subtest**	**Description of Item**
Information	How many wings does a bird have?	Picture arrangement	Arrange a series of cartoon panels to make a meaningful story.
Digit span	Repeat from memory a series of digits, such as 3 1 0 6 7 4 2 5, after hearing it once.	Picture completion	What is missing from these pictures?
General comprehension	What is the advantage of keeping money in a bank?	Block design	Copy designs with blocks 
Arithmetic	If 2 apples cost 15¢, what will be the cost of a dozen apples?		
Similarities	In what way are a lion and a tiger alike?		
Vocabulary	This test consists simply of asking, "What is a ________?" or "What does ________ mean?" The words cover a wide range of difficulty or familiarity.	Object assembly	Put together a jigsaw puzzle.
		Digit symbol	Fill in the symbols: 1 2 3 4 / X III I O 3 4 1 3 4 2 1 2 / (blank boxes)

One advantage of the Wechsler scales is their ability to identify intellectual strengths in nonverbal as well as verbal areas. Wechsler also believed that differences in a person's scores on the various verbal and performance subtests could be used for diagnostic purposes. In fact, the Wechsler Memory Scale (WMS-R) is frequently used to assess memory function in adults and to evaluate patients with epilepsy (Cañizares et al., 2000).

Group Intelligence Tests: Testing More Than One at a Time Administering individual intelligence tests such as the Stanford–Binet and Wechsler scales is expensive and time-consuming. The tests must be given to one person at a time by a qualified professional. For testing large numbers of people in a short period of time on a limited budget, group intelligence tests are the answer. Group intelligence tests, such as the California Test of Mental Maturity, the Cognitive Abilities Test, and the Otis–Lennon Mental Ability Test, are widely used.

Requirements of Good Tests: Reliability, Validity, and Standardization

What do the terms *reliability, validity,* and *standardization* mean?

If your watch gains 6 minutes one day and loses 3 or 4 minutes the next day, it is not reliable. You want a watch that you can rely on to give the correct time day after day. Like a watch, an intelligence test must have **reliability;** the test must consistently yield nearly the same score when the same people are tested and then retested on the same test or an alternative form of the test. The higher the correlation between the two scores, the more reliable the test. A correlation coefficient of 1.0 would indicate perfect reliability. Most widely used tests, such as the Stanford–Binet and Wechsler scales and the Scholastic Assessment Test (SAT), boast high reliabilities of about .90. Some researchers, however, have stated that the index scores for WISC-III should be interpreted cautiously: When used with children who are not members of the mainsteam cultural group on whom the tests were normed, the scores have poor reliability (Caruso & Cliff, 2000).

Tests can be highly reliable but worthless if they are not valid. **Validity** is the ability or power of a test to measure what it is intended to measure. For example, a thermometer is a valid instrument for measuring temperature; a bathroom scale is valid for measuring weight. But no matter how reliable your bathroom scale is, it will not take your temperature. It is valid only for weighing. The validity of some of the WISC III subtests as social intelligence measures has been questioned. Some researchers have claimed that the picture arrangement subtest is unrelated to social functioning and that the general comprehension subtest has limited clinical significance when used with children who have attention-deficit/hyperactivity disorder (ADHD) (Beebe et al., 2000).

Aptitude tests are designed to predict a person's probable achievement or performance at some future time. Selecting students for admission to college or graduate schools is based partly on the predictive validity of aptitude tests, such as the Scholastic Assessment Test (SAT), the American College Testing Program (ACT), and the Graduate Record Examination (GRE). How well do SAT scores predict success in college? Moderately at best. The correlation between SAT scores and the grades of college freshmen is about .40 (Linn, 1982).

Once a test is proven to be valid and reliable, the next requirement is **standardization.** There must be standard procedures for administering and scoring the test. Exactly the same directions must be given, whether written or oral, and the same amount of time must be allowed for every test taker. Even more important, standardization means establishing norms by which all scores are interpreted. A test is standardized by administering it to a large sample of people representative of those who will be taking the test in the future. The group's scores are analyzed, and then the average score, standard deviation, percentile rankings, and other measures are computed. These comparative scores become the norms used as the standard against which all other scores on that test are measured.

After studying the performance of Black and White South African children on WISC-R (the predecessor of WISC-III), researchers claimed that the validity of such traditional tests is questionable for cultural groups other than those with whom the tests were normed (Skuy et al., 2000). Test items that are valid in one cultural context may lose their validity in a different context (Knowles & Condon, 2000). Moreover, intelligence tests must undergo continuous revision to maintain their validity. The wording of test items is critical, especially since some items may be as old or older than the grandparents of today's young test takers (Strauss et al., 2000). Also, the nature of the U.S. population is changing rapidly. Thus, when new tests are normed and standardized or when existing tests are renormed, the increasing diversity of the test takers must be considered. Researchers Okazaki and Sue (2000) point out that Asian Americans, in particular, have been severely underrepresented in the validation studies of the Wechsler scales.

reliability: The ability of a test to yield nearly the same score when the same people are tested and then retested on the same test or an alternative form of the test.

validity: The ability of a test to measure what it is intended to measure.

aptitude test: A test designed to predict a person's achievement or performance at some future time.

standardization: Establishing norms for comparing the scores of people who will take a test in the future; administering tests using a prescribed procedure.

The Range of Intelligence

What are the ranges of IQ scores considered average, superior, and in the range of mental retardation?

When large populations are measured on intelligence or on physical characteristics such as height or weight, the test scores or results usually conform to the bell-shaped distribution known as the *normal curve.* The majority of the scores cluster around the mean (average). The farther scores deviate, or move away, from the mean, either above or below, the fewer there are.

The average IQ test score for all people in the same age group is arbitrarily assigned an IQ score of 100. On the Wechsler intelligence tests, approximately 50% of the scores are in the average range, between 90 and 110. About 68% of the scores fall between 85 and 115, and about 95% fall between 70 and 130. Some 2% of the scores are above 130, which is considered superior, and about 2% fall below 70, in the range of mental retardation (see Figure 8.2 on p. 286).

Figure 8.2

The Normal Curve

When a large number of test scores are compiled, they are typically distributed in a normal (bell-shaped) curve. On the Wechsler scales, the average or mean IQ score is set at 100. As the figure shows, about 68% of the scores fall between 15 IQ points (1 standard deviation) above and below 100 (from 85 to 115), and about 95.5% of the scores fall between 30 points (2 standard deviations) above and below 100 (from 70 to 130).

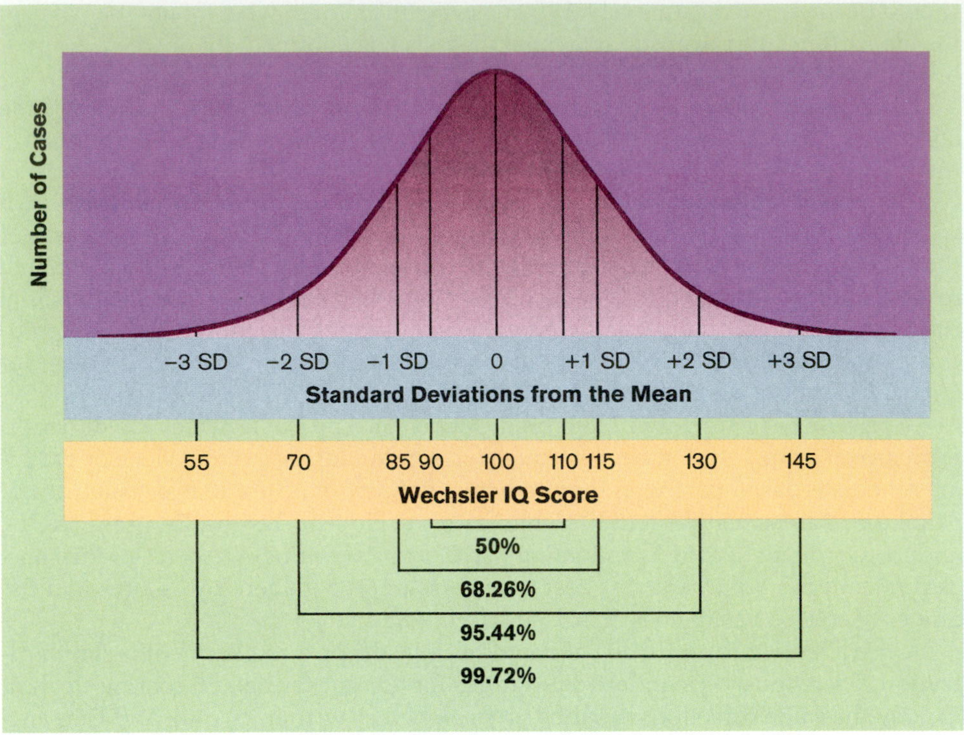

According to the Terman study, how do the gifted differ from the general population?

Terman's Study of the Gifted: 1,528 Geniuses and How They Grew In 1921 Lewis M. Terman (1925) launched a longitudinal study, now a classic, in which 1,528 gifted students were selected and measured at different ages throughout their lives. Tested on the Stanford–Binet, the participants, 857 males and 671 females, had unusually high IQs, ranging from 135 to 200, with an average of 151. Terman assumed the Stanford–Binet measured innate intelligence and that IQ was fixed at birth (Cravens, 1992).

Terman's early findings put an end to the myth that mentally superior people are more likely to be physically inferior. In fact, Terman's gifted participants excelled in almost all of the abilities he studied—intellectual, physical, emotional, moral, and social. Terman also exploded many other myths about the mentally gifted (Terman & Oden, 1947). For example, you may have heard the saying that there is a thin line between genius and madness. Actually Terman's gifted group enjoyed better mental health than the general population. Also, you may have heard that mentally gifted people are long on "book sense" but short on "common sense." In reality, Terman's participants earned more academic degrees, achieved higher occupational status and higher salaries, were better adjusted both personally and socially, and were healthier than their less mentally gifted peers. However, most women at that time did not pursue careers outside of the home, so the findings related to occupational success applied primarily to the men. Terman (1925) concluded that "there is no law of compensation whereby the intellectual superiority of the gifted is offset by inferiorities along nonintellectual lines" (p. 16).

The Terman study continues today, with the surviving participants in their 80s or 90s. In a report on Terman's study, Shneidman (1989) states its basic findings—that "an unusual mind, a vigorous body, and a relatively well-adjusted personality are not at all incompatible" (p. 687).

Who Are the Gifted? Beginning in the early 1920s, the term *gifted* was used to describe the intellectually superior—those with IQs in the upper 2–3% of the U.S. population. Today the term includes both the exceptionally creative and those who excel in the visual or performing arts.

Table 8.2 Mental Retardation as Measured on the Wechsler Scales

Classification	IQ Range	Percentage of the Mentally Retarded	Characteristics of Retarded Persons at Each Level
Mild	55–70	90%	Are able to grasp learning skills up to 6th-grade level. They may become self-supporting and can be profitably employed in various vocational occupations.
Moderate	40–55	6%	Probably are not able to grasp more than 2nd-grade academic skills but can learn self-help skills and some social and academic skills. They may work in sheltered workshops.
Severe	25–40	3%	Can be trained in basic health habits; can learn to communicate verbally. Learn through repetitive habit training.
Profound	Below 25	1%	Rudimentary motor development; may learn very limited self-help skills.

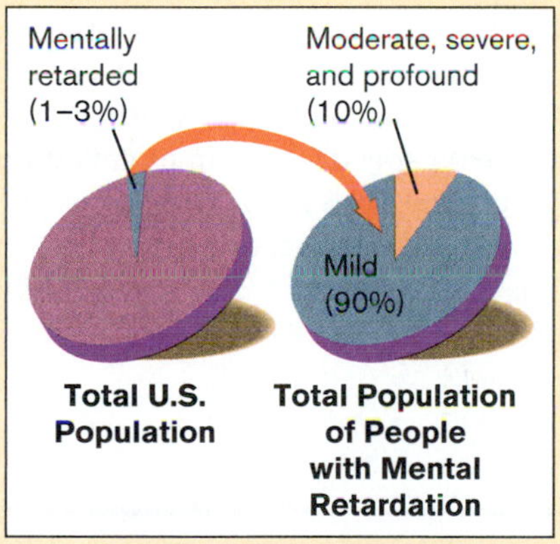

Traditionally, special programs for the gifted have involved either acceleration or enrichment. Acceleration enables students to progress at a rate that is consistent with their ability. Students may skip a grade, progress through subject matter at a faster rate, be granted advanced placement in college courses, or enter college early. Enrichment programs aim to broaden students' knowledge by giving them special courses in foreign language, music appreciation, and the like, or by providing special experiences designed to foster advanced thinking skills.

The Mentally Retarded At the opposite end of the continuum from the intellectually gifted are the 2% of the U.S. population whose IQ scores place them in the range of **mental retardation.** Individuals are not classified as mentally retarded unless (1) their IQ score is below 70 and (2) they have a severe deficiency in everyday adaptive functioning—the ability to care for themselves and relate to others (Grossman, 1983). There are degrees of retardation from mild to profound. Individuals with IQs ranging from 55 to 70 are considered mildly retarded; from 40 to 55, moderately retarded; from 25 to 40, severely retarded; and below 25, profoundly retarded. Table 8.2 shows the level of functioning expected for various categories of mental retardation.

What two criteria must one meet to be classified as mentally retarded?

mental retardation: Subnormal intelligence reflected by an IQ below 70 and by adaptive functioning severely deficient for one's age.

mainstreaming: Educating mentally retarded students in regular rather than special schools by placing them in regular classes for part of the day or having special classrooms in regular schools.

There are many causes of mental retardation, including brain injuries, chromosomal abnormalities such as Down syndrome, chemical deficiencies, and hazards present during fetal development. And studies continue to document the enduring mental deficits produced by early exposure to lead (Garavan et al., 2000; Morgan et al., 2000).

Before the late 1960s, mentally retarded children in the United States were educated almost exclusively in special schools. Since then there has been a movement toward **mainstreaming**—educating mentally retarded students in regular schools. Mainstreaming may involve placing these students in classes with nonhandicapped students for part of the day or in special classrooms in regular schools.

Resources spent on training programs for the mentally retarded are proving to be sound investments. Such programs rely heavily on behavior modification techniques and are making it possible for some retarded citizens to become employed workers earning the minimum wage or better. Everyone benefits—the individual, the family, and society as well.

Intelligence and Neural Processing

What is the relationship between intelligence and the efficiency and speed of neural processing?

Recently, researchers have sought to understand more fully the relationships between neural processing and intelligence. Using PET scan studies, researchers are comparing the *efficiency* and *speed* of neural processing in people with a range of intelligence levels. A PET scan, as you will recall from Chapter 2, reveals the location and amount of brain activity by measuring how much glucose and oxygen are used during the performance of various mental tasks.

What about the relationship of intelligence to speed of neural processing? Researchers have reported that the speed at which certain simple mental tasks are performed is related to intelligence test scores (Neisser et al., 1996). Many people perform less well on intelligence tests than they otherwise could because they are inefficient in terms of processing speed, sometimes called inspection time. Spending too much time agonizing over the answer to a single question robs many test takers of time they could be using on other questions that they might be able to answer correctly immediately. The *Try It!* lets you check your own processing speed on a few sample test questions.

Try It!

Have someone time you while you answer these practice test items. You have only 60 seconds.

1. Two ducks and two dogs have a total of fourteen legs. (true/false)
2. A pie can be cut into more than seven pieces by making only four cuts that run along a diameter. (true/false)
3. Two of the following numbers add up to thirteen: 1, 6, 3, 5, 11. (true/false)

If you answered all three questions correctly in 60 seconds or less, you would probably do quite well on a conventional intelligence test. If it took you considerably longer, you may want to try to improve your processing speed by practicing on similar test items.

Answers: 1. false 2. true 3. false

Some researchers have found that processing speed is related to intelligence, and that processing speed accelerates as children get older (Fry & Hale, 1996). But studies of processing speed have a methodological problem. It is hard to separate neural processing time from physical reaction time (Brody, 1992). For example, a participant must decide whether two objects flashed on a screen are the same or different and then respond physically by pushing one of two buttons, labeled "S" and "D." Consequently, the time taken for the mental task (processing speed) may be affected by the time needed for the physical task (reaction time) and that physical factor may have nothing to do with intelligence. A research technique that measures *inspection time* is a better way to gauge processing speed (Deary & Stough, 1996; Scheuffgen et al., 2000).

A typical inspection-time task is shown in Figure 8.3. An image of the incomplete stimulus, part (a) is flashed to the participant very briefly and then immediately masked by a stimulus that covers it, part (b). The subject then is asked whether the long side of the original stimulus appeared on the left or the right. Of course, the experiment is very simple, but the relevant factor is how much inspection time (from a few hundred milliseconds to 10 milliseconds or less) is needed for a participant to consistently achieve a given level of accuracy, say 75% or 85%. The shorter the inspection time, the greater the "speed of intake of information" (Deary & Stough, 1996). Is inspection time (perceptual speed) related to intelligence? Apparently so. Deary and Stough claim that "inspection time is, to date, the only single information-processing index that accounts for approximately 20% of intelligence-test variance" (p. 599). Even so, experts in intelligence still lack a sufficient understanding of the relationship between inspection time and intelligence (Brody, 1992).

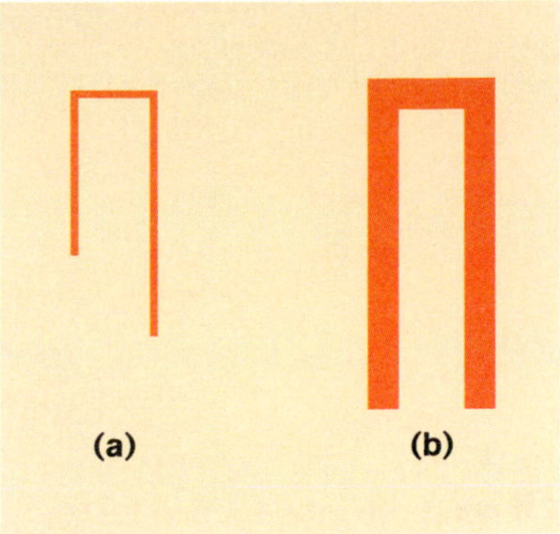

Figure 8.3

A Typical Inspection-Time task

(From Deary & Stough, 1996.)

Remember It!

1. The first successful attempt to measure intelligence was made by
   a. Binet and Simon. c. Wechsler.
   b. Spearman. d. Terman.
2. According to Stern's formula, as revised by Terman, what is the IQ of a child with a mental age of 12 and a chronological age of 8?
   a. 75 b. 150 c. 125 d. 100
3. The Stanford–Binet and Wechsler intelligence tests must be administered individually, rather than in groups. (true/false)
4. Wechsler developed intelligence tests for adults and children. (true/false)
5. In which range will the largest percentage of people taking an IQ test score?
   a. 80–100 b. 90–110 c. 100–130 d. 65–90
6. In his study of the gifted, Terman found that mentally superior individuals tend to be physically smaller and weaker. (true/false)
7. People are considered mentally retarded if they are clearly deficient in adaptive functioning and their IQ is below
   a. 100. b. 90. c. 80. d. 70.
8. A test that measures what it claims to measure has (reliability, validity); a test that gives consistent results has (reliability, validity).
9. People who are more intelligent generally use less mental energy and employ a faster neural processing speed than do less intelligent people. (true/false)

Answers: 1. a 2. b 3. true 4. true 5. b 6. false 7. d 8. validity, reliability 9. true

THE IQ CONTROVERSY: BRAINY DISPUTE

The Uses and Abuses of Intelligence Tests

Intelligence testing has become a major growth industry. And many Americans have come to believe that a "magical" number—an IQ score, a percentile rank, or some other derived score—unfalteringly portrays a person's intellectual capacity, ability, or potential. In many cases, the score has served as the ticket of admission to or the mark of rejection from educational and occupational opportunities.

Of what are intelligence tests good predictors?

Intelligence Test Scores: Can They Predict Success and Failure? What can intelligence tests really reveal? IQ scores are fairly good predictors of academic performance. The correlation between school grades and IQ scores is about .50, which means that about 25% of the variance in school grades can be accounted for by IQ score. Consequently, the remaining 75% must be explained by factors other than IQ alone. According to Neisser and others (1996), "successful school learning depends on many personal characteristics other than intelligence, such as persistence, interest in school, and willingness to study" (p. 81).

Is there a high correlation between IQ and success in life? Although the average IQ score of people in the professions (doctors, dentists, lawyers) tends to be higher than that of people in lower-status occupations, the exact relationship between IQ score and occupational status is not clearly understood. Nevertheless, studies indicate that intelligence test scores are related to a wide range of social outcomes, including job performance, income, social status, and years of education completed (Neisser et al., 1996).

Teenagers who score higher on intelligence tests are significantly less likely than their lower-scoring peers to engage in early sexual activity (Halpern et al., 2000). In fact, a higher IQ score appears to be a protective factor against a wide spectrum of risky sexual behavior among 7th to 12th graders, while a lower score represents a risk factor for such behavior. The frequent consequences of early sexual behavior are unwanted pregnancies and sexually transmitted diseases, which can ruin young lives.

What are some abuses of intelligence tests?

The Abuses of Intelligence Tests: Making Too Much of a Single Number Abuses occur when scores on intelligence or aptitude tests are the only or even the major criterion for admitting people to various educational programs. Intelligence tests do not measure attitude and motivation, critical ingredients of success. Many people are admitted to educational programs who probably should not be, while others are denied admission who could profit from them and possibly make significant contributions to society. Consider Dr. Robert Jarvik, described at the beginning of this chapter.

Early categorization based solely on IQ scores can doom children to slow-track educational programs that are not appropriate for them. Many poor and minority children (particularly those for whom English is a second language) and visually or hearing impaired children have been erroneously placed in special education programs. IQ tests predicted that they were not mentally able to profit from regular classroom instruction. There would be no problem if IQ test results were unfailingly accurate, but in fact they are not. In some states IQ tests are banned altogether. In others it is now illegal to place children in classes for the mentally retarded based solely on their IQ scores without additional testing of their level of adaptive functioning in daily life.

culture-fair intelligence test: An intelligence test that uses questions that will not penalize those whose culture differs from that of the middle or upper classes.

Another problem with intelligence tests is that they are sometimes created in such a way that they are culturally biased. However, several attempts have been made to develop **culture-fair intelligence tests.** In general, the questions on such tests do not penalize individuals whose cultural background and/or language dif-

Figure 8.4

An Example of an Item on a Culture-Fair Test

This culture-fair test item does not penalize test takers whose language or cultural experiences differ from those of the urban middle or upper classes. Subjects are to select, from the six samples in the right, the patch that would complete the pattern. Patch number 3 is the correct answer. (Adapted from the Raven Standard Progressive Matrices Test.)

fers from that of the middle and upper classes. An example of a test question that might be culturally unfair is

> Choose the best answer to complete the analogy below.
>
> *Caesar* is to *salad* as ______________ is to *brandy*.
> a. Churchill b. Napoleon c. Hitler d. Lincoln

If the test takers' cultures did not expose them to Caesar salad and Napoleon brandy, this question could prove more difficult than intended. See Figure 8.4 for an example of the type of test items found on culture-fair intelligence tests.

Recently, a comparative study using a culture-fair nonverbal ability test with 7,890 participants revealed only small differences between matched samples of White Americans (2,306) and African Americans (2,306). Minimal differences were also found between Whites (1,176) and Hispanics (1,176) and between Whites (466) and Asians (466). Scores on the test, the Naglieri Nonverbal Ability Test, correlated moderately well with achievement for the total sample. Results of the study suggest that this nonverbal ability test provides a means of fair assessment for both White and minority children (Naglieri & Ronning, 2000).

nature–nurture controversy: The debate over whether intelligence and other traits are primarily the result of heredity or environment.

behavioral genetics: A field of research that investigates the relative effects of heredity and environment on behavior and ability.

twin study method: Studying identical and fraternal twins to determine the relative effects of heredity and environment on a variety of characteristics.

identical twins: Twins with identical genes; monozygotic twins.

fraternal twins: Twins who are no more alike genetically than ordinary brothers and sisters; dizygotic twins.

The Nature–Nurture Controversy: Battle of the Centuries

How does the nature–nurture controversy apply to intelligence?

Even though it has been debated for about 130 years, the **nature–nurture controversy** is still very much alive. British researcher Sir Francis Galton (1874) initiated the debate over whether intelligence is predominantly the result of heredity (nature) or the environment (nurture). Galton coined the phrase *nature–nurture controversy,* and after studying many prominent English families, he concluded that intelligence is inherited—that nature, not nurture, is responsible for intelligence. Environmentalists disputed Galton's claim and just as strongly insisted that intelligence is the product of one's environment—the result of nurture. Today, most psychologists agree that both nature and nurture contribute to intelligence, but they continue to debate the relative contributions of these two factors.

What is behavioral genetics, and what are the primary methods used in the field today?

Behavioral Genetics: Investigating Nature and Nurture

Behavioral genetics is a field of research that investigates the relative effects of heredity and environment on behavior and ability (Plomin et al., 1997). Two of the primary methods used by behavioral geneticists are the twin study method, first used by Galton (1875) in his studies of heredity, and the adoption method.

In the **twin study method,** researchers study **identical twins** (monozygotic twins) and **fraternal twins** (dizygotic twins) to determine how much they resemble each other on a variety of characteristics. Identical twins have exactly the same genes because a single sperm cell of the father fertilizes a single egg of the mother, forming

heritability: An index of the degree to which a characteristic is estimated to be influenced by heredity.

adoption method: A method researchers use to study the relative effects of heredity and environment on behavior and ability in children adopted shortly after birth, by comparing them with their biological and adoptive parents.

a cell that then splits and forms two human beings—"carbon copies." But fraternal twins are no more alike genetically than any two siblings born to the same parents. In the case of fraternal twins, two separate sperm cells fertilize two separate eggs that happen to be released at the same time during ovulation.

Twins who are raised together, whether identical or fraternal, have similar environments. If identical twins raised together are found to be more alike than fraternal twins on a certain trait, then that trait is assumed to be more influenced by heredity. But if identical and fraternal twins from similar environments do not differ on a trait, then that trait is assumed to be influenced more by environment. The term **heritability** is an index of the degree to which a characteristic is estimated to be influenced by heredity. Figure 8.5 shows estimates of genetic and environmental factors contributing to intelligence.

In the **adoption method,** behavioral geneticists study children adopted shortly after birth. By comparing their abilities and personality traits to those of their adoptive family members with whom they live and those of their biological parents whom they may never have met, researchers can disentangle the effects of heredity and environment (Plomin et al., 1988).

How do twin studies support the view that intelligence is inherited?

A Natural Experiment: Identical Twins Reared Apart

Minnesota—home of the twin cities and the Minnesota Twins—is also, fittingly, the site of the most extensive U.S. study of identical and fraternal twins. The Minnesota Center for Twin and Adoption Research has assembled the Minnesota Twin Registry, which in 1998 included more than 10,000 twin pairs (Bouchard, 1998).

Probably the best way to assess the relative contributions of heredity and environment is to study identical twins who have been separated at birth and raised apart. Although it seems amazing, researchers have found that identical twins who grow up in the same family are no more alike as adults than identical twins who are reared apart. When separated twins are found to have strikingly similar traits, it is assumed that heredity has been a major contributor to those traits. When separated twins differ on a given trait, the influence of the environment is thought to be greater.

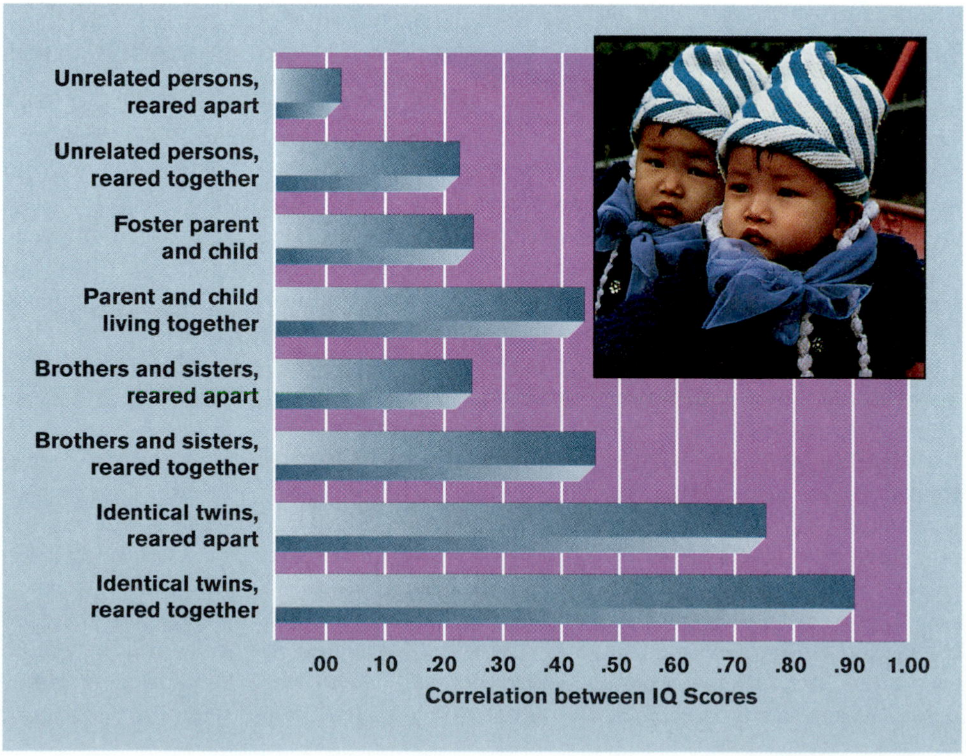

Figure 8.5

Correlations between the IQ Scores of Persons with Various Relationships

The more closely related two individuals are, the more similar their IQ scores tend to be. Thus, there is a strong genetic contribution to intelligence. (Based on data from Bouchard & McGue, 1981; Erlenmeyer-Kimling & Jarvik, 1963.)

Since 1979 the Minnesota researchers headed by Thomas Bouchard have studied about 60 pairs of fraternal twins and 80 pairs of identical twins who were reared apart. Of all the traits Bouchard and his colleagues studied, the most heritable trait turned out to be intelligence. Bouchard (1997) reports that various types of twin studies have consistently yielded heritability estimates of .60 to .70 for intelligence. (The heritability of some personality traits is discussed in Chapter 14.)

Not all researchers agree with Bouchard's heritability estimate for intelligence. Combining data from a number of twin studies, Plomin and others (1994) found the heritability estimate for general intelligence to be .52. Similar findings emerged from meta-analyses using dozens of adoption studies and twin studies involving more than 10,000 pairs of twins. These analyses concluded that the heritability of general cognitive ability was about .50 (McClearn et al., 1997). Psychologists who consider environmental factors as the chief contributors to differences in intelligence also take issue with Bouchard's findings. They claim that most separated identical twins are raised by adoptive parents who have been matched as closely as possible to the biological parents. This fact, the critics say, could account for the similarity in IQ. In response to his critics, Bouchard (1997) points out that children who are not related biologically but are raised in the same home are no more similar in intelligence once they reach adulthood than complete strangers.

Adoption studies reveal that children adopted shortly after birth have IQs more closely resembling those of their biological parents than those of their adoptive parents. The family environment has an influence on IQ early in life, but that influence seems to diminish. Twin and adoption studies indicate that as people reach adulthood, it is genes that are most closely correlated with IQ (Loehlin et al., 1988, 1989; McCartney et al., 1990; Plomin & Rende, 1991). In fact, the influence of the genes seems to increase predictably as people age: there is a heritability of .30 in infancy, .40 in childhood, .50 in adolescence, and about .60 in adulthood (McGue et al., 1993). A large study in Sweden of pairs of identical twins and same-sex fraternal twins who had been reared together and had reached the age of 80 or more revealed a heritability estimate of .62 for general cognitive ability (McClearn et al., 1997).

Bouchard and others (1990) claim that "although parents may be able to affect their children's rate of cognitive skill acquisition, they may have relatively little influence on the ultimate level attained" (p. 225). A great deal of convincing research does argue for the importance of genes in determining intelligence, including language skills (Plomin & Dale, 2000). But a great deal of room is still left for environmental forces to have a significant influence. Thus, the nature–nurture controversy remains unresolved.

What are Jensen's and Herrnstein and Murray's controversial views on race and IQ?

Race and IQ: The Controversial Views of Jensen and of Herrnstein and Murray Some studies during the past several decades have reported that, on the average, African Americans score about 15 points lower than Whites on standardized IQ tests (Herrnstein & Murray, 1994; Jensen, 1985; Loehlin et al., 1975). In 1969 psychologist Arthur Jensen published an article in which he attributed the IQ gap to genetic differences between the races. Further, he claimed that the genetic influence on intelligence is so strong that the environment cannot make a significant difference. Almost immediately, Jensen's views on race and intelligence sent a shock wave through the scientific community.

Herrnstein and Murray (1994) added fresh fuel to the controversy with their book *The Bell Curve.* They argue that IQ differences among people and between groups explain how those at the top in U.S. society got there and why those at the lower rungs of society's ladder remain there. Herrnstein and Murray (1994) largely attribute the social ills of modern society—poverty, welfare dependency, crime, illegitimacy—to low IQ, which they imply is primarily genetic and largely immune to change by environmental intervention. Yet they offer their own estimate that 60% of IQ is genetically inherited, "which, by extension, means that IQ is about 40% a matter of environment" (p. 105). That 40% would seem to leave a lot of room for improvement.

The Bell Curve offers correlational data to show a relationship between IQ and many other variables—poverty, for example. Critics of *The Bell Curve* were quick to point out that correlational data cannot be used to conclude that low IQ causes poverty—or, for that matter, that poverty causes low IQ (Kamin, 1995). Herrnstein and Murray's most ominous conclusion rests heavily on the notion that IQ is destiny, and their book warns of castelike divisions in modern society based on IQ. The highest 5–10% of the intelligence distribution will be even more firmly entrenched at the top of society, they write. And those with low IQs will remain a permanent underclass. But the frightening outcomes envisioned by Herrnstein and Murray are inescapable only to the degree that IQ is *not* affected by environmental factors.

Jensen's and Herrnstein and Murray's views run counter to the belief that an enriched, stimulating environment can overcome the deficits of poverty and cultural disadvantage and thus reduce the IQ deficit.

Is the Gap Caused by Race Alone? If average IQ differences were genetically determined by race, then the mean IQ scores of mixed-race individuals should fall somewhere between the mean scores for African Americans and Whites. But studies over the decades have not found such a relationship between IQ and mixed ancestry (Loehlin et al., 1973; Scarr et al., 1977). At the end of World War II, American soldiers stationed in Germany, both African American and White, fathered thousands of children with German women. Fifteen years later, Eyeferth (1961) randomly selected samples of these children. The mean IQs of the two groups were virtually identical. Having a White father conferred no measurable IQ advantage at all.

Intelligence: Is It Fixed or Changeable?

What kinds of evidence suggest that IQ is changeable rather than fixed?

Probably the most important issue in intelligence is whether IQ is fixed or changeable. Clearly, the high degree of similarity in the intelligence scores of identical twins who have been reared apart makes a strong case for the powerful influence of genetics. But even Bouchard and his colleagues (1990) caution against trying to generalize their findings to people raised in disadvantaged environments. Bouchard (1997) states: "A child raised in crushing poverty by illiterate parents is unlikely to score well on IQ tests, no matter what his mental inheritance. . . . Twin studies tend to attract few subjects in such dire straits, so their findings may not always apply to people exposed to extremes of deprivation or privilege" (p. 56).

The idea that a behavior or characteristic that is genetic in origin cannot be changed is a myth. According to Richard Weinberg (1989):

> Genes do not fix behavior. Rather, they establish a range of possible reactions to the range of possible experiences that environments can provide. . . . How people behave or what their measured IQs turn out to be or how quickly they learn depends on the nature of their environments *and* on their genetic endowments bestowed at conception. (p. 101)

Actress Mia Farrow has adopted several children from diverse cultures. Will Farrow's high socioeconomic status have an effect on the IQ scores of these children?

Adoption Studies: Enriched Environments Boost IQs Several studies indicate that IQ test scores are not fixed but can be modified with an enriched environment. More than a quarter-century ago, Sandra Scarr and Richard Weinberg (1976) studied 130 African-American and interracial children who had been adopted by highly educated, upper-middle-class White families; 99 of the children had been adopted in the first year of life. The adoptees were fully exposed to middle-class cultural experiences and vocabulary, the "culture of the tests and the school" (p. 737).

How did the children perform on IQ and achievement tests? The average IQ score of the 130 adoptees was 106.3. And their achievement test scores were slightly above the national average, not below. On the average, the earlier the children were adopted, the higher their IQs.

The mean IQ score of the 99 early adoptees was 110.4, about 10 IQ points above the average for Whites. Studies in France have also shown that IQ scores and achievement are substantially higher when children from lower-class environments are adopted by middle-class and upper-middle-class families (Duyme, 1988; Schiff and Lewontin, 1986).

Changes in Standard of Living Other evidence also suggests that environmental factors have a strong influence on IQ scores. Americans and similarly advantaged populations all over the world have gained about 3 IQ points per decade since 1940. James Flynn (1987) analyzed 73 studies involving some 7,500 participants ranging in age from 12 to 48 and found that "every Binet and Wechsler sample from 1932 to 1978 has performed better than its predecessor" (p. 225). This consistent improvement in IQ scores over time is known as the *Flynn effect.* The average IQ in Western industrialized nations is currently about 15 IQ points, or 1 standard deviation, higher than 50 years ago. Regarding the Black–White IQ gap among U.S. adults, Flynn (1987) asserts that "the environmental advantage Whites enjoy over Blacks is similar to what Whites (adults) of today enjoy over their own parents or grandparents of 50 years ago" (p. 226).

Zajonc and Mullally (1997) suggest that the Flynn effect might be attributable to the fact that family size has decreased over the decades. First- and second-born children tend to do better on intelligence and achievement tests than children born later in larger families. The decrease in average family size has increased the proportions of first- and second-born people in the population as a whole.

Researcher Ken Vincent (1991) presents data suggesting that the Black–White IQ gap is narrowing in younger children—to about 7 or 8 IQ points. Vincent (1993) attributes the rapid mean gains by African American children to environmental changes in economic and educational opportunity.

It should not be surprising that enriched environments can help alter traits that are highly heritable. Consider the fact that American and British adolescents are several inches taller on average than their counterparts a century and a half ago (Tanner, 1962). Height has the same heritability (.90) today as it did in the mid–19th century. So a significant average gain in height is entirely attributable to environmental influences: better health, better nutrition, and so on. The highest heritability estimates for intelligence are far lower than those for height. It seems clear then that environmental influences have the power to affect intelligence and achievement. Poverty affects nutrition. And research clearly shows that malnutrition, especially early in life, can harm intellectual development (Brown & Pollitt, 1996).

Poverty is a strong factor in perpetuating other environmental differences between American Blacks and Whites. According to Donald Campbell (1996), opportunities—or the lack thereof—to learn the vocabulary used on intelligence and achievement tests and to gain other cognitive skills expected in school are enough to explain group differences on test scores.

The environmental influences that affect people for good or ill are transmitted through culture. Are there identifiable cultural values related to academic achievement?

Expectations, Effort, and Academic Achievement: A Cross-Cultural Comparison

Stevenson and others (1986) compared the math ability of randomly selected elementary school children from three comparable cities—Taipei in Taiwan, Sendai in Japan, and Minneapolis in the United States. By the fifth grade, the Asian students were outscoring the Americans by about 15 points in math ability, roughly 1 standard deviation. And the Asian superiority held firmly from the highest to the lowest achievement levels. The Japanese children scored the highest of the three groups in fifth grade, and even the lowest-scoring Japanese classes did better than the top-scoring classes in the United States.

Asian students consistently score higher on math achievement tests than their American counterparts. It appears that the reasons for this difference are cultural and relate to parental expectations.

How can such differences in achievement in children from different cultures be explained? Researchers such as Jensen (1985) and Galton before him, and more recently Herrnstein and Murray (1994), would point to genetic differences. But Stevenson and others (1990) suggest that cultural, rather than genetic, differences may be a major factor in explaining the gap in math ability. Their study was conducted with first and fifth graders from the same three cities and included 1,440 students (480 from each of the three countries). The children were tested in reading and mathematics and interviewed along with their mothers. In a follow-up study 4 years later, the first graders (now fifth graders) were tested again, and again they and their mothers were interviewed.

The interviews revealed significant differences between the Asian and American cultures. The Chinese and Japanese mothers considered academic achievement to be *the most important* pursuit of their children, whereas American parents did not value it as a central concern. The Asian, but not the American, families structured their home activities to promote academic achievement as soon as their first child started elementary school. The Asian parents downplayed the importance of innate ability but emphasized the value of hard work and persistence (Stevenson, 1992). American parents, in contrast, believed more firmly in genetic limitations on ability and achievement. Stevenson states, "When parents believe success in school depends for the most part on ability rather than effort, they are less likely to foster participation in activities related to academic achievement" (p. 73). Also, American mothers tended to overestimate the cognitive abilities of their children, but the Chinese and Japanese mothers did not. Asian mothers held their children to higher standards while giving more realistic assessments of their children's abilities (see Figure 8.6).

In follow-up studies, Stevenson and others (1993) found that the achievement gap between Asian and American students persisted over a 10-year period. Differences in high-school achievement were explained in part by the fact that the American students spent more time working at part-time jobs and socializing than their Asian counterparts did (Fuligni & Stevenson, 1995). But do Asian students pay a psychological price for their stunning academic achievement? Are they more likely than students in the United States to be stressed and heavily burdened by pressures to maintain academic excellence? A large cross-cultural study comparing 11th-grade students from Japan, Taiwan, and the United States did find a correlation between achievement in mathematics and psychological distress—but, surprisingly, for the American students, not the Asian students (Crystal et al., 1994).

Figure 8.6

Mothers' Satisfaction with Their Children's Academic Performance

Even though American students had by far the poorest achievement record of the children studied in the United States, Taiwan, and Japan, American mothers expressed much higher satisfaction with their children's academic performance than did mothers from the two Asian countries. (From Stevenson, 1992.)

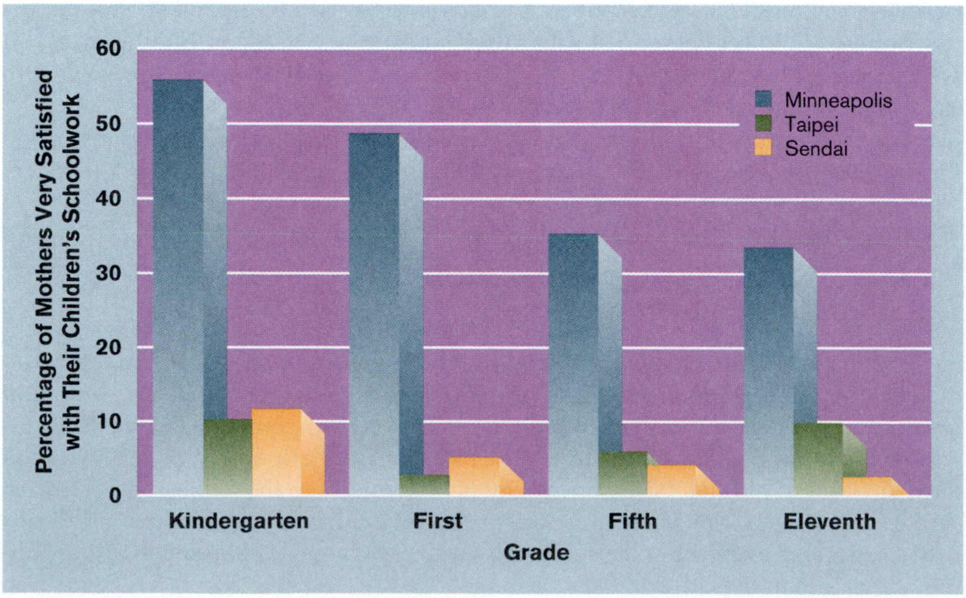

Why should high-achieving American students, but not Asian students, pay a price in terms of psychological distress? The researchers found that Asian teenagers typically enjoy support and encouragement for their academic achievement from family and peers alike. In contrast, high-achieving teenagers in the United States are often torn between studying harder to excel academically and pursuing nonacademic social interests. Such interests may be strongly encouraged by their peers and often by parents who want their children to be "well-rounded."

Which of these two cultural tendencies is more likely to maximize the development of one's intellectual potential, whether large or modest? Perhaps the answer to the stunning record of academic achievement of Asian students lies not in their genes, but in the cultural values that nurture them.

Remember It!

1. IQ tests are good predictors of success in school. (true/false)
2. What field of research investigates the relative effects of heredity and environment on behavior and ability?
   a. genetics
   b. behavioral genetics
   c. biology
   d. physiology
3. Twin studies suggest that environment is stronger than heredity as a factor in shaping IQ differences. (true/false)
4. Jensen and Herrnstein and Murray claim that the Black–White IQ gap is caused primarily by
   a. genetics.
   b. environment.
   c. discrimination.
   d. racism.
5. Several adoption studies have revealed that when infants from disadvantaged environments are adopted by middle- and upper-middle-class parents, their IQ scores are raised about 15 points. (true/false)

Answers: 1. true 2. b 3. false 4. a 5. true

EMOTIONAL INTELLIGENCE

The concept of emotional intelligence has grown in popularity and gained acceptance since the work of Peter Salovey, John Mayer, and Peter Caruso (Mayer, Caruso, & Salovey, 2000; Mayer, Salovey, & Caruso, 2000; Salovey & Mayer, 1990). **Emotional intelligence** refers to a set of capabilities that are separate from IQ but are necessary for success in life—in the workplace, in intimate personal relations, and in social interactions. According to Daniel Goleman (1995), emotional intelligence may more strongly influence success in life than IQ.

Personal Components of Emotional Intelligence

What are the personal components of emotional intelligence?

The foundation of emotional intelligence is said to be self-knowledge, which involves an awareness of emotions, an ability to manage those emotions, and self-motivation.

Awareness of One's Emotions Being aware of our own emotions—recognizing and acknowledging feelings as they happen—is at the very heart of emotional intelligence. And it means being aware not only of our moods, but of thoughts about those moods as well. People who are able to monitor their feelings as they arise are less likely to be ruled by them and are thus better able to manage their emotions.

emotional intelligence: A type of intelligence that includes an awareness of and an ability to manage one's own emotions, the ability to motivate oneself, empathy, and the ability to handle relationships successfully.

Managing One's Emotions Managing emotions does not mean suppressing them; nor does it mean giving free rein to every feeling. Goleman (1995) insists that the goal is balance and that every feeling has its value and significance. Goleman says, "A life without passion would be a dull wasteland of neutrality, cut off and isolated from the richness of life itself" (p. 56). Thus, we manage our emotions by expressing them in an appropriate manner. People high in emotional intelligence have learned how to regulate their moods and not let anger, boredom, or depression ruin their day (or their lives). Emotions can be managed by activities that cheer us up, soothe our hurts, reassure us, or otherwise temper an inappropriate or out-of-control emotion.

If negative emotions become too troublesome, are there any simple, inexpensive ways to manage them? Yes, according to Goleman. We can purposely schedule pleasant, distracting activities—going out with friends, watching an entertaining movie, working on an interesting project, or doing any other activity that provides pleasant distraction. Also, we can challenge the unwanted thoughts that are plunging us into a blue mood, or fueling our anger, or ushering in fear and worry.

Self-Motivation: Controlling One's Impulses *Self-motivation* refers to a strength of emotional self-control that enables a person to get moving and pursue worthy goals, persist at tasks even when frustrated, and resist the temptation to act on impulse. Resisting impulsive behavior is, according to Goleman (1995), "the root of all emotional self-control" (p. 81).

Of all the attributes of emotional intelligence, the ability to postpone immediate gratification and to persist in working toward some greater future gain is most closely related to success—whether one is trying to build a business, get a college degree, or even stay on a diet. One researcher has found that 4-year-old children who have mastered the art of delaying instant gratification in order to advance toward some greater future goal are "far superior as students" upon high-school graduation compared with four-year-olds who are not able to resist the impulse to satisfy their immediate wishes (Shoda et al., 1990).

Interpersonal Components of Emotional Intelligence

What are the interpersonal components of emotional intelligence?

The interpersonal aspects of emotional intelligence are the sensitivity to and understanding of others' emotions and the ability to handle relationships.

Empathy: Recognizing Emotions in Others *Empathy,* a sensitivity toward the needs and feelings of others, appears to be a higher level of development that springs from self-awareness. If we have no insight into our own emotions, it is unlikely that we will develop sensitivity and understanding of those of others.

One key indicator, or hallmark, of the empathy component of emotional intelligence is the ability to read and interpret nonverbal behavior—the gestures, vocal inflections, tones of voice, and facial expressions of others. Nonverbal behavior is, in a sense, the language of the emotions, because our feelings are most genuinely expressed this way. People may fail to communicate their feelings verbally or even lie about them, but their nonverbal behavior will most often reveal their true feelings.

A person with high emotional intelligence shows empathy—recognizing nonverbal signals from others and making appropriate responses.

Handling Relationships For most people, hardly anything in life is more important than their relationships—intimate love relationship, family, professional, and work relationships, and relationships with friends. Without rewarding relationships, life would be lonely indeed. And emotional intelligence has a great deal to do with forming and maintaining successful relationships.

Two components of emotional intelligence that are prerequisites for handling relationships are (1) the ability to manage one's own emotions, and (2) empathy, or the ability to perceive, understand, and relate to the emotions of others. These two components combine to produce the ability to respond appropriately to emotions in others.

Those who are high in emotional intelligence often emerge as leaders. Successful leaders can empathize with their followers, understand their needs and wants. If you want to be an influential leader, a top salesperson, a therapist, or a marriage counselor, or if you want to have fulfilling intimate relationships, learn to understand and manage your own emotions and to understand and respond appropriately to the emotions of others. To find out what your Emotional Quotient (EQ) is, do the *Try It!*

Try It!

Check one response for each item.

1. I'm always aware of even subtle feelings as I have them.

   ___ Always ___ Usually ___ Sometimes ___ Rarely ___ Never

2. I can delay gratification in pursuit of my goals instead of getting carried away by impulse.

   ___ Always ___ Usually ___ Sometimes ___ Rarely ___ Never

3. Instead of giving up in the face of setbacks or disappointments, I stay hopeful and optimistic.

   ___ Always ___ Usually ___ Sometimes ___ Rarely ___ Never

4. My keen sense of others' feelings makes me compassionate about their plight.

   ___ Always ___ Usually ___ Sometimes ___ Rarely ___ Never

5. I can sense the pulse of a group or relationship and state unspoken feelings.

   ___ Always ___ Usually ___ Sometimes ___ Rarely ___ Never

6. I can soothe or contain distressing feelings, so that they don't keep me from doing things I need to do.

   ___ Always ___ Usually ___ Sometimes ___ Rarely ___ Never

Score your responses as follows: Always = 4 points, Usually = 3 points, Sometimes = 2 points, Rarely = 1 point, Never = 0 points). The closer your total number of points is to 24, the higher your EQ probably is.

Optimism Although it is not one of the five main domains of emotional intelligence identified by Salovey and Mayer (1990), *optimism* appears to be a component of emotional intelligence. People who are optimistic have a "strong expectation in general [that] things will turn out all right in life" (p. 88). The most significant aspect of optimism in the context of emotional intelligence is the way in which optimists explain their successes and failures. When optimists fail, they attribute their failure to something in the situation that can be changed. Thus, they believe that by trying harder, they can succeed the next time. But when pessimists fail, they blame themselves and attribute their failure to some personal characteristic or flaw that cannot be changed.

This one attribute of emotional intelligence appears to have far-reaching effects. Martin Seligman (1990), whose classic work on learned helplessness was discussed in Chapter 5, has also studied optimism. His research has shown that optimism, as measured by students' scores on a test, is a more accurate predictor of actual first-year college grades than SAT scores or high school GPAs. Fortunately, optimism can be learned. We will discuss Seligman's learned optimism in more detail in Chapter 14.

Remember It!

1. Identify the category in which each component of emotional intelligence belongs.

   ____ (1) empathy — a. personal

   ____ (2) awareness of one's own emotions — b. interpersonal

   ____ (3) self-motivation

   ____ (4) ability to handle relationships

2. Which one of the following does *not* demonstrate emotional intelligence?

   a. Feeling depressed and distracted, Marcus takes a break from studying and surfs the Internet.

   b. When she fails a test, Whitney thinks to herself, "It was my boyfriend's fault for being so needy and demanding so much of my time."

   c. Carlos notices that his boss is in a bad mood and stays out of her way.

   d. Danielle really knows how to motivate her team to meet the department's quarterly goals.

Answers: 1. (1) b (2) a (3) a (4) b 2. b

CREATIVITY: UNIQUE AND USEFUL PRODUCTIONS

What is creativity, and how is it related to intelligence?

Creativity can be thought of as the ability to produce original, appropriate, and valuable ideas and/or solutions to problems. Is creativity related to intelligence? Research to date indicates that there is only a modest correlation between creativity and IQ. Highly creative people do tend to be well above average in intelligence, but in the upper IQ ranges (over 120) there seems to be little correlation between IQ and creativity (Barron & Harrington, 1981).

Remember the young geniuses studied by Lewis Terman? Not a single one of them has produced a highly creative work (Terman & Oden, 1959). No Nobel laureates, no Pulitzer prizes. Geniuses, yes; creative geniuses, no. Thus, high intelligence is a necessary but not sufficient condition for high creativity.

The Creative Process

What are the four stages in the creative process?

Where does creativity originate? Cartoonists often illustrate creative thinking as a flash of insight, a lightbulb that suddenly turns on in the mind. But research studies indicate that useful and genuine creativity rarely appears in the form of sudden flashes (Haberlandt, 1997). For the most part, creative ideas that come to conscious awareness have been incubating for some time. And most experts agree that genuine creativity "is an accomplishment born of intensive study, long reflection, persistence and interest" (Snow, 1993, p. 1033).

There are four basic stages in the creative problem-solving process (Goleman et al., 1992):

- *Preparation*—searching for information that may help solve the problem
- *Incubation*—letting the problem "sit" while the relevant information is digested

creativity: The ability to produce original, appropriate, and valuable ideas and/or solutions to problems.

- *Illumination*—being suddenly struck by the right solution
- *Translation*—transforming the new insight into useful action

The incubation stage, perhaps the most important part of the process, takes place below the level of awareness.

divergent thinking: The ability to produce multiple ideas, answers, or solutions to a problem for which there is no agreed-on solution.

The Nature of Creative Thinking

How does creative thinking differ from conventional thought? According to psychologist J. P. Guilford (1967), who studied creativity for several decades, creative thinkers are highly proficient at divergent thinking. **Divergent thinking** is the ability to produce multiple ideas, answers, or solutions to a problem for which there is no agreed-on solution (Guilford, 1967). More broadly, divergent thinking is *novel,* or original, and involves the synthesis of an unusual association of ideas; it is *flexible,* in that it involves switching quickly and smoothly from one stream of thought or set of ideas to another; and it requires *fluency,* or the ability to formulate an abundance of ideas (Csikszentmihalyi, 1996). In contrast to divergent thinking, Guilford labeled more conventional thought "convergent thinking." *Convergent thinking* is the type of mental activity measured by IQ and achievement tests, and it consists of solving precisely defined, logical problems for which there is a known correct answer.

In order to be creative, a person must develop divergent thinking. But divergent thinking alone is not enough. A creative person must be able to recognize the difference between a good divergent idea and a bad one, and this requires convergent thinking (Csikszentmihalyi, 1996).

Researchers are identifying the different brain areas involved in convergent and divergent thinking. In general, convergent thinking is characterized by greater activity in the left frontal cortex, while divergent thinking is marked by higher levels of activity in the right frontal cortex (Razoumnikova, 2000). Other studies show that processes involved in convergent thinking, such as searching for patterns in events, are carried out in the left hemisphere (Wolford et al., 2000). And studies by Carlsson and others (2000) that measured regional cerebral blood flow (rCBF) revealed striking differences in frontal lobe activity between participants who were engaged in highly creative thinking and those who were not engaged in creative thinking. Figure 8.7 (a) shows the frontal lobe activity during highly creative thinking. There is activity in both hemispheres but a significantly greater amount in the right frontal cortex. In contrast, Figure 8.7 (b) shows that the left frontal lobe is most active during periods without creative thinking, and there is very little activity in the right hemisphere.

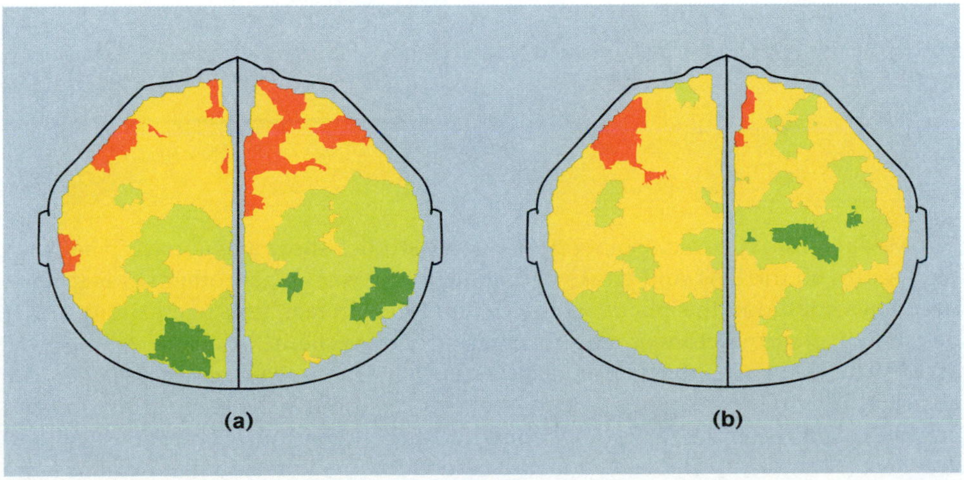

Figure 8.7

Color Maps of Regional Cerebral Blood Flow (rCBF)

(a) Highly creative thinking is associated with activity in both hemispheres, but with significantly higher levels in the right hemisphere (red indicates activity). (b) During thinking that is not creative, activity is largely restricted to the left hemisphere. (Adapted from Carlsson and others, 2000.)

But is the ability to think in divergent ways a sufficient condition for the production of creative thinking? No! All creative thought is divergent, but not all divergent thought is creative. Novelty is not synonymous with creativity. It is not surprising, then, that high scores on tests of divergent production do not have a very high correlation with creative production in real life. Guilford (1967) himself admitted that in studies of students from elementary through high school, the correlations of his divergent-production tests with actual creative production were not spectacular.

Measuring Creativity: Are There Reliable Measures?

What kinds of tests have been used to measure creativity, and how good are they as predictors of creativity?

Tests designed to measure creativity emphasize novel or original approaches to arriving at solutions for open-ended problems or to producing artistic works (Gregory, 1996). One creativity test, the *Unusual Uses Test,* asks respondents to name as many uses as possible for an ordinary object (such as a brick). Another creativity measure is the *Consequences Test,* which asks test takers to list as many consequences as they can that would be likely to follow some basic change in the world (such as the force of gravity being reduced by 50%).

Other researchers have also tried to design tests to measure creative ability. Mednick and Mednick (1967) reasoned that the essence of creativity consists of the creative thinker's ability to fit together ideas that to the noncreative thinker might appear remote or unrelated. To measure creative ability, they created the *Remote Associates Test* (RAT). Test your creativity with the *Try It!*

Try It!

One indication of creativity may be the ability to make associations among several elements that seem only remotely related or unrelated. Test your ability to find associations for these 10 sets of words, which are similar to those on the Remote Associates Test. Think of a fourth word that is related in some way to all three of the words in each row. For example, the words *keeper, text,* and *worm* are related to the word *book* and become *bookkeeper, textbook,* and *bookworm.*

1. sales, collector, income
2. flower, room, water
3. red, shot, dog
4. ball, hot, stool
5. rock, man, classical
6. story, true, sick
7. news, plate, waste
8. stuffed, sleeve, sweat
9. class, temperature, bath
10. wrist, man, stop

Answers: 1. tax 2. bed 3. hot 4. foot 5. music 6. love 7. paper 8. shirt 9. room 10. watch

Mednick and Mednick point out that some studies show a relationship between high scores on the RAT and creative thinking in the workplace; other studies, however, have not found this relationship (Matlin, 1983). In fact, tests of creativity are, at best, mediocre predictors of real-life creative achievements (Hocevar & Bachelor, 1989). The main weakness of such tests is that they measure creativity in the abstract. They treat creativity as a general trait, as though the same set of abilities could explain the creative accomplishments of the inventor, composer, artist, and architect (Amabile, 1983, 1990). It is rare indeed for one individual to excel in more than one creative domain.

Characteristics of Creative People

Creative people share a number of characteristics that distinguish them from less creative individuals. Among the most important of these traits are expertise, openness to experience, independence of mind, intrinsic motivation, and perseverance.

What are some characteristics of creative people?

Expertise Expertise in a specific area of endeavor is built up over years of disciplined practice. Although expertise alone does not produce creativity, genuine creative accomplishments are rooted in this quality (Ericsson & Charness, 1994). Benjamin Bloom (1985) and his associates studied 120 case histories of people who had made notable creative contributions in six different fields. Every one of these individuals had unquestioned expertise, based on high-quality training, and unyielding determination.

Openness to Experience Creative individuals are open to experience and will entertain, at least initially, even seemingly irrational thoughts that uncreative people might dismiss. Creative people are typically less close-minded and less inhibited than others in their feelings and fantasies (McCrae, 1987). Moreover, they seem to be inherently curious and inquisitive (Sternberg, 1985a). They are comfortable with ambiguity and don't seem to need immediate resolution of conflicting and contradictory ideas. During the early stages of creative work, these individuals are not on a quest for certainty, but rather a quest of discovery. And along the way they are not bothered by loose or dead ends. Rather, they work their way through failures and out of blind alleys, persisting until they succeed.

One characteristic of creative people is intrinsic motivation. They enjoy the process of creation for its own sake—the end result may be a whimsical toy rather than a practical tool.

Independence of Mind Creative people tend to be independent thinkers. They cherish this independence and, especially in their area of creative expertise, prefer to go their own way. They can easily spend long periods alone and are not influenced by the opinions of others as much as their less creative counterparts are. They will take unpopular stands if they must and are often seen as nonconformists. But then, by its very nature, creativity is unconventional and uncommon. Such unconventionality is, however, typically confined to the work of creative people. Otherwise, they do not appear to be especially eccentric or out-of-the-ordinary.

Intrinsic Motivation Unlike people who are readily influenced by the opinions of others and motivated by extrinsic (external) rewards, the creative are more likely to be intrinsically (internally) motivated. Creative people are moved by—and sometimes carried away with—the anticipation, excitement, and enjoyment of their work, whether it is inventing, producing works of art, or advancing scientific knowledge. For creative people, the sheer joy of creative activity itself carries its own reward. In short, they "enjoy the process of creation for its own sake" (Csikszentmihalyi, 1996, p. 40).

Perseverance Creative endeavor requires intelligence and hard work. Creativity is not poured from empty vessels, nor fashioned by idle hands. Thomas A. Edison, who held 1,093 patents, claimed that his magnificently creative contributions were accomplished by 2% inspiration and 98% perspiration. Albert Einstein published 248 papers and persevered (perspired) for 10 years on his theory of relativity before it was finished. And Mozart, when he died at age 35, had created 609 musical compositions (Haberlandt, 1997).

Can creativity be learned? There is some evidence that creative abilities can be learned, or at least improved. To learn some techniques for stimulating your own creativity, read the *Apply It!* at the end of this chapter.

Savant Syndrome: A Special Form of Creativity

Savant syndrome, a curious combination of retardation and genius, is a condition that allows an individual whose level of general intelligence is very low to perform certain highly creative mental feats. Arthur is such a person.

savant syndrome: A condition that allows an otherwise mentally retarded individual to perform an amazing mental feat or display a remarkable specific skill (such as computation, music, or art).

> "Arthur, how much is 6,427 times 4,234?" Arthur turned his head in my direction and said slowly but without hesitation, "27 million, 211 thousand, 918." His voice was stilted but precise. His eyes never lost their blank stare, and now he returned to gazing into space, without seeing anything, a handsome, impassive 8-year-old. (Rimland, 1978, p. 69)

Arthur can multiply multi-digit numbers in his head faster than you could do it on a calculator, and he never makes a mistake. Yet his measured IQ is extremely low.

People who can perform certain amazing mental feats or who possess remarkable specific skills, but whose level of general intelligence is very low, are known as *idiot savants.* The French term *idiot* means "poorly informed or untutored" and *savant* means "wise one." Such a person's thinking is a curious combination of retardation and genius.

Alonzo Clemons is not able to speak in complete sentences, cannot read or count, and, at almost 50 years of age, has the mental ability of the average 6-year-old child. He lives in a facility for the retarded near Denver. But Alonzo, the retarded genius, is making a name for himself in the art world, creating bronze sculptures, which collectors are eagerly buying for hundreds of dollars each—or more for special pieces. In only 4 months after his first show, Alonzo the sculptor sold $30,000 worth of his work through a Denver art gallery.

Another rare combination of genius and low IQ is Arnold, who is identified as an *autistic savant.* Although his IQ of 80 is low, it is too high to allow him to be considered retarded. Arnold is employed at a Goodwill store, doing assembly work. But his mother describes him this way:

> He reads and understands books on electronics and uses the theories to build devices. He recently put together a tape recorder, a fluorescent light, and a small transistor radio with some other components, so that music from the tape was changed to light energy in the light and then back to music in the radio. By passing his hand between the recorder and the light, he could stop the music. He understands the concepts of electronics, astronomy, music, navigation and mechanics. He knows an astonishing amount about how things work and is familiar with technical terms. (Rimland, 1978, p. 70)

Here are cases of truth being far stranger than fiction. Although the puzzle of savant syndrome is yielding its secrets to scientists only slowly, perhaps the unraveling of such mental mysteries will eventually provide clues that will lead to a clearer understanding of intelligence, thinking, and creativity.

Remember It!

1. Geniuses are typically highly creative. (true/false)
2. The stages in the creative problem-solving process occur in the following sequence:
   a. illumination, incubation, preparation, translation
   b. incubation, illumination, preparation, translation
   c. preparation, incubation, illumination, translation
   d. translation, preparation, incubation, illumination
3. Divergent-production tests and the Remote Associates Test are used to measure
   a. emotional intelligence.
   b. intelligence.
   c. problem-solving ability.
   d. creativity.

Answers: 1. false 2. c 3. d

Apply It!

Stimulating Creativity

Creativity is certainly not limited to "special" people who are naturally gifted with flair and imagination. Everyone has some potential for creativity. What can you do to become more creative? Psychologists have suggested a variety of techniques for stimulating creativity.

- *"Tune in" to your own creativity and have confidence in it.* The more you develop the habit of thinking of yourself as a creative person and the higher you value creativity as a personal goal, the more likely you will be to come up with creative ideas and solutions to problems (Hennessey & Amabile, 1988).
- *Challenge yourself to develop your special interests.* Do you enjoy cooking or photography? Whatever your creative interest, set small challenges for yourself. Go beyond simply cooking a tasty meal or taking pictures of friends and family. Start inventing new recipes or photographing new subjects in original ways. The more you stretch yourself beyond the ordinary, the more creative you will become.
- *Broaden yourself.* The more knowledge and expertise you acquire, the greater potential for creative output you will develop (Epstein, 1996).
- *Use problem finding as a stimulus to creativity.* Instead of being upset by everyday inconveniences and annoyances, consider such problems to be opportunities for devising creative solutions (Getzels & Csikszentmihalyi, 1976).
- *Change your normal routine.* Have lunch at a different time. Take a new route to school or work. Seek out someone you've never talked to and strike up a conversation. Don't ask yourself why you're making the change; just do it for the sake of change.
- *Spend more time with creative people.* This will stimulate whatever creativity abilities you might have (Amabile, 1983).
- *Be flexible and open to new possibilities.* Free your thoughts from arbitrary restraints. Learn to avoid *mental set*—the failure to consider alternative solutions to common problems.
- *Avoid self-censorship.* Ignore the inner voice that tells you something can't possibly work. Don't be critical of your thoughts or efforts during the early stages of the creative process. Fretting over the correctness of the output inhibits the very process itself (Amabile, 1983).
- *Don't be afraid to make mistakes.* For the creative person, mistakes are valuable learning experiences, not something to be feared and avoided at all costs. In fact, creative people tend to make more mistakes than less imaginative people. Why? Because they make more attempts, try more experiments, and come up with more ideas to be tested (Goleman et al., 1992).
- *Capture your creative thoughts.* Become more attentive to your creative thoughts, and be prepared to preserve them no matter where you might be (Epstein, 1996). Use a notepad, sketchpad, tape recorder, or any other device or method to capture your good ideas when you get them. It is highly unlikely that they will reappear in the same form at a more convenient time.
- *Relax.* One way to stimulate creative thinking is to relax. Go for a walk, take a long shower, sit in a comfortable chair and daydream, lie on the beach. Relaxing gives the unconscious mind a chance to play with ideas and combine them in new ways. The result may be a flash of insight like the one that led Archimedes to leap from his bath and exclaim "Eureka!" (Greek for "I've found it!") when he figured out why heavy objects float in water.

In group settings, creativity appears to be fostered by humor. Groups whose members joke, kid around, and laugh easily often have been found to be more creative than groups whose members interact more formally. One technique used to stimulate creativity in group settings is *brainstorming,* in which group members try to generate as many ideas as possible, no matter how wild or unusual. Because anxiety and self-consciousness can inhibit the free flow of suggestions, all judgment or evaluation is prohibited until everyone's ideas have been presented.

But Margaret Matlin (1994) and other psychologists are skeptical of the value of brainstorming. She points out that the product of group creativity is often of lower quality than creative ideas offered by individuals working independently.

Organizations that seek to encourage creativity and innovation should allow employees more leeway in solving problems and more control over performance of assigned tasks. Moreover, employees should be given sufficient time to do quality work, should be allowed to work independently where appropriate, and should be free of continuous monitoring.

THINKING CRITICALLY

Evaluation

Which of the theories of intelligence best fits your notion of intelligence? Why?

Point/Counterpoint

Prepare an argument supporting each of the following positions:

a. Intelligence tests should be used in the schools.
b. Intelligence tests should not be used in the schools.

Psychology in Your Life

Give several examples of how you might bring more creativity into your educational and personal life.

SUMMARY AND REVIEW

THE NATURE OF INTELLIGENCE

What factors underlie intelligence, according to Spearman and Thurstone?

Spearman believed that intelligence is composed of a general ability (*g* factor), which underlies all intellectual functions, and a number of specific abilities (*s* factors). Thurstone points to seven primary mental abilities, which singly or in combination are involved in all intellectual activities.

What types of intelligence did Gardner and Sternberg identify?

Gardner claims that there are eight independent types of intelligence. Sternberg's triarchic theory of intelligence identifies three types: componential (conventional intelligence), experiential (creative intelligence), and contextual (practical intelligence).

Key Terms
intelligence (p. 278); *g* factor (p. 279); primary mental abilities (p. 279); triarchic theory of intelligence (p. 280)

MEASURING INTELLIGENCE

What is Binet's major contribution to psychology?

Binet's major contribution to psychology is the concept of mental age and a method for measuring it—the intelligence test.

What is the Stanford–Binet Intelligence Scale?

The Stanford–Binet Intelligence Scale is a highly regarded individual intelligence test for those aged 2 to 23. It yields one overall IQ score.

What does IQ mean, and how has the method for calculating it changed over time?

IQ stands for *intelligence quotient*, an index of intelligence originally derived by dividing a person's mental age by his or her chronological age and then multiplying by 100. Now it is derived by comparing an individual's score with the scores of others of the same age.

What did Wechsler's tests provide that the Stanford–Binet did not?

David Wechsler developed the first successful individual intelligence test for adults, the Wechsler Adult Intelligence Scale (WAIS-III). His tests for adults, children, and preschoolers yield separate verbal and performance (nonverbal) IQ scores as well as an overall IQ score.

What do the terms *reliability, validity,* and *standardization* mean?

Reliability is the ability of a test to yield nearly the same score each time a person takes the test or an alternative form of the test. Validity is the power of a test to measure what it is intended to measure. Standardization refers to prescribed procedures for administering a test and to established norms that provide a means of evaluating test scores.

What are the ranges of IQ scores considered average, superior, and in the range of mental retardation?

Fifty percent of the U.S. population have IQ scores ranging from 90 to 110; 2% have scores above 130, considered superior; and 2% have scores below 70, in the range of mental retardation.

According to the Terman study, how do the gifted differ from the general population?

Terman's longitudinal study revealed that, in general, the gifted enjoy better physical and mental health and are more successful than the general population.

What two criteria must a person meet to be classified as mentally retarded?

To be classified as mentally retarded, an individual must have an IQ score below 70 and show severe deficiencies in everyday adaptive functioning.

What is the relationship between intelligence and the efficiency and speed of neural processing?

People who are more intelligent generally use less mental energy and have a faster neural processing speed than less intelligent people.

Key Terms
norms (p. 283); Stanford–Binet Intelligence Scale (p. 283); intelligence quotient (IQ) (p. 283); deviation score (p. 283); Wechsler Adult Intelligence Scale (WAIS-III) (p. 283); reliability (p. 284); validity (p. 285); aptitude test (p. 285); standardization (p. 285); mental retardation (p. 287); mainstreaming (p. 288)

THE IQ CONTROVERSY: BRAINY DISPUTE

Of what are intelligence tests good predictors?

IQ tests are good predictors of academic achievement and success in school.

What are some abuses of intelligence tests?

Abuses occur when IQ tests are the only criterion for admitting people to educational programs, for tracking children, or for placing them in classes for the mentally retarded. Many people claim that IQ tests are biased in favor of the urban middle or upper class.

How does the nature–nurture controversy apply to intelligence?

The nature–nurture controversy is the debate over whether intelligence is primarily determined by heredity or environment.

What is behavioral genetics, and what are the primary methods used in the field today?

Behavioral genetics is the study of the relative effects of heredity and environment on behavior and ability. The twin study method and the adoption method are the primary methods used.

How do twin studies support the view that intelligence is inherited?

Twin studies provide evidence that intelligence is primarily inherited because identical twins are more alike in intelligence than fraternal twins, even if they have been reared apart.

What are Jensen's and Herrnstein and Murray's controversial views on race and IQ?

These researchers claim that the Black–White IQ gap is due to genetic differences between the races that cannot be changed significantly through environmental intervention.

What kinds of evidence suggest that IQ is changeable rather than fixed?

Several adoption studies have revealed that when infants from disadvantaged environments are adopted by middle- and upper-middle-class parents, their IQ scores are higher on average than would otherwise be expected. Also, IQ scores have been rising steadily over the past 60 years in Western industrialized nations, presumably because of increases in the standard of living and educational opportunities.

Key Terms

culture-fair intelligence test (p. 290); nature–nurture controversy (p. 291); behavioral genetics (p. 291); twin study method (p. 291); identical twins (p. 291); fraternal twins (p. 291); heritability (p. 292); adoption method (p. 292)

EMOTIONAL INTELLIGENCE

What are the personal components of emotional intelligence?

The personal components of emotional intelligence are an awareness of and an ability to control one's own emotions and the ability to motivate oneself.

What are the interpersonal components of emotional intelligence?

The interpersonal components of emotional intelligence are empathy and the ability to handle relationships.

Key Term

emotional intelligence (p. 297)

CREATIVITY: UNIQUE AND USEFUL PRODUCTIONS

What is creativity, and how is it related to intelligence?

Creativity is the ability to produce original, appropriate, and valuable ideas and/or solutions to problems. Highly creative people tend to have well above average intelligence, but there seems to be little correlation between very high IQ (above 120) and creativity.

What are the four stages in the creative process?

The four stages in the creative process are preparation, incubation, illumination, and translation.

What kinds of tests have been used to measure creativity, and how good are they as predictors of creativity?

Some tests used to measure creativity are the Unusual Uses Test, the Consequences Test, and the Remote Associates Test. They are only mediocre as predictors of creativity.

What are some characteristics of creative people?

Creative people share some characteristics that distinguish them: expertise, openness to experience, independence of mind, intrinsic motivation, and perseverance.

Key Terms

creativity (p. 300); divergent thinking (p. 301); savant syndrome (p. 303)

Surf It!

Want to be sure you've absorbed the material in Chapter 8, "Intelligence and Creativity," before the big test? Visiting *www.abacon.com/wood* can put a top grade within your reach. The site is loaded with free practice tests, flashcards, activities, and links to help you review your way to an A. To enliven that inevitable study break, the site also offers personality assessment quizzes and a psychology career corner.

9 Child Development

In 1984 Ugandan soldiers retreating through the African jungle came upon one of the strangest sights they had ever seen. They were accustomed to the numerous monkeys living in the jungle, hopping, chattering, and leaping from place to place and avoiding humans who alarmed them. But with one group of monkeys, the soldiers saw a larger creature who was unlike the others but was playfully hopping around with them. Intrigued, the soldiers came closer and were amazed to discover a human child.

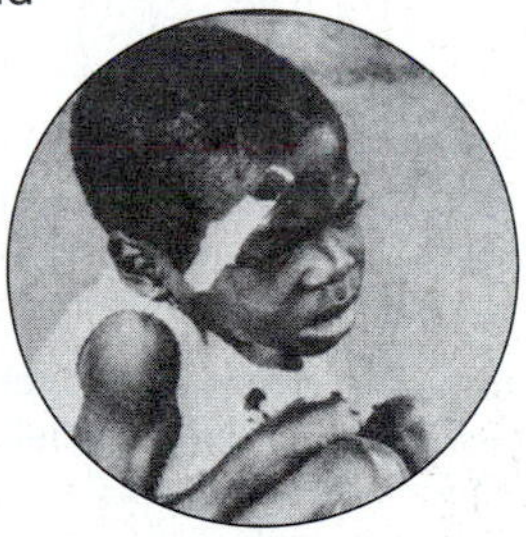

The soldiers captured the young boy and brought him to an orphanage in Kampala, Uganda. Here staff members named him Robert, estimated him to be between 5 and 7 years old, and were amazed by his behavior. He squealed and grunted but could not speak. He didn't walk normally but jumped from one place to another the way a monkey would. He scratched people when they approached him; he ate grass or any other edible thing he could find. And he did not sit but squatted when he was not moving around. Small for his age, Robert was only 2½ feet tall when he was found and weighed only 22 pounds.

Foreign relief workers stationed in Uganda at the time were afraid that other children might be living as wild creatures in the jungle where Robert was found. They suspected this because hundreds of orphaned children had been discovered wandering around in nearby villages after the end of the civil war, which had disturbed the peace and beauty of Uganda for many years. Those who studied Robert's case believed that his parents had been slaughtered when he was about 1 year old. Somehow he had managed to escape the massacre and make his way deep into the jungle.

Even though Robert's behavior was more like that of the monkeys that nurtured him, he is, genetically, as fully human as any other person. Cases like Robert's are intriguing to developmental psychologists because they demonstrate the profound effects that extreme environmental conditions (nurture) can have on the course of human development. Researchers continue to study the effects of severe early deprivation on infants and children from war-torn countries, such as Romania, who were adopted by families in the United States and other countries (O'Connor et al., 2000).

DEVELOPMENTAL PSYCHOLOGY: BASIC ISSUES AND METHODOLOGY

Developmental psychology is the study of how humans grow, develop, and change throughout the life span. Some developmental psychologists specialize in the study of a particular age group within the continuum from infancy, childhood, and adolescence through early, middle, and late adulthood, to the end of the life span. Others concentrate on a specific area of interest, such as physical, cognitive, or language development or emotional or moral development.

developmental psychology: The study of how humans grow, develop, and change throughout the life span.

nature–nurture controversy: The debate concerning the relative influences of heredity and environment on development.

longitudinal study: A type of developmental study in which the same group of participants is followed and measured at different ages.

cross-sectional study: A type of developmental study in which researchers compare groups of participants of different ages on certain characteristics to determine age-related differences.

genes: The segments of DNA that are located on the chromosomes and are the basic units for the transmission of all hereditary traits.

Controversial Issues in Developmental Psychology

All developmental psychologists must consider several controversial issues that continue to influence the field.

1. *To what degree do heredity and environment influence development?* For centuries thinkers have debated the influences of heredity and environment on human development—a debate called the **nature–nurture controversy.** Some thinkers have taken the nature side in the debate, believing that people's abilities are determined almost exclusively by heredity and are transmitted through the genes. Others have taken the nurture position, maintaining that environment—the circumstances in which individuals are raised—determines what they become. Today the debate is not about nature *versus* nurture, but about the degree to which each influences various aspects of development.

Obviously, heredity imposes some limits on what a person can become. The best possible home environment, education, and nutrition cannot produce an Einstein or a Marilyn Mach vos Savant–Jarvik (whose 230 IQ is the highest ever recorded). But parental neglect, poor nutrition, ill health, abuse, and lack of education can prevent even the brightest among us from becoming the best our genes would allow. Robert, devoid of all human contact, suffered such extreme deprivation that he failed to develop in ways most characteristically human. But surely nature and nurture are not opposing forces in the course of our development; they are partners. Together they exert a shared influence, forging and shaping us into the individuals we become (Bouchard, 1997; Maccoby, 2000; Plomin et al., 1994).

To what degree do personality traits (aggressiveness, passivity, etc.) change or remain stable during childhood? Developmental psychologists conduct research studies to answer such questions.

2. *Is development continuous, or does it occur in stages?* Physical growth during middle childhood is usually gradual, continuous, and cumulative. Children change quantitatively as they grow taller, heavier, and stronger. Are other aspects of development—cognitive and moral development, for example—best understood in terms of gradual, continuous, cumulative change? Or does change in some aspects of development occur in spurts in the form of stages, with one stage *qualitatively* different from the next? We will explore two stage theories in this chapter: Piaget's theory of cognitive development and Erikson's theory of psychosocial development.

3. *To what extent are personal traits stable over time?* In various later chapters we will discuss whether certain personal traits (intelligence, aggression, and aspects of temperament, for example) tend to be stable or changeable over time. How do developmental psychologists study changes over the life span?

Approaches to Studying Developmental Change

What are two types of studies developmental psychologists use to investigate age-related changes?

impact of DNA which we receive our key traits 23rd pair - sex chromosomes

Developmental psychologists use the longitudinal study and the cross-sectional study to investigate age-related changes. A **longitudinal study** is one in which the same group of participants is followed and measured at different ages, and it may take years to complete. There are some drawbacks to the longitudinal study. It is time-consuming and expensive, and participants may drop out of the study or die, possibly leaving the researcher with a biased sample.

A **cross-sectional study** is a less expensive and less time-consuming method in which researchers compare groups of participants of different ages on various characteristics to determine age-related differences. But in the cross-sectional study, differences found in age groups are based on group averages, so this approach is not able to provide answers to some questions. For example, it could not be used to determine if individual temperament is stable over time. Moreover, there may be certain relevant differences in groups of participants that have less to do with the participants' ages than with the eras in which they grew up. Figure 9.1 (on p. 312) illustrates longitudinal and cross-sectional studies.

Development is a fascinating and remarkable process that begins even before birth, and we will trace its course from the very beginning.

HEREDITY AND PRENATAL DEVELOPMENT

The Mechanism of Heredity: Genes and Chromosomes

How are hereditary traits transmitted?

Genes are the biological blueprints that determine and direct the transmission of all hereditary traits. Genes are segments of DNA located on each of the rod-shaped structures called **chromosomes** that are found in the nuclei of body cells. Normal body cells, with two exceptions, have 23 pairs of chromosomes (46 chromosomes in all). The two exceptions are the sperm cells and the mature egg cells, each of which has 23 single chromosomes. At conception the sperm adds its 23 single chromosomes to the 23 of the egg. From this union a single cell called a *zygote* is formed, with the full

chromosomes: Rod-shaped structures in the nuclei of body cells, which contain all the genes and carry all the hereditary information.

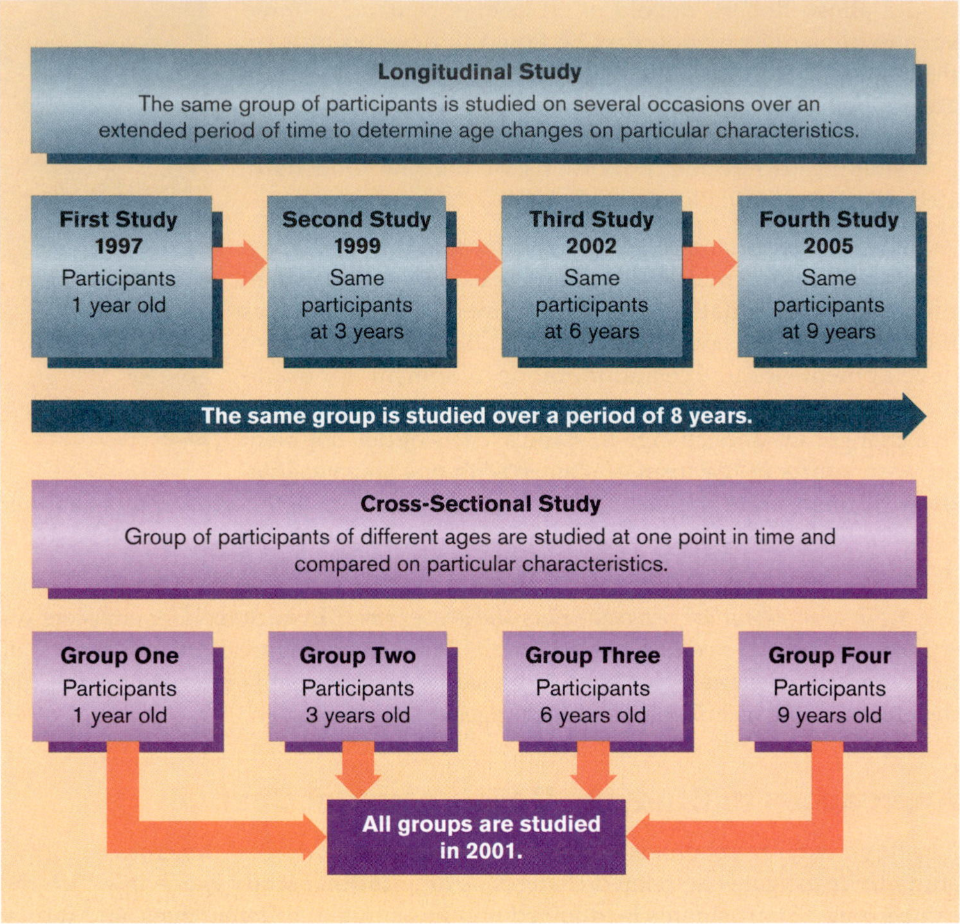

Figure 9.1

A Comparison of Longitudinal and Cross-Sectional Studies

To study age-related changes using a longitudinal study, researchers examine the same group of participants at several times over an extended period. When using a cross-sectional study, researchers examine and compare groups of different ages at one point in time.

complement of 46 chromosomes (23 pairs), which contain about 30,000 genes (Baltimore, 2001). Surprisingly, these genes carry all of the genetic information needed to make a human being.

Twenty-two of the 23 pairs of chromosomes are matching pairs, called *autosomes,* and each member of these pairs carries genes for particular physical and mental traits. The 23rd pair are called **sex chromosomes** because they carry the genes that determine a person's sex; primary and secondary sex characteristics; and other sex-linked traits, such as red-green color blindness, male pattern baldness, and hemophilia.

The sex chromosomes of females consist of two X chromosomes (XX); males have an X chromosome and a Y chromosome (XY). The egg cell always contains an X chromosome. Therefore, the sex of a child will depend on whether the egg is fertilized by a sperm carrying an X chromosome, which produces a female, or a sperm carrying a Y chromosome, which produces a male. Half of a man's sperm cells carry an X chromosome, and half carry a Y. It is not the Y chromosome itself, but a single gene found only on Y chromosomes that causes a fetus to become a male. This gene, which has been labeled Sry, initiates and orchestrates the development of the male sex organs (Capel, 2000). If the Sry gene is absent from the Y chromosome for any reason (mutation, etc.), the fetus will develop as a female.

In some cases, a single gene from each pair of chromosomes provides the genetic influence for a particular trait. In many other cases, such as intelligence, height, and weight, a number of genes collectively produce the genetic influence for a particular trait or ability. The Human Genome Project is aimed at identifying the functions of all the genes and locating them on the chromosomes. Its ultimate goal is to decipher the complete instructions for making a human being.

sex chromosomes: The 23rd pair of chromosomes, which carries the genes that determine one's sex, primary and secondary sex characteristics, and other sex-linked traits.

dominant gene: The gene that is expressed in the individual.

recessive gene: A gene that will not be expressed if paired with a dominant gene but will be expressed if paired with another recessive gene.

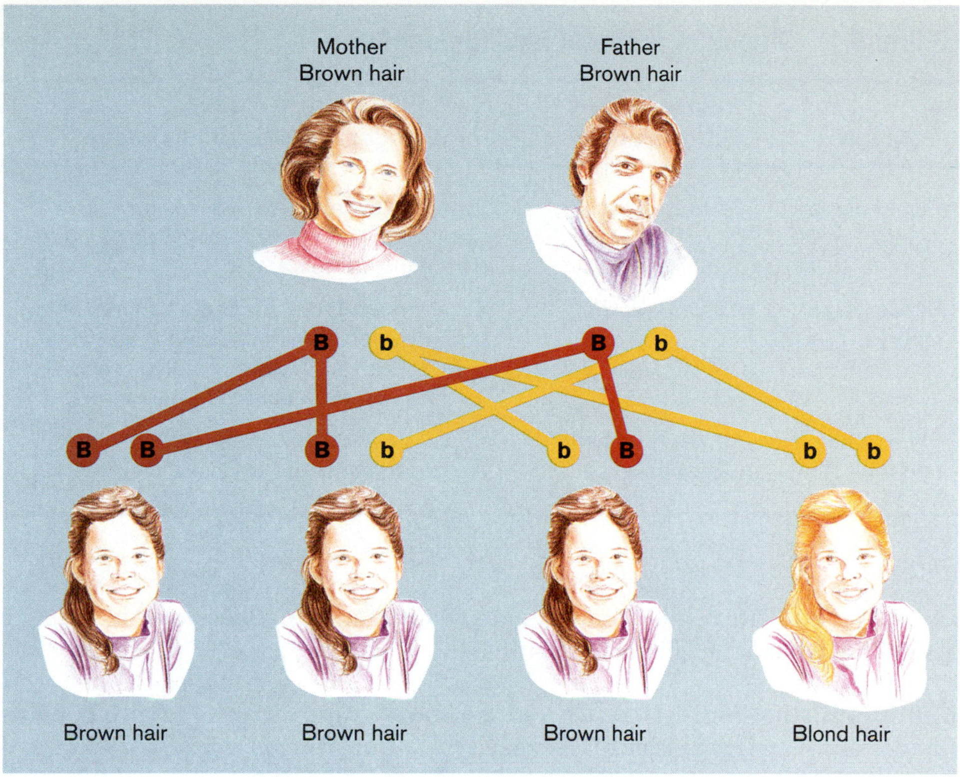

Figure 9.2

Gene Transmission for Hair Color

This figure shows all the possible combinations in children when both parents carry a dominant gene for brown hair (B) and a recessive gene for blond hair (b). The chance of their having a blond-haired child (bb) or a brown-haired child (BB) is 25% in each case. There is a 50% chance of having a brown-haired child who carries both the dominant gene (B) and the recessive gene (b).

Dominant and Recessive Genes: Dominants Call the Shots When two different genes are transmitted for the same trait, one is usually a **dominant gene,** causing the dominant trait to be expressed in the individual. The gene for brown hair, for example, is dominant over the gene for blond hair. A person having one gene for brown hair and one gene for blond hair will have brown hair. And, of course, two dominant genes will produce brown hair (see Figure 9.2).

The gene for blond hair is recessive. A **recessive gene** will be expressed if it is paired with another recessive gene. Therefore, blond people have two recessive genes for blond hair. A recessive gene will *not* be expressed if it is paired with a dominant gene. Yet a person with such a pair can still pass either the recessive gene or the dominant gene along to his or her offspring.

When are dominant or recessive genes expressed in an individual's traits?

What are the three stages of prenatal development?

The Stages of Prenatal Development: Unfolding According to Plan

Conception occurs the moment a sperm cell fertilizes the ovum (egg cell), forming the single-celled zygote. Conception usually takes place in one of the fallopian tubes, and within the next 2 weeks the zygote travels to the uterus and attaches itself to the uterine wall. During this 2-week period, called the **period of the zygote,** rapid cell division occurs. At the end of this first stage of **prenatal** development, the zygote is only the size of the period at the end of this sentence.

The second stage is the period of the **embryo,** when the major systems, organs, and structures of the body develop. Lasting from week 3 through week 8, this period ends when the first bone cells form. Only 1 inch long and weighing ⅐ of an ounce, the embryo already resembles a human being, with limbs, fingers, toes, and many internal organs that have begun to function.

The final stage of prenatal development, called the period of the **fetus,** lasts from the end of the second month until birth. It is a time of rapid growth and further development of the structures, organs, and systems of the body. Table 9.1 (on p. 314) describes the characteristics of each stage of prenatal development.

period of the zygote: The approximately 2-week-long period from conception to the attachment of the zygote to the uterine wall.

prenatal: Occurring between conception and birth.

embryo: The developing human organism during the period (week 3 through week 8) when the major systems, organs, and structures of the body develop.

fetus: The developing human organism during the period (week 9 until birth) when rapid growth and further development of the structures, organs, and systems of the body occur.

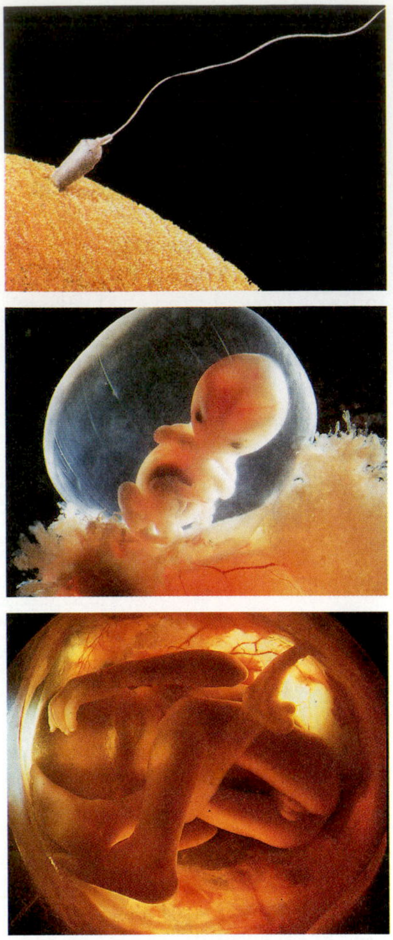

This sequence of photos shows the fertilization of an egg by a sperm (top), an embryo at 7 weeks (middle), and a fetus at 22 weeks (bottom).

Table 9.1 Stages of Prenatal Development

Stage	Time after Conception	Major Activities of the Stage
Period of the zygote	1 to 2 weeks	Zygote attaches to the uterine lining. At 2 weeks, zygote is the size of the period at the end of this sentence.
Period of the embryo	3 to 8 weeks	Major systems, organs, and structures of the body develop. Period ends when first bone cells appear. At 8 weeks, embryo is about 1 inch long and weighs ⅐ of an ounce.
Period of the fetus	9 weeks to birth (38 weeks)	Rapid growth and further development of the body structures, organs, and systems.

This is how life begins for most of us, with a single egg fertilized by a single sperm. But what occurs in multiple births?

Multiple Births: More Than One at a Time In the case of **identical twins (monozygotic twins),** one egg is fertilized by one sperm, but the zygote splits and develops into two embryos with identical genetic codes. Thus, identical twins are always of the same sex. This splitting of the zygote seems to be a chance occurrence accounting for about 4 in 1,000 births.

Fraternal twins (dizygotic twins) develop when two eggs are released during ovulation and are fertilized by two different sperm. The two zygotes develop into two siblings who are no more alike genetically than ordinary brothers and sisters. The likelihood of fraternal twins increases if there is a family history of multiple births, if the mother is between ages 35 and 40, or if the mother has recently stopped taking birth control pills. Also, fertility drugs often cause the release of more than one egg.

Of course, twins are not the only type of multiple births. Triplets, quadruplets, and on up to septuplets can result when multiple eggs are released during ovulation, when one or more eggs split before or after fertilization, or when a combination of these events occurs.

Negative Influences on Prenatal Development: Sabotaging Nature's Plan

What are some negative influences on prenatal development, and during what time is their impact greatest?

Teratogens are agents in the prenatal environment that can have a negative impact on prenatal development, causing birth defects and other problems. A teratogen's impact depends on both its intensity and the time during prenatal development when it is present. Drugs, environmental hazards such as X rays or toxic waste, and diseases such as rubella generally have their most devastating consequences during the first 3 months of development (the first trimester). During this time there are **critical periods** when certain body structures develop. If drugs or infections interfere with development during a critical period, the structure or body part will not form properly, nor will it develop later (Kopp & Kaler, 1989).

Exposure to risks during the second trimester of pregnancy—the fourth to sixth month—is more likely to result in various types of intellectual and social impairments than to cause physical abnormalities.

Prenatal malnutrition can harm the developing embryo and fetus and can have particularly severe effects on brain development during the final trimester. The belief that a baby can get all the nutrition it needs from the mother regardless of her diet is simply not true. The number of newborns in the United States who are seriously undernourished at birth is estimated to be between 80,000 and 100,000 annually (Children's Defense Fund, 1996). A woman should have proper nutrition and take appropriate multivitamin supplements before as well as during pregnancy (Bendich & Keen, 1993). On the other hand, maternal obesity can also be a danger, increasing the risk of congenital malformations in the central nervous system (Prentice & Goldberg, 1996).

The Hazard of Drugs: What the Pregnant Mother Takes, the Baby Gets Too

Many drugs cross the placental barrier and directly affect the unborn child. Consequently, both prescription and nonprescription drugs (for example, aspirin, nasal sprays, laxatives, douches, reducing aids, baking soda, and vitamin supplements) should be taken only with the consent of a doctor (Apgar & Beck, 1982). Some prescription drugs, such as certain antibiotics, tranquilizers, and anticonvulsants, are known to cause specific damage in the unborn.

Heroin, Cocaine, and Crack The use of crack cocaine during pregnancy has been linked to miscarriage, fetal death, prematurity, low birthweight, and physical birth defects, as well as to later breathing difficulties and sleep disturbances in children (Richardson et al., 2000; Scher et al., 2000). And some studies reveal less well-developed brain regions not only at birth but in follow-up studies 1 year later (Scher et al., 2000). Cocaine use by the father at the time of conception also can be harmful because tiny specks of cocaine can bind to sperm and "piggyback" their way into the zygote (Yazigi et al., 1991).

A recent study indicated that babies born to mothers who took heroin during pregnancy had significantly lower birthweights and were less mature in physical development than babies not exposed to heroin. More than half (55%) of the heroin babies required a period of intensive special nursery care, and their hospital stays were significantly longer than those of other infants (Kelly et al., 2000).

Most people realize that pregnant women should not take hard drugs, but fewer people are aware of the potential dangers of alcohol and cigarettes.

Alcohol Few mothers would think of giving their newborns beer, wine, or hard liquor. But this is precisely what they are doing when they drink alcohol during pregnancy. Alcohol crosses the placental barrier, and alcohol levels in the fetus almost match the levels in the mother's blood (Little et al., 1989). Alcohol can alter brain development throughout pregnancy (Streissguth et al., 1989). And it doesn't take a lot of alcohol to have an effect. The fetal brain can be damaged if a woman drinks only moderate amounts of alcohol (Golden, 2000). And those who drink heavily during pregnancy risk having babies with **fetal alcohol syndrome.** Babies with this syndrome are mentally retarded and have abnormally small heads, short noses, wide-set eyes, and reduced visual acuity (Hug et al., 2000). Fetal alcohol syndrome is not reversible and leaves affected children with life-long abnormalities in growth, health, behavior, and cognitive ability (Hannigan & Armant, 2000). The longer a fetus is exposed to alcohol, the more severe the consequences (Autti-Ramo, 2000).

The Surgeon General warns women to abstain from drinking alcohol altogether during pregnancy, but about 20% ignore the warnings (Braun, 1996). In addition, there is some evidence that when men ingest large amounts of alcohol, changes in sperm cells occur that can inhibit conception or cause complications in development (Cicero, cited in Dryden, 1994).

Smoking Smoking decreases the amount of oxygen and increases the amount of carbon monoxide crossing the placental barrier. This is especially serious when a woman is pregnant with twins, because of the increased oxygen demand due to two fetuses (Pollack et al., 2000). Smoking increases the probability of premature birth, low birthweight, stillbirth, and sudden infant death syndrome. Mothers who continue to smoke during pregnancy place their offspring at significantly greater risk for depression and anxiety and increase the likelihood that they will engage in early

Drinking alcohol during pregnancy can result in the birth of an infant with fetal alcohol syndrome, a permanent condition that involves mental retardation and physical and behavioral abnormalities.

identical (monozygotic) twins: Twins with exactly the same genes, who develop after one egg is fertilized by one sperm, and the zygote splits into two parts.

fraternal (dizygotic) twins: Twins, no more alike genetically than ordinary siblings, who develop after two eggs are released during ovulation and fertilized by two different sperm.

✓**teratogens:** Harmful agents in the prenatal environment, which can have a negative impact on prenatal development or even cause birth defects.

critical period: A period that is so important to development that a harmful environmental influence at that time can keep a bodily structure from developing normally or can impair later intellectual or social development.

fetal alcohol syndrome: A condition, caused by maternal alcohol intake during pregnancy, in which the baby is born mentally retarded, with a small head and facial, organ, and behavioral abnormalities.

low-birthweight baby: A baby weighing less than 5.5 pounds.

preterm infant: An infant born before the 37th week and weighing less than 5.5 pounds; a premature infant.

tobacco use by more than five times (Cornelius et al., 2000). Still other studies have reported a relationship between tobacco use during the first trimester of pregnancy and increased risk for cleft lip and cleft palate (Lorente et al., 2000). In addition, Olds and others (1994) found that 3- and 4-year-old children of mothers who smoked 10 cigarettes a day or more during pregnancy scored 4 IQ points lower, on average, than children of nonsmokers.

Caffeine Some researchers have reported that heavy caffeine consumption (more than than 300 milligrams, or the equivalent of three cups of coffee, per day) is related to low birthweight and miscarriage (Dlugosz & Bracken, 1992; Eskenazi, 1993). Other researchers have concluded that adverse outcomes of pregnancy cannot be definitely linked to caffeine (Hinds et al., 1996). Because the jury is still out on this question, it would be prudent for pregnant women to restrict caffeine consumption to less than 300 milligrams daily.

Low-Birthweight Babies: Newborns at High Risk The infant mortality rate in the United States is 7.2 per 1,000 live births. The rate is 6.0 per 1,000 live births among White Americans, but it is more than twice as high—14.3 per 1,000 live births—among African Americans (National Center for Health Statistics, 2000). Sixty-five percent of these deaths involve the 6–7% of newborns who are **low-birthweight babies**—babies weighing less than 5.5 pounds. Infants of this weight born at or before the 37th week are considered **preterm infants.** The smaller and more premature the baby, the greater the risk (Lukeman & Melvin, 1993). The handicaps of prematurity range from subtle learning and behavior problems, in babies closer to normal birthweight, to "severe retardation, blindness, hearing loss, and even death," in the smallest newborns (Apgar & Beck, 1982, p. 69).

Poor nutrition, poor prenatal care, smoking, drug use, and maternal infection all increase the likelihood of having a low-birthweight baby with complications. But even with good prenatal care and nutrition and no drug use, 14- to 17-year-olds appear to be at higher risk of having very small babies (Fraser et al., 1995).

Remember It!

1. The cross-sectional study takes longer to complete than the longitudinal study. (true/false)
2. In humans, genes are located on how many pairs of chromosomes?

   a. 22 b. 23 c. 44 d. 46
3. Females have an X and a Y chromosome. (true/false)
4. A dominant gene will not be expressed if the individual carries
   a. two dominant genes for the trait.
   b. one dominant and one recessive gene for the trait.
   c. two recessive genes for the trait.
   d. either one or two dominant genes for the trait.
5. Fraternal twins are no more alike genetically than ordinary brothers and sisters. (true/false)
6. Match the stage of prenatal development with its description.

   ____ (1) first 2 weeks of life
   ____ (2) rapid growth and further development of body structures and systems
   ____ (3) development of major systems, organs, and structures of the body

   a. period of the fetus
   b. period of the embryo
   c. period of the zygote
7. Negative influences such as drugs, illnesses, and environmental hazards cause the most devastating consequences during the ______________ trimester.

   a. first b. second c. third d. second or third

Answers: 1. false 2. b 3. false 4. c 5. true 6. (1) c (2) a (3) b 7. a

PHYSICAL DEVELOPMENT AND LEARNING IN INFANCY

You may already know a great deal about physical development in infants. You can test your knowledge of their motor development by filling in the blanks in the *Try It!*

Try It!

At what age, on average, do infants achieve each of the following developmental milestones?

1. Lifts head up ____ months
2. Rolls over ____ months
3. Sits alone ____ months
4. Stands holding on ____ months
5. Stands alone ____ months
6. Walks ____ months

Answers: See Figure 9.4 on page 320 for the correct ages.

The Neonate: Seven Pounds of Beauty?

Although **neonates** (newborn babies) may be beautiful to their parents, they do not yet resemble the babies who pose for Gerber or Johnson & Johnson ads. Newborns measure about 20 inches long, weigh about 7½ pounds, and have a head one-quarter the length of the body. They arrive with dry and wrinkled skin, a rather flat nose, and an elongated forehead—the temporary result of the journey through the birth canal. Nevertheless, newborns come equipped with an impressive range of **reflexes**—built-in responses to certain stimuli that are needed to ensure survival in their new world.

Reflexes: Built-In Responses Sucking, swallowing, coughing, and blinking are some important behaviors that newborns can perform right away. Newborns will move an arm, a leg, or other body part away from a painful stimulus and will try to remove a blanket or cloth placed over the face. Stroke a baby on the cheek and you will trigger the rooting reflex—the baby opens its mouth and actively searches for a nipple. Neonates also have some reflexes that serve no apparent function, and these reflexes are believed to be remnants of humans' evolutionary past. As the brain develops, some behaviors that were initially reflexive (controlled by the lower brain centers) gradually come under the voluntary control of the higher brain centers. The presence of these reflexes at birth and their disappearance between the second and fourth months provide researchers with a means of assessing development of the nervous system.

What are the perceptual abilities of the newborn?

Perceptual Development in Infancy

The five senses, although not fully developed, are functional at birth, and the newborn already has preferences for certain odors, tastes, sounds, and visual configurations. Hearing is much better developed than vision in the neonate and is functional even before birth (Busnel et al., 1992). A newborn is able to turn the head in the direction of a sound and shows a general preference for female voices. Shortly after

neonate: Newborn infant up to 1 month old.

reflexes: Inborn, unlearned, automatic responses (such as blinking, sucking, and grasping) to certain environmental stimuli.

Figure 9.3
Results of Fantz's Study

Using a device called a *viewing box* to observe and record infants' eye movements, Fantz (1961) found that they preferred faces, to black-and-white abstract patterns.

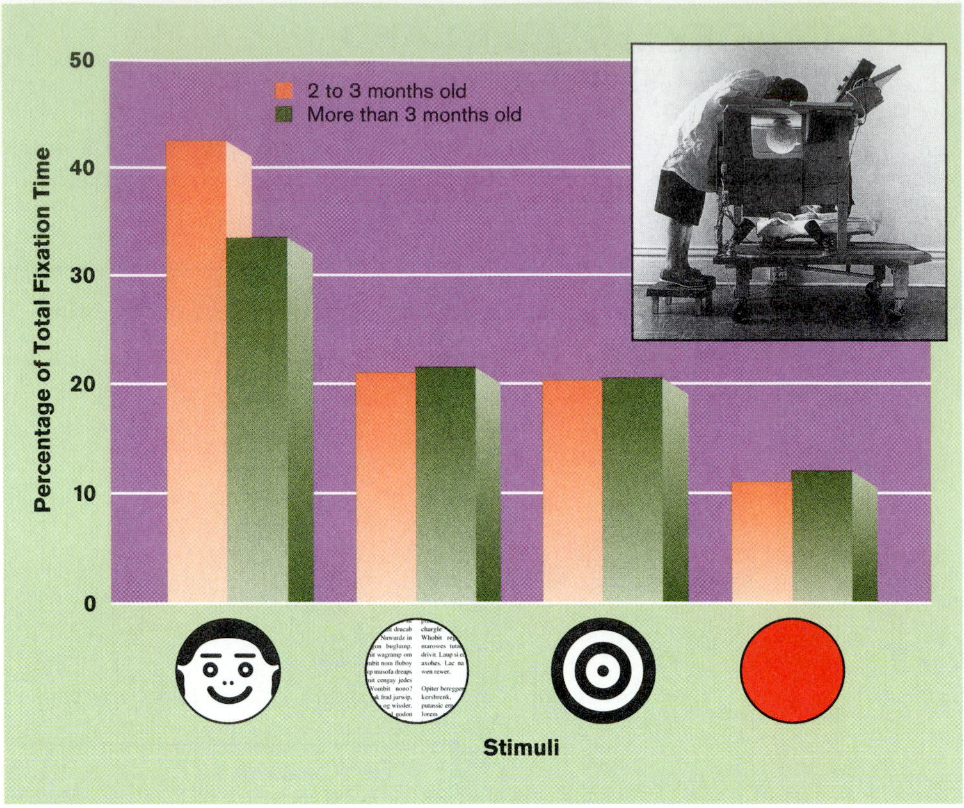

birth, infants prefer their own mother's voice to that of an unfamiliar female (DeCasper & Fifer, 1980), although a preference for the father's voice over a strange male voice does not develop until later. Newborns are able to discriminate among and show preferences for certain odors and tastes (Bartoshuk & Beauchamp, 1994; Leon, 1992). They show a favorable response to sweet tastes and are able to differentiate between salty, bitter, and sour solutions. Newborns are also sensitive to pain (Porter et al., 1988) and are particularly responsive to touch, reacting positively to stroking and fondling.

Robert Fantz (1961) made a major breakthrough when he realized that a baby's interest in an object can be gauged by the length of time it fixates on it. An infant's visual preferences can be assessed with eye-tracking devices that measure what the baby looks at and for how long. Fantz demonstrated that infants prefer the image of a human face to other patterns, such as black-and-white abstract patterns (see Figure 9.3). Fantz's study and others have shown that newborns have clear preferences and powers of discrimination, and even memory recognition and learning ability.

When placed on the visual cliff, most infants older than 6 months will not crawl out over the deep side, indicating that they can perceive depth.

Vision: What Newborns Can See At birth, an infant's vision is about 20/600, and it doesn't reach an adult level until the child is about 2 years old (Courage & Adams, 1990; Held, 1993). Newborns focus best on objects about 9 inches away, and they can follow a slowly moving object. Infants 22 to 93 hours old already indicate a preference for their own mother's face over that of an unfamiliar female (Field et al., 1984). Although newborns prefer colored stimuli to gray ones, they can't distinguish all of the colors adults normally can until they are about 2 months old (Brown, 1990). Then they prefer red, blue, green, and yellow (Bornstein & Marks, 1982).

One famous experiment was devised to study depth perception in infants and other animals. Gibson and Walk (1960) designed an apparatus called the **visual cliff,** consisting of "a board laid across a sheet of heavy glass, with a patterned material directly beneath the glass on one side and several feet below it on the other" (p. 65). This arrangement made it appear that there was a sudden drop-off, or "visual cliff," on one side. When 36 babies aged 6 to 14 months were placed on the center board, most could be coaxed by their mothers to crawl to the shallow side, but only three would crawl onto the deep side. Gibson and Walk concluded that most babies "can discriminate depth as soon as they can crawl" (p. 64).

Using the visual cliff, Campos and others (1970) found that 6-week-old infants had distinct changes in heart rate when they faced the deep side of the cliff, but no change when they faced the shallow side. The change in heart rate indicated interest and showed that the infants could perceive depth.

visual cliff: An apparatus used to test depth perception in infants and young animals.

habituation: A decrease in response or attention to a stimulus as an infant becomes accustomed to it.

maturation: Changes that occur according to one's genetically determined, biological timetable of development.

Learning in Infancy

What types of learning occur in the first few days of life?

attatch

Mary Ainesworth
strange
situation
test bonding
seperation
Anxieties

Harry Carlow
monkeys
wire
all living things
need contact

When are babies first capable of learning? If you say from the moment of birth, you are underestimating them. Learning begins even before birth, because infants' experiences in the womb can affect their preferences shortly after birth. DeCasper and Spence (1986) had 16 pregnant women read *The Cat in the Hat* to their developing fetuses twice a day during the final 6½ weeks of pregnancy. A few days after birth the infants could adjust their sucking on specially designed, pressure-sensitive nipples to hear their mother reading either *The Cat in the Hat* or *The King, the Mice, and the Cheese,* a story they had never heard before. Which story did the infants prefer? You guessed it—by their sucking behavior they showed a clear preference for the familiar sound of *The Cat in the Hat.*

Researchers have demonstrated both classical conditioning and operant conditioning in infants in the first few days of life (Lipsitt, 1990). Sansavini and others (1997) found that newborns quickly learned to suck a pressure-sensitive nipple faster in order to view preferred visual patterns or hear music and the sound of human voices. But the simplest evidence of learning in infants is the phenomenon of **habituation.** When presented with a new stimulus, they respond with a general quieting, their heart rate slows, and they fixate on the stimulus. But when infants become accustomed to the stimulus, they stop responding—that is, they habituate to it. Later, if the familiar stimulus is presented along with a new stimulus, they will usually pay more attention to the new stimulus, indicating that they remember the original stimulus but prefer the new one. Memory can be measured by (1) the speed with which habituation occurs and (2) the relative amounts of time infants spend looking at or listening to a new and an old stimulus.

Swain and others (1993) demonstrated that 3-day-old newborns could retain in memory for 24 hours a speech sound that had been presented repeatedly the day before. When the same sound was repeated the following day, the babies quickly showed habituation by turning their head away from the familiar sound and toward a novel sound. And infants 2 to 3 months old can form memories of their past experience lasting for days and even longer as they get older (Rovee-Collier, 1990).

Amazing as it may seem, Meltzoff and Moore (1977) found that babies only 42 minutes old could imitate gestures such as sticking out the tongue or opening and closing the mouth. And infants averaging 42 hours old can imitate head movements (Meltzoff & Moore, 1989). More recently, the ability of newborns to imitate facial expressions has been demonstrated in many different ethnic groups and cultures (Meltzoff & Kuhl, 1994). However, Anisfeld (1996) reviewed nine studies and concluded that only tongue protrusion was consistently matched by newborns.

A study by Meltzoff (1988a) demonstrated observational learning in 14-month-olds. After watching an adult on television handling "a novel toy in a particular way," the babies were able to imitate the behavior when presented with the toy 24 hours later. Perhaps parents should be more particular about the TV programs their babies watch.

Motor Development in Infancy

What is the primary factor influencing attainment of the major motor milestones?

Babies undergo rapid change during the first few years of life. Some changes are due to maturation, others to learning. **Maturation** occurs naturally according to the infant's own genetically determined, biological timetable of development. Many motor milestones, such as sitting, standing, and walking (shown in Figure 9.4) are primarily a result of maturation and ultimately depend on the growth and development of the central nervous system. But the rate at which these milestones are achieved is delayed when an infant is subjected to extremely unfavorable environmental conditions such as severe malnutrition or maternal and sensory deprivation. Cross-cultural research reveals that in some African cultures in Uganda and Kenya, mothers use special motor training techniques that enable their infants to attain some of the major motor milestones earlier than most infants in the United States (Kilbride & Kilbride, 1975; Super, 1981). But speeding up the attainment of motor skills has no lasting impact on development. Babies will walk, talk, and be toilet trained according to their own developmental schedules.

Although infants follow their own individual timetables, the basic motor skills usually appear in a particular sequence. Physical and motor development proceeds from the head downward to the trunk and legs. So, babies lift their heads before they sit, and they sit before they walk. Development also proceeds from the center of the body outward—trunk to shoulders to arms to fingers. Thus, control of the arms develops before control of the fingers.

The second process affecting development is learning, but learning cannot take place until particular areas of the brain mature. In other words, the child must be physically and neurologically ready to learn.

Figure 9.4

The Progression of Motor Development

Most infants develop motor skills in the sequence shown in the figure. The ages indicated are only averages, so normal, healthy infants may develop any of these milestones a few months earlier or several months later than the average. (From Frankenburg et al., 1992.)

Remember It!

1. Compared with a neonate, the number of reflexes you possess is
   a. much larger. c. the same.
   b. slightly larger. d. smaller.
2. Which of the following statements about infant sensory development is *not* true?
   a. Vision, hearing, taste, and smell are all fully developed at birth.
   b. Vision, hearing, taste, and smell are all functional at birth.
   c. Infants can show preferences in what they want to look at, hear, taste, and smell shortly after birth.
   d. Hearing is better developed at birth than vision.
3. Classical and operant conditioning and observational learning occur in the first few days of life. (true/false)
4. Two-month-old Carter likes to look at the soft, multicolored ball in his crib, but the new black-and-white ball has recently gained his attention. Habituation has occurred, meaning that
   a. Carter has gotten used to a stimulus (the multicolored ball).
   b. Carter no longer remembers the stimulus he has seen previously.
   c. Carter has a short attention span.
   d. a complex form of learning has taken place.
5. The primary factor influencing the attainment of the major motor milestones is
   a. experience. c. learning.
   b. maturation. d. habituation.

Answers: 1. d 2. a 3. true 4. a 5. b

EMOTIONAL DEVELOPMENT IN INFANCY

Temperament: How and When Does It Develop?

What is temperament, and what are the three temperament types identified by Thomas, Chess, and Birch?

José is usually cheerful, easygoing, and adaptable. Anna is always on the go, and she sticks with a problem until it is solved, but she gets upset easily. Their parents say the two children have always been that way. Is each baby born with an individual behavior style or characteristic way of responding to the environment—a particular **temperament**?

The New York Longitudinal Study was undertaken in 1956 to investigate temperament and its effect on development. Thomas, Chess, and Birch (1970) studied 2- to 3-month-old infants and followed them into adolescence and adulthood using observation, interviews with parents and teachers, and psychological tests. They found that "children do show distinct individuality in temperament in the first weeks of life independently of their parents' handling or personality style" (p. 104). Three general types of temperament emerged from the study.

"Easy" children—40% of the group—had generally pleasant moods, were adaptable, approached new situations and people positively, and established regular sleeping, eating, and elimination patterns. "Difficult" children—10% of the group—had generally unpleasant moods, reacted negatively to new situations and people, were intense in their emotional reactions, and showed irregularity of bodily functions. "Slow-to-warm-up" children—15% of the group—tended to withdraw, were slow to adapt, and were "somewhat negative in mood." The remaining 35% of the children studied were too inconsistent to categorize.

Thomas and others (1970) believe that personality is molded by the continuous interaction of temperament and environment. Although the environment can intensify, diminish, or modify inborn behavioral tendencies, "the original characteristics of temperament tend to persist in most children over the years" (p. 104). However, more recent studies suggest that even though temperament is believed to be heavily

temperament: A person's behavioral style or characteristic way of responding to the environment.

influenced by genes, environmental factors such as parents' childrearing style also strongly affect temperament (Richter et al., 2000). An easy child usually elicits a positive response from the parents, which reinforces the child's behavior and increases the likelihood that the behavioral style will continue. A difficult child, on the other hand, may stimulate hostility and resentment in parents and others, which, in turn, may perpetuate negative behavior.

Some aspects of temperament appear to be less persistent than others. Jerome Kagan (1996, 1997) studied high and low emotional reactivity provoked by unexpected and unfamiliar events in 462 infants and followed them through their preschool years. High-reactive infants became distressed, timid, fearful, and emotionally subdued in response to unfamiliar people and situations. Low-reactive infants were relatively bold, outgoing, and sociable in response to new situations.

Studies now suggest that temperament in early childhood can be a predictor of various behavioral problems that may appear later in childhood or in adolescence (Pierrehumbert et al., 2000). Children who are undercontrolled or impulsive at a young age tend to become aggressive, danger-seeking, impulsive adolescents (Hart et al., 1997) with strong negative emotions (Caspi & Silva, 1995). On the other hand, overcontrolled children have been found to be "more prone to social withdrawal" (Hart et al., 1997) and lacking in social potency as adolescents; that is, "they were submissive, not fond of leadership roles, and had little desire to influence others" (Caspi & Silva, 1995, p. 495).

Activity level seems to show the most consistency over time (Goldsmith et al., 1987; Korner et al., 1985). Researchers conducting twin studies (Emde et al., 1992; Plomin et al., 1990; Saudino et al., 1996) and adoption studies (Braungart et al., 1992) have found a genetic influence on activity level and on other aspects of temperament, such as mood/extraversion, inhibition to the unfamiliar (shyness), and task orientation.

Attachment

One of the most important concepts in developmental psychology is **attachment.** Attachment has to do with the impact of the early, close relationships formed between infants and their caregivers (Thompson, 2000). Human newborns are among the most helpless and dependent of all animal babies; thus, forming a strong attachment to a caregiver, often called *bonding,* is critically important to an infant's survival (Brazelton et al., 1975).

What precisely is the glue that binds infants and caregivers in the first place and sustains the bond over time? For many years it was believed that the main ingredient in infant–caregiver attachment was the fact that the caregiver provides the infant with the nourishment that sustains life. However, a series of classic studies conducted by psychologist Harry Harlow on attachment in rhesus monkeys suggests that physical nourishment alone is not enough to bind infants to their primary caregivers.

What did Harlow's studies reveal about maternal deprivation and attachment in infant monkeys?

attachment: The strong affectionate bond a child forms with the mother or primary caregiver.

surrogate: Substitute; someone or something that stands in place of someone or something else.

Attachment in Infant Monkeys: Like Humans in So Many Ways

Harlow found that the behavior of monkeys deprived of mothering was not unlike that of children raised in orphanages. Motherless monkeys would "sit in their cages and stare fixedly into space, circle their cages in a repetitive stereotyped manner and clasp their heads in their hands or arms and rock for long periods of time" (Harlow & Harlow, 1962, p. 138).

To investigate systematically the nature of attachment and the effects of maternal deprivation on infant monkeys, Harlow constructed two **surrogate** (artificial) monkey "mothers." One was a plain wire-mesh cylinder with a wooden head; the other was a wire-mesh cylinder that was padded, covered with soft terry cloth, and fitted with a somewhat more monkey-like head. A baby bottle could be attached to either surrogate mother for feeding.

Newborn monkeys were placed in individual cages where they had equal access to a cloth surrogate and a wire surrogate. The source of their nourishment (cloth or wire surrogate) was unimportant. "The infants developed a strong attachment to the cloth mothers and little or none to the wire mothers" (Harlow & Harlow, 1962, p. 141). Harlow found that it was contact comfort—the comfort supplied by bodily contact—rather than nourishment that formed the basis of the infant monkey's attachment to its mother.

The monkeys formed the same type of attachment to the cloth mothers as normal monkeys did to their real mothers. In both cases monkeys would cling to their mothers many hours each day and "run to them for comfort or reassurance when they are frightened" (Harlow, 1959, p. 73). If the cloth mother was not present when unfamiliar objects were placed in the cage, the monkey would huddle in the corner, clutching its head, rocking, sucking its thumb or toes, and crying in distress. But when the cloth mother was present, it would first cling to her and then explore and play with the unfamiliar objects.

If infant monkeys were placed with the cloth mother for the first 5½ months of life, their attachment was so strong that it persisted even after an 18-month separation. Their attachment to the cloth mother was almost identical to the attachment normal monkeys have to their real mothers, but their emotional development was not like that of normal monkeys. They would not interact with other monkeys, and they showed inappropriate aggression. Their sexual behavior was grossly abnormal, and they would not mate. If impregnated artificially, they became terrible mothers whose behavior ranged from ignoring their babies to violently abusing them (Harlow et al., 1971). The only aspect of development not affected was learning ability.

Harlow found that infant monkeys developed a strong attachment to a cloth-covered surrogate mother and little or no attachment to a wire surrogate mother—even when the wire mother provided nourishment.

The Necessity for Love Harlow's research reveals the disastrous effects of maternal deprivation on infant monkeys. Human infants, too, need love in order to grow physically and psychologically. Between 1900 and 1920 in the United States, the majority of infants under 1 year old who were placed in orphanages did not survive, even with adequate food and medical care (Montagu, 1962). Usually kept in cribs, the sides draped with sheets, these unfortunate infants were left to stare at the ceiling. Lacking a warm, close, personal caregiver and the all-important ingredient love, the infants who survived their first year failed to gain weight and grow normally—a condition known as *deprivation dwarfism* (Gardner, 1972). And they were severely retarded in their mental and motor development (Spitz, 1946). Another less extreme but still serious developmental disorder—*failure to thrive*—also results from insufficient attention and lack of affection. Studies continue to show that early and chronic sensory deprivation and separation from the primary caregiver are associated with impaired brain development (Anand & Scalzo, 2000).

For their very survival, infants need to become attached to someone. That person is most often the mother.

The Development of Attachment in Humans A close emotional relationship between the infant and the primary caregiver (typically the mother) is not present at birth but develops gradually. Such behavior appears to be driven more by nurture than by nature (van Ijzendoorn et al., 2000). The primary caregiver holds, strokes, and talks to the baby and responds to the baby's needs. In turn, the baby gazes at, listens to, and moves in synchrony with the caregiver's voice (Condon & Sander, 1974; Lester et al., 1985). Even crying can promote attachment: The caregiver is motivated to relieve the baby's distress and feels rewarded when the crying stops. Like Harlow's monkeys, babies cling to their mothers and when old enough to crawl, will move to stay near them.

According to Bowlby, when does the infant have a strong attachment to the mother?

John Bowlby (1951), a leading theorist on attachment, believes that to grow up mentally healthy, infants and young children "should experience a warm, intimate, and continuous relationship" that is mutually satisfying and enjoyable with their mother or a permanent mother substitute (p. 13). The infant's attachment to the mother develops over time and is usually quite strong by age 6 to 8 months (Bowlby, 1969). According to Bowlby, attachment behavior serves the evolutionary function of protecting the infant from danger (Bretherton, 1992).

separation anxiety: The fear and distress shown by toddlers when their parent leaves, occurring from 8 to 24 months and reaching a peak between 12 and 18 months.

stranger anxiety: A fear of strangers common in infants at about 6 months and increasing in intensity until about 12½ months, and then declining in the second year.

Once the attachment has formed, infants show **separation anxiety**—fear and distress when the parent leaves them. Occurring from about age 8 to 24 months, separation anxiety peaks between ages 12 and 18 months (Fox & Bell, 1990). Toddlers who previously voiced no distress when their parents left them with a babysitter may now scream when their parents leave.

At about 6 or 7 months of age, infants develop a fear of strangers called **stranger anxiety,** which increases in intensity until 12½ months and then declines in the second year (Marks, 1987). Stranger anxiety is greater in an unfamiliar setting, when the parent is not close at hand, and when a stranger abruptly approaches or touches the child. Interestingly, stranger anxiety is not directed at unfamiliar children until ages 19 to 30 months (P. K. Smith, 1979).

Stranger anxiety and separation anxiety in infants are not just Western phenomena. They are found in Israeli kibbutzim and in cultures as diverse as those of the Kung bushmen, rural Ganda, Navajo, and Guatemalan Maya (Super, 1981).

What are the four attachment patterns identified in infants?

Ainsworth's Study of Attachment: The Importance of Being Securely Attached

Practically all infants reared in a family develop an attachment to a familiar caregiver by the age of 2. But there are vast differences in the quality of attachment. In a classic study of mother–child attachment, Mary Ainsworth (1973, 1979) observed mother–child interactions in the home during the infants' first year and then again at age 12 months in a laboratory using a procedure called the "strange situation." Based on infants' reactions to their mothers after brief periods of separation, Ainsworth and others (1978; Main & Solomon, 1990) identified four patterns of attachment: secure, avoidant, resistant, and disorganized/disoriented.

Secure Attachment Securely attached infants (about 65% of American infants), although usually distressed when separated from their mother, eagerly seek to re-establish the connection and then show an interest in play. Moreover, securely attached infants use the mother as a safe base of operation from which to explore, much as Harlow's monkeys did when unfamiliar objects were placed in their cages. Securely attached infants are typically more responsive, obedient, cooperative, and content and also cry less than other infants.

Securely attached infants are likely to grow up to be more sociable, more effective with peers, more interested in exploring the environment, and generally more competent than less securely attached infants (Masters, 1981). Their interactions with friends tend to be more harmonious and less controlling (Park & Waters, 1989). Attachment style even seems to have an impact on the quality of adult love relationships (Collins, 1996).

Fathers of securely attached infants tend to be more agreeable and extroverted and to have happier marriages than fathers of insecurely attached infants (Belsky, 1996). Mothers of securely attached infants are typically more sensitive, accepting, affectionate, and responsive to their infants' cries and needs (Isabella et al., 1989; Pederson et al., 1990). This observation contradicts the notion that mothers who respond promptly to their infant's cries end up with a spoiled baby who cries more. And, contrary to some speculations, the facial appearance of infants who have been disfigured by cleft lip or cleft palate does not appear to have any adverse effect on early infant–mother relationships. In fact, one study indicated that most of the infants with clefts enjoyed a secure maternal attachment throughout the first 2 years of life (Maris et al., 2000).

Avoidant Attachment Infants with an avoidant attachment pattern (approximately 20% of American infants) are usually not responsive to their mother when she is present and not troubled when she leaves. When the parent returns, the infant may actively avoid contact with her or, at least, not be quick to greet her. In short, these infants do not act much more attached to a parent than to a stranger. Mothers of avoidant infants tend to show little affection and to be generally unresponsive to their infants' needs and cries.

Resistant Attachment Prior to a period of separation, infants who show resistant attachment (10–15% of American infants) seek and prefer close contact with their mother. Yet they do not tend to branch out and explore like securely attached infants. And when the mother returns to the room after a period of separation, the resistant infant displays anger and may push the mother away or hit her. When picked up, the infant is hard to comfort and may continue crying.

Disorganized/Disoriented The disorganized/disoriented attachment pattern (5–10% of American infants) is the most puzzling and apparently the least secure pattern. When reunited with the mother, the infant exhibits contradictory and disoriented responses. Rather than looking at the mother while being held, the child may purposely look away or approach the mother with an expressionless or depressed demeanor. Also characteristic are a dazed and vacant facial expression and a peculiar, frozen posture after being calmed by the mother.

Some studies show that certain psychological disorders in the mothers of infants can affect the nature of attachment between the mother and child. Studies of the patterns of mother–infant interaction indicate that depression is related to insecure attachment (Hipwell et al., 2000). Other researchers have studied infant–caregiver attachment in foster relationships. In these settings, the primary factor affecting attachment seems to be the age of the infant at the time of placement in a foster home. Children who were less than 1 year old when placed tended to develop secure attachments, while those who were older than 1 year when placed were more likely to develop insecure attachments (Stovall and Dozier, 2000).

Secure attachment is the most common pattern across cultures. However, cross-cultural research revealed a higher incidence of insecure attachment patterns in Israel, Japan, and West Germany than in the United States (Collins & Gunnar, 1990). Ainsworth's procedure may not be valid for all cultures.

The Father–Child Relationship

What are the typical differences in the ways mothers and fathers interact with their children?

Mother–child rather than father–child relationships have been the traditional focus of research. But this is changing because of the greater child-rearing responsibility some fathers are assuming. Some fathers even elect to stay home with the children, while the mother works outside the home (Grbich, 1994). Fathers can be as responsive and competent as mothers when they voluntarily assume child-rearing responsibilities (Parke et al., 1972; Roberts & Moseley, 1996), and their attachments can be just as strong. Yet even when attachment to both parents is strong, infants in the first year tend to prefer their mothers for comfort when they are in distress (Hartup, 1989). In general, fathers do not appear to be as affectionate as mothers (Berndt et al., 1993; Hoosain & Roopnarine, 1994).

In the United States, as well as in many other cultures around the world, mothers spend more time in caretaking—feeding, bathing, changing—and fathers generally spend more time playing with their infants (Lamb, 1987). Mother play and father play also seem to differ. Fathers engage in more exciting and arousing physical play (McCormick & Kennedy, 2000); mothers tend to talk more to their children, provide toys, and play more conventional games with them. Mothers are more likely to cushion their children against overstimulation, while fathers tend to pour it on, producing a wider range of arousal. Fathers tend "to get children worked up, negatively or positively, with fear as well as delight, forcing them to learn to regulate their feelings" (Lamb, quoted in Roberts & Moseley, 1996, p. 53).

There appear to be qualitative differences in the ways mothers and fathers typically interact with their infants. Mothers primarily comfort, reassure, and provide a safe harbor from which the infant may launch out and then return to. Fathers primarily stimulate, challenge, and help children develop a sense of individual identity (Moradi, cited in Adler, 1997). While a mother may instill a sense of caution in a child—"be careful"—a father may encourage the child (especially if male) to be more daring. Generally, fathers appear to be more likely than mothers to give children "a longer leash," letting them crawl farther away, up to twice as far as mothers usually allow. And fathers remain farther away as the infant explores novel stimuli and situations; mothers tend to move in closer when the child confronts the unknown.

Fathers provide an important influence on children's development. They tend to engage in more physical play with their children, especially boys, and encourage them to be active and daring.

Ideally, children need both sets of influences. Father–child interaction has many enduring positive influences on children. Children who experience regular interaction with their fathers tend to have higher IQs, and to do better in social situations and at coping with frustration than children lacking such interaction. They also persist longer in solving problems, and are less impulsive and less likely to become violent (Adler, 1997; Bishop & Lane, 2000; Roberts & Moseley, 1996).

When the mother and the father have a good relationship, fathers tend to spend more time with and interact more with their children (Willoughby & Glidden, 1995). Furthermore, they tend to develop a more intense and positive relationship with the infant (Lamb & Elster, 1985) and to maintain it in middle childhood (Brody et al., 1986). But, sadly, about 38% of American children live apart from their biological fathers today—more than twice the percentage (17.5%) who did in 1960. And more than half of American children will not have a father present for at least part of their childhood (Shapiro & Schrof, 1995). Some research suggests that absence of the father is associated with various negative outcomes in American families. Among these are cognitive deficits that can lead to poorer school performance, lower grade point average, lower school attendance, and higher dropout rate. Father absence is also related to children's reduced self-confidence in problem solving, low self-esteem, depression, suicidal thoughts, and behavioral problems such as aggression and delinquency (Bishop & Lane, 2000).

Remember It!

1. Which statement best describes Thomas, Chess, and Birch's thinking about temperament?
   a. Temperament develops gradually as a result of parental handling and personality.
   b. Temperament is inborn and is not influenced by the environment.
   c. Temperament is inborn but can be modified by the family and the environment.
   d. Temperament is set at birth and is unchangeable.
2. Infants raised with adequate physical care but without the attention of a close, personal caregiver often become mentally and/or physically retarded. (true/false)
3. Which of the following was *not* true of infant monkeys raised with surrogate mothers?
   a. They showed inappropriate aggression.
   b. They would not interact with other monkeys.
   c. Their learning ability was impaired.
   d. They became abusive mothers.
4. A strong attachment between infant and mother usually occurs shortly after birth. (true/false)
5. Ainsworth found that most infants had secure attachment. (true/false)
6. The most common type of interaction most fathers have with their infants is in the context of caregiving–feeding, changing, and bathing. (true/false)

Answers: 1. c 2. true 3. c 4. false 5. true 6. false

PIAGET'S THEORY OF COGNITIVE DEVELOPMENT

How does a child's mind differ from an adult's? Thanks to the work of Swiss psychologist Jean Piaget (PEE-ah-ZHAY), psychologists have gained insights into the cognitive, or mental, processes of children—how they think, perceive, and gain knowledge about the world.

Piaget maintained that children are active participants in their own cognitive development. Rather than being empty vessels that can be filled with knowledge, children discover and construct knowledge through their own activity. According to Piaget, cognitive development begins with a few basic **schemas**—cognitive structures or concepts used to identify and interpret objects, events, and other information in the environment. Confronted with new objects, events, experiences, and information, children try to fit them into their existing schemas, a process known as **assimilation.** But not everything can be assimilated into the existing schemas. If children call a stranger "Daddy" or the neighbor's cat "doggie," assimilation has led them to make an error. When parents and others correct them, or when they discover for themselves that something cannot be assimilated into an existing schema, children will use a process known as accommodation. In **accommodation,** existing schemas are modified or new schemas are created to process new information. It is through the processes of assimilation and accommodation, then, that schemas are formed, differentiated, and broadened.

schema: Piaget's term for a cognitive structure or concept used to identify and interpret information.

assimilation: The process by which new objects, events, experiences, or information are incorporated into existing schemas.

accommodation: The process by which existing schemas are modified and new schemas are created to incorporate new objects, events, experiences, or information.

sensorimotor stage: Piaget's first stage of cognitive development (ages birth to 2 years), culminating with the development of object permanence and the beginning of representational thought.

The Cognitive Stages of Development: Climbing the Steps to Cognitive Maturity

What did Piaget claim regarding the stages of cognitive development?

Piaget formulated a comprehensive theory that systematically describes and explains how intellect develops (Piaget, 1963b, 1964; Piaget & Inhelder, 1969). He claimed that cognitive development occurs in a sequence of four stages: sensorimotor, preoperational, concrete operations, and formal operations. These stages occur in a fixed sequence in which the accomplishments of one stage provide the foundation for the next stage. Yet each stage represents a qualitatively different way of thinking, reasoning, and understanding the world. Piaget believed that children around the world progress through the four stages in the same order, but that there are individual differences in the rate at which they pass through them. The transition from one stage to another is not abrupt, but gradual, and during such a transition, children may show characteristics of both stages.

What occurs during Piaget's sensorimotor stage?

The Sensorimotor Stage (Ages Birth to 2 Years) In the first stage, the **sensorimotor stage,** infants gain an understanding of the world through their senses and their motor activities (actions or body movements), hence the name *sensorimotor.* At this stage, the child's intelligence is one of action rather than of thought, and it is confined to objects that are present and events that are directly perceived. The child learns to respond to and manipulate objects and to use them in goal-directed activity.

Developed toward the end of his career, Piaget's theory of action reflected a change in his thinking that elevated action to the level of being the primary source of knowledge. Perception and language were assigned more secondary roles. To Piaget, action—so prominent in the sensorimotor stage of development—is not random, but has organization, as well as logic. Action in the sensorimotor stage is physical at first but becomes transformed into "mental action" and mental representation (Beilin & Fireman, 1999).

At birth, infants are incapable of thought, and they are unable to differentiate themselves from others or from the environment. Living in a world of the here and

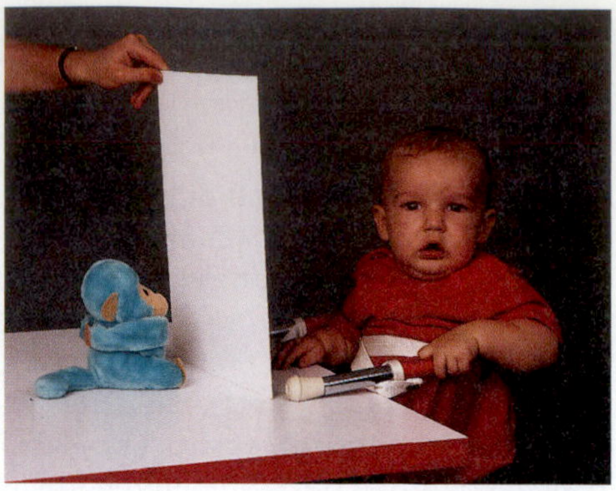

According to Piaget, this infant has not yet developed object permanence—the understanding that objects continue to exist even when they are out of sight. He makes no attempt to look for the toy behind the screen.

now, infants are aware that objects exist only when they can actually see them. Take a stuffed animal away from a 5-month-old and it ceases to exist, as far as the child is concerned. At this age, out of sight is always out of mind.

The major achievement of the sensorimotor stage is the development of **object permanence,** which is the realization that objects (including people) continue to exist even when they are out of sight. The concept of object permanence develops gradually and is complete when the child is able to represent objects mentally in their absence. The attainment of this ability marks the end of the sensorimotor period.

What cognitive limitations characterize a child's thinking during the preoperational stage?

The Preoperational Stage (Ages 2 to 7 Years) The **preoperational stage** is a period of rapid development in language. Children become increasingly able to represent objects and events mentally with words and images. Their thinking is no longer restricted to objects and events that are directly perceived and present in the environment. Evidence of representational thought is a child's ability to imitate the behavior of a person who is no longer present (*deferred imitation*). Other evidence is the child's ability to engage in imaginary play using one object to stand for another, such as using a broom to represent a horse.

Although thinking at the preoperational stage is more advanced than at the previous stage, it is still quite restricted. Thinking is dominated by perception, and children at this stage exhibit egocentrism in thought. They believe that everyone sees what they see, thinks as they think, and feels as they feel.

At this stage children also show *animistic thinking,* believing that inanimate objects such as a tree, the sun, and a doll are alive and have feelings and intentions (Piaget, 1960, 1963a). That explains why 2-year-old Austin says "hello" to his food before he eats it, and why 3-year-old Hannah shows distress when her brother throws her doll into her toy box. Children at this stage also believe that all things, even the moon and clouds, are made for and usually by people.

The preoperational stage is so named because children are not yet able to perform mental operations (manipulations) that follow logical rules. Children at this stage are not aware that a given quantity of matter (a given number, mass, area, weight, or volume of matter) remains the same if it is rearranged or changed in its appearance, as long as nothing is added or taken away. This concept is known as **conservation.**

If you know a child of preschool age, try the conservation experiment illustrated in the *Try It!* at the top of the next page.

Centration and reversibility are two restrictions in children's thinking that lead them to wrong conclusions. **Centration** is the tendency to focus on only one dimension of a stimulus and ignore the other dimensions. For example, in the *Try It!* the child focuses on the tallness of the glass and fails to notice that it is also narrower. At this stage, taller means more.

Preoperational children have not developed **reversibility** in thinking—the realization that after any change in its shape, position, or order, matter can be returned

object permanence: The realization that objects continue to exist even when they can no longer be perceived.

preoperational stage: Piaget's second stage of cognitive development (ages 2 to 7 years), characterized by rapid development of language and thinking governed by perception rather than logic.

conservation: The concept that a given quantity of matter remains the same despite rearrangement or change in its appearance, as long as nothing is added or taken away.

centration: A preoperational child's tendency to focus on only one dimension of a stimulus and ignore other dimensions.

reversibility: The realization that any change in the shape, position, or order of matter can be reversed mentally.

Try It!

Show a preschooler two glasses of the same size and then fill them with the same amount of juice. After the child agrees they are the same, pour the juice from one glass into a taller, narrower glass and place that glass beside the other original one. Now ask the child if the two glasses have the same amount of juice, or if one glass has more than the other. Children at this stage will insist that the taller, narrower glass has more juice, although they will quickly agree that you neither added juice nor took any away.

mentally to its original state. In the *Try It!* the preoperational child cannot mentally return the poured juice to the original glass and realize that the two glasses of juice are equal.

Children at the preoperational stage also have difficulty classifying objects—that is, deciding which ones are similar enough to be in the same category. Piaget called this *class inclusion*. You can observe this concept in action by doing the next *Try It!*

Try It!

Ask a child aged 2–7 to look at the flowers shown below. Ask the child, "Are there more yellow flowers or more flowers?" The preoperational child will respond, "More yellow flowers," because he or she fails to understand that both yellow and blue flowers are included in the category "flowers." (Adapted from Berk, 2001 p. 225.)

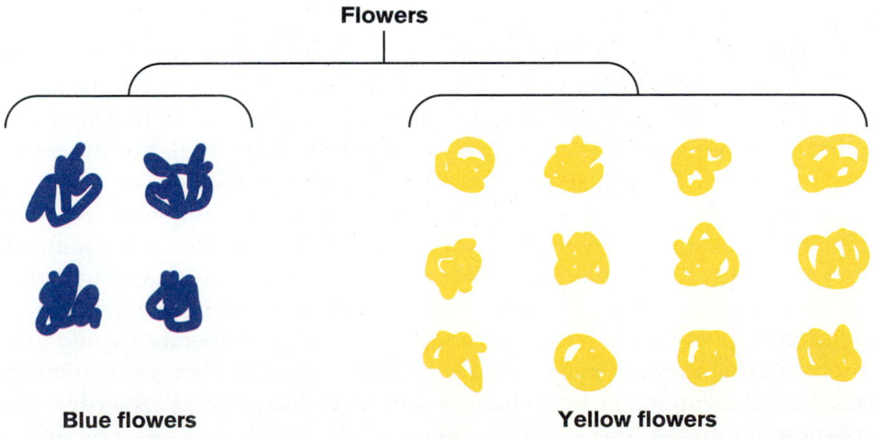

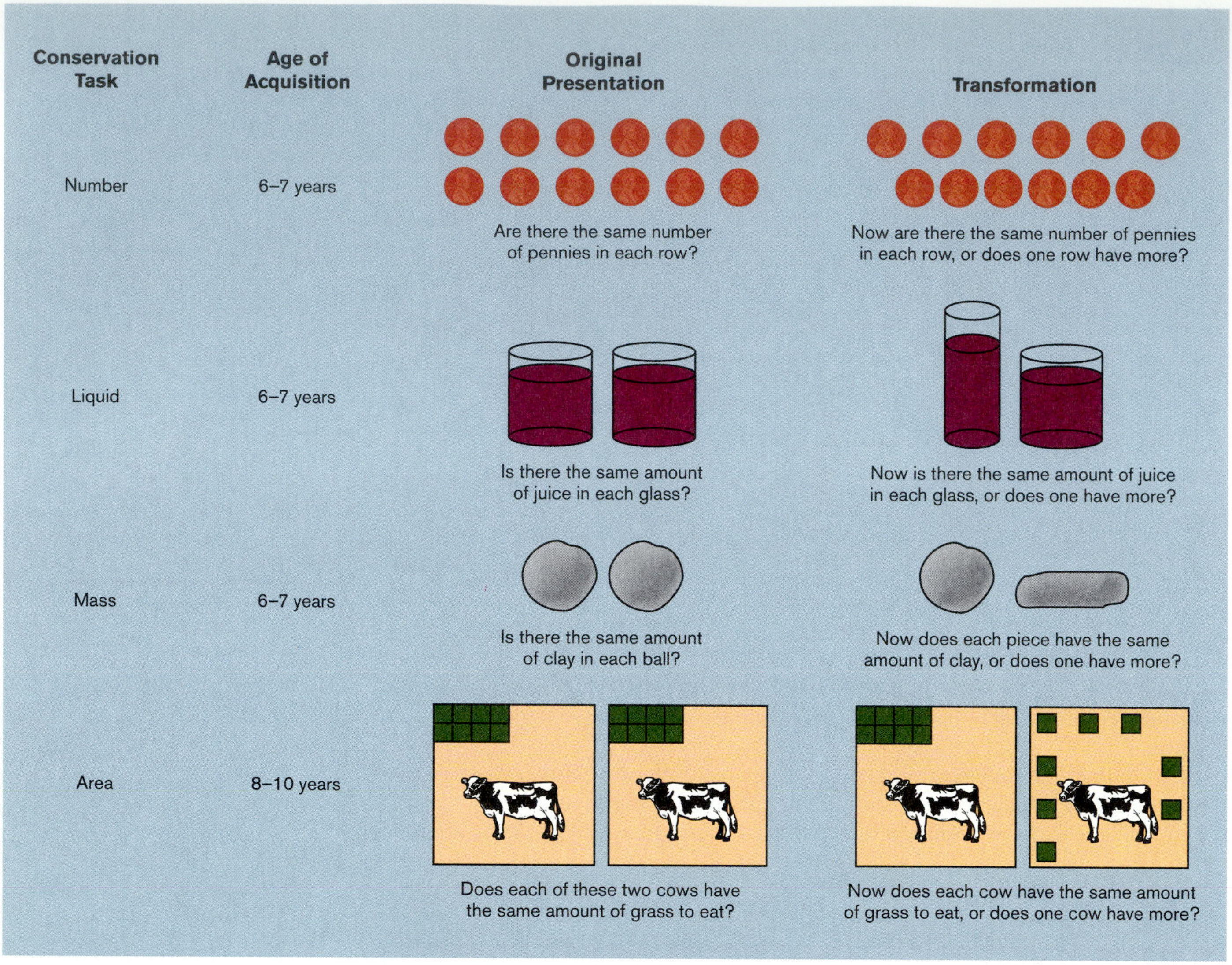

Figure 9.5

Piaget's Conservation Tasks

Pictured here are several of Piaget's conservation tasks. The ability to answer correctly develops over time, according to the ages indicated for each task. (From Berk, 1994a.)

What cognitive abilities do children acquire during the concrete operations stage?

concrete operations stage: Piaget's third stage of cognitive development (ages 7 to 11 years), during which a child acquires the concepts of reversibility and conservation and is able to apply logical thinking to concrete objects.

The Concrete Operations Stage (Ages 7 to 11 or 12 Years) In the third stage, the **concrete operations stage,** children gradually overcome the obstacles to logical thought associated with the preoperational period. Their thinking is less egocentric, and they come to realize that other people have thoughts and feelings that may be different from their own. Children acquire the ability to carry out mentally the operations essential for logical thought. They are able to *decenter* their thinking, that is, to attend to two or more dimensions of a stimulus at the same time. They can also understand the concept of reversibility, which is crucial in problem solving. Finally, during this stage children acquire the concept of conservation.

Children at this stage, however, are able to apply logical operations only to concrete problems that they can perceive directly. They cannot apply these mental operations to verbal, abstract, or hypothetical problems. Surprisingly the concepts of conservation of number, substance (liquid or mass), length, area, weight, and volume are not all acquired at once. They come in a certain sequence and usually at specific ages (see Figure 9.5).

Review & Reflect 9.1 Piaget's Stages of Cognitive Development

↓ know these

Stage		Description
Sensorimotor (0 to 2 years)		Infants experience the world through their senses, actions, and body movements. At the end of this stage, toddlers develop the concept of object permanence and can mentally represent objects in their absence.
Preoperational (2 to 7 years)		Children are able to represent objects and events mentally with words and images. They can engage in imaginary play (pretend), using one object to represent another. Their thinking is dominated by their perceptions, and they are unable to consider more than one dimension of an object at the same time (centration). Their thinking is egocentric; that is, they fail to consider the perspective of others.
Concrete operational (7 to 11 or 12 years)		Children at this stage become able to think logically in concrete situations. They acquire the concepts of conservation and reversibility, can order objects in a series, and can classify them according to multiple dimensions.
Formal operational (11 or 12 years and beyond)		At this stage, adolescents learn to think logically in abstract situations, learn to test hypotheses systematically, and become interested in the world of ideas. Not all people attain full formal operational thinking.

The Formal Operations Stage (Ages 11 or 12 Years and Beyond) The **formal operations stage** is Piaget's fourth and final stage of cognitive development. At this stage adolescents can apply reversibility and conservation to abstract, verbal, or hypothetical situations and to problems in the past, present, or future. Teenagers can comprehend abstract subjects such as philosophy and politics. They become interested in the world of ideas, and they begin to formulate theories.

Not all people attain full formal operational thinking (Kuhn, 1984; Neimark, 1981), but high school math and science experience seems to facilitate it (Sharp et al., 1979). Failure to achieve formal operational thinking has been associated with below-average scores on intelligence tests (Inhelder, 1966).

Review & Reflect 9.1 provides a summary of Piaget's four stages.

What new capability characterizes the formal operations stage?

formal operations stage: Piaget's fourth and final stage, characterized by the ability to apply logical thinking to abstract problems and hypothetical situations.

An Evaluation of Piaget's Contribution

Although Piaget's genius and his monumental contribution to scientists' knowledge of mental development are rarely disputed, his methods and some of his findings and conclusions have been criticized (Halford, 1989). It now seems clear that children are more advanced cognitively and adults are less competent cognitively than Piaget believed (Flavell, 1985, 1992; Mareschal, 2000; Siegler, 1991).

Piaget was limited in the information he could gather about infants, because he relied on observation and on the interview technique, which depended on verbal responses. Newer techniques requiring nonverbal responses—sucking, looking, heart-rate changes, reaching, and head turning—have shown that infants and young children are more competent than Piaget proposed (Flavell, 1992; Johnson, 2000). For example, recent research indicates that an infant's knowledge of hidden objects may be more advanced than Piaget originally believed (Mareschal, 2000). And there are some signs that awareness of object permanence may begin as early as 3½ months (Baillargeon & DeVos, 1991). And whereas Piaget claimed that deferred imitation begins in the preoperational stage, some research (Heimann & Meltzoff, 1996; Meltzoff, 1988b) has demonstrated that even 9-month-olds are able to imitate actions they have observed as long as 24 hours earlier.

Other studies have shown that preoperational children are able to take the perspective of another. For example, 4-year-old children can adjust their speech when talking to 2-year-olds (Shatz & Gelman, 1973), and they can understand the emotions of characters in a story (Ford, 1979).

Few developmental psychologists believe that cognitive development takes place in the general stagelike fashion proposed by Piaget. If it did, children's cognitive functioning would be similar across all cognitive tasks and content areas (Flavell, 1992). Neo-Piagetians believe that while there are important general patterns in cognitive development, there is also more variability in how children perform on certain tasks than Piaget described (Case, 1992). This variability results from expertise children acquire in different content areas through extensive practice and experience (Flavell, 1992). Even adults who use formal operational reasoning fall back on concrete operational reasoning when they approach a task outside their areas of expertise.

Cross-cultural studies have affirmed the universality of the types of reasoning and the sequence of stages formulated by Piaget. But cross-cultural research has also revealed differences in the rates of cognitive development in various domains. Whereas Piaget's subjects began to acquire the concept of conservation between ages 5 and 7, Australian Aboriginal children show this change between the ages of 10 and 13 (Dasen, 1994). Yet the Aboriginal children function at the concrete operations stage earlier on spatial tasks than on quantification (counting) tasks, while the reverse is true for Western children.

According to Flavell (1996), "Piaget's greatest contribution was to found the field of cognitive development as we currently know it" (p. 200). However, Piaget's theories, remain works in progress because of their continuing impact on psychology and education (Beilin & Fireman, 1999).

VYGOTSKY'S SOCIOCULTURAL VIEW OF COGNITIVE DEVELOPMENT

In Vygotsky's view, how do private speech and scaffolding contribute to cognitive development?

Russian psychologist Lev Vygotsky (1896–1934) strongly rejected Piaget's individualistic view and offered his own theory that each individual's quest for cognitive growth and development is forged within a sociocultural environment.

Vygotsky (1934/1986) maintained that human infants come equipped with basic skills such as perception, the ability to pay attention, and certain capacities of memory not unlike those of many other animal species. During the first 2 years of life, these skills grow and develop naturally through direct experiences and interactions with the child's sociocultural world. In due course, children develop the mental ability to represent objects, activities, ideas, people, and relationships in a variety of ways, but primarily through language (speech). With their new ability to represent ideas, activities, and so on through speech, children are often observed "talking to themselves." Vygotsky believed that talking to oneself—*private speech*—is a key component in cognitive development. Through private speech, children can specify the components of a problem and verbalize steps in a process to help them work through puzzling activities and situations. As young children develop greater competence, private speech fades into barely audible mumbling and muttering, and finally becomes simply thinking.

Vygotsky saw a strong connection among social experience, speech, and cognitive development. He also maintained that a child's readiness to learn resides within a zone of proximal (or potential) development. This zone, according to Vygotsky, is a range of cognitive tasks that the child cannot yet perform alone but can learn to perform with the instruction, help, and guidance of a parent, teacher, or more advanced peer. Laura Berk (1994b) explains it well: "As children engage in cooperative dialogues with more mature partners, they take the language of these dialogues, make it part of their private speech, and use this speech to organize their independent efforts in the same way" (p. 256).

Followers of Vygotsky advocate the use of an instructional technique known as *scaffolding*—in which a teacher or parent adjusts the quality and degree of help to fit the child's present level of ability or performance. In scaffolding, more direct instruction is given, at first, for unfamiliar tasks (Maccoby, 1992). But as the child shows increasing competence, the scaffolder (teacher or parent) gradually withdraws from direct and active teaching, and the child may continue toward independent mastery of the task.

Contemporary researchers have found widespread evidence to support many of Vygotsky's ideas (Berk, 1994b).

This father teaching his daughter to ride a bike is using Vygotsky's technique called scaffolding. *A parent or other teacher provides direct and continuous instruction at the beginning of the learning process and then gradually withdraws from active teaching as the child becomes more proficient at the new task or skill.*

COGNITIVE DEVELOPMENT: THE INFORMATION-PROCESSING APPROACH

What three cognitive abilities have information-processing researchers studied extensively?

Piaget's perspective on cognitive development took the form of a single, unified theory of how children learn to reason. But many researchers have pointed to inadequacies in Piaget's theory. Prominent among them are psychologists who study cognitive development using the information-processing approach (Klahr, 1992; Kuhn, 1992). As we discussed in Chapter 6, the information-processing approach views the human mind as an exceedingly complex system that functions like a computer in many ways.

Developmental psychologists using this approach study how information-processing capabilities develop and change with age. Researchers using the information-processing have done extensive work on three cognitive abilities: attention, memory, and metacognition.

Attention

Preschool children have a short attention span and are easily distracted (except perhaps when they are watching a TV show like *Blue's Clues*). But the ability to focus and sustain attention on an appropriate, narrow range of stimuli develops rapidly throughout childhood. Attention becomes less random and more controlled, less reactive and more actively planned. During the course of their development, children learn to become more selective in where they focus their attention, their attention span increases, and they become increasingly capable of filtering out meaningless or irrelevant stimuli in order to concentrate on the information that matters most.

Memory

The one aspect of cognition that seems most closely analogous to computer processing is memory. As you recall from Chapter 6, the three processes in memory are encoding, storage, and retrieval. All three are necessary for creating and retrieving a memory—or a file in a computer. Like other aspects of cognitive development, memory develops and improves as individuals mature.

Short-term memory develops dramatically during an infant's first year. Babies under 8 months of age who watch an object being hidden have trouble remembering its location if they are distracted for a short time and are not allowed to reach for the object immediately—out of sight, out of short-term memory. At 15 months, though, children's short-term memory has developed to the point that they can remember where an object is hidden even when they are not allowed to reach for it until 10 seconds have passed (Bell & Fox, 1992).

Children use strategies for improving memory increasingly as they mature cognitively. One universal strategy for holding information in short-term memory is *rehearsal*—mentally repeating information over and over. You use rehearsal when you silently repeat a new phone number long enough to dial it. Certain aspects of rehearsal may be observed in preschoolers, but generally they have not learned how to use it effectively to help them retain information (Bjorklund & Coyle, 1995). But rehearsal becomes a more valuable strategy for storing information by the time children reach age 6, and the majority of children use rehearsal routinely by age 8 (Lovett & Flavell, 1990).

Organization is a very practical strategy for storing information in such a way that it can be retrieved without difficulty. By about age 9, children tend to use organization to help them remember. *Elaboration,* another useful strategy, is not widely used until age 11 or older (Schneider & Pressley, 1989). Elaboration requires creating relationships or connections between items that are to be remembered but are not of the same category and thus have no inherent connection.

Metacognition: Theory of Mind

A fundamental developmental task for children is coming to understand how people may differ greatly in what they know and what they believe (Miller, 2000). Reaching a level of cognitive maturity in which an individual is aware of his or her own thoughts and has an understanding about the nature of thought (how "thinking" operates) involves acquiring what is referred to as a *theory of mind.* More broadly, this state of mental maturity is known as *metacognition.* We use metacognition when we see ourselves and others as having various mental states such as beliefs, perceptions, and desires (Johnson, 2000). Children learn very young (at about 3 years old) that people, including themselves, have different mental states during thinking, remembering, forgetting, pretending, wishing, imagining, guessing, and daydreaming. In short, they can distinguish between thinking and other mental states.

Some research suggests that children as young as 1½ are aware when adults are imitating their behavior, gestures, or words and have been observed purposely testing the adults to see if the "imitation" will continue (Aspendorf et al., 1996). Children older than 2½ know the difference between reality and pretending. And 3-year-olds typically know that thinking is an activity that occurs inside one's head and that they can think about something without seeing, hearing, or touching it (Flavell et al., 1995). Deficits in the development of metacognition have been identified in children with autism (Jarrold et al., 2000) and schizophrenia (Pilowsky et al., 2000; Sarfati, 2000).

Even though it has some shortcomings, the information-processing approach appears promising as a means for expanding scientific knowledge of cognitive development.

Remember It!

1. Which statement reflects Piaget's thinking about the stages of cognitive development?
   a. All people pass through the same stages but not necessarily in the same order.
   b. All people progress through the stages in the same order but not at the same rate.
   c. All people progress through the stages in the same order and at the same rate.
   d. Very bright children sometimes skip stages.
2. Three-year-old Samuel says "airplane!" when he sees a helicopter for the first time. He is using the process Piaget called (assimilation/accommodation).
3. Four-year-old Madeleine rolls a ball of clay into a sausage shape to make "more" clay. Her actions demonstrate that she has *not* acquired the concept of
   a. reversibility. c. centration.
   b. animism. d. conservation.
4. Not all individuals reach the stage of formal operations. (true/false)
5. Match the stage with the relevant concept(s).

   ____ (1) abstract thought
   ____ (2) conservation, reversibility
   ____ (3) object permanence
   ____ (4) egocentrism, centration

   a. concrete operations stage
   b. sensorimotor stage
   c. formal operations stage
   d. preoperational stage
6. Vygotsky believed that children's private speech slows their cognitive growth. (true/false)
7. Researchers who focus on how attention, memory, and metacognition develop and change with age are using the ______________ approach.

Answers: 1. b 2. assimilation 3. d 4. true 5. (1) c (2) a (3) b (4) d 6. false 7. information-processing

LANGUAGE DEVELOPMENT

At birth, the infant's only means of communication is crying, but at age 17, the average high school graduate has a vocabulary of 80,000 words (Miller & Gildea, 1987). From age 18 months to 5 years, the child acquires about 14,000 words, an amazing average of 9 new words per day (Rice, 1989). The fact that children acquire language so rapidly is one of the most enduring mysteries of human cognition (Gómez & Gerken, 2000).

But children do much more than simply add new words to their vocabulary. In the first 5 years of life, they also acquire an understanding of the way words are put together to form sentences (syntax) and the way language is used in social situations. Children acquire most of their language without any formal teaching and discover the rules of language on their own.

The Stages of Language Development: The Orderly Progression of Language

What are the stages of language development from cooing through the acquisition of grammatical rules?

Infants begin to communicate long before they utter their first words. During their first few months, they communicate distress or displeasure through crying, although this is not actually their intent (Shatz, 1983). The cry is simply their innate reaction to an unpleasant internal state, such as hunger, thirst, discomfort, or pain. Intentional or not, the cry usually gets results from a parent or caretaker who is motivated to relieve the baby's discomfort and end the auditory assault.

Cooing and Babbling During the second or third month, infants begin cooing—repeatedly uttering vowel sounds such as "ah" and "oo." Even at this young age, the infant can carry on conversations with a parent or caregiver, each vocalizing in turn, and the infant moving in synchrony with the adult's voice.

At about 6 months, infants begin **babbling.** They utter **phonemes**—the basic speech sounds of any language, which form words when combined. Consonant–vowel combinations are repeated in a string, like "ma-ma-ma" or "ba-ba-ba." During the first part of the babbling stage, infants babble all the basic speech sounds that occur in all the languages of the world. Language up to this point seems to be biologically determined, because all babies throughout the world, even deaf children, vocalize this same range of speech sounds.

At about 8 months, babies begin to focus attention on those speech sounds (phonemes) common to their native tongue and on the rhythm and intonation of the language. Gradually they cease making the sounds not found in their native language. At about 1 year, a French-speaking child's babbling sounds like French, and an English-speaking child's babbling sounds like English (Levitt & Wang, 1991). Deaf children who are exposed to sign language from birth babble manually. That is, they make the hand movements that represent the phonemes in sign language (Petitto & Marentette, 1991).

The One-Word Stage At about 1 year, the babbling stage gives way to the one-word stage, and infants utter their first real words. The first words usually represent objects that move or those that infants can act on or interact with. Early words usually include food, animals, and toys—"cookie," "mama," "dada," "doggie," and "ball," to name a few (Nelson, 1973).

Sometimes infants use one-word sentences, called *holophrases,* in which a single word is used to convey different meanings depending on the context. For example, "cookie" can mean "This is a cookie," "I want a cookie," or, if the child is looking down from a high chair, "The cookie is on the floor."

From 13 to 18 months of age, children markedly increase their vocabulary (Woodward et al., 1994), and by 2 years it consists of about 270 words (Brown, 1973). Initially a child's understanding of words differs from that of an adult. On the basis of some shared feature and because they lack the correct word, children may apply a word to a broader range of objects than is appropriate. This is known as **overextension.** For example, any man may be called "dada," any four-legged animal, "doggie." **Underextension** occurs, too, when children fail to apply a word to other members of the class. The family's poodle is a "doggie," but the German shepherd next door is not.

The Two-Word Stage and Telegraphic Speech Between 18 and 20 months, when the vocabulary is about 50 words, children begin to put nouns, verbs, and adjectives together in two-word phrases and sentences. At this stage children depend to a great extent on gesture, tone, and context to convey their meaning (Slobin, 1972). Depending on intonation, their sentences may indicate questions, statements, or possession. Children adhere to a rigid word order. You might hear "mama drink," "drink milk," or "mama milk," but not "drink mama," "milk drink," or "milk mama."

At about 2½ years, children begin to use short sentences, which may contain three or more words. Labeled **telegraphic speech** by Roger Brown (1973), these short sentences follow a rigid word order and contain only essential content words, leaving out plurals, possessives, conjunctions, articles, and prepositions. Telegraphic speech reflects the child's understanding of syntax—the rules governing how words are ordered in a sentence. When a third word is added to a sentence, it usually fills in the word missing from the two-word sentence (for example, "Mama drink milk").

Suffixes, Function Words, and Grammatical Rules After using telegraphic speech for a time, children gradually begin to add modifiers to make words more precise. Suffixes and function words—pronouns, articles, conjunctions, and preposi-

babbling: Vocalization of the basic speech sounds (phonemes), which begins between 4 and 6 months.

phonemes: The basic speech sounds in any language that, when combined, form words.

overextension: The act of using a word, on the basis of some shared feature, to apply to a broader range of objects than appropriate.

underextension: Restricting the use of a word to only a few, rather than to all, members of a class of objects.

telegraphic speech: Short sentences that follow a strict word order and contain only essential content words.

Table 9.2 Language Development during the First 3 Years of Life

Age	Language Activity
2–3 months	Makes cooing sounds when alone; responds with smiles and cooing when talked to
20 weeks	Mixes various vowel and consonant sounds with cooing
6 months	Babbles; utters phonemes of all languages
8 months	Focuses on the phonemes, rhythm, and intonation of native tongue
12 months	Says single words; mimics sounds; understands some words
18–20 months	Uses two-word sentences; has vocabulary of about 50 words; overextension common
24 months	Has vocabulary of about 270 words; acquires suffixes and function words in a fixed sequence
30 months	Uses telegraphic speech
36 months	Begins acquisition of grammar rules; overregularization common

tions—are acquired in a fixed sequence, although the rate of acquisition varies (Brown, 1973; Maratsos, 1983).

Children pick up grammatical rules intuitively and apply them rigidly. **Overregularization** is the kind of error that results when a grammatical rule is misapplied to a word that has an irregular plural or past tense (Marcus, 1996). Thus, children who have correctly used the words "went," "came," and "did" incorrectly apply the rule for past tenses and begin to say "goed," "comed," and "doed." What the parents see as a regression in speech actually means that the child has acquired a grammatical rule. Most children, but not all, acquire grammatical rules with relative ease. Since the relationship between the spoken and written forms of English is not very close or straightforward, children whose language abilities are compromised can experience great difficulty in developing literacy (Simpson, 2000).

Table 9.2 provides a summary of the early stages of language development.

Theories of Language Development: How Is Language Acquired?

How do learning theory and the nativist position explain the acquisition of language?

There is no disagreement among theorists that children's learning of language is a truly amazing feat. But theorists do disagree about *how* children are able to accomplish such a feat. Several theories have been proposed to explain language acquisition. Some theories emphasize the role of learning and experience (nurture); some propose a biological explanation, emphasizing maturation (nature); and others suggest an interaction between maturation and experience. "There is currently no consensus of support for any one of them" (Rice, 1989, p. 150).

Learning Theory Learning theorists have long maintained that language is acquired in the same way as other behaviors are acquired—as a result of learning through reinforcement and imitation. B. F. Skinner (1957) asserted that language is shaped through reinforcement. He claimed that parents selectively criticize incorrect speech and reinforce correct speech through praise, approval, and attention. Thus, the child's utterances are progressively shaped in the direction of grammatically correct speech. Others believe that children acquire vocabulary and sentence construction mainly through imitation (Bandura, 1977a).

overregularization: The act of inappropriately applying the grammatical rules for forming plurals and past tenses to irregular nouns and verbs.

There are some problems, however, with learning theory as the sole explanation for language acquisition. Imitation cannot account for patterns of speech such as telegraphic speech or for systematic errors such as overregularization. Children do not hear telegraphic speech in everyday life, and "I comed" and "he goed" are not forms commonly used by parents.

There are also problems with reinforcement as an explanation for language acquisition. First, parents seem to reward children more for the content of the utterance than for the correctness of the grammar (Brown et al., 1968). And parents are much more likely to correct them for saying something untrue than for making a grammatical error. Regardless, correction has little impact on a child's grammar. But reinforcement still plays an important part in language learning. Responsiveness to infants' vocalizations increases the amount of vocalization, and reinforcement can help children with language deficits improve (Whitehurst et al., 1989).

The Nativist Position Noam Chomsky (1957) believes that language ability is largely innate, and he has proposed a very different theory. Chomsky (1968) maintains that the brain contains a *language acquisition device (LAD),* which enables children to acquire language and discover the rules of grammar easily and naturally. Language develops in stages that occur in a fixed order and appear at about the same time in most normal children—babbling at about 6 months, the one-word stage at about 1 year, and the two-word stage at 18 to 20 months. Deaf children exposed to sign language from birth proceed along the same schedule (Meier, 1991; Petitto & Marentette, 1991). Lenneberg (1967) claims that biological maturation underlies language development in much the same way that it underlies physical and motor development.

Very young infants do seem to have an innate mechanism that allows them to perceive and differentiate phonemes present in any language (Christophe & Morton, 1994; Eimas, 1985; Jusczyk & Aslin, 1995). But by the end of the first year, their power to distinguish between speech sounds that do not differentiate words in their own language is greatly reduced (Kuhl et al., 1992). This is why adults whose native tongue is Japanese have so much difficulty discriminating between the *r* and *l* sounds in English.

The nativist position is better able than learning theory to account for the fact that children throughout the world go through the same basic stages in language development. It can account, too, for the similar errors all children make when they are first learning to form plurals, past tenses, and negatives—errors not acquired through imitation or reinforcement. However, there are several aspects of language development that the nativist position cannot explain.

Deaf mothers use sign language to communicate with their young children, but they do so in "motherese," signing slowly and with frequent repetitions.

Nature and Nurture: An Interactionist Perspective The interactionist perspective acknowledges the critical importance of both nature and nurture for language learning (Chapman, 2000). One's native language, after all, is acquired in a social setting, where the experiences one has must have some influence on language development. And, of course, genetics plays a role in every human capability.

Recent research reveals that language learning proceeds in a piecewise fashion, which calls into question the assumptions of Chomsky's nativist approach (Tomasello, 2000). Children learn concrete language expressions they hear around them, and then they imitate and build on those. Recall that even though Robert, the boy in the chapter opening story, could not use use human language, he had learned the vocal expressions of the monkeys he lived with. That is, he vocalized the sounds he heard in his social setting, even though those sounds were nonhuman ones.

Parents can facilitate language acquisition by adjusting their speech to their infant's level of development. Parents often use *motherese*—highly simplified speech with shorter phrases and sentences and simpler vocabulary, which is uttered slowly, at a high pitch, and with exaggerated intonation and much repetition (Fernald, 1993). Deaf mothers communicate with their infants in a similar way, signing more slowly and with exaggerated hand and arm movements and frequent repetition (Masataka, 1996).

Reading to children and with them supports language development. Parents should comment and expand on what the child says and encourage the child to say more by asking questions. According to Rice (1989), "Most children do not need to be taught language, but they do need opportunities to develop language" (p. 155).

Unfortunately, parents from lower socioeconomic classes tend to talk to their children less, to expose them to a less diverse vocabulary, and to discourage them from talking more often (Walker et al., 1994). This disadvantage in language experience not only slows early language development (Hart & Risley, 1992) but may negatively affect later intellectual development (Walker et al., 1994).

Remember It!

1. Match the linguistic stage with the example.

____ (1) "ba-ba-ba"	a. telegraphic speech
____ (2) "He eated the cookies."	b. holophrase
____ (3) "Mama see ball"	c. overregularization
____ (4) "oo," "ah"	d. babbling
____ (5) "kitty," meaning a lion	e. overextension
____ (6) "ball," meaning "look at the ball"	f. cooing

2. Learning theory is better able than the nativist position to account for how language development can be encouraged. (true/false)

3. The nativist position does *not* suggest that
   a. language ability is largely innate.
   b. language is acquired in stages that occur in a fixed order.
   c. reinforcement and imitation are the primary factors influencing language acquisition.
   d. most normal children around the world acquire language in the same stages and at the same ages.

4. Which explanation best accounts for the early stages of babbling and telegraphic speech?
   a. reinforcement
   b. imitation
   c. cognitive mapping
   d. the nativist position

Answers: 1. (1) d (2) c (3) a (4) f (5) e (6) b 2. true 3. c 4. d

SOCIALIZATION OF THE CHILD

To function effectively and comfortably in society, children must come to know the patterns of behavior considered to be desirable and appropriate. The process of learning socially acceptable behaviors, attitudes, and values is called **socialization.** Although parents have the major role in socialization, peers, school, the media, and religion are all important influences as well.

What is Erikson's theory of psychosocial development?

Erikson's Theory of Psychosocial Development

Erik Erikson (1902–1994) proposed the only major theory of development to include the entire life span. He was the first to stress the part that society and individuals themselves play in their own personality development, rather than focusing exclusively on the influence of parents.

According to Erikson, individuals progress through eight **psychosocial stages** during the life span. Each stage is defined by a conflict involving the individual's relationship with the social environment, which must be resolved satisfactorily in order for healthy development to occur. The stages are named for a "series of alternative basic attitudes," which result depending on how the conflict is resolved (Erikson, 1980). Erikson believed that a healthy personality depends on acquiring

socialization: The process of learning socially acceptable behaviors, attitudes, and values.

psychosocial stages: Erikson's eight developmental stages through the life span, each defined by a conflict that must be resolved satisfactorily in order for healthy personality development to occur.

basic trust versus basic mistrust: Erikson's first stage (ages birth to 1 year), when infants develop trust or mistrust based on the quality of care, love, and affection provided.

autonomy versus shame and doubt: Erikson's second stage (ages 1 to 3 years), when infants develop autonomy or shame based on how parents react to their expression of will and their wish to do things for themselves.

initiative versus guilt: Erikson's third stage (ages 3 to 6 years), when children develop a sense of initiative or guilt depending on how parents react to their initiation of play, their motor activities, and their questions.

industry versus inferiority: Erikson's fourth stage (ages 6 years to puberty), when children develop a sense of industry or inferiority based on how parents and teachers react to their efforts to undertake projects.

the appropriate basic attitudes in the proper sequence. Although failure to resolve a conflict impedes later development, resolution may occur at a later stage and reverse any damage done previously.

Stage 1: Basic Trust versus Basic Mistrust (Ages Birth to 1 Year) During the first stage, **basic trust versus basic mistrust,** infants develop a sense of trust or mistrust depending on the degree and regularity of care, love, and affection they receive from the mother or primary caregiver. Erikson (1980) considered "basic trust as the cornerstone of a healthy personality" (p. 58).

Stage 2: Autonomy versus Shame and Doubt (Ages 1 to 3 Years) During the second stage, **autonomy versus shame and doubt,** children are developing their physical and mental abilities and want to do things for themselves. They begin to express their independence and develop a "sudden violent wish to have a choice" (Erikson, 1963, p. 252). "No!" becomes one of their favorite words. Erikson believed that parents must set appropriate limits, but at the same time facilitate the child's desire for autonomy by encouraging appropriate attempts at independence. If parents are impatient or overprotective, they may make children feel shame and doubt about their efforts to exercise their own will and explore their environment.

Stage 3: Initiative versus Guilt (Ages 3 to 6 Years) In the third stage, **initiative versus guilt,** children go beyond merely expressing their autonomy and begin to develop initiative. Enjoying their new locomotor and mental powers, children initiate play and motor activities and ask questions.

> If the child is made to feel that his motor activity is bad, that his questions are a nuisance and that his play is silly and stupid, then he may develop a sense of guilt over self-initiated activities in general that will persist through later life stages. (Elkind, 1970, pp. 87, 89)

If appropriate attempts at initiative are encouraged and inappropriate attempts are handled firmly but sensitively, children will leave this stage with a sense of initiative that will form "a basis for a high and yet realistic sense of ambition and independence" (Erikson, 1980, p. 78).

In Erikson's fourth stage—industry versus inferiority—children enjoy and take pride in making things.

Stage 4: Industry versus Inferiority (Ages 6 Years to Puberty) During the fourth stage, **industry versus inferiority,** children begin to enjoy and take pride in making things and doing things.

> When children are encouraged in their efforts to make, do, or build practical things . . . , are allowed to finish their products, and are praised and rewarded for the results, then the sense of industry is enhanced. But parents who see their children's efforts at making and doing as "mischief," and as simply "making a mess," help to encourage in children a sense of inferiority. (Elkind, 1970, pp. 89–90)

The encouragement of teachers as well as parents is important for a positive resolution of this stage.

Review & Reflect 9.2 describes Erikson's first four stages. Erikson's next four stages, which cover adolescence through adulthood, are discussed in Chapter 10.

The Parents' Role in the Socialization Process

What are the three parenting styles identified by Baumrind, and which did she find most effective?

The parents' role in the socialization process is to set examples, to teach, and to provide discipline. Parents are usually more successful if they are loving, warm, nurturant, and supportive (Maccoby & Martin, 1983). In fact, a longitudinal study that followed individuals from age 5 to age 41 revealed that "children of warm, affectionate parents were more likely to be socially accomplished adults who, at age 41, were mentally healthy, coping adequately, and psychosocially mature in work, relationships, and

Review & Reflect 9.2 Erikson's Psychosocial Stages of Development

↓ know these.

Stage	Ages	Description
Trust vs. mistrust	Birth to 1 year	Infants learn to trust or mistrust depending on the degree and regularity of care, love, and affection provided by parents or caregivers.
Autonomy vs. shame and doubt	1 to 3 years	Children learn to express their will and independence, to exercise some control, and to make choices. If not, they experience shame and doubt.
Initiative vs. guilt	3 to 6 years	Children begin to initiate activities, to plan and undertake tasks, and to enjoy their developing motor and other abilities. If not allowed to initiate or if made to feel stupid and considered a nuisance, they may develop a sense of guilt.
Industry vs. inferiority	6 years to puberty	Children develop industriousness and feel pride in accomplishing tasks, making things, and doing things. If not encouraged or if rebuffed by parents and teachers, they may develop a sense of inferiority.
Identity vs. role confusion	Adolescence	Described in Chapter 10.
Intimacy vs. isolation	Young adulthood	
Generativity vs. stagnation	Middle adulthood	
Ego integrity vs. despair	Late adulthood	

generativity" (Franz et al., 1991, p. 593). Families are dysfunctional when the roles are reversed, and the children nurture and control their parents (Maccoby, 1992).

To be effective, socialization must ultimately result in children coming to regulate their own behavior. The attainment of this goal is undermined when parents control their children's behavior by asserting power over them (Maccoby, 1992). Diane Baumrind (1971, 1980, 1991) studied the continuum of parental control and identified three parenting styles—the authoritarian, the authoritative, and the permissive. She related these styles to different patterns of behavior in predominantly white, middle-class children.

Authoritarian Parents **Authoritarian parents** make the rules, expect unquestioned obedience from their children, punish misbehavior (often physically), and value obedience to authority. Rather than giving a rationale for a rule, authoritarian parents consider "because I said so" a sufficient reason for obedience. Parents using this parenting style tend to be uncommunicative, unresponsive, and somewhat distant. Baumrind (1967) found preschool children disciplined in this manner to be withdrawn, anxious, and unhappy.

Parents' failure to provide a rationale for rules makes it hard for children to see any reason for following them. Saying "Do it because I said so" or "Do it or you'll be punished" may succeed in making the child do what is expected when the parent is present, but it is ineffective when the parent is not around. The authoritarian style has been associated with low intellectual performance and lack of social skills, especially

authoritarian parents: Parents who make arbitrary rules, expect unquestioned obedience from their children, punish transgressions, and value obedience to authority.

authoritative parents: Parents who set high but realistic standards, reason with the child, enforce limits, and encourage open communication and independence.

permissive parents: Parents who make few rules or demands and allow children to make their own decisions and control their own behavior.

in boys (Maccoby & Martin, 1983). Also, if not blindly obeyed, extremely authoritarian parents tend to respond with anger, which has potentially negative long-term consequences. In fact, anger is precisely the wrong emotion to direct at children if they are to thrive, to achieve, to be well adjusted and happy, and to become effective parents in the next generation (Denham et al., 2000).

Authoritative Parents **Authoritative parents** set high but realistic and reasonable standards, enforce limits, and at the same time encourage open communication and independence. They are willing to discuss rules and supply rationales for them. Knowing why the rules are necessary makes it easier for children to internalize them and to follow them, whether in the presence of their parents or not. Authoritative parents are generally warm, nurturant, supportive, and responsive, and they show respect for their children and their opinions. Their children are the most mature, happy, self-reliant, self-controlled, assertive, socially competent, and responsible. The authoritative parenting style is associated with higher academic performance, independence, higher self-esteem, and internalized moral standards in middle childhood and adolescence (Lamborn et al., 1991; Steinberg et al., 1989).

More recent research continues to show a strong relationship between authoritative parenting and high achievement and feelings of high self-worth. Children who experience authoritative parenting also tend to expect success, not failure, and to be active rather than passive (Aunola et al., 2000).

Permissive Parents Although they are rather warm and supportive, **permissive parents** make few rules or demands and usually do not enforce those that are made. They allow children to make their own decisions and control their own behavior. Children raised in this manner are the most immature, impulsive, and dependent, and they seem to be the least self-controlled and self-reliant.

Permissive parents also come in the indifferent, unconcerned, uninvolved variety (Maccoby & Martin, 1983). This parenting style is associated with drinking problems, promiscuous sex, delinquent behavior, and poor academic performance in adolescents.

Peer Relationships

How do peers contribute to the socialization process?

Infants begin to show an interest in each other at a very young age. At only 6 months of age, they already demonstrate an interest in other infants by looking, reaching, touching, smiling, and vocalizing (Vandell & Mueller, 1980). Friendships begin to develop by 3 or 4 years, and relationships with peers become increasingly important. By middle childhood, membership in a peer group is central to a child's happiness. Peer groups are usually composed of children of the same race, sex, and social class (Schofield & Francis, 1982).

The peer group serves a socializing function by providing models of behavior, dress, and language. It is a continuing source of both reinforcement for appropriate behavior and punishment for deviant behavior. The peer group also provides an objective measure against which children can evaluate their own traits and abilities—how smart or how good at sports they are, for example. In their peer groups children learn how to get along with age-mates—how to share and cooperate, develop social skills, and regulate aggression.

Physical attractiveness is a major factor in peer acceptance even in children as young as 3 to 5 years, although it seems to be more important for girls than for boys (Krantz, 1987; Langlois, 1985). Negative traits are often attributed to unattractive children. Athletic ability and academic success in school are also valued by the peer group. The more popular children are usually energetic, happy, cooperative, sensitive, and thoughtful. Popular children have social skills that lead to positive social outcomes and facilitate the goals of their peers. But they are also able to be assertive and aggressive when the situation calls for it (Newcomb et al., 1993). Also, popular children tend to have parents who use an authoritative parenting style (Dekovic & Janssens, 1992).

Low acceptance by peers is an important predictor of later mental health problems (Kupersmidt et al., 1990). Most often excluded from the peer group are neglected children, who are shy and withdrawn, and rejected children, who typically exhibit aggressive and inappropriate behavior and who are likely to start fights (Dodge, Cole, et al., 1990). Children abused at home tend to be unpopular with their classmates, who typically view them as aggressive and uncooperative (Salzinger et al., 1993). Rejection by peers is linked to unhappiness, alienation, and poor achievement, and in middle childhood with delinquency and dropping out of school (Kupersmidt & Coie, 1990; Parker & Asher, 1987).

Television as a Socializing Agent: Does It Help or Hinder?

What are some of the positive and negative effects of television?

Television is a powerful influence on young children. They spend more time watching television than on any other activity except sleeping (Tuncer & Yalcin, 2000). By the time the average American child is 2 years old, he or she watches about 27 hours of television per week (Cooke, 1992). And, on average, American children have viewed more than 100,000 violent acts on television by the time they finish elementary school (Gerbner & Signorielli, 1990). Even the youngest children prefer to watch cartoons that are violent in nature. Literally thousands of studies suggest that TV violence leads to aggressive behavior in children and teenagers (Slaby et al., 1995). Other studies show that excessive TV viewing is linked to childhood obesity (Tuncer & Yalcin, 2000). Still other research has reported a relationship between too much television watching and sleep disturbances (Owens et al., 2000).

Television shapes the child's view of the world, and heavy viewers perceive the world as a "mean and scary place" (Donnerstein et al., 1994). Children's preferences and beliefs are easily manipulated by television programming, and television socializes children to become active consumers. Moreover, the socializing effect of television begins before that of schools, religious institutions, and peers.

Television has a strong influence on most children, beginning before they go to school and teaching them much about social behavior—unfortunately, perhaps more about aggression than about affection.

Television, however, can be an effective educational medium. *Mister Rogers' Neighborhood* has been found to increase prosocial behavior, imaginative play, and task persistency in preschoolers (Stein & Friedrich, 1975). Children viewing *Sesame Street* at ages 3 and 4 had larger vocabularies and better prereading skills at age 5 (Rice et al., 1990). Jerome and Judith Singer (cited in Leland, 1997) found that *Barney* encouraged creative play among 2- to 3-year-olds, but *Power Rangers* led to fighting.

Racial and ethnic minorities make up more than 30% of the U.S. population, and although their numbers seem to be increasing on television, they are still underrepresented. Even today, racial and sexual stereotypes and stereotypic views of the elderly and the mentally ill continue to appear on television. Minorities are often cast as criminals or victims of crime, and they are more likely to be cast in lower-class jobs than in professional or executive roles, although shows such as *NYPD Blue, The Practice,* and *ER* seem to be challenging this stereotype to some extent. And there are relatively few Hispanics, Asian Americans, or Native Americans appearing on national newscasts as anchors, reporters, or newsmakers or as those cited as authorities.

Much of children's commercial programming is marked by rapid activity and change and an "intense auditory and visual barrage" (Wright & Huston, 1983, p. 837). Singer and Singer (1979) suggest that such programming can lead to a shortened attention span. Others contend that television "promotes passive rather than active learning, induces low-level cognitive processing, and takes away time and energy from more creative or intellectually stimulating activities" (Wright and Huston, 1983, p. 835).

We have seen that many factors contribute to child development. And for all of life, from conception onward, it is the interplay of nature and nurture that drives and shapes us. In the next chapter we will continue to explore human development, moving from adolescence through old age.

Remember It!

1. According to Erikson, if the basic conflict of a given stage is *not* resolved satisfactorily,
   a. a person will not enter the next stage.
   b. development at the next stage will be adversely affected.
   c. a person will be permanently damaged regardless of future experiences.
   d. a person will revert to the previous stage.
2. Match the psychosocial stage with the phrase that describes the child in that stage.

____ (1) needs regular care and love	a. basic trust versus mistrust
____ (2) initiates play and motor activities, asks questions	b. industry versus inferiority
____ (3) strives for sense of independence	c. initiative versus guilt
____ (4) undertakes projects, makes things	d. autonomy versus shame and doubt

3. Match the parenting style with the approach to discipline.

____ (1) expecting unquestioned obedience	a. permissive
____ (2) setting high standards, giving rationale for rules	b. authoritative
____ (3) setting few rules or limits	c. authoritarian

4. The peer group usually has a negative influence on social development. (true/false)
5. Which is *not* an effect of television on children?
   a. reducing racial and sexual stereotypes
   b. shortening attention span
   c. contributing to childhood obesity
   d. increasing aggressive behavior through exposure to TV violence

Answers: 1. b 2. (1) a (2) c (3) d (4) b 3. (1) c (2) b (3) a 4. false 5. a

Apply It!

The Importance of Prenatal Care

Are you pregnant or planning to become pregnant? If so, the first thing you should do is see your doctor. Good prenatal care is essential to your health and your baby's, both during pregnancy and after the baby is born.

Prenatal medical care usually begins with an initial visit that includes a complete physical examination, followed by monthly checkups early in the pregnancy and weekly ones toward the end. These regular exams, which include blood and urine tests, are critical to the early detection and treatment of complications that may arise during pregnancy.

Unfortunately, many woman do not seek prenatal medical care. They may consider it unnecessary, may be ambivalent about their pregnancy, or may lack health insurance. This is particularly true of minority women: White women are twice as likely as Hispanic and African American women to receive prenatal care. As a result, minority women and their babies are at risk for health problems such as premature delivery and low birthweight. In addition, African American women are four times more likely to die from pregnancy complications than are other women.

In addition to medical care, prenatal care also involves a variety of maternal health practices. These include good nutrition, exercise, and avoidance of cigarettes, alcohol, and any drugs that might harm the fetus. It is also important to reduce stress during pregnancy.

Nutrition. Although it is commonplace to say that a pregnant woman is "eating for two," a woman's nutritional needs actually increase by only 300 calories a day during pregnancy. Those extra calories should come from the major food groups and be supplemented with an extra serving of milk or other dairy product (to provide calcium for bone formation) and about 10 more grams of protein (for cell formation). Fats should not be increased beyond the recommended 30% or less of total calories. In other words, during pregnancy it's important to "eat twice as well, not twice as much" (OnHealth, 2000). One way to add nutrition without eating twice as much is to eat small snacks at various times during the day. For example, a snack of cheese or yogurt will provide extra calcium.

Expectant mothers also need additional vitamin C and folic acid. And their iron intake needs to increase to 30 milligrams because of increased blood volume. Most physicians therefore recommend a prenatal vitamin supplement containing iron. Finally, a pregnant woman should drink at least eight 8-ounce glasses of water every day to avoid dehydration, muscle cramps, and urinary tract infections.

Exercise. Pregnancy is a normal condition, not an illness, and there is no reason for pregnant women to stop exercising. Moderate aerobic exercise increases the flow of oxygen and nutrients to the fetus and reduces fluid retention, hemorrhoids, and varicose veins in the mother.

It's important to exercise safely, though, by walking, cycling, or swimming, for example. Activities that might lead to falls such as skiing, rollerblading, and horseback riding should be avoided.

Smoking. If you are a smoker and planning to become a mother, there couldn't be a better time to stop. Smoking has a variety of effects on the reproductive system, including lowering a woman's ability to conceive and making a man's sperm less viable. It is also hazardous to the health of the fetus. A woman who smokes is almost twice as likely as one who doesn't to have a low-birthweight baby. Smoking can also cause a miscarriage, stillbirth, or premature birth. Children born to mothers who smoke tend to have respiratory problems such as chronic coughing and are twice as likely to develop asthma. They may also be retarded in their physical and intellectual development. In short, the evidence is overwhelming: A pregnant woman should not smoke or be exposed to secondhand smoke.

Alcohol consumption. Alcohol reaches the fetus in the same concentration found in the mother's blood, and alcohol consumed during pregnancy has a direct effect on the baby. A major effect of excessive alcohol consumption during pregnancy is fetal alcohol syndrome, which produces physical abnormalities such as widely spaced eyes, small eye openings, a small nose, and a small upper lip. These children are usually mentally retarded.

Experts disagree on what constitutes "excessive" drinking and cannot accurately predict the effect that even light drinking will have on a fetus. The American Academy of Pediatrics therefore recommends that women avoid alcohol altogether during pregnancy (McAnulty & Burnette, 2001).

Drugs. Every drug a woman takes during pregnancy reaches the fetus. This means that before taking any drug, even a common one like aspirin, a pregnant woman should consult a physician about the potential effects. Some prescription drugs can have devastating effects on the fetus; an example is the sedative thalidomide, which caused malformations of the legs and arms in thousands of babies before it was withdrawn from the market. More recently, Accutane, a drug used to treat acne, was found to cause birth defects in many cases. Although these drugs are no longer prescribed to pregnant women, they serve as a reminder of the potential for ill effects when any medication is taken during pregnancy.

Also harmful to the fetus are illegal drugs such as cocaine and heroin. Use of these drugs can lead to several dangerous conditions, including premature birth, cerebral hemorrhage, and sudden infant death syndrome. Fetuses of heroin users become addicted themselves and may suffer withdrawal symptoms as newborns. In recent years women who use drugs that are known to harm the fetus have increasingly been subject to prosecution for child abuse.

Maternal stress. All of the above seems to indicate that a pregnant woman has many things to worry about. But, ironically, worry itself can cause problems. Job stress, for example, puts a woman at risk for preeclampsia (pregnancy-induced high blood pressure), and anxiety during pregnancy has been linked to premature birth and low birthweight.

What can you do to reduce stress? First, try to find some time to relax each day. Choose a time when you are unlikely to be interrupted and an activity you enjoy, and put everything else aside. You can also reduce stress by exercising and by spending time with friends and relatives. If you find it difficult to relax, you may be able to attend a relaxation course at a hospital or other organization in your community.

In sum, having regular medical checkups, watching your diet, exercising, avoiding harmful substances, and reducing the stress in your life, will put you on track for a healthy pregnancy, a trouble-free delivery, and a healthy baby.

THINKING CRITICALLY

Evaluation

Evaluate Erikson's first four stages of psychosocial development, explaining what aspects of his theory seem most convincing and least convincing. Support your answer.

Point/Counterpoint

Using your knowledge of both learning theory and the nativist position on language development, prepare an argument in favor of each position and a counterargument against each.

Psychology in Your Life

Using Baumrind's categories, classify the parenting style your mother and/or father or guardian used in rearing you.

a. Cite examples of techniques they used that support your classification.
b. Do you agree with Baumrind's conclusions about the effects of that parenting style on children? Why or why not?

SUMMARY AND REVIEW

DEVELOPMENTAL PSYCHOLOGY: BASIC ISSUES AND METHODOLOGY

What are two types of studies developmental psychologists use to investigate age-related changes?

To investigate age-related changes, developmental psychologists use the longitudinal study and the cross-sectional study.

HEREDITY AND PRENATAL DEVELOPMENT

How are hereditary traits transmitted?

Hereditary traits are transmitted by the genes, which are located on each of the 23 pairs of chromosomes.

When are dominant or recessive genes expressed in an individual's traits?

When there are alternate forms of a gene for a specific trait, the dominant gene will be expressed. A recessive gene is expressed when it is paired with another recessive gene.

What are the three stages of prenatal development?

The three stages of prenatal development are the period of the zygote, the period of the embryo, and the period of the fetus.

What are some negative influences on prenatal development, and during what time is their impact greatest?

Some common negative influences on prenatal development include certain prescription and nonprescription drugs, psychoactive drugs, poor maternal nutrition, and maternal infections and illnesses. Their impact is greatest during the first trimester.

Key Terms
developmental psychology (p. 310); nature–nurture controversy (p. 310); longitudinal study (p. 311); cross-sectional study (p. 311); genes (p. 311); chromosomes (p. 311); sex chromosomes (p. 312); dominant gene (p. 313); recessive gene (p. 313); period of the zygote (p. 313); prenatal (p. 313); embryo (p. 313); fetus (p. 313); identical (monozygotic) twins (p. 314); fraternal (dizygotic) twins (p. 314); teratogens (p. 314); critical period (p. 314); fetal alcohol syndrome (p. 315); low-birth-weight baby (p. 316); preterm infant (p. 316)

PHYSICAL DEVELOPMENT AND LEARNING IN INFANCY

What are the perceptual abilities of the newborn?

All of the newborn's senses are functional at birth, and he or she already shows preferences for certain odors, tastes, sounds, and visual patterns.

What types of learning occur in the first few days of life?

Newborns are capable of habituation, and they can acquire new responses through classical and operant conditioning and observational learning.

What is the primary factor influencing attainment of the major motor milestones?

Maturation is the primary factor influencing attainment of the major motor milestones.

Key Terms
neonate (p. 317); reflexes (p. 317); visual cliff (p. 318); habituation (p. 319); maturation (p. 319)

EMOTIONAL DEVELOPMENT IN INFANCY

What is temperament, and what are the three temperament types identified by Thomas, Chess, and Birch?

Temperament refers to an individual's characteristic way of responding to the environment. The three temperament types are easy, difficult, and slow-to-warm-up.

What did Harlow's studies reveal about maternal deprivation and attachment in infant monkeys?

Harlow found that the basis of attachment in infant monkeys is contact comfort, and that monkeys raised with surrogate mothers showed normal learning ability but abnormal social, sexual, and emotional behavior.

According to Bowlby, when does the infant have a strong attachment to the mother?

The infant has usually developed a strong attachment to the mother at age 6 to 8 months.

What are the four attachment patterns identified in infants?

The four attachment patterns identified in infants are secure, avoidant, resistant, and disorganized/disoriented.

What are the typical differences in the ways mothers and fathers interact with their children?

Mothers tend to spend more time caretaking, and fathers spend more time playing with their children.

Key Terms
temperament (p. 321); attachment (p. 322); surrogate (p. 322); separation anxiety (p. 324); stranger anxiety (p. 324)

PIAGET'S THEORY OF COGNITIVE DEVELOPMENT

What did Piaget claim regarding the stages of cognitive development?

Piaget claimed that cognitive ability develops in four stages, each representing a qualitatively different form of reasoning and understanding. He believed the stages to be universal and sequencial, although children may progress through them at different rates.

What occurs during Piaget's sensorimotor stage?

During the sensorimotor stage (ages birth to 2 years), infants gain knowledge and understanding of the world through their senses and motor activities. The major accomplishment of the stage is object permanence.

What cognitive limitations characterize a child's thinking during the preoperational stage?

Children at the preoperational stage (ages 2 to 7 years) are increasingly able to represent objects and events mentally, but they exhibit egocentrism and centration and have not developed the concepts of reversibility and conservation.

What cognitive abilities do children acquire during the concrete operations stage?

When working on concrete problems, children at the concrete operations stage (ages 7 to 11 or 12 years) become able to decenter their thinking and to understand the concepts of reversibility and conservation.

What new capability characterizes the formal operations stage?

At the formal operations stage (ages 11 or 12 years and beyond) adolescents are able to apply logical thinking to abstract problems and hypothetical situations.

Key Terms

schemas (p. 327); assimilation (p. 327); accommodation (p. 327); sensorimotor stage (p. 327); object permanence (p. 328); preoperational stage (p. 328); conservation (p. 328); centration (p. 328); reversibility (p. 328); concrete operations stage (p. 330); formal operations stage (p. 331)

VYGOTSKY'S SOCIOCULTURAL VIEW OF COGNITIVE DEVELOPMENT

In Vygotsky's view, how do private speech and scaffolding contribute to cognitive development?

Private speech, or self-guided talk, helps children to direct their actions and solve problems. Scaffolding is an instructional technique in which a teacher or parent adjusts the quality and degree of help to fit the child's ability. It allows a child gradually to become independent.

COGNITIVE DEVELOPMENT: THE INFORMATION-PROCESSING APPROACH

What three cognitive abilities have information-processing researchers studied extensively?

The three cognitive abilities studied extensively by information-processing researchers are attention, memory, and metacognition.

LANGUAGE DEVELOPMENT

What are the stages of language development from cooing through the acquisition of grammatical rules?

The stages of language development are cooing (age 2 to 3 months), babbling (beginning at age 6 months), single words (about age 1 year), two-word sentences (age 18 to 20 months), and telegraphic speech (age 2½ years), followed by the acquisition of grammatical rules.

How do learning theory and the nativist position explain the acquisition of language?

Learning theory suggests that language is acquired through imitation and reinforcement. The nativist position is that language ability is largely innate, because it is acquired in stages that occur in a fixed order at the same ages in most normal children throughout the world.

Key Terms

babbling (p. 336); phonemes (p. 336); overextension (p. 336); underextension (p. 336); telegraphic speech (p. 336); overregularization (p. 337)

SOCIALIZATION OF THE CHILD

What is Erikson's theory of psychosocial development?

Erikson believed that individuals progress through eight psychosocial stages during the life span, and each stage is defined by a conflict with the social environment, which must be resolved. The four stages in childhood are basic trust versus basic mistrust (ages birth to 2 years), autonomy versus shame and doubt (ages 1 to 3 years), initiative versus guilt (ages 3 to 6 years), and industry versus inferiority (ages 6 years to puberty).

What are the three parenting styles identified by Baumrind, and which did she find most effective?

The three parenting styles identified by Baumrind are the authoritarian, the permissive, and the authoritative. She found the authoritative style to be the most effective.

How do peers contribute to the socialization process?

The peer group serves a socializing function by modeling and reinforcing behaviors it considers appropriate, by punishing inappropriate behavior, and by providing an objective measure against which children can evaluate their own traits and abilities.

What are some of the positive and negative effects of television?

Television can increase prosocial behavior and improve prereading and number skills, but it can lead to a shortened attention span, promote racial and sexual stereotypes, and reinforce aggressive behavior.

Key Terms

socialization (p. 339); psychosocial stages (p. 339); basic trust versus basic mistrust (p. 340); autonomy versus shame and doubt (p. 340); initiative versus guilt (p. 340); industry versus inferiority (p. 340); authoritarian parents (p. 341); authoritative parents (p. 342); permissive parents (p. 342)

Surf It!

Want to be sure you've absorbed the material in Chapter 9, "Child Development," before the big test? Visiting *www.abacon.com/wood* can put a top grade within your reach. The site is loaded with free practice tests, flashcards, activities, and links to help you review your way to an A. To enliven that inevitable study break, the site also offers personality assessment quizzes and a psychology career corner.

10 Adolescence and Adulthood

personal fable
imaginary audience
early + late maturing
boys + girls
how morality is passed
Lawrence Colberg

Adolescence: Physical and Cognitive Development

Adolescence: Moral and Social Development

Erikson's Psychosocial Theory: Adolescence through Adulthood

Other Theories of Adulthood

Early and Middle Adulthood

Later Adulthood

parenting styles
Diane 3 kinds

As a child, Rafer Johnson lived with his family in a boxcar–no lights, no heat, no indoor toilet or running water. He also lived in fear of a drunken, abusive father. But Johnson overcame these disadvantages, in large part because he was poor only in material things. He was rich in physical ability, as well as intellectual accomplishment. Along with a forgiving spirit, these qualities enabled him to transcend poverty and abuse. Rafer determined that in everything he did in life, he would be the best he could be.

His dedication paid off. In 1958, Rafer broke the Olympic and world records in the decathlon. Two years later, he won the gold medal for the decathlon at the 1960 Olympics in Rome.

But the honor that meant the most to him was being named torch lighter for the opening ceremonies of the Los Angeles Olympics in 1984. It was then that his young daughter, Jenny, finally realized the significance of her father's accomplishments.

Now, nearly two decades later, Jenny Johnson Jordan is also a talented athlete. In 1999, Jenny and

Annett Buckner Davis (shown in action together in the chapter opening photo) became the top-ranked beach volleyball team in the United States, ranking second in the world. Then Jenny and Annett spiked their way into the quarterfinals of the 2000 Olympics in Sydney, Australia. Now Jenny has her eye set on the 2004 Olympics.

What explains these tremendous athletic accomplishments by one family? Did Jenny's genes destine her to become an Olympian like her father? Did her environment influence the development of her skills?

Jenny was born with a better-than-average chance of exceling at sports. But beyond that her genes may have also influenced her mind-set throughout her life. Genetics partly explains why her father overcame the bad environment of his youth, and those same qualities—perseverance, perfectionism, and optimism—may have helped propel Jenny to the Olympics, too.

It's easy to imagine that Jenny might have felt pressure to measure up to her father's impressive athletic record. But she says that he never pressured her to participate in athletics, let alone to excel. Instead, he inspired her with love and encouragement, as well as his accomplishments. "Ever since I understood what he had done, and what a great experience it was for him, I wanted it for myself," Jenny says (NBC Olympics, 1999).

As Jenny ages, do you think she will attempt to pass along her volleyball skills to another generation? Would you expect Jenny's and Rafer's physical, cognitive, and social skills to remain intact longer than those of the average nonathlete?

Development is a lifelong process. And Rafer Johnson serves as an example showing how one can overcome severe disadvantages in early life and not only survive, but thrive and develop into a heroic role model. This chapter continues our study of human development, from adolescence through adulthood and old age. We will consider the ways in which individuals change over time and the ways in which they remain much the same. We will trace physical, cognitive, social, and personality development from adolescence to the end of life. We begin by entering the developmental world of the adolescent.

ADOLESCENCE: PHYSICAL AND COGNITIVE DEVELOPMENT

How difficult is adolescence for most teenagers?

Many people have quite negative associations with the word *adolescence,* picturing a life filled with rebellion and stormy and stressful relationships with parents and other family members. Others picture strong peer-group conformity, which may include unorthodox dress, tattoos, piercings of body parts, drug dependency, and worse.

Is this view of adolescence supported by research? The answer might surprise you. **Adolescence** is the developmental stage that spans the period from the end of childhood to the beginning of adulthood. A person does not go to sleep one night as a child and awaken as an adult the next morning, at least not in contemporary American society. But some cultures have designed elaborate ceremonies known as rites of passage or puberty rites, which publicly mark the passage from childhood to adulthood. At the end of the ceremony, the young person becomes an "instant adult," ready to assume adult responsibilities and to marry.

adolescence: The developmental stage that begins at puberty and encompasses the period from the end of childhood to the beginning of adulthood.

puberty: A period of rapid physical growth and change that culminates in sexual maturity.

adolescent growth spurt: A period of rapid physical growth that peaks in girls at about age 12 and in boys at about age 14.

The concept of adolescence did not exist until psychologist G. Stanley Hall first wrote about it in his book by that name in 1904. He portrayed this stage in life as one of "storm and stress," the inevitable result of biological changes occurring during the period. Anna Freud (1958), daughter of Sigmund Freud, even considered a stormy adolescence a necessary part of normal development. And though it does appear to be true that "storm and stress" are associated with adolescence more than with any other period of human development, Hall and Freud overstated their case (Arnett, 1999).

Although adolescence poses a great risk to healthy development for about one-fourth of teenagers, for at least one-half of them the period is marked by healthy development (Takanishi, 1993). On average, adolescents enjoy good relationships with their families and friends, and researchers say that the majority of them are happy and self-confident (Diener & Diener, 1996).

Contrary to popular belief, adolescence is not stormy and difficult for most teenagers.

Children at highest risk for a troubled adolescence seem to be those who have a tendency toward depression or aggressive behavior or who come from particularly negative environments, such as those filled with family conflict (Buchanan et al., 1992). According to Ebata (1987), adolescent boys who experience turmoil are likely to have had difficulties before they reached adolescence, whereas girls are more likely to experience psychological difficulties for the first time in adolescence. Research also suggests that there are gender differences in the coping strategies adolescents use to deal with conflict, turmoil, and difficulties. Boys tend to use more direct, physically active coping strategies, while girls rely more on an interpersonal coping style (Recklitis & Noam, 1999).

Physical Development during Adolescence: Growing, Growing, Grown

Adolescence begins with the onset of **puberty**—a period of rapid physical growth and change that culminates in sexual maturity (Rice, 1992). Although the average onset of puberty is age 10 for girls and age 12 for boys, the normal range extends from age 7 to age 14 for girls and from 9 to 16 for boys (Chumlea, 1982). Every person's individual timetable for adolescence is influenced primarily by heredity, although environmental factors also exert some influence.

The Physical Changes of Puberty: Flooding Hormones Jump-Start Growth

What physical changes occur during puberty?

Puberty begins with a surge in hormone production, which in turn causes a number of physical changes. The most startling change during puberty is the marked acceleration in growth known as the **adolescent growth spurt.** Who doesn't remember that time in life when the girls were towering over boys of the same age? On the average, the growth spurt occurs from age 10½ to 13 in girls and about 2 years later in boys, from age 12½ to 15 (Tanner, 1961). Because various parts of the body grow at different rates, the adolescent often has a lanky, awkward appearance. Girls attain their full height between ages 16 and 17, and boys, between ages 18 and 20 (Roche & Davila, 1972).

During puberty the reproductive organs in both sexes mature, and **secondary sex characteristics** appear—those physical characteristics not directly involved in reproduction that distinguish the mature male from the mature female. In girls the breasts develop and the hips round; in boys the voice deepens, and facial and chest hair appears; and in both sexes there is growth of pubic and underarm (axillary) hair.

The major landmark of puberty for males is the first ejaculation, which occurs, on average, at age 13 (Jorgensen & Keiding, 1991). And for females it is **menarche**—the onset of menstruation—which occurs at an average age of 12½, although from 10 to 15½ is considered within the normal range (Tanner, 1990). Some research suggests that environmental stress, such as parental divorce or conflict, is related to an earlier onset of menarche (Belsky et al., 1991; Wierson et al., 1993).

What are the psychological effects of early and late maturation for boys and girls?

The Timing of Puberty: Early and Late Maturation

Probably at no other time in life does physical appearance have such a strong impact on self-image and self-esteem as during adolescence. Girls want to be slim and attractive; boys want to be tall, broad-shouldered, and muscular. The timing of puberty can have important psychological consequences, coming as it does at a time when a sense of security is gained from being like other members of the peer group.

Early- and Late-Maturing Boys For males, early maturation seems to bestow important advantages and enhanced status in the peer group (Mussen & Jones, 1957; Peterson, 1987). Early-maturing boys, taller and stronger than their classmates, have an advantage in sports and capture admiring glances from the girls. They are likely to have a positive body image, to feel confident, secure, independent, and happy, and to be more successful academically as well (Alsaker, 1995; Blyth et al., 1981; Peterson, 1987). Early maturers are also viewed more favorably by adults. They are perceived as being more attractive and are given more responsibility and freedom than their less physically mature counterparts (Jones & Bayley, 1950).

Judged as less attractive by both peers and adults, late-maturing boys are often at a disadvantage socially and athletically. They are self-conscious about their size and lack the physical traits of manliness—a deep voice and a developing beard. To make matters worse, they are often teased by their peers and treated like "kids." Late-maturing boys are frequently subjected to bullying, at school and in their neighborhoods. Research indicates that many of these victims of bullying have poor skills in emotional regulation, which would help them cope with provocations and reduce the stress of negative emotions. Boys who lack such skills tend to employ a coping style that perpetuates or even escalates the bullying (Wilton et al., 2000).

Early- and Late-Maturing Girls The social advantages and disadvantages of early and late maturation are less clear for girls. Early-maturing girls, who may tower over their peers, feel more self-conscious about their developing bodies and their size. In addition, they have to deal with the sexual advances of older boys before they are emotionally or psychologically mature (Peterson, 1987). In addition to having earlier sexual experiences and more unwanted pregnancies than late-maturing girls, early-maturing girls are more likely to be exposed to alcohol and drug use (Caspi et al., 1993). And, having had such experiences, early-maturing girls, not surprisingly, tend to perform less well academically than their age mates (Stattin & Magnusson, 1990). By later adolescence, when their peers have caught up, early maturers tend to be shorter and heavier than later maturers and, therefore, more likely to be unhappy with their physical appearance (Simmons et al., 1983).

Late-maturing girls often experience considerable stress when they fail to develop physically along with their peers. But there is a compensation for the late-maturing girl. Eventually she is likely to be taller and slimmer than her early-maturing age mates.

---

secondary sex characteristics: Those physical characteristics that are not directly involved in reproduction but distinguish the mature male from the mature female.

menarche (men-AR-kee): The onset of menstruation.

formal operations stage: Piaget's final stage of cognitive development, characterized by the ability to use logical reasoning in abstract situations.

imaginary audience: A belief of adolescents that they are or will be the focus of attention in social situations and that others will be as critical or approving as they are of themselves.

personal fable: An exaggerated sense of personal uniqueness and indestructibility, which may be the basis for adolescent risk taking.

Cognitive Development in Adolescence: Piaget's Formal Operations Stage

What cognitive abilities develop during the formal operations stage?

The most striking achievement in cognitive development during adolescence is the ability to think abstractly. Jean Piaget (1972; Piaget & Inhelder, 1969) believed that young people typically enter the final stage of cognitive development, the **formal operations stage,** at age 11 or 12, when they become able to use logical reasoning in abstract situations. Remember that, according to Piaget, preadolescents are able to apply logical thought processes only in concrete situations. Once they become capable of fully operational thinking, adolescents are able to attack problems by systematically testing hypotheses and drawing conclusions through deductive reasoning.

When high school students develop formal operational thinking, they are able to unravel the mysteries of algebra and to decipher analogies and metaphors in English literature. With formal operations comes the ability to explore the world of ideas, to look at religion and moral values in a new light, and to consider different philosophies and political systems. Formal operational thinking enables adolescents to think hypothetically; that is, they can think of what *might* be. Given this new ability, it is not surprising that they begin to conceive of "perfect" solutions to the world's problems.

Formal operational thought does not develop automatically, and it may be virtually absent in some primitive cultures (Dasen, 1972). One longitudinal study of American adolescents and adults concluded that only 30% of those studied attained formal operations (Kuhn et al., 1977). Not only do many people fail to show formal operational thinking, but those who do attain it usually apply it only in those areas in which they are most proficient (Ault, 1983; Martorano, 1977). Some studies suggest that even very intelligent, well-educated adults think best when thinking concretely (Neimark, 1975). According to John Flavell (1992), adults appear less competent, and infants and young children more competent, than developmental psychologists once believed.

Adolescent Egocentrism: On Center Stage, Unique, and Indestructible

David Elkind (1967, 1974) claims that the early teenage years are marked by adolescent egocentrism, which takes two forms—the imaginary audience and the personal fable. Do you remember, as a teenager, picturing how your friends would react to the way you looked when you made your grand entrance at a big party? At this stage of life, it never occurs to teens that most of the people at the party are preoccupied not with others, but with the way *they* look and the impression *they* are making. This **imaginary audience** of admirers (or critics) that adolescents conjure up exists only in their imagination; "but in the young person's mind, he/she is always on stage" (Buis & Thompson, 1989, p. 774).

Teenagers also have an exaggerated sense of their own uniqueness and indestructibility that Elkind calls the **personal fable.** They cannot fathom that anyone has ever felt as deeply as they feel or has ever loved as they love. Elkind suggests that this compelling sense of personal uniqueness may cause many adolescents to believe that they are somehow indestructible and protected from the misfortunes that befall others, such as unwanted pregnancies, auto accidents, or drug overdoses. Belief in the personal fable may account for much of the risk taking during adolescence.

Adolescents frequently engage in high-risk behaviors even though they understand the risks involved. What underlying factors might explain this behavior?

In another study, however, Quadrel and others (1993) found that both high-risk adolescents (from group homes or juvenile centers) and middle-class, low-risk adolescents actually perceived themselves as *more* likely to experience certain negative events—injury in an auto accident, alcohol dependency, mugging, and so forth—than did adults.

Remember It!

1. Adolescence is a stormy period for most teenagers. (true/false)
2. The secondary sex characteristics
   a. are directly involved in reproduction.
   b. appear at the same time in all adolescents.
   c. distinguish mature males from mature females.
   d. include the testes and the ovaries.
3. Which of the following provides the most advantages?
   a. early maturation in girls
   b. early maturation in boys
   c. late maturation in girls
   d. late maturation in boys
4. The ability to apply logical reasoning in abstract situations characterizes Piaget's formal operations stage. (true/false)
5. The teenager's personal fable includes all of the following *except*
   a. a sense of personal uniqueness.
   b. a belief that he or she is indestructible and protected from misfortunes.
   c. a belief that no one has ever felt so deeply before.
   d. a feeling that he or she is always on stage.

Answers: 1. false 2. c 3. b 4. true 5. d

ADOLESCENCE: MORAL AND SOCIAL DEVELOPMENT

Kohlberg's Theory of Moral Development

Lawrence Kohlberg (1981, 1984, 1985) believed, as did Piaget before him, that moral reasoning is closely related to cognitive development and that it, too, evolves in stages. Kohlberg (1969) studied moral development by presenting a series of moral dilemmas to male participants from the United States and other countries. Read one of his best-known dilemmas, and *Try It!*

Try It!

In Europe a woman was near death from a special kind of cancer. There was one drug the doctors thought might save her. It was a form of radium that a druggist in the same town had recently discovered. The drug was expensive to make, and the druggist was charging ten times what it cost him. He paid $200 for the radium and charged $2,000 for a small dose of the drug. The sick woman's husband, Heinz, went to everyone he knew to borrow the money, but he could only get together $1,000, which was half of what the drug cost. He told the druggist that his wife was dying and asked him to sell it cheaper or let him pay later. But the druggist said, "No, I discovered the drug, and I am going to make money from it." So Heinz got desperate and broke into the man's store to steal the drug for his wife (Colby et al., 1983, p. 77).

What moral judgment would you make about the dilemma? Should Heinz have stolen the drug? Why or why not?

Levels of Moral Reasoning Kohlberg was less interested in whether the participants judged Heinz's behavior (as described in the *Try It!*) right or wrong than in the *reasons* for their responses. He found that moral reasoning could be classified into three levels, with each level having two stages.

What are Kohlberg's three levels of moral reasoning?

The Preconventional Level At the first level of moral reasoning, the **preconventional level,** moral reasoning is governed by the standards of others rather than one's own internalized standards of right and wrong. An act is judged good or bad based on its physical consequences. In Stage 1 "right" is whatever avoids punishment; in Stage 2 "right" is whatever is rewarded, benefits the individual, or results in a favor being returned. "You scratch my back and I'll scratch yours" is the thinking common at this stage. Children through age 10 usually function at the preconventional level.

The Conventional Level At the second level of moral reasoning, the **conventional level,** the individual has internalized the standards of others and judges right and wrong in terms of those standards. At Stage 3, sometimes called the "good boy–nice girl" orientation, "good behavior is that which pleases or helps others and is approved by them" (Kohlberg, 1968, p. 26). At Stage 4 the orientation is toward "authority, fixed rules, and the maintenance of the social order. Right behavior consists of doing one's duty, showing respect for authority, and maintaining the given social order for its own sake" (p. 26). Kohlberg believed that a person must function at Piaget's concrete operations stage to reason morally at the conventional level.

The Postconventional Level Kohlberg's highest level is the **postconventional level,** which requires the ability to think at Piaget's stage of formal operations. Postconventional reasoning is most often found among middle-class, college-educated people. At this level, people do not simply internalize the standards of others. Instead, they weigh moral alternatives, realizing that at times the law may conflict with basic human rights. At Stage 5 the person believes that laws are formulated to protect both society and the individual and should be changed if they fail to do so. At Stage 6 ethical decisions are based on universal ethical principles, which emphasize respect for human life, justice, equality, and dignity for all people. People who reason morally at Stage 6 believe that they must follow their conscience even if it results in a violation of the law.

Could this kind of moral reasoning provide a convenient justification for doing anything a person feels like doing at any time? Not according to Kohlberg, who insisted that an action must be judged in terms of whether it is right and fair from the perspective of everyone involved. In other words, the person must be convinced that the action would be proper even if he or she had to change positions with any individual, from the most favored to the least favored, in the society. Later Kohlberg had second thoughts about this sixth stage and was unsure whether it exists except as a matter of theoretical speculation (Levine et al., 1985).

Review & Reflect 10.1 summarizes Kohlberg's six stages of moral development.

The Development of Moral Reasoning Kohlberg claimed that people progress through moral stages one stage at a time in a fixed order. An individual does not skip stages, and if movement occurs, it is to the next higher stage. Postconventional reasoning is not possible, Kohlberg said, until people fully attain Piaget's level of formal operations. They must be able to think in terms of abstract principles and be able to think through and apply ethical principles in hypothetical situations (Kohlberg & Gilligan, 1971; Kuhn et al., 1977). Attaining a high level of cognitive development, however, does not guarantee advanced moral reasoning. And, as Kohlberg came to realize, discussion of moral dilemmas does not reliably improve moral behavior. He eventually agreed that direct teaching of moral values is necessary and compatible with his theory (Higgins, 1995; Power et al., 1989).

preconventional level: Kohlberg's lowest level of moral reasoning, based on the physical consequences of an act; "right" is whatever avoids punishment or gains a reward.

conventional level: Kohlberg's second level of moral reasoning, in which right and wrong are based on the internalized standards of others; "right" is whatever helps or is approved of by others, or whatever is consistent with the laws of society.

postconventional level: Kohlberg's highest level of moral reasoning, in which moral reasoning involves weighing moral alternatives; "right" is whatever furthers basic human rights.

Review & Reflect 10.1 Kohlberg's Stages of Moral Development

Level	Stage
Level I: Preconventional level (Ages 4–10) Moral reasoning is governed by the standards of others; an act is good or bad depending on its physical consequences–whether it is punished or rewarded.	**Stage 1** The stage in which behavior that avoids punishment is right. Children obey out of fear of punishment. **Stage 2** The stage of self-interest. What is right is what benefits the individual or gains a favor in return. "You scratch my back and I'll scratch yours."
Level II: Conventional level (Ages 10–13) The child internalizes the standards of others and judges right and wrong according to those standards.	**Stage 3** The morality of mutual relationships. The "good boy–nice girl" orientation. Child acts to please and help others. **Stage 4** The morality of the social system and conscience. Orientation toward authority. Morality is doing one's duty, respecting authority, and maintaining the social order.
Level III: Postconventional level (After age 13, at young adulthood, or never) Moral conduct is under internal control; this is the highest level and the mark of true morality.	**Stage 5** The morality of contract; respect for individual rights and laws that are democratically agreed on. Rational valuing of the wishes of the majority and the general welfare. Belief that society is best served if citizens obey the law. **Stage 6** The highest stage of the highest social level. The morality of universal ethical principles. The person acts according to internal standards independent of legal restrictions or opinions of others.

What do cross-cultural studies reveal about the universality of Kohlberg's theory?

Research on Kohlberg's Theory In a review of 45 studies of Kohlberg's theory conducted in 27 countries, Snarey (1985) found support for the virtual universality of Stages 1 through 4, and for the invariant sequence of these stages in all groups studied. Although extremely rare, Stage 5 was found in almost all samples from urban or middle-class populations and was absent in all of the tribal or village folk societies studied. And Snarey's more recent research (1995) supports the conclusions he and his colleagues reached a decade earlier.

One controversy concerns possible gender bias in Kohlberg's stages. Kohlberg indicated that the majority of women remain at Stage 3, while most men attain Stage 4. Do men typically attain a higher level of moral reasoning than women? Carol Gilligan (1982) asserts that Kohlberg's theory is sex-biased. Not only did Kohlberg fail to include females in his original research, Gilligan points out, but he limited morality to abstract reasoning about moral dilemmas. And, at his highest level, Stage 6, Kohlberg emphasized justice and equality but not mercy, compassion, love, or concern for others. Gilligan suggests that females, more than males, tend to view moral behavior in terms of compassion, caring, and concern for others. More recent evidence suggests that females do tend to emphasize care and compassion in resolving moral dilemmas, while males tend to stress justice or at least to give it equal standing with caring (Garmon et al., 1996; Wark & Krebs, 1996). But, females score as high as males in moral reasoning (Walker, 1989).

In a cross-cultural study of the moral reasoning of adults and children from India and the United States, Miller and Bersoff (1992) found great differences between the two cultures. The postconventional moral reasoning common in India stressed interpersonal responsibilities over obligations to further justice. In contrast, Americans emphasized a personal or rights-oriented view over individual responsibilities to others—a view that the world would be more just if each person, without fail, got exactly what he or she deserved, no more, no less. But would such a world be more moral? Are mercy and compassion less moral than objective, emotionless justice?

Regardless of whether we agree with Kohlberg's theory, most of us would agree moral individuals make moral societies.

Parental Relationships: Their Quality and Influence

Some research indicates that teens begin to distance themselves from their parents at puberty and that conflict increases, particularly with the mother (Paikoff & Brooks-Gunn, 1991). Yet, most adolescents have good relationships with their parents (Steinberg, 1990).

The conventional notion that conflict between parent and child is healthy has not been supported. In fact, a high level of conflict is related to drug abuse, dropping out of school, early pregnancy and marriage, running away, suicide attempts, and the development of psychiatric disorders (Peterson, 1988). Also, there is growing support for the assertion that the father is an important ingredient for the healthy development of children and adolescents. As was mentioned in Chapter 9, father absence is related to aggression and delinquency in adolescence (Bishop & Lane, 2000)

Most adolescents and their parents have good relationships and enjoy doing things together.

Parental involvement is a key ingredient in fostering adolescents' academic success. And researchers have recently found indications that parents tend to be more involved with the education of their adolescent daughters than with that of their sons. This finding may be explained in part by current social conditions (delayed marriage of young people, higher divorce rate, etc.), which demand that females develop a career and be more financially self-sufficient, rather than expecting to rely on a husband (Carter & Wojtkiewicz, 2000). Although parental involvement clearly encourages academic success, it does seem to be the most important factor in teenagers' perception of fair treatment, especially when there are siblings in a family. In one study, whether siblings perceived their parents' treatment of them as fair depended more on each sibling's self-concept and the quality of the relationship between the siblings' than on the parents' time involvement, personal warmth, and allocation of household chores (Updegraff et al., 2000).

What outcomes are often associated with the authoritative, authoritarian, and permissive parenting styles?

The Three Parenting Styles Revisited Of the three parenting styles discussed in Chapter 9—authoritative, authoritarian, and permissive—the authoritative is most effective and the permissive least effective for adolescents (Baumrind, 1991; Steinberg et al., 1994). In a study of about 2,300 adolescents, those with permissive parents were more likely to use alcohol and drugs and to have conduct problems and less likely to be engaged in school than were those with authoritative or authoritarian parents (Lamborn et al., 1991). The authoritarian style was related to more psychological distress and less self-reliance and self-confidence in adolescents. The authoritative parenting style was associated with psychosocial competence for adolescents of all racial and ethnic groups and with academic success for those who are White and middle-class (Aunola et al., 2000; Steinberg et al., 1994). And female adolescents who perceive their parents as authoritative have higher levels of involvement in community activities. Moreover, a parent's relationship with his or her adolescent daughter's peers and their parents is related to the daughter's involvement in extracurricular school activities (Fletcher & Shaw, 2000).

But the authoritative style was not found to be associated with high academic achievement in African American and Asian American adolescents (Steinberg, 1992). Why not? Steinberg (1992) suggests that White middle-class students benefit both from an authoritative parenting style and from peer support for academic achievement. And although Asian American adolescents typically have authoritarian parents, several factors may explain why they outperform other groups academically. First, academic achievement is highly valued by both their families and their peers, and second, they believe strongly that academic excellence is a prerequisite for future occupational success. But African American and Hispanic adolescents typically lack peer support for academic excellence and are less likely to see it as necessary for their occupational future. In fact, according to Steinberg (1992), "African American students are more likely than others to be caught in a bind between performing well in school and being popular among their peers" (p. 728). Thus, when peer values and norms do not support academic pursuits, the peer influences often negate parental influence.

The Peer Group

What are some of the useful functions of the adolescent peer group?

At a time when adolescents feel the need to become more independent from their parents, friends become a vital source of emotional support and approval. Adolescents usually choose friends of the same sex and race (Clark & Ayers, 1992), who have similar values, interests, and backgrounds (Duck, 1983; Epstein, 1983; Hamm, 2000).

Interactions with peers are critical while young people are fashioning their identities. Adolescents can try out different roles and observe the reactions of their friends to their behavior and their appearance. The peer group provides teenagers with a standard of comparison for evaluating their own assets as well as a vehicle for developing social skills (Berndt, 1992).

A controversial book, *The Nurture Assumption,* by Judith Harris (1998), suggests that peers have more influence on young people than parents do. But such a claim implies that the environmental influence of peers is strong enough to override both parents' genetic contribution (nature), and their environmental influence (nurture). In fact, peer and parental influences are not necessarily opposing forces. Often parents know and like the friends of their teenage children. Moreover, adolescents are not assigned to peer groups at random; as mentioned above, they usually choose to associate with those similar to themselves. For example, an academically inclined teen is likely to gravitate to a peer group with academic interests. The relationship between parent and child also affects the selection of a peer group. Thus, teens differ greatly in the degree to which they are influenced by their peers (Collins et al., 2000).

For males and females, popularity within the peer group is based largely on good looks and personality. For boys, athletic ability is often an important factor in popularity with both sexes (Savin-Williams, 1980). And conformity appears to be another important ingredient in popularity for both sexes (Sebald, 1981).

Sexuality and Adolescence

Before the 1960s the surging sex drive of adolescents was held in check primarily because most societal influences—parents, religious leaders, the schools, and the media—were all preaching the same message: Premarital sex is wrong. Then sexual attitudes began to change.

The acceptance by teenagers of cohabitation and even having babies without being married has risen dramatically over the last few decades. Less than one-third of teenage girls and slightly more than one-third of teenage boys believe that people will have happier and richer lives if they marry, rather than simply live with someone (Poponoe & Whitehead, 2000). Today, more than 60% of teens agree, or mostly agree, that it is a good idea for a couple to live together before getting married.

Early premarital intercourse is associated with an increased risk of pregnancy (Morgan et al., 1995) and of sexually transmitted diseases and with a higher number of sexual partners. Teens who tend to be less experienced sexually are those who attend religious services frequently and live with both biological parents, who are neither too permissive nor too strict in their discipline and rules (White & DeBlassie, 1992). Early intercourse is less prevalent among adolescents whose academic achievement is above average and whose parents have a harmonious relationship (Brooks-Gunn & Furstenberg, 1989).

Teenage Pregnancy: Too Much Too Soon

Young women in the United States are not more sexually active than their European counterparts. Yet the incidence of pregnancy among 15- to-19-year-old females is higher in this country than in any other developed nation (Ambuel, 1995; Creatsas et al., 1995; Kaufman, 1996). About 10% of the 10 million adolescent girls in the United States become pregnant each year ("Rate of Births," 1995). What happens to their babies? Approximately 40% of these 1 million teenage pregnancies are terminated by abortion, and another 13% end in miscarriage (Jaskiewics & McAnamey, 1994). Of course, some of these teenage mothers are married, but about 70% of them are not, according to the Children's Defense Fund (1996). And nearly one-third of the unwed teenage mothers in the United States will find themselves in the same condition again within 2 years (Alan Guttmacher Institute, 1991).

Recently, out-of-wedlock births accounted for 32% of U.S. births (U.S. Bureau of the Census, 1997). In contrast, only 15% of American babies were born to unwed mothers in 1960 (National Research Council, 1993). Why the dramatic increase in out-of-wedlock births? The explanation lies in rapidly changing attitudes. In the past females had always been less willing than males to have babies outside of marriage. But this is no longer true. Today, 54% of teenage girls see nothing wrong in having babies without being married, compared with 49% of teenage boys (Poponoe & Whitehead, 2000).

What are some of the disturbing consequences of teenage pregnancy?

The Consequences for Mother and Child Early pregnancy can have serious physical consequences. Pregnant teens are more likely to come from poor backgrounds and less likely to receive early prenatal medical care and adequate nutrition. As a result, they are at higher risk for miscarriage, stillbirth, and complications during delivery. They are also more likely to deliver premature or low-birthweight babies, who have a higher infant mortality rate (Fraser et al., 1995; Goldenberg & Klerman, 1995; Scholl et al., 1996).

Among young women who give birth before age 18 and choose to keep their babies, half never complete high school. As a group, their earning power is about half that of their counterparts who did not have babies at this early age (National Research Council, 1993), and many eventually depend on welfare (Grogger & Bronars, 1993). Because many teenage mothers are single parents living in poverty, their children often suffer from inadequate parenting, nutrition, and health care, and are more likely to be abused and neglected. In school, these children typically score lower on intelligence tests, have poor achievement records, and are more likely to exhibit disruptive behavior (Berk, 1997). Furthermore, teenage parents often misinterpret their child's behavior. Research has shown that adolescent mothers who use coercive parenting practices tend to interpret their child's emotional expressions as angry ones and assume that the child is being defiant (Strassberg, 2000).

Relatively little research has focused on teenage fathers. A young father is more likely to marry the mother of his child if he can find a job that provides enough income to support a family. However, few such jobs are available to young people who have not completed high school. One-third of pregnant teenagers do marry their baby's father, but the divorce rate for these marriages is two to three times higher than the national average.

Part-Time Jobs for Adolescents: A Positive or a Negative?

In general, what is the impact on adolescents of working more than 15 to 20 hours a week during the school year?

For several decades it was assumed that adolescents benefit from part-time jobs, because they develop a work ethic, earn money, and become better prepared to enter the world of work. Several very large studies indicate that for teenagers the consequences of working more than 15 to 20 hours weekly are primarily negative. In a study of more than 70,000 high school seniors, Bachman and Schulenberg (1993) found working long hours was "positively correlated with smoking cigarettes, drinking alcohol, using illicit drugs, interpersonal aggression, theft, victimization, trouble with police, arguments with parents, lack of sleep, and lack of exercise" (p. 230). Furthermore, rather than earning and saving, the typical adolescent with a job was more likely to earn and spend.

In a study of 1,800 high school students, Steinberg and others (1993) found that working students spent less time on homework and had poorer class attendance. Also, students who worked long hours were more likely to have used drugs and to have lacked interest in school even before their employment. Moreover, their intensive work schedule made their existing problems worse.

Studies have shown that working more than 15–20 hours per week during the school year typically has negative consequences for teenagers.

Remember It!

1. Match Kohlberg's level of moral reasoning with the rationale for engaging in a behavior.

   ____ (1) to avoid punishment or gain a reward — a. conventional
   ____ (2) to ensure that human rights are protected — b. preconventional
   ____ (3) to gain approval or to follow the law — c. postconventional

2. Most teenagers have good relationships with their parents. (true/false)
3. For adolescents, the most effective parenting style is the ______________; the least effective is the ______________.
   a. authoritative; authoritarian
   b. authoritarian; permissive
   c. authoritative; permissive
   d. permissive; authoritarian
4. For most adolescents, the peer group serves some useful functions. (true/false)
5. Although teen pregnancy has many negative consequences for the mother, it has relatively few for the child. (true/false)
6. Overall, the impact of working long hours during high school is positive. (true/false)

Answers: 1. (1) b (2) c (3) a 2. true 3. c 4. true 5. false 6. false

ERIKSON'S PSYCHOSOCIAL THEORY: ADOLESCENCE THROUGH ADULTHOOD

Erik Erikson distinguished himself as a psychoanalyst and personality theorist. He won a Pulitzer Prize for his writing, and his books still sell by the thousands. Even in his 90s, Erikson continued with his wife, Joan (an artist and author), to make scholarly contributions. They both served as models of the successful resolution of the eight stages of human development that he proposed.

Chapter 9 presented the first four stages of Erikson's psychosocial theory of development. Each of Erikson's stages is built around a conflict that involves the individual's relationship with the social environment. The stages themselves are named for the two opposite basic attitudes that may be formed, depending on how the conflicts are resolved. To preserve the continuity of the theory, we will consider the remaining four stages together. All eight stages are described in *Review & Reflect 10.2.*

Review & Reflect 10.2 Erikson's Psychosocial Stages of Development

Stage	Ages	Description
Trust vs. mistrust	Birth to 1 year	Infants learn to trust or mistrust depending on the degree and regularity of care, love, and affection provided by parents or caregivers.
Autonomy vs. shame and doubt	1 to 3 years	Children learn to express their will and independence, to exercise some control, and to make choices. If not, they experience shame and doubt.
Initiative vs. guilt	3 to 6 years	Children begin to initiate activities, to plan and undertake tasks, and to enjoy developing motor and other abilities. If not allowed to initiate or if made to feel stupid and considered a nuisance, they may develop a sense of guilt.
Industry vs. inferiority	6 years to puberty	Children develop industriousness and feel pride in accomplishing tasks, making things, and doing things. If not encouraged or if rebuffed by parents and teachers, they may develop a sense of inferiority.
Identity vs. role confusion	Adolescence	Adolescents must make the transition from childhood to adulthood, establish an identity, develop a sense of self, and consider a future occupational identity. Otherwise, role confusion can result.
Intimacy vs. isolation	Young adulthood	Young adults must develop intimacy–the ability to share with, care for, and commit themselves to another person. Avoiding intimacy brings a sense of isolation and loneliness.
Generativity vs. stagnation	Middle adulthood	Middle-aged people must find some way of contributing to the development of the next generation. Failing this, they may become self-absorbed and emotionally impoverished and reach a point of stagnation.
Ego integrity vs. despair	Late adulthood	Individuals review their lives, and if they are satisfied and feel a sense of accomplishment, they will experience ego integrity. If dissatisfied, they may sink into despair.

Identity versus Role Confusion: Erikson's Stage for Adolescence

How did Erikson explain the fifth psychosocial stage–identity versus role confusion?

Erikson's fifth stage of psychosocial development, **identity versus role confusion,** is the developmental struggle of adolescence. "Who am I?" becomes the critical question at this stage, as adolescents seek to establish their identity and find values to guide their lives (Erikson, 1963). At this point, for the first time, adolescents are seriously looking to the future and considering an occupational identity—what they will choose as their life's work. Erikson (1968) believed that "in general it is the inability to settle on an occupational identity which most disturbs young people" (p. 132). The danger at this stage, he said, is that of role confusion—not knowing who you are or where you belong.

Erikson used the term *identity crisis* to portray the disturbance adolescents experience in forging an identity. But research does not support the notion that most young people experience a crisis (Blyth & Traeger, 1983). Although Erikson (1980) considered establishing an identity to be the focus of adolescence, he recognized that "identity *formation* neither begins nor ends with adolescence: it is a lifelong development" (p. 122).

Intimacy versus Isolation: Erikson's Stage for Early Adulthood

What is Erikson's psychosocial task for early adulthood?

Erikson contended that if healthy development is to continue into adulthood, it is necessary for a young adult to establish intimacy in a relationship. This sixth stage of psychosocial development he called **intimacy versus isolation.** For Erikson, intimacy meant the ability of young adults to form strong emotional attachments—that is, to share with, care for, make sacrifices for, and commit themselves to another person. He believed that avoiding intimacy results in a sense of isolation and loneliness.

Erikson (1980) argued that young adults must establish their own identity before true intimacy is possible. He said, "The condition of a true twoness is that one must first become oneself" (p. 101). Several studies support Erikson's notion that a stable identity is a necessary prerequisite for an intimate relationship (Tesch & Whitbourne, 1982; Vaillant, 1977).

Generativity versus Stagnation: Erikson's Stage for Middle Adulthood

What changes did Erikson believe are essential for healthy personality development in middle age?

Erikson's seventh psychosocial stage is called **generativity versus stagnation.** Erikson (1980) claimed that in order to maintain good mental health into middle adulthood, individuals must develop generativity—an "interest in establishing and guiding the next generation" (p. 103). There is some research support for Erikson's claim about generativity. In a study of mid-life adults, generativity was positively related to satisfaction in life and work, and it was a strong predictor of emotional well-being (Ackerman et al., 2000). People who do not develop generativity become self-absorbed and "begin to indulge themselves as if they were their own one and only child" (Erikson, 1980, p. 103). Personal impoverishment and a sense of stagnation often accompany such self-absorption.

According to Erikson, in middle adulthood, people develop generativity—an interest in guiding the next generation.

Ego Integrity versus Despair: Erikson's Final Stage

Psychosocial development continues into later adulthood, but its course is usually an extension of the former life pattern. The outcome of Erikson's eighth stage, **ego integrity versus despair,** depends primarily on whether a person has resolved the conflicts at previous stages (Erikson et al., 1986). Those who have a sense of ego integrity believe their life has had meaning. They look back with satisfaction and a sense of accomplishment and do not have major regrets.

What is the key to a positive resolution of Erikson's eighth psychosocial stage–ego integrity versus despair?

> At the other extreme is the individual who looks back upon his life as a series of missed opportunities and missed directions; now in the twilight years he realizes that it is too late to start again. For such a person the inevitable result is a sense of despair at what might have been. (Elkind, 1970, p. 112)

Erikson's Theory: Does Research Support It?

Whitbourne and others (1992) studied three different age groups to measure change over a 22-year period from early to middle adulthood. Their research supported Erikson's claim that a favorable resolution of the psychosocial crisis at one stage depends on the successful resolution of earlier crises. However, the researchers found participants often continued to show changes associated with previous stages, particularly the stage of industry versus inferiority.

In a cross-sectional study of young, midlife, and older adults, McAdams and others (1993) found that compared with younger and older adults, middle-aged adults express more generative concern—a conscious concern for "having a positive and enduring impact on the next generation" (p. 227). But these adults' concerns were not matched with actions, because they did not engage in significantly more behaviors that would foster this end.

Remember It!

1. Which of the following was *not* identified by Erikson as a developmental task in his psychosocial stage for adolescence?
   a. forming an intimate relationship
   b. planning for an occupation
   c. forming an identity
   d. finding values to live by
2. Erikson claimed that an interest in guiding the next generation is necessary for good mental health in
   a. adolescence.
   b. young adulthood.
   c. middle age.
   d. old age.
3. Erikson believed the main task in young adulthood is to
   a. develop generativity.
   b. forge an identity.
   c. start a family.
   d. form an intimate relationship.
4. According to Erikson, older people who feel they did not reach many of their goals or contribute positively to others experience
   a. stagnation.
   b. despair.
   c. isolation.
   d. inferiority.

Answers: 1. a 2. c 3. d 4. b

identity versus role confusion: Erikson's fifth psychosocial stage, when adolescents need to establish their own identity and to form values to live by; failure can lead to an identity crisis.

intimacy versus isolation: Erikson's sixth psychosocial stage, when the young adult must establish intimacy in a relationship in order to avoid feeling a sense of isolation and loneliness.

generativity versus stagnation: Erikson's stage for middle age, when people become increasingly concerned with guiding the next generation rather than stagnating.

ego integrity versus despair: Erikson's stage for old age, when people look back on their lives with satisfaction or with major regrets.

OTHER THEORIES OF ADULTHOOD

While Erikson's theory covers developmental stages throughout the life span, other theories focus on stages of adult development.

Levinson's Seasons of Life

How is Levinson's concept of life structure related to his proposed stages of development?

Daniel Levinson formulated a stage theory of adult development based on extensive interviews of 40 men between the ages of 35 and 45. They were "hourly workers in industry, business executives, university biologists and novelists"—of diverse racial, ethnic, and religious origins and social classes (Levinson et al., 1978). Levinson identified four eras, or seasons, in the life cycle: preadulthood (childhood and adolescence), early adulthood, middle adulthood, and late adulthood. Participants went through stable periods lasting from 6 to 10 years. During these periods they made certain key choices that formed the basis of their **life structure**—the basic pattern of their life at a given time, including their relationships and activities.

Between these stable 6- to 10-year periods were transitional periods lasting 4 to 5 years. A transitional period might be a time for minor changes in the life structure or drastic changes, such as divorce, remarriage, changing jobs or occupations, or moving to another part of the country. Levinson called a particularly difficult transitional period a *crisis.*

Following are descriptions of some of Levinson's proposed stages:

- *Early Adult Transition* (ages 17 to 22): During this period of transition between adolescence and early adulthood, young people begin to separate psychologically from parents and other aspects of the pre-adult world in preparation for entry into the adult world.
- *Entering the Adult World* (ages 22 to 28): Young adults typically choose an occupation, form love relationships, marry and have a family, and try to turn their dream of the kind of life they want into reality.
- *Age 30 Transition* (ages 28 to 33): This period is a time for modifying the first adult life structure and creating "the basis for a more satisfactory structure within which to complete the era of early adulthood" (1978, p. 58).
- *Settling Down* (ages 33 to 40): Adults build a second life structure and anchor themselves more firmly in family or community. They seek to advance in their occupation and climb the ladder of success.
- *Midlife Transition* (ages 40 to 45): During this transition period people develop "a heightened awareness of . . . mortality and a desire to use the remaining time more wisely" (1978, p. 192). Some people make few external changes; others make drastic ones involving "divorce, remarriage, major shifts in occupation and lifestyle" (p. 194). Levinson reported that 80% of his participants experienced a moderate or severe **midlife crisis.**
- *Middle Adult Era* (ages 45 to 60): Having become senior members in their own world, individuals feel a responsibility for "the development of the current generation of young adults who will soon enter the dominant generation" (Levinson, 1986, p. 6).
- *Late Adult Transition* (ages 60 to 65): In the transition into late adulthood, individuals must face the coming retirement years. The life structure must once again be modified to allow for work no longer being the central focus. Much more time can be spent pursuing personal interests, such as hobbies, community service, or travel, and personal relationships with grandchildren, other family members, or friends.

life structure: Levinson's term for the basic pattern of one's life at any given time, including one's relationships and activities and the significance they have for the individual.

midlife crisis: A period of turmoil usually occurring in a person's 40s and brought on by an awareness of one's mortality; characterized by a reassessment of one's life and a decision to make changes, either drastic or moderate, in order to make the remaining years better.

Although his first study included only men, Levinson later studied 45 women. His findings convinced him that his theory is applicable to females as well. On the basis of his research and that of others, Levinson claims that his theory "holds for men and women of different cultures, classes, and historical epochs" (Levinson, 1986, p. 8).

Does research support Levinson's claim of the existence of a midlife crisis? Not according to researchers McCrae and Costa (1990) at the National Institute of Aging. Using their *Midlife Crisis Scale,* they assessed 350 men, whose ages ranged from 30 to 60. Finding no evidence at all for a midlife crisis, they administered the scale to another 300 men and then also used it along with a measure of emotional instability to assess almost 10,000 men and women. Again, they found no evidence that distress typically peaks during midlife, producing a crisis.

Reinke and Others: The Life Course in Women

What did the study of middle-class women by Reinke and others reveal about major transitional periods in the life cycle?

Reinke and her colleagues (1985) interviewed 124 middle-class women aged 30 to 60 to gain information about their marriages, families, employment, life satisfactions and dissatisfactions, and life changes. Like Levinson, the researchers found major transitional periods in which participants seemed to reappraise their lives and consider changes. Some of these changes were related to specific chronological ages, but the researchers believe that women's development is examined most profitably in relation to six phases in the family cycle: (1) the *no children phase,* (2) the *starting a family–preschool phase,* (3) the *school age phase,* (4) the *adolescent phase,* (5) the *launching phase* (beginning when the first child leaves home and ending when the last child leaves), and (6) the *postparental phase.*

Changes were reliably associated with each of the six family-cycle phases, regardless of whether women had experienced major transitions. Women experiencing a major transition at the family–preschool phase were more likely to report changes in themselves, as well as marital separation or divorce. The 40% of participants who reported a transition at the launching phase became more introspective and assertive, but very few experienced the *empty nest syndrome* (feelings of emptiness and depression when children grow up and leave home).

Life Stages: Fact or Fiction?

Not all researchers accept the notion of stages in adult development. For example, Bernice Neugarten (1982), one of the most respected researchers in adult development, warns against assuming that Levinson's findings apply to all adults. For many people, life is one long crisis. For someone facing chronic unemployment, a midlife crisis that involved choosing to change a job or vocation would be considered a luxury.

When their children leave home to go to college or get a job, most parents do not experience the sadness associated with the "empty nest syndrome" but instead are able to adjust successfully.

Remember It!

1. Levinson claims that as people make the transition from one era in the life cycle to another, they reexamine and modify their
   a. life maps.
   b. personal schemas.
   c. lifestyles.
   d. life structures.
2. Levinson found that the transition most likely to cause a crisis was the
   a. early adult transition.
   b. age 30 transition.
   c. midlife transition.
   d. late adult transition.
3. Research on thousands of men and women indicates that most people experience a midlife crisis. (true/false)
4. Reinke and others believe that the best way to examine life changes in a woman's life is in relation to
   a. changes in her marital status.
   b. phases in the family cycle relating to her children.
   c. alternating stable and transitional periods.
   d. young adulthood, middle adulthood, and older adulthood.

Answers: 1. d 2. c 3. false 4. b

EARLY AND MIDDLE ADULTHOOD

The long period of some 40 to 45 years known as adulthood is generally divided into three parts—young or early adulthood (ages 20 to 40 or 45), middle adulthood (ages 40 or 45 to 65), and late adulthood (after age 65 or 70). Obviously, some things change during adulthood, but in many ways people remain much the same throughout this period. The most obvious changes are usually physical ones.

Physical Changes in Adulthood

What are the physical changes associated with middle age?

Opinions vary about what period should be called the "prime of life," but it is clear that the *physical* prime of life occurs early. Most people in their 20s and 30s enjoy good general health and vitality, but the decade of the 20s is the period of top physical condition, when physical strength, reaction time, reproductive capacity, and manual dexterity all peak. During the 30s, there is a slight decline in these physical capacities, which is barely perceptible to most people other than professional athletes.

Middle-aged people often complain about a loss of physical vigor and endurance. But such losses have to do less with aging than with exercise, diet, and health habits. Some fine professional athletes, such as star pitcher Nolan Ryan and heavyweight champion George Foreman, were competing into their 40s. One unavoidable change in the mid- to late 40s is **presbyopia,** a condition in which the lenses of the eyes no longer accommodate adequately for near vision, and reading glasses or bifocals are required for reading.

In middle age, people are more susceptible to diseases, especially life-threatening ones. Heart disease is responsible for a little over 31% and cancer nearly 31% of all deaths among men between ages 45 and 54 (U.S. Bureau of the Census, 1997). Cancer, usually of the lungs or breast, accounts for about 43% and heart disease 21% of the deaths of women in this age group. Consequently, during middle age, people become more aware of their mortality. By the time we reach 50, as one researcher has put it, "We must accept that life's seesaw has tipped; that there are now more yesterdays than tomorrows" (Vaillant, 1977, p. 233).

The major biological event for women during middle age is **menopause**—the cessation of menstruation, which usually occurs between ages 45 and 55 and marks the end of reproductive capacity. Although life expectancy for females in developed countries increased by 30 years during the 20th century, the fertile years, during

presbyopia (prez-bee-O-pee-uh): A condition, occurring in the mid- to late 40s, in which the lenses of the eyes no longer accommodate adequately for near vision, and reading glasses or bifocals are required for reading.

menopause: The cessation of menstruation, occurring between ages 45 and 55 and signifying the end of reproductive capacity.

which women can conceive, have not increased. The span of woman's reproductive capability is apparently unaffected by the factors that control longevity (Brody et al., 2000).

The most common symptom associated with menopause and the sharp decrease in the level of estrogen is *hot flashes*—sudden feelings of being uncomfortably hot. Some women also experience symptoms such as anxiety, irritability, and/or mood swings, and about 10% become depressed. However, most women do not experience psychological problems in connection with menopause (Busch et al., 1994; Matthews, 1992).

Although men do not have a physical event equivalent to menopause, they do experience a gradual decline in testosterone from age 20 until about age 60. During late middle age, many men also experience a reduction in semen production and in the sex drive. However, though women are not able to conceive after menopause, many men can and do father children during late adulthood. In 1997, actor Tony Randall became a father at age 73.

Intellectual Capacity during Early and Middle Adulthood

In general, can adults look forward to an increase or a decrease in intellectual performance from their 20s to their 60s?

Conventional wisdom has held that intellectual ability reaches its peak in the late teens or early 20s, and that it's all downhill after that. Fortunately, conventional wisdom is wrong. It is true that younger people do better on tests requiring speed or rote memory. But on tests measuring general information, vocabulary, reasoning ability, and social judgment, older participants usually do better than younger ones because of their greater experience and education (Horn, 1982). Adults actually continue to gain knowledge and skills over the years, particularly when they lead intellectually challenging lives.

Schaie (1994, 1995) analyzed data from the Seattle Longitudinal Study, which assessed the intellectual abilities of some 5,000 participants. Many of the participants were tested six times over the course of 35 years. Schaie found that in five areas—verbal meaning, spatial orientation, inductive reasoning, number, and word fluency—participants showed modest gains from young adulthood to the mid-40s (see Figure 10.1). Decline did not occur, on average, until after age 60, and even then the decline was modest until the 80s. Half of the participants, even at age 81, showed no decline over the previous 7 years. The study also revealed several gender differences. Females performed better on tests of verbal meaning and inductive reasoning, while males tended to do better on tests of number and spatial orientation. The

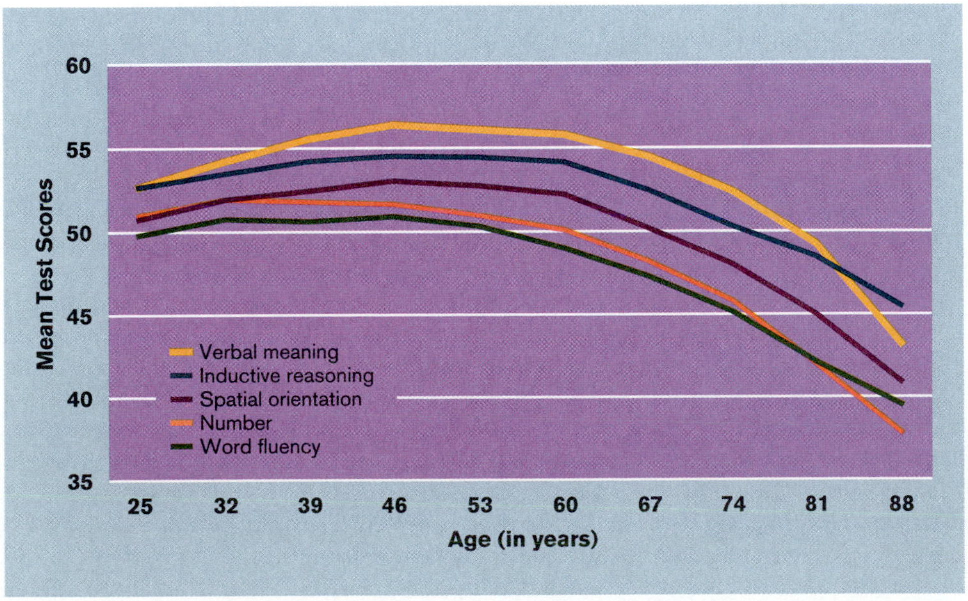

Figure 10.1

Age Differences in Performance on Tests of Five Mental Abilities

This graph shows the average scores of subjects in the Seattle Longitudinal Study on tests of five mental abilities. Participants were tested six times over a period of 35 years and showed gains through young adulthood until their mid-40s. Very little decline occurred until after age 60. (Based on Schaie, 1994.)

only ability found to show a continuous decline from the mid-20s to the 80s was perceptual speed.

Dennis (1968) looked at the productivity of 738 persons who had lived at least 79 years and had attained eminence as scholars or in the sciences or the arts. For almost every one, the decade of the 40s was most productive. Historians, philosophers, and literary scholars enjoyed high productivity from the 40s all the way through the 70s. Scientists were highly productive from their 40s through their 60s, but showed a significant decline in productivity in their 70s. Those in the arts peaked earliest and showed a dramatic decline in their 70s. But, of course, the researchers did not interview Michelangelo, Pablo Picasso, Georgia O'Keeffe, Duke Ellington, Irving Berlin, and many others who were artistically potent and vital into their 70s, 80s, and 90s.

Lifestyle Patterns in Adulthood

What are some of the trends in lifestyle patterns in young adulthood?

Is the "average household" in the United States still headed by a married couple? Yes, for about two-thirds of the population. The majority of people (66%) live in a household headed by a married couple who may or may not have children under age 18 (U.S. Bureau of the Census, 1997). Figure 10.2 illustrates the percentages of the U.S. population living in various household arrangements. Let's consider some of these lifestyle patterns.

Singles: Playing the Field About 26.8% of males and 19.9% of females over age 18 are single (U.S. Bureau of the Census, 1997). Some people believe that if unburdened by a spouse, they will be able to pursue their careers and their interests and have a more interesting and exciting life. Yet the happiest singles seem to be those who have relationships that provide emotional support.

Some single people who want a relationship choose living together rather than making the commitment of marriage. The U.S. Bureau of the Census (1997) labels them "unmarried couples." From 1970 to 1996 there was almost a fifteenfold increase in cohabitation among people under age 25. Such arrangements usually last 1 or 2 years, with one-third of the couples marrying and the rest breaking up. Surprisingly, the divorce rate among these couples is higher than the divorce rate for couples who do not live together before marriage (DeMaris & Rao, 1992).

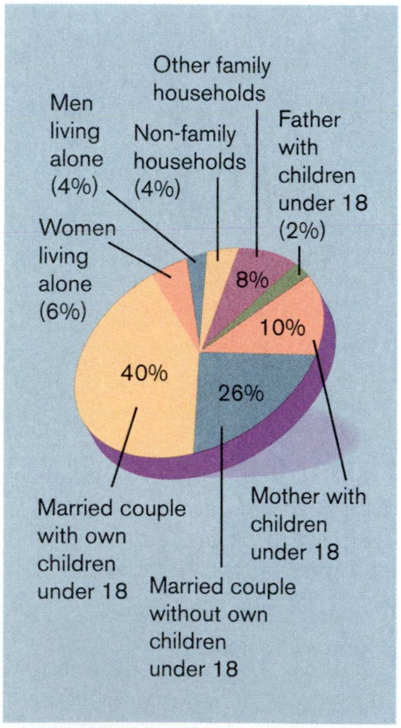

Figure 10.2

Household Arrangements among U.S. Population

Although U.S. households headed by married couples have decreased over the last several decades, 66% of the population lives in such households. About 14% live alone or with non–family members. (Data from U.S. Bureau of the Census, 1997.)

Marriage: Tying the Knot The mating culture of today's singles is not as oriented toward marriage as it was in the past. A recent major report of The National Marriage Project, sponsored by Rutgers University, is entitled "The State of Our Unions 2000." The report suggests that the dating scene today is one of low commitment, a culture of "sex without strings, relationships without rings." Most young singles, 66% of the men and 58.5% of the women, were in favor of living together before marriage, in order to find out more about each other prior to making a commitment. And 54% of the women said they would consider unwed motherhood if they could not find a suitable man to marry (Poponoe & Whitehead, 2000). Furthermore, the age at first marriage keeps rising for both males and females. In 1960, the median age at first marriage was 20 for females and 23 for males. Today, the median age is 25 for females and 27 for males (Poponoe & Whitehead, 2000).

In a review of 93 studies, Wood and others (1989) found that married people report much higher levels of well-being than unmarried people, and that married women report slightly higher levels than married men. Inglehart (1990) analyzed studies done in Europe and North America and reported that married couples are happier than people who are unmarried, separated, or divorced. Lesbian couples, too, report being happier than lesbian women living alone (Wayment & Peplau, 1995).

Divorce: Untying the Knot According to a 1989 Gallup poll, half of those who have ever been married have experienced severe marital problems or divorce, and 26% have been divorced at least once (Colasanto & Shriver, 1989). The reasons given for divorce were basic personality differences or incompatibility (47%); infidelity (17%); a drug or alcohol problem (16%); disputes about money, family, or children (10%); and physical abuse (5%). People aged 35 to 54 experienced the most severe marital discord, and those over age 55, the least. Today's divorce rate is more than twice that of 40 years ago. In 1960, there were 9 divorces per 1,000 married women age 15 and older. Today, there are approximately 20 divorces per 1,000 married women age 15 and older (Poponoe & Whitehead, 2000). The chances are very high—between 40% and 50%—that a marriage entered into today will end in divorce or permanent separation.

The marriages most likely to fail are marriages between teenagers, nonreligious marriages in which the bride was pregnant, and marriages of people whose parents had divorced (Poponoe & Whitehead, 2000). But the marriages that do survive are not necessarily happy. Many couples stay together for reasons other than love—because of religious beliefs, for the sake of the children, for financial reasons, or out of fear of facing the future alone.

But even for the "miserable marrieds," divorce does not always solve the problems. "Alcoholism, drug abuse, depression, psychosomatic problems, and accidents are more common among divorced than nondivorced adults" (Hetherington et al., 1989, pp. 307–308). Yet most people who do get divorced are not soured on the institution of marriage, because the majority of them do remarry.

What effect does parenthood have on marital satisfaction?

Parenthood: Passing Along the Genes Although satisfaction with marriage does tend to decline after the birth of the first child (Belsky et al., 1989; Cowan & Cowan, 1992; Hackel & Ruble, 1992), women in general find the period of child rearing the least satisfying time of marriage. The problem centers mainly on the division of work—who does what. Even though men are helping with children more than in the past, child care still generally ends up being primarily the responsibility of the woman. Unless she holds very traditional views of sex roles, a woman's dissatisfaction after the birth of the first child often relates to the discrepancy between how much help with child care and housework she had expected from her husband and how much help she actually receives (Hackel & Ruble, 1992).

Parenthood can cause stress and conflict in a marriage, but it is also immensely satisfying for most couples.

Glass and Fujimoto (1994) found that time spent in housework was related to an increase in depression for both husbands and wives. It is also related to a more negative view of the marriage and an increase in marital conflict (Crouter et al., 1987). In contrast, other researchers have found that equitable sharing of responsibilities yields a more satisfying marriage, which translates, in turn, into better relationships between parents and children (Erel & Burman, 1995).

Almost 59% of new mothers enter the labor force before their child is a year old (U.S. Bureau of the Census, 1997). Figure 10.3 (on p. 370) shows the percentage of married women in the U.S. labor force according to the age of their youngest child.

Remaining Childless: No Bundles of Joy Some couples are choosing not to have children, leaving themselves free to devote their time, energy, and money to pursuing their own interests and careers. A few studies indicate that such couples are happier and find their marriages more satisfying than couples with children (Campbell, 1975). However, this same sense of satisfaction may not continue into middle and old age, when couples may wonder if their decision to remain childless was a good one. A 1990 Gallup poll found that only about 4% of Americans are "antichildren"—that is, they don't have any children, they don't want any, or they are glad they never had any (Gallup & Newport, 1990c). In spite of the tremendous emotional and financial investment children require, most parents find their children provide a major source of satisfaction and meaning in their lives and that the investment has been a good one.

Figure 10.3

Percentage of the U.S. Labor Force Made Up of Married Women with Children

The percentage of the U.S. labor force consisting of married women with children continues to rise. About 59% of women with children 1 year of age or under, and about 66% of women with children 3 to 5 years old, are employed. (Data from U.S. Bureau of the Census, 1997.)

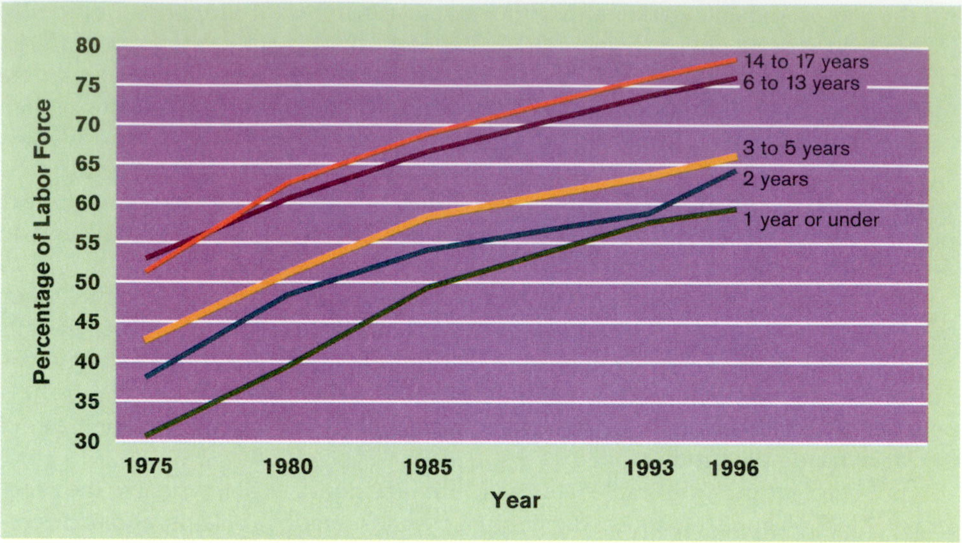

Career Choice: A Critical Life Decision Probably no other part of life is so central to identity and self-esteem as a person's occupation or profession, with the possible exception of motherhood for some women. Although the majority of Americans seem satisfied with their jobs, job satisfaction is higher for middle-aged adults than for young adults (Kohut & DeStefano, 1989). However, young adults are probably less likely than middle-aged adults to be permanently situated in jobs and careers they will continue to follow. In fact, nearly one out of three young adults (in their 20s and 30s) will not only change jobs, but will even change occupational field (Phillips & Blustein, 1994).

One of the most profound changes in employment patterns has been the tremendous increase of women in the workplace. In 1996 women made up 46.2% of the civilian labor force (U.S. Bureau of the Census, 1997). But women are not rushing into the workplace primarily to find self-fulfillment. Most are there out of economic necessity.

Contrary to what one might expect, in middle-class, dual-career couples, positive and negative job experiences have similar effects on the mental health of men and women (Barnett et al., 1995). But changes in the quality of the marital relationship affect women's mental health more than men's. If their marriage deteriorates, women experience more distress; if it improves, women's mental health improves as well (Barnett et al., 1995).

Personality and Social Development in Middle Age

Why is middle age often considered the prime of life?

A generation ago, researcher Bernice Neugarten (1968) stated that society "may be oriented towards youth," but it is "controlled by the middle-aged" (p. 93). People aged 40 to 60 are the decision makers in industry, government, and society. This is even more true now that the majority of baby boomers have reached middle age. Neugarten found that very few at this time of life "express a wish to be young again" (p. 97). As a participant in one of her studies said, "There is a difference between wanting to *feel* young and wanting to *be* young" (p. 97).

Reaching middle age, men and women begin to express personality characteristics they had formerly suppressed. Men generally become more nurturant and women more assertive. For many women, middle age is a time of increased freedom.

Wink and Helson (1993) found that after children leave home, most women work at least part-time and tend to experience an increase in self-confidence and a heightened sense of competence and independence. Contrary to the conventional notion of the empty nest syndrome, most parents seem to be happier when their children are on their own (Norris & Tindale, 1994). It is when the children do *not* leave home that a crisis occurs (for both parent and child)" (Neugarten, 1982, p. 163).

Remember It!

1. During which decade do people reach their peak physically?
   a. teens b. 20s c. 30s d. 40s
2. From the 20s to the 40s, intellectual performance tends to
   a. increase. c. remain the same.
   b. decrease. d. show continuous fluctuation.
3. The majority of people in the United States live in households headed by a married couple. (true/false)
4. Higher levels of life satisfaction are reported by (singles, married people).
5. Most middle-aged people have difficulty adjusting when their children grow up and leave home. (true/false)

Answers: 1. b 2. a 3. true 4. married people 5. false

LATER ADULTHOOD

Age 65 or 70 is generally considered the beginning of old age, and 12.7% of the U. S. population is now over age 65 (U.S. Bureau of the Census, 1997). What are your perceptions of life after 65? Before reading further, complete the *Try It!*

Try It!

Are the following statements true (T) or false (F)?

____ 1. Older adults tend to express less satisfaction with life in general than younger adults do.

____ 2. A lack of money is a serious problem for most people over age 65.

____ 3. Marital satisfaction declines in old age.

____ 4. Mandatory retirement forces most workers out of jobs before they are ready to leave.

____ 5. The majority of retirees do not adjust well to retirement.

____ 6. A large percentage of individuals over age 85 end up in nursing homes or institutions.

Answers: All of the statements are false!

Physical Changes in Later Adulthood

What are some physical changes generally associated with later adulthood?

It was long assumed that the number of neurons declined sharply in later adulthood, but this assumption appears to be false (Gallagher & Rapp, 1997). Research has shown that the shrinking volume of the aging cortex is due more to breakdown of the myelin that covers the axons in the white matter than to loss of the neurons that make up the gray matter (Peters et al., 1994; Wickelgren, 1996). As you learned in Chapter 2, the myelin sheath allows for the rapid conduction of neural impulses. The breakdown of myelin thus explains one of the most predictable characteristics of aging—the slowing of behavior (Birren & Fisher, 1995). With degeneration of the myelin, the brain takes longer to process information, and reaction time is slower. However, these age-related cognitive impairments occur gradually (Sauzeon et al., 2000), and they are accompanied by age-related losses that primarily affect the performance of working memory (Haut et al., 2000).

With advancing age, people typically become more farsighted and have increasingly impaired night vision (Long & Crambert, 1990). They suffer hearing loss in the higher frequencies and often have difficulty following a conversation when there is competing background noise (Slawinski et al., 1993). They may have trouble with balance because of a deterioration in the vestibular sense.

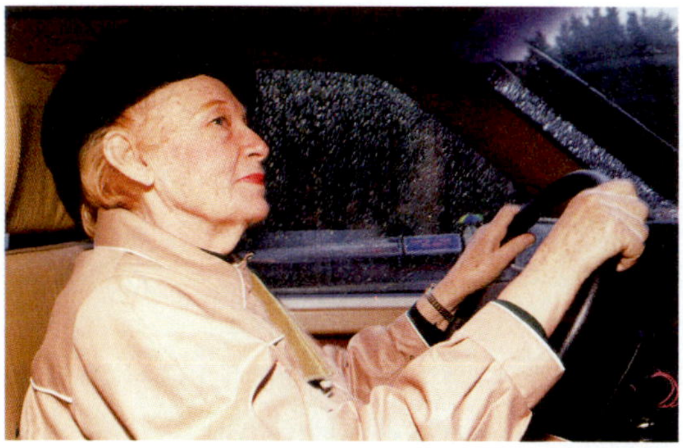

Sensory and other physical deficits develop as people age. Some older people experience impaired night vision, making driving after dark dangerous for themselves and others.

Older adults can expect a decline in heart, lung, kidney, and muscle function, and they typically have less energy and stamina. Joints become stiffer, and bones lose calcium and become more brittle, increasing the risk of fractures from falls.

About 80% of Americans over age 65 have one or more chronic conditions such as arthritis, rheumatism, heart problems, or high blood pressure. For both males and females, the three leading causes of death are heart disease, cancer, and stroke. A high ratio of total cholesterol to high-density lipoprotein (HDL) increases the risk of mortality from all causes (heart disease, cancer, stroke, etc.) in men aged 65 and older. But an increased level of HDL (good cholesterol) alone seems to protect against mortality from all causes in men between 65 and 74. For women, no associations were found between any of the cholesterol measures studied and mortality from all causes (Chyou & Eaker, 2000).

The vast majority of people over age 65 consider their health good. One-half of those aged 75 to 84 and more than one-third of those over 85 do not have to curb their activities because of health problems (Toufexis, 1988). In fact, the majority of older adults are active, healthy, and self-sufficient (Schaie & Willis, 1996). Not only are the elderly more numerous now, but more of them are enjoying life in relatively good health (Morley & van den Berg, 2000).

An interesting study of the "oldest old"—those over 95—revealed that they are often in better mental and physical condition than those 20 years younger (Perls, 1995). They often remain employed and sexually active through their 90s and carry on "as if age were not an issue" (p. 70). How do they do it? They appear to have a genetic advantage that makes them particularly resistant to the diseases that kill or disable most people at younger ages.

Are there personality characteristics that predict longevity? Friedman and others (1995) examined data from Terman's 7-decade longitudinal study (discussed in Chapter 8) and found that the childhood personality trait in males that best predicted a long life was conscientiousness. Those participants who ranked in the top 25% on conscientiousness could expect to live, on average, 2 years longer than those who ranked in the lowest 25%. The researchers also found that parental divorce during childhood and unstable marriage patterns during adulthood were associated with shorter life spans.

One of the greatest fears among the elderly is that they will spend their last years in a nursing home. Yet, even among those 85 and older, this "greatest fear" comes to pass for only 15% of males and 25% of females.

Fitness and Aging Men and women in their 60s and 70s who exercise properly and regularly can have the energy and fitness of someone 20 to 30 years younger (deVries, 1986). Recent research suggests that physical exercise has a favorable effect on the functioning of the cardiovascular system of aging adults (Kasch et al., 1999).

"People rust out faster from disuse than they wear out from overuse" (Horn & Meer, 1987, p. 83). In one study, 100 frail nursing-home residents, average age 87, exercised their thigh and hip muscles vigorously on exercise machines for 45 minutes three times a week. At the end of 10 weeks, they had increased their stair-climbing power by 28.4% and their walking speed by 12%, and four were able to exchange their walkers for canes (Fiatarone et al., 1994). For most of us, remaining fit and vigorous as we age lies within our power.

crystallized intelligence: Aspects of intelligence, including verbal ability and accumulated knowledge, that tend to increase over the life span.

fluid intelligence: Aspects of intelligence involving abstract reasoning and mental flexibility, which peak in the early 20s and decline slowly as people age.

senile dementia: A state of mental deterioration caused by physical deterioration of the brain and characterized by impaired memory and intellect and by altered personality and behavior; senility.

Sex and the Senior Citizen Masters and Johnson (1966) studied the sexual response in older men and women and found that regular sexual relations are necessary to maintain effective sexual performance. In a survey of adults aged 80 to 102 who were not taking medication, 70% of the men and 50% of the women admitted fantasizing about intimate sexual relations often or very often. But 63% of the men and 30% of the women were doing more than fantasizing—they were still having sex (McCarthy, 1989). And, remember, they were between 80 and 102.

Cognitive Development in Later Adulthood

What happens to mental ability in later adulthood?

Intellectual decline in late adulthood is *not* inevitable. Older adults who keep mentally and physically active tend to retain their mental skills. They do well on tests of vocabulary, comprehension, and general information, and their ability to solve practical problems is generally higher than that of young adults.

Researchers often distinguish between two types of intelligence (Horn, 1982). **Crystallized intelligence**—one's verbal ability and accumulated knowledge—tends to increase over the life span. **Fluid intelligence**—abstract reasoning and mental flexibility—peaks in the early 20s and declines slowly as people age. The rate at which people process information also slows gradually with age (Hertzog, 1991; Lindenberger et al., 1993; Salthouse, 1996). This explains, in part, why older adults perform more poorly on tests requiring speed.

Is it accurate to equate old age with forgetfulness? In laboratory memory tasks, older people do as well or almost as well as younger people on recognition tasks (Hultsch & Dixon, 1990) and on recall of information in their areas of expertise (Charness, 1989). But in tasks requiring speed of processing in short-term memory or recall of items that hold no particular meaning for them, younger participants do significantly better than older ones (Verhaeghen et al., 1993). Older adults also perform less well than their younger counterparts on tests of spatial memory (recalling the locations of objects) (Newman & Kaszniak, 2000).

Two of the most common and annoying age-related memory complaints are inability to recall a name and difficulty in coming up with a word needed in a conversation (Lovelace & Twohig, 1990). Researchers have also noted some decline in *prospective memory*—remembering to perform an action in the future, such as mailing a letter or taking medicine (Hultsch & Dixon, 1990).

Several factors are positively correlated with good cognitive functioning in the elderly. They are education level (Anstey et al., 1993), a complex work environment, a long marriage to an intelligent spouse, and a higher income (Schaie, 1990). And gender is a factor as well; women not only outlive men, they generally show less cognitive decline during old age. But intellectual functioning can be hampered by physical problems (Manton et al., 1986) or by psychological problems such as depression (Flint & Rifat, 2000). A study by Shimamura and others (1995) revealed that people who continue to lead intellectually stimulating and mentally active lives are far less likely to suffer mental decline as they age.

What is Alzheimer's disease?

Alzheimer's Disease and Other Types of Dementia **Senile dementia**, or senility, is a state of severe mental deterioration marked by impaired memory and intellect, as well as by altered personality and behavior. It afflicts about 5–8% of adults over age 65, 15–20% of those over 75, and 25–50% of those over 85 (American

As Alzheimer's disease worsens, those afflicted with it need constant reminders of the locations and names of common household items if they are to perform any routine tasks.

Psychiatric Association, 1997). Senility is caused by physical deterioration of the brain. It can result from cerebral arteriosclerosis (hardening of the arteries in the brain), chronic alcoholism, and irreversible damage by a series of small strokes. About 50–60% of all cases of senility, however, result from Alzheimer's disease.

In **Alzheimer's disease** there is a progressive deterioration of intellect and personality that results from widespread degeneration of brain cells. In fact, Alzheimer's patients suffer substantial tissue loss in the middle (medial) area of the temporal lobe, which of course impairs memory (Rombouts et al., 2000). At present, about 4 million people in the United States suffer from this incurable disorder (Khachaturian, 1997). At first, victims show a gradual impairment in memory and reasoning, and in their efficiency in carrying out everyday tasks. Many have difficulty finding their way around in familiar locations. Alzheimer's patients, even in early stages, have difficulty with temporal memory (time sequences) especially when distractors are present (Putzke et al., 2000). As the disorder progresses, Alzheimer's patients become confused and irritable, tend to wander away from home, and become increasingly unable to care for themselves. Eventually their speech becomes unintelligible, and they become unable to control bladder and bowel functions. If they live long enough, they reach a stage where they do not respond when spoken to and no longer recognize even spouse or children.

Compared with nondemented people of similar age, Alzheimer's patients in one study averaged 68% fewer neurons in parts of the hippocampus, the area of the brain important in the formation and retention of memories (West et al., 1994). Alzheimer's patients also show memory impairment beyond that involving the hippocampal region. Eventually, even implicit or nondeclarative memory functions such as motor skills, habits, and simple classically conditioned responses are impaired as well (Bäckman et al., 2000). Autopsies of Alzheimer's patients reveal that the cerebral cortex and particularly the hippocampus contain neurons clogged with twisted stringy masses (called *neurofibrillary tangles*) and surrounded by plaques (de Leon et al., 1996; Peskind, 1996). Researchers are using sophisticated brain-imaging techniques to view hippocampal changes in the early stages of Alzheimer's, and such studies may have some diagnostic value (de Leon et al., 1996). A consistent characteristic of Alzheimer's disease is the excessive amounts of amyloid beta protein in the brain, which forms the core of the plaques (Soininen & Riekkinen, 1996).

Alzheimer's disease (ALZ-hye-merz): An incurable form of dementia characterized by progressive deterioration of intellect and personality, resulting from widespread degeneration of brain cells.

Heredity is a major factor in early-onset Alzheimer's, which accounts for about 10% of the disease's victims and develops before age 65—in some cases as early as the 40s. Heredity is also a major factor in late-onset Alheimer's, which generally affects people over age 65 (Bergem et al., 1997). Alzheimer's has been linked to genes on chromosomes 1, 14, 19, and 21 (Selkoe, 1997).

Results from a multiethnic community sample of older Americans suffering from Alzheimer's disease showed that African Americans were less debilitated than their Asian, White, and Hispanic counterparts. Compared to the other ethnic groups, African Americans had less depression, less anxiety, and fewer sleep problems (Chen et al., 2000).

Can Alzheimer's disease be delayed? According to Alexander and others (1997), a high IQ coupled with life-long intellectual activity may delay or lessen the symptoms of Alzheimer's in those who are at risk for the disease. Tang and others (1996) reported that postmenopausal women who had taken estrogen supplements for 10 years reduced their risk of developing Alzheimer's by almost 40%. And certain anti-inflammatory drugs (such as ibuprofen) and the antioxidant vitamin E may provide a measure of protection (Nash, 1997; Sano et al., 1997). Clinical trials with a non-steroidal anti-inflammatory drug called indomethacin are showing promising results (Hull et al., 1999).

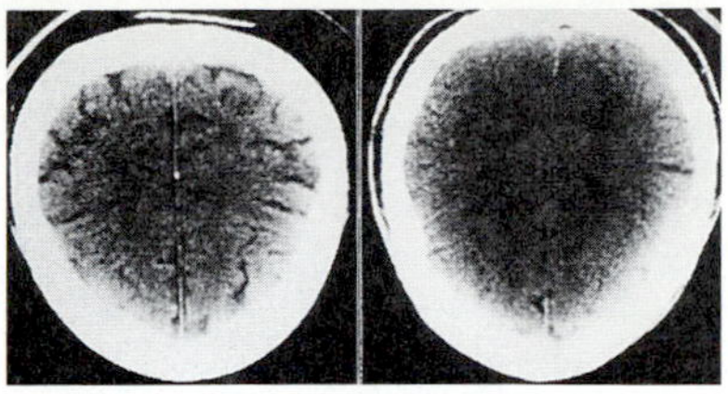

Compared with a normal adult brain (right), the brain of an Alzheimer's patient (left) has a smaller volume and many twisted stringy masses called neurofibrillary tangles.

motivation
Sternberg -
Love.

Social Development and Adjustment in Later Adulthood

It may surprise you to learn that in several major national surveys life satisfaction and feelings of well-being were about as high in older adults as in younger ones (Inglehart, 1990) (see Figure 10.4). Life satisfaction appears to be most strongly related to good health, as well as to a feeling of control over one's life (Schulz & Heckhausen, 1996). A large meta-analysis combined findings from 286 studies on the relationship of socioeconomic status, social networks, and feelings of competence to older adults' life satisfaction. Income was associated more strongly than education with high life satisfaction, and the "quality" of social contacts was more significant than the number of social contacts (Pinquart & Sörensen, 2000). Life satisfaction after retirement also appears to be related to participation in community service and in social activities (Harlow & Cantor, 1996). Participation in religious activities also has a beneficial effect on psychological well-being. Furthermore, religious doubt is associated with psychological distress and diminished feelings of well-being. But religious doubt causes more distress for younger adults than for older ones (Krause et al., 1999). Levenson and others (1993) found

Figure 10.4

Age and Life Satisfaction

Surveys including participants from many nationalities reveal that levels of life satisfaction and happiness remain much the same and relatively high (approximately 80%) throughout life. (Data from Inglehart, 1990.)

that older couples tended to be happier in their marriages than middle-aged couples, experiencing less conflict and more sources of pleasure than their younger counterparts.

Much has been said about the elderly poor. About 10.5% of Americans over age 65 live below the poverty line, and among them are disproportionately high numbers of African Americans (25.4%) and Hispanic Americans (23.5%) (U.S. Bureau of the Census, 1997). And elderly persons, especially those with cognitive or physical impairments who are struggling to live on small incomes, are especially vulnerable to financial exploitation (Tueth, 2000). But many adults in the 65-plus group live comfortably. With homes that are paid for and no children to support, people over 65 tend to view their financial situation more positively than do younger adults.

Yet old age undoubtedly involves many losses. Health declines, friends die, and some who do not wish to retire must do so because of company policies or for health reasons. When life becomes more burdensome than enjoyable, an older person can fall victim to depression, a serious problem affecting about 15% of the elderly. This depression can even be deadly. White males over age 75 have the highest suicide rate of any age group in this society (U.S. Bureau of the Census, 1997). But the rate of major depression seems to be lower among the elderly than among younger persons (Benazzi, 2000).

Retirement: Leaving the World of Work To many people, retirement marks the end of middle age and the beginning of old age. Younger people tend to see retirement as a time when one is forced to leave the workforce and is "put out to pasture"—an event that is seen as leading to premature death. Perceptions of the "appropriate" age for retirement varied among young, middle-aged, and elderly adults. Generally, the younger the person being interviewed, the lower the perceived "appropriate" age for retirement (Joulain et al., 2000). Also, those who have not yet retired worry more about it than those who have already retired. And women worry significantly more than men (Skarborn & Nicki, 2000). However, most retirees are happy to leave the world of work. Generally, the people most reluctant to retire are those who are better educated, hold high-status jobs with a good income, and find fulfillment in their work. Bosse and others (1991) found that only 30% of retirees reported finding retirement stressful, and of those who did, most were likely to be in poor health and to have financial problems.

Losing a Spouse: The Hardest Blow For most people, losing a spouse is the most stressful event in a lifetime, and more women than men experience this loss. In 1996, 63.6% of women over age 65 had lost a spouse compared with only 32.5% of men. There were only about 69.5 males for every 100 females aged 65 and older (U.S. Bureau of the Census, 1997). Both widows and widowers are at a greater risk for health problems due to suppressed immune function and have a higher mortality rate, particularly within the first 6 months, than their age mates who are not bereaved (Martikainen & Valkonen, 1996).

Losing a spouse leaves a great void in the life of the survivor. This loss seems to be more emotionally distressing for men than for women (Umberson et al., 1992). Women experience greater financial strains, but most men have the strain of learning to manage a household.

Cultural Differences in Care for the Elderly

The fastest-growing segment of the U.S. population consists of those 85 and older (Thomas, 1992). Are there cultural differences in the ways older family members are viewed, treated, and cared for?

Older African Americans as well as older Asian and Hispanic Americans are more likely to live with and be cared for by their adult children than are other elderly Americans. African Americans are more likely than Whites to regard elderly persons with respect and to feel that children should help their older parents (Mui, 1992). Still, multigenerational households are by no means commonplace among most racial groups in the United States. For the most part, older Americans have a strong preference for maintaining their independence and living in their own homes, although they and their adult children express a desire to live near each other (Bengtson et al., 1990).

The living arrangements of American families are not typical of other countries around the world. Economic and social necessity often dictate living arrangements. In many Latin American countries, the majority of elderly people live in the same household with younger generations in an extended family setting (De Vos, 1990). In Korea, 80% of the elderly are cared for by family members (Sung, 1992). And three-generation households have been the rule rather than the exception among the Japanese.

How do attitudes toward providing care for aged relatives differ between the United States and Japan? Elaine Brody and others (1984) studied the attitudes of three generations of American women toward providing care for their aged relatives. Her study was replicated with a comparable sample of three generations of Japanese women in Tokyo (Campbell & Brody, 1985). Women's attitudes were studied because the care of aged relatives is typically provided by female family members in both countries. The American women expressed a stronger sense of obligation toward elderly members of their family, such as helping them with household chores, than the Japanese women did. Campbell and Brody (1985) point out, however, that in Japan daughters-in-law, not daughters, most often care for elderly family members, who are more likely to live in the home of their oldest son. Relations between daughters and parents are likely to be more positive than relations between daughters-in-law and parents-in-law.

Brody and others (1992) found that married daughters experienced less strain and less depression resulting from parent care than those who were single, divorced, or widowed. Also, African Americans caring for elderly relatives suffering from Alzheimer's report less stress and depression than do their White counterparts (Hayley et al., 1996).

Death and Dying

One of the developmental tasks for every elderly person is to accept the inevitability of death and to prepare for it. At no time does this task become more critical than when an individual faces a terminal illness.

According to Kübler-Ross, what stages do terminally ill patients experience as they come to terms with death?

Kübler-Ross on Death and Dying: The Final Exit Elisabeth Kübler-Ross (1969) interviewed some 200 terminally ill people and found they shared common reactions to their impending death. In her book *On Death and Dying* she identifies five stages people go through in coming to terms with death.

In the first stage, denial, most patients react to the diagnosis of their terminal illness with shock and disbelief. (Surely, the doctors must be wrong.) The second stage, anger, is marked by feelings of anger, resentment, and envy of those who are young and healthy. In the third stage, bargaining, the person attempts to postpone death in return for a promise of "good behavior." An individual may offer God some special service or a promise to live a certain kind of life in exchange for an opportunity to attend a child's wedding or a grandchild's graduation. The fourth stage, depression, brings a great sense of loss and may take two forms—depression over past losses and depression over impending losses. Given enough time, patients may reach the final stage, acceptance, in which they stop struggling against death and contemplate its coming without fear or despair. Kübler-Ross claims that the family also goes through stages similar to those experienced by the patient.

Dr. Jack Kevorkian, shown here with his controversial apparatus, has helped many terminally ill people commit suicide.

Critics deny the universality of Kübler-Ross's proposed stages and their invariant sequence (Butler & Lewis, 1982; Kastenbaum, 1992). Each person is unique. The reactions of all the terminally ill cannot be expected to conform to some rigid sequence of stages.

What are some benefits of hospice care?

Decisions about Death: When? Death comes too soon for most people, but not soon enough for others. Some who are terminally ill and subject to intractable pain would welcome an end to their suffering. Should dying patients be left with no choice but to suffer to the end? In answer to this highly controversial question, Dr. Jack Kevorkian has said "No!" and has defied both laws and criticism and helped many terminally ill patients end their lives. Although Dr. Kevorkian was convicted and jailed for his work, he brought to the nation's attention the plight of many hopelessly, terminally ill individuals who wish to end their lives. Today, physician-assisted suicide ("requested death") has become the focus of a social movement (McInerney, 2000). The state of Oregon legalized physician-assisted suicide in 1997. Most patients who "request" death cite as their reasons loss of control of bodily functions, loss of autonomy, and inability to take part in activities that make life enjoyable (Sullivan, Hedberg, et al., 2000).

To avoid leaving surviving family members with staggering medical bills, many people today write *living wills.* Under the terms of most living wills, hospitals and medical professionals are not to use heroic measures or life-support systems to delay the death of patients who cannot possibly recover, but may linger indefinitely in a comatose state.

Decisions about Death: Where? A rapidly growing alternative to hospitals and nursing homes is *hospice care.* Hospices are agencies that care for the needs of the dying more humanely and affordably than hospitals can. A hospice follows a set of guidelines that make it more attuned to patients' personal needs and preferences. These guidelines include the following:

- The patient and his or her family will control decisions about the patient's care.
- The patient's pain will be managed so that the patient's remaining time is more livable.
- Professional personnel will be available as needed, any time of the day or night.
- Facilities will be less clinical and more homelike than typical hospital environments are.

- Family members may work with the hospice team as caregivers.
- Family members may receive counseling before and after the patient dies and be helped through the grieving process.

Bereavement: The Grieving Process Many of us have experienced the grieving process—the period of bereavement that follows the death of a loved one and sometimes lingers long after the person has gone. Contrary to what many believe, bereaved individuals who suffer the most intense grief initially, who weep inconsolably and feel the deepest pain, do not get through their bereavement more quickly than others (Bonanno et al., 1995). According to one proposed model for how people cope with bereavement, the grieving spouse at times actively confronts and at other times avoids giving full vent to grief. This *dual-process coping* provides for doses of grieving as well as periods of relief in dealing with the stress of losing a spouse (Stroebe & Schut, 1999).

Researchers have looked at the bereavement of those who care for loved ones dying of AIDS. Folkman and her colleagues (1996) interviewed male partners who were caregivers for AIDS patients. From several interviews conducted both before and after the patient's death, they concluded that the grieving process for those partners was very similar to that experienced by spouses.

Death and dying are not pleasant subjects, but you should remember that life itself is a terminal condition, and each day of life should be treasured like a precious gift.

Remember It!

1. Which of the following statements is true of older adults?
   a. They are considerably less satisfied with life than young adults are.
   b. Their financial situation is considerably worse than that of younger adults.
   c. Most retirees are happy to be retired.
   d. A large percentage of adults over 85 end up in nursing homes.
2. Alzheimer's disease is curable if diagnosed in its very earliest stages. (true/false)
3. Compared with older adults who are mentally and physically active, younger adults do better on
   a. tests requiring speed.
   b. comprehension tests.
   c. general information tests.
   d. practical problem solving.
4. According to Kübler-Ross, the first stage experienced by terminally ill patients in coming to terms with death is ______________; the last stage is ______________.
   a. anger; depression
   b. denial; depression
   c. bargaining; acceptance
   d. denial; acceptance
5. An agency that is an alternative to a hospital or nursing home as a provider of care for the dying is a ______________.

Answers: 1. c 2. false 3. a 4. d 5. hospice

Apply It!

Building a Good Relationship

Decide whether each of the following statements about intimate relationships is true (T) or false (F):

____ The best relationships are free from conflict.

____ Voicing complaints to one's partner undermines happiness in the relationship.

____ Anger in all its forms is a negative emotion that is destructive in a relationship.

____ The best way to maintain a relationship is to have a realistic view of one's partner.

All of these statements are true, right? Wrong! Every one of them is false. Recent research has offered some surprising findings about the dynamics of successful relationships. Perhaps the most significant finding is that some conflict is necessary for long-term survival of a close relationship. How can this be so?

In studies of couples married 20 years or more, John Gottman (1994) and his colleagues have found that many couples equate lack of conflict with happiness and are proud that they "never fight." However, these marriages may suffer from a lack of communication. In reality, "a certain amount of conflict is necessary to help couples weed out actions and ways of dealing with each other that can harm the marriage in the long run" (p. 67). Couples who do not resolve the conflicts that are inevitable in any relationship run the risk of becoming mired in negative emotions and eventually breaking up. And since the formation of intimate relationships is a crucial task of young adulthood, it is important for couples to learn how to communicate effectively and resolve their conflicts.

Complaints, criticism, contempt, and anger. Gottman points out that a common barrier to effective communication is criticism. Although criticizing and complaining are often equated, the difference between them is crucial to any relationship. A complaint is limited to a specific situation and states how you feel: "I am upset because you didn't take out the garbage tonight." Complaints may actually make a relationship stronger. In fact, Gottman believes that complaining "is one of the healthiest activities that can occur in a marriage" (1994, p. 73). Why? Because it is better to express feelings through complaints than to let them seethe until they crystallize into deep-seated resentment.

This is not to say that all complaining is useful. *Cross-complaining,* in which you counter your partner's complaint with one of your own and ignore what your partner has said, obviously serves no useful purpose. And spouting off a long list of complaints all at once—what Gottman calls *kitchen-sinking*—is not productive either.

A criticism differs from a complaint in that it heaps blame on the other person. A complaint is likely to begin with "I," but criticisms typically begin with "you": "You never remember to take out the trash. You promised you would do it, and you broke your promise again!" Criticisms also tend to be global, often including the word *always* or *never:* "You never take me anywhere"; "You're always finding fault with me." Criticizing thus goes beyond merely stating a feeling; a criticism is an accusation, sometimes even a personal attack. Frequent criticism can destroy a relationship.

Even more damaging than criticism is contempt. As Gottman points out, "what separates *contempt* from criticism is the *intention to insult* and *psychologically abuse* your partner" (1994, p. 79). Contempt basically adds insult to criticism. The insult can take a variety of forms, including name-calling, hostile humor, mockery, and body language such as sneering and rolling the eyes. According to Gottman, words such as *bitch, jerk, fat,* and *stupid* "are such dangerous assault weapons that they ought to be outlawed" (1994, p. 80).

While criticism and contempt definitely have negative effects on relationships, anger does not. Anger has negative effects on a relationship only if it is expressed along with criticism or contempt. In fact, according to Gottman, "expressing anger and disagreement—airing a complaint—though rarely pleasant, makes the [relationship] stronger in the long run than suppressing the complaint" (1994, p. 73).

Hints for resolving conflicts. How can you make good use of your knowledge about the varying effects of complaining, criticism, contempt, and anger? Apply the the following guidelines for resolving conflicts:

- *Be gentle with complaints.* Kindness works wonders when stating a complaint. And remember to avoid criticism.
- *Don't get defensive when your partner makes requests.* Remain positive, and comply willingly and as quickly as possible.
- *Stop conflicts before they get out of hand.* Don't let negative thoughts about your partner grow into criticism or contempt. Do whatever it takes to put the brakes on negativity. Replay in memory and relish the happiest moments you and your partner have spent together.

Of course, none of this will work if you have a thoroughly negative attitude toward your partner. In fact, it helps to have a positive, even idealistic, perception of one's partner. Research by Sandra Murray and her colleagues (1996a, 1996b) has shown that in the best relationships partners overlook each other's faults and embellish each other's virtues. A full and accurate assessment of one's partner's frailties leads to dissatisfaction.

Love, then, is only half-blind. Partners in intimate relationships are blind to each other's negative qualities, while magnifying each other's virtues far beyond reality.

THINKING CRITICALLY

Evaluation

In your opinion, do Erikson's psychosocial stages for adolescence and early adulthood accurately represent the major conflicts of these periods of life? Why or why not?

Point/Counterpoint

Levinson's theory of adult development, for both men and women, includes stages and transitional periods occurring at certain ages. The theory of Reinke and others revolves around phases in the family cycle. Prepare an argument supporting each of the following positions:

a. Levinson's theory is superior to that of Reinke and others in explaining development in women.
b. The theory of Reinke and others is superior to Levinson's in explaining development in women.

Psychology in Your Life

Think back to your junior high school and high school years. To what degree did early or late maturation seem to affect how boys and girls were treated by their peers, their parents, or their teachers? Did early or late maturation affect their adjustment? Explain your answer.

SUMMARY AND REVIEW

ADOLESCENCE: PHYSICAL AND COGNITIVE DEVELOPMENT

How difficult is adolescence for most teenagers?

Although about one-fourth of teenagers experience a troubled adolescence, at least half enjoy a period of healthy development and good relationships with family and friends.

What physical changes occur during puberty?

Puberty is characterized by the adolescent growth spurt, further development of the reproductive organs, and the appearance of the secondary sex characteristics.

What are the psychological effects of early and late maturation for boys and girls?

Early maturation provides enhanced status for boys, because of their early advantage in sports and greater attractiveness to girls. Late maturation puts the boys at a disadvantage in these areas, resulting in a lack of confidence that can persist into adulthood. Early-maturing girls are more likely to be exposed prematurely to alcohol and drug use and to have early sexual experiences and unwanted pregnancies.

What cognitive abilities develop during the formal operations stage?

During the formal operations stage, adolescents develop the ability to think abstractly, to attack problems by systematically testing hypotheses, to draw conclusions through deductive reasoning, and to think hypothetically.

Key Terms
adolescence (p. 351); puberty (p. 351); adolescent growth spurt (p. 351); secondary sex characteristics (p. 352); menarche (p. 352); formal operations stage (p. 353); imaginary audience (p. 353); personal fable (p. 353)

ADOLESCENCE: MORAL AND SOCIAL DEVELOPMENT

What are Kohlberg's three levels of moral reasoning?

At the preconventional level, moral reasoning is based on the physical consequences of an act—"right" is whatever averts punishment or brings a reward. At the conventional level, right and wrong are based on the internalized standards of others—"right" is whatever helps or is approved of by others, or whatever is consistent with the laws of society. Postconventional moral reasoning involves weighing moral alternatives—"right" is whatever furthers basic human rights.

What do cross-cultural studies reveal about the universality of Kohlberg's theory?

Cross-cultural studies support the universality of Kohlberg's Stages 1 through 4 as well as their invariant sequence. Stage 5 was found in almost all of the urban or middle-class samples but was absent in tribal and village folk societies.

What outcomes are often associated with the authoritative, authoritarian, and permissive parenting styles?

Authoritative parenting is most effective and is associated with psychosocial competence in all groups and with academic success in White middle-class youth. Adolescents with authoritarian parents are typically the most psychologically distressed and the least self-reliant and self-confident. Permissive parenting is least effective and is often associated with adolescent drug use and behavior problems.

What are some of the useful functions of the adolescent peer group?

The adolescent peer group (usually composed of teens of the same sex and race and similar social background) provides a vehicle for developing social skills and a standard of comparison against which teens' attributes can be evaluated.

What are some of the disturbing consequences of teenage pregnancy?

Teens are at higher risk for delivering premature or low-birthweight babies. Half of teenage mothers never finish high school, and many eventually depend on welfare. Their children are more likely to receive inadequate parenting, nutrition, and health care and to have behavior and academic problems in school.

In general, what is the impact on adolescents of working more than 15 to 20 hours a week during the school year?

Working long hours negatively affects schoolwork, promotes an "earn and spend" pattern, and is associated with drug use and behavior problems.

Key Terms
preconventional level (p. 355); conventional level (p. 355); postconventional level (p. 355)

ERIKSON'S PSYCHOSOCIAL THEORY: ADOLESCENCE THROUGH ADULTHOOD

How did Erikson explain the fifth psychosocial stage–identity versus role confusion?

In this stage adolescents seek to establish their identity and to find values to guide their lives. Difficulty at this stage can result in an identity crisis.

What is Erikson's psychosocial task for early adulthood?

In Erikson's sixth stage, intimacy versus isolation, young adults must establish intimacy in a relationship to avoid a sense of isolation and loneliness.

What changes did Erikson believe are essential for healthy personality development in middle age?

Erikson's seventh stage, generativity versus stagnation, occurs during middle age. To avoid stagnation, individuals must develop generativity—an interest in establishing and guiding the next generation.

What is the key to a positive resolution of Erikson's eighth stage–ego integrity versus despair?

Erikson's psychosocial stage for old age is a time for reflection. People look back on their lives with satisfaction and a sense of accomplishment or have major regrets about mistakes and missed opportunities.

Key Terms
identity versus role confusion (p. 362); intimacy versus isolation (p. 362); generativity versus stagnation (p. 362); ego integrity versus despair (p. 363)

OTHER THEORIES OF ADULTHOOD

How is Levinson's concept of life structure related to his proposed stages of development?

According to Levinson's theory of adult development, all people go through a fixed set of stages. During transitional periods, individuals review and evaluate their life and their life structure. During stable periods, they make choices that form the basis of a revised life structure and then proceed to pursue their goals within the new structure.

What did the study of middle-class women by Reinke and others reveal about major transitional periods in the life cycle?

Reinke and others found that middle-class women go through major transitional periods that can be related more easily to phases in the family cycle than to chronological age.

Key Terms
life structure (p. 364); midlife crisis (p. 364)

EARLY AND MIDDLE ADULTHOOD

What are the physical changes associated with middle age?

Physical changes associated with middle age are a need for reading glasses, a greater susceptibility to life-threatening diseases, and the end of reproductive capacity (menopause) in women and a decline in testosterone levels and often sex drive in men.

In general, can adults look forward to an increase or a decrease in intellectual performance from their 20s to their 60s?

Although younger people tend to do better on tests requiring speed or rote memory, the intellectual performance of adults shows modest gains until the mid-40s. A modest decline occurs from the 60s to the 80s.

What are some of the trends in lifestyle patterns in young adulthood?

About 66% of the U.S. population live in households headed by a married couple with or without children under 18. Couples are waiting longer to have children, and 66% of married women with children under age 6 hold full-time or part-time jobs outside the home.

What effect does parenthood have on marital satisfaction?

Even though most couples want children, satisfaction with marriage, particularly in women, tends to decline after children arrive. This decline can be explained in part by the unequal workload carried by mothers employed outside the home.

Why is middle age often considered the prime of life?

The decision makers in society are usually aged 40 to 60. When children grow up and leave home, parents have more time and money to pursue their own goals and interests.

Key Terms
presbyopia (p. 366); menopause (p. 366)

LATER ADULTHOOD

What are some physical changes generally associated with later adulthood?

Physical changes generally associated with later adulthood include a general slowing, a decline in sensory capacity and in heart, lung, kidney, and muscle function, and an increase in the number of chronic conditions such as arthritis, heart problems, and high blood pressure.

What happens to mental ability in later adulthood?

Crystallized intelligence shows no significant age-related decline; fluid intelligence does decline. Although older adults perform tasks more slowly, if they keep mentally and physically active, they can usually maintain their mental skills as long as their health holds out.

What is Alzheimer's disease?

Alzheimer's disease is an incurable form of dementia characterized by a progressive deterioration of intellect and personality, resulting from widespread degeneration of brain cells.

According to Kübler-Ross, what stages do terminally ill patients experience as they come to terms with death?

Kübler-Ross maintains that terminally ill patients go through five stages in coming to terms with death: denial, anger, bargaining, depression, and acceptance.

What are some benefits of hospice care?

Hospice agencies care for the needs of the dying more humanely and affordably than hospitals do, and they also provide support for family members.

Key Terms
crystallized intelligence (p. 373); fluid intelligence (p. 373); senile dementia (p. 373); Alzheimer's disease (p. 374)

Surf It!

Want to be sure you've absorbed the material in Chapter 10, "Adolescence and Adulthood," before the big test? Visiting *www.abacon.com/wood* can put a top grade within your reach. The site is loaded with free practice tests, flashcards, activities, and links to help you review your way to an A. To enliven that inevitable study break, the site also offers personality assessment quizzes and a psychology career corner.

11 Motivation and Emotion

For much of his adult life, millions recognized actor Christopher Reeve as "Superman." Then, in 1995, a tragic horseback-riding accident left him paralyzed from the neck down, unable even to breathe unassisted for long. Today, Reeve is called upon to be a "man of steel" in an emotional sense, as he strives to lead a happy, productive life despite his circumstances.

What is daily life like for Reeve, his wife Dana, and their family? First, it is a challenge simply to get through each day. Everyday activities—having dinner, bathing, even breathing—are far from routine. Reeve must exercise 3 hours every day to prevent his muscles from wasting away and to coax from every muscle as much cooperation as possible for each daily task. Ironically, in the late 1970s Reeve had to exercise 3 hours daily to add some 30 pounds of muscle mass for his starring role in the four *Superman* films. So, although the workouts are nothing new for him, the circumstances are.

But apart from these challenges of daily living and what Dana describes as a "production" every time they leave the house, the Reeves are busy running the Christopher Reeve Paralysis Foundation. The foundation supports research toward effective treatment and the search for a cure for paralysis from spinal cord and other nervous system disorders. Reeve makes 40 or more speaking engagements every year, as well as countless visits to other victims of paralysis. He lobbies tirelessly for the severely disabled and recently won praise for helping add $2 billion to the budget of the National Institutes of Health. The *Wall Street Journal* called him "perhaps the most effective medical fund-raiser on the planet." But that's not all. He's still acting and directing. In 1999 he starred in a remake of the film *Rear Window* for ABC, and in 1997 he directed *In the Gloaming* for HBO, which won him an Emmy nomination. Quite a lot of living for a man who, in the emotional devastation after his injury, told his wife, "Maybe I should just check out."

In an era that often finds Hollywood heroes in short supply, Christopher Reeve stands out as an inspiration, proving himself to be, indeed, a super man.

Are those who are handicapped destined to live a life of misery and sadness? No. Many who are severely handicapped, like Christopher Reeve, have an abundant supply of one of life's most positive emotions—happiness. But what motivates some people to propel themselves toward great accomplishments? Can everyone choose to be happy, regardless of the circumstances? (Be sure to read the *Apply It!* at the end of this chapter for more on this question.)

Many psychologists consider motivation and emotion to be fascinating subjects of study. Some of their findings, and some of the questions that remain to be answered, are discussed in this chapter.

INTRODUCTION TO MOTIVATION

What is the difference between intrinsic and extrinsic motivation?

In this chapter on **motivation,** we will look at the underlying processes that initiate, direct, and sustain behavior in order to satisfy physiological and psychological needs. At any given time your behavior might be explained by one or a combination of **motives**—needs or desires that energize and direct behavior toward a goal. Motives can arise from an internal need, such as when we are hungry and are motivated to find something to eat. In this case we are pushed into action from within. Other motives originate from outside, as when some external stimulus, or **incentive,** pulls or entices us to act. After finishing a huge meal, some people yield to the temptation of a delicious dessert. At times like this, it is the enticement of the external tempter, not the internal need for food, that provides the motive.

Three primary characteristics of motivation are activation, persistence, and intensity (Geen, 1995). *Activation* is the initiation of motivated behavior; it involves taking the first steps required to achieve a goal or complete a project. *Persistence* is the faithful and continued effort put forth in order to achieve a goal or finish a project. *Intensity* refers to the focused energy and attention applied in order to achieve a goal or complete a project.

Sometimes activities are pursued as ends in themselves, simply because they are enjoyable, not because any external reward is attached. This type of motivation

motivation: The process that initiates, directs, and sustains behavior to satisfy physiological or psychological needs or wants.

motives: Needs or desires that energize and direct behavior toward a goal.

incentive: An external stimulus that motivates behavior (examples: money, fame).

Table 11.1 Intrinsic and Extrinsic Motivation

	Description	Examples
Intrinsic motivation	An activity is pursued as an end in itself because it is enjoyable and rewarding.	A person anonymously donates a large sum of money to a university to fund scholarships for deserving students. A child reads several books each week because reading is fun.
Extrinsic motivation	An activity is pursued to gain an external reward or to avoid an undesirable consequence.	A person agrees to donate a large sum of money to a university for the construction of a building, provided it will bear the family name. A child reads two books each week to avoid losing TV privileges.

is known as **intrinsic motivation.** On the other hand, when we act in order to gain some external reward or to avoid some undesirable consequence, we are pulled by **extrinsic motivation.** If you are working hard in this course solely because you find the subject interesting, then your motivation is intrinsic. But if you are studying only to keep from getting kicked out of school, your motivation is extrinsic. In real life, the motives for many activities are both intrinsic and extrinsic. You may love your job, but you would probably be motivated to leave if your salary, an important extrinsic motivator, were taken away. Table 11.1 gives examples of intrinsic and extrinsic motivation.

What do researchers say about the motives for behavior? Let's consider some theories of motivation.

THEORIES OF MOTIVATION

Obviously, both inborn and external forces influence us, but theories of motivation differ in the relative power they attribute to each. The most thoroughly biological theories of motivation are the instinct theories.

Instinct Theories of Motivation

How do instinct theories explain motivation?

Scientists have learned much about instincts by observing animal behavior. Spiders instinctively spin their intricate webs without being taught the technique by other spiders. It is neither a choice they make nor a task they learn, but an **instinct**—an inborn, unlearned, fixed pattern of behavior that is characteristic of an entire species. An instinct does not improve with practice, and an animal will behave in that same way even if it has never seen another member of its species. Even when their web-spinning glands are removed, spiders still perform the complex spinning movements and then lay their eggs in the imaginary webs they have spun. So instincts explain much of animal behavior.

But can human motivation be explained by **instinct theory**—the notion that human behavior is motivated by certain innate, unlearned tendencies or instincts that are shared by all individuals? Instinct theory was widely accepted by William James, Sigmund Freud, and others through the first 20 or 30 years of the 20th century. Over those decades, the list of instincts expanded until thousands of instincts were being proposed to explain human behavior. Most psychologists today reject

intrinsic motivation: The desire to perform an act because it is satisfying or pleasurable in and of itself.

extrinsic motivation: The desire to perform an act to gain a reward or to avoid an undesirable consequence.

instinct: An inborn, unlearned, fixed pattern of behavior that is characteristic of an entire species.

instinct theory: The notion that human behavior is motivated by certain innate tendencies, or instincts, shared by all individuals.

Figure 11.1

Drive-Reduction Theory

Drive-reduction theory is based on the biological concept of homeostasis–the natural tendency of a living organism to maintain a state of internal balance, or equilibrium. When the equilibrium becomes disturbed (by a biological need such as thirst), a drive (internal state of arousal) emerges. Then the organism is motivated to take action to satisfy the need, thus reducing the drive and restoring equilibrium.

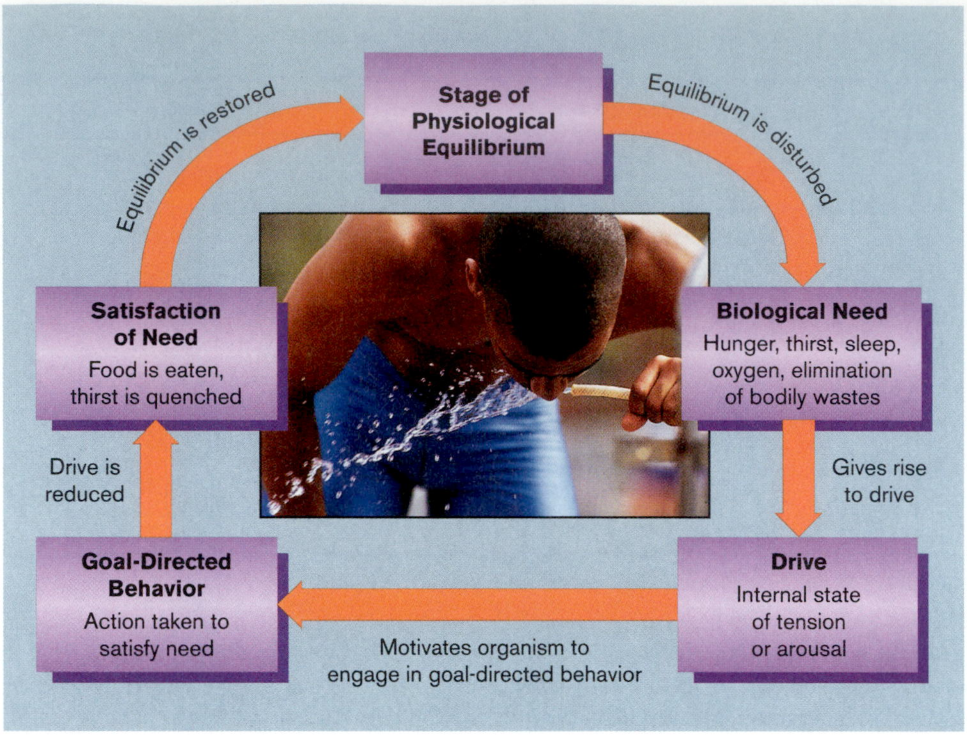

instinct theory as an explanation of human motivation. They do not deny that genetic or biological predispositions affect the character and nature of motivation and behavior. However, observation alone suggests that human behavior is too richly diverse, and often too unpredictable, to be considered fixed and invariant across the entire species.

Drive-Reduction Theory: Striving to Keep a Balanced Internal State

How does drive-reduction theory explain motivation?

Another major attempt to explain motivation is the **drive-reduction theory,** or drive theory, which was popularized by Clark Hull (1943). According to Hull, all living organisms have certain biological needs that must be met if they are to survive. A need gives rise to an internal state of tension or arousal called a **drive,** and the person or organism is motivated to reduce it. For example, when you are deprived of food or go too long without water, your biological need causes a state of tension, in this case the hunger or thirst drive. You become motivated to seek food or water to reduce the drive and satisfy your biological need.

Drive-reduction theory is derived largely from the biological concept of **homeostasis**—the tendency of the body to maintain a balanced, internal state in order to ensure physical survival. Body temperature, blood sugar, water balance, oxygen—in short, everything required for physical existence—must be maintained in a state of equilibrium, or balance. When this state is disturbed, a drive is created to restore the balance, as shown in Figure 11.1. But drive-reduction theory cannot fully account for the broad range of human motivation.

It is true that people are sometimes motivated to reduce tension, as drive-reduction theory states, but often they are just as motivated to increase it. Why do people seek activities that actually create a state of tension—hang-gliding, horror movies, and bungee-jumping? Why do animals and humans alike engage in exploratory behavior when it does not serve to reduce any primary drive?

drive-reduction theory: A theory of motivation suggesting that a need creates an unpleasant state of arousal or tension called a drive, which impels the organism to engage in behavior that will satisfy the need and reduce the tension.

drive: A state of tension or arousal brought about by an underlying need, which motivates an organism to engage in behavior that will satisfy the need and reduce the tension.

homeostasis: The tendency of the body to maintain a balanced internal state with regard to oxygen level, body temperature, blood sugar, water balance, and so forth.

Review & Reflect 11.1 Theories of Motivation

Theory	View	Example
Instinct theory	Behavior is the result of innate, unlearned tendencies. (This view has been rejected by most modern psychologists.)	Two people fighting because of their aggressive instinct
Drive-reduction theory	Behavior results from the need to reduce an internal state of tension or arousal.	Eating to reduce hunger
Arousal theory	Behavior results from the need to maintain an optimal level of arousal.	Climbing a mountain for excitement; listening to classical music for relaxation

Arousal Theory: Striving for an Optimal Level of Arousal

How does arousal theory explain motivation?

Arousal theory can answer some of the puzzling questions that drive-reduction theory cannot answer. **Arousal** refers to a person's state of alertness and mental and physical activation. Arousal levels can range from no arousal (when a person is comatose), to moderate arousal (when pursuing normal day-to-day activities), to high arousal (when excited and highly stimulated).

Unlike drive-reduction theory, **arousal theory** does not suggest that people are always motivated to reduce arousal or tension. Arousal theory states that people are motivated to maintain an *optimal* level of arousal. If arousal is less than the optimal level, we do something to stimulate it; if arousal exceeds the optimal level, we seek to reduce the stimulation.

Biological needs, such as the need for food and water, increase arousal. But people also become aroused when they encounter new stimuli or when the intensity of stimuli is increased, as with loud noises, bright lights, or foul odors. And, of course, certain kinds of drugs—stimulants such as caffeine, nicotine, amphetamines, and cocaine—also increase arousal.

Review & Reflect 11.1 summarizes three major motivation theories that we have discussed: instinct theory, drive-reduction theory, and arousal theory.

Stimulus Motives: Increasing Stimulation When arousal is too low, **stimulus motives,** such as curiosity and the motives to explore, to manipulate objects, and to play, cause humans and other animals to increase stimulation. Young monkeys will play with mechanical puzzles for long periods just for the stimulus of doing so (Harlow, 1950). A very early study found that rats will explore intricate mazes when they are neither thirsty nor hungry and when no reinforcement is provided (Dashiell, 1925). According to Berlyne (1960), rats will spend more time exploring novel objects than familiar objects. So will humans.

Arousal and Performance There is often a close link between arousal and performance. According to the **Yerkes–Dodson law,** performance on tasks is best when arousal level is appropriate to the difficulty of the task. Performance on simple tasks is better when arousal is relatively high. Tasks of moderate difficulty are best accomplished when arousal is moderate; complex or difficult tasks, when arousal is lower (see Figure 11.2 on p. 390). But performance suffers when arousal level is either too high or too low for the task. You may have experienced too much or too little

arousal: A state of alertness and mental and physical activation.

arousal theory: A theory suggesting that the aim of motivation is to maintain an optimal level of arousal.

stimulus motives: Motives that cause humans and other animals to increase stimulation and that appear to be unlearned (examples: curiosity and the need to explore, manipulate objects, and play).

Yerkes–Dodson law: The principle that performance on tasks is best when the arousal level is appropriate to the difficulty of the task—higher arousal for simple tasks, moderate arousal for tasks of moderate difficulty, and lower arousal for complex tasks.

Figure 11.2

The Yerkes–Dodson Law

The optimal level of arousal varies according to the difficulty of the task. Arousal levels should be relatively high for simple tasks, moderate for moderately difficult tasks, and lower for difficult tasks.

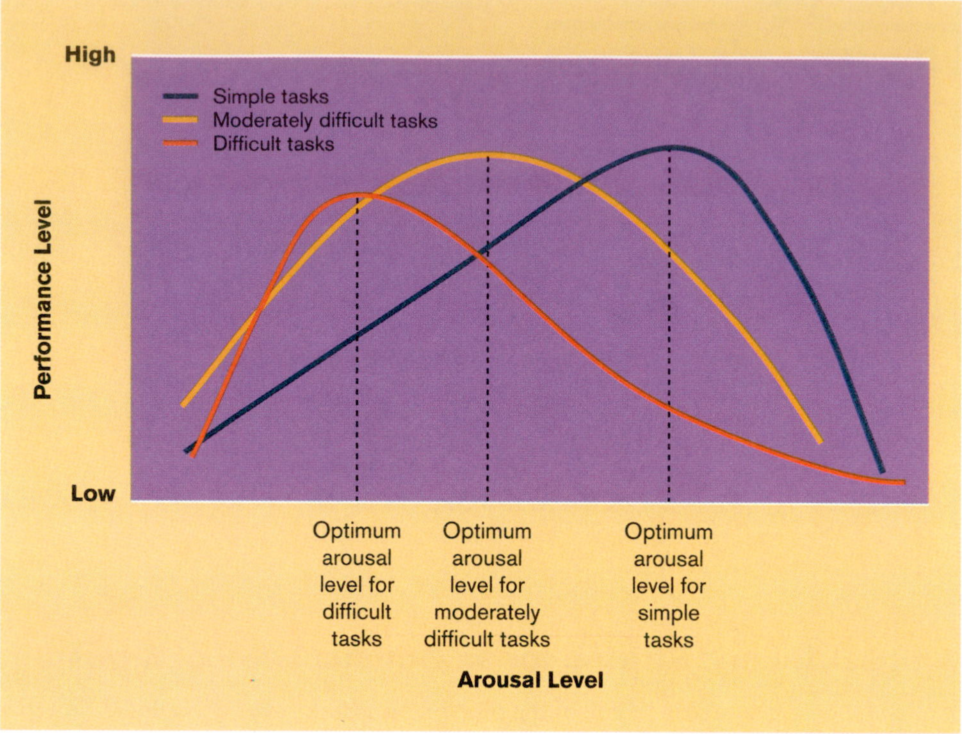

arousal when taking an exam. Perhaps your arousal was so low that your mind was sluggish and you didn't finish the test; or you might have been so keyed up that you couldn't remember much of what you had studied.

Individual Differences in Arousal: Too Much for One Is Too Little for Another People differ in the level of arousal they normally prefer. Some people are sensation seekers, who love the thrill of new experiences and adventure. Sensation seekers are willing, even eager, to take risks. They are easily bored and experience little fear or uncertainty (McCourt et al., 1993). Other people are the opposite: They enjoy the routine and the predictable, avoid risk, and fare best when arousal is relatively low.

Individuals vary widely in their scores on tests that measure sensation seeking. And there may be gender and cultural differences in sensation-seeking tendencies as well. Researchers have found that males tend to score higher than females, and White Americans tend to score higher than African Americans (Zuckerman, 1979).

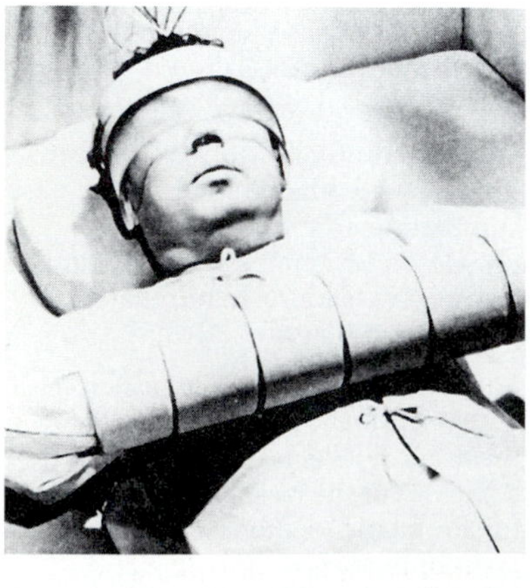

Sensory stimulation is reduced to the minimum for participants in sensory deprivation experiments.

The Effects of Sensory Deprivation: Sensory Nothingness How do you suppose it would feel to have no stimulation at all? In an early experiment, Bexton and others (1954) at McGill University gave student volunteers the opportunity to find out when they studied the effects of **sensory deprivation**—a condition in which sensory stimulation is reduced to a minimum or eliminated.

Students had to lie motionless in a specially designed sensory deprivation chamber in which sensory stimulation was severely restricted. They wore translucent goggles that reduced visual input to a diffused light. Their hands were placed in cotton gloves, and cardboard cuffs were placed over their lower arms, preventing the sensation of touch. The only sound they heard was the hum of an air conditioner through a foam-rubber headpiece. The participants could eat, drink, and go to the bathroom when they wanted to. Occasionally they would take tests of motor and mental function. Otherwise they were confined to their sensationless prison.

Did they enjoy the experience? Hardly! Half the participants quit the experiment after the first 2 days. Eventually the remaining participants became irritable, confused, and unable to concentrate. They began to have visual hallucinations. Some began to hear imaginary voices and music and felt as if they were receiving electric shocks or being hit by pellets. Their performance on motor and cognitive tasks deteriorated, and none of the participants said they liked the experiment.

Other studies using milder forms of sensory deprivation, known as *sensory restriction,* have produced some beneficial effects. Positive results range from improved concentration (Lilly, 1956) to better control over cigarette smoking (Suedfeld, 1990) and other addictions (Borrie, 1991). Some studies have shown that sensory restriction has beneficial effects for autistic children (Harrison & Barabasz, 1991).

Researchers who study motivation are typically not searching for a general theory that explains all types of motivation. Rather, they assume that a variety of factors—biological, cognitive, behavioral, social, and cultural—in various combinations influence the motivation underlying any given behavior. Researchers today are thus more likely to study particular kinds of motivated behavior (Petri, 1996).

Remember It!

1. When you engage in an activity in order to gain a reward or to avoid an unpleasant consequence, your motivation is (intrinsic, extrinsic).
2. Drive-reduction theory focused primarily on ______________ needs and the drives they produce.
   a. cognitive c. biological
   b. psychological d. emotional
3. Which of the following suggests that human behavior is motivated by certain innate, unlearned tendencies that are shared by all individuals?
   a. arousal theory c. Yerkes-Dodson law
   b. instinct theory d. drive-reduction theory
4. According to arousal theory, people seek ______________ arousal.
   a. minimized c. decreased
   b. increased d. optimal

Answers: 1. extrinsic 2. c 3. b 4. d

THE PRIMARY DRIVES: HUNGER AND THIRST

Drive-reduction theory suggests that motivation is based largely on the **primary drives,** those that are unlearned and that serve to satisfy biological needs. Two of the most important primary drives are thirst and hunger.

Thirst: There Are Two Kinds

Under what kinds of conditions do the two types of thirst occur?

Thirst is a basic biological drive, for all animals must have a continuous supply of fluid. Adequate fluid is critical because the body itself is about 75% water. Without any intake of fluids, a person can survive only about 4 or 5 days.

But how do you know when you are thirsty? When you have a dry mouth and throat, or a powerful urge to drink? Yes, but thirst is more complex than that. There are two types of thirst. One type (extracellular thirst) occurs when fluid is lost from the body tissues rather than from the body cells. If you are exercising heavily or doing almost anything in hot weather, you will perspire and lose bodily fluid. Bleeding, vomiting, and diarrhea also rob your body of fluid. Extracellular fluid loss takes fluid from the surrounding tissues, rather than from the body's cells. It is not a good idea to drink a cold beer or any other type of alcohol to quench your thirst on

sensory deprivation: A condition in which sensory stimulation is reduced to a minimum or eliminated.

primary drive: A state of tension or arousal arising from a biological need; one not based on learning.

a very hot day, because alcohol increases extracellular fluid loss. This is why people awaken with a powerful thirst after drinking heavily the night before.

Another type of thirst (intracellular thirst) involves the loss of water from inside the body cells. When you eat a lot of salty food, the water–sodium balance in the blood and in the tissues outside the cells is disturbed. The salt cannot readily enter the cells, so the cells release some of their own water to restore the balance. As the body cells become dehydrated, thirst is stimulated and you drink to increase the water volume (Robertson, 1983). This explains why so many bars offer customers free salted nuts, chips, or pretzels.

The Biological Basis of Hunger: Internal Hunger Cues

What are the roles of the lateral hypothalamus and the ventromedial hypothalamus in the regulation of eating behavior?

Hunger is a biological drive operating in all animals, including humans. What happens in the body to make you feel hungry, and what causes satiety—the feeling of being full or satisfied?

The Role of the Hypothalamus: The Feeding and Satiety Centers Researchers have found two areas of the hypothalamus that are of central importance in regulating eating behavior and thus affect the hunger drive (Steffens et al., 1988). As researchers discovered long ago, the **lateral hypothalamus (LH)** acts as a feeding center to excite eating. Stimulating the feeding center causes animals to eat even when they are full (Delgado & Anand, 1953). And when the feeding center is destroyed, animals initially refuse to eat (Anand & Brobeck, 1951).

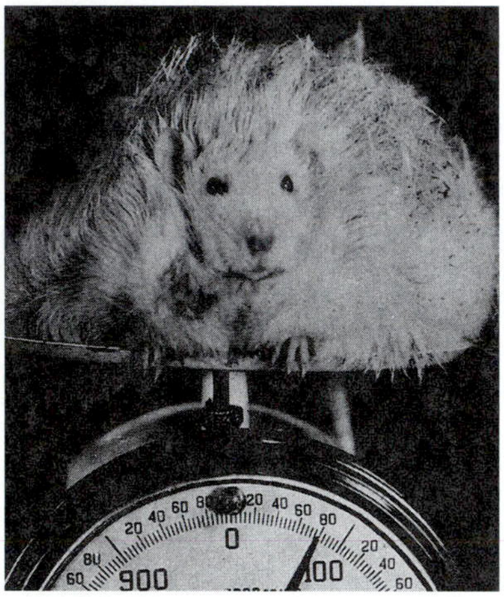

A rat whose satiety center has been destroyed can weigh up to six times as much as a normal rat—in this case, 1080 grams, enough to exceed the capacity of the scale.

The **ventromedial hypothalamus (VMH)** apparently acts as a satiety center, and when active, it inhibits eating (Hernandez & Hoebel, 1989). If the satiety center is electrically stimulated, animals stop eating (Duggan & Booth, 1986). If the VMH is surgically removed, animals soon eat their way to gross obesity (Hetherington & Ranson, 1940; Parkinson & Weingarten, 1990). One rat whose satiety center was destroyed weighed nearly six times as much as a normal rat. In human terms this would be like a 150-pound person ballooning up to 900 pounds.

Gorging to obesity or refusing to eat altogether occurs immediately after the destruction of a rat's VMH or LH. Some time after the surgery, the rat begins to establish more normal eating patterns. But the obese rats continue to maintain above-average body weight, and the noneating rats eventually establish a below-average body weight (Hoebel & Teitelbaum, 1966). Some researchers believe that destruction of the VMH causes animals to lose the ability to adjust their metabolism and thereby stabilize their body weight (Vilberg & Keesey, 1990).

Other organs and substances in the body also play a role in our feelings of hunger and satiety.

What are some of the body's hunger and satiety signals?

The Role of the Stomach: Hunger Pangs The fullness of the stomach affects feelings of hunger. The stomach has a capacity of about 1 pint when empty and stretches to hold 2½ pints when full (Avraham, 1989). Generally, the more full or distended the stomach, the less hunger is felt (Pappas et al., 1989).

How do you know when you are hungry? Do you have stomach contractions called hunger pangs? In a classic experiment, Cannon and Washburn (1912) demonstrated a close correlation between stomach contractions and the perception of hunger. But their discovery does not necessarily mean that the sensation of hunger is caused by stomach contractions. Humans and other animals continue to experience hunger even when it is impossible for them to feel stomach contractions. Cancer and ulcer patients who have had their stomachs removed entirely still report feeling hunger pangs (Janowitz & Grossman, 1950).

If animals and humans without stomachs continue to experience hunger and satiety, then there must be other hunger and satiety signals besides stomach contractions. The search for these signals moved from the stomach to the blood, because the bloodstream is the means of transporting the products of digestion to sustain all the cells of the body.

lateral hypothalamus (LH): The part of the hypothalamus that acts as a feeding center and, when activated, signals an animal to eat; when the LH is destroyed, the animal refuses to eat.

ventromedial hypothalamus (VMH): The part of the hypothalamus that acts as a satiety center and, when activated, signals an animal to stop eating; when the VMH is destroyed, the animal overeats, becoming obese.

Other Hunger and Satiety Signals In an early study, Templeton and Quigley (1930) found that the blood of an animal that has eaten its fill is different from the blood of an excessively hungry animal. In one study, blood was taken from a very hungry dog and from a dog that had recently eaten. The blood taken from each dog was given in a transfusion to the other. After the transfusions, the dog that had previously eaten began having stomach contractions even though its stomach was full. When the hungry dog that had been experiencing stomach contractions received the blood transfusion, its stomach contractions stopped.

The question is: What was in the blood that signaled hunger and satiety? Researchers began investigating factors such as the blood levels of glucose—a simple sugar resulting from the digestion of carbohydrates.

Glucose and Hunger Blood levels of glucose are monitored by nutrient detectors in the liver that send this information to the brain (Friedman et al., 1986). Hunger is stimulated when the brain receives the message that blood levels of glucose are low.

Insulin Levels in the Blood Insulin, a hormone produced by the pancreas, chemically converts glucose into energy that is usable by the cells. Elevations in insulin cause an increase in hunger, in food intake, and in a desire for sweets (Rodin et al., 1985). Chronic oversecretion of insulin stimulates hunger and often leads to obesity.

Satiety Signals Released from the Gastrointestinal Tract Some of the substances secreted by the gastrointestinal tract during digestion are released into the blood and act as satiety signals (Flood et al., 1990). The hormone cholecystokinin (CCK) is one satiety signal that causes people to limit the amount of food they eat during a meal (Bray, 1991; Woods & Gibbs, 1989).

But we are motivated to eat not only by the internal hunger drive. There are also external factors that stimulate hunger.

Other Factors Influencing Hunger: External Eating Cues

What are some nonbiological factors that influence what and how much people eat?

Apart from internal hunger, there are external factors influencing what, where, and how much people eat. Sensory cues such as the taste, smell, and appearance of food stimulate the appetite. For many, the hands of the clock alone, signaling mealtime, are enough to prompt a quest for food. Even eating with other people tends to stimulate people to eat more than they would if they were eating alone (de Castro & de Castro, 1989).

Susceptibility to External Eating Cues: Can You Resist Them? Are we all equally susceptible to external eating cues? Stanley Schachter and colleagues suggested that overweight people are overly responsive to these external cues and are therefore more likely to overeat (Schachter & Gross, 1968). Normal-weight individuals, on the other hand, were thought to be more affected by internal rather than external cues, eating when they actually needed food. But later studies showed that the degree of external or internal responsiveness was not strongly correlated with the degree of overweight (Rodin, 1981).

Just the sight of mouth-watering foods can make us want to eat, even when we aren't actually hungry.

However, external cues *can* trigger internal processes that motivate a person to eat. The sight and smell of appetizing food can trigger the release of insulin, particularly in those who are externally responsive (Rodin et al., 1977). Even in rats, environmental cues previously associated with food cause an increase in insulin level (Detke et al., 1989). For some individuals, simply seeing or thinking about food can cause an elevated level of insulin, and such people have a greater tendency to gain weight (Rodin, 1985). To find out why you eat, do the *Try It!*

When you do eat, which do you prefer—biscuits or bagels, egg-drop soup or creole gumbo, chicken curry or chicken and dumplings? You might say it is a matter of taste, but researchers say that taste itself is largely a matter of culture (Rozin, 1996). All cultures have distinctive preferences when it comes to food. For example,

Try It!

For 48 hours, keep a diary of everything you eat. Record what and how much you ate, the time you ate, whether or not you felt physically hungry, and, if you didn't, what motivated you to eat. A partial diary might look like this:

8:45 A.M.	2 donuts	Not hungry–ate because I didn't want to get hungry during 9 o'clock class
1:15 P.M.	2 sandwiches, salad, 1 cookie	Hungry–stomach was growling

Based on your diary, what typically motivates you to eat? Do you more often follow your stomach or your head? If you are overweight and you find that your motivation to eat is usually not hunger-based, you may want to continue your diary and start paying attention to internal, rather than external, hunger cues. If you eat only when you feel physically hungry, you will lose weight.

some Native American tribes traditionally flavored their soup with dirt, and many Eskimos consider whale blubber a treat.

Table 11.2 summarizes the factors that stimulate and inhibit eating.

Understanding Body Weight: Why Does It Vary So Widely?

What are some factors that account for variations in body weight?

Pencil-thin models seen in TV commercials and fashion magazines have come to represent the ideal body for many American women. But most of these models have only 10–15% body fat, far below the 22–26% considered normal for women (Brownell, 1991). Fat has become a negative term, even though some body fat is nec-

Table 11.2 Biological and Environmental Factors That Inhibit and Stimulate Eating

	Biological	Environmental
Factors that inhibit eating	Activity in ventromedial hypothalamus	Unappetizing smell, taste, or appearance of food
	Raised blood glucose levels	Acquired taste aversions
	Distended (full) stomach	Learned eating habits
	CCK (hormone that acts as satiety signal)	Desire to be thin
	Sensory-specific satiety	Reaction to stress, unpleasant emotional state
Factors that stimulate eating	Activity in lateral hypothalamus	Appetizing smell, taste, or appearance of food
	Low blood levels of glucose	Acquired food preferences
	Increase in insulin	Being around others who are eating
	Stomach contractions	Foods high in fat and sugar
	Empty stomach	Learned eating habits
		Reaction to boredom, stress, unpleasant emotional state

essary. Men need 3% and women, 12%, just to survive. And in order for a woman's reproductive system to function properly, she must maintain 20% body fat.

Extremes in either fatness or thinness can pose health risks. An abnormal desire for thinness can result in eating disorders such as the self-starvation of anorexia nervosa and the pattern of binging and purging seen with bulimia nervosa. At the other extreme are some 34 million Americans suffering from obesity—excessive fatness. In the United States, 20% of men and 25% of women are obese, and obesity is becoming more common on every continent (Kopelman, 2000). Many researchers find this trend alarming: "Obesity should no longer be regarded simply as a cosmetic problem affecting certain individuals, but an epidemic that threatens global well-being" (Kopelman, 2000, p. 365). Approximately 300,000 obese Americans die annually as a result of the damaging effects of eating too much and moving too little (Gibbs, 1996). People who have excess fat in the waist and stomach (the so-called apple pattern) are at much greater risk than those whose fat is deposited in the hips and thighs (the pear pattern) (Shapiro, 1997).

In 1994 the third in a series of studies (the most recent of their kind)—the National Health and Nutrition Examination Surveys—was published, bearing the bad news that for all racial and ethnic groups combined, a full one-third of American adults aged 20 and older are overweight (Flegal, 1996; Kuczmarski et al., 1994). For men, being overweight is defined as 24% above their desirable weight; for women, 20% above. Adults in the United States were 8% heavier in the mid-1990s than they were in 1976 (Flegal, 1996). Americans add about 1 pound each year, on average, from early adulthood to late middle age (Wood, 1996), and weight gain is strongly correlated with decreasing physical fitness (Lewis et al., 1997). The incidence of obesity is much higher and fat intake is generally greater in lower socioeconomic classes than in higher ones in the United States (Jeffrey & French, 1996). However, fatness, particularly in women, is associated with affluence in some developing countries (Cogan et al., 1996).

Lara Flynn Boyle (left), who appears on the popular TV series The Practice, *has been criticized for being too thin, while Camryn Mannheim (right), her costar, is said to be too heavy. Numerous health risks are associated with both extremes of body weight.*

metabolic rate (meh-tuh-BALL-ik): The rate at which the body burns calories to produce energy.

Although both excessive thinness and obesity result from a long-term imbalance between energy (food) intake and energy expenditure, the cause is not simply insufficient or excessive food intake. Obesity is usually caused by a combination of factors that include heredity, metabolic rate, activity level, number of fat cells, and eating habits.

The Role of Genetic Factors in Body Weight How strong is the genetic influence on body mass? Knowledge about this topic has grown enormously in recent years (Barsh et al., 2000). One review of studies encompassed more than 100,000 participants and found that 74% of identical twin pairs have a similar body weights. Only 32% of fraternal twins, however, have comparable body weights. The researchers reported an estimated heritability for body weight of between .50 and .90 (Barsh et al., 2000).

A human obesity gene map has been constructed (Perusse et al., 1999), which contains information about 15 different chromosome regions. More than 40 genes appear to be related to obesity and body weight regulation (Barsh et al., 2000). Once the functioning of such genes is clearly understood, perhaps new weight-loss drugs can be developed that are virtually tailor-made to fit individuals' genetic makeup.

Across all weight classes, from very thin to very obese, children adopted from birth tend to resemble their biological parents more than their adoptive parents in body size. In adoptees, thinness seems to be even more influenced by genes than obesity is (Costanzo & Schiffman, 1989). Also, people may inherit their resting metabolic rate, their tendency to store surplus calories primarily as muscle or fat, and even the pattern of where fat is deposited (Bouchard et al., 1990). Nevertheless, Bouchard (1997) found evidence "that environmental conditions and lifestyle characteristics make an even stronger contribution than the genes" to overall body mass (p. S25).

Researchers Friedman and colleagues identified the hormone leptin, which directly affects the feeding and satiety centers in the brain's hypothalamus and is known to be a key element in the regulation of body weight (Friedman, 1997, 2000). Leptin is produced by the body's fat tissues, and the amount produced is a direct measure of body fat: The more leptin produced, the higher the level of body fat. Decreases in body fat cause lower levels of leptin in the body, and lower levels of leptin stimulate food intake. When leptin levels increase sufficiently, energy expenditure exceeds food intake, and people lose weight. Obese mice injected with leptin lost 30% of their body weight within 2 weeks (Halaas et al., 1995). In humans, a mutation of the leptin receptor gene can cause obesity as well as pituitary abnormalities (Clément et al., 1998). Changes in the body's leptin levels can affect the immune and reproductive systems as well as the processes involved in bone formation. Thus, leptin plays a key role in linking nutrition to overall human physiology (Friedman, 2000).

Researchers have discovered that hormones that play a key role in stress are also important in eating behavior. These stress-related hormones not only coordinate human and animal responses to stress, but are essential for the sustained or long-term suppression of appetite and feeding (Coste et al., 2000).

Metabolic Rate: Burning Energy–Slow or Fast *Metabolism* refers to all the physical and chemical processes that are carried out in the body to sustain life. And food is the source of energy required to carry out these processes. The rate at which the body burns calories to produce energy is called the **metabolic rate.** Physical activity uses up only about one-third of your energy intake; the other two-thirds is consumed by the maintenance processes that keep you alive. When there is an imbalance between energy intake (how much you eat) and output (how much energy you use), your weight changes. Generally, if your caloric intake exceeds your daily energy requirement, you gain weight. If your daily energy requirement exceeds your caloric intake, you lose weight. Researchers studying human metabolism from the perspective of thermodynamics have learned that obesity can result when energy intake (eating) exceeds energy expenditure (body heat and exercise) by only a small amount over an extended time period (Lowell & Spiegelman, 2000). There are, however, significant individual differences in the efficiency with which energy is burned. Even if two people are the same age and weight and have the same build and level of activity, one may be able to consume more calories each day without gaining weight.

fat cells: Cells that serve as storehouses for liquefied fat in the body and that number from 25 to 35 billion in normal-weight individuals; with weight loss, they decrease in size but not in number.

set point: The weight the body normally maintains when one is trying neither to gain nor to lose weight; if weight falls below the normal level, appetite increases and metabolic rate decreases; if weight is gained, appetite decreases and metabolic rate increases to its original level.

Fat-Cell Theory: Tiny Storage Tanks for Fat Fat-cell theory proposes that fatness is related to the number of **fat cells** (adipose cells) in the body. It is estimated that people of normal weight have between 25 and 35 billion fat cells, while those whose weight is twice normal may have between 100 and 125 billion fat cells (Brownell & Wadden, 1992). The number is determined by both genes and eating habits (Grinker, 1982). Fat cells serve as storehouses for liquefied fat. When you lose weight, you do not lose the fat cells themselves. You lose the fat that is stored in them, and the cells simply shrink (Dietz, 1989).

Researchers once believed that all the fat cells a person would ever have were formed early in life. This is no longer the accepted view. Now researchers believe that when people overeat beyond the fat cells' capacity, the number of fat cells continues to increase (Rodin & Wing, 1988).

How does set point affect body weight?

Set-Point Theory: Thin/Fat Thermostat Set-point theory suggests that humans are genetically programmed to carry a certain amount of body weight (Keesey, 1988). **Set point**—the weight the body maintains when one is trying neither to gain nor to lose weight—is affected by the number of fat cells in the body and by metabolic rate, both of which are influenced by the genes (Gurin, 1989). Yet people with a genetic propensity to be thin can become overweight if they continually overeat, because over the years they will develop a high set point for body fat.

According to set-point theory, an internal homeostatic system functions to maintain set-point weight, much as a thermostat works to keep temperature near the point at which it is set. Whether an individual is lean, overweight, or average, when body weight falls below set point, appetite increases. When weight climbs above set point, appetite decreases so as to restore the original weight. The rate of energy expenditure is also adjusted to maintain the body's set-point weight (Keesey & Powley, 1986). When people gain weight, metabolic rate increases (Dietz, 1989). But when they restrict calories to lose weight, the metabolic rate lowers, causing the body to burn fewer calories and thus making further weight loss more difficult. Increasing the amount of physical activity—exercising during and after weight loss—is the one method recommended for lowering the set point so that the body will store less fat (Forey et al., 1996).

Dieting: A National Obsession

At any given time, one out of five adults in the United States is on some kind of reducing diet, but a far larger number—51% of women and 43% of men—perceive themselves as overweight (Gallup & Newport, 1990a). According to Rodin (1992), the struggle for "the perfect body is like most wars, a costly one—emotionally and physically, to say nothing of financially. It leaves most of us feeling frustrated, ashamed, and defeated" (p. 59). Most diets do produce an initial weight loss—but not a permanent one (Serdula et al., 1993; Wadden, 1993). In fact, little of the weight lost in diet programs is kept off over the long term (Williams et al., 1996). But one behavior that separates those who keep the pounds off from those who regain them is regular exercise (Wadden et al., 1997). Furthermore, dieters who are self-motivated to participate in weight loss programs are much more likely to maintain their lower weight than those who feel pressured or coerced to lose weight (Williams et al., 1996).

Why is it almost impossible to maintain weight loss by cutting calories alone?

Why Diets Don't Work The high complexity of the processes involved in appetite regulation and energy metabolism helps explain why diets often do not work (Campbell & Dhand, 2000). To be effective, any weight-loss program must help people decrease energy intake (eat less), increase energy expenditure (exercise more), or both (Bray & Tartaglia, 2000). Unfortunately, most people who are trying to lose weight focus only on cutting calories. At first, when overweight people begin to diet and cut their calories, they do lose weight. But after a few pounds are shed initially, the dieter's metabolic rate slows down as if to conserve the remaining fat store because fewer calories are being consumed (Hirsch, 1997).

What can overweight people do to reach their desired weight and then maintain it? The answer, according to Bouchard (1996), is to adopt a physically active lifestyle coupled with a diet containing no more than 30% fat. Reasonable calorie restriction must be coupled with increased exercise and activity to counteract the body's tendency to maintain a lower metabolic rate when fewer calories are consumed (Blair, 1993). Starvation diets are self-defeating in the long run. When a person restricts calories too severely, even exercise cannot reverse the body's drastic lowering of metabolism and its natural tendency to conserve remaining fat (Ballor et al., 1990). Women should consume at least 1,000 calories a day, and men 1,500 calories a day, unless they are under a doctor's supervision.

Some encouraging news for overweight exercisers is that the more they weigh, the more calories they burn during exercise, compared with thinner people. And exercise does not increase the appetite. Sometimes exercise alone, without a restriction in diet, can result in weight loss (Frey-Hewitt et al., 1990).

Yo-Yo Dieting Many dieters go through repeated cycles of weight gain and loss called *weight cycling*, or *yo-yo dieting*. Some studies have suggested that frequent dieting causes the body to become an increasingly efficient energy conserver, and thus the dieter loses weight more slowly and regains it more quickly with each succeeding weight cycle (Archambault et al., 1989). But more recent research casts doubt on the notion that, in general, yo-yo dieters find it progressively more difficult to lose weight (Brownell & Rodin, 1994).

Changing Eating Habits: A Long-Term Solution Dieting is not a long-term solution to the problem of being overweight. Many people believe that once the weight is lost, the diet is no longer necessary and old eating habits can be resumed. But because the old habits caused much of the weight problem, returning to those habits is a sure-fire formula for weight gain.

Some evidence suggests that successful weight loss involves more than simply counting calories. It seems that calories eaten in the form of fat are more likely to be stored as body fat than calories eaten as carbohydrates. Miller and others (1990) found that even when obese and thin people have the same caloric intake, thin people derive about 29% of their calories from fats, while obese people average 35% from fat. Recent research suggests that the optimal fat intake appropriate for the average American is approximately 30% of the total calories consumed (Grundy, 1999). The composition of the diet may have as much to do with weight gain as the amount of food eaten and the lack of exercise. Counting and limiting the grams of fat may be more beneficial than counting calories to help a person achieve and maintain a desirable body weight. Low-fat diets are healthier, too!

Eating Disorders: The Tyranny of the Scale

Over the past quarter century, the "ideal" female figure, as portrayed in the media and by the fashion and entertainment industries, has become ever thinner, often to the point of emaciation. Accompanying this trend has been an increase in the incidence of eating disorders, such as anorexia nervosa and bulimia nervosa (Halmi, 1996).

What are the symptoms of anorexia nervosa?

Anorexia Nervosa **Anorexia nervosa** is characterized by an overwhelming, irrational fear of gaining weight or becoming fat, compulsive dieting to the point of self-starvation, and excessive weight loss. Some anorexics lose as much as 20–25% of their original body weight.

Anorexia typically begins in adolescence, and most of those afflicted are females. About 1% of females between ages 12 and 40 suffer from this disorder (Johnson et al., 1996). The greater prevalence of eating disorders among females appears to be a general phenomenon, rather than a culturally specific one. In a large sample of Norwegian adults, for example, women were twice as likely as men to have an eating disorder (Augestad, 2000). Although it has been established that females are significantly more at risk for eating disorders than males are, a study of the relationship of eating problems to self-concept and other emotional/behavioral measures found that 20% of the females and, surprisingly, 10% of the males in a sample of 471 college students had symptoms of anorexia. This study, although small, suggests that eating disorders may be more prevalent among males than current estimates (Nelson et al., 1999).

Anorexia often begins with dieting, which gradually develops into an obsession. Anorexic individuals continue to feel hunger and are overly preoccupied with food. And their perception of their body size is grossly distorted. No matter how emaciated they become, they continue to perceive themselves as fat. Frequently, they not only starve themselves but also exercise relentlessly in an effort to accelerate the weight loss. Among young women, progressive and significant weight loss eventually results in *amenorrhea* (cessation of menstruation). Anorexics may also develop low blood pressure, impaired heart function, dehydration, electrolyte disturbances, and sterility (American Psychiatric Association, 1993a), as well as decreases in the gray matter volume in the brain, which are thought to be irreversible (Lambe et al., 1997). Unfortunately, up to 20% of those suffering from anorexia nervosa eventually die of starvation or complications from organ damage (Brotman, 1994).

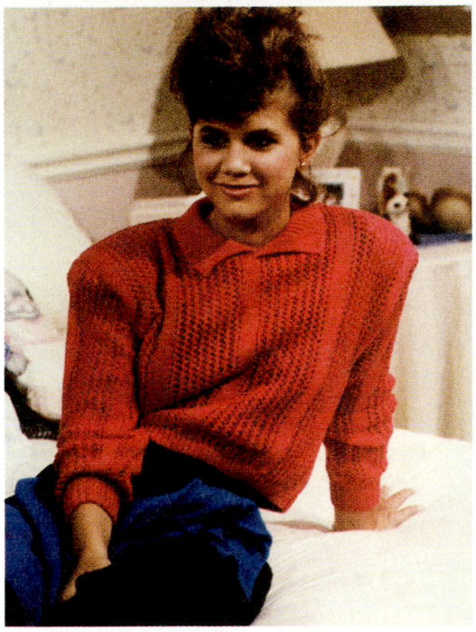

Actress Tracey Gold developed an eating disorder while she was one of the stars of the hit TV series Growing Pains, *which ran from 1985 to 1992. Virtually ignoring food, she would "chain drink" diet soda and iced tea. Today, Tracey has recovered and is doing well.*

It is difficult to pinpoint the cause of this disorder. Most anorexic individuals are well-behaved and academically successful (Vitousek & Manke, 1994). Psychological risk factors for eating disorders include being overly concerned about physical appearance, worrying about perceived attractiveness, and feeling social pressure in favor of thinness (Whisenhunt et al., 2000). Some investigators believe that young women who refuse to eat are attempting to control a portion of their lives, which they may feel unable to control in other respects.

Anorexia is very difficult to treat. Most anorexics are steadfast in their refusal to eat, while insisting that nothing is wrong with them. The main thrust of treatment, therefore, is to get the anorexic individual to gain weight. The patient may be admitted to a hospital, fed a controlled diet, and given rewards for small weight gains and increases in food intake. The treatment usually includes some type of psychotherapy and/or a self-help group.

What are the symptoms of bulimia nervosa?

Bulimia Nervosa Up to 50% of anorexics also develop **bulimia nervosa,** a chronic disorder characterized by repeated and uncontrolled (and often secretive) episodes of binge eating (American Psychiatric Association, 1993a). An episode of binge eating has two main features: (1) the consumption of much larger amounts of food than most people would eat during the same period of time, and (2) a feeling that one cannot stop eating or control the amount eaten. Binges—which generally involve foods that are rich in carbohydrates, such as cookies, cake, and candy—are frequently followed by purging. Purging consists of self-induced vomiting and/or the use of large quantities of laxatives and diuretics. Bulimics may also engage in excessive dieting and exercise. Athletes are especially susceptible to this disorder. But many bulimics are of average size and purge after an eating binge simply to maintain their weight.

Bulimia nervosa can cause a number of physical problems. The stomach acid in vomit eats away at the teeth and may cause them to rot, and the delicate balance of body chemistry is destroyed by excessive use of laxatives and diuretics. The bulimic may have a chronic sore throat as well as a variety of other symptoms, including dehydration, swelling of the salivary glands, kidney damage, and hair loss. The disorder also has a strong emotional component; the bulimic person is aware that the eating pattern is abnormal and feels unable to control it. Depression, guilt, and

anorexia nervosa: An eating disorder characterized by an overwhelming, irrational fear of being fat, compulsive dieting to the point of self-starvation, and excessive weight loss.

bulimia nervosa: An eating disorder characterized by repeated and uncontrolled episodes of binge eating, usually followed by purging, that is, self-induced vomiting and/or the use of large quantities of laxatives and diuretics.

Athletes have been found to be susceptible to bulimia, and this young woman's excessive thinness suggests that she might have an eating disorder.

shame accompany both bingeing and purging. "Bulimia nervosa is most likely to develop in dieters who are at risk of obesity and psychiatric disorder in general" (Fairburn et al., 1997). Some evidence suggests that decreased function of the neurotransmitter serotonin appears to contribute to this disorder (Jimerson et al., 1997).

Bulimia nervosa tends to appear in the late teens and affects about 1 in 25 women (Kendler et al., 1991). An even larger number of young women regularly binge and purge, but not frequently enough to warrant the diagnosis of bulimia nervosa (Drewnowski et al., 1994). About 10–15% of all bulimics are males, and homosexuality or bisexuality seems to increase the risk for bulimia in males (Carlat et al., 1997). In addition, researchers are finding more evidence of a cultural component to bulimia. Westernized attitudes in Turkey, for example, are clashing with the country's traditional values and, according to researchers, creating an increase in cases of bulimia (Elal et al., 2000). Apparently, some Turkish citizens succumb to Western media pressure to have an ultrathin body.

Bulimia, like anorexia, is difficult to treat. Sometimes treatment is complicated by the fact that a person with an eating disorder is likely to have a personality disorder as well (Rosenvinge et al., 2000). Some behavior modification programs have helped extinguish bulimic behavior (Traverso et al., 2000), and cognitive-behavioral therapy has been used successfully to help bulimics modify their eating habits and their abnormal attitudes about body shape and weight (Halmi, 1996; Johnson et al., 1996). Certain antidepressant drugs have been found to reduce the frequency of binge eating and purging and to result in significant attitudinal change (Agras et al., 1994; "Eating disorders," 1997).

Remember It!

1. Body cells lose water and become dehydrated when a person
   a. perspires heavily.
   b. consumes too much salt.
   c. has diarrhea or vomiting.
   d. drinks too much alcohol.
2. The lateral hypothalamus (LH) acts as a (feeding, satiety) center; the ventromedial hypothalamus (VMH) acts as a (feeding, satiety) center.
3. All of the following are hunger signals *except*
   a. activity in the lateral hypothalamus.
   b. low levels of glucose in the blood.
   c. the hormone CCK.
   d. a high insulin level.
4. Foods that are sweet and high in fat tend to stimulate the appetite. (true/false)
5. Which factor is *most* responsible for how fast your body burns calories to produce energy?
   a. calories consumed
   b. fat cells
   c. eating habits
   d. metabolic rate
6. According to set-point theory, the body works to (increase, decrease, maintain) body weight.
7. Fat cells never decrease in number. (true/false)
8. Adopted children are more likely to be very thin or obese if their (biological, adoptive) parents are very thin or obese.
9. Increased exercise during dieting is important to counteract the body's tendency to
   a. increase the fat in the fat cells.
   b. increase the number of fat cells.
   c. lower its metabolic rate.
   d. raise its metabolic rate.
10. Compulsive dieting to the point of self-starvation is the defining symptom of ______________; binge eating followed by purging is the main symptom of ______________.

Answers: 1. b 2. feeding, satiety 3. c 4. true 5. d 6. maintain 7. true 8. biological 9. c 10. anorexia nervosa; bulimia nervosa

SOCIAL MOTIVES

What is Murray's contribution to the study of motivation?

Do you have a strong need to be with other people (affiliation) or a need for power or achievement? These needs are three examples of **social motives,** which we learn or acquire through social and cultural experiences.

Henry Murray (1938) identified and defined a list of social motives, or needs, such as the need for achievement, recognition, affiliation, dominance, or order. Murray believed that people have social motives in differing degrees. To investigate the strength of various needs, Murray developed the **Thematic Apperception Test (TAT),** which consists of a series of pictures of ambiguous situations. The person taking the test is asked to write a story about each picture—to describe what is going on in the picture, what the person or persons pictured are thinking about, what they may be feeling, and what is likely to be the outcome of the situation. The stories are presumed to reveal the test taker's needs and the strength of those needs. (The TAT has also been used as a more general personality test, as described in Chapter 14.)

The Need for Achievement: The Drive to Excel

What is the need for achievement?

Murray (1938) defined the **need for achievement** (abbreviated *n* Ach) as the motive "to accomplish something difficult. . . . To overcome obstacles and attain a high standard. To excel one's self. To rival and surpass others. To increase self-regard by the successful exercise of talent" (p. 164). The need for achievement, rather than being satisfied with accomplishment, seems to grow as it is fed, not to diminish.

The need for achievement has been researched more vigorously than any other of Murray's needs, and researchers David McClelland and John Atkinson have conducted many of these studies (McClelland et al., 1953; McClelland, 1958, 1961, 1985). (Unfortunately, their participants were almost exclusively male.) To assess achievement motivation, McClelland and Atkinson had participants view four to six ambiguous pictures from the Thematic Apperception Test and then write stories about them. The content of the participants' stories was analyzed for references to achievement. Participants who consistently included achievement themes were scored as being high in achievement motivation. On the basis of a meta-analysis of 105 research studies, Spangler (1992) found support for the TAT as a valid measure of achievement motivation.

Complete the *Try It!* which describes a game that is said to reveal high or low achievement motivation.

Try It!

Imagine yourself involved in a ring-toss game. You have three rings to toss at any of the six pegs pictured here. You will be paid a few pennies each time you are able to ring a peg.

Which peg would you try to ring with your three tosses—peg 1 or 2 nearest you, peg 3 or 4 at a moderate distance, or peg 5 or 6 at the far end of the row?

social motives: Motives acquired through experience and interaction with others.

Thematic Apperception Test (TAT): A projective test consisting of drawings of ambiguous situations, which the test taker describes; thought to reveal inner feelings, conflicts, and motives.

need for achievement (*n* Ach): The need to accomplish something difficult and to perform at a high standard of excellence.

Illusionist David Blaine entombed himself in a block of ice for 62 hours and was once buried alive in a Plexiglas coffin for 7 days. His accomplishment of such difficult tasks seems to indicate a high need for achievement. However, Blaine's pursuit of high-risk goals makes him unlike most people with high n *Ach, who prefer moderate risks.*

What are some characteristics shared by people who are high in achievement motivation?

Characteristics of Achievers: Successful People Possess Them High achievers differ from low achievers in several ways. People with a high *n* Ach tend to set goals of moderate difficulty. They pursue goals that are challenging, yet attainable through hard work, ability, determination, and persistence. Goals that are too easy, those anyone can reach, offer no challenge and hold no interest, because success would not be rewarding (McClelland, 1985). Impossibly high goals and high risks are also not pursued, because they offer little chance of success and are considered a waste of time. People high in *n* Ach enjoy taking moderate risks in situations that depend on their ability, but they are not gamblers. To become wealthy, businesspeople high in achievement motivation often take moderate risks, which are more likely to pay off, rather than very high risks offering little or no chance of success.

People with low *n* Ach, the researchers claim, are not willing to take chances when it comes to testing their own skills and abilities. They are motivated more by their fear of failure than by their hope and expectation of success. This is why they set either ridiculously low goals, which anyone can attain, or else impossibly high goals (Geen, 1984). After all, who can fault a person for failing to reach a goal that is impossible for almost anyone?

In view of this description, which peg in the ring-toss game in the *Try It!* would people low in achievement motivation try for? If you guessed peg 1 or 2, or peg 5 or 6, you are right. People low in achievement motivation are likely to stand right over peg 1 so they can't possibly fail. Or they may toss the rings at peg 6, hoping that they might be lucky. If they failed, no one could blame them for not attaining a nearly impossible goal. A chance to win a few cents is certainly no incentive for people with a high need for achievement, so they tend to toss their rings at peg 3 or 4, an intermediate distance that offers some challenge. Which pegs did you choose?

People with high *n* Ach see their success as a result of their own talents, abilities, persistence, and hard work (Kukla, 1972). They typically do not credit luck or the influence of other people for their successes, or blame luck or others for their failures. When people with low *n* Ach fail, they usually give up quickly. They believe that luck or fate, rather than effort and ability, is responsible for accomplishment (Weiner, 1974).

In a young person, the need for achievement may be expressed as a need to excel in school. Neumann and others (1988) found that high achievement motivation is related to college students' accomplishments and grades. And those who were underachievers in high school showed less persistence later in completing college, keeping a job, and sustaining a successful marriage (McCall, 1994).

In adulthood those high in *n* Ach are often drawn to business, sometimes starting their own, and to other occupations and professions in which their own efforts can result in high achievement. According to McClelland, it is primarily the achievement motive rather than the profit motive that drives entrepreneurs. They are interested in profits and personal income mainly because those serve as measures of their competence. Money becomes a symbol of success. This is probably true of Bill Gates, someone who is very high in *n* Ach.

But what about those who want to be achievers, who dream of being rich and famous, yet who are not willing to put forth the effort to achieve their dreams? The person with high *n* Ach does not fit this picture. People high in achievement motivation may indeed be dreamers, but they are doers as well.

Developing Achievement Motivation: Can You Learn It? If achievement motivation, like the other social motives, is primarily learned, how is it learned? Some experts believe that child-rearing practices and values in the home are important factors in developing achievement motivation (McClelland & Pilon, 1983). Parents can foster *n* Ach if they give their children responsibilities, teach them to think and act independently from the time they are very young, stress excellence, persistence, and independence, and praise them sincerely for their accomplishments (Ginsberg & Bronstein, 1993; Gottfried et al., 1994). Birth order appears to be related to achievement motivation, with first-born and only children showing higher *n* Ach than younger siblings (Falbo & Polit, 1986). Younger siblings, however, tend to be more sociable and likable than first-born or only children, and this has its rewards, too.

Do some people lack achievement motivation because they fear success?

Fear of Success

Have you ever purposely done less than your best to avoid being called a "brain"? Are there some people who are actually afraid of success, or are there other reasons why people prefer to conceal their abilities and lower their performance?

Researcher Matina Horner (1969) conducted an early study on fear of success. She found that women seem to have a "motive to avoid success," which she defined as "the fear that success in competitive achievement situations will lead to negative consequences such as unpopularity and the loss of femininity" (p. 38). In follow-up studies, however, researchers found that men reveal as much fear of success as women (Kearney, 1984; Tresemer, 1977).

One study by Balkin (1987) reports that fear of success in female college students was related to whether their close friends attended college. Of those whose friends attended college, only 10% showed fear of success, compared with 42% of those with few or no close friends attending college. Such results led Balkin to speculate that fear of success might involve the "fear of disapproval and rejection from significant others, namely, family and friends" (p. 40). Balkin suggests that the same explanation could apply to males.

Work Motivation

What is work motivation, and what are two effective techniques for increasing it?

Psychologists who apply their knowledge in the workplace are known as **industrial/organizational (I/O) psychologists.** Although I/O psychologists are involved in many aspects of the workplace—organizational design, decision making, personnel selection, training and evaluation, work-related stress—they are vitally interested in work motivation and job performance.

Work motivation can be thought of as "the conditions and processes that account for the arousal, direction, magnitude, and maintenance of effort in a person's job" (Katzell & Thompson, 1990, p. 144). Two of the most effective ways to increase employee motivation and improve performance are reinforcement and goal setting.

To use reinforcement, I/O psychologists help design behavior modification techniques to increase performance and productivity. Reinforcers or incentives include bonuses, recognition awards, praise, time off, posting of individual performance, better offices, more impressive titles, and/or promotions. Companies may discourage ineffective behaviors through such measures as docking the pay of employees who miss work.

A second technique for increasing performance is goal setting. Establishing specific, difficult goals leads to higher levels of performance than simply telling people to do their best in the absence of assigned goals (Locke & Latham, 1990). An organization can enhance employees' commitment to goals (1) by having them participate in the goal setting; (2) by making goals specific, attractive, difficult, and attainable; (3) by providing feedback on performance; and (4) by rewarding the employees for attaining the goals (Katzell & Thompson, 1990).

industrial/organizational (I/O) psychologists: Psychologists who focus on the relationship between the workplace or organization and the worker.

work motivation: The conditions and processes responsible for the arousal, direction, magnitude, and maintenance of effort one puts forth in one's job.

Several theories have been applied to research on work motivation. According to one of these, expectancy theory, motivation to engage in a given activity is determined by (1) *expectancy*—a person's belief that more effort will result in improved performance; (2) *instrumentality*—the person's belief that doing a job well will be noticed and rewarded; and (3) *valence*—the degree to which a person values the rewards that are offered. Several studies have supported the assumptions of expectancy theory (Tubbs et al., 1993; van Eerde & Thierry, 1996). Employees work harder when they believe that more effort will improve their performance, when they think that a good performance will be acknowledged and rewarded, and when they value the rewards that are offered.

Job Satisfaction and Performance The aspects of a job workers consider most rewarding are interesting work, good pay, sufficient resources and authority, and friendly and cooperative co-workers. Supervisors' beliefs can affect job satisfaction. Supervisors led to believe that certain employees were intrinsically motivated gave those employees more autonomy and were more supportive of them (Pelletier & Vallerand, 1996). In addition, some studies show that the impact of stress on the job, which affects job satisfaction and performance, is buffered by social support. Workers who have social support still experience stress, but without the significant increases in heart rate or blood pressure seen in workers who lack such support (Steptoe, 2000).

I/O psychologists redesign jobs to make them more interesting, satisfying, and attractive—an approach termed *job enrichment*. For example, assembly-line workers might become involved in the production of a whole item instead of repeating the same single task day after day. And workers might be given a greater voice in how their work will be accomplished. Job enrichment improves worker attitudes but not necessarily job performance (Locke et al., 1981; Stone, 1986). On-the-job productivity tends to be higher when workers are given incentives, when they think their work is important, and when the effort level required is challenging but not excessive (Shepperd, 1993).

Remember It!

1. Social motives are mostly unlearned. (true/false)
2. According to Atkinson, which of the following is *not* a major factor in determining whether a person high in *n* Ach approaches a goal?
   a. the strength of the need for achievement
   b. the expectation of success
   c. how much pride would result from achieving the goal as opposed to how upsetting failure would be
   d. the financial reward attached to the goal
3. Which statement is *not* true of people high in *n* Ach?
   a. They set very high goals, which will be extremely difficult to attain.
   b. They set goals of moderate difficulty.
   c. They attribute their success to their talents, abilities, and hard work.
   d. They are likely to choose careers as entrepreneurs.
4. According to the text, two of the most effective ways I/O psychologists improve employee motivation and performance are
   a. reinforcement and goal setting.
   b. counseling and guidance.
   c. evaluation and feedback.
   d. training and evaluation.

Answers: 1. false 2. d 3. a 4. a

THE WHAT AND WHY OF EMOTIONS

Motivation and Emotion: What Is the Connection?

Motivation does not occur in a vacuum. Much of our motivation to act is fueled by emotional states. In fact, the root of the word **emotion** means "to move," indicating the close relationship between motivation and emotion. The emotion of disgust, for example, may motivate us to avoid contamination, disease, and illness. Observing the emotion of sadness in another often elicits feelings of empathy and may motivate us to acts of altruism (helping behavior). Interest motivates exploration, play, and learning, and anger motivates aggressive actions of defense or protection. Fear motivates us either to flee and escape danger or to take actions that will provide security and safety (Izard, 1992). And among the positive emotions, happiness motivates us to continue performing pleasant activities. The daily events we experience are closely related to our emotions, and our emotional experiences play a key role in linking everyday life to cognitive well-being (Robinson, 2000). Emotions also enable us to communicate feelings and intentions more effectively and thus make it more likely that others will respond. But what, precisely, are emotions?

The Components of Emotions: The Physical, the Cognitive, and the Behavioral

What are the three components of emotions?

Nothing more than feelings—is that what emotions are? We may say that we feel lonely or sad, happy or content, embarrassed or afraid. We normally describe emotions in terms of feeling states, but there is, in fact, a key distinction between emotions and feelings. All of the emotions we experience—fear, anger, surprise, disgust, sadness, and happiness—are expressed physically and in ways that other people can observe. Feelings, on the other hand, are our conscious perceptions of all these bodily changes as well as the mood states we feel internally (Damasio, 1999). Typically, psychologists have studied emotions in terms of arousal and have included three components—the physical, the cognitive, and the behavioral (Wilken et al., 2000).

The physical component is the physiological arousal (the internal body state) that accompanies the emotion. Without the physiological arousal, the emotion would not be felt in all its intensity. The surge of powerful feeling we know as emotion is due largely to the physiological arousal we experience. In a recent study, participants who were better at detecting changes in their own arousal level (sensing heartbeat variations) were found to experience emotions (anger, fear, amusement) with greater intensity than participants who were not as good at detecting such arousal changes (Wiens et al., 2000).

The cognitive component—the way we perceive or interpret a stimulus or situation—determines the specific emotion we feel. If you are home alone and the wind is banging a tree limb on your roof, you may become fearful if you perceive the knocking and the banging as a burglar trying to break into your house. An emotional response to an imaginary threat is every bit as powerful as a response to a real threat. Perceptions make it so. Have you ever worked yourself into a frenzy before a first date, a job interview, or an oral presentation for one of your classes? If so, you have experienced the powerful influence your own thinking has on your emotional state.

The behavioral component of emotions is the outward expression of the emotions. Facial expressions, gestures, body posture, and tone of voice stem from and convey the emotions felt within. Some of the facial expressions that accompany emotions are innate and are the same across cultures. But some emotional expressions are more influenced by culture and its rules for displaying emotion.

emotion: A feeling state involving physiological arousal, a cognitive appraisal of the situation arousing the state, and an outward expression of the state.

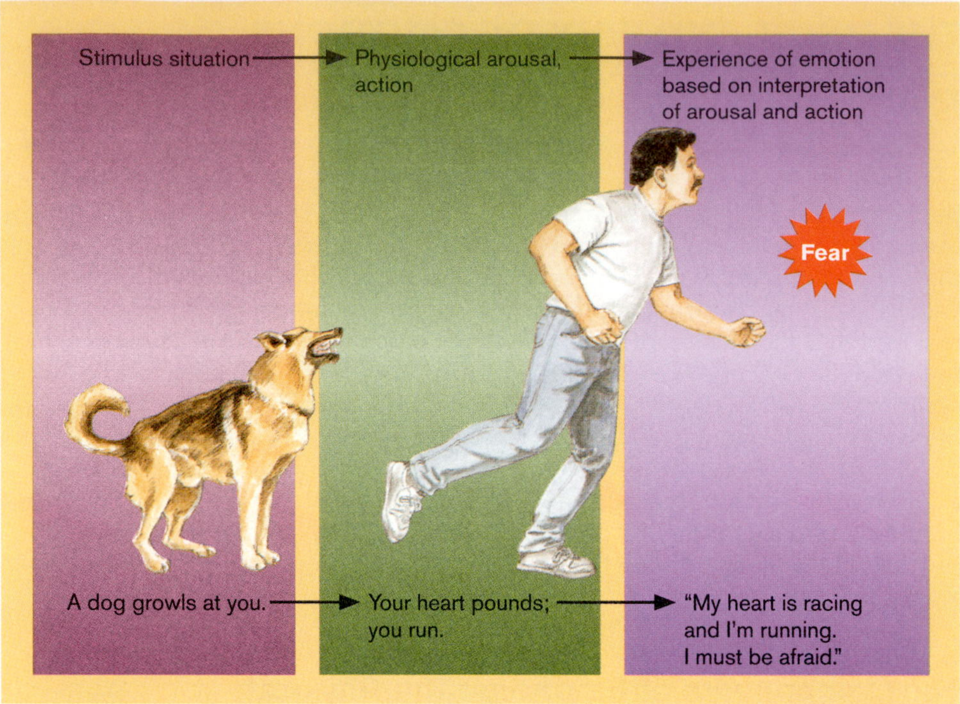

Figure 11.3

The James–Lange Theory of Emotion

The James–Lange theory of emotion is the exact opposite of what subjective experience tells us. If a dog growls at you, the James–Lange interpretation is that the dog growls, your heart begins to pound, and only after perceiving that your heart is pounding do you conclude that you must be afraid.

Theories of Emotion: Which Comes First, the Thought or the Feeling?

There is no doubt that we react to certain experiences with emotion. For example, if you think you are making a fool of yourself in front of your friends, the emotion you feel is embarrassment, which triggers a physiological response that may cause you to blush. This explanation of your embarrassed reaction seems logical—it seems to fit with everyday experience. But is this sequence of events the course that an emotional experience really follows? Not according to psychologist William James.

According to the James–Lange theory, what sequence of events occurs when an individual experiences an emotion?

James–Lange theory of emotion: The theory that emotional feelings result when an individual becomes aware of a physiological response to an emotion-provoking stimulus (for example, feeling fear because of trembling).

The James–Lange Theory American psychologist William James (1884) argued that the sequence of events in an emotional experience is exactly the reverse of what subjective experience tells us. James claimed that first an event causes physiological arousal and a physical response. Only then does the individual perceive or interpret the physical response as an emotion. In other words, saying something stupid causes you to blush, and you interpret your physical response, blushing, as an emotion, embarrassment. James (1890) went on to suggest that "we feel sorry *because* we cry, angry *because* we strike, afraid *because* we tremble" (p. 1066).

At about the same time that James proposed his theory, a Danish physiologist and psychologist, Carl Lange, independently formulated nearly the same theory. The **James–Lange theory** of emotion (Lange & James, 1922) suggests that different patterns of arousal in the autonomic nervous system produce the different emotions people feel, and that the physiological arousal appears before the emotion is perceived. See Figure 11.3.

But if the physical arousal itself causes what we know as emotion, there would have to be distinctly different bodily changes associated with each emotion. Otherwise, you wouldn't know whether you were sad, embarrassed, frightened, or happy.

The Cannon–Bard Theory Another early theory of emotion that challenged the James–Lange theory was proposed by Walter Cannon (1927), who did pioneering work on the fight-or-flight response and the concept of homeostasis. Cannon claimed that the bodily changes caused by the various emotions are not sufficiently distinct to allow people to distinguish one emotion from another.

What is the Cannon–Bard theory of emotion?

Cannon's original theory was later expanded by physiologist Philip Bard (1934). The **Cannon–Bard theory** suggests that the following chain of events occurs when we feel an emotion: Emotion-provoking stimuli are received by the senses and are then relayed simultaneously to the cerebral cortex, which provides the conscious mental experience of the emotion, and to the sympathetic nervous system, which produces the physiological state of arousal. In other words, your feeling of emotion (fear, for example) occurs at about the same time that you experience physiological arousal (a pounding heart). One does not cause the other.

The Schachter–Singer Theory Stanley Schachter believed that the early theories of emotion left out a critical component—the subjective cognitive interpretation of why a state of arousal has occurred. Schachter and Singer (1962) proposed a two-factor theory. According to the **Schachter–Singer theory,** two things must happen in order for a person to feel an emotion: (1) The person must first experience physiological arousal. (2) Then there must be a cognitive interpretation or explanation of the physiological arousal so that the person can label it as a specific emotion. Thus, Schachter concluded, a true emotion can occur only if a person is physically aroused *and* can find some reason for it. When people are in a state of physiological arousal but do not know why they are aroused, they tend to label the state as an emotion that is appropriate to their situation at the time.

According to the Schachter–Singer theory, what two factors must occur in order for a person to experience an emotion?

Some attempts to replicate the findings of Schachter and Singer have been unsuccessful (Marshall & Zimbardo, 1979). Also, the notion that arousal is general rather than specific has been questioned by later researchers who have identified some distinctive patterns of arousal for some of the basic emotions (Ekman et al., 1983; Levenson, 1992; Scherer & Wallbott, 1994).

The Lazarus Theory The theory of emotion that most heavily emphasizes the cognitive aspect has been proposed by Richard Lazarus (1991a, 1991b, 1995). According to the **Lazarus theory,** a cognitive appraisal is the first step in an emotional response, and all other aspects of an emotion, including physiological arousal, depend on the cognitive appraisal. This theory is most compatible with the subjective experience of an emotion's sequence of events—the sequence that William James reversed long ago. Faced with a stimulus—an event—a person first appraises it. This cognitive appraisal determines whether the person will have an emotional response and, if so, what type of response. The physiological arousal and all other aspects of the emotion flow from the appraisal. In short, Lazarus contends that emotions are provoked when cognitive appraisals of events or circumstances are positive or negative—but not neutral.

According to Lazarus, what sequence of events occurs when an individual feels an emotion?

Critics of the Lazarus theory point out that some emotional reactions are instantaneous—occurring too rapidly to pass through a cognitive appraisal (Zajonc, 1980, 1984). Lazarus (1984, 1991) responds that some mental processing occurs without conscious awareness. And there must be some form of cognitive realization, however brief, or else a person would not know what he or she is responding to or what emotion to feel—fear, happiness, embarrassment, and so on.

Review & Reflect 11.2 (on p. 408) summarizes the four major theories of emotion: James–Lange, Cannon–Bard, Schachter–Singer, and Lazarus.

Cannon–Bard theory of emotion: The theory that an emotion-provoking stimulus is transmitted simultaneously to the cortex, providing the feeling of an emotion, and to the sympathetic nervous system, causing the physiological arousal.

Schachter–Singer theory of emotion: A two-stage theory stating that for an emotion to occur, there must be (1) physiological arousal and (2) an explanation for the arousal.

Lazarus theory of emotion: The theory that an emotion-provoking stimulus triggers a cognitive appraisal, which is followed by the emotion and the physiological arousal.

Review & Reflect 11.2 Theories of Emotion

Theory	View	Example
James–Lange theory	An event causes physiological arousal. You experience an emotion only *after* you interpret the physical response.	You are walking home late at night and hear footsteps behind you. Your heart pounds and you begin to tremble. You interpret these physical responses as *fear.*
Cannon–Bard theory	An event causes a physiological *and* an emotional response simultaneously. One does not cause the other.	You are walking home late at night and hear footsteps behind you. Your heart pounds, you begin to tremble, *and* you feel afraid.
Schachter–Singer theory	An event causes physiological arousal. You must then be able to identify a reason for the arousal in order to label the emotion.	You are walking home late at night and hear footsteps behind you. Your heart pounds and you begin to tremble. You know that walking alone at night can be dangerous, and so you feel afraid.
Lazarus theory	An event occurs, a cognitive appraisal is made, and then the emotion and physiological arousal follow.	You are walking home late at night and hear footsteps behind you. You think it could be a mugger. So you feel afraid, and your heart starts to pound and you begin to tremble.

Emotion and the Brain

What brain structure processes the emotion of fear?

More than any other emotion, fear has stimulated research by neuroscientists (LeDoux, 1996, 2000). And the brain structure most closely associated with fear is the amygdala. (See Figure 11.4.) Information comes to the amygdala directly from all five of the senses and is acted on there immediately, without initial involvement of the primary "thinking" area of the brain, the cortex. But, as with reflex actions, the cortex does become involved as soon as it "catches up" with the amygdala (LeDoux, 2000). Thus, our emotions can be stirred up even before the cortex knows what is going on.

When the emotion of fear first materializes, much of the brain's processing is nonconscious. We become conscious of it later, of course, but the amygdala is activated before we are aware that a threat is present (Damasio, 1994, 1999). Interestingly, the amygdala becomes more highly activated when a person looks at photos of angry- or fearful-looking faces than it does when the person views photos of happy faces (LeDoux, 2000).

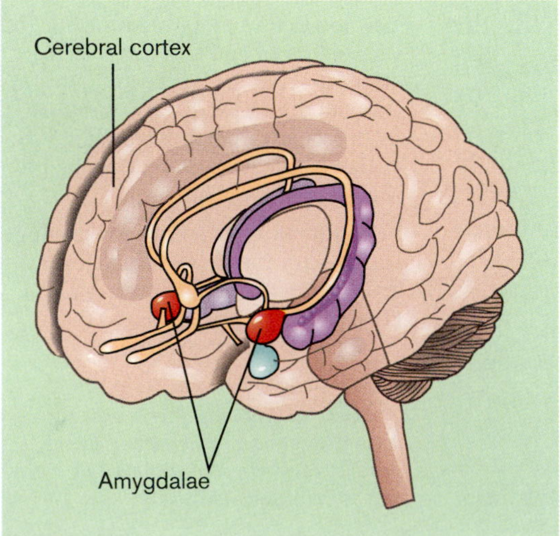

Figure 11.4
Emotion and the Amygdala
The amygdala plays an important role in emotion. It is activated by fear before any direct involvement of the cerebral cortex occurs.

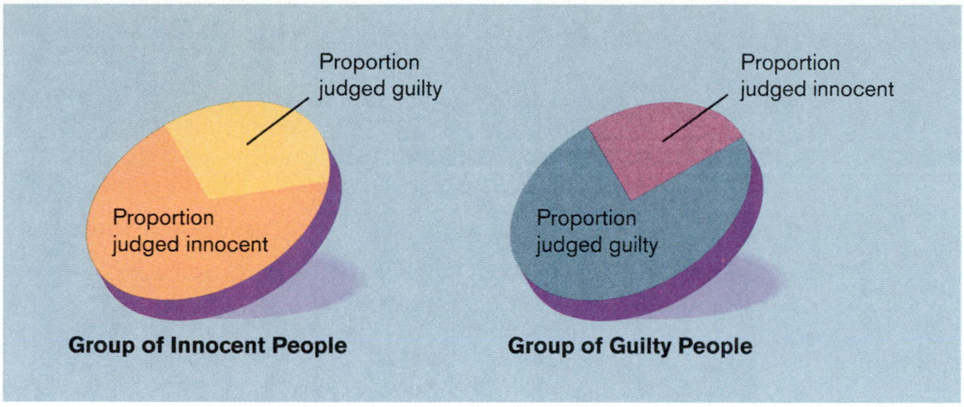

Figure 11.5

The Unreliability of Polygraph Tests

Polygraph tests are far from infallible. In one study, one out of three innocent people were judged guilty and one out of four guilty people were judged innocent. People who can lie easily often show little physical arousal and therefore may come across as telling the truth.

The Polygraph: Lie Detector or Emotion Detector?

What does a polygraph measure?

Do you suppose a distinctive pattern of arousal is associated with lying? The existence of such a connection was the basis for the invention of the polygraph, or lie detector. A **polygraph** is a device designed to detect changes in heart rate, blood pressure, respiration rate, and the skin conductance response that typically accompany the anxiety a person experiences when telling a lie. Could a polygraph indicate that you were telling the truth if you were lying? And could it indicate that you were lying if you were telling the truth? The answer is yes to both of these questions.

A polygraph is not really a lie detector. It can detect only physiological changes associated with emotional arousal. It cannot distinguish lying from fear, sexual arousal, anxiety, anger, or general emotional arousal. The assumption is that when people lie, they feel anxious, and their anxiety causes physiological changes in blood pressure, heart rate, breathing, and perspiration (Rosenfeld, 1995).

How accurate is the polygraph? Some experts say that the percentage of innocent people falsely accused of lying may be as high as one out of three, as illustrated in Figure 11.5 (Kleinmuntz & Szucko, 1984). What about guilty people? One out of four who lied on a polygraph test were judged to be telling the truth. Does this mean it's possible to beat the lie detector? Inveterate, or habitual, liars—those who lie easily without any emotional disturbance or physiological arousal—are more likely to be evaluated as telling the truth. It has been suggested that failing to pay close attention or being distracted during questioning also lowers physiological responses.

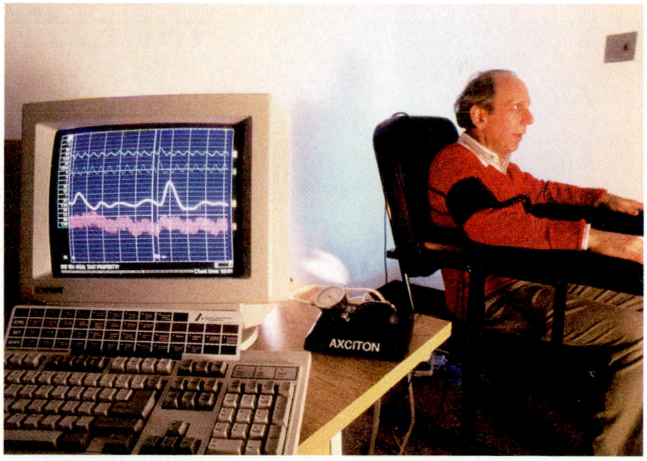

The polygraph can detect only the physiological changes associated with emotional arousal.

In one study, volunteer participants distracted themselves by counting backward by sevens throughout the examination, and they were able to lie without being detected more often than when they were not using such distraction (Waid et al., 1981). Lykken (1981) found that increasing arousal by tensing muscles and thinking about something exciting during neutral questions could also alter the results. Apparently even taking tranquilizers before the test can reduce the physiological response that usually accompanies lying.

The less-than-satisfactory reliability of lie detectors has led to increasing restrictions in their use. Evidence from a polygraph is not admissible in most of the states in the United States (Lykken, 1985).

polygraph: A device designed to detect changes in heart rate, blood pressure, respiration rate, and the skin conductance response that typically accompany the anxiety that occurs when a person lies.

Remember It!

1. According to the text, emotions have all of following *except* a ______________ component.
   a. physical c. sensory
   b. cognitive d. behavioral
2. Which theory of emotion holds that you feel a true emotion only when you become physically aroused and can identify some cause for the arousal?
   a. Schachter–Singer theory
   b. James–Lange theory
   c. Cannon–Bard theory
   d. Lazarus theory
3. Which theory of emotion suggests that you would feel fearful *because* you were trembling?
   a. Schachter–Singer theory c. Cannon–Bard theory
   b. James–Lange theory d. Lazarus theory
4. Which theory suggests that the feeling of emotion and the physiological response to an emotional situation occur at about the same time?
   a. Schachter–Singer theory c. Cannon–Bard theory
   b. James–Lange theory d. Lazarus theory
5. Which theory suggests that the physiological arousal and the emotion flow from a cognitive appraisal of an emotion-provoking event?
   a. Schachter–Singer theory c. Cannon–Bard theory
   b. James–Lange theory d. Lazarus theory
6. When fear strikes, the (amygdala, cortex) is activated before the (amygdala, cortex).
7. A polygraph measures
   a. lies. c. honesty. b. integrity. d. arousal.

Answers: 1. c 2. a 3. b 4. c 5. d 6. amygdala; cortex 7. d

THE EXPRESSION OF EMOTION

Expressing emotions comes as naturally to humans as breathing. No one has to be taught how to smile or frown, or how to express fear, sadness, surprise, or disgust. And the facial expressions of the basic emotions are similar in all cultures.

The Range of Emotion: How Wide Is It?

What are basic emotions?

How many emotions are there? The number of emotions people list depends on their culture, the language they speak, and other factors. Two leading researchers on emotion, Paul Ekman (1993) and Carroll Izard (1992), insist that there are a limited number of basic emotions. **Basic emotions** are unlearned and universal; that is, they are found in all cultures, are reflected in the same facial expressions, and emerge in children according to their own biological timetable of development. Fear, anger, disgust, surprise, joy or happiness, and sadness or distress are usually considered basic emotions. Izard (1992, 1993) suggests that there are distinct neural circuits that underlie each of the basic emotions, and Levenson and others (1990) point to specific autonomic nervous system activity associated with the basic emotions. Panksepp (1992) believes there is strong evidence for emotional systems in the brain that, at a minimum, underlie rage, fear, expectancy, and panic. Not all researchers, however, subscribe to the notion of basic emotions (Turner & Ortony, 1992).

basic emotions: Emotions that are found in all cultures, that are reflected in the same facial expressions across cultures, and that emerge in children according to their biological timetable; fear, anger, disgust, surprise, happiness, and distress are usually considered basic emotions.

In studying the range of emotion, Ekman (1993) has suggested considering emotions as families. Clearly there are gradients, or degrees, of intensity within a single emotion. A person could experience fear, for example, in various degrees, from being mildly apprehensive to being afraid, scared, or terrified. The anger family might range from annoyed to irritated, angry, livid, and finally enraged. Furthermore, if perceived as a family, anger should also include various forms of its expression, according to Ekman (1993). Resentment, for example, is a form of anger "in which there is a sense of grievance" (p. 386). Other forms are indignation and outrage, which seem to be justifiable anger focused on a wrongful or unjust action against self or others. Vengefulness is anger that retaliates, or gets revenge for an injustice or misdeed by another. And in its most intense form, anger may be expressed as blind rage, in which a person loses control and may commit brutal atrocities against the target of the rage.

It takes little imagination to picture the facial expression of annoyance being quite different from the facial expression of rage, but can you imagine 60 different facial expressions for the different types and intensities of anger? Ekman and Friesen identified 60 anger expressions, with subtle differences, but all sharing the basic properties of the face of anger (Ekman, 1993). Just as there are many words in the English language to describe the variations in the range of any emotion, Ekman and Friesen claim there are subtle distinctions in the facial expression of a single emotion that convey its intensity.

Research continues to show that people have stronger emotional reactions to negative stimuli than to positive ones (National Advisory Mental Health Council, 1995). In one study, participants who were highly responsive to their own emotions showed greater increases in blood pressure and heart rate when their emotions were negative than when they were positive. These individuals also reported less satisfaction with the social support in their lives and had higher levels of perceived daily stress, anxiety, and symptoms of depression (Carels et al., 2000). When we make decisions that turn out to be wrong or less than satisfactory, we often experience negative emotions such as regret and disappointment. Then the anticipation of regret and disappointment can, in turn, influence our later decision making (Zeelenberg et al., 2000). Moreover, the ability to shift from one emotion to a different one takes longer if the first emotion is a negative one (Compton, 2000). In social interactions, a person's feelings about another individual are typically influenced more by a single negative attribute than by a collection of positive qualities. And some research suggests that positive emotional experiences in a marriage must outnumber negative ones by about 5 to 1 for a satisfactory relationship to be sustained (Gottman, 1994).

From the vantage point of evolution, such findings are logical. Survival may depend on avoiding noxious stimuli and dangerous situations that provoke negative emotions. But with respect to one's mental health, it is important to guard against the power of negative emotions by balancing them with positive ones.

How do we learn to express emotions? Or do we learn? There is considerable evidence that the basic emotions (fear, anger, sadness, happiness, disgust, and surprise), or at least the facial expressions we make when we feel them, are biologically rather than culturally determined.

The Development of Facial Expressions in Infants: Smiles and Frowns Come Naturally

How does the development of facial expressions of different emotions in infants suggest a biological basis for emotional expression?

Like the motor skills of crawling and walking, facial expressions of emotions develop naturally, according to a biological timetable of maturation. Even newborns are capable of expressing certain emotions—specifically, distress, pleasure, and interest in the environment. By 3 months, babies can express happiness and sadness (Lewis, 1995), and laughter appears somewhere around 3½ to 4 months (Provine, 1996). Between the ages of 4 and 6 months, the emotions of anger and surprise appear, and by about 7 months, infants show fear. The self-conscious emotions do not emerge until later. Between 18 months and 3 years, children begin to show first empathy, envy, and embarrassment, followed by shame, guilt, and pride (Lewis, 1995).

Another strong indication that the facial expressions of emotion are biologically determined, rather than learned, results from research on children who were blind and deaf since birth. Their smiles and frowns, laughter and crying, and facial expressions of anger, surprise, and pouting were the same as those of children who could hear and see (Eibl-Eibesfeldt, 1973).

Although recent studies have contributed much to scientists' understanding of facial expressions, the biological connection between emotions and facial expressions was proposed many years ago.

Facial Expressions for the Basic Emotions: A Universal Language

The relationship between emotions and facial expressions was first studied by Charles Darwin (1872/1965). He believed that the facial expression of emotion was an aid to survival, because it enabled people to communicate their internal states and react to emergencies before they developed language. Darwin maintained that most emotions and the facial expressions that convey them are genetically inherited and characteristic of the entire human species. To test his belief, he asked missionaries and people of different cultures around the world to record the facial expressions that accompany the basic emotions. Based on those data, he concluded that facial expressions were similar across cultures. Modern researchers agree that Darwin was right.

Convincing evidence that the facial expressions of emotion are universal was provided by Ekman and Friesen (1971). They showed photographs portraying facial expressions of the primary emotions—sadness, surprise, happiness, anger, fear, and disgust—to members of the Fore tribe in a remote area in New Guinea. The Fore people were able to identify the emotional expressions of happiness, sadness, anger, and disgust, although they had difficulty distinguishing fear and surprise.

In later research Ekman and others (Ekman, 1982; Ekman & Friesen, 1975; Ekman et al., 1987) used participants from the United States, Argentina, Japan, Brazil, and Chile, who viewed photographs showing the same basic emotions. Could people from widely diverse cultures name the emotions conveyed by the facial expressions of Americans? Yes, to an amazing degree. Ekman (1992) believes that such research results provide strong support for a biological explanation of facial expression. More recently, Russell (1994) reviewed 11 cross-cultural studies spanning a period of 12 years (1980–1992), and all of the studies concluded that the human face reveals emotions that are universally recognized.

Even though we acknowledge and appreciate cultural differences and human diversity, people are, after all, one species. And facial expressions of basic emotion are much the same around the world. Try Ekman's test and see if you can identify the faces of emotion in the *Try It!*

Try It!

Look carefully at the six photographs. Which basic emotion is portrayed in each? Match the number of the photograph with the basic emotion it conveys.

a. happiness b. sadness c. fear d. anger e. surprise f. disgust

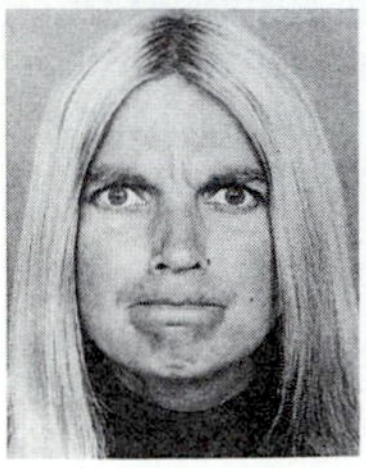

1. ____________

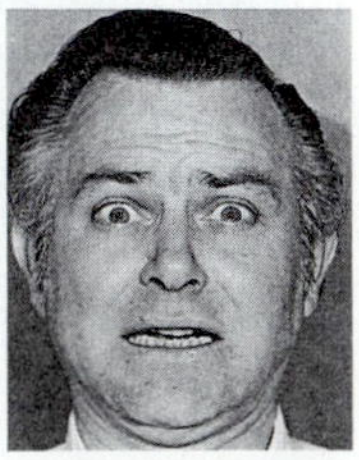

2. ____________

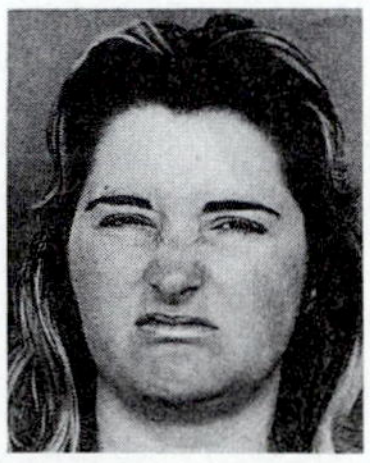

3. ____________

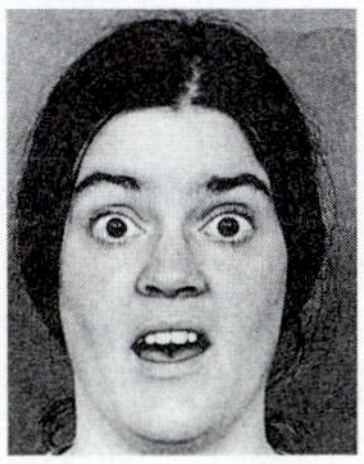

4. ____________

5. ____________

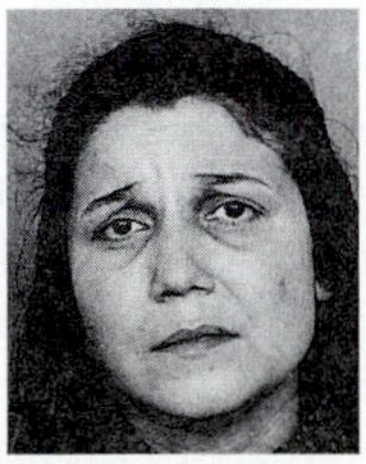

6. ____________

Answers: 1. d 2. c 3. f 4. e 5. a 6. b

Other research finds evidence for universality, as Darwin and Ekman and others did, but evidence for cultural variations as well. Scherer and Wallbott (1994) found very extensive overlap in the patterns of emotional experiences reported across cultures in 37 different countries on 5 continents. They also found important cultural differences in the ways emotions are elicited and regulated and in how they are shared socially.

Even though communicating emotional states via facial expressions is universal, don't assume that such communication is simple or primitive. Research suggests that facial expressions alone can convey meaning at a level comparable to verbal communication (Wierzbicka, 2000). Still animals and humans are able to quickly and accurately perceive and interpret many facial expressions. Shouldn't artificial intelligence systems be able to do so, too? Today, researchers are using psychologists' and cognitive scientists' findings to develop systems capable of interpreting the sometimes subtle emotional states conveyed by various facial expressions (Lisetti & Schiano, 2000).

display rules: Cultural rules that dictate how emotions should be expressed, and when and where their expression is appropriate.

Cultural Rules for Displaying Emotion

While the facial expressions of the basic emotions are much the same in cultures around the world, each culture can have very different **display rules**—cultural rules that dictate how emotions should generally be expressed and where and when their expression is appropriate (Ekman, 1993; Ekman & Friesen, 1975; Scherer & Wallbott, 1994). One significant cultural difference concerns the tendency to have an independent, disengaged Western emotional style (as in the United States) as opposed to an interdependent, socially engaged Eastern emotional style (as in Japan) (Kitayama et al., 2000).

Often a society's display rules require people to give evidence of certain emotions that they may not actually feel or to disguise their true feelings. For example, we are expected to look sad at funerals, to hide disappointment when we lose, and to refrain from making facial expressions of disgust if the food we are served tastes bad. In one study, Cole (1986) found that 3-year-old girls, when given an unattractive gift, smiled nevertheless. They had already learned a display rule and signaled an emotion they very likely did not feel. Davis (1995) found that among first to third graders, girls were better able to hide disappointment than boys were.

Different cultures, neighborhoods, and even families may have very different display rules. Display rules in Japanese culture dictate that negative emotions must be disguised when other people are present (Ekman, 1972; Triandis, 1994). In many societies in the West, women are expected to smile often, whether they feel happy or not. And in East Africa, young males from traditional Masai society are expected to appear stern and stony-faced and to "produce long, unbroken stares" (Keating, 1994). So it appears that much emotion that is displayed is not authentic, not truly felt, but merely reflects compliance with display rules.

Not only can emotions be displayed but not felt, they can also be felt but not displayed (Russell, 1995). Consider Olympic medalists waiting to receive their gold, silver, or bronze. Though obviously flooded with happiness, the athletes display few smiles until their medals have been presented and they are interacting with the authorities and responding to the crowd (Fernández-Dols & Ruiz-Belda, 1995).

Most of us learn display rules very early and abide by them most of the time. Yet you may not be fully aware that the rules you have learned dictate where, when, how, and even how long certain emotions should be expressed. You will learn more about reading emotions and detecting the probable motives of others when we explore nonverbal behavior—the language of facial expressions, gestures, and body positions—in Chapter 17.

There are many situations in which people must disguise their emotions to comply with the display rules of their culture, which dictate when and how feelings should be expressed. For example, these soccer players—both winners and losers—are expected to be good sports, even if it means hiding their true feelings.

Emotion as a Form of Communication: Cultural, Evolutionary, and Technological Views

Why is emotion considered a form of communication?

The ways in which we feel and express emotions actually represent a form of communication. Emotions enable us to communicate our desires, intentions, and needs more effectively than just words alone and thus make it more likely that others will respond. And researchers maintain that not only are people biologically wired to convey certain emotional signals but there is evidence that they are biologically predisposed to read and interpret them as well (Dimberg, 1990; Oatley & Jenkins, 1992).

Communicating emotions can motivate action by others. If you communicate sadness or distress, then people close to you are likely to be sympathetic and try to help. Emotional expressions allow infants to communicate their feelings and needs before they are able to speak. In an early study Katherine Bridges (1932) observed emotional expression in Canadian infants over a period of months. She reported that the first emotional expression to appear is that of distress. In survival terms, the expression of distress enables helpless newborns to get the attention of their caretakers so that their needs can be met.

Do you feel happier when you are around others who are happy? You may already know that emotions are contagious. Infants will usually begin to cry when they hear another infant cry. Your emotional expressions can infect others with the same emotion. Mothers seem to know this intuitively when they display happy expressions in an effort to infect their babies with happy moods (Keating, 1994). Researchers have found that mothers in many cultures—Trobriand Island, Yanomamo, Greek, German, Japanese, and American—attempt to regulate the moods of their babies through facial communication of emotions (Kanaya et al., 1989; Keller et al., 1988; Termine & Izard, 1988).

From an evolutionary perspective, the ability to interpret various states instantly and reliably and then emulate them has survival value. In many species, if a single member of the group or herd senses a predator and communicates the emotion of fear, the other members also become afraid, preparing them to flee for their lives. For humans, too, quick and accurate recognition of facial expressions communicating anger or threat clearly has adaptive value. And new research indicates that such recognition is indeed fast and efficient (Fox et al., 2000b).

Humans perceive the emotions of others early in the first year of life and use this information to guide behavior. Infants pay close attention to the facial expressions of others, especially their mothers. And when they are confronted with an ambiguous situation, they use the mother's emotion as a guide to whether they should approach or avoid the situation. This phenomenon is known as *social referencing* (Klinnert et al., 1983).

You had to identify the emotions associated with the facial expressions in the photographs in the *Try It!* without any help from context. But in real life you use information provided by the situation or context in addition to the facial expression itself to help determine the emotion being conveyed (Carroll & Russell, 1996). But what if false emotions are being conveyed and you are being deceived?

Evolutionary psychologists, who (as Chapter 1 noted) study how humans adapt their behavior for the purpose of passing on their genes, have presented evidence indicating that both males and females use emotional deception in the context of mating behavior. In a study involving some 200 male and female university students, women admitted that they had flirted with, smiled at, and played up to men, leading them on when they had no romantic interest in the men or any intention of having sex with them. Men admitted intentionally deceiving women about the depth of their emotional commitment. Asked whether they had ever exaggerated the depth of their feelings for a partner to get sex, more than 70% of the male students said yes, compared with 39% of the female students. When asked whether a man had ever exaggerated his feelings to get sex, a staggering 97% of the female subjects said yes (Buss, 1994, 1999).

Evolutionary psychologists would say that this study shows how males have adapted their behavior so that they can mate with as many females as possible and pass on their genes to the offspring. Females, on the other hand, seek to gain emotional commitment from males *before* procreation, so the resulting children will be provided for. Devastating negative emotions can therefore result if a woman consents to having sex with a man and later learns that he was lying about his emotional commitment. False emotions are almost always detected, so emotional honesty is the best policy in any relationship.

Remember It!

1. Which of the following is *not* true of the basic emotions?
   a. They are reflected in distinctive facial expressions.
   b. They are found in all cultures.
   c. They number in the hundreds.
   d. They are unlearned.
2. Which of the following is *not* one of the emotions represented by a distinctive facial expression?
   a. happiness b. hostility c. surprise d. sadness
3. Facial expressions associated with the basic emotions develop naturally according to a child's own biological timetable of maturation. (true/false)
4. People show stronger emotional reactions to positive stimuli than to negative stimuli. (true/false)
5. All of the following are true of display rules *except* that they
   a. are the same in all cultures.
   b. dictate when and where emotions should be expressed.
   c. dictate what emotions should not be expressed.
   d. often cause people to display emotions they do not feel.
6. Which of the following statements is *not* true about emotion as a form of communication?
   a. Emotions can communicate feelings better than words alone do.
   b. Emotions can communicate intentions.
   c. Emotions are often contagious.
   d. Infants under 1 year of age are unable to use the emotions of others to guide their behavior.
7. Evolutionary psychologists found that ______________ produces negative emotions in both men and women.
   a. angriness c. noncommitment
   b. unkindness d. deception

Answers: 1. c 2. b 3. true 4. false 5. a 6. d 7. d

EXPERIENCING EMOTION

How is the expression of emotion related to the experience of emotion? Some researchers go so far as to suggest that the facial expression alone can actually produce the experience.

The Facial-Feedback Hypothesis: Does the Face Cause the Feeling?

What is the facial-feedback hypothesis?

Researcher Sylvan Tomkins (1962, 1963), like Darwin, agreed that facial expressions of the basic emotions are genetically programmed. But Tomkins went a step further. He claimed that the facial expression itself—that is, the movement of the facial muscles producing the expression—triggers both the physiological arousal

facial-feedback hypothesis: The idea that the muscular movements involved in certain facial expressions trigger the corresponding emotions (for example, smiling makes one feel happy).

and the conscious feeling associated with the emotion. The notion that the muscular movements involved in certain facial expressions produce the corresponding emotion is called the **facial-feedback hypothesis** (Izard, 1971, 1977, 1990; Strack et al., 1988).

In an extensive review of research on the facial-feedback hypothesis, Adelmann and Zajonc (1989) found impressive evidence to support the association between facial expression and the subjective experience of an emotion. In addition, they found considerable support for the notion that simply making the facial expression can initiate the subjective feeling of the emotion. If this is true, you should be able to feel more understanding and empathy for others if you mirror their facial expressions with your own.

Do you think that making particular facial expressions can affect your emotions? A simple experiment you can try alone or with friends or classmates is described in the *Try It!*

Try It!

Hold a pencil between your lips with your mouth closed, as shown in the left-hand drawing, for about 15 seconds. Pay attention to your feelings. Now hold the pencil between your teeth, letting your teeth show, as shown in the right-hand drawing, for about 15 seconds. Did you have more pleasant feelings with the pencil between your lips or between your teeth? Why do you think that was so? (Adapted from Strack et al., 1988.)

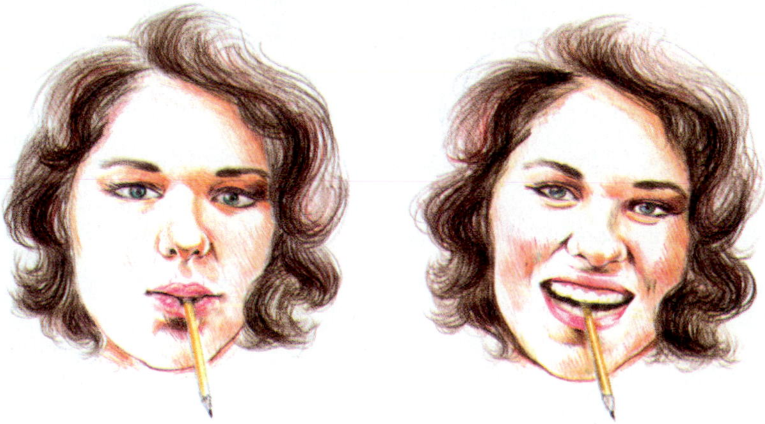

In the *Try It!* activity, when you held a pencil between your teeth, you activated the facial muscles used to express happiness.

The Simulation of Facial Expressions: Put On a Happy Face Nearly 125 years ago Darwin wrote, "Even the simulation of an emotion tends to arouse it in our minds" (1872/1965, p. 365). Ekman and colleagues (1983) put this notion to the test using 16 participants (12 professional actors and 4 scientists). The participants were guided to contract specific muscles in the face so that they could assume the facial expressions of six basic emotions—surprise, disgust, sadness, anger, fear, and happiness. They were never actually told to smile, frown, or put on an angry face, however.

The participants were monitored by electronic instruments, which recorded physiological changes in heart rate, galvanic skin response (to measure perspiring), muscle tension, and hand temperature. Measurements were taken as the participants made each facial expression. The participants were also asked to imagine or relive an experience in which they had felt each of the six emotions.

Ekman reported that a distinctive physiological response pattern emerged for the emotions of fear, sadness, anger, and disgust, whether the participants relived one of their emotional experiences or simply made the corresponding facial expression. In fact, in some cases the physiological measures of emotion were greater when the actors and scientists made the facial expression than when they imagined an emotional experience (Ekman et al., 1983). The researchers found that both anger and fear accelerate heart rate, but fear produces colder fingers than does anger.

Controlling Facial Expressions to Regulate Feelings If facial expressions can activate emotions, is it possible that intensifying or weakening a facial expression might intensify or weaken the corresponding feeling state? In 1872 Darwin wrote:

> The free expression by outward signs of an emotion intensifies it. On the other hand, the repression . . . of all outward signs softens our emotions. He who gives way to violent gestures will increase his rage; he who does not control the signs of fear will experience fear in greater degree. (p. 365)

Izard (1990) believes that learning to self-regulate emotional expression can help in controlling emotions. You might learn to change the intensity of an emotion by inhibiting, weakening, or amplifying its expression. Or you might change the emotion itself by simulating the expression of another emotion. Izard proposes that this approach to the regulation of emotion might be a useful adjunct to psychotherapy. Regulating or modifying an emotion by simulating an expression of its opposite may be effective if the emotion is not unusually intense.

Gender Differences in Experiencing Emotion: The Evolutionary Psychologists' Perspective

Do females and males differ significantly in the way they experience their emotions? Do women tend to be more intensely emotional than men? According to evolutionary psychologists, the answer to both questions is yes. Intense emotions are frequently experienced in the context of sexual behavior, and evolutionary psychologist David Buss (1999, 2000b) has reported that women are far more likely to feel anger when their partner is sexually aggressive. Men, on the other hand, experience greater anger than women when their partner withholds sex.

There are other gender differences with respect to the emotion of anger. According to the evolutionary perspective, your answer to the following question is likely to be gender-specific: What emotion would you feel first if you were betrayed or harshly criticized by another person? When asked to respond to this question, male research participants were more likely to report that they would feel angry, while female participants were more likely to say that they would feel hurt, sad, or disappointed (Brody, 1985). Of course, both males and females express anger, but typically not in the same ways. Women are just as likely as men to express anger in private (at home) but much less likely than men to express it publicly (Cupach & Canary, 1995).

Research by evolutionary psychologists also suggests clear and consistent differences between the sexes concerning feelings of jealousy. Men, more than women, experience jealousy over evidence or suspicions of sexual infidelity. A woman, however, is more likely than a man to be jealous of her partner's emotional attachment and commitment to another and over the attention, time, and resources diverted from the relationship (Buss, 1999, 2000a; White & Mullen, 1989).

Within married couples, women appear to be more finely tuned to the relationship's overall emotional climate and are more likely to be its "emotional manager" (Gottman, 1994).

The most puzzling gender difference in emotional experience is the following: In surveys of happiness, women report greater happiness and life satisfaction than men report (Wood et al., 1989). Paradoxically, women also report more sadness than men, are twice as likely to report being depressed, and admit to greater fear than men (Scherer et al., 1986). How can women be both happier and sadder than men? Another gender difference may explain it. Researchers have found sex differences in the intensity of emotional response. Grossman and Wood (1993) tested male and female participants for the intensity of emotional responses on five basic emotions—joy, love, fear, sadness, and anger. They found that "women reported more intense and more frequent emotions than men did, with the exception of anger" (p. 1013).

More joy, more sadness, more fear, more love! But these were self-reports. How did Grossman and Wood know that the female participants actually *felt* four of the five emotions more intensely than the males? The researchers also measured physiological arousal. The participants viewed slides depicting the various emotions while they were hooked up to an electromyograph to measure tension in the facial muscles. The researchers found that "women not only reported more intense emotional experience than men, but they also generated more extreme physiological reactions" (p. 1020). Other researchers agree that, in general, women respond with greater emotional intensity than men and thus can experience both greater joy and greater sorrow (Fujita et al., 1991).

An AIDS Memorial Quilt display evoked strong feelings of grief and sadness in both of these people, but the woman's visible emotional reaction is more intense.

In a recent study, men were found to process emotions, especially positive ones, predominantly in the left hemisphere of the brain. Women, however, were found to use both cerebral hemispheres more equally for processing emotions (Coney & Fitzgerald, 2000), which could account for some of the emotional differences between the genders.

Love: The Strongest Emotional Bond

The emotion of love comes in many varieties. And although people often use the term rather loosely or casually—"I love ice cream," "I love to dance"—love is usually experienced as a deep and abiding affection for our parents, our children, and ideally our friends and neighbors and other fellow humans. There is also love of country and love of learning.

How many components are there to this thing called love?

Romantic Love: Lost in Each Other When you say you have "fallen" in love, it is probably romantic love you have fallen into. Romantic love (sometimes called *passionate love*) is an intense emotional response to another person, coupled with sexual arousal and a tremendous longing for that person. But when the passion fades, couples may find that they do not have the similar backgrounds, attitudes, values, and interests that often form the basis for a more enduring relationship. Fortunately, there is more to love than passion, important though it is. In fact, passion may be only one of three parts of an ideal love relationship.

How does Sternberg's triangular theory of love account for the different kinds of love?

Sternberg's Theory of Love: Three Components, Seven Types Robert Sternberg (1986b, 1987), whose triarchic theory of intelligence was discussed in Chapter 8, proposes a **triangular theory of love.** Its three components are intimacy, passion, and commitment. Sternberg explains intimacy as "those feelings in a relationship that promote closeness, bondedness, and connectedness" (1987, p. 339). Passion refers to those drives in a loving relationship "that lead to romance, physical attraction, [and] sexual consummation" (1986b, p. 119). The decision/commit-

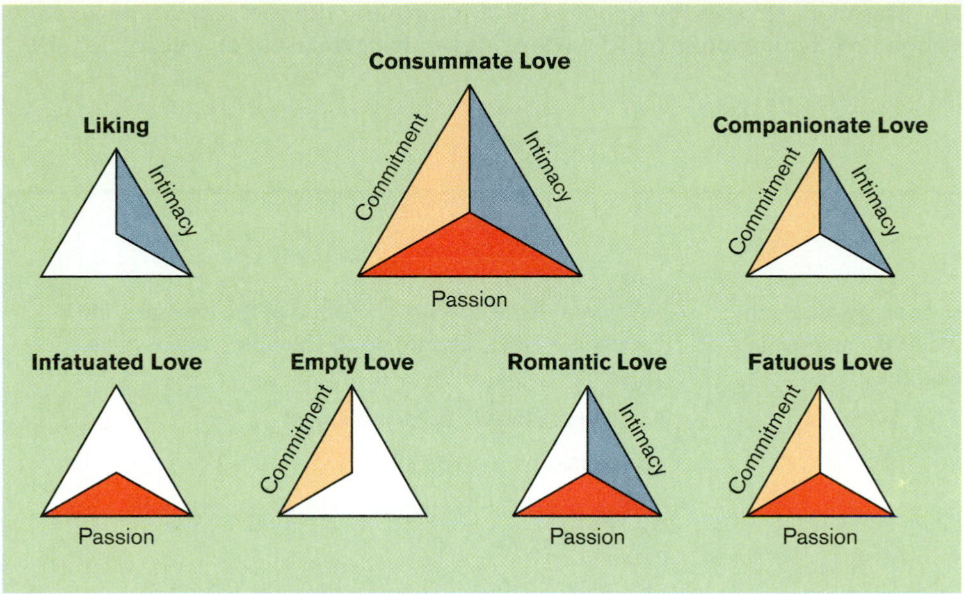

Figure 11.6

Sternberg's Triangular Theory of Love

Sternberg identifies three components of love–passion, intimacy, and commitment–and shows how the three, singly and in various combinations, produce seven different kinds of love. Consummate love, the most complete form of love, has all three components. (Based on Sternberg, 1986b.)

ment component consists of (1) a short-term aspect—the decision that one loves another person—and (2) a long-term aspect—a commitment to maintaining that love over time.

Sternberg proposes that these three components, singly and in various combinations, produce seven different kinds of love (see Figure 11.6):

- *Liking* has only one of the love components—intimacy. In this case, *liking* is not used in a trivial sense. Sternberg says that this intimate liking characterizes true friendships, in which a person feels a bondedness, a warmth, and a closeness with another but not intense passion or long-term commitment.
- *Infatuated love* consists solely of passion and is often what is felt as "love at first sight." But without the intimacy and the decision/commitment components of love, infatuated love may disappear suddenly.
- *Empty love* consists of the decision/commitment component without intimacy or passion. Sometimes a stronger love deteriorates into empty love—the commitment remains, but the intimacy and passion have died. In cultures in which arranged marriages are common, relationships often begin as empty love.
- *Romantic love* is a combination of intimacy and passion. Romantic lovers are bonded emotionally (as in liking) and physically through passionate arousal.
- *Fatuous love* has the passion and the decision/commitment components but not the intimacy. This type of love can be exemplified by a whirlwind courtship and marriage in which a commitment is motivated largely by passion without the stabilizing influence of intimacy.
- *Companionate love* consists of intimacy and commitment. This type of love is often found in marriages in which the passion has gone out of the relationship, but a deep affection and commitment remain.
- *Consummate love* is the only type that has all three components—intimacy, decision/commitment, and passion. **Consummate love** is the most complete form of love, and it represents the ideal love relationship for which many people strive but which apparently few achieve. Sternberg cautions that maintaining a consummate love may be even harder than achieving it.

triangular theory of love: Sternberg's theory that three components—intimacy, passion, and decision/commitment—singly and in various combinations produce seven different kinds of love.

consummate love: According to Sternberg's theory, the most complete form of love, consisting of three components—intimacy, passion, and decision/commitment.

Sternberg stresses the importance of translating the components of love into action. "Without expression," he warns, "even the greatest of loves can die" (1987, p. 341).

Remember It!

1. The idea that making a happy, sad, or angry face can actually trigger the physiological response and feeling associated with the emotion is called the
   a. emotion production theory.
   b. emotion control theory.
   c. facial-feedback hypothesis.
   d. facial expression theory.
2. Heightened emotion tends to facilitate rational thinking. (true/false)
3. Some research supports the notion that women tend to experience emotions more intensely than men. (true/false)
4. Which of the following is *not* one of the central components of love, according to Sternberg's triangular theory?
   a. compatibility
   b. passion
   c. commitment
   d. intimacy
5. What is the complete form of love, according to Sternberg?
   a. romantic love
   b. fatuous love
   c. companionate love
   d. consummate love

Answers: 1. c 2. false 3. true 4. a 5. d

Apply It!

The Quest for Happiness

"Life, Liberty and the pursuit of Happiness"—these ringing words from the Declaration of Independence are familiar to most of us, and most of us would agree that happiness is a desirable goal. But what exactly is happiness, and how can one attain it? These questions are not as easily answered as you might expect.

Psychologists usually equate happiness with the feeling of well-being, the pervasive sense that life is good. As David G. Myers, a leader in the field of happiness research, puts it, well-being "is an ongoing perception that this time of one's life, or even life as a whole, is fulfilling, meaningful, and pleasant" (1992, p. 23). Happiness is closely related to life satisfaction—people who feel happy also tend to believe that their lives are satisfying.

Happiness does not appear to be associated with age, gender, race, or geographical location. Instead, it is related to self-satisfaction. Researchers have found that happy people tend to be energetic, decisive, flexible, creative, and sociable. They are more trusting, loving, and responsive than sad people, tend to look at the brighter side of life, and are more willing to help those in need. Happy people have high self-esteem and a sense of personal control, are optimistic, and enjoy social support—that is, they have a large circle of friends and often engage in rewarding social activities.

Although it is commonly believed that money can't buy happiness, there is a connection between money and a sense of well-being. When asked what would improve their quality of life, most people answer, "More money." It is true that many poor people are far from happy, but there are limits to the amount of happiness that money can buy. A survey of 49 wealthy Americans, all with net worths well over $100 million, found them to be only slightly happier than average. (Diener et al., 1985).

An important factor affecting happiness is the tendency to compare one's situation with that of other people. If you feel that you are struggling to make ends meet while everyone around you appears to be living in comfort and security, you will feel less joy and more stress. Indeed, surveys have shown that perceived wealth matters more than absolute wealth. As Myers points out, "actual income doesn't much influence happiness; how *satisfied* we are with our income does. If we're content with our income, regardless of how much it is, we're likely to say we're happy." To put it another way, "satisfaction isn't so much getting what you want as wanting what you have" (1992, p. 39).

If good fortune in the form of wealth cannot buy certain and enduring happiness, does a life-shattering experience destroy all hope of future happiness? Surprisingly, no. People who have suffered a tragic accident leading to blindness or paralysis (like Christopher Reeve, who was featured in this chapter's opening story) tend to return to a near-normal state of day-to-day happiness after a period of adjustment.

What can you do to make yourself happier from day to day? For one thing, you can smile more. Smiling really does induce feelings of happiness. Smile at other people—even people you don't like a lot. As the song goes, "Put on a happy face." Don't worry if it feels like pretending; after a while it will come naturally. "Act as if you like someone and soon you may," Myers notes (1992, p. 125).

Another way to make your life happier is to make the most of social occasions—phone calls, visits, meals with friends. Such occasions often require you to behave as if you were happy, which can actually serve to free you from unhappiness.

There are inevitably times when happiness seems far removed from life in the real world—times when you feel bored or anxious, overwhelmed by work, relationships, or life in general. However, there are also times when you are so caught up in an activity that you become oblivious to your surroundings and time seems to fly by. Psychologists refer to this feeling as *flow.* To be in flow is to be unselfconsciously absorbed (Csikszentmihalyi, 1990). People who are engaged in some activity that engages their skills—whether it is work, play, or simply driving a car—report more positive feelings. "To experience flow," says Myers, "we need to find challenge and meaning in our work, and to seek experiences that fully engage our talents" (1992, p. 134). So, pursue happiness by living more *intentionally*—devoting more time to the things you do best and find most meaningful, while avoiding activities that waste time and bring little satisfaction, such as sleeping late, hanging out, and watching television.

In short, there are many things you can do to try to become happier. Myers sums them up in these words:

> You and I can *decide* to exercise, to allow enough hours for sleep, to make comparisons that remind us of our blessings, to manage our time in ways that boost our sense of control, . . . to initiate relationships, to devote effort to maintaining love rather than taking it for granted, to plan involving rather than passive leisure activities, . . . and even to begin working at reshaping our culture in ways that will promote the well-being that fame and fortune can't buy. (1992, p. 207; emphasis added)

THINKING CRITICALLY

Evaluation

1. In your view, which theory better explains motivation: drive-reduction theory or arousal theory? Which theory do you find less convincing? Support your answers.
2. Using what you have learned about body weight and dieting, select any well-known weight-loss plan (for example, Weight Watchers, Jenny Craig, Slim Fast) and evaluate it, explaining why it is or is not an effective way to lose weight and keep it off.

Point/Counterpoint

Present a convincing argument for each of these positions:

a. Polygraph testing should not be allowed in the legal system or in business and industry.
b. Polygraph testing should be allowed in the legal system and in business and industry.

Psychology in Your Life

Considering what you have learned about Murray's need for achievement (n Ach), do you think you have a high, moderate, or low n Ach? If low, how might you increase your n Ach?

SUMMARY AND REVIEW

INTRODUCTION TO MOTIVATION

What is the difference between intrinsic and extrinsic motivation?

With intrinsic motivation, an act is performed because it is satisfying or pleasurable in and of itself; with extrinsic motivation, an act is performed in order to bring a reward or to avert an undesirable consequence.

Key Terms
motivation (p. 386); motives (p. 386); incentive (p. 386); intrinsic motivation (p. 387); extrinsic motivation (p. 387)

THEORIES OF MOTIVATION

How do instinct theories explain motivation?

Instinct theories suggest that human behavior is motivated by certain innate, unlearned tendencies, or instincts, which are shared by all people.

How does drive-reduction theory explain motivation?

Drive-reduction theory suggests that a biological need creates an unpleasant state of arousal or tension called a drive, which impels the organism to engage in behavior that will satisfy the need and reduce the tension.

How does arousal theory explain motivation?

Arousal theory suggests that the aim of motivation is to maintain an optimal level of arousal. If arousal is less than optimal, a person engages in activities that stimulate arousal; if arousal exceeds the optimal level, the person seeks to reduce stimulation.

Key Terms
instinct (p. 387); instinct theory (p. 387); drive-reduction theory (p. 388); drive (p. 388); homeostasis (p. 388); arousal (p. 389); arousal theory (p. 389); stimulus motives (p. 389); Yerkes–Dodson law (p. 389); sensory deprivation (p. 390)

THE PRIMARY DRIVES: HUNGER AND THIRST

Under what kinds of conditions do the two types of thirst occur?

One type of thirst results from a loss of bodily fluid that can be caused by perspiring, vomiting, bleeding, diarrhea, or excessive intake of alcohol. Another type of thirst results from excessive intake of salt, which disturbs the water–sodium balance in the blood and tissues.

What are the roles of the lateral hypothalamus and the ventromedial hypothalamus in the regulation of eating behavior?

The lateral hypothalamus (LH) apparently acts as a feeding center—when it is activated, it signals the animal to eat; when it is destroyed, the animal refuses to eat. The ventromedial hypothalamus (VMH) evidently acts as a satiety center—when it is activated, it signals the animal to stop eating; when it is destroyed, the animal overeats, becoming obese.

What are some of the body's hunger and satiety signals?

Some of the body's hunger signals are stomach contractions, low blood glucose levels, and high insulin levels. Some satiety signals are a full stomach, high blood glucose levels, and the presence in the blood of other satiety substances (such as CCK), secreted by the gastrointestinal tract during digestion.

What are some nonbiological factors that influence what and how much people eat?

External eating cues such as the taste, smell, and appearance of food, the variety of food offered, as well as the time of day, can cause people to eat more food than they actually need.

What are some factors that account for variations in body weight?

Variations in body weight are influenced by genes, metabolic rate, activity level, number of fat cells, and eating habits.

How does set point affect body weight?

Set-point theory suggests an internal homeostatic system that functions to maintain body weight by adjusting appetite and metabolic rate.

Why is it almost impossible to maintain weight loss by cutting calories alone?

It is almost impossible to maintain weight loss by cutting calories alone because a dieter's metabolic rate slows down to compensate for the lower intake of calories. Exercise both prevents the lowering of metabolic rate and burns up additional calories.

What are the symptoms of anorexia nervosa?

The symptoms of anorexia nervosa are an overwhelming, irrational fear of being fat, compulsive dieting to the point of self-starvation, and excessive weight loss.

What are the symptoms of bulimia nervosa?

The symptoms of bulimia nervosa are repeated and uncontrolled episodes of binge eating, usually followed by purging, that is, self-induced vomiting and/or the use of large quantities of laxatives and diuretics.

Key Terms
primary drive (p. 391); lateral hypothalamus (LH) (p. 392); ventromedial hypothalamus (VMH) (p. 392); metabolic rate (p. 396); fat cells (p. 397); set point (p. 397); anorexia nervosa (p. 398); bulimia nervosa (p. 399)

SOCIAL MOTIVES

What is Murray's contribution to the study of motivation?

Murray defined a list of social motives, or needs, and developed the Thematic Apperception Test (TAT) to assess a person's level of these needs.

What is the need for achievement?

The need for achievement (*n* Ach) is the need to accomplish something difficult and to perform at a high standard of excellence.

What are some characteristics shared by people who are high in achievement motivation?

People high in achievement motivation enjoy challenges and like to compete. They tend to set goals of moderate difficulty, are more motivated by hope of success than fear of failure, attribute their success to their ability and hard work, and are most often drawn to business, frequently becoming entrepreneurs.

What is work motivation, and what are two effective techniques for increasing it?

Work motivation can be thought of as the conditions and processes responsible for the arousal, direction, magnitude, and maintenance of effort on the job. Two effective techniques for increasing work motivation are reinforcement and goal setting.

Key Terms
social motives (p. 401); Thematic Apperception Test (TAT) (p. 401); need for achievement (*n* Ach) (p. 401); industrial/organizational (I/O) psychologists (p. 403); work motivation (p. 403)

THE WHAT AND WHY OF EMOTIONS

What are the three components of emotions?

An emotion is a feeling state that involves physiological arousal, cognitive appraisal of the situation, and outward expression of the emotion.

According to the James–Lange theory, what sequence of events occurs when an individual experiences an emotion?

According to the James–Lange theory, environmental stimuli produce a physiological response, and then awareness of this response causes the emotion to be experienced.

What is the Cannon–Bard theory of emotion?

The Cannon–Bard theory suggests that emotion-provoking stimuli received by the senses are relayed simultaneously to the cortex, providing the mental experience of the emotion, and to the sympathetic nervous system, producing the physiological arousal.

According to the Schachter–Singer theory, what two factors must occur in order for a person to experience an emotion?

The Schachter–Singer theory states that for an emotion to occur (1) there must be physiological arousal, and (2) the person must perceive some reason for the arousal in order to label the emotion.

According to Lazarus, what sequence of events occurs when an individual feels an emotion?

An emotion-provoking stimulus triggers a cognitive appraisal, which is followed by the emotion and the physiological arousal.

What brain structure processes the emotion of fear?

The emotion of fear is processed by the amygdala, without initial involvement of the brain's cortex.

What does a polygraph measure?

A polygraph monitors changes in heart rate, blood pressure, respiration rate, and galvanic skin response, which typically accompany the anxiety that occurs when a person lies.

Key Terms
emotion (p. 405); James–Lange theory (p. 406); Cannon–Bard theory (p. 407); Schachter–Singer theory (p. 407); Lazarus theory (p. 407); polygraph (p. 409)

THE EXPRESSION OF EMOTION

What are basic emotions?

The basic emotions (happiness, sadness, disgust, and so on) are those that are unlearned and that are reflected in the same facial expressions in all cultures.

How does the development of facial expressions of different emotions in infants suggest a biological basis for emotional expression?

The facial expressions of different emotions develop in a particular sequence in infants and seem to be the result of maturation rather than learning. The same sequence occurs even in children who have been blind and deaf since birth.

Why is emotion considered a form of communication?

Emotions enable people to communicate desires, intentions, and needs more effectively than just words alone and thus make it more likely that others will respond.

Key Terms
basic emotions (p. 410); display rules (p. 413)

EXPERIENCING EMOTION

What is the facial-feedback hypothesis?

The facial-feedback hypothesis suggests that the muscular movements involved in certain facial expressions trigger the corresponding emotions (for example, smiling triggers happiness).

How does Sternberg's triangular theory of love account for the different kinds of love?

In his triangular theory of love, Sternberg proposes that, singly and in various combinations, three components—intimacy, passion, and decision/commitment—produce seven different kinds of love: infatuated, empty, romantic, fatuous, companionate, and consummate love, as well as liking.

Key Terms
facial-feedback hypothesis (p. 416); triangular theory of love (p. 418); consummate love (p. 419)

Surf It!

Want to be sure you've absorbed the material in Chapter 11, "Motivation and Emotion," before the big test? Visiting *www.abacon.com/wood* can put a top grade within your reach. The site is loaded with free practice tests, flashcards, activities, and links to help you review your way to an A. To enliven that inevitable study break, the site also offers personality assessment quizzes and a psychology career corner.

12 Human Sexuality and Gender

Do you find it difficult to understand how someone could sit down at a computer, presumably to work, play games, or check email—and instead get sexually aroused? It may or may not surprise you, but it's happening more and more often, as the number of visits to sexually explicit websites and chat rooms increases. In 1998, approximately 70,000 sex-related websites existed—allowing surfers to log onto "The Fetish Room" and "The Dominance and Submission Room" among others. And an estimated 200 new sex sites are added every day.

Visiting sexually oriented websites may seem a relatively harmless adult recreational pursuit—in fact, some prime-time TV shows such as *Ally McBeal* have used virtual sex as a lighthearted storyline. But for some people, the psychological need to enter the world of cybersex has become a compulsion—some might say an addiction.

Although the great majority of cybersex addicts are men, women also participate. But the genders differ in their preferences regarding type of cybersex activity. Men are predominantly drawn to pornographic photos and videos, demonstrating an interest in visual stimulation with no commitment demands. In contrast, women are most often attracted to cybersex chat rooms, where those who enter are turned on by the "talk." This indicates that women tend to look for companionship and relationships in their online use.

So what's the harm? Virtual sex is safe—no sexually transmitted diseases. And cybersex addicts are not *really* cheating on their partners—are they? Experts say that even if cybersex remains confined to the virtual world, never consummated physically and existing only in the imagination, its consequences can be devastating. One woman caught her cybersex-addicted husband viewing what she termed "graphically repulsive images." After that, she felt uncomfortable and threatened in their sexual relationship.

Further, cybersex addiction *can* lead to an actual affair. One man, devastated after losing his wife of 24 years to a 1-month online-chat affair, constructed a website specifically to help others recognize and prevent Internet infidelity in their mates.

Another negative effect of cybersex is reality avoidance. Some studies show that although sexual stimulation may be the initial reason for engaging in virtual sex, people become addicted to the "high" or the feeling of escape over time. Kimberly Young, one of the first psychologists to study Internet addictions, suggests that three factors—anonymity, convenience, and escape—coax many individuals with no history of sexual deviance into the unreal world of cybersex and often keep them there. Warning signs of addiction include preferring cybersex over a real-life partner as a primary source of sexual fufillment, feeling preoccupied with finding cybersexual partners via the Internet, and communicating anonymously during online sexual fantasies, says Young.

Why do some people engage in cybersex and others do not? What drives people's sexual desires, appetites, and attitudes? Why do men and women have differing sexual needs? Psychologists are interested in all aspects of sex, and we will explore the many facets of sex and gender in this chapter.

We begin by considering the biological processes and factors leading up to the first announcement of a proud parent—"It's a girl!" or "It's a boy!" In other words, we start by exploring what people *are* sexually, as males and as females, then move on to how people *behave* sexually as men and as women, depending on sexual orientation.

WHAT MAKES A MALE, A MALE OR A FEMALE, A FEMALE?

The Sex Chromosomes: X's and Y's

What are the biological factors that determine whether a person is male or female?

The **sex chromosomes**—XX in females and XY in males—initially determine one's **biological sex.** A female's eggs all carry an X sex chromosome, but sperm cells in the male can carry either an X or a Y chromosome. If a Y-bearing sperm cell unites with the egg, the developing embryo will be XY—a male. If a sperm cell carrying an X chromosome fertilizes the egg, the result will be XX—a female.

But the pairing of two sex chromosomes at conception is only the beginning of the many developmental processes that forge the differences between males and females. At 6 weeks after conception, the primitive **gonads** (sex glands) are the same in males and females. During the 7th week, however, if a Y chromosome is present, the gonads develop into primitive testes. However, it is not the Y chromosome itself that determines the sex of the fetus, but a single gene found only on the Y chromosome (Capel, 2000). Mentioned in Chapter 9, this gene, known as Sry, sets in motion the forces that cause the undifferentiated gonads to form testes (Hanley et al., 2000). If the Sry gene is absent or nonfunctional for any reason, the gonads will develop into ovaries about 12 weeks after conception (Wertz & Herrmann, 2000). But the story does not end here. Later in development, the sex hormones can alter the initial genetic determination of male or female.

sex chromosomes: The pair of chromosomes that determines the sex of a person (XX in females and XY in males).

biological sex: Physical and physiological status as male or female.

gonads: The sex glands; the ovaries in females and the testes in males.

androgens: Male sex hormones.

genitals (JEN-uh-tulz): The internal and external reproductive organs.

primary sex characteristics: The internal and external reproductive organs; the genitals.

secondary sex characteristics: The physical characteristics that are not directly involved in reproduction but that develop at puberty and are associated with sexual maturity.

gender (JEN-der): Psychological and sociocultural definition of masculinity or femininity based on the expected behaviors for males and females.

gender roles: Cultural expectations about the behavior appropriate to each gender.

The Sex Hormones: Contributing to Maleness and Femaleness

In the male embryo, the primitive testes produce and secrete **androgens,** the male sex hormones that cause the male **genitals**—the penis, testes, and scrotum—to develop. If androgens are not present, female genitals—the ovaries, uterus, and vagina—develop (Breedlove, 1994). The prenatal exposure to androgens permanently transforms body tissues and organs other than the genitalia, such as the brain (Martin, 2000). The presence or absence of androgens determines whether an embryo develops male or female genitals—**primary sex characteristics.** A genetic male (XY) can develop female genitals if androgens are absent, and a genetic female (XX) can develop male genitals if too much androgen is present.

Androgens affect more than the physical development of the genitals. These hormones also have a tremendous influence on the brain during fetal development, causing the male and female brains to diverge and begin to develop in their own separate ways (S. Kelly et al., 2000; Lazar, 2000). The presence or absence of androgens in the fetus determines whether a part of the brain, the hypothalamus, becomes male- or female-differentiated (Swaab & Hofman, 1995). The hypothalamus, through its control of the pituitary gland, plays a major part in controlling the production and release of the sex hormones.

At puberty the hypothalamus sends a signal to the pituitary, which in turn sets in motion the maturing of the internal and external genitals and the appearance of the **secondary sex characteristics.** These are the physical characteristics associated with sexual maturity—pubic and underarm hair in both sexes, breasts in females, and facial and chest hair and a deepened voice in males.

Gender-role typing begins early in life, when girls and boys learn to engage in activities that are considered typically female or male.

GENDER-ROLE DEVELOPMENT

Setting aside strictly physiological determinants of sex brings us into the more ambiguous realm of **gender**—the psychological and sociocultural definition of masculinity or femininity based on the expected behaviors for males and females.

What are the prevailing cultural stereotypes about masculine and feminine **gender roles**—those behaviors associated with males or females? Traditionally, males have been expected to be strong, dominant, independent, competitive, assertive, logical, decisive, confident, and unemotional; females have been expected to be warm, nurturant, caring, sensitive, supportive, emotional, passive, submissive, and dependent.

Why is it that:

- By age 15 to 26 months, children already exhibit clear preferences for toys considered appropriate for their gender?
- By age 2½ years, children already have formed stereotypes concerning what boys and girls do and do not do, and what they like and dislike?
- By age 2 to 3 years, children already consider some jobs to be for men and others for women?

Here is another area of study in psychology that involves the nature–nurture controversy. To what degree are gender differences influenced by nature (biological factors) and by nurture (environmental factors)?

Biological Influences on Gender Typing

What is gender typing, and what role do biological influences play in it?

How do people acquire the traits, behaviors, attitudes, preferences, and interests that the culture considers appropriate for their gender? This process is known as **gender typing.** The majority of psychologists attribute gender typing primarily to learning within a social or cultural context. But according to the biological view, the genes and the influence of prenatal sex hormones play an important role in laying the groundwork for a variety of gender differences in behavior.

In a review of studies on the effects of prenatal androgens (male sex hormones) Collaer and Hines (1995) found that these hormones have a reasonably strong influence on tendencies toward aggression and on sexual orientation. Their strongest influence is on children's play behavior, especially rough-and-tumble play and toy and playmate preferences. Girls exposed to prenatal androgens are more likely than girls not exposed to these hormones to prefer to play with toys favored by boys—such as trucks, cars, and fire engines (Berenbaum & Snyder, 1995). And more recent clinical evidence suggests that androgen-derived steroids lead to irritability and increased aggression (Johansson et al., 2000).

Prenatal androgens are also known to affect brain development and functioning in humans and many other animal species (Beyenburg et al., 2000). Women tend to use both hemispheres of the brain in performing certain language tasks, while men are more likely to use one hemisphere, primarily the left. And men and women typically use different brain areas to perform rhyming tasks (Shaywitz, 1996; Shaywitz et al., 1995). Although research has uncovered these and other gender-related brain differences, such as a differently shaped corpus callosum in males versus females, it has yet to be clearly determined whether such differences have behavioral significance (Kelly, Ostrowski, et al., 2000).

Environmental Influences on Gender Typing

What are the environmental factors that contribute to gender typing?

Parents, peers, teachers, television, and other environmental influences play a powerful role in promoting gender typing after birth.

The Parents' Role: Pink and Blue Blankets and Gender-Typed Toys Although parents vary widely in their efforts to influence gender-role development, virtually all parents, consciously or unconsciously, create somewhat different environments for sons and daughters from birth on. At birth, boys are not wrapped in pink blankets and dressed in pink clothes. And from infancy on, children may receive some presents that are gender-neutral, but most are not—dolls and doll houses, tea sets, and jewelry are considered appropriate for girls; toy cars and trucks, construction toys, and sports equipment for boys.

What part do parents play in the continuation of gender typing as their children grow and develop? According to researchers Lytton and Romney (1991), who did a meta-analysis of 172 studies on the role of parents in gender typing, both parents

gender typing: The process by which individuals acquire the traits, behaviors, attitudes, preferences, and interests that the culture considers appropriate for their gender.

encourage gender-typed activities. And fathers tend to differentiate more between boys and girls than mothers do. Fathers typically encourage their sons to be competent, competitive, and assertive and to control their emotions. And some studies indicate that fathers pressure sons to achieve more than they pressure daughters (Gervai et al., 1995). Daughters are reinforced for being affectionate, nurturant, and obedient (Lamb, 1981). Boys are punished more than girls, and girls are treated with more warmth and gentleness. Boys are encouraged to engage in large-muscle activities and to be more independent than girls (Fagot, 1982; Maccoby & Jacklin, 1974a).

Parents' expectations about how well their children will perform in a range of academic subjects also reveal gender-based differences. Longitudinal research on more than 2,000 families with school-aged children revealed that parents rated sons as more capable than daughters in sports and math, and daughters as more competent than sons in English (Eccles et al., 1990). And these perceptions prevailed even though the boys and girls in the sample actually performed about equally well in English and math, as measured by grades and achievement test scores. Predictably, the more stereotypic the parents' beliefs about gender-specific capabilities were, the more likely they were to perceive their children as being endowed with talent and/or expertise in "appropriate" areas. And parents' gender-specific expectations can even set up a self-fulfilling prophecy in that their children lack confidence in their ability to succeed in other than gender-typical areas (Eccles et al., 1989; Jacobs, 1991).

If fathers and mothers play different roles in the gender typing of their children, what happens when children are raised in single-parent homes headed by the mother? The effects of father absence seem to be most pronounced in boys under age 5 (Stevenson & Black, 1988). Boys whose fathers are present are more stereotypically gender-typed than boys whose fathers are absent and more likely to choose masculine toys and activities. But, by the time they reach adolescence, father-absent boys are more stereotypically gender-typed and more aggressive than father-present boys. Father-absent girls do tend to be slightly less feminine, but this might be the effect of having mothers who are less stereotypically feminine (Kurdek & Siesky, 1980).

Other Environmental Influences on Gender Typing Peers also play an important role in enforcing conformity to gender-roles. For example, the reaction of peers to the selection of a gender-inappropriate toy can be very strong.

Parents, peers, and teachers put much stronger pressure on boys to avoid feminine activities—such as playing with dolls and dishes and dressing up in mother's clothes—than they put on girls to avoid masculine activities (Levy et al., 1995). While a girl may feel complimented if someone calls her a "tomboy," almost every boy considers it an insult to be called a "sissy" (Doyle & Paludi, 1995). The masculine role is more highly esteemed than the feminine role by children of both sexes (Unger & Crawford, 1996). Carol Martin (1990) suggests that adults react more negatively to cross-gender behavior in boys because they fear that boys may be less likely to outgrow it.

Psychological Theories of Gender-Role Development

What are three theories of gender-role development?

Three psychological theories are currently used to explain, in part, how gender-role development occurs—social learning theory, cognitive developmental theory, and gender-schema theory.

Social Learning Theory: Learning by Observing According to **social learning theory,** observation, imitation, and reinforcement are the mechanisms that explain gender typing (Mischel, 1966). Children are usually reinforced for imitating behaviors considered appropriate for their gender. When behaviors are not appropriate (a boy puts on lipstick, or a girl pretends to shave her face), children are quickly informed, often in a tone of reprimand, that boys or girls do not do that. Through reinforcement and punishment, children are led to engage in gender-appropriate behavior. They need not have knowledge about gender to acquire gender-typed preferences.

social learning theory: A theory that explains the process of gender typing in terms of observation, imitation, and reinforcement.

Children also learn gender-appropriate behaviors from television, peers, teachers, and books. They observe the actions of others and the consequences of those actions. Even the praise or scorn others receive for gender-appropriate or inappropriate actions can provide memorable lessons for children as to which behaviors are acceptable and which are not (Bussey & Bandura, 1999).

Children are particularly influenced by the gender roles depicted in the popular media. Men and women are commonly portrayed in traditional occupational roles on television (Signorielli, 1990). Advertisements further reinforce gender-role stereotypes. And not only are males portrayed as more competent in various TV series, but experts appearing on TV news shows are predominantly male, as are the majority of the news reporters (Evan, 1991). Study gender roles on television for yourself in the *Try It!*

Try It!

Take an informal sample of 20 TV commercials. Record how many males and females are represented (include voiceovers) and briefly describe the role of each. Pay attention to which characters are perceived as leaders or experts, and which are perceived as helpless, passive, or sexy. Do any patterns emerge? If so, what conclusions can you draw from the patterns?

Cognitive Developmental Theory: Understanding Gender in Stages **Cognitive developmental theory,** proposed by Lawrence Kohlberg (1966; Kohlberg & Ullian, 1974) suggests that children play an active role in their own gender typing, but that an understanding of gender is a prerequisite. According to Kohlberg, children go through a series of stages in acquiring the concept of gender. Between ages 2 and 3, children acquire **gender identity**—their sense of being a male or a female. Between ages 4 and 5, children acquire the concept of *gender stability*—awareness that boys are boys and girls are girls for a lifetime. Finally, between ages 6 and 8, children understand gender constancy—that gender does not change regardless of the activities people engage in or the clothes they wear. Moreover, according to Kohlberg, when children realize their gender is permanent, they are motivated to seek out same-sex models and learn to act in ways considered appropriate for their gender. Cross-cultural studies reveal that Kohlberg's stages of gender identity, gender stability, and gender constancy occur in the same order in cultures as different as those in Samoa, Kenya, Nepal, and Belize (Munroe et al., 1984).

Although attaining an understanding of gender constancy is a necessary part of gender-role development, children have a great deal of gender-role knowledge long before they reach that point (Levy & Carter, 1989; Serbin & Sprafkin, 1986). Gender constancy may be acquired between 6 and 8 years, as Kohlberg suggests, but this theory fails to explain why many gender-appropriate behaviors and preferences are observed in children as young as age 2 or 3 (Bussey & Bandura, 1999; Jacklin, 1989; Martin & Little, 1990).

Gender-Schema Theory: Forming Gender Stereotypes **Gender-schema theory,** proposed by Sandra Bem (1981), combines elements of both social learning and cognitive developmental theory. Like social learning theory, gender-schema theory suggests that young children are motivated to pay attention to and behave in a way consistent with gender-based standards and stereotypes of the culture. Like cognitive developmental theory, gender-schema theory stresses that children begin to use gender as a way to organize and process information (Bussey & Bandura, 1999). But gender-schema theory holds that this process occurs earlier, when gender

cognitive developmental theory: A theory suggesting that when children realize their gender is permanent, they are motivated to seek out same-sex models and learn to act in ways considered appropriate for their gender.

gender identity: One's sense of being a male or a female.

gender-schema theory: A theory suggesting that young children are motivated to attend to and behave in ways consistent with gender-based standards and stereotypes of the culture.

identity rather than gender constancy is attained (Bem, 1985). According to Martin and Little (1990), "Once children can accurately label the sexes, they begin to form gender stereotypes and their behavior is influenced by these gender-associated expectations" (p. 1438). They develop strong preferences for sex-appropriate toys and clothing, and they favor same-sex peers over those of the other sex (Powlishta, 1995). Fagot and others (1992) found gender labeling and gender stereotyping to occur in children 2 to 3 years old.

Children learn which activities and traits are most important for males and females and then evaluate themselves in relation to those traits. They first learn the characteristics appropriate to their own sex, and later those appropriate to the other sex (Martin et al., 1990). To a large extent, their own self-concepts and self-esteem depend on the match between their abilities and behaviors and the cultural definition of what is desirable for their gender. Bem (1993) believes that we all view our social world through "the lenses of gender."

Remember It!

1. The sex chromosomes in a male are ______________; the sex chromosomes in a female are ______________.
   a. XX; XY b. YY; XX c. XX; YY d. XY; XX
2. The Y sex chromosome must be present for the testes to develop; the ovaries will develop if the Y chromosome is absent. (true/false)
3. If androgens are not present, the female genitals will develop regardless of whether the sex chromosomes are XY or XX. (true/false)
4. What is the process by which individuals acquire the traits, behaviors, attitudes, preferences, and interests that the culture considers gender appropriate?
   a. gender differentiation c. gender constancy
   b. sexual enculturation d. gender typing
5. In the family, the mother usually plays the major role in gender typing. (true/false)
6. Which theory of gender-role development explains the process of gender typing in terms of observation, imitation, and reinforcement?
   a. gender-schema theory
   b. androgyny theory
   c. social learning theory
   d. cognitive developmental theory
7. Cognitive developmental theory offers a better explanation of how very young children acquire gender-appropriate behaviors than does gender-schema theory. (true/false)

Answers: 1. d 2. true 3. true 4. d 5. false 6. c 7. false

GENDER DIFFERENCES: FACT OR MYTH?

Males and females are indeed different, but in what ways and to what degree? Let's look more closely into gender differences.

The Evolutionary Psychology Perspective on Gender Differences

Evolutionary psychologists have a great deal to say about gender differences, which is not surprising. The basic goal is identical for males and females, according to evolutionary psychology—to pass as many of their genes into the future as possible—but the behavior required for achieving the goal differs greatly for males and females. A male can maximize the number of copies of his genes by sowing his seed as "wildly" as he can, having sex with as many different women as possible, as often as possible. But a female, as a result of nature's constraints, has a limited number of eggs carrying her genes and a limited window of opportunity during which she can conceive. Further biological restrictions dictate that she spend nearly a year bringing a single pregnancy to term. A male can sire hundreds of offspring during that time.

Such biological differences forge a number of gender differences through natural selection, according to evolutionary psychologists (Buss, 1999, 2000b). And central among these gender differences are the differing mate selection strategies of men and women. Males typically seek females that are young, healthy (physical attractiveness is taken as a sign of good health), and well suited for child bearing. A female tends to prefer a male who is somewhat older, more stable and with sufficient resources, generous, emotionally attached, and strong enough to protect her and their children (Buss, 1999). These and related gender differences are apparently not culture-specific, but are found in 37 different countries around the world (Buss, 1994).

Other researchers question whether reported mate-selection preferences of females are thoroughly biological in nature. Wouldn't females prefer very attractive mates, too, under circumstances of greater gender equity in financial resources? Yes, according to researchers Eagly and Wood (1999), who contend that gender differences in mate preference are significantly smaller when economic and social conditions for males and females are more equal, as they are becoming in developed countries in the 21st century.

Gender Differences in Cognitive Abilities

For what cognitive abilities have gender differences been proven?

What does research say about cognitive differences and gender? Eleanor Maccoby and Carol Jacklin (1974a) examined 1,600 studies on gender differences. They found evidence that males had a slight advantage in mathematics and spatial skills, while females had a slight advantage in verbal ability. For many years after Maccoby and Jacklin's study, researchers believed that, on average, females were superior in verbal skills and males were superior in mathematics and spatial skills. Concerning gender differences in cognitive abilities, there are two important points to keep in mind:

1. In general, the differences within each gender are greater than the differences between the genders.
2. Even though gender differences in cognitive abilities have been generally small on average, there tends to be more variation in such abilities among males than among females (that is, the range of test scores is typically greater for males).

Gender Differences in Verbal Ability: Are Females Better with Words?

Using meta-analysis, researchers Janet Hyde and Marcia Linn (1988) examined 165 studies reporting test results on verbal ability for approximately 1.5 million males and females. But they found no significant gender differences in verbal ability. Hedges and Nowell (1995) analyzed the results of the National Assessment of Educational Progress, which has tested a nationally representative sample of 70,000 to 100,000 9-, 13-, and 17-year-olds annually in reading comprehension, writing, math, and science. The researchers compared the achievement of the 17-year-olds from 1971 through 1992 and reported that females outperformed males in reading and writing, while males did better in science and math. Although average gender differences were small, there was one prominent exception: "Females performed substantially better than males in writing every year" (p. 44). Furthermore, Hedges and Nowell reported that more males than females were near the bottom of the distribution, not only in writing, but in reading comprehension as well. Finally, in high school, girls are generally more fluent verbally than boys are (Halpern, 1992) and do considerably better in spelling (Lubinsky & Benbow, 1992).

Gender Differences in Math Ability: Do Males Have the Edge? In one of the largest studies conducted on gender differences in mathematics, Hyde and others (1990) performed a meta-analysis of 100 studies, which together represented test results for more than 3 million participants. They found no significant gender difference in the understanding of mathematical concepts among the various age groups. Although females did slightly better in mathematical problem solving in elementary and middle school, males scored moderately higher in high school and college. Benbow and Stanley (1980, 1983) found a significant male superiority in a select segment of the population—the brightest of the bright in mathematics ability. There were twice as many boys as girls scoring above 500 on the SAT, and 13 times as many scoring above 700. Hedges and Nowell (1995) reported that twice as many boys as girls were in the top 3% of the Project Talent Mathematics total scale, and seven times as many were in the top 1%.

Parents often expect boys to do better than girls in math (Lummis & Stevenson, 1990). Could such expectations become a self-fulfilling prophecy, leading girls to lack confidence in their math ability and to decide not to pursue advanced math courses? Yes, say Eccles & Jacobs (1986). The American Association of University Women Education Foundation provided evidence that many science teachers and some math teachers as well tend to pay noticeably more attention to boys than to girls (Chira, 1992). Such treatment might discourage girls with math or science aptitude from choosing careers in these areas.

Gender Differences in Spatial Ability Researchers have found that, in general, males tend to perform somewhat better than females on tests of spatial skills (Kimura, 1992, 2000; Linn & Hyde, 1989; Linn & Peterson, 1985). This gender difference has been found on some but not all of the various spatial tasks (Geary, 1996; Kimura, 1992, 2000). Some research has shown that spatial abilities appear to be enhanced by prenatal exposure to high levels of androgens (Berenbaum et al., 1995). However, this finding does not minimize the role of social experiences and expectations in shaping children's abilities and interests.

Gender differences are revealed most often on mental rotation tasks, in which three-dimensional figures must be quickly and accurately rotated mentally (Voyer et al., 1995). Casey and others (1995) found that mental rotation ability was a predictor of math aptitude for female students.

What gender differences are found in social behavior and personality?

Figure 12.1 (on p. 434) shows problem-solving tasks, some of which are more easily solved by females, others by males.

Gender Differences in Social Behavior and Personality

Are there any significant gender differences in social behavior and personality? Yes, in certain specific areas, according to a number of research studies.

While boys show higher levels of physical aggression, girls tend to use indirect forms of aggression, such as gossiping about and rejecting another individual.

Gender Differences in Aggression: The Clearest Difference Most researchers agree that greater physical aggression in males is one of the most consistent and significant gender differences (Bogard, 1990; Harris, 1992). Such a conclusion is hardly surprising. Just consider the number of men in prison for violent crimes compared with the number of women. Gender differences have been found in virtually every culture where aggressive behavior has been studied. And recent research by Knight and others (1996) suggests that "the gender differences in aggression appear to be remarkably stable" (p. 410).

Greater aggression can usually be observed in boys from the time they are 2 to 2½ years old. They are more likely than girls to engage in mock fighting and rough-and-tumble play and to have aggressive fantasies (Maccoby & Jacklin, 1974b). But females can be aggressive, too. They may be even more likely than males to use *indirect*

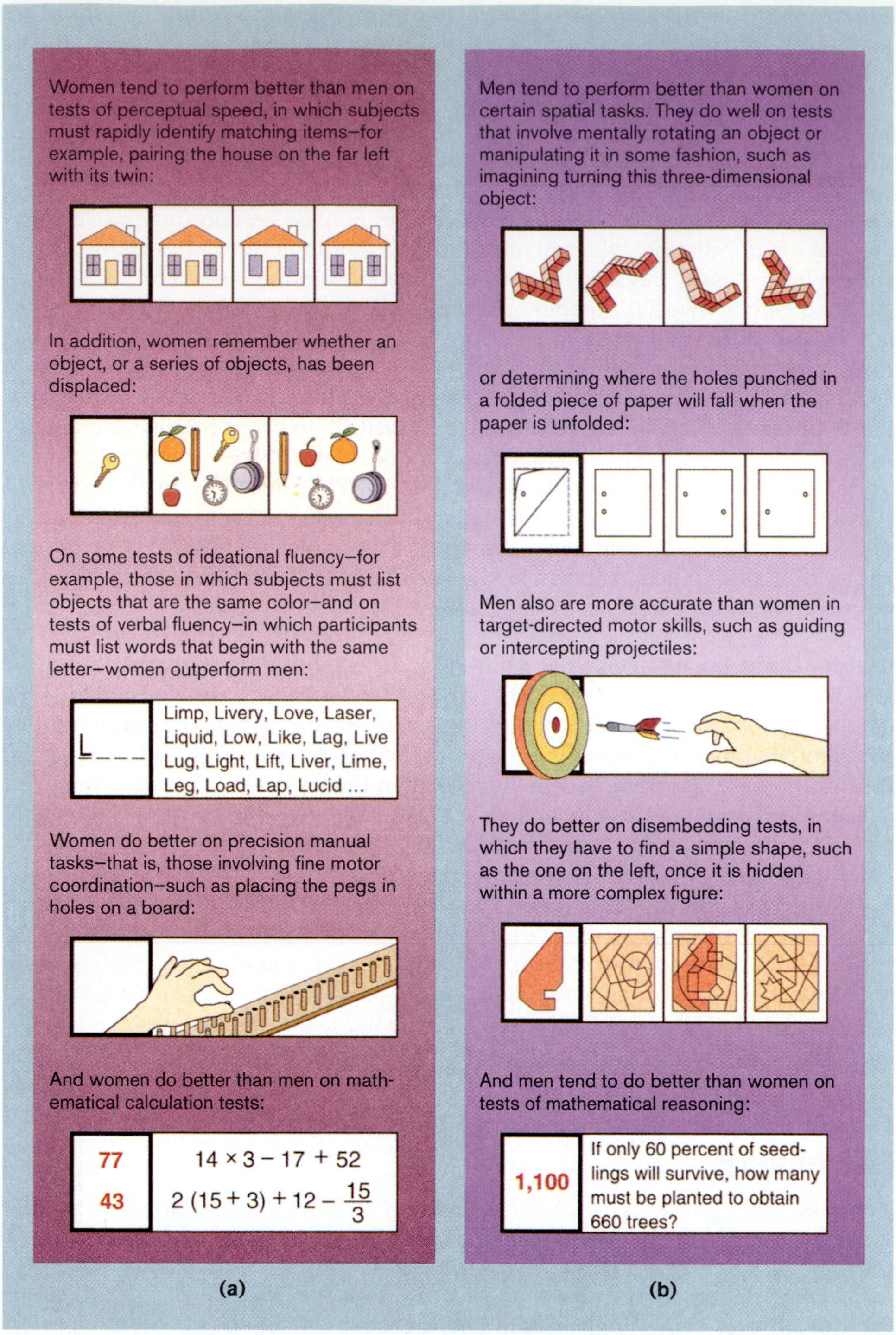

Figure 12.1

Problem-Solving Tasks Favoring Women and Men

(a) A series of problem-solving tasks on which women generally do better than men. (b) Tasks on which men do better. (From Kimura, 1992.)

forms of aggression, such as gossip, spreading rumors, and rejecting, ignoring, or avoiding the target of aggression (Björkqvist et al., 1992).

Research rather dramatically shows that men are far more willing than women to act aggressively in the absence of provocation (Bettencourt & Miller, 1996). And men are more likely than women to interpret an ambiguous situation as a provocation (Crick & Dodge, 1994). However, with respect to willingness to use aggression when clearly provoked, the differences between men and women are considerably smaller (Bettencourt & Miller, 1996). Females seem to feel more guilt and anxiety about engaging in aggressive behavior and to feel more fearful that they will be the target of retaliation (Eagly & Steffen, 1986). However, when women are provoked and feel that aggression is justified, and their fear of retaliation is minimal, they too are likely to behave aggressively and to feel less guilty about doing so (Bettencourt & Miller, 1996).

Gender differences in aggression have been linked to testosterone levels in a number of animal studies, especially with rats and primates (Maccoby & Jacklin, 1980). And, in humans, Gladue (1991) found that both heterosexual and gay men with higher blood levels of testosterone were more likely to engage in physical and verbal aggression than men with lower blood levels.

Other Social and Personality Differences Most aspects of personality appear to show no significant gender differences. But there are indications that important differences may exist in a few areas. Are females typically more nurturant than males? Are males generally more assertive than females? Some researchers (Feingold, 1994; Helgeson, 1994) answer yes to both these questions. From results of a meta-analysis, Alice Eagly (1995) concluded that some apparent gender differences are consistent with long-held gender stereotypes. "In general, women tend to manifest behaviors that can be described as socially sensitive, friendly, and concerned with others' welfare, whereas men tend to manifest behaviors that can be described as dominant, controlling, and independent" (Eagly, 1995, p. 154).

Women in general appear to be more attuned to others' verbal and nonverbal expressions of feelings and less reluctant than men to discuss their personal experiences and reveal their own feelings (Dindia & Allen, 1992). Some evidence suggests that females tend to be relatively more people-oriented and males relatively more object-oriented. And this gender difference appears to hold across the life span (McGuinness, 1993).

As children, from the time they enter school, males are more likely to dominate classroom discussions (Sadker & Sadker, 1994). And as adults, they tend to interrupt others more, to be more willing to change the topic of conversation, and to smile less than females (Deaux, 1985; Hall 1984). Gender differences are also apparent in the preference for cooperation versus competition. As children, males tend to favor competitive activities and situations, while females are more likely to prefer cooperative ones (Geary, 1996). Males are more apt to thrive and females to suffer when exposed to highly competitive work or school environments (Hoyenga & Hoyenga, 1993).

Gender differences are not purely biological or purely environmental. "The major importance of this fact is that sex differences can be manipulated—magnified, minimized, or even reversed—by appropriate manipulations of the relevant environmental factors and developmental experiences" (Hoyenga & Hoyenga, 1993, p. 400).

Adjustment and Gender Typing: Feminine, Masculine, or Androgynous?

Do good adjustment and high self-esteem seem to be related to masculine, feminine, or androgynous traits?

Traditionally, masculinity and femininity have been considered opposite ends of a continuum. But must we think of masculine traits and feminine traits as mutually exclusive? Must an individual be either independent, competent, and assertive or nurturant, sensitive, and warm? Sandra Bem (1974, 1977, 1985) proposed that "masculine" and "feminine" characteristics are separate and independent dimensions of personality rather than opposite ends of a continuum. A person can be high or low on one or both dimensions. People who are low on both "masculine" and "feminine" dimensions are labeled *undifferentiated.* **Androgyny** is a combination of the desirable male and female characteristics in one person, who is said to be *androgynous.* There is some evidence that African American women are more androgynous than White women (Binion, 1990).

Some researchers claim that androgynous individuals have a wider range of possible behavioral characteristics at their disposal. Consequently, such individuals are said to be better equipped to meet the challenges of the work world and their personal relationships (Bem, 1975). Is this true? Are androgynous persons better adjusted than those who adopt a more traditional masculine or feminine role

androgyny (an-DROJ-uh-nee): A combination of the desirable male and female characteristics in one person.

consistent with their gender? There is some evidence that a combination of positive masculine traits and positive feminine traits in males is correlated with success in intimate relationships (Coleman & Ganong, 1985). But research suggests that for both males and females, masculine traits are most strongly associated with self-esteem and adjustment (Aubé & Koestner, 1992). Jones and others (1978) found that "the more adaptive, flexible, unconventional, and competent patterns of responding occurred among more masculine subjects independent of their gender" (p. 311). To the extent that androgynous people possess the desired masculine traits, they are likely to be better adjusted and have higher self-esteem than people who are feminine or undifferentiated. Males displaying feminine interests and behaviors and the "undesirable" feminine traits (submissiveness, gullibility, and so on) are found to have the lowest self-esteem (O'Heron & Orlofsky, 1990; Pryor, 1994).

Gender Bias in the Workplace

Research refutes the notion that women's personality traits or attitudes make them less suited for upper-level positions in businesses.

As we entered the 21st century, women were reported to be holding 53% of the more than 20 million professional jobs in the United States. Even so, the majority of those jobs—such as public school teaching and nursing—pay only moderately well. More than 8 million professional jobs pay much better, providing average annual incomes exceeding $40,000, but women hold only slightly over 28% of those higher-paying jobs. Figure 12.2 charts the percentages of women who were holding those better-paying jobs through 1998 and shows women's earnings as a percentage of men's earnings for each job (Doyle, 2000).

More than a decade ago, a study by the U.S. Department of Labor (1991) stated that a barrier described as a "glass ceiling" prevents American women from advancing to top corporate management positions. The study pointed out that there were only two female CEOs at U.S. Fortune 1000 companies in 1978. Eighteen years later, in 1996, that number had doubled—to four! Why are there so few women in top (upper management) positions in U.S. corporations? Various explanations, or more accurately, justifications, have been offered. Many corporate leaders

Figure 12.2

Representation of Women in Jobs and Professions in the United States, 1950–2000

Although women are increasing their representation in the U.S. labor force overall, they still make up less than half of all civilian workers. (From Doyle, 2000.)

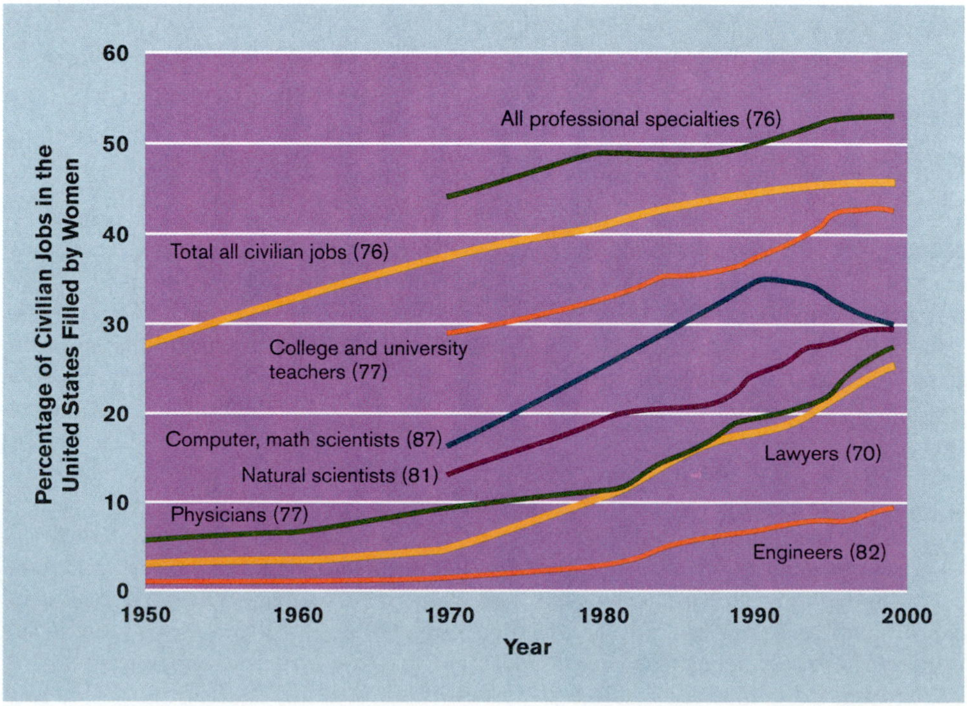

define a good manager as tough, decisive, logical, and unemotional—qualities said to fit the male stereotype. And some people point to women's so-called deficiencies in these male personality traits and attitudes as justification for the virtual absence of women from top management. On the other hand, the pull of motherhood certainly competes with some women's climb up the career ladder—often by their own choice. Still, today women's share of jobs in medicine and law is on the rise as females earn a higher proportion of degrees in these fields (Doyle, 2000).

Remember It!

1. In general, differences in cognitive abilities are greater within each gender than between the genders. (true/false)
2. For each cognitive ability, indicate whether males or females, in general, tend to score higher on tests of that ability.

   ____ (1) writing a. males

   ____ (2) science b. females

   ____ (3) spatial ability

   ____ (4) reading comprehension

   ____ (5) mathematics
3. Physical aggression is believed to be more typical of (males, females).
4. Males and females thrive equally well in competitive classrooms. (true/false)
5. Women are (overrepresented/underrepresented) in the upper tier of better-paying jobs in the United States.

Answers: 1. true 2. (1) b (2) a (3) a (4) b (5) a 3. males 4. false 5. underrepresented

Alfred Johnson. Theory of sexual human response cycle. STD's 2 kinds viral bacterial

SEXUAL ATTITUDES AND BEHAVIOR

Few would disagree that society's attitudes about sexual behavior are more liberal now than in decades past. In the 1940s and 1950s, virtually all societal institutions officially frowned on sex before marriage. Sex was not considered an appropriate subject for serious investigation, nor was it discussed openly in polite society. But all that began to change when Alfred Kinsey came on the scene.

The Kinsey Surveys: The First In-Depth Look at Sexual Behavior

What were the famous Kinsey surveys?

In the 1940s Alfred Kinsey and his associates undertook a monumental survey that helped to bring the subject of sex out in the open. They interviewed thousands of men and women about their sexual behaviors and attitudes, and their results were published in a two-volume report—*Sexual Behavior in the Human Male* (1948) and *Sexual Behavior in the Human Female* (1953). The public was stunned by what Kinsey's participants said they had done and were doing. It appeared that a lot of Americans had a head start on the sexual revolution way back in the 1940s and

coitus (KOeh-tis): Penile-vaginal intercourse.

1950s. And there was a great gulf between what people were practicing in private and what they were admitting openly.

Kinsey's interviews revealed the following:

- About 50% of the females and nearly 90% of the males reported having sexual intercourse, **coitus,** before marriage.
- Over 40% of the college-educated couples said that they engaged in oral sex.
- The majority of women and virtually all males reported that they had masturbated.
- About 26% of the married women and half of the married men admitted having had extramarital affairs.

But was Kinsey's study valid? Was it scientific? People attacked the findings for a variety of reasons. Unfortunately, Kinsey's sample was not broadly representative. He reported no information on African Americans. Elderly people, rural residents, and those with only grade school educations were underrepresented; Protestants, the college-educated, the middle class, and urban residents were overrepresented. Above all, we must keep in mind that Kinsey's studies were not direct studies of behavior. All of his data were based on interviews, or self-reports—what people *said* they were doing. Kinsey's participants could have been exaggerating (in either direction), trying to tell the researcher what they thought he or she wanted to hear, or trying to present themselves in a good light (known as the *social desirability response,* explained in the section on survey research in Chapter 1). So whatever weight we give to Kinsey's research must take into account the somewhat subjective nature of his data.

Have sexual attitudes and behavior changed much since Kinsey's surveys half a century ago?

Sexual Attitudes and Behavior Today: The New Sexual Revolution

The most comprehensive survey of sexual behavior since Kinsey was published in 1994. *The Social Organization of Sexuality* by Laumann and others (1994) is believed to be the most valid and reliable survey of its kind to date. The findings were based on interviews of a nationwide representative sample composed of 3,432 males and females aged 18 to 59. The major findings are summarized below and in Figure 12.3.

- People with one sexual partner are happier than people with none or more than one.
- Married people have sex more frequently and are more likely to have orgasms than noncohabiting men and women.
- On average, over the course of a lifetime, men have six sex partners and women have two.
- Almost 75% of men and 90% of women reported that they had been faithful to their spouses.
- About 54% of men and 19% of women reported thinking about sex every day or several times a day; 4% of men and 14% of women reported either never thinking of sex or thinking of it less than once a month.
- About 27% of men and 8% of women said that they had masturbated at least once a week during the previous 12 months; 37% of men and 58% of women said they had not masturbated.

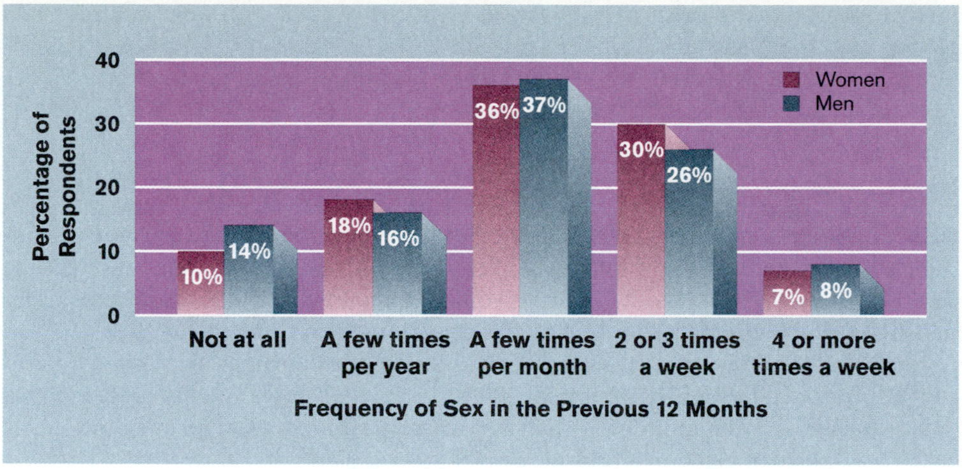

Figure 12.3

Some Results of a 1994 U.S. Sex Survey

Contrary to what is generally portrayed in the media, most Americans are having sex a few times a month or less. Of the respondents to the survey, 83% reported having either one or no sex partner during the past 12 months.

- Of women, 22.8% reported having been forced to do something sexual that they did not want to do, while only 2.8% of men reported forcing a woman to engage in a sexual act.

Throughout all age groups in the United States today, men report having had more sex partners and express a more permissive attitude toward casual premarital sex than women (Oliver & Hyde, 1993). According to Sprecher and Hatfield (1996), African American students tend to have more permissive premarital sexual standards than White students, while Mexican American students have more conservative sexual standards than White students do.

In general, males are likely to be more interested in purely physical sex, and "females tend to be more interested . . . in love, nurturant relationships, and lasting social bonds" (Baldwin & Baldwin, 1997, p. 182). Males tend to be less inhibited than females of the same age about masturbation—and to do it far more often. Perhaps this explains, in part, why males, more than females, can think of sex as a quick, easy, casual release without any emotional commitment (Baldwin & Baldwin, 1997).

In a study of first-year college students, Cohen and Shotland (1996) found that the men expected sexual intercourse to become part of a dating relationship far sooner than the women did. Nearly all of the men in the study expressed a willingness to have sex on a basis of physical attraction only, with no emotional involvement; fewer than two-thirds of the women were willing to do so. And approximately one-third of the men but only 5% of the women admitted to having had sex with someone they were neither attracted to nor emotionally involved with. Another interesting finding was that the research participants reported believing that "the average person of their gender was considerably more permissive" in sexual matters than they were (p. 291). Another study found that college men with numerous sex partners tend to have a positive attitude toward sexual activities, to be physically attractive, to have high testosterone levels, to be sensation-seekers, and even to have antisocial tendencies (Bogaert & Fisher, 1995).

From 1990 to 1995, researchers Sprecher and Regan (1996) surveyed college students who were virgins to determine their reasons for and feelings about their virginity. For both men and women, it was not lack of sexual desire that prompted their decision to remain virgins. The main reason given was not having found the "right" person, followed by fear of pregnancy or other potential negative consequences of sexual activity, including AIDs and other sexually transmitted diseases. Moral and religious beliefs also influenced the decision for some of the students. And some of the men felt inadequate and insecure about initiating sex. The women surveyed felt more pride and happiness about being virgins, while the men were more inclined to experience embarrassment or guilt. But in the more recent years of the study, the men reported greater pride in their status. This, the researchers suggest, might be a response to the "greater number of publicly visible virginal role models to emulate" (p. 12), such as the well-known male athletes in the group Athletes for Abstinence.

Sexual Desire and Arousal: Driving the Sex Drive

According to Masters and Johnson, what are the four phases of the human sexual response cycle?

Virginia Johnson and William Masters were pioneers in the study of the human sexual response.

Masters and Johnson and the Human Sexual Response Cycle Kinsey conducted the first major survey of sexual behavior, but what if the act of intercourse could be monitored in the laboratory? Wouldn't this be more scientific than simply relying on self-reports? These were the questions asked by sex researchers Dr. William Masters and Virginia Johnson. To answer them, they planned and conducted the first laboratory investigations of the human sexual response in 1954. They monitored their volunteer participants, who engaged in sex while connected to electronic sensing devices.

Masters and Johnson (1966) concluded that the human sexual response is quite similar for males and females. Two major physiological changes occur in both sexes—the flow of blood into the genitals (and the breasts in females) and an increase in neuromuscular tension.

Both males and females experience a **sexual response cycle** with four phases: (1) the excitement phase, (2) the plateau phase, (3) the orgasm, and (4) the resolution phase. Masters and Johnson studied more than "10,000 complete cycles of sexual response" in 382 women and 312 men (1966, p. 15). They found that these phases apply not only to sexual intercourse but also to other types of sexual activity.

The Excitement Phase The **excitement phase** is the beginning of the sexual response. It can be triggered by direct physical contact as well as by psychological arousal—thoughts, emotions, and a variety of sensory stimuli. For both partners, muscular tension increases, heart rate quickens, and blood pressure rises. As additional blood is pumped into the genitals, the male's penis becomes erect and the female feels a swelling of the clitoris. Vaginal lubrication occurs as the inner two-thirds of the vagina expands and the inner lips of the vagina enlarge. In women especially, the nipples harden and stand erect.

The Plateau Phase After the excitement phase, the individual enters the **plateau phase,** when excitement continues to mount. Blood pressure and muscle tension increase still more, and breathing becomes heavy and more rapid. The man's testes swell, and drops of liquid, which could contain live sperm cells, may drip from the penis. The outer part of the woman's vagina swells as the increased blood further engorges the area. The clitoris withdraws under the clitoral hood, its skin covering, and the breasts become engorged with blood. Excitement builds steadily during the plateau phase.

The Orgasm The **orgasm,** the shortest of the phases, is the highest point of sexual pleasure, marked by a sudden discharge of accumulated sexual tension. Involuntary muscle contractions may seize the entire body during orgasm, and the genitals contract rhythmically.

Orgasm is a two-stage experience for the male. First is his awareness that ejaculation is near and that he can do nothing to stop it; second is the ejaculation itself, when semen is released from the penis in forceful spurts.

The experience of orgasm in women builds in much the same way as for men. Marked by powerful, rhythmic contractions, the female's orgasm usually lasts longer than that of the male. About 40–50% of women regularly experience orgasm during intercourse (Wilcox & Hager, 1980). Although vaginal orgasms and clitoral orgasms may feel different, according to the research conducted by Masters and Johnson (1966), the actual physiological response in the female is the same.

sexual response cycle: The four phases—excitement, plateau, orgasm, and resolution—that Masters and Johnson found are part of the human sexual response in both males and females.

excitement phase: The first stage in the sexual response cycle, characterized by an erection in males and a swelling of the clitoris and vaginal lubrication in females.

plateau phase: The second stage of the sexual response cycle, during which muscle tension and blood flow to the genitals increase in preparation for orgasm.

orgasm: The third phase in the sexual response cycle, marked by rhythmic muscular contractions and a sudden discharge of accumulated sexual tension.

resolution phase: The final stage of the sexual response cycle, during which the body returns to an unaroused state.

The Resolution Phase The orgasm gives way to the **resolution phase,** a tapering-off period, when the body returns to its unaroused state. Men experience a *refractory period* in the resolution phase, during which they cannot have another orgasm. The refractory period may last from only a few minutes for some men to as much as several hours for others. Women do not have a refractory period and may, if restimulated, experience another orgasm right away.

The Role of Hormones in Sexual Desire and Arousal: Sexual Substances

What are the male and female sex hormones, and how do they affect sexual desire and activity in males and females?

In most animal species, sexual activity does not occur unless the female is "in heat." Thus, most animals behave sexually in response to hormones, odors, and biologically determined sexual cycles. But human sexual desire can be aroused at practically any time, independent of rhythmic biological cycles. And humans engage in far more sex than is required to continue the species.

The sex glands themselves manufacture hormones—**estrogen** and **progesterone** in the ovaries, and androgens in the testes. The adrenal glands in both sexes also produce small amounts of these hormones. Females have considerably more estrogen and progesterone than males do, so these are known as the female sex hormones. Males have considerably more androgens—the male sex hormones. **Testosterone,** the most important androgen, influences the development and maintenance of male sex characteristics as well as sexual motivation.

Testosterone and Sexual Desire Males must have a sufficient level of testosterone in order to maintain sexual interest and have an erection. It is more than coincidence that at puberty, when testosterone levels increase dramatically, sexual thoughts and fantasies, masturbation, and nocturnal emissions also increase significantly. Udry and colleagues (1985) found that adolescents with high blood levels of testosterone spend more time thinking about sex. Thus, they are more likely to engage in masturbation, coitus, or other sexual activity than their counterparts with lower levels of testosterone.

As men age, the level of testosterone declines, and usually there is also a decline in sexual interest and activity and in sexual fantasies (Leitenberg & Henning, 1995). The decline in sexual interest and activity can sometimes be reversed with the use of testosterone patches (which are similar to nicotine patches) (Meyer, 1997). Castration (removal of the testes, which produce 95% of the male's androgens) usually lowers sexual desire and activity dramatically.

Females, too, need small amounts of testosterone in the bloodstream to maintain sexual interest and responsiveness (Anderson & Cyranowski, 1995). But hormones and other biological processes are not the only factors that drive sexual arousal. Psychological factors are important, as well, in producing and maintaining sexual arousal.

Psychological and Cultural Factors in Sexual Arousal

What psychological and cultural factors influence sexual arousal?

Psychological factors play a large role in sexual arousal. Part of the psychological nature of sexual behavior stems from those preferences and practices people learn from their culture. And cultural norms on sexual behavior vary widely, covering everything from the age at which initiation of sexual behavior is proper to the partners, conditions, settings, positions, and specific sexual acts that are considered acceptable. Moreover, what is perceived as sexually attractive in the male and the female may differ dramatically from culture to culture. In the United States, movie stars and models are often regarded as the ultimate in sexual desirability.

Sometimes, as a result of conditioning, men and women find certain stimuli sexually arousing (Dekker & Everaerd, 1989; O'Donohue & Plaud, 1994). The stimuli might be specific settings, certain kinds of music, particular objects or articles of clothing, or even the scent of a certain perfume or cologne.

Men and women differ in the ways they become sexually aroused. Men are more aroused by what they see; visual cues like watching a woman undress are likely to arouse them. Tender, loving touches coupled with verbal expressions of love arouse women more readily than visual stimulation. Men can become aroused almost instantly, while arousal for women may be a more gradual, building process.

estrogen (ES-truh-jen): A female sex hormone that promotes the secondary sex characteristics in females and controls the menstrual cycle.

progesterone (pro-JES-tah-rone): A female sex hormone that plays a role in the regulation of the menstrual cycle and prepares the lining of the uterus for possible pregnancy.

testosterone (tes-TOS-tah-rone): The most powerful androgen secreted by the testes and adrenal glands in males and by the adrenal glands in females; influences the development and maintenance of male sex characteristics and sexual motivation; associated with male aggressiveness.

Psychological factors play an important role in sexual attraction and arousal. Such factors involve preferences and attitudes we learn from our culture.

Sexual Fantasy: The Brain as a Sexual Organ In a review of the literature on sexual fantasy, Leitenberg and Henning (1995) point out that "one's brain is at least as important a sexual organ as one's genitals" (p. 469). The motivation to fantasize generally arises, not from a state of sexual deprivation, but rather from the desire to stimulate or heighten sexual arousal. Both men and women are likely to fantasize during intercourse. But men engage in sexual fantasies more frequently because they tend to fantasize during other activities, including masturbation, which they do far more often than women do.

Most often sexual fantasies involve conventional imagery about one's current or past partner or an imaginary lover. There are consistent gender differences in fantasies: "Men more than women imagine doing something sexual to their partner, whereas women more than men imagine something sexual being done to them" (Leitenberg and Henning, 1995, p. 491). Men's fantasies generally involve more specific visual imagery, while women's fantasies have more emotional and romantic content.

Although 95% of males and females admit to having sexual fantasies, about 25% experience strong guilt about them (Leitenberg & Henning, 1995). But research seems to suggest an association between a higher incidence of sexual fantasies and a more satisfactory sex life and fewer sexual problems. Guilt over fantasies seems to be related to having fewer fantasies and more sexual problems.

Stimulating Arousal through Explicit Sexual Materials Men are more likely to seek out sexual stimulation and arousal in magazines such as *Playboy,* in X-rated movies, and in adult bookstores. Some studies reveal that people may come to value their partner and relationship less after exposure to erotic sexual material. Male college students who agreed to view sexually explicit films showing highly attractive females reported being less pleased with their wives or girlfriends than were control groups of college men who did not view such materials (Kenrick & Gutierres, 1980; Weaver et al., 1984). Also, people may feel disappointed with their own sexual performance after comparing it to the performance portrayed by actors.

Sexuality and Commitment: Where the Best Sex Is Found The physiology of the sex act is certainly important, but there is much more to sex than the physical response. Many people view sex as a casual recreational activity that has little to do with love. Masters and Johnson have been accused of reducing the sex act to its clinical, physical components, but their book *The Pleasure Bond* (1975) argues strongly against separating the physical act of sex from the context of love and commitment. They are critical of those who "consider the physical act of intercourse as something in and of itself, a skill to be practiced and improved . . . an activity to exercise the body, or a game to be played." "To reduce sex to a physical exchange," they say, "is to strip it of richness and subtlety and, even more important, ultimately means robbing it of all emotional value." In Masters and Johnson's view it is a couple's "total commitment, in which all sense of obligation is linked to mutual feelings of loving concern, [that] sustains a couple sexually over the years" (1975, p. 268).

Although sex is one of life's greatest physical and emotional pleasures, it can also be a crime.

Child Sexual Abuse

To many people, child sexual abuse is perhaps the worst of crimes. Trust is violated; innocence is stolen. And children who are sexually abused may suffer emotional and social problems, often continuing into adulthood.

The number of cases of child sexual abuse reported each year in the United States exceeds 200,000. And the statistics do not tell the whole story, because child sexual abuse is vastly underreported. A nationwide survey found that at least 15% of girls and 9% of boys under the age of 19 had experienced a completed or attempted act of sexual intercourse with an adult (Finkelhor et al., 1990).

Sexual abuse begins very early in the lives of some victims and may continue for years (Burkhardt & Rotatori, 1995). It is well known that the vast majority of sexual abusers of both boys and girls are male. And in most cases, the abuser is not a stranger, but someone the child trusts—a family member, relative by blood or by marriage, a family friend, or a neighbor (Waterman & Lusk, 1986). Sexual abuse by a family member is, of course, *incest*. And while most of the cases that become known are father–daughter incest, brother–sister incest is more common. The rarest type is mother–daughter incest (Waterman & Lusk, 1986).

Children who live in poverty and/or who live in a highly unstable household where adults have a rapidly changing series of new sexual partners (especially live-in boyfriends) are at greater risk of being sexually abused. But child sexual abuse occurs in economically advantaged households as well.

What are some of the enduring problems victims of child sexual abuse are likely to face? Depression is a common problem, along with low self-esteem, anger, guilt, eating disorders, and problems in personal relationships. Sexually abused children are likely to live in fear and to experience sleep disorders and loss of appetite. As they enter adolescence, victims of sexual abuse may become sexually active at a relatively young age and even promiscuous, may abuse drugs and alcohol, and may have suicidal thoughts and tendencies. Some become delinquent or run away to escape their abusive environment (Kendall-Tackett et al., 1993).

Some researchers have suggested that a tendency toward *pedophilia* (a preference for children as sexual partners) may be the result of hypersexuality due to a brain disorder, especially in the front part of the right temporal lobe (Mendez et al., 2000). Therapies to treat those who sexually abuse children are likely to focus on the abuser's deviant sexual fantasies, which are believed to serve as "triggers" pushing the abuser to act (Swaffer et al., 2000).

Remember It!

1. Who conducted the first major surveys of sexual attitudes and behaviors of American males and females?
   a. Alfred Kinsey
   b. Masters and Johnson
   c. George Gallup
   d. Laumann and others
2. Men and women have equally permissive attitudes toward premarital sex. (true/false)
3. Which of the following statements about the human sexual response cycle is *false*?
   a. It consists of four phases.
   b. It occurs in sexual intercourse and can occur in other types of sexual activity.
   c. It is quite different in males and females.
   d. It was researched by Masters and Johnson.
4. Androgens, estrogen, and progesterone are present in both males and females. (true/false)
5. Testosterone plays a role in maintaining sexual interest in males and females. (true/false)
6. Sexual fantasies are most common among those with unsatisfactory sex lives. (true/false)
7. In child sexual abuse, the abuser is typically someone the child knows, rather than a stranger. (true/false)
8. The most common form of incest is (father–daughter, brother–sister).

Answers: 1. a 2. false 3. c 4. true 5. true 6. false 7. true 8. brother–sister

SEXUAL ORIENTATION

What is meant by sexual orientation?

So far we have discussed many aspects of human sexual response and sexual arousal, but we have not considered **sexual orientation**—the direction of an individual's sexual preference, erotic feelings, and sexual activity. In heterosexuals, the human sexual response is oriented toward members of the opposite sex; in homosexuals, toward those of the same sex; and in bisexuals, toward members of both sexes.

Homosexuality has been reported in all societies throughout recorded history (Carrier, 1980; Ford & Beach, 1951). Kinsey and his associates (1948, 1953) estimated that 4% of the male participants had nothing but homosexual relations throughout life, and about 2–3% of the female participants had been in mostly or exclusively lesbian relationships. Gay and lesbian rights groups, however, claim that about 10% of the U.S. population is predominantly homosexual. In what is said to be the most definitive and reliable sex survey to date, Laumann and others (1994) reported that the percentages of people who identified themselves as homosexual or bisexual were 2.8% of men and 1.4% of women. But 5.3% of men and 3.5% of women said that they had had a sexual experience with a person of the same sex at least once since puberty. And even larger percentages of those surveyed—10% of males and 8–9% of females—said that they had felt some same-sex desires. Notably, all estimates suggest that homosexuality is twice as prevalent in males as in females.

A gay rights demonstration gives lesbians and gay men and their supporters the chance to show pride and solidarity.

Until recent years, most gay men and lesbians kept their sexual orientation a secret rather than risk shame and discrimination. But more are "coming out," preferring to acknowledge and express their sexual orientation rather than having to lead a double life (Gorman, 1991).

Determinants of Sexual Orientation: Physiological or Psychological?

What are the various biological factors that have been suggested as possible determinants of a gay or lesbian sexual orientation?

Psychologists continue to debate whether sexual orientation is biologically fixed or acquired through learning and experience. A few decades ago, many experts believed that a homosexual orientation is learned (Gagnon & Simon, 1973; Masters & Johnson, 1979). Many now believe that biological factors largely determine sexual orientation (Bailey & Pillard, 1994; Isay, 1989; LeVay, 1993). And still others lean toward an interaction—the theory that both nature and nurture play a part (Breedlove, 1994; Byne, 1994; Patterson, 1995). Could hormones play a role?

Some have suggested that abnormal levels of androgens during prenatal development might influence sexual orientation (Collaer & Hines, 1995). Too much or too little androgen at critical periods of brain development might masculinize or feminize the brain of the developing fetus, making a homosexual orientation more likely (Berenbaum & Snyder, 1995). A few studies have revealed an increase in the incidence of lesbianism among females who had been exposed prenatally to synthetic estrogen (Meyer-Bahlburg et al., 1995) or to an excess of androgens (Ehrhardt et al., 1968; Money & Schwartz, 1977).

Definitive answers to nature–nurture questions are always elusive, but some recent research suggests that biological factors may play a part in homosexuality.

Sexual Orientation and the Brain Neuroscientist Simon LeVay (1991) reported that an area in the hypothalamus governing sexual behavior is about twice as large in heterosexual men as in homosexual men. This part of the hypothalamus, no larger than a grain of sand, is about the same size in heterosexual females as in homosexual males. LeVay admits that his research offers no direct evidence that the brain differences he found cause homosexuality (LeVay & Hamer, 1994). Critics

sexual orientation: The direction of one's sexual preference—toward members of the opposite sex (heterosexuality), toward one's own sex (homosexuality), or toward both sexes (bisexuality).

were quick to point out that all of the gay men included in LeVay's sample died of AIDS. It is known that AIDS is associated with abnormalities affecting certain brain areas. Some researchers questioned whether the brain differences LeVay observed might have resulted from AIDS, rather than being associated with sexual orientation (Byne, 1993). Others have suggested that the brain differences could be the cause or the consequence of variables as yet unidentified that may interact with the brain in determining sexual orientation.

Swaab & Hofman (1995) contend that structural differences in the hypothalamus might be related to sexual orientation and that sexual differentiation of the hypothalamus takes place between about 4 years of age and puberty. However, the researchers caution that these observations await further confirmation, and their exact functional implications are not yet understood. Bailey and Zucker (1995) maintain that there is empirical evidence to support the notion that "childhood sex-typed behavior and sexual orientation are subject to similar hormonal influences (whether or not they are affected by the same brain structures)" (p. 50).

Sexual Orientation: Is There a Genetic Connection? Researchers looking for a genetic contribution to sexual orientation suggest that a number of "feminizing" genes work together to shift male brain development in the female direction (Miller, 2000). If only a few of these feminizing genes are acting, males who inherit them are more tender-minded and sensitive. But if many such genes are active during development, their effect probably contributes to homosexuality. Moreover, a similar effect may occur with other genes, resulting in lesbianism in females (Miller, 2000). In earlier research on the influence of heredity on sexual orientation, Bailey and Pillard (1991) studied gay males who had twin brothers. They found that 52% of the gay identical twins and 22% of the gay fraternal twins had a gay twin brother. Of the gay twins who had adoptive brothers, however, only 11% shared a homosexual orientation. In a similar study, Whitam and others (1993) found that 66% of the identical twins and 30% of the fraternal twins of gay males studied were also gay. Such studies indicate a substantial genetic influence on sexual orientation, but suggest that nongenetic influences are at work as well.

According to Bailey and Benishay (1993), "female homosexuality appears to run in families" (p. 277). They found that 12.1% of their lesbian participants had a sister who was also lesbian, compared with 2.3% of heterosexual female participants. Bailey and others (1993) report that in a study of lesbians, 48% of their identical twins, 16% of their fraternal twins, 14% of their nontwin biological sisters, and 6% of their adopted sisters were also lesbian. Bailey and Pillard (1994) claim that, according to their statistical analysis, the heritability of sexual orientation is about 50%.

Hamer and others (1993) found that brothers of gay participants had a 13.5% chance of also being gay. Furthermore, male relatives on the participants' mother's side of the family, but not on the father's side, had a significantly higher rate of homosexuality. This led the researchers to suspect that a gene influencing sexual orientation might be located on the X chromosome, the sex chromosome contributed by the mother. After studying the DNA on the X chromosomes of 40 pairs of gay brothers, the researchers found that 33 of the pairs carried matching genetic information on the end tip of the X chromosome. But an exact gene has not been identified from among the several hundred genes carried on that end tip. And precisely how the gene might influence sexual orientation is not known (LeVay & Hamer, 1994). Some researchers have questioned the validity of Hamer's findings, and a colleague has charged that Hamer excluded from the study some pairs of brothers whose sexual orientations contradicted his findings (Horgan, 1995).

Do the findings of LeVay, Hamer and others, and Bailey and Pillard provide convincing evidence that sexual orientation is biologically determined? Some researchers (Byne, 1993; Byne & Parsons, 1993, 1994) maintain that, in the absence of studies of identical twins reared *apart,* the influence of environment cannot be ruled out as the cause of a higher incidence of homosexuality in certain families. Furthermore, they suggest that if one or more genes are involved, they may not be genes directly influencing sexual orientation. Rather, they could be genes affecting personality or temperament that could influence how people react to environmental stimuli (Byne, 1994). Let's explore early environmental influences.

The Developmental Experiences of Gay Men and Lesbians

What does the study by Bell, Weinberg, and Hammersmith reveal about the developmental experiences of gay men and lesbians?

Some evidence suggests that sexual orientation, whether homosexual or heterosexual, is established by early childhood (Marmor, 1980; Money, 1987).

The Bell, Weinberg, and Hammersmith Study Bell, Weinberg, and Hammersmith (1981) conducted extensive face-to-face interviews with 979 homosexual participants (293 women, 686 men) and 477 heterosexual controls. The researchers found no single condition of family life that in and of itself appeared to be a factor in either homosexual or heterosexual development. But, as children, the homosexuals they interviewed did not feel they were like others of their sex.

Early Effeminate Behavior in Boys: What Does It Mean? Some researchers have suggested that boys and girls who do not show typical gender-role behavior, but rather are seen as sissies or tomboys, may be more likely to be homosexual (Green, 1985, 1987). Zuger (1990) believes that, in many cases, early and extreme effeminate behavior in boys is an early stage of homosexuality. Such effeminate behavior might include a boy's cross-dressing, expressing the desire to be a girl or insisting that he is in fact a girl, and/or preferring girls as playmates and girls' games over boys' games and sports.

This early effeminate pattern is not characteristic of all gay males by any means. In a study of sexual orientation and childhood memories of gender-conforming and nonconforming behaviors, Phillips and Over (1992) found that 36% of gay males (22 out of 61 participants) recalled "few, if any, of the gender conforming behaviors, and most, if not all, of the gender nonconforming behaviors" (p. 543). But, like heterosexual men, about 30% of the gay men (18 of the 61 participants) recalled gender-conforming childhood experiences. In another study, Bailey and others (1995) found a strong association between sexual orientation and sex-typed behavior in childhood as recalled by both gay men and their mothers. However, some gay men exhibited masculine sex-typed behavior, and some heterosexual men were "feminine" boys.

In another study of recalled childhood experiences and sexual orientation, Phillips and Over (1995) found that heterosexual women could be distinguished from lesbian women with 80% accuracy, on the basis of recalled childhood experiences. The lesbian women were more likely to recall imagining themselves as males, preferring boy's games and being called "tomboys." Yet, some heterosexual women recalled childhood experiences similar to those of the majority of lesbians, and some lesbians recalled experiences more like those of the majority of heterosexual women. Using meta-analysis, Bailey and Zucker (1995) found that cross-gender behavior could be a predictor of homosexuality for both females and males.

Researchers continue to disagree on the genesis of sexual orientation. Psychologist Charlotte Patterson (1995) suggests that the relationship between sexual orientation and human development can be studied more profitably as a complex interaction of nature and nurture.

Social Attitudes toward Gays and Lesbians: From Celebration to Condemnation

homophobia: An intense, irrational hostility toward or fear of homosexuals.

The American Psychiatric Association considered homosexuality a disorder until 1973, but now views it as such only if the individual considers it a problem. Lesbians and gay men appear to be as healthy psychologically as their heterosexual counterparts (Strickland, 1995).

In contrast to most researchers who remain open-minded, many people are homophobic. **Homophobia** is an intense, irrational hostility toward or fear of homosexuals; in its extreme form homophobia can lead to ridicule, beatings, and even murder (Greer, 1986).

Negative attitudes toward homosexuality are common in U.S. society (Katz, 1995). In one survey, 45% of male respondents believed gays should "stay in the closet"; only 30% of female respondents expressed such a belief (Moore, 1993). Thirty-four percent of males, compared with 42% of females, considered homosexuality an acceptable lifestyle (Hugick, 1992). Heterosexual male college students hold more negative attitudes about gay males than about lesbians (Louderback & Whitley, 1997). Whitley and Kite (1995) reported results of a meta-analysis that found that heterosexual men *did* have more negative attitudes toward homosexuality than heterosexual women did. Both White and Black heterosexuals who believe that sexual orientation is chosen have more negative attitudes toward homosexuality than those who believe it is inborn (Herek & Capitanio, 1995).

Marsiglio (1993) found that Hispanic males were more likely than non-Hispanic males to say that they would befriend a gay male. The variable most predictive of positive attitudes toward gay males, according to Herek and Glunt (1993), was whether the person reported interpersonal contact with gay men.

Social attitudes toward homosexuality appear to be moving slowly toward acceptance. In the United States today, men continue to hold more negative attitudes about homosexuality than women do.

Remember It!

1. The direction of one's sexual preference—toward members of the opposite sex or members of one's own sex—is termed
   a. sexual role.
   b. sexual identification.
   c. sexual leaning.
   d. sexual orientation.
2. Statistics suggest that homosexuality is twice as common in males as in females. (true/false)
3. Which of the following factors has the *least* research support as a biological explanation of sexual orientation?
   a. genetic factors
   b. variations in adult levels of androgens and estrogen
   c. levels of androgens during prenatal development
   d. structural differences in an area of the hypothalamus in gay males
4. Which of the following did Bell, Weinberg, and Hammersmith's study reveal about their gay and lesbian participants?
   a. They were likely to have been seduced or molested by adult homosexuals.
   b. As adolescents, they did not have normal opportunities for dating.
   c. As children, they did not feel that they were like others of their gender.
   d. As children, they had disturbed relationships with their parents.
5. As children, lesbians and gay men were usually more interested in (gender-conforming, gender-nonconforming) activities?

Answers: 1. d 2. true 3. b 4. c 5. gender-nonconforming

sexual dysfunction: A persistent or recurrent problem that causes marked distress and interpersonal difficulty and that may involve some combination of the following: sexual desire, sexual arousal or the pleasure associated with sex, or orgasm.

hypoactive sexual desire disorder: A sexual dysfunction marked by little or no sexual desire or interest in sexual activity.

sexual aversion disorder: A sexual desire disorder characterized by an aversion to or a desire to avoid genital contact with a sexual partner.

SEXUAL DYSFUNCTIONS

Like the course of true love, the course of sexual functioning is not always smooth. Although most people experience sexual problems some of the time, a sizable number of women and men are plagued with sexual dysfunctions, which eliminate or at least decrease the pleasures of sex (see Figure 12.4). A **sexual dysfunction** is a persistent or recurrent problem that may involve any or a combination of the following: sexual desire, sexual arousal or the pleasure associated with sex, or orgasm.

Sexual dysfunctions cause much distress and interpersonal difficulty, but can be treated through behavioral or biological therapy. The most widely used system for classifying these dysfunctions is found in the American Psychiatric Association's *Diagnostic and Statistical Manual of Mental Disorders-IV* (DSM-IV) (1994). This manual groups sexual dysfunctions into four main categories: sexual desire disorders, sexual arousal disorders, orgasmic disorders, and sexual pain disorders.

Sexual Desire Disorders: Form Disinterest to Aversion

What are two sexual desire disorders and their defining features?

Disorders of sexual desire involve a lack of sexual desire and/or an aversion to genital sexual contact. One of the most common complaints of people who see sex therapists is low or nonexistent sexual desire or interest in sexual activity. This condition is known as **hypoactive sexual desire disorder** (Beck, 1995). Such people may be unreceptive to the sexual advances of their partners, or they may participate in spite of their lack of desire. Loss of desire or lack of interest could stem from depression, emotional stress, marital dissatisfaction, or repeated unsuccessful attempts at intercourse. In men who are middle-aged and older, a decline in sexual interest may be related to a decline in testosterone levels that occurs as men age (Brody, 1995).

A more severe problem is **sexual aversion disorder**—an "aversion to and active avoidance of genital contact with a sexual partner" (American Psychiatric Association, 1994, p. 499). People with this condition experience emotions ranging from anxiety or fear to disgust when confronted with a sexual situation. In some cases, a sexual aversion stems from a sexual trauma such as rape or incest.

Sexual Arousal Disorders

What are the sexual arousal disorders and their defining features?

Sexual arousal disorders are characterized by a persistent inability to attain or maintain psychophysiological arousal until the completion of sexual activity.

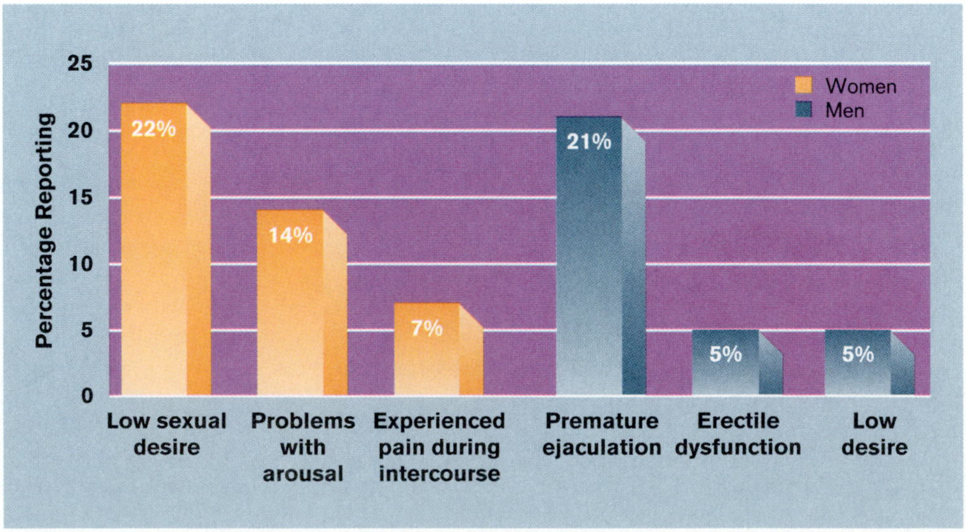

Figure 12.4

Types of Sexual Dysfunction Reported by Women and Men

Today, more women than men report experiencing some type of sexual dysfunction. And the most common problem cited by woman is lack of desire for sex. (American Medical Association, 1995–2000)

A woman with **female sexual arousal disorder** may not feel sexually aroused in response to sexual stimulation, or she may be unable to achieve or sustain "an adequate lubrication-swelling response to sexual excitement" (American Psychiatric Association, 1994, p. 500). The problem may stem from the trauma of rape or childhood sexual abuse, from resentment toward one's partner, or from vaginal dryness due to reduced estrogen production.

A common sexual dysfunction reported in men is **male erectile disorder**—the repeated inability to have or sustain an erection firm enough for coitus. This disorder (more widely known as impotence or erectile dysfunction) can take different forms: the inability to have an erection at all, having one but losing it, or having a partial erection that is not adequate for intercourse. Some men have firm erections under some conditions but not under others (with one sexual partner but not with another, or during masturbation but not during intercourse). The term *erectile disorder* does not apply to the failures all males have on occasion as a result of fear or anxiety, physical fatigue, illness, or drinking too much alcohol.

In a study of 1,290 men aged 40 to 70, 52% were found to have some degree of erectile disorder, with the likelihood increasing with age. The prevalence of complete erectile disorder ranged from 5% in men aged 40 to 15% in men aged 70 (Feldman et al., 1994). Male erectile disorder may be physical or psychological in origin, but most cases involve some combination of the two (Ackerman & Carey, 1995; Rosen, 1996). Physical causes may include diabetes, alcoholism, and drugs such as cocaine, amphetamines, barbiturates, tranquilizers, and blood pressure medication. When the cause is physical, the problem usually develops gradually over a period of months or years, and the man *always* has difficulty achieving an erection, in all circumstances (Lizza & Cricco-Lizza, 1990). But if a man awakens to find himself with an erection, even occasionally, he can usually rule out a physical cause.

The most common cause of erectile disorder is *performance anxiety.* When a man fails repeatedly to achieve an erection, his worst psychological enemy is the fear that he will not be able to have an erection when he most wants one. A number of medical treatments have been found to be effective in treating this problem (Rosen, 1996).

female sexual arousal disorder: A sexual dysfunction in which a woman may not feel sexually aroused in response to sexual stimulation or may be unable to achieve or sustain an adequate lubrication-swelling response to sexual excitement.

male erectile disorder: The repeated inability to have or sustain an erection firm enough for coitus; erectile dysfunction, or impotence.

female orgasmic disorder: The persistent inability of a woman to reach orgasm, or a delay in reaching orgasm despite adequate sexual stimulation.

male orgasmic disorder: A sexual dysfunction in which there is an absence of ejaculation, or in which ejaculation occurs only after strenuous effort over a prolonged period.

premature ejaculation: A chronic or recurring orgasmic disorder in which orgasm and ejaculation occur with little stimulation, before, during, or shortly after penetration and before the person desires it.

Orgasmic Disorders

What are the three orgasmic disorders and the defining features of each?

Three disorders involve a persistent and recurrent problem at the orgasm stage of the sexual response cycle. They are female orgasmic disorder, male orgasmic disorder, and premature ejaculation.

The most common sexual dysfunction in women is **female orgasmic disorder**—a persistent inability to reach orgasm or a delay in reaching orgasm despite adequate sexual stimulation. Some women have never been able to reach orgasm; others who were formerly orgasmic no longer can achieve orgasm. Some women are able to have orgasms only under certain circumstances or during certain types of sexual activity, while others have orgasms only from time to time. Women with this disorder may be uninterested in sex, or they may still find it exciting, satisfying, and enjoyable, despite the lack of orgasms.

In **male orgasmic disorder** there is an absence of ejaculation, or ejaculation occurs only after strenuous effort over an extremely prolonged period. Sometimes both partners may nearly collapse from exhaustion before the male finally reaches orgasm or gives up. The delay in or absence of ejaculation usually occurs during intercourse, rather than during manual or oral stimulation or during masturbation. Suspected causes are alcoholism or use of drugs (illicit or prescription), an overly strict religious background, stressful or traumatic life situations, or fear of impregnating one's partner (Kaplan, 1974).

The most common sexual dysfunction in males is **premature ejaculation**—a chronic or recurring condition in which orgasm and ejaculation occur with little stimulation, before, during, or shortly after penetration and before the man wishes (American Psychiatric Association, 1994). This condition sometimes results when a

dyspareunia (dis-PAH-roo-nee-yah): A sexual pain disorder marked by genital pain associated with sexual intercourse, more comon in females than in males.

vaginismus (VAJ-ah-NIZ-mus): A sexual pain disorder in which involuntary muscle contractions tighten and close the vagina, making intercourse painful or impossible.

sexually transmitted diseases (STDs): Infections that are spread primarily through intimate sexual contact.

man feels hostility toward his partner. It may also have its origins in early sexual experiences that called for quick ejaculation, such as hurried masturbation or fast, impersonal sexual release with a prostitute. Some recent research suggests that SSRI antidepressants (those that increase the action of the neurotransmitter serotonin) are effective in helping some men with this problem (Balon, 1996).

Sexual Pain Disorders

Sexual pain disorders are common in women but infrequent in men (Rosen & Leiblum, 1995). **Dyspareunia,** genital pain associated with sexual intercourse, is much more common in women. Inadequate lubrication is the major cause, although vaginal infections, sexually transmitted diseases, and various psychological factors may also be involved.

Vaginismus is a sexual dysfunction in which involuntary muscle contractions tighten and even close the vagina, making intercourse painful or impossible. The problem may stem from a rigid religious upbringing in which sex was looked on as sinful and dirty. It may also stem from past experiences of extremely painful intercourse or from a fear of men, rape, or other traumatic experiences associated with intercourse (Kaplan, 1974).

Remember It!

Match the appropriate description with each sexual disorder.

____ (1) male erectile disorder	a. inability to reach orgasm
____ (2) vaginismus	b. inability to control ejaculation
____ (3) premature ejaculation	c. lack of sexual interest
____ (4) female orgasmic disorder	d. inability to have or maintain an erection
____ (5) female sexual arousal disorder	e. an involuntary closing of the vagina
____ (6) hypoactive sexual desire disorder	f. inability to feel sexually excited and to lubricate sufficiently

Answers: 1. d 2. e 3. b 4. a 5. f 6. c

SEXUALLY TRANSMITTED DISEASES: THE PRICE OF CASUAL SEX

What are the major bacterial and viral infections known as sexually transmitted diseases?

Sexually transmitted diseases (STDs) are infections spread primarily through sexual contact. The incidence of many sexually transmitted diseases has increased dramatically since the early 1970s. This can be explained in part by more permissive attitudes toward sex and an increase in sexual activity among young people, some of whom have sexual contact with multiple partners (Turner et al., 1995). Another factor is the greater use of nonbarrier methods of contraception such as the pill. Barrier methods, such as condoms and vaginal spermicide, provide some protection against STDs.

Some of the serious sexually transmitted diseases are bacterial infections such as chlamydia, gonorrhea, and syphilis, which are curable; and viral infections such as genital warts, genital herpes, and AIDS, which are not curable.

Each year about 12 million Americans contract a sexually transmitted disease (Tanfer, 1994), and 56 million Americans—one in five—already have been infected with an incurable STD-causing virus other than HIV (Barringer, 1993). Minority populations in U.S. inner cities are experiencing an epidemic in STDs, as are people in developing countries (Piot & Islam, 1994). Worldwide, 250 million people contract STDs each year (Quinn, 1994).

How much do you already know about the major sexually transmitted diseases? To find out, complete the *Try It!*

Try It!

Choose the correct answer to each item.

1. 40 million Americans currently have ______________.
   a. HIV/AIDS b. herpes c. chlamydia
2. Which of the following bacterial STDs do experts call the "silent epidemic"?
   a. scabies b. chlamydia c. trichomoniasis
3. Which of the following groups is at greatest risk for STDs?
   a. men under 25 b. women under 25 c. men 25 to 40
4. Which STD should sexually active young people be immunized against?
   a. chlamydia b. herpes c. hepatitis B
5. Which of the following STDs can be cured?
   a. herpes b. ghonorrhea c. genital warts
6. For women, the most common symptom of chlamydia or gonorrhea infection is ______________.
   a. vaginal discharge b. genital sores/blisters c. a lack of symptoms

Answers: 1. b 2. b 3. b 4. c 5. b 6. c

The Bacterial Infections: The Curable STDs

Chlamydia Many people have never heard of **chlamydia,** but 478,000 new cases were reported in the United States in 1996 (U.S. Bureau of the Census, 1997). About 10% of all college students have chlamydia, and it is highly infectious. Women have a 70% risk of contracting chlamydia from an infected man in any single sexual encounter; men have a 25–50% risk in a single encounter.

Why do chlamydia and gonorrhea pose a greater threat to women than to men?

chlamydia (klah-MIH-dee-uh): The most common bacterial STD found in both sexes, and one that can cause infertility in females.

pelvic inflammatory disease (PID): An infection in the female pelvic organs, which can result from untreated chlamydia or gonorrhea and can cause pain, scarring of tissue, and even infertility or ectopic pregnancy.

Men with chlamydia are likely to have symptoms that alert them to the need for treatment, but they suffer no adverse reproductive consequences from the infection. Women, on the other hand, typically have only mild symptoms or no symptoms at all when chlamydia begins in the lower reproductive tract. Therefore, the infection often goes untreated and spreads to the upper reproductive tract, where it can cause **pelvic inflammatory disease (PID)**. PID often produces scarring of tissue in the fallopian tubes, which can result in infertility or ectopic pregnancy—a pregnancy in which the fertilized ovum is implanted outside of the uterus (Temmerman, 1994; Weström, 1994). Fortunately, chlamydia can be cured with antibiotics, which should be given to both partners.

Gonorrhea In 1998, in the United States, 355,131 cases of **gonorrhea** were reported to the Centers for Disease Control; this number represented nearly 133 cases per 100,000 population. The rate rose from 122 cases per 100,000 population in 1997 (National Center for Health Statistics, 1998). A woman having intercourse one time with an infected partner runs a 50% risk of contracting gonorrhea (Platt et al., 1983); a male has a 20–25% chance of developing gonorrhea after one such exposure.

Within the first 2 weeks after contracting gonorrhea, 95% of men develop a discharge from the penis and experience painful urination (Schwebke, 1991a). Most seek treatment and are cured. If there are no symptoms present or if the individual does not seek treatment within 2 to 3 weeks, the infection may spread to the internal reproductive organs and eventually cause sterility. The bad news for women is that 50–80% of women who contract gonorrhea do not have early symptoms. The infection spreads from the cervix through the other internal reproductive organs, causing inflammation and scarring. About 20% of women with untreated gonorrhea develop pelvic inflammatory disease which carries the risk of sterility and ectopic pregnancy (Schwebke, 1991a). Gonorrhea can be cured with antibiotics (Levine et al., 1994).

Syphilis About 69,000 cases of **syphilis** were reported in the United States in 1996 (U.S. Bureau of the Census, 1997). The rate is particularly high "among inner city ethnic groups of low socioeconomic status" (Schwebke, 1991b, p. 44). Syphilis has been linked to the use of illicit drugs, particularly crack, because addicts often exchange sex for drugs (Gunn et al., 1995).

Left untreated, syphilis progresses in predictable stages. In the primary stage, a painless sore, or chancre (pronounced "shanker"), appears where the syphilis *spirochete*—the microorganism that causes syphilis—entered the body. This sore may go unnoticed, but even without treatment it will heal. In the second stage—secondary syphilis—a painless rash appears on the body, usually accompanied by a fever, sore throat, loss of appetite, fatigue, and headache. Again, without treatment these symptoms eventually disappear. Then the spirochetes enter the various tissues and organs of the body, where they may be inactive for anywhere from several years to a lifetime. About 30–50% of people with syphilis who remain untreated enter the final and terrible third stage, in which blindness, paralysis, heart failure, mental illness, and death result.

A pregnant woman in any stage of syphilis will infect the fetus. But syphilis can be stopped at any point in its development, except in the final stage, with strong doses of penicillin (Levine et al., 1994).

The Viral Infections: The Incurable STDs

Unlike the bacterial infections, the viral infections—genital warts, genital herpes, and AIDS—are incurable.

Genital Warts **Genital warts** are caused by a common sexually transmitted virus—the *human papillomavirus* (HPV). Genital warts, often resembling cauliflower in appearance, are found most often in the genital and anal regions. Blakeslee (1992) estimated that almost half of female teenagers in a number of U.S. cities are infected with HPV. And approximately 1 million new cases are reported annually (Penn, 1993).

Genital warts are caused by one of several different strains of HPV, and even after the warts are removed or disappear spontaneously, the virus remains latent in the body for years, making recurrences likely. Some strains of HPV that remain in the system are strongly related to genital cancer, particularly cervical cancer (Koutsky et al., 1992; Tinkle, 1990). In fact, HPVs may be linked to 85% or more of the cervical cancer cases in the United States (Ochs, 1994).

gonorrhea (gahn-ah-REE-ah): An STD that, in males, causes a puslike discharge from the penis; if untreated, females can develop pelvic inflammatory disease and possible infertility.

syphilis (SIF-ih-lis): An STD that progresses through three stages; if untreated, it can eventually be fatal.

genital warts: Growths that are caused by *human papillomavirus* (HPV), that often resemble cauliflower, and that are most often found in the genital and anal regions.

genital herpes (HER-peez): An STD caused by the herpes simplex virus (usually type 2) that results in painful blisters on the genitals; presently incurable, the infection usually recurs and is highly contagious during outbreaks.

acquired immune deficiency syndrome (AIDS): A devastating and incurable illness that is caused by HIV and progressively weakens the body's immune system, leaving the person vulnerable to opportunistic infections that usually cause death.

Genital Herpes In 1995 there were 500,000 new cases of **genital herpes** in the United States (Ubell, 1996). Already more than 30 million Americans are infected with this incurable virus (Catotti et al., 1993).

Why is genital herpes particularly upsetting to those who have it?

Genital herpes can be caused by two forms of the herpes simplex virus. The type 1 virus usually causes oral herpes—cold sores and fever blisters in the mouth—but as a result of oral sex may produce blisters on the genitals. The type 2 virus produces 80–90% of the cases of genital herpes and is transmitted through direct contact with infected genitals (Peter et al., 1982).

In genital herpes, painful blisters form on the genitals (or around the anus in homosexual men), fill with pus, and then burst, leaving open sores. It is at this point that a person is most contagious. After the blisters heal, the virus travels up nerve fibers to an area around the base of the spinal cord, where it remains in a dormant state but can flare up anew at any time. The first herpes episode is usually the most severe (Apuzzio, 1990); recurring attacks are typically milder and briefer. Although genital herpes is most contagious during an outbreak, it can be transmitted even when an infected person has no symptoms (Dawkins, 1990).

A survey of over 2,940 people with genital herpes revealed that its impact can be "serious and long-lasting," leaving people depressed, fearing rejection, and feeling isolated (Catotti et al., 1993).

Acquired Immune Deficiency Syndrome (AIDS) No sexually transmitted disease generates more fear or has more devastating consequences than **acquired immune deficiency syndrome (AIDS).** Although the first case was diagnosed in this country in 1981, there is still no cure for AIDS and no vaccine to protect against it. By the end of 1996, 581,429 cases of AIDS and 362,000 deaths from AIDS had been reported to the Centers for Disease Control (1997). According to the World Health Organization, worldwide statistics are that almost 6 million people have died from AIDS and 28 million people are infected with HIV (Mertens & Low-Beer, 1996).

What happens to a person from the time of infection with HIV to the development of full-blown AIDS?

You may already know a great deal about AIDS. Test your knowledge by completing the *Try It!*

Try It! Answer true or false for each statement.

1. AIDS is a single disease. (true/false)
2. AIDS symptoms vary widely from country to country, and even from risk group to risk group. (true/false)
3. Those at greatest risk for getting AIDS are people who have sex without using condoms, drug users who share needles, and infants born to AIDS-infected mothers. (true/false)
4. AIDS is one of the most highly contagious diseases. (true/false)
5. One way to avoid contracting AIDS is to use an oil-based lubricant with a condom. (true/false)

Answers:

1. False: AIDS is not a single disease. Rather, a severely impaired immune system leaves a person with AIDS highly susceptible to a whole host of infections and diseases.
2. True: In the United States and Europe, AIDS sufferers may develop Kaposi's sarcoma (a rare form of skin cancer), pneumonia, and tuberculosis. In Africa, people with AIDS usually waste away with fever, diarrhea, and symptoms caused by tuberculosis.
3. True: Those groups are at greatest risk. Screening of blood donors and testing of donated blood have greatly reduced the risk of contracting AIDS through blood transfusions. Today, women make up the fastest-growing group of infected people worldwide, as AIDS spreads among heterosexuals, especially in Africa.
4. False: AIDS is not among the most highly infectious diseases. You cannot get AIDS from kissing, shaking hands, or using objects handled by people who have AIDS.
5. False: *Do not* use oil-based lubricants, which can eat through condoms. Latex condoms with an effective spermicide are safer. Learn the sexual history of any potential partner, including HIV test results. Don't have sex with prostitutes.

Rudy Galindo, who has announced that he is HIV-positive, is shown here competing at the World Professional Figure Skating Championship in December 1999.

AIDS is caused by **HIV,** the **human immunodeficiency virus,** often referred to as the *AIDS virus.* When a person is first infected, HIV enters the bloodstream. This initial infection usually causes no symptoms, and the immune system begins to produce HIV antibodies. It is these antibodies that are detected in the AIDS test. Individuals then progress to the asymptomatic *carrier state,* in which they experience no symptoms whatsoever and thus can unknowingly infect others.

HIV attacks the immune system until it becomes essentially nonfunctional. The diagnosis of AIDS is made when the immune system is so damaged that victims develop rare forms of cancer or pneumonia or other so-called opportunistic infections. Such infections would not usually be serious in people with normal immune responses, but in those with a very impaired immune system, these infections can be serious and even life-threatening. At this point patients typically experience progressive weight loss, weakness, fever, swollen lymph nodes, and diarrhea, and 25% develop a rare cancer that produces reddish-purple spots on the skin. Other infections develop as the immune system weakens further.

Before developing a full-blown case of AIDS, some people develop less severe immune-system symptoms such as unexplained fevers, chronic diarrhea, and weight loss. The average time from infection with HIV to advanced AIDS is about 10 years, but the time may range from 2 years to as long as 15 years or more (Nowak & McMichael, 1995). The disease progresses faster in smokers, in the very young, in people over 50, and apparently, in women. AIDS also progresses faster in those who are repeatedly exposed to the virus and in those who were infected by someone in an advanced stage of the disease.

Currently researchers are testing drugs on people infected with HIV, and early detection of HIV infection can lead to life-prolonging medical intervention. Researchers have discovered that drugs known as *protease inhibitors,* in combination with some drugs such as AZT, can cause significant reductions in blood levels of HIV (Collier et al., 1996).

How is AIDS transmitted?

The Transmission of AIDS Researchers believe that HIV is transmitted primarily through the exchange of blood, semen, or vaginal secretions during sexual contact or when IV (intravenous) drug users share contaminated needles or syringes. In the United States about 22.6% of those with AIDS are IV drug users (U.S. Bureau of the Census, 1997). An estimated 50% of IV drug users are infected with HIV, whereas 20% of gay men carry the virus ("AIDS and Mental Health," 1994).

The rate of AIDS among gay men is high because many gay men have multiple sex partners, and because gay men are likely to have anal intercourse. Anal intercourse is more dangerous than coitus, because rectal tissue often tears during penetration, allowing HIV ready entry into the bloodstream.

It is a mistake to view AIDS as a disease confined to gay men, however. About 25% of the AIDS cases reported in the United States in 1996 were females, 40% of whom contracted it through heterosexual contact and 35.4% through IV drug abuse (U.S. Bureau of the Census, 1997). In Africa, where AIDS is believed to have originated, it strikes men and women equally, and heterosexual activity is believed to be the primary means of transmission (Abramson & Herdt, 1990). AIDS is transmitted 12 times more easily from infected men to women than vice versa (Padian et al., 1991).

About one-third of babies born to mothers with HIV will be infected before or during birth or as a result of breast feeding (Valleroy et al., 1990). The blood-bank industry claims that the chance of acquiring HIV from a blood transfusion is now 1 in 75,000 (Altman, 1992).

Figure 12.5 summarizes the means of transmission for male AIDS cases in the United States.

HIV (human immunodeficiency virus): The virus that causes AIDS.

The Psychological Impact of HIV Infection and AIDS What are the psychological effects on people who struggle to cope with this fearsome plague? The reaction to the news that one is HIV-positive is frequently a state of shock, bewilderment, confusion, or disbelief. Stress reactions to the news are typically so common and so

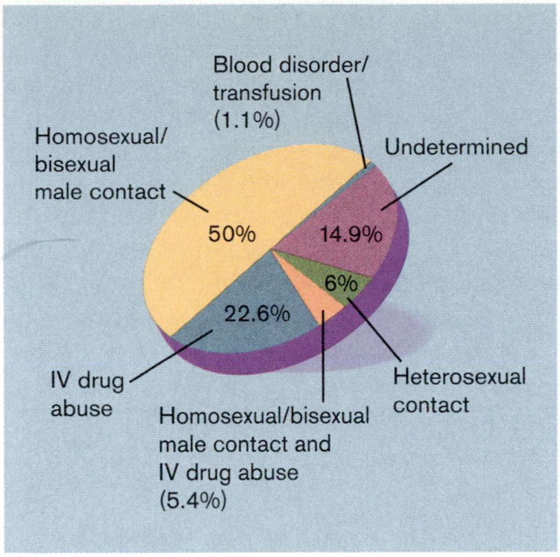

Figure 12.5

How HIV Was Transmitted in Adult/Adolescent AIDS Cases Reported in the United States

The primary means of transmission of HIV is through homosexual/bisexual male contact (50%). IV drug abuse (sharing needles) accounts for 22.6% of the AIDS cases in the United States. (U.S. Bureau of the Census, 1997)

acute that experts strongly recommend pretest counseling so that those who do test positive may know in advance what to expect (Maj, 1990). Another common reaction is anger—at past or present sexual partners, family members, health care professionals, or society in general. Often the response includes guilt, a sense that one is being punished for homosexuality or drug abuse. Other patients exhibit denial, ignoring medical advice and continuing to act as if nothing has changed in their lives. Then, of course, there is fear—of death, of mental and physical deterioration, of rejection by friends, family, or co-workers, of sexual rejection, of abandonment.

To cope psychologically, AIDS patients and those infected with HIV need education and information about the disease. They can be helped by psychotherapy, self-help groups, and medications such as antidepressants and antianxiety drugs. Self-help groups and group therapy may serve as a substitute family for some patients. An ever-present concern voiced by patients in psychotherapy is whether to tell others, and if so, what to tell them and how. Patients may feel a compelling need to confide in others and, at the same time, to conceal their condition.

Protection against Sexually Transmitted Diseases: Minimizing Risk

What are the most effective methods of protection against sexually transmitted diseases?

There are only two foolproof ways to protect oneself from becoming infected with a sexually transmitted disease through intimate sexual contact. The first is obvious—abstain from sexual contact. The second is to have a mutually faithful (monogamous) relationship with a partner free of infection. Anything short of these two courses of action will place a person at risk.

Discharges, blisters, sores, rashes, warts, odors, or any other unusual symptoms are warning signs of sexually transmitted diseases. Yet many people who have no visible symptoms carry STDs. And what you don't know *can* hurt you. People who choose to practice risky sex cannot be safe but can reduce the risks by using a latex condom along with a spermicide such as an intravaginal contraceptive foam, jelly, or cream.

The potential for risky sexual behavior is increased when people are under the influence of alcohol and other drugs (Leigh & Stall, 1993). People are putting themselves at risk for AIDS when they have multiple sex partners or if they have sex with prostitutes, IV drug users, or anyone carrying HIV. This potential risk was dramatically confirmed by basketball star Magic Johnson when he announced that he had tested positive for HIV. Several recent studies reveal that most young people, even those engaging in high-risk behavior, are ignoring the warnings about AIDS (Yam, 1995a). Despite intense efforts to promote the use of condoms, only a minority of sexually active individuals use condoms regularly (Catania et al., 1992).

Not only is it wise to have regular medical checkups, but anyone who fears that he or she might have been exposed to an STD should go to a doctor or clinic to be tested. Many STDs are easily treated, and serious complications can be avoided if the treatment is prompt. Obviously, anyone who has an STD should tell his or her partner so that the partner can be checked and treated.

STDs were curable until herpes and AIDS came on the scene. But today engaging in sexual intimacy with multiple partners or casual acquaintances is indeed a dangerous way to satisfy the sex drive. Much has been written in recent decades about the joy of sex. It is true that the pleasures sex brings to life are many—but chlamydia, gonorrhea, syphilis, genital warts, herpes, and AIDS are not among them.

Remember It!

1. Which STD causes painful blisters on the genitals and is usually recurring, highly contagious during outbreaks, and incurable?
   a. syphilis   c. genital herpes
   b. chlamydia   d. gonorrhea
2. Which of the following STDs, if left untreated, can eventually be fatal?
   a. syphilis   c. genital herpes
   b. gonorrhea   d. chlamydia
3. The two STDs most likely to cause infertility and ectopic pregnancy are
   a. syphilis and gonorrhea.
   b. syphilis and chlamydia.
   c. genital herpes and chlamydia.
   d. chlamydia and gonorrhea.
4. Since symptoms of STDs are usually more readily apparent in males, males are more likely to seek treatment and be cured. (true/false)
5. HIV eventually causes a breakdown in the ______________ system.
   a. circulatory   c. immune
   b. vascular   d. respiratory
6. The incidence of AIDS in the United States is highest among
   a. homosexuals and IV drug users.
   b. homosexuals and hemophiliacs.
   c. homosexuals and bisexuals.
   d. heterosexuals, IV drug users, and hemophiliacs.

Answers: 1. c 2. a 3. d 4. true 5. c 6. a

Apply It!

How to Improve Your Date-Seeking Skills

All right, so you think you have found Mr. or Ms. Right. So what do you do? How do you go about making a date?

Psychologists have learned that we can enhance our social skills, including our date-seeking skills, through the technique of *successive approximations.* That means that we can practice a series of tasks that are *graded in difficulty.* We can hone our social skills and gain self-confidence at each step. We can try out some of our skills on friends. Friends can role-play the prospective date and give honest feedback about our behavior.

Here is a series of graduated (step-by-step) tasks that may help you sharpen your own date-seeking skills.

Easy Practice Level

- Select a person with whom you are friendly but whom you have no desire to date. Practice making small talk about the weather, new films, TV shows, concerts, museum shows, political events, and personal hobbies.
- Select a person you might have some interest in dating. Smile when

you pass this person at work, school, or elsewhere, and say, "Hi." Engage in this activity with other people of both genders to increase your skills at greeting others.

- Speak into your mirror, using behavior rehearsal and role playing. Pretend you are in the process of sitting next to the person you would like to date, say, at lunch or in the laundry room. Say "Hello" with a broad smile, and introduce yourself. Work on the smile until it looks inviting and genuine. Make some comment about the food or the setting—the cafeteria, the office, whatever. Use a family member or confidant to obtain feedback about the effectiveness of the smile, your tone of voice, posture, and choice of words.

Medium Practice Level

- Sit down next to the person you want to date, and engage in small talk. If you are in a classroom, talk about a homework assignment, the seating arrangement, or the instructor (be kind). If you are at work, talk about the building or some recent interesting event in the neighborhood. Ask your intended date how he or she feels about the situation. If you are at a group meeting, such as Parents Without Partners, tell the other person that you are there for the first time and ask for advice on how to relate to the group.
- Engage in small talk about the weather and local events. Channel the conversation into an exchange of personal information. Give your "name, rank, and serial number"—who you are, your major field or your occupation, where you're from, why or how you came to the school or company. The other person is likely to reciprocate and provide equivalent information. Ask how he or she feels about the class, place of business, city, hometown, and so on.
- Rehearse asking the person out before your mirror, a family member, or a confidant. You may wish to ask the person out for a cup of coffee or to a film. It is somewhat less threatening to ask someone out to a gathering at which "some of us will be getting together." Or you may rehearse asking the person to accompany you to a cultural event, such as an exhibition at a museum or a concert—it's "sort of" a date, but also less anxiety-inducing.

Target Behavior Level

- Ask the person out on a date in a manner that is consistent with your behavior rehearsal. If the person says he or she has a previous engagement or can't make it, you might wish to say something like, "That's too bad" or "I'm sorry you can't make it" and add something like, "Perhaps another time." You should be able to get a feeling for whether the person you asked out was just seeking an excuse or has a genuine interest in you and, as claimed, could not in fact accept the specific invitation.
- Before asking the date out again, pay attention to his or her apparent comfort level when you return to small talk on a couple of occasions. If there is still a chance, the person should smile and return your eye contact. The other person might also offer you an invitation. In any event, if you are turned down twice, do not ask a third time. And don't make a catastrophe out of the refusal. Look up. Note that the roof hasn't fallen in. The birds are still chirping in the trees. You are still paying taxes. Then give someone else a chance to appreciate your fine qualities. (From Rathus et al., 2000)

THINKING CRITICALLY

Evaluation

What are some of the potential problems with information about sexual behavior and attitudes derived from surveys?

Point/Counterpoint

List the most persuasive arguments you can think of to justify each of the following:

a. Today it is easier to be a man than a woman.
b. Today it is easier to be a woman than a man.

Psychology in Your Life

Mary has sex with several partners, and she takes birth control pills to prevent pregnancy. She believes that she is careful in her choice of partners and that condoms are therefore not necessary in her case. Has Mary overlooked anything that could put her at risk?

SUMMARY AND REVIEW

WHAT MAKES A MALE, A MALE, OR A FEMALE, A FEMALE?

What are the biological factors that determine whether a person is male or female?

At conception the sex chromosomes are set—XY in males and XX in females. The primitive gonads develop into testes if the Y chromosome is present or into ovaries if it is absent. If sufficient levels of androgens are present, male genitals develop; if not, female genitals develop.

Key Terms
sex chromosomes (p. 426); biological sex (p. 426); gonads (p. 427); androgens (p. 427); genitals (p. 427); primary sex characteristics (p. 427); secondary sex characteristics (p. 427)

GENDER-ROLE DEVELOPMENT

What is gender typing, and what role do biological influences play in it?

Gender typing is the process by which people acquire the traits, behaviors, attitudes, preferences, and interests that the culture considers appropriate for their biological sex. Prenatal androgens are thought to influence brain development and tendencies toward aggression, sexual orientation, and children's play behavior.

What are the environmental factors that contribute to gender typing?

Parents, peers, the school, and the media each play a role in gender typing.

What are three theories of gender-role development?

Three theories of gender-role development are social learning theory, cognitive developmental theory, and gender-schema theory.

Key Terms
gender (p. 427); gender roles (p. 427); gender typing (p. 428); social learning theory (p. 429); cognitive developmental theory (p. 430); gender identity (p. 430); gender-schema theory (p. 430)

GENDER DIFFERENCES: FACT OR MYTH?

For what cognitive abilities have gender differences been proven?

Females outperform males in reading and writing; males seem to do better in science, math, and some spatial tasks. More males than females are found at the very highest levels of mathematics ability.

What gender differences are found in social behavior and personality?

The most consistent and significant gender difference is that males tend to be more physically aggressive than females. Females are more likely to use indirect aggression, to be more nurturant, more attuned to the feelings of others, and more people-oriented. Males tend to be more dominant, controlling, more object-oriented, and more competitive.

Do good adjustment and high self-esteem seem to be related to masculine, feminine, or androgynous traits?

Masculine traits appear to be related to better adjustment and high self-esteem in both males and females.

Key Term
androgyny (p. 435)

SEXUAL ATTITUDES AND BEHAVIOR

What were the famous Kinsey surveys?

In the 1940s and 1950s Alfred Kinsey and associates conducted the first major surveys of the sexual attitudes and behaviors of American men and women.

According to Masters and Johnson, what are the four phases of the human sexual response cycle?

The sexual response cycle consists of four phases: excitement phase, plateau phase, orgasm, and resolution phase.

What are the male and female sex hormones, and how do they affect sexual desire and activity in males and females?

The female sex hormones are estrogen and progesterone; the male sex hormones are the androgens, the most important of which is testosterone. Testosterone affects sexual interest and the ability to have an erection in males, and small amounts are necessary for females to maintain sexual interest and responsiveness.

What psychological and cultural factors influence sexual arousal?

Sexual arousal is influenced by the preferences and practices people learn from their culture. As a result of conditioning, individuals find certain stimuli sexually arousing. Males and females use sexual fantasies to heighten arousal, and men are more likely to seek out sexual stimulation from magazines or X-rated movies.

Key Terms
coitus (p. 438); sexual response cycle (p. 440); excitement phase (p. 440); plateau phase (p. 440); orgasm (p. 440); resolution phase (p. 441); estrogen (p. 441); progesterone (p. 441); testosterone (p. 441)

SEXUAL ORIENTATION

What is meant by sexual orientation?

Sexual orientation refers to the direction of a person's sexual preference—toward members of the opposite sex (heterosexuality), toward one's own sex (homosexuality), or toward both sexes (bisexuality).

What are the various biological factors that have been suggested as possible determinants of a gay or lesbian sexual orientation?

The biological factors suggested as possible causes of a gay or lesbian sexual orientation are (1) abnormal levels of androgens during prenatal development, which could masculinize or feminize the brain of the developing fetus; (2) structural differences in an area of the hypothalamus of gay men; and (3) genetic factors.

What does the study by Bell, Weinberg, and Hammersmith reveal about the developmental experiences of gay men and lesbians?

In comparing gay men and lesbians with heterosexual controls, Bell, Weinberg, and Hammersmith were unable to trace differences between the two groups to problems in parental relationships. The only commonality was that as children, gays did not feel that they were like others of their sex.

Key Terms
sexual orientation (p. 444); homophobia (p. 447)

SEXUAL DYSFUNCTIONS

What are two sexual desire disorders and their defining features?

Hypoactive sexual desire disorder is characterized by little or no sexual desire or interest; sexual aversion disorder, by an aversion to genital contact with a sexual partner.

What are the sexual arousal disorders and their defining features?

A woman with female sexual arousal disorder may not feel sexually aroused or become sufficiently lubricated in response to sexual stimulation. Male erectile disorder, or impotence, involves the repeated inability to have or sustain an erection firm enough for coitus.

What are the three orgasmic disorders and the defining features of each?

Female orgasmic disorder is the persistent inability of a woman to reach orgasm or a delay in reaching orgasm despite adequate sexual stimulation. In male orgasmic disorder there is an absence of ejaculation, or it occurs only after strenuous effort over a prolonged period. In premature ejaculation the male ejaculates with little stimulation, before he desires it.

Key Terms
sexual dysfunction (p. 448); hypoactive sexual desire disorder (p. 448); sexual aversion disorder (p. 448); female sexual arousal disorder (p. 449); male erectile disorder (p. 449); female orgasmic disorder (p. 449); male orgasmic disorder (p. 449); premature ejaculation (p. 449); dyspareunia (p. 450); vaginismus (p. 450)

SEXUALLY TRANSMITTED DISEASES: THE PRICE OF CASUAL SEX

What are the major bacterial and viral infections known as sexually transmitted diseases?

The major sexually transmitted diseases are chlamydia, gonorrhea, and syphilis (all curable bacterial infections), and genital warts, genital herpes, and AIDS (viral infections that presently are not curable).

Why do chlamydia and gonorrhea pose a greater threat to women than to men?

Chlamydia and gonorrhea pose a particular threat to women because, unlike men, women with these infections typically have no symptoms or very mild symptoms, making prompt treatment less likely. If the infection spreads, it may result in infertility or ectopic pregnancy.

Why is genital herpes particularly upsetting to those who have it?

Genital herpes causes painful blisters on the genitals, is usually recurring and highly contagious during outbreaks, and is incurable.

What happens to a person from the time of infection with HIV to the development of full-blown AIDS?

When a person is initially infected with HIV, the body begins to produce HIV antibodies, eventually detectable in a blood test. For a period of time the victim is without symptoms, but HIV gradually renders the immune system nonfunctional. The diagnosis of AIDS is made when the person succumbs to various opportunistic infections.

How is AIDS transmitted?

AIDS is transmitted primarily through the exchange of blood or semen during sexual contact or through the sharing of contaminated needles and syringes among IV drug users.

What are the most effective methods of protection against sexually transmitted diseases?

Abstinence or a monogamous relationship with a partner free of infection is the only foolproof way to protect yourself from acquiring an STD through intimate sexual contact. Failing this, avoid sex with multiple or anonymous partners, be on the lookout for symptoms of these diseases in a potential partner, and use a latex condom with a spermicide.

Key Terms
sexually transmitted diseases (STDs) (p. 450); chlamydia (p. 451); pelvic inflammatory disease (PID) (p. 451); gonorrhea (p. 452); syphilis (p. 452); genital warts (p. 452); genital herpes (p. 452); acquired immune deficiency syndrome (AIDS) (p. 453); HIV (human immunodeficiency virus) (p. 454)

Surf It!

Want to be sure you've absorbed the material in Chapter 12, "Human Sexuality and Gender," before the big test? Visiting *www.abacon.com/wood* can put a top grade within your reach. The site is loaded with free practice tests, flashcards, activities, and links to help you review your way to an A. To enliven that inevitable study break, the site also offers personality assessment quizzes and a psychology career corner.

13 Health and Stress

Many of us were introduced to him in the late 1980s as Alex P. Keaton, an endearing, Republican-to-the-core teen on the hit TV series *Family Ties.* Others loved him as Marty McFly, racing through time in a DeLorean in the *Back to the Future* trilogy. Still others came to know him best when he returned to prime time in 1996, portraying Michael Flaherty, New York's deputy mayor, on ABC's *Spin City.* A rich and famous, award-winning actor, with millions of adoring fans, Michael J. Fox's future looked bright.

Then, at the age of 30, Fox was diagnosed with Parkinson's disease, a debilitating degenerative disease that strikes the neural circuits in the brain that control movement. Symptoms of Parkinson's are slow or jerky movements, tremor, and garbled speech. This progressive disease worsens with time, and it is terminal.

For 7 long years, Fox kept his disease a secret from everyone but his family. He continued with his career at full tilt, appearing in more than a dozen films and TV shows, while also producing and directing. Later, in his testimony to a Senate subcommittee, Fox said, "While the changes in my life were profound and progressive, I kept them to myself for a number of reasons: fear, denial for sure, but I also felt that it was important for me to just quietly 'soldier on.'"

Can you imagine the heavy load of stress he endured to keep his illness a secret while constantly in the public eye? And what about the stress on his wife and children as well?

Finally, in 1998, Fox disclosed his condition to his friends and to the world. Two years later, he announced his retirement from *Spin City*, saying that he had decided to shift his focus away from the demanding world of producing and performing in a TV series. Instead, he wanted to spend time with his family and help find a cure for Parkinson's. Amid a flood of emotions, Fox waved good-bye to adoring fans after taping his 100th and final episode of *Spin City*.

Michael J. Fox is more than just a successful actor. He is an admirable man who has turned tragedy into triumph, and who now spends his time, his considerable financial resources, and his talents in the service of others. He chairs the Michael J. Fox Foundation for Parkinson's Disease Research to raise awareness about the disease and to search for a cure. He knows, first-hand, that one's health is far more important than fame or fortune.

Would you have advised Fox to keep his disease a secret? Why or why not? How would you cope with the stress of fighting a disease while working in the public eye?

In this chapter we discuss the many issues connected with health and stress. We begin our exploration by looking at stress, which we all experience and which is necessary for our survival, but which can disable or kill us if it is chronic and excessive.

STRESS: WHAT IS IT?

What is stress?

stress: The physiological and psychological response to a condition that threatens or challenges a person and requires some form of adaptation or adjustment.

fight-or-flight response: A response to stress in which the sympathetic nervous system and the endocrine glands prepare the body to fight or flee.

Most psychologists define **stress** as the physiological and psychological response to a condition that threatens or challenges an individual and requires some form of adaptation or adjustment. The word *stress* has mostly negative connotations in everyday life, but the stress response is an evolutionary reaction to danger that is absolutely essential for survival. During the stress response, or **fight-or-flight response,** first described by Walter Cannon in 1932, our bodies produce and release stress hormones. These include epinephrine (adrenaline) and other hormones that set in motion the forces that increase our heart rate and prepare our muscles to move us out of harm's way (Gold, 2000). Clearly, the stress response is adaptive and helpful when we are in danger. But if the stress response becomes a chronic state—that is, if it turns on but does not turn off appropriately—it can cause a number of health problems.

EVALUATING LIFE STRESS: MAJOR LIFE CHANGES, HASSLES, AND UPLIFTS

There are two major approaches to evaluating life stress and its relation to illness. One approach focuses on major life events, which cause life changes that require adaptation. A second approach focuses on life's daily hassles.

Holmes and Rahe's Social Readjustment Rating Scale: Adding Up the Stress Score

What was the Social Readjustment Rating Scale designed to reveal?

Researchers Holmes and Rahe (1967) developed the **Social Readjustment Rating Scale (SRRS)** to measure stress by ranking different life events from most to least stressful and assigning a point value to each event. Life events that produce the greatest life changes and require the greatest adaptation are considered the most stressful, regardless of whether the events are positive or negative. The 43 life events range from death of a spouse (assigned 100 stress points), to such items as divorce (73 points), death of a close family member (63 points), marriage (50 points), and pregnancy (40 points), to minor law violations such as getting a traffic ticket (11 points). Add up the number of stress points in your life—complete the *Try It!* on page 464.

Holmes and Rahe claim that there is a connection between the degree of life stress and major health problems. People who score 300 or more on the SRRS, the researchers say, run about an 80% risk of suffering a major health problem within the next 2 years. And those who score between 150 and 300 have a 50% chance of becoming ill within a 2-year period (Rahe et al., 1964).

Most researchers, however, do not consider a high score on the SRRS a reliable predictor of future health problems (Krantz et al., 1985; McCrae, 1984). One of the main shortcomings of the SRRS is that it assigns a point value to each life change without taking into account whether the change is for better or worse. For example, life changes such as divorce, pregnancy, retirement from work, and changing jobs or residences may be either welcome or unwelcome events.

Even positive life events, such as getting married, can cause stress.

The Hassles of Life: Little Things Stress a Lot

What roles do hassles and uplifts play in the stress of life, according to Lazarus?

Richard Lazarus disagrees with the rationale behind Holmes and Rahe's scale. He contends that life events cannot be assessed and assigned a numerical value for stressfulness without considering their meaning to the individual. Furthermore, he believes that the little stressors, which he calls **hassles,** add up to more stress than major life events.

Daily hassles are the "irritating, frustrating, distressing demands and troubled relationships that plague us day in and day out" (Lazarus & DeLongis, 1983, p. 247). Kanner and others (1981) developed the Hassles Scale to assess various categories of hassles. Unlike the Holmes and Rahe scale, the Hassles Scale takes into account that items may or may not represent stressors and that the amount of stress produced by an item varies from person to person. People completing the scale indicate the items that have been a hassle for them and rate the items for severity on a 3-point scale. Table 13.1 (on p. 465) shows the ten hassles most frequently reported by college students.

DeLongis and others (1988) studied 75 American couples over a 6-month period and found that daily stress (as measured on the Hassles Scale) related significantly to present and future "health problems such as flu, sore throat, headaches, and backaches" (p. 486). Several studies reveal that scores on the Hassles Scale are better than SRRS scores at predicting illness (DeLongis et al., 1982; Weinberger et al., 1987) and at predicting psychological symptoms such as anxiety and depression (Kanner

Social Readjustment Rating Scale (SRRS): Holmes and Rahe's stress scale, which ranks 43 life events from most to least stressful and assigns a point value to each.

hassles: Little stressors that include the irritating demands and troubled relationships that can occur daily and that, according to Lazarus, cause more stress than do major life changes.

Try It!

To assess your life in terms of life changes, check all of the events listed that have happened to you in the past year. Add up the points to derive your life stress score. (Based on data from Holmes & Masuda, 1974.)

Rank	Life Event	Life Change Unit Value	Your Points
1	Death of spouse	100	____
2	Divorce	73	____
3	Marital separation	65	____
4	Jail term	63	____
5	Death of close family member	63	____
6	Personal injury or illness	53	____
7	Marriage	50	____
8	Getting fired at work	47	____
9	Marital reconciliation	45	____
10	Retirement	45	____
11	Change in health of family member	44	____
12	Pregnancy	40	____
13	Sex difficulties	39	____
14	Gain of new family member	39	____
15	Business readjustment	39	____
16	Change in financial state	38	____
17	Death of close friend	37	____
18	Change to different line of work	36	____
19	Change in number of arguments with spouse	35	____
20	Taking out loan for major purchase (e.g., home)	31	____
21	Foreclosure of mortgage or loan	30	____
22	Change in responsibilities at work	29	____
23	Son or daughter leaving home	29	____
24	Trouble with in-laws	29	____
25	Outstanding personal achievement	28	____
26	Spouse beginning or stopping work	26	____
27	Beginning or ending school	26	____
28	Change in living conditions	25	____
29	Revision of personal habits	24	____
30	Trouble with boss	23	____
31	Change in work hours or conditions	20	____
32	Change in residence	20	____
33	Change in schools	20	____
34	Change in recreation	19	____
35	Change in church activities	19	____
36	Change in social activities	18	____
37	Taking out loan for lesser purchase (e.g., car or TV)	17	____
38	Change in sleeping habits	16	____
39	Change in number of family get-togethers	15	____
40	Change in eating habits	15	____
41	Vacation	13	____
42	Christmas	12	____
43	Minor violation of the law	11	____
		Life stress score:	____

Table 13.1 The Ten Most Common Hassles for College Students

Hassle	Percentage of Times Checked
1. Troubling thoughts about future	76.6
2. Not getting enough sleep	72.5
3. Wasting time	71.1
4. Inconsiderate smokers	70.7
5. Physical appearance	69.9
6. Too many things to do	69.2
7. Misplacing or losing things	67.0
8. Not enough time to do the things you need to do	66.3
9. Concerns about meeting high standards	64.0
10. Being lonely	60.8

Source: From Kanner et al., 1981.

et al., 1981). More recent research indicates that minor hassles that accompany stressful major life events are better predictors of the level of psychological distress than the major life events themselves (Pillow et al., 1996).

According to Lazarus, "a person's morale, social functioning, and health don't hinge on hassles alone, but on a balance between the good things that happen to people—that make them feel good—and the bad" (quoted in Goleman, 1979, p. 52). Fortunately, the **uplifts,** or positive experiences in life, may neutralize or cancel out the effect of many of the hassles. Lazarus and his colleagues also constructed an Uplifts Scale. As with the Hassles Scale, people completing the scale make a cognitive appraisal of what they consider an uplift. Items viewed as uplifts by some people may actually be stressors for other people. Kanner and others (1981) found that for middle-aged people, uplifts were often health- or family-related, whereas for college students uplifts often came in the form of having a good time.

Remember It!

1. On the Social Readjustment Rating Scale, only negative life changes are considered stressful. (true/false)
2. The Social Readjustment Rating Scale takes account of the individual's perceptions of the stressfulness of the life change in assigning stress points. (true/false)
3. According to Lazarus, hassles typically account for more life stress than major life changes. (true/false)
4. Lazarus's approach to measuring hassles and uplifts considers individual perceptions of stressful events. (true/false)

Answers: 1. false 2. false 3. true 4. true

uplifts: The positive experiences in life, which can neutralize the effects of many of the hassles.

SOURCES OF STRESS: THE COMMON AND THE EXTREME

Some stressors produce temporary stress, while others produce chronic stress—a state of stress that continues unrelieved over time. Chronic health problems, physical handicaps, poverty, and unemployment are sources of chronic stress. The burden of chronic stress is disproportionately heavy for the poor, for minorities, and for the elderly.

Everyday Sources of Stress

How do approach–approach, avoidance–avoidance, and approach–avoidance conflicts differ?

Everyday sources of stress can range from the need to make choices to the perception of a lack of control over one's life. And some people experience added stress from being a member of a minority group within the larger culture.

When we know we want to purchase a particular item but must choose between two similar versions of it, we are caught in the middle of an approach–approach conflict.

Making Choices: Should I or Shouldn't I? Sometimes conflicting motives can be sources of stress. When a person must make a choice between two desirable alternatives, known as an **approach–approach conflict,** stress may be the result. Some approach–approach conflicts are minor, such as deciding which movie to see. Others can have major consequences, such as the conflict between building a promising career or interrupting the career to raise a child. In approach–approach conflicts, both choices are desirable.

In an **avoidance–avoidance conflict** a person must choose between two undesirable alternatives. You may want to avoid studying for an exam, but at the same time you want to avoid failing the test. **Approach–avoidance conflicts** include both desirable and undesirable features in the same choice. The person facing this type of conflict is simultaneously drawn to and repelled by a choice—wanting to take a wonderful vacation but having to empty a savings account to do so.

How do the unpredictability and lack of control over a stressor affect its impact?

Unpredictability and Lack of Control Unpredictable stressors are more difficult to cope with than predictable stressors. Laboratory tests have shown that rats receiving electric shocks without warning develop more ulcers than rats given shocks just as often but only after a warning (Weiss, 1972). Likewise, humans who are warned of a stressor before it occurs and have a chance to prepare themselves for it experience less stress than those who must cope with an unexpected stressor.

Our physical and psychological well-being is profoundly influenced by the degree to which we feel a sense of control over our lives (Rodin & Salovey, 1989). Langer and Rodin (1976) studied the effects of control on nursing-home residents. Residents in one group were given some measure of control over their lives, such as choices in arranging their rooms and in the times they could see movies. They showed improved health and well-being and had a lower death rate than another group who were not given control. Within 18 months, 30% of the residents given no choices had died, compared with only 15% of those who had been given some control over their lives. Control is important for cancer patients, too. Some researchers suggest that for cancer patients a sense of control over their daily physical symptoms and emotional reactions may be even more important than control over the course of the disease itself (Thompson et al., 1993).

Several studies suggest that we are less subject to stress when we have the power to do something about it, whether we exercise that power or not. Glass and Singer (1972) subjected two groups of participants to the same loud noise. One group was told that they could, if necessary, terminate the noise by pressing a switch. This group (which had the control) suffered less stress even though they never did exercise the control they were given. Friedland and others (1992) suggest that when people experience a loss of control because of a stressor, they are motivated to try to reestablish control in the stressful situation. Failing this, they often attempt to increase their sense of control in other areas of their lives.

approach–approach conflict: A conflict arising from having to choose between desirable alternatives.

avoidance–avoidance conflict: A conflict arising from having to choose between undesirable alternatives.

approach–avoidance conflict: A conflict arising when the same choice has both desirable and undesirable features.

The Stress of Being Different A significant source of everyday stress is being a member of a minority group in a majority culture. A study of White and Black participants' responses to a questionnaire about ways of coping revealed that a person may experience *racial stress* from simply being one of the few or only members of a particular race in any of a variety of settings, such as a classroom, the workplace, or a social situation. The feeling of stress experienced in such situations can be intense, even in the absence of racist attitudes, discrimination, or any other overt evidence of racism (Plummer & Slane, 1996). Similarly, being gay or lesbian in straight majority settings is often stressful.

Stress in the Workplace

In the modern workplace, too many people find their jobs a source of chronic stress. Assembly-line workers and piece-goods workers must endure boring and repetitive jobs; doctors, nurses, and emergency ambulance personnel must deal with life and death every day. Even workers who hold more ordinary jobs can be subject to intense stress—the salesperson struggling to reach a quota, the manager fretting over the bottom line for the upcoming quarterly financial report. And employees in any field working under managers who hassle or threaten them may suffer from excessive work-related stress.

Occupational stress can be especially problematic for women, because of sex-specific stressors including sex discrimination and sexual harassment in the workplace and problems combining work and family roles. These added stressors have been shown to increase the negative effects of occupational stress on the health and well-being of working women (Swanson, 2000).

For people to function effectively and find satisfaction on the job, what nine variables should fall within their comfort zone?

Variables in Work Stress Everyone who works is subject to certain amounts of job-related stress, but the amount and sources of stress differ, depending on the type of job and the kind of organization. Albrecht (1979) suggests that if people are to function effectively and find satisfaction on the job, the following nine variables must fall within their comfort zone (also summarized in Figure 13.1 on p. 468):

- *Workload.* An overload of work—too much to do and too little time to do it in—causes people to feel anxious, frustrated, and unrewarded. Interestingly, just the opposite—work underload—produces similar feelings.
- *Clarity of job description and evaluation criteria.* The lack of a clearly defined role or confusion about performance criteria often causes anxiety and stress in workers. At the other extreme, a role that is too rigidly defined may leave insufficient room for creativity or individual initiative and may result in worker stress.
- *Physical variables.* Temperature, noise, humidity, pollution, and amount of work space should fall within a person's comfort zone. Being confined to a desk or having to work in fatiguing positions can also create stress.
- *Job status.* Extremes in job status can produce stress. People with very low status—garbage collectors, or janitors, for example—may feel psychological discomfort. At the other extreme, those with celebrity status often cannot handle the stress that fame brings.
- *Accountability.* Accountability has to do with the relationship between the perceived importance of the job and the amount of control a person has over its outcome. Accountability underload occurs when workers perceive their jobs as meaningless. Extreme overload occurs when people have responsibility for the

Figure 13.1
Variables in Work Stress

For a person to function effectively and find satisfaction on the job, these nine variables should fall within the person's comfort zone. (Based on Albrecht, 1979.)

physical or psychological well-being of others but only a limited degree of control, such as air-traffic controllers and emergency-room nurses and doctors.

- *Task variety.* Jobs can be deadly boring, repetitive, and monotonous. To function well, people need a comfortable amount of variety and stimulation.
- *Human contact.* Some workers have virtually no human contact on the job (forest-fire lookouts); others have almost continuous contact with others (welfare and employment-office workers). People vary greatly in how much interaction they enjoy or even tolerate.
- *Physical challenge.* Jobs range from physically demanding (construction work, professional sports) to those requiring no physical activity. Some jobs (fire fighting, police work) involve physical risk as well.
- *Mental challenge.* Jobs that tax people beyond their mental capability or training cause feelings of inadequacy and frustration. Yet jobs that require too little mental challenge are also frustrating.

Decision Latitude: A Critical Factor in Job Stress **Decision latitude** refers to the degree to which employees may exercise initiative and use their skills to control their working conditions. Jobs that involve a large workload but little latitude in or control over the pace and manner in which the work will be completed are highly stressful (Karasek & Theorell, 1990). According to Sauter and others (1990), machine-paced assembly workers report "the highest levels of anxiety, depression, and irritation, as well as more frequent somatic [bodily] complaints" (p. 1150).

In contrast are jobs like those of executives and professionals, in which high demand is coupled with a high degree of control over how the work will be done. In this case high demand is likely to be viewed as challenging and rewarding.

How much stress have you experienced in jobs you have had? Rate your stress in the *Try It!*

What are some of the psychological and health consequences of job stress?

decision latitude: The degree to which employees have the opportunity to exercise initiative and use their skills to control their working conditions.

Psychological and Health Consequences of Job Stress Job stress can have a variety of consequences. Perhaps the most frequent is reduced effectiveness on the job. But stress can also lead to absenteeism, tardiness, accidents, substance abuse, and lower morale. Workers who are experiencing stress often become alienated from their co-workers and may also suffer from headaches, exhaustion, back problems, insomnia, and indigestion. Stress can even lead to more serious illnesses, such as depression, high blood pressure, and cardiovascular disease.

Try It!

What are the sources of stress in a job you have now or have had in the past? Rate the job by indicating whether there is or was too little, too much, or about the right amount of each of the job dimensions listed. (Adapted from Albrecht, 1979.)

Job Dimension	Too Little	About Right	Too Much
Workload	________	________	________
Decision latitude	________	________	________
Clarity of job description	________	________	________
Task variety	________	________	________
Mental challenge	________	________	________
Physical demand	________	________	________
Human contact	________	________	________
Job status	________	________	________
Job security	________	________	________

Burnout When job stress is intense and unrelieved, many people suffer from **burnout,** a condition in which they become pessimistic, dissatisfied, inefficient on the job, and debilitated psychologically. Energy reserves are depleted, resistance to illness is lowered, and interest in work wanes. In the final stages of burnout, people may be unable to function. "Job burnout is not a symptom of work stress, it is the end of unmanaged work stress" (Rice, 1987, p. 223).

What is burnout?

Catastrophic Events and Chronic Intense Stress

How do people typically react to catastrophic events?

Environmental, social, physical, and emotional stressors are a fact of life for most people, but some people also experience catastrophic events such as plane crashes, fires, or earthquakes. Panic reactions are rare, except in situations such as fires in which people feel that they will survive only if they escape immediately. Many victims of catastrophic events react initially with such shock that they appear dazed, stunned, and emotionally numb. They seem disoriented and may wander about aimlessly, often unaware of their own injuries, attempting to help neither themselves nor others. Following this stage, victims show a concern for others, and although unable to act efficiently on their own, they are willing to follow the directions of rescue workers.

As victims begin to recover, the shock is replaced by generalized anxiety. Recovering victims typically have recurring nightmares and feel a compulsive need to talk about the event repeatedly. Reexperiencing the event through dreaming and retelling seems to help desensitize victims to the horror of the experience.

What is posttraumatic stress disorder?

Posttraumatic Stress Disorder: The Trauma Is Over, but the Stress Remains

Posttraumatic stress disorder (PTSD) is a prolonged and severe stress reaction to a catastrophic event (such as a plane crash or an earthquake) or to chronic intense stress (such as occurs in combat or imprisonment as a hostage or POW). Breslau and others (1991) found that 9% of a random sample of 1,007 adults aged 20 to 30 in metropolitan Detroit had suffered from posttraumatic stress disorder from a variety of events; 80% of the women with PTSD had been raped. Some researchers estimate

burnout: The result of intense, unrelieved, and unmanaged job stress; a condition in which an individual becomes pessimistic, dissatisfied, inefficient on the job, and debilitated psychologically.

posttraumatic stress disorder (PTSD): A prolonged and severe stress reaction to a catastrophic event or to chronic intense stress.

When writer Pico Iyer's home was destroyed by arson, he saved only his cat and his manuscript. A fairly common reaction to such catastrophic events is posttraumatic stress disorder.

that between 1% and 2% of Americans meet the diagnostic criteria for PTSD (Foa & Meadows, 1997). The disorder may show up immediately, or it may not occur until 6 months or more after the traumatic experience, in which case it is called *delayed posttraumatic stress disorder.* More than 400,000 Vietnam veterans were found to suffer from PTSD (Goldberg et al., 1990). And for female veterans, not only war trauma, but sexual trauma as well, was a contributing factor (Fontana et al., 1997). The most serious cases of PTSD have resulted from witnessing brutal atrocities, whether among Vietnam veterans, Cambodian refugees, Holocaust survivors, or victims of state-sanctioned terrorism and torture.

People with posttraumatic stress disorder often have flashbacks, nightmares, or intrusive memories that make them feel as though they are actually reexperiencing the traumatic event. They suffer increased anxiety and startle easily, particularly in response to anything that reminds them of the trauma (Green et al., 1985). Many survivors of war or catastrophic events experience survivor guilt because they lived while others died. Some feel that perhaps they could have done more to save others. Extreme combat-related guilt in Vietnam veterans is a risk factor for suicide or preoccupation with suicide (Hendin & Haas, 1991). And a study of women with PTSD revealed that they were twice as likely as women without PTSD to experience first-onset depression and three times as likely to develop alcohol use disorder (Breslau et al., 1997).

Research on 4,042 identical and fraternal twin pairs who were Vietnam veterans suggests a genetic susceptibility to posttraumatic stress symptoms. Identical twins were much more similar than fraternal twins in the posttraumatic stress symptoms they had in response to similar combat experiences (True et al., 1993). Moreover, some research has revealed that high intelligence seems to protect against symptoms of PTSD (McNally & Shin, 1995).

Can anything lessen the stress that follows a major trauma? According to Bloche and Eisenberg (1993), "Belief systems that give life a sense of purpose and meaning can prevent emotional damage" (p. 5).

Remember It!

1. Rick cannot decide whether to go out or stay home and study for his test. What kind of conflict does he have?
   a. approach–approach conflict
   b. avoidance–avoidance conflict
   c. approach–avoidance conflict
   d. ambivalence–ambivalence conflict
2. What factor or factors increase stress, according to research on the topic?
   a. predictability of the stressor
   b. unpredictability of the stressor
   c. predictability of and control over the stressor
   d. unpredictability of and lack of control over the stressor
3. In general, an assembly-line worker suffers more stress than a business executive because
   a. the workload is higher.
   b. the workload is lower.
   c. the decision latitude is higher.
   d. the decision latitude is lower.
4. Victims of catastrophic events typically want to talk about their experience. (true/false)
5. Posttraumatic stress disorder is a prolonged and severe stress reaction that results when a number of common sources of stress occur simultaneously. (true/false)

Answers: 1. c 2. d 3. d 4. true 5. false

THEORIES OF STRESS

Two leading theories of stress are the physiological theory of Hans Selye and the cognitive theory of Richard Lazarus.

stressor: Any stimulus or event capable of producing physical or emotional stress.

general adaptation syndrome (GAS): The predictable sequence of reactions (alarm, resistance, and exhaustion stages) that organisms show in response to stressors.

alarm stage: The first stage of the general adaptation syndrome, when there is emotional arousal and the defensive forces of the body are prepared for fight or flight.

resistance stage: The second stage of the general adaptation syndrome, when there are intense physiological efforts to either resist or adapt to the stressor.

Selye and the General Adaptation Syndrome

What is the general adaptation syndrome?

Hans Selye (1907–1982), the researcher most prominently associated with the effects of stress on health, established the field of stress research. Selye knew that all living organisms are constantly confronted with **stressors**—stimuli or events that place a demand on the organism to adapt or readjust. Each stressor causes both specific and nonspecific responses. Extreme cold, for example, causes the specific response of shivering. Apart from the specific response, the body makes a common, or nonspecific, response to a wide variety of stressors. The heart of Selye's concept of stress is the **general adaptation syndrome (GAS),** his term for the nonspecific response to stress. The syndrome consists of three stages: the alarm stage, the resistance stage, and the exhaustion stage (Selye, 1956). (See Figure 13.2.)

The body's first response to a stressor is the **alarm stage,** when emotional arousal occurs and the defensive forces of the body are prepared to meet the threat. In the alarm stage the sympathetic nervous system, through the release of hormones, mobilizes the body to fight or flee. Specifically, the hypothalamus signals the pituitary gland to release a hormone (ACTH), which in turn stimulates the adrenal cortex to release hormones known as *glucocorticoids.* The short-term effects of the glucocorticoids are essential for protecting the body from harm caused by stressors. Glucocorticoids raise blood-sugar levels, thereby supplying a burst of energy that helps the person deal with the stressful situation (Pennisi, 1997).

If the stressor cannot be quickly conquered or avoided, the organism enters the **resistance stage,** characterized by intense physiological efforts to either resist or adapt to the stressor. During the resistance stage the adrenal cortex continues to release the glucocorticoids to help the body resist stressors. Resistance may last a long time, but according to Selye, the length of the resistance stage depends both on the strength or intensity of the stressor and on the body's power to adapt. Seyle found that the most harmful effects of stress are due to the prolonged secretion of glucocorticoids. Such prolonged secretion can increase blood pressure, suppress the immune system, damage muscle tissue, weaken the body's ability to fight inflammation, and even cause damage to the hippocampus (Stein-Behrens et al., 1994).

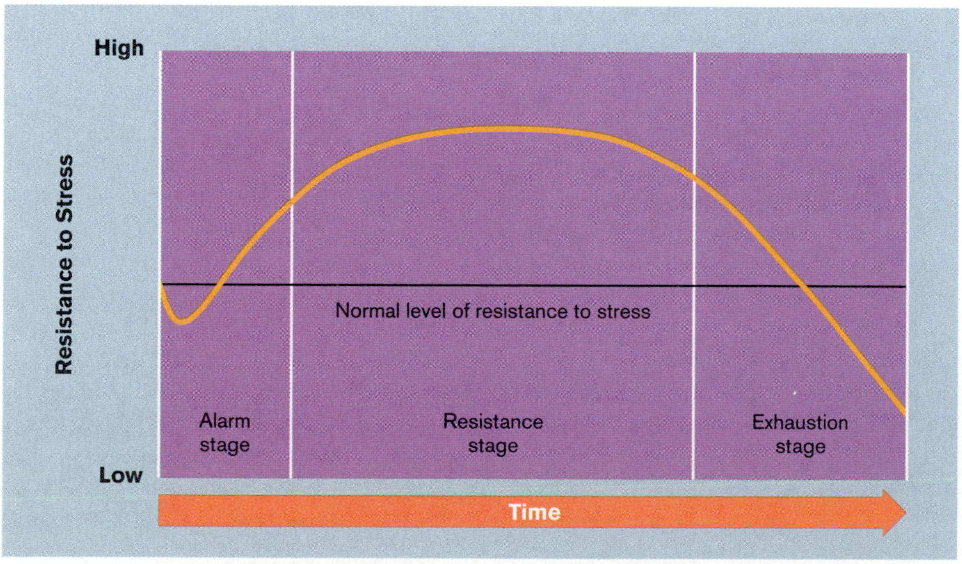

Figure 13.2

The General Adaptation Syndrome

The three stages in Hans Selye's general adaptation syndrome are (1) the alarm stage, during which there is emotional arousal and the defensive forces of the body are mobilized for fight or flight; (2) the resistance stage, in which intense physiological efforts are exerted to resist or adapt to the stressor; and (3) the exhaustion stage, when the organism fails in its efforts to resist the stressor. (Based on Selye, 1956.)

If the organism finally fails in its efforts to resist, it reaches the **exhaustion stage.** Selye (1974) wrote, "The stage of exhaustion after a temporary demand upon the body, is reversible, but the complete exhaustion of all stores of deep adaptation energy is not" (p. 29). If exposure to the stressor continues, all the stores of deep energy are depleted, and disintegration and death follow.

Selye claimed that any event requiring a readjustment, positive or negative, will produce stress in an organism. He did, however, differentiate between the positive and negative aspects of stress. "Eustress" is positive or good stress, including exhilaration, excitement, and the thrill of accomplishment. "Distress" is damaging or unpleasant stress, such as frustration, inadequacy, loss, disappointment, insecurity, helplessness, or desperation.

Thanks to Selye, the connection between extreme, prolonged stress and certain diseases is now widely accepted by medical experts. Critics pointed out that Selye's model was primarily formulated from research on laboratory rats. In addition, his theory does not provide for a psychological component—how a person perceives and evaluates the stressor. This criticism led to the development of the cognitive theory of stress.

Lazarus's Cognitive Theory of Stress

What are the roles of primary and secondary appraisal when a person is confronted with a potentially stressful event?

Richard Lazarus (1966; Lazarus & Folkman, 1984) contends that it is not the stressor itself that causes stress, but a person's perception of the stressor. Because Lazarus emphasizes the importance of perceptions and appraisal of stressors, his is a cognitive theory of stress and coping. Lazarus (1993) believes that physiological and psychological stress must be analyzed differently. Selye's model describes how the body copes with physiological stress; Lazarus's model focuses on how people cope with psychological stressors.

The Cognitive Appraisal of Stressors: Evaluating the Stressor and Considering the Options According to Lazarus, when people are confronted with a potentially stressful event, they engage in a cognitive process that involves a primary and a secondary appraisal. A **primary appraisal** is an evaluation of the meaning and significance of a situation—whether its effect on one's well-being is positive, irrelevant, or negative. An event appraised as stressful could involve (1) harm or loss—damage that has already occurred; (2) threat—the potential for harm or loss; or (3) challenge—the opportunity to grow or to gain. An appraisal of threat, harm, or loss can occur in relation to anything important to you—a friendship, a part of your body, your property, your finances, or your self-esteem.

The same event can be appraised differently by different people. Some students may welcome the opportunity to give an oral presentation in class, seeing it as a challenge and a chance to impress their professor and raise their grade. Other students may feel threatened, fearing that they may embarrass themselves in front of their classmates and lower their grade in the process. Still others may view the assignment as both a challenge and a threat. When people appraise a situation as involving harm, loss, or threat, they experience negative emotions such as anxiety, fear, anger, or resentment (Folkman, 1984). A challenge appraisal, on the other hand, is usually accompanied by positive emotions such as excitement, hopefulness, and eagerness. Stress for younger people is more likely to take the form of challenges; for older people, losses and threats are more common (El-Shiekh et al., 1989).

When people assess an event as stressful, they engage in a **secondary appraisal.** During secondary appraisal, if they judge the situation to be within their control, they make an evaluation of available coping resources—physical (health, energy, stamina), social (support network), psychological (skills, morale, self-esteem), material (money, tools, equipment), and time. Then they consider the options and decide how to deal with the stressor. The level of stress they feel is largely a function of whether their resources are adequate to cope with the threat, and how severely those resources will be taxed in the process.

exhaustion stage: The final stage of the general adaptation syndrome, occurring if the organism fails in its efforts to resist the stressor.

primary appraisal: An evaluation of the significance of a potentially stressful event according to how it will affect one's well-being—whether it is perceived as irrelevant or as involving harm or loss, threat, or challenge.

secondary appraisal: An evaluation of one's coping resources prior to deciding how to deal with a stressful event.

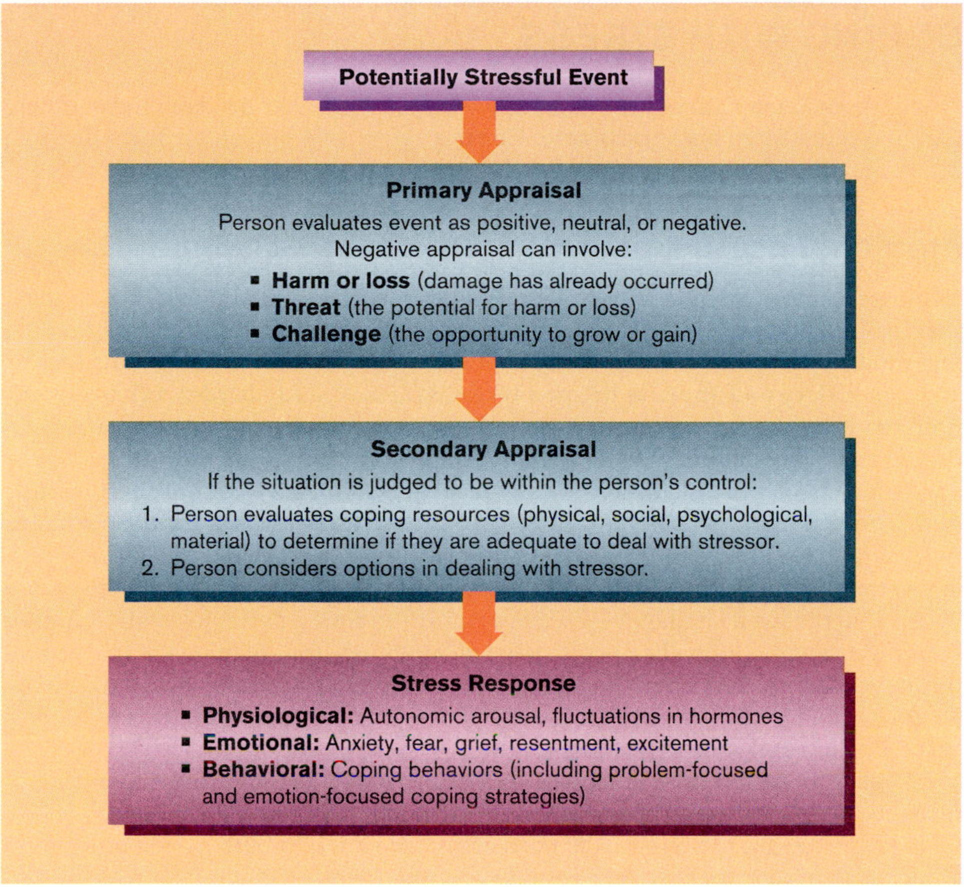

Figure 13.3

Lazarus and Folkman's Psychological Model of Stress

Lazarus and Folkman emphasize the importance of a person's perceptions and appraisal of stressors. The stress response depends on the outcome of the primary and secondary appraisals, whether the person's coping resources are adequate to cope with the threat, and how severely the resources are taxed in the process. (From Folkman, 1984.)

Figure 13.3 summarizes the Lazarus and Folkman psychological model of stress. There is research support for Lazarus and Folkman's claim that the physiological, emotional, and behavioral reactions to stressors depend partly on whether the stressors are appraised as challenging or threatening.

Remember It!

1. The stage of the general adaptation syndrome marked by intense physiological efforts to adapt to the stressor is the (alarm, resistance) stage.
2. Susceptibility to illness increases during the (alarm, exhaustion) stage of the general adaptation syndrome.
3. During secondary appraisal, a person
   a. evaluates his or her coping resources and considers options in dealing with the stressor.
   b. determines whether an event is positive, neutral, or negative.
   c. determines whether an event involves loss, threat, or challenge.
   d. determines whether an event causes physiological or psychological stress.
4. Selye focused on the (psychological, physiological) aspects of stress; Lazarus focused on the (psychological, physiological) aspects of stress.

Answers: 1. resistance 2. exhaustion 3. a 4. physiological; psychological

COPING WITH STRESS

When we encounter stressful situations, we try either to alter or to reinterpret them to make them seem more favorable. **Coping** refers to a person's efforts through action and thought to deal with demands perceived as taxing or overwhelming.

Problem-Focused and Emotion-Focused Coping

What is the difference between problem-focused and emotion-focused coping?

Coping strategies fall into two categories—problem-focused and emotion-focused (Lazarus & Folkman, 1984). **Problem-focused coping** is direct; it consists of reducing, modifying, or eliminating the source of stress itself. If you are getting a poor grade in history and appraise this as a threat, you may study harder, talk over your problem with your professor, form a study group with other class members, get a tutor, or drop the course.

But what can people do when they face stress that they cannot fight, escape from, avoid, or modify in any way? They can use **emotion-focused coping** to change the way they respond emotionally. Emotion-focused coping may involve reappraising a stressor. If you lose your job, you may decide that it isn't a major tragedy and instead view it as a challenge—an opportunity to find a better job with a higher salary. To cope emotionally, people may use anything from religious faith, wishful thinking, humor, or denial, to alcohol, drugs, or promiscuous sex (Lazarus & DeLongis, 1983). But misguided emotion-focused coping efforts can themselves become additional sources of stress.

Well-functioning people use a combination of problem-focused and emotion-focused coping in almost every stressful situation. Folkman and Lazarus (1980) studied the coping patterns of 100 participants over a 12-month period and found that both types of coping were used in 98% of the 1,300 stressful life events the participants had confronted. Not surprisingly, problem-focused coping strategies increased in situations participants appraised as changeable, and emotion-focused coping techniques increased in situations appraised as not changeable.

These ideas about coping have been tested in the workplace. Ninety volunteers in a high-stress media organization were given therapy training for 3 months. They were trained in acceptance commitment therapy (emotion-focused coping) and innovation promotion therapy (problem-focused coping). The participants learned to identify and change the causes of stress that were susceptible to change and to accept those that were unchangeable and, thus, reduce their stress on the job (Bond & Bunce, 2000).

The two types of coping are summed up well in an ancient prayer you may have heard: "Lord, grant me the strength to change those things that I can change [problem-focused coping], the grace to accept those things that I cannot change [emotion-focused coping], and the wisdom to know the difference."

coping: Efforts through action and thought to deal with demands that are perceived as taxing or overwhelming.

problem-focused coping: A response aimed at reducing, modifying, or eliminating a source of stress.

emotion-focused coping: A response aimed at reducing the emotional impact of the stressor.

proactive coping: Efforts or actions taken in advance of a potentially stressful situation to prevent its occurrence or to minimize its consequences.

Proactive Coping: Dealing with Stress in Advance

Most of our discussion of coping has explored ways of coping once stress has begun. Although stress is inevitable in life, many of the stressful situations people must endure are self-imposed, a result of a lack of planning. Some stressful situations can be anticipated in advance, allowing active measures to be taken to avoid or minimize them. Such active measures are known as *proactive coping* (Aspinwall & Taylor, 1997). **Proactive coping** consists of efforts or actions taken in advance of a potentially stressful situation to prevent its occurrence or to minimize its consequences.

The important feature of proactive coping is action itself. Proactive copers anticipate and then prepare for upcoming stressful events and situations, including those that are certain and those that are only likely. Worrying and dread are not ingredients of proactive coping. Worrying works only if it moves a person to plan and to act—that is, to use proactive coping.

The next time you feel stressed, use the coping technique featured in the *Try It!* This technique, known as *stress-inoculation training*, was designed by Donald Meichenbaum (1977). This program teaches people to recognize their own negative thoughts and to replace them with positive ones. In other words, people learn to talk to themselves using positive coping statements, which dispel worry and provide self-encouragement.

Try It!

Write a corresponding positive thought to replace each negative thought below. (Adapted from Meichenbaum, 1977.)

Negative Thought	Positive Thought
1. This problem is just too overwhelming.	______________________
2. When my boss confronts me about my mistake, I will be too intimidated to say anything intelligent.	______________________
3. I've got so many things on my mind, I know I won't get anything done today.	______________________
4. I'm too worked up to handle this situation well.	______________________
5. Managing my stress today was easier than I thought it would be. It must have been a fluke.	______________________

Suggested Answers:
1. I can come up with a plan to handle the problem.
2. If I feel fear, I will simply pause, consider what I want to say, and then say it calmly and confidently.
3. I will keep my mind focused on the present, on what is happening now, and just concentrate on what I have to do.
4. I will take a few slow, deep breaths and relax. Then I will consider the situation rationally.
5. I am really making progress. My efforts are paying off.

Remember It!

1. Coping aimed at reducing, modifying, or eliminating a source of stress is called (emotion-focused, problem-focused) coping; that aimed at reducing an emotional reaction to stress is called (emotion-focused, problem-focused) coping.
2. People typically use a combination of problem-focused and emotion-focused coping when dealing with a stressful situation. (true/false)
3. Proactive coping involves taking action (before, after) a stressor occurs.

Answers: 1. problem-focused; emotion-focused 2. true 3. before

HEALTH AND ILLNESS

Two Approaches to Health and Illness

How do the biomedical and biopsychosocial models differ in their approaches to health and illness?

Medical doctors and researchers are increasingly recognizing the part that nonbiological factors play in health and illness. For many decades the predominant view in medicine was the **biomedical model,** which focuses on illness rather than on health. It explains illness in terms of biological factors without considering psychological and social factors that might contribute to the condition.

Another approach is the **biopsychosocial model,** which focuses on health as well as illness. It holds that both are determined by a combination of biological, psychological, and social factors (Engel, 1977, 1980; Schwartz, 1982). It is this model that most health psychologists endorse. The biopsychosocial model is depicted in Figure 13.4.

But first, what is health psychology? **Health psychology** is "the field within psychology devoted to understanding psychological influences on how people stay healthy, why they become ill, and how they respond when they do get ill" (Taylor, 1991, p. 6). Health psychologists study psychological factors associated with health and illness, and they promote interventions that foster good health and aid recovery from illness.

Why do people become ill in the modern age? At the beginning of the 20th century, the primary causes of death in the United States were pneumonia and infectious diseases such as diphtheria and tuberculosis. Medical research has virtually conquered these diseases, with the exception of some new strains of tuberculosis.

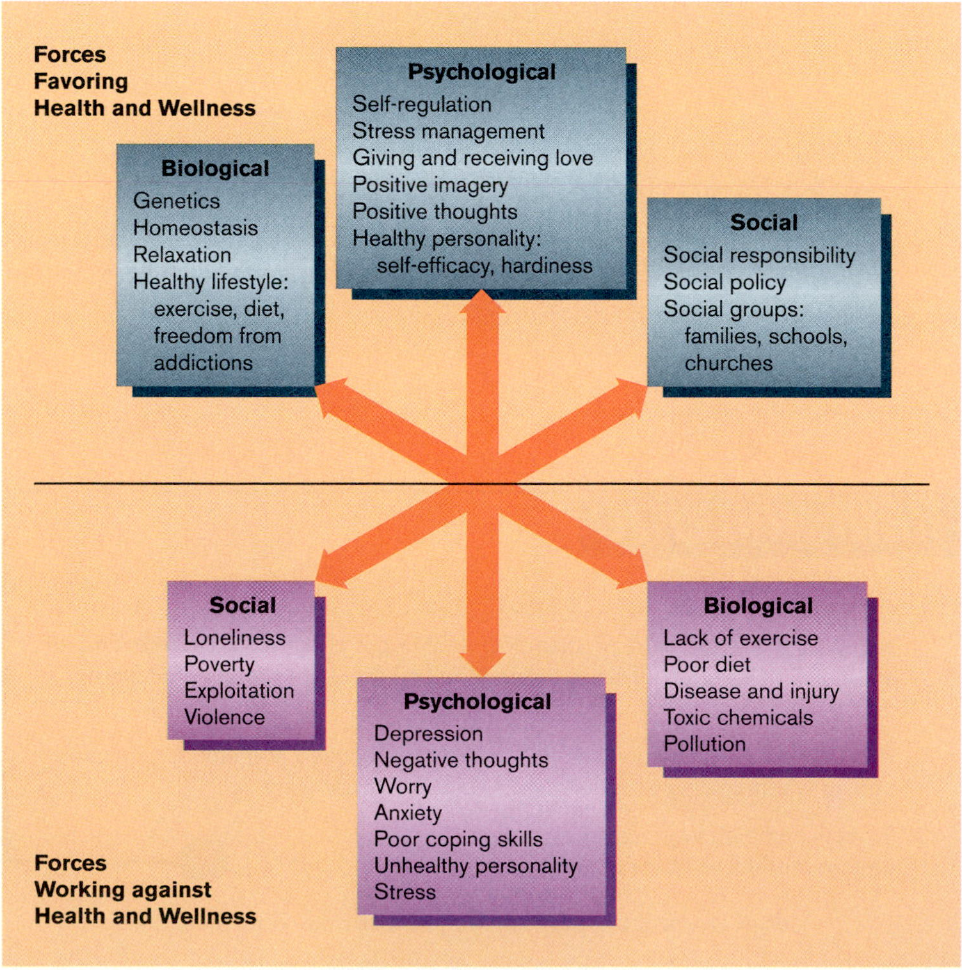

Figure 13.4

The Biopsychosocial Model of Health and Wellness

The biopsychosocial model focuses on health as well as on illness and holds that both are determined by a combination of biological, psychological, and social factors. Most health psychologists endorse the biopsychosocial model. (From Green & Shellenberger, 1990.)

The health menaces of modern times are diseases related to unhealthy lifestyle and stress (Taylor & Repetti, 1997). The price of an unhealthy lifestyle coupled with the added burden of stress is high indeed—heart attack, stroke, hardening of the arteries, cancer, and cirrhosis of the liver.

biomedical model: A perspective that focuses on illness rather than on health, explaining illness in terms of biological factors without regard to psychological and social factors.

biopsychosocial model: A perspective that focuses on health as well as illness and holds that both are determined by a combination of biological, psychological, and social factors.

health psychology: The field concerned with the psychological factors that contribute to health, illness, and recovery.

sedentary lifestyle: A lifestyle that includes less than 20 minutes of exercise three times a week.

Responding to Illness

Health psychologists study the myriad ways in which people respond to illness and the factors that affect whether they seek treatment. How do people tend to respond to illness?

When people recognize symptoms and interpret them as potentially serious, they seek treatment—or do they? Several factors determine who is likely to seek treatment and use health services. Gender is one: Women use medical services more frequently than men. The reasons are not clear, and even when visits involving pregnancy and childbirth are factored out, women still seek health services more than men. It has been suggested that women may be more sensitive to bodily changes and able to detect symptoms more readily than men (Taylor, 1991). Cultural norms and expectations may also partly explain why women seek treatment more than men (Bishop, 1984).

Socioeconomic class is related to seeking treatment because the lower socioeconomic classes have less to spend on health care. The poor are likely to seek treatment only in emergencies and are far less likely than middle- or upper-class people to have a regular physician.

When people do receive medical treatment, do they always comply with the treatment regimen? Do they take all the medicine prescribed as the doctor instructed or stop taking it when their symptoms disappear? A review of some 250 studies indicates that up to 50% of patients fail to follow their doctors' orders (Adler & Stone, 1984). Even among patients with chronic disorders, at least half do not comply fully with their prescribed treatment regimen (Taylor, 1991). It is even less likely that patients will comply with lifestyle changes that promote better health. Health professionals and researchers have discovered many more effective treatments than people are willing to follow.

Coronary Heart Disease: The Leading Cause of Death

In order to survive, the heart muscle requires a steady, sufficient supply of oxygen and nutrients carried by the blood. Coronary heart disease is caused by the narrowing or the blockage of the coronary arteries—the arteries that supply blood to the heart muscle. Although coronary heart disease remains the leading cause of death in the United States, responsible of 31% of all deaths, the death rate due to this cause has declined 50% during the past 30 years (National Center for Health Statistics, 2000).

Air traffic controllers have an incredibly high-stress job. The on-the-job stress they experience increases the risk of coronary heart disease and stroke.

A health problem of modern times, coronary heart disease is largely attributable to lifestyle and is therefore an important field of study for health psychologists. A **sedentary lifestyle**—one that includes less than 20 minutes of exercise three times per week—is the primary modifiable risk factor contributing to death from coronary heart disease. High levels of stress and job strain have also been associated with increased risk for coronary heart disease and stroke (Rosengren et al., 1991; Siegrist et al., 1990). Other risk factors are high serum cholesterol levels, cigarette smoking, obesity, high blood pressure, and diabetes. Though not modifiable, another important risk factor is a family history of heart disease.

What are the Type A and Type B behavior patterns?

The Type A and Type B Behavior Patterns: In a Hurry or Laid Back Is personality related to heart disease? After extensive research, cardiologists Meyer Friedman and Ray Rosenman (1974) concluded that there are two types of personality—Type A, associated with a high rate of coronary heart disease, and Type B, commonly found in persons unlikely to develop heart disease. Are your characteristics more like those of a Type A or a Type B person? Before reading further, complete the *Try It!* and find out.

Try It!

Answer true (T) or false (F) for each of the statements below. (Adapted from Friedman and Rosenman, 1974.)

____ 1. I forcefully emphasize key words in my everyday speech.

____ 2. I usually walk and eat quickly.

____ 3. I get irritated and restless around slow workers.

____ 4. When talking to others, I get impatient and try to hurry them along.

____ 5. I get very irritated, even hostile, when the car in front of me drives too slowly.

____ 6. When others are talking, I often think about my own concerns.

____ 7. I usually think of or do at least two things at the same time.

____ 8. I get very impatient when I have to wait.

____ 9. I usually take command and move the conversation to topics that interest me.

____ 10. I usually feel guilty when I relax and do nothing.

____ 11. I am usually too absorbed in my work to notice my surroundings.

____ 12. I keep trying to do more and more in less time.

____ 13. I sometimes punctuate my conversation with forceful gestures such as clenching my fists or pounding the table.

____ 14. My accomplishments are due largely to my ability to work faster than others.

____ 15. I don't play games just for fun. I play to win.

____ 16. I am more concerned with acquiring things than with becoming a better person.

____ 17. I usually use numbers to evaluate my own activities and the activities of others.

People with the **Type A behavior pattern** have a strong sense of time urgency and are impatient, excessively competitive, hostile, and easily angered. They are "involved in a *chronic, incessant* struggle to achieve more and more in less and less time" (Friedman & Rosenman, 1974, p. 84). Type A's would answer "true" to most or all of the questions in the *Try It!* The Type A person may be a driven executive, a competitive mortician, or a stressed blue collar employee.

In stark contrast to Type A's, people with the **Type B behavior pattern** are relaxed and easygoing and do not suffer from a sense of time urgency. They are not impatient or hostile and are able to relax without guilt. They play for fun and relaxation rather than to exhibit superiority over others. Yet the Type B individual may be as bright and ambitious as the Type A, and more successful as well. Type B's would answer "false" to most or all of the *Try It!* questions.

What aspect of the Type A behavior pattern is most clearly linked to coronary heart disease?

Type A behavior pattern: A behavior pattern marked by a sense of time urgency, impatience, excessive competitiveness, hostility, and anger; considered a risk factor in coronary heart disease.

Type B behavior pattern: A behavior pattern marked by a relaxed, easygoing approach to life; not associated with coronary heart disease.

Research on Behavior Pattern and Heart Disease Using meta-analysis, Miller and others (1991) found that 70% of middle-aged men with coronary heart disease were Type A, compared to 46% of healthy middle-aged men. Some researchers speculate that it may not be the whole Type A behavior pattern that leads to heart disease. Dembroski and others (1985) point to anger and hostility as the toxic components. Redford Williams of Duke University Medical School also suggests that hostility is the real culprit, particularly a cynical, distrustful attitude (Barefoot et al., 1983; Williams, 1989). More recent research supports earlier findings that the lethal core of the Type A personality is not time urgency but anger and hostility, which fuel an aggressive, reactive temperament (Miller et al., 1996; Williams,

1993). Hostility is not only highly predictive of coronary heart disease but also associated with ill health in general (Miller et al., 1996).

While anger and hostility clearly place male heart-attack survivors at greater risk of dying from heart disease, just the opposite may be the case for females. Powell and others (1993) found that among women who have survived a heart attack, those who suppress unpleasant emotions such as anger, resentment, loneliness, and dissatisfaction tend to be at greatest risk of death. Women who died of heart disease were also more likely to be divorced, to lack a college education, and to be working full-time but earning less than $20,000. Financial and emotional stress and the lack of an intimate relationship appeared to be associated with increased risk of dying of coronary heart disease.

Moser and Dracup (1996) found that of patients who had suffered heart attacks, those who had high levels of anxiety were almost five times more likely to experience further complications than those with lower levels of anxiety. Apparently the effects of stress may enter the bloodstream almost as if they were injected intravenously. Malkoff and others (1993) report that after an experimental group of participants had experienced laboratory-induced stress, their blood platelets (special clotting cells) released large amounts of a substance that promotes the buildup of plaque in blood vessels and may lead to heart attack and stroke. No changes were found in the blood platelets of unstressed control-group participants.

Cancer: A Dreaded Disease

Cancer is the second leading cause of death in the United States, accounting for 23% of all deaths (National Center for Health Statistics, 2000). Cancer strikes frequently in the adult population, and about 30% of Americans—over 75 million people—will develop cancer at some time in their lives. The young are not spared the scourge of cancer, for it takes the lives of more children aged 3 to 14 than any other disease.

We speak of cancer as a single disease, but actually it is a complicated collection of diseases. It can invade cells in any part of a living organism—humans, other animals, and even plants. It always starts small, because it is a disease of the body's cells. Normal cells in all parts of the body divide, but fortunately they have built-in instructions about when to stop dividing. If they did not, every part of the body would continue to grow throughout life. Unlike normal cells, cancer cells do not stop dividing. And unless caught in time and destroyed, they continue to grow and spread, eventually killing the organism.

Health psychologists warn that an unhealthy diet, smoking, excessive alcohol consumption, promiscuous sexual behavior, or becoming sexually active in the early teens (especially for females) are all behaviors that increase the risk of cancer.

The 1 million people in the United States who are diagnosed with cancer each year have the difficult task of adjusting to a potentially life-threatening disease and the chronic stressors associated with it. Patients must cope with difficult therapies, "continued emotional distress, disrupted life tasks, social and interpersonal turmoil and fatigue and low energy" (Anderson et al., 1994, p. 390). Patients need more than medical treatment for cancer, say researchers. Their therapy should include help with psychological and behavioral factors that can influence their quality of life. Researchers Carver and others (1993) found that 3 months and 6 months after surgery, breast-cancer patients who maintained an optimistic outlook, accepted the reality of their situation, and maintained a sense of humor experienced less distress. Patients who used denial—refusal to accept the reality of their situation—and had thoughts of giving up experienced much higher levels of

This group of cancer patients is apparently benefiting from art therapy, which is believed to lower the stress level associated with having a serious illness.

distress. Dunkel-Schetter and others (1992) found that the most effective elements of a strategy for coping with cancer were social support (such as through self-help groups), a focus on the positive, and distraction. Avoidant coping strategies such as fantasizing, denial, and social withdrawal were associated with more emotional distress.

Health in the United States

The quality of health and the leading health risk factors are not the same for all Americans. They differ among various cultural and ethnic groups and according to gender, age, and socioeconomic status as well. The mortality rate is higher among people from lower socioeconomic levels for virtually all major causes of death (Taylor & Repetti, 1997).

African Americans As the largest minority group in the United States, African Americans make up 12.3% of the population (U.S. Bureau of the Census, 2000). They are represented in every socioeconomic group from the poorest to the richest, but their overall poverty rate is about three times higher than that of the White population. As a result, many African Americans are at higher risk for disease and death and are more likely to suffer from inadequate health care. Their life expectancy trailed behind that of the total U.S. population throughout the 20th century. African-American infants are at twice the risk of death within their first year of life as White infants.

Compared to White Americans, African Americans have higher rates of diabetes, arthritis, and high blood pressure (Kington & Smith, 1997). And the rate of AIDS is more than three times higher among African Americans than among Whites. African-American women are from 10 to 15 times more likely than White women to contract AIDS (Public Health Service, 1991).

Hispanic Americans By 1999, Hispanic Americans, the fastest-growing and second-largest of U.S. minority groups, had increased to about 11.5% of the total population (U.S. Bureau of the Census, 2000). While some Hispanic Americans are immigrants, the Census Bureau estimates that 90.5% are native-born. Most Hispanics, about 63%, are Mexican Americans.

Hypertension and diabetes are more prevalent among Hispanic Americans than among non-Hispanic Whites, whereas heart problems are less prevalent (Kington & Smith, 1997). Cigarette smoking and alcohol abuse are more common among Hispanic teenagers than among other teenagers, White or Black. Hispanic Americans are at high risk of death from accidental injuries (from automobile accidents and other causes), homicide, cirrhosis and other chronic liver diseases, and AIDS (Public Health Service, 1991).

Partly because of a lower average socioeconomic level, Hispanic Americans and other minorities often have less access than White Americans to adequate health care.

Asian Americans Asian Americans, who make up 1.6% of the U.S. population, are comparatively very healthy. The overall age-adjusted death rate for Asian-American males is 40% lower than that for White males, but Asian-American males' death rate from stroke is 8% higher. Of all U.S. ethnic groups, infant mortality is lowest for Chinese Americans, at 3 deaths per 1,000 births, compared with 7 per 1,000 for the overall population (National Center for Health Statistics, 2000).

Native Americans Native Americans, the smallest of the defined minority groups in the United States, number about 2 million. A large proportion of Native Americans die before the age of 45. This fact partly accounts for their statistically low rates of heart disease and cancer, which are more common among older people.

Alcohol represents a serious rick factor for Native Americans and is a leading factor in their high homicide and suicide rates. Native Americans under age 35 are at least 10 times more likely than other Americans to die from diseases directly related to alcoholism (Sandfur et al., 1996).

Obesity is common among many Native-American tribes and contributes to extremely high rates of diabetes. According to the Indian Health Service (1988), more than one-fifth of the members of some tribes suffer from diabetes. Among members of the Pima tribe over age 35, the rate is more than 50% (Sandfur et al., 1996).

The Gender Gap in America's Health Care American society also has significant health disparities that are related neither to poverty nor to racial or ethnic differences (Holloway, 1994). There has been a serious gender gap in health care and medical research in the United States. Most medical research in the past, much of it funded by the U.S. government, rejected women as participants in favor of men (Matthews et al., 1997). Women are slighted as well in health care and treatment (Rodin & Ickovics, 1990). Physicians are more likely to see women's health complaints as "emotional" in nature rather than due to physical causes (Council on Ethical and Judicial Affairs, AMA, 1991). The American Medical Association released a major report in 1991 revealing that of men and women who received an abnormal reading on a heart scan, 40% of the men but only 4% of the women were referred for further testing and possible bypass surgery. Women are less likely than men to receive kidney dialysis and 30% less likely to receive a kidney transplant (Council on Ethical and Judicial Affairs, AMA, 1991).

The good news is that efforts to erase the gender and race disparities in medical research and treatment are now underway. The National Institutes of Health created offices of Research on Women's Health and of Minority Programs. Every application for research funding from the National Institutes of Health must now include women and minorities unless there is a good rationale for not doing so. Studies of hypertension and coronary disease in African Americans have been funded. And a study of 164,000 postmenopausal women is examining the effects of estrogen replacement therapy and nutrition on cardiovascular health and the prevention of breast cancer and osteoporosis (Matthews et al., 1997).

The Immune System: An Army of Cells to Fight Off Disease

Most researchers do not question the notion that stress and health are closely related (Kiecolt-Glaser & Glaser, 1992). People who experience stress may indeed be more susceptible to coronary heart disease, stroke, and poorer pregnancy outcomes (Adler & Matthews, 1994). But even more ominous is the growing evidence that stress can impair the functioning of the immune system itself.

The immune system, known to be one of the most complex systems of the body, protects against infection and disease. An army of highly specialized cells and organs, the immune system works to identify and search out and destroy bacteria, viruses, fungi, parasites, and any other foreign matter that may enter the body. This is why organ transplants—foreign tissue to the recipient's body—are rejected by the immune system unless powerful immune-suppressing drugs are administered to prevent the rejection (Fischbein et al., 2000).

The key components of the immune system are white blood cells known as **lymphocytes,** which include B cells and T cells. B cells are so named because they are produced in the bone marrow. T cells derive their name from the thymus gland where they are produced. All cells foreign to the body, such as bacteria, viruses, and so on, are known as *antigens.* B cells produce proteins called *antibodies,* which are highly effective in destroying antigens that live in the bloodstream and in the fluid surrounding body tissues (Paul, 1993). But for defeating harmful foreign invaders that have taken up residence inside the body's cells, T cells are critically important.

During wartime, when recognition and communication systems fail, troops may attack and kill their own soldiers—a phenomenon referred to as "friendly fire." Likewise, the immune system may turn on healthy self cells or specific organs and

lymphocytes: The white blood cells—including B cells and T cells—that are key components of the immune system.

attack them, as happens in autoimmune diseases such as juvenile diabetes, multiple sclerosis, rheumatoid arthritis, and lupus.

The most feared disease related to the immune system is AIDS, which is caused by the human immunodeficiency virus (HIV). The virus attacks the T cells, gradually but relentlessly weakening the immune system until it is essentially nonfunctional. See Chapter 12 for a detailed discussion of HIV and AIDS.

What are the effects of stress and depression on the immune system?

Stress and the Immune System **Psychoneuroimmunology** is a field of study in which psychologists, biologists, and medical researchers combine their expertise to learn the effects of psychological factors—emotions, thinking, and behavior—on the immune system (Cohen, 1996). Researchers now know that the immune system is not merely a separate system to fight off foreign invaders. Rather, it is an incredibly complex, interconnected defense system working with the brain to keep the body healthy (Ader, 2000).

Psychological factors, emotions, and stress are all related to immune system functioning. The immune system exchanges information with the brain, and what goes on in the brain can apparently influence the immune system for good or ill. In one study researchers gave volunteers nasal drops containing a cold virus. Within the next few days, symptoms of the viral infection rose sharply in some of the 151 women and 125 men who participated in the study, but less so or not at all in others. Participants with a rich social life in the form of frequent interactions with others—spouses, children, parents, co-workers, friends, and volunteer and religious groups—seemed to enjoy a powerful shield of protection against the virus infection. And this pattern of protection held across age and racial groups, for both sexes, at all educational levels, and at every season of the year (Ader, 2000; Cohen et al., 1997).

Close social ties—to family, friends, and others—apparently have good effects on the immune system. Ill effects often come from stress. High periods of stress are correlated with increased symptoms of many infectious diseases, including oral and genital herpes, mononucleosis, colds, and flu. And stress has caused decreased levels of the immune system's B and T cells. Kiecolt-Glaser and others (1996) found that elderly men and women experiencing chronic stress due to years of caring for a spouse with Alzheimer's disease showed an impaired immune response to flu shots. Physicians have long observed that stress and anxiety can worsen autoimmune diseases. And "if fear can produce relapses [in autoimmune diseases], then even the fear of a relapse may become a self-fulfilling prophecy" (Steinman, 1993, p. 112). Reviews of studies also show that stress is associated with an increase in illness behaviors—reporting physical symptoms and seeking medical care (Cohen & Herbert, 1996; Cohen & Williamson, 1991).

Stress has the power to suppress the immune system long after the stressful experience is over. An experimental group of medical students who were enduring the stress of major exams was compared with a control group of medical students who were on vacation from classes and exams. When tested for the presence of disease-fighting antibodies, participants in the exam group, but not those in the control group, had a significant reduction in their antibody count because of the stress. The lowered antibody count was still present 14 days after the exams were over. At that point the students were not even aware that they were still stressed and reported feeling no stress (Deinzer et al., 2000).

In addition to academic pressures, poor marital relationships and sleep deprivation have been linked to lowered immune response (Kiecolt-Glaser et al., 1987; Maier & Laudenslager, 1985). Several researchers have reported that severe, incapacitating depression is also related to lowered immune activity (Herbert & Cohen, 1993). For several months after the death of a spouse, the widow or widower suffers weakened immune system function and is at a higher risk of mortality. Severe bereavement weakens the immune system, increasing a person's chance of suffering from a long list of physical and mental ailments for up to 2 years following a partner's death (Prigerson et al., 1997).

psychoneuroimmunology (sye-ko-NEW-ro-IM-you-NOLL-oh-gee): A field in which psychologists, biologists, and medical researchers study the effects of psychological factors on the immune system.

Personal Factors Reducing the Impact of Stress and Illness

Researchers have identified four personal factors that may contribute to better health: optimism, psychological hardiness, religious involvement, and social support.

What four personal factors are associated with health and resistance to stress?

Optimism and Pessimism People who are generally optimistic tend to cope more effectively with stress, and this in turn may reduce their risk of illness (Seligman, 1990). An important characteristic optimists share is that they generally expect good outcomes. And such positive expectations help make them more stress-resistant than pessimists, who tend to expect bad outcomes. An especially lethal form of pessimism is hopelessness. A longitudinal study of a large number of Finnish men revealed that participants who reported feeling moderate to high hopelessness died from all causes at two to three times the rates of those reporting low or no hopelessness (Everson et al., 1996).

Optimists are more likely to use problem-focused coping, to seek social support, and to find the positive aspects of a stressful situation (Carver et al., 1993; Scheier & Carver, 1992). Pessimists, on the other hand, are more likely to use denial or to focus on their stressful feelings (Scheier et al., 1986). In a study of college students, Scheier and Carver (1985) found that at the end of the semester, optimistic students reported fewer physical symptoms than those who were pessimistic. And another study, of patients who had undergone coronary bypass surgery, revealed that optimists recovered faster during their hospitalization and were able to resume their normal activities sooner after discharge than pessimists (Scheier et al., 1989). Optimists are more likely to take preventive action against illness and to get treatment once illness strikes (Seligman, 1990). Apparently, happy thoughts are healthy thoughts.

Psychological Hardiness: Commitment, Challenge, and Control Suzanne Kobasa (1979; Kobasa et al., 1982) wondered why some people under great stress succumb to illness while others do not. Studying male executives with high levels of stress, she found three psychological characteristics that distinguished those who remained healthy from those who had a high incidence of illness. The three qualities, which she referred to collectively as **hardiness,** were *commitment, control,* and *challenge.*

Hardy individuals feel a strong sense of commitment to both their work and their personal life. They see themselves not as victims of whatever life brings, but as people who have control over consequences and outcomes. They act to solve their own problems. And they welcome challenges in life, viewing them not as threats but as opportunities for growth and improvement.

Florian and others (1995) found that commitment and control alone are apparently sufficient to produce hardiness. In stressful situations, commitment and control are compatible, complementary attributes. Commitment ensures a continuing involvement in the situation and provides the staying power to see it through. A person who is committed does not give up. Control provides the confidence that the person is in charge of the situation and capable of finding the right solution to solve the problems at hand.

Religious Involvement: The Power of Faith Religion has been and it continues to be important in the lives of most Americans (McCullough et al., 2000). Some 96% of Americans say that they believe in God or a supreme universal being, and about 42% attend religious services regularly (Gallup, 1995).

Does religious faith help people cope with negative life events? Several studies indicate that in the majority of cases, it does. Koenig and others (1992) studied a large sample of hospitalized elderly men who had been suffering from a range of serious medical problems. They found that the more these patients turned to religious coping, the less likely they were to be depressed. One longitudinal study (conducted over a period of 28 years) revealed that frequent attendance at religious services is correlated with better health habits (Strawbridge et al., 1997).

hardiness: A combination of three psychological qualities shared by people who can undergo high levels of stress yet remain healthy: a sense of control over one's life, commitment to one's personal goals, and a tendency to view change as a challenge rather than as a threat.

Do people who are religious tend to live longer? They do, according to one very large recent study. This meta-analysis of 42 separate studies combined data on some 126,000 individuals and revealed that religious involvement is positively associated with measures of physical health and lower rates of cancer, heart disease, and stroke (McCullough et al., 2000). Also, measures of religious involvement were reliable predictors of greater longevity when all causes of mortality were considered. The specific measures of religious involvement most closely related to a lower mortality rate were regular attendance at worship services, religious orthodoxy, and a personal sense of comfort and strength from one's religion (McCullough et al., 2000). This study and others have found the association between religious involvement and lower mortality to be stronger for women than for men (Hummer, 1999; Strawbridge et al., 1997).

Social Support: Help in Time of Need Another factor contributing to better health is **social support** (Cohen, 1988; Kaplan et al., 1994). Social support is support provided, usually in time of need, by a spouse or other family members or by friends, neighbors, colleagues, support groups, or others. It can involve tangible aid, information, and advice, as well as emotional support. It can also be viewed as the feeling of being loved, valued, and cared for by those for whom we feel a mutual obligation.

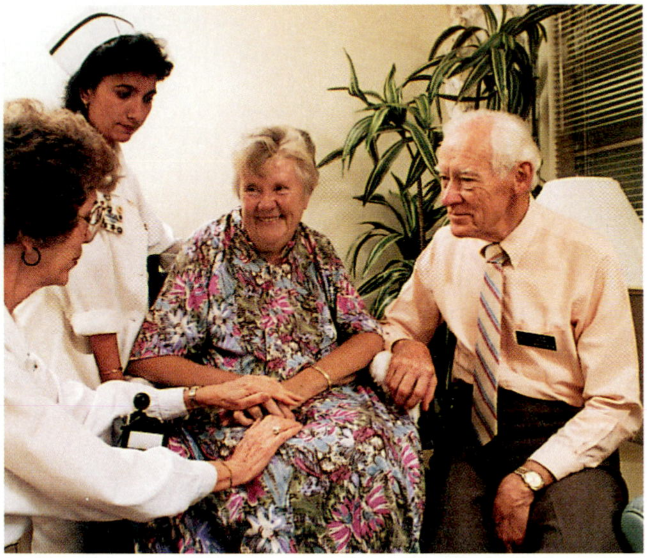

A strong social support network can help a person recover faster from an illness.

Social support appears to have positive effects on the body's immune system as well as on the cardiovascular and endocrine systems (Uchino et al., 1996). Social support may help encourage health-promoting behaviors and reduce the impact of stress so that people will be less likely to resort to unhealthy methods of coping, such as smoking or drinking.

Social support has been shown to reduce the impact of stress from unemployment, long-term illness, retirement, and bereavement. And a large study of soldiers who had enlisted in the U.S. Army showed that a high level of social support from peers was an essential ingredient in reducing stress (Bliese & Castro, 2000). People with social support recover more quickly from illnesses and lower their risk of death from specific diseases. Social support may even increase the probability of surviving a heart attack because it buffers the impact of stress on cardiovascular function (Steptoe, 2000). A longitudinal study of 4,775 people over a 9-year period found that those low in social support died at twice the rate of those high in social support (Berkman & Syme, 1979).

Research on natural disasters reveals that initial social support is common but that the support tends to deteriorate, because the needs of victims overwhelm the tangible and emotional resources of friends and family. Similarly, chronic physical or mental illness may deplete resources and lead to burnout in those supplying care and social support.

In a study of 821 pairs of female twins, Kessler and others (1992) found that both genetic and environmental factors appear to influence social support or the perception of social support. The perception that social support exists is very powerful in promoting psychological health and in providing protection during times of stress. Some research has found that perceived support has even more positive effects than received support (Norris & Kaniasty, 1996). Other research has shown that high levels of perceived social support are associated with lower levels of depression and even with recovery from depression (Lara et al., 1997).

Personality factors such as extroversion influence a person's tendency to make friends and to perceive them as being supportive. One study on extroversion and social support found that a high level of extroversion, both when entering college and at midlife, correlated positively with perceived social support later in adulthood (Von Dras & Siegler, 1997).

social support: Tangible support, information, advice, and/or emotional support provided in time of need by family, friends, and others; the feeling of being loved, valued, and cared for.

Remember It!

1. The biomedical model focuses on ______________; the biopsychosocial model focuses on ______________.
   a. illness; illness
   b. health and illness; illness
   c. illness; health and illness
   d. health and illness; health and illness
2. Recent research suggests that the most toxic component of the Type A behavior pattern is
   a. hostility. c. a sense of time urgency.
   b. impatience. d. perfectionism.
3. Most research has pursued the connection between the Type A behavior pattern and
   a. cancer. c. stroke.
   b. coronary heart disease. d. ulcers.
4. Lowered immune response has been associated with
   a. stress. c. stress and depression.
   b. depression. d. neither stress nor depression.
5. Some research suggests that optimists are more stress-resistant than pessimists. (true/false)
6. Which of the following is *not* a dimension of psychological hardiness?
   a. a feeling that adverse circumstances can be controlled and changed
   b. a sense of commitment and deep involvement in personal goals
   c. a tendency to look on change as a challenge rather than a threat
   d. close, supportive relationships with family and friends
7. Social support tends to reduce stress but is unrelated to health outcomes. (true/false)

Answers: 1. c 2. a 3. b 4. c 5. true 6. d 7. false

LIFESTYLE AND HEALTH

What constitutes an unhealthy lifestyle, and how serious a factor is lifestyle in illness and disease?

For most Americans, health enemy number one is their own habits. As Figure 13.5 shows, 53.5% of all deaths in the United States are attributable to unhealthy behavior or lifestyle (Powell et al., 1986). What are these unhealthy behaviors? The culprits are all well known—lack of exercise, too little sleep, alcohol or drug abuse, an unhealthy diet, and overeating. A longitudinal study on the health consequences of

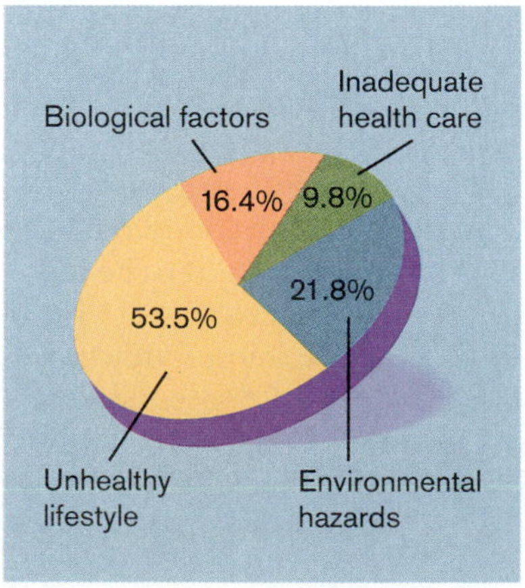

Figure 13.5

Factors Contributing to Death before Age 65

The number one factor leading to premature death in the United States is unhealthy lifestyle. Fortunately your own lifestyle is more completely under your control than are any of the other factors contributing to premature death. (Based on Powell et al., 1986.)

certain lifestyle factors tracked nearly 117,000 female nurses from 1976 through 1992. The study showed that the overweight nurses were from 2 to 2.5 times more likely to suffer a stroke than were their leaner counterparts. But the most dangerous unhealthy behavior of all is smoking.

Smoking: Hazardous to Your Health

Why is smoking considered the single most preventable cause of death?

The Surgeon General continues to warn that smoking remains the number one cause of preventable disease and death in the United States (U.S. Department of Health and Human Services, 2000). That message appears to be taking root because the prevalence of smoking among American adults has been decreasing and is now under 25% (National Center for Health Statistics, 2000). But there are wide variations in smoking habits according to gender and ethnic group. The highest rates of smoking are found among Native-American men (41%) and women (29%), while the lowest rates are reported for Asian-American men (18%) and women (11%) (U.S. Department of Health and Human Services, 2000).

Even though the prevalence of smoking is decreasing, every year more than 1 million young Americans become regular smokers, and more than 400,000 American adults die from diseases related to tobacco use (U.S. Department of Health and Human Services, 2000). Smoking increases the risk for heart disease, lung cancer, other cancers that are smoking-related, and emphysema. And it is now known that smoking suppresses the action of pulmonary T cells, increasing susceptibility to respiratory tract infections and tumors (McCue et al., 2000).

Millions of nonsmokers who must breathe smoke-filled air suffer the ill effects of this passive, or second-hand, smoke. Research indicates that nonsmokers who are regularly exposed to passive smoke have twice the risk of heart attack of those who are not exposed (Kawachi et al., 1997). And think of the suffering of millions from chronic bronchitis, emphysema, and other respiratory diseases; the deaths and injuries from fires caused by smoking; and the low birthweight and retarded fetal development in babies born to smoking mothers. Furthermore, mothers who smoke during pregnancy tend to have babies who are at greater risk for anxiety and depression and are five times more likely to become smokers themselves (Cornelius et al., 2000).

Because smoking is so addictive, smokers have great difficulty breaking the habit. Even so, 90% of ex-smokers quit smoking on their own (Novello, 1990). The average smoker makes five or six attempts to quit before finally succeeding (Sherman, 1994). Some aids, such as nicotine gum and the nicotine patch, help many people kick the habit. A meta-analysis involving 17 studies and over 5,000 participants revealed that 22% of people who used the nicotine patch were smoke-free compared with only 9% of those who received a placebo. And 27% of those receiving the nicotine patch plus antismoking counseling or support remained smoke-free (Fiore, cited in Sherman, 1994). But even with the patch, quitting is difficult, because the patch only lessens withdrawal symptoms, which typically last 2 to 4 weeks (Hughes, 1992). Half of all relapses occur within the first 2 weeks after people quit, and relapses are most likely when people are experiencing negative emotions or are using alcohol. It takes just one cigarette, sometimes only one puff, to cause a relapse.

Researchers have found smoking rates to be high in people suffering from drug and alcohol abuse and schizophrenia. Furthermore, a link has been found between smoking and a history of major depression, both of which are thought to be influenced by genetic factors (Breslau et al., 1993; Kendler, Neale, MacLean, et al., 1993). Some smokers who try to quit are at higher risk for major depression. Withdrawal brings on depression in more than 85% of those with a history of depression compared with only 20% of those with no such history (Glassman, 1993). Consequently, depressed smokers are much less likely to succeed at quitting (Borrelli et al., 1996; Stage et al., 1996).

Alcohol: A Problem for Millions

What are some health risks of alcohol abuse?

Although smoking is directly related to a greater number of deaths, alcohol abuse undoubtedly causes more misery. The health and social costs of alcohol abuse are staggering—fatalities, medical bills, lost work, family problems. According to Rodin and Salovey (1989), alcohol is one of the three main causes of death in modern societies. Some 18 million Americans have a serious drinking problem (Lord et al., 1987), and about 10 million are alcoholics (Neimark et al., 1994). And binge drinking on campus is a growing health problem in the United States, according to a large national survey involving more than 14,000 students at 119 colleges in 40 states (Wechsler & Kuo, 2000). Alcohol abuse and dependence is three times more prevalent in males than in females (Grant et al., 1991). And people who begin drinking before age 15 are four times more likely than those who begin later to become alcoholics (Grant & Dawson, 1998). Although a higher percentage of white-collar workers use alcohol, the percentage of problem drinkers is higher among blue-collar workers (Harford et al., 1992). For many, alcohol provides a method of coping with life stresses they feel powerless to control (Seeman & Seeman, 1992).

As many as 80% of men and women who are alcoholics complain of episodes of depression. A large study of almost 3,000 alcoholics concluded that some depressive episodes are independent of alcohol, whereas others are substance-induced (Schuckit et al., 1997).

Alcohol can damage virtually every organ in the body, but it is especially harmful to the liver and is the major cause of cirrhosis, which kills 26,000 people each year (Neimark et al., 1994). Alcohol can also cause stomach problems—indigestion, nausea, diarrhea, and ulcers. One-half of long-term, heavy drinkers suffer damage to their skeletal muscles, and one-third sustain damage to their heart muscle (Urbano-Marquez et al., 1989). Alcohol increases the risk of many cancers, including cancer of the liver, mouth, throat, tongue, and voice box. Pregnant women should avoid all alcohol because of its potentially disastrous effects on the developing fetus. (See Chapter 9 for a discussion of fetal alcohol syndrome.)

Shrinkage in the cerebral cortex of alcoholics has been found by researchers using magnetic resonance imaging (Jernigan et al., 1991). CT scans also show brain shrinkage in a high percentage of alcoholics, even in young subjects and in those who appear to be intact mentally (Lishman, 1990). Moreover, heavy drinking can cause cognitive impairment (Goldman, 1983) and seizures (Ng et al., 1988). The only good news in recent studies is that some of the effects of alcohol on the brain seem to be partially reversible with prolonged abstinence.

An all too common scene in the United States is the tragic aftermath of an alcohol-related, fatal car accident.

Alcoholism's toll goes beyond the physical damage to the alcoholic. In 1995 alcohol was involved in 41% of the traffic fatalities in the United States, which numbered almost 17,300 (National Safety Council, 1997). Alcohol has been implicated in 40% of criminal victimization cases ("Alcoholism: A factor," 1998), 20–36% of suicides, 53% of falls, and 48% of burns (U.S. House, Committee on Energy and Commerce, 1991).

Alcoholism: Causes and Treatment The American Medical Association maintains that alcoholism is a disease, and once an alcoholic, always an alcoholic. According to this view, even a small amount of alcohol can cause an irresistible craving for more, leading alcoholics to lose control of their drinking (Jellinek, 1960). Thus, total abstinence is seen as the only acceptable and effective method of treatment. The medical establishment and Alcoholics Anonymous endorse both the disease concept and the total abstinence approach to treatment. And there is a drug that may make abstinence somewhat easier. German researchers report that the drug acamprosate helps prevent relapse in recovering alcoholics (Sass et al., 1996).

controlled drinking: A behavioral approach to the treatment of alcoholism, designed to teach the skills necessary so that alcoholics can drink socially without losing control.

aerobic exercise (ah-RO-bik): Exercise that uses the large muscle groups in continuous, repetitive action and increases oxygen intake and breathing and heart rates.

Some studies suggest a genetic factor in alcoholism and lend support to the disease model. According to Goodwin (1985), about one-half of hospitalized alcoholics have a family history of alcohol abuse. Adoption studies have revealed that "sons of alcoholics were three or four times more likely to be alcoholic than were sons of nonalcoholics, whether raised by their alcoholic biologic parents or by nonalcoholic adoptive parents" (Goodwin, 1985, p. 172).

A large study by McGue and others (1992) involving 356 pairs of identical and fraternal twins revealed a substantial genetic influence for males when the first symptoms of alcoholism appear before age 20. And a study of 1,000 pairs of female identical and fraternal twins by Kendler, Neale, and others (1994) found that alcoholism in women has a heritability of 50–60%, a rate similar to that for male alcoholics. Some studies, however, indicate that familial risk factors need to be defined more specifically than the high-risk/low-risk categories often used when studying heritability and alcoholism (Alterman et al., 2000).

Is alcoholism a disease? Some experts reject the disease concept and contend that alcoholism can take various forms and have various causes (Pattison, 1982). Even in people who are genetically predisposed, researchers caution against overlooking the environmental contribution to alcoholism (Searles, 1988). Family and cultural influences are apparently the dominant factors in men whose drinking problems appear after adolescence.

Some experts stress the role of behavioral, social, and cultural factors in alcoholism and advocate various approaches to treatment. One approach—*cue exposure*—systematically exposes the problem drinker to cues that have stimulated a craving for alcohol and triggered drinking in the past (Neimark et al., 1994). The person is prevented from drinking in the presence of those cues and gradually becomes less responsive to them.

In another approach—*network therapy*—the therapist meets with the alcoholic and a small group of friends and family members at regular intervals (Galanter, 1993). The group focuses on helping the alcoholic face the distorted perceptions and manipulative behaviors that have enabled him or her to deny the drinking problem. The group learns to provide the necessary support to help the drinker develop a drug-free life. It also can present a united front, showing disapproval of the behaviors that lead to relapse.

With behavior therapy, some (not all) problem drinkers can learn the skills necessary to drink socially without losing control (Peele, 1992; Sobell & Sobell, 1978). Advocates of this treatment—**controlled drinking**—generally suggest that it is most successful with younger drinkers who have less serious drinking problems and who are not yet physically dependent on alcohol (Marlatt, 1983; Polich et al., 1981).

Whatever treatment approach is used, social support is essential. It can be provided by friends, family members, therapists, or self-help groups. Alcoholics who have such support are often able to quit on their own, without any formal treatment. The key seems to be to develop the motivation to quit drinking with the encouragement of others. Abstinence remains the surest solution to alcoholism (Nathan, 1992).

Exercise: Keeping Fit Is Healthy

What are some benefits of regular aerobic exercise?

For years medical experts, especially health psychologists, have promoted regular exercise. Yet most Americans exercise irregularly, if at all (Hurrell, 1997). Some 60% of the U.S. population does not engage in enough physical activity to remain healthy, according to a 1996 Surgeon General's report. Many studies show that regular **aerobic exercise** pays rich dividends in the form of physical and mental fitness. Aerobic exercise (such as running, swimming, brisk walking, bicycling, rowing, and jumping rope) is exercise that uses the large muscle groups in continuous, repetitive action and increases oxygen intake and breathing and heart rates. To improve cardiovascular fitness and endurance and to lessen the risk of heart attack, aerobic exercise should be performed regularly. This means three or four times a week for 20–30 minutes, with additional 5–10 minute warm-up and cool-down periods (Alpert et al., 1990; Shepard, 1986). Less than 20 minutes of aerobic exercise 3 times a week has "no measurable effect on the heart," and more than 3 hours per week "is not known to reduce cardiovascular risk any further" (Simon, 1988, p. 3).

Regular aerobic exercise improves cardiovascular fitness in people of all ages.

Regular aerobic exercise is beneficial for people of all ages. Even preschoolers have been shown to receive cardiovascular benefits from planned exercise (Alpert et al., 1990). At the other end of the age spectrum, regular, planned exercise yields dramatic increases in muscle and bone strength in older people. Exercisers between the ages of 87 and 96 who were on a weight-lifting program for only 2 months showed the same absolute gains in rate of muscular strength as younger people (Allison, 1991). Strenuous workouts would not have transformed George Burns into Arnold Schwarzenegger, but significant increases in muscle strength have been recorded even in people pushing 100.

A large study on the health benefits of physical fitness is compelling enough to convince couch potatoes of all ages to get up and get moving. Steven Blair and colleagues (1989) studied 13,344 men and women of different age groups, 20 years and older. The participants were tested for physical fitness and then assigned to one of five physical fitness levels based on age, sex, and performance on a treadmill test. Follow-up continued for a little more than 8 years, and during that time 283 participants (240 men and 43 women) died. And the number of deaths from all causes was significantly related to fitness level for both men and women.

You do not need to become a marathon runner or spend several hours a day sweating and grunting in a fitness center in order to enjoy the maximum benefits of health and longevity. Exercise need not be strenuous. Low-intensity physical training improves physical fitness in older adults (De Vito et al., 1997). Even a brisk daily walk of 30 minutes or more helps to reduce stress and yields the fitness standard associated with a much lower death rate. In a study of 137 stressed male business executives, Kobasa and her colleagues (1982) found that those who exercised had lower rates of illness. The more stress the men suffered, the more important exercise was in the prevention of illness.

In case you are not yet convinced, consider the following benefits of exercise:

- Increases the efficiency of the heart, enabling it to pump more blood with each beat; reduces the resting pulse rate and improves circulation
- Raises HDL (the good blood cholesterol) levels, which (1) helps rid the body of LDL (the bad blood cholesterol) and (2) removes plaque buildup on artery walls
- Burns up extra calories, enabling you to lose weight or maintain your weight
- Makes bones denser and stronger, helping to prevent osteoporosis in women
- Moderates the effects of stress
- Gives you more energy and increases your resistance to fatigue
- Benefits the immune system by increasing natural killer cell activity (Fiatarone et al., 1988)

Remember It!

1. Which is the most important factor leading to disease and death?
   a. unhealthy lifestyle
   b. a poor health care system
   c. environmental hazards
   d. genetic disorders
2. Which health-compromising behavior is responsible for the most deaths?
   a. overeating
   b. smoking
   c. lack of exercise
   d. excessive alcohol use
3. (Alcohol, Smoking) damages virtually every organ in the body.
4. To improve cardiovascular fitness, aerobic exercise should be done
   a. 15 minutes daily.
   b. 1 hour daily.
   c. 20 to 30 minutes daily.
   d. 20 to 30 minutes three or four times a week.

Answers: 1. a 2. b 3. Alcohol 4. d

Apply It!

Dealing with Road Rage

It's Monday morning, and you're late for class. Traffic is heavy. You find yourself in an open lane and speed up, but suddenly another car cuts in front of you. "Blankety-blank," you mutter, leaning on the horn. Apparently trying to punish you for honking, the other car slows down. By now you're furious and want to teach that annoying driver a lesson. Then the other car signals a turn and leaves the highway. You arrive in class with a flushed face and a racing pulse.

As in this case, most incidents of road rage end without causing harm to anyone except the angry driver. But sometimes an episode can end in violence, even tragedy. Drivers have been seen getting out of their cars and fighting each other, deliberately bumping or ramming other cars, and even shooting at other drivers.

What is road rage, and what causes it? Road rage is deliberate, violent behavior in response to a real or imagined traffic offense; it involves using a car like a weapon or physically assaulting another driver. It is closely related to aggressive driving–operating a motor vehicle in a manner that endangers or is likely to endanger a person or property. Both aggressive driving and road rage are growing problems on U.S. highways (Archbold, 2000).

Aggressive driving has been attributed to crowded highways, ignorance, and bad manners (Koch, 1997). Some experts believe that people learn aggressive driving habits by observing other drivers and by watching TV programs and commercials that feature dangerous driving. According to psychologist Leon James (1997), these explanations are inadequate. In his view, aggressive driving stems from the central role of the automobile in American society. James points out that our cars have become extensions of our selves.

How does aggressive driving lead to road rage? The process starts when another driver interferes with the feeling of freedom and well-being that comes from achieving control over one's environment. When a car suddenly moves in front of you, you are forced to change your behavior. This frustrates you and causes an emotional response. You may feel hostile, and hostility may escalate to anger (James, 1997).

What can be done? Proposals for reducing aggressive driving include building more and better roads, mounting public education campaigns, and increasing enforcement of traffic regulations. Dealing with road rage presents a greater challenge. People who are prone to emotional explosions on the road need to learn how to manage their anger. Those who encounter angry drivers need to learn how to deflect that anger before it escalates.

Suppose you're on the receiving end of a road rage episode. What can you do to defuse the situation? Leon James suggests avoiding eye contact, verbal replies, and other forms of provocation. Road rage is the result of a cycle of hostility in which each person reinforces the other's anger. The longer the cycle continues, the more intense it becomes. If you can avoid giving the other driver an opportunity to vent his or her anger, you may be able to keep the situation from getting out of hand (James, 1997).

If you are an aggressive driver and feel that you may be prone to road rage, there are some things you can do to manage your own anger. You can start by tape recording your thoughts and feelings while driving in traffic. This technique, called *self-witnessing*, can help aggressive drivers see themselves from other drivers' point of view. This insight can help reduce angry thoughts and feelings and thus help modify aggressive driving behavior (James, 1997).

A key feature of aggressive driving is an unforgiving attitude toward drivers who make mistakes. (Check your self-witnessing tape. Does it refer to drivers who make mistakes as "idiots," "morons," or worse?) But a driver who makes mistakes may not be stupid or careless–just momentarily confused or unprepared. Most drivers appear incompetent to others at one time or another–for example, if they are unfamiliar with the road or are experiencing temporary physical difficulties. An intelligent driver recognizes that there are a variety of drivers on the road, with varying skill levels, reaction times, and amounts of control over their emotions. Rather than calling other drivers idiots or morons, it is more realistic to think of alternative explanations for their mistakes (James, 1997).

Whether you're the source or the target of road rage, the next time you're on the road, remember the Golden Rule: Treating other drivers the way you want to be treated could save a life–maybe your own.

THINKING CRITICALLY

Evaluation

In your view, which is more effective for evaluating stress—the Social Readjustment Rating Scale or the Hassle Scale? Explain the advantages and disadvantages of each.

Point/Counterpoint

Prepare two arguments—one supporting the position that alcoholism is a genetically inherited disease, and the other supporting the position that alcoholism is not a medical disease but results from learning.

Psychology in Your Life

Choose several stress-producing incidents from your life and explain what problem-focused and emotion-focused coping strategies you used. From the knowledge you have gained in this chapter, list other coping strategies that might have been more effective.

SUMMARY AND REVIEW

STRESS: WHAT IS IT?

What is stress?

Stress is the physiological and psychological response to a condition that threatens or challenges an individual and requires some form of adaptation or adjustment.

Key Terms
stress (p. 462); fight-or-flight response (p, 462)

EVALUATING LIFE STRESS: MAJOR LIFE CHANGES, HASSLES, AND UPLIFTS

What was the Social Readjustment Rating Scale designed to reveal?

The SRRS assesses stress in terms of life events that necessitate life change. Holmes and Rahe found a relationship between degree of life stress (as measured on the scale) and major health problems.

What roles do hassles and uplifts play in the stress of life, according to Lazarus?

According to Lazarus, daily hassles typically cause more stress than major life changes. The positive experiences in life—the uplifts—can neutralize the effects of many of the hassles.

Key Terms
Social Readjustment Rating Scale (SRRS) (p. 463); hassles (p. 463); uplifts (p. 465)

SOURCES OF STRESS: THE COMMON AND THE EXTREME

How do approach–approach, avoidance–avoidance, and approach–avoidance conflicts differ?

In an approach–approach conflict, a person must decide between equally desirable alternatives; in an avoidance–avoidance conflict, between two undesirable alternatives. In an approach–avoidance conflict, a person is both drawn to and repelled by a choice.

How do the unpredictability and lack of control over a stressor affect its impact?

Stressors that are unpredictable and uncontrollable are more stressful than those that are predictable and controllable.

For people to function effectively and find satisfaction on the job, what nine variables should fall within their comfort zone?

Nine variables that should fall within a worker's comfort zone are workload, clarity of job description and evaluation criteria, physical variables, job status, accountability, task variety, human contact, and physical and mental challenge.

What are some of the psychological and health consequences of job stress?

Job stress can cause serious illnesses, such as depression, high blood pressure, and cardiovascular disease; it can also cause headaches, exhaustion, back problems, insomnia, and indigestion. Other consequences may include absenteeism, reduced productivity, tardiness, accidents, substance abuse, low morale, and alienation from co-workers.

What is burnout?

Burnout is the result of intense, unrelieved, and unmanaged job stress; a person experiencing burnout becomes pessimistic, dissatisfied, inefficient on the job, and debilitated psychologically.

How to people typically react to catastrophic events?

Victims of catastrophic events are initially dazed and stunned. When they begin to recover from the shock, they typically experience anxiety, nightmares, and a compulsive need to recount the event over and over.

What is posttraumatic stress disorder?

Posttraumatic stress disorder (PTSD) is a prolonged, severe stress reaction to a catastrophic event.

Key Terms
approach–approach conflict (p. 466); avoidance–avoidance conflict (p. 466); approach–avoidance conflict (p. 466); decision latitude (p. 468); burnout (p. 469); posttraumatic stress disorder (PTSD) (p. 469)

THEORIES OF STRESS

What is the general adaptation syndrome?

The general adaptation syndrome is the predictable sequence of reactions that organisms show in response to stressors. It consists of the alarm stage, the resistance stage, and the exhaustion stage.

What are the roles of primary and secondary appraisal when a person is confronted with a potentially stressful event?

Lazarus maintains that when confronted with a potentially stressful event, a person engages in a cognitive appraisal process consisting of (1) a primary appraisal, to evaluate the relevance of the event to one's well-being (whether it will be positive; will be irrelevant; or will involve harm or loss, threat, or challenge); and (2) a secondary appraisal to determine how to cope with the stressor.

Key Terms
stressor (p. 471); general adaptation syndrome (GAS) (p. 471); alarm stage (p. 471); resistance stage (p. 471); exhaustion stage (p. 472); primary appraisal (p. 472); secondary appraisal (p. 472)

COPING WITH STRESS

What is the difference between problem-focused and emotion-focused coping?

Problem-focused coping is a response aimed at reducing, modifying, or eliminating the source of stress; emotion-focused coping is aimed at reducing the emotional impact of the stressor.

Key Terms
coping (p. 474); problem-focused coping (p. 474); emotion-focused coping (p. 474); proactive coping (p. 474)

HEALTH AND ILLNESS

How do the biomedical and biopsychosocial models differ in their approaches to health and illness?

The biomedical model focuses on illness rather than on health and explains illness in terms of biological factors. The biopsychosocial model focuses on health as well as on illness and holds that both are determined by a combination of biological, psychological, and social factors.

What are the Type A and Type B behavior patterns?

The Type A behavior pattern, often cited as a risk factor for coronary heart disease, is characterized by a sense of time urgency, impatience, excessive competitive drive, hostility, and easily aroused anger. The Type B behavior pattern is characterized by a relaxed, easygoing approach to life.

What aspect of the Type A behavior pattern is most clearly linked to coronary heart disease?

Hostility is the aspect of the Type A pattern most clearly linked to coronary heart disease.

What are the effects of stress and depression on the immune system?

Both stress and depression have been associated with lowered immune response, and stress has been linked with increased symptoms of various infectious diseases.

What four personal factors are associated with health and resistance to stress?

Personal factors related to health and resistance to stress are optimism, psychological hardiness, religious involvement, and social support.

Key Terms
biomedical model (p. 476); biopsychosocial model (p. 476); health psychology (p. 476); sedentary lifestyle

(p. 477); Type A behavior pattern (p. 478); Type B behavior pattern (p. 478); lymphocytes (p. 481); psychoneuroimmunology (p. 482); hardiness (p. 483); social support (p. 484)

LIFESTYLE AND HEALTH

What constitutes an unhealthy lifestyle, and how serious a factor is lifestyle in illness and disease?

Slightly over 50% of all deaths in this country can be attributed to unhealthy lifestyle factors, which include smoking, overeating, an unhealthy diet, too much alcohol, drug abuse, and/or too little exercise and rest.

Why is smoking considered the single most preventable cause of death?

Smoking is considered the single most preventable cause of death because it is directly related to 434,000 deaths each year, including deaths from heart disease, cancer, lung disease, and stroke.

What are some health risks of alcohol abuse?

Alcohol abuse damages virtually every organ in the body, including the liver, stomach, skeletal muscles, heart, and brain; and it is involved in over 50% of motor vehicle accidents.

What are some benefits of regular aerobic exercise?

Regular aerobic exercise reduces the risk of cardiovascular disease, increases muscular strength, moderates the effects of stress, makes bones denser and stronger, and helps one maintain a desirable weight.

Key Terms
controlled drinking (p. 488); aerobic exercise (p. 488)

Surf It!

Want to be sure you've absorbed the material in Chapter 13, "Health and Stress," before the big test? Visiting *www.abacon.com/wood* can put a top grade within your reach. The site is loaded with free practice tests, flashcards, activities, and links to help you review your way to an A. To enliven that inevitable study break, the site also offers personality assessment quizzes and a psychology career corner.

14 Personality Theory and Assessment

What makes us the way we are? Are the personality characteristics we exhibit influenced more markedly by genes or by the environment in which we live, grow, and develop? Environments can be strikingly different. Consider the environments described in the next two paragraphs.

Oskar Stohr was raised as a Catholic by his grandmother in Nazi Germany. As part of Hitler's youth movement, Oskar was expected to be an obedient Nazi. Book burnings, military parades, hatred of Jews, and the right hand raised with the salute "Heil Hitler" were all part of Oskar's early environment. How did this environment affect his personality?

Jack Yufe, the same age as Oskar, was raised by his Jewish father on the island of Trinidad. Far removed from the goose-stepping storm troopers in Nazi Germany, Jack enjoyed all of the educational advantages and social supports of a middle-class Jewish upbringing. How did Jack's environment affect his personality?

Though raised in starkly different environments, Oskar and Jack are amazingly alike. They have quick tempers, are domineering toward women, enjoy surprising people by faking sneezes in elevators, and flush the toilet before using it. They both read magazines from back to front, store rubber bands on their wrists, like spicy foods and sweet liqueurs, and dip buttered toast in their coffee.

The list of similarities between Oskar and Jack is much longer, but there is a good reason for them. The men are identical twins. They were separated shortly after birth when their father took Jack with him to the island of Trinidad, and their maternal grandmother raised Oskar in Germany.

Researchers at the Minnesota Center for Twin and Adoption Research are studying the effects of genetics and environment on identical twins reared apart. When Oskar and Jack first arrived at the center to take part in the study, they looked almost exactly alike physically, and both of them were wearing double-breasted blue shirts with epaulets, identical neatly trimmed mustaches, and wire-rimmed glasses. How powerfully the genes influence personality!

Joan Gardiner and Jean Nelson are another pair of identical twins in the Minnesota study. They were also raised apart, but their environments did not differ so markedly. Joan's adoptive mother and Jean's adoptive father were sister and brother, so the twins were together quite often.

Like Oskar and Jack, Joan and Jean have many similarities and a few differences. But one difference between the twins is so unusual that researchers are especially intrigued by it. Joan is musical; Jean is not. Although her adoptive mother was a piano teacher, Jean does not play. But Joan, whose adoptive mother was not a musician, plays piano very well—so well, in fact, that she has performed with the Minnesota Symphony Orchestra. Joan's mother made her practice piano several hours every day, while Jean's mother allowed her to pursue whatever interests she chose.

Duplicate genes but differences in musical ability—how do the researchers explain this? David Lykken of the Minnesota Center suggests that both twins have the same genetic musical capability, but the reason one plays and the other does not shows the effects produced by the environment. How powerfully the environment influences personality!

personality: A person's characteristic patterns of behavior, thinking, and feeling.

It is often said that no two people are exactly alike, that each of us is unique. When most people talk about someone's uniqueness, they are referring to the personality. **Personality** is defined as an individual's characteristic patterns of behaving, thinking, and feeling (Carver & Scheier, 1996). During the 2000 presidential election, people made inferences about the personalities of candidates George W. Bush and Al Gore. Gore was perceived to be somewhat stiff and less approachable than Bush, who was seen as warmer, more personable, and more natural. Such perceptions may or may not be accurate. What do psychologists know about personality?

There are a number of theories that attempt to account for personality differences and explain how people come to be the way they are. In this chapter we explore some of the major personality theories and a variety of tests and inventories used to assess personality.

SIGMUND FREUD AND PSYCHOANALYSIS

To what two aspects of Freud's work does the term *psychoanalysis* apply?

Most textbooks begin their exploration of personality theory with Sigmund Freud, and for good reason. Freud created one of the first and most controversial personality theories. Using information gained while treating his patients and from his own life experiences, Freud developed the theory of **psychoanalysis.** When you hear the term *psychoanalysis,* you may picture a psychiatrist treating a troubled patient on a couch. But psychoanalysis is much more than that. The term refers not only to a therapy for treating psychological disorders (which we will explore in Chapter 16) but also to a personality theory.

Sigmund Freud (1856–1939), with his daughter Anna.

Freud's theory of psychoanalysis is neither the extension of an earlier theory nor a reaction against one. It is largely original, and it was revolutionary and shocking to the 19th- and early 20th-century European audience to which it was introduced. The major components of Freud's theory, and perhaps the most controversial, are (1) the central role of the sexual instinct, (2) the concept of infantile sexuality, and (3) the dominant part played by the unconscious in moving and shaping human thought and behavior. Freud's theory assumes a psychic determinism, the view that there is a cause for every thought, idea, feeling, action, or behavior. Nothing happens by chance or accident; everything we do and even everything we forget to do has a cause behind it.

A married man vacationing alone in Hawaii sends his wife a postcard and writes, "Having a wonderful time! Wish you were her." The husband, no doubt, would protest that he was writing hurriedly and accidentally left off the *e.* His wife might suspect otherwise, and Freud would agree. The "her" was no accident. It was a Freudian slip. Slips of the tongue, slips of the pen, and forgetting appointments—incidents we often call accidental—are not accidental at all, according to Freud (1901/1960).

The Conscious, the Preconscious, and the Unconscious: Levels of Awareness

What are the three levels of awareness in consciousness?

Freud believed that there are three levels of awareness in consciousness: the conscious, the preconscious, and the unconscious. The **conscious** consists of whatever we are aware of at any given moment—a thought, a feeling, a sensation, or a memory. When attention shifts, there is a change in the content of the conscious.

Freud's **preconscious** is very much like long-term memory. It contains all the memories, feelings, experiences, and perceptions that we are not consciously thinking about at the moment, but that may be brought to consciousness. Where did you go to high school? In what year were you born? This information resides in your preconscious but can easily be brought to consciousness.

The most important of the three levels is the **unconscious,** which Freud believed to be the primary motivating force of human behavior. The unconscious holds memories that once were conscious but were so unpleasant or anxiety-provoking that they were repressed (involuntarily removed from consciousness). The unconscious also contains all of the instincts (sexual and aggressive), wishes, and desires that have never been allowed into consciousness. Freud traced the roots of psychological disorders to these impulses and repressed memories.

psychoanalysis (SY-co-ah-NAL-ih-sis): Freud's term for his theory of personality and his therapy for treating psychological disorders.

conscious (KON-shus): The thoughts, feelings, sensations, or memories of which a person is aware at any given moment.

preconscious: The thoughts, feelings, and memories that a person is not consciously aware of at the moment but that may be brought to consciousness.

unconscious (un-KON-shus): For Freud, the primary motivating force of behavior, containing repressed memories as well as instincts and wishes that have never been conscious.

The Id, the Ego, and the Superego: Warring Components of the Personality

What are the roles of the id, the ego, and the superego?

In 1920, when he was nearly 65 years old, Freud (1923/1961) proposed a new conception of the personality, one that contained three systems—the id, the ego, and the superego. These systems do not exist physically; they are only concepts, or ways of looking at personality.

The **id** is the only part of the personality that is present at birth. It is inherited, primitive, inaccessible, and completely unconscious. The id contains (1) the life instincts, which are the sexual instincts and the biological urges such as hunger and thirst, and (2) the death instinct, which accounts for aggressive and destructive impulses (Freud, 1933/1965). The id operates according to the **pleasure principle;** that is, it tries to seek pleasure, avoid pain, and gain immediate gratification of its wishes. The id is the source of the **libido,** the psychic energy that fuels the entire personality; yet the id cannot act on its own. It can only wish, image, fantasize, demand.

The **ego** is the logical, rational, realistic part of the personality. The ego evolves from the id and draws its energy from the id. One of the ego's functions is to satisfy the id's urges. But the ego, which is mostly conscious, acts according to the reality principle. It must consider the constraints of the real world in determining appropriate times, places, and objects for gratification of the id's wishes. The art of the possible is its guide, and sometimes compromises must be made—settling for a McDonald's hamburger instead of steak or lobster.

When a child is age 5 or 6, the **superego**—the moral component of the personality—is formed. The superego has two parts: (1) The "conscience" consists of all the behaviors for which the child has been punished and about which he or she feels guilty; (2) the "ego ideal" contains the behaviors for which the child has been praised and rewarded and about which he or she feels pride and satisfaction. At first the superego reflects only the parents' expectations of what is good and right, but it expands over time to incorporate teachings from the broader social world. In its quest for moral perfection, the superego sets guidelines that define and limit the ego's flexibility. A harsher judge than any external authority, including one's parents, the superego judges not only behavior, but also thoughts, feelings, and wishes.

Figure 14.1 describes the three systems of the personality.

What is a defense mechanism?

id (IHD): The unconscious system of the personality, which contains the life and death instincts and operates on the pleasure principle.

pleasure principle: The principle by which the id operates to seek pleasure, avoid pain, and obtain immediate gratification.

libido (lih-BEE-doe): Freud's name for the psychic or sexual energy that comes from the id and provides the energy for the entire personality.

ego (EE-go): In Freudian theory, the rational, largely conscious system of personality, which operates according to the reality principle.

superego (sue-per-EE-go): The moral system of the personality, which consists of the conscience and the ego ideal.

defense mechanism: An unconscious, irrational means used by the ego to defend against anxiety; involves self-deception and the distortion of reality.

repression: Involuntarily removing an unpleasant memory or barring disturbing sexual and aggressive impulses from consciousness.

Defense Mechanisms: Protecting the Ego

All would be well if the id, the ego, and the superego had compatible aims. But the id's demands for sensual pleasure are often in direct conflict with the superego's desire for moral perfection. At times the ego needs some way to defend itself against the anxiety created by the excessive demands of the id, by the harsh judgments of the superego, or by the sometimes threatening conditions in the environment. Often the ego can relieve anxiety by solving its problems rationally and directly. When it cannot do so, it must resort to irrational defenses against anxiety, called *defense mechanisms.* Freud's daughter Anna, also a psychoanalyst, contributed much to the understanding of defense mechanisms (A. Freud, 1966).

A **defense mechanism** is a technique used to defend against anxiety and to maintain self-esteem, but it involves self-deception and an altering of "perception of both internal and external reality" (Vaillant, 1994). People use defense mechanisms to protect themselves from failure and from guilt-producing desires or actions. Defense mechanisms are like painkillers. They lessen the pain of anxiety, but do not cure the problem; and if they are to work, they must be unconscious. All people use defense mechanisms to some degree; it is only their overuse that is considered abnormal. But there is a price to be paid. Psychic energy is required to keep defenses in place—energy that could be used more profitably in other ways.

Repression: Out of Mind, Out of Sight According to Freud, **repression** is the most important and the most frequently used defense mechanism, and it is present

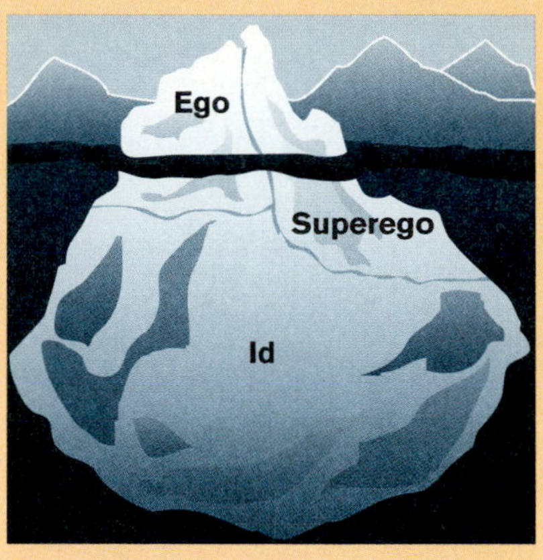

Figure 14.1

Freud's Conception of Personality

According to Freud, personality, which may be conceptualized as a giant iceburg, is composed of three structures: the id, the ego, and the superego. The id, completely unconscious, is wholly submerged, floating beneath the surface. The ego is largely conscious and visible, but partly unconscious. The superego also operates at both the conscious and unconscious levels.

to some degree in all other defense mechanisms. Repression operates in two ways: (1) It can remove painful or threatening memories, thoughts, ideas, or perceptions from consciousness and keep them in the unconscious; (2) it can prevent unconscious but disturbing sexual and aggressive impulses from breaking into consciousness.

What are two ways in which repression operates?

Even though they are repressed, the memories lurk in the unconscious and exert an active influence on personality and behavior. In fact, Freud (1933/1965) said repressed memories are "virtually immortal; after the passage of decades, they behave as though they had just occurred" (p. 74). This is why repressed traumatic events of childhood can cause psychological disorders (neuroses) in adults. Freud believed that the way to cure such disorders was to bring the repressed material back to consciousness. This was what he tried to accomplish through his system of therapy, psychoanalysis.

Other Defense Mechanisms: Excuses, Substitutions, and Denials There are several other defense mechanisms that people may use from time to time. They use **projection** when they attribute their own undesirable impulses, thoughts, personality traits, or behavior to others, or when they minimize the undesirable in themselves and exaggerate it in others. Projection allows people to avoid acknowledging unacceptable traits and thereby to maintain self-esteem, but it seriously distorts their perception of the external world. A sexually promiscuous husband or wife may accuse the partner of being unfaithful. A dishonest businessperson may think everyone is out to cheat him or her.

What are some other defense mechanisms?

Denial is a refusal to acknowledge consciously or to believe that a danger or a threatening condition exists. Many people who abuse alcohol and drugs deny that they have a problem. Yet denial is sometimes useful as a temporary means of getting through a crisis until a more permanent adjustment can be made, such as when people initially deny the existence of a terminal illness.

Rationalization occurs when a person unconsciously supplies a logical, rational, or socially acceptable reason rather than the real reason for an action or event. Rationalization can be used to justify past, present, or future behaviors or to soften the disappointment connected with not attaining a desired goal. When people rationalize, they make excuses for, or justify, failures and mistakes. A student who did not study and then failed a test might complain, "The test was unfair."

Sometimes, when frustrated or anxious, people may use **regression** and revert to behavior that might have reduced anxiety at an earlier stage of development. A 5-year-old child with a new baby sister or brother may regress and suck her thumb or drag a blanket around the house. An adult may have a temper tantrum, rant and rave, or throw things.

Reaction formation is at work when people express exaggerated ideas and emotions that are the opposite of their disturbing, unconscious impulses and desires. In

projection: Attributing one's own undesirable thoughts, impulses, traits, or behaviors to others.

denial: Refusing to acknowledge consciously the existence of danger or a threatening condition.

rationalization: Supplying a logical, rational, socially acceptable reason rather than the real reason for an action.

regression: Reverting to a behavior characteristic of an earlier stage of development.

reaction formation: Denying an unacceptable impulse, often a sexual or aggressive one, by giving strong conscious expression to its opposite.

Review & Reflect 14.1 Defense Mechanisms

Defense Mechanism	Description	Example
Repression	Involuntarily removing an unpleasant memory from consciousness or barring disturbing sexual and aggressive impulses from consciousness	Jill forgets a traumatic incident from childhood.
Projection	Attributing one's own undesirable traits or impulses to another	A very lonely divorced woman accuses all men of having only one thing on their minds.
Denial	Refusing to acknowledge consciously the existence of danger or a threatening situation	Amy fails to take a tornado warning seriously and is severely injured.
Rationalization	Supplying a logical, rational reason rather than the real reason for an action or event	Fred tells his friend that he didn't get the job because he didn't have connections.
Regression	Reverting to a behavior characteristic of an earlier stage of development	Susan bursts into tears whenever she is criticized.
Reaction formation	Expressing exaggerated ideas and emotions that are the opposite of disturbing, unconscious impulses and desires	A former purchaser of pornography, Bob is now a tireless crusader against it.
Displacement	Substituting a less threatening object for the original object of an impulse	After being spanked by his father, Bill hits his baby brother.
Sublimation	Rechanneling sexual and aggressive energy into pursuits that society considers acceptable or even admirable	Tim goes to a gym to work out when he feels hostile and frustrated.

reaction formation the conscious thought or feeling masks the unconscious one. Unconscious hatred may be expressed as love and devotion, cruelty as kindness. A reaction formation may be suspected when a behavior is extreme, excessive, and compulsive, as when a former chain smoker becomes irate and complains loudly at the faintest whiff of cigarette smoke. Reaction formation can be viewed as a barrier a person unconsciously erects to keep from acting on an unacceptable impulse.

Displacement occurs when a person substitutes a less threatening object or person for the original object of a sexual or aggressive impulse. If your boss makes you angry, you may take out your hostility on your boyfriend or girlfriend, husband or wife.

With **sublimation,** people rechannel sexual or aggressive energy into pursuits or accomplishments that society considers acceptable or even praiseworthy. An aggressive person may rechannel the aggression and become a football or hockey player, a boxer, a surgeon, or a butcher. Freud viewed sublimation as the only completely healthy ego defense mechanism. In fact, Freud (1930/1962) considered all advancements in civilization to be the result of sublimation.

Review & Reflect 14.1 summarizes the defense mechanisms

displacement: Substituting a less threatening object for the original object of an impulse.

sublimation: Rechanneling sexual or aggressive energy into pursuits that society considers acceptable or admirable.

Remember It!

1. Psychoanalysis is both a theory of personality and a therapy for the treatment of psychological disorders. (true/false)
2. Freud considered the (conscious, unconscious) to be the primary motivating force of human behavior.
3. The part of the personality that would make you want to eat, drink, and be merry is your

   a. id. b. ego. c. superego. d. ego ideal.
4. You just found a gold watch in a darkened movie theater. Which part of your personality would urge you to turn it in to the lost-and-found?

   a. id b. ego c. superego d. ego ideal
5. The part of the personality that determines appropriate ways to satisfy biological urges is the

   a. id. b. ego. c. superego. d. ego ideal.
6. Defense mechanisms are used only by psychologically unhealthy individuals. (true/false)
7. Match the defense mechanism and the example.

   ____ (1) sublimation
   ____ (2) repression
   ____ (3) displacement
   ____ (4) rationalization

   a. forgetting a traumatic childhood experience
   b. supplying a logical reason for arriving late
   c. crafting a creative work (art, music, writing, etc.)
   d. venting anger on a friend or spouse after getting a speeding ticket from a police officer

Answers: 1. true 2. unconscious 3. a 4. c 5. b 6. false 7. (1) c (2) a (3) d (4) b

The Psychosexual Stages of Development: Centered on the Erogenous Zones

What are the psychosexual stages, and why did Freud consider them so important in personality development?

The sex instinct, Freud said, is the most important factor influencing personality; but it does not suddenly appear full-blown at puberty. It is present at birth and then develops through a series of **psychosexual stages.** Each stage centers on a particular erogenous zone, a part of the body that provides pleasurable sensations and around which a conflict arises (1905/1953b; 1920/1963b). If the conflict is not resolved without undue difficulty, the child may develop a **fixation.** This means that a portion of the libido (psychic energy) remains invested at that stage, leaving less energy to meet the challenges of future stages. Overindulgence at a stage may leave a person unwilling psychologically to move on to the next stage. But too little gratification may leave the person trying to make up for previously unmet needs. Freud believed that certain personality characteristics develop as a result of difficulty at one or another of the stages.

psychosexual stages: A series of stages through which the sexual instinct develops; each stage is defined by an erogenous zone that becomes the center of new pleasures and conflicts.

fixation: Arrested development at a psychosexual stage occurring because of excessive gratification or frustration at that stage.

oral stage: Freud's first psychosexual stage (birth to 1 or 1½ years), in which sensual pleasure is derived mainly through stimulation of the mouth.

anal stage: Freud's second psychosexual stage (ages 1 or 1½ to 3 years), in which the child derives sensual pleasure mainly from expelling and withholding feces.

The Oral Stage (Birth to 12 or 18 Months) During the **oral stage,** the mouth is the primary source of an infant's sensual pleasure, which Freud (1920/1963b) considered to be an expression of infantile sexuality. The conflict at this stage centers on weaning. Too much or too little gratification may result in an oral fixation—an excessive preoccupation with oral activities such as eating, drinking, smoking, gum chewing, nail biting, and even kissing. (Freud's 20-cigars-a-day habit probably qualifies as an oral fixation, according to his theory.) Freud claimed that difficulties at the oral stage can result in personality traits such as either excessive dependence, optimism, and gullibility (tendency to "swallow" anything) or extreme pessimism, sarcasm, hostility, and aggression.

The Anal Stage (1 or 1½ to 3 Years) During the **anal stage,** children derive sensual pleasure, Freud believed, from expelling and withholding feces. But a conflict arises when toilet training begins, because this is one of the parents' first

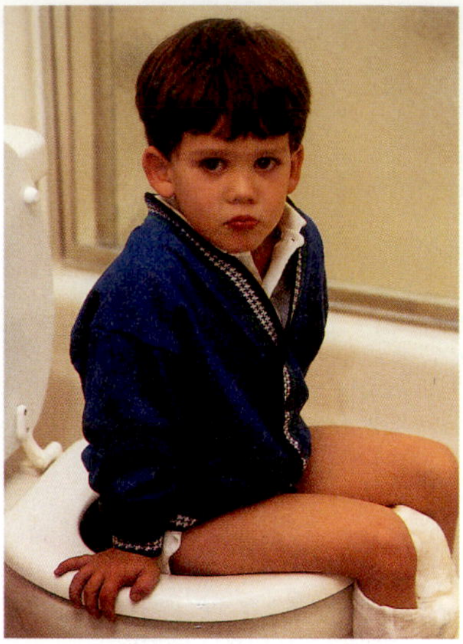

Freud believed that a fixation at the anal stage, resulting from harsh parental pressure, could lead to an anal retentive personality—characterized by excessive stubbornness, rigidity, and neatness.

attempts to have children give up or postpone gratification. When parents are harsh in their approach, children may rebel openly, defecating whenever and wherever they please. This may lead to an anal expulsive personality—someone who is sloppy, irresponsible, rebellious, hostile, and destructive. Other children may defy their parents and gain attention by withholding feces. They may develop anal retentive personalities, gaining security through what they possess and becoming stingy, stubborn, rigid, excessively neat and clean, orderly, and precise (Freud, 1933/1965). Do these patterns remind you of Felix and Oscar of the old TV series *The Odd Couple*?

What is the Oedipus complex?

The Phallic Stage (3 to 5 or 6 Years) During the **phallic stage,** children learn that they can derive pleasure from touching their genitals, and masturbation is common. They become aware of the anatomical differences in males and females and may begin to "play doctor."

The conflict that develops at this stage is a sexual desire for the parent of the opposite sex and a hostility toward the same-sex parent, a conflict Freud called the **Oedipus complex** (after the central character in the Greek tragedy *Oedipus Rex,* by Sophocles). "Boys concentrate their sexual wishes upon their mother and develop hostile impulses against their father as being a rival" (1925/1963a, p. 61). But the young boy eventually develops castration anxiety—an intense fear that his father might retaliate and harm him by cutting off his penis, the offending organ (1933/1965). This fear becomes so intense, Freud believed, that the boy usually resolves the Oedipus complex by identifying with his father and repressing his sexual feelings for his mother. With identification, the child takes on his father's behaviors, mannerisms, and superego standards, and in this way the superego develops (Freud, 1930/1962).

Girls experience a similar internal Oedipal conflict that is often referred to as the Electra complex, although Freud did not use that term. When young girls discover they have no penis, they develop "penis envy," Freud claimed, and they turn to their father because he has the desired organ (1933/1965). They feel sexual desires for him and develop jealousy and rivalry toward their mother. But eventually girls, too, experience anxiety as a result of their hostile feelings. They repress their sexual feelings toward the father and identify with the mother, leading to the formation of their superego (Freud, 1930/1962).

According to Freud, failure to resolve these conflicts can have serious consequences for both boys and girls. Freud thought that tremendous guilt and anxiety could be carried over into adulthood and cause sexual problems, great difficulty relating to members of the opposite sex, and even homosexuality.

The Latency Period (5 or 6 Years to Puberty) Following the stormy phallic stage, the **latency period** is one of relative calm. The sex instinct is repressed and temporarily sublimated in school and play activities, hobbies, and sports. And children prefer same-sex friends and playmates.

The Genital Stage (from Puberty On) In the **genital stage,** the focus of sexual energy gradually shifts to the opposite sex for the vast majority of people, culminating in heterosexual love and the attainment of full adult sexuality. Freud believed that the few who reach the genital stage without having fixations at earlier stages can achieve the state of psychological health that he equated with the ability to love and work.

Review & Reflect 14.2 provides a summary of Freud's psychosexual stages.

According to Freud, what are the two primary sources of influence on the personality?

Freud's Explanation of Personality

According to Freud, personality is almost completely formed at age 5 or 6, when the Oedipal conflict is resolved and the superego is formed. He believed that there are two primary sources of influence on personality: (1) the traits that develop because of fixations at any of the psychosexual stages, and (2) the relative strengths of the id, the ego, and the superego. In psychologically healthy people, there is a balance

phallic stage: Freud's third psychosexual stage (ages 3 to 5 or 6 years), during which sensual pleasure is derived mainly through touching the genitals, and the Oedipus complex arises.

Oedipus complex (ED-uh-pus): Occurring in the phallic stage, a conflict in which the child is sexually attracted to the opposite-sex parent and feels hostility toward the same-sex parent.

latency period: The period following Freud's phallic stage (ages 5 or 6 years to puberty), in which the sex instinct is largely repressed and temporarily sublimated in school and play activities.

genital stage: Freud's final psychosexual stage (from puberty on), in which for most people the focus of sexual energy gradually shifts to the opposite sex, culminating in the attainment of full adult sexuality.

Review & Reflect 14.2 Freud's Psychosexual Stages of Development

Stage	Erogenous Zone	Conflicts/Experiences	Adult Traits Associated with Problems at This Stage
Oral (birth to 12–18 months) 	Mouth	Weaning Oral gratification from sucking, eating, biting	Optimism, gullibility, dependency, pessimism, passivity, hostility, sarcasm, aggression
Anal (12–18 months to 3 years) 	Anus	Toilet training Gratification from expelling and withholding feces	Excessive cleanliness, orderliness, stinginess, messiness, rebelliousness, destructiveness
Phallic (3 to 5–6 years) 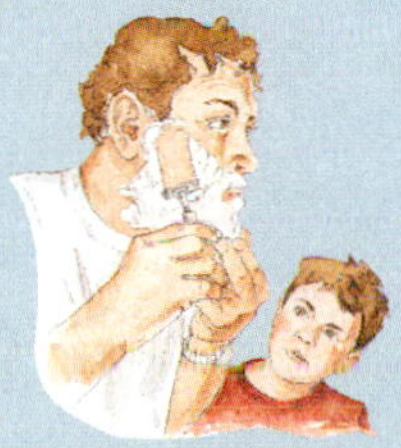	Genitals	Oedipal conflict Sexual curiosity Masturbation	Flirtatiousness, vanity, promiscuity, pride, chastity
Latency (5–6 years to puberty) 	None	Period of sexual calm Interest in school, hobbies, same-sex friends	
Genital (puberty onward) 	Genitals	Revival of sexual interests Establishment of mature sexual relationships	

among the three components. If the id is too strong and the superego too weak, people will take pleasure and gratify desires, no matter who is hurt or what the cost, and not feel guilty. But a tyrannical superego will leave people with perpetual guilt feelings, unable to enjoy sensual pleasure.

Evaluating Freud's Contribution

Freud's theory is so comprehensive (he wrote more than 24 volumes) that its elements must be evaluated separately. His beliefs that women are inferior to men sexually, morally, and intellectually and that they suffer penis envy seem ridiculous today. Also, research contradicts Freud's notion that personality is almost completely formed by age 5 or 6. However, psychology is indebted to him for emphasizing the influence of early childhood experiences on later development.

Critics charge that much of Freud's theory defies scientific testing. How, they ask, can a conceptual framework based on Freud's analysis of his own life and the case histories of his disturbed patients provide a theory of personality generalizable to the larger population? The most serious flaw critics find is that Freud's theory interprets and explains behavior after the fact and lacks the power to predict behavior (Stanovich, 1989). In too many cases, any act of behavior or even no act of behavior at all can be interpreted to support Freud's theory. Some critics even go so far as to say that Freud's entire theory can be neither supported scientifically nor justified therapeutically (Crews, 1996; Erwin, 1996; Webster, 1995). Perhaps this is why most managed health care providers pay for only a limited amount of psychoanalytic therapy.

Freud believed that his concepts of the unconscious and the principles by which it operated were his most important work. In fact, the primary aim of psychoanalysis is to bring unconscious thoughts, wishes, and desires to consciousness. Leading scholars today do not dispute the existence of unconscious processes (Loftus & Klinger, 1992). However, they do not see the unconscious as envisioned by Freud. Rather, unconscious mental activity is viewed more broadly as information processing that takes place below the level of awareness. For example, certain aspects of stereotypic thinking, though unconscious, strongly influence the way people process information related to themselves and others (Bargh, 1997). And research by Motley (1985) indicates that although the unconscious is sometimes at work in Freudian slips, most slips of the tongue should be attributed to misfirings in the brain and its verbal mechanisms. Today, some researchers who hold the psychoanalytic view see psychoanalytic theory as primarily a cognitive theory, whose goal is to gain a fuller understanding of how the human mind functions (Blatt & Auerbach, 2000).

Today there are very few strict Freudians left, and for most psychoanalysts, Freud's techniques constitute only a part of the therapeutic arsenal. Sigmund Freud has been both worshipped and ridiculed, but his standing as a pioneer in psychology cannot be denied. Even today, when members of the general public are asked to name a famous psychologist, it is Freud's name that most readily comes to mind.

Remember It!

1. According to Freud, the sex instinct arises at (birth, puberty).
2. Which of the following lists presents Freud's psychosexual stages in the order in which they occur?
   a. anal; oral; genital; phallic
   b. genital; anal; oral; phallic
   c. oral; phallic; anal; genital
   d. oral; anal; phallic; genital
3. Matt's excessive concern with cleanliness and order could indicate a fixation at the ______________ stage.
   a. oral b. anal c. phallic d. genital
4. When a young boy develops sexual feelings toward his mother and hostility toward his father, he is said to have a conflict called the ______________.
5. According to Freud, which of the following represents a primary source of influence on personality?
   a. heredity
   b. life experiences after beginning school
   c. the relative strengths of the id, ego, and superego
   d. the problems experienced during adolescence

Answers: 1. birth 2. d 3. b 4. Oedipus complex 5. c

THE NEO-FREUDIANS

Several personality theorists, referred to as *neo-Freudians*, started their careers as followers of Freud but began to disagree on certain basic principles of psychoanalytic theory. Freud was rather intolerant of any differing perspectives on psychoanalysis (Slipp, 1999), and so these followers split with him. They modified aspects of the theory and presented their own original ideas about personality. We will discuss Carl Jung (analytical psychology), Alfred Adler (individual psychology), and Karen Horney.

Carl Gustav Jung (1875–1961)

Carl Gustav Jung: Delving into the Collective Unconscious

Carl Jung (1875–1961) differed with Freud on many major points. He did not consider the sexual instinct to be the main factor in personality; nor did he believe that the personality is almost completely formed in early childhood. For Jung (1933), middle age was an even more important period for personality development. He also disagreed with Freud on the basic structure of personality.

Jung's View of the Personality: A Different View of the Unconscious Jung conceived of the personality as consisting of three parts: the ego, the personal unconscious, and the collective unconscious. He saw the ego as the conscious component of personality, which carries out normal daily activities. Like Freud, he believed the ego to be secondary in importance to the unconscious.

The **personal unconscious** develops as a result of one's own experience and is therefore unique to each person. It contains all the experiences, thoughts, and perceptions accessible to the conscious, as well as repressed memories, wishes, and impulses. The personal unconscious resembles a combination of Freud's preconscious and unconscious.

The **collective unconscious** is the deepest and most inaccessible layer of the unconscious. Jung thought that the universal experiences of humankind throughout evolution are transmitted to each of us and reside in the collective unconscious. This is how he accounted for the similarity of certain myths, dreams, symbols, and religious beliefs in cultures widely separated by distance and time.

Figure 14.2 (on p. 506) provides a summary of Jung's conception of the personality.

Archetypes: Unconscious Predispositions The collective unconscious contains what Jung called *archetypes*. An **archetype** is an inherited tendency to respond to universal human situations in particular ways. Jung would say that the tendencies of people to believe in a god, a devil, evil spirits, and heroes, and to have a fear of the dark and of snakes, all result from inherited archetypes that reflect the shared experience of humankind.

Jung named several archetypes that exert a major influence on the personality: the persona, the shadow, the anima and animus, and the self. The *persona* is the public face one shows to the world—"a kind of mask, designed on the one hand to make a definite impression on others, and, on the other, to conceal the true nature of the individual" (Jung, 1966, p. 192). The persona is consistent with the roles people play, and helps them to function socially. But problems result if people confuse the persona (the mask) with the real person behind it.

The *shadow* is a powerful archetype that represents "the 'negative side' of the personality, the sum of all those unpleasant qualities we like to hide" (Jung, 1917/1953, par. 103). To deny the shadow, or to fail to be conscious of it, gives it more power. And ironically, the qualities we condemn most in others may be lurking in our own shadow, unadmitted and unknown.

While Jung saw differences in the psychology of males and females, he believed that each of us has within the unconscious qualities and images of the opposite sex, although usually in an underdeveloped state. The *anima* is Jung's term for the "inner feminine figure" within the unconscious of every man, and the *animus*, the "inner

According to Jung, what are the three components of personality?

What are five archetypes that Jung believed have a major influence on the personality?

personal unconscious: In Jung's theory, the layer of the unconscious containing all of the thoughts and experiences that are accessible to the conscious, as well as repressed memories and impulses.

collective unconscious: In Jung's theory, the most inaccessible layer of the unconscious, which contains the universal experiences of humankind transmitted to each individual.

archetype (AR-keh-type): Existing in the collective unconscious, an inherited tendency to respond in particular ways to universal human situations.

Figure 14.2

Jung's Conception of Personality

Like Freud, Carl Jung saw three components in personality. The ego and the personal unconscious are unique to each individual. The collective unconscious accounts for the similarity of myths and beliefs in diverse cultures.

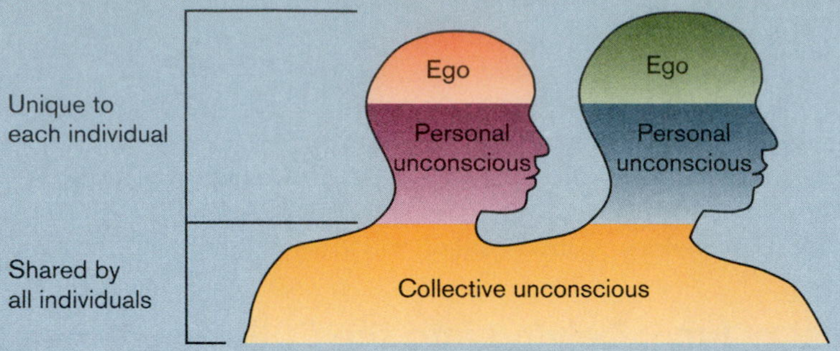

Structure	Characteristics
Ego	The conscious component of personality; carries out normal daily activities.
Personal unconscious	The component containing all the individual's memories, thoughts, and feelings that are accessible to consciousness, and all repressed memories, wishes, and impulses; similar to a combination of Freud's preconscious and unconscious.
Collective unconscious	The most inaccessible layer of the unconscious, shared by all people; contains the universal experiences of humankind throughout evolution, as well as the archetypes.

masculine figure" within the unconscious of every woman (Jung, 1961, p. 186). Both the masculine and feminine qualities must be consciously acknowledged and integrated, Jung thought, for a healthy personality to develop. Jung's work was a forerunner of more recent research on psychological androgyny (see Chapter 12).

The *self* represents the full development of the personality and is attained only when the opposing forces within are integrated and balanced. The self encompasses the conscious and the unconscious, the persona, the shadow, the masculine and feminine qualities, and the tendency toward extraversion or introversion (terms originated by Jung). **Extroversion** (Jung spelled it "extraversion") is the tendency to be outgoing, adaptable, and sociable; **introversion** is the tendency to focus inward and to be reflective, retiring, and nonsocial. A recent large cross-cultural study of extroversion identified its fundamental feature. Lucas and others (2000) studied more than 6,450 men and women from 39 nations, virtually covering the globe. The majority of the participants (some 83%) were between 18 and 25 years old. The researchers found some evidence that a strong motivation or desire for reward may be the link that holds the dimensions of extroversion together. They concluded that even "sociability," a key component of extroversion, may be a by-product of this desire.

Jung believed that the balancing and integration of the opposing forces of the personality begins in midlife. For some, the beginning of change may be accompanied by a midlife crisis, which Jung himself experienced. Because he emphasized personality development in midlife, many consider Jung the conceptual founder of the psychology of adult development (Moraglia, 1994).

Alfred Adler: Overcoming Inferiority

extroversion: The tendency to be outgoing, adaptable, and sociable.

introversion: The tendency to focus inward; to be reflective, retiring, and nonsocial.

Alfred Adler (1870–1937) disagreed with most of Freud's basic beliefs; on many points his views were the exact opposite. Adler emphasized the unity of the personality rather than the separate warring components of id, ego, and superego. He believed that human behavior is motivated more by the conscious than by the unconscious and that people are influenced more by future goals than by early childhood experiences.

What did Adler consider to be the driving force of the personality?

Unlike Freud, who claimed that unconscious sexual and aggressive impulses are the primary motivators, Adler (1927, 1956) maintained that people are driven by the need to compensate for inferiority and to strive for superiority or significance. For him, feelings of weakness and inferiority are an inevitable experience in every child's early life. (Adler himself had felt a particularly keen sense of inferiority as a child. He was small, sickly, and unable to walk until he was 4, because of rickets.) Adler (1964/1933) also maintained that *birth order* influences personality, making first-born children more likely than their younger siblings to be high achievers.

According to Adler (1956), people at an early age develop a "style of life"—a unique way in which the child and later the adult will go about the struggle to achieve superiority. Sometimes inferiority feelings are so strong that they prevent personal development, and Adler originated a term to describe this condition—the "inferiority complex" (Dreikurs, 1953). Because Adler's theory stressed the uniqueness of each individual's struggle to achieve superiority and referred to the "creative self," a conscious, self-aware component of the individual's personality, it is known as *individual psychology.*

Karen Horney: Championing Feminine Psychology

Why is Horney considered a pioneer in psychology?

—due to parenting skills

The work of Karen Horney (1885–1952) centered on two main themes—the neurotic personality (Horney, 1937, 1945, 1950) and feminine psychology (Horney, 1967). Horney considered herself a disciple of Freud, accepting his emphasis on unconscious motivation and the basic tools of psychoanalysis. However, she disagreed with many of his basic beliefs. She did not accept his division of personality into id, ego, and superego, and she flatly rejected his psychosexual stages and the concepts of the Oedipus complex and penis envy. Furthermore, Horney thought Freud overemphasized the role of the sexual instinct and neglected cultural and environmental influences on personality. While she did stress the importance of early childhood experiences, Horney (1939) believed that personality could continue to develop and change throughout life. Horney argued forcefully against Freud's notion that a woman's desire to have a child and a man are nothing more than a conversion of the unfulfilled wish for a penis.

Horney insisted that, rather than envying the male's penis, women really want the same opportunities, the same rights and privileges society grants to males. Freud did not respond directly to Horney's arguments, but implied that her challenge to his theory was merely a manifestation of her own penis envy. Horney prevailed and continued her pioneering efforts for women. She argued convincingly that women must be free to find their own personal identities, to develop their abilities, and to pursue careers if they choose.

Horney (1945) believed that in order to be psychologically healthy, we all need safety and satisfaction. But these needs can be frustrated in early childhood by parents

More than half a century ago, psychologist Karen Horney insisted that, rather than envying the penis, as Freud believed, women really want the same opportunities and privileges as men—to play sports at the Olympic and professional level, for example, and to pursue whatever careers they choose.

who are indifferent, unaffectionate, rejecting, or hostile. Such early experiences may cause a child to develop basic anxiety—"the feeling a child has of being isolated and helpless in a potentially hostile world" (p. 41). To minimize this basic anxiety and satisfy the need for safety, children develop coping strategies that form their basic attitude toward life—either moving toward people, moving against people, or moving away from people. Normal people move in all three ways as different situations demand. But a neurotic person will use only one way to reduce anxiety, and will use it excessively and inappropriately.

If we cannot tolerate ourselves the way we are, said Horney, we may repress all our negative attributes and replace them with an idealized image, perfect and unblemished. As long as this image remains real to us, we feel superior and entitled to make all kinds of demands and claims. Horney (1950) believed that the idealized self brings with it the "tyranny of the should"—unrealistic demands for personal perfection, which "no human being could fulfill" (p. 66). The irrational, neurotic thinking that may spring from the "tyranny of the should" is an important part of Horney's theory. Her influence may be seen in modern cognitive-behavioral therapies, which we will explore in Chapter 16.

Remember It!

1. In Jung's theory, the inherited part of the personality that stores the experiences of humankind is the (collective, personal) unconscious.
2. Match the archetype with its description.

____ (1) self	a. the dark side of one's nature
____ (2) anima or animus	b. one's public face
____ (3) shadow	c. the full development of the integrated and balanced personality
____ (4) persona	d. the qualities and images of the opposite sex carried within each person

3. Which personality theorist believed that the basic human drive is to overcome and compensate for inferiority feelings and strive for superiority and significance?
   a. Sigmund Freud
   b. Carl Jung
   c. Alfred Adler
   d. Karen Horney
4. Horney traced the origin of psychological maladjustment to
   a. the inferiority feelings of childhood.
   b. basic anxiety resulting from the parents' failure to satisfy the child's needs for safety and satisfaction.
   c. excessive frustration or overindulgence of the child at early stages of development.
   d. the failure to balance opposing forces in the personality.

Answers: 1. collective 2. (1) c (2) d (3) a (4) b 3. c 4. b

TRAIT THEORIES

What are trait theories of personality?

trait: A personal characteristic that is used to describe or explain personality.

How would you describe yourself—cheerful, moody, talkative, quiet, shy, friendly, outgoing? When you describe your personality or that of someone else, you probably list several relatively consistent personal characteristics called **traits.** Traits are the qualities or characteristics that make it possible for us to face a wide variety of situational demands and deal with unforeseen circumstances (De Raad & Kokkonen, 2000). There is not widespread agreement among psychologists concerning how many characteristics should be considered traits, but traits are useful for describing how people differ. **Trait theories** are attempts to explain personality and differences between people in terms of their personal characteristics.

trait theories: Theories that attempt to explain personality and differences between people in terms of their personal characteristics.

cardinal trait: Allport's name for a personal quality that is so strong a part of a person's personality that he or she may become identified with that trait.

central trait: Allport's name for the type of trait that might be mentioned in an accurate letter of recommendation.

Gordon Allport: Personality Traits in the Brain

How did Allport differentiate between cardinal and central traits?

Gordon Allport (1897–1967) claimed that personality traits are real entities, physically located somewhere in the brain (Allport & Odbert, 1936). Each person inherits a unique set of raw materials for given traits, which are then shaped by experiences. Traits describe the particular way an individual responds to the environment and the consistency of that response. Shy people respond to strangers differently than friendly people; self-confident people approach tasks differently than people who feel inferior. Some research in behavioral genetics supports the notion that certain personality characteristics are influenced by the genes (Finkel & McGue, 1997).

Allport (1961) identified two main categories of traits—common traits and individual traits. Common traits are those we share or hold in common with most others in our own culture. The quiet, polite behavior often seen in Asian people is a common trait of those cultures. More important to Allport were three types of individual traits: cardinal, central, and secondary traits.

A **cardinal trait** is "so pervasive and so outstanding in a life that . . . almost every act seems traceable to its influence" (Allport, 1961, p. 365). It is so strong a part of a person's personality that he or she may become identified with or known for that trait. We even describe people who, to some degree, exhibit the cardinal traits of well-known characters as being a Don Juan or a Scrooge, for example. **Central traits** are those, said Allport (1961), that we would "mention in writing a careful letter of recommendation" (p. 365). Do the *Try It!* to learn more about central traits.

Try It!

Which adjectives in this list best describe you? Which characterize your mother? Your father? In Allport's terms you are describing your or their central traits.

decisive	outgoing	generous	industrious
funny	inhibited	sloppy	deceptive
intelligent	religious	laid-back	cooperative
disorganized	arrogant	rebellious	reckless
shy	loyal	calm	sad
fearful	competitive	good-natured	honest
jealous	liberal	nervous	happy
controlled	friendly	serious	selfish
responsible	compulsive	humble	organized
rigid	quick	lazy	quiet

People also have secondary traits, but these are less obvious, less consistent, and not as critical in defining personality as the cardinal and central traits. Secondary traits are such things as food and music preferences and specific attitudes. Each of us has many more secondary traits than cardinal or central traits.

Raymond Cattell's 16 Personality Factors

How did Cattell differentiate between surface and source traits?

Raymond Cattell (1950) considered personality to be a pattern of traits providing the key to understanding and predicting a person's behavior. Cattell identified two types: surface traits and source traits.

surface traits: Cattell's name for observable qualities of personality, such as those used to describe a friend.

source traits: Cattell's name for the traits that make up the most basic personality structure and cause behavior.

If you were asked to describe your best friend, you might say that she is kind, honest, helpful, generous, and so on. These observable qualities of personality Cattell called **surface traits.** (Allport called these qualities central traits.) Using observations and questionnaires, Cattell studied thousands of people and found certain clusters of surface traits that appeared together time after time. He thought these were evidence of deeper, more general, underlying personality factors. Using factor analysis, a statistical technique, Cattell tried to identify these factors, which he called *source traits.*

Source traits make up the most basic personality structure and, according to Cattell, cause behavior. Even though these traits are common to everyone, people differ in the degree to which they possess each trait. Intelligence is a source trait, and every person has a certain amount of it, but obviously not exactly the same amount or the same kind. How intelligent people are can influence whether they pursue a college degree, what profession or job they choose, what type of leisure activities they enjoy, and what kind of friends they have.

Cattell found 23 source traits in normal individuals, 16 of which he studied in great detail. Cattell's Sixteen Personality Factor Questionnaire, commonly called *the 16 PF,* yields a personality profile (Cattell et al., 1950, 1977). A Cattell personality profile can be used to provide a better understanding of a single individual or to compare one person's traits with those of others. When later researchers tried to confirm Cattell's 16 factors, however, no one could find more than 7 factors, and most found 5 (Digman, 1990). You can chart your own source traits in the *Try It!*

Try It!

This hypothetical personality profile is based on Cattell's Sixteen Personality Factor Questionnaire. Along each of the 16 dimensions of bipolar traits, circle the point you think would apply to you if you took the 16 PF. (From Cattell, 1993.)

Reserved	■ ■ ■ ■ ■ ■ ■ ■ ■ ■	Warm
Concrete	■ ■ ■ ■ ■ ■ ■ ■ ■ ■	Abstract
Reactive	■ ■ ■ ■ ■ ■ ■ ■ ■ ■	Emotionally stable
Avoids conflict	■ ■ ■ ■ ■ ■ ■ ■ ■ ■	Dominant
Serious	■ ■ ■ ■ ■ ■ ■ ■ ■ ■	Lively
Expedient	■ ■ ■ ■ ■ ■ ■ ■ ■ ■	Rule-conscious
Shy	■ ■ ■ ■ ■ ■ ■ ■ ■ ■	Socially bold
Utilitarian	■ ■ ■ ■ ■ ■ ■ ■ ■ ■	Sensitive
Trusting	■ ■ ■ ■ ■ ■ ■ ■ ■ ■	Suspicious
Practical	■ ■ ■ ■ ■ ■ ■ ■ ■ ■	Imaginative
Forthright	■ ■ ■ ■ ■ ■ ■ ■ ■ ■	Private
Self-assured	■ ■ ■ ■ ■ ■ ■ ■ ■ ■	Apprehensive
Traditional	■ ■ ■ ■ ■ ■ ■ ■ ■ ■	Open to change
Group-oriented	■ ■ ■ ■ ■ ■ ■ ■ ■ ■	Self-reliant
Tolerates disorder	■ ■ ■ ■ ■ ■ ■ ■ ■ ■	Perfectionistic
Relaxed	■ ■ ■ ■ ■ ■ ■ ■ ■ ■	Tense

Hans Eysenck: Stressing Two Factors

What does Eysenck consider to be the two most important dimensions of personality?

British psychologist Hans Eysenck (1990) has always believed that personality is largely determined by the genes, and that environmental influences are slight at best. Although Eysenck claims that three higher-order factors, or dimensions, are needed to capture the essence of personality, he places particular emphasis on two of those dimensions—Extroversion (extroversion versus introversion) and Neuroticism (emotional stability versus instability). Extroverts are sociable, outgoing, and active, whereas introverts are withdrawn, quiet, and introspective. (Jung originally introduced the terms *introversion* and *extraversion.*) Emotionally stable people are calm, even-tempered, and often easygoing, while emotionally unstable people are anxious, excitable, and easily distressed.

Eysenck (1981) believes that individual variability on the two dimensions may be partly due to differences in nervous system functioning. He suggests that extroverts have a lower level of cortical arousal than introverts and as a result actively seek out more stimulation to increase arousal. Introverts are more easily aroused and thus more likely to show emotional instability. Stelmack (1990) suggests that rather than having a higher base rate of arousal, "introverts exhibit greater reactivity to sensory stimulation than extroverts" (p. 293).

The Five-Factor Theory of Personality: The Big Five

What are the Big Five personality dimensions in the five-factor theory as described by McCrae and Costa?

Today, the most talked-about personality theory is the **five-factor theory,** also known as the Big Five (Wiggins, 1996). Each of the five broad personality factors is composed of a constellation of traits. As Goldberg (1993; Goldberg & Saucier, 1995) puts it, the five-factor theory seeks to provide a scientifically accurate framework for organizing the many individual differences that characterize humankind.

Some researchers who accept these five broad dimensions of personality still disagree as to what they should be named. We will consider the Big Five dimensions using the names assigned by Robert McCrae and Paul Costa (1987; McCrae, 1996), the most influential proponents of the five-factor theory:

- *Extroversion.* This dimension contrasts such traits as sociable, outgoing, talkative, assertive, persuasive, decisive, and active with more introverted traits such as withdrawn, quiet, passive, retiring, and reserved.
- *Neuroticism.* People high on Neuroticism are prone to emotional instability. They tend to experience negative emotions and to be moody, irritable, nervous, and inclined to worry. Neuroticism differentiates people who are anxious, excitable, and easily distressed from those who are emotionally stable and thus calm, even-tempered, easygoing, and relaxed.
- *Conscientiousness.* This factor differentiates individuals who are dependable, organized, reliable, responsible, thorough, hard-working, and persevering from those who are undependable, disorganized, impulsive, unreliable, irresponsible, careless, negligent, and lazy.
- *Agreeableness.* This factor is composed of a collection of traits that range from compassion to antagonism toward others. A person high on Agreeableness would be a pleasant person, good-natured, warm, sympathetic, and cooperative; one low on Agreeableness would tend to be unfriendly, unpleasant, aggressive, argumentative, cold, even hostile and vindictive.
- *Openness to Experience.* This factor contrasts individuals who seek out varied experiences and who are imaginative, intellectually curious, and broad-minded with those who are concrete-minded and practical and whose interests are narrow. Researchers have found that being high on Openness to Experience is a requirement for creative accomplishment (King et al., 1996).

According to the five-factor theory of personality, people who are extroverts are sociable, outgoing, and active. What are some characteristics of introverts?

To measure the Big Five dimensions of personality, Costa and McCrae (1985, 1992a, 1997) developed the NEO Personality Inventory (NEO-PI) and, more recently, the Revised NEO Personality Inventory (NEO-PI-R).

Researchers from many different traditions have found five factors when they have subjected self-ratings, observer ratings, and peer ratings to factor analysis. Five factors have emerged, as well, from cross-cultural studies involving participants from Canada, Finland, Poland, Germany, Russia, and Hong Kong (Paunonen et al., 1996). Based on studies of a wide variety of cultures, McCrae and Costa (1997) "strongly suggest that personality trait structure is universal" (p. 509). In more

five-factor theory: A trait theory that attempts to explain personality using five broad dimensions, each of which is composed of a constellation of personality traits.

recent studies, McCrae and Costa and their colleagues have found universal changes in the strength of some personality factors as people age. Some 7,360 participants from five diverse cultures (Croatia, Italy, Germany, Portugal, and South Korea) were found to undergo changes in the relative strength of Neuroticism, Extroversion, and Openness to Experience, all of which tended to weaken between college age and middle adulthood. During the same period, Agreeableness and Conscientiousness strengthened somewhat for these participants. Similar maturational, or age-related, changes were reported for participants in the United States (McCrae et al., 2000).

Using meta-analysis, Sulloway (1996, 1997) found evidence of a relationship between birth order and the Big Five traits. First-borns were more likely than later-borns to be extroverted and conscientious, but less likely to be emotionally stable, agreeable, and open to experience.

Are there correlations between the Big Five personality dimensions and sensitivity to daily hassles? A 3-year longitudinal study among university students revealed that Neuroticism, Extroversion, and Conscientiousness were correlated with high levels of reported frustration due to daily hassles. There was only a small correlation of hassled feelings with Openness to Experience and none at all with Agreeableness (Vollrath, 2000).

Arguing from the evolutionary perspective, Buss (1991) suggests that humans evolved who were able to pay attention to, interpret, and act upon dimensions of their social world related to these traits and thus gain a better chance of survival. Others who hold the evolutionary perspective point to long-standing evidence of substantial heritability of certain personality factors, Neuroticism and Extroversion, for example.

Although acceptance for it is growing, the five-factor model has its critics. Block (1995) maintains that there is inconsistency in "the way the five-factor advocates represent the Big Five or say the factors ought to be understood" (p. 208). And Paunonen and Jackson (2000) have stated that there are many other dimensions of personality beyond the Big Five.

But the Big Five may be helpful in predicting general trends of behavior in a wide variety of situations. It has proved useful in predicting job performance in the United States (Costa, 1996) and Europe (Salgado, 1997). In fact, upon entering the job market, today's college students are likely to be asked to complete a personality inventory before they are hired.

Evaluating the Trait Perspective

Do people possess stable and enduring traits that predictably guide the way they will act over time and across changing situations? Critics of trait theories say no and maintain that there is very little consistency of behavior across situations and that behavior is not predictable on the basis of personality traits. In a recent study, Shoda and Mischel (2000) point out that for many behaviors of interest to social and personality psychologists, it is variability, not consistency, across situations that seems to be the norm. Initially, one of the severest critics of trait theories, Walter Mischel (1968), concluded that the situation, not a person's traits, determines behavior. His position stimulated the person–situation debate over relative importance of factors within the person and factors within the situation that account for behavior (Rowe, 1987). Mischel (1973, 1977) later modified his original position and admitted that behavior is influenced by both the person *and* the situation. Mischel views a trait as a conditional probability that a particular action will occur in response to a particular situation (Wright & Mischel, 1987).

Support for trait theories has come from longitudinal studies. McCrae and Costa (1990) studied personality traits of subjects over time and found them to be stable for periods of 3 to 30 years. Typically, personality changes very little with age. As McCrae (1993) puts it, "Stable individual differences in basic dimensions are a universal feature of adult personality" (p. 577). A large meta-analysis was performed recently to determine the consistency of personality traits from childhood into old age. The consistency of personality traits increased from .31 in childhood to .54 for college students, rose to .64 by age 30, and peaked at .74 between the ages of 50 and 70 (Roberts & DelVecchio, 2000).

The weight of evidence supports the view that there are internal traits that strongly influence behavior across situations (Carson, 1989; McAdams, 1992). At the same time, many situations in life call forth similar behavior from most people, even though internal traits differ drastically. Even the most talkative and boisterous among us tend to be quiet during a religious service, a funeral, or another solemn occasion. Characteristic traits, say the trait theorists, determine how we behave *most* of the time, not *all* of the time. Even the most optimistic, happy, and outgoing people have "down" days, fall ill, and frown occasionally.

Research on personality suggests that some traits, such as agreeableness, tend to change very little with age.

Remember It!

1. According to Allport, the kind of trait that is a defining characteristic of one's personality is a ______________ trait.
   a. common b. source c. secondary d. cardinal
2. According to Cattell, the differences between people are explained by the number of source traits they possess. (true/false)
3. Who claimed that psychologists can best understand personality by assessing people on two major dimensions, Extroversion and Neuroticism?
   a. Hans Eysenck c. Raymond Cattell
   b. Gordon Allport d. Carl Jung
4. The text suggests that, according to a growing consensus among trait theorists, there are ______________ major dimensions of personality.
   a. 3 b. 5 c. 7 d. 16

Answers: 1. d 2. false 3. a 4. b

LEARNING THEORIES AND PERSONALITY

According to the learning perspective, personality consists of the learned tendencies that have been acquired over a lifetime.

The Behaviorist View of B. F. Skinner

How did Skinner account for what most people refer to as personality?

B. F. Skinner and other strict behaviorists have an interesting view of personality. They deny that there is any such thing. What people call personality, they believe, is nothing more or less than a collection of learned behaviors or habits that have been reinforced in the past. Skinner denied that a personality or self initiates and directs behavior. The causes of behavior, he stated, lie outside the person, and they are

Figure 14.3

Albert Bandura's Reciprocal Determinism

Albert Bandura takes a social-cognitive view of personality. He suggests that three components–the environment, behavior, and personal/cognitive factors such as beliefs, expectancies, and personal dispositions–play reciprocal roles in determining personality and behavior.

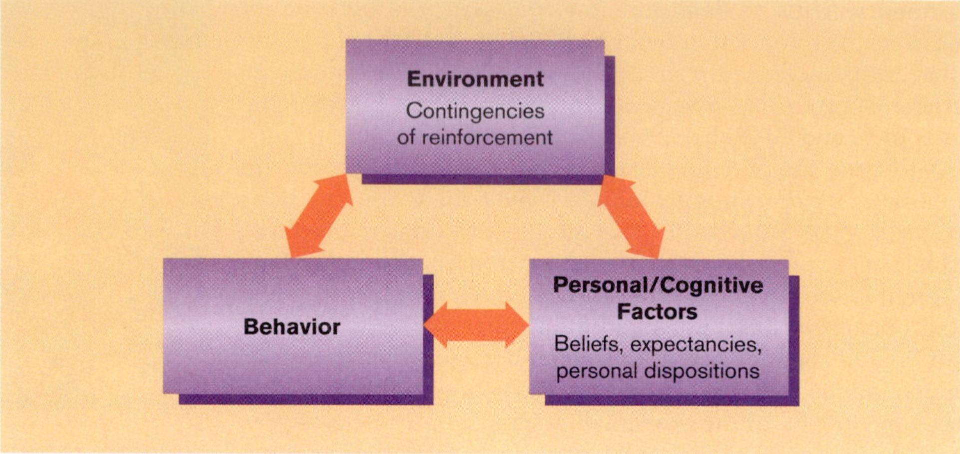

based on past and present rewards and punishments. Thus, Skinner did not use the term *personality*. He simply described the variables in the environment that shape an individual's observable behavior. Healthy experiences in a healthy environment make a healthy person.

But what about the psychologically unhealthy individual? Skinner (1953) believed that psychologically unhealthy people have been reinforced by the environment for behaving abnormally. For example, an overly dependent person may have been punished by her parents for asserting her independence and reinforced for dependency. If behavior is to change, then, the environment must be restructured to reinforce normal rather than abnormal behavior. What a contrast to psychoanalytic theory and trait theory, which see internal forces as the major shapers and determiners of behavior.

The Social-Cognitive Theorists: Expanding the Behaviorist View

Much of human behavior can be traced to classical and operant conditioning; but can all of personality, or even all of learning, be explained in this way? Not according to social-cognitive theorists, who consider both the environment *and* personal/cognitive factors in their attempts to understand personality and behavior. Personal/cognitive factors include personal dispositions, feelings, expectations, perceptions, and cognitions, such as thoughts, beliefs, and attitudes.

What are the components of Bandura's concept of reciprocal determinism, and how do they interact?

Albert Bandura's Views on Personality A chief advocate of the social-cognitive theory is Albert Bandura (1977a, 1986). He maintains that personal/cognitive factors, one's behavior, and the external environment all influence each other and are influenced by each other (Bandura, 1989). This mutual relationship Bandura calls **reciprocal determinism** (see Figure 14.3).

Consider how Bandura's concept of reciprocal determinism might work in the following situation: A waiter who normally works in a section of a restaurant where good tippers habitually sit, is reassigned to tables in an area where tips are normally poor. This new environment influences the waiter's beliefs and expectancies (personal/cognitive factors). Now, because he believes that good service will not be appropriately rewarded, his behavior changes. He is inattentive, is not very pleasant, and provides poor service. Consequently, the waiter's attitude and behavior have a reciprocal effect on the customers, influencing their thinking, feelings, and attitudes. And these, in turn, affect their behavior. Not surprisingly, these customers *do* tip poorly. Can you recall examples in your own life where your thinking, expectancies, and attitudes, your behavior, and external environmental factors worked reciprocally to your benefit—or to your detriment?

reciprocal determinism: Bandura's concept that behavior, personal/cognitive factors, and environment all influence and are influenced by each other.

One of the personal/cognitive factors Bandura (1997a; 1997b) considers especially important is self-efficacy. **Self-efficacy** is the perception people hold of their ability to perform competently and successfully in whatever they attempt. And this, Bandura believes, affects how they behave in a variety of situations. People high in self-efficacy will approach new situations confidently, set high goals, and persist in their efforts because they believe success is likely. They are less likely to suffer stress and depression because they believe they can handle threatening or difficult situations. People low in self-efficacy, on the other hand, will expect failure and avoid challenges, will "give up in the face of difficulty, recover slowly from setbacks, and easily fall victim to stress and depression" (Bandura, 1997a, p. 5). Apparently, one's sense of self-efficacy can become a self-fulfilling prophecy.

self-efficacy: A person's belief in his or her ability to perform competently in whatever is attempted.

locus of control: A concept used to explain how people account for what happens in their lives—people with an *internal* locus of control see themselves as primarily in control of their behavior and its consequences; those with an *external* locus of control perceive what happens to be in the hands of fate, luck, or chance.

Julian Rotter and Locus of Control Julian Rotter proposes another concept—**locus of control**—which provides additional insight into why people behave as they do. Some people see themselves as primarily in control of their behavior and its consequences. This perception Rotter (1966, 1971, 1990) defines as an *internal* locus of control. Others perceive that whatever happens to them is in the hands of fate, luck, or chance. They exhibit an *external* locus of control and may claim that it does not matter what they do because "whatever will be, will be." Rotter contends that people with an external locus of control are less likely to change their behavior as a result of reinforcement, because they do not see reinforcers as being tied to their own actions.

What does Rotter mean by the terms *internal* and *external locus of control*?

Locus of control is closely tied to achievement and success in life. Where is your locus of control? To find out, complete the *Try It!*

Try It!

For each statement, indicate which choice best expresses your view.

1. Heredity determines most of a person's personality.
   a. strongly disagree b. disagree c. neutral d. agree e. strongly agree
2. Chance has a lot to do with being successful.
   a. strongly disagree b. disagree c. neutral d. agree e. strongly agree
3. Whatever plans you make, something will always interfere.
   a. strongly disagree b. disagree c. neutral d. agree e. strongly agree
4. Being at the right place at the right time is essential for getting what you want in life.
   a. almost never b. rarely c. sometimes d. quite often e. most of the time
5. Intelligence is a given, and it cannot be improved.
   a. strongly disagree b. disagree c. neutral d. agree e. strongly agree
6. If I successfully accomplish a task, it's because it was an easy one.
   a. strongly disagree b. disagree c. neutral d. agree e. strongly agree
7. You cannot change your destiny.
   a. strongly disagree b. disagree c. neutral d. agree e. strongly agree
8. School success is mostly a result of one's socioeconomic background.
   a. strongly disagree b. disagree c. neutral d. agree e. strongly agree
9. People are lonely because they are not given the chance to meet new people.
   a. strongly disagree b. disagree c. neutral d. agree e. strongly agree
10. If you set realistic goals, you can succeed at almost anything.
   a. strongly agree b. agree c. neutral d. disagree e. strongly disagree

Score your responses as follows: a = 10 points, b = 7.5, c = 5, d = 2.5, e = 0. A perfect score is 100 points, and the higher your total score, the more internal your locus of control is. The more internal your locus of control, the more likely you are to succeed in life!

Evaluating the Social-Cognitive Perspective The social-cognitive perspective cannot be criticized for lacking a strong research base. Yet some of its critics claim that the social-cognitive perspective continues to weigh the situation too heavily. These critics ask: What about unconscious motives or internal dispositions (traits) that people exhibit fairly consistently across many different situations? Other critics point to mounting evidence of a genetic influence on personality, which may explain 40–50% or more of the variation in personality characteristics (Bouchard, 1994).

Remember It!

1. According to Skinner, behavior is initiated by inner forces called personality. (true/false)
2. Bandura's concept of reciprocal determinism refers to the mutual effects of:
   a. a person's behavior, personality, and thinking.
   b. a person's feelings, attitudes, and thoughts.
   c. a person's behavior, personal/cognitive factors, and the environment.
   d. classical and operant conditioning and observational learning.
3. Which statement is *not* true of people low in self-efficacy?
   a. They persist in their efforts.
   b. They lack confidence.
   c. They expect failure.
   d. They avoid challenge.
4. Who proposed the concept of locus of control?
   a. B. F. Skinner
   b. Albert Bandura
   c. Hans Eysenck
   d. Julian Rotter

Answers: 1. false 2. c 3. a 4. d

HUMANISTIC PERSONALITY THEORIES

Who were the two pioneers in humanistic psychology, and how did they view human nature?

Humanistic psychology seeks to give a more complete and positive picture of the human personality than the two other major forces in psychology—behaviorism and psychoanalysis. Humanistic psychologists are critical of psychoanalysis because it is based primarily on Freud's work with patients who were psychologically unhealthy. Moreover, the humanists take issue with behaviorism because of its almost exclusive concern with observable behavior, to the neglect of what is going on inside the person.

But the early humanistic psychologists did more than simply react against psychoanalysis and behaviorism. They developed their own unique view of human nature, a view that is considerably more flattering. Human nature is seen as innately good, and people are assumed to have a natural tendency toward growth and the realization of their fullest potential. The humanists largely deny a dark or evil side of human nature. They do not believe that we are shaped strictly by the environment or ruled by mysterious unconscious forces. Rather, as creative beings with an active, conscious free will, we can chart our own course in life.

Humanistic psychology is sometimes called the "third force" in psychology. (Behaviorism and psychoanalysis are the other two forces.) The pioneering humanistic psychologists were Abraham Maslow and Carl Rogers.

Abraham Maslow: The Self-Actualizing Person

What is self-actualization, and how did Maslow study it?

For Abraham Maslow (1970), motivational factors were at the root of personality. Maslow constructed a hierarchy of needs, ranging from physiological needs at the bottom upward to safety needs, belonging and love needs, esteem needs, and finally to the highest need—for self-actualization. **Self-actualization** means developing to one's fullest potential. A healthy person is ever growing and becoming all that he or she can be.

Maslow claimed that if you want to know what makes a healthy personality, you must study people who are healthy. He wrote, "the study of the crippled, stunted, immature, and unhealthy specimens can yield only a cripple psychology." So Maslow studied people he believed were using their talents and abilities to their fullest—in other words, those who exemplified self-actualization. He studied some historical figures, such as Abraham Lincoln and Thomas Jefferson, and figures who made significant contributions during his own lifetime—Albert Einstein, Eleanor Roosevelt, and Albert Schweitzer. After examining the lives of such people, Maslow identified characteristics that self-actualizing persons seem to share.

Abraham Maslow (1908–1970)

Maslow found self-actualizers to be accurate in perceiving reality—able to judge honestly and to spot quickly the fake and the dishonest. Self-actualizers are comfortable with life; they accept themselves and others, and nature as well, with good humor and tolerance. Most of them believe they have a mission to accomplish or the need to devote their life to some larger good. Self-actualizers tend not to depend on external authority or other people but seem to be inner-driven, autonomous, and independent. They feel a strong fellowship with humanity, and their relationships with others are characterized by deep and loving bonds. They can laugh at themselves, and their sense of humor, though well developed, never involves hostility or criticism of others. Finally, the hallmark of self-actualizers is frequently occurring *peak experiences*—experiences of deep meaning, insight, and harmony within and with the universe.

Maslow concluded that each of us has the capacity for self-actualization. If we apply our talent and energy to doing our best in whatever endeavor we choose, then we, too, can lead creative lives and be self-actualizing.

Carl Rogers: The Fully Functioning Person

According to Rogers, why don't all people become fully functioning persons?

Like Freud, Carl Rogers (1951, 1961) developed his theory of personality through insights gained from his patients in therapy sessions. Yet he saw something very different from what Freud and the psychoanalysts observed. Rogers viewed human nature as basically good. If left to develop naturally, he thought, people would be happy and psychologically healthy.

According to Rogers, we each live in our own subjective reality, which he called the *phenomenological field.* It is in this personal, subjective field (rather than in the objective, real, physical environment) that we act and think and feel. In other words, the way we see things is the way they are—for us. Gradually a part of the phenomenological field becomes differentiated as the self. The self concept emerges as a result of repeated experiences involving such terms as "I," "me," and "mine." With the emerging self comes the need for positive regard. We need warmth, love, acceptance, sympathy, and respect from the people who are significant in our lives. But there are usually strings attached to positive regard from others.

Our parents do not view us positively regardless of our behavior. They set up **conditions of worth**—conditions on which their positive regard hinges. Conditions of worth force us to live and act according to someone else's values rather than our own. In our efforts to gain positive regard, we deny our true self by inhibiting some of our behavior, denying and distorting some of our perceptions, and closing ourselves to parts of our experience. In so doing, we experience stress and anxiety, and our whole self-structure may be threatened.

humanistic psychology: An approach to psychology that stresses the uniquely human attributes and a positive view of human nature.

self-actualization: Developing to one's fullest potential.

conditions of worth: Conditions on which the positive regard of others rests.

For Rogers, a major goal of psychotherapy is to enable people to open themselves up to experiences and begin to live according to their own values rather than according to the values of others in order to gain positive regard. He calls his therapy "person-centered therapy," preferring not to use the term *patient* (Rogers's therapy will be discussed in Chapter 16). Rogers believes that the therapist must give

unconditional positive regard: Unqualified caring and nonjudgmental acceptance of another.

the client **unconditional positive regard,** that is, positive regard no matter what the client says, does, has done, or is thinking of doing. Unconditional positive regard is designed to reduce threat, eliminate conditions of worth, and bring the person back in tune with his or her true self. If successful, the therapy helps the client become what Rogers calls a *fully functioning person*—one who is functioning at an optimal level and living fully and spontaneously according to his or her own inner value system.

Evaluating the Humanistic Perspective

Humanism has become much more than a personality theory and an approach to therapy. Its influence has spread significantly as a social movement in the schools and in society in general. Some of its severest critics are religious and moral leaders who see the philosophy of humanism as a powerful threat to traditional moral values and the Judeo-Christian ethic. Others charge that an all-consuming personal quest for self-fulfillment can lead to a self-centered, self-serving, self-indulgent personality, lacking moral restraint or genuine concern for others (Campbell & Sprecht, 1985; Wallach & Wallach, 1983).

Humanistic psychologists do not accept such criticisms as valid. By and large, they trust in the inherent goodness of human nature, and their perspective on personality is consistent with that trust. But how do humanists explain the evil we see around us—assaults, murder, rape? Where does this originate? Carl Rogers (1981) replied, "I do not find that this evil is inherent in human nature" (p. 16). Of psychological environments that nurture growth and choice, Rogers said, "I have never known an individual to choose the cruel or destructive path. . . . So my experience leads me to believe that it is cultural influences which are the major factors in our evil behaviors" (p. 16).

Even some humanists disagree about the nature of human nature. In an open letter to Carl Rogers, psychologist Rollo May (1982) wrote, "Who makes up the culture except persons like you and me? . . . The culture is not something made by fate and foisted upon us. . . . The culture is evil as well as good because we, the human beings who constitute it, are evil as well as good" (pp. 12–13).

Though humanists have been criticized for being unscientific and for seeing, hearing, and finding no evil within the human psyche, they have inspired the study of the positive qualities—altruism, cooperation, love, acceptance of others, and self-esteem. Complete the *Try It!* to estimate your current level of self-esteem.

Try It!

For each statement below, write in the blank the letter that best reflects your feelings.

a. strongly agree b. agree c. neutral d. disagree e. strongly disagree

____ 1. I feel confident in most social situations.

____ 2. I believe I have something worthwhile to offer in life.

____ 3. I feel that others respect my opinion.

____ 4. I compare favorably with most people I know.

____ 5. I feel that, on the whole, other people like me.

____ 6. I deserve the love and respect of others.

Compute your score as follows: a = 4 points, b = 3, c = 2, d = 1, e = 0. A total score of 20–24 points indicates that you have excellent self-esteem; 15–19 means good, 10–14 is fair, and below 10 indicates that you could work on this quality.

Self-esteem is a highly variable state. Many people esteem themselves more highly than they should, and probably even more people esteem themselves too low. Fortunately, self-esteem is changeable. If you'd like to raise your self-esteem, how could you go about it?

First, translate self-esteem into self-respect. Now consider the three or four qualities or attributes you respect most in others. If you respect people who keep their promises, ask yourself where you stand with regard to that quality. Do you keep your promises to others? Would your self-respect increase if you followed through on more of your promises to others and refused to make promises you could not, or did not intend to, keep?

If you wish, work on one or two self-respect qualities as a "take home" *Try It!* If you do, you may be surprised at how quickly your self-esteem and others' respect for you will grow.

Remember It!

1. Humanistic psychologists would *not* say that
   a. human nature is innately good.
   b. human beings have a natural tendency toward self-actualization.
   c. human beings have free will.
   d. researchers should focus primarily on observable behavior.
2. Which psychologist studied individuals he believed exemplified self-actualization in order to identify characteristics that self-actualizing persons share?
   a. Carl Rogers
   b. Gordon Allport
   c. Abraham Maslow
   d. Hans Eysenck
3. Which psychologist believed that individuals often do not become fully functioning persons because, in childhood, they fail to receive unconditional positive regard from their parents?
   a. Carl Rogers
   b. Gordon Allport
   c. Abraham Maslow
   d. Hans Eysenck

Answers: 1. d 2. c 3. a

PERSONALITY: IS IT IN THE GENES?

What has research in behavioral genetics revealed about the influence of the genes and the environment on personality?

Behavioral genetics is a field of research that investigates the relative effects of heredity and environment on behavior and ability.

The Twin Study Method: Studying Identical and Fraternal Twins

An ideal way to assess the relative contribution of heredity and environment to personality is to study identical twins who have been separated at birth and reared apart. When identical twins who were reared apart have strikingly similar traits, as in the case of Oskar and Jack, introduced at the beginning of this chapter, it is assumed that heredity has been a major contributor. When twins differ on a given trait, as Joan and Jean do, the influence of the environment is thought to be greater.

In the Minnesota twin study, Tellegen and others (1988) found that identical twins are quite similar on several personality factors regardless of whether they are

behavioral genetics: The field of research that investigates the relative effects of heredity and environment on behavior and ability.

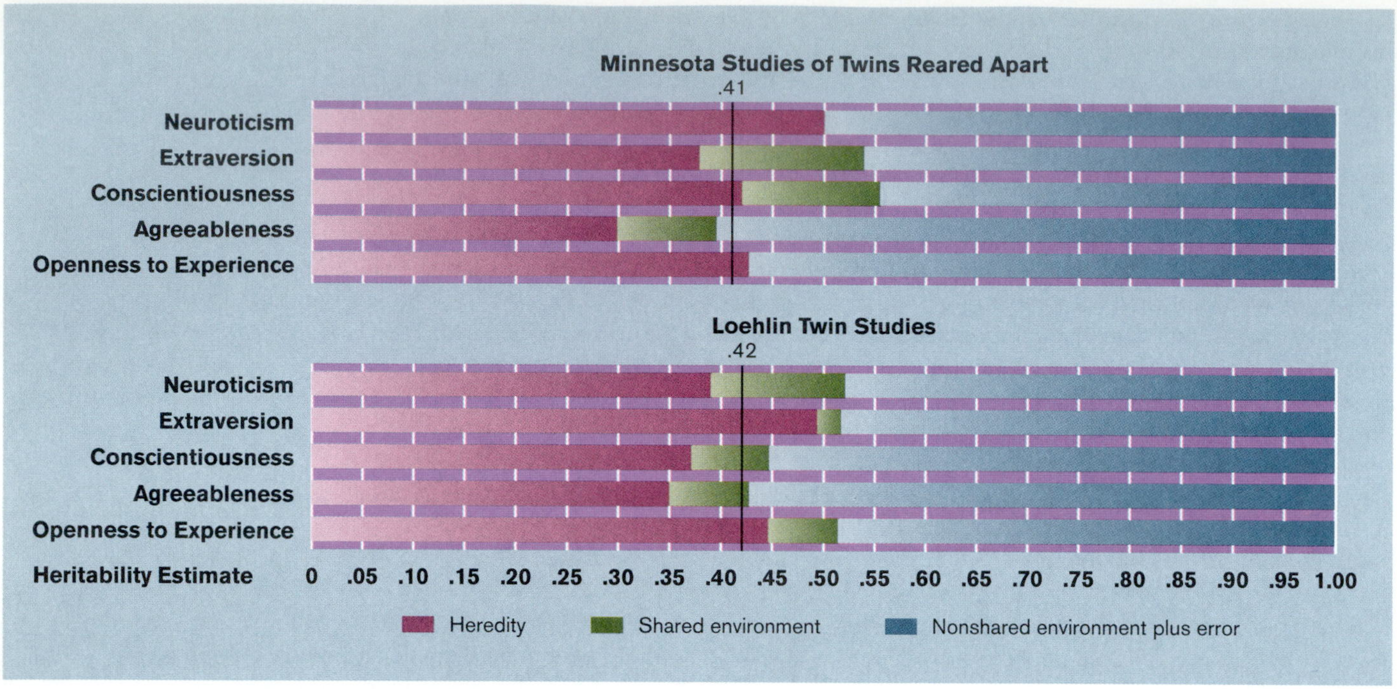

Figure 14.4

Estimated Influence of Heredity and Environment on the Big Five Personality Factors

The Minnesota studies of twins reared apart yield an average heritability estimate of .41 (41%) for the Big Five personality factors; the Loehlin twin studies, a heritability estimate of .42 (42%). Both studies found the influence of the shared environment to be only about .07 (7%). The remaining percentage represents a combination of nonshared environmental influences and measurement error. (Adapted from Bouchard, 1994.)

raised together or apart. The term **heritability** refers to the degree to which a characteristic is estimated to be influenced by heredity. After studying heritability of traits in 573 adult twin pairs, Rushton and colleagues (1986) found that nurturance, empathy, and assertiveness are substantially influenced by heredity. Even altruism and aggressiveness, traits one would expect to be strongly influenced by parental upbringing, were actually more heavily influenced by heredity. A meta-analysis by Miles and Carey (1997) revealed that the heritability of aggressiveness may be as high as .50 (or 50%).

Twin studies have also revealed a genetic influence on social attitudes such as traditionalism—whether a person endorses traditional moral values and follows rules and authority (Finkel & McGue, 1997). The risk of divorce appears to have a heritability of .55 for women and .59 for men. This is not to say that there is a gene for divorce; rather, the risk derives from the genetic influence on certain personality factors (Jockin et al., 1996). Genes also influence personality factors that correlate with psychological disorders as measured by the Minnesota Multiphasic Personality Inventory (DiLalla et al., 1996). There even seems to be a genetic influence on people's sense of well being (Lykken & Tellegen, 1996), their interests (Lykken et al., 1993), how they tend to view their environment (Chipuer et al., 1993), and how they perceive life events, particularly controllable ones (Plomin & Rende, 1991).

Evidence from behavioral genetics suggests that the average heritability of the Big Five personality factors is about .41 to .42, somewhat less than the earlier twin study estimates of around .50 (Bouchard, 1994). Figure 14.4 shows the heritability estimates for the Big Five from the Minnesota studies of twins reared apart and the Loehlin twin studies (Loehlin, 1992).

heritability: An index of the degree to which a characteristic is estimated to be influenced by heredity.

How can heritability estimates vary so much from study to study? The reason is that researchers can only estimate statistically how much variability is due to genetics in a particular group of research participants. And their estimates apply to that sample only. When different researchers find similar heritabilities, however, psychologists have more confidence in the findings.

Taken together, these data show that personality factors are significantly influenced by heredity. But even with a heritability estimate as high as .50, the remaining 50% of the variance has to be attributed to nongenetic (environmental) factors plus measurement error. The behavioral genetics studies, then, leave a great deal of room for environmental forces to shape personality. Plomin and others (1994) claim that "nongenetic factors generally account for as much variance as genetic factors" (p. 1736). So personality is a product of nature *and* nurture working together.

The Shared and Nonshared Environment

Have you ever wondered why siblings raised in the same household often seem to have totally different personalities? To explain why, researchers point out that environmental influences are produced in two different forms: through the shared environment and through the nonshared environment. The shared environment consists of those environmental influences that tend to make family members similar. If the shared environmental influences were high, then you would expect siblings raised in the same household to be more alike than different. But the shared environmental influences on personality are modest at best, about 7% (Bouchard, 1994; Loehlin, 1992).

The nonshared environment consists of influences that operate in different ways among children in the same family (Rowe, 1994). These influences "cause family members to differ regardless of whether the locus of influence is the family (such as differential treatment by parents) or outside the family (such as different experiences at school or with peers)" (Plomin & Daniels, 1987, p. 7). Nonshared influences can occur because individual children tend to elicit different responses from their parents for a variety of reasons—their temperament, gender, or birth order, or accidents and illnesses they may have had (Plomin, 1989). Bouchard claims that twins can experience nonshared environmental influences even in the womb if the positioning of the twin embryos in the uterus leads to differences in fetal nutrition (Aldhous, 1992).

It is important to keep in mind that people are not merely acted on by their environment but also, given the opportunity, select and shape it (Revelle, 1995). Says Bouchard (1997), "A person predisposed to religion, in other words, is likely to find her way into the company of other religious people, even if her parents are confirmed atheists" (p. 56).

We are impressed by the similarities between identical twins separated at birth, but striking similarities are sometimes found even between total strangers. And although several thousand pairs of twins have been studied, most have been raised in middle-class environments. Might the differences between twins have been greater, particularly between identical twins reared apart, if their nonshared environments had differed more drastically?

The Adoption Method

Another method used to disentangle the effects of heredity and environment is to study children adopted shortly after birth. Loehlin and others (1987) assessed the personalities of 17-year-olds who had been adopted at birth and came to this startling conclusion: "Adopted children do not resemble their adoptive family members in personality, despite having lived with them from birth, but they do show a modest degree of resemblance to their genetic mothers, whom they had never known" (p. 968). When the adopted children were compared to other children in the family, the researchers found that the shared family environment had virtually no influence on their personalities. Other researchers studying adopted children have come to the same basic conclusion (Scarr et al., 1981). Loehlin and colleagues (1990) measured change in personality of adoptees over a 10-year period and found that children tended "to change on the average in the direction of their genetic parents' personalities" (p. 221). The prevailing thinking in behavioral genetics, then, is that the shared environment plays a negligible role in the formation of personality (Loehlin et al., 1988), although there have been a few dissenting voices (Rose et al., 1988).

The genetic influences we have been discussing are not the result of one or even a few genes. Rather, they involve many genes, each with small effects (Plomin et al., 1994). While these findings indicate that most personality traits are influenced by genes, "behavioral genetic research clearly demonstrates that both nature and nurture are important in human development" (Plomin, 1989, p. 110).

To learn that most psychological traits are significantly heritable does not lessen the value or reduce the importance of environmental factors such as family influences, parenting, culture, and education (Bouchard et al., 1990). Furthermore, Bouchard and colleagues (1990) state that their findings "do not imply that parenting is without lasting effects" (p. 227).

Personality and Culture

There is general agreement that nature and nurture together influence the formation of personality. Important among the influences of nurture are the diverse cultures in which humans live and work.

Hofstede (1980, 1983) analyzed questionnaire responses measuring the work-related values of more than 100,000 IBM employees in 53 countries around the world. Factor analysis revealed four separate dimensions related to culture and personality, but one factor, the individualism/collectivism dimension, is of particular interest here.

"Individualist cultures emphasize independence, self-reliance, [and] creativity" (Triandis et al., 1993, p. 368). Individualists "see themselves as more differentiated and separate from others, and place more importance on asserting their individuality" (Bochner, 1994, p. 274). More emphasis is placed on individual achievement than on group achievement. High-achieving individuals are accorded honor and prestige in individualist cultures. People in collectivist cultures, on the other hand, tend to be more interdependent and define themselves and their personal interests in terms of their group membership. Asians, for example, have highly collectivist cultures, and collectivism is compatible with Confucianism, the predominant religion of these Eastern cultures. In fact, according to the Confucian values, the individual finds his or her identity in interrelatedness, as a part of, not apart from, the larger group. Moreover, this interrelatedness is an important ingredient of happiness for Asians (Kitayama & Markus, 2000).

Hofstede rank-ordered the 53 countries on each of the four dimensions. It should hardly be surprising that the United States ranked as the most individualist culture in the sample, followed by Australia, Great Britain, Canada, and the Netherlands. At the other end of the continuum were the most collectivist, or least individualist, cultures—Guatemala, Ecuador, Panama, Venezuela, and Colombia, all Latin American countries.

Although, according to Hofstede, the United States ranks first in individualism, there are many distinct minority cultural groups in the United States, which may be decidedly less individualistic.

Native Americans number close to 2 million, but even within this relatively small cultural group, there are over 200 different tribes, and no single language, religion, or culture (Bennett, 1994). Yet Native Americans have many shared values—collectivist values—such as the importance of family, community, cooperation, and generosity. Native Americans value a generous nature as evidenced by gift giving and helpfulness. Such behaviors bring more honor and prestige than accumulating property and building individual wealth.

For these native Alaskans, participating in the traditional blanket toss ceremony is one manifestation of their culture's values related to community and cooperation.

Hispanic Americans, who number almost 28.3 million (U.S. Bureau of the Census, 1997), also tend to be more collectivist than individualist. While there are significant cultural differences among various Hispanic American groups, there are striking similarities as well. The clearest shared cultural value is a strong identification with and attachment to the extended family. Another important value is *simpatía*—the desire for smooth and harmonious social relationships, which includes respect for the dignity of others, avoidance of confrontation, and avoidance of words or actions that might hurt the feelings of another (Marín, 1994).

But to observe that the Native American and Hispanic cultures value collectivist more than individualist interests does not mean that any one member of these cultures is necessarily less individualistic than any given member of the majority American culture. Moreover, many people could value both orientations, being individualistic at work, for example, and collectivistic in the home and community (Kagitcibasi, 1992).

The influences of culture on personality become more important social considerations as societies become more multicultural and economies become increasingly global.

Remember It!

1. Many behavioral geneticists believe that personality may be as much as ______________ inherited.
   a. 10–20% c. 40–50%
   b. 25–35% d. 65–75%
2. Behavioral geneticists have found that the (shared, nonshared) environment has the greater effect on personality.
3. Children adopted at birth are more similar in personality to their adoptive parents than to their biological parents. (true/false)
4. (All, The majority of) individuals in a collectivist society have a collectivist orientation.

Answers: 1. c 2. nonshared 3. false 4. The majority of

PERSONALITY ASSESSMENT

What are the three major methods used in personality assessment?

Just as there are many different personality theories, there are many different methods for measuring personality. Various personality tests are used by clinical and counseling psychologists, psychiatrists, and counselors in the diagnosis of patients and in the assessment of progress in therapy. Personality assessment is also used in business and industry to aid in hiring decisions and by counselors for vocational and educational counseling.

Personality assessment methods can be grouped in a few broad categories: (1) observation, interviews, and rating scales, (2) personality inventories, and (3) projective tests.

Observation, Interviews, and Rating Scales

Observation We all use observation informally, to form opinions about other people. Psychologists, too, use observation in personality assessment and evaluation in a variety of settings—hospitals, clinics, schools, and workplaces.

Behaviorists, in particular, prefer observation to other methods of personality assessment. Using an observational technique known as *behavioral assessment,* psychologists can count and record the frequency of particular behaviors. This method is often used in behavior modification programs in settings such as mental hospitals, where psychologists may chart the patients' progress in reducing aggressive acts or other undesirable or abnormal behaviors.

Although much can be learned from observation, it has its shortcomings; it is time-consuming and expensive, and observers must be trained and paid. What is observed may be misinterpreted, and two observers can view the same event and interpret it differently. Probably the most serious limitation is that the very presence of the observer can alter the behavior being observed.

The Interview Another personality assessment technique is the interview. Clinical psychologists and psychiatrists use interviews to help in the diagnosis and treatment of patients. Counselors use interviews to screen applicants for admission to college or other special programs, and employers use them to evaluate job applicants and employees for job promotions.

Interviewers consider not only a person's answers to questions but the person's tone of voice, speech, mannerisms, gestures, and general appearance as well. Professionals use both structured and unstructured interviews in making their assessments. In unstructured situations, the direction the interview will take and the questions to be asked are not all planned beforehand, and so the interview can be highly personalized. But the unstructured interview may be so loose that little objective information is gained. Also, it is hard to compare people unless some of the same questions are asked of everyone.

For this reason interviewers often use a structured interview, in which the content of the questions and even the manner in which they are asked are carefully planned ahead of time. The interviewer tries not to deviate in any way from the structured format so that more reliable comparisons can be made between different subjects.

Rating Scales Sometimes examiners use rating scales to record data from interviews or observations. Rating scales are useful because they provide a standardized format, including a list of traits or behaviors to evaluate. The rating scale helps to focus the rater's attention on all the relevant traits to be considered so that none is overlooked or weighed too heavily.

But there are problems with rating scales, too. Often there is little agreement among raters in their evaluation of the same individual. If you have watched Olympic events such as figure skating on television, you have sometimes noticed

Job interviews today are likely to include personality tests. Many companies ask job candidates to complete an interest inventory, to determine the type of position a candidate is best suited for, or a vocational preference inventory, to assess how well the person's traits and interests relate to specific jobs.

wide variations in the several judges' scoring of the same performance. One way to overcome this problem is to train the judges or raters to a point where high agreement can be achieved when rating the same person or event.

Another problem in evaluation is the **halo effect**—the tendency of raters to be excessively influenced in their overall evaluation of a person by one or a few favorable or unfavorable traits. Often traits or attributes that are not even on the rating scale, such as physical attractiveness or similarity to the rater, heavily influence a rater's perception of a subject.

Personality Inventories: Taking Stock

What is an inventory, and what are the MMPI-2 and the CPI designed to reveal?

There is an objective method for measuring personality, a method in which the personal opinions and ratings of observers or interviewers do not unduly influence the results. This method is the **inventory,** a paper-and-pencil test with questions about an individual's thoughts, feelings, and behaviors, which measures several dimensions of personality and can be scored according to a standard procedure. Psychologists favoring the trait approach prefer the inventory because it reveals where people fall on various dimensions of personality and yields a personality profile. Of the many personality inventories available, none has been more widely used than the Minnesota Multiphasic Personality Inventory.

The MMPI and MMPI-2 The **Minnesota Multiphasic Personality Inventory (MMPI)** and its revision, the **MMPI-2,** for years have been the most popular, the most heavily researched, and the most widely used personality tests for screening and diagnosing psychiatric problems and disorders, and for use in psychological research (Butcher & Rouse, 1996).

There have been more than 115 recognized translations of the MMPI, and it is used in more than 65 countries (Butcher & Graham, 1989). Published in 1943 by researchers McKinley and Hathaway, the MMPI was originally intended to identify tendencies toward various types of psychiatric disorders. The researchers administered over 1,000 questions about attitudes, feelings, and specific psychiatric symptoms to selected groups of psychiatric patients who had been clearly diagnosed with various specific disorders and to a control group of normal men and women. They retained the 550 items that differentiated the specific groups of psychiatric patients from the group of participants considered to be normal.

Because the original MMPI had become outdated, the MMPI-2 was published in 1989 (Butcher et al., 1989). Most of the original test items were retained, but new items were added to more adequately cover areas such as alcoholism, drug abuse, suicidal tendencies, eating disorders, and Type A personality. New norms were established to reflect national census data and thus achieve a better geographical, racial, and cultural balance (Ben-Porath & Butcher, 1989).

halo effect: The tendency of raters to be excessively influenced in their overall evaluation of a person by one or a few favorable or unfavorable traits.

inventory: A paper-and-pencil test with questions about a person's thoughts, feelings, and behaviors, which can be scored according to a standard procedure.

Minnesota Multiphasic Personality Inventory (MMPI): The most extensively researched and widely used personality test; used to screen and diagnose psychiatric problems and disorders; revised as MMPI-2.

Table 14.1 The Clinical Scales of the MMPI-2

Scale Name	Interpretation
1. Hypochondriasis (Hs)	High scorers exhibit an exaggerated concern about their physical health.
2. Depression (D)	High scorers are usually depressed, despondent, and distressed.
3. Hysteria (Hy)	High scorers complain often about physical symptoms that have no apparent organic cause.
4. Psychopathic deviate (Pd)	High scorers show a disregard for social and moral standards.
5. Masculinity/femininity (Mf)	High scorers show "traditional" masculine or feminine attitudes and values.
6. Paranoia (Pa)	High scorers demonstrate extreme suspiciousness and feelings of persecution.
7. Psychasthenia (Pt)	High scorers tend to be highly anxious, rigid, tense, and worrying.
8. Schizophrenia (Sc)	High scorers tend to be socially withdrawn and to engage in bizarre and unusual thinking.
9. Hypomania (Ma)	High scorers are usually emotional, excitable, energetic, and impulsive.
10. Social introversion (S)	High scorers tend to be modest, self-effacing, and shy.

Table 14.1 shows the 10 clinical scales of the MMPI-2. Following are examples of questions on the test, which are to be answered "true," "false," or "cannot say."

I wish I were not bothered by thoughts about sex.
When I get bored I like to stir up some excitement.
In walking I am very careful to step over sidewalk cracks.
If people had not had it in for me, I would have been much more successful.

A high score on any of the scales does not necessarily mean that a person has a problem or a psychiatric symptom. Rather, the psychologist looks at the individual's MMPI profile—the pattern of scores on all the scales—and then compares it to the profiles of normal individuals and those with various psychiatric disorders.

But what if someone lies on the test in order to appear mentally healthy? Embedded in the test to provide a check against lying are questions such as these:

Once in a while I put off until tomorrow what I ought to do today.
I gossip a little at times.
Once in a while, I laugh at a dirty joke.

Most people would almost certainly have to answer "true" in response to such items—unless, of course, they were lying. Another scale controls for people who are faking psychiatric illness, as in the case of someone hoping to be judged not guilty of a crime by reason of insanity. Research seems to indicate that the validity scales in the MMPI-2 are effective in detecting test takers who were instructed to fake psychological disturbance or to lie to make themselves appear more psychologically healthy (Bagby et al., 1994; Butcher et al., 1995). Even when given specific information about various psychological disorders, test takers could not produce profiles similar to those of people who actually suffered from the disorder (Wetter et al., 1993).

Evaluating the MMPI-2 The MMPI-2 is reliable, easy to administer and score, and inexpensive to use. It is useful in the screening, diagnosis, and clinical description of abnormal behavior, but does not reveal differences among normal personalities very well. The MMPI had often been unreliable for African Americans, women, and adolescents (Levitt & Duckworth, 1984). But this problem has been addressed, and norms have been established for the MMPI-2 that are more representative of the national population. A special form of the test, the MMPI-A, was developed for adolescents in 1992. The MMPI-A has some items that are especially relevant to adolescents, such as those referring to eating disorders, substance abuse, and problems with school and family.

The MMPI-2 has been translated for use in Belgium, Chile, China, France, Hong Kong, Israel, Korea, Italy, Japan, Norway, Russia, Spain, and Thailand (Butcher, 1992). Lucio and others (1994) administered the Mexican (Spanish) version of MMPI-2 to more than 2,100 Mexican college students. They found the profiles of these students "remarkably similar" to profiles of U.S. college students.

The California Psychological Inventory What instruments are available for assessing the personality of a normal person? The **California Psychological Inventory (CPI)** is a highly regarded personality test developed especially for normal populations aged 13 and older.

Similar to the MMPI, the CPI even has many of the same questions, but it does not include any questions designed to reveal psychiatric illness (Gough, 1987). The CPI is valuable for predicting behavior, and it has been "praised for its technical competency, careful development, cross-validation and follow-up, use of sizable samples and separate sex norms" (Domino, 1984, p. 156). The CPI was revised in 1987, to make it provide "a picture of the subject's life-style and the degree to which his or her potential is being realized" (McReynolds, 1989, p. 101). The CPI is particularly useful in predicting school achievement in high school and beyond; leadership and executive success; and effectiveness of police, military personnel, and student teachers (Gregory, 1996).

The Myers–Briggs Type Indicator (MBTI) The **Myers–Briggs Type Indicator (MBTI)** is a personality inventory based on Jung's theory. The MBTI is a forced-choice, self-report inventory that is scored on four separate bipolar dimensions:

Extraversion (E) .... Introversion (I)
Sensing (S) .... Intuition (N)
Thinking (T) .... Feeling (F)
Judging (J) .... Perceptive (P)

A person could score anywhere along each continuum of the four bipolar dimensions, and these individual scores are usually summarized according to a typology. Sixteen types of personality profiles can be derived from the possible combinations of the four bipolar dimensions. For example, a person whose scores were more toward the Extraversion, Intuition, Feeling, and Perceptive poles would be labeled an ENFP personality type, which is described as follows:

> Relates more readily to the outer world of people and things than to the inner world of ideas (E); prefers to search for new possibilities over working with known facts and conventional ways of doing things (N); makes decisions and solves problems on the basis of personal values and feelings rather than relying on logical thinking and analysis (F); and prefers a flexible, spontaneous life to a planned and orderly existence (P). (Gregory, 1996)

California Psychological Inventory (CPI): A highly regarded personality test used to assess the normal personality.

Myers–Briggs Type Indicator (MBTI): An inventory for classifying personality types based on Jung's theory of personality.

The MBTI is growing in popularity, especially in business and industry and in schools. Critics point to the absence of rigorous, controlled validity studies of the inventory (Pittenger, 1993). And it has been criticized for being interpreted too often by unskilled examiners, who have been accused of making overly simplistic interpretations (Gregory, 1996). However, sufficiently sophisticated methods for interpreting the MBTI do exist, as revealed by almost 500 research studies to date. And interest in this tool continues to be strong (Allen, 1997).

Projective Tests: Projections from the Unconscious

How do projective tests provide insight into personality, and what are some of the most commonly used projective tests?

Responses on interviews and questionnaires are conscious responses and, for this reason, are less useful to therapists who wish to probe the unconscious. Such therapists may choose a completely different technique called a projective test. A **projective test** is a personality test consisting of inkblots, drawings of ambiguous human situations, or incomplete sentences for which there are no obvious correct or incorrect responses. People respond by projecting their own inner thoughts, feelings, fears, or conflicts into the test materials.

The Rorschach Inkblot Method: What Do You See? One of the oldest and most popular projective tests is the **Rorschach Inkblot Method** developed by Swiss psychiatrist Hermann Rorschach (ROR-shok) in 1921. It consists of 10 inkblots, which the test taker is asked to describe (see Figure 14.5).

To develop his test, Rorschach put ink on paper and then folded the paper so that symmetrical patterns would result. Earlier, psychologists had used standardized series of inkblots to study imagination and other variables, but Rorschach was the first to use inkblots to investigate personality. He experimented with thousands of inkblots on different groups of people and found that 10 of the inkblots could be used to discriminate among different diagnostic groups, such as manic depressives, paranoid schizophrenics, and so on. These 10 inkblots—5 black and white, and 5 with color—were standardized and are still widely used.

The Rorschach can be used to describe personality, make differential diagnoses, plan and evaluate treatment, and predict behavior (Ganellen, 1996; Weiner, 1997). For the last 20 years, it has been second in popularity to the MMPI for use in research and clinical assessment (Butcher & Rouse, 1996).

Administration and Scoring of the Rorschach The test taker is shown the 10 inkblots and asked to tell everything that each inkblot looks like or resembles. The examiner writes down the test taker's responses and then goes through the cards again, asking questions to clarify what the test taker has reported.

In scoring the Rorschach, the examiner considers whether the test taker uses the whole inkblot in the description or only parts of it. The test taker is asked whether the shape of the inkblot, its color, or something else prompted the response. The

Figure 14.5

An Inkblot Similar to One Used for the Rorschach Inkblot Method

tester also considers whether the test taker sees movement, human figures or parts, animal figures or parts, or other objects in the inkblots.

Until the 1990s, the main problem with the Rorschach was that the results were too dependent on the interpretation and judgment of the examiner. In response to such criticisms, Exner (1993) has developed the Comprehensive System—a more reliable system for scoring the Rorschach. It provides some normative data so that the responses of a person taking the test can be compared to those of others with known personality characteristics. Using this system, some researchers have found high agreement among different raters interpreting the same responses (interrater agreement) (McDowell & Acklin, 1996). Others believe that more research is necessary before it can be concluded that the Comprehensive System yields reliable and valid results (Wood et al., 1996). However, a number of meta-analyses indicate that the Rorschach Inkblot Method has "psychometric soundness and practical utility" (Weiner, 1996).

The Thematic Apperception Test: Seeing Oneself in Scenes of Others

Another projective test is the **Thematic Apperception Test (TAT)** developed by Henry Murray and his colleagues in 1935 (Morgan & Murray, 1935; Murray, 1938). The TAT consists of 1 blank card and 19 other cards showing vague or ambiguous black-and-white drawings of human figures in various situations. "The test is based upon the well-recognized fact that when a person interprets an ambiguous social situation he is apt to expose his own personality as much as the phenomenon to which he is attending" (Morgan & Murray, 1962, p. 531).

If you were tested on the TAT, this is what you would be told:

> This is a test of your creative imagination. I shall show you a picture, and I want you to make up a plot or story for which it might be used as an illustration. What is the relation of the individuals in the picture? What has happened to them? What are their present thoughts and feelings? What will be the outcome? (Morgan & Murray, 1962, p. 532)

What does the story you write have to do with your personality or your problems or motives? Murray (1965) stresses the importance of "an element or theme that recurs three or more times in the series of stories" (p. 432). For example, if many of a person's story themes are about illness, sex, fear of failure, aggression, power, or interpersonal conflict, such a recurring theme is thought to reveal a problem in the person's life. Murray (1965) also claims that the strength of the TAT is "its capacity to reveal things that the patient is unwilling to tell or is unable to tell because he [or she] is unconscious of them" (p. 427).

The TAT is time-consuming and difficult to administer and score. Although it has been used extensively in research, it suffers from the same weaknesses as other projective techniques: (1) It relies heavily on the interpretation skills of the examiner, and (2) it may reflect too strongly a person's temporary motivational and emotional state and not get at the more permanent aspects of personality. Because Murray was trained as a Freudian and Jungian analyst, it is not surprising that he developed an instrument to assess unconscious motivation (Triplet, 1992).

The Sentence Completion Method: Filling in the Blanks Another projective technique, the sentence completion method, may be one of the most valid projective techniques of all. It consists of a number of incomplete sentences to be completed by the test taker, such as these:

> I worry a great deal about ______________.
> I sometimes feel ______________.
> I would be happier if ______________.
> My mother ______________.

projective test: A personality test in which people respond to inkblots, drawings of ambiguous human situations, incomplete sentences, and the like, by projecting their own inner thoughts, feelings, fears, or conflicts onto the test materials.

Rorschach Inkblot Method (ROR-shok): A projective test composed of 10 inkblots to which a test taker responds; used to reveal unconscious functioning and the presence of psychiatric disorders.

Thematic Apperception Test (TAT): A projective test consisting of drawings of ambiguous human situations, which the test taker describes; thought to reveal inner feelings, conflicts, and motives, which are projected onto the test materials.

In a comprehensive review, Goldberg (1965) summarized 50 validity studies and concluded that sentence completion is a valuable technique appropriate for widespread clinical and research use.

Review & Reflect 14.3 summarizes the various personality tests.

Review & Reflect 14.3 Three Approaches to Personality Assessment

Method	Examples	Description
Observation and rating	Observation Interviews Rating scales	Performance (behavior) is observed in a specific situation, and personality is assessed based on the observation. In interviews, the responses to questions are taken to reveal personality characteristics. Rating scales are used to score or rate test takers on the basis of traits, behaviors, or results of interviews. Assessment is subjective, and accuracy depends largely on the ability and experience of the evaluator.
Inventories	Minnesota Multiphasic Personality Inventory–2 (MMPI-2) California Personality Inventory (CPI) Myers–Briggs Type Indicator (MBTI)	Test takers reveal their beliefs, feelings, behavior, and/or opinions on paper-and-pencil tests. Scoring procedures are standardized, and responses of test takers are compared to group norms.
Projective tests	Rorschach Inkblot Method Thematic Apperception Test (TAT) Sentence completion method	Test takers respond to ambiguous test materials and presumably reveal elements of their own personalities by what they report they see in inkblots, by themes they write about scenes showing possible conflict, or by how they complete sentences. Scoring is subjective (less so for the sentence completion method than for the other two), and accuracy depends largely on the ability and experience of the evaluator.

Personality Theories: A Final Comment

In this chapter, we have explored the major theories of personality, which are summarized in *Review & Reflect 14.4*. By now you may be wondering which perspective best captures the elusive concept of personality. Some psychologists adhere strictly to single theories and are followers of Freud, for example, or Skinner or Rogers. However, it seems clear that all of the theories contribute to scientific knowledge, but that none taken alone can adequately explain the whole of human personality.

Review & Reflect 14.4 Summary of Approaches to Personality

Approach	Associated Theorist(s)	Assumptions about Behavior	Assessment Techniques	Research Methods
Psychoanalytic	Freud	Behavior arises mostly from unconscious conflicts between pleasure-seeking id and moral-perfectionist superego with reality-oriented ego as mediator.	Projective tests to tap unconscious motives; interviews for purposes of analysis	Case studies
Trait	Allport Cattell Eysenck McCrae and Costa	Behavior springs from personality traits that may be influenced by both heredity and environment.	Self-report inventories; adjective checklists; inventories	Analysis of test results for identifying strength of various traits
Learning behaviorist	Skinner	Behavior is determined strictly by environmental influences.	Direct observation of behavior; objective tests; interviews; rating scales; self-reports	Analysis of observations of behavior; quantifying of behaviors; analysis of person–situation interactions
Social-cognitive	Bandura Rotter	Behavior results from an interaction between internal cognitive factors and environmental influences.	Direct observation of behavior; objective tests; interviews; self-reports	Analysis of interactions between internal cognitive factors and evironmental influences
Humanistic	Maslow Rogers	Behavior springs from the person's own unique perception of reality and conscious choices. Humans are innately good.	Interviews and tests designed to assess the person's self-concept and perceptions of control	Analysis of the relationship between the person's feelings or perceptions and behavior

Remember It!

1. Match the personality test with its description.

____ (1) MMPI-2
____ (2) Rorschach
____ (3) TAT
____ (4) CPI
____ (5) MBTI

a. inventory used to diagnose psychopathology
b. inventory used to assess normal personality
c. projective test using inkblots
d. projective test using drawings of ambiguous human situations
e. inventory to assess personality types

2. Two experts in personality assessment would be most likely to agree on interpreting results from the

a. Rorschach. c. TAT.
b. MMPI-2. d. sentence completion method.

3. George has an unconscious resentment toward his father. Which test might best detect this?

a. MMPI-2 c. Rorschach
b. CPI d. TAT

4. Which of the following items might appear on the MMPI-2?

a. What is happening in the picture?
b. Hand is to glove as foot is to ______________.
c. My mother was a good person.
d. What is your favorite food?

Answers: 1. (1) a (2) c (3) d (4) b (5) e 2. b 3. d 4. c

Apply It!

How to Practice Positive Psychology

Most people spend their lives searching for happiness, for that elusive pot of gold at the end of the rainbow. But how many of us actually attain it? Positive psychologists suggest that we should look for the pot of gold in our own backyards rather than in some faraway place or time.

What makes people happy? So why are some people happy while others are not? Life circumstances have less to do with it than you might think, says David G. Myers, who has examined thousands of studies on this topic from all over the world. According to Myers (1992) these studies show that happy people have four inner characteristics that predispose them to a cheery attitude:

- *Self-esteem.* Myers says, "Defensive people maintain self-esteem by managing the impressions they create and by denying threats and pain." By contrast, "a healthier self-esteem is positive but realistic . . . because it is based on the genuine achievement of realistic ideals, and on feeling accepted for what one is" (1992, p. 113). Simply put, happy people like themselves.
- *Sense of personal control.* George Bernard Shaw wrote, "Hell is to drift, heaven is to steer." Those who feel both in control of their lives and satisfied with themselves (15% of all people) agree with him, reporting "extraordinarily positive feelings of happiness" (Myers, 1992, p. 113). Happy people typically plan and fill their schedules, and they are on time and efficient. Unhappy people's schedules are open and uncommitted. They procrastinate and do things inefficiently.
- *Extroversion.* Studies show that outgoing, sociable people report more happiness and life satisfaction than introverts do. Myers (1992) attributes this partly to extroverts' innate high-spiritedness and partly to their larger circle of friends. Nurturing a strong social group can contribute to feelings of happiness.
- *Optimism.* An optimistic outlook seems to be conducive to achievement. Optimists do better in school, succeed more often at work, and win more elections than pessimists do. What's the connection? According to Martin Seligman, who has conducted extensive studies of optimistic and pessimistic people,

"Success requires persistence, the ability to not give up in the face of failure. I believe that an optimistic explanatory style is the key to persistence" (1990, p. 101).

Optimists versus pessimists. By "explanatory style," Seligman means the way people explain what happens to them. Pessimists tend to believe that bad events will last a long time, will undermine everything they do, and are their own fault. Pessimism can thus stand in the way of achievement and a happy and productive life. Optimists, in contrast, tend to believe that a bad event is just a temporary setback, that its causes are unique, and that it is due to circumstances, bad luck, or other people.

The ABC method. If you get discouraged easily, get depressed more often than you would like, and fail more than you think you should, you may need to change your explanatory style.

Seligman believes that an individual can *learn* to be more optimistic and thereby improve his or her general health and sense of well-being. But contrary to what you might expect, this is not a matter of learning to say positive things to yourself. "What *is* crucial," Seligman notes, "is what you think when you fail. . . . Changing the destructive things you say to yourself when you experience the setbacks that life deals all of us is the central skill of optimism" (1990, p. 15).

Seligman has developed a method for learning optimism that he calls the *ABC method,* for *a*dversity, *b*eliefs, and *c*onsequences. Here is how this method might work:

- *Adversity* (anything that causes you to feel discouraged): I decided to join a gym, and when I walked into the place I saw nothing but firm, toned bodies all around me.
- *Belief* (how you explain the adversity): What am I doing here? I look like a beached whale compared to these people! I should get out of here while I still have my dignity.
- *Consequences* (the way you feel about the adverse event): I felt totally self-conscious and ended up leaving after 15 minutes. (Seligman, 1990, pp. 214–215.)

What you can do. If your reactions to adversity consistently follow a pessimistic pattern, you can do several specific things to change your thought patterns. Seligman has identified three useful techniques: distraction, disputation, and distancing.

- *Distraction.* Start by attempting to distract yourself—slap your hand against the wall and shout "Stop!" Then try to think about something else.
- *Disputation.* Argue with yourself about the adverse event. Take a close look at the facts. "The most convincing way of disputing a negative belief is to show that it is factually incorrect" (1990, p. 221). An advantage of this technique is that it is realistic. Learned optimism is based on accuracy, not merely on making positive statements. For example, a student whose grades are somewhat below expectations might say, "I'm blowing things out of proportion. I hoped to get all As, but I got a B, a B+, and a B−. Those aren't awful grades. I may not have done the best in the class, but I didn't do the worst in the class either" (Seligman, 1990, p. 219).
- *Distancing.* Still another way of dealing with pessimistic beliefs is distancing. Try to dissociate yourself from your pessimistic thoughts, at least long enough to judge their accuracy objectively. Recognize that simply believing something doesn't make it so.

Once you have challenged your pessimistic beliefs and convinced yourself that bad events are temporary and will not affect everything you do for the rest of your life, you will be able to look forward to better times in the future. Along with Little Orphan Annie, you will be confident that "The sun will come out tomorrow!"

THINKING CRITICALLY

Evaluation

In your opinion, which of the major personality theories discussed in this chapter is the most accurate, reasonable, and realistic? Which is the least accurate, reasonable, and realistic? Give reasons to support your answers.

Point/Counterpoint

Are personality characteristics mostly learned? Or are they mostly transmitted through the genes? Using what you have learned in this chapter and other evidence you can gather, make a case for each position. Support your answers with research and expert opinion.

Psychology in Your Life

Consider your own behavior and personality attributes from the standpoint of each of the theories: psychoanalysis, trait theory, and the learning, humanistic, and genetic perspectives. Which theory or theories best explain your personality? Why?

SUMMARY AND REVIEW

SIGMUND FREUD AND PSYCHOANALYSIS

To what two aspects of Freud's work does the term *psychoanalysis* apply?

Psychoanalysis is the term Freud used for both his theory of personality and his therapy for the treatment of psychological disorders.

What are the three levels of awareness in consciousness?

The three levels of awareness in consciousness are the conscious, the preconscious, and the unconscious.

What are the roles of the id, the ego, and the superego?

The id is the primitive, unconscious part of the personality, which contains the instincts and operates on the pleasure principle. The ego is the rational, largely conscious system, which operates according to the reality principle. The superego is the moral system of the personality, consisting of the conscience and the ego ideal.

What is a defense mechanism?

A defense mechanism is an unconscious, irrational means that the ego uses to defend against anxiety and to maintain self-esteem; it involves self-deception and the distortion of reality.

What are two ways in which repression operates?

Through repression, (1) painful memories, thoughts, ideas, or perceptions are involuntarily removed from consciousness, and (2) disturbing sexual or aggressive impulses are prevented from breaking into consciousness.

What are some other defense mechanisms?

Other defense mechanisms include projection, denial, rationalization, regression, reaction formation, displacement, and sublimation.

What are the psychosexual stages, and why did Freud consider them so important in personality development?

Freud believed that the sexual instinct is present at birth, develops through a series of psychosexual stages, and provides the driving force for thought and activity. The psychosexual stages are the oral stage, anal stage, phallic stage (followed by the latency period), and genital stage.

What is the Oedipus complex?

The Oedipus complex, occurring in the phallic stage, is a conflict in which the child is sexually attracted to the opposite-sex parent and feels hostility toward the same-sex parent.

According to Freud, what are the two primary sources of influence on the personality?

Freud believed that differences in personality result from the relative strengths of the id, the ego, and the superego and from the personality traits that develop as a result of problems during the psychosexual stages.

Key Terms
personality (p. 496); psychoanalysis (p. 497); conscious (p. 497); preconscious (p. 497); unconscious (p. 497); id (p. 498); pleasure principle (p. 498); libido (p. 498); ego (p. 498); superego (p. 498); defense mechanism (p. 498); repression (p. 498); projection (p. 499); denial (p. 499); rationalization (p. 499); regression (p. 499); reaction formation (p. 500); displacement (p. 500); sublimation (p. 500); psychosexual stages (p. 501); fixation (p. 501); oral stage (p. 501); anal stage (p. 501); phallic stage (p. 502); Oedipus complex (p. 502); latency period (p. 502); genital stage (p. 502)

THE NEO-FREUDIANS

According to Jung, what are the three components of personality?

Jung conceived of the personality as having three parts: the ego, the personal unconscious, and the collective unconscious.

What are five archetypes that Jung believed have a major influence on the personality?

Jung believed that the persona, shadow, anima, animus, and self are five archetypes that exert a major influence on personality.

What did Adler consider to be the driving force of the personality?

Adler claimed that the predominant force of the personality is the drive to overcome and compensate for feelings of weakness and inferiority and to strive for superiority or significance.

Why is Horney considered a pioneer in psychology?

Horney took issue with Freud's sexist view of women and added the feminine dimension to the world of psychology.

Key Terms
personal unconscious (p. 505); collective unconscious (p. 505); archetype (p. 505); extroversion (p. 506); introversion (p. 506)

TRAIT THEORIES

What are trait theories of personality?

Trait theories of personality are attempts to explain personality and differences between people in terms of their personal characteristics.

How did Allport differentiate between cardinal and central traits?

Allport defined a cardinal trait as a personal quality that is so strong a part of a person's personality that he or she may become identified with that trait or known for it. A central trait is the type you might mention when writing a letter of recommendation.

How did Cattell differentiate between surface and source traits?

Cattell used the term *surface traits* to refer to observable qualities of personality, which you might use in describing a friend. *Source traits* underlie the surface traits, exist in all of us in varying degrees, make up the most basic personality structure, and cause behavior.

What does Eysenck consider to be the two most important dimensions of personality?

Eysenck considers the two most important dimensions of personality to be Extroversion (extroversion versus introversion) and Neuroticism (emotional stability versus instability).

What are the Big Five personality dimensions in the five-factor theory as described by McCrae and Costa?

According to McCrae and Costa, the Big Five factors are Neuroticism, Extroversion, Conscientiousness, Agreeableness, and Openness to Experience.

Key Terms
trait (p. 508); trait theories (p. 509); cardinal trait (p. 509); central trait (p. 509); surface traits (p. 510); source traits (p. 510); five-factor theory (p. 511)

LEARNING THEORIES AND PERSONALITY

How did Skinner account for what most people refer to as personality?

B. F. Skinner viewed personality as simply a collection of behaviors and habits that have been reinforced in the past.

What are the components of Bandura's concept of reciprocal determinism, and how do they interact?

The external environment, behavior, and personal/cognitive factors are the three components of reciprocal determinism, each influencing and being influenced by the others.

What does Rotter mean by the terms *internal* and *external locus of control*?

According to Rotter, people with an internal locus of control see themselves as primarily in control of their behavior and its consequences; those with an external locus of control believe their destiny is in the hands of fate, luck, or chance.

Key Terms
reciprocal determinism (p. 514); self-efficacy (p. 515); locus of control (p. 515)

HUMANISTIC PERSONALITY THEORIES

Who were the two pioneers in humanistic psychology, and how did they view human nature?

Abraham Maslow and Carl Rogers, the two pioneers in humanistic psychology, believed that human nature is innately good and that people have free will and a tendency toward growth and realization of their potential.

What is self-actualization, and how did Maslow study it?

Self-actualization means developing to one's fullest potential. Maslow studied people who had made significant contributions in their lifetimes and who exemplified self-actualization to determine what characteristics they shared.

According to Rogers, why don't all people become fully functioning persons?

Individuals often do not become fully functioning persons because in childhood they did not receive unconditional positive regard from their parents. To gain positive regard, they had to meet their parents' conditions of worth.

Key Terms
humanistic psychology (p. 516); self-actualization (p. 517); conditions of worth (p. 517); unconditional positive regard (p. 518)

PERSONALITY: IS IT IN THE GENES?

What has research in behavioral genetics revealed about the influence of the genes and the environment on personality?

Research in behavioral genetics has revealed that about 40–50% of personality can be attributed to the genes, and that the environmental influences on personality are mainly from the nonshared environment.

Key Terms
behavioral genetics (p. 519); heritability (p. 520)

PERSONALITY ASSESSMENT

What are the three major methods used in personality assessment?

The three major methods used in personality assessment are (1) observation, interviews, and rating scales, (2) inventories, and (3) projective tests.

What is an inventory, and what are the MMPI-2 and the CPI designed to reveal?

An inventory is a paper-and-pencil test with questions about a person's thoughts, feelings, and behaviors, which can be scored according to a standard procedure. The MMPI-2 is designed to screen and diagnose psychiatric problems, and the CPI is designed to assess the normal personality.

How do projective tests provide insight into personality, and what are some of the most commonly used projective tests?

In a projective test, people respond to inkblots, drawings of ambiguous human situations, incomplete sentences, and the like by projecting their own inner thoughts, feelings, fears, or conflicts onto the test materials. Examples are the Rorschach Inkblot Method, the Thematic Apperception Test (TAT), and the sentence completion method.

Key Terms
halo effect (p. 525); inventory (p. 525); Minnesota Multiphasic Personality Inventory (MMPI) (p. 525); California Psychological Inventory (CPI) (p. 527); Myers–Briggs Type Indicator (MBTI) (p. 527); projective test (p. 528); Rorschach Inkblot Method (p. 528); Thematic Apperception Test (TAT) (p. 529)

Surf It!

Want to be sure you've absorbed the material in Chapter 14, "Personality Theory and Assessment," before the big test? Visiting *www.abacon.com/wood* can put a top grade within your reach. The site is loaded with free practice tests, flashcards, activities, and links to help you review your way to an A. To enliven that inevitable study break, the site also offers personality assessment quizzes and a psychology career corner.

15 Psychological Disorders

It was early in January, and Sybil Dorsett was working with other students in the chemistry lab at Columbia University in New York. Suddenly the loud crash of breaking glass made her heart pound and her head throb. The room seemed to be whirling around, and the acrid smell of chemicals filled the air, stinging her nostrils.

That smell—so like the old drugstore back in her native Wisconsin—and the broken glass—like a half-forgotten, far-off memory of being at home in her dining room when she was a little girl. Again Sybil heard the accusing voice, "You broke it." Frantically she seized her chemistry notes, stuffed them into her brown zipper folder, and ran for the door with the eyes of the professor and the other students following her in astonishment.

Sybil ran down the long, dark hall on the third floor of the chemistry building, pushed the elevator button, and waited. Seconds seemed like hours.

The next thought that entered Sybil's awareness was that of clutching for her folder, but it was gone. Gone, too, were the elevator she was waiting for and the long, dark hallway. She found herself walking down a dark, deserted street in a strange city. An icy wind whipped her face, and thick snowflakes filled the air. This wasn't New York. Where could she be? And how could she have gotten here in the few seconds between

psychological disorders have a physical cause, such as genetic inheritance, biochemical abnormalities or imbalances, structural abnormalities within the brain, and/or infection. Consequently, those taking the biological perspective generally favor biological treatments, which may include drugs, electroconvulsive therapy (shock treatment), or psychosurgery.

The Biopsychosocial Perspective It is important to keep in mind as you read this chapter that even when there is strong evidence of a genetic factor in a psychological disorder, people do not inherit the disorder directly. They inherit a predisposition toward it. Whether they actually develop the disorder will depend on other conditions in their lives. The biopsychosocial perspective acknowledges these facts. It recognizes the important roles played by biological, psychological, and social factors in the study, identification, and treatment of psychological disorders.

The Psychodynamic Perspective What does the psychodynamic perspective see as the cause of psychological disorders? Originally proposed by Freud, the psychodynamic perspective maintains that psychological disorders stem from early childhood experiences and unresolved, unconscious conflicts, usually of a sexual or aggressive nature. The cause assumed by the psychodynamic approach also suggests the cure—psychoanalysis—which Freud developed to uncover and resolve such unconscious conflicts.

The Learning Perspective According to the learning perspective, psychological disorders are not symptoms of an underlying disorder; the behavioral symptoms are themselves the disorder. Get rid of the symptoms (the abnormal behavior), and the problem is solved. Many abnormal behaviors are thought to be learned and sustained in the same way as any other behavior. According to this view, people who exhibit abnormal behavior either are victims of faulty learning or have failed to learn appropriate patterns of thinking and acting. Behavior therapists use learning principles to eliminate distressing behavior and to establish new, more appropriate behavior in its place.

The Cognitive Perspective The cognitive perspective suggests that faulty thinking or distorted perceptions can contribute to some types of psychological disorders. For example, negative thinking is intimately involved in depression and anxiety. Treatment consistent with this perspective is aimed at changing thinking and perceptions, which presumably will lead to a change in behavior.

The Humanistic Perspective The humanistic perspective views human nature as inherently good and rational and as naturally moving toward self-actualization (the fulfillment of each person's potential). According to this view, psychological disorders result when a person's natural tendency toward self-actualization is blocked (Maslow, 1970; Rogers, 1961). Remove the psychological blocks, and the person can move toward self-actualization.

Review & Reflect 15.1 summarizes the six perspectives on psychological disorders. Each perspective has its place in the description, analysis, and treatment of certain of these disorders.

Although mental health professionals often disagree about the causes of abnormal behavior and the best treatments, there is less disagreement about diagnosis. A standard set of criteria has been established and is used by the majority of mental health professionals to diagnose psychological disorders.

Defining and Classifying Psychological Disorders

What is the *DSM-IV*?

In 1952 the American Psychiatric Association published a manual providing a diagnostic system for describing and classifying psychological disorders. Over the years

Review & Reflect 15.1 Perspectives on Psychological Disorders

Perspective	Cause of Psychological Disorders	Treatment
Biological perspective	A psychological disorder is a symptom of an underlying physical disorder caused by a structural or biochemical abnormality in the brain, by genetic inheritance, or by infection.	Diagnose and treat like any other physical disorder Drugs, electroconvulsive therapy, or psychosurgery
Biopsychosocial perspective	Psychological disorders result from a combination of biological, psychological, and social causes.	An eclectic approach employing treatments from one or more of the other perspectives
Psychodynamic perspective	Psychological disorders stem from early childhood experiences; unresolved, unconscious sexual or aggressive conflicts; and/or imbalance among id, ego, and super ego.	Bring disturbing repressed material to consciousness and help patient work through unconscious conflicts Psychoanalysis
Learning perspective	Abnormal thoughts, feelings, and behaviors are learned and sustained like any other behaviors, or there is a failure to learn appropriate behaviors.	Use classical and operant conditioning and modeling to extinguish abnormal behaviors and to increase adaptive behavior Behavior therapy, behavior modification
Cognitive perspective	Faulty and negative thinking can cause psychological disorders.	Change faulty, irrational, and/or negative thinking Beck's cognitive therapy, rational-emotive therapy
Humanistic perspective	Psychological disorders result from blocking of normal tendency toward self-actualization.	Increase self-acceptance and self-understanding; help patient become more inner-directed Client-centered therapy, Gestalt therapy

the manual has been revised several times. The most recent edition, the *Diagnostic and Statistical Manual of Mental Disorders,* (Fourth Edition), commonly known as the ***DSM-IV,*** appeared in 1994. It contains descriptions of about 290 specific psychological disorders and lists criteria that must be met in order to make a particular diagnosis. The *DSM-IV,* the most widely accepted diagnostic system in the United States, is used by researchers, therapists, mental health workers, and most insurance companies. It enables professionals to speak the same language when diagnosing, treating, researching, and conversing about a variety of psychological disorders (Clark et al., 1995). The task force that compiled the *DSM-IV* acknowledges that it is a work in progress, that it describes mental disorders rather than providing an explanation of their causes.

Table 15.1 summarizes the major categories of disorders in the *DSM-IV.*

DSM-IV: The *Diagnostic and Statistical Manual of Mental Disorders,* Fourth Edition, a manual published by the American Psychiatric Association, which describes about 290 mental disorders and their symptoms.

Table 15.1 Major *DSM-IV* Categories of Mental Disorders

Disorder	Symptoms	Examples
Schizophrenia and other psychotic disorders	Disorders characterized by the presence of psychotic symptoms including hallucinations, delusions, disorganized speech, bizarre behavior, or loss of contact with reality	Schizophrenia, paranoid type Schizophrenia, disorganized type Schizophrenia, catatonic type Delusional disorder, jealous type
Mood disorders	Disorders characterized by periods of extreme or prolonged depression or mania or both	Major depressive disorder Bipolar disorder
Anxiety disorders	Disorders characterized by anxiety and avoidance behavior	Panic disorder Social phobia Obsessive compulsive disorder Posttraumatic stress disorder
Somatoform disorders	Disorders in which physical symptoms are present that are psychological in origin rather than due to a medical condition	Hypochondriasis Conversion disorder
Dissociative disorders	Disorders in which one handles stress or conflict by forgetting important personal information or one's whole identity, or by compartmentalizing the trauma or conflict into a split-off alter personality	Dissociative amnesia Dissociative fugue Dissociative identity disorder
Personality disorders	Disorders characterized by long-standing, inflexible, maladaptive patterns of behavior beginning early in life and causing personal distress or problems in social and occupational functioning	Antisocial personality disorder Histrionic personality disorder Narcissistic personality disorder Borderline personality disorder
Substance-related disorders	Disorders in which undesirable behavioral changes result from substance abuse, dependence, or intoxication	Alcohol abuse Cocaine abuse Cannabis dependence
Disorders usually first diagnosed in infancy, childhood, or adolescence	Disorders that include mental retardation, learning disorders, communication disorders, pervasive developmental disorders, attention-deficit and disruptive behavior disorders, tic disorders, and elimination disorders	Conduct disorder Autistic disorder Tourette's syndrome Stuttering
Eating disorders	Disorders characterized by severe disturbances in eating behavior	Anorexia nervosa Bulimia nervosa

Source: Based on the *DSM-IV* (American Psychiatric Association, 1994).

You have heard the terms *neurotic* and *psychotic* used in relation to mental disturbances. Before 1980 the American Psychiatric Association grouped psychological disorders into two broad, general categories labeled *neuroses* and *psychoses* (plurals of neurosis and psychosis). Although now obsolete, the term **neurosis** was applied to disorders that cause people considerable personal distress and some impairment in functioning, without causing them to lose contact with reality or to violate important social norms. In contrast, a **psychosis** is a more serious disturbance that greatly impairs the ability to function in everyday life. It can cause people to lose touch with reality, possibly suffer from delusions and/or hallucinations, and sometimes require hospitalization. The term *psychosis* is still used by mental health professionals, most often in discussing the most serious psychological disorder, schizophrenia.

neurosis (new-RO-sis): An obsolete term for a disorder causing personal distress and some impairment in functioning but not causing loss of contact with reality or violation of important social norms.

psychosis (sy-CO-sis): A severe psychological disorder, marked by loss of contact with reality and a seriously impaired ability to function.

Remember It!

1. It is relatively easy to differentiate normal behavior from abnormal behavior. (true/false)

2. The *DSM-IV* is a manual that is published by the American Psychiatric Association and used to

   a. diagnose psychological disorders.

   b. explain the causes of psychological disorders.

   c. outline treatments for various psychological disorders.

   d. assess the effectiveness of treatment programs.

3. Match the perspective with its suggested cause of abnormal behavior.

____ (1) faulty learning	a. psychodynamic
____ (2) unconscious, unresolved conflicts	b. biological
____ (3) blocking of the natural tendency toward self-actualization	c. learning
	d. humanistic
____ (4) genetic inheritance or biochemical or structural abnormalities in the brain	e. biopsychosocial
	f. cognitive
____ (5) faulty thinking	
____ (6) a combination of biological, psychological, and social factors	

Answers: 1. false 2. a 3. (1) c (2) a (3) d (4) b (5) f (6) e

SCHIZOPHRENIA: THE MOST SERIOUS PSYCHOLOGICAL DISORDER

Schizophrenia is so far removed from common, everyday experience that it is all but impossible for most of us to imagine what it is like to be schizophrenic. Consider the case of Eric, whose normal childhood and youth turned into a nightmare when he lost touch with reality during his senior year in high school.

> Now in his thirties, he lives in his parents' wood-paneled basement. Usually sitting with a blanket covering his head, Eric is oblivious to the normal world. His world consists of the voices he hears inside his head and the visual hallucinations he takes to be real. Eric insists that he talks to God and to Satan, and at times he believes that he is Jesus Christ. If he refuses to take his antipsychotic medication, he is likely to become violent, and two times he has tried to take his own life. "His parents live in fear of what tomorrow will bring as they muddle through discouraging todays. There is seldom a moment without stress, an hour with peace of mind." (Bartimus, 1983, p. D1)

Schizophrenia is the most serious of the psychological disorders and probably the most devastating because of the social disruption and misery it causes for both the people who suffer from it and their families. "One should never underestimate the depth of their pain, even though the illness itself may diminish their ability to convey it" (Keith, 1993, p. 1617).

schizophrenia (SKIT-soh-FREE-nee-ah): A severe psychological disorder characterized by loss of contact with reality, hallucinations, delusions, inappropriate or flat affect, some disturbance in thinking, social withdrawal, and/or other bizarre behavior.

Schizophrenia affects about 1 person in 100, and one-half of all the mental hospital beds in this country are occupied by schizophrenic patients. The disorder usually begins in adolescence or early adulthood, although it can appear later in life.

The Symptoms of Schizophrenia: Many and Varied

What are some of the major positive and negative symptoms of schizophrenia?

Any given individual with schizophrenia may have one or more of its major symptoms, yet there is not one single symptom or brain abnormality shared by all people with the disorder. The symptoms of schizophrenia are classified into two categories—positive symptoms and negative symptoms.

Positive Symptoms Positive symptoms are *not* so named because they are desirable. Rather, they are the abnormal behaviors that are present in people with schizophrenia. Positive symptoms include hallucinations and delusions, as well as disorganized thinking and speech and grossly disorganized or bizarre behavior (McGlashan & Fenton, 1992).

Hallucinations One of the clearest positive symptoms of schizophrenia is the presence of **hallucinations**—imaginary sensations. Schizophrenic patients may see, hear, feel, taste, or smell strange things in the absence of any stimulus in the environment, but hearing voices is the most common type of hallucination. Patients may think they hear the voice of God or Satan, the voices of family members or friends, unknown voices, and even their own voice broadcasting aloud what they are thinking. Most often the voices accuse or curse the patients or engage in a running commentary on their behavior. Sometimes there are *command hallucinations,* in which the voices give instructions such as "Go outside" (Zisook et al., 1995, p. 462). At other times a menacing voice may order the patient to kill someone or take his or her own life.

Because there is increased activity in Broca's area of the brain when schizophrenics report hearing voices, the voices may be simply the person's own inner speech, not recognized as such (McGuire et al., 1993). These auditory hallucinations stimulate the primary auditory cortex much as real sounds do (Tiihonen et al., 1992).

Visual hallucinations, less common than auditory hallucinations, are usually in black and white and commonly take the form of friends, relatives, God, Jesus, or the devil. Schizophrenics also may experience exceedingly frightening and painful bodily sensations and feel they are being beaten, burned, or sexually violated. One schizophrenic complained that "spiders were crawling all through his heart and vessels, eating his brain, and . . . crawling on his skin" (Salama & England, 1990, p. 86).

Delusions Imagine how upset you would be if you believed that your every thought was being broadcast aloud for everyone to hear. What if you were convinced that some strange agent was stealing your thoughts or inserting other thoughts in your head? These are examples of **delusions**—false beliefs not generally shared by others in the culture. Usually patients cannot be persuaded that their beliefs are false, even in the face of strong evidence.

Delusions may take different forms. Schizophrenics with **delusions of grandeur** may believe they are a famous person (the president or Jesus Christ, for example) or a powerful or important person who possesses some great knowledge, ability, or authority. Those with **delusions of persecution** have the false notion that some person or agency is trying to harass, cheat, spy on, conspire against, injure, kill, or in some other way harm them.

Disturbances in the Form of Thought or Speech Schizophrenia is often marked by a disturbance in the form of thought. Most common is the loosening of associations, or *derailment,* when a person does not follow one line of thought to completion, but on the basis of vague connections shifts from one subject to another.

hallucination: A sensory perception in the absence of any external sensory stimulus; an imaginary sensation.

delusion: A false belief, not generally shared by others in the culture, that cannot be changed despite strong evidence to the contrary.

delusion of grandeur: A false belief that one is a famous person or a person who has some great knowledge, ability, or authority.

delusion of persecution: A false belief that a person or group is trying in some way to harm one.

> I am writing on paper. The pen I am using is from a factory called "Perry & Co." This factory is in England. . . . The city of London is in England. I know this from my school-days. Then, I always liked geography. My last teacher in that subject was . . . a man with black eyes. I also like black eyes. There are also blue and gray eyes and other sorts, too. I have heard it said that snakes have green eyes. All people have eyes. There are some, too, who are blind. (Bleuler, 1911/1950, p. 17)

Research by Docherty and others (1996) suggests that derailment seems to be related to weaknesses in working memory and attention.

The speech of schizophrenics is often difficult or even impossible to understand. The content of the message may be extremely vague, or the person may invent words or use them inappropriately.

Grossly Disorganized Behavior Grossly disorganized behavior can include such things as childlike silliness, inappropriate sexual behavior (masturbating in public), disheveled appearance, and peculiar dress. There may also be unpredictable agitation, including shouting and swearing, and unusual or inappropriate motor behavior, including strange gestures, facial expressions, or postures.

Inappropriate Affect Schizophrenics may display **inappropriate affect;** that is, their facial expressions, tone of voice, and gestures may not reflect the emotion that would be expected under the circumstances. A person might cry when watching a TV comedy and laugh when watching a news story showing bloody bodies at the scene of a fatal automobile accident.

inappropriate affect: A symptom common in schizophrenia in which a person's behavior (including facial expression, tone of voice, and gestures) does not reflect the emotion that would be expected under the circumstances; for example, a person laughs at a tragedy or cries at a joke.

Negative Symptoms A negative symptom of schizophrenia is a loss of or deficiency in thoughts and behaviors that are characteristic of normal functioning. Negative symptoms include social withdrawal, apathy, loss of motivation, lack of goal-directed activity, very limited speech, slowed movements, and poor hygiene and grooming (Skrabalo, 2000). Some schizophrenic patients have *flat affect*—showing practically no emotional response at all, even though they often report feeling the emotion. These patients may speak in a monotone, have blank and emotionless facial expressions, and act and move more like robots than humans.

Schizophrenics with negative symptoms seem to have the poorest outcomes (Fenton & McGlashan, 1994). Negative symptoms are predictors of impaired overall social and vocational functioning. Schizophrenics tend to withdraw from normal social contacts and retreat into their own world. They have difficulty relating to people, and often their functioning is too impaired for them to hold a job or even to care for themselves.

Brain Abnormalities in Some Schizophrenics Several abnormalities in brain structure and function have been found in schizophrenic patients. Among these are defects in the neural circuitry of the cerebral cortex and the limbic system (Benes, 2000; McGlashan & Hoffman, 2000). PET scans have revealed abnormally low neural activity in the frontal lobes (Glantz & Lewis, 2000; Kim et al., 2000). And schizophrenia, itself, may result in brain damage and hasten the progression of the disorder (Stahl, 1997). Other studies have revealed a decreased volume of the hippocampus and the amygdala (Nelson et al., 1998), and the thalamus (Buchsbaum et al., 1996). In many schizophrenics, there is a reduced volume of frontal lobe cortical gray matter, and the ventricles—fluid-filled cavities in the brain—are larger than in a normal brain (Gur et al., 2000; Sanfilippo et al., 2000; Staal et al., 2000). See Figure 15.1 (on p. 546). This particular abnormality was found in the brain of John Hinckley, Jr., the man who tried to assassinate Ronald Reagan.

Types of Schizophrenia

What are the four types of schizophrenia?

Even though various symptoms are commonly shared by schizophrenics, certain features distinguish one type of schizophrenia from another. The four types of schizophrenia are paranoid, disorganized, catatonic, and undifferentiated.

Figure 15.1
MRI Scans of Identical Twins

(a) This twin is healthy and has a normal MRI scan. (b) Note the enlarged ventricles (at tips of red arrows) in the brain of this twin, who has schizophrenia. (From Clinical Brain Disorders Branch, National Institute of Mental Health.)

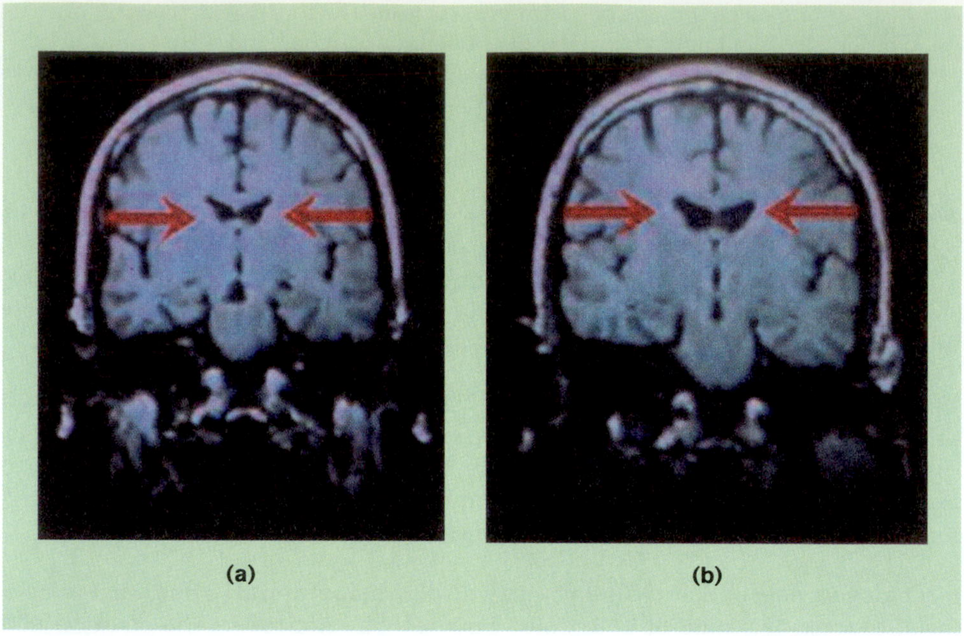

A person with catatonic schizophrenia may become frozen in an unusual position, like a statue, for hours at a time.

People with **paranoid schizophrenia** usually suffer from delusions of grandeur or persecution. They may be convinced that they have an identity other than their own—that they are the president, the Virgin Mary, or God—or that they possess great ability or talent. They may feel that they are in charge of the hospital or on a secret assignment for the government. Paranoid schizophrenics often show exaggerated anger and suspiciousness. If they have delusions of persecution and feel that they are being harassed or threatened, they may become violent in an attempt to defend themselves against their imagined persecutors. Usually the behavior of the paranoid schizophrenic is not so obviously disturbed as that of the catatonic or disorganized type, and the chance for recovery is better.

Disorganized schizophrenia, the most serious type, tends to occur at an earlier age than the other types and is marked by extreme social withdrawal, hallucinations, delusions, silliness, inappropriate laughter, grimaces, grotesque mannerisms, and other bizarre behavior. These patients show flat or inappropriate affect and are frequently incoherent. They often exhibit obscene behavior, may masturbate openly, and swallow almost any kind of object or material. Disorganized schizophrenia results in the most severe disintegration of the personality, and its victims have the poorest chance of recovery (Fenton & McGlashan, 1991).

Persons with **catatonic schizophrenia** may display complete stillness and stupor, or great excitement and agitation. Frequently they alternate rapidly between the two. They may become frozen in a strange posture or position, as shown in the photograph, and remain there for hours without moving.

Undifferentiated schizophrenia is the general catchall category used when schizophrenic symptoms either do not conform to the criteria of any schizophrenia type or conform to more than one type.

The Causes of Schizophrenia

What are some suggested causes of schizophrenia?

The primary causes of schizophrenia have been identified as genetic inheritance, environmental factors, and excessive dopamine activity. It is thought that the various causes interact somehow in most cases of the disorder.

Genetic Inheritance Schizophrenia does tend to run in families, and genetic factors play a major role (Cannon et al., 1998; Gottesman, 1991; Kendler & Diehl, 1993).

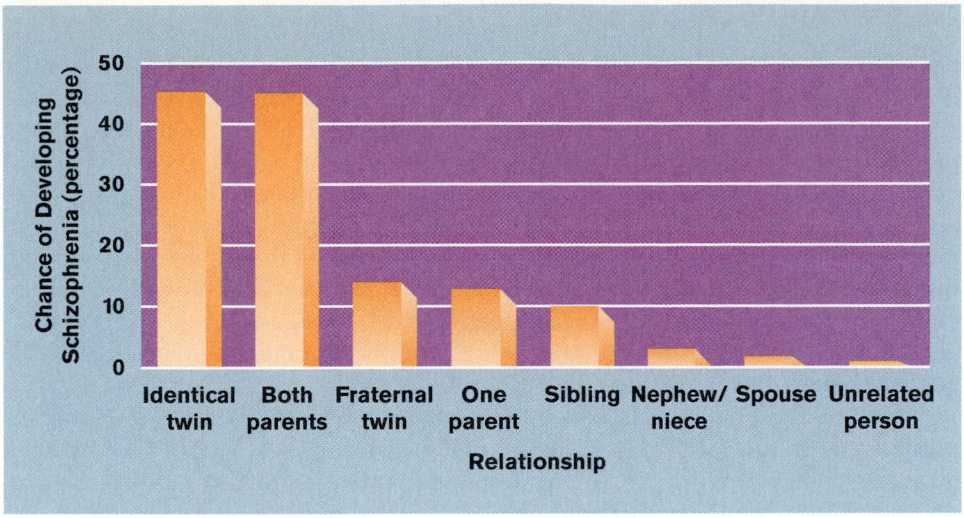

Figure 15.2

Genetic Similarity and Probability of Developing Schizophrenia

Research strongly indicates a genetic factor operating in many cases of schizophrenia. Identical twins have identical genes, and if one twin develops schizophrenia, the other twin has a 46% chance of developing it also. In fraternal twins the chance is only 14%. A person with one schizophrenic parent has a 13% chance of developing schizophrenia, but a 46% chance if both parents are schizophrenic. (Data from Nicol & Gottesman, 1983.)

The chance of a person in the United States developing schizophrenia is about 1 in 100 (Jeste, 1994). However, people with one schizophrenic parent have about a 13% chance of developing the disorder; those with two schizophrenic parents have roughly a 46% chance. If one identical twin develops schizophrenia, the other twin has about a 46% chance of having it as well (Nicol & Gottesman, 1983). Figure 15.2 shows how the chance of developing schizophrenia varies with the degree of relationship to a schizophrenic person. Still more evidence for a genetic factor comes from adoption studies showing that adoptees have ten times the risk of developing schizophrenia if their biological parent rather than their adoptive parent is schizophrenic (Kendler et al., 1994; Kety et al., 1994). Exactly what is the genetic connection? According to genetic theorists, what is inherited is not schizophrenia itself, but a predisposition or tendency to develop it (Zubin & Spring, 1977).

Environmental Factors The biopsychosocial perspective suggests that schizophrenia develops when there is *both* a genetic predisposition toward the disorder and more stress than a person can handle. The excessive stress can occur in the womb, during the birth process, or during childhood, adolescence, or adulthood. Any environmental factor that can interfere with normal brain development brings an increased risk for schizophrenia. Among these stressors are prenatal malnutrition, viruses, or injury, and brain infections in infancy or early childhood (Karp et al., 2001; McDonald & Murray, 2000). Trauma during labor and delivery, especially when labor is prolonged, can also lead to the abnormalities in brain structures associated with schizophrenia (McNeil et al., 2000).

Schizophrenics are particularly vulnerable to stress, and whether predisposed people develop the disorder may depend on their life circumstances (Fowles, 1992; Johnson, 1989). Schizophrenia is more common in highly urbanized areas of the United States than in rural areas. Perhaps the cause is the greater stress of city life coupled with higher exposure to pollutants, toxins, and infectious diseases (Torrey & Bowler, 1990).

Excessive Dopamine Activity Abnormal activity in the brain's dopamine system is found in many schizophrenics. Such altered dopamine activity sometimes results from cocaine abuse, which can pose an increased risk for schizophrenia (Benes, 2000; Tzschentke, 2001). Much of the brain's dopamine activity occurs in the limbic system, which is involved in human emotions. Drugs that are effective in reducing the symptoms of schizophrenia block dopamine action, although about one-third of the patients who are given them do not show improvement with such drugs.

paranoid schizophrenia (PAIR-uh-noid): A type of schizophrenia characterized by delusions of grandeur or persecution.

disorganized schizophrenia: The most serious type of schizophrenia, marked by inappropriate affect, silliness, laughter, grotesque mannerisms, and bizarre behavior.

catatonic schizophrenia (KAT-uh-TAHN-ik): A type of schizophrenia characterized by complete stillness or stupor and/or periods of great agitation and excitement; patients may assume an unusual posture and remain in it for long periods.

Gender and Schizophrenia

Gender has an effect on the risk factors for schizophrenia. Schizophrenia is more likely to strike men than women. Men also tend to develop the disorder at an earlier age (Takahashi et al., 2000), they do not respond as well to treatment, they spend more time in mental hospitals, and they are more likely to relapse. The earlier age of onset of the disorder among males appears to be independent of culture and socioeconomic variables. Studies of male and female schizophrenics conducted in Japan more than 40 years apart (in the 1950s and 1990s) revealed that Japanese males with the disorder had an earlier onset than Japanese females and that the average age of onset did not change over the 40-year period. Thus, the age of onset was not influenced by the dramatic cultural and socioeconomic changes in Japan during the postwar period (Takahashi et al., 2000).

Why are there such significant gender differences in the prevalence of schizophrenia and in the age of onset? Recent evidence strongly suggests that estrogen hormones, which females produce in abundance, provide protection against schizophrenia (Garcia-Segura et al., 2001).

Remember It!

1. Match the symptom of schizophrenia with the example.

____ (1) Bill believes he is Moses.
____ (2) Cristina thinks her family is spreading rumors about her.
____ (3) Sal hears voices cursing him.
____ (4) Ophelia laughs at tragedies and cries when she hears a joke.

a. delusions of grandeur
b. hallucinations
c. inappropriate affect
d. delusions of persecution

2. There is substantial research evidence that all of the following have roles as causes of schizophrenia *except*

a. genetic factors.
b. stress in people predisposed to the disorder.
c. excessive dopamine activity.
d. unhealthy family interaction patterns.

3. Match the subtype of schizophrenia with the example:

____ (1) Katy stands for hours in the same strange position.
____ (2) Vu believes the CIA is plotting to kill him.
____ (3) Ethan makes silly faces, laughs a lot, and masturbates openly.
____ (4) Pam has the symptoms of schizophrenia but does not fit any one type.

a. paranoid schizophrenia
b. disorganized schizophrenia
c. catatonic schizophrenia
d. undifferentiated schizophrenia

Answers: 1. (1) a (2) d (3) b (4) c 2. d 3. (1) c (2) a (3) b (4) d

MOOD DISORDERS: EMOTIONAL HIGHS AND LOWS

mood disorders: Disorders characterized by extreme and unwarranted disturbances in feeling or mood.

Mood disorders involve moods or emotions that are extreme and unwarranted. In the most serious of these disorders, mood ranges from the depths of severe depression to the heights of extreme elation. Mood disorders fall into two broad categories: depressive disorders and bipolar disorders.

Major Depressive Disorder

What are the symptoms of major depressive disorder?

It is normal to feel blue, sad, or depressed in response to many of life's common experiences—death of a loved one, divorce, loss of a job, or an unhappy ending to a long-term relationship. Major depression, however, is not normal. People with **major depressive disorder** feel an overwhelming sadness, despair, and hopelessness, and they usually lose their ability to experience pleasure. They may have changes in appetite, weight, or sleep patterns, loss of energy, and difficulty in thinking or concentrating. Key symptoms of major depressive disorder are psychomotor disturbances (Sobin & Sackeim, 1997). For example, body movements, reaction time, and speech may be so slowed that some depressed people seem to be doing everything in slow motion. Others experience the opposite extreme and are constantly moving and fidgeting, wringing their hands, and pacing. Depression can be so severe that its victims suffer from delusions or hallucinations, which are symptoms of psychotic depression. And the more deeply a person descends into depression over an extended period, the greater his or her deficit of social activities becomes (Judd et al., 2000). The most common of all *serious* mental disorders, depression strikes people of all social classes, cultures, and nations around the world.

Diversity and Depression Major depression, the number one cause of disability in the United States and around the world (National Institute of Mental Health, 1999c), affects nearly 10% of Americans aged 18 and over each year. In most countries the rate of depression for females is about twice that of males (Culbertson, 1997). Before boys reach puberty, they are more likely than girls to be depressed, but at adolescence a dramatic reversal in the gender-related depression rates takes place (Cyranowski et al., 2000). Not only are women more likely to suffer from depression, they are also more likely to be affected by negative consequences as a result. Early-onset depressive disorder adversely affects the educational attainment and earning power of women, but not men (Berndt et al., 2000). However, the overall depression rate for women is not twice as high across all ethnic groups. Among Jews, males are equally as likely as females to have major depression (Levav et al., 1997).

Major depressive disorder, the most common of the serious psychological disorders, is found in all cultures and social classes. Women are about twice as likely as men to suffer from depression.

In recent years there has been an increase in depression among adolescents, particularly in adolescent girls, and perhaps in Native American and homosexual young people as well (Peterson et al., 1993). Studies have also revealed high rates of mood disorders in writers and artists (Jamison, 1995; Schildkraut et al., 1994), composers, and entertainers (Ludwig, 1995, 1996). But the highest rates of depression appear to be among patients experiencing chronic pain (Banks & Kerns, 1996).

A large study involving participants from ten countries revealed that the lifetime risk for developing depression varied greatly around the world, with Asian countries (Taiwan and Korea) having significantly lower rates of the disorder (Weissman et al., 1996). See Figure 15.3 (on p. 550).

Recurrence of Depression and Recovery from It Some people suffer only one major depressive episode, but 50–60% will have a recurrence. Risk of recurrence is greatest for females (Winokur et al., 1993), for those with an onset of depression before age 20 (Giles et al., 1989), and for those with a family history of mood disorders (Akiskal, 1989). People who experience their first episode of depression when they are young, especially if they are younger than 15 years of age, are at greater risk of having multiple episodes of depression throughout life (Brown, 1996). Recurrences may be frequent or infrequent, and for 20–35% of patients, the episodes

major depressive disorder: A mood disorder marked by feelings of great sadness, despair, guilt, worthlessness, and hopelessness.

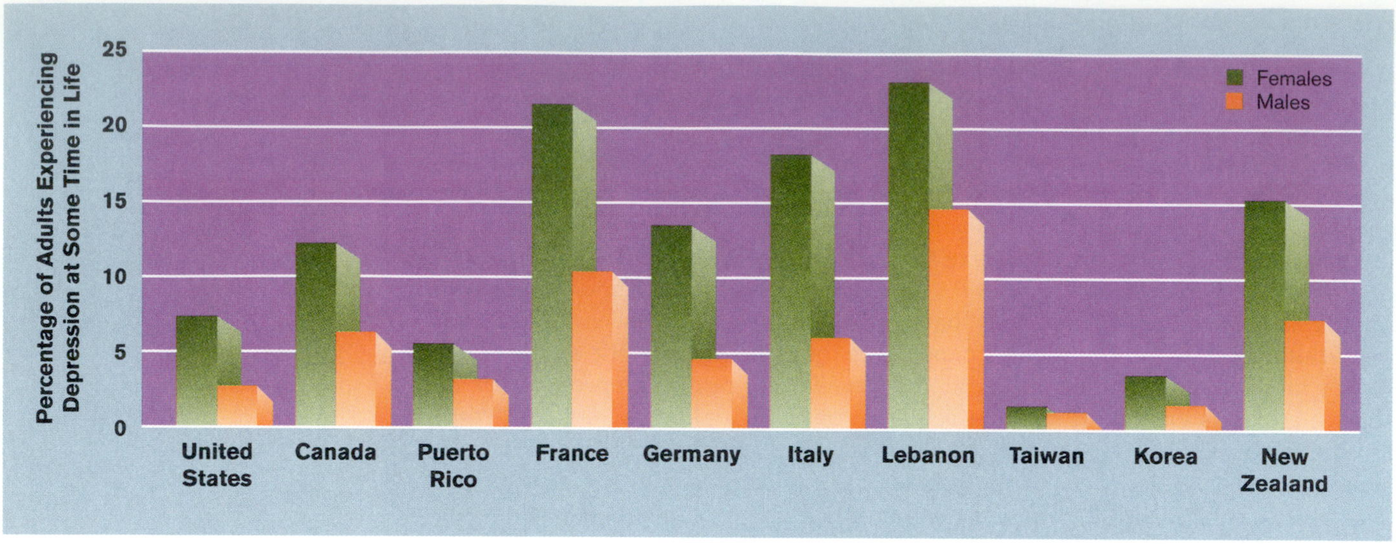

Figure 15.3

Lifetime Risk for Developing Depression in 10 Countries

The lifetime prevalence of depression for 38,000 men and women in 10 different countries reveals that women are more susceptible to depression worldwide. (Data from Weissman et al., 1996.)

The depressed moods of seasonal affective disorder (SAD) usually occur during the winter, when days are short, and can be improved using light therapy.

seasonal affective disorder (SAD): A mood disorder in which depression comes and goes with the seasons.

are chronic, lasting 2 years or longer. Recurring episodes tend to be increasingly more severe and long-lasting (Greden, 1994; Maj et al., 1992). According to the American Psychiatric Association (1994), 1 year after their initial diagnosis of major depressive disorder, 40% of patients are without symptoms; 40% are still suffering from major depression; and 20% are depressed, but not enough to warrant a diagnosis of major depression. Slightly less than one-half of those hospitalized for major depressive disorder are fully recovered after 1 year (Keitner et al., 1992). Unfortunately, about 80% of those suffering from depression never even receive treatment (Holden, 1986), and about 15% of people with major depressive disorder commit suicide (Coppen, 1994).

Dysthymia Many people who suffer from a milder form of depression called *dysthymia* experience depressed mood but have fewer of the associated symptoms common in major depressive disorder. This does not mean that dysthymia is not serious. It is a chronic disorder that lasts 2 years or longer. The risk of relapse is high, and nearly all people suffering from this disorder experience episodes of major depression (Klein et al., 2000).

Seasonal Depression Many people find that their moods seem to change with the seasons (Kasper et al., 1989). But people suffering from **seasonal affective disorder (SAD)** experience a significant depression that tends to come and go with the seasons (Wehr & Rosenthal, 1989). A spring/summer depression that remits in winter does exist, but the more common type, winter depression, seems to be triggered by light deficiency. During the winter months, when the days are shorter, some people become very depressed and tend to sleep and eat more, gain weight, and crave carbohydrates (Rosenthal et al., 1986; Wurtman & Wurtman, 1989). However, during the spring and summer months, they are in higher spirits, become more energetic, and claim to function better (Wehr et al., 1986). Molin and others (1996) found a correlation between the depression ratings of SAD patients and the minutes of sunshine and of daylight from September through May.

Reasoning that the obvious difference between the seasons was the amount and intensity of light, Rosenthal and colleagues (1985) exposed patients with winter

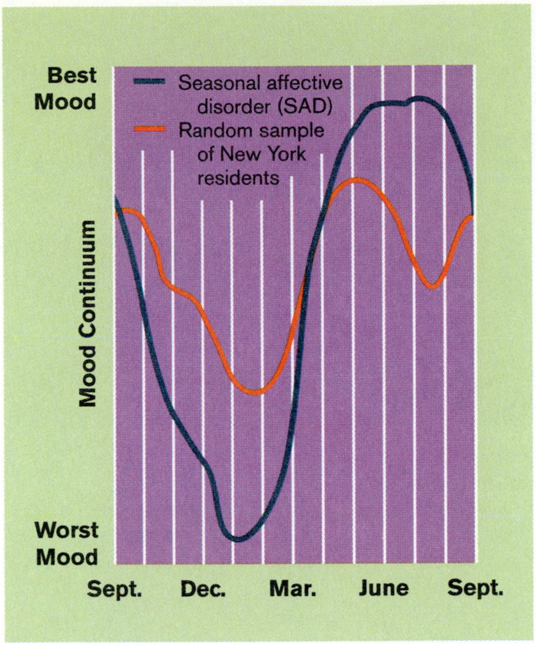

Figure 15.4

Seasonal Mood Changes

Many people report feeling best during May and June and worst during January and February. People with seasonal affective disorder (SAD) experience wider mood fluctuations—higher highs in June, July, and August and lower lows in December, January, and February. (Based on data from Wurtman & Wurtman, 1989.)

depression to bright light, which simulated the longer daylight hours of summer. After several days of the light treatment, most of the subjects improved. Even exposure to normal outdoor light during a walk helped people with SAD (Wirz-Justice et al., 1996). Figure 15.4 shows the difference in mood fluctuations between seasonal-affective-disorder patients and a random sample of New York residents.

Bipolar Disorder

What are the extremes of mood suffered by those with bipolar disorder?

Another type of mood disorder is **bipolar disorder,** in which patients experience two radically different moods—extreme highs called *manic episodes* (or *mania*) and the extreme lows of major depression—usually with relatively normal periods in between. A **manic episode** is marked by excessive euphoria, inflated self-esteem, wild optimism, and hyperactivity. During a manic episode people are wound up and full of energy. They frantically engage in a flurry of activity, rarely sleep, and talk loud and fast, skipping from one topic to another.

What is wrong with being euphoric, energetic, and optimistic? Obviously nothing, as long as the state is warranted. But people in a manic state have temporarily lost touch with reality and frequently have delusions of grandeur along with their euphoric highs. Their high-spirited optimism is not merely irrational, it is delusional. They may go on wild spending sprees or waste large sums of money on grand get-rich-quick schemes. If family members try to stop them or to convince them to abandon their irrational plans, they are likely to become irritable, hostile, enraged, or even dangerous. Quite often patients must be hospitalized during manic episodes to protect them and others from the disastrous consequences of their poor judgment.

The excessive euphoria, boundless energy, and delusions of grandeur are all apparent in this description of a manic episode experienced by Edward O, a 27-year-old high school teacher:

> One day Edward O's behavior suddenly became bizarre. He charged into the principal's office and outlined his plan for tearing down the school building and having his students rebuild it from the ground up over the weekend. The school principal called the police and had Edward taken to a hospital. There Edward paced up and down for two days, would not sleep or eat, and spoke excitedly about his plans to take over administration of the hospital. On the third day he demanded paper and

bipolar disorder: A mood disorder in which manic episodes alternate with periods of depression, usually with relatively normal periods in between.

manic episode (MAN-ik): A period of extreme elation, euphoria, and hyperactivity, often accompanied by delusions of grandeur and by hostility if activity is blocked.

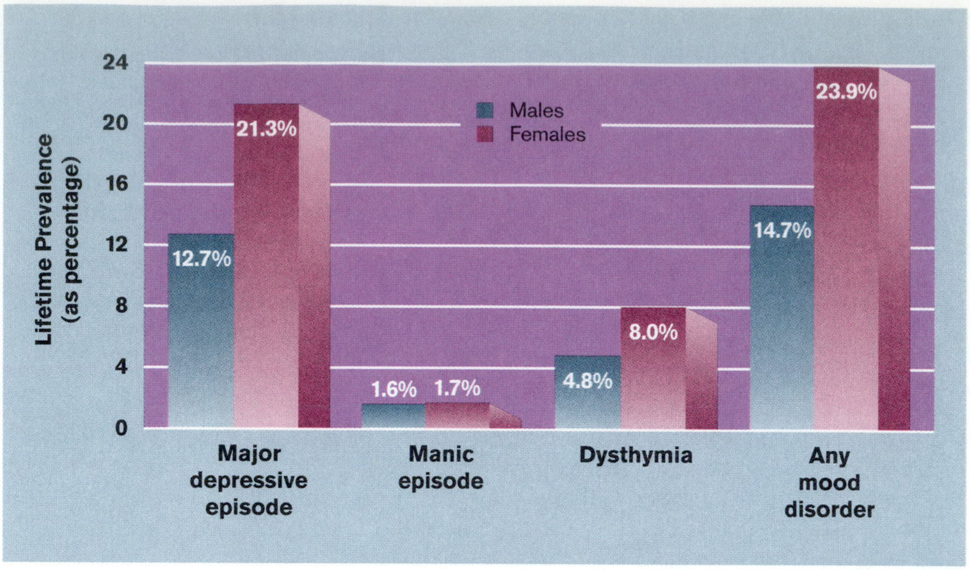

Figure 15.5

Lifetime Prevalence of Mood Disorders

The percentages of males and females in the United States who have suffered from various mood disorders during their lifetime are based on the findings of the National Comorbidity Survey. (Data from Kessler et al., 1994.)

> pens and, in a frenzy, wrote 100 letters, one to each U.S. senator. He cursed the pens for not writing faster and threw them against the wall, demanding new ones. When staff members tried to stop him, Edward flew into a rage, so they decided to let him "run out of steam." After the fourth day he collapsed, totally exhausted. (Adapted from Goldenberg, 1977)

Bipolar disorder is much less common than major depressive disorder, affecting about 1% of the U.S. population in any given year, and the lifetime prevalence rates are about the same for males and females (National Institute of Mental Health, 2000). Bipolar disorder tends to appear in late adolescence or early childhood, and, unfortunately, about 90% of those with the disorder have recurrences, and half experience another episode within a year of recovering from a previous one. The good news is that 70–80% of the patients return to normal after an episode (American Psychiatric Association, 1994). But some are "rapid cyclers"—experiencing four or more episodes per year.

Figure 15.5 shows the percentages of American females and males who have suffered from manic episodes and other mood disorders during their lifetime.

Causes of Major Depressive Disorder and Bipolar Disorder

What are some suggested causes of major depressive disorder and bipolar disorder?

The biological and cognitive perspectives offer some insight into the causes of mood disorders and suggest treatments that have proven helpful to many people suffering from these disorders.

The Biological Perspective Biological factors such as genetic inheritance and abnormal brain chemistry play a major role in bipolar disorder and major depressive disorder. PET scans have revealed abnormal patterns of brain activity in both of these disorders (George et al., 1993). Drevets and others (1997) located a brain area that may trigger both the sadness of major depression and the mania of bipolar disorder. A small, thimble-size patch of brain tissue in the lower prefrontal cortex (about 2–3 inches behind the bridge of the nose) is a striking 40–50% smaller in people with hereditary depression. Earlier research established that this area of the brain plays a key role in the control of emotions.

The Role of Genetic Inheritance Does depression tend to run in families? Apparently so, because people who have relatives with mood disorders are at higher risk of developing mood disturbances, and this risk is due to shared genetic factors rather than shared environmental factors (Kendler, Walters, et al., 1994). Based on a study of 1,721 identical and fraternal female twins, Kendler, Neale, Kessler, and others (1993) estimated the heritability of major depression to be 70% and the contribution of environment to be 30%.

Adoption studies have shown that among adult adoptees who had developed depression, there was 8 times more major depression and 15 times more suicide in biological than in adoptive family members (Wender et al., 1986). The genetic link is even stronger for bipolar disorder than for depression. Also, earlier-onset and more severe depression is more heavily influenced by genetic factors.

The Role of Serotonin and Norepinephrine It is common knowledge that substances can alter mood—alcohol, caffeine, other uppers and downers, and a host of additional psychoactive substances. Researchers now know that moods are also altered and regulated by biochemicals occurring naturally in the body. Norepinephrine and serotonin are two neurotransmitters that play important roles in mood disorders (Lambert et al., 2000). Both are localized in the limbic system and the hypothalamus, parts of the brain that help regulate emotional behavior. Too little norepinephrine is associated with depression, and too much is related to mania. Amphetamines, which cause an emotional "high," are reported to stimulate the release of both serotonin and norepinephrine. And hypersecretion of cortisol in response to stress can cause suppression of norepinephrine and serotonin (Dinan, 1996).

An important unanswered question remains. Do these biochemical differences in the brain *cause* psychological changes or *result* from them? Theorists who emphasize psychological causes see the biochemical changes as results, not causes, of mood disorders.

The Cognitive Perspective According to the cognitive perspective, depression results from distortions in thinking (Haaga et al., 1991). Depressed individuals view themselves, their world, and their future all in negative ways (Beck, 1967, 1991). They see their interactions with the world as a series of burdens and obstacles that usually end in failure. Depressed persons believe they are deficient, unworthy, and inadequate, and they attribute their perceived failures to their own physical, mental, or moral inadequacies. Finally, according to the cognitive theory, depressed patients believe that their future holds no hope. They may reason: "Everything always turns out wrong." "I never win." "Things will never get better." "It's no use."

The cognitive perspective offers a great deal of insight that can be applicable in daily life. For example, one step toward healthy thinking is to recognize and avoid five cognitive traps.

- *Cognitive Trap 1: The "Tyranny of the Should."* One sure path to unhappiness is to set unrealistic, unachievable standards for yourself. Karen Horney (1950) called this cognitive trap the "tyranny of the should." Have you ever been tyrannized by "shoulds" like these? I "should always be the perfect friend, lover, spouse, parent, student, teacher, [or] employee," or I "should never feel hurt" and "should always be calm" (Horney, 1950, pp. 64–66).
- *Cognitive Trap 2: Negative, "What If" Thinking.* Much unhappiness stems from a preoccupation with what might be. These are examples of "what if" thinking: "What if she/he turns me down for a date?" "What if I lose my job?" And if a "what if" comes to pass, the third cognitive trap may be sprung.
- *Cognitive Trap 3: Making Mountains Out of Molehills.* A molehill becomes a mountain when a single negative event is perceived as catastrophic or allowed to become a definition of total worth. "I failed this test" might become "I'll never pass this course."
- *Cognitive Trap 4: The Perfection–Failure Dichotomy.* Only on the rarest occasions can anyone's performance be considered absolutely perfect or a total failure. In reality,

outcomes will fall somewhere on a continuum between these two extremes. But people who fall into this cognitive trap judge anything short of perfection as total failure.

- *Cognitive Trap 5: Setting Impossible Conditions for Happiness.* Don't let your happiness hinge on perfection in yourself and others. Not everyone will love you or even like you, approve of you, or agree with you. If any of these are conditions on which your happiness depends, you are setting the stage for disappointment or even depression.

The Psychodynamic Explanation Psychodynamic theorists propose another cause for mood disorders. They suggest that when people cannot effectively express aggressive or negative feelings, they may turn those feelings inward (repress them) and thus experience depression.

Social Factors Even though heredity is the best predictor of depression over a lifetime, Kendler and others (1995) found that social factors such as getting divorced or losing a job are the best short-term predictors of depression, and for those who are genetically predisposed, the risk is much greater. The vast majority of first episodes of depression strike after major life stress (Brown et al., 1994; Frank et al., 1994). Cui and Vaillant (1996), in a longitudinal study of Harvard graduates that continued for over 40 years, found that negative life events as well as family history played significant roles in the development of mood disorders. This seems particularly true of women, who are more likely to have experienced a severe negative life event just prior to the onset of depression (Spangler et al., 1996). Yet recurrences of depression, at least in people who are biologically predisposed, often occur without significant life stress (Brown et al., 1994).

Why are women so much more likely to suffer from depression than men? The National Task Force on Women and Depression suggests that the higher rate of depression in women is largely due to social and cultural factors. In fulfilling her many roles—mother, wife, lover, friend, daughter, neighbor—a woman is likely to put the needs of others ahead of her own. Having young children poses a particular risk, and women suffer other stresses disproportionately, such as poverty and physical and sexual abuse.

Some depressed people commit the ultimate act of desperation—suicide. What are some of the risk factors for suicide, and what can be done to help prevent a person from committing suicide?

Suicide and Gender, Race, and Age

In March 1999, David Strickland, an actor known for his role on NBC's *Suddenly Susan,* commited suicide by hanging himself. He was 29 years old. Why would any person commit this final act of desperation?

Who Commits Suicide? Between 30,000 and 31,000 suicides are reported annually in the United States, and more than 72% of the victims are white males. Together, white males and white females account for more than 90% of all suicides (U.S. Bureau of the Census, 1999). Why do so many more males than females commit suicide? This question is complicated by the fact that females are at least three times more likely than males to *attempt* suicide (Garland & Zigler, 1993). More women try, but men are four times more likely to *succeed* at taking their own lives.

Mood disorders and schizophrenia, along with substance abuse, are major risk factors for suicide in all age groups (Mościcki, 1995; Shaffer et al., 1996). There is also evidence that suicidal behavior runs in families (Brent et al., 1996). Older Americans are at far greater risk for suicide than younger people. White males aged 85 and over have the highest recorded suicide rate, with over 75 suicides for every 100,000 people in that age group, more than six times the average national suicide rate of 12.2 per 100,000 (U.S. Bureau of the Census, 1999). Poor general health, serious illness, loneliness (often due to the death of a spouse), and decline in social and economic status are conditions that may push many older Americans, especially those aged 75 and over, to commit suicide.

For teenagers and young adults aged 15 through 24, suicide is now the third leading cause of death, with accidents ranking first and homicides second (U.S. Bureau of the Census, 1999). For college students, however, suicide ranks second. According to Garland and Zigler (1993), 6–13% of adolescents and 10.4% of college students have made a suicide attempt. Up to 40% of those who attempt suicide will try again, and 5–15% will eventually succeed (Rudd et al., 1996).

The rate of suicide among 15- to 19-year-olds has nearly doubled over the last few decades, an increase that may be due to increases in alcohol and drug abuse, psychiatric disorders, antisocial behavior, and disturbed home life. In addition, an underlying psychiatric condition or a precipitating circumstance such as the breakup of a relationship, family conflict, a disciplinary crisis, or school problems may push a teenager "over the edge" (Gould et al., 1996; Heikkinen et al., 1993). There is also an elevated risk of suicide among adolescents who have been in trouble with the police or incarcerated.

Among adults, suicide rates are lowest for married persons, lower in women who have children, and lower still for pregnant women. And the suicide rate is highest for persons who have made a previous suicide attempt. People suffering from psychiatric disorders, particularly depression, schizophrenia, panic disorder, and alcoholism or drug abuse, are at higher risk. In fact, 70% of suicides are associated with depression.

Figure 15.6 shows the differences in U.S. suicide rates according to race, gender, and age.

Evidence suggests that suicidal behavior tends to run in families. Les Franklin founded the Shaka Franklin Foundation for Youth, a suicide prevention organization, in memory of his son Shaka, who had killed himself. Then, 10 years later Franklin's other son, Jamon, also committed suicide.

Preventing Suicide Although there are cultural differences in the rates, the methods used, and the reasons for committing suicide, the warning signs are very similar across racial, gender, and age groups.

Most suicidal persons communicate their intent; in fact, about 90% of them leave clues (Shneidman, 1994). They may communicate verbally: "You won't be seeing

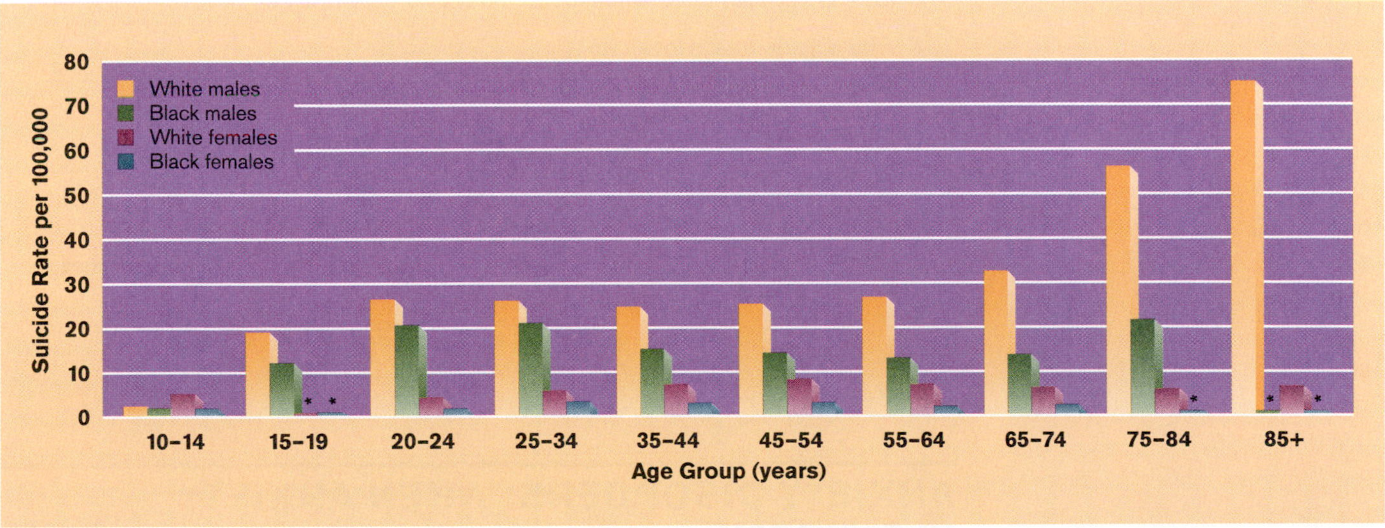

Figure 15.6

Differences in Suicide Rate According to Race, Gender, and Age

In every age group the suicide rate is highest for White males and second highest for Black males. The general conclusion is that males are more likely to commit suicide than females, and Whites are more likely than Blacks. Suicide rates indicated by asterisks (*) are too low to be statistically reliable. (Data from U.S. Bureau of the Census, 1994.)

me again." "You won't have to worry about me any more." They may show behavioral clues, such as giving away their most valued possessions; withdrawing from friends, family, and associates; taking unnecessary risks; showing personality changes; acting and looking depressed; and losing interest in favorite activities. These warning signs should always be taken seriously.

Hopelessness is a common characteristic of suicidal individuals (Beck et al., 1990). Proposing solutions or alternatives that could lessen hopelessness may lower the likelihood of suicide. Most people contemplating suicide are not totally committed to self-destruction. This may explain why many potential victims leave warnings or use less lethal means in attempting suicide.

If you are dealing with a suicidal person, the best service you can render is to encourage the person to get professional help. There are 24-hour suicide hotlines all over the country. A call might save a life.

Remember It!

1. Jamal has periods in which he is so depressed that he becomes suicidal. At other times he is energetic and euphoric. He would probably receive the diagnosis of

   a. dysthymia. c. bipolar disorder.

   b. seasonal mood disorder. d. major depressive disorder.

2. Match the theory of depression with the proposed cause.

   ____ (1) negative thoughts about oneself, the world, and one's future

   ____ (2) hereditary predisposition or biochemical imbalance

   ____ (3) turning resentment and hostility inward

   a. psychodynamic perspective

   b. cognitive perspective

   c. biological perspective

3. Stress appears to be unrelated to depression. (true/false)

4. The suicide rate is lower for

   a. males than for females.

   b. African Americans than for White Americans.

   c. the elderly than for teenagers.

   d. people who suffer psychological disorders than for those who do not.

Answers: 1. c 2. (1) b (2) c (3) a 3. false 4. b

ANXIETY DISORDERS: WHEN ANXIETY IS EXTREME

When is anxiety normal, and when is it abnormal?

Among the most common psychological disorders are the **anxiety disorders. Anxiety** is a vague, general uneasiness or an ominous feeling that something bad is about to happen. This feeling may be associated with a particular situation—a big exam, a job interview, or a first date, for example. Sometimes, however, anxiety is free-floating—not associated with anything specific.

Some anxiety is normal and appropriate. Imagine driving on a highway late at night and noticing that your gas gauge is on empty. The anxiety you would feel in this situation is normal anxiety—a response to a real threat. Normal anxiety would prompt you to take useful action—to look for a gas station. But anxiety serves no useful purpose and is abnormal if it is all out of proportion to the seriousness of the situation, if it does not soon fade once the danger is past, or if it occurs in the absence of real danger.

Psychological disorders characterized by severe anxiety are generalized anxiety disorder, panic disorder, phobias, and obsessive compulsive disorder. Take a minute right now to complete the anxiety disorder checklist in the *Try It!*

Try It!

Read each of the four descriptions below and place a checkmark beside each description that sounds like you or someone you know.

____ 1. You are always worried about things, even when there are no signs of trouble. You have frequent aches and pains that can't be traced to physical illness or injury. You tire easily, and yet you have trouble sleeping. Your body is constantly tense.

____ 2. Out of the blue, your heart starts pounding. You feel dizzy. You can't breathe. You feel like you are about to die. You've had these symptoms over and over again.

____ 3. Every day you fear you will do something embarrassing. You've stopped going to parties because you're afraid to meet new people. When other people look at you, you break out in a sweat and shake uncontrollably. You stay home from work because you're terrified of being called on in a staff meeting.

____ 4. You are so afraid of germs that you wash your hands repeatedly until they are raw and sore. You can't leave the house until you check the locks on every window and door over and over again. You are terrified that you will harm someone you care about. You just can't get those thoughts out of your head.

As you continue through this section of the chapter, you'll learn which anxiety disorders these symptoms represent. (From National Institute of Mental Health, 1999a.)

Generalized Anxiety Disorder: Chronic Worrying

Generalized anxiety disorder is the diagnosis given to people who are plagued by chronic, excessive, worry for 6 months or more. These unfortunate people expect the worst; their worrying is either unfounded or greatly exaggerated, and, thus, difficult to control. They may be unduly worried about their finances, their own health or that of family members, their performance at work, or their ability to function socially. Their excessive anxiety may cause them to feel tense, tired, and irritable, and to have difficulty concentrating and sleeping. Other symptoms may include trembling, palpitations, sweating, dizziness, nausea, diarrhea, or frequent urination. This disorder affects twice as many women as men and leads to considerable distress and impairment (Brawman-Mintzer & Lydiard, 1996, 1997; Kranzler, 1996). The heritability of generalized anxiety disorder is estimated to be about 30% (Kendler et al., 1992b). But, as troubling as this disorder is, it is less severe than panic disorder.

anxiety disorders: Psychological disorders characterized by severe anxiety (e.g., panic disorder, phobias, general anxiety disorder, obsessive compulsive disorder).

anxiety: A general uneasiness or ominous feeling that may be associated with a particular object or situation or may be free-floating, not associated with anything specific.

generalized anxiety disorder: An anxiety disorder in which people experience excessive anxiety or worry that they find difficult to control.

Panic Disorder: Disabling Attacks of Fear

What are the symptoms of panic disorder?

> Mindy Markowitz is young, attractive, and successful. An art director for a trade magazine, she came seeking treatment for panic attacks she had suffered over the past year. Now occurring as often as two or three times a day, the panic attacks would appear, seemingly out of nowhere, as a sudden, intense wave of terrible fear, sometimes during the day and sometimes at night, waking her from sleep. During the attacks Mindy would begin to tremble, feel nauseated, and sweat profusely. She "feels as though she is gagging," she said, but even worse is the horrible fear that "she will lose control and do something crazy, like run screaming into the street." (Spitzer et al., 1989, p. 154)

During **panic attacks**—attacks of overwhelming anxiety, fear, or terror—people commonly report a pounding heart, uncontrollable trembling or shaking, and sensations of choking or smothering. Some say they believe they are going to die or are "going crazy." Recent studies have revealed that the more catastrophic such beliefs are, the more intense the panic attack is likely to be (Hedley et al., 2000).

Mindy Markowitz was diagnosed with **panic disorder**—a disorder characterized by recurrent, unpredictable panic attacks that cause apprehension about the occurrence and consequences of further attacks. This apprehension can lead people to avoid situations that have been associated with previous panic attacks. About 2% of men and 5% of women in the United States suffer from panic disorder (Kessler et al., 1994).

What causes panic disorder? It is currently believed that multiple factors are responsible. These include heredity, other biological factors, excessive stress, and so-called catastrophic thinking, or the tendency to misinterpret common internal bodily sensations as dangerous. This assumption of multiple causes is consistent with the biopsychosocial perspective.

Panic disorder can have significant social and health consequences (Sherbourne et al., 1996). Panic-disorder patients tend to overuse the health care system (Katon, 1996) and are at increased risk for abuse of alcohol and other drugs (Marshall, 1997a). In a study of panic disorder involving 40,000 patients in 10 countries (the United States, Canada, Puerto Rico, France, Germany, Italy, Lebanon, Korea, New Zealand, and Taiwan), Weissman and others (1997) found a similar incidence, age of onset, and male/female ratio in all countries except Taiwan, where the incidence was considerably lower.

Phobias: Persistent, Irrational Fears

What are the characteristics of the three categories of phobias?

A person suffering from a **phobia** experiences a persistent, irrational fear of some specific object, situation, or activity that poses no real danger (or whose danger is blown all out of proportion). Phobics realize their fears are irrational, but they nevertheless feel compelled to avoid the feared objects or situations. There are three classes of phobias—agoraphobia, social phobia, and specific phobia.

Agoraphobia The phobia most likely to drive people to seek professional help is **agoraphobia.** Agoraphobics have an intense fear of being in a situation from which immediate escape is not possible or in which help would not be available if the person should become overwhelmed by anxiety or experience a panic attack or panic-like symptoms. In some cases a person's entire life must be planned around avoiding feared situations such as busy streets, crowded stores, restaurants, and/or public transportation. An agoraphobic often will not leave home unless accompanied by a friend or family member and, in severe cases, not even then. Women are four times more likely than men to be diagnosed with agoraphobia (Bekker, 1996).

Although agoraphobia can occur without panic attacks, it typically begins during the early adult years with repeated panic attacks (Horwath et al., 1993). The intense fear of having another attack causes the person to avoid any place or situation where previous attacks have occurred. Some researchers believe that agoraphobia is actually an extreme form of panic disorder (Sheehan, 1983). *Panic disorder with agoraphobia (PDA)* is one of the most debilitating of psychological disorders and

---

panic attack: An attack of overwhelming anxiety, fear, or terror.

panic disorder: An anxiety disorder in which a person experiences recurrent unpredictable attacks of overwhelming anxiety, fear, or terror.

phobia (FO-bee-ah): A persistent, irrational fear of an object, situation, or activity that the person feels compelled to avoid.

agoraphobia (AG-or-uh-FO-bee-uh): An intense fear of being in a situation from which immediate escape is not possible or in which help is not immediately available in case of incapacitating anxiety.

---

it is more common in women than in men. It can affect most areas of life—physical, psychological, social, occupational, interpersonal, and economic.

People are at greater risk of developing agoraphobia when other family members have it—the closer the relative, the higher the risk. Some agoraphobics have been treated successfully with psychotherapy (Shear & Weiner, 1997); others have responded well to antidepressants (Marshall, 1997c).

Although incredibly talented, Barbra Streisand suffers from extreme performance anxiety, which kept her from appearing live in concerts for many years.

Social Phobia Is someone you know always missing at your holiday parties? People who are consistently absent at social gatherings may be suffering from **social phobia.** These individuals are intensely afraid of any social or performance situation in which they might embarrass or humiliate themselves in front of others—where they might shake, blush, sweat, or in some other way appear clumsy, foolish, or incompetent. About one-third of social phobics fear only speaking publicly (Kessler et al., 1998). The rest may fear speaking, performing, or writing in public, eating with others, or using public restrooms (Greist, 1995). Can you imagine being unable to cash a check, or even take notes or a written exam in class because you feared writing in front of others?

Social phobia typically develops by adolescence (Hirschfeld, 1995; Jefferson, 1996) and may have its origins in childhood shyness and a traumatic event such as a very embarrassing social evaluation (Stemberger et al., 1995). It affects 11.1% of males and 15.5% of females at some time in their lives (Kessler et al., 1994), and genetic factors appear to play a role.

Social phobia may take the form of specific performance anxiety, commonly experienced by musicians, as well as many successful politicians, actors, comedians, and singers. Barbra Streisand's extreme performance anxiety kept her from appearing live in concert for many years. Even many people who have not been diagnosed as social phobics fear speaking in public. In fact, one-third of 449 survey respondents said they would experience excessive anxiety if they had to speak in front of a large audience (Stein et al., 1996). If you are one of the millions who are afraid of public speaking, see the *Apply It!* at the end of this chapter for advice on overcoming your fear.

Although less debilitating than agoraphobia, social phobia can be a disabling disorder (Stein & Kean, 2000). In its extreme form, it can seriously affect people's performance at work, prevent them from advancing in their careers or pursuing an education, and severely restrict their social lives (Greist, 1995; Stein & Kean, 2000). And often those with social phobia turn to alcohol and tranquilizers to lessen their anxiety in social situations. Mickey Mantle, for example, used alcohol to calm himself when making public appearances (Jefferson, 1996).

Specific Phobia **Specific phobia**—a marked fear of a specific object or situation—is a catchall category for any phobias other than agoraphobia and social phobia. This type usually begins in childhood. The categories of specific phobias, in order of frequency of occurrence, are (1) situational phobias (fear of elevators, airplanes, enclosed places, heights, tunnels, or bridges); (2) fear of the natural environment (storms or water); (3) animal phobias (fear of dogs, snakes, insects, or mice); and (4) blood–injection–injury phobia (fear of seeing blood or an injury, or of receiving an injection) (Fredrikson et al., 1996). Two types of situational phobias—claustrophobia (fear of closed spaces) and acrophobia (fear of heights)—are the specific phobias treated most often by therapists.

People with specific phobias usually fear the same things others fear, but their fears are greatly exaggerated. To be considered a phobia, a fear must cause great distress or interfere with a person's life in a major way.

Faced with the object or situation they fear, phobics experience intense anxiety, even to the point of shaking or screaming. They will go to great lengths to avoid the feared object or situation. Some people with blood–injection–injury phobia will not seek medical care even if it is a matter of life and death (Marks, 1988). And those with a severe dental phobia will actually let their teeth rot rather than visit the dentist. John Madden, well-known former coach of the Oakland Raiders and TV sports commentator, certainly went to great lengths to avoid his phobia—fear of flying.

social phobia: An irrational fear and avoidance of social situations in which one might embarrass or humiliate oneself by appearing clumsy, foolish, or incompetent.

specific phobia: A marked fear of a specific object or situation; a catchall category for any phobia other than agoraphobia and social phobia.

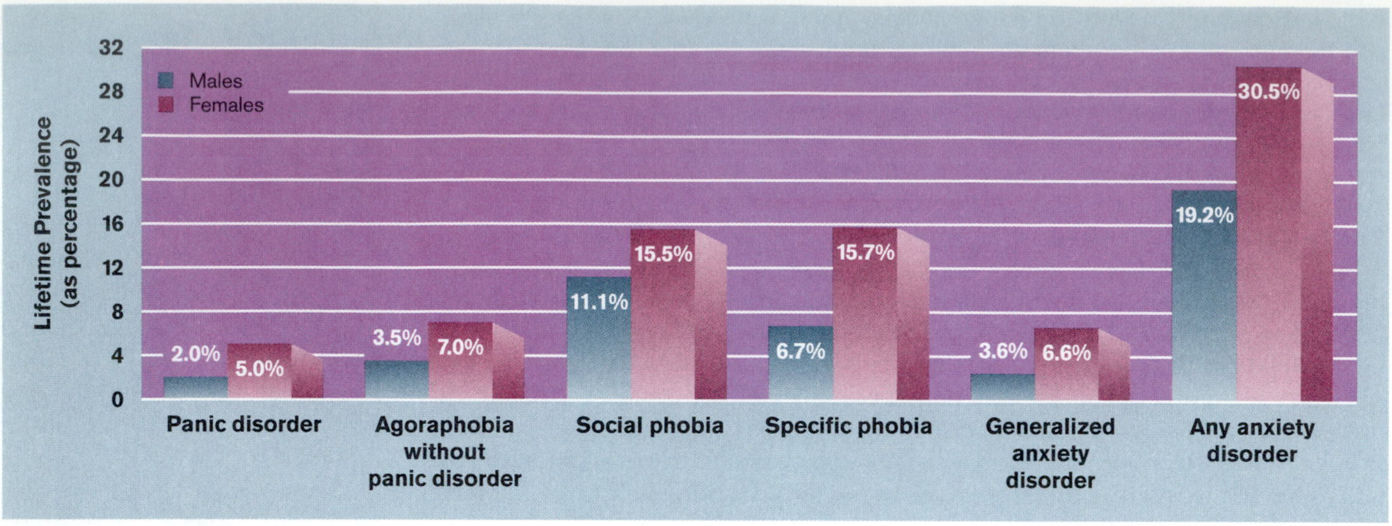

Figure 15.7

Lifetime Prevalence of Anxiety Disorders

The percentages of males and females in the United States who have suffered from various anxiety disorders during their lifetime are based on the findings of the National Comorbidity Survey. (Data from Kessler et al., 1994.)

When his team played a game at home in California one week and one in New York the following week, he preferred to spend the entire week driving from Oakland to the East Coast in his mobile home (the "Madden Mobile") rather than get on an airplane and be there in hours.

Figure 15.7 shows the percentages of males and females who have suffered from phobias and other anxiety disorders during their lifetime.

What do psychologists see as probable causes of phobias?

Causes of Phobias Most specific and social phobias probably are learned through direct conditioning, modeling, or the transmission of information (Rachman, 1997). Virtually all dog phobias can be attributed to one or the other of these learning pathways (King et al., 1997). Frightening experiences set the stage for phobias, although not all phobics recall the experience producing the phobia. A person with a dental phobia may be able to trace its beginning to a previous traumatic experience during a visit to the dentist. Or a person humiliated by performing poorly in front of others may develop a social phobia.

Phobias may be acquired, as well, through observational learning. For example, children who hear their parents talk about frightening experiences with the dentist or with bugs or snakes or thunderstorms may develop similar fears themselves. In many cases phobias are acquired through a combination of conditioning and observational learning (Merckelbach et al., 1996).

Genes appear to play a role in all classes of phobias. A person has three times the risk of developing a phobia if a close relative suffers from one (Fyer, 1993).

From the psychodynamic perspective, people develop phobias primarily as a defense against the anxiety they feel when sexual or aggressive impulses threaten to break into consciousness. For example, a single person who has strong repressed sexual urges may develop a fear of going out at night as an unconscious defense against acting on these urges.

Obsessive Compulsive Disorder

What is obsessive compulsive disorder?

What is wrong with people who are endlessly counting, checking, or performing other time-consuming rituals over and over? What causes some people to wash their hands 100 times a day until they are raw and bleeding? The answer is **obsessive compulsive disorder (OCD),** another form of anxiety disorder in which people suffer from recurrent obsessions or compulsions, or both.

Obsessions If you have ever had a tune or the words of a song run through your mind over and over without being able to stop it, you have experienced obsessive thinking in a mild form. But imagine how miserable you would be if every time you touched something you thought you were being contaminated, or if the thought of stabbing your mother kept popping into your mind. **Obsessions** are persistent, recurring, involuntary thoughts, images, or impulses that invade consciousness and cause a person great distress.

People with obsessions might worry about contamination or about whether they performed a certain act, such as turning off the stove or locking the door (Insel, 1990). Other types of obsessions center on aggression, religion, or sex. One minister reported obsessive thoughts of running naked down the church aisle and shouting obscenities at his congregation.

Do people ever act on their obsessive thoughts? It is rare for people actually to carry out obsessive thoughts. Yet many people are so horrified by their obsessions that they think they are losing their mind.

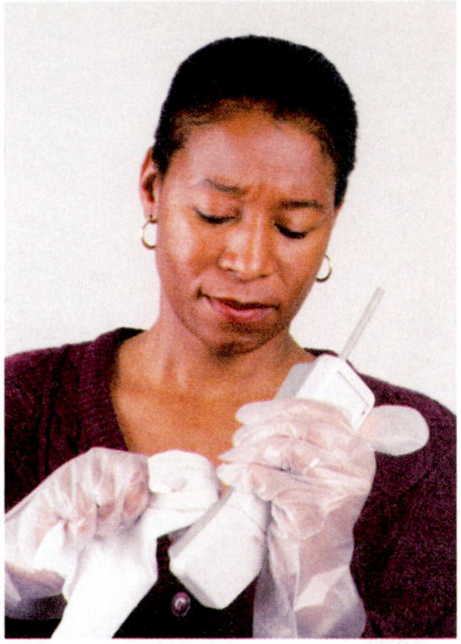

Like this woman, many people with obsessive compulsive disorder take great pains to avoid contamination from germs and dirt.

Compulsions A person with a **compulsion** feels literally compelled to repeat certain acts or perform specific rituals over and over. The individual knows such acts are irrational and senseless but cannot resist performing them without experiencing an intolerable buildup of anxiety—anxiety that can be relieved only by yielding to the compulsion. Many of us have engaged in compulsive behavior like stepping over cracks on the sidewalk, counting stairsteps, or performing little rituals from time to time. The behavior becomes a psychological problem only if the person cannot resist performing it, if it is very time-consuming, and if it interferes with the person's normal activities and relationships with others.

Compulsions usually involve cleaning and washing behaviors, counting, checking, touching objects, hoarding, and excessive organizing. These cleaning and checking compulsions affect 75% of OCD patients receiving treatment (Ball et al., 1996). Sometimes compulsive acts or rituals resemble magical thinking and must be performed faithfully to ward off some danger.

People with OCD do not enjoy the time-consuming rituals—the endless counting, checking, or cleaning. They realize that their behavior is not normal; but they simply cannot help themselves, as shown in the following example.

> Mike, a 32-year-old patient, performed checking rituals that were preceded by a fear of harming other people. When driving, he had to stop the car often and return to check whether he had run over people, particularly babies. Before flushing the toilet, he had to check to be sure that a live insect had not fallen into the toilet, because he did not want to be responsible for killing a living thing. At home he repeatedly checked to see that the doors, stoves, lights, and windows were shut or turned off. . . . Mike performed these and many other checking rituals for an average of 4 hours a day. (Kozak et al., 1988, p. 88)

Are there many Mikes out there, or is his case unusual? Mike's checking compulsion is quite extreme, but it has been estimated that perhaps 2–3% of the U.S. population will suffer from OCD at some time in life. Fairly similar rates have been reported in studies in Canada, Puerto Rico, Germany, Korea, and New Zealand (Weissman et al., 1994).

About 70% of people in treatment for OCD have both obsessions and compulsions. But surveys of OCD in the general population reveal that 50% of the cases involve obsessions only, 34% compulsions only, and 16% both obsessions and compulsions (Weissman et al., 1994). When both occur together, the compulsion usually serves to relieve the anxiety caused by the obsession. All age groups with this disorder—children, adolescents, and adults—show strikingly similar thoughts and rituals (Swedo et al., 1989).

obsessive compulsive disorder (OCD): An anxiety disorder in which a person suffers from obsessions and/or compulsions.

obsession: A persistent, recurring, involuntary thought, image, or impulse that invades consciousness and causes great distress.

compulsion: A persistent, irresistible, irrational urge to perform an act or ritual repeatedly.

Causes of Obsessive Compulsive Disorder For many years obsessive compulsives were seen as extremely insecure people who viewed the world as threatening and unpredictable. Ritualistic behavior was thought to be their method of imposing some order, structure, and predictability on their world.

OCD is not caused by attitudes developed in childhood or by parents who are overly zealous about such things as cleanliness (National Institute of Mental Health, 1999b). However, there are environmental causal factors for OCD. Recent studies have shown that early autoimmune system diseases, early strep infections, and changes in the brain caused by infection may predispose a person to develop OCD (Giedd et al., 2000; Hamilton & Swedo, 2001).

Research evidence points to a biological basis for obsessive compulsive disorder in some people, and several twin and family studies suggest that a genetic factor is involved (Nestadt et al., 2000; Rasmussen & Eisen, 1990). PET scans of OCD patients have revealed abnormally high rates of glucose consumption in two brain regions involved in emotional reactions—the orbitofrontal cortex (the part of the frontal lobes just above the eye sockets) and the cingulate cortex (a part of the limbic system) (Rauch et al., 1994). Other brain-imaging studies with OCD patients show normal brain activity during a resting state and heightened activity in certain neural circuits after exposure to contaminants or something else that triggers the compulsion. After the patients have received drugs or other therapies, brain activity is again reduced (Trivedi, 1996).

The most significant finding seems to be that many OCD patients have abnormal serotonin functioning (Pigott, 1996). Such patients are often helped by an antidepressant medication, which increases the availability of serotonin in the synapses. Also, a form of behavior therapy known as *exposure and response prevention* has been successful in treating some cases of OCD. Here, patients are taught how to postpone and ultimately avoid performing their compulsive rituals. Then they are deliberately and directly exposed to whatever triggers their obsessive thoughts, so that they can practice the response prevention.

Remember It!

1. Match the psychological disorder with the example.

   ____ (1) René refuses to eat in front of others for fear her hand will shake.

   ____ (2) John is excessively anxious about his health and his job, even though there is no concrete reason to be.

   ____ (3) Tawana has been housebound for 4 years.

   ____ (4) Jackson gets hysterical when a dog approaches him.

   ____ (5) Ling has incapacitating attacks of anxiety that come on her suddenly.

   ____ (6) Max repeatedly checks his doors, windows, and appliances before he goes to bed.

   a. panic disorder
   b. agoraphobia
   c. specific phobia
   d. generalized anxiety disorder
   e. social phobia
   f. obsessive compulsive disorder

2. Anxiety serves no useful function. (true/false)
3. Most phobias result from frightening experiences and observational learning. (true/false)
4. Obsessive compulsive disorder appears to be caused primarily by psychological rather than biological factors. (true/false)

Answers: 1. (1) e (2) d (3) b (4) c (5) a (6) f 2. false 3. true 4. false

SOMATOFORM AND DISSOCIATIVE DISORDERS

Somatoform Disorders: Physical Symptoms with Psychological Causes

What are two somatoform disorders, and what symptoms do they share?

The **somatoform disorders** involve bodily symptoms that cannot be identified as any of the known medical conditions. Although their symptoms are psychological in origin, patients are sincerely convinced that they spring from real physical disorders. People with somatoform disorders are not consciously faking illness to avoid work or other activities. Two types of somatoform disorders are hypochondriasis and conversion disorder.

Hypochondriasis People with **hypochondriasis** are overly concerned about their health and fear that their bodily symptoms are a sign of some serious disease. A person with this disorder "might notice a mole and think of skin cancer or read about Lyme disease and decide it might be the cause of that tired feeling" (Barsky, 1993, p. 8). Yet their symptoms are not usually consistent with known physical disorders, and even when a medical examination reveals no physical problem, they are not convinced. Hypochondriacs may "doctor shop," going from one physician to another, seeking confirmation of their worst fears. Unfortunately, hypochondriasis is not easily treated, and there is usually a poor chance for recovery.

Conversion Disorder: When Thoughts and Fears Can Paralyze A man is suddenly struck blind, or an arm, a leg, or some other part of his body becomes paralyzed. Extensive medical tests find nothing wrong—no physical reason that could possibly cause the blindness or the paralysis. How can this be?

A person is diagnosed with a **conversion disorder** when there is a loss of motor or sensory functioning in some part of the body that is not due to a physical cause but that solves a psychological problem. A person may become blind, deaf, or unable to speak or may develop a paralysis in some part of the body. Many of Freud's patients suffered from conversion disorder, and he believed that they unconsciously developed a physical disability to help resolve an unconscious sexual or aggressive conflict.

Modern-day psychologists think that conversion disorder can act as an unconscious defense against any intolerable anxiety situation that the person cannot otherwise escape. For example, a soldier who desperately fears going into battle might escape the anxiety by developing a paralysis or some other physically disabling symptom.

You would expect normal persons to show great distress if they suddenly lost their sight or hearing or became paralyzed. But this is not true of many patients with conversion disorder; they seem to exhibit a calm and cool indifference to their symptoms, called "la belle indifference." Furthermore, many seem to enjoy the attention, sympathy, and concern their disability brings them.

Conversion disorder is two to ten times more common in women than in men and is seen more often in people with limited medical knowledge (American Psychiatric Association, 1994).

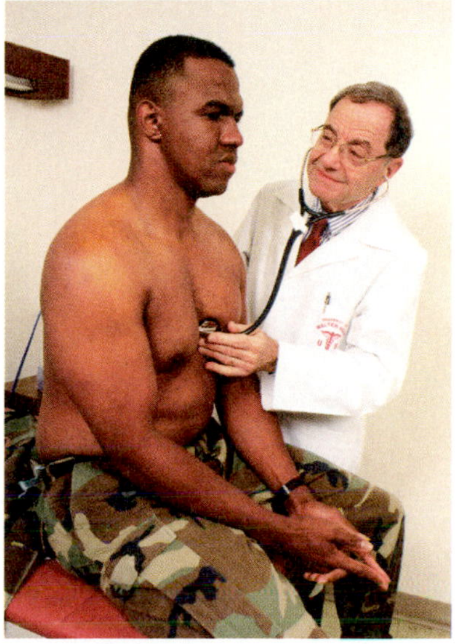

A soldier who continually complains of various symptoms and seeks medical treatment for them, even though doctors can discover nothing physically wrong, may be suffering from conversion disorder due to an intense fear of battle.

somatoform disorders (so-MAT-uh-form): Disorders in which physical symptoms are present that are due to psychological rather than physical causes.

hypochondriasis (HI-poh-kahn-DRY-uh-sis): A somatoform disorder in which persons are preoccupied with their health and convinced they have some serious disorder despite reassurance from doctors to the contrary.

conversion disorder: A somatoform disorder in which a person suffers a loss of motor or sensory functioning in some part of the body; the loss has no physical cause but solves some psychological problem.

dissociative disorders: Disorders in which, under stress, one loses the integration of consciousness, identity, and memories of important personal events.

Dissociative Disorders: Mental Escapes

Day in and day out we are consciously aware of who we are, and we are able to recall important events in our lives. Our memories, our identity, our consciousness, and our perception of the environment are integrated. But in response to unbearable stress, some people develop a **dissociative disorder** and lose this integration. Their consciousness becomes dissociated from their identity or their memories of important personal events, or both. Dissociative disorders provide a mental escape from intolerable circumstances. Three types of dissociative disorders are dissociative amnesia, dissociative fugue, and dissociative identity disorder (commonly known as multiple personality).

What are dissociative amnesia and dissociative fugue?

Dissociative Amnesia: "Who Am I?" Amnesia is a complete or partial loss of the ability to recall personal information or identify past experiences that cannot be attributed to ordinary forgetfulness or substance use. Popular books, movies, and TV shows have used amnesia as a plot element: characters—usually after a blow to the head—cannot remember who they are or anything about their past. But with **dissociative amnesia,** no physical cause is present. Instead, a traumatic experience—a psychological blow, so to speak—or a situation that creates unbearable anxiety causes the person to escape by "forgetting." Patients with dissociative amnesia can have a loss of memory of specific periods of their life or a complete loss of memory of their entire identity. For example, soldiers who experienced the trauma of watching a friend blown apart on the battlefield, might protect themselves from that trauma by developing some form of dissociative amnesia. Yet such people do not forget everything. They forget only items of personal reference such as their name, age, and address, and may fail to recognize their parents, other relatives, and friends. But they do not forget how to read and write or solve problems, and their basic personality structure remains intact.

Dissociative Fugue: "Where Did I Go and What Did I Do?" Even more puzzling than dissociative amnesia is **dissociative fugue.** In a fugue state, people not only forget their identity, they also travel away from home. Some take on a new identity that is usually more outgoing and uninhibited than their former identity. The fugue state may last for hours, days, or even months. The fugue is usually a reaction to some severe psychological stress, such as a natural disaster, a serious family quarrel, a deep personal rejection, or military service in wartime.

For most people, recovery from dissociative fugue is rapid, although they may have no memory of the initial stressor that brought on the fugue state. And when people recover from the fugue, they often have no memory of events that occurred during the episode.

What are some of the identifying symptoms of dissociative identity disorder?

Dissociative Identity Disorder: Multiple Personality In **dissociative identity disorder (DID),** two or more distinct, unique personalities exist in the same individual, and there is severe memory disruption concerning personal information about the other personalities. In 50% of the cases, there are more than 10 different personalities (Sybil Dorsett had 16). The change from one personality to another often occurs suddenly and usually during stress.

The personality in control of the body the largest percentage of time is known as the *host personality* (Kluft, 1984). The alternate personalities, or *alter personalities,* may differ radically in intelligence, speech, accent, vocabulary, posture, body language, hairstyle, taste in clothes, manners, and even handwriting. And incredibly, within the same individual, the alter personalities may differ in gender, age, and even sexual orientation. Some alters may be right-handed; others left-handed. Some may need different prescription glasses, have specific food allergies, or show different responses to alcohol or medications (Putnam et al., 1986). And there are usually promiscuous alters who act on forbidden impulses (Putnam, 1992).

Many DID patients report hearing voices in their heads and sometimes the sounds of crying or screaming or laughter. For this reason, they have often been misdiagnosed as schizophrenic.

In 80% of the cases of dissociative identity disorder, the host personality does not know of the alter personalities, but the alters have varying levels of awareness of each other (Putnam, 1989, p. 114). The host and alter personalities commonly show amnesia for certain periods of time or for important life events such as a graduation or wedding. There is the common complaint of "lost time"—periods for which a given personality has no memory because he or she was not in control of the body.

Causes of Dissociative Identity Disorder Dissociative identity disorder usually begins in early childhood but is rarely diagnosed before adolescence (Vincent & Pickering, 1988). About 90% of the treated cases have been women (Ross et al., 1989), and more than 95% of the patients reveal early histories of severe physical

dissociative amnesia: A dissociative disorder in which there is a loss of memory of limited periods in one's life or of one's entire identity.

dissociative fugue (FEWG): A dissociative disorder in which one has a complete loss of memory of one's entire identity, travels away from home, and may assume a new identity.

dissociative identity disorder (DID): A dissociative disorder in which two or more distinct personalities occur in the same person, each taking over at different times; also called multiple personality.

and/or sexual abuse (Coons, 1994; Putnam, 1992). The splitting off of separate personalities is apparently a way of coping with the intolerable abuse. Recent research has found corroborating evidence to confirm the severe trauma and abuse suffered by many patients with DID (Gleaves, 1996).

How do researchers account for the 5% of multiple personality patients who were not abused? The psychodynamic perspective suggests that alternate personalities may come forth to express forbidden sexual or aggressive impulses that would be unacceptable to the original personality.

The Incidence of Dissociative Identity Disorder There is no general consensus on the incidence of dissociative identity disorder. Some clinicians believe that it is extremely rare or nonexistent (Chodoff, 1987; Thigpen & Cleckley, 1984). Spanos (1994) believes that people who receive a diagnosis of dissociative identity disorder merely "behave as if they have two or more distinct identities" (p. 143) and are motivated mainly by gaining attention. Other skeptics suggest that patients may simply assume the role of a person with multiple personalities to explain their deviant behavior and have the role reinforced by a therapist (McHugh, 1993). Or therapists may be uncovering personalities in gullible patients for financial gain (Aldridge-Morris, 1989).

Other clinicians believe that the disorder is even more common than reported and claim that it is widely misdiagnosed and underdiagnosed (Bliss & Jeppsen, 1985; Kluft, 1993). Dramatic increases in the number of cases have been reported in the United States (Putnam & Loewenstein, 1993). And more cases are also being reported in Puerto Rico (Martinez-Taboas, 1991) and in a number of other countries—Canada (Ross et al., 1991), Switzerland (Modestin, 1992), the Netherlands, and Turkey (Şar et al., 1996), and 11 other countries outside of North America (Coons et al., 1991). But DID can be treated, often by psychotherapy, and empirical evidence indicates that DID patients respond well to treatment (Ellason & Ross, 1997).

Remember It!

1. Match the psychological disorder with the example.

    ____ (1) Tyra is convinced she has some serious disease although her doctors can find nothing physically wrong.

    ____ (2) David is found far away from his home town, calling himself by another name and having no memory of his past.

    ____ (3) Theresa suddenly loses her sight, but doctors can find no physical reason for the problem.

    ____ (4) Manuel has no memory of being in the boat with other family members the day his older brother drowned.

    ____ (5) Nadia has no memory for blocks of time in her life and often finds clothing in her closet that she cannot remember buying.

    a. dissociative identity disorder
    b. dissociative fugue
    c. dissociative amnesia
    d. hypochondriasis
    e. conversion disorder

2. Somatoform disorders have physiological rather than psychological causes. (true/false)

3. Dissociative disorders are psychological in origin. (true/false)

Answers: 1. (1) d (2) b (3) e (4) c (5) a 2. false 3. true

OTHER PSYCHOLOGICAL DISORDERS

As you have seen, there are a variety of mental disorders, with causes ranging from the biological or the genetic to life events and one's environment. As you will see in Chapter 16, there are a variety of treatments as well.

Sexual and Gender Identity Disorders

What are the sexual and gender identity disorders?

Most psychologists define sexual disorders as those that are destructive, guilt- or anxiety-producing, compulsive, or a cause of discomfort or harm to one or both parties involved. The *DSM-IV* has two categories of sexual disorders: sexual dysfunctions (discussed in Chapter 12) and paraphilias. As Chapter 12 explained, **sexual dysfunctions** are persistent, recurrent, and distressing problems involving sexual desire, sexual arousal, or the pleasure associated with sex or orgasm. **Paraphilias** are disorders in which a person experiences recurrent sexual urges, fantasies, or behaviors involving children, other nonconsenting partners, nonhuman objects, or the suffering or humiliation of the individual or a partner. To be diagnosed as having a paraphilia, the person must experience considerable psychological distress or an impairment in functioning in an important area of his or her life. **Gender identity disorders** involve a problem accepting one's identity as male or female; children either express a desire to be or insist that they are the other gender. They show a preference for the clothes, games, pastimes, and playmates of the opposite sex.

Table 15.2 shows a number of the sexual disorders listed in the *DSM-IV.* Please note that homosexuality is *not* considered a sexual disorder.

Table 15.2 *DSM-IV* Categories of Sexual Disorders

Type of Disorder	Symptoms
Sexual dysfunctions	Disorders involving low sexual desire; the inability to attain or maintain sexual arousal; a delay or absence of orgasm; premature ejaculation; or genital pain associated with sexual activity
Paraphilias	Disorders in which recurrent sexual urges, fantasies, and behavior involve nonhuman objects, children, other nonconsenting persons, or the suffering or humiliation of the individual or his/her partner
Fetishism	A disorder in which sexual urges, fantasies, and behavior involve an inanimate object, such as women's undergarments or shoes
Pedophilia	A disorder in which sexual urges, fantasies, and behavior involve sexual activity with a prepubescent child or children
Exhibitionism	A disorder in which sexual urges, fantasies, and behavior involve exposing one's genitals to an unsuspecting stranger
Voyeurism	A disorder in which sexual urges, fantasies, and behavior involve watching unsuspecting people naked, undressing, or engaging in sexual activity
Sexual masochism	A disorder in which sexual urges, fantasies, and behavior involve being beaten, humiliated, bound, or otherwise made to suffer
Sexual sadism	A disorder in which sexual urges, fantasies, and behavior involve inflicting physical or psychological pain and suffering on another
Other paraphilias	Disorders in which sexual urges, fantasies, and behavior involve, among other things, animals, feces, urine, corpses, filth, or enemas
Sexual identity disorders	Problems accepting one's identity as male or female

Source: Based on the *DSM-IV* (American Psychiatric Association, 1994).

Table 15.3 Examples of *DSM-IV* Categories of Personality Disorders

Type of Disorder	Symptoms
Antisocial personality disorder	Person shows callous disregard for the rights and feelings of others; is manipulative, impulsive, selfish, aggressive, irresponsible, reckless; is willing to break the law, lie, cheat, or exploit others for personal gain, without remorse; fails to hold a job.
Paranoid personality disorder	Person is highly suspicious, untrusting, guarded, hypersensitive, easily slighted, lacking in emotion; holds grudges.
Histrionic personality disorder	Individual seeks attention and approval; is overly dramatic, self-centered, shallow; is demanding, manipulative, easily bored, suggestible; craves excitement; often, is attractive and sexually seductive.
Narcissistic personality disorder	Person has exaggerated sense of self-importance and entitlement and is self-centered, arrogant, demanding, exploitive, envious; craves admiration and attention; lacks empathy.
Borderline personality disorder	Individual is unstable in mood, behavior, self-image, and social relationships; has intense fear of abandonment; exhibits impulsive and reckless behavior, inappropriate anger; makes suicidal gestures and performs self-mutilating acts.

Source: Based on the *DSM-IV* (American Psychiatric Association, 1994).

Personality Disorders: Troublesome Behavior Patterns

What characteristics are shared by most people with personality disorders?

Do you know people who are impossible to get along with—people who always seem to be at odds with themselves, their environment, their family, and others? Such a person may have a **personality disorder**—a long-standing, inflexible, maladaptive pattern of behaving and relating to others, which usually begins early in childhood or adolescence (Widiger et al., 1988). People with personality disorders tend to have problems in their social relationships and at work, and may experience personal distress as well. Some of these people know that their behavior causes problems in their lives, yet they seem unable to change. But more commonly, they are self-centered and do not see themselves as responsible for their difficulties. Instead, they tend to blame other people or situations for their problems.

The *DSM-IV* lists ten categories of personality disorders; five are explained briefly in Table 15.3. Of particular interest is antisocial personality disorder.

People with **antisocial personality disorder** have a "pervasive pattern of disregard for, and violation of, the rights of others that begins in childhood or early adolescence and continues into adulthood" (American Psychiatric Association, 1994, p. 645). As children they lie, steal, vandalize, initiate fights, skip school, run away from home, and may be physically cruel to others. By early adolescence they usually drink excessively, use drugs, and engage in promiscuous sex. And in adulthood they cannot keep a job, act as a responsible parent, honor financial commitments, or obey the law.

Many antisocial types are intelligent and may seem charming and very likable at first. They are good con men, and they are more often men—as many as 5.8% of the U.S. male population, compared to less than 1.3% of the female population (Kessler et al., 1994). Checkley (1941), one of the first to study antisocial personality, revealed that persons with the disorder seem to lack the ability to love or feel loyalty and compassion toward others. They do not appear to have a conscience and feel little or no guilt or remorse no matter how cruel or despicable their actions might be. As Hare (1995) puts it, they "use charm, manipulation, intimidation, and violence to control others and satisfy their own selfish needs" (p. 4). Ted Bundy, the infamous serial killer executed in 1990, was thought to have antisocial personality disorder.

sexual dysfunction: A persistent or recurrent problem that causes marked distress and interpersonal difficulty and that may involve any or some combination of the following: sexual desire, sexual arousal, or the pleasure associated with sex or orgasm.

paraphilia: A sexual disorder in which sexual urges, fantasies, and behavior generally involve children, other nonconsenting partners, nonhuman objects, or the suffering and humiliation of oneself or one's partner.

gender identity disorders: Disorders characterized by a problem accepting one's identity as male or female.

personality disorder: A continuing, inflexible, maladaptive pattern of inner experience and behavior that causes great distress or impaired functioning and differs significantly from the patterns expected in the person's culture.

antisocial personality disorder: A disorder marked by lack of feeling for others; selfish, aggressive, irresponsible behavior; and willingness to break the law, lie, cheat, or exploit others for personal gain.

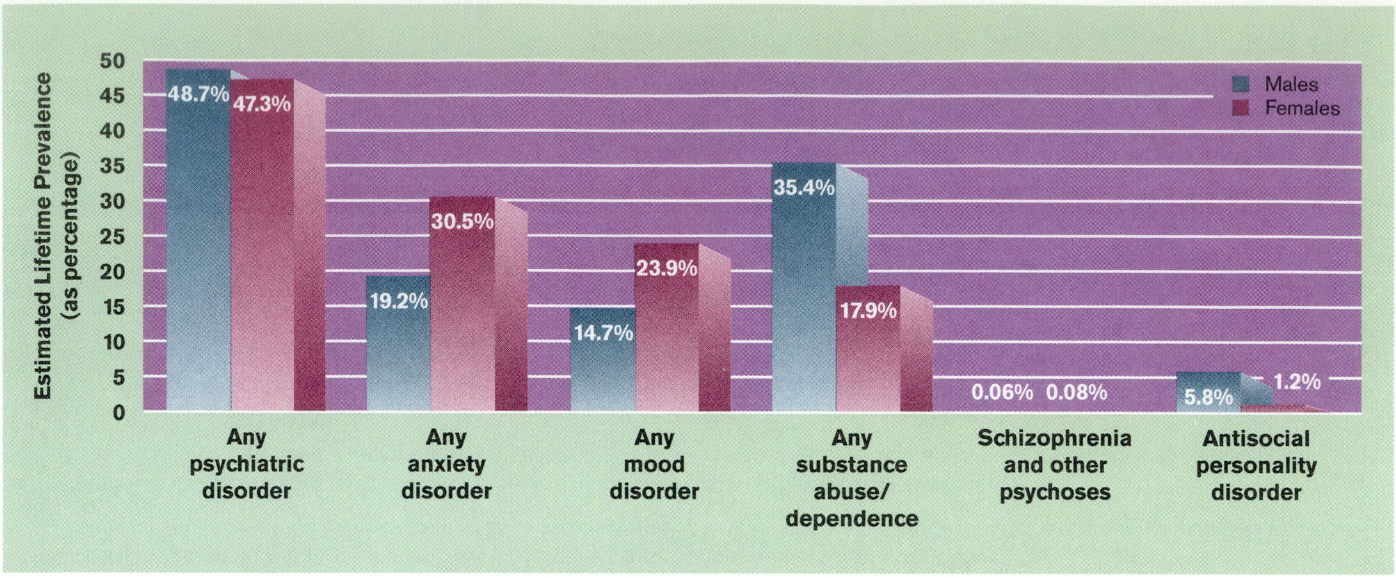

Figure 15.8

Lifetime Prevalence of Psychological Disorders

The percentages of males and females in the United States who suffer from various psychological disorders during their lifetime are based on the findings of the National Comorbidity Survey. Almost 50% of the respondents interviewed in this large national survey suffered from at least one psychological disorder in their lifetime. Males and females had about the same rate for experiencing some type of disorder. Males had higher rates for substance abuse and dependence and antisocial personality disorder. Females had higher rates for anxiety disorders and mood disorders. (Data from Kessler et al., 1994.)

Although the *DSM-IV* does not include this characteristic, some experts believe that antisocial types fail to experience anxiety as normal people do. They seem fearless, oblivious to danger to themselves and unconcerned about the possible, even likely, consequences of their actions; and they appear to be unable to profit from experience (Chesno & Kilmann, 1975; Hare, 1970, 1995). Several adoption studies indicate a genetic factor in antisocial personality disorder (Loehlin et al., 1988). Other studies of adoptees have provided strong evidence of an interaction between heredity and environment accounting for this disorder (Rutter, 1997).

Brain-imaging studies suggest that people with antisocial personality disorder do not comprehend the emotional significance of words and images (Hare, 1995). They show the same level of arousal, measured by EEG recordings of brain electrical potentials, whether confronting neutral stimuli (words such as *chair, table,* and *stone*) or emotionally charged stimuli (words such as *cancer, rape,* and *murder*). Such findings suggest a neurophysiological basis for "the characteristic lack of empathy or guilt, shallow emotions, and cold-blooded cruelty" (Hare, 1995, p. 5).

Years ago people with antisocial personality disorder were referred to as *psychopaths* or *sociopaths*. Con men, quack doctors, impostors, and today many drug pushers, pimps, delinquents, and criminals could be diagnosed as having this disorder. Some come to the attention of the authorities and end up serving time (about 15–20% of U.S. prisoners); others do not (Hare, 1995).

Figure 15.8 shows the estimated lifetime prevalence in the United States of antisocial personality disorder and other disorders we have discussed.

By now, you should know a great deal about psychological disorders. Apply your knowledge in the *Try It!*

Try It!

Make a list of movies, TV shows, or plays you have seen or heard about in which a character with a psychological disorder plays a prominent role. One example is given to get you started.

As Good As It Gets	Jack Nicholson	Obsessive compulsive disorder

Remember It!

1. (Sexual dysfunctions, Paraphilias) are disorders in which sexual urges, fantasies, and behaviors involve children, other nonconsenting partners, or nonhuman objects.
2. Which statement is true of personality disorders?
   a. Personality disorders usually begin in adulthood.
   b. Persons with these disorders usually realize that they have a problem.
   c. Personality disorders typically cause problems in social relationships and at work.
   d. Persons with these disorders typically seek professional help.
3. Tim lies, cheats, and exploits others without feeling guilty. His behavior best fits the diagnosis of _______________ personality disorder.
   a. avoidant
   b. histrionic
   c. antisocial
   d. narcissistic

Answers: 1. Paraphilias 2. c 3. c

Apply It!

Overcoming the Fear of Public Speaking

Do you break out in a cold sweat and start trembling when you have to speak in public? If so, cheer up; you're in good company. As a young lawyer in South Africa, Mahatma Gandhi fainted from anxiety the first time he had to present a case in court. And Kim Basinger, Barbra Streisand, and Carly Simon are among the many entertainers who have suffered such severe stage fright that they have been unable to perform. In fact, fear of public speaking is the number one fear reported by American adults in surveys: More people fear public speaking than flying, sickness, or even death!

What Is It? Fear of public speaking is a form of *performance anxiety,* a common type of social phobia. It goes beyond the mild anxiety most people feel when called upon to speak to a group. People with intense fear of public speaking may experience symptoms of panic, including heart palpitations, trembling, rapid breathing, and dizziness. They may blush or sweat and have great difficulty concentrating.

Much of the fear of public speaking stems from fear of being embarrassed or of being judged negatively by others. Some people cope with this fear by trying to avoid situations in which they may be required to speak in public. This adversely affects their professional lives and closes off opportunities to advance in their careers (In the SpotLight, 2001). A more practical approach is to examine the fear more closely in order to determine its causes, and then take specific steps to overcome it.

What Causes It? Fear of public speaking stems from a variety of incorrect beliefs—starting with the belief that speaking in public is inherently stressful and therefore experiencing stress when called upon to speak to a group is inevitable. In reality, there is no reason for public speaking to be more stressful than any other aspect of everyday life, and thousands of people are able to speak in public without feeling any stress at all.

Here are some other incorrect beliefs associated with public speaking (Orman, 1996):

- To succeed, you need to be perfect. (Not true; no audience expects perfection.)
- A good speaker presents as many facts and details about the subject as possible. (Not true; all you need is two or three main points.)
- If some members of the audience aren't paying attention, you need to do something about it. (Not true; you can't please everyone, and it's a waste of time to try to do so.)
- The more you prepare, the better you will do. (Not true; while preparation is useful for any public appearance, overpreparation can have detrimental effects.)

What Can You Do? There are many specific, easy steps you can take to remove the stress from public speaking and increase your chances of a successful performance. Some of these steps deal with how you present yourself to your audience; others focus on what's going on inside you. Here are some of the many suggestions offered by experts (In the SpotLight, 2001; Toastmasters International, 2001):

- *Know your material well.* Practice aloud and revise your speech if necessary. Practice, practice, practice.
- *Visualize your speech.* Imagine yourself giving your speech in a confident, clear manner.
- *Relax.* Reduce your tension by doing deep breathing or relaxation exercises.
- *Be familiar with the place where you will speak.* Arrive early and practice using the microphone and any other equipment you plan to use.
- *Connect with the audience.* Greet some members of the audience as they arrive; then speak to them as if they were a group of friends.
- *Project confidence through your posture.* Stand or sit in a self-assured manner, smile, and make eye contact with the audience.
- *Focus on your message, not on yourself.* Turn your attention away from your nervousness and focus on the purpose of your speech, which is to transmit information to your audience.
- *Remember that the audience doesn't expect you to be perfect.* Don't apologize for any problems you think you have with your speech. Just be yourself.

Applying these few simple tips, you can overcome nervousness and speak confidently on any topic—even on the spur of the moment.

THINKING CRITICALLY

Evaluation

Some psychological disorders are more common in women (depression, agoraphobia, and simple phobia), and some are more common in men (antisocial personality disorder and substance abuse and dependence). Give some possible reasons for such gender differences in the prevalence of these disorders. Support your answer.

Point/Counterpoint

There is continuing controversy over whether specific psychological disorders are chiefly biological in origin (nature) or result primarily from learning and experience (nurture). Select any two disorders from this chapter and prepare arguments for both the nature and nurture positions for both disorders.

Psychology in Your Life

Formulate a specific plan for your own life that will help you to recognize and avoid the five cognitive traps that contribute to unhealthy thinking. You might enlist the help of a friend to monitor your negative statements.

SUMMARY AND REVIEW

WHAT IS ABNORMAL?

What criteria might be used to differentiate normal from abnormal behavior?

Behavior might be considered abnormal if it deviates radically from what is considered normal in one's own culture, if it leads to personal distress or impaired functioning, or if it results in one's being a danger to self and/or others.

What are six current perspectives that attempt to explain the causes of psychological disorders?

Six current perspectives on the causes of psychological disorders are the biological perspective, the biopsychosocial perspective, the psychodynamic perspective, the learning perspective, the cognitive perspective, and the humanistic perspective.

What is the *DSM-IV*?

The *DSM-IV*, published by the American Psychiatric Association, is the system most widely used in the United States to diagnose psychological disorders.

Key Terms
psychological disorder (p. 538); *DSM-IV* (p. 541); neurosis (p. 542); psychosis (p. 542)

SCHIZOPHRENIA: THE MOST SERIOUS PSYCHOLOGICAL DISORDER

What are some of the major positive and negative symptoms of schizophrenia?

The positive symptoms of schizophrenia are abnormal behaviors and characteristics including hallucinations, delusions, disorganized thinking and speech, bizarre behavior, and inappropriate affect. The negative symptoms represent deficiencies in thoughts and behavior and include social withdrawal, apathy, loss of motivation, very limited speech, slowed movements, flat affect, and poor hygiene and grooming.

What are the four types of schizophrenia?

The four types of schizophrenia are paranoid, disorganized, catatonic, and undifferentiated schizophrenia.

What are some suggested causes of schizophrenia?

Some suggested causes of schizophrenia are a genetic predisposition, sufficient stress in people who are predisposed to the disorder, and excessive dopamine activity in the brain.

Key Terms
schizophrenia (p. 543); hallucination (p. 544); delusion (p. 544); delusion of grandeur (p. 544); delusion of persecution (p. 544); inappropriate affect (p. 545); paranoid schizophrenia (p. 546); disorganized schizophrenia (p. 546); catatonic schizophrenia (p. 546)

MOOD DISORDERS: EMOTIONAL HIGHS AND LOWS

What are the symptoms of major depressive disorder?

Major depressive disorder is characterized by feelings of great sadness, despair, guilt, worthlessness, hopelessness, and, in extreme cases, suicidal intentions.

What are the extremes of mood suffered by those with bipolar disorder?

Bipolar disorder is a mood disorder in which a person suffers from manic episodes (periods of extreme elation, euphoria, and hyperactivity) alternating with major depression, usually with relatively normal periods in between.

What are some suggested causes of major depressive disorder and bipolar disorder?

Some of the proposed causes are (1) a genetic predisposition; (2) an imbalance in the neurotransmitters norepinephrine and serotonin; (3) a tendency to turn hostility and resentment inward rather than expressing it; (4) distorted and negative views of oneself, the world, and the future; and (5) stress.

Key Terms
mood disorders (p. 548); major depressive disorder (p. 549); seasonal affective disorder (SAD) (p. 550); bipolar disorder (p. 551); manic episode (p. 551)

ANXIETY DISORDERS: WHEN ANXIETY IS EXTREME

When is anxiety normal, and when is it abnormal?

Anxiety—a generalized feeling of apprehension, fear, or tension—is healthy if it is a response to a real danger or threat, and it is unhealthy if it is inappropriate or excessive.

What are the symptoms of panic disorder?

Panic disorder is marked by recurrent, unpredictable panic attacks—attacks of overwhelming anxiety, fear, or terror, during which people experience palpitations, trembling or shaking, choking or smothering sensations, and the feeling that they are going to die or lose their sanity.

What are the characteristics of the three categories of phobias?

The three categories of phobias are (1) agoraphobia, fear of being in situations where escape is impossible or help is not available in case of incapacitating anxiety; (2) social phobia, fear of social situations where one might be embarrassed or humiliated by appearing clumsy or incompetent; and (3) specific phobia, a marked fear of a specific object or situation and a catchall category for all phobias other than agoraphobia or social phobia.

What do psychologists see as probable causes of phobias?

Phobias result primarily from frightening experiences or through observational learning. Genes may also play a role.

What is obsessive compulsive disorder?

Obsessive compulsive disorder is characterized by obsessions (persistent, recurring, involuntary thoughts, images, or impulses that cause great distress) and/or compulsions (persistent, irresistible, irrational urges to perform an act or ritual repeatedly).

Key Terms
anxiety disorders (p. 556); anxiety (p. 556); generalized anxiety disorder (p. 557); panic attack (p. 558); panic disorder (p. 558); phobia (p. 558); agoraphobia (p. 558); social phobia (p. 559); specific phobia (p. 559) obsessive compulsive disorder (OCD) (p. 560); obsession (p. 561); compulsion (p. 561)

SOMATOFORM AND DISSOCIATIVE DISORDERS

What are two somatoform disorders, and what symptoms do they share?

Somatoform disorders involve bodily symptoms that cannot be identified as any of the known medical conditions. Hypochondriasis involves a persistent fear that bodily symptoms are the sign of some serious disease, and conversion disorder involves a loss of motor or sensory functioning in some part of the body, such as paralysis or blindness.

What are dissociative amnesia and dissociative fugue?

People with dissociative amnesia have a loss of memory for limited periods of their life or for their entire personal identity. In dissociative fugue people forget their entire identity, travel away from home, and may assume a new identity somewhere else.

What are some of the identifying symptoms of dissociative identity disorder?

Dissociative identity disorder (often called multiple personality) is one in which two or more distinct, unique personalities occur in the same person, each taking over at different times. Most patients are female and victims of early, severe physical and/or sexual abuse.

Key Terms
somatoform disorders (p. 563); hypochondriasis (p. 563); conversion disorder (p. 563); dissociative disorders (p. 563); dissociative amnesia (p. 564); dissociative fugue (p. 564); dissociative identity disorder (p. 564)

OTHER PSYCHOLOGICAL DISORDERS

What are the sexual and gender identity disorders?

Three categories of sexual disorders are sexual dysfunctions (problems with sexual desire, sexual arousal, or orgasm); paraphilias (needing unusual or bizarre objects, conditions, or acts for sexual gratification); and gender identity disorders (having a problem accepting one's identity as male or female).

What characteristics are shared by most people with personality disorders?

People with personality disorders have long-standing, inflexible, maladaptive patterns of behavior that cause problems in their social relationships and at work and often cause personal distress. Such people seem unable to change and blame others for their problems.

Key Terms
sexual dysfunction (p. 566); paraphilia (p. 566); gender identity disorders (p. 566); personality disorder (p. 567); antisocial personality disorder (p. 567)

Surf It!

Want to be sure you've absorbed the material in Chapter 15, "Psychological Disorders," before the big test? Visiting *www.abacon.com/wood* can put a top grade within your reach. The site is loaded with free practice tests, flashcards, activities, and links to help you review your way to an A. To enliven that inevitable study break, the site also offers personality assessment quizzes and a psychology career corner.

20p. 90cts

16 Therapies

Bill, a 21-year-old college student, suffers from a debilitating phobia, an intense fear of any kind of sudden loud noise—fireworks, gunshots, cars backfiring, and especially the sound of popping balloons. His fear of the sound of balloons bursting has extended to balloons themselves, and he cannot bear to touch or even stand within several feet of a balloon.

One day two people lead Bill into a small room that is filled with 100 large balloons of every imaginable color. Already Bill is visibly shaking, and he huddles near the door. One person stands close to Bill, while the other person explains that he is going to begin popping the balloons. While some 50 balloons are popped with a pin, Bill shakes uncontrollably. Tears stream down his face, he turns pale, and his legs shake so hard that a chair has to be provided so he can sit down. The remaining balloons are popped, making even more frightening sounds as the person steps on them. Although this upsets Bill even more, he must endure the popping of another 250 balloons before he is allowed to leave. And he must return for the next 2 days for still more balloon popping.

What is going on here? Torture? An initiation? A sadistic ritual? No—it is a therapy session. Bill is undergoing treatment for his phobia, and the therapists are using a rapid treatment technique known as *flooding.*

Flooding is a form of behavior therapy in which the patient agrees to be instantly and totally immersed in the feared situation or surrounded by the feared object—in Bill's case, balloons.

Although Bill was doing well in college—he maintained a respectable B average—he hardly had a social life at all. Because of his phobia, Bill avoided all social situations where there was even the remotest possibility that balloons might be present—parties, dances, weddings, athletic events, concerts. But he did have a girlfriend, and it was she who referred him to the therapists who treated his phobia.

During the course of the 3 days, Bill became progressively less fearful in the presence of balloons and was even able to join in stepping on hundreds of balloons and popping them. In a 1-year follow-up, Bill reported that he experienced no distress in the presence of balloons and no longer avoided situations where he might encounter them. In fact, according to his girlfriend, balloons were on the table at one formal event they attended, yet it didn't bother Bill. Neither was he ill at ease when he sat relatively near a fireworks display on the Fourth of July. (Adapted from Houlihan et al., 1993.)

Flooding is a behavioral therapy technique known to be effective in treating various types of phobias (Coles & Heinberg, 2000). But flooding is only one of the many effective therapies you will learn about in this chapter.

What comes to mind when you hear the word *psychotherapy*? Many people picture a patient on a couch talking to a gray-haired, bearded therapist who has a heavy accent. But that picture is hopelessly out of date, as you will see. **Psychotherapy** uses psychological rather than biological means to treat emotional and behavioral disorders, and it usually involves a conversation between the patient (or client) and a therapist. But psychotherapy has grown and changed enormously since its beginnings in the days of Freud, more than 100 years ago. Now it seems that there is a therapy for every trouble, a technique for every taste—over 400 different psychotherapies (Kingsbury, 1995). Today, for the most part, the couch has been replaced by a comfortable chair, and instead of involving years of treatment, psychotherapy is usually relatively brief in this era of managed care (Frei et al., 2000). Furthermore, psychotherapy today is not completely dominated by men, as more women are becoming therapists.

psychotherapy: The treatment for psychological disorders that uses psychological rather than biological means and primarily involves conversations between patient and therapist.

In this chapter we will explore insight therapies, which use talk, thought, reasoning, understanding, and analysis to treat psychological problems. Next we will look at behavior therapies, which are based on principles of learning theory. Finally, we will examine biological therapies—drug therapy, electroconvulsive therapy, and psychosurgery.

INSIGHT THERAPIES

Some forms of psychotherapy are collectively referred to as **insight therapies** because their assumption is that psychological well-being depends on self-understanding—understanding of one's own thoughts, emotions, motives, behavior, and coping mechanisms. Because of this focus on subjective analysis, the insight therapies have been criticized for being, or appearing to be, less objective than other psychotherapies. One critic recently questioned their "scientific status" (Jopling, 2001). The major insight therapies are psychoanalysis, person-centered therapy, and Gestalt therapy.

insight therapy: Any type of psychotherapy based on the notion that psychological well-being depends on self-understanding.

psychoanalysis (SY-ko-uh-NAL-ul-sis): The psychotherapy that uses free association, dream analysis, and analysis of resistance and transference to uncover repressed memories, impulses, and conflicts thought to cause psychological disorders.

free association: A psychoanalytic technique used to explore the unconscious by having patients reveal whatever thoughts or images come to mind.

resistance: In psychoanalytic therapy, the patient's attempts to avoid expressing or revealing painful or embarrassing thoughts or feelings.

Psychodynamic Therapies: Freud's Perspective

As we saw in Chapter 15, Sigmund Freud originally proposed the psychodynamic perspective on abnormal behavior. His theory assumed that the causes of psychological disorders were rooted in childhood experiences in the form of repressed impulses and unresolved, unconscious conflicts—usually of a sexual or aggressive nature. The treatment, or therapy, that Freud developed was **psychoanalysis.** Psychoanalysis, the first formal psychotherapy, was the dominant therapeutic approach in the middle of the 20th century. Today, in the new millennium, very few therapists practice Freudian psychoanalysis, but many of Freud's techniques are still used in modified form (Epstein et al., 2001). What were Freud's therapeutic techniques?

What are the four basic techniques of psychoanalysis, and how are they used to help disturbed patients?

Psychoanalysis: Freud's Therapeutic Techniques

Freudian psychoanalysis used four basic techniques: free association, analysis of resistance, dream analysis, and analysis of transference.

Free Association The central technique of psychoanalytic therapy is **free association,** in which the patient is asked to reveal whatever thoughts, feelings, or images come to mind no matter how trivial, embarrassing, or terrible they might appear. Freud believed that free association allows important unconscious material to surface, such as repressed memories, threatening impulses, and traumatic episodes of childhood.

The patient lies comfortably on a couch, and the analyst sits out of the patient's view. This setting is presumed to minimize distractions that might interfere with the patient's free flow of thoughts and speech. The analyst pieces together the free-flowing associations, explains their meaning, and helps patients gain insight into the thoughts and behavior that are troubling them.

Freud's famous couch was used by his patients during psychoanalysis.

Analysis of Resistance How do you think you would react if an analyst told you to express *everything* that came into your mind? Would you try to avoid revealing certain painful or embarrassing thoughts? Freud's patients did, and he called this **resistance.** Freud (1920/1963b) said:

> The patient attempts to escape from it by every possible means. First he says nothing comes into his head, then that so much comes into his head that he can't grasp any of it. . . . He betrays it by the long pauses which occur in his talk. At last he admits that he really cannot say something, he is ashamed to. (p. 254)

If the patient hesitates, balks, or becomes visibly upset about any topic, the analyst assumes the topic is emotionally significant for him or her. Freud also pointed out other forms of resistance, such as "forgetting" appointments with the analyst or arriving late.

Dream Analysis Freud believed that areas of emotional concern repressed in waking life are sometimes expressed in symbolic form in dreams. He called dreams "the

transference: An intense emotional reaction during psychoanalysis, when the patient displays feelings and attitudes toward the analyst that were present in a significant relationship in the past.

person-centered therapy: A nondirective, humanistic therapy in which the therapist creates a warm, accepting climate, freeing clients to be themselves and releasing their natural tendency toward positive growth.

royal road to the unconscious" because they often convey hidden meanings and identify important repressed thoughts, memories, and emotions.

Analysis of Transference Freud claimed that at some point during psychoanalysis, the patient inevitably begins to react to the analyst with the same feelings and attitudes that were present in another significant relationship—usually with the mother or father. This reaction he called **transference.**

> In every analytic treatment there arises . . . an intense emotional relationship between the patient and the analyst. . . . It can be of a positive or of a negative character and can vary between the extremes of a passionate, completely sensual love and the unbridled expression of an embittered defiance and hatred. (Freud, 1925/1963a, p. 71)

Transference allows the patient to relive or reenact troubling experiences from the past with the analyst as parent substitute. Then the unresolved childhood conflicts can be replayed in the present, but this time with a parent figure who does not reject, provoke guilt, or punish as the actual parent did.

Psychodynamic Therapy Today: The New View Traditional psychoanalysis can be a long and costly undertaking. Patients attend four or five therapy sessions per week for 2 to 4 years. But by the mid-1980s, only about 2% of people undergoing psychotherapy chose classical psychoanalysis (Goode, 1987). And today the number is steadily declining. Psychoanalysis is most suitable for those with average or higher intelligence who are not severely disturbed but are interested in extensive self-exploration.

Many psychoanalysts practice brief psychodynamic therapy, which is also aimed at gaining insight into unconscious conflicts. The therapist and patient decide on the issues to explore at the outset rather than waiting for them to emerge in the course of treatment. The therapist assumes a more active role and places more emphasis on the present than in traditional psychoanalysis. Brief psychodynamic therapy may require only one or two visits per week for as few as 12 to 20 weeks. In a meta-analysis of 11 well-controlled studies, Crits-Christoph (1992) found brief psychodynamic therapy to be as effective as other psychotherapies. And more recent research has also shown brief psychodynamic therapy to be comparable to other forms of psychotherapy (Hager et al., 2000).

Criticisms of Psychoanalytic Therapy Traditional psychoanalysis has been criticized for its emphasis on the unconscious and the past and its virtual neglect of the conscious and the present. Furthermore, the focus on unconscious motives as the major determinants of behavior minimizes patients' responsibility for their behavior and their choices. And from a practical standpoint, research does not suggest that the tremendous cost of psychoanalysis yields results superior to briefer, less costly therapy.

Humanistic Therapies

Based on a more optimistic and hopeful picture of human nature and human potential, humanistic therapies stand in stark contrast to psychoanalysis. Individuals are viewed as unique and basically self-determining, with the ability and freedom to lead rational lives and make rational choices. Humanistic therapists encourage personal growth and seek to teach clients how to fulfill their potential and to take responsibility for their behavior and for what they become in life. The focus is primarily on current relationships and experiences.

What are the role and the goal of the therapist in person-centered therapy?

Person-Centered Therapy: The Patient Becomes the Person **Person-centered therapy,** developed by Carl Rogers (1951) (and formerly called *client-centered therapy*), is based on the humanistic view of human nature. According to this view, people are innately good and if allowed to develop naturally, they will grow toward **self-actualization**—the realization of their inner potential.

If people grow naturally toward self-actualization, then why is everyone not self-actualized? The humanistic perspective suggests that psychological disorders result when a person's natural tendency toward self-actualization is blocked. Rogers (1959) insisted that individuals themselves block their natural tendency toward growth and self-actualization when they act in ways inconsistent with their true selves in order to gain the positive regard of others.

In person-centered therapy the focus is on conscious thoughts and feelings. The therapist attempts to create a warm, accepting climate in which clients are free to be themselves so that their natural tendency toward growth can be released. Person-centered therapy is a **nondirective therapy;** that is, the direction of the therapy sessions is controlled by the client. The therapist acts as a facilitator of growth, giving understanding, support, and encouragement rather than proposing solutions, answering questions, or actively directing the course of therapy. Rogers rejected all forms of therapy that cast the therapist in the role of expert and clients in the role of patients who expect the therapist to tell them something or prescribe something that "cures" their problem.

In Rogers' view, there are only three conditions required of therapists. First, they must have unconditional positive regard for, or total acceptance of, the client, regardless of the client's feelings, thoughts, or behavior. In this atmosphere of unconditional positive regard, clients will feel free to reveal their weakest points, to relax their defenses, and to begin to accept and value themselves. Second, therapists' expressions of their feelings toward their clients must be genuine, or congruent—no facade, no putting up a professional front. Third, therapists must have empathy with the clients—the ability to put themselves in the clients' place. Therapists must show that they comprehend the clients' feelings, emotions, and experiences, and that they understand and see the clients' world as the clients see it. When clients speak, the therapist follows by restating or reflecting back their ideas and feelings. In this way clients begin to see themselves more clearly and eventually resolve their own conflicts and make positive decisions about their lives. The following is an excerpt from a 21-year-old woman's first session of person-centered therapy.

> *Therapist:* I really know very little as to why you came in. Would you like to tell me something about it?
>
> *Client:* It is a long story. I can't find myself. Everything I do seems to be wrong. . . . If there is any criticism or anyone says anything about me I just can't take it. . . .
>
> *Therapist:* You feel things are all going wrong and that you're just crushed by criticism.
>
> *Client:* Well, it doesn't even need to be meant as criticism. It goes way back. In grammar school I never felt I belonged. . . .
>
> *Therapist:* You feel the roots go back a long way but that you have never really belonged, even in grammar school. (Rogers, 1977, p. 199)

In the 1940s and 1950s, person-centered therapy enjoyed a strong following among psychologists. Even as late as the 1980s, a survey of 400 psychologists and counselors revealed that Carl Rogers was considered the most influential figure in counseling and psychotherapy (Smith, 1982).

Gestalt Therapy: Getting in Touch with Your Feelings **Gestalt therapy,** developed by Fritz Perls (1969), emphasizes the importance of clients' fully experiencing, in the present moment, their feelings, thoughts, and actions and then taking responsibility for them. Perls maintained that many of us block out aspects of our experience and are often not aware of how we really feel.

self-actualization: Developing to one's fullest potential.

nondirective therapy: An approach in which the therapist acts to facilitate growth, giving understanding and support rather than proposing solutions, answering questions, or actively directing the course of therapy.

Gestalt therapy: A therapy that was originated by Fritz Perls and that emphasizes the importance of clients' fully experiencing, in the present moment, their feelings, thoughts, and actions and taking personal responsibility for their behavior.

Carl Rogers (at upper right) facilitates discussion in a therapy group.

What is the major emphasis in Gestalt therapy?

directive therapy: An approach to therapy in which the therapist takes an active role in determining the course of therapy sessions and provides answers and suggestions to the patient.

Gestalt therapy is a **directive therapy,** one in which the therapist takes an active role in determining the course of therapy sessions. The well-known phrase "getting in touch with your feelings" is an ever-present objective of the Gestalt therapist, who helps, prods, or badgers clients to experience their feelings as deeply and genuinely as possible and then admit responsibility for them.

Perls suggested that those of us who are in need of therapy carry around a heavy load of unfinished business, which may be in the form of resentment toward or conflicts with parents, siblings, lovers, employers, or others. If not resolved, these conflicts are carried forward into our present relationships. One method for dealing with unfinished business is the "empty chair" technique (Paivio & Greenberg, 1995). The client sits facing an empty chair and imagines, for example, that a wife, husband, father, or mother sits there and proceeds to tell the chair what he or she truly feels about that person. Then the client trades places and sits in the empty chair and role-plays what the imagined person's response would be to what the client has said.

The goal of Gestalt therapy is not merely to relieve symptoms, but to help clients achieve a more integrated self and become more authentic and self-accepting. In addition, they must learn to assume personal responsibility for their behavior rather than blame society, past experiences, parents, or others.

Remember It!

1. In psychoanalysis the technique whereby a patient reveals every thought, idea, or image that comes to mind is called ______________; the patient's attempt to avoid revealing certain thoughts is called ______________.
   a. transference; resistance
   b. free association; transference
   c. revelation; transference
   d. free association; resistance
2. (Person-centered, Gestalt) therapy is the directive therapy that emphasizes the importance of the client's fully experiencing, in the present moment, his or her thoughts, feelings, and actions.
3. (Person-centered, Gestalt) therapy is the nondirective therapy developed by Carl Rogers in which the therapist creates a warm, accepting climate so that the client's natural tendency toward positive change can be released.
4. (Psychodynamic, Humanistic) therapy presumes that the cause of the patient's problems are repressed memories, impulses, and conflicts.

Answers: 1. d 2. Gestalt 3. Person-centered 4. Psychodynamic

Therapies Emphasizing Interaction with Others

Some therapies look not only at the individual's internal struggles but also at interpersonal relationships.

What four problems commonly associated with major depression is interpersonal therapy designed to treat?

Interpersonal Therapy: Short Road to Recovery **Interpersonal therapy (IPT)** is a brief psychotherapy that has proven very effective in the treatment of depression (Elkin et al., 1989, 1995; Klerman et al., 1984). IPT is designed specifically to help patients cope with four types of problems commonly associated with major depression:

1. *Unusual or severe responses to the death of a loved one.* The therapist and patient discuss the patient's relationship with the deceased person and feelings (such as guilt) that may be associated with the death. The therapist tries to help the patient release the past and develop an active interest in the present.

2. *Interpersonal role disputes.* Depression is often associated with mutually incompatible expectations about roles or responsibilities between patients and their spouses, children, parents, friends, co-workers, or employers. These may be a source of conflict, resentment, and even hostility in that neither party discusses the problem openly and honestly or really tries to understand the other's point of view. The therapist helps the patient to understand what is at stake for those involved and to explore options for bringing about change. If the problem involves a family member, it is often helpful for that person also to attend a therapy session.

3. *Difficulty in adjusting to role transitions such as divorce, career change, and retirement.* Role transitions may involve a loss, such as a life change resulting from an illness or injury or the loss of a job. Other role transitions involve positive events, such as marriage, a new baby, or a promotion. Patients are helped to see the change not as a threat but as a challenge and an opportunity for growth that they can master.

4. *Deficits in interpersonal skills.* Some people lack the skills to make friends and to sustain intimate relationships. Such deficits may lead to loneliness, isolation, and depression. Through role-playing and analysis of the patient's communication style, the therapist tries to help the patient develop the interpersonal skills necessary to initiate and sustain relationships.

Interpersonal therapy is relatively brief, consisting of 12 to 16 weekly sessions. A large study conducted by the National Institute of Mental Health found IPT to be an effective treatment even for severe depression and one with a low dropout rate (Elkin et al., 1989, 1995). Research also indicates that patients who recover from major depression can enjoy a longer period without relapse when they continue with monthly sessions of IPT (Frank et al., 1991).

interpersonal therapy (IPT): A brief psychotherapy designed to help depressed people better understand and cope with problems relating to their interpersonal relationships.

family therapy: Therapy involving an entire family, based on the assumption that an individual's problem is caused and/or maintained in part by problems within the family unit.

Family and Couple Therapy: Healing Interpersonal Relationships Even the best of families sometimes have problems, and there are therapists of all types who specialize in treating the troubled family. Families may come to therapists for help with troubled or troublesome teenagers, alcoholic parents, abusive situations, or other problems. In **family therapy,** parents and children enter therapy as a group with one or more family therapists (called *conjoint therapy*). Sometimes therapists work with only one or a few family members at a time.

Therapists working with couples pay attention to the dynamics between the two people—how they communicate, act toward each other, and view each other.

The therapist pays attention to the dynamics of the family unit—how family members communicate, how they act toward one another, and how they view each other. Is there a power struggle? Are unreasonable demands being made? The goal of the therapist is to help the family members reach agreement on certain changes that will help heal the wounds of the family unit, improve communication patterns, and create more understanding and harmony within the group.

Marriages often have problems, too. Nearly half of the couples who decide to tie the knot will later decide to untie it. Some therapists work with couples to help them resolve their difficulties and stay together; or they may work to ease the emotional turmoil if a break-up is the best answer for the couple.

Family or couple therapy appears to have positive effects in treating a number of disorders and clinical problems (Lebow & Gurman, 1995). As an adjunct to medication, family therapy can be beneficial in the treatment of schizophrenia and can reduce relapse rates (Carpenter, 1996). Schizophrenic patients are more likely to relapse if their family members express emotions, attitudes, and behaviors that involve criticism, hostility, or emotional overinvolvement (Linszen et al., 1997). This pattern is labeled *high in expressed emotion,* or *high EE* (Falloon, 1988; Jenkins & Karno, 1992). Family therapy can help other family members modify their behavior toward the patient. Family therapy also seems to be the most favorable setting for treating adolescent drug abuse (Lebow & Gurman, 1995).

What are some advantages of group therapy?

Group Therapy: Helping One at a Time, Together **Group therapy** is a form of therapy in which several clients (usually 7–10) meet regularly with one or more therapists to resolve personal problems. It took root in the military nearly 60 years ago, during World War II. The armed services ran short of therapists and tried to handle more patients with group therapy. Besides being less expensive than individual therapy, group therapy has other advantages. It gives the individual a sense of belonging and an opportunity to express feelings, to get feedback from other members, and to give and receive help and emotional support. Learning that others also share their problems leaves people feeling less alone and ashamed. The American Psychiatric Association (1993b) has endorsed group therapy as particularly useful for depression associated with bereavement or chronic illness.

Self-help groups such as Alateen (a version of Alcoholics Anonymous for teenagers) are not, strictly speaking, a form of psychotherapy, but they have helped many of their participants deal with personal problems.

Self-Help Groups: Let's Do It Ourselves Many Americans seek help for their problems from sources other than mental health professionals. Millions of people get support from some kind of self-help group, a special type of group offering help for specific problems. Unlike other group therapy approaches we have discussed, self-help groups usually are not led by professional therapists. They are simply groups of people who share a common problem and meet to give and receive support. About 12 million people in the United States participate in roughly 500,000 self-help groups.

One of the oldest and best-known self-help groups is Alcoholics Anonymous, which claims 1.5 million members worldwide. Other self-help groups patterned after Alcoholics Anonymous have been formed to help individuals overcome many other addictive behaviors, from overeating (Overeaters Anonymous) to gambling (Gamblers Anonymous). There are self-help groups for people with a variety of physical and mental illnesses, and groups to help people deal with crises, from divorce and bereavement to victimization. In addition, there are groups to help relatives and friends of people having such problems.

Self-help groups offer comfort because people can talk about their problems with others who have "been there" and learn that their painful emotional reactions are normal. They can exchange useful information, discuss their coping strategies, and gain hope by seeing people who are coping with the same problems successfully. After reviewing a number of studies of self-help groups, Lieberman (1986) concluded that the results tend to be positive. For problems such as alcoholism and obesity, self-help groups are often as effective as psychotherapy (Zilbergeld, 1986). A recent study indicated that people suffering from anxiety-based problems were helped by a commercial multimedia self-help program called "Attacking Anxiety." Of the 176 individuals who participated in the study, 62 were reported to have achieved clinically significant improvement, and another 40 reported some improvement (Finch et al., 2000). According to Jacobs and Goodman (1989), "the self-help group is becoming a serious rival to psychotherapy as a major method for coping with mental health problems" (p. 544).

Review & Reflect 16.1 compares the insight therapies and the therapies that emphasize interaction with others.

group therapy: A form of therapy in which several clients (usually 7–10) meet regularly with one or more therapists to resolve personal problems.

Review & Reflect 16.1 Summary and Comparison of Insight Therapies and Therapies Emphasizing Interaction with Others

Type of Therapy	Perceived Cause of Disorder	Goals of Therapy	Methods Used	Primary Disorders Treated
Psychoanalysis	Unconscious sexual and aggressive urges or conflicts; fixations; weak ego	Help patient bring disturbing, repressed material to consciousness and work through unconscious conflicts; strengthen ego functions	Psychoanalyst analyzes and interprets dreams, free associations, resistances, and transference.	General feelings of unhappiness; unresolved problems from childhood
Person-centered therapy	Blocking of normal tendency toward self-actualization; incongruence between real and desired self; overdependence on positive regard of others	Increase self-acceptance and self-understanding; help patient become more inner-directed; increase congruence between real and desired self; enhance personal growth	Therapist shows empathy, unconditional positive regard, and genuineness, and reflects client's expressed feelings back to client.	General feelings of unhappiness; interpersonal problems
Interpersonal therapy	Difficulty with relationships and/or life transitions, as well as possible biological causes	Adjust to bereavement; overcome interpersonal role disputes; improve interpersonal skills; adjust to role transitions such as divorce, career change, and retirement	Therapist helps patient (1) release the past and become actively interested in the present, (2) explore options for changing excessive role expectations (often involving other family members), (3) view change as a challenge rather than a threat, and/or (4) improve interpersonal skills, using techniques such as role-playing.	Depression
Family and couple therapy	Problems caused by faulty communication patterns, unreasonable role expectations, drug and/or alcohol abuse, and so on	Create more understanding and harmony within the relationships; improve communication patterns; adjust to the emotional turmoil of divorce	Therapist sees clients individually or several family members at a time and explores such things as communication patterns, power struggles, and unreasonable demands and expectations.	Family problems such as marriage or relationship problems, troubled or troublesome teenagers, abusive relationships, drug or alcohol problems, schizophrenic family member

Remember It!

1. Which depressed person would be *least* likely to be helped by interpersonal therapy (IPT)?
   a. Kirk, who is unable to accept the death of his wife
   b. Martha, who has been depressed since she was forced to retire
   c. Sharon, who was sexually abused by her father
   d. Tony, who feels isolated and alone because he has difficulty making friends
2. Which of the following is *not* true of group therapy?
   a. It allows people to get feedback from other members.
   b. It allows individuals to receive help and support from other members.
   c. It is not conducted by trained therapists.
   d. It is less expensive than individual therapy.
3. Self-help groups are generally ineffective, because they are not led by professionals. (true/false)

Answers: 1. c 2. c 3. false

BEHAVIOR THERAPIES: UNLEARNING THE OLD, LEARNING THE NEW

What is a behavior therapy?

A **behavior therapy** is a treatment approach consistent with the learning perspective on psychological disorders—that abnormal behavior is learned. According to the behaviorists, unless people are suffering from some physiological disorder, such as brain pathology, those who seek therapy need it for one of two reasons: (1) they have learned inappropriate or maladaptive responses, or (2) they never had the opportunity to learn appropriate behavior in the first place. Instead of viewing the maladaptive behavior as a symptom of some underlying disorder, the behavior therapist sees the behavior itself as the disorder. If a person comes to a therapist with a fear of flying, that fear of flying is seen as the problem.

Behavior therapies use the principles of operant conditioning, classical conditioning, and/or observational learning theory to eliminate inappropriate or maladaptive behaviors and replace them with more adaptive responses. Sometimes this type of approach is referred to as **behavior modification.** The goal is to change the troublesome behavior, not to change the individual's personality structure or to search for the origin of the problem behavior. "Behavior therapy is educational rather than 'healing'" (Thorpe & Olson, 1990, p. 15). The therapist's role is active and directive.

Behavior Modification Techniques Based on Operant Conditioning

How do behavior therapists modify behavior using operant conditioning techniques?

Behavior modification techniques based on operant conditioning seek to control the consequences of behavior. Extinction of an undesirable behavior is accomplished by terminating, or withholding, the reinforcement that is maintaining that behavior (Lerman & Iwata, 1996). Behavior therapists also seek to reinforce any desirable behavior in order to increase its frequency, and they use reinforcement, as well, to shape entirely new behaviors. The process works best when it is applied consistently. Institutional settings such as hospitals, prisons, and school classrooms are well suited to these techniques, because they provide a restricted environment where the consequences (or contingencies) of behavior can be more strictly controlled.

Token Economies: What Would You Do for a Token? Some institutions use behavior modification programs called **token economies** that reward appropriate behavior with tokens such as poker chips, play money, gold stars, or the like. These tokens can later be exchanged for desired goods (candy, gum, cigarettes) and/or privileges (weekend passes, free time, participation in desirable activities). Sometimes individuals are fined a given number of tokens for undesirable behavior. For decades mental hospitals have successfully used token economies with chronic schizophrenics to improve their self-care skills and social interaction (Ayllon & Azrin, 1965, 1968). Patients tend to perform chores when reinforced but not when reinforcement is discontinued. Schizophrenic symptoms such as delusions and hallucinations, of course, are not affected.

Time Out: All Alone with No Reinforcers Another effective method used to eliminate undesirable behavior, especially in children and adolescents, is **time out** (Brantner & Doherty, 1983). The principle is simple. Children are told in advance that if they engage in certain undesirable behaviors, they will be removed calmly from the situation and will have to pass a period of time (usually no more than 15 minutes) in a place containing no reinforcers (no television, books, toys, friends, and so on). Theoretically, the undesirable behavior will stop if it is no longer followed by attention or any other positive reinforcers.

Stimulus Satiation: Too Much of a Good Thing Another behavior modification technique, **stimulus satiation,** attempts to change problem behaviors by giving people too much of whatever they find reinforcing. The idea is that the reinforcer will lose its attraction and become something to be avoided.

The stimulus satiation technique was used successfully with a 47-year-old chronic schizophrenic woman who would collect and hoard large numbers of towels.

> At the beginning of treatment, the nurses would bring a towel to the patient in her room several times throughout the day, and without any comment, simply hand it to her. "The first week she was given an average of 7 towels daily, and by the third week this number was increased to 60." (Ayllon, 1977, p. 358)
>
> At first, she seemed to enjoy folding and stacking her towels, but finally, when the patient had 625 towels in her room, she could stand it no longer and began saying to the nurses: "Don't give me no more towels. I've got enough." "Take them towels away. . . . I can't sit here all night and fold towels." . . . Within a few weeks the patient was angrily demanding, "Get these dirty towels out of here." (p. 359)

During the following 12 months, no more than one or two towels could be found in the patient's room.

The Effectiveness of Operant Approaches: Do They Work? Behavior therapies based on operant conditioning have been particularly effective in modifying some behaviors of seriously disturbed people. Although these techniques do not presume to cure schizophrenia, autism, or mental retardation, they can increase the frequency of desirable behaviors and decrease the frequency of undesirable behaviors. Sometimes modifying some of the more extreme and bizarre behaviors enables family members to accept and care for the patient themselves.

Behavior modification techniques can also be used by people who want to break bad habits such as smoking and overeating or to develop good habits such as a regular exercise regime. If you want to modify any of your behaviors, devise a reward system for desirable behaviors, and remember the principles of shaping. Reward gradual changes in the direction of your ultimate goal. If you are trying to develop better eating habits, don't try to change a lifetime of bad habits all at once. Begin with a small step such as substituting frozen yogurt for ice cream. Set realistic weekly goals that you are likely to be able to achieve.

behavior therapy: A treatment approach employing the principles of operant conditioning, classical conditioning, and/or observational learning theory to eliminate inappropriate or maladaptive behaviors and replace them with more adaptive responses.

behavior modification: The systematic application of learning principles to help a person eliminate undesirable behaviors and/or acquire more adaptive behaviors; also called behavior therapy.

token economy: A behavior modification technique that reinforces desirable behaviors with tokens that can be exchanged later for desired objects, activities, and/or privileges.

time out: A behavior modification technique used to decrease the frequency of undesirable behavior by withdrawing an individual from all reinforcement for a period of time.

stimulus satiation (say-she-A-shun): A behavior modification technique that involves giving a patient so much of a stimulus that it becomes something the patient wants to avoid.

Therapies Based on Classical Conditioning

What behavior therapies are based on classical conditioning?

Some behavior therapies are based mainly on the principles of classical conditioning, which can account for how we acquire many of our emotional reactions. In Chapter 5 you learned how Little Albert came to fear the white rat when it was presented along with a frightening loud noise. In classical conditioning, a neutral stimulus—some object, person, or situation that initially does not elicit any strong positive or negative emotional reaction—is paired with either a very positive or a very negative stimulus. After conditioning, the person's strong feeling toward the positive or negative stimulus is transferred to the original, neutral stimulus.

Therapies based on classical conditioning can be used to rid people of fears and other undesirable behaviors. We will discuss four types of therapy based primarily on classical conditioning: systematic desensitization, flooding, exposure and response prevention, and aversion therapy.

How do therapists use systematic desensitization to rid people of fears?

Systematic Desensitization: Overcoming Fears One Step at a Time Have you ever been both afraid and relaxed at the same time? Psychiatrist Joseph Wolpe (1958, 1973) came to the conclusion that these two responses are incompatible; that is, one inhibits the other. On the basis of this idea, Wolpe developed a therapy to treat fears and phobias. He reasoned that if he could get people to relax and stay relaxed while they thought about a feared object, person, place, or situation, they could conquer their fear or phobia.

In Wolpe's therapy, **systematic desensitization,** clients are trained in deep muscle relaxation. Then they confront a hierarchy of fears—a graduated series of anxiety-producing situations—either *in vivo* (in real life) or in imagination, until they can remain relaxed even in the presence of the most feared situation. The technique can be used for everything from fear of animals to claustrophobia, test anxiety, and social and other situational fears.

What do you fear most? Many college students would say that they fear taking tests. If that were your fear and you went to a behavior therapist who used systematic desensitization, this is what would happen: First the therapist would ask you to identify the fear causing your anxiety and everything connected with it. Then all the aspects of the fear would be arranged on a hierarchy from least to most anxiety-producing.

After preparing the hierarchy, you would be taught deep muscle relaxation, progressively relaxing parts of your body until you achieved a completely relaxed state. During the actual desensitization procedure, you would be asked to picture, as vividly as possible, the least fear-producing item on your hierarchy—for example, reading in your course syllabus that a test will be given. When you were able to remain relaxed while visualizing this item, the therapist would have you move one step up the hierarchy and picture the next item. This procedure would be followed until you reached the top of the hierarchy and could remain calm and relaxed while you imagined vividly the most fear-producing stimulus—actually taking the test in class. If, during the desensitization process, anxiety should creep in as you imagined items on the hierarchy, you would signal the therapist. The therapist would instruct you to stop thinking about that item. You would then clear your mind, come back to a state of complete relaxation, and begin again. Try creating your own hierarchy in the *Try It!*

systematic desensitization: A behavior therapy that is used to treat phobias and that involves training clients in deep muscle relaxation and then having them confront a graduated series of anxiety-producing situations (real or imagined) until they can remain relaxed while confronting even the most feared situation.

How effective is systematic desensitization? Many experiments, demonstrations, and case reports confirm that systematic desensitization is a highly successful treatment for eliminating fears and phobias in a relatively short time (Kalish, 1981; Rachman & Wilson, 1980). It has proved effective for specific problems such as test anxiety, stage fright, and anxiety related to sexual disorders.

The critical element in systematic desensitization is the patient's exposure to the feared stimulus. Even relaxation, an important part of Wolpe's treatment, is appar-

Try It!

Use what you have learned about systematic desensitization to create a step-by-step approach to help someone overcome a fear of taking tests. The person's hierarchy of fears begins with reading in the syllabus that a test will be given and culminates in actually taking the test. Fill in successive steps, according to a possible hierarchy of fears, that will lead to the final step. One set of possible steps is given below.

Suggested Answers: (1) Preparing for each class session by reading the assigned material and/or completing any homework assignments. (2) Attending each class session and taking notes on the material the test will cover. (3) Reviewing the new notes after each class period. (4) Reviewing all class materials beginning one week before the test. (5) Reciting key information from memory the day before the test. (6) Arriving early to take the test, having gotten a good night's sleep.

ently not essential. But relaxation does help to keep especially fearful patients from jumping up and running away from the fear-provoking stimulus.

There are several other therapies that use exposure as the key therapeutic element to treat phobias and obsessive compulsive disorder.

What is flooding?

Flooding: Confronting Fears All at Once **Flooding,** a behavior therapy used in the treatment of phobias, was the type of therapy used to help Bill, who was featured in this chapter's opening story. It involves exposing clients to the feared object or event (or asking them to vividly imagine it) for an extended period until their anxiety decreases. Flooding is almost the opposite of systematic desensitization. The person is exposed to the fear all at once, not gradually and certainly not while in a state of relaxation. An individual with a fear of heights, for example, might have to go onto the roof of a tall building and remain there until the fear subsided. A person with a cat phobia might be told: "Visualize the cat all over you, perhaps scratching you, its eyes right up against yours, its hair all over you" (Sheehan, 1983, pp. 158–159).

What is the key to success in flooding? It is not that a person must be frightened to death in order for flooding to work. And it is not necessary for the person to become physically comfortable in the presence of the fear (Lang & Craske, 2000). If the exposure to the feared stimulus is too brief, anxiety simply intensifies, and patients get worse instead of better. Flooding sessions typically last from 30 minutes

flooding: A behavioral therapy used to treat phobias, during which clients are exposed to the feared object or event (or asked to imagine it vividly) for an extended period until their anxiety decreases.

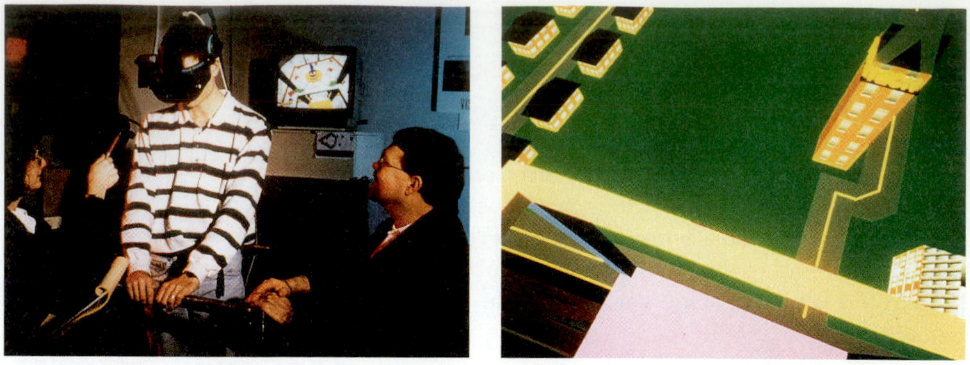

An acrophobic client wears a virtual-reality headset, which exposes him to the view from a high balcony (right) but allows him to experience moving toward or away from the railing. Such a realistic but safe exposure to the feared stimulus allows many people to overcome their phobias.

to 2 hours and should not be terminated until patients are markedly less afraid than they were at the beginning of the session. Additional sessions are required until the fear response is extinguished or reduced to an acceptable level. It is rare for a patient to need more than six treatment sessions (Marshall & Segal, 1988).

In vivo flooding, the real-life experience, works faster and is more effective than simply imagining the feared object (Chambless & Goldstein, 1979; Marks, 1972). Flooding may be quite painful for the patient, as it was for Bill. And it is certainly not the treatment of choice for phobics with a weak heart. But flooding often works where other therapies have failed, and it works faster as well.

How does exposure and response prevention help people with obsessive compulsive disorder?

Exposure and Response Prevention: Cutting the Tie That Binds Fears and Rituals **Exposure and response prevention** has been successful in treating obsessive compulsive disorder (Baer, 1996; Foa, 1995; Rhéaume & Ladouceur, 2000). The therapy consists of two components. The first involves *exposure*—exposing patients to objects or situations they have been avoiding because they trigger obsessions and compulsive rituals. The second component is *response prevention,* in which patients agree to resist performing their compulsive rituals for progressively longer periods of time.

Initially the therapist identifies the thoughts, objects, or situations that trigger the compulsive ritual. For example, touching a doorknob, a piece of unwashed fruit, or garbage might ordinarily send people with a fear of contamination to the nearest bathroom to wash their hands. Patients are gradually exposed to stimuli they find more and more distasteful and anxiety-provoking. They must agree not to perform the normal ritual (hand washing, bathing, or the like) for a specified period of time after exposure. Gradually patients learn to tolerate the anxiety evoked by the various "contaminants."

A typical treatment course—about 10 sessions over a period of 3 to 7 weeks—can bring about considerable improvement in 60–70% of patients (Jenike, 1990). And patients treated with exposure are less likely to relapse after treatment than those treated with drugs alone (Greist, 1992).

A behavior therapy alone can produce physical changes in the brain. In many studies of patients for whom behavior therapy was effective, PET scans showed significant changes in glucose and metabolic activity in the area of the brain involved in obsessive compulsive disorder (Baxter et al., 1992; Rauch et al., 1995). But these changes were *not* seen when the therapy was ineffective (Schwartz et al., 1996).

Systematic desensitization, flooding, and exposure help people stop avoiding feared objects or situations. Even treatments using *virtual reality* as the means of exposure have been successful. Virtual reality has been proven effective in treating spider phobias (Carlin et al., 1997) and fear of flying (Rothbaum et al., 1996). But what if the person's problem is just the opposite—bad habits, addictions, and other such behaviors that *should* be avoided? Aversion therapy is designed to help people

exposure and response prevention: A behavior therapy that exposes patients with obsessive compulsive disorder to stimuli generating increasing anxiety; patients must agree not to carry out their normal rituals for a specified period of time after exposure.

break bad habits, overcome addictions, and learn to avoid situations that trigger harmful behavior.

How does aversion therapy rid people of a harmful or undesirable behavior?

Aversion Therapy: Making Clients Sick to Make Them Better **Aversion therapy** is used to rid clients of a harmful or socially undesirable behavior by pairing it with a painful, sickening, or otherwise aversive stimulus. Electric shock, emetics (which cause nausea and vomiting), or other unpleasant stimuli are paired with the undesirable behavior time after time until a strong negative association is formed and the person comes to avoid that behavior, habit, or substance. Treatment continues until the bad habit loses its appeal and becomes associated with pain or discomfort.

Alcoholics are sometimes given a nausea-producing substance such as Antabuse, which reacts violently with alcohol and causes a person to retch and vomit until the stomach is empty. But for most problems, aversion therapy need not be so intense as to make a person physically ill. A controlled comparison of treatments for chronic nail biting revealed that mild aversion therapy—painting a bitter-tasting substance on the fingernails—yielded significant improvement (Allen, 1996).

Therapies Based on Observational Learning Theory: Just Watch *This!*

How does participant modeling help people overcome fears?

Much of what we learn in life, we learn from watching others and then copying or imitating the behaviors modeled for us. Much positive behavior is learned this way; but so are bad habits, aggressive behaviors, and fears or phobias. Therapies derived from Albert Bandura's work on observational learning are based on the belief that people can overcome fears and acquire social skills through modeling.

For example, therapists have effectively treated fears and phobias by having clients watch a model (on film or in real life) responding to a feared situation in appropriate ways with no dreaded consequences. Usually the model approaches the feared object in gradual steps. Bandura (1967) describes how nursery school children lost their fear of dogs after watching a film depicting a child who was not afraid of dogs first approach a dog, then play with it, pet it, and so on. Modeling films have been used to reduce the fears of children who must undergo surgery (Melamed & Siegel, 1975) and to reduce children's fear of the dentist (Shaw & Thoresen, 1974).

The most effective type of therapy based on observational learning theory is called **participant modeling** (Bandura, 1977a; Bandura et al., 1975, 1977). In this therapy, not only does the model demonstrate the appropriate response in graduated steps, but the client attempts to imitate the model step by step, while the therapist gives encouragement and support. This technique provides the additional benefit of exposure to the feared stimulus.

Suppose you had a snake phobia, for example, and sought treatment. A therapist using participant modeling would first calmly approach a cage containing a snake and would encourage you to do the same. Then she would show you how easy it is to handle a snake while it is in the cage. Next the therapist would urge you to touch the snake, perhaps suggesting how surprised you will be to find that it does not feel at all slimy. Next she would remove the snake from the cage and have you observe her holding it for a period of time with no adverse results. In this manner your behavior would gradually imitate hers until you reached the point of actually holding the snake.

Most specific phobias can be extinguished in only 3 or 4 hours of modeling therapy when the client participates. Participant modeling has proved more effective in treating snake phobias than simple observation of a filmed or live model, and more effective than systematic desensitization (Bandura et al., 1969).

aversion therapy: A behavior therapy in which an aversive stimulus is paired with an undesirable behavior until the behavior becomes associated with pain and discomfort.

participant modeling: A behavior therapy in which an appropriate response is modeled in graduated steps and the client attempts each step, encouraged and supported by the therapist.

Remember It!

1. Techniques based on (classical, operant) conditioning are used to change behavior by reinforcing desirable behavior and removing reinforcers for undesirable behavior.
2. Behavior therapies based on classical conditioning are used mainly to
   a. shape new, more appropriate behaviors.
   b. rid people of fears and undesirable behaviors or habits.
   c. promote development of social skills.
   d. demonstrate appropriate behaviors.
3. Exposure and response prevention is a treatment for people with
   a. panic disorder.
   b. phobias.
   c. generalized anxiety disorder.
   d. obsessive compulsive disorder.
4. Match the description with the therapy.
   ____ (1) flooding
   ____ (2) aversion therapy
   ____ (3) systematic desensitization
   ____ (4) participant modeling
   a. practicing deep muscle relaxation during gradual exposure to feared object
   b. imagining painful or sickening stimuli associated with undesirable behavior
   c. being exposed directly to a feared object without relaxation
   d. imitating a model responding appropriately in a feared situation

Answers: 1. operant 2. b 3. d 4. (1) c (2) b (3) a (4) d

COGNITIVE THERAPIES: IT'S THE THOUGHT THAT COUNTS

We have seen that behavior therapies based on classical and operant conditioning and modeling are effective in eliminating many types of troublesome behavior. But what if the problem is in a person's thinking, attitudes, false beliefs, or poor self-concept? There are therapies for these problems as well. *Cognitive therapies,* based on the cognitive perspective, assume that maladaptive behavior can result from irrational thoughts, beliefs, and ideas, which the therapist tries to change. The emphasis of cognitive therapies is on conscious rather than unconscious processes and on the present rather than the past. We will explore rational-emotive therapy and cognitive therapy.

Rational-Emotive Therapy: Challenging False Beliefs

What is the aim of rational-emotive therapy?

rational-emotive therapy: A directive, confrontational therapy developed by Albert Ellis and designed to challenge and modify the irrational beliefs thought to cause personal distress.

Picture this scenario: Harry received two free tickets to a Saturday-night concert. Excited, Harry called Sally, whom he had dated a couple of times, to ask her to go to the concert with him. To his surprise, she turned him down without even giving a reason. He was shocked and became dejected. "How could she do this to me?" he wondered. As the week dragged on, he became more and more depressed.

What caused Harry's depression? Sally's turning him down? Not according to Albert Ellis (1961, 1977, 1993), a clinical psychologist who developed **rational-emotive therapy** in the 1950s. Rational-emotive therapy is based on Ellis's ABC theory. The A refers to the *activating event,* the B to the person's *belief* about the event, and the C

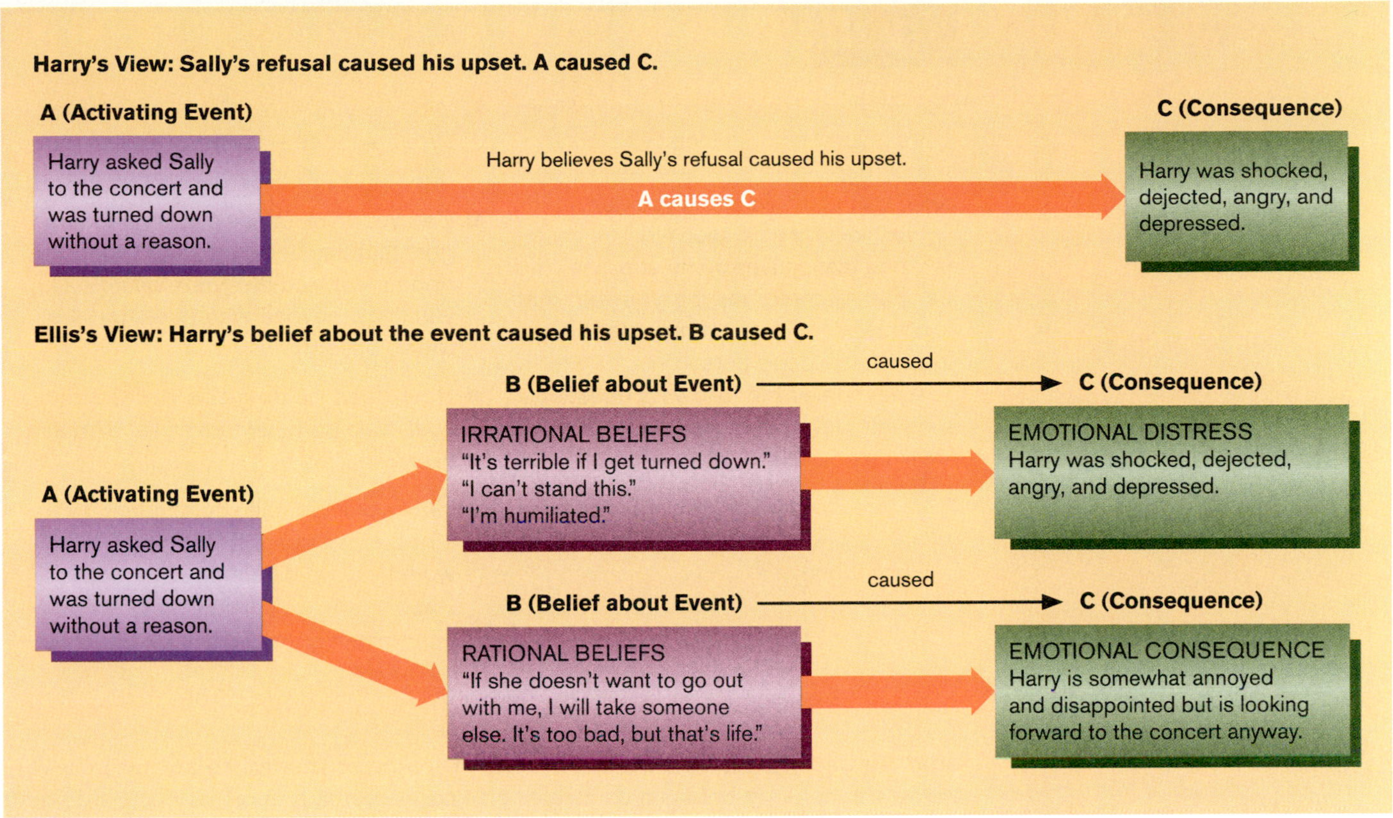

Figure 16.1

The ABCs of Rational-Emotive Therapy

Rational-emotive therapy teaches clients that it is not the activating event (A) that causes the upsetting consequences (C). Rather, it is the client's beliefs (B) about the activating event. Irrational beliefs cause emotional distress, according to Albert Ellis. Rational-emotive therapists help clients identify their irrational beliefs and replace them with rational ones.

to the emotional *consequence* that follows. Ellis claims that it is not the event itself that causes the emotional consequence, but rather the person's belief about the event. In other words, A does not cause C; B causes C. If the belief is irrational, then the emotional consequence can be extreme distress, as illustrated in Figure 16.1.

"Everyone should love me!" "I have to be perfect!" Reality does not conform to these and other irrational beliefs, and people who hold them are doomed to frustration and unhappiness. Irrational beliefs cause people to see an undesirable event as a catastrophe rather than as a disappointment or an inconvenience. Irrational beliefs cause people to feel depressed, worthless, or enraged instead of simply disappointed or annoyed. Even worse, they go on to feel "anxious about their anxiety" and "depressed about their depression" (Ellis, 1987, p. 369).

Rational-emotive therapy is a directive, confrontational form of psychotherapy designed to challenge clients' irrational beliefs about themselves and others. As clients begin to replace irrational beliefs with rational ones, their emotional reactions become more appropriate, less distressing, and more likely to lead to constructive behavior. Try challenging an irrational belief of your own in the *Try It!* on page 592.

Most clients in rational-emotive therapy see a therapist individually, once a week, for 5 to 50 sessions. In stark contrast to person-centered therapists (and most

Try It!

Use what you have learned about Albert Ellis's rational-emotive therapy to identify—and perhaps even eliminate—an irrational belief that you hold about yourself.

First, identify an irrational belief, preferably one that causes some stress in your life. For example, maybe you feel that you must earn all A's in order to think of yourself as a good person.

Ask yourself the following questions, and write down your answers in as much detail as possible.

- Where does this belief come from? Can you identify the time in your life when it began?
- Why do you think this belief is true? What evidence can you think of that "proves" your belief?
- Can you think of any evidence to suggest that this belief is false? What evidence contradicts your belief? Do you know anyone who does not cling to this belief?
- How does holding this belief affect your life, both negatively and positively?
- How would your life be different if you stopped holding this belief? What would you do differently?

other therapists, for that matter), "rational-emotive therapists do not believe a warm relationship between counselee and counselor is a necessary or a sufficient condition for effective personality change" (Ellis, 1979, p. 186). In Ellis's view, "Giving a client RET with a good deal of warmth, approval and reassurance will tend to help this client 'feel better' rather than 'get better'" (p. 194).

One meta-analysis of 28 studies showed that patients receiving rational-emotive therapy did better than those receiving no treatment or a placebo, and about the same as those receiving systematic desensitization (Engles et al., 1993).

Cognitive Therapy: Overcoming "The Power of Negative Thinking"

How does cognitive therapy help people overcome depression and anxiety disorders?

"In order to be happy, I have to be successful in whatever I undertake."
"To be happy, I must be accepted (liked, admired) by all people at all times."
"If people disagree with me, it means they don't like me."

If you agree with all of these statements, you probably spend a good part of your time upset and unhappy. Psychiatrist Aaron T. Beck (1976) claims that much of the misery endured by a depressed and anxious person can be traced to **automatic thoughts**—unreasonable but unquestioned ideas that rule the person's life. Beck (1991) believes that depressed persons hold "a negative view of the present, past, and future experiences" (p. 369). They tend to view themselves as "deficient, defective, and/or undeserving"; their environment as "unduly demanding, depriving, and/or rejecting"; and their future as "without promise, value, or meaning" (Karasu, 1990a, p. 138). These persons notice only negative, unpleasant things and jump to upsetting conclusions. Anxious people expect the worst; they see negative events as catastrophes and at the same time underestimate their coping ability.

automatic thoughts: Unreasonable and unquestioned ideas that rule a person's life and lead to depression and anxiety.

cognitive therapy: A therapy designed to change maladaptive behavior by changing the person's irrational thoughts, beliefs, and ideas.

The goal of **cognitive therapy** is to help patients stop their negative thoughts as they occur and replace them with more objective thoughts. The focus is on the present rather than on the past, and no attempt is made to uncover hidden meanings in the patients' thoughts and responses. After challenging patients' irrational thoughts, the therapist sets up a plan and guides patients so that their own experience can provide actual evidence in the real world to refute their false beliefs. Patients are given homework assignments, such as keeping track of automatic thoughts and the feelings evoked by them and substituting more rational thoughts. When cognitive therapy is combined with behavioral techniques such as relaxation training or exposure, it is called *cognitive-behavioral therapy.*

Cognitive therapy is brief, usually lasting only 10 to 20 sessions, and is therefore less expensive than many other types of therapy (Beck, 1976). This therapy has been researched extensively and is reported to be highly successful in the treatment of mild to moderately depressed patients (Antonuccio et al., 1995; Thase et al., 1991). There is some evidence that depressed people who have received cognitive therapy are less likely to relapse than those who have been treated with antidepressant drugs (Evans et al., 1992; Scott, 1996).

Aaron T. Beck, early proponent of cognitive therapy, blames automatic thoughts for much of the misery endured by people suffering from depression or anxiety.

Cognitive therapy has also been shown to be effective for treating panic disorder (Barlow, 1997; Power et al., 2000). Cognitive therapy teaches patients to change the catastrophic interpretations of their symptoms and thereby prevent the symptoms from escalating into panic. Studies have shown that after 3 months of cognitive therapy, about 90% of patients with panic disorder are panic-free (Robins & Hayes, 1993). Not only does cognitive therapy have a low dropout rate and a low relapse rate, but often patients continue to improve even after treatment is completed (Öst & Westling, 1995). Also, cognitive therapy has proved effective for generalized anxiety disorder (Beck, 1993), OCD (Abramowitz, 1997), cocaine addiction (Carroll et al., 1994), and bulimia (Agras et al., 2000). Some research even indicates that cognitive therapy is effective in treating both negative and positive symptoms of schizophrenia in patients who were helped only modestly by standard antipsychotic drugs (Sensky et al., 2000).

Review & Reflect 16.2 compares behavior therapy and cognitive therapy.

Review & Reflect 16.2 Summary and Comparison of Behavior Therapy and Cognitive Therapy

Type of Therapy	Perceived Cause of Disorder	Goals of Therapy	Methods Used	Primary Disorders Treated
Behavior therapy	Learning of maladaptive behaviors or failure to learn appropriate behaviors	Extinguish maladaptive behaviors and replace with more adaptive ones; help patient acquire needed social skills	Therapist uses methods based on classical and operant conditioning and modeling, which include systematic desensitization, flooding, exposure and response prevention, aversion therapy, and reinforcement.	Fears, phobias, panic disorder, obsessive compulsive disorder, bad habits
Cognitive therapy	Irrational and negative assumptions and ideas about self and others	Change faulty, irrational, and/or negative thinking	Therapist helps client identify irrational and negative thinking and substitute rational thinking.	Depression, anxiety, panic disorder, general feelings of unhappiness

Remember It!

1. Cognitive therapists believe that, for the most part, emotional disorders
   a. have physical causes.
   b. result from unconscious conflicts and motives.
   c. result from faulty and irrational thinking.
   d. result from environmental stimuli.
2. Rational-emotive therapy is a nondirective therapy that requires a warm, accepting therapist. (true/false)
3. The goal of cognitive therapy is best described as helping people
   a. develop effective coping strategies.
   b. replace automatic thoughts with more objective thoughts.
   c. develop an external locus of control.
   d. develop realistic goals and aspirations.
4. Cognitive therapy has proved very successful in the treatment of
   a. depression and mania.
   b. suicidal tendencies.
   c. fears and phobias.
   d. anxiety disorders and depression.

Answers: 1. c 2. false 3. b 4. d

THE BIOLOGICAL THERAPIES

What are the three main biological therapies?

Professionals who favor the biological perspective—the view that psychological disorders are symptoms of underlying physical disorders—usually favor a **biological therapy.** The three main biological therapies are drug therapy, electroconvulsive therapy, and psychosurgery.

biological therapy: A therapy (drug therapy, ECT, or psychosurgery) that is based on the assumption that most mental disorders have physical causes.

Drug Therapy: Pills for Psychological Ills

The favorite and by far the most frequently used biological treatment is drug therapy. Capable of relieving the debilitating symptoms of schizophrenia, depression, bipolar disorder, and some anxiety disorders, modern drug therapy has had a tremendous impact on the treatment of psychological disorders. In some cases drugs are used in conjunction with psychotherapy. Drug therapy is more likely to be integrated with behavior and cognitive therapies than with psychodynamic therapies (Zogg, 2000).

Schizophrenia As we saw in Chapter 15, schizophrenia is a serious psychological disorder that severely limits a person's ability to function (Kawanishi et al., 2000). Before the middle of the 20th century, efforts to treat schizophrenia were woefully inadequate. Many schizophrenic patients were confined to locked wards where padded cells, straitjackets, and other restraints were widely used. Then, shortly after the introduction of antipsychotic drugs in 1955, the picture suddenly changed. The breakthrough in drug therapy, coupled with the federal government's effort to reduce involuntary hospitalization of mental patients, enabled many schizophrenics who had been locked in mental institutions to be discharged into the community. In fact, the mental hospital patient population decreased from about 559,000 in 1955, when the drugs were introduced, to about 100,000 by 1990 and continued to drop throughout the 1990s (see Figure 16.2).

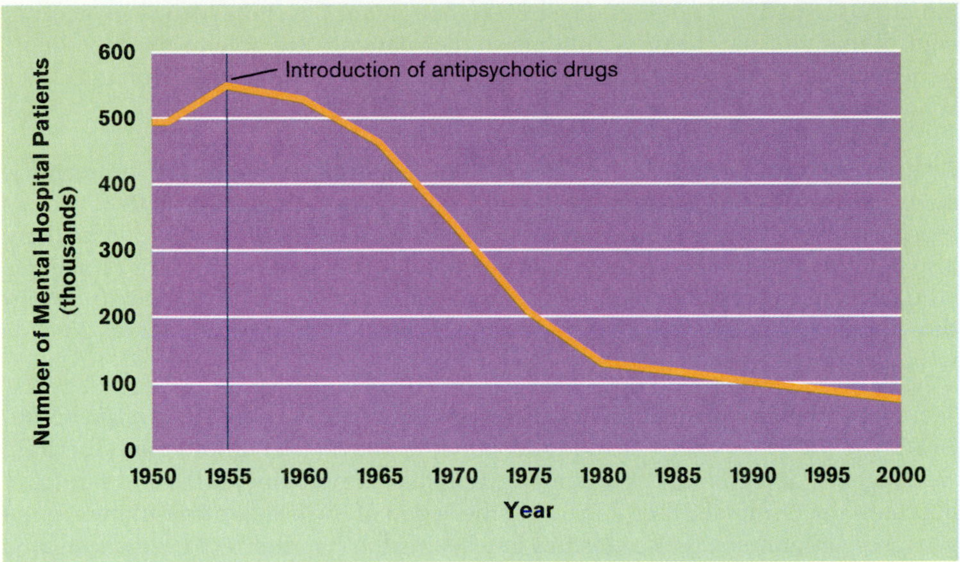

Figure 16.2

Decrease in Patient Populations in State and County Mental Hospitals (1950–2000)

State and county mental hospital patient populations peaked at approximately 560,000 in 1955. In the same year the antipsychotic drugs were introduced. The drugs, coupled with the federal government's efforts to reduce involuntary hospitalization of mental patients, resulted in a dramatic decrease in the patient population—down to about 100,000 in 1990 and lower than that in 2000.

How do antipsychotic drugs help schizophrenic patients?

Antipsychotic Drugs **Antipsychotic drugs** known as *neuroleptics* (sometimes called *major tranquilizers*) are prescribed primarily for schizophrenia. Their purpose is to control the severe psychotic symptoms of this psychological disorder, including hallucinations, delusions, disorganized speech, and disorganized behavior, which are the classic positive symptoms (Andreasen et al., 1995). You may have heard of these drugs by their brand names—Thorazine, Stelazine, Compazine, and Mellaril. The neuroleptics work primarily by inhibiting the activity of the neurotransmitter dopamine. The levels of dopamine at the synapses in the brains of people with schizophrenia tend to be at least twice as high as in the brains of normal persons (Seeman, 2001). About 50% of patients have a good response to the standard antipsychotics (Kane, 1996). But many patients, particularly those with an early onset of schizophrenia, are not helped by them (Meltzer et al., 1997), and others show only slight or modest improvement in symptoms. The long-term use of typical antipsychotic drugs carries a high risk of the most severe side effect, *tardive dyskinesia*—almost continual twitching and jerking movements of the face and tongue, and squirming movements of the hands and trunk (Glazer et al., 1993).

As troublesome as the positive symptoms of schizophrenia are, the negative symptoms are even more serious and more debilitating. Negative symptoms are deficits in behavior or affect—the schizophrenic person tends to be unresponsive, emotionally flat, unmotivated, and socially withdrawn, often with long periods of no movement (Kirkpatrick et al., 2000). Newer antipsychotic drugs called *atypical neuroleptics* can treat not only the positive symptoms of schizophrenia but the negative symptoms as well, leading to marked improvement in patients' quality of life (Worrel et al., 2000). Atypical neuroleptics such as clozapine, risperidone, and olanzipine target both dopamine neurotransmitter receptors and seratonin receptors (Kawanishi et al., 2000). About 10% of patients who take clozapine find the results so dramatic that they almost feel as though they have been reborn. Clozapine produces fewer side effects than standard neuroleptics, and patients taking it are less likely to develop tardive dyskinesia (Casey, 1996). However, clozapine is extremely expensive, and without careful monitoring it can cause a fatal blood defect in 1–2% of patients who take it. Risperidone appears to be effective and safe and has fewer side effects than standard neuroleptics (Marder, 1996a; Tamminga, 1996). Yet another advantage is that risperidone is much more effective than other neuroleptics in treating the negative symptoms of schizophrenia (Marder, 1996a).

Schizophrenics who were hospitalized in the past could expect to stay for weeks or months. Now, thanks to the antipsychotics, the average stay of such

antipsychotic drugs: Drugs used to control severe psychotic symptoms, such as the delusions and hallucinations of schizophrenics; also known as neuroleptics or major tranquilizers.

patients is usually a matter of days. Even though antipsychotic drugs reduce and control many of the major symptoms so that patients are able to function, most patients must continue to take them in order to avoid relapse (Carpenter, 1996; Schooler et al., 1997).

For what conditions are antidepressants prescribed?

Antidepressant Drugs Not long after the antipsychotic drugs came on the scene, the **antidepressants** were introduced. Antidepressants act effectively as mood elevators for people who are severely depressed (Elkin et al., 1995) and are also helpful in the treatment of certain anxiety disorders. About 65–75% of patients who take antidepressants find themselves significantly improved, and 40–50% of those are essentially completely recovered (Frazer, 1997). But this leaves 25–35% who show only minimal improvement.

Tricyclics The first generation of antidepressants are known as the *tricyclics* (Nutt, 2000). The tricyclics, which include amitriptyline (Elavil) and imipramine (Tofranil), work against depression by blocking the reuptake of norepinephrine and serotonin into the axon terminals, thus enhancing the action of these neurotransmitters in the synapses. Imipramine is also effective in relieving the symptoms of generalized anxiety disorder (Rickels, Downing et al., 1993) and panic disorder and agoraphobia (Clum et al., 1993). In fact, Aronson (1987) found that 88% of patients who could tolerate the drug stopped having panic attacks.

But tricyclics can have some unpleasant side effects—sedation, dizziness, nervousness, fatigue, dry mouth, forgetfulness, and weight gain (Frazer, 1997). Progressive weight gain (an average of more than 20 pounds) is the main reason people stop taking tricyclics, in spite of the relief these drugs provide from distressing psychological symptoms.

Selective Serotonin Reuptake Inhibitors (SSRIs) The second-generation antidepressants, the *selective serotonin reuptake inhibitors (SSRIs),* block the reuptake of the neurotransmitter serotonin, increasing its availability at the synapses in the brain (Nutt, 2000; Vetulani & Nalepa, 2000). SSRIs have fewer side effects (Nelson, 1997) and are safer in overdose than tricyclics (Thase & Kupfer, 1996). SSRIs have been found to be promising in treating obsessive compulsive disorder (Goodwin, 1996), social phobia (Jefferson, 1995), panic disorder (Coplan et al., 1997; Jefferson, 1997), and binge eating (Hudson et al., 1996). SSRIs include such drugs as fluoxetine (sold as Prozac) and clomipramine (Anafranil). By 1994 more than 28 million people worldwide had used Prozac (Avenoso, 1997); more than 1 million prescriptions were being written for it each month, making it the most widely used antidepressant (Mauro, 1994). Prozac's popularity is due not to greater effectiveness than the tricyclics but to milder side effects (Pen et al., 1994). But Prozac can cause sexual dysfunction, although normal sexual functioning returns when the drug is discontinued.

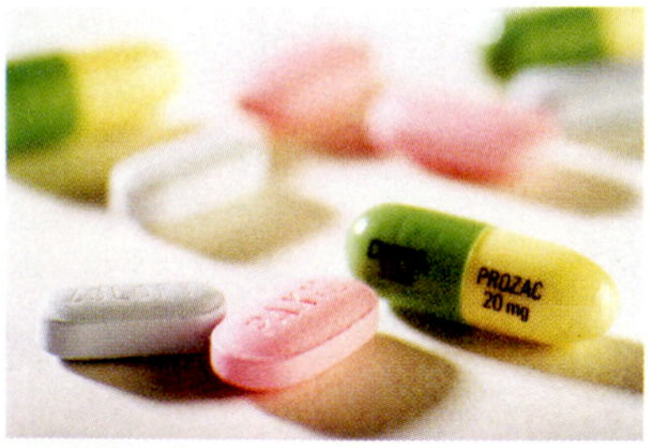

Prozac, the leading SSRI, has milder side effects than other SSRIs but is a highly effective antidepressant that is also prescribed for obsessive-compulsive disorder and posttraumatic stress disorder.

Prozac has been proved to be an effective treatment for less severe depression, with 50–60% of patients showing improvement (Nelson, 1991). It is also effective in the treatment of obsessive compulsive disorder, which has been associated with a serotonin imbalance (Rapoport, 1989). With an adequate trial of Prozac, the large majority of OCD patients are at least moderately better, and some become symptom-free. But about 30% have little or no response to the drug (Rasmussen et al., 1993; Tollefson et al., 1994). Prozac has also been effective in the treatment of compulsive buying (Black et al., 1997) and shows promise as a treatment for posttraumatic stress disorder (Lydiard et al., 1996). Early publicity that Prozac increases the risk of suicide has not been substantiated (Warshaw & Keller, 1996).

Monoamine Oxidase Inhibitors (MAO Inhibitors) Another line of treatment for depression is the monoamine oxidase inhibitors. By blocking the action of an enzyme that breaks down norepinephrine and serotonin in the synapses, MAO inhibitors increase the availability of norepinephrine and serotonin. MAO inhibitors (sold under the names Marplan, Nardil, and Parnate) are usually prescribed for depressed patients who do not respond to other antidepressants (Thase et al., 1992). They are also effec-

antidepressants: Drugs that are prescribed to treat depression and some anxiety disorders.

tive in treating panic disorder (Sheehan & Raj, 1988) and social phobia (Marshall et al., 1994). But MAO inhibitors have many of the same unpleasant side effects as tricyclic antidepressants, and patients taking MAO inhibitors must avoid certain foods or run the risk of stroke.

Lithium: A Natural Salt That Evens Moods **Lithium,** a naturally occurring salt, is considered a wonder drug for 40–50% of patients suffering from bipolar disorder (Thase & Kupfer, 1996). It is said to begin to quiet the manic state within 5 to 10 days. This is an amazing accomplishment, because the average episode, if untreated, lasts about 3 to 4 months. A proper maintenance dose of lithium yields reductions in depressive episodes as well as manic ones. Published reports over a period of three decades show that the clinical effectiveness of lithium for treating depression and bipolar disorder is unmatched (Ross et al., 2000). But 40–60% of those who take a maintenance dose will experience a recurrence (Thase & Kupfer, 1996). Also, careful monitoring of the lithium level in the patient's system is necessary every 2 to 6 months to guard against lithium poisoning and permanent damage to the nervous system (Schou, 1997).

How does lithium help patients with bipolar disorder?

The Minor Tranquilizers The family of minor tranquilizers called *benzodiazepines* includes, among others, the well-known drugs sold as Valium and Librium and the newer high-potency drug Xanax (pronounced ZAN-ax). Used primarily to treat anxiety, benzodiazepines are prescribed more often than any other class of psychoactive drugs (Medina et al., 1993). They have been found to be an effective treatment for panic disorder (Davidson, 1997; Noyes et al., 1996) and generalized anxiety disorder (Lydiard et al., 1996).

Xanax, the largest selling psychiatric drug (Famighetti, 1997), appears to be particularly effective in relieving anxiety and depression. Xanax is effective in the treatment of panic disorder (Noyes et al., 1996), and it works faster and has fewer side effects than antidepressants (Ballenger et al., 1993; Jonas & Cohon, 1993). However, if patients discontinue treatment, relapse is likely (Rickels, Schweizer et al., 1993). And there is a downside to Xanax. Many patients, once they are panic-free, find themselves unable to discontinue the drug because they experience moderate to intense withdrawal symptoms, including intense anxiety (Otto et al., 1993). Valium seems to be just as effective as Xanax for treating panic disorder, and withdrawal is easier. Although withdrawal is a problem with benzodiazepines, the abuse and addiction potential of these drugs is fairly low (Romach et al., 1995).

Some Problems with Drug Therapy Having read this far, you might conclude that drug therapy is the simplest and possibly the most effective way of treating schizophrenia, depression, panic disorder, and obsessive compulsive disorder. There are, however, a number of potential problems with the use of drugs. Antipsychotics and antidepressants have side effects that can be so unpleasant that a number of patients stop treatment before they experience a reduction in symptoms. Other patients discontinue treatment even if they believe the drugs are helping to relieve their psychological distress.

What are some of the problems with drug therapy?

Antipsychotics, antidepressants, and lithium do not cure psychological disorders, so patients usually experience a relapse if they stop taking the drugs when their symptoms lift. Maintenance doses of antidepressants following a major depression reduce the probability of recurrences (Prien & Kocsis, 1995). Maintenance doses are usually required with anxiety disorders as well, or symptoms are likely to return (Rasmussen et al., 1993).

People who have not been helped by drug therapy may have been given too low a dosage for too short a period of time (Keller, 1989). When the same drugs are administered in the same dose to different people, there can be a 40-fold difference in blood levels of the antipsychotics (Torrey, 1983) and a 30-fold difference in blood levels of the tricyclics (Preskorn, 1993). This means that the correct dose for one patient may be too much or too little for another. "Many 'nonresponders' to antidepressant

lithium: A drug used in bipolar disorder to control the symptoms in a manic episode and to even out the mood swings and reduce recurrence of future manic or depressive states.

drugs may become responders with a higher dosage and/or longer duration of treatment" (Joyce & Paykel, 1989, p. 94).

The main problem with antidepressants is that they are relatively slow-acting. In addition, more often than not, depressed patients have to try several different antidepressants before finding one that is effective. A severely depressed patient would need at least 2 to 6 weeks to obtain relief, and 30% don't respond at all. This can be too risky for suicidal patients. Thus, antidepressant drugs are not the treatment of choice if suicide is an imminent danger. In such cases many experts consider electroconvulsive therapy the preferred treatment.

Electroconvulsive Therapy: The Controversy Continues

For what purpose is electroconvulsive therapy (ECT) used, and what is its major side effect?

Electroconvulsive therapy (ECT), or electric shock, was introduced as a treatment for mental disorders by two Italian physicians, Cerletti and Bini, in 1938. ECT was widely used as a treatment for several mental disorders until the introduction of the antipsychotic and antidepressant drugs in the 1950s. ECT developed a bad reputation, partly because it was misused and overused in the 1940s and 1950s. Often it was misused simply to make troublesome patients easier to handle, and some patients received hundreds of shock treatments.

If you were to have electroconvulsive therapy, what could you expect? Electrodes would be placed on your head, and a mild electric current would be passed through your brain for 1–2 seconds. Immediately after the shock was administered, you would lose consciousness and experience a seizure lasting about 30 seconds to 1 minute. Apparently the seizure is necessary if ECT is to have any effect. The complete ECT procedure takes about 5 minutes, and medical complications following the procedure are said to be rare. Usually there is no pain associated with the treatment, and patients have no memory of the experience when they wake up.

The way ECT is administered has changed drastically since it was introduced more than 65 years ago. For many years the electric current was passed through both cerebral hemispheres, a procedure known as *bilateral ECT.* Today electric current is administered to the right hemisphere only, and the procedure is called *unilateral ECT.* Research suggests that unilateral ECT is as effective as the more intense bilateral ECT while producing milder cognitive effects (Sackeim et al., 2000). Also, a patient undergoing ECT today is given anesthesia, controlled oxygenation, and a muscle relaxant. As it is currently used, ECT is a highly effective treatment for major depression (Folkerts, 2000). And depressed patients who are 75 and older tolerate the procedure as well as younger patients do and reap comparable therapeutic benefits (Tew et al., 1999).

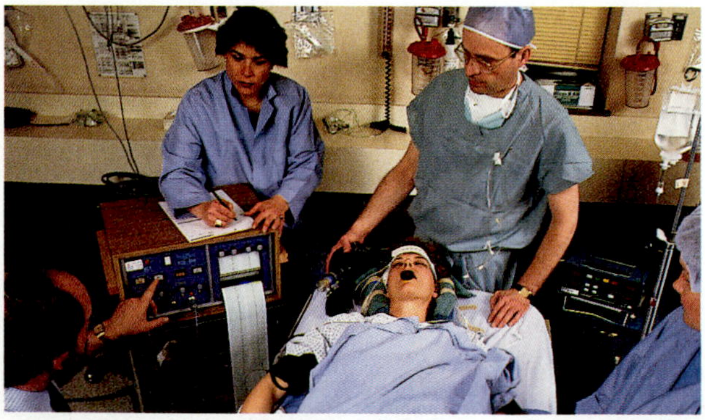

In electroconvulsive therapy a mild electric current is passed through the brain for 1–2 seconds, causing a brief seizure.

Although ECT can cut depression short, it is not a cure. Experts think that the seizure temporarily changes the biochemical balance in the brain, which in turn results in a lifting of depression. When ECT is effective, cerebral blood flow in the prefrontal cortex is reduced, and delta waves (usually associated with slow-wave sleep) appear (Sackeim et al., 1996).

Some psychiatrists and neurologists have spoken out against the use of ECT, claiming that it causes pervasive brain damage and memory loss. But advocates of ECT say that claims of brain damage are based on animal studies in which dosages of ECT were much higher than those now used in human patients. No structural brain damage from ECT has been revealed in studies comparing MRI or CT scans before and after a series of treatments (Devanand et al., 1994).

While its pros and cons continue to be debated, a majority of psychiatrists believe that there is a legitimate place for ECT in the treatment of severely depressed patients who are suicidal or who have not been helped by any other therapy (Folkerts, 2000).

Rapid Transcranial Magnetic Stimulation Apart from electrical shock, are there other methods of physically stimulating the brain that might be useful in treat-

Review & Reflect 16.3 Summary of the Biological Therapies

Type of Therapy	Perceived Cause of Disorder	Goals of Therapy	Methods Used	Primary Disorders Treated
Biological therapies	Underlying physical disorder caused by structural or biochemical abnormality in the brain; genetic inheritance	Eliminate or control biological cause of abnormal behavior; restore balance of neurotransmitters	Physician prescribes drugs such as antipsychotics, antidepressants, lithium, or tranquilizers; ECT; or psychosurgery.	Schizophrenia, depression, bipolar disorder, anxiety disorders

ing depression? Toward the end of the 20th century, a new therapy known as *rapid transcranial magnetic stimulation (rTMS)* appeared. This magnetic therapy is not invasive in any way. It is performed on patients who are not sedated; it causes no seizures, no memory loss, and has no known side effects. Its therapeutic value is similar to that of ECT, and it is much more accepted by the public (Vetulani & Nalepa, 2000). This therapy has also been used effectively in conjunction with SSRIs in treating depressed patients (Conca et al., 2000).

Psychosurgery: Cutting to Cure

What is psychosurgery, and for what problems is it used?

An even more drastic procedure than ECT is **psychosurgery**—brain surgery performed strictly to alleviate serious psychological disorders, such as severe depression, severe anxiety, or obsessions, or to provide relief from unbearable chronic pain. Psychosurgery is *not* the same as other brain surgery performed to correct a physical problem, such as removing a tumor or blood clot.

The first experimental brain surgery for human patients was developed by Portuguese neurologist Egas Moniz in 1935 to treat severe phobias, anxiety, and obsessions. In his technique, the **lobotomy,** surgeons severed the neural connections between the frontal lobes and the deeper brain centers involved in emotion. But no brain tissue was removed. At first the procedure was considered a tremendous contribution, and it won for Moniz the Nobel Prize in Medicine in 1949. Not everyone considered it a positive contribution, however. One of Moniz's lobotomized patients curtailed the surgeon's activities by shooting him in the spine, leaving him paralyzed on one side.

Neurosurgeons performed tens of thousands of frontal lobotomies in the United States and elsewhere from 1935 until 1955. But eventually it became apparent that this treatment was no cure-all. Although the surgery was effective in calming many of the patients, it often left them in a severely deteriorated condition. Apathy, impaired intellect, loss of motivation, and a change in personality kept many from resuming a normal life.

In the mid-1950s, when antipsychotic drugs came into use, psychosurgery virtually stopped. Since that time there has been a "second wave" of psychosurgical procedures that are far less drastic than the lobotomies of decades past. Some of the most modern procedures result in less intellectual impairment because, rather than using conventional surgery, surgeons deliver electric currents through electrodes to destroy a much smaller, more localized area of brain tissue. In one procedure, called a *cingulotomy,* electrodes are used to destroy the cingulum, a small bundle of nerves connecting the cortex to the emotional centers of the brain. Several procedures, including cingulotomy, have been helpful for some extreme cases of obsessive compulsive disorder (Baer et al., 1995; Trivedi, 1996).

But even today the results of psychosurgery are still not predictable, and for better or for worse, the consequences are irreversible. For this reason, the treatment is considered experimental and absolutely a last resort.

Review & Reflect 16.3 summarizes the biological therapies.

electroconvulsive therapy (ECT): A treatment in which an electric current is passed through the brain, causing a seizure; usually reserved for severely depressed patients who are either suicidal or unresponsive to other treatment.

psychosurgery: Brain surgery to treat some severe, persistent, and debilitating psychological disorder or severe chronic pain.

lobotomy: A psychosurgery technique in which the nerve fibers connecting the frontal lobes to the deeper brain centers are severed.

Remember It!

1. For the most part, advocates of biological therapies assume that psychological disorders have a physical cause. (true/false)
2. Match the disorder with the drug most often used for its treatment.

   ____ (1) panic disorder and agoraphobia
   ____ (2) schizophrenia
   ____ (3) bipolar disorder
   ____ (4) depression
   ____ (5) obsessive compulsive disorder

   a. lithium
   b. antipsychotic
   c. antidepressant
3. Medication that relieves the symptoms of schizophrenia is thought to work by blocking the action of
   a. serotonin. c. norepinephrine.
   b. dopamine. d. epinephrine.
4. Which of the following is *not* true of drug therapy for psychological disorders?
   a. It is often difficult to determine the proper dose.
   b. Drugs often have unpleasant side effects.
   c. Patients often relapse if they stop taking the drugs.
   d. Drugs are usually not very effective.
5. For which disorder is ECT typically used?
   a. severe depression c. anxiety disorders
   b. schizophrenia d. panic disorder
6. Psychosurgery techniques are now so precise that the exact effects of the surgery can be predicted in advance. (true/false)

Answers: 1. true 2. (1) c (2) b (3) a (4) c (5) c 3. b 4. d 5. a 6. false

THERAPIES AND THERAPISTS: MANY CHOICES

Evaluating the Therapies: Do They Work?

How effective is psychotherapy? Several hundred studies have compared the effectiveness of several psychotherapies against no treatment at all. What do these studies show on average? Researchers Smith, Glass, and Miller (1980) tried to answer this question by reanalyzing 475 studies, which involved 25,000 patients. Using meta-analysis, they were able to combine the findings of the studies and compare various psychotherapies against no treatment. They concluded that "the average person who receives therapy is better off at the end of it than 80% of the persons who do not" (p. 87). Figure 16.3 shows the comparative effectiveness of various psychotherapies as reported by Smith and others (1980). Although this study revealed that psychotherapy is better than no treatment, it did not indicate that one type of therapy was clearly more effective than another. In other words, the different types of therapy—behavioral, psychodynamic, and cognitive—appeared to be more or less equally effective. Moreover, neither the length of treatment nor the therapists' years of experience appeared to be related to the effectiveness of treatment.

Hans Eysenck (1994) takes issue with the conclusion that Smith and others (1980) reached in their meta-analysis. According to Eysenck's analysis of the data, psychodynamic, person-centered, Gestalt, and rational-emotive therapies were not significantly more effective than a placebo treatment. He found them to be significantly less effective than systematic desensitization, flooding, behavior modification, and cognitive therapy.

An even larger meta-analysis—a combined study of 302 other meta-analyses—revealed that psychological, educational, and behavioral treatment generally had "a strong, dramatic pattern of positive overall effects" (Lipsey & Wilson, 1993).

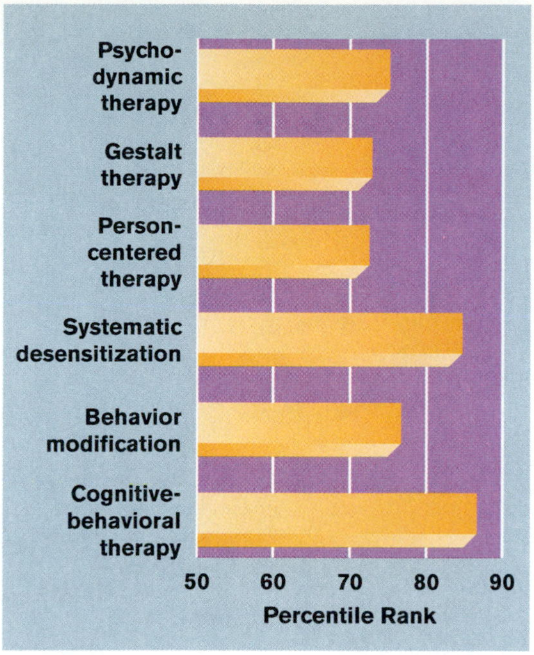

Figure 16.3

The Effectiveness of Different Types of Psychotherapy

Using meta-analysis, Smith, Glass, and Miller were able to combine the results of 475 studies involving 25,000 patients. These researchers compared the results of various psychotherapies against no treatment and concluded that, on the average, the people who received therapy were better off than about 80% of the people who received no therapy. The percentile ranks indicate how much better off those patients who received each type of therapy were than those who did not receive any therapy. (Data from Smith et al., 1980.)

It is one thing for researchers to assess the comparative value of different therapies, but how do the patients themselves rate the therapies? To answer this question, *Consumer Reports* (1995) conducted the largest survey to date on patient attitudes toward psychotherapy. Martin Seligman (1995, 1996), a consultant for the study, summarized its findings:

- Overall, patients believed that they benefited substantially from psychotherapy.
- Patients seemed equally satisfied with their therapy, whether it was provided by a psychologist, a psychiatrist, or a social worker.
- Specifically, patients who were in therapy for more than 6 months did considerably better; generally, the longer patients stayed in therapy, the more they improved.
- Patients who took a drug such as Prozac or Xanax believed they were helped, but overall, psychotherapy alone seemed to work about as well as psychotherapy plus drugs.

According to Seligman (1995), under some conditions patients did not fare so well. "Patients whose length of therapy or choice of therapist was limited by insurance and managed care did worse" (p. 965).

Factors other than the type of therapy contribute to patient outcomes. One is the *therapeutic alliance*—the quality of the relationship between the individual patient and the therapist (Blatt et al., 1996). This factor affected treatment outcomes even when the patient received only drugs with no additional psychotherapy, according to one large study of depression (Krupnick et al., 1996). This study also revealed that 20% of individual differences in treatment outcome were accounted for by a close and positive relationship between patient and therapist. And a recent review of empirical studies suggests that the relationship between the patient and the therapist also affects the outcome of behavior therapy (Keijsers et al., 2000).

Mental Health Professionals: How Do They Differ?

What different types of mental health professionals conduct psychotherapy?

According to one of the most comprehensive studies of the use of mental health services in the United States, 15 million people sought help during a recent year for substance use and mental health problems (Horgan, 1996). Troubled people turned to a

Figure 16.4

Where People Go for Help

People with mental health and substance use problems seek help from a variety of professional or volunteer sources. (Adapted from Narrow et al., 1993.)

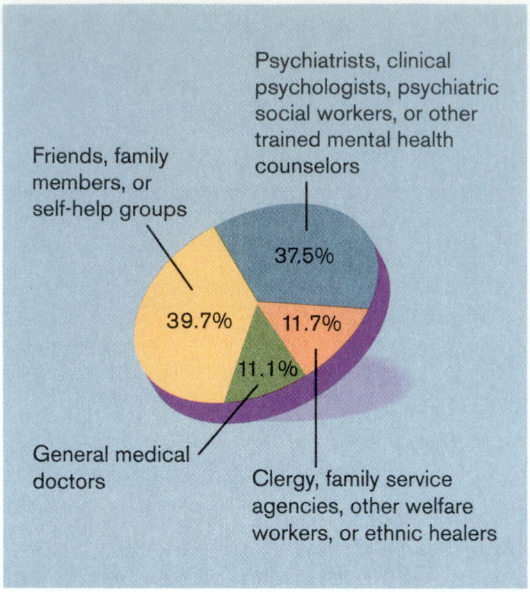

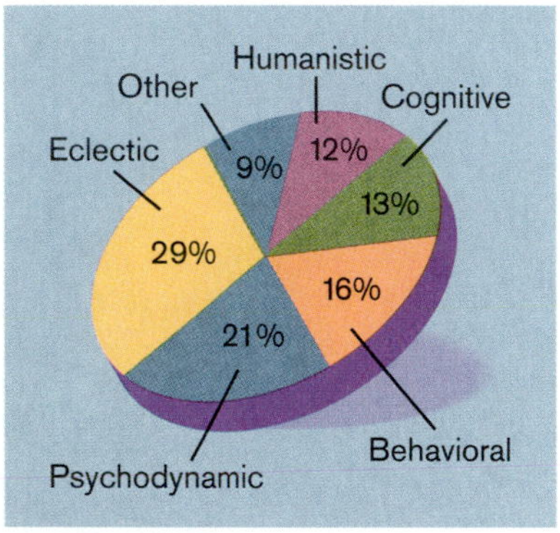

Figure 16.5

Primary Psychotherapeutic Approach Used by a Sample of Clinical Psychologists

Of 579 clinical psychologists who are members of the American Psychological Association, the largest percentage (29%) are eclectic, using a variety of therapies in their practice. (Based on Norcross et al., 1989.)

clinical psychologist: A psychologist, usually with a PhD, whose training is in the diagnosis, treatment, or research of psychological and behavioral disorders.

psychiatrist: A medical doctor with a specialty in the diagnosis and treatment of mental disorders.

psychoanalyst (SY-ko-AN-ul-ist): A professional, usually a psychiatrist, with special training in psychoanalysis.

variety of sources for help. As shown in Figure 16.4, 37.5% of all visits to professional or volunteer sources were made to psychiatrists, clinical psychologists, psychiatric social workers, and other trained mental health counselors. Practicing in the United States are 60,000 psychologists, 40,000 psychiatrists, 75,000 social workers, and relatively few who call themselves psychoanalysts (Horgan, 1996). Who are these mental health professionals, and for what problems are their services most appropriate?

For serious psychological disorders, a clinical psychologist or psychiatrist is the best source of help. A **clinical psychologist** specializes in the assessment, treatment, and/or research of psychological problems and behavioral disturbances, and usually has a PhD in clinical psychology. Clinical psychologists use various types of psychotherapy to treat a variety of psychological disorders and adjustment problems. Although clinical psychologists are not allowed to prescribe medications, the American Psychological Association is working toward gaining them this privilege (Kingsbury, 1996). While many psychologists applaud the APA's effort (DeLeon & Wiggins, 1996; Klein, 1996), others do not (DeNelsky, 1996; Hayes & Heiby, 1996).

A **psychiatrist** is a medical doctor with a specialty in the diagnosis and treatment of mental disorders. Psychiatrists can prescribe drugs and other biological treatments, and many also provide psychotherapy. A **psychoanalyst** is usually, but not always, a psychiatrist with specialized training in psychoanalysis from a psychoanalytic institute.

For clients with other psychological problems, such as adjustment disorders, substance abuse, and marital or family problems, the choice of mental health professionals widens and includes counseling psychologists, counselors, and psychiatric social workers. A counseling psychologist usually has a PhD in clinical or counseling psychology or a doctor of education degree (EdD) with a major in counseling. A counselor typically has a master's degree in psychology or counselor education. Often employed by colleges and universities, counseling psychologists and counselors help students with personal problems and/or test or counsel them in academic or vocational areas. A psychiatric social worker usually has a master's degree in social work (MSW) with specialized training in psychiatric problems, and may practice psychotherapy.

The entire range of mental health professionals may be found in private practice, in social agencies, or in hospital or clinic settings. There are hundreds of types of therapy and a trend among therapists toward *eclecticism*—incorporating techniques from many different therapies as appropriate, rather than practicing only one type of therapy exclusively. Figure 16.5 shows the percentages of clinical psychologists practicing various types of psychotherapy.

Selecting a Therapy: Finding One That Fits

What therapy, if any, has proved to be the most effective in treating psychological disorders?

Is one therapy really better, on average, than other therapies? It seems obvious to ask which therapy, if any, is likely to be best for a specific person with a particular disorder, under the given circumstances.Therapists do not treat "average" persons; they treat people individually, and some therapies are more effective than others for treating certain disorders.

Insight therapies are often more effective for general feelings of unhappiness and interpersonal problems. Various types of behavior therapy are usually best for people with a specific problem behavior they want to change, such as a fear, phobia, bad habit, or some socially undesirable behavior. Specific phobias are successfully treated with flooding and systematic desensitization. Social phobia is better treated with cognitive-behavioral therapy or exposure therapy (DeRubeis & Crits-Christoph, 1998), a high-potency benzodiazepine such as Xanax (Marshall et al., 1994), or an SSRI (Jefferson, 1995). Tricyclic antidepressants and benzodiazepines such as Xanax and Valium often relieve the symptoms of panic disorder (Davidson, 1997; Noyes et al., 1996). Cognitive or behavioral therapy also works well for panic disorder, and patients are less likely to relapse when therapy is complete than are patients treated with drugs alone (Pollack & Otto, 1997; Sharp et al., 1996). Obsessive compulsive disorder is best treated with exposure and response prevention (Foa, 1995) and/or SSRIs (Goodwin, 1996).

For depression, a variety of treatments have proved successful—tricyclic antidepressants, SSRIs, MAO inhibitors, cognitive therapy, and interpersonal therapy (DeRubeis & Crits-Christoph, 1998; Stahl, 1998). ECT is often effective for severely depressed people for whom other treatments have not worked and for suicidal individuals who need immediate help and cannot wait for the standard treatments to take effect. For bipolar disorder, lithium is the treatment of choice.

Conventional antipsychotics (neuroleptics) are prescribed for people suffering from schizophrenia. When these drugs are not effective or the patient cannot tolerate the side effects, atypical neuroleptics such as clozapine and resperidone are often helpful (Daniel & Whitcomb, 1998).

Therapy and Race, Ethnicity, and Gender

Why is it important to consider multicultural variables in the therapeutic setting?

There is a growing awareness that psychotherapists need to consider multicultural variables such as race, ethnicity, and gender in diagnosing and treating psychological disorders (Bernal & Castro, 1994). According to Kleinman and Cohen (1997), people experience and suffer from psychological and biological disorders within a cultural context in which the meaning of symptoms, outcomes, and responses to therapy may differ dramatically. The APA (1993) has issued "Guidelines for Providers of Psychological Services to Ethnic, Linguistic, and Culturally Diverse Populations." And for the first time, the American Psychiatric Association's *Diagnostic and Statistical Manual of Mental Disorders (Fourth Edition) (DSM-IV)* includes a section headed "Specific Culture, Age, and Gender Features" for most psychological disorders and a description of disorders specific to particular cultures. Nevertheless, most graduate students in clinical and counseling psychology are not adequately trained to work with minority clients (Allison et al., 1994; Bernal & Castro, 1994).

When the cultures of the therapist and patient (client) differ markedly, behavior that is normal for the patient can be misinterpreted as abnormal by the therapist (Lewis-Fernández & Kleinman, 1994). Psychologists Sue and Sue (1990) identified four cultural barriers that hinder effective counseling: *cultural values, social class, language,* and *nonverbal communications* (gestures, facial expressions, and the like). For example, "an Asian American client who values restraint of strong feelings may be viewed by a counselor as repressed, inhibited, or unassertive" (Sue, 1994, p. 293).

When therapist and client have the same racial or ethnic background, they are more likely to share cultural values and communication styles, which can facilitate the counseling process.

There is dramatic evidence that language can pose a problem in both diagnosis and treatment. When a group of Puerto Rican patients took the Thematic Apperception Test (TAT) in English, their pauses and the choices of words they used to describe the TAT pictures were interpreted as indications of psychological problems. In fact, the patients' "problems" were with the language, which was not their native tongue (Suarez, 1983). A group of Mexican Americans interviewed in English were perceived as having more disorders in thinking and more emotional disorders than when they were interviewed in Spanish (Martinez, 1986).

Nonverbal behavior has different meanings for different cultural and ethnic groups. For example, making direct eye contact, which is presumed by many in the U.S. majority culture to connote honesty, interest, and self-confidence, is a gesture of disrespect among many Native Americans. The misinterpretation of this and other nonverbal communications partly helps to explain why so many Native Americans (over 50%) never return to non–Native American therapists after the first visit (Heinrich et al., 1990).

Race also accounts for some differences in the diagnosis and treatment of psychological disorders. Strakowski and others (1995) found that "Black patients were significantly more likely to be diagnosed with schizophrenia and substance abuse than similar White patients" (p. 101). And Blacks are more likely to be hospitalized involuntarily than their White counterparts under similar circumstances (Lawson et al., 1994).

The ability to generalize treatments to minority populations is compromised by the high volume of research studies that use only White populations in controlled settings (Matt & Navarro, 1997). For example, there are significant racial and gender differences in optimal therapeutic doses of some drugs used to treat mental disorders, including schizophrenia and bipolar disorder. Researcher Ken-Ming Lin discovered that a 2-milligram dose of the antipsychotic haloperidol relieved symptoms of schizophrenia in Asian patients, whereas 10 times that dose was required for White patients (Holden, 1991). And women generally need lower doses of most psychiatric drugs than men do (Yonkers & Hamilton, 1995). In spite of this difference, research to establish the dosage of drugs has been conducted largely on men, even though women use the drugs more often.

In therapy, one size does *not* fit all.

Remember It!

1. What is true regarding the effectiveness of therapies?
   a. All are equally effective for any disorder.
   b. Specific therapies have proved effective in treating particular disorders.
   c. Insight therapies are consistently best.
   d. Therapy is no more effective than no treatment for emotional and behavioral disorders.
2. Match the problem with the most appropriate therapy.
   ____ (1) eliminating fears, bad habits
   ____ (2) schizophrenia
   ____ (3) general unhappiness, interpersonal problems
   ____ (4) severe depression

   a. behavior therapy
   b. insight therapy
   c. drug therapy
3. One must have a medical degree to become a
   a. clinical psychologist.
   b. psychoanalyst.
   c. psychiatrist.
   d. clinical psychologist, psychiatrist, or psychoanalyst.
4. The responses and outcomes of patients in therapy are (significantly, slightly) influenced by multicultural factors.

Answers: 1. b 2. (1) a (2) c (3) b (4) c 3. c 4. significantly

Apply It!

E-Therapy: Is It Right for You?

Kenny Evans was depressed. He knew he needed help, but since he is partially paralyzed, it was difficult for him to secure face-to-face psychotherapy. For him, online psychotherapy was the answer. Without leaving his home, he could exchange e-mail messages with a trained therapist (Roan, 2000). Martha Ainsworth was experiencing a major life problem while on an extensive business trip. She found a therapist on the Internet and ended up communicating with him daily for about 2 years. "It was probably one of the most significant and powerful relationships I have ever had," she comments (Walker, 2000).

Evans and Ainsworth are among the thousands who are turning to *e-therapy*—ongoing online interaction with a trained therapist. It typically involves the exchange of e-mail messages over a period of hours or days, and therefore is more limited than traditional psychotherapy. However, e-therapy—also called *life coaching, psychoeducation,* or *e-mail counseling*—can be therapeutic. Like many other kinds of relationships, relationships formed online between a therapist and a client can be intimate, intense, and emotionally healing (Ainsworth, 2000; Roan, 2000).

Advantages and disadvantages. Besides being convenient, e-therapy enables clients to be much less inhibited than they might be in a face-to-face situation. It is also less expensive than traditional therapy (Roan, 2000). Another advantage is that the therapist and the client do not have to be in the same place at the same time. The client can write to the therapist whenever he or she feels like it and can keep accurate records of "sessions" (e-mail correspondence) to refer to later (Ainsworth, 2000; Stubbs, 2000).

On the other hand, because of the anonymity of the Internet, it is easy for imposters to pose as therapists. So far there is no system for regulating or licensing e-therapists. In addition, e-therapy poses some potential ethical problems, such as the possibility of breaches of confidentiality. But like all reputable therapists, the best e-therapists do everything they can to protect clients' privacy and confidentiality—except when necessary to protect them or someone else from immediate harm (Ainsworth, 2000).

Perhaps the most serious drawback of e-therapy is the fact that the therapist cannot see the client and therefore cannot use the visual and auditory cues to determine when the person is becoming anxious or upset. This reduces the effectiveness of treatment (Roan, 2000; Walker, 2000).

Should you choose e-therapy over face-to-face therapy? E-therapy is not for everyone. Most important, *it is not appropriate for someone who is in the midst of a serious crisis.* There are better ways to get immediate help, such as suicide hotlines. E-therapy is also not effective for people with extremely complex problems. Some researchers (Ainsworth, 2000; Walker, 2000), however, claim that e-therapy can be a valuable alternative to psychotherapy for individuals such as these:

- People who are often away from home or have full schedules
- People who cannot afford traditional therapy
- People who live in rural areas and do not have access to mental health care
- People with disabilities
- People who are too timid or embarrassed to make an appointment with a therapist

To participate in e-therapy, you need to be a reasonably good writer, able to write expressively and in some detail. You must also be willing to reveal your feelings to the therapist. If you conceal important feelings, you cannot benefit fully from the therapist's insights (Ainsworth, 2000).

Finding an e-therapist. A reputable therapist will provide his or her name, credentials, location, and telephone number. With this information, you can determine whether he or she is a qualified psychotherapist. In return, the therapist will probably ask you to provide your name, address, and phone number so that he or she can help you if you experience a crisis (Ainsworth, 2000).

If you wish to locate an e-therapist, the best place to start is http://www.metanoia.org. The site lists online therapists whose credentials have been checked by Mental Health Net. It provides information about the location of the therapist, the services offered, payment method, and so forth (Roan, 2000). When choosing a therapist, be sure to do the following (Ainsworth, 2000):

- Make sure the person's credentials have been verified by a third party.
- Get real-world contact information.
- Verify that you'll receive a personal reply to your messages.
- Find out in advance how much the therapist charges.

If you decide to contact an e-therapist, bear this in mind: While e-therapy may be a good way to get started, if you have persistent problems, it would be wise in the long run to obtain traditional psychotherapy (Roan, 2000).

THINKING CRITICALLY

Evaluation

What are the major strengths and weaknesses of the following approaches to therapy: psychoanalysis, person-centered therapy, behavior therapy, cognitive therapy, and drug therapy?

Point/Counterpoint

From what you have learned in this chapter, prepare a strong argument to support each of these positions:

a. Psychotherapy is generally superior to drug therapy in the treatment of psychological disorders.
b. Drug therapy is generally superior to psychotherapy in the treatment of psychological disorders.

Psychology in Your Life

If you were considering therapy for yourself or advising a friend or family member, would you try or recommend e-therapy? Make a list of the reasons why you would or would not consider e-therapy as an option.

SUMMARY AND REVIEW

INSIGHT THERAPIES

What are the four basic techniques of psychoanalysis, and how are they used to help disturbed patients?

The four basic techniques of psychoanalysis are free association, analysis of resistance, dream analysis, and analysis of transference. They are used to uncover the repressed memories, impulses, and conflicts presumed to be the cause of the patient's problems.

What are the role and the goal of the therapist in person-centered therapy?

Person-centered therapy is a nondirective therapy in which the therapist provides a climate of unconditional positive regard where clients are free to be themselves so that their natural tendency toward positive growth will be released.

What is the major emphasis in Gestalt therapy?

Gestalt therapy emphasizes the importance of clients' fully experiencing, in the present moment, their feelings, thoughts, and actions, and taking personal responsibility for their behavior.

What four problems commonly associated with major depression is interpersonal therapy designed to treat?

Interpersonal therapy (IPT) is designed to help depressed patients cope with severe responses to the death of a loved one, interpersonal role disputes, difficulties in adjusting to role transitions, and deficits in interpersonal skills.

What are some advantages of group therapy?

Group therapy is less expensive than individual therapy and gives people an opportunity to express feelings and get feedback from other group members and to give and receive help and emotional support.

Key Terms

psychotherapy (p. 576); insight therapy (p. 577); psychoanalysis (p. 577); free association (p. 577); resistance (p. 577); transference (p. 578); person-centered therapy (p. 578); self-actualization (p. 579); nondirective therapy (p. 579); Gestalt therapy (p. 579); directive therapy (p. 580); interpersonal therapy (IPT) (p. 580); family therapy (p. 581); group therapy (p. 582)

BEHAVIOR THERAPIES: UNLEARNING THE OLD, LEARNING THE NEW

What is a behavior therapy?

A behavior therapy is a treatment approach that employs the principles of operant conditioning, classical conditioning, and/or observational learning theory to replace inappropriate or maladaptive behaviors with more adaptive responses.

How do behavior therapists modify behavior using operant conditioning techniques?

Operant conditioning techniques involve the withholding of reinforcement to eliminate undesirable behaviors, as in time out, or the use of reinforcement to shape or increase the frequency of desirable behaviors, as in token economies.

What behavior therapies are based on classical conditioning?

Behavior therapies based on classical conditioning are systematic desensitization, flooding, exposure and response prevention, and aversion therapy.

How do therapists use systematic desensitization to rid people of fears?

Therapists using systematic desensitization train clients in deep muscle relaxation and then have them confront a series of graduated anxiety-producing situations, either real or imagined, until they can remain relaxed even in the presence of the most feared situation.

What is flooding?

With flooding, clients are exposed to the feared object or event or asked to imagine it vividly for an extended period until their anxiety decreases and they realize that none of the dreaded consequences come to pass.

How does exposure and response prevention help people with obsessive compulsive disorder?

In exposure and response prevention, people with OCD are exposed to the anxiety-generating stimulus but gradually increase the time before they begin their compulsive rituals and thus learn to tolerate their anxiety.

How does aversion therapy rid people of a harmful or undesirable behavior?

Aversion therapy pairs the unwanted behavior with an aversive stimulus until the bad habit becomes associated with pain or discomfort.

How does participant modeling help people overcome fears?

In participant modeling, an appropriate response is modeled in graduated steps and the client is asked to imitate each step with the encouragement and support of the therapist.

Key Terms
behavior therapy (p. 584); behavior modification (p. 584); token economy (p. 585); time out (p. 585); stimulus satiation (p. 585); systematic desensitization (p. 586); flooding (p. 587); exposure and response prevention (p. 588); aversion therapy (p. 589); participant modeling (p. 589)

COGNITIVE THERAPIES: IT'S THE THOUGHT THAT COUNTS

What is the aim of rational-emotive therapy?

Rational-emotive therapy is a directive form of therapy designed to challenge and modify the client's irrational beliefs, which are believed to be the cause of personal distress.

How does cognitive therapy help people overcome depression and anxiety disorders?

Cognitive therapy helps people overcome depression and anxiety disorders by pointing out the irrational thoughts causing them misery and by helping them learn other, more realistic ways of looking at themselves and their experience.

Key Terms
rational-emotive therapy (p. 590); automatic thoughts (p. 592); cognitive therapy (p. 592)

THE BIOLOGICAL THERAPIES

What are the three main biological therapies?

The three main biological therapies are drug therapy, ECT, and psychosurgery.

How do antipsychotic drugs help schizophrenic patients?

Antipsychotic drugs control the major symptoms of schizophrenia by inhibiting the activity of dopamine.

For what conditions are antidepressants prescribed?

Antidepressants are prescribed for depression, generalized anxiety disorder, panic disorder, agoraphobia, and obsessive compulsive disorder.

How does lithium help patients with bipolar disorder?

Lithium is used to control the symptoms in a manic episode and to even out the mood swings in bipolar disorder.

What are some of the problems with drug therapy?

Some problems are the drugs' unpleasant or dangerous side effects, the difficulty in establishing the proper dosages, and the fact that relapse is likely if the drug therapy is discontinued.

For what purpose is electroconvulsive therapy (ECT) used, and what is its major side effect?

ECT is a treatment of last resort for people with severe depression, and it is most often reserved for those who are in imminent danger of committing suicide. Some memory loss is its major side effect.

What is psychosurgery, and for what problems is it used?

Psychosurgery is brain surgery performed strictly to relieve some severe, persistent, and debilitating psychological disorder; it is considered experimental and highly controversial.

Key Terms
biological therapy (p. 594); antipsychotic drugs (p. 595); antidepressants (p. 596); lithium (p. 597); electroconvulsive therapy (ECT) (p. 598); psychosurgery (p. 599); lobotomy (p. 599)

THERAPIES AND THERAPISTS: MANY CHOICES

What different types of mental health professionals conduct psychotherapy?

Professionals trained to conduct psychotherapy fall into these categories: clinical psychologists, psychiatrists, psychoanalysts, counseling psychologists, counselors, and psychiatric social workers.

What therapy, if any, has proved to be the most effective in treating psychological disorders?

Although, overall, no one therapeutic approach has proved generally superior, specific therapies have proven effective in treating particular disorders.

Why is it important to consider multicultural variables in the therapeutic setting?

Multicultural variables such as race, ethnicity, and gender have a profound influence on patients' responses to the therapy and the therapist and on therapists' responses to patients.

Key Terms
clinical psychologist (p. 602); psychiatrist (p. 602); psychoanalyst (p. 602)

Surf It!

Want to be sure you've absorbed the material in Chapter 16, "Therapies," before the big test? Visiting *www.abacon.com/wood* can put a top grade within your reach. The site is loaded with free practice tests, flashcards, activities, and links to help you review your way to an A. To enliven that inevitable study break, the site also offers personality assessment quizzes and a psychology career corner.

17 Social Psychology

In the 1960s, an advertisement appeared in newspapers in New Haven, Connecticut, and other communities near Yale University. It read: "Wanted: Volunteers to serve as subjects in a study of memory and learning at Yale University."

Many people responded to the ad, and 40 male participants between the ages of 20 and 50 were selected, among them "postal clerks, high school teachers, salesmen, engineers, and laborers" (Milgram, 1963, p. 372). Yet no experiment on memory and learning was to take place. Instead, a staged drama was planned in which only one actual participant would be involved at a time. Imagine that you are one of the naive participants selected for the experiment.

The researcher actually wants to know how far you will go in obeying orders to administer what you believe to be increasingly painful electric shocks to a "learner" who misses questions on a test. The cast of characters is as follows:

The Experimenter: A 31-year-old high school biology teacher dressed in a gray laboratory coat who assumes a stern and serious manner

The Learner: A pleasant, heavyset accountant about 50 years of age (an accomplice of the experimenter)

The Teacher: You—the only naive member of the cast

The experimenter leads you and the learner into one room, where the learner is strapped into an electric-chair apparatus. You, the teacher, are delivered a sample shock of 45 volts, which stings you and is supposedly for the purpose of testing the equipment and showing you what the learner will feel. The learner complains of a heart condition and says that he hopes the electric shocks will not be too painful. The experimenter admits that the stronger shocks will hurt but hastens to add, "Although the shocks can be extremely painful, they cause no permanent tissue damage" (p. 373).

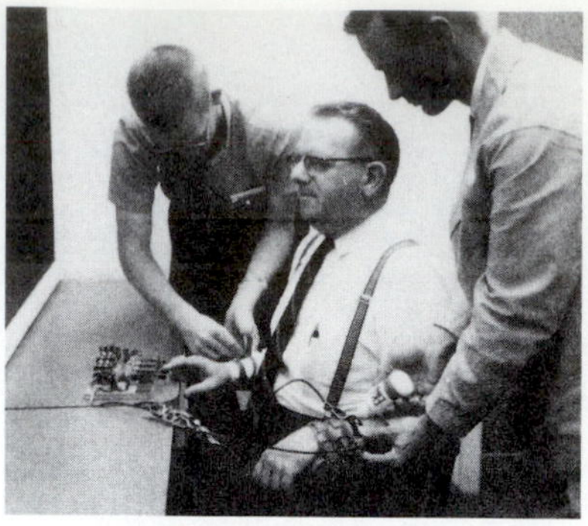

Then the experimenter takes you to an adjoining room, out of sight of the learner. The experimenter seats you in front of an instrument panel with 30 lever switches arranged horizontally across the front. The first switch on the left, you are told, delivers only 15 volts, but each successive switch is 15 volts stronger than the last–30 volts, 45 volts, and so on up to the last switch, which carries 450 volts. The switches on the instrument panel are labeled with designations ranging from "Slight Shock" to "Danger: Severe Shock."

The experimenter explains that you are to read a list of word pairs to the learner and then test his memory. When the learner makes the right choice, you go on to the next pair. If the learner misses a question, you are to flip a switch and shock him, moving one switch to the right–delivering 15 additional volts–each time he misses a question. The learner does well at first but then begins missing about three out of every four questions. You begin flipping the switches, which you believe are delivering stronger and stronger shocks for each incorrect answer. When you hesitate, the experimenter urges you, "Please continue" or "Please go on." If you still hesitate, the experimenter orders you, "The experiment requires that you continue," or more strongly, "You have no other choice, you *must* go on" (p. 374).

At the 20th switch, 300 volts, the learner pounds on the wall and screams, "Let me out of here, let me out, my heart's bothering me, let me out!" (Meyer, 1972, p. 461). From this point on, the learner answers no more questions. Alarmed, you protest to the experimenter that the learner, who is pounding the wall frantically, does not want to continue. The experimenter answers, "Whether the learner likes it or not, you must go on" (Milgram, 1963, p. 374). Even if the learner fails to respond, you are told to count that as an incorrect response and shock him again.

Do you continue? If so, you flip the next switch–315 volts–and hear only groans from the learner. You look at the experimenter, obviously distressed, your palms sweating, your heart pounding. The experimenter states firmly, "You have no other choice, you *must* go on" (p. 374). If you refuse at this point, the experiment is ended. Would you refuse, or would you continue to shock a silent learner nine more times until you delivered the maximum of 450 volts?

You have just read a description of a classic experiment that was designed to learn just how far ordinary people would go to obey an authority figure, even if it meant injuring another person. We will explore this and other interesting questions in this chapter as we study social psychology.

social psychology: The study of how the actual, imagined, or implied presence of others influences the thoughts, feelings, and behavior of individuals.

confederate: Someone who is posing as a participant in an experiment but is actually assisting the experimenter.

naive subject: A person who has agreed to participate in an experiment but is not aware that deception is being used to conceal its real purpose.

INTRODUCTION TO SOCIAL PSYCHOLOGY

Social psychology is the area of study that attempts to explain how the actual, imagined, or implied presence of others influences the thoughts, feelings, and behavior of individuals. No human being lives in a vacuum, alone and apart from other people. We are truly social animals, and our social nature—how we think about, respond to, and interact with other people—provides the territory that social psychology explores. Research in social psychology yields some surprising and provocative answers to puzzling human behavior, from the atrocious to the altruistic.

This chapter explores social perception—how people form impressions of others, and try to understand why they behave as they do. What are the factors involved in attraction? What draws people to one another, and how do friendships and romantic relationships develop? We will look at factors influencing conformity and obedience, and we'll examine groups and their influence on performance and decision making. We will also discuss attitudes and learn how they can be changed, and then we will explore prejudice and discrimination. Finally, we will look at the conditions under which people are likely to help each other (prosocial behavior) and hurt each other (aggression).

To start, let's consider how social psychologists conduct their studies. You may have seen the TV show *Candid Camera,* which showed people "caught in the act of being themselves." Secretly videotaped by a hidden camera, ordinary individuals caught in various social situations provided the humorous, sometimes hilarious, material for the show. This is precisely what researchers in social psychology must do in most of their studies—catch people in the act of being themselves. For this reason deception has traditionally played a prominent part in their research. To accomplish this deception, the researcher often must use one or more **confederates**—people who pose as participants in a psychology experiment but who are actually assisting the experimenter. A **naive subject** is an actual participant who has agreed to participate but is not aware that deception is being used to conceal the real purpose of the experiment. Both confederates and naive subjects were used in the Milgram experiment, described at the beginning of this chapter, and you will continue to see why it is often necessary to conceal the purpose of an experiment as you read about other classic studies in social psychology.

SOCIAL PERCEPTION

Are you often surprised by the behavior of other people—the things they say or do? Are you curious about their motives, expectations, or intentions? Other people can be puzzling, but our ability to understand others is important because we live in a social world. The process we use to obtain critically important social information about others is known as *social perception* (Allison et al., 2000).

What first impression have you formed of the person shown here?

Impression Formation: Sizing Up the Other Person

When we meet people for the first time, we begin forming impressions about them right away, and, of course, they are busily forming impressions of us. Naturally we notice the obvious attributes first—gender, race, age, dress, and how physically attractive or unattractive someone appears (Shaw & Steers, 2001). Physical attractiveness, as shallow as it might seem, has a definite impact on first impressions. Beyond noticing physical appearance, we may wonder: What is her occupation? Is he married? Answers to such questions, combined with conscious or unconscious

primacy effect: The tendency for an overall impression of another to be influenced more by the first information that is received about that person than by information that comes later.

assessments of people's verbal and nonverbal behavior, all play their part in forming first impressions. Moods also play a part—when we are happy, our impressions of others are usually more positive than when we are unhappy. And recent research shows that a firm handshake still makes a powerful first impression (Chaplin et al., 2000). It conveys that a person is positive, confident, and outgoing, not shy or weak-willed. Even how frequently people blink their eyes has an impact on the impression they make. Those who blink frequently tend to be rated as more nervous and less intelligent (Omori & Miyata, 1996). First impressions are powerful and can color many of the later impressions we form about people.

Why are first impressions so important and enduring?

First Impressions: Put Your Best Foot Forward–First If we gave you a list of a certain individual's characteristics or traits and asked you to write your impressions of the person, would it matter which traits were listed first? Solomon Asch (1946) gave one group of participants the following list of traits: intelligent, industrious, impulsive, critical, stubborn, and envious. He then asked the participants to write their impression of the person. Asch gave another group the same list but in reverse order. Participants who responded to the list with the positive traits first gave more favorable evaluations than participants whose list began with the negative traits.

Why should first impressions be so important? A number of studies reveal that an overall impression or judgment of another person is influenced more by the first information received about the person than by information that comes later (Luchins, 1957). This phenomenon is called the **primacy effect.** It seems that we attend to initial information more carefully, and once an impression is formed, it provides the framework through which we interpret later information. Any information that is consistent with the first impression is likely to be accepted, thus strengthening the impression. Information that does not fit with the earlier information is more likely to be disregarded.

Remember, any time you list your personal traits or qualities, always list your most positive qualities first. It pays to put your best foot forward—first.

Expectancies: Seeing What You Expect to See Sometimes expectations about how other persons will act in a situation become a self-fulfilling prophecy and actually influence the way they do act. Expectations may be based on a person's gender, age, racial or ethnic group, social class, role or occupation, personality traits, past behavior, relationship to us, and so on. Once formed, our expectancies affect how we perceive the behavior of others—what we pay attention to and ignore. But expectations may also color our attitude and manner toward, and treatment of a person in such a way that we partly bring about the very behavior we expect (Jones, 1986; Miller & Turnbull, 1986).

Attribution: Explaining Behavior

What is the difference between a situational attribution and a dispositional attribution for a specific behavior?

Why do people do the things they do? To answer this question, we all make **attributions**—that is, we assign or attribute causes to explain the behavior of others and to explain our own behavior as well. People are particularly interested in the causes of behaviors when the behaviors are unexpected, when goals are not attained (Weiner, 1985), or when actions are not socially desirable (Jones & Davis, 1965).

Although we can actually observe others' behavior, we can usually only infer its cause or causes. In trying to determine why you or someone else behaved in a certain way, you might make a **situational attribution** (an external attribution) and attribute the behavior to some external cause or factor operating within the situation. After failing an exam, you might say, "The test was unfair" or "The professor didn't give us enough time." Or you might make a **dispositional attribution** (an internal attribution) and attribute the behavior to some internal cause such as a personal trait, motive, or attitude. You might attribute a poor grade to lack of ability or to a poor memory.

How do the kinds of attributions people tend to make about themselves differ from those they make about other people?

Attributional Biases: Different Attributions for Self and Others There are basic differences in the way people make attributions about their own behavior and that of others (Jones, 1976, 1990; Jones & Nisbett, 1971). We tend to use situational attributions to explain our own behavior, because we are aware of factors in the situation that influenced us to act as we did. Also, being aware of our past behavior, we know whether our present actions are typical or atypical.

In explaining the behavior of others, however, people have a consistent tendency to focus more on personal factors than on the factors operating within the situation (Gilbert & Malone, 1995; Leyens et al., 1996). Not knowing how a person has behaved in different situations in the past, we assume a consistency in the behavior. Thus we are likely to attribute the behavior to some personal quality. In the United States, the plight of the homeless and of people on welfare is often attributed to laziness, an internal attribution, rather than to factors in their situation that might explain their condition.

The tendency to attribute our own behavior primarily to situational factors and the behavior of others to internal or dispositional factors is known as the **actor–observer effect.** Members of both Catholic and Protestant activist groups in Northern Ireland are subject to the actor–observer effect. Each group attributes the violence of the other group to internal or dispositional characteristics (they are murderers, they have evil intentions, etc.). And each group attempts to justify its own violence by attributing it to external or situational causes (we were just protecting ourselves, we were only retaliating, etc.) (Hunter et al., 2000).

There is one striking inconsistency in the way we view our own behavior: the self-serving bias. We use the **self-serving bias** when we attribute our successes to internal or dispositional causes and blame our failures on external or situational causes (Baumgardner et al., 1986; Brown & Rogers, 1991). If we interview for a job and get it, it is probably because we have the right qualifications. If someone else gets the job, it is probably because he or she knew the right people. The self-serving bias allows us to take credit for our successes and shift the blame for our failures to the situation.

Roesch and Amirkhan (1997) analyzed statements by professional athletes quoted in newspaper articles for evidence of the self-serving bias. And, indeed, athletes did tend to credit their wins to internal factors (their own skills) and to attribute their losses to situational factors (bad luck, poor referees). The self-serving bias was more frequently used by beginning professional athletes than by veterans and by individual athletes (golfers, tennis players) than by members of teams.

attribution: An inference about the cause of one's own or another's behavior.

situational attribution: Attributing a behavior to some external cause or factor operating in the situation; an external attribution.

dispositional attribution: Attributing a behavior to some internal cause, such as a personal trait, motive, or attitude; an internal attribution.

actor–observer effect: The tendency to attribute one's own behavior primarily to situational factors and the behavior of others primarily to internal or dispositional factors.

self-serving bias: The tendency to attribute personal successes to dispositional causes and failures to situational causes.

Remember It!

1. Which of the following statements about first impressions is *false*?
   a. People usually pay closer attention to early information they receive about a person than to later information.
   b. Early information forms a framework through which other information is interpreted.
   c. First impressions often serve as self-fulfilling prophecies.
   d. The importance of first impressions is greatly overrated.
2. People tend to make ______________ attributions to explain their own behavior and ______________ attributions to explain the behavior of others.
   a. situational; situational
   b. situational; dispositional
   c. dispositional; situational
   d. dispositional; dispositional
3. The tendency of people to attribute their own behavior primarily to situational factors and the behavior of others primarily to internal causes is called the
   a. actor–observer effect.
   b. false consensus error.
   c. self-serving bias.
   d. external bias error.
4. Attributing Mike's poor grade to his lack of ability is a dispositional attribution. (true/false)

Answers: 1. d 2. b 3. a 4. true

ATTRACTION

Think for a moment about the people you consider to be your closest friends. What causes you to like or even love one person yet ignore or react negatively to someone else? What factors influence interpersonal attraction—the degree to which people are drawn to or like one another?

Factors Influencing Attraction: Magnets That Draw People Together

Some of the factors influencing attraction are within the situation and some are within the person.

Why is proximity an important factor in attraction?

Proximity: Closeness Counts One major factor influencing the choice of friends is physical **proximity,** or geographic closeness. If you live in an apartment complex, you are probably more friendly with people who live next door or only a few doors away. The same is true in a dormitory. What about the people you like best in your classes? Do they sit next to you or not more than a seat or two away?

Why is proximity so important? It is much less trouble to make friends or even fall in love with people who are close at hand. Physical proximity also increases the frequency of interaction, and mere exposure to people, objects, and circumstances usually increases our liking for them (Zajonc, 1968). The **mere-exposure effect** is the tendency to feel more positively toward stimuli with repeated exposure. People, food, songs, and styles become more acceptable the more we are exposed to them. Advertisers rely on the positive effects of repeated exposure to increase people's liking for products and even for political candidates.

There are exceptions to the mere-exposure effect, however. If your initial reaction to a person is highly negative, frequent exposure can make you feel even more negatively toward the person. In addition, those who value privacy may react less favorably when proximity results in repeated contacts with people.

Liking through Association: A Case of Classical Conditioning Our moods and emotions, whether positive or negative, can influence how much we are attracted to people we meet. And sometimes we may develop positive or negative feelings toward others simply because they are present when very good or very bad things happen to us. Through classical conditioning, other people can become associated with the pleasant or unpleasant event and the resulting good or bad feelings may rub off on them.

Reciprocal Liking: Liking Those Who Like You We tend to like the people who also like us—or who we *believe* like us. Curtis and Miller (1986) falsely led participants to believe that another person either liked or disliked them after an initial encounter. This false information became a self-fulfilling prophecy. When the participants met the person again, those who believed they were liked "self-disclosed more, disagreed less, expressed dissimilarity less, and had a more positive tone of voice and general attitude than subjects who believed they were disliked" (p. 284). These positive behaviors, in turn, actually caused the other person to view them positively. The moral of this story seems easy to grasp: If you want others to like you, like them first!

How important is physical attractiveness in attraction?

Attractiveness: Good Looks Attract Although people are quick to deny that mere physical appearance is the main factor that attracts them to someone initially, a substantial body of evidence indicates that it is. People of all ages have a strong tendency to prefer physically attractive people (Langlois et al., 2000). Even 6-month-old infants, when given the chance to look at a photograph of an attractive or an unattractive woman, man, or infant, will spend more time looking at the attractive face. More than 2,000 years ago Aristotle said, "Beauty is a greater recommendation than any letter of introduction." Apparently, it still is.

What constitutes physical beauty? Researchers Langlois and Roggman (1990) reported that physical beauty consists not of rare physical qualities but of facial features that are approximately the mathematical average of the features in a given general population. And the more faces the researchers averaged, the more attractive the computer-generated composite representing the average face became. But Perrett and others (1994) found that simply averaging facial features can only partially account for facial beauty. These researchers generated two composite images, one of 60 White female faces and another of the most attractive 15 of the 60 faces. Then, by exaggerating the differences between the two composite images, they derived the most attractive image, with larger eyes, higher cheekbones, and a thinner jaw. Averaging faces tends to make them more symmetrical. And symmetrical faces and bodies, are seen as more attractive and sexually appealing (Singh, 1995b; Thornhill & Gangestad, 1994).

The halo effect—the attribution of other favorable qualities to those who are attractive—helps explain why physical attractiveness is so important.

Do males and females across different cultures have similar ideas about the physical attractiveness of members of the opposite sex? Yes, they do, report Langlois and others (2000), based on the results of 11 meta-analyses. When native Asian, Hispanic, and White American male students rated photographs of Asian, Hispanic, Black, and White females on attractiveness, Cunningham and others (1995) reported a very high mean correlation (.93) among the groups in attractiveness ratings. When Black and White American men rated photos of Black women, their agreement on facial features was also very high—a correlation of .94. But the Black and White men differed in their ratings of the women's attractiveness from the neck down; Black men were more attracted than White men to women with heavier figures.

Feingold (1992) reported a most intriguing finding. He discovered a positive correlation between a person's *self-rated* physical attractiveness and many attributes—self-esteem, popularity with the opposite sex, social comfort, extroversion, mental health, and sexual experience. The moral of this story seems to be that if you believe you are physically attractive, others will also perceive you as attractive.

Is a person's sense of happiness (subjective well-being) related to physical attractiveness? Diener and others (1995) found that people are able to reach comparable levels of subjective well-being whether they are attractive or unattractive. But those already high in subjective well-being *think* they are more attractive.

Other than "believing" you are physically attractive, what else can you do to increase your attractiveness to others? Try smiling more. A study by Reis and others (1990) revealed that smiling increases the perceived attractiveness of others and makes them appear more sincere, sociable, and competent.

Attractiveness and the Halo Effect Why is physical attractiveness so important? When people have one trait or quality that we either admire or dislike very much, we often assume that they also have other admirable or negative traits—a phenomenon known as the **halo effect** (Nisbett & Wilson, 1977). Dion and others (1972) found that people generally attribute other favorable qualities to those who are attractive. Attractive people are seen as more exciting, personable, interesting, and socially desirable than unattractive people.

Eagly and others (1991) analyzed 76 studies of the physical attractiveness stereotype. They found that physical attractiveness has its greatest impact on judgments of popularity and sociability and less impact on judgments of adjustment and intellectual competence. They did find one negative, however. Attractive people are perceived as more vain and less modest than less attractive people.

Job interviewers are more likely to recommend highly attractive people (Dipboye et al., 1975), and attractive people have their written work evaluated more favorably (Landy & Sigall, 1974). A meta-analysis by Vicki Ritts and others (1992) "indicated that physically attractive students are usually judged more favorably by

proximity: Geographic closeness; a major factor in attraction.

mere-exposure effect: The tendency of people to develop a more positive evaluation of some person, object, or other stimulus with repeated exposure to it.

halo effect: The tendency to infer generally positive or negative traits in a person as a result of observing one major positive or negative trait.

teachers on a number of dimensions, including intelligence, academic potential, grades, and various social skills" (p. 413). Even the evaluation of the attractiveness of a person's voice is affected by the person's physical appearance (Zuckerman et al., 1991).

Being attractive is an advantage to children and adults, to males and females; but according to some studies, women's looks contribute more to how they are judged on other personal qualities than do men's looks (Feingold, 1990). Physical attractiveness seems to have its greatest impact in the context of romantic attraction, particularly in initial encounters (Hatfield & Sprecher, 1986). Attractiveness is even an advantage for infants. According to Langlois and others (1995), mothers of attractive infants are more playful and affectionate with them than are mothers of less attractive infants. Mothers with less attractive infants have more negative attitudes toward them than do mothers with attractive infants.

Does this mean that unattractive people don't have a chance? Fortunately not. Eagly and her colleagues (1991) suggest that the impact of physical attractiveness is strongest in the perception of strangers. But once we get to know people, other qualities assume more importance. In fact, as we come to like people, they begin to look more attractive to us, while people with undesirable personal qualities begin to look less attractive.

Are people, as a rule, more attracted to those who are opposite or to those who are similar to them?

Similarity: A Strong Basis of Attraction To sum up research on attraction, the saying "Birds of a feather flock together" is more accurate than "Opposites attract." Beginning in elementary school and continuing through life, people are more likely to pick friends of the same age, gender, race, and socioeconomic class. Choosing friends who are similar to us could be related to proximity—the fact that we tend to come into contact with people who are similar to us in a variety of ways.

Liking people who have similar attitudes begins early in childhood and continues throughout life in both sexes (Griffitt et al., 1972). We are likely to choose friends and lovers who have similar views on most things that are important to us. Similar interests and attitudes toward leisure-time activities make it more likely that time spent together is rewarding. Not only is similarity in attitudes an important ingredient in attraction (Newcomb, 1956), but people often have negative feelings toward others whose attitudes differ from their own (Byrne et al., 1986; Smeaton et al., 1989). People who share our attitudes validate our judgments; those who disagree with us suggest the possibility that we are wrong and arouse negative feelings in us. It is similarities, then, not differences, that usually stimulate liking and loving (Alicke & Largo, 1995).

Romantic Attraction

The Matching Hypothesis: Peas in a Pod Can you imagine reading this ad in the personals column of your newspaper?

> Moderately attractive, unskilled, unemployed, 50-year-old divorced man with 7 children seeks beautiful, wealthy, exciting woman between the ages of 20 and 30 for companionship, romance, and possible marriage. No smokers or drinkers please.

Even though most of us may be attracted to handsome or beautiful people, the **matching hypothesis** suggests that we are likely to end up with someone similar to ourselves in attractiveness and other assets (Berscheid et al., 1971; Feingold, 1988; Walster & Walster, 1969). Furthermore, couples mismatched in attractiveness are more likely to end the relationship (Cash & Janda, 1984).

matching hypothesis: The notion that people tend to have spouses, lovers, or friends who are approximately equivalent in social assets such as physical attractiveness.

It has been suggested that we estimate our social assets and realistically expect to attract someone with approximately equal assets. In terms of physical attractiveness, some people might consider a movie star or supermodel to be the ideal man or woman, but they do not seriously consider the ideal to be a realistic, attainable possibility. Fear of rejection keeps many people from pursuing those who are much more attractive than they are. But instead of marrying an extremely handsome man, a very beautiful woman may sacrifice physical attractiveness for money and social status. Extremely handsome men have been known to make similar "sacrifices."

What about same-sex friendships? The matching hypothesis is generally applicable to such friendships (Cash & Derlega, 1978), although it is more true of males than of females (Feingold, 1988). A person's perceived attractiveness seems to be affected in part by the attractiveness of his or her friends (Geiselman et al., 1984).

Mate Selection: The Mating Game

Robert Winch (1958) proposes that men and women tend to choose mates with needs and personalities that are complementary rather than similar to their own. Winch sees complementary needs not necessarily as opposite, but as needs that supply what the partner lacks. A talkative person may seek a quiet mate who prefers to listen. There is some support for this view (Dryer & Horowitz, 1997).

The weight of research, however, indicates that similarity in needs is mainly what attracts (Buss, 1984; Phillips et al., 1988). Similarity in personality and in "physical characteristics, cognitive abilities, age, education, religion, ethnic background, attitudes and opinions, and socioeconomic status" is related to marital choice (O'Leary & Smith, 1991, p. 196). And similarity in needs and in personality appears to be related to marital success as well as to marital choice (O'Leary & Smith, 1991). Similarities wear well.

If you were to select a marriage partner, what qualities would attract you? Complete the *Try It!* to evaluate your own preferences.

Try It!

In your choice of a mate, which qualities are most and least important to you? Rank these 18 qualities of a potential mate from most important (1) to least important (18) to you.

___ Ambition and industriousness

___ Chastity (no previous sexual intercourse)

___ Desire for home and children

___ Education and intelligence

___ Emotional stability and maturity

___ Favorable social status or rating

___ Good cooking and housekeeping skills

___ Similar political background

___ Similar religious background

___ Good health

___ Good looks

___ Similar education

___ Pleasing disposition

___ Refinement/neatness

___ Sociability

___ Good financial prospects

___ Dependable character

___ Mutual attraction/love

How do your selections in the *Try It!* compare with those of men and women from 33 countries and 5 major islands around the world? Generally men and women across cultures rate these four qualities as most important in mate selection: (1) mutual attraction/love, (2) dependable character, (3) emotional stability and maturity, and (4) pleasing disposition (Buss et al., 1990). Aside from these first four choices, however, women and men differ somewhat in the attributes they prefer. According to Buss (1994), "Men prefer to mate with beautiful young women, whereas women prefer to mate with men who have resources and social status" (p. 239). These preferences, he claims, have been adaptive in human evolutionary history. To a male, beauty and youth suggest health and fertility—the best opportunity to send his genes into the next generation. To a female, resources and social status provide security for her and her children (Buss, 2000b). Thus, the clearest research on attraction and especially mate selection has come from research by evolutionary psychologists (Buss, 1999, 2000b). For further discussion of their work, see Chapters 11 and 12.

Remember It!

1. Match each term with a description at the left.

____ (1) Brian sees Susan at the library often and begins to like her.

____ (2) Liane assumes that because Boyd is handsome, he must be popular and sociable.

____ (3) Alan and Carol are going together and are both very attractive.

a. matching hypothesis

b. halo effect

c. mere-exposure effect

2. Physical attractiveness is a very important factor in initial attraction. (true/false)

3. People are usually drawn to those who are more opposite than similar to themselves. (true/false)

Answers: 1. (1) c (2) b (3) a 2. true 3. false

SOCIAL INFLUENCE

Conformity: Going Along with the Group

To conform or not to conform—that is not the question for most of us. Rather, the question is, to *what* will we conform? **Conformity** is changing or adopting a behavior or an attitude in order to be consistent with the social norms of a group or the expectations of other people. **Social norms** are the standards of behavior and the attitudes that are expected of members of the group. Some conformity is necessary if we are to have a society at all. We cannot drive on any side of the street we please, park any place we want, or drive as fast as we choose when in a hurry.

Because we need other people, we must conform to their expectations, to some extent, in order to have their esteem, their love, or even their company. It is easy to see why people conform to social norms and standards of groups that are important to them, such as their family, peer group, social group, or team. But to an amazing degree, people also conform to the majority opinion, even when they are among a group of strangers.

What did Asch find in his famous experiment on conformity?

conformity: Changing or adopting an attitude or behavior to be consistent with the social norms of a group or the expectations of other people.

social norms: The attitudes and standards of behavior expected of members of a particular group.

Asch's Experiment: The Classic on Conformity The best-known experiment on conformity was conducted by Solomon Asch (1951, 1955), who designed the simple test shown in Figure 17.1. Look at the standard line, and then pick the line—1, 2, or 3—that is the same length. Did you pick line 2? Can you imagine any circumstances in which a person might tell the experimenter that either line 1 or line 3 matched the standard line? This is exactly what happened in Asch's classic experiment, even with tests so simple that participants who were not being influenced by others could pick the correct line over 99% of the time.

Eight male participants were seated around a large table and were asked, one by one, to tell the experimenter which of the three lines matched the standard line as in Figure 17.1. But only one of the eight was an actual participant; the others were confederates assisting the experimenter. There were 18 trials—18 different lines to be matched. During 12 of these trials, the confederates all gave the same wrong answer, which of course puzzled the naive participant. Would that participant con-

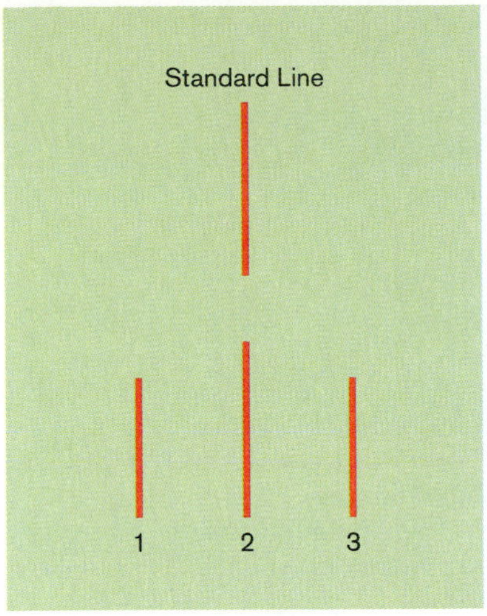

Figure 17.1

Asch's Classic Study of Conformity

If you were one of eight participants in the Asch experiment who were asked to pick the line (1, 2, or 3) that matched the standard line shown above them, which line would you choose? If the other participants all chose line 3, would you conform and answer line 3? (Based on Asch, 1955.)

tinue to believe his eyes and select the correct line, or would he feel pressure to conform to the group selections and give the wrong answer himself?

Asch found that 5% of the subjects conformed to the incorrect, unanimous majority *all* of the time, 70% conformed *some* of the time, but 25% remained completely independent and were *never* swayed by the group.

Asch wondered how group size would influence conformity. Varying the experiment with groups of 2, 3, 4, 8, and 10–15, he found that the tendency to "go along" with the majority opinion was in full force even when there was a unanimous majority of only 3 confederates. Surprisingly, unanimous majorities of 15 produced no higher conformity rate than did those of 3. Asch also discovered that if just one other person voices a dissenting opinion, the tendency to conform is not as strong. When just one confederate in the group disagreed with the incorrect majority, the naive subjects' errors dropped drastically, from 32% to 10.4%.

In this scene from Asch's experiment on conformity, all but one of the "subjects" were really confederates of the experimenter. They deliberately chose the wrong line to try to influence the naive subject (second from right) to go along with the majority.

Other research on conformity reveals that people of low status are more likely to conform than those of high status (Eagly, 1987); but, contrary to the conventional wisdom, women are no more likely to conform than men (Eagly & Carli, 1981). And conformity is greater if the sources of influence are perceived as belonging to one's own group (Abrams et al., 1990).

Even so, those who hold minority opinions on an issue have more influence in changing a majority view if they present a well-organized, clearly stated argument and if they are especially consistent in advocating their views (Wood et al., 1994).

Obedience: Following Orders

Some obedience is necessary if civilized society is to function, but unquestioned obedience can cause humans to commit unbelievably horrible acts. One of the darkest chapters in human history was due to the obedience of officials in Nazi Germany in carrying out Adolph Hitler's orders to exterminate Jews and other "undesirables." The civilized world was stunned and sickened by the revelations of the Nazi death camps, and nearly everyone wondered what type of person could be capable of committing such atrocities.

What did Milgram find in his classic study of obedience?

The Milgram Study: The Classic on Obedience Stanley Milgram, a young researcher at Yale University in 1961, wondered, too. He designed the study you read about at the beginning of this chapter to investigate how far ordinary citizens

Figure 17.2

The Results of Milgram's Classic Experiment on Obedience

In his classic study, Stanley Milgram showed that a large majority of participants would obey authority even if obedience caused great pain or was life-threatening to another. Milgram reported that 87.5% of the participants continued to administer what they thought were painful electric shocks of 300 volts to a victim who complained of a heart condition. Amazingly, 65% of the participants obeyed authority to the bitter end and continued to deliver what they thought were dangerous, severe shocks to the maximum of 450 volts. (Data from Milgram, 1963.)

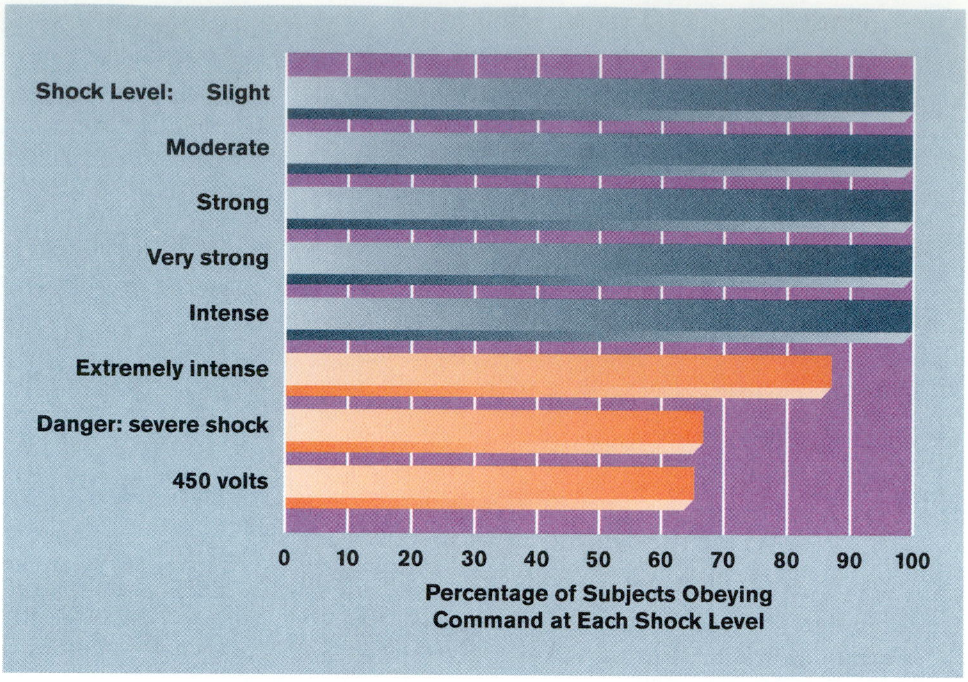

would go to obey orders, even if obedience meant the injury or possible death of a fellow human being.

How many of the 40 participants in the Milgram study do you think obeyed the experimenter to the end—450 volts? Not a single participant stopped before the 20th switch, supposedly 300 volts, when the learner began pounding the wall. Amazingly, 26 participants—65% of the sample—obeyed the experimenter to the bitter end, as shown in Figure 17.2. But this experiment took a terrible toll on the participants. They "were observed to sweat, tremble, stutter, bite their lips, groan, and dig their fingernails into their flesh. These were characteristic rather than exceptional responses to the experiment" (Milgram, 1963, p. 375).

The Milgram experiment dramatically revealed the extent of the human capacity to obey, even to the extreme of harming others. All of the participants in the study were thoroughly debriefed at the end of the experiment; they were assured that no electric shocks were actually given and that no harm had come to anyone. None of the participants felt they were harmed by the experience, and some said they were pleased to have participated. However, a study like Milgram's could not be performed today because it would violate the American Psychological Association's code of conduct governing ethics in research.

Variations of the Milgram Study Would the same results have occurred if the experiment had not been conducted at a famous university like Yale? The same experiment was carried out in a three-room office suite in a run-down building identified by a sign, "Research Associates of Bridgeport." Even there, 48% of the participants administered the maximum shock compared to 65% in the Yale setting (Meyer, 1972).

Milgram (1965) conducted a variation of the original experiment in which each trial involved three teachers, two of whom were confederates and the other, a naive participant. One confederate was instructed to refuse to continue after 150 volts, and the other confederate after 210 volts. In this situation 36 out of 40 naive participants (90%) defied the experimenter before the maximum shock could be given, compared with only 14 participants in the original experiment (Milgram, 1965). In Milgram's experiment, as in Asch's conformity study, the presence of another person who refused to go along gave many of the participants the courage to defy the authority.

Compliance: Giving In to Requests

There are many times when people act, not out of conformity or obedience, but in accordance with the wishes, suggestions, or direct requests of another person. This type of action is called **compliance.** Almost daily we are confronted with people who make requests of one sort or another. Do we comply with requests and yield to appeals? Often the answer is yes, and people use several techniques to gain our compliance.

What are three techniques used to gain compliance?

The Foot-in-the-Door Technique: Upping the Ante One strategy, the **foot-in-the-door technique,** is designed to gain a favorable response to a small request first. The intent is to make the person more likely to agree later to a larger request (the result desired from the beginning). In one study a researcher claiming to represent a consumers' group called a number of homes and asked whether the people answering the phone would mind answering a few questions about the soap products they used. Then a few days later, the same person called those who had agreed to the first request and asked if he could send five or six of his assistants to conduct an inventory of the products in their home. The researcher told the people that the inventory would take about 2 hours, and that the inventory team would have to search all drawers, cabinets, and closets in the house. Would you agree to such an imposition?

Nearly 53% of those asked preliminary questions agreed to the larger request, compared to 22% of a control group who were contacted only once with the request (Freedman & Fraser, 1966). A review of many studies on the foot-in-the-door approach suggests that it is highly effective (Beaman et al., 1983; DeJong, 1979). But, strangely enough, exactly the opposite approach works just as well.

The Door-in-the-Face Technique: An Unreasonable Request First With the **door-in-the-face technique,** a large, unreasonable request is made first. The expectation is that the person will refuse but will then be more likely to respond favorably to a smaller request later (the result desired from the beginning). In one of the best-known studies on the door-in-the-face technique, college students were approached on campus. They were asked to agree to serve without pay as counselors to juvenile delinquents for 2 hours each week for a minimum of 2 years. As you would imagine, not a single person agreed (Cialdini et al., 1975). Then the experimenters countered with a much smaller request, asking if the students would agree to take a group of juveniles on a 2-hour trip to the zoo. Half the students agreed, a fairly high compliance rate. The researchers used another group of college students as controls, asking them to respond only to the smaller request, the zoo trip. Only 17% agreed when the smaller request was presented alone.

The Low-Ball Technique: Not Telling the Whole Truth Up Front Another method used to gain compliance is the **low-ball technique.** A very attractive initial offer is made to get people to commit themselves to an action, and then the terms are made less favorable. College students were asked to enroll in an experimental course for which they would receive credit. But they were low-balled: Only after the students had agreed to participate were they informed that the class would meet at 7:00 A.M. But 55% of the low-balled group agreed to participate anyway. When another group of students were told up front that the class would meet at 7:00 A.M., only about 25% agreed to take the class (Cialdini et al., 1978).

Other Techniques to Gain Compliance Recent research suggests that the wording of requests is all important in gaining compliance (Guéguen & Pascual, 2000). Wording an appeal for a charitable donation to clearly convey that it is indeed a request and not a demand is important. Simply adding to the appeal a statement such as "but you are free to accept or refuse" serves to increase compliance and the average amount of contributions.

compliance: Acting in accordance with the wishes, the suggestions, or the direct request of another person.

foot-in-the-door technique: A strategy designed to secure a favorable response to a small request at first, with the aim of making the person more likely to agree later to a larger request.

door-in-the-face technique: A strategy in which someone makes a large, unreasonable request with the expectation that the person will refuse but will then be more likely to respond favorably to a smaller request at a later time.

low-ball technique: A strategy to gain compliance by making a very attractive initial offer to get a person to agree to an action and then making the terms less favorable.

Guilt, too, may motivate compliance in response to charitable appeals. An appeal ending with a statement indicating dire need, such as "Even a dollar will help," tends to elicit more compliance than the direct, negative appeal "Won't you help us?" (Guéguen & Pascual, 2000).

Have you seen infomercials on television that use the *"But that's not all" technique*? A salesperson presents a product at a certain price and then pauses while the viewer considers the offer. Then the salesperson announces, "But that's not all," and improves the deal by including an extra product and/or slashing the price if the viewer orders immediately. If the frequency of its appearance on television is any indication of its success, the "But that's not all" technique gains wide compliance.

Remember It!

1. Match the technique for gaining compliance with the appropriate example.

   ____ (1) Julie agrees to sign a letter supporting an increase in taxes for road construction. Later she agrees to make 100 phone calls urging people to vote for the measure.

   ____ (2) Bart refuses a phone request for a $24 donation to send four needy children to the circus but does agree to give $6.

   ____ (3) Hue agrees to babysit for her next-door neighbors and then is informed that their three nephews will be there, too.

   a. door-in-the-face technique
   b. low-ball technique
   c. foot-in-the-door technique

2. What percentage of the subjects in the original Asch study never conformed to the majority's unanimous incorrect response?

   a. 70% b. 33% c. 25% d. 5%

3. What percentage of the subjects in Milgram's original obedience experiment administered what they thought was the maximum 450-volt shock?

   a. 85% b. 65% c. 45% d. 25%

Answers: 1. (1) c (2) a (3) b 2. c 3. b

GROUP INFLUENCE

It is obvious that being in a group influences our behavior and our performance. We behave differently in a variety of ways when we are alone and when we are part of a group, small or large.

The Effects of the Group on Individual Performance

A person's performance on tasks can be enhanced or impaired by the mere presence of others, and the decisions the person reaches as part of a group can be quite different from those she or he would make if acting alone.

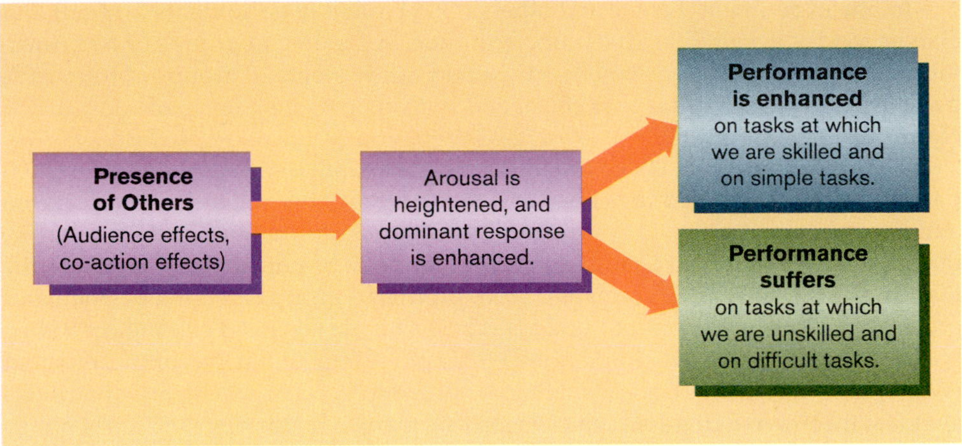

Figure 17.3

Social Facilitation: Performing in the Presence of Others

The presence of others (either as an audience or as co-actors engaged in the same task) may have opposite effects, either helping or hindering an individual's performance. Why? Robert Zajonc explained that (1) the presence of others heightens arousal, and (2) heightened arousal leads to better performance on tasks we are good at and worse performance on tasks that are difficult for us. (Based on Zajonc & Sales, 1966.)

Under what conditions does social facilitation have either a positive or a negative effect on performance?

Social Facilitation: Performing in the Presence of Others In certain cases individual performance can be either helped or hindered by the mere physical presence of others. The term **social facilitation** refers to any effect on performance, whether positive or negative, that can be attributed to the presence of others. Research on this phenomenon has focused on two types of effects: (1) **audience effects**—the impact of passive spectators on performance; and (2) **co-action effects**—the impact on performance caused by the presence of other people engaged in the same task.

In one of the first studies in social psychology, Norman Triplett (1898) looked at co-action effects. He had observed in official bicycle records that bicycle racers pedaled faster when they were pedaling against other racers than when they were racing against the clock. Was this pattern of performance peculiar to competitive bicycling? Or was it part of a more general phenomenon whereby people would work faster and harder in the presence of others than when performing alone? Triplett set up a study in which he told 40 children to wind fishing reels as quickly as possible under two conditions: (1) alone, or (2) in the presence of other children performing the same task. He found that the children worked faster when other reel turners were present than when they performed alone.

Later studies on social facilitation found just the opposite effect—that the presence of others, whether co-acting or just watching, could hurt or diminish individual performance. Robert Zajonc (1965; Zajonc & Sales, 1966) proposed an explanation for these seemingly contradictory effects. He reasoned that we become aroused by the presence of others and that arousal facilitates the dominant response—the one most natural to us. On simple tasks and on tasks at which we are skilled, the dominant response is to perform effectively. However, on tasks that are difficult or tasks we are just learning, the incorrect response (making a mistake) is dominant. This reasoning accounts for the repeated findings that, in the presence of others, performance improves on tasks that people do easily, but suffers on difficult tasks (Michaels et al., 1982). See Figure 17.3.

Other researchers have suggested that concern over the observers' evaluation is what most affects people's performance, particularly if they expect a negative evaluation (Sanna & Shotland, 1990).

What is social loafing, and what factors lessen or eliminate it?

Social Loafing: Not Pulling Your Weight What happens in cooperative tasks when two or more people are working together? Do they increase their effort or slack off? Researcher Bibb Latané used the term **social loafing** to refer to people's tendency to exert less effort when working with others on a common task than when they are working alone. Social loafing occurs in situations where no one person's contribution to the group can be identified and individuals are neither praised for a good performance nor blamed for a poor one (Williams et al., 1981).

social facilitation: Any positive or negative effect on performance due to the presence of others, either as an audience or as co-actors.

audience effects: The impact of passive spectators on performance.

co-action effects: The impact on performance of the presence of others engaged in the same task.

social loafing: The tendency to put forth less effort when working with others on a common task than when working alone.

In one experiment, Latané and others (1979) asked male students to shout and clap as loudly as possible, first alone and then in groups. In groups of two, individuals made only 71% of the noise they had made alone; in groups of four, each person put forth 51% of his solo effort; and with six persons each made only a 40% effort.

Harkins and Jackson (1985) found that social loafing disappeared when participants in a group were led to believe that each person's output could be monitored and his or her performance evaluated. Even the possibility that the group performance may be evaluated against some standard can be sufficient to eliminate the loafing effect (Harkins & Szymanski, 1989). When a group is relatively small and group evaluation is important, some members will even expend extra effort if they know that some of their co-workers are either unwilling, unreliable, or incompetent (Williams & Karau, 1991). Social loafing is not likely to occur when participants can evaluate their own individual contribution (Szymanski & Harkins, 1987), when they have a personal stake in the outcome, when they feel that the task is challenging (Brickner et al., 1986), or when they are working with close friends or teammates (Karau & Williams, 1993).

Does Culture Affect Social Loafing? Some 80 experimental studies have been conducted on social loafing in diverse cultures, including those of Taiwan, Japan, Thailand, India, China, and the United States. Social loafing on a variety of tasks was evident to some degree in all of the cultures studied. But it appears to be more common in individualistic Western cultures such as the United States (Karau & Williams, 1993).

The Effects of the Group on Decision Making

We have seen that group influences—the mere presence of others—can positively affect performance on tasks that are easy for us and negatively affect performance on tasks that are difficult for us. Also, we have learned that we may be subject to social loafing and exert less personal effort when acting with others on a group task than when acting alone. How do groups influence decision making? Are group decisions typically more moderate and well reasoned than individual decisions? It turns out that group attitudes going into a discussion can have profound and predictable effects on decision making.

How are the initial attitudes of group members likely to affect group decision making?

Group Polarization: When Group Decisions Become More Extreme It is commonly believed that groups tend to make more moderate, conservative decisions than individuals make, but some research in social psychology suggests otherwise.

Group discussion often causes members of a group to shift to a more extreme position in whatever direction the group was leaning initially—a phenomenon known as **group polarization** (Isenberg, 1986; Lamm, 1988). The group members, it seems, will decide to take a greater risk if they were leaning in a risky direction to begin with, but they will shift toward a more cautious position if they were, on the average, somewhat cautious at the beginning of the discussion (Myers & Lamm, 1975). Myers and Bishop (1970) found that as a result of group polarization, group discussions of racial issues can either increase or decrease prejudice.

group polarization: The tendency of members of a group, after group discussion, to shift toward a more extreme position in whatever direction they were leaning initially—either more risky or more cautious.

Why, then, aren't all group decisions either very risky or very cautious? The reason is that the members of a group do not always all lean in the same direction at the beginning of a discussion. When evidence both for and against a particular stand on a given topic is presented, group polarization is an infrequent consequence (Kuhn & Lao, 1996). Moreover, when subgroups within a larger group hold opposing views, compromise rather than polarization is the likely outcome (Vinokur & Burnstein, 1978).

Groupthink: When Group Cohesiveness Leads to Bad Decisions Group cohesiveness refers to the degree to which group members are attracted to the group and experience a feeling of oneness. **Groupthink** is the term social psychologist Irving Janis (1982) applies to the decisions often reached by overly cohesive groups. When a tightly knit group is more concerned with preserving group solidarity and uniformity than with objectively evaluating all possible alternatives in decision-making, individual members may hesitate to voice any dissent. The group may also discredit opposing views from outsiders and begin to believe it is incapable of making mistakes. Even plans bordering on madness can be hatched and adopted when groupthink prevails.

To guard against groupthink, Janis suggests that the group encourage an open discussion of alternative views and encourage the expression of any objections and doubts. He further recommends that outside experts sit in and challenge the views of the group. At least one group member should take the role of devil's advocate whenever a policy alternative is evaluated. Finally, to avoid groupthink in the workplace, managers should withhold their own opinions when problem-solving and decision-making strategies are being considered (Bazan, 1998).

So, to summarize, the mere presence of others can increase arousal and thereby affect individual performance, can induce social loafing on a group task, and can even influence the decisions we reach. But groups exert an even more powerful influence on individuals through their prescribed social roles.

Social Roles

The group is indispensable to human life. We are born into a family group, a culture, a racial and ethnic group, and usually a religious group. And as we grow and mature, there are many other groups that we may choose to join, such as social groups and professional groups. We all fulfill a number of social roles within various groups to which we belong.

Social roles are socially defined behaviors that are considered appropriate for individuals occupying certain positions within a given group. Roles are useful because they tell us beforehand how people are likely to act toward us in many situations, even people we have never met before. If you have ever been stopped for speeding by a police officer, you were at that moment unwillingly cast in the role of speeder, and you had few doubts about the role the officer would play. But both you and the police officer assume many different roles in life—family roles, social roles, work roles, and so on—and your behavior can differ dramatically as you shift from role to role.

Some of the social roles we take on may initially seem unnatural or phony, somewhat like pretending. But roles can shape our behavior, sometimes quickly and dramatically. Consider an experiment in which the participants' roles were either almost absolutely powerful (prison guard) or virtually powerless (prisoner). Philip Zimbardo (1972) simulated a prison experience in which college student volunteers were randomly assigned to be either guards or prisoners. The guards, wearing uniforms and carrying small clubs, strictly enforced harsh rules. The prisoners were stripped naked, searched, and deloused. Then they were given prison uniforms, assigned numbers, and locked away in small, bare cells. The guards quickly adopted their role, some even to the point of becoming heartless and sadistic. One guard remembered forcing prisoners to clean toilets with their bare hands. Prisoners began to behave like *real* prisoners, acting debased and subservient. The role playing became all too real—so much so that the experiment had to be ended in only six days. This study helps us to understand how, during some fraternity initiations, college students can assume roles that are reminiscent of those of Zimbardo's guards and prisoners.

groupthink: The tendency for members of a very cohesive group to feel such pressure to maintain group solidarity and to reach agreement on an issue that they fail to weigh available evidence adequately or to consider objections and alternatives.

social roles: Socially defined behaviors considered appropriate for individuals occupying certain positions within a group.

Remember It!

1. Which of the following statements regarding the effects of social facilitation (the presence of other people) is true?
   a. Performance improves on all tasks.
   b. Performance worsens on all tasks.
   c. Performance improves on easy tasks and worsens on difficult tasks.
   d. Performance improves on difficult tasks and worsens on easy tasks.
2. Social loafing is most likely to occur when
   a. individual output is monitored.
   b. individual output is evaluated.
   c. a task is challenging.
   d. individual output cannot be identified.
3. When group polarization occurs following group discussion, the group will decide to take a greater risk
   a. if members are initially leaning in a cautious direction.
   b. if members are initially leaning in a risky direction.
   c. if members are initially leaning in different directions.
   d. regardless of the initial position of the members.
4. What occurs when members of a very cohesive group are more concerned with preserving group solidarity than with evaluating all possible alternatives in making a decision?
   a. groupthink
   b. group polarization
   c. social facilitation
   d. social loafing

Answers: 1. c 2. d 3. b 4. a

ATTITUDES AND ATTITUDE CHANGE

Can you imagine someone who lacks any definite attitudes, who is neutral about everything—family, friends, school or job, even food and clothes? Of course not. We all have attitudes, some of them very strong. But what are attitudes?

Attitudes: Cognitive, Emotional, and Behavioral Patterns

What are the three components of an attitude?

Essentially, **attitudes** are relatively stable evaluations of persons, objects, situations, or issues along a continuum ranging from positive to negative (Petty et al., 1997). Most attitudes have three components: (1) a cognitive component—thoughts and beliefs about the attitudinal object; (2) an emotional component—feelings toward the attitudinal object; and (3) a behavioral component—predispositions concerning actions toward the object (Breckler, 1984). Figure 17.4 shows these three components of an attitude.

Attitudes enable us to appraise people, objects, and situations, and provide structure and consistency in the social environment (Fazio, 1989). Attitudes also help us process social information (Pratkanis, 1989), guide our behavior (Sanbonmatsu & Fazio, 1990), and influence our social judgments and decisions (Jamieson & Zanna, 1989).

How do people form attitudes? Some attitudes are acquired through firsthand experience with people, objects, situations, and issues. Others are acquired vicariously. When children hear parents, family, friends, and teachers express positive or negative attitudes toward certain issues or people, they may adopt the same attitudes as their own. The mass media, including advertising, influence people's attitudes and reap billions of dollars annually for their efforts. As you might expect, however, the attitudes that people form through their own direct experience are

attitude: A relatively stable evaluation of a person, object, situation, or issue.

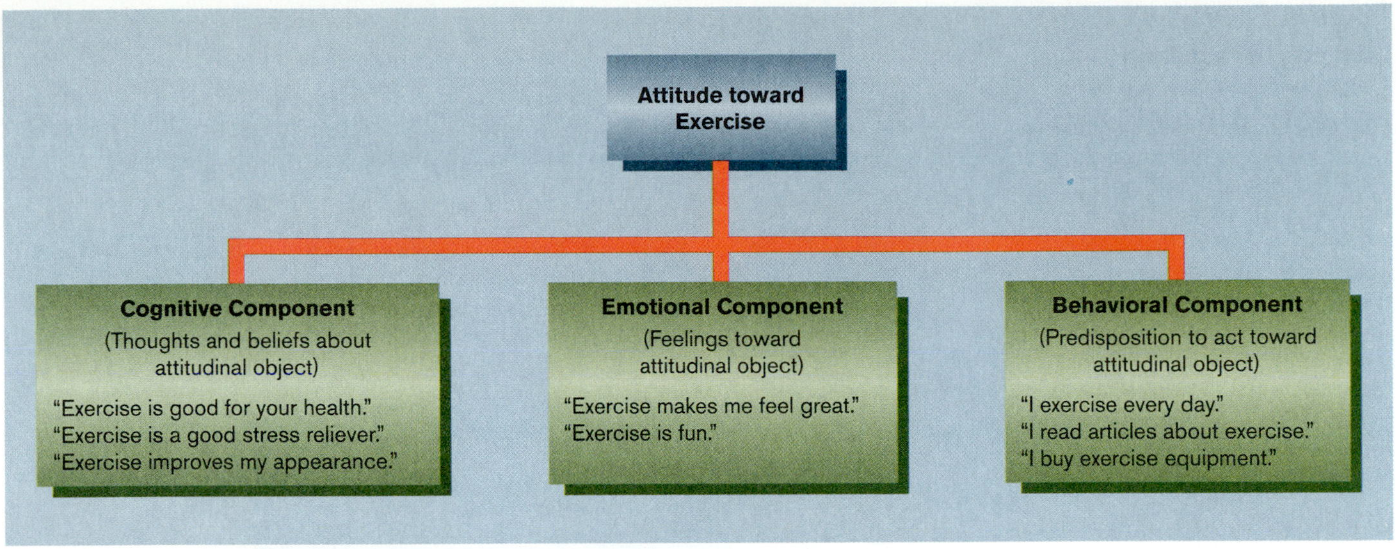

Figure 17.4

The Three Components of an Attitude

An attitude is a relatively stable evaluation of a person, object, situation, or issue. Most of our attitudes have (1) a cognitive component, (2) an emotional component, and (3) a behavioral component.

stronger than those they acquire vicariously, and they are also more resistant to change (Wu & Shaffer, 1987).

Some research indicates that attitudes, such as a distaste for snakes, may have a partly genetic basis (Lykken et al., 1993). Tesser (1993) found that the greater the degree to which particular attitudes could be attributed to genetic influence, the more resistant those attitudes were to conformity pressures. But the controversial claim for a genetic influence on attitudes contradicts more conventional findings that emphasize the roles of learning and experience in attitude formation (Petty et al., 1997).

It is widely thought that attitudes grow even stronger with time and are thus less susceptible to change as people grow older. But an analysis of six studies questions this notion (Visser & Krosnick, 1998). Apparently, attitude strength is greatest in middle adulthood, and attitudes are more susceptible to change in both early and late adulthood.

Some of our attitudes do change over time, but do they change easily, naturally, and completely? Or do remnants of our old attitudes linger below our level of awareness, only to resurface at unguarded moments? In other words, does a new attitude simply replace the old one? Some research suggests that when a new attitude overrides an old attitude, the old one may not be entirely discarded. In other words, we are left with a mixed attitude toward an object or issue (T. Wilson et al., 2000).

The Relationship between Attitudes and Behavior In the first half of the 20th century, the general consensus among social scientists was that attitudes govern behavior (Allport, 1935). But toward the end of the 1960s, one study after another failed to reveal a strong relationship between people's beliefs as reported on attitude measurement scales and their actual behavior. Attitudes seemed to predict observed behavior only about 10% of the time (Wicker, 1969).

Why aren't attitude measures better predictors of behavior? Attitude measures may often be too general to predict specific behaviors. People may express strong attitudes in favor of protecting the environment and conservation of resources, yet

Figure 17.5

Methods of Reducing Cognitive Dissonance

Cognitive dissonance can occur when people become aware of inconsistencies in their attitudes or between their attitudes and their behavior. People try to reduce dissonance by (1) changing their behavior, (2) changing their attitude, (3) explaining away the inconsistency, or (4) reducing its importance. Here are examples of how a smoker might use these methods to reduce the cognitive dissonance created by his or her habit.

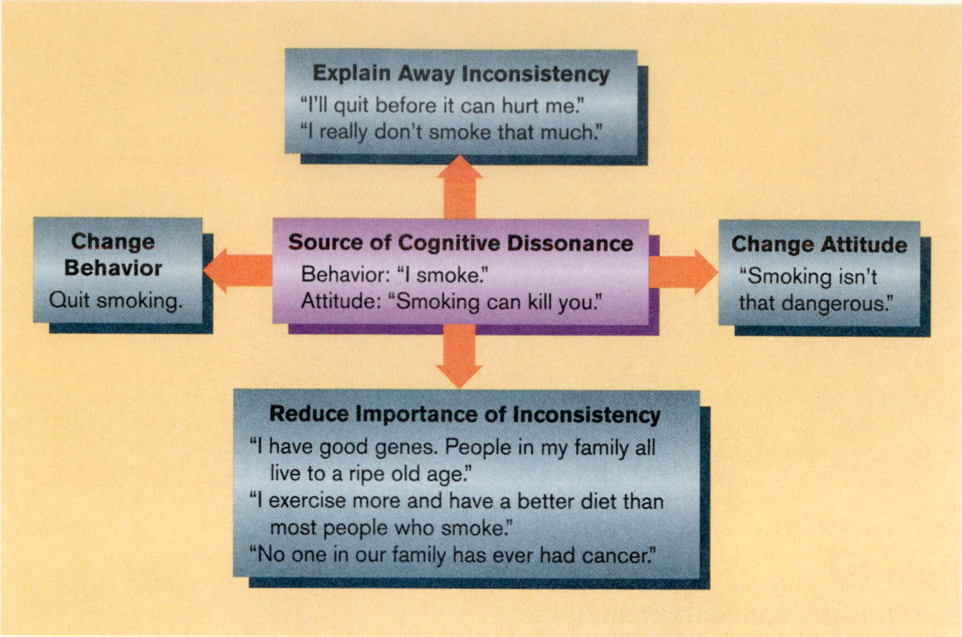

not take their aluminum cans to a recycling center or join carpools. But when attitude measures correspond very closely to specific behaviors of interest, they actually become good predictors of that behavior (Ajzen & Fishbein, 1977). Finally, attitudes are better predictors of behavior if they are strongly held, are readily accessible in memory (Bassili, 1995; Fazio & Williams, 1986; Kraus, 1995), and vitally affect the holder's interests (Sivacek & Crano, 1982). Attitudes toward a social category (politicians or media stars, for example) and attitude–behavior consistency are affected by the specific exemplars (members of that social category) that most readily come to mind (Sia et al., 1997).

What is cognitive dissonance, and how can it be resolved?

Cognitive Dissonance: The Mental Pain of Inconsistency If people discover that some of their attitudes are in conflict with others or that their attitudes are not consistent with their behavior, they are likely to experience an unpleasant state. Leon Festinger (1957) called this **cognitive dissonance.** People usually try to reduce the dissonance by changing the behavior or the attitude, or by somehow explaining away the inconsistency or reducing its importance (Aronson, 1976; Festinger, 1957). A change in attitudes does seem to reduce the discomfort caused by dissonance (Elliot & Devine, 1994).

Smoking is a perfect situation for cognitive dissonance. What are smokers to do? The healthiest, but perhaps not the easiest, way to reduce cognitive dissonance is to change the behavior—quit smoking. Another way is to change the attitude—to convince themselves that smoking is not as dangerous as it is said to be. Smokers can also tell themselves that they will stop smoking long before any permanent damage is done, or that medical science is advancing so rapidly that a cure for cancer or emphysema is just around the corner. Figure 17.5 illustrates the methods a smoker can use to reduce cognitive dissonance.

Researchers have found that if people voluntarily make a statement or take a position that is counter to what they believe, they will experience cognitive dissonance because of the inconsistency. To resolve this dissonance, they are likely to change their belief to make it more consistent with their behavior (Festinger & Carlsmith, 1959). Cognitive dissonance can also be reduced by trivializing or minimizing the dissonant cognitions instead of changing one's attitudes (Simon et al., 1995).

cognitive dissonance: The unpleasant state that can occur when people become aware of inconsistencies between their attitudes or between their attitudes and their behavior.

Justifying a Sacrifice Following Festinger's work, Aronson and Mills (1959) found broader applications for the cognitive dissonance theory. They reasoned that the more people have to sacrifice, give up, or suffer to become a member of an organization, say a fraternity or sorority, the more positive their attitudes are likely to become toward the group, in order to justify their sacrifice. Members of cults are often required to endure hardships and make great sacrifices, such as severing ties with their families and friends and turning over their property and possessions to the group. Such extreme sacrifice can then be justified only by a strong and radical defense of the cult, its goals, and its leaders.

Persuasion: Trying to Change Attitudes

What are the four elements of persuasion?

Persuasion is a deliberate attempt to influence the attitudes and/or the behavior of another person. Attempts at persuasion are pervasive parts of work experience, social experience, and even family life.

Researchers have identified four elements of persuasion: (1) the source of the communication (who is doing the persuading), (2) the audience (who is being persuaded), (3) the message (what is being said), and (4) the medium (the means by which the message is transmitted). The attitudes people hold are instrumental in their resistance to persuasion. And resistance is stronger if attitudes are infused with intense feeling (the emotional component) as well as being based on sufficient, accurate knowledge (the cognitive component) (Zuwerink & Devine, 1996).

What qualities make a source most persuasive?

The Source: Look Who's Talking Some factors that make the source (the communicator) more persuasive are credibility, attractiveness, and likability. Credibility refers to how believable a source is. A credible communicator is one who has expertise (knowledge of the topic at hand) and trustworthiness (truthfulness and integrity). The influence of a credible source is even greater if the audience knows the communicator's credentials beforehand. Moreover, people attach greater credibility to sources who have nothing to gain from persuading them or, better yet, who seem to be arguing against their own best interest. For example, arguments against pornography are more persuasive if they are made by a source known to be generally opposed to censorship.

Persuasion is a deliberate attempt to influence the attitudes and/or behavior of another person. What tactics do you use when trying to persuade others?

In matters that involve personal tastes and preferences rather than issues, attractive people and celebrities can be very persuasive. Movie and TV stars, athletes, and even unknown but attractive fashion models have long been used by advertisers to persuade consumers to buy certain products. Likable, down-to-earth, ordinary people who are perceived to be similar to the audience are sometimes even more effective persuaders than famous experts, attractive models, or movie stars. Political candidates attempt to appear more likable and more like the voters when they don hard hats and visit construction sites and coal mines, kiss babies, and pose with farmers. But researcher Elliot Aronson (1999) maintains that our own influence with ourselves—or *self-persuasion*—is especially powerful in affecting long-term changes in attitudes and behavior.

The Audience and the Message Persuaders must consider the nature of their audience before they attempt to use persuasion. In general, people with low intelligence are easier to persuade than those who are highly intelligent (Rhodes & Wood, 1992). Research evidence suggests that a one-sided message is usually most persuasive if the audience is not well informed on the issue, is not overly intelligent, or already agrees with the point of view. A two-sided message (where both sides of an issue are mentioned) works best when the audience is well informed on the issue, is fairly

persuasion: A deliberate attempt to influence the attitudes and/or behavior of another.

intelligent, or is initially opposed to the point of view. A two-sided appeal will usually sway more people than a one-sided appeal (Hovland et al., 1949; McGuire, 1985).

People tend to scrutinize arguments that are contrary to their existing beliefs more carefully and exert more effort refuting them; they are also more likely to judge such arguments as weaker than those that support their beliefs (Edwards & Smith, 1996).

A message can be well reasoned, logical, and unemotional ("just the facts"); a message can be strictly emotional ("scare the hell out of them"); or it can be a combination of the two. Which type of message works best? Arousing fear seems to be an effective method for persuading people to adopt healthier attitudes and behaviors. High-fear appeals have been found to be more effective than low-fear appeals in antismoking presentations, seat-belt safety campaigns, and appeals urging regular chest X rays. Appeals based on fear are most effective when the presentation outlines definite actions the audience can take to avoid the feared outcomes (Buller et al., 2000; Stephenson & Witte, 1998).

When using appeals based on fear, persuaders need to be certain exactly *what* the audience actually fears. Public service announcements against drinking and driving typically warn of the consequences of death or injury in their high-fear messages. Yet research reveals that for college students the most feared consequence of drinking and driving is being charged with driving under the influence (Gotthoffer, 1999).

Another important factor in persuasion is repetition. The more often a product or a point of view is presented, the more people will be persuaded to buy it or embrace it. Advertisers apparently believe in the mere-exposure effect, for they repeat their messages over and over (Bornstein, 1989). But messages are likely to be less persuasive if they include vivid elements (colorful language, striking examples) that hinder the reception of the content (Frey & Eagly, 1993).

Remember It!

1. Which of the following is *not* one of the three components of an attitude?
   a. cognitive component
   b. emotional component
   c. physiological component
   d. behavioral component
2. All of the following are ways to reduce cognitive dissonance *except*
   a. changing an attitude.
   b. changing a behavior.
   c. explaining away the inconsistency.
   d. strengthening the attitude and behavior.
3. People who have made a great sacrifice to join a group usually decrease their liking for the group. (true/false)
4. Credibility relates most directly to the communicator's
   a. attractiveness.
   b. expertise and trustworthiness.
   c. likability.
   d. personality.
5. With a well-informed audience, two-sided messages are more persuasive than one-sided messages. (true/false)
6. High-fear appeals are more effective than low-fear appeals if they provide definite actions that people can take to avoid dreaded outcomes. (true/false)

Answers: 1. c 2. d 3. false 4. b 5. true 6. true

PREJUDICE AND DISCRIMINATION

Increasing cultural diversity is a fact of life in the United States. Can we learn to live and work peacefully with our fellow Americans, no matter what racial, ethnic, cultural, or other differences exist among us? The answer is a conditional yes—if we can learn how to combat prejudice and discrimination.

The Roots of Prejudice and Discrimination

What is the difference between prejudice and discrimination?

Prejudice consists of attitudes (usually negative) toward others based on their gender, religion, race, or membership in a particular group. Prejudice involves beliefs and emotions (not actions) that can escalate into hatred. **Discrimination** consists of behavior—actions (usually negative) toward members of a group. Many Americans have experienced prejudice and discrimination—minority racial groups (racism), women (sexism), the elderly (ageism), the handicapped, homosexuals, religious groups, and others. What are the roots of prejudice and discrimination?

The Realistic Conflict Theory: When Competition Leads to Prejudice One of the oldest explanations offered for the genesis of prejudice is competition among various social groups who must struggle against each other for scarce resources—good jobs, homes, schools, and so on. Commonly called the **realistic conflict theory,** this view suggests that as competition increases, so do prejudice, discrimination, and hatred among the competing groups. Some historical evidence supports the realistic conflict theory. Prejudice and hatred were high between the American settlers and the Native Americans who struggled over land during the westward expansion. The multitudes of Irish and German immigrants who came to the United States in the 1830s and 1840s felt the sting of prejudice and hatred from other Americans who were facing economic scarcity. As many nations around the world experience hard economic times in the new millennium, will prejudice and discrimination increase? The realistic conflict theory predicts that they will. But prejudice and discrimination are attitudes and actions too complex to be explained solely by economic conflict and competition. What are some other causes?

What is meant by the terms *in-group* and *out-group*?

Us versus Them: Dividing the World into In-Groups and Out-Groups Prejudice can also spring from the distinct social categories into which people divide the world—*us versus them* (Turner et al., 1987). An **in-group** is a social group with a strong feeling of togetherness and from which others are excluded. Members of college fraternities and sororities often exhibit strong in-group feelings. The **out-group** consists of individuals or groups specifically identified by the in-group as not belonging. Us-versus-them thinking can lead to excessive competition, hostility, prejudice, discrimination, and even war. Prejudiced individuals who most strongly identify with their racial in-group are most reluctant to admit others to the group if there is the slightest doubt about their racial purity (Blasovich et al., 1997).

A famous study by Sherif and Sherif (1967) shows how in-group/out-group conflict can escalate into prejudice and hostility rather quickly, even between groups that are very much alike. The researchers set up their experiment at the Robber's Cave summer camp. Their subjects were 22 bright, well-adjusted, 11- and 12-year-old white middle-class boys from Oklahoma City. Divided into two groups and housed in separate cabins, the boys were kept apart for all their daily activities and games. During the first week, in-group solidarity, friendship, and cooperation developed within each of the groups. One group called itself "the Rattlers"; the other group took the name "Eagles."

During the second week of the study, competitive events were purposely scheduled so that the goals of one group could be achieved "only at the expense of the other group" (Sherif, 1958, p. 353). The groups were happy to battle each other, and

prejudice: Negative attitudes toward others based on their gender, religion, race, or membership in a particular group.

discrimination: Behavior, usually negative, directed toward others based on their gender, religion, race, or membership in a particular group.

realistic conflict theory: The notion that prejudices arise when social groups must compete for scarce resources and opportunities.

in-group: A social group with a strong sense of togetherness and from which others are excluded.

out-group: A social group specifically identified by the in-group as not belonging.

Can you perceive differences among the young girls shown here? Research shows that people typically perceive more variability among members of groups to which they belong and more similarity among members of groups with which they are unfamiliar.

intergroup conflict quickly emerged. Name-calling began, fights broke out, and accusations were hurled back and forth. During the third week of the experiment, the researchers tried to put an end to the hostility and to turn rivalry into cooperation. They simply brought the groups together for pleasant activities such as eating meals and watching movies. "But far from reducing conflict, these situations only served as opportunities for the rival groups to berate and attack each other. . . . They threw paper, food and vile names at each other at the tables" (Sherif, 1956, pp. 57–58).

Finally, the last stage of the experiment was set in motion. The experimenters manufactured a series of crises that could be solved only if all the boys combined their efforts and resources and cooperated. The water supply, sabotaged by the experimenters, could be restored only if all the boys worked together. After a week of several activities requiring cooperation, cut-throat competition gave way to cooperative exchanges. Friendships developed between groups, and before the end of the experiment, peace was declared. Working together toward shared goals had turned hostility into friendship.

How does prejudice develop, according to the social learning theory?

The Social Learning Theory: Acquiring Prejudice through Modeling and Reinforcement According to the social learning theory, people learn attitudes of prejudice and hatred the same way they learn other attitudes. If children hear their parents, teachers, peers, and others openly express prejudices toward different racial, ethnic, or cultural groups, they may be quick to learn such attitudes. And if parents, peers, and others reward children with smiles and approval for parroting their own prejudices (operant conditioning), children may learn these prejudices even more quickly.

Phillips and Ziller (1997) suggest that people learn to be nonprejudiced. These researchers conceptualize *nonprejudice* as a set of attitudes about interpersonal relations that lead people to selectively pay attention to and emphasize the similarities between themselves and others, rather than the differences.

What are stereotypes?

social cognition: Mental processes that people use to notice, interpret, understand, remember, and apply information about the social world and that enable them to simplify, categorize, and order that world.

stereotypes: Widely shared beliefs about the characteristic traits, attitudes, and behaviors of members of various social groups (racial, ethnic, religious), including the assumption that the members of such groups are usually all alike.

Social Cognition: Natural Thinking Processes Can Lead to Prejudice Emotion- and learning-based views help explain how prejudice develops. But a more recent view suggests that social cognition plays a role in giving birth to prejudice. **Social cognition** refers to the ways in which people typically process social information—the natural thinking processes used to notice, interpret, and remember information about the social world. The very processes we use to simplify, categorize, and order the social world are the same processes that distort our views of it. So prejudice may arise not only from heated negative emotions and hatred toward other social groups, but also from cooler cognitive processes that govern how we think and process social information (Kunda & Oleson, 1995).

One way people simplify, categorize, and order the world is by using stereotypes. **Stereotypes** are widely shared beliefs about the characteristics of members of various social groups (racial, ethnic, religious), which include the assumption that "they" are usually all alike. Macrae and colleagues (1994) suggest that people apply stereotypes in their interactions with others because doing so requires less mental energy than trying to understand others as individuals. Stereotyping allows people to make quick, automatic (thoughtless) judgments about others and apply their mental resources to other activities (Forgas & Fiedler, 1996). Research by Anderson and others (1990) showed that participants could process information more efficiently and answer questions faster when they were using stereotypes.

Do you use stereotypes in your thinking? To find out, complete the *Try It!*

Try It!

Can you list characteristics for each of the following groups?

African Americans	Hispanic Americans
White, male top-level executives	Jews
Native Americans	Arabs
Homosexuals	Italians
Members of fundamentalist religious groups	Germans

In the *Try It!* how many group characteristics could you list? If you listed traits thought to represent any group, you are probably demonstrating stereotypic thinking. We know that not *all* members of a group possess the same traits or characteristics, but we tend to use stereotypic thinking nonetheless.

Some research has revealed that social stereotypes involve more than overgeneralization about the traits or characteristics of members of certain groups (Judd et al., 1991). People tend to perceive more diversity, more variability, within the groups to which they belong (in-groups), but they see more similarity among members of other groups (out-groups) (Ostrom et al., 1993). Whites see more diversity among themselves but more sameness within groups of African Americans or Asians. This tendency in thinking can extend from race to gender to age or any other category of persons. Another study showed that young college students believed there was much more variability or diversity in 100 of their group than in a group of 100 elderly Americans, whom the students perceived to be much the same (Linville et al., 1989). What about the elderly subjects? They perceived even more variability within their own group and less variability among 100 college students. Age stereotypes can be even more pronounced and negative than gender stereotypes (Kite et al., 1991).

Some research indicates that prejudice and stereotyping (whether conscious or not) may be means of bolstering one's self-image by disparaging others (Fein & Spencer, 1997). Moreover, some minority group members may protect their self-esteem by attempting to minimize discrimination or by denying its significance (Ruggiero & Taylor, 1997).

Stereotypes can be positive or negative, but all are distortions of reality. And stereotypic thinking can result in discrimination.

Discrimination in the Workplace

Research conducted at Princeton University by Word and others (1974) indicates that stereotypic thinking can govern people's expectancies. And often what we expect is what we get, regardless of whether our expectancies are high or low.

One form of discrimination in the workplace that African Americans may face as job applicants is a tendency for White interviewers to use an interviewing style based on stereotypic thinking.

Participants in one study were White undergraduates who were to interview White and African American job applicants (actually confederates of the experimenters). The researchers secretly videotaped the interviews and studied the tapes to see if the student interviewers had treated the African American and White applicants differently. The researchers found substantial differences in the interviews based on the race of the applicants. The interviewers spent less time with the African American applicants, maintained a greater physical distance from them, and generally were less friendly and outgoing. During interviews with these applicants, the interviewers' speech deteriorated—they made more errors in grammar and pronunciation.

In a follow-up study the same researchers trained White confederates to copy the two different interview styles used in the first study. The confederates then used the different styles to interview a group of White job applicants. These interviews were videotaped as well, and later a panel of judges evaluated the tapes. The judges agreed that applicants who were subjected to the interview style for African Americans were more nervous and performed more poorly than applicants interviewed according to the "White" style. The experimenters concluded that as a result of the interview style they experienced, the African American confederates from the first study were not given the opportunity to demonstrate their skills and qualifications to the best of their ability. Thus they were subjected to a subtle form of discrimination in which their performance was hampered by the expectancies of the original interviewers.

Discrimination is also evident after the job interviews have been completed and people take their positions in the workplace. How do women and minorities fare in the world of work in the new millennium? Even though federal legislation forbids hiring, promoting, laying off, or awarding benefits to workers on the basis of sex, race, color, national origin, or religion, studies continue to show discrimination exists (Renzetti & Curran, 1992). A considerable body of research refutes the notion that gender and race deficiencies explain why so few women and minorities are in upper management (Morrison & Von Glinow, 1990). Nevertheless, the mere perception of deficiencies, if held by the dominant corporate leaders, is sufficient to produce bias and discrimination.

Morrison and Von Glinow (1990) claim that "discrimination occurs in part because of the belief by White men that women and people of color are less suited for management than White men" (p. 202). The dominant group's belief that customers, employees, and others are more comfortable dealing with or working for White male managers may lead to discrimination. In such cases these managers may be less willing to promote women and minorities to sensitive, responsible management positions.

Tokenism is a subtle form of discrimination in which people are hired or promoted primarily because they represent a specific group or category rather than strictly on the basis of their qualifications. Female and minority employees may be perceived by the White majority as "tokens," especially as they move up in the ranks of management. But "tokens" are interchangeable. If placed in a position solely to meet a company's affirmative action goals, one token is as good as another as long as he or she represents the right category. No matter how eminently qualified an employee may be, if the employee perceives that he or she is a token, the individual suffers and so does the organization.

Combating Prejudice and Discrimination

What are several strategies for reducing prejudice and discrimination?

Given that prejudice and discrimination may grow from many roots, are there effective ways to reduce them? Many experts believe there are. One way is through education. To the extent that prejudice is learned, it can also be unlearned. Sustained educational programs designed to increase teachers' and parents' awareness of the damage caused by prejudice and discrimination can be very effective (Aronson, 1990).

Direct Contact: Bringing Diverse Groups Together Can we reduce our prejudices and stereotypic thinking by increasing our contact and interaction with others from diverse groups? Yes, according to the **contact hypothesis.**

Increased contacts with members of groups that we view stereotypically can teach us that members of those groups are not all alike. But the contact hypothesis works to reduce prejudice *only* under certain conditions. In fact, if people from diverse groups are simply thrown together, prejudice and even hostility are likely to increase rather than decrease, as you learned from Sherif's Robber's Cave experiment. Sherif outlined the conditions under which intergroup contact reduces prejudice, and his findings have been confirmed and extended by others (Aronson, 1990; Finchilescu, 1988).

The contact hypothesis will work to reduce prejudice most effectively under the following conditions:

- Interacting groups should be approximately equal in social and economic status and in their ability on the tasks to be performed.
- The intergroup contact must be cooperative (not competitive) in nature, and work should be confined to shared goals.
- The contact should be informal, so that friendly interactions develop more easily and group members get to know each other individually.
- The contact situation should be one in which conditions favor group equality.
- The individuals involved should perceive each other as typical members of the groups to which they belong.

When these conditions are met, intergroup friendships can form and prejudice can be reduced. Fortunately, people tend to generalize reduced prejudice toward one group to other groups (Pettigrew, 1997). Moreover, feelings of empathy for a particular member of a stigmatized group, such as a young woman with AIDS or a homeless man, can improve feelings for the group as a whole (Batson et al., 1997).

Us versus Them: Extending the Boundaries of Narrowly Defined Social Groups As we have seen, people's tendency to separate themselves into social categories (in-groups and out-groups) creates an us-versus-them mentality. This mentality heightens prejudice, stereotypic thinking, and discrimination—our group (our college, our country, our race, our religion) is better than theirs. But the boundary lines between us and them are not eternally fixed. If such boundaries can be extended, prejudice and in-group/out-group conflict can be reduced. You saw in Sherif's study that the Rattlers and the Eagles became a larger "us" group when they were brought together to work cooperatively on shared goals.

If your college or university wins the state championship in a competitive event, then in-state rival colleges and universities will often join your "us" group as you represent the state in national competition. Many researchers have shown that working cooperatively, rather than in competition, reduces us-versus-them bias and prejudice (Gaertner et al., 1990; Wright et al., 1990).

Prejudice: Is It Increasing or Decreasing?

Few people would readily admit to being prejudiced. Gordon Allport (1954), a pioneer in research on prejudice, said, "Defeated intellectually, prejudice lingers

contact hypothesis: The notion that prejudice can be reduced through increased contact among members of different social groups.

emotionally" (p. 328). Even those who are sincerely intellectually opposed to prejudice may still harbor some prejudiced feelings (Devine, 1989).

Is there any evidence that prejudice is decreasing in U.S. society? Gallup polls reveal that Whites in the United States are becoming more racially tolerant than they were in decades past (Gallup & Hugick, 1990). When Whites were asked in 1990 whether they would move if African Americans were to move next door to them, 93% said no, compared with 65% 25 years earlier. Even if African Americans were to move into their neighborhood in great numbers, 68% of Whites still said they would not move.

School integration, which in the past created a storm of controversy, seems to be less of an issue for most Whites today. Only 10% of Gallup's White respondents said they would object to sending their children to an integrated school in which up to one-half of the children were African American. Also, the majority of African Americans polled (two-thirds) believed that their children have the same opportunity as White children to get a good education.

People still show marked differences of opinion about equality of job opportunities, availability of housing, and other areas of life in which race might be an issue. When asked whether the quality of life for African Americans has gotten better, stayed the same, or gotten worse over the last 10 years, 46% of African Americans and 62% of Whites believed conditions had improved. Twenty-five percent of both races believed the quality of life had stayed the same. But 23% of African Americans, compared to only 6% of Whites, believed the quality of life was worse now than it was 10 years ago.

We can make things better for all by examining our own attitudes and actions, and then by using what we have learned to combat our own prejudice and discrimination. Prejudice has no virtues. It immediately harms those who feel its sting and ultimately harms those who practice it.

Remember It!

1. Match the example on the left with the term on the right.

   ____ (1) José was promoted because the firm needed one Hispanic manager.

   ____ (2) Darlene thinks all Whites are racists.

   ____ (3) Betty's salary is $5,000 less than that of her male counterpart.

   ____ (4) Bill can't stand Jews.

   a. stereotypic thinking
   b. discrimination
   c. prejudice
   d. tokenism

2. Members of an in-group often like out-group members as individuals. (true/false)

3. The social learning theory suggests that prejudice develops and is maintained through

   a. competition and ambition.
   b. us-versus-them thinking.
   c. modeling and reinforcement.
   d. genetic inheritance.

4. Researchers have found that bringing diverse social groups together almost always decreases hostility and prejudice. (true/false)

Answers: 1. (1) d (2) a (3) b (4) c 2. false 3. c 4. false

PROSOCIAL BEHAVIOR: BEHAVIOR THAT BENEFITS OTHERS

bystander effect: The fact that as the number of bystanders at an emergency increases, the probability that the victim will receive help decreases, and help, if given, is likely to be delayed.

diffusion of responsibility: The feeling among bystanders at an emergency that the responsibility for helping is shared by the group, so each person feels less compelled to act than if he or she alone bore the total responsibility.

> Kitty Genovese was returning home alone late one night. But this was no ordinary night. Nearly 40 of her neighbors who lived in the apartment complex nearby watched as she was attacked and stabbed, but they did nothing. The attacker left. Kitty was still screaming, begging for help, and then . . . he returned. He dragged her around, stabbing her again while her neighbors watched. Some of them turned off their bedroom lights to see more clearly, pulled up chairs to the window, and watched. Someone yelled, "Leave the girl alone," and the attacker fled again. But even then, no one came to her aid. A third time the attacker returned, more stabbing and screaming, and they watched. Finally, Kitty Genovese stopped screaming. When he had finally killed her, the attacker fled for the last time. (Adapted from Rosenthal, 1964.)

This actual event might not seem so unusual today, but it was a rare occurrence back in the early 1960s. So rare, in fact, that people wondered how her neighbors could have been so callous and cold-hearted, to do nothing but watch as Kitty Genovese begged for help that never came. Social psychologists Bibb Latané and John Darley looked deeper for an explanation. Perhaps certain factors in the situation itself would help explain why so many people just stood or sat there.

The Bystander Effect: The More Bystanders, the Less Likely They Are to Help

What is the bystander effect, and what factors have been suggested to explain why it occurs?

If you were injured or ill and needed help, would you feel safer if one or two other people were near, or if a large crowd of onlookers were present? You may be surprised to learn of the **bystander effect:** As the number of bystanders at an emergency increases, the probability that the victim will receive help from them decreases, and the help, if given, is likely to be delayed.

Why should this be? Darley and Latané (1968a) set up a number of experiments to study helping behavior. In one study, participants were placed one at a time in a small room and told that they would be participating in a discussion group by means of an intercom system. It was explained that because personal problems were being discussed, a face-to-face group discussion might be inhibiting. Some participants were told that they would be communicating with only one other participant, some believed that two other participants would be involved, and some were told that five other people would participate. There really were *no* other participants in the study—only the prerecorded voices of confederates assisting the experimenter.

Shortly after the discussion began, the voice of one confederate was heard over the intercom calling for help, indicating that he was having an epileptic seizure. Of the participants who believed that they alone were hearing the victim, 85% went for help before the end of the seizure. When participants believed that one other person heard the seizure, 62% sought help. But when they believed that four other people were aware of the emergency, only 31% tried to get help before the end of the seizure. Figure 17.6 (on p. 638) shows how the number of bystanders affects both the number of people who try to help and the speed of response.

Latané and Darley suggest two possible explanations for the bystander effect—diffusion of responsibility and the influence of apparently calm bystanders.

Why do people often ignore someone who is unconscious on the sidewalk? Diffusion of responsibility is one possible explanation.

Diffusion of Responsibility: An Explanation for the Bystander Effect When bystanders are present in an emergency, they generally feel that the responsibility for helping is shared by the group, a phenomenon known as **diffusion of responsibility.** Consequently each person feels less compelled to act than if she or he were alone and felt the total responsibility. Kitty Genovese's neighbors were aware that

Figure 17.6
The Bystander Effect

In their intercom experiment, Darley and Latané showed that the more people a participant believed were present during an emergency, the longer it took the participant to respond and help a person in distress. (Data from Darley & Latané, 1968a.)

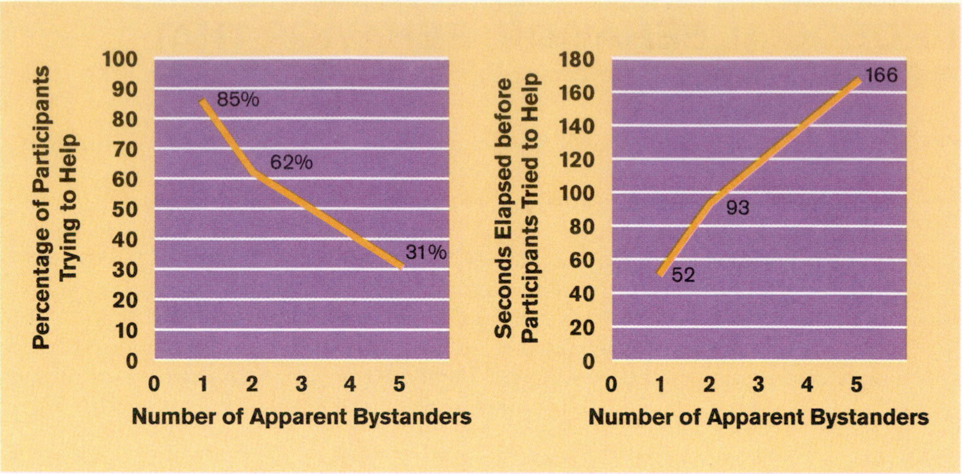

other people were watching because they saw lights go off in the other apartments. They did not feel that the total responsibility for action rested only on their shoulders, or they may have thought that "somebody else must be doing something" (Darley & Latané, 1968a).

The Influence of Apparently Calm Bystanders: When Faces Deceive Sometimes real emergencies occur in rather ambiguous situations. Bystanders may not be sure if an actual emergency exists. At the risk of appearing foolish, they often hesitate to react with alarm until they are sure that intervention is appropriate (Clark & Word, 1972). So the bystanders may stand there watching other calm-appearing bystanders and conclude that nothing is really wrong and no intervention is necessary (Darley & Latané, 1968b).

More than a few people have died while many potential helpers stood and watched passively because of the bystander effect. Picture an orthopedic surgeon's large waiting room in which eight patients are waiting to see the doctor. In one chair a middle-aged man sits slumped over, yet he does not appear to be sleeping. His position resembles that of a person who is unconscious. If you were a patient in such a setting, would you check on the man's condition or just continue sitting?

This was the actual scene one of the authors entered a few years ago as a patient. She sat down and immediately noticed the man slumped in his chair. She scanned the faces of the other waiting patients but saw no sign of alarm or even concern. Was there really no emergency, or was this a case of the bystander effect? Knowing that the reaction of onlookers is a poor indicator of the seriousness of a situation, she quickly summoned the doctor, who found that the man had suffered a heart attack. Fortunately, the doctor's office was attached to a large hospital complex, and almost immediately a hospital team appeared and rushed the victim to the emergency room.

People Who Help in Emergencies

There are many kinds of **prosocial behavior**—behavior that benefits others, such as helping, cooperation, and sympathy. Such impulses arise early in life. Researchers agree that young children respond sympathetically to companions in distress, usually before their second birthday (Hay, 1994; Kochanska, 1993).

The term **altruism** is usually reserved for behavior aimed at helping others that requires some self-sacrifice and is not performed for personal gain. What motivates us to help or not to help in an emergency? Batson and colleagues (1989) believe that we help out of *empathy*—the ability to take the perspective of others—to put oneself in their place. Some studies show that girls show more empathy than boys and older children show more than younger ones (Litvak-Miller et al., 1997).

prosocial behavior: Behavior that benefits others, such as helping, cooperation, and sympathy.

altruism: Behavior aimed at helping another, requiring some self-sacrifice and not designed for personal gain.

Cultures vary in their norms for helping others—that is, their social responsibility norms. According to Miller and others (1990), people in the United States tend to feel an obligation to help family, friends, and even strangers in life-threatening circumstances, but only family in moderately serious situations. In contrast, in India the social responsibility norm extends to strangers whose needs are only moderately serious or even minor.

In spite of the potentially high costs of helping, accounts of people who have risked their lives to help others are numerous. During World War II, thousands of Christians risked their lives to protect Jews from extermination in Nazi Germany. Are there common factors that might explain such uncommon risks in the service of others? A study of 406 of these rescuers revealed that they did not consider themselves heroes, and that different motives led to their altruistic behavior. Some rescuers were motivated by strong convictions about how human beings should be treated; others, by empathy for the particular person or persons they rescued (Fogelman & Wiener, 1985; Oliner & Oliner, 1988). Still others were acting based on norms of their family or social group that emphasized helping others.

In what conditions or circumstances might a person be more likely to receive help? People are more likely to receive help if they are physically attractive (Benson et al., 1976), if they are perceived by potential helpers as similar to them (Dovidio, 1984), and if they are not considered responsible for their plight (Schmidt & Weiner, 1988). Potential helpers are more likely to help if they have specialized training in first aid or police work, if they are not in a hurry, if they have been exposed to a helpful model (Bryan & Test, 1967), if they are in a positive mood (Carlson et al., 1988), and if the weather is good (Cunningham, 1979).

Oskar Schindler risked his life to save hundreds of Jews from the Nazis during the Holocaust in World War II. An exemplar of altruism, Schindler was the subject of the well-known movie Schindler's List.

Remember It!

1. The bystander effect is influenced by all of the following *except*
   a. the number of bystanders.
   b. the personalities of bystanders.
   c. whether the bystanders appear calm.
   d. whether the situation is ambiguous.
2. Altruism is one form of prosocial behavior. (true/false)
3. As the number of bystanders at an emergency increases, the probability that the victim will receive help decreases. (true/false)
4. In an ambiguous situation, a good way to determine if an emergency exists is to look at the reactions of other bystanders. (true/false)

Answers: 1. b 2. true 3. true 4. false

AGGRESSION: INTENTIONALLY HARMING OTHERS

Humanity has a long history of **aggression**—intentionally inflicting physical or psychological harm on others. Consider the tens of millions of people killed by other humans in wars and even in times of peace. In 1999, in the United States alone, there were reported about 17,000 homicides, 93,000 rapes, 447,000 robberies, and 974,000 assaults (Federal Bureau of Investigation, 1999). And the crime clock, timing acts of aggression, continues to tick into the 21st century (see Figure 17.7).

aggression: The intentional infliction of physical or psychological harm on another.

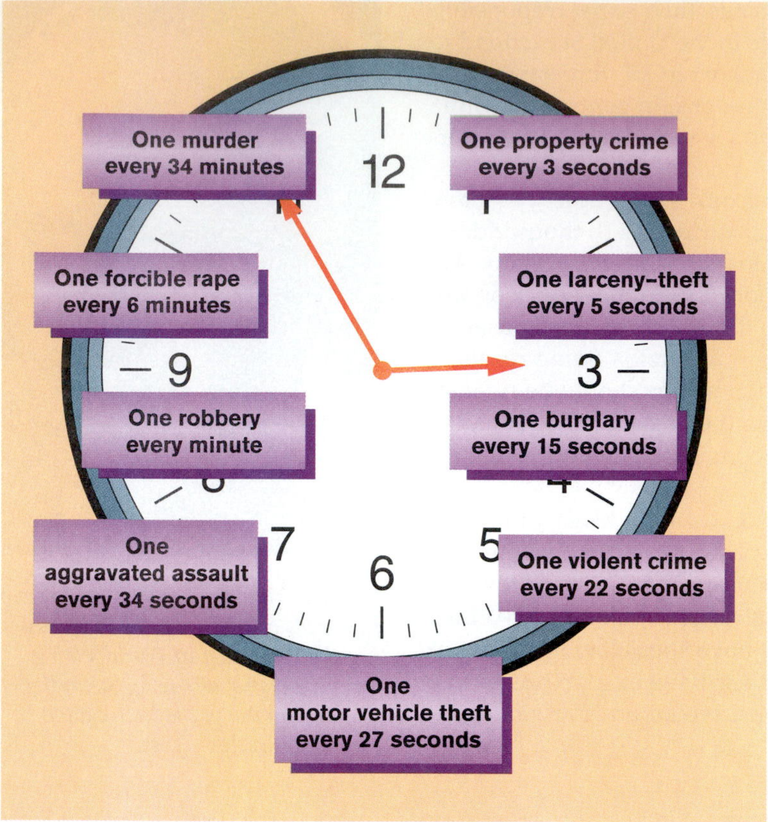

Figure 17.7

The Crime Clock

This clock shows the frequency at which certain crimes occur in the United States. (Federal Bureau of Investigation, 1999.)

Where Aggression Occurs

Aggression and violence can be found anywhere humans gather—in the home (domestic violence), in the workplace, in schools and on campus, and on the road.

Domestic Violence *Partner abuse,* a form of domestic violence, has been gaining attention since several well-known people, including entertainer Tina Turner, revealed their experiences of it.

Some research indicates that abusers use violence as a strategy to gain power and impose control over their partner or family (Walker, 1999). In a study involving 2,000 violent couples, Jacobson and Gottman (1998) identified two kinds of male abusers: (1) *Pit Bulls,* males whose anger and emotions quickly come to the boiling point, and (2) *Cobras,* males who inflict pain and humiliation on their partners in a cool and methodical manner.

Women, too, are capable of aggression and abuse. Among young heterosexual couples, some studies have found that women are slightly more likely than men to use physically aggressive acts. But, overall, men are significantly more likely to inflict an injury. In fact, of people injured by a partner, some 62% are women (Archer, 2000).

Violence in the Workplace On December 26, 2000, Michael McDermott, a software tester from Wakefield, Massachusetts, methodically shot to death seven of his co-workers. On February 5, 2001, one day before he was to report to prison for stealing from his employer, William Baker, a former factory worker from suburban Chicago, killed four of his former co-workers and wounded four others. Then he put a gun to his head and killed himself.

Workplace violence is a serious public health problem (LaMar et al., 1998). The number of violent incidents in the workplace is currently estimated to be as high as 2 million per year, and it is on the rise (Fletcher et al., 2000; Peek-Asa, 2001). Acts of violence include physical assault, assault or threat with a weapon, suicide, and murder (Eisele et al., 1998). Less violent but still aggressive are verbal threats and assaults, harassment, and vandalism.

Workplace homicide rates are highest for men, older and self-employed workers, minorities, and those in certain high-risk occupations such as taxi drivers, health care professionals, and municipal workers who must enforce regulations and provide services in unsecured settings (Peek-Asa, 2001). Women who are murdered in the workplace are most likely to be killed by an estranged partner (Moracco et al., 2000).

Violence in School Mention aggression and violence in school, and it is likely that Columbine High School in Littleton, Colorado will come to mind. There, in April 1999, two teenagers armed with bombs and guns attacked their school and classmates, resulting in the deaths of 15 people. Far from being an isolated event, the Columbine High School massacre was just one of eight multiple killings by young students in U.S. schools within a 2-year period. We may never know precisely why, but such brutal acts may be symptoms of widespread social problems in the schools, which seem to permeate student life. Out-group students like the Columbine killers experience years of being excluded, rejected, taunted, and bullied by the popular students, day after day. Some experts believe that the stress of being routinely and predictably humiliated, harassed, and ostracized has been a major factor in recent school killings (Aronson, 1999).

Fraternity Initiations and Athletic Team Hazing College fraternities and sororities have a long tradition of initiation practices. And those rites of passage to membership can range from the merely humiliating to the gruesome, dangerous, and even deadly. Many sports teams across college campuses in the United States subject new team members to similar practices known as *hazing*. Student athletes have been tied up, beaten, or forced to drink alcohol until they vomit and then drink more. Others have been stripped naked and marched around campus (Rossellini, 2000).

Hazing is anything but harmless amusement; it is sadistic and dangerous. Almost all of the National Collegiate Athletic Association member schools have banned it, and 42 states have passed laws against it.

Road Rage Jack Nicholson reaches for his golf club, gets out of his car at a red light and repeatedly strikes the roof and windshield of the Mercedes-Benz that just cut him off. This is not a movie scene. It is a real-life example of *road rage*—violence in response to minor collisions, near misses, or disagreements between drivers. Acts of road rage range from verbal assaults to physical assaults and even murder.

The majority of perpetrators of these violent acts are poorly educated, 18- to 26-year-old males with a history of violence or drug or alcohol problems. But many of the perpetrators have no such problems; they can be young, old, rich, poor, White, Black, male, or female.

A growing number of men, women, and children suffer injury or death at the hands of aggressive drivers who use guns, bats, fists, knives, and even the cars themselves as weapons (Pepper, 1997). For drivers who are already angry, hostile, or frustrated, a minor traffic altercation can be the last straw. To see if you are an aggressive driver who might bring out the road rage in others or be susceptible to it yourself, complete the *Try It!*

Try It!

Write in each blank the letter that indicates how often you engage in the action specified while you are behind the wheel.

a. frequently b. occasionally c. rarely or never

____ 1. Knowingly cutting off another driver

____ 2. Zigzagging through traffic

____ 3. Swearing and/or using aggressive or obscene gestures

____ 4. Tailgating

____ 5. Braking suddenly to scare a tailgater

____ 6. Flashing your lights in anger

____ 7. Blowing your horn in anger

____ 8. Cutting into lanes where other drivers are waiting to exit

Compute your score as follows: a = 2 points, b = 1, c = 0.

If your total is 12–16 points, you qualify as a very aggressive driver; 5–11 points means you are aggressive; less than 5 points, not aggressive.

Several measures can be taken to lessen road rage. In addition to avoiding the behaviors in the *Try It!* you should try not to make eye contact with aggressive drivers, try not to block passing lanes or right-turn lanes, and try to be forgiving of other drivers' errors. You have probably made some yourself. For more about road rage, read the *Apply It!* at the end of Chapter 13.

The Causes of Aggression

What causes aggression? One of the earliest explanations of aggression was the *instinct theory*—that human beings, along with other animal species, are genetically programmed for such behavior. Sigmund Freud believed that humans have an aggressive instinct that can be turned inward as self-destruction or outward as aggression or violence toward others. A Nobel Prize–winning researcher in animal behavior, Konrad Lorenz (1966) claimed that aggression springs from an inborn fighting instinct common in many animal species. Most social psychologists, however, consider human behavior too complex to attribute to instincts.

Biological Factors in Aggression: Genes, Hormones, and Brain Damage

What biological factors are thought to be related to aggression?

While rejecting the instinct theory of aggression, many psychologists do concede that biological factors are involved. A meta-analysis of 24 twin and adoption studies of several personality measures of aggression revealed a heritability estimate of about .50 for aggression (Miles & Carey, 1997). However, rather than finding that genes are a direct cause of aggression, research is more likely to find specific genes that increase the risk for the expression of violence (Alsobrook & Pauls, 2000). Twin and adoption studies have revealed a genetic link for criminal behavior (DiLalla & Gottesman, 1991). Cloninger and others (1982) found that adoptees with a criminal biological parent were four times as likely as members of the general population to commit crimes, while adoptees with a criminal adoptive parent were at twice the risk of committing a crime. But adoptees with both a criminal biological and a criminal adoptive parent were 14 times as likely to commit crimes, indicating the power of the combined influences of nature and nurture.

One biological factor that seems very closely related to aggression is low arousal level of the autonomic nervous system (Raine, 1996). Low arousal level (low heart rate and lower reactivity) has been linked to antisocial and violent behavior (Brennan et al., 1997). People with low arousal levels tend to seek stimulation and excitement and often exhibit fearlessness, even in the face of danger.

Men are more physically aggressive than women (Green et al., 1996), and the male hormone testosterone is involved. In fact, the primary biological variable related to domestic violence (both verbal and physical abuse) appears to be high testosterone levels, which are highly heritable (Soler et al., 2000). A correlation between high testosterone level and aggressive behavior has been found in males (Archer, 1991; Dabbs & Morris, 1990). Harris and others (1996) found testosterone levels in male and female college students to be positively correlated with aggression and negatively correlated with prosocial behavior. But abnormally low testosterone levels have also been linked to aggression (Angier, 1995). And violent behavior has been associated with low levels of the neurotransmitter serotonin (Gartner & Whitaker-Azmitia, 1996; Mitsis et al., 2000).

Brain damage, brain tumors, and temporal lobe epilepsy have all been related to aggressive and violent behavior (Mednick et al., 1988; van Elst et al., 2000). A study of 15 death row inmates revealed that all had histories of severe head injuries (Lewis et al., 1986). According to Eronen and others (1996) homicide rates are eight times higher in men with schizophrenia and ten times higher in men with antisocial personality disorder. The risk of violence is even greater when individuals with these disorders abuse alcohol (Hodgins et al., 1996; Tiihonen et al., 1997). In children, high levels of lead exposure (Needleman et al., 1996) and low IQ and problems paying attention (Loeber & Hay, 1997) are related to aggressive behavior and delinquency.

Alcohol and aggression are also frequent partners. A meta-analysis of 30 experimental studies indicated that alcohol is related to aggression (Bushman & Cooper, 1990). Alcohol and other drugs that affect the brain's prefrontal cortex lead to aggressive behavior in humans and other animals by disrupting normal executive functions (Lyvers, 2000). Ito and others (1996) found that alcohol intoxication is particularly likely to lead to aggression in response to frustration. People who are intoxicated commit the majority of murders, spouse beatings, stabbings, and instances of physical child abuse.

Aggression in Response to Frustration: Sometimes, but Not Always

What is the frustration–aggression hypothesis?

Does **frustration**—the blocking of an impulse, or interference with the attainment of a goal—lead to aggression? The **frustration–aggression hypothesis** suggests that frustration produces aggression (Dollard et al., 1939; Miller, 1941). If a traffic jam delayed you and you were frustrated, would you lean on your horn, shout obscenities out of your window, or just sit patiently and wait? Frustration doesn't always cause aggression, but it is especially likely to if it is intense and seems to be unjustified (Doob & Sears, 1939; Pastore, 1950). Berkowitz (1988) points out that even if frustration is justified and not aimed specifically at an individual, it can cause aggression if it arouses negative emotions.

Aggression in response to frustration is not always aimed at the people causing it. If the preferred target is too threatening or not available, the aggression may be displaced. For example, children who are angry with their parents may take out their frustrations on a younger sibling. Sometimes minorities and others who have not been responsible for a frustrating situation become targets of displaced aggression, a practice known as **scapegoating** (Koltz, 1983). Recent research suggests that displaced aggression is more likely to occur when the aggressor and the victim are in an unpleasant, stressful setting. And the more stressful the setting, the stronger the displaced aggression is likely to be (Marcus-Newhall et al., 2000).

Aggression in Response to Aversive Events: Pain, Heat, Noise, and Crowding

What kinds of aversive events and unpleasant emotions have been related to aggression?

Aggression in response to frustration is only one special case of a broader phenomenon—aggression resulting from unpleasant or aversive events in general, says a leading researcher on aggression, Leonard Berkowitz (1988, 1989). People often become aggressive when they are in pain (Berkowitz, 1983) or are exposed to loud noise, foul odors (Rotton et al., 1979), irritating cigarette smoke, or crowding. Extreme heat has been linked to aggression in several studies (Anderson & Anderson, 1996; Rotton & Cohn, 2000).

These and other studies lend support to the cognitive–neoassociationistic model proposed by Berkowitz (1990). He has suggested that anger and aggression result from aversive events and from unpleasant emotional states such as sadness, grief, and depression. "The core notion in this model is that negative affect is the basic source of anger and angry aggression" (Berkowitz, 1990, p. 494). Negative emotions (negative affect) tend to activate angry feelings, thoughts, and memories, as well as tendencies toward aggression or escape. The cognitive component of Berkowitz's model occurs when the angered person makes an appraisal of the aversive situation and makes attributions about the motives of the people involved. As a result of the cognitive appraisal, the initial reaction of anger can be intensified or reduced or suppressed. This process will make the person either more or less likely to act on the aggressive tendency.

frustration: Interference with the attainment of a goal, or the blocking of an impulse.

frustration–aggression hypothesis: The hypothesis that frustration produces aggression.

scapegoating: Displacing aggression onto minority groups or other innocent targets not responsible for the frustrating situation.

Figure 17.8

Social and Spatial Density

Social density increases as the number of people in a given space increases, as illustrated in (a). Spatial density increases as the amount of space for a given number of people decreases, as shown in (b).

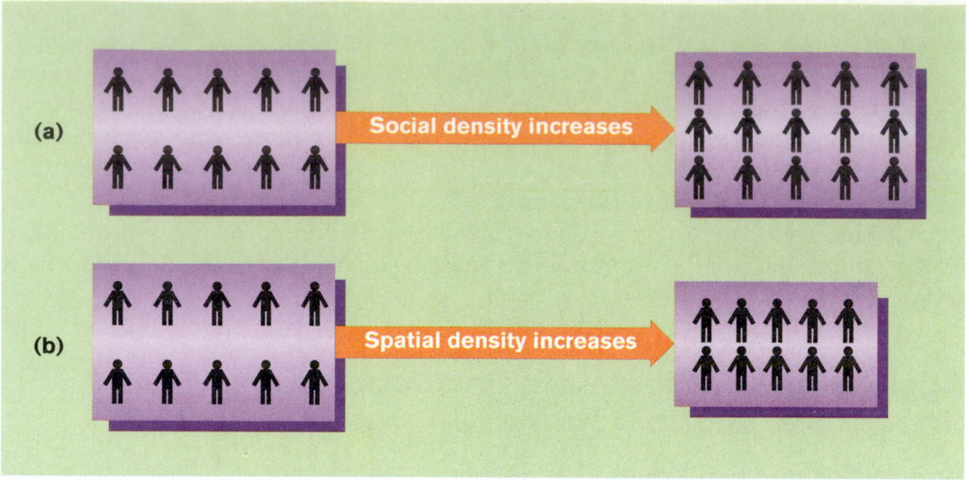

Crowding **Personal space** is an area surrounding each individual, much like an invisible bubble, that the person considers part of himself or herself and uses to regulate the closeness of interactions with others. Personal space serves to protect personal privacy and to regulate the level of intimacy with others. The size of personal space varies according to the person or persons with whom an individual is interacting and the nature of the interaction. And when personal space is reduced, aggression can result.

What is the difference between density and crowding?

Most psychologists draw a distinction between **density**—the number of people occupying a defined physical space—and crowding. **Crowding** is subjective and refers to the perception that there are too many people in a defined space. A hermit would probably feel crowded if one other person was anywhere in sight.

Psychologists further differentiate between social density and spatial density (Baum & Valins, 1977), and a sense of crowding is affected by both. Social density increases as the number of people in a fixed space increases. If five relatives came to live in your house for several weeks, social density would increase and you might feel crowded. Conversely, social density decreases as the number of people in a fixed space decreases. With spatial density, the number of people remains constant, but the space they occupy increases or decreases. If you have ever taken a family vacation in a car, you have felt the effects of increasing spatial density. Figure 17.8 illustrates the difference between social density and spatial density.

What are some psychological effects of crowding?

Sometimes it is enjoyable and exciting to be densely packed with other people at a sports event, a concert, or a party. But what if the crowd followed you home and you could not escape to your own private world even for a moment? In many parts of the world, people have little or no privacy. They must live under continuously crowded conditions, where day and night they are subjected to the sights, the sounds, and the smells of too many other people.

Does crowding lead to increased aggression? Comparing records from four state prisons, Paulus and others (1988) found that death rates, suicides, disciplinary actions, and psychological problems resulting in psychiatric commitment all increased as the prison population increased. The more inmates per cell, the greater the number of problems. But keep in mind that a prison is an atypical environment with an atypical population.

Crowding may or may not be stressful depending on the situation—waiting in a crowded airport terminal is more likely to be perceived as stressful than being part of a large crowd at a rally on Martin Luther King, Jr. Day.

Diversity and Crowding Crowding often leads to higher physiological arousal, and males typically experience its effects more negatively than females do. The effects of crowding also vary across cultures and situations. Researchers have studied its effects on such diverse populations as male heads of households in India and middle-class male and female college students in the United States (Evans & Lepore, 1993). In both of these studies psychological distress was linked to household crowding.

The Social Learning Theory of Aggression: Learning to Be Aggressive

According to social learning theory, what causes aggressive behavior?

The social learning theory of aggression holds that people learn to behave aggressively by observing aggressive models and by having their aggressive responses reinforced (Bandura, 1973). It is well known that aggression is higher in groups and subcultures that condone violent behavior and accord high status to aggressive members. A leading advocate of the social learning theory of aggression, Albert Bandura (1976), claims that aggressive models in the subculture, the family, and the media all play a part in increasing the level of aggression in society.

Abused children certainly experience aggression and see it modeled day after day. And the rate of physical abuse is seven times greater in families where there is a stepparent (Daly & Wilson, 1996). "One of the most commonly held beliefs in both the scholarly and popular literature is that adults who were abused as children are more likely to abuse their own children" (Widom, 1989, p. 6). There is some truth to this belief. On the basis of original research and an analysis of 60 other studies, Oliver (1993) concludes that one-third of people who are abused go on to become abusers, one-third do not, and the final third may become abusers if their lives are highly stressful.

Most abusive parents, however, were not abused as children (Widom, 1989). Although abused and neglected children are at higher risk of becoming delinquent, criminal, or violent, the majority do not (Widom & Maxfield, 1996). Several researchers suggest that the higher risk for aggression may not be due solely to an abusive family environment but may be partly influenced by the genes (DiLalla & Gottesman, 1991). Some abused children become withdrawn and isolated rather than aggressive and abusive (Dodge, Bates, & Pettit, 1990).

The Media and Aggression: Is There a Connection? By the time the average American child completes elementary school, he or she will have watched over 8,000 murders and more than 100,000 various other acts of violence (Huston et al., 1992). But is there a causal link between viewing aggressive acts and committing them? The research evidence overwhelmingly supports a relationship between TV violence and viewer aggression (Huesmann & Moise, 1996; Singer et al., 1999). And the negative effects of TV violence are even worse for individuals who are, by nature, highly aggressive (Bushman, 1995).

According to Eron (1987, p. 438), "One of the best predictors of how aggressive a young man would be at age 19 was the violence of the TV programs he preferred when he was 8 years old." A longitudinal study conducted in Finland also found that the viewing of TV violence was related to criminality in young adulthood (Viemerö, 1996).

A review of 28 studies of the effects of media violence on children and adolescents revealed that "media violence enhances children's and adolescents' aggression in interactions with strangers, classmates, and friends" (Wood et al., 1991, p. 380). It may stimulate physiological arousal, lower inhibitions, cause unpleasant feelings, and decrease sensitivity to violence and make it more acceptable to people.

Black and Bevan (1992) administered an aggression inventory to moviegoers attending violent and nonviolent movies. Higher aggression scores were found (both before and after the movie) for moviegoers attending violent movies than for moviegoers attending nonviolent movies. Are violent episodes of TV shows in which the "good guys" finally get the "bad guys" less harmful? Not according to Berkowitz (1964), who claims that justified aggression is the type most likely to encourage the viewer to express aggression.

personal space: An area surrounding each individual, much like an invisible bubble, that is considered to belong to the person and used to regulate the closeness of interactions with others.

density: A measure referring to the number of people occupying a unit of space.

crowding: A subjective perception that there are too many people in a defined space.

Researchers have found a correlation between playing violent video games and aggression (Anderson & Dill, 2000). Moreover, aggressiveness increases as more time is spent playing such games (Colwell & Payne, 2000). Researchers in the Netherlands found that boys who chose aggressive video games tended to be more aggressive, less intelligent, and less prosocial in their behavior (Weigman & van Schie, 1998).

Violence in music videos is another source of concern. White females are most frequently represented as the victims in such videos, and, in proportion to their population in the United States, Black males are overrepresented as both aggressors and victims. As a consequence, these videos may strengthen stereotypes of Black males as aggressive and White females as victims (Rich et al., 1998).

Can aggression can be reduced in American society? Not by letting off steam vicariously through watching aggression or violence in sports or the media, and not by engaging in aggressive but nonviolent behavior (Berkowitz, 1964; Josephson, 1987). The best hope is to find ways to reduce aggression in families, eliminate reinforcement for aggression, and remove excessive violence from the media (Eron, 1980).

Remember It!

1. The social learning theory of aggression emphasizes all of the following *except* that
   a. aggressive responses are learned from the family, the subculture, and the media.
   b. aggressive acts are learned through modeling.
   c. most aggression results from frustration.
   d. when aggressive responses are reinforced, they are more likely to continue.
2. Pain, extreme heat, loud noise, and foul odors have all been associated with an increase in aggressive responses. (true/false)
3. Social psychologists generally believe that aggression stems from an aggressive instinct. (true/false)
4. According to the frustration–aggression hypothesis, frustration ______________ leads to aggression.
   a. always b. often c. rarely d. never
5. Which of the following statements is *not* true of personal space?
   a. It functions to protect privacy and regulate intimacy.
   b. How much personal space a person requires is affected by culture, race, gender, and personality.
   c. The size of a person's personal space is fixed.
   d. Invasions of personal space are usually perceived as unpleasant.
6. Research suggests that media violence is probably related to increased aggression. (true/false)
7. Research tends to support the notion that a person can drain off aggressive energy by watching others behave aggressively in sports or on television. (true/false)

Answers: 1. c 2. true 3. false 4. b 5. c 6. true 7. false

Apply It!

Nonverbal Behavior: The Silent Language

There is some truth to the old saying "It's not what you say, it's how you say it." When you speak, what emotional impact does the verbal message alone, the words themselves, have on your listeners? Very little, according to Albert Mehrabian (1968), who claims that the emotional impact of a communication is influenced only slightly (about 7%) by the verbal message itself. More than five times as powerful is what he calls the vocal message—tone of voice, pronunciation, stress on words, vocal inflections, and the length and frequency of pauses—which provides 38% of the impact. If you were 30 minutes late for class and your professor said in a sarcastic tone, "We're so happy that you could join us today," would you believe the vocal message (the sarcastic tone) or the verbal message?

But the most powerful effect of all comes not from the verbal or the vocal message, but from *nonverbal behavior*—facial expressions, gestures, posture, and so on—which provides an amazing 55% of the emotional impact of a message. If the nonverbal behavior and the verbal message do not match, which one is more likely to be attended to? Almost every time, the nonverbal message comes across as the real one.

Communicating feelings through nonverbal cues. Nonverbal behavior can communicate anger, liking, love, happiness, sadness, anxiety, impatience, deception, and difference in status among people. But it is important to avoid attributing meaning to an isolated clue apart from its context.

People are best at reading nonverbal behavior that signals anger and a possible threat to their well-being. Cold stares will make almost anyone tense and uncomfortable.

Nonverbal behavior often reveals attitudes toward others. Encountering people or objects you like, you tend to move closer to them, lean toward them, and look directly at them. Your pupils dilate as if to take in more of them. The opposite occurs when you confront something or someone you dislike. Your pupils constrict, you tend to stand farther away or look away, and you often assume a closed position with arms and/or legs crossed.

Two people who are romantically involved cannot easily conceal their feelings. Their nonverbal behavior usually sends a clear message. They often gaze into each other's eyes and generally position themselves closer to each other than do friends or acquaintances. They exchange touches, lean toward one another, and often mirror each other's body language. When two people meet at a party and find each other attractive, they usually communicate their feelings to each other, although often unconsciously. Dilated pupils, extended eye contact, bodies leaning toward each other, and preening behavior—stroking the hair, readjusting the clothes—are all signs of interest.

Touch can be a sign of warmth and intimacy, a sign of sexual interest, or a means of conveying higher status (Major et al., 1990). Higher-status persons are more likely to touch lower-status persons than vice versa (Henley, 1973). In nonintimate settings, men are more likely to touch women than the reverse (Major et al., 1990).

Nonverbal behavior can reveal deceit. In his book *Telling Lies,* Ekman (1985) states that failure to look you in the eye is not necessarily a sign of lying but can indicate that a person is uncomfortable under scrutiny. More telling cues are overly long smiles, frowns, or looks of disbelief. Genuine expressions don't last longer than 4 or 5 seconds. True feelings often slip through in the form of fleeting microexpressions that are quickly replaced by the expression meant to deceive (Ekman et al., 1988). In deception there are discrepancies among the verbal, vocal, and nonverbal messages. Finally, when people are lying, they often have more pauses in their speech and begin sentences, stop, then begin again (Stiff et al., 1989).

Gestures—different meanings in different countries. When traveling in another country, most tourists find a phrase book indispensable, and some even make an effort to learn another language. But even if tourists learn to speak a foreign language like natives, few will recognize that the gestures they use in communicating may convey something entirely different in another country.

For instance, after a wonderful dinner in Naples, Italy, an American, wishing to thank his waiter for fine food and expert service, flashed a big smile and the A-okay sign. The stunned waiter turned pale and rushed to the restaurant manager, and the two of them discussed excitedly whether they should call the police and have the American arrested for obscene and vulgar behavior in a public place. The A-okay gesture is not a friendly one in all cultures. The smiling American tourist had unwittingly used a sign that called his waiter a name that is a crude and vulgar reference to the anal opening. In Turkey and Greece the same gesture signals a lewd, insulting sexual invitation.

Ironically, if we are trying to communicate with people who speak a different language, we are even more likely to use an abundance of gestures. Gestures are powerful communication tools, but travelers should use them with care in cultures other than their own.

THINKING CRITICALLY

Evaluation

In recent history, many Americans were surprised when the majority of people in the Soviet Union rejoiced at the downfall of the Communist system. Using what you have learned about attribution bias and conformity, explain why many Americans had mistakenly believed that the Soviet masses preferred Communism.

Point/Counterpoint

Prepare a convincing argument supporting each of these positions:

a. The Milgram study should have been conducted because it provided vitally important information about the troubling human tendency to inflict pain and suffering on others in obedience to authority figures.
b. Despite the value of the knowledge the Milgram study provided, it should never have been conducted because it subjected research participants to tremendous stress.

Psychology in Your Life

Review the factors influencing impression formation and attraction discussed in this chapter. Prepare a dual list of behaviors indicating what you should and should not do if you wish to make a better impression on other people and to increase their liking for you.

SUMMARY AND REVIEW

INTRODUCTION TO SOCIAL PSYCHOLOGY

Key Terms
social psychology (p. 611); confederate (p. 611); naive subject (p. 611)

SOCIAL PERCEPTION

Why are first impressions so important and enduring?

First impressions are important because people attend more carefully to the first information they receive about another person; and because, once formed, an impression acts as a framework through which later information is interpreted.

What is the difference between a situational attribution and a dispositional attribution for a specific behavior?

An attribution is an inference about the cause of one's own or another's behavior. In making situational attributions, people attribute the cause of behavior to some factor in the environment. With dispositional attributions, the inferred cause is internal—some personal trait, motive, or attitude.

How do the kinds of attributions people tend to make about themselves differ from those they make about other people?

People tend to attribute their own behavior primarily to situational factors and the behavior of others primarily to internal or dispositional factors, a tendency known as the actor–observer effect.

Key Terms
primacy effect (p. 612); attribution (p. 612); situational attribution (p. 612); dispositional attribution (p. 612); actor–observer effect (p. 613); self-serving bias (p. 613)

ATTRACTION

Why is proximity an important factor in attraction?

Proximity influences attraction because it is easier to develop relationships with people close at hand. Also, proximity increases the likelihood that there will be repeated contacts, and mere exposure tends to increase attraction (the mere-exposure effect).

How important is physical attractiveness in attraction?

Physical attractiveness is a major factor in attraction for people of all ages. People attribute positive qualities to those who are physically attractive—a phenomenon called the halo effect.

Are people, as a rule, more attracted to those who are opposite or to those who are similar to them?

People are generally attracted to those who have similar attitudes and interests, and who are similar in economic status, race, and age.

Key Terms
proximity (p. 614); mere-exposure effect (p. 614); halo effect (p. 615); matching hypothesis (p. 616)

SOCIAL INFLUENCE

What did Asch find in his famous experiment on conformity?

In Asch's classic study on conformity, 5% of the participants went along with the incorrect, unanimous majority all the time; 70% went along some of the time; and 25% remained completely independent.

What did Milgram find in his classic study of obedience?

In Milgram's classic study of obedience, 65% of the participants obeyed the experimenter's orders to the end of the experiment and administered what they believed to be increasingly painful shocks to the learner, up to the maximum of 450 volts.

What are three techniques used to gain compliance?

Three techniques used to gain compliance are the foot-in-the-door technique, the door-in-the-face technique, and the low-ball technique.

Key Terms
conformity (p. 618); social norms (p. 618); compliance (p. 621); foot-in-the-door technique (p. 621); door-in-the-face technique (p. 621); low-ball technique (p. 621)

GROUP INFLUENCE

Under what conditions does social facilitation have either a positive or a negative effect on performance?

When others are present, either as an audience or as co-actors, a person's performance on easy tasks is usually improved, but performance on difficult tasks is usually impaired.

What is social loafing, and what factors lessen or eliminate it?

Social loafing is people's tendency to put forth less effort when they are working with others on a common task than when working alone. It is less likely to occur when individual output can be monitored or when people have a personal stake in the outcome.

How are the initial attitudes of group members likely to affect group decision making?

Following group discussions, group decisions usually shift to a more extreme position in whatever direction the members were leaning toward initially—a phenomenon known as group polarization.

Key Terms
social facilitation (p. 623); audience effects (p. 623); co-action effects (p. 623); social loafing (p. 623); group polarization (p. 624); groupthink (p. 625); social roles (p. 625)

ATTITUDES AND ATTITUDE CHANGE

What are the three components of an attitude?

An attitude usually has a cognitive, an emotional, and a behavioral component.

What is cognitive dissonance, and how can it be resolved?

Cognitive dissonance is an unpleasant state that can occur when people become aware of inconsistencies among their attitudes or between their attitudes and their behavior. People can resolve cognitive dissonance by rationalizing away the inconsistency or by changing the attitude or the behavior.

What are the four elements of persuasion?

The four elements of persuasion are the source, the audience, the message, and the medium.

What qualities make a source most persuasive?

Persuasive attempts are most successful when the source is credible (expert and trustworthy), attractive, and likable.

Key Terms
attitude (p. 626); cognitive dissonance (p. 628); persuasion (p. 629)

PREJUDICE AND DISCRIMINATION

What is the difference between prejudice and discrimination?

Prejudice consists of attitudes (usually negative) toward others based on their gender, religion, race, or membership in a particular group. Discrimination consists of actions against others based on the same factors.

What is meant by the terms *in-group* and *out-group*?

An in-group is a social group with a strong sense of togetherness and from which others are excluded; an out-group consists of individuals or groups specifically identified by the in-group as not belonging.

How does prejudice develop, according to the social learning theory?

According to this theory, prejudice is learned the same way other attitudes are—through modeling and reinforcement.

What are stereotypes?

Stereotypes are widely shared beliefs about the characteristics of members of various social groups (racial, ethnic, religious), including the assumption that the members of such groups are usually all alike.

What are several strategies for reducing prejudice and discrimination?

Several strategies for reducing prejudice include (1) arranging appropriate educational experiences for children and (2) providing situations in which diverse social groups can interact under certain favorable conditions.

Key Terms
prejudice (p. 631); discrimination (p. 631); realistic conflict theory (p. 631); in-group (p. 631); out-group (p. 631); social cognition (p. 632); stereotypes (p. 632); contact hypothesis (p. 635)

PROSOCIAL BEHAVIOR: BEHAVIOR THAT BENEFITS OTHERS

What is the bystander effect, and what factors have been suggested to explain why it occurs?

The bystander effect means that as the number of bystanders at an emergency increases, the probability that the victim will receive help decreases, and help, if given, is likely to be delayed. The bystander effect may be due in part to diffusion of responsibility or, in ambiguous situations, to the assumption that no emergency exists.

Key Terms
bystander effect (p. 637); diffusion of responsibility (p. 637); prosocial behavior (p. 638); altruism (p. 638)

AGGRESSION: INTENTIONALLY HARMING OTHERS

What biological factors are thought to be related to aggression?

Biological factors thought to be related to aggression are a genetic link in criminal behavior, high testosterone levels, low levels of serotonin, and brain damage.

What is the frustration–aggression hypothesis?

The frustration–aggression hypothesis holds that frustration produces aggression and that this aggression may be directed at the frustrater or displaced onto another target, as in scapegoating.

What kinds of aversive events and unpleasant emotions have been related to aggression?

Aggression has been associated with aversive conditions such as pain, heat, loud noise, foul odors, and crowding, and with unpleasant emotional states such as sadness, grief, and depression.

What is the difference between density and crowding?

Density is an objective measure of the number of people occupying a defined physical space. Crowding is subjective and refers to the perception that there are too many people in a defined space.

What are some psychological effects of crowding?

Reported psychological effects of crowding include social withdrawal, decreased willingness to give or receive social support, and increased arousal level.

According to social learning theory, what causes aggressive behavior?

According to social learning theory, people acquire aggressive responses by observing aggressive models in the family, the subculture, and the media, and by having aggressive responses reinforced.

Key Terms
aggression (p. 639); frustration (p. 643); frustration–aggression hypothesis (p. 643); scapegoating (p. 643); personal space (p. 644); density (p. 644); crowding (p. 644)

Surf It!

Want to be sure you've absorbed the material in Chapter 17, "Social Psychology," before the big test? Visiting *www.abacon.com/wood* can put a top grade within your reach. The site is loaded with free practice tests, flashcards, activities, and links to help you review your way to an A. To enliven that inevitable study break, the site also offers personality assessment quizzes and a psychology career corner.

Appendix: Statistical Methods

Comedian Tim Conway, who appeared on *The Carol Burnett Show* many years ago, once did a humorous skit as an inept sports announcer. Reporting the daily baseball scores, he said, "And now here are the scores in the National League—6 to 4, 3 to 0, 2 to 1, 8 to 3, and 5 to 2." Conway's report of baseball scores may have been humorous, but it was not very informative. Numbers alone tell us very little.

Psychologists must deal with mountains of data in conducting their studies. The data they compute would be just as meaningless as Conway's baseball scores unless some methods were available to organize and describe the data. Fortunately, there are such methods. *Statistics,* a branch of mathematics, enables psychologists and other scientists to organize, describe, and draw conclusions about the quantitative results of their studies. We will explore the two basic types of statistics that psychologists use—descriptive statistics and inferential statistics.

DESCRIPTIVE STATISTICS

Descriptive statistics are statistics used to organize, summarize, and describe data. Descriptive statistics include measures of central tendency, variability, and relationship.

Measures of Central Tendency

A **measure of central tendency** is a measure or score that describes the center, or middle, of a distribution of scores. The most widely used and the most familiar measure of central tendency is the mean, which is short for arithmetic mean. The **mean** is the arithmetic average of a group of scores. One computes the mean by adding up all the single scores and dividing the sum by the number of scores.

Carl, a student who sometimes studies and does well in his classes, occasionally procrastinates and fails a test. Table A.1 shows how Carl performed on the seven tests in his psychology class last semester. Carl computes his mean score by adding up all his test scores and dividing the sum by the number of tests. Carl's mean, or average, score is 80.

Table A.1 Carl's Psychology Test Scores

Test 1	98
Test 2	74
Test 3	86
Test 4	92
Test 5	56
Test 6	68
Test 7	86
Sum:	560
Mean: 560 ÷ 7 = 80	

The mean is an important and widely used statistical measure of central tendency, but it can be misleading when a group of scores contains one or several extreme scores. For example, in one group of 10 people, the mean annual income last year was $124,700. In this case, the figure for the mean income alone covers up more than it reveals. Table A.2 lists the annual incomes of the 10 people in rank order. When a million-dollar income is averaged with several other, more modest incomes, the mean does not provide a true picture of the group.

Therefore, when one or a few individuals score far above or below the middle range of a group, a different measure of central tendency should be used. The **median** is the middle value or score when a group of scores are arranged from highest to lowest. When there are an odd number of scores, the score in the middle is the median. When there are an even number of scores, the median is the average of the two middle scores.

For the 10 incomes arranged from highest to lowest in Table A.2, the median is $27,000, which is the average of the middle incomes, $28,000 and $26,000. The median income—$27,000—is a truer reflection of the comparative income of the

Table A.2 Annual Income for 10 People

Person	Annual Income	
1	$1,000,000	
2	$50,000	
3	$43,000	
4	$30,000	
5	$28,000	$27,000 = Median
6	$26,000	
7	$22,000	Mode
8	$22,000	
9	$16,000	
10	$10,000	
Sum:	$1,247,000	

Mean: $1,247,000 ÷ 10 = $124,700

Median: $27,000

Mode: $22,000

group than is the $124,700 mean. It is important to select the measure of central tendency that most accurately reflects the group being studied.

Another measure of central tendency is the mode. The **mode** is easy to find, because it is the score that occurs most frequently in a group of scores. The mode of the annual-income group is $22,000.

Describing Data with Tables and Graphs

A researcher tested 100 students for recall of 20 new vocabulary words. The students were tested 24 hours after they had memorized the list. The raw scores (number of words recalled), arranged from lowest to highest, for the 100 students are as follows.

2	4	4	5	5	6	6	6	6	7
7	7	7	7	7	7	7	8	8	8
8	8	8	8	8	8	8	9	9	9
9	9	9	9	9	9	9	10	10	10
10	10	10	10	10	10	10	10	10	10
11	11	11	11	11	11	11	11	11	11
11	11	12	12	12	12	12	12	12	12
12	12	12	13	13	13	13	13	13	13
13	13	14	14	14	14	14	14	14	14
15	15	15	15	15	16	16	16	17	19

The raw data reveal that one student remembered only 2 words (the lowest score) and that one student remembered 19 words (the highest score). We can also observe that the most frequently occurring score, the mode, is 10.

descriptive statistics: Statistics used to organize, summarize, and describe information gathered from actual observations.

measure of central tendency: A measure or score that describes the center, or middle, of a distribution of scores (example: mean, median, or mode).

mean: The arithmetic average of a group of scores; calculated by adding up all the single scores and dividing the sum by the number of scores.

median: The middle value or score when a group of scores are arranged from highest to lowest.

mode: The score that occurs most frequently in a group of scores.

frequency distribution: An arrangement showing the numbers of scores that fall within equal-sized class intervals.

histogram: A bar graph that depicts the number of scores within each class interval in a frequency distribution.

frequency polygon: A line graph that depicts the frequency or number of scores within each class interval in a frequency distribution.

Table A.3 Frequency Distribution of 100 Vocabulary Test Scores

Class Interval	Tally of Scores in Each Class Interval	Number of Scores in Each Class Interval (Frequency)
1–2	|	1
3–4	||	2
5–6	~~||||~~ |	6
7–8	~~||||~~ ~~||||~~ ~~||||~~ |||	18
9–10	~~||||~~ ~~||||~~ ~~||||~~ ~~||||~~ |||	23
11–12	~~||||~~ ~~||||~~ ~~||||~~ ~~||||~~ |||	23
13–14	~~||||~~ ~~||||~~ ~~||||~~ ||	17
15–16	~~||||~~ |||	8
17–18	|	1
19–20	|	1

The researcher organized the scores in a **frequency distribution**—an arrangement showing the numbers of scores that fall within equal-sized class intervals. To organize the 100 test scores, the researcher decided to use intervals of two points each. (A different class interval—three points, for example—could have been chosen instead.) Next the researcher tallied the frequency (number of scores) within each two-point interval. Table A.3 presents the resulting frequency distribution.

The researcher then made a histogram, a more graphic representation of the frequency distribution. A **histogram** is a bar graph that depicts the number of scores within each class interval in the frequency distribution. The intervals are plotted along the horizontal axis, and the frequency of scores in each interval is plotted along the vertical axis. Figure A.1 shows the histogram for the 100 test scores.

Another common method for representing frequency data is the **frequency polygon.** As in a histogram, the class intervals are plotted along the horizontal axis and the frequencies are plotted along the vertical axis. However, in a frequency polygon, each graph point is placed at the middle (midpoint) of a class interval so that its vertical distance above the horizontal axis shows the frequency of that interval. Lines are drawn to connect the points, as shown in Figure A.2. The histogram and the frequency polygon are simply two different ways of presenting data.

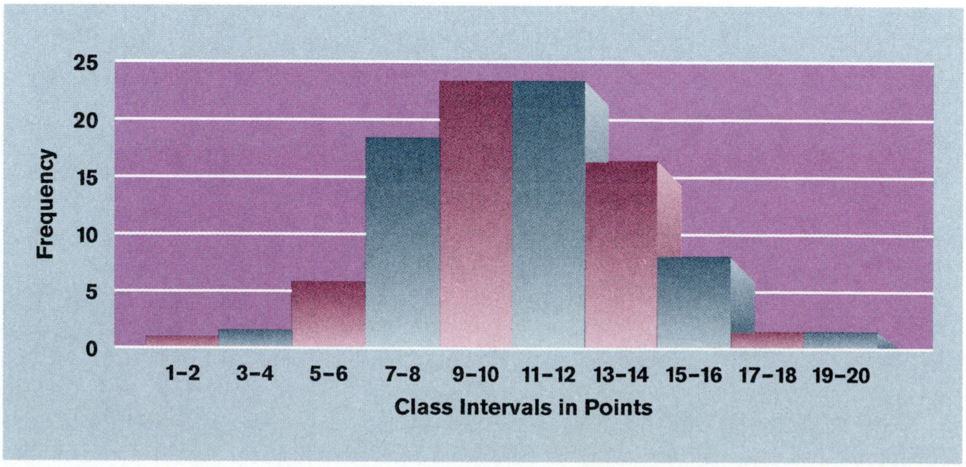

Figure A.1

A Frequency Histogram

Vocabulary test scores from the frequency distribution in Table A.3 are plotted here in the form of a frequency histogram. Class intervals of 2 points each appear on the horizontal axis. Frequencies of the scores in each class interval are plotted on the vertical axis.

Measures of Variability

Researchers usually need more information than measures of central tendency can provide. Often they need to know the **variability** of a set of scores—how much the scores spread out, away from the mean. There can be tremendous differences in variability even when the mean and the median of two sets of scores are exactly the same, as you can see in Table A.4.

Both groups in Table A.4 have a mean and a median of 80. However, the scores in Group II cluster tightly around the mean, while the scores in Group I vary widely from the mean. Simply looking at the data is not sufficient for determining variability. Fortunately, researchers have statistical techniques for measuring variability with great precision.

The Range The simplest measure of variability is the **range**—the difference between the highest and lowest scores in a distribution of scores. Table A.4 reveals that Group I has a range of 47, indicating high variability, while Group II has a range of only 7, showing low variability. Unfortunately the range is as limited as it is simple. It reveals the difference between the lowest score and the highest score but tells nothing about the scores in between. A more sophisticated measure of variability is the standard deviation.

The Standard Deviation The **standard deviation** is a descriptive statistic reflecting the average amount that scores in a distribution deviate, or vary, from their mean. The larger the standard deviation, the greater the variability in a distribution of scores. Refer to Table A.4 and note the standard deviations for the two distributions of test scores. In Group I the relatively large standard deviation of 18.1 reflects the wide variability in that distribution. By contrast, the small standard

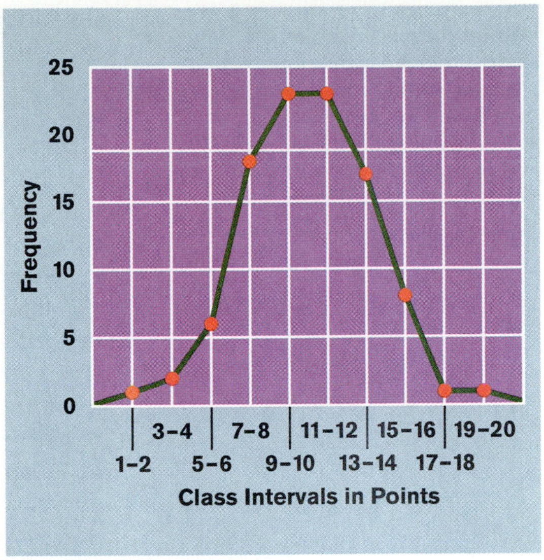

Figure A.2
A Frequency Polygon
Vocabulary test scores from the frequency distribution in Table A.3 are plotted here in the form of a frequency polygon. Class intervals of 2 points each appear on the horizontal axis. Frequencies of the scores in each class interval are plotted on the vertical axis.

Table A.4 Comparison of Range and Standard Deviation for Two Small Groups of Scores Having Identical Means and Medians

Group I			Group II		
Test	**Score**		**Test**	**Score**	
1	99		1	83	
2	99		2	82	
3	98		3	81	
4	80	Median	4	80	Median
5	72		5	79	
6	60		6	79	
7	52		7	76	
Sum:	560		Sum:	560	
Mean:	$\frac{560}{7} = 80$		Mean:	$\frac{560}{7} = 80$	
Median:	80		Median:	80	
Range: $99 - 52 = 47$			Range: $83 - 76 = 7$		
Standard deviation: 18.1			Standard deviation: 2.14		

variability: How much the scores in a distribution spread out, away from the mean.

range: The difference between the highest score and the lowest score in a distribution of scores.

standard deviation: A descriptive statistic reflecting the average amount that scores in a distribution deviate, or vary, from their mean.

deviation of 2.14 in Group II indicates that the variability is low, and you can see that the scores cluster tightly around the mean.

normal curve: A symmetrical, bell-shaped frequency distribution that represents how scores are normally distributed in a population; most scores fall near the mean, and fewer and fewer scores occur in the extremes either above or below the mean.

The Normal Curve

Psychologists and other scientists use descriptive statistics most often in connection with an important type of frequency distribution known as the normal curve, pictured in Figure A.3. The **normal curve** is a symmetrical, bell-shaped theoretical curve that represents how scores are normally distributed in a population.

If a large number of people are measured on any of a wide variety of traits, the majority of scores will fall near the mean of the distribution. There will be progressively fewer and fewer scores toward the extremes either above or below the mean. Even the small distribution of the 100 test scores in the histogram in Figure A.1 would yield a roughly bell-shaped curve. With increasingly larger numbers of scores in a distribution, the shape of the curve will more strongly resemble the ideal normal curve. On most variables researchers might measure (such as height or IQ score), the great majority of values will cluster in the middle, with fewer and fewer individuals measuring extremely low or high on these variables. The normal distribution with its bell-shaped curve is a potent statistical concept with many very useful, practical applications.

Using the properties of the normal curve and knowing the mean and the standard deviation of a normal distribution, we can find where any score stands (how high or low) in relation to all the other scores in the distribution. Look again at Figure A.3. You will note that slightly over 68% of the scores in a normal distribution fall within 1 standard deviation of the mean (34.13% within 1 standard deviation above the mean, and 34.13% within 1 standard deviation below the mean). Almost 95.5% of the scores in a normal distribution lie between 2 standard deviations above and below the mean. Theoretically the tails of the bell-shaped curve extend indefinitely, never touching the base line of the curve. Yet the vast majority of scores in a normal distribution, almost 99.75%, fall between 3 standard deviations above and below the mean.

On the Wechsler intelligence scales, the mean IQ is 100 and the standard deviation is 15. Thus, 99.72% of the population would have an IQ score within 3 standard deviations above and below the mean, ranging from an IQ of 55 to an IQ of 145. Recall from Chapter 8 that the highest IQ score ever recorded was an unbelievable 230 on the Stanford–Binet Intelligence Scale, scored by Marilyn Mach vos Savant. To

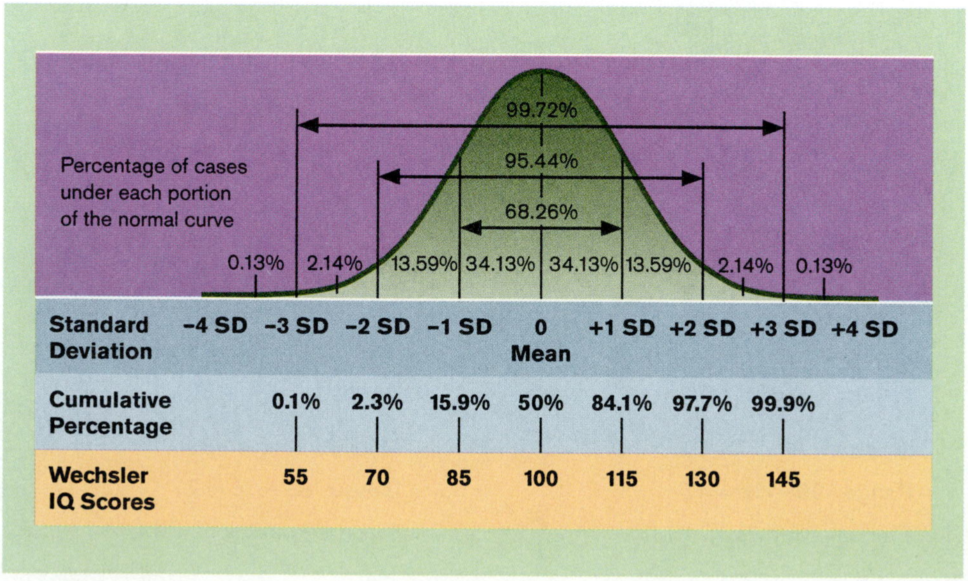

Figure A.3

The Normal Curve

The normal curve is a symmetrical, bell-shaped curve that represents how scores are normally distributed in a population. Slightly over 68% of the scores in a normal distribution fall within 1 standard deviation above and below the mean. Almost 95.5% of the scores lie between 2 standard deviations above and below the mean, and about 99.75% fall between 3 standard deviations above and below the mean.

plot her score on the normal curve, we would need to count 8½ standard deviations above the mean, so far up the right tail of the curve that her score would be in a standard deviation of its own. The next highest IQ score of 210 would be almost 7 standard deviations above the mean.

The statistical methods we have discussed so far, the measures of central tendency and the measures of variation, are designed to consider only one variable, such as test scores. What if researchers are interested in knowing whether two or more different variables are related to each other? The descriptive statistic used to show relationships between variables is the correlation coefficient.

correlation coefficient: A numerical value indicating the strength and direction of relationship between two variables, which ranges from +1.00 (a perfect positive correlation) to −1.00 (a perfect negative correlation).

positive correlation: A relationship between two variables in which both vary in the same direction.

negative correlation: A relationship between two variables in which an increase in one variable is associated with a decrease in the other variable.

The Correlation Coefficient

A **correlation coefficient** is a number that indicates the degree and direction of relationship between two variables. Correlation coefficients can range from +1.00 (a perfect positive correlation) to .00 (no correlation) to −1.00 (a perfect negative correlation). (See Figure A.4.) A **positive correlation** indicates that two variables vary in the same direction. An increase in one variable is associated with an increase in the other variable, or a decrease in one variable is associated with a decrease in the other. There is a positive correlation between the number of hours college students spend studying and their grades. The more hours they study, the higher their grades are likely to be.

A **negative correlation** means that an increase in one variable is associated with a decrease in the other variable. As we saw in Chapter 1, there is a negative correlation between cigarette smoking and life expectancy. When cigarette smoking increases, the number of years the smoker lives tends to decrease, and vice versa. There may be a negative correlation between the number of hours you spend watching television and studying. The more hours you spend watching TV, the fewer hours you may spend studying, and vice versa.

The sign + or − merely tells whether the two variables vary in the same or opposite directions. (If no sign appears, the correlation is assumed to be positive.) The number in a correlation coefficient indicates the relative strength of the relationship between two variables—the higher the number, the stronger the relationship. For example, a correlation of −.70 is higher than a correlation of +.56; a correlation of −.85 is just as strong as one of +.85. A correlation of .00 indicates that no relationship exists between the variables. IQ and shoe size are examples of two variables that are not correlated.

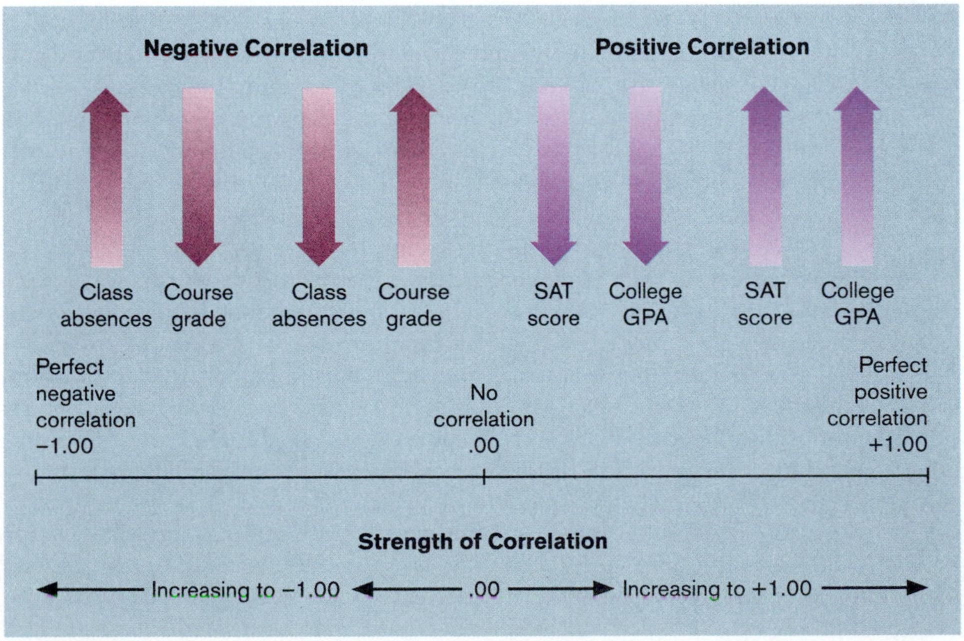

Figure A.4

Understanding Correlation Coefficients

Correlation coefficients can range from −1.00 (a perfect negative correlation) through .00 (no correlation) to +1.00 (a perfect positive correlation). As the arrows indicate, a negative correlation exists when an increase in one variable is associated with a decrease in the other variable, and vice versa. A positive correlation exists when both variables tend to either increase or decrease together.

Table A.5 High School and College GPAs for 11 Students

Student	High School GPA (Variable X)	College GPA (Variable Y)
1	2.0	1.8
2	2.2	2.5
3	2.3	2.5
4	2.5	3.1
5	2.8	3.2
6	3.0	2.2
7	3.0	2.8
8	3.2	3.3
9	3.3	2.9
10	3.5	3.2
11	3.8	3.5

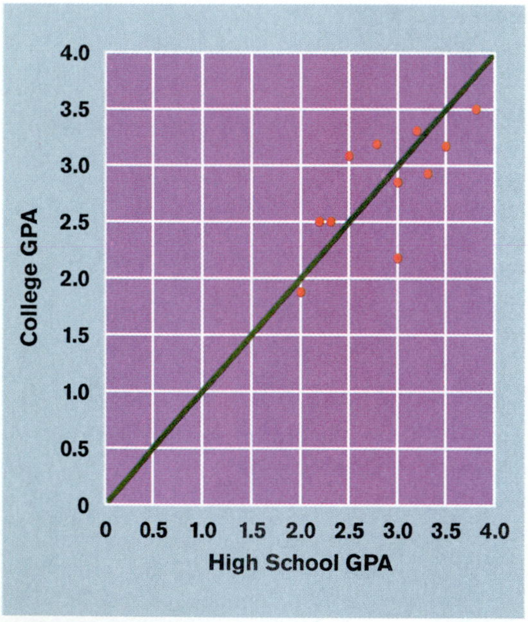

Figure A.5

A Scatterplot

A scatterplot reveals a relatively high positive correlation between the high school and college GPAs of the 11 students listed in Table A.5. One dot is plotted for each of the 11 students at the point where high school GPA (plotted on the horizontal axis) and college GPA (plotted on the vertical axis) intersect.

Table A.5 shows the measurements of two variables—high school GPA and college GPA for 11 college students. Most college and university admissions officers use high school grades along with standardized tests and other criteria to predict academic success in college.

Looking at the scores in Table A.5, we can observe that 6 of the 11 students had a higher GPA in high school, while 5 of the students had a higher GPA in college. A clearer picture of the actual relationship is shown by the scatterplot in Figure A.5. High school GPA (variable X) is plotted on the horizontal axis, and college GPA (variable Y) is plotted on the vertical axis.

One dot is plotted for each of the 11 students at the point where high school GPA, variable X, and college GPA, variable Y, intersect. For example, the first student's high school and college GPAs intersect at 2.0 on the horizontal (x) axis and at 1.8 on the vertical (y) axis. The scatterplot in Figure A.5 reveals a relatively high correlation between high school and college GPAs because the dots cluster near the diagonal line. It also shows that the correlation is positive because the dots run diagonally upward from left to right. The correlation coefficient for the high school and college GPAs of these 11 students is .71. If the correlation were perfect (1.00), all the dots would fall exactly on the diagonal line.

A scatterplot shows whether a correlation is low, moderate, or high and whether it is positive or negative. Scatterplots that run diagonally up from left to right reveal a positive correlation. Scatterplots that run diagonally down from left to right indicate a negative correlation. The closer the dots are to the diagonal line, the higher the correlation. The scatterplots in Figure A.6 depict a variety of correlations.

It is important to remember that correlation does not demonstrate cause and effect. Even a perfect correlation (+1.00 or −1.00) does not mean that one variable causes or is caused by the other. Correlation shows only that two variables are related.

Not all relationships between variables are positive or negative. The relationships between some variables are said to be *curvilinear.* A curvilinear relationship exists when two variables correlate positively (or negatively) up to a certain point and then change direction. For example, there is a positive correlation between physical strength and age up to about 40 or 45 years of age. As age increases from childhood to middle

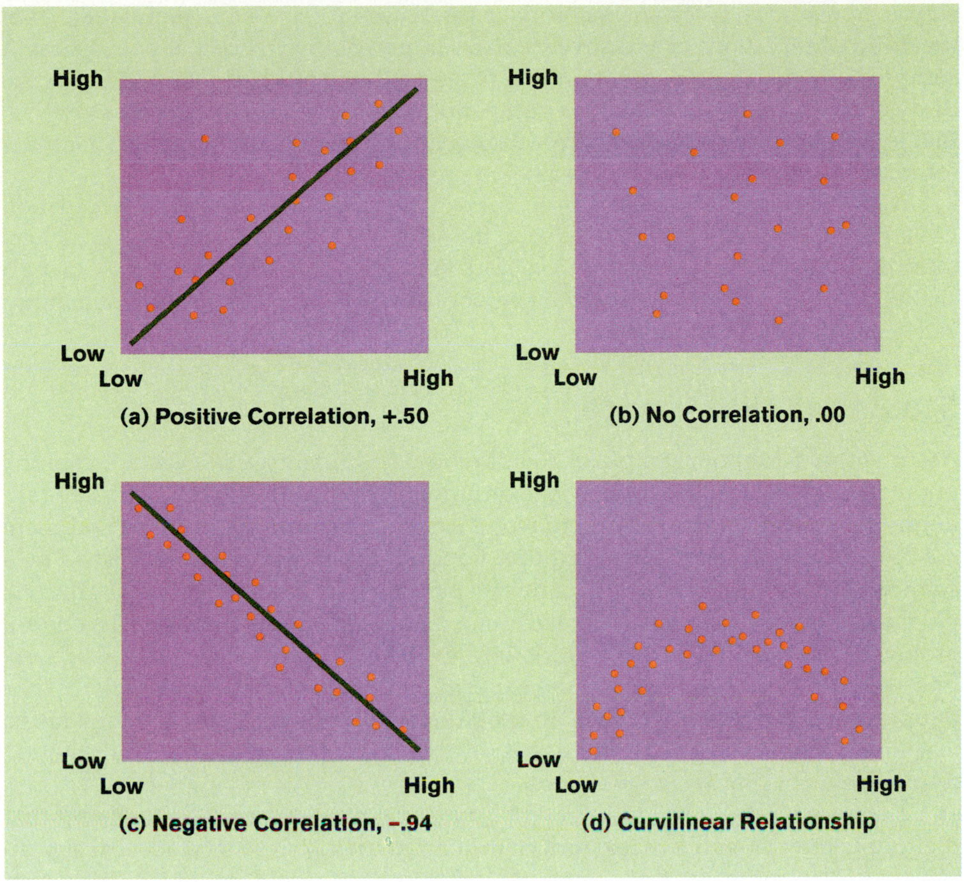

Figure A.6

A Variety of Scatterplots

Scatterplots moving diagonally up from left to right as in (a) indicate a positive correlation. Scatterplots moving diagonally down from the left to right as in (c) indicate a negative correlation. The more closely the dots cluster around a diagonal line, the higher the correlation. Scatterplot (b) indicates no correlation. Scatterplot (d) shows a curvilinear relationship that is positive up to a point and then becomes negative. Age and strength of handgrip have a curvilinear relationship: Handgrip increases in strength up to about age 40 and then decreases with continued aging.

age, so does the strength of handgrip pressure. But beyond middle adulthood, the relationship becomes negative, and increasing age is associated with decreasing handgrip strength. Figure A.6(d) shows a scatterplot of this curvilinear relationship.

INFERENTIAL STATISTICS

We have seen that measures of central tendency, variability, and correlation are important in describing characteristics of data and in describing relationships between sets of data. Often, however, investigators wish to make inferences beyond the relatively small groups of subjects they actually measure. **Inferential statistics** allow researchers (1) to make inferences about the characteristics of the larger population from their observations and measurements of a sample, and (2) to derive estimates of how much faith or confidence can be placed in those inferences.

In statistical theory a **population** is the entire group that is of interest to researchers—the group to which they wish to apply their findings. For example, a population could be all the registered voters in the United States, all the members of a religious denomination or political party, and so on. On a smaller scale, a population might consist of all the female students, the entire senior class, or all the psychology professors at your college or university. A population need not consist of persons. It can be all the chihuahuas in California, all the automobile tires manufactured in the United States, or all the oranges grown in Florida in a given year. In short, a population is all members of any group a researcher may define for study.

Usually researchers cannot directly measure and study the entire population of interest, because the population may be extremely large or inaccessible, or studying the whole population may be too costly in time and money. But thanks to inferential

inferential statistics: Statistical procedures that allow researchers (1) to make inferences about the characteristics of the larger population from observations and measurements of a sample, and (2) to derive estimates of how much confidence can be placed in those inferences.

population: The entire group of interest to researchers and to which they wish to generalize their findings; the group from which a sample is selected.

sample: The portion of any population that is selected for study and from which generalizations are made about the entire population.

random sample: A sample of subjects selected in such a way that every member of the population has an equal chance of being included in the sample; its purpose is to obtain a sample that is representative of the population of interest.

statistical methods, researchers can make inferences about a large population from the direct observations of a relatively small sample selected from that population. A **sample** is the part of a population that is selected and studied. For researchers to draw conclusions about the larger population, the sample must be representative; that is, its characteristics must mirror those of the larger population. (See Chapter 1 for more information about representative samples.)

A **random sample** is selected in such a way that every member of the population has an equal chance of being included in the sample. To accomplish this, researchers must have a list of all members of the population. Then the sample is selected using a chance procedure such as pulling names out of a hat or using a table of random numbers generated by a computer.

Statistical Significance

Assume that a random sample of 200 psychology students was selected from the population of students at your college or university. Then the 200 students are randomly assigned to either the experimental group or the control group so that there are 100 students in each of these groups. Random assignment is accomplished by a chance procedure such as drawing names out of a hat. The experimental group is taught psychology with innovative learning materials for one semester. The control group receives the traditional instruction. At the end of the semester, researchers find that the mean test scores of the experimental group are considerably higher than those of the control group. Can the researchers conclude that the innovative learning program worked? No, not until they can show that the experimental results were not simply due to chance.

The researchers must use inferential statistical procedures to be confident that the results they observe are real (not chance occurrences). Tests of statistical significance yield an estimate of how often the experimental results could have occurred by chance alone. The estimates derived from tests of statistical significance are stated as probabilities. A probability of .05 means that the experimental results would be expected to occur by chance no more than 5 times out of 100. The .05 level of significance is usually required as a minimum for researchers to conclude that their findings are statistically significant. Often the level of significance reached is even more impressive, such as the .01 level. The .01 level means that the probability is no more than 1 in 100 that the results occurred by chance.

The inferences researchers make are not absolute. They are based on probability, and there is always a possibility, however small, that experimental results could occur by chance. For this reason replication of research studies is recommended.

References

Note: Bracketed numbers following references indicate chapter(s) in which they are cited.

Abbot, N. C., Stead, L. F., White, A. R., Barnes, J., & Ernst, E. (2000). Hypnotherapy for smoking cessation. *Cochrane Database System Review, 2,* CD001008. [4]

Abbott, N. J., & Raff, M. C. (1991). Preface. *Annals of the New York Academy of Sciences, 633,* xiii–xv. [2]

Abramov, I., & Gordon, J. (1994). Color appearance: On seeing red—or yellow, or green, or blue. *Annual Review of Psychology, 45,* 451–485. [3]

Abramowitz, J. S. (1997). Effectiveness of psychological and pharmacological treatments for obsessive-compulsive disorder: A quantitative review. *Journal of Consulting and Clinical Psychology, 65,* 44–52. [16]

Abrams, D., Wetherell, M., Cochrane, S., Hogg, M. A., & Turner, J. C. (1990). Knowing what to think by knowing who you are: Self-categorization and the nature of norm formation, conformity and group polarization. *British Journal of Social Psychology, 29*(Pt. 2), 97–119. [17]

Abramson, P., & Herdt, G. (1990). The assessment of sexual practices relevant to the transmission of AIDS: A global perspective. *Journal of Sex Research, 27,* 215–232. [12]

Ackerman, M. D., & Carey, M. P. (1995). Psychology's role in the assessment of erectile dysfunction: Historical precedents, current knowledge, and methods. *Journal of Consulting and Clinical Psychology, 63,* 862–876. [12]

Ackerman, S., Zuroff, D. C., & Moskowitz, D. S. (2000). Generativity in midlife and young adults: Links to agency, communion and subjective well-being. *International Journal of Aging and Human Development, 50,* 17–41. [10]

Adams, J. H., Graham, D. I., & Jennett, B. (2000). The neuropathology of the vegetative state after an acute brain insult. *Brain, 123,* 1327–1338. [2]

Adelmann, P. K., & Zajonc, R. B. (1989). Facial efference and the experience of emotion. *Annual Review of Psychology, 40,* 249–280. [11]

Ader, D. N., & Johnson, S. B. (1994). Sample description, reporting, and analysis of sex in psychological research: A look at APA and APA division journals in 1990. *American Psychologist, 49,* 216–218. [1]

Ader, R. (1985). CNS immune systems interactions: Conditioning phenomena. *Behavioral and Brain Sciences, 9,* 760–763. [5]

Ader, R. (2000). On the development of psychoneuroimmunology. *European Journal of Pharmacology, 405,* 167–176. [13]

Ader, R., & Cohen, N. (1982). Behaviorally conditioned immunosuppression and murine systemic *Lupus erythematosus. Science, 215,* 1534–1536. [5]

Ader, R., & Cohen, N. (1993). Psychoneuroimmunology: Conditioning and stress. *Annual Review of Psychology, 44,* 53–85. [5]

Adler, A. (1927). *Understanding human nature.* New York: Greenberg. [14]

Adler, A. (1956). In H. L. Ansbacher & R. R. Ansbacher (Eds.), *The individual psychology of Alfred Adler: A systematic presentation in selections from his writings.* New York: Harper & Row. [14]

Adler, A. (1964). *Social interest: A challenge to mankind.* New York: Capricorn. (Originally published 1933). [14]

Adler, J. (1997, Spring/Summer). It's a wise father who knows . . . . *Newsweek* [Special Edition], p. 73. [9]

Adler, N., & Matthews, K. (1994). Health psychology: Why do some people get sick and some stay well? *Annual Review of Psychology, 45,* 229–259. [13]

Adler, N., & Stone, G. (1984). Psychology and the health system. In J. Ruffini (Ed.), *Advances in medical social science.* New York: Gordon & Breach. [13]

Agras, W. S., Rossiter, E. M., Arnow, B., Telch, C. F., Raeburn, S. D., Bruce, B., & Koran, L. M. (1994). One-year follow-up of psychosocial and pharmacologic treatments for bulimia nervosa. *Journal of Clinical Psychiatry, 55,* 179–183. [11]

Agras, W. S., Walsh, T., Fairburn, C. G., Wilson, T., & Kraemer, H. C. (2000). A multicenter comparison of cognitive-behavioral therapy and interpersonal psychotherapy for bulimia nervosa. *Archives of General Psychiatry, 57,* 459–466. [16]

Ahmad, S. (1994, November). *Culturally sensitive caregiving for the Pakistani woman.* Lecture presented at the Medical College of Virginia Hospitals, Richmond, VA. [3]

AIDS and Mental Health—Part II. (1994). *Harvard Mental Health Letter, 10*(8), 1–4. [12]

Aiken, L. R. (1997). *Psychological testing and assessment* (9th ed.). Boston: Allyn & Bacon. [8]

Ainsworth, M. (2000). ABCs of "internet therapy." *Metanoia* [Online]. Available: www.metanoia.org [16]

Ainsworth, M. D. S. (1973). The development of infant-mother attachment. In B. Caldwell & H. Ricciuti (Eds.), *Review of child development research* (Vol. 3). Chicago: University of Chicago Press. [9]

Ainsworth, M. D. S. (1979). Infant-mother attachment. *American Psychologist, 34,* 932–937. [9]

Ainsworth, M. D. S., Blehar, M. C., Walters, E., & Wall, S. (1978). *Patterns of attachment.* Hillsdale, NJ: Erlbaum. [9]

Ajzen, I., & Fishbein, M. (1977). Attitude-behavior relations: A theoretical analysis and review of empirical research. *Psychological Bulletin, 84,* 888–918. [17]

Åkerstedt, T. (1990). Psychological and psychophysiological effects of shift work. *Scandinavian Journal of Work and Environmental Health, 16,* 67–73. [4]

Akiskal, H. S. (1989). New insights into the nature and heterogeneity of mood disorders. *Journal of Clinical Psychiatry, 50*(5, Suppl.), 6–10. [15]

Alan Guttmacher Institute. (1991). *Facts in brief.* New York: Author. [10]

Albert, M. L., & Helm-Estabrooks, N. (1988). Diagnosis and treatment of aphasia: Part II. *Journal of the American Medical Association, 259,* 1205–1210. [2]

Albrecht, K. (1979). *Stress and the manager: Making it work for you.* Englewood Cliffs, NJ: Prentice-Hall. [13]

Aldhous, P. (1992). The promise and pitfalls of molecular genetics. *Science, 257,* 164–165. [14]

Aldridge-Morris, R. (1989). *Multiple personality disorder: An exercise in deception.* London: Lawrence Erlbaum Associates. [15]

Alexander, G. E., Furey, M. L., Grady, C. L., Pietrini, P., Brady, D. R., Mentis, M. J., & Schapiro, M. B. (1997). Association of premorbid intellectual function with cerebral metabolism in Alzheimer's disease: Implications for the cognitive reserve hypotheses. *American Journal of Psychiatry, 154,* 165–172. [10]

Alicke, M. D., & Largo, E. (1995). The role of the self in the false consensus effect. *Journal of Experimental Social Psychology, 31,* 28–47. [17]

Allen, B. P. (1997). *Personality theories: Development, growth, and diversity* (2nd ed.). Boston: Allyn & Bacon. [14]

Allen, G., Buxton, R. B., Wong, E. C., & Courchesne, E. (1997). Attentional activation of the cerebellum independent of motor involvement. *Science, 275,* 1940–1943. [2]

Allen, K. W. (1996). Chronic nailbiting: a controlled comparison of competing response and mild aversion treatments. *Behaviour Research and Therapy, 34,* 269–272. [16]

Allison, K. W., Crawford, I., Echemendia, R., Robinson, L., & Knepp, D. (1994). Human diversity and professional competence: Training in clinical and counseling psychology revisited. *American Psychologist, 49,* 792–796. [16]

Allison, M. (1991, February). Improving the odds. *Harvard Health Letter, 16*, 4–6. [13]

Allison, T., Puce, A., & McCarthy, G. (2000). Social perception from visual cues: Role of the STS region. *Trends in Cognitive Sciences, 4*, 267–278. [17]

Allport, G. W. (1935). Attitudes. In C. Murchison (Ed.), *Handbook of social psychology*. Worcester, MA: Clark University Press. [17]

Allport, G. W. (1954). *The nature of prejudice*. Reading, MA: Addison-Wesley. [17]

Allport, G. W. (1961). *Pattern and growth in personality*. New York: Holt, Rinehart & Winston. [14]

Allport, G. W., & Odbert, J. S. (1936). Trait names: A psycholexical study. *Psychological Monographs, 47*(1, Whole No. 211), 1–171. [14]

Alpert, B., Field, T., Goldstein, S., & Perry, S. (1990). Aerobics enhances cardiovascular fitness and agility in preschoolers. *Health Psychology, 9*, 48–56. [13]

Alsaker, F. D. (1995). Timing of puberty and reactions to pubertal changes. In M. Rutter (Ed.), *Psychosocial disturbances in young people* (pp. 37–82). New York: Cambridge University Press. [10]

Alsobrook, J. P., & Pauls, D. L. (2000). Genetics and violence. *Child & Adolescent Psychiatric Clinics, 9*, 765–776. [17]

Alterman, A. I., Renner, B. J., Cacciola, J. S., Mulvaney, F. D., & Rutherford, M. J. (2000). Familial risk for alcoholism and self-reported psychopathology. *Psychology of Addictive Behaviors, 14*, 19–28. [13]

Altman, L. K. (1992, April 9). Ashe received a transfusion before blood supply was tested for H.I.V. *The New York Times*, p. B15. [12]

Amabile, T. M. (1983). *The social psychology of creativity*. New York: Springer-Verlag. [8]

Amabile, T. M. (1990). Within you, without you: The social psychology of creativity, and beyond. In M. A. Runco & R. S. Albert (Eds.), *Theories of creativity*. Newbury Park, CA: Sage. [8]

Ambuel, B. (1995). Adolescents, unintended pregnancy, and abortion: The struggle for a compassionate social policy. *Current Directions in Psychological Science, 4*, 1–5. [10]

American Medical Association (1994) *Report of the Council on Scientific Affairs: Memories of childhood abuse.* CSA Report 5-A-94. [6]

American Psychiatric Association. (1993). *Statement approved by the Board of Trustees, December 12, 1993.* Washington, DC: Author. [6]

American Psychiatric Association. (1993a). Practice guideline for eating disorders. *American Journal of Psychiatry, 150*, 212–228. [11]

American Psychiatric Association. (1993b). Practice guideline for major depressive disorder in adults. *American Journal of Psychiatry, 150*(4, Suppl.), 1–26. [15, 16]

American Psychiatric Association. (1994). *Diagnostic and statistical manual of mental disorders* (4th ed.). Washington DC: Author. [4, 11, 12, 15]

American Psychiatric Association. (1997). Practice guideline for the treatment of patients with Alzheimer's disease and other dementias of late life. *American Journal of Psychiatry, 154*, 1–39. [10]

American Psychological Association. (1992a). *Demographic characteristics of APA members by membership status, 1991.* Washington, DC: Office of Demographic, Employment, and Educational Research, APA Education Directorate. [1]

American Psychological Association. (1992b). Ethical principles of psychologists and code of conduct. *American Psychologist, 47*, 1597–1611. [1]

American Psychological Association. (1993). Guidelines for providers of psychological services to ethnic, linguistic, and culturally diverse populations. *American Psychologist, 48*, 45–48. [16]

American Psychological Association. (1994). *Interim report of the APA Working Group on Investigation of Memories of Childhood Abuse.* Washington, DC: Author. [6]

Anagnostaras, S. B., Josselyn, S. A., Frankland, P. W., & Silva, A. J. (2000). Computer-assisted behavioral assessment of Pavlovian fear conditioning in mice. *Learning & Memory, 7*, 48–57. [5]

Anand, B. K., & Brobeck, J. R. (1951). Hypothalamic control of food intake in rats and cats. *Yale Journal of Biological Medicine, 24*, 123–140. [11]

Anand, K. J. S., & Scalzo, F. M. (2000). Can adverse neonatal experiences alter brain development and subsequent behavior? *Biology of the Neonate, 77*, 69–82. [9]

Andersen, B. L., & Cyranowski, J. M. (1995). Women's sexuality: Behaviors, responses, and individual differences. *Journal of Consulting and Clinical Psychology, 63*, 891–906. [12]

Anderson, B. L., Kiecolt-Glaser, J. K., & Glaser, R. (1994). A biobehavioral model of cancer stress and disease course. *American Psychologist, 49*, 389–404. [13]

Anderson, C. A., & Anderson, K. B. (1996). Violent crime rate studies in philosophical context: A destructive testing approach to heat and southern culture of violence effects. *Journal of Personality and Social Psychology, 70*, 740–756. [17]

Anderson, C. A., & Dill, K. E. (2000). Video games and aggressive thoughts, feelings, and behavior in the laboratory and in life. *Journal of Personality & Social Psychology, 78*, 772–790. [17]

Anderson, S. M., Klatzky, R. L., & Murray, J. (1990). Traits and social stereotypes: Efficiency differences in social information processing. *Journal of Personality and Social Psychology, 59*, 192–201. [17]

Andreasen, N. C., & Black, D. W. (1991). *Introductory textbook of psychiatry.* Washington, DC: American Psychiatric Press. [4]

Andreasen, N. C., Arndt, S., Alliger, R., Miller, D., & Flaum, M. (1995). Symptoms of schizophrenia: Methods, meanings, and mechanisms. *Archives of General Psychiatry, 52*, 341–351. [15, 16]

Andreasen, N. C., Cohen, G., Harris, G., Cizaldlo, T., Parkkinen, J., Rezai, K., & Swayze, V. W. (1992). Image processing for the study of brain structure and function: Problems and programs. *Journal of Neuropsychiatry and Clinical Neurosciences, 4*, 125–133. [2]

Andreasen, N. C., Flaum, M., Swayze, V., O'Leary, D. S., Alliger, R., Cohen, G., Ehrhardt, J., & Yuh, W. T. C. (1993). Intelligence and brain structure in normal individuals. *American Journal of Psychiatry, 150*, 130–134. [2]

Angeleri, F., Angeleri, V. A., Foschi, N., Giaquinto, S., Nolfe, G., Saginario, A., & Signorino, M. (1997). Depression after stroke: An investigation through catamnesis. *Journal of Clinical Psychiatry, 58*, 261–265. [2]

Anisfeld, M. (1996). Only tongue protrusion modeling is matched by neonates. *Developmental Review, 16*, 149–161. [9]

Annett, M. (1985). *Left, right hand and brain: The right shift theory.* London: Lawrence Erlbaum Associates. [2]

Anstey, K., Stankov, L., & Lord, S. (1993). Primary aging, secondary aging, and intelligence. *Psychology and Aging, 8*, 562–570. [10]

Antoniadis, E. A., & McDonald, R. J. (2000). Amygdala, hippocampus and discriminative fear conditioning to context. *Behavioural Brain Research, 108*, 1–19. [5]

Antonuccio, D. O., Danton, W. G., & DeNelsky, G. Y. (1995). Psychotherapy versus medication for depression: Challenging the conventional wisdom with data. *Professional psychology: Research and Practice, 26*, 574–585. [16]

Apgar, V., & Beck, J. (1982). A perfect baby. In H. E. Fitzgerald & T. H. Carr (Eds.), *Human Development 82/83* (pp. 66–70). Guilford, CT: Dushkin. [9]

Apuzzio, J. J. (1990, February). A patient guide: Genital herpes. *Medical Aspects of Human Sexuality, 24*, 15–16. [12]

Archambault, C. M., Czyzewski, D., Cordua y Cruz, G. D., Foreyt, J. P., & Mariotto, M. J. (1989). Effects of weight cycling in female rats. *Physiology and Behavior, 46*, 417–421. [11]

Archbold, M. (2000, December 10). Putting the brakes on road rage: Dangerous drivers apt to repeat. *Eastside Journal.* [13]

Archer, J. (1991). The influence of testosterone on human aggression. *British Journal of Social Psychology, 82*(Pt. 1), 1–28. [17]

Archer, J. (1996). Sex differences in social behavior: Are the social role and evolutionary explanations compatible? *American Psychologist, 51*, 909–917. [1]

Archer, J. (2000). Sex differences in aggression between heterosexual partners: A meta-analytic review. *Psychological Bulletin, 126*, 651–680. [17]

Arnett, J. J. (1999). Adolescent storm and stress, reconsidered. *American Psychologist, 54*, 317–326. [10]

Aronson, E. (1976). Dissonance theory: Progress and problems. In E. P. Hollander & R. C. Hunt (Eds.), *Current perspectives in social psychology* (4th ed., pp. 316–328). New York: Oxford University Press. [17]

Aronson, E. (1990). Applying social psychology to desegregation and energy conservation. *Personality and Social Psychology Bulletin, 16,* 118–132. [17]

Aronson, E. (1999). The power of self-persuasion. *American Psychologist, 54,* 875–886. [17]

Aronson, E., & Mills, J. (1959). The effect of severity of initiation on liking for a group. *Journal of Abnormal and Social Psychology, 59,* 177–181. [17]

Aronson, T. A. (1987). A naturalistic study of imipramine in panic disorder and agoraphobia. *American Journal of Psychiatry, 144,* 1014–1019. [16]

Asch, S. E. (1946). Forming impressions of personality. *Journal of Abnormal and Social Psychology, 41,* 258–290. [17]

Asch, S. E. (1951). Effects of group pressure upon the modification and distortion of judgments. In H. Guetzkow (Ed.), *Groups, leadership, and men.* Pittsburgh, PA: Carnegie Press. [17]

Asch, S. E. (1955). Opinions and social pressure. *Scientific American, 193,* 31–35. [17]

Aspendorf, J. B., Warkentink, V., & Baudonniere, P. M. (1996). Self-awareness and other-awareness II: Mirror self-recognition, social contingency awareness, and synchronic imitation. *Developmental Psychology, 32,* 313–321. [9]

Aspinwall, L. G., & Taylor, S. E. (1997). A stitch in time: Self-regulation and proactive coping. *Psychological Bulletin, 121,* 417–436. [13]

Atkinson, R. C., & Shiffrin, R. M. (1968). Human memory: A proposed system and its controlled processes. In K. W. Spence & J. T. Spence (Eds.), *The psychology of learning and motivation* (Vol. 2, pp. 89–195). New York: Academic. [6]

Au, J. G., & Donaldson, S. I. (2000). Social influences as explanations for substance use differences among Asian-American and European-American adolescents. *Journal of Psychoactive Drugs, 32,* 15–23. [4]

Aubé, J., & Koestner, R. (1992). Gender characteristics and adjustment: A longitudinal study. *Journal of Personality and Social Psychology, 63,* 485–493. [12]

Augestad, L. B. (2000). Prevalence and gender differences in eating attitudes and physical activity among Norwegians. *Eating and Weight Disorders: Studies on Anorexia, Bulimia, and Obesity, 5,* 62–72. [11]

Ault, R. L. (1983). *Children's cognitive development* (2nd ed.). Oxford: Oxford University Press. [10]

Aunola, K., Stattin, H., & Nurmi, J. E. (2000). Parenting styles and adolescents' achievement strategies. *Journal of Adolescence, 23,* 2205–2222. [9, 10]

Autti-Ramo, I. (2000). Twelve-year follow-up of children exposed to alcohol in utero. *Developmental Medicine and Child Neurology, 42,* 406–441. [9]

Avenoso, K. (1997, September 14). A decade of Prozac. *The Boston Globe,* pp. 12–13, 25–35. [16]

Avraham, R. (1989). *The digestive system.* New York: Chelsea House. [11]

Axel, R. (1995, October). The molecular logic of smell. *Scientific American, 273,* 154–159. [3]

Axelsson, A., & Jerson, T. (1985). Noisy toys: A possible source of sensorineural hearing loss. *Pediatrics, 76,* 574–578. [3]

Ayllon, T. (1977). Intensive treatment of psychotic behaviour by stimulus satiation and food reinforcement. In S. J. Morse & R. I. Watson, Jr. (Eds.), *Psychotherapies: A comparative casebook* (pp. 355–362). New York: Holt, Rinehart & Winston. [16]

Ayllon, T., & Azrin, N. (1965). The measurement and reinforcement of behavior of psychotics. *Journal of the Experimental Analysis of Behavior, 8,* 357–383. [5, 16]

Ayllon, T., & Azrin, N. (1968). *The token economy: A motivational system for therapy and rehabilitation.* New York: Appleton-Century-Crofts. [5, 16]

Azrin, N. H., & Holz, W. C. (1966). Punishment. In W. K. Honig (Ed.), *Operant behavior: Areas of research and application.* New York: Appleton-Century-Crofts. [5]

Bach, M., & Hoffman, M. B. (2000). Visual motion detection in man is governed by non-retinal mechanisms. *Vision Research, 40,* 2379–2385. [3]

Bachman, J. G., & Schulenberg, J. (1993). How part-time work intensity relates to drug use, problem behavior, time use, and satisfaction among high school seniors: Are these consequences or merely correlates? *Developmental Psychology, 29,* 220–235. [10]

Bäckman, L., Almkvist, O., Nyberg, L., & Anderson, J. (2000). Functional changes in brain activity during priming in Alzheimer's disease. *Journal of Cognitive Neuroscience, 12,* 134–141. [10]

Baddeley, A. D. (1982). *Your memory: A user's guide.* New York: Macmillan. [6]

Baddeley, A. D. (1990). *Human memory.* Boston, MA: Allyn & Bacon. [6]

Baddeley, A. D. (1992). Working memory. *Science, 255,* 556–559. [6]

Baddeley, A. D. (1995) Working memory. In M. S. Gazzaniga (Ed.), *The cognitive neurosciences.* Cambridge, MA: MIT Press.

Baddeley, A. D., & Andrade, J. (2000). Working memory and the vividness of imagery. *Journal of Experimental Psychology: General, 129,* 107–129. [7]

Baer, L. (1996). Behavior theory: Endogenous serotonin therapy? *Journal of Clinical Psychiatry, 57*(6, Suppl.), 33–35. [16]

Baer, L., Rauch, S. L., Ballantine, T., Jr., Martuza, R., Cosgrove, R., Cassem, E., Giriunas, I., Manzo, P. A., Dimino, C., & Jenike, M. A. (1995). Cingulotomy for intractable obsessive-compulsive disorder. *Archives of General Psychiatry, 52,* 384–392. [16]

Bagby, R. M., Rogers, R., & Buis, T. (1994). Detecting malingered and defensive responding on the MMPI-2 in a forensic inpatient sample. *Journal of Personality Assessment, 62,* 191–203. [14]

Bahrick, H. P., Bahrick, P. O., & Wittlinger, R. P. (1975). Fifty years of memory for names and faces: A cross-sectional approach. *Journal of Experimental Psychology: General, 104,* 54–75. [6]

Bahrick, H. P., Hall, L. K., & Berger, S. A. (1996). Accuracy and distortion in memory for high school grades. *Psychological Science, 7,* 265–271. [6]

Bailey, J. M., & Benishay, D. S. (1993). Familial aggregation of female sexual orientation. *American Journal of Psychiatry, 150,* 272–277. [12]

Bailey, J. M., & Pillard, R. C. (1991). A genetic study of male sexual orientation. *Archives of General Psychiatry, 48,* 1089–1096. [12]

Bailey, J. M., & Pillard, R. C. (1994). The innateness of homosexuality. *Harvard Mental Health Letter, 10*(7), 4–6. [12]

Bailey, J. M., & Zucker, K. J. (1995). Childhood sex-typed behavior and sexual orientation: A conceptual analysis and quantitative review. *Developmental Psychology, 31,* 43–55. [12]

Bailey, J. M., Nothnagel, J., & Wolfe, M. (1995). Retrospectively measured individual differences in childhood sex-typed behavior among gay men: Correspondence between self- and maternal reports. *Archives of Sexual Behavior, 24,* 613–622. [12]

Bailey, J. M., Pillard, R. C., Neale, M. C., & Agyei, Y. (1993). Heritable factors influence sexual orientation in women. *Archives of General Psychiatry, 50,* 217–223. [12]

Baillargeon, R., & DeVos, J. (1991). Object permanence in young infants: Further evidence. *Child Development, 62,* 1227–1246. [9]

Baldwin, J. D., & Baldwin, J. I. (1997). Gender differences in sexual interest. *Archives of Sexual Behavior, 26,* 181–210. [12]

Balkin, J. (1987). Contributions of friends to women's fear of success in college. *Psychological Reports, 61,* 39–42. [11]

Ball, C. G., & Grinker, J. A. (1981). Overeating and obesity. In S. J. Mule (Ed.), *Behavior in excess* (pp. 194–220). New York: Free Press. [11]

Ball, S. G., Baer, L., & Otto, M. W. (1996). Symptom subtypes of obsessive-compulsive disorder in behavioral treatment studies: A quantitative review. *Behaviour Research and Therapy, 34,* 47–51. [15]

Ballenger, J. C., Pecknold, J., Rickels, K., & Sellers, E. M. (1993). Medication discontinuation in panic disorder. *Journal of Clinical Psychiatry, 54*(10, Suppl.), 15–21. [16]

Ballor, D. L., Tommerup, L. J., Thomas, D. P., Smith, D. B., & Keesey, R. E. (1990). Exercise training attenuates diet-induced reduction in metabolic rate. *Journal of Applied Physiology: Respiratory, Environmental, and Exercise Physiology, 68,* 2612–2617. [11]

Balon, R. (1996). Antidepressants in the treatment of premature ejaculation. *Journal of Sex and Marital Therapy, 22,* 85–96. [12]

Baltimore, D. (2000). Our genome unveiled. *Nature, 409,* 814–816. [9]

Band, G. P., & Kok, A. (2000). Age effects on response monitoring in a mental-rotation task. *Biological Psychology, 51,* 201–221. [7]

Bandura, A. (1967). Behavioral psychotherapy. *Scientific American, 216,* 78–82. [16]

Bandura, A. (1969). *Principles of behavior modification.* New York: Holt, Rinehart & Winston. [5]

Bandura, A. (1973). *Aggression: A social learning analysis.* Englewood Cliffs, NJ: Prentice-Hall. [17]

Bandura, A. (1976). On social learning and aggression. In E. P. Hollander & R. C. Hunt (Eds.), *Current perspectives in social psychology* (4th ed., pp. 116–128). New York: Oxford University Press. [17]

Bandura, A. (1977a). *Social learning theory.* Englewood Cliffs, NJ: Prentice-Hall. [5, 9, 14, 16]

Bandura, A. (1977b). Self-efficacy: Toward a unifying theory of behavioral change. *Psychological Review, 84,* 191–215. [14]

Bandura, A. (1986). *Social functions of thought and action: A social-cognitive theory.* Englewood Cliffs, NJ: Prentice-Hall. [5, 14]

Bandura, A. (1989). Social cognitive theory. *Annals of Child Development, 6,* 1–60. [14]

Bandura, A. (1997a, March). Self-efficacy. *Harvard Mental Health Letter, 13*(9), 4–6. [14]

Bandura, A. (1997b). *Self-efficacy: The exercise of control.* New York: Freeman. [14]

Bandura, A., Adams, N. E., & Beyer, J. (1977). Cognitive processes mediating behavioral change. *Journal of Personality and Social Psychology, 35,* 125–139. [16]

Bandura, A., Blanchard, E. B., & Ritter, B. J. (1969). The relative efficacy of desensitization and modeling therapeutic approaches for inducing behavioral, affective and attitudinal changes. *Journal of Personality and Social Psychology, 13,* 173–199. [16]

Bandura, A., Jeffery, R. W., & Gajdos, E. (1975). Generalizing change through participant modeling with self-directed mastery. *Behaviour Research and Therapy, 13,* 141–152. [16]

Bandura, A., Ross, D., & Ross, S. A. (1961). Transmission of aggression through imitation of aggressive models. *Journal of Abnormal and Social Psychology, 63,* 575–582. [5]

Bandura, A., Ross, D., & Ross, S. A. (1963). Imitation of film-mediated aggressive models. *Journal of Abnormal and Social Psychology, 66,* 3–11. [5]

Banks, S. M., & Kerns, R. D. (1996). Explaining high rates of depression in chronic pain: A diathesis-stress framework. *Psychological Bulletin, 119,* 95–110. [15]

Barber, T. X. (1970, July). Who believes in hypnosis? *Psychology Today,* pp. 20–27, 84. [4]

Bard, P. (1934). The neurohumoral basis of emotional reactions. In C. A. Murchison (Ed.), *Handbook of general experimental psychology.* Worcester, MA: Clark University Press. [11]

Barefoot, J. C., Dahlstrom, W. D., & Williams, R. B. (1983). Hostility, CHD incidence, and total mortality: A 25-year follow-up study of 255 physicians. *Psychosomatic Medicine, 45,* 59–63. [13]

Bargh, J. A. (1997). The automaticity of everyday life. In R. S. Wyer, Jr. (Ed.), *Advances in social cognition,* Vol. 10. Mahwah, NJ: Erlbaum. [14]

Bargmann, C. (1996). From the nose to the brain. *Nature, 384,* 512–513. [3]

Barinaga, M. (1997). How jet-lag hormone does double duty in the brain. *Science, 277,* 480. [4]

Barlow, D. H. (1997). Cognitive-behavioral therapy for panic disorder: Current status. *Journal of Clinical Psychiatry, 58*(6, Suppl.), 32–36. [16]

Barnett, R. C., Raudenbush, S. W., Brennan, R. T., Pleck, J. H., & Marshall, N. L. (1995). Change in job and marital experiences and change in psychological distress: A longitudinal study of dual-earner couples. *Journal of Personality and Social Psychology, 69,* 839–850. [10]

Barringer, F. (1993, April 1). Viral sexual diseases are found in 1 of 5 in U.S. *The New York Times,* pp. A1, B9. [12]

Barron, F., & Harrington, D. M. (1981). Creativity, intelligence, and personality. *Annual Review of Psychology, 32,* 439–476. [8]

Barsh, G. S., Farooqi, I. S., & O'Rahilly, S. (2000). Genetics of body-weight regulation. *Nature, 404,* 644–651. [11]

Barsky, A. J. (1993, August). How does hypochondriasis differ from normal concerns about health? *Harvard Mental Health Letter, 10*(3), 8. [15]

Bartimus, T. (1983, March 1). One man's descent into schizophrenia. *St. Louis Post-Dispatch,* pp. D1, 7. [15]

Bartlett, F. C. (1932). *Remembering: A study in experimental and social psychology.* London: Cambridge University Press. [6]

Bartoshuk, L. (1989). Taste: Robust across the age span? *Annals of the New York Academy of Sciences, 561,* 65–75. [3]

Bartoshuk, L. M., & Beauchamp, G. K. (1994). Chemical senses. *Annual Review of Psychology, 45,* 419–449. [3, 9]

Bartoshuk, L. M., Fast, K., Karrer, T. A., Marino, S., Price, R. A., & Reed, D. A. (1992). PROP supertasters and the perception of sweetness and bitterness. *Chemical Senses, 17,* 594 (Abstract). [3]

Bartoshuk, L., Desnoyers, S., Hudson, C., Marks, L., O'Brien, M., Catalanotto, F., Gent, J., Williams, D., & Ostrum, K. M. (1987). Tasting on localized areas. *Annals of the New York Academy of Sciences, 510,* 166–168. [3]

Basic Behavioral Science Task Force of the National Advisory Mental Health Council. (1996). Basic behavioral science research for mental health: Perception, attention, learning, and memory. *American Psychologist, 51,* 133–142. [5, 6]

Bass, E., & Davis, L. (1988). *The courage to heal.* New York: Harper & Row. [6]

Bassili, J. N. (1995). Response latency and the accessibility of voting intentions: What contributes to accessibility and how it affects vote choice. *Personality and Social Psychology Bulletin, 21,* 686–695. [17]

Bateson, G. (1982). Totemic knowledge in New Guinea. In U. Neisser (Ed.), *Memory observed: Remembering in natural contexts.* San Francisco: W. H. Freeman. [6]

Batson, C. D., Batson, J. G., Griffitt, C. A., Barrientos, S., Brandt, J. R., Sprengelmeyer, P., & Bayly, M. J. (1989). Negative-state relief and the empathy-altruism hypothesis. *Journal of Personality and Social Psychology, 56,* 922–933. [17]

Batson, C. D., Polycarpou, M. R., Harmon-Jones, E., Imhoff, H. J., Mitchener, E. C., Bednar, L. L., Klein, T. R., & Highberger, L. (1997). Empathy and attitudes: Can feeling for a member of a stigmatized group improve feelings toward the group? *Journal of Personality and Social Psychology, 72,* 105–118. [17]

Baum, A., & Valins, S. (1977). *Architecture and social behavior: Psychological studies of social density.* Hillsdale, NJ: Erlbaum. [17]

Baumgardner, A. H., Heppner, P. P., & Arkin, R. M. (1986). Role of causal attribution in personal problem solving. *Journal of Personality and Social Psychology, 50,* 636–643. [17]

Baumrind, D. (1967). Child care practices anteceding three patterns of preschool behavior. *Genetic Psychology Monographs, 75,* 43–88. [9]

Baumrind, D. (1971). Current patterns of parental authority. *Developmental Psychology Monographs, 4*(1, Pt. 2). [9]

Baumrind, D. (1980). New directions in socialization research. *American Psychologist, 35,* 639–652. [9]

Baumrind, D. (1985). Research using intentional deception: Ethical issues revisited. *American Psychologist, 40,* 165–174. [1]

Baumrind, D. (1991). The influence of parenting style on adolescent competence and substance use. *Journal of Early Adolescence, 11,* 56–95. [9, 10]

Baxter, L. R., Jr., Schwartz, J. M., Bergman, K. S., Szuba, M. P., Guze, B. H., Mazziotta, J. C., Alazraki, A., Selin, C. E., Ferng, H-K., Munford, P., & Phelps, M. E. (1992). Caudate glucose metabolic rate changes with both drug and behavior therapy for obsessive-compulsive disorder. *Archives of General Psychiatry, 49,* 681–689. [16]

Bazan, S. (1998). Enhancing decision-making effectiveness in problem-solving teams. *Clinical Laboratory Management Review, 12,* 272–276. [17]

Beaman, A. L., Cole, C. M., Preston, M., Klentz, B., & Steblay, N. M. (1983). Fifteen years of foot-in-the-door research: A meta-analysis. *Personality and Social Psychology Bulletin, 9,* 181–196. [17]

Beatty, J. (1995). *Principles of behavioral neuroscience.* Dubuque, IA: Brown & Benchmark. [3]

Bechara, A., Damasio, H., & Damasio, A. R. (2000). Emotion, decision making and the orbitofrontal cortex. *Cerebral Cortex, 10,* 295–307. [4]

Beck, A. T. (1967). *Depression: Causes and treatment.* Philadelphia: University of Pennsylvania Press. [15]

Beck, A. T. (1976). *Cognitive therapy and the emotional disorders.* New York: New American Library. [15, 16]
Beck, A. T. (1991). Cognitive therapy: A 30-year retrospective. *American Psychologist, 46,* 368–375. [15, 16]
Beck, A. T. (1993). Cognitive therapy: Past, present, and future. *Journal of Consulting and Clinical Psychology, 61,* 194–198. [16]
Beck, A. T., Brown, G., Berchick, R. J., Stewart, B. L., & Steer, R. A. (1990). Relationship between hopelessness and ultimate suicide: A replication with psychiatric outpatients. *American Journal of Psychiatry, 147,* 190–195. [15]
Beck, J. G. (1995). Hypoactive sexual desire disorder: An overview. *Journal of Consulting and Clinical Psychology, 63,* 919–927. [12]
Beebe, D. W., Pfiffner, L. J., & McBurnett, K. (2000). Evaluation of the validity of the Wechsler Intelligence Scale for Children—Third Edition comprehension and picture arrangement subtests as measures of social intelligence. *Psychological Assessment, 12,* 197–201. [8]
Begg, I. M., Needham, D. R., & Bookbinder, M. (1993). Do backward messages unconsciously affect listeners? No. *Canadian Journal of Experimental Psychology, 47,* 1–14. [3]
Beilin, H. (1992). Piaget's enduring contribution to developmental psychology. *Developmental Psychology, 28,* 191–204. [9]
Beilin, H., & Fireman, G. (1999). The foundation of Piaget's theories: Mental and physical action. *Advances in Child Development and Behavior, 27,* 221–246. [9]
Békésy, G. von (1957). The ear. *Scientific American, 197,* 66–78. [3]
Bekker, M. H. J. (1996). Agoraphobia and gender: A review. *Clinical Psychology Review, 16,* 129–146. [15]
Bell, A. P., Weinberg, M. S., & Hammersmith, S. K. (1981). *Sexual preference: Its development in men and women.* Bloomington: Indiana University Press. [12]
Bell, J. (1991). *Evaluating psychological information: Sharpening your critical thinking skills.* Boston: Allyn & Bacon. [1]
Bell, M. A., & Fox, N. A. (1992). The relationship between frontal brain electrical activity and cognitive development during infancy. *Child Development, 63,* 1142–1163. [9]
Belsky, J. (1996). Parent, infant, and social-contextual antecedents of father-son attachment security. *Developmental Psychology, 32,* 905–913. [9]
Belsky, J., & Rovine, M. J. (1988). Nonmaternal care in the first year of life and the security of infant-parent attachment. *Child Development, 59,* 157–167. [9]
Belsky, J., Rovine, M., & Fish, M. (1989). The developing family system. In M. Gunnar (Ed.), *Minnesota symposium on child psychology: Vol. 22. Systems and development.* Hillsdale, NJ: Erlbaum. [10]
Belsky, J., Steinberg, L., & Draper, P. (1991). Childhood experience, interpersonal development, and reproductive strategy: An evolutionary theory of socialization. *Child Development, 62,* 647–670. [10]
Bem, S. L. (1974). The measurement of psychological androgyny. *Journal of Consulting and Clinical Psychology, 42,* 155–162. [12]
Bem, S. L. (1975). Sex role adaptability: One consequence of psychological androgyny. *Journal of Personality and Social Psychology, 31,* 634–643. [12]
Bem, S. L. (1977). On the utility of alternative procedures for assessing psychological androgyny. *Journal of Consulting and Clinical Psychology, 45,* 196–205. [12]
Bem, S. L. (1981). Gender schema theory: A cognitive account of sex typing. *Psychological Review, 88,* 354–364. [12]
Bem, S. L. (1985). Androgyny and gender schema theory: A conceptual and empirical integration. In T. B. Sonderegger (Ed.), *Nebraska symposium on motivation: Psychology of gender* (Vol. 32, pp. 179–226). Lincoln: University of Nebraska Press. [12]
Bem, S. L. (1993). *The lenses of gender.* New Haven: Yale University Press. [12]
Benazzi, F. (2000). Late-life atypical major depressive episode: A 358-case study in outpatients. *American Journal of Geriatric Psychiatry, 8,* 117–122. [10]
Benbow, C. P., & Stanley, J. C. (1980). Sex differences in mathematical ability: Fact or artifact? *Science, 210,* 1262–1264. [12]
Benbow, C. P., & Stanley, J. C. (1983). Sex differences in mathematical reasoning ability: More facts. *Science, 222,* 1029–1031. [2, 12]
Bendich, A., & Keen, C. L. (1993). Influence of maternal nutrition on pregnancy outcome: Public policy issues: Introduction to Part V. *Annals of the New York Academy of Sciences, 678,* 284–285. [9]
Benes, F. M. (2000). Emerging principles of altered neural circuitry in schizophrenia. *Brain Research Reviews, 31,* 251–269. [15]
Bengtson, V., Rosenthal, C., & Burton, L. (1990). Families and aging: Diversity and heterogeneity. In R. H. Binstock & L. K. George (Eds.), *Handbook of aging and the social sciences* (3rd ed., pp. 263–287). San Diego: Academic. [10]
Benjamin, L. T. (2000). The psychology laboratory at the turn of the 20th century. *American Psychologist, 55,* 318–321. [1]
Bennett, M. E., Miller, J. H., & Woodall, W. G. (1999). Drinking, binge drinking, and other drug use among Southwestern undergraduates: Three-year trends. *American Journal of Drug and Alcohol Abuse, 25,* 331–350. [4]
Bennett, M. R. (2000). The concept of long-term potentiation of transmission at synapses. *Progress in Neurobiology, 60,* 109–137. [6]
Bennett, M. V. L. (2000). Seeing is relieving: Electrical synapses between visualized neurons. *Nature Neuroscience, 3,* 7–9. [2]
Bennett, S. K. (1994). The American Indian: A psychological overview. In W. J. Lonner & R. Malpass (Eds.), *Psychology and culture* (pp. 35–39). Boston: Allyn & Bacon. [14]
Bennett, W. I. (1990, November). Boom and doom. *Harvard Health Letter, 16,* 1–4. [3]
Ben-Porath, Y. S., & Butcher, J. N. (1989). The comparability of MMPI and MMPI–2 scales and profiles. *Psychological Assessment: A Journal of Consulting and Clinical Psychology, 1,* 345–347. [14]
Benson, H. (1975). *The relaxation response.* New York: Avon. [4]
Benson, P. L., Karabenick, S. A., & Lerner, R. M. (1976). Pretty pleases: The effects of physical attractiveness, race, and sex on receiving help. *Journal of Personality and Social Psychology, 12,* 409–415. [17]
Berenbaum, S. A., & Snyder, E. (1995). Early hormonal influences on childhood sex-typed activity and playmate preferences: Implications for the development of sexual orientation. *Developmental Psychology, 31,* 31–42. [12]
Berenbaum, S. A., Korman, K., & Leveroni, C. (1995). Early hormones and sex differences in cognitive abilities. *Learning and Individual Differences, 7,* 303–321. [12]
Bergem, A. L. M., Engedal, K., & Kringlen, E. (1997). The role of heredity in late-onset Alzheimer's disease and vascular dementia. *Archives of General Psychiatry, 54,* 264–270. [10]
Berk, L. E. (1994a). *Child development* (3rd ed.). Boston: Allyn & Bacon. [9]
Berk, L. E. (1994b). Why children talk to themselves. *Scientific American, 271,* 78–83. [9]
Berk, L. E. (1997). *Child development* (4th ed.). Boston: Allyn & Bacon. [9, 10]
Berk, L. E. (2001). *Development through the lifespan* (2nd ed., p. 225). Boston: Allyn & Bacon. [9]
Berkman, L. F., & Syme, S. L. (1979). Social networks, host resistance, and mortality: A nine-year followup study of Alameda County residents. *American Journal of Epidemiology, 109,* 184–204. [13]
Berkowitz, L. (1964). The effects of observing violence. *Scientific American, 210,* 35–41. [17]
Berkowitz, L. (1983). Aversively stimulated aggression: Some parallels and differences in research with animals and humans. *American Psychologist, 38,* 1135–1144. [17]
Berkowitz, L. (1988). Frustrations, appraisals, and aversively stimulated aggression. *Aggressive Behavior, 14,* 3–11. [17]
Berkowitz, L. (1989). Frustration-aggression hypothesis: Examination and reformulation. *Psychological Bulletin, 106,* 59–73. [17]
Berkowitz, L. (1990). On the formation and regulation of anger and aggression: A cognitive-neoassociationistic analysis. *American Psychologist, 45,* 494–503. [17]
Berlin, B., & Kay, P. (1969). *Basic color terms: Their universality and evolution.* Berkeley: University of California Press. [7]
Berlyne, D. E. (1960). *Conflict, arousal, and curiosity.* New York: McGraw-Hill. [11]
Bernal, M. E., & Castro, F. G. (1994). Are clinical psychologists prepared for service and research with ethnic minorities? Report of a decade of progress. *American Psychologist, 49,* 797–805. [16]

Berndt, E. R., Koran, L. M., Finkelstein, S. N., Gelenberg, A. J., Kornstein, S. G., Miller, I. M., Thase, M. E., Trapp, G. A., & Keller, M. B. (2000). Lost human capital from early-onset chronic depression. *American Journal of Psychiatry, 157,* 940–947. [15]

Berndt, T. J. (1992). Friendship and friends' influence in adolescence. *Current Directions in Psychological Science, 1,* 156–159. [10]

Berndt, T. J., Cheung, P. C., Lau, S., Hau, K. T., & Lew, W. J. F. (1993). Perceptions of parenting in mainland China, Taiwan, and Hong Kong: Sex differences and societal differences. *Developmental Psychology, 29,* 156–164. [9]

Bernstein, I. L. (1985). Learned food aversions in the progression of cancer and its treatment. *Annals of the New York Academy of Sciences, 443,* 365–380. [5]

Bernstein, I. L., Webster, M. M., & Bernstein, I. D. (1982). Food aversions in children receiving chemotherapy for cancer. *Cancer, 50,* 2961–2963. [5]

Berquier, A., & Aston, R. (1992). Characteristics of the frequent nightmare sufferer. *Journal of Abnormal Psychology,* 101, 246–250. [4]

Berreby, D. (1994, January/February). Figures of speech: The rise and fall and rise of Chomsky's linguistics. *The Sciences,* 44–49. [7]

Berscheid, E., Dion, K., Walster, E., & Walster, G. W. (1971). Physical attractiveness and dating choice: A test of the matching hypothesis. *Journal of Experimental Social Psychology, 7,* 173–189. [17]

Bettencourt, B. A., & Miller, N. (1996). Gender differences in aggression as a function of provocation: A meta-analysis. *Psychological Bulletin, 119,* 422–447. [12]

Bexton, W. H., Herron, W., & Scott, T. H. (1954). Effects of decreased variation in the sensory environment. *Canadian Journal of Psychology, 8,* 70–76. [11]

Beyenburg, S., Watzka, M., Clusmann, H., Blümcke, I., Bidlingmaier, F., Stoffel-Wagner, C. E. E., & Stoffel-Wagner, B. W. (2000). Androgen receptor mRNA expression in the human hippocampus. *Neuroscience Letters, 294,* 25–28. [12]

Billiard, M., Pasquiré-Magnetto, V., Heckman, M., Carlander, B., Besset, A., Zachariev, Z., Eliaou, J. F., & Malafosse, A. (1994). Family studies in narcolepsy. *Sleep, 17,* S54–S59. [4]

Binion, V. J. (1990). Psychological androgyny: A Black female perspective. *Sex Roles, 22,* 487–507. [12]

Birren, J. E., & Fisher, L. M. (1995). Aging and speed of behavior: Possible consequences for psychological functioning. *Annual Review of Psychology, 46,* 329–353. [10]

Bishop, G. D. (1984). Gender, role, and illness behavior in a military population. *Health Psychology, 3,* 519–534. [13]

Bishop, J., & Lane, R. C. (2000). Father absence and the attitude of entitlement. *Journal of Contemporary Psychotherapy, 30,* 105–117. [9, 10]

Bisiach, E. (1996). Unilateral neglect and the structure of space representation. *Current Directions in Psychological Science, 5,* 62–65. [2]

Bjork, D. W. (1993). *B. F. Skinner: A life.* New York: Basic Books. [5]

Bjorklund, D. F., Cassel, W. S., Bjorklund, B. R., Brown, R. D., Park, C. L., Ernst, K., & Owen, F. A. (2000). Social demand characteristics in children's and adults' memory and suggestibility: The effect of different interviewers on free recall and recognition. *Applied Cognitive Psychology, 14,* 421–433. [6]

Bjorklund, D. F., & Coyle, T. R. (1995). Utilization deficiencies in the development of memory strategies. In F. E. Weinert & W. Schneider (Eds.), *Research on memory development: State of the art and future directions.* Hillsdale, NJ: Erlbaum. [9]

Björkqvist, K., Lagerspetz, K. M. J., & Kaukiainen, A. (1992). Do girls manipulate and boys fight? Developmental trends in regard to direct and indirect aggression. *Aggressive Behavior, 18,* 117–127. [12]

Black, D. W., Monahan, P., & Gabel, J. (1997). Fluvoxamine in the treatment of compulsive buying. *Journal of Clinical Psychiatry, 58,* 159–163. [16]

Black, S. L., & Bevan, S. (1992). At the movies with Buss and Durkee: A natural experiment on film violence. *Aggressive Behavior, 18,* 37–45. [17]

Blair, S. N. (1993). Evidence for success of exercise in weight loss and control. *Annals of Internal Medicine, 119,* 702–706. [11]

Blair, S. N., Kohl, H. W., III, Paffenbarger, R. S., Jr., Clark, D. G., Cooper, K. H., & Gibbons, L. W. (1989). Physical fitness and all-cause mortality: A prospective study of healthy men and women. *Journal of the American Medical Association, 262,* 2395–2401. [13]

Blakeslee, S. (1992, January 22). An epidemic of genital warts raises concern but not alarm. *The New York Times,* p. C12. [12]

Blanchette, I., & Dunbar, K. (2000). How analogies are generated: The roles of structural and superficial similarity. *Memory and Cognition, 28,* 108–124. [7]

Blascovich, J., Wyer, N. A., Swart, L. A., & Kibler, J. L. (1997). Racism and racial categorization. *Journal of Personality and Social Psychology, 72,* 1364–1372. [17]

Blatt, S. J., & Auerbach, J. S. (2000). Psychoanalytic models of the mind and their contributions to personality research. *European Journal of Personality, 14,* 429–447. [14]

Blatt, S. J., Sanislow, C. A., III, Zuroff, D. C., & Pilkonis, P. A. (1996). Characteristics of effective therapists: Further analyses of data from the National Institute of Mental Health Treatment of Depression Collaborative Research Program. *Journal of Consulting and Clinical Psychology, 64,* 1276–1284. [16]

Blau, A. (1946). *The master hand.* New York: American Ortho-Psychiatric Association. [2]

Bleuler, E. (1950). *Dementia praecox, or the group of schizophrenias.* (J. Zinkin & N. D. C. Lewis, Trans.). New York: International Universities Press, 1950. (Original work published 1911). [15]

Bliese, P. D., & Castro, C. A. (2000). Role clarity, work overload and organizational support: Multilevel evidence of the importance of support. *Work & Stress, 14,* 65–73. [13]

Bliss, E. L., & Jeppsen, E. A. (1985). Prevalence of multiple personality among inpatients and outpatients. *American Journal of Psychiatry, 142,* 250–251. [15]

Bliss, T. V., & Lomo, T. (2000). Plasticity in a monosynaptic cortical pathway. *Journal of Physiology, 207,* 61. [6]

Bloche, M. G., & Eisenberg, C. (1993). The psychological effects of state-sanctioned terror. *Harvard Mental Health Letter, 10*(5), 4–6. [13]

Block, J. (1995). A contrarian view of the five-factor approach to personality description. *Psychological Bulletin, 117,* 187–215. [14]

Bloom, B. S. (Ed.). (1985). *Developing talent in young people.* New York: Ballantine. [8]

Bloomer, C. M. (1976). *Principles of visual perception.* New York: Van Nostrand Reinhold. [3]

Blyth, D. A., & Traeger, C. M. (1983). The self-concept and self-esteem of early adolescents. *Theory into Practice, 22,* 91–97. [10]

Blyth, D. A., Simmons, R. G., Bulcroft, R., Felt, D., VanCleave, E. F., & Bush, D. M. (1981). The effects of physical development on self-image and satisfaction with body-image for early adolescent males. In R. G. Simmons (Ed.), *Research in community and mental health* (Vol. 2). Greenwich, CT: JAI. [10]

Bochner, S. (1994). Cross-cultural differences in the self concept: A test of Hofstede's individualism/collectivism distinction. *Journal of Cross-Cultural Psychology, 25,* 273–283. [11, 14]

Bogaert, A. F., & Fisher, W. A. (1995). Predictors of university men's number of sexual partners. *Journal of Sex Research, 32,* 119–130. [12]

Bogard, N. (1990). Why we need gender to understand human violence. *Journal of Interpersonal Violence, 5,* 132–135. [12]

Bogen, J. E., & Vogel, P. J. (1963). Treatment of generalized seizures by cerebral commissurotomy. *Surgical Forum, 14,* 431. [2]

Bohannon, J. N., III. (1988). Flashbulb memories for the Space Shuttle disaster: A tale of two theories. *Cognition, 29,* 179–196. [6]

Boivin, D. B., Czeisler, C. A., Dijk, D-J., Duffy, J. F., Folkard, S., Minors, D. S., Totterdell, P., & Waterhouse, J. M. (1997). Complex interaction of the sleep-wake cycle and circadian phase modulates mood in healthy subjects. *Archives of General Psychiatry, 54,* 145–152. [4]

Bonanno, G. A., Keltner, D., Holen, A., & Horowitz, M. J. (1995). When avoiding unpleasant emotions might not be such a bad thing: Verbal-autonomic response dissociation and midlife conjugal bereavement. *Journal of Personality and Social Psychology, 69,* 975–989. [10]

Bond, F. W., & Bunce, D. (2000). Mediators of change in emotion-focused and problem-focused worksite stress management interventions. *Journal of Occupational Health Psychology, 5,* 1156–1163. [13]

Bonnet, M. H., & Arand, D. L. (1995). We are chronically sleep deprived. *Sleep, 18,* 908–911. [4]

Bonnet, M. H., Gomez, S., Wirth, O., & Arand, D. L. (1995). The use of caffeine versus prophylactic naps in sustained performance. *Sleep, 18,* 97–104. [4]

Borbely, A. A. (1984). Sleep regulation: Outline of a model and its implications for depression. In A. A. Borbely & J. L. Valatx (Eds.), *Sleep mechanisms.* Berlin: Springer-Verlag. [4]

Borbely, A. A., Achermann, P., Trachsel, L., & Tobler, I. (1989). Sleep initiation and initial sleep intensity: Interactions of homeostatic and circadian mechanisms. *Journal of Biological Rhythms, 4,* 149–160. [4]

Borg, E., & Counter, S. A. (1989). The middle-ear muscles. *Scientific American, 261,* 74–80. [3]

Bornstein, M. H., & Marks, L. E. (1982, January). Color revisionism. *Psychology Today,* pp. 64–73. [9]

Bornstein, R. F. (1989). Exposure and affect: Overview and meta-analysis of research, 1968–1987. *Psychological Bulletin, 106,* 265–289. [17]

Borod, J. C. (1992). Interhemispheric and intrahemispheric control of emotion: A focus on unilateral brain damage. *Journal of Consulting and Clinical Psychology, 60,* 339–348. [2]

Borrelli, B., Niaura, R., Keuthen, N. J., Goldstein, M. G., DePue, J. D., Murphy, C., & Abrams, D. B. (1996). Development of major depressive disorder during smoking-cessation treatment. *Journal of Clinical Psychiatry, 57,* 534–538. [13]

Borrie, R. A. (1991). The use of restricted environmental stimulation therapy in treating addictive behaviors. *International Journal of the Addictions, 25,* 995–1015. [11]

Bosse, R., Aldwin, C. M., Levenson, M. R., & Workman-Daniels, K. (1991). How stressful is retirement? *Journal of Gerontology, 46,* 9–14. [10]

Bouchard, C. (1996). Can obesity be prevented? *Nutrition Reviews, 54,* S125–S130. [11]

Bouchard, C. (1997). Human variation in body mass: Evidence for a role of the genes. *Nutrition Reviews, 55,* S21–S30. [11]

Bouchard, C., Tremblay, A., Despres, J-P., Nadeau, A., Lupien, P. J., Theriault, G., Dussault, J., Moorjani, S., Pinault, S., & Fournier, G. (1990). The response to long-term overfeeding in identical twins. *New England Journal of Medicine, 322,* 1477–1482. [11]

Bouchard, T. J., Jr. (1994). Genes, environment, and personality. *Science, 264,* 1700–1701. [14]

Bouchard, T. J., Jr. (1997, September/October). Whenever the twain shall meet. *The Sciences, 37,* 52–57. [8, 9, 14]

Bouchard, T. J., Jr. (1998, May 13). Personal communication. [8]

Bouchard, T. J., Jr., & McGue, M. (1981). Familial studies of intelligence: A review. *Science, 212,* 1055–1058. [8]

Bouchard, T. J., Jr., Lykken, D. T., McGue, M., Segal, N. L., & Tellegen, A. (1990). Sources of human psychological differences: The Minnesota study of twins reared apart. *Science, 250,* 223–228. [8, 14]

Bouton, M. E. (1993). Context, time, and memory retrieval in the interference paradigms of Pavlovian learning. *Psychological Bulletin, 114,* 80–89. [5]

Bouton, M. E., & Ricker, S. T. (1994) Renewal of extinguished responding in a second context. *Animal Learning and Behavior, 22,* 317–324. [5]

Bovbjerg, D. H., Redd, W. H., Maier, L. A., Holland, J. C., Lesko, L. M., Niedzwiecki, D., Rubin, S. C., & Hakes, T. B. (1990). Anticipatory immune suppression and nausea in women receiving cyclic chemotherapy for ovarian cancer. *Journal of Consulting and Clinical Psychology, 58,* 153–157. [5]

Bower, G. H. (1973, October). How to . . . uh . . . remember! *Psychology Today,* pp. 63–70. [6]

Bower, G. H., Thompson-Schill, S., & Tulving E. (1994). Reducing retroactive interference: An interference analysis. *Journal of Experimental Psychology: Learning, Memory, and Cognition, 20,* 51–66. [6]

Bowers, K. S. (1992). Imagination and dissociative control in hypnotic responding. *International Journal of Clinical and Experimental Hypnosis, 40,* 253–275. [4]

Bowers, K. S., & Farvolden, P. (1996). Revisiting a century-old Freudian slip—from suggestion disavowed to the truth repressed. *Psychological Bulletin, 119,* 355–380. [6]

Bowers, K. S., & Woody, E. Z. (1996). Hypnotic amnesia and the paradox of intentional forgetting. *Journal of Abnormal Psychology, 105,* 381–390. [4]

Bowlby, J. (1951). Maternal care and mental health. *World Health Organization Monograph* (Serial No. 2). [9]

Bowlby, J. (1969). *Attachment and loss* (Vol. 1). New York: Basic Books. [9]

Bradshaw, J. L. (1989). *Hemispheric specialization and psychological function.* New York: Wiley. [2]

Brain imaging and psychiatry—Part I. (1997, January). *Harvard Mental Health Letter, 13*(7), 1–4. [2]

Bramblett, D. A. (1997, October). Personal communication. [3]

Brantner, J. P., & Doherty, M. A. (1983). A review of time out: A conceptual and methodological analysis. In S. Axelrod & J. Apsche (Eds.), *The effects of punishment on human behavior* (pp. 87–132). New York: Academic Press. [16]

Braun, S. (1996). New experiments underscore warnings on maternal drinking. *Science, 273,* 738–739. [9]

Braungart, J. M., Plomin, R., DeFries, J. C., & Fulker, D. W. (1992). Genetic influence on tester-rated infant temperament as assessed by Bayley's Infant Behavior Record: Nonadoptive and adoptive siblings and twins. *Developmental Psychology,* 28, 40–47. [9]

Brawman-Mintzer, O., & Lydiard, R. B. (1996). Generalized anxiety disorder: Issues in epidemiology. *Journal of Clinical Psychiatry, 57*(7, Suppl.), 3–8. [15]

Brawman-Mintzer, O., & Lydiard, R. B. (1997). Biological basis of generalized anxiety disorder. *Journal of Clinical Psychiatry, 58*(3, Suppl.), 16–25. [15]

Bray, G. A. (1991). Weight homeostasis. *Annual Review of Medicine, 42,* 205–216. [11]

Bray, G. A., & Tartaglia, L. A. (2000). Medicinal strategies in the treatment of obesity. *Nature, 404,* 672–677. [11]

Brazelton, T. B., Tronick, E., Adamson, L., Als, H., & Wise, S. (1975). *Early mother-infant interaction. In Parent-Infant Interaction, Ciba Symposium 33.* Amsterdam: Assoc. Science Publ. [9]

Breckler, S. J. (1984). Empirical validation of affect, behavior, and cognition as distinct attitude components. *Journal of Personality and Social Psychology, 47,* 1191–1205. [17]

Breedlove, S. M. (1994). Sexual differentiation of the human nervous system. *Annual Review of Psychology, 45,* 389–418. [12]

Breland, K., & Breland, M. (1961). The misbehavior of organisms. *American Psychologist, 16,* 681–684. [5]

Brembs, F., & Heisenberg, M. (2000). The operant and the classical in conditioned orientation of *Drosophila melanogaster* at the flight simulator. *Learning & Memory, 7,* 104–115. [5]

Brennan, P. A., Raine, A., Schulsinger, F., Kirkegaard-Sorensen, L., Knop, J., Hutchings, B., Rosenberg, R., & Mednick, S. A. (1997). Psychophysiological protective factors for male subjects at high risk for criminal behavior. *American Journal of Psychiatry, 154,* 853–855. [17]

Brent, D. A., Bridge, J., Johnson, B. A., & Connolly, J. (1996). Suicidal behavior runs in families: A controlled family study of adolescent suicide victims. *Archives of General Psychiatry, 53,* 1145–1152. [15]

Breslau, N., Davis, G. C., Andreski, P., & Peterson, E. (1991). Traumatic events and posttraumatic stress disorder in an urban population of young adults. *Archives of General Psychiatry, 48,* 216–222. [13]

Breslau, N., Davis, G. C., Peterson, E. L., & Schultz, L. (1997). Psychiatric sequelae of posttraumatic stress disorder in women. *Archives of General Psychiatry, 54,* 81–87. [13]

Breslau, N., Kilbey, M. N., & Andreski, P. (1993). Nicotine dependence and major depression: New evidence from a prospective investigation. *Archives of General Psychiatry, 50,* 31–35. [13]

Bretherton, I. (1992). The origins of attachment theory: John Bowlby and Mary Ainsworth. *Developmental Psychology, 28,* 759–775. [9]

Brickner, M. A., Harkins, S. G., & Ostrom, T. M. (1986). Effects of personal involvement: Thought-provoking implications for social loafing. *Journal of Personality and Social Psychology, 51,* 763–769. [17]

Bridges, K. M. B. (1932). Emotional development in early infancy. *Child Development, 3,* 324–341. [11]

Brigham, J. C., & Wolfskeil, M. P. (1983). Opinions of attorneys and law enforcement personnel on the accuracy of eyewitness identifications. *Law and Human Behavior, 7,* 337–349. [6]

Broadbent, D. E. (1958). *Perception and communication.* New York: Pergamon Press. [6]

Brody, E. M., Johnson, P. T., & Fulcomer, M. C. (1984). What should adult children do for elderly parents? Opinions and preferences of three generations of women. *Journal of Gerontology, 39,* 736–746. [10]

Brody, E. M., Litvin, S. J., Hoffman, C., & Kleban, M. H. (1992). Differential effects of daughters' marital status on their parent care experiences. *The Gerontologist, 32,* 58–67. [10]

Brody, G., Pillegrini, A., & Sigel, I. (1986). Marital quality and mother-child and father-child interactions with school-aged children. *Developmental Psychology, 22,* 291–296. [9]

Brody, J. A., Grant, M. D., Frateschi, L. J., Miller, S. C., & Zhang, H. (2000). Reproductive longevity and increased life expectancy. *Age and Ageing, 29,* 75–78. [10]

Brody, J. E. (1995, August 30). Hormone replacement therapy for men: When does it help? *The New York Times,* p. C8. [12]

Brody, L. R. (1985). Gender differences in emotional development: A review of theories and research. *Journal of Personality, 53,* 102–149. [11]

Brody, N. (1992). *Intelligence* (2nd ed.). San Diego, CA: Academic. [8]

Brooks-Gunn, J., & Furstenberg, F. F. (1989). Adolescent sexual behavior. *American Psychologist, 44,* 249–257. [10]

Brotman, A. W. (1994). What works in the treatment of anorexia nervosa? *Harvard Mental Health Letter, 10*(7), 8. [11]

Brou, P., Sciascia, T. R., Linden, L., & Lettvin, J. Y. (1986). The colors of things. *Scientific American, 255,* 84–91. [3]

Broughton, R. J., & Shimizu, T. (1995). Sleep-related violence: A medical and forensic challenge. *Sleep, 18,* 727–730. [4]

Broughton, W. A., & Broughton, R. J. (1994). Psychosocial impact of narcolepsy. *Sleep, 17,* S45–S49. [4]

Brown, A. (1996, Winter). Mood disorders in children and adolescents. *NARSAD Research Newsletter,* pp. 11–14. [15]

Brown, A. M. (1990). Development of visual sensitivity to light and color vision in human infants: A critical review. *Vision Research, 30,* 1159–1188. [9]

Brown, G. W., Harris, T. O., & Hepworth, C. (1994). Life events and endogenous depression: A puzzle reexamined. *Archives of General Psychiatry, 51,* 525–534. [15]

Brown, J. D., & Rogers, R. J. (1991). Self-serving attributions: The role of physiological arousal. *Personality and Social Psychology Bulletin, 17,* 501–506. [17]

Brown, J. L., & Pollitt, E. (1996). Malnutrition, poverty and intellectual development. *Scientific American, 274,* 38–43. [8]

Brown, R. (1973). *A first language: The early stages.* Cambridge, MA: Harvard University Press. [9]

Brown, R., & Kulik, J. (1977). Flashbulb memories. *Cognition, 5,* 73–99. [6]

Brown, R., & McNeil, D. (1966). The "tip of the tongue" phenomenon. *Journal of Verbal Learning and Verbal Behavior, 5,* 325–337. [6]

Brown, R., Cazden, C., & Bellugi, U. (1968). The child's grammar from I to III. In J. P. Hill (Ed.), *Minnesota symposium on child psychology* (Vol. 2, pp. 28–73). Minneapolis: University of Minnesota Press. [9]

Brown, R. J., & Donderi, D. C. (1986). Dream content and self-reported well-being among recurrent dreamers, past-recurrent dreamers, and nonrecurrent dreamers. *Journal of Personality and Social Psychology, 50,* 612–623. [4]

Brown, W. A. (1998, January). The placebo effect. *Scientific American, 278,* 90–95. [3]

Brownell, K. (1991). Dieting and the search for the perfect body: Where physiology and culture collide. *Behavior Therapy, 22,* 1–12. [11]

Brownell, K. D., & Rodin, J. (1994). The dieting maelstrom: Is it possible and advisable to lose weight? *American Psychologist, 49,* 781–791. [11]

Brownell, K. D., & Wadden, T. A. (1992). Etiology and treatment of obesity: Understanding a serious, prevalent, and refractory disorder. *Journal of Consulting and Clinical Psychology, 60,* 505–517. [11]

Brownlee, S., & Schrof, J. M. (1997, March 17). The quality of mercy. *U.S. News & World Report,* pp. 54–67. [3]

Bryan, J. H., & Test, M. A. (1967). Models and helping: Naturalistic studies in aiding behavior. *Journal of Personality and Social Psychology, 6,* 400–407. [17]

Buchanan, C. M., Eccles, J. S., & Becker, J. B. (1992). Are adolescents the victims of raging hormones? Evidence for activational effects of hormones on moods and behavior at adolescence. *Psychological Bulletin, 111,* 62–107. [10]

Büchel, C., & Dolan, R. J. (2000). Classical fear conditioning in functional neuroimaging. *Current Opinion in Neurobiology, 10,* 219–223. [5]

Buchsbaum, M. S., Someya, T., Teng, C. Y., Abel, L., Chin, S., Najafi, A., Haier, R. J., Wu, J., & Bunney, W. E., Jr. (1996). PET and MRI of the thalamus in never-medicated patients with schizophrenia. *American Journal of Psychiatry, 153,* 191–199. [15]

Buck, L. B. (1996). Information coding in the vertebrate olfactory system. *Annual Review of Neuroscience, 19,* 517–544. [3]

Buckhout, R., Eugenio, P., Licitra, T., Oliver, L., & Kramer, T. H. (1981). Memory, hypnosis, and evidence: Research on eyewitnesses. *Social Action and the Law, 7,* 67–72. [6]

Buckingham, H. W., Jr., & Kertesz, A. (1974). A linguistic analysis of fluent aphasics. *Brain and Language, 1,* 29–42. [2]

Buffenstein, A., Heaster, J., & Ko, P. (1999). Chronic psychotic illness from amphetamine. *American Journal of Psychiatry, 156,* 662. [4]

Buis, J. M., & Thompson, D. N. (1989). Imaginary audience and personal fable: A brief review. *Adolescence, 24,* 773–781. [10]

Buller, D. B., Burgoon, M., Hall, J. R., Levine, N., Taylor, A. M., Beach, B. H., Melcher, C., Buller, M. K., Bowen, S. L., Hunsaker, F. G., & Bergen, A. (2000). Using language intensity to increase the success of a family intervention to protect children from ultraviolet radiation: Predictions from language expectancy theory. *Preventive Medicine, 30,* 103–113. [17]

Buonomano, D. V., & Merzenich, M. M. (1995). Temporal information transformed into a spatial code by a neural network with realistic properties. *Science, 267,* 1028–1030. [7]

Burke, A., Heuer, F., & Reisberg, D. (1992). Remembering emotional events. *Memory and Cognition, 20,* 277–290. [6]

Burkhardt, S. A., & Rotatori, A. F. (1995). *Treatment and prevention of childhood sexual abuse.* Washington, DC: Taylor & Francis. [12]

Burns, B. D. (1996). Meta-analogical transfer: Transfer between episodes of analogical reasoning. *Journal of Experimental Psychology: Learning, Memory, and Cognition, 22,* 1032–1048. [7]

Burt, D. B., Zembar, M. J., & Niederehe, G. (1995). Depression and memory impairment: A meta-analysis of the association, its pattern, and specificity. *Psychological Bulletin, 117,* 285–305. [6]

Busch, C. M., Zonderman, A. B., & Costa, P. T. (1994). Menopausal transition and psychological distress in a nationally representative sample: Is menopause associated with psychological distress? *Journal of Aging and Health, 6,* 209–228. [10]

Bushman, B. J. (1995). Moderating role of trait aggressiveness in the effects of violent media on aggression. *Journal of Personality and Social Psychology, 69,* 950–960. [17]

Bushman, B. J., & Cooper, H. M. (1990). Effects of alcohol on human aggression: An integrative research review. *Psychological Bulletin, 107,* 341–354. [17]

Busnel, M. C., Granier-Deferre, C., & Lecanuet, J. P. (1992). Fetal audition. *Annals of the New York Academy of Sciences, 662,* 118–134. [9]

Buss, D. M. (1984). Marital assortment for personality dispositions: Assessment with three different data sources. *Behavioral Genetics, 14,* 111–123. [17]

Buss, D. M. (1991). Evolutionary personality psychology. *Annual Review of Psychology, 42,* 459–491. [11, 14]

Buss, D. M. (1994). The strategies of human mating. *American Scientist, 82,* 238–249. [12, 17]

Buss, D. M. (1999). *Evolutionary psychology: The new science of the mind.* Boston: Allyn & Bacon. [1, 5, 12, 17]

Buss, D. M. (2000a). *The dangerous passion: Why jealousy is as necessary as sex and love.* New York: Free Press. [1, 5]

Buss, D. M. (2000b). Desires in human mating. *Annals of the New York Academy of Sciences, 907,* 39–49. [1, 11, 12, 17]

Buss, D. M., Abbott, M., Angleitner, A., Asherian, A., Biaggio, A., Blanco-Villasenor, A., Bruchon-Schweitzer, M., et al. (1990). International preferences in selecting mates: A study of 37 cultures. *Journal of Cross-Cultural Psychology, 21,* 5–47. [1, 17]

Buss, D. M., Larson, R., Westen, D., & Semmelroth, J. (1992). Sex differences in jealousy: Evolution, physiology, and psychology. *Psychological Science, 3,* 251–255. [1]

Bussey, K., & Bandura, A. (1999). Social cognitive theory of gender development and differentiation. *Psychological Review, 106,* 676–713. [12]

Butcher, J. N. (1992, October). International developments with the MMPI–2. *MMPI–2 News & Profiles, 3*, 4. [14]
Butcher, J. N., & Graham, J. R. (1989). *Topics in MMPI–2 interpretation.* Minneapolis: Department of Psychology, University of Minnesota. [14]
Butcher, J. N., & Rouse, S. V. (1996). Personality: Individual differences and clinical assessment. *Annual Review of Psychology, 47*, 89–111. [14]
Butcher, J. N., Dahlstrom, W. G., Graham, J. R., Tellegen, A., & Kaemmer, B. (1989). *Manual for the restandardized Minnesota Multiphasic Personality Inventory: MMPI–2. An administrative and interpretive guide.* Minneapolis: University of Minnesota Press. [14]
Butcher, J. N., Graham, J. R., & Ben-Porath, Y. S. (1995). Methodological problems and issues in MMPI, MMPI-2, and MMPI-A research. *Psychological Assessment, 7*, 320–329. [14]
Butler, R., & Lewis, M. (1982). *Aging and mental health* (3rd ed.). St. Louis: Mosby. [10]
Buunk, B. P., Angleitner, A., Oubaid, V., & Buss, D. M. (1996). Sex differences in jealousy in evolutionary and cultural perspective: Tests from the Netherlands, Germany and the United States. *Psychological Science, 7*, 359–363. [1]
Byne, W. (1993). Human sexual orientation: The biologic theories reappraised. *Archives of General Psychiatry, 50*, 228–239. [12]
Byne, W. (1993). Sexual orientation and brain structure: Adding up the evidence. Paper presented at the annual meeting of the International Academy of Sex Research. Pacific Grove, CA. [12]
Byne, W. (1994). The biological evidence challenged. *Scientific American, 270*, 50–55. [12]
Byne, W., & Parsons, B. (1993). Human sexual orientation: The biologic theories reappraised. *Archives of General Psychiatry, 50*, 228–239. [12]
Byne, W., & Parsons, B. (1994). Biology and human sexual orientation. *Harvard Mental Health Letter, 10*(8), 5–7. [12]
Byrne, D., Clore, G. L., & Smeaton, G. (1986). The attraction hypothesis: Do similar attitudes affect anything? *Journal of Personality and Social Psychology, 51*, 1167–1170. [17]

Cahill, L., Babinsky, R., Markowitsch, H. J., & McGaugh, J. L. (1995). The amygdala and emotional memory. *Nature, 377*, 295–296. [2, 6]
Caldwell, J. L. (2000). The use of melatonin: An information paper. *Aviation Space and Environmental Medicine, 71*, 238–244. [4]
Callahan, J. (1997, May–June). Hypnosis: Trick or treatment? You'd be amazed at what modern doctors are tackling with an 18th century gimmick. *Health, 11*, 52–54. [4]
Camp, D. S., Raymond, G. A., & Church, R. M. (1967). Temporal relationship between response and punishment. *Journal of Experimental Psychology, 74*, 114–123. [5]
Campbell, A. (1975, May). The American way of mating: Marriage si, children only maybe. *Psychology Today*, pp. 37–43. [10]
Campbell, D. T. (1996). Unresolved issues in measurement validity: An autobiographical overview. *Psychological Assessment, 8*, 363–368. [8]
Campbell, D. T., & Sprecht, J. C. (1985). Altruism: Biology, culture, and religion. *Journal of Social and Clinical Psychology, 3*, 33–42. [14]
Campbell, P., & Dhand, R. (2000). Obesity. *Nature, 404*, 631. [11]
Campbell, R., & Brody, E. M. (1985). Women's changing roles and help to the elderly: Attitudes of women in the United States and Japan. *The Gerontologist, 25*, 584–592. [10]
Campbell, S. S. (1985). Spontaneous termination of ad libitum sleep episodes with special reference to REM sleep. *Electroencephalography & Clinical Neurophysiology, 60*, 237–242. [4]
Campbell, S. S. (1995). Effects of timed bright-light exposure on shift-work adaptation in middle-aged subjects. *Sleep, 18*, 408–416. [4]
Campbell, S. S., & Murphy, P. J. (1998). Extraocular circadian phototransduction in humans. *Science, 279*, 396–399. [4]
Campos, J. J., Langer, A., & Krowitz, A. (1970). Cardiac responses on the visual cliff in prelocomotor human infants. *Science, 170*, 196–197. [9]
Cañizares, S., Boget, T., Salamero, M., Rumià, J., Elices, E., & Arroyo, S. (2000). Reliability and clinical usefulness of the short forms of the Wechsler memory scale (revised) in patients with epilepsy. *Epilepsy Research, 41*, 97–106. [8]
Cannon, T. D., Kaprio, J., Lönnqvist, J., Huttunen, M., & Koskenvuo, M. (1998). The genetic epidemiology of schizophrenia in a Finnish twin cohort: A population-based modeling study. *Archives of General Psychiatry, 55*, 67–74. [15]
Cannon, W. B. (1927). The James-Lange theory of emotions: A critical examination as an alternative theory. *American Journal of Psychology, 39*, 106–112. [11]
Cannon, W. B. (1929). *Bodily changes in pain, hunger, fear and rage* (2nd ed.). New York: Appleton. [2]
Cannon, W. B. (1932). *The wisdom of the body.* New York: Norton. [13]
Cannon, W. B. (1935). Stresses and strains of homeostasis. *American Journal of Public Health, 189*, 1–14. [2]
Cannon, W. B., & Washburn, A. L. (1912). An explanation of hunger. *American Journal of Physiology, 29*, 441–454. [11]
Capel, B. (2000). The battle of the sexes. *Mechanisms of Development, 92*, 89–103. [9, 12]
Cardena, E. (2000). Hypnosis in the treatment of trauma: A promising, but not fully supported, efficacious intervention. *International Journal of Clinical Experimental Hypnosis, 48*, 225–238. [4]
Cardoso, S. H., de Mello, L. C., & Sabbatini, R. M. E. (2000). How nerve cells work. [On-line]. Available: http://www.epub.org.br/cm/n09/fundamentos/transmissao/voo_i.htm [2]
Carels, R. A., Blumenthal, J. A., & Sherwood, A. (2000). Emotional responsivity during daily life: Relationship to psychosocial functioning and ambulatory blood pressure. *International Journal of Psychophysiology, 36*, 25–33. [11]
Carlat, D. J., Camargo, C. A., Jr., & Herzog, D. B. (1997). Eating disorders in males: A report on 135 patients. *American Journal of Psychiatry, 154*, 1127–1132. [11]
Carlin, A. S., Hoffman, H. G., & Weghorst, S. (1997). Virtual reality and tactile augmentation in the treatment of spider phobia: a case report. *Behaviour Research and Therapy, 35*, 153–158. [16]
Carlson, M., Charlin, V., & Miller, N. (1988). Positive mood and helping behavior: A test of six hypotheses. *Journal of Personality and Social Psychology, 55*, 211–229. [17]
Carlson, N. R. (1994). *Physiology of behavior* (5th ed.). Boston: Allyn & Bacon. [3]
Carlson, N. R. (1998). *Foundations of physiological psychology* (4th ed.). Boston: Allyn & Bacon. [4]
Carlsson, I., Wendt, P. E., & Risberg, J. (2000). On the neurobiology of creativity. Differences in frontal activity between high and low creative subjects. *Neuropsychologia, 38*, 873–885. [8]
Carpenter, W. T., Jr. (1996). Maintenance therapy of persons with schizophrenia. *Journal of Clinical Psychiatry, 57*(9, Suppl.), 10–18. [16]
Carrier, J. (1980). Homosexual behavior in cross-cultural perspective. In J. Marmor (Ed.), *Homosexual behavior* (pp. 100–122). New York: Basic Books. [12]
Carroll, J. M., & Russell, J. A. (1996). Do facial expressions signal specific emotions? Judging emotion from the face in context. *Journal of Personality and Social Psychology, 70*, 205–218. [11]
Carroll, K. M., Rounsaville, B. J., Nich, C., Gordon, L. T., Wirtz, P. W., & Gawin, F. (1994). One-year follow-up of psychotherapy and pharmacotherapy for cocaine dependence: Delayed emergence of psychotherapy effects. *Archives of General Psychiatry, 51*, 989–997. [16]
Carskadon, M. A., & Dement, W. C. (1989). Normal human sleep: An overview. In M. H. Kryger, T. Roth, & W. C. Dement (Eds.), *Principles and practice of sleep medicine* (pp. 3–13). Philadelphia: W. B. Saunders. [4]
Carskadon, M. A., & Rechtschaffen, A. (1989). Monitoring and staging human sleep. In M. H. Kryger, T. Roth, & W. C. Dement (Eds.), *Principles and practice of sleep medicine* (pp. 665–683). Philadelphia: W. B. Saunders. [4]
Carson, R. C. (1989). Personality. *Annual Review of Psychology, 40*, 227–248. [14]
Carter, R. S., & Wojtkiewicz, R. A. (2000). Parental involvement with adolescents' education: Do daughters or sons get more help? *Adolescence, 35*, 29–44. [10]
Caruso, J. C., & Cliff, N. (2000). Increasing the reliability of Wechsler Intelligence Scale for Children—Third Edition difference scores with reliable component analysis. *Psychological Assessment, 12*, 189–196. [8]

Carver C. S., Pozo, C., Harris, S. D., Noriega, V., Scheier, M. F., Robinson, D. S., Ketcham, A. S., Moffat, F. L., Jr., & Clark, K. C. (1993). How coping mediates the effect of optimism on distress: A study of women with early stage breast cancer. *Journal of Personality and Social Psychology, 65,* 375–390. [13]

Carver, C. S., & Scheier, M. F. (1996). *Perspectives on personality* (3rd ed.). Boston: Allyn & Bacon. [14]

Case, R. (Ed.). (1992). *The mind's staircase: Exploring the conceptual underpinnings of children's thought and knowledge.* Hillsdale, NJ: Erlbaum. [9]

Casey, D. E. (1996). Side effect profiles of new antipsychotic agents. *Journal of Clinical Psychiatry, 57*(11, Suppl.), 40–45. [16]

Casey, M. B., Nuttall, R., Pezaris, E., & Benbow, C. P. (1995). The influence of spatial ability on gender differences in mathematics college entrance test scores across diverse samples. *Developmental Psychology, 31,* 697–705. [12]

Cash, T. F., & Derlega, V. J. (1978). The matching hypothesis: Physical attractiveness among same-sexed friends. *Personality and Social Psychology Bulletin, 4,* 240–243. [17]

Cash, T. F., & Janda, L. H. (1984, December). The eye of the beholder. *Psychology Today,* pp. 46–52. [17]

Caspi, A., & Silva, P. A. (1995). Temperamental qualities at age three predict personality traits in young adulthood: Longitudinal evidence from a birth cohort. *Child Development, 66,* 486–498. [9]

Caspi, A., Lynam, D., Moffitt, T. E., & Silva, P. A. (1993). Unraveling girls' delinquency: Biological, dispositional, and contextual contributions to adolescent misbehavior. *Developmental Psychology, 29,* 19–30. [10]

Catania, J. A., et al. (1992). Prevalence of AIDS-related risk factors and condom use in the United States. *Science, 258,* 1101–1106. [12]

Catlin, F. I. (1986). Noise-induced hearing loss. *American Journal of Otology, 7,* 141–149. [3]

Catotti, D. N., Clarke, P., & Catoe, K. E. (1993). Herpes revisited: Still a cause of concern. *Sexually Transmitted Diseases, 20*(2), 77–80. [12]

Cattell, R. B. (1950). *Personality: A systematic, theoretical, and factual study.* New York: McGraw-Hill. [14]

Cattell, R. B. (1993). *16PF® fifth edition profile sheet.* Champaign, IL: Institute for Personality and Ability Testing. [14]

Cattell, R. B., Eber, H. W., & Tatsuoka, M. M. (1977). *Handbook for the 16 personality factor questionnaire.* Champaign, IL: Institute of Personality and Ability Testing. [14]

Cattell, R. B., Saunders, D. R., & Stice, G. F. (1950). *The 16 personality factor questionnaire.* Champaign, IL: Institute of Personality and Ability Testing. [14]

Challis, B. H. (1996). Implicit memory research in 1996: Introductory remarks. *Canadian Journal of Experimental Psychology, 50,* 1–4. [6]

Chambless, D. L., & Goldstein, A. J. (1979). Behavioral psychotherapy. In R. J. Corsini (Ed.), *Current psychotherapies* (2nd ed., pp. 230–272). Itasca, IL: F. E. Peacock. [16]

Changeux, J-P. (1993). Chemical signaling in the brain. *Scientific American, 269,* 58–62. [2]

Chaplin, W. F., Philips, J. B., Brown, J. D., Clanton, N. R., & Stein, J. L. (2000). Handshaking, gender, personality, and first impressions. *Journal of Personality and Social Psychology, 19,* 110–117. [17]

Chapman, R. S. (2000). Children's language learning: An interactionist perspective. *Journal of Child Psychology & Psychiatry, 41,* 133–154. [9]

Charness, N. (1989). Age and expertise: Responding to Talland's challenge. In L. W. Poon, D. C. Rubin, & B. A. Wilson (Eds.), *Everyday cognition in adulthood and old age.* New York: Cambridge University Press. [10]

Chase, M. H., & Morales, F. R. (1990). The atonia and myoclonia of active (REM) sleep. *Annual Review of Psychology, 41,* 557–584. [4]

Chaudhari, N., Landin, A. M., & Roper, S. D. (2000). A metabotropic glutamate receptor variant functions as a taste receptor. *Nature Neuroscience, 3,* 113–119. [3]

Checkley, H. (1941). *The mask of sanity.* St. Louis: Mosby. [15]

Chen, J. C., Borson, S., & Scanlan, J. M. (2000). Stage-specific prevalence of behavioral symptoms in Alzheimer's disease in a multi-ethnic community sample. *American Journal of Geriatric Psychiatry, 8,* 123–133. [10]

Cheng, L. S., Swan, G. E., & Carmelli, D. (2000). A genetic analysis of smoking behavior in family members of older adult males. *Addiction, 95,* 427–435. [4]

Chen-Sea, M.-J. (2000). Validating the Draw-A-Man Test as a personal neglect test. *American Journal of Occupational Therapy, 54,* 391–397. [2]

Chesno, F. A., & Killman, P. R. (1975). Effects of stimulation on sociopathic avoidance learning. *Journal of Abnormal Psychology, 84,* 144–150. [15]

Children's Defense Fund. (1996). *The state of America's children yearbook, 1996.* Washington, DC: Author. [9, 10]

Chipuer, H. M., Plomin, R., Pedersen, M. L., McClearn, G. E., & Nesselroade, J. R. (1993). Genetic influence on family environment: The role of personality. *Developmental Psychology, 29,* 110–118. [14]

Chira, S. (1992, February 12). Bias against girls is found rife in schools, with lasting damage. *The New York Times,* pp. A1, A23. [12]

Chodoff, P. (1987). More on multiple personality disorder. *American Journal of Psychiatry, 144,* 124. [15]

Chollar, S. (1989). Conversation with the dolphins. *Psychology Today, 23,* 52–57. [7]

Chomsky, N. (1957). *Syntactic structures.* The Hague: Mouton. [9]

Chomsky, N. (1968). *Language and mind.* New York: Harcourt, Brace & World. [9]

Chomsky, N. (1986). *Knowledge of language: Its nature, origin, and use.* New York: Praeger. [7]

Chomsky, N. (1990). On the nature, use and acquisition of language. In W. G. Lycan (Ed.), *Mind and cognition* (pp. 627–646). Oxford, England: Blackwell. [7]

Christensen, L. B. (1997). *Experimental methodology* (7th ed.). Boston: Allyn & Bacon. [1]

Christensen, L. B. (2001). *Experimental methodology* (8th ed.). Boston: Allyn & Bacon. [1]

Christianson, S-Å. (1992). Emotional stress and eyewitness memory: A critical review. *Psychological Bulletin, 112,* 284–309. [6]

Christophe, A., & Morton, J. (1994). Comprehending baby-think. *Nature, 370,* 250–251. [9]

Chu, S., & Downes, J. J. (2000). Long live Proust: The odour-cued autobiographical memory bump. *Cognition, 75,* B41–B50. [3]

Chumlea, W. C. (1982). Physical growth in adolescence. In B. B. Wolman (Ed.), *Handbook of developmental psychology.* Englewood Cliffs, NJ: Prentice-Hall. [10]

Church R. M. (1963). The varied effects of punishment on behavior. *Psychological Review, 70,* 369–402. [5]

Church, R. M. (1989). Theories of timing behavior. In S. P. Klein & R. Mowrer (Eds.), *Contemporary learning theories: Instrumental conditioning theory and the impact of biological constraints on learning.* Hillsdale, NJ: Erlbaum. [5]

Chyou, P. H., & Eaker, E. D. (2000). Serum cholesterol concentrations and all-cause mortality in older people. *Age and Ageing, 29,* 69–74. [10]

Cialdini, R. B., Cacioppo, J. T., Basset, R., & Miller, J. A. (1978). Lowball procedure for producing compliance: Commitment then cost. *Journal of Personality and Social Psychology, 36,* 463–476. [17]

Cialdini, R. B., Vincent, J. E., Lewis, S. K., Catalan, J., Wheeler, D., & Darby, B. L. (1975). Reciprocal concessions procedure for inducing compliance: The door-in-the-fact technique. *Journal of Personality and Social Psychology, 31,* 206–215. [17]

Cipolli, C., Bolzani, R., Cornoldi, C., De Beni, R., & Fagioli, I. (1993). Bizarreness effect in dream recall. *Sleep, 16,* 163–170. [4]

Clapp, J. D., Shillington, A. M., & Segars, L. B. (2000). Deconstructing contexts of binge drinking among college students. *American Journal of Drug and Alcohol Abuse, 26,* 139–154. [4]

Clark, D. M., & Teasdale, J. D. (1982). Diurnal variation in clinical depression and accessibility of memories of positive and negative experiences. *Journal of Abnormal Psychology, 91,* 87–95. [6]

Clark, L. A., Watson, D., & Reynolds, S. (1995). Diagnosis and classification of psychopathology: Challenges to the current system and future directions. *Annual Review of Psychology, 46,* 121–153. [15]

Clark, M. L., & Ayers, M. (1992). Friendship similarity during early adolescence: Gender and racial patterns. *Journal of Psychology, 126,* 393–405. [10]

Clark, R. D., III, & Word, L. E. (1972). Why don't bystanders help? Because of ambiguity? *Journal of Personality and Social Psychology, 24,* 392–400. [17]

Classen, J., Liepert, J., Wise, S., Hallett, M., & Cohen, L. (1998). Rapid plasticity of human cortical movement representation induced by practice. *Journal of Neurophysiology, 79,* 1117–1123. [2]

Clayton, K. N. (1964). T-maze choice learning as a joint function of the reward magnitudes for the alternatives. *Journal of Comparative and Physiological Psychology, 58,* 333–338. [5]

Clayton, N. S. (1998). Memory and the hippocampus in food-storing birds: A comparative approach. *Neuropharmacology, 37,* 441–452. [6]

Clément, K., Vaisse, C., Lahlou, N., Cabrol, S., Pelloux, V., Cassuto, D., Gourmelen, M., Dina, C., Chambaz, J., Lacorte, J-M., Basdevant, A., Bougnères, P., Lubouc, Y., Froguel, P., & Guy-Grand, B. (1998). A mutation in the human leptin receptor gene causes obesity and pituitary dysfunction. *Nature, 392,* 398–401. [11]

Clifford, E. (2000). Neural plasticity: Merzenich, Taub, and Greenough. *Harvard Brain* [Special Issue], *6,* 16–20. [2]

Cloninger, C. R., Sigvardsson, S., Bohman, M., & von Knorring, A. L. (1982). Predispositions to petty criminality in Swedish adoptees, II. Cross-fostering analysis of gene-environment interaction. *Archives of General Psychiatry, 39,* 1242–1249. [17]

Clum, G. A., Clum, G. A., & Surls, R. (1993). A meta-analysis of treatments for panic disorder. *Journal of Consulting and Clinical Psychology, 61,* 317–326. [16]

Cogan, J. C., Bhalla, S. K., Sefa-Dedeh, A., & Rothblum, E. D. (1996). A comparison study of United States and African students on perceptions of obesity and thinness. *Journal of Cross-Cultural Psychology, 27,* 98–113. [11]

Cohen, A. (1997, September 8). Battle of the binge. *Time,* p. 54–56. [4]

Cohen, L. L., & Shotland, R. L. (1996). Timing of first sexual intercourse in a relationship: Expectations, experiences, and perceptions of others. *Journal of Sex Research, 33,* 291–299. [12]

Cohen, M. S., Kosslyn, S. M., Breiter, H. C., DiGirolamo, G. J., Thompson, W. L., Anderson, A. K., Bookheimer, S. Y., Rosen, B. R., & Belliveau, J. W. (1996). Changes in cortical activity during mental rotation: A mapping study using functional MRI. *Brain, 119,* 89–100. [7]

Cohen, S. (1988). Psychosocial models of the role of social support in the etiology of physical disease. *Health Psychology, 7,* 269–297. [13]

Cohen, S. (1996). Psychological stress, immunity, and upper respiratory infections. *Current Directions in Psychological Science, 5,* 86–89. [13]

Cohen, S., & Herbert, T. B. (1996). Health psychology: Psychological factors and physical disease from the perspective of human psychoneuroimmunology. *Annual Review of Psychology, 47,* 113–142. [13]

Cohen, S., & Williamson, G. M. (1991). Stress and infectious disease in humans. *Psychological Bulletin, 109,* 5–54. [13]

Cohen, S., Doyle, W. J., Skoner, D. P., Rabin, B. S., & Gwaltney, J. M., Jr. (1997). Social ties and susceptibility to the common cold. *Journal of the American Medical Association, 277,* 1940–1944. [13]

Colasanto, D., & Shriver, J. (1989, May). Mirror of America: Middle-aged face marital crisis. *Gallup Report, No. 284,* 34–38. [10]

Colby, A., Kohlberg, L., Gibbs, J., & Lieberman, M. (1983). A longitudinal study of moral judgment. *Monographs of the Society for Research in Child Development, 48*(1–2, Serial No. 200). [10]

Cole, P. M. (1986). Children's spontaneous control of facial expression. *Child Development, 57,* 1309–1321. [11]

Coleman, M., & Ganong, L. H. (1985). Love and sex role stereotypes: Do macho men and feminine women make better lovers? *Journal of Personality and Social Psychology, 49,* 170–176. [12]

Coles, M. E., & Heinberg, R. G. (2000). Patterns of anxious arousal during exposure to feared situations in individuals with social phobia. *Behaviour Research & Therapy, 38,* 405–424. [16]

Collaer, M. L., & Hines, M. (1995). Human behavioral sex differences: A role for gonadal hormones during early development. *Psychological Bulletin, 118,* 55–107. [12]

Collier, A. C., Coombs, R. W., Schoenfeld, D. A., Bassett, R. L., Timpone, J., Baruch, A., Jones, M., Facey, K., Whitacre, C., McAuliffe, V. J., Friedman, H. M., Merigan, T. C., Reichman, R. C., Hooper, C., & Corey, L. (1996). Treatment of human immunodeficiency virus infection with saquinavir, zidovudine, and zalcitabine. *New England Journal of Medicine, 334,* 1011–1017. [12]

Collins, N. L. (1996). Working models of attachment: Implications for explanation, emotion, and behavior. *Journal of Personality and Social Psychology, 71,* 810–832. [9]

Collins, W. A., & Gunnar, M. R. (1990). Social and personality development. *Annual Review of Psychology, 41,* 387–416. [9, 11]

Collins, W. A., Maccoby, E. E., Steinberg, L., Hetherington, E. M., & Bornstein, M. H. (2000). Contemporary research on parenting. *American Psychologist, 55,* 218–232. [10]

Colombo, M., & Broadbent, N. (2000). Is the avian hippocampus a functional homologue of the mammalian hippocampus? *Neuroscience and Biobehavioral Reviews, 24,* 465–484. [6]

Colón, I., & Wuollet, C. A. (1994). Homeland, gender and Chinese drinking. *Journal of Addictive Diseases, 13,* 59–67. [4]

Colwell, J., & Payne, J. (2000). Negative correlates of computer game play in adolescents. *British Journal of Psychology, 91*(Pt. 3), 295–310. [17]

Compton, R. J. (2000). Ability to disengage attention predicts negative affect. *Cognition and Emotion, 14,* 401–415. [11]

Conca, A., Swoboda, E., König, P., Koppi, S., Beraus, W., Künz, A., et al. (2000). Clinical impacts of single transcranial magnetic stimulation (sTMS) as an add-on therapy in severely depressed patients under SSRI treatment. *Human Psychopharmacology: Clinical and Experimental, 15,* 429–438. [16]

Condon, W. S., & Sander, L. W. (1974). Neonatal movement is synchronized with adult speech: Interactional participation and language acquisition. *Science, 183,* 99–101. [9]

Coney, J., & Fitzgerald, J. (2000). Gender differences in the recognition of laterally presented affective nouns. *Cognition and Emotion, 14,* 325–339. [11]

Conrad, R. (1964). Acoustic confusions in immediate memory. *British Journal of Psychology, 55,* 75–84. [6]

Consumer Reports. (1995, Novmber) Mental health: Does therapy help? pp. 734–739. [16]

Conway, M. A., Cohen, G., & Stanhope, N. (1991). On the very long-term retention of knowledge acquired through formal education: Twelve years of cognitive psychology. *Journal of Experimental Psychology: General, 120,* 395–409. [6]

Conway, M. A., Collins, A. F., Gathercole, S. E., & Anderson, S. J. (1996). Recollections of true and false autobiographical memories. *Journal of Experimental Psychology: General, 125,* 69–95. [6]

Cook, M., Mineka, S., Wolkenstein, B., & Laitsch, K. (1985). Observational conditioning of snake fear in unrelated rhesus monkeys. *Journal of Abnormal Psychology, 94,* 591–610. [5]

Cooke, P. (1992, December/January). TV or not TV. *Health,* pp. 33–43. [9]

Coons, P. M. (1994). Confirmation of childhood abuse in child and adolescent cases of multiple personality disorder and dissociative disorder not otherwise specified. *Journal of Nervous and Mental Disease, 182,* 461–464. [15]

Coons, P. M., Bowman, E. S., Kluft, R. P., & Milstein, V. (1991). The cross-cultural occurrence of MPD: Additional cases from a recent survey. *Dissociation, 4,* 124–128. [15]

Cooper, L. A., & Shepard, R. N. (1984). Turning something over in the mind. *Scientific American, 251,* 106–114. [7]

Cooper, R. (1994). Normal sleep. In R. Cooper (Ed.), *Sleep.* New York: Chapman & Hall. [4]

Coplan, J. D., Papp, L. A., Pine, D., Marinez, J., Cooper, T. Rosenblum, L. A., Klein, D. F., & Gorman, J. M. (1997). Clinical improvement with fluxetine therapy and noradrenergic function in patients with panic disorder. *Archives of General Psychiatry, 54,* 643–648. [16]

Coppen, A. (1994). Depression as a lethal disease: Prevention strategies. *Journal of Clinical Psychiatry, 55*(4, Suppl.), 37–45. [15]

Corballis, M. C. (1989). Laterality and human evolution. *Psychological Review, 96,* 492–509. [2]

Coren, S. (1989). Left-handedness and accident-related injury risk. *American Journal of Public Health, 79,* 1–2. [2]

Coren, S. (1993). *The left-hander syndrome: The causes and consequences of left-handedness.* New York: Vintage Books. [2]

Coren, S. (1996a). Accidental death and the shift to daylight savings time. *Perceptual and Motor Skills, 83,* 921–922. [4]

Coren, S. (1996b). Daylight savings time and traffic accidents. *New England Journal of Medicine, 334,* 924. [4]

Coren, S., & Halpern, D. F. (1991). Left-handedness: A marker for decreased survival fitness. *Psychological Bulletin, 109,* 90–106. [2]

Cork, L. C., Clarkson, T. B., Jacoby, R. O., Gaertner, D. J., Leary, S. L., Linn, J. M., Pakes, S. P., Ringler, D. H., Strandberg, J. D., & Swindle, M. M. (1997). The costs of animal research: Origins and options. *Science, 276,* 758–759. [1]

Cornelius, M. D., Leech, S. L., Goldschmidt, L., & Day, N. L. (2000). Prenatal tobacco exposure: Is it a risk factor for early tobacco experimentation? *Nicotine & Tobacco Research, 2,* 45–52. [9, 13]

Cornish, J. L., & Kalivas, P. W. (2000). Glutamate transmission in the nucleus accumbens mediates relapse in cocaine addiction. *Journal of Neuroscience, 20,* RC89. [4]

Cosmides, L., & Tooby, J. (2000). Evolutionary psychology and the emotions. In M. Lewis, Jr., & J. M. Haviland-Jones (Eds.), *Handbook of emotions* (2nd ed.). New York: Guilford. [1]

Costa, P. T., Jr. (1996). Work and personality: Use of the NEO-PI-R in industrial/organisational psychology. *Applied Psychology: An International Review, 45,* 225–241. [14]

Costa, P. T., Jr., & McCrae, R. R. (1985). *The NEO Personality Inventory.* Odessa, FL: Psychological Assessment Resources. [14]

Costa, P. T., Jr., & McCrae, R. R. (1992a). *NEO-PI-R: Revised NEO Personality Inventory (NEO-PI-R).* Odessa, FL: Psychological Assessment Resources. [14]

Costa, P. T., Jr., & McCrae, R. R. (1997). Stability and change in personality assessment: The Revised NEO Personality Inventory in the year 2000. *Journal of Personality Assessment, 68,* 8694. [14]

Costanzo, P. R., & Schiffman, S. S. (1989). Thinness—not obesity—has a genetic component. *Neuroscience and Biobehavioral Reviews, 13,* 55–58. [11]

Coste, S. C., Kesterson, R. A., Heldwein, K. A., Stevens, S. L., Heard, A. D., Hollis, J. H., et al. (2000). Abnormal adaptations to stress and impaired cardiovascular function in mice lacking corticotropin-releasing hormone receptor-2. *Nature Genetics, 24,* 403–409. [11]

Costa E Silva, J. A., Chase, M., Sartorius, N., & Roth, T. (1996). Special report from a symposium held by the World Health Organization and the World Federation of Sleep Research Societies: An overview of insomnias and related disorders—recognition, epidemiology, and rational management. *Sleep, 19,* 412–416. [4]

Cotman, C. W., & Lynch, G. S. (1989). The neurobiology of learning and memory. *Cognition, 33,* 201–241. [6]

Council on Ethical and Judicial Affairs, American Medical Association. (1991). Gender disparities in clinical decision making. *Journal of the American Medical Association, 266,* 559–562. [13]

Courage, M. L., & Adams, R. J. (1990). Visual acuity assessment from birth to three years using the acuity card procedures: Cross-sectional and longitudinal samples. *Optometry and Vision Science, 67,* 713–718. [9]

Courtney, S. M., Ungerleider, L. G., Keil, K., & Haxby, J. V. (1997). Transient and sustained activity in a distributed neural system for human working memory. *Nature, 386,* 608–611. [6]

Covey, E. (2000). Neural population coding and auditory temporal pattern analysis. *Physiology and Behavior, 69,* 211–220. [3]

Cowan, C. P., & Cowan, P. A. (1992, July/August). Is there love after baby? *Psychology Today,* 58–63. [10]

Cowan, N. (1988). Evolving conceptions of memory storage, selective attention, and their mutual constraints within the human information-processing system. *Psychological Bulletin, 104,* 163–191. [6]

Coyle, J., & Draper, E. S. (1996). What is the significance of glutamate for mental health? *Harvard Mental Health Letter, 13*(6), 8. [2]

Craik, F. I. M., & Lockhart, R. S. (1972). Levels of processing: A framework for memory research. *Journal of Verbal Learning and Verbal Behavior, 11,* 671–684. [6]

Craik, F. I. M., & Tulving, E. (1975). Depth of processing and the retention of words in episodic memory. *Journal of Experimental Psychology: General, 104,* 268–294. [6]

Craik, F. I. M., & Watkins, M. J. (1973). The role of rehearsal in short-term memory. *Journal of Verbal Learning and Verbal Behavior, 12,* 599–607. [6]

Crasilneck, H. B. (1992). The use of hypnosis in the treatment of impotence. *Psychiatric Medicine, 10,* 67–75. [4]

Cravens, H. (1992). A scientific project locked in time: The Terman genetic studies of genius, 1920s–1950s. *American Psychologist, 47,* 183–189. [8]

Craver-Lemley, C., & Reeves, A. (1992). How visual imagery interferes with vision. *Psychological Bulletin, 99,* 633–649. [7]

Creatsas, G. K., Vekemans, M., Horejsi, J., Uzel, R., Lauritzen, C., & Osler, M. (1995). Adolescent sexuality in Europe: A multicentric study. *Adolescent and Pediatric Gynecology, 8,* 59–63. [10]

Crespi, L. P. (1942). Quantitative variation of incentive and performance in the white rat. *American Journal of Psychology, 55,* 467–517. [5]

Crews, F. (1996). The verdict on Freud. *Psychological Science, 7,* 63–68. [14]

Crick, F., & Mitchison, G. (1983). The function of dream sleep. *Nature, 304,* 408–416. [4]

Crick, F., & Mitchison, G. (1995). REM sleep and neural nets. *Behavioural Brain Research, 69,* 147–155. [4]

Crick, N. R., & Dodge, K. A. (1994). A review and reformulation of social information-processing mechanisms in children's social adjustment. *Psychological Bulletin, 115,* 74–101. [12]

Crits-Christoph, P. (1992). The efficacy of brief dynamic psychotherapy: A meta-analysis. *American Journal of Psychiatry, 149,* 151–158. [16]

Crouter, A. C., Perry-Jenkins, M., Huston, T. L., & McHale, S. M. (1987). Processes underlying father involvement in dual-earner and single-earner families. *Developmental Psychology, 23,* 431–440. [10]

Crowder, R. G. (1992) Sensory memory. In L. R. Squire (Ed.), *Encyclopedia of learning and memory.* New York: Macmillan. [6]

Crowe, L. C., & George, W. H. (1989). Alcohol and human sexuality: Review and integration. *Psychological Bulletin, 105,* 374–386. [4]

Cruz, A., & Green, B. G. (2000). Thermal stimulation of taste. *Nature, 403,* 889–892. [3]

Crystal, D. S., Chen, C., Fulligni, A. J., Stevenson, H. W., Hsu, C-C., Ko, H-J., Kitamura, S., & Kimura, S. (1994). Psychological maladjustment and academic achievement: A cross-cultural study of Japanese, Chinese, and American high school students. *Child Development, 65,* 738–753. [8]

Csikszentmihalyi, M. (1990). *Flow: The psychology of optimal experience.* Cambridge, England: Cambridge University Press. [11]

Csikszentmihalyi, M. (1996, July/August). The creative personality. *Psychology Today, 29,* 36–40. [8]

Cui, X-J., & Vaillant, G. E. (1996). Antecedents and consequences of negative life events in adulthood: A longitudinal study. *American Journal of Psychiatry, 153,* 21–26. [15]

Culbertson, F. M. (1997). Depression and gender: An international review. *American Psychologist, 52,* 25–31. [15]

Cull, W. L. (2000). Untangling the benefits of multiple study opportunities and repeated testing for cued recall. *Applied Cognitive Psychology, 14,* 215–235. [6]

Cunningham, M. R. (1979). Weather, mood, and helping behavior: Quasi experiments with the sunshine Samaritan. *Journal of Personality and Social Psychology, 37,* 1947–1956. [17]

Cunningham, M. R., Roberts, A. R., Barbee, A. P., Druen, P. B., & Wu, C-H. (1995). "Their ideas of beauty are, on the whole, the same as ours": Consistency and variability in the cross-cultural perception of female physical attractiveness. *Journal of Personality and Social Psychology, 68,* 261–279. [17]

Cupach, W. R., & Canary, D. J. (1995). Managing conflict and anger: Investigating the sex stereotype hypothesis. In P. J. Kalbfleisch & M. J. Cody (Eds.), *Gender, power, and communication in human relationships.* Hillsdale, NJ: Erlbaum. [11]

Curran, P. J., Stice, E., & Chassin, L. (1997). The relation between adolescent alcohol use and peer alcohol use: A longitudinal random coefficients model. *Journal of Consulting and Clinical Psychology, 65,* 130–140. [4]

Curtis, R. C., & Miller, K. (1986). Believing another likes or dislikes you: Behaviors making the beliefs come true. *Journal of Personality and Social Psychology, 51,* 284–290. [17]

Cyranowski, J. M., Frand, E., Young, E., & Shear, M. K. (2000). Adolescent onset of the gender difference in lifetime rates of major depression. *Archives of General Psychiatry, 57,* 21–27. [15]

Dabbs, J. M., Jr., & Morris, R. (1990). Testosterone, social class, and antisocial behavior in a sample of 4,462 men. *Psychological Science, 1,* 209–211. [17]

Dakof, G. A. (2000). Understanding gender differences in adolescent drug abuse: Issues of comorbidity and family functioning. *Journal of Psychoactive Drugs, 32,* 25–32. [4]

Dale, N., & Kandel, E. R. (1990). Facilitatory and inhibitory transmitters modulate spontaneous transmitter release at cultured Aplysia sensorimotor synapses. *Journal of Physiology, 421,* 203–222. [6]

Daly, M., & Wilson, M. I. (1996). Violence against stepchildren. *Current Directions in Psychological Science, 5,* 77–81. [17]

Damasio, A. R. (1994). *Descartes' error: Emotion, reason, and the human brain.* New York: Lyons Press. [11]

Damasio, A. R. (1999). *The feeling of what happens: Body and emotion in the making of consciousness.* New York: Harcourt. [11]

Daniel, D. G., & Whitcomb, S. R. (1998). Treatment of the refractory schizophrenic patient. *Journal of Clinical Psychiatry, 59*(1, Suppl.), 13–19. [16]

Darley, J. M., & Latané, B. (1968a). Bystander intervention in emergencies: Diffusion of responsibility. *Journal of Personality and Social Psychology, 8,* 377–383. [17]

Darley, J. M., & Latané, B. (1968b, December). When will people help in a crisis? *Psychology Today,* pp. 54–57, 70–71. [17]

Darwin, C. (1965). *The expression of emotion in man and animals.* Chicago: University of Chicago Press. (Original work published 1872). [11]

Dasen, P. R. (1972). Cross-cultural Piagetian research: A summary. *Journal of Cross-Cultural Psychology, 3,* 23–29. [10]

Dasen, P. R. (1994). Culture and cognitive development from a Piagetian perspective. In W. J. Lonner & R. Malpass (Eds.), *Psychology and culture* (pp. 145–149). Boston: Allyn & Bacon. [9]

Dashiell, J. F. (1925). A quantitative demonstration of animal drive. *Journal of Comparative Psychology, 5,* 205–208. [11]

Davidson, J. R. T. (1997). Use of benzodiazepines in panic disorder. *Journal of Clinical Psychiatry, 58*(2, Suppl.), 26–28. [16]

Davis, S., Butcher, S. P., & Morris, R. G. M. (1992). The NMDA receptor antagonist D-2-amino-5-phosphonopentanoate (D-AP5) impairs spatial learning and LTP in vivo at intracerebral concentrations comparable to those that block LTP in vitro. *Journal of Neuroscience, 12,* 21–34. [6]

Davis, T. L. (1995). Gender differences in masking negative emotions: Ability or motivation? *Developmental Psychology, 31,* 660–667. [11]

Dawkins, B. J. (1990). Genital herpes simplex infections. *Primary Care: Clinics in Office Practice, 17,* 95–113. [12]

Dawson, D., Encel, N., & Lushington, K. (1995). Improving adaptation to simulated night shift: Timed exposure to bright light versus daytime melatonin administration. *Sleep, 18,* 11–21. [4]

D'Azevedo, W. A. (1982). Tribal history in Liberia. In U. Neisser (Ed.), *Memory observed: Remembering in natural contexts.* San Francisco: W. H. Freeman. [6]

Deary, I. J., & Stough, C. (1996). Intelligence and inspection time: Achievements, prospects, and problems. *American Psychologist, 51,* 599–608. [8]

Deaux, K. (1985). Sex and gender. *Annual Review of Psychology, 36,* 49–81. [12]

DeCasper, A. J., & Fifer, W. P. (1980). Of human bonding: Newborns prefer their mothers' voices. *Science, 208,* 1174–1176. [9]

DeCasper, A. J., & Spence, M. J. (1986). Prenatal maternal speech influences newborns' perception of speech sounds. *Infant Behavior and Development, 9,* 133–150. [9]

de Castro, J. M., & de Castro, E. S. (1989). Spontaneous meal patterns of humans: Influence of the presence of other people. *Journal of Clinical Nutrition, 50,* 237–247. [11]

Deci, E. L., Koestner, R., & Ryan, R. M. (1999). A meta-analytic review of experiments examining the effects of extrinsic rewards on intrinsic motivation. *Psychological Bulletin, 125,* 627–668. [5]

Deese, J. (1959). On the prediction of occurrence of particular verbal intrusions in immediate recall. *Journal of Experimental Psychology, 58,* 17–22. [6]

Deinzer, R., Kleineidam, C., Stiller-Winkler, R., Idel, H., & Bachg, D. (2000). Prolonged reduction of salivary immunoglobulin (sIgA) after a major academic exam. *International Journal of Psychophysiology, 37,* 219–232. [13]

DeJong, W. (1979). An examination of self-perception mediation of the foot-in-the-door effect. *Journal of Personality and Social Psychology, 37,* 2221–2239. [17]

Dekker, J., & Everaerd, W. (1989). Psychological determinants of sexual arousal: A review. *Behaviour Research and Therapy, 27,* 353–364. [12]

Dekovic, M., & Janssens, J. M. A. M. (1992). Parents' child-rearing style and child's sociometric status. *Developmental Psychology, 28,* 925–932. [9]

Del Monte, M. M. (2000). Retrieved memories of childhood sexual abuse. *British Journal of Medical Psychology, 73*(Pt. 1), 1–13. [6]

de Leon, M. J., Convit, A., George, A. E., Golomb, J., de Santi, S., Tarshish, C., Rusinek, H., Bobinski, M., Ince, C., Miller, D., & Wisniewski, H. (1996). *In vivo* structural studies of the hippocampus in normal aging and in incipient Alzheimer's disease. *Annals of the New York Academy of Sciences, 777,* 1–13. [10]

DeLeon, P. H., & Wiggins, J. G., Jr. (1996). Prescription privileges for psychologists. *American Psychologist, 51,* 225–229. [16]

Delgado, J. M. R. (1969). *Physical control of the mind: Toward a psychocivilized society.* New York: Harper & Row. [2]

Delgado, J. M. R., & Anand, B. K. (1953). Increased food intake induced by electrical stimulation of the lateral hypothalamus. *American Journal of Physiology, 172,* 162–168. [11]

DeLongis, A., Coyne, J. C., Dakof, G., Folkman, S., & Lazarus, R. S. (1982). Relationship of daily hassles, uplifts, and major life events to health status. *Health Psychology, 1,* 119–136. [13]

DeLongis, A., Folkman, S., & Lazarus, R. S. (1988). The impact of daily stress on health and mood: Psychological and social resources as mediators. *Journal of Personality and Social Psychology, 54,* 486–495. [13]

DeMaris, A., & Rao, K. V. (1992). Premarital cohabitation and subsequent marital stability in the United States: A reassessment. *Journal of Marriage and the Family, 54,* 178–190. [10]

Dembroski, T. M., MacDougall, J. M., Williams, R. B., Haney, T. I., & Blumenthal, J. A. (1985). Components of Type A hostility and anger in relationship to angiographic findings. *Psychosomatic Medicine, 47,* 219–233. [13]

Dement, W. C. (1974). *Some must watch while some must sleep.* San Francisco: W. H. Freeman. [4]

Dement, W., & Kleitman, N. (1957). The relation of eye movements during sleep to dream activity: An objective method for the study of dreaming. *Journal of Experimental Psychology, 53,* 339–346. [4]

DeNelsky, G. Y. (1996). The case against prescription privileges for psychologoists. *American Psychologist, 51,* 207–212. [16]

Denham, S. A., Workman, E., Cole, P. M., Weissbrod, C., Kendziora, K. T., & Zahn-Waxler, C. (2000). Prediction of externalizing behavior problems from early to middle childhood: The role of parental socialization and emotion expression. *Developmental Psychopathology, 12,* 123–145. [9]

Dennis, W. (1968). Creative productivity between the ages of 20 and 80. In B. L. Neugarten (Ed.), *Middle age and aging* (pp. 106–114). Chicago: University of Chicago Press. [10]

Deovell, L. Y., Bentin, S., & Soroker, N. (2000). Electrophysiological evidence for an early (pre-attentive) information processing deficit in patients with right hemisphere damage and unilateral neglect. *Brain, 123,* 353–365. [2]

De Raad, B., & Kokkonen, M. (2000). Traits and emotions: A review of their structure and management. *European Journal of Personality, 14,* 477–496. [14]

DeRubeis, R. J., & Crits-Christoph, P. (1998). Empirically supported individual and group psychological treatments for adult mental disorders. *Journal of Consulting and Clinical Psychology, 66,* 37–52. [16]

Detke, M. J., Brandon, S. E., Weingarten, H. P., Rodin, J., & Wagner, A. R. (1989). Modulation of behavioral and insulin responses by contextual stimuli paired with food. *Physiology and Behavior, 45,* 845–851. [11]

De Valois, R. L., & De Valois, K. K. (1975). Neural coding of color. In E. C. Carterette & M. P. Friedman (Eds.), *Handbook of perception* (Vol. 5). New York: Academic. [3]

Devanand, D. P., Dwork, A. J., Hutchinson, M. S. E., Bolwig, T. G., & Sackeim, H. A. (1994). Does ECT alter brain structure? *American Journal of Psychiatry, 151,* 957–970. [16]

Devine, P. G. (1989). Stereotypes and prejudice: Their automatic and controlled components. *Journal of Personality and Social Psychology, 56,* 5–18. [17]

Devine, P. G., Monteith, M. J., Zuwerink, J. R., & Elliot, A. J. (1991). Prejudice with and without compunction. *Journal of Personality and Social Psychology, 60,* 817–830. [17]

De Vito, G., Hernandez, R., Gonzalez, V., Felici, F., & Figura, F. (1997). Low intensity physical training in older subjects. *Journal of Sports Medicine and Physical Fitness, 37,* 72–77. [13]

De Vos, S. (1990). Extended family living among older people in six Latin American countries. *Journal of Gerontology: Social Sciences, 45,* S87–94. [10]

deVries, H. A. (1986). *Fitness after 50.* New York: Scribner's. [10]

Dewsbury, D. A. (2000). Introduction: Snapshots of psychology circa 1900. *American Psychologist, 55,* 255–259. [1]

Di Chiara, G. (1997). Alcohol and dopamine. *Alcohol Health & Research World, 21,* 108–114. [4]

Diener, E., & Diener, C. (1996). Most people are happy. *Psychological Science, 7,* 181–185. [10]

Diener, E., Horwitz, J., & Emmons, R. A. (1985). Happiness of the very wealthy. *Social Indicators, 16,* 263–274. [11]

Diener, E., Wolsic, B., & Fujita, F. (1995). Physical attractiveness and subjective well-being. *Journal of Personality and Social Psychology, 69,* 120–129. [17]

Dietz, W. H. (1989). Obesity. *Journal of the American College of Nutrition, 8*(Suppl.), 139–219. [11]

Digman, J. M. (1990). Personality structure: Emergence of the five-factor model. *Annual Review of Psychology, 41,* 417–440. [13]

DiLalla, D. L., Carey, G., Gottesman, I. J., & Bouchard, T. J., Jr. (1996). Heritability of MMPI personality indicators of psychopathology in twins reared apart. *Journal of Abnormal Psychology, 105,* 491–499. [14]

DiLalla, L. F., & Gottesman, I. I. (1991). Biological and genetic contributors to violence—Widom's untold tale. *Psychological Bulletin, 109,* 125–129. [17]

Dimberg, U. (1990). Facial electromyography and emotional reactions. *Psychophysiology, 27,* 481–494. [11]

Dinan, T. G. (1996). Noradrenergic and serotonergic abnormalities in depression: Stress-induced dysfunction? *Journal of Clinical Psychiatry, 57*(4, Suppl.), 14–18. [15]

Dindia, K., & Allen, M. (1992). Sex differences in self-disclosure: A meta-analysis. *Psychological Bulletin, 112,* 106–124. [12]

Dion, K., Berscheid, E., & Walster, E. (1972). What is beautiful is good. *Journal of Personality and Social Psychology, 24,* 285–290. [17]

Dipboye, R. L., Fromkin, H. L., & Wilback, K. (1975). Relative importance of applicant sex, attractiveness, and scholastic standing in evaluation of job applicant resumes. *Journal of Applied Psychology, 60,* 39–43. [17]

Dlugosz, L., & Bracken, M. B. (1992). Reproductive effects of caffeine: A review and theoretical analysis. *Epidemiological Review, 14,* 83–100. [9]

Dobb, E. (1989, November/December). The scents around us. *The Sciences, 29,* 46–53. [3]

Dobelle Institute. (2000). Dobelle Institute's artificial vision system. Device stimulates visual cortex of the totally blind [On-line]. Available: http://lionhrtpub.com/ISR/isr-3-00/cover.html [7]

Dobie, R. A. (1987, December). Noise-induced hearing loss: The family physician's role. *American Family Physician,* pp. 141–148. [3]

Docherty, N. M., Hawkins, K. A., Hoffman, R. E., Quinlan, D. M., Rakfeldt, J., & Sledge, W. H. (1996). Working memory, attention, and communication disturbances in schizophrenia. *Journal of Abnormal Psychology, 105,* 212–219. [15]

Dodge, K. A., Bates, J. E., & Pettit, G. S. (1990). Mechanisms in the cycle of violence. *Science, 250,* 1678–1683. [17]

Dodge, K. A., Cole, J. D., Pettit, G. S., & Price, J. M. (1990). Peer status and aggression in boys' groups: Developmental and contextual analyses. *Child Development, 61,* 1289–1309. [9]

Dodson, C. S., Koutstaal, W., & Schacter, D. L. (2000). Escape from illusion: Reducing false memories. *Trends in Cognitive Sciences, 4,* 391–397. [6]

Dollard, J., Doob, L. W., Miller, N., Mowrer, O. H., & Sears, R. R. (1939). *Frustration and aggression.* New Haven: Yale University Press. [17]

Domino, G. (1984). California Psychological Inventory. In D. J. Keyser & R. C. Sweetland (Eds.), *Test Critiques* (Vol. 1, pp. 146–157). Kansas City: Test Corporation of America. [14]

Domjan, M, & Purdy, J. E. (1995). Animal research in psychology: More than meets the eye of the general psychology student. *American Psychologist, 50,* 496–503. [1]

Donnerstein, E., Slaby, R. G., & Eron, L. D. (1994). The mass media and youth aggression. In L. D. Eron, J. H. Gentry, & P. Schlegel (Eds.), *Reason to hope: A psychosocial perspective on violence and youth* (pp. 219–250). Washington, DC: American Psychological Association. [9]

Doob, L. W., & Sears, R. R. (1939). Factors determining substitute behavior and the overt expression of aggression. *Journal of Abnormal and Social Psychology,* 34, 293–313. [17]

Dovidio, J. F. (1984). Helping behavior and altruism: An empirical and conceptual overview. In L. Berkowitz (Ed.), *Advances in experimental social psychology* (Vol. 17, pp. 361–427). New York: Academic Press. [17]

Doyle, J. A., & Paludi, M. A. (1995). *Sex and gender* (3rd ed.). Madison, WI: Brown & Benchmark. [12]

Doyle, R. (2000). Women and the professions. *Scientific American, 282,* 30. [12]

Dreikurs, R. (1953). *Fundamentals of Adlerian psychology.* Chicago: Alfred Adler Institute. [14]

Drevets, W. C., Price, J. L., Simpson, J. R., Jr., Todd, R. D., Reich, T., Vannier, M., & Raichle, M. E. (1997). Subgenual prefrontal cortex abnormalities in mood disorders. *Nature, 386,* 824–827. [2, 15]

Drevets, W. C., Videen, T. O., Price, J. L., Preskorn, S. H., Carmichael, S. T., & Raichle, M. E. (1992). A functional anatomical study of unipolar depression. *Journal of Neuroscience, 12,* 3628–3641. [15]

Drewnowski, A., Yee, D. K., Kurth, C. L., & Krahn, D. D. (1994). Eating pathology and DSM-III-R bulimia nervosa: A continuum of behavior. *American Journal of Psychiatry, 151,* 1217–1219. [11]

Druckman, D., & Bjork, R. A. (Eds.) (1994). *Learning, remembering, believing: Enhancing human performance.* Washington, DC: National Academy Press. [4]

Drummond, S. P. A., Brown, G. G., Gillin, J. C., Stricker, J. L., Wong, E. C., & Buxton, R. B. (2000). Altered brain response to verbal learning following sleep deprivation. *Nature, 403,* 655–657. [4]

Dryden, J. (1994, September 8). Alcohol use by fathers may affect fetal development. *Washington University Record,* p. 2. [9]

Dryer, D. C., & Horowitz, L. M. (1997). When do opposites attract? Interpersonal complementarity versus similarity. *Journal of Personality and Social Psychology, 72,* 592–603. [17]

Duck, S. (1983). *Friends for life: The psychology of close relationships.* New York: St. Martin's Press. [10]

Dudai, Y. (2000). Neurobiology: The shaky trace. *Nature, 406,* 686–687. [6]

Duggan, J. P., & Booth, D. A. (1986). Obesity, overeating, and rapid gastric emptying in rats with ventromedial hypothalamic lesions. *Science, 231,* 609–611. [11]

Duncan, J., Seitz, R. J., Kolodny, J., Bor, D., Herzog, H., Ahmed, A., Newell, F. N., & Emslie, H. (2000). A neural basis for general intelligence. *Science, 289,* 457–460. [8]

Dunkel-Schetter, C., Feinstein, L. G., Taylor, S. E., & Falke, R. L. (1992). Patterns of coping with cancer. *Health Psychology, 11,* 79–87. [13]

Duyme, M. (1988). School success and social class: An adoption study. *Developmental Psychology, 24,* 203–209. [8]

Dywan, J., & Bowers, K. (1983). The use of hypnosis to enhance recall. *Science, 222,* 184–185. [4, 6]

Eagly, A. H. (1987). *Sex differences in social behavior: A social-role interpretation.* Hillsdale, NJ: Erlbaum. [17]

Eagly, A. H. (1995). The science and politics of comparing women and men. *American Psychologist, 50,* 145–158. [12]

Eagly, A. H., & Carli, L. (1981). Sex of researchers and sex-typed communications as determinants of sex differences in influence-ability: A meta-analysis of social influence studies. *Psychological Bulletin, 90,* 1–20. [17]

Eagly, A. H., & Steffen, V. J. (1986). Gender and aggressive behavior: A meta-analytic review of the social psychological literature. *Psychological Bulletin, 100,* 309–330. [12]
Eagly, A. H., & Wood, W. (1999). The origins of sex differences in human behavior: Evolved dispositions versus social roles. *American Psychologist, 54,* 408–423. [12]
Eagly, A. H., Ashmore, R. D., Makhijani, M. G., & Longo, L. C. (1991). What is beautiful is good . . . : A meta-analytic review of research on the physical attractiveness stereotype. *Psychological Bulletin, 110,* 109–128. [17]
Eastman, C. I., Liu, L., & Fogg, L. F. (1995). Circadian rhythm adaptation to simulated night shift work: Effect of nocturnal bright-light duration. *Sleep, 18,* 399–407. [4]
Easton, C. J., Swann, S., & Sinha, R. (2000). Prevalence of family violence in clients entering substance abuse treatment. *Journal of Substance Abuse Treatment, 18,* 23–28. [4]
Eating disorders—part II. (1997, November). *Harvard Mental Health Letter, 14*(5), 1–5. [11]
Ebata, A. T. (1987). A longitudinal study of psychological distress during early adolescence. Unpublished doctoral dissertation, Pennsylvania State University. [10]
Ebbinghaus, H. E. (1964). *Memory: A contribution to experimental psychology* (H. A. Ruger & C. E. Bussenius, Trans.). New York: Dover. (Original work published 1885). [6]
Eccles, J. S., & Jacobs, J. E. (1986). Social forces shape math attitudes and performance. *Signs, 11,* 367–389. [12]
Eccles, J. S., Jacobs, J. E., & Harold, R. D. (1990). Gender-role stereotypes, expectancy effects, and parents' role in the socialization of gender differences in self-perceptions and skill acquisition. *Journal of Social Issues, 46,* 183–201. [12]
Eccles, J. S., Wigfield, A., Flanagan, C., Miller, C., Reuman, D., & Yee, D. (1989). Self-concepts, domain values, and self-esteem: Relations and changes at early adolescence. *Journal of Personality and Social Psychology, 57,* 283–310. [12]
Edwards, K., & Smith, E. E. (1996). A disconfirmation bias in the evaluation of arguments. *Journal of Personality and Social Psychology, 71,* 5–24. [17]
Efron, R. (1990). *The decline and fall of hemispheric specialization.* Hillsdale, NJ: Erlbaum. [2]
Egeth, H. E. (1993). What do we not know about eyewitness identification? *American Psychologist, 48,* 577–580. [6]
Ehrhardt, A. A., Evers, K., & Money, J. (1968). Influence of androgen and some aspects of sexual dimorphic behavior in women with the late-treated adrenogenital syndrome. *Johns Hopkins Medical Journal, 123,* 115–122. [12]
Eibl-Eibesfeldt, I. (1973). The expressive behavior of the deaf-and-blind-born. In M. von Cranach & I. Vine (Eds.), *Social communication and movement.* New York: Academic Press. [11]
Eich, E., Macaulay, D., & Ryan, L. (1994). Mood dependent memory for events of the personal past. *Journal of Experimental Psychology: General, 123,* 201–215. [6]
Eich, J. E. (1980). The cue dependent nature of state-dependent retrieval. *Memory and Cognition, 8,* 157–173. [6]
Eichenbaum, H. (1997). Declarative memory: Insights from cognitive neurobiology. *Annual Review of Psychology, 48,* 547–572. [2, 6]
Eichenbaum, H., & Otto, T. (1993). LTP and memory: Can we enhance the connection? *Trends in Neurosciences, 16,* 163. [6]
Eimas, P. D. (1985). The perception of speech in early infancy. *Scientific American, 252,* 46–52. [9]
Eisele, G. R., Watkins, J. P., & Matthews, K. O. (1998). Workplace violence at government sites. *American Journal of Industrial Medicine, 33,* 485–492. [17]
Ekman, P. (1972). Universals and cultural differences in facial expression of emotion. In J. Cole (Ed.), *Nebraska symposium on motivation* (Vol. 19). Lincoln: University of Nebraska Press. [11]
Ekman, P. (1982). *Emotion and the human face* (2nd ed.). New York: Cambridge University Press. [11]
Ekman, P. (1985). *Telling lies: Clues to deceit in the marketplace, marriage, and politics.* New York: Norton. [17]
Ekman, P. (1992). Are there basic emotions? *Psychological Review, 99,* 550–553. [11]
Ekman, P. (1993). Facial expression and emotion. *American Psychologist, 48,* 384–392. [11]
Ekman, P., & Friesen, W. V. (1971). Constants across cultures in the face and emotion. *Journal of Personality and Social Psychology, 17,* 124–129. [11]
Ekman, P., & Friesen, W. V. (1975). *Unmasking the face: A guide to recognizing emotions from facial clues.* Englewood Cliffs, NJ: Prentice-Hall. [11]
Ekman, P., Friesen, W. V., & O'Sullivan, M. (1988). Smiles when lying. *Journal of Personality and Social Psychology, 54,* 414–420. [17]
Ekman, P., Friesen, W. V., O'Sullivan, M., Chan, A., Diacoyanni-Tarlatzis, I., Heider, K., Krause, R., LeCompte, W. A., Pitcairn, T., Ricci-Bitti, P. E., Scherer, K., Tomita, M., & Tzavaras, A. (1987). Universals and cultural differences in the judgments of facial expressions of emotion. *Journal of Personality and Social Psychology, 53,* 712–717. [11]
Ekman, P., Levenson, R. W., & Friesen, W. V. (1983). Autonomic nervous system activity distinguishes among emotions. *Science, 221,* 1208–1210. [11]
Elal, G., Altug, A., Slade, P., & Tekcan, A. (2000). Factor structure of the Eating Attitudes Test (EAT) in a Turkish university sample. *Eating and Weight Disorders: Studies on Anorexia, Bulimia, and Obesity, 5,* 46–50. [11]
Elbert, T., Pantev, C., Wienbruch, C., Rockstroh, B., & Taub, E. (1995). Increased cortical representation of the fingers of the left hand in string players. *Science, 270,* 305–307. [2]
Elkin, I., Gibbons, R. D., Shea, M. T., Sotsky, S. M., Watkins, J. T., Pikonis, P. A., & Hedeker, D. (1995). Initial severity and differential treatment outcome in the National Institute of Mental Health Treatment of Depression Collaborative Research Program. *Journal of Consulting and Clinical Psychology, 63,* 841–847. [16]
Elkin, I., Shea, M. T., Watkins, J. T., et al. (1989). National Institute of Mental Health Treatment of Depression Collaborative Research Program: General effectiveness of treatments. *Archives of General Psychology, 46,* 971–982. [16]
Elkind, D. (1967). Egocentrism in adolescence. *Child Development, 38,* 1025–1034. [10]
Elkind, D. (1970, April 5). Erik Erikson's eight ages of man. *The New York Times Magazine,* pp. 25–27, 84–92, 110–119. [9, 10]
Elkind, D. (1974). *Children and adolescents: Interpretive essays on Jean Piaget* (2nd ed.). New York: Oxford University Press. [10]
Ellason, J. W., & Ross, C. A. (1997). Two-year follow–up of inpatients with dissociative identity disorder. *American Journal of Psychiatry, 154,* 832–839. [15]
Elliot, A. J., & Devine, P. G. (1994). On the motivational nature of cognitive dissonance: Dissonance as psychological discomfort. *Journal of Personality and Social Psychology, 67,* 382–394. [17]
Elliott, R., Friston, K. J., & Dolan, R. J. (2000). Dissociable neural responses in human reward systems. *Journal of Neuroscience, 20,* 6159–6165. [5]
Ellis, A. (1961). *A guide to rational living.* Englewood Cliffs, NJ: Prentice-Hall. [16]
Ellis, A. (1977). The basic clinical theory of rational-emotive therapy. In A. Ellis & R. Grieger (Eds.), *Handbook of rational-emotive therapy* (pp. 3–33). New York: Springer. [16]
Ellis, A. (1979). Rational-emotive therapy. In R. J. Corsini (Ed.), *Current psychotherapies* (2nd ed., pp. 185–229). Itasca, IL: F. E. Peacock. [16]
Ellis, A. (1987). The impossibility of achieving consistently good mental health. *American Psychologist, 42,* 364–375. [16]
Ellis, A. (1993). Reflections on rational-emotive therapy. *Journal of Consulting and Clinical Psychology, 61,* 199–201. [16]
El-Shiekh, M., Klacynski, P. A., & Valaik, M. E. (1989). Stress and coping across the life course. *Human Development, 32,* 113–117. [13]
Embick, D., Marantz, A., Miyashita, Y., O'Neil, W., & Sakai, K. L. (2000). A syntactic specialization for Broca's area. *Proceedings of the National Academy of Science, 97,* 6150–6154. [2]
Emde, R. N., Plomin, R., Robinson, J., Corley, R., DeFries, J., Fulker, D. W., Reznick, J. S., Campos, J., Kagan, J., & Zahn-Waxler, C. (1992). Temperament, emotion, and cognition at fourteen months: The MacArthur Longitudinal Twin Study. *Child Development, 63,* 1437–1455. [9]
Engel, G. L. (1977). The need for a new medical model: A challenge for biomedicine. *Science, 196,* 126–129. [13]
Engel, G. L. (1980). The clinical application of the biopsychosocial model. *American Journal of Psychiatry, 137,* 535–544. [13]

Engen, T. (1982). *The perception of odors.* New York: Academic Press. [3]

Engles, G. I., Garnefski, N., & Diekstra, R. F. W. (1993). Efficacy of rational-emotive therapy: A quantitative analysis. *Journal of Consulting and Clinical Psychology, 61,* 1083–1090. [16]

Epstein, J. (1983). Examining theories of adolescent friendships. In J. Epstein & N. Karweit (Eds.), *Friends in school.* New York: Academic Press. [10]

Epstein, J., Stern, E., & Silbersweig, D. (2001). Neuropsychiatry at the millennium: The potential for mind/brain integration through emerging interdisciplinary research strategies. *Clinical Neuroscience Research, 1,* 10–18. [16]

Epstein, R. (1996, July/August). Capturing creativity. *Psychology Today, 29,* 41–43, 75–78. [8]

Erel, O., & Burman, B. (1995). Interrelatedness of marital relations and parent-child relations: A meta-analytic review. *Psychological Bulletin, 118,* 108–132. [10]

Ericsson, K. A., & Charness, N. (1994). Expert performance: Its structure and acquisition. *American Psychologist, 49,* 725–747. [8, 17]

Erikson, E. H. (1963). *Childhood and society* (2nd ed.). New York: Norton. [9, 10]

Erikson, E. H. (1968). *Identity: Youth and crisis.* New York: Norton. [10]

Erikson, E. H. (1980). *Identity and the life cycle.* New York: Norton. [9, 10]

Erikson, E. H., Erikson, J. M., & Kivnick, H. Q. (1986). *Vital involvement in old age: The experience of old age in our time.* New York: W. W. Norton. [10]

Erlenmeyer-Kimling, L., & Jarvik, L. F. (1963). Genetics and intelligence: A review. *Science, 142,* 1477–1479. [8]

Eron, L. D. (1980). Prescription for reducing aggression. *American Psychologist, 35,* 244–252. [17]

Eron, L. D. (1987). The development of aggressive behavior from the perspective of a developing behaviorism. *American Psychologist, 42,* 435–442. [17]

Eronen, M., Hakola, P., & Tiihonen, J. (1996). Mental disorders and homicidal behavior in Finland. *Journal of Personality and Social Psychology, 53,* 497–501. [17]

Erwin, E. (1996). *A final accounting: Philosophical and empirical issues in Freudian psychology.* Cambridge, MA: MIT Press. [14]

Eskenazi, B. (1993). Caffeine during pregnancy: Grounds for concern? *Journal of the American Medical Association, 270,* 2973–2974. [9]

Estes, W. K. (1994). *Classification and cognition.* New York: Oxford University Press. [7]

Evan, D. (1991). *The great divide.* New York: Poseidon Press. [12]

Evans, D., & Zarate, O. (2000). *Introducing evolutionary psychology.* New York: Totem Books. [1]

Evans, G. W., & Lepore, S. J. (1993). Household crowding and social support: A quasiexperimental analysis. *Journal of Personality and Social Psychology, 65,* 308–316. [17]

Evans, M. D., Hollon, S. D., DeRubeis, R. J., Piasecki, J. M., Grove, W. M., Garvey, M. J., & Tuason, V. B. (1992). Differential relapse following cognitive therapy and pharmacotherapy for depression. *Archives of General Psychiatry, 49,* 802–808. [16]

Everson, S. A., Goldberg, D. E., Kaplan, G. A., Cohen, R. D., Pukkala, E., Tuomilehto, J., & Salonen, J. T. (1996). Hopelessness and risk of mortality and incidence of myocardial infarction and cancer. *Psychosomatic Medicine, 58,* 113–121. [13]

Ewin, D. M. (1992). Hypnotherapy for warts (*Verruca vulgaris*): 41 consecutive cases with 33 cures. *American Journal of Clinical Hypnosis, 35,* 1–10. [4]

Exner, J. E. (1993). *The Rorschach: A comprehensive system: Vol. 1. Basic foundations* (3rd ed.). New York: Wiley. [14]

Exton, M. S., von Auer, A. K., Buske-Kirschbaum, A., Stockhorst, U., Göbel, U., & Schedlowski, M. (2000). Pavlovian conditioning of immune function: Animal investigation and the challenge of human application. *Behavioural Brain Research, 110,* 129–141. [5]

Eyeferth, K. (1961). Leistungen verschiedener Gruppen von Besatzungskindern in Hamburg-Wechsler Intelligenztest für Kinder (HAWIK). *Archir für die Gesamte Psychologie, 113,* 224–241. [8]

Eysenck, H. J. (1981). *A model for personality.* Berlin: Springer-Verlag. [14]

Eysenck, H. J. (1990). Genetic and environmental contributions to individual differences: The three major dimensions of personality. *Journal of Personality, 58,* 245–261. [14]

Eysenck, H. J. (1994). The outcome problem in psychotherapy: What have we learned? *Behaviour Research and Therapy, 32,* 477–495. [16]

Fackelmann, K. (1997). Marijuana on trial: Is marijuana a dangerous drug or a valuable medicine? *Science News, 151,* 178–179, 183. [4]

Fagiolini, M., & Hensch, T. K. (2000). Inhibitory threshold for critical-period activation in primary visual cortex. *Nature, 404,* 183–186. [3]

Fagot, B. I. (1982). Adults as socializing agents. In T. M. Field (Ed.), *Review of human development.* New York: Wiley. [12]

Fagot, B. I., Leinbach, M. D., & O'Boyle, C. (1992). Gender labeling, gender stereotyping, and parenting behaviors. *Developmental Psychology, 28,* 225–230. [12]

Fairburn, C. G., Welch, S. L., Doll, H. A., Davies, B. A., & O'Connor, M. E. (1997). Risk factors for bulimia nervosa: A community-based case-control study. *Archives of General Psychiatry, 54,* 509–517. [11]

Falbo, T., & Polit, D. F. (1986). Quantitative review of the only child literature: Research evidence and theory development. *Psychological Bulletin, 100,* 176–189. [11]

Falloon, I. R. H. (1988). Expressed emotion: Current status. *Psychological Medicine, 18,* 269–274. [16]

Famighetti, R. (Ed.). (1997). *The world almanac and book of facts 1998.* Mahwah, NJ: World Almanac Books. [11, 16]

Fantz, R. L. (1961). The origin of form perception. *Scientific American, 204,* 66–72. [9]

Farah, M. J. (1988). Is visual imagery really visual? Overlooked evidence from neuropsychology. *Psychological Review, 95,* 307–317. [7]

Farah, M. J. (1995). The neural bases of mental imagery. In M. S. Gazzaniga (Ed.), *The cognitive neurosciences.* Cambridge, MA: MIT Press. [7]

Farde, L. (1996). The advantage of using positron emission tomography in drug research. *Trends in Neurosciences, 19,* 211–214. [2]

Faw, H. W. (1990). Memory for names and faces: A fair comparison. *American Journal of Psychology, 103,* 317–326. [6]

Fawcett, J. C. (1992). Intrinsic neuronal determinants of regeneration. *Trends in Neurosciences, 15,* 5–8. [2]

Fazio, R. H. (1989). On the power and functionality of attitudes: The role of attitude accessibility. In A. R. Pratkanis, S. J. Breckler, & A. G. Greenwald (Eds.), *Attitude structure and function* (pp. 153–179). Hillsdale, NJ: Erlbaum. [17]

Fazio, R. H., & Williams, C. J. (1986). Attitude accessibility as a moderator of the attitude perception and attitude-behavior relations: An investigation of the 1984 presidential election. *Journal of Personality and Social Psychology, 51,* 505–514. [17]

Federal Bureau of Investigation. (1999). United States crime rates 1960–1998 [On-line]. Available: http://www.disastercenter.com/crime/uscrime.htm [17]

Fein, S., & Spencer, S. J. (1997). Prejudice as self-image maintenance: Affirming the self through derogating others. *Journal of Personality and Social Psychology, 73,* 31–44. [17]

Feingold, A. (1988). Matching for attractiveness in romantic partners and same-sex friends: A meta-analysis and theoretical critique. *Psychological Bulletin, 104,* 226–235. [17]

Feingold, A. (1990). Gender differences in effects of physical attractiveness on romantic attraction: A comparison across five research paradigms. *Journal of Personality and Social Psychology, 59,* 981–993. [17]

Feingold, A. (1992). Good-looking people are not what we think. *Psychological Bulletin, 111,* 304–341. [17]

Feingold, A. (1994). Gender differences in personality: A meta-analysis. *Psychological Bulletin, 116,* 429–456. [12]

Feldman, H. A., Goldstein, I., Hatzichristou, D. G., Krane, R. J., & McKinlay, J. B. (1994). Impotence and its medical and psychosocial correlates: Results of the Massachusetts male aging study. *Journal of Urology, 151,* 54–61. [12]

Fenton, W. S., & McGlashan, T. H. (1991). Natural history of schizophrenia subtypes: I. Longitudinal study of paranoid, hebephrenic, and undifferentiated schizophrenia. *Archives of General Psychiatry, 48,* 969–977. [15]

Fenton, W. S., & McGlashan, T. H. (1994). Antecedents, symptom progression, and long-term outcome of the deficit syndrome in schizophrenia. *American Journal of Psychiatry, 151,* 351–356. [15]

Fernald, A. (1993). Approval and disapproval: Infant responsiveness to vocal affect in familiar and unfamiliar languages. *Child Development, 64,* 637–656. [9]

Fernández-Dols, J.-M., & Ruiz-Belda, M.-A. (1995). Are smiles a sign of happiness? Gold medal winners at the Olympic games. *Journal of Personality and Social Psychology, 69,* 1113–1119. [11]

Festinger, L. (1957). *A theory of cognitive dissonance.* Evanston, IL: Row, Peterson. [17]

Festinger, L., & Carlsmith, J. M. (1959). Cognitive consequences of forced compliance. *Journal of Abnormal and Social Psychology, 58,* 203–210. [17]

Fiatarone, M. A., Morley, J. E., Bloom, E. T., Benton, D., Makinodan, T., & Solomon, G. F. (1988). Endogenous opioids and the exercise-induced augmentation of natural killer cell activity. *Journal of Laboratory and Clinical Medicine, 112,* 544–552. [13]

Fiatarone, M. A., O'Neill, E. F., Ryan, N. D., Clements, K. M., Solares, G. R., Nelson, M. E., Roberts, S. B., Kehayias, J. J., Lipsitz, L. A., & Evans, W. J. (1994). Exercise training and nutritional supplementation for physical frailty in very elderly people. *New England Journal of Medicine, 330,* 1769–1775. [10]

Field, T., Schanberg, S. M., Scfidi, F., Bauer, C. R., Vega-Lahr, N., Garcia, R., Nystrom, J., & Kuhn, C. (1986, May). Tactile/kinesthetic stimulation effects on preterm neonates. *Pediatrics, 77,* 654–658. [3]

Field, T. M., Cohen, D., Garcia, R., & Greenberg, R. (1984). Mother-stranger face discrimination by the newborn. *Infant Behavior and Development, 7,* 19–25. [9]

Fiez, J. A. (1996). Cerebellar contributions to cognition. *Neuron, 16,* 13–15. [2]

Fiez, J. A. (2000). Sound and meaning: How native language affects reading strategies. *Nature Neuroscience, 3,* 3–5. [7]

Finch, A. E., Lambert, M. J., & Brown, G. (2000). Attacking anxiety: A naturalistic study of a multimedia self-help program. *Journal of Clinical Psychology, 56,* 11–21. [16]

Finchilescu, G. (1988). Interracial contact in South Africa within the nursing context. *Journal of Applied Social Psychology, 18,* 1207–1221. [17]

Finke, R. A. (1985). Theories relating mental imagery to perception. *Psychological Bulletin, 98,* 236–259. [7]

Finkel, D., & McGue, M. (1997). Sex differences and nonadditivity in heritability of the Multidimensional Personality Questionnaire scales. *Journal of Personality and Social Psychology, 72,* 929–938. [14]

Finkelhor, D., et al. (1990). Sexual abuse in a national survey of adult men and women: Prevalence, characteristics, and risk factors. *Child Abuse and Neglect, 14,* 19–28. [12]

Fiorito, G., & Scotto, P. (1992). Observational learning in Octopus vulgaris. *Science, 256,* 545–547. [5]

Fischbach, G. D. (1992). Mind and brain. *Scientific American, 267,* 48–56. [6]

Fischbein, M. P., Ardehali, A., Yun, J., Schoenberger, S., Laks, H., Irie, Y., Dempsey, P., Cheng, G., Fishbein, M. C., & Bonavida, B. (2000). CD40 signaling replaces CD4+ lymphocytes and its blocking prevents chronic rejection of heart transplants. *Journal of Immunology, 165,* 7216–7322. [13]

Fixx, J. F. (1978). *Solve It! A perplexing profusion of puzzles.* New York: Doubleday. [7]

Flavell, J. H. (1985). *Cognitive development.* Englewood, NJ: Prentice-Hall. [9]

Flavell, J. H. (1992). Cognitive development: Past, present, and future. *Developmental Psychology, 28,* 998–1005. [9, 10]

Flavell, J. H. (1996). Piaget's legacy. *Psychological Science, 7,* 200–203. [9]

Flavell, J. H., Green, F. L., & Flavell, E. R. (1995). Young children's knowledge about thinking. *Monographs of the Society for Research in Child Development, 60*(1, Serial No. 243). [9]

Flegal, K. M. (1996). Trends in body weight and overweight in the U.S. population. *Nutrition Reviews, 54,* S97–S100. [11]

Fleming, J. D. (1974, July). Field report: The state of the apes. *Psychology Today,* pp. 31–46. [7]

Fletcher, A. C., & Shaw, R. A. (2000). Sex differences in associations between parental behaviors and characteristics and adolescent social integration. *Social Development, 9*(2). [10]

Fletcher, J. M., Page, B., Francis, D. J., Copeland, K., Naus, M. J., Davis, C. M., Morris, R., Krauskopf, D., & Satz, P. (1996). Cognitive correlates of long-term cannabis use in Costa Rican men. *Archives of General Psychiatry, 53,* 1051–1057. [4]

Fletcher, T. A., Brakel, S. J., & Cavanaugh, J. L. (2000). Violence in the workplace: New perspectives in forensic mental health services in the USA. *British Journal of Psychiatry, 176,* 339–344. [17]

Flint, A. J., & Rifat, S. L. (2000). Maintenance treatment for recurrent depression in late life: A four-year outcome study. *American Journal of Geriatric Psychiatry, 8,* 112–116. [10]

Flood, J. F., Silver, A. J., & Morley, J. E. (1990). Do peptide-induced changes in feeding occur because of changes in motivation to eat? *Peptides, 11,* 265–270. [11]

Florian, V., Mikulincer, M., & Taubman, O. (1995). Does hardiness contribute to mental health during a stressful real-life situation? The roles of appraisal and coping. *Journal of Personality and Social Psychology, 68,* 687–695. [13]

Flynn, J. R. (1987). Race and IQ: Jensen's case refuted. In S. Modgil, & C. Modgil (Eds.), *Arthur Jensen: Consensus and controversy.* New York: Palmer Press. [8]

Foa, E. B. (1995). How do treatments for obsessive-compulsive disorder compare? *Harvard Mental Health Letter, 12*(1), 8. [16]

Foa, E. B., & Meadows, E. A. (1997). Psychosocial treatments for posttraumatic stress disorder: A critical review. *Annual Review of Psychology, 48,* 449–480. [13]

Fogelman, E., & Wiener, V. L. (1985, August). The few, the brave, the noble. *Psychology Today,* pp. 60–65. [17]

Foley, D. J., Monjan, A. A., Brown, S. L., Simonsick, E. M., Wallace, R. B., & Blazer, D. G. (1995). Sleep complaints among elderly persons: An epidemiologic study of three communities. *Sleep, 18,* 425–432. [4]

Folkard, S. (1990). Circadian performance rhythms: Some practical and theoretical implications. *Philosophical Transactions of the Royal Society of London. Series B: Biological Sciences, 327,* 543–553. [4]

Folkerts, H. (2000). Electroconvulsive therapy of depressive disorders. *Ther. Umsch, 57,* 290–294. [16]

Folkman, S. (1984). Personal control and stress and coping processes: A theoretical analysis. *Journal of Personality and Social Psychology, 46,* 839–852. [13]

Folkman, S., & Lazarus, R. S. (1980). An analysis of coping in a middle-aged community sample. *Journal of Health and Social Behavior, 21,* 219–239. [13]

Folkman, S., Chesney, M., Collette, L., Boccellari, A., & Cooke, M. (1996). Postbereavement depressive mood and its prebereavement predictors in HIV^+ and HIV^- gay men. *Journal of Personality and Social Psychology, 70,* 336–348. [10]

Fontana, A., Schwartz, L. S., & Rosenheck, R. (1997). Posttraumatic stress disorder among female Vietnam veterans: A causal model of etiology. *American Journal of Public Health, 87,* 169–175. [13]

Ford, C. S., & Beach, F. A. (1951). *Patterns of sexual behavior.* New York: Harper & Row. [12]

Ford, M. E. (1979). The construct validity of egocentrism. *Psychological Bulletin, 86,* 1169–1188. [9]

Forey, J. P., Walker, S., Poston, C., II, & Goodrick, G. K. (1996). Future directions in obesity and eating disorders. *Addictive Behaviors, 21,* 767–778. [11]

Forgas, J. P., & Fiedler, K. (1996). Us and them: Mood effects on intergroup discrimination. *Journal of Personality and Social Psychology, 70,* 28–40. [17]

Foulkes, D. (1996). Sleep and dreams: Dream research: 1953–1993. *Sleep, 19,* 609–624. [4]

Fowles, D. C. (1992). Schizophrenia: Diathesis-stress revisited. *Annual Review of Psychology, 43,* 303–336. [15]

Fox, A. M., Michie, P. T., Wynne, C. D. L., & Maybery, M. T. (2000a). ERP correlates of response inhibition to elemental and configural stimuli in a negative patterning task. *Clinical Neurophysiology, 111,* 1045–1053. [5]

Fox, E., Lester, V., Russo, R., Bowles, R. J., Pichler, A., & Dutton, K. (2000b). Facial expressions of emotion: Are angry faces detected more efficiently? *Cognition and Emotion, 14,* 61–92. [11]

Fox, N. A., & Bell, M. A. (1990). Electrophysiological indices of frontal lobe development: Relations to cognitive and affective behavior in human infants over the first year of life. *Annals of the New York Academy of Sciences, 608,* 677–698. [9]

Frank, E., Anderson, B., Reynolds, C. F., III, Ritenour, A., & Kupfer, D. J. (1994). Life events and the research diagnostic criteria endogenous subtype. *Archives of General Psychiatry, 51,* 519–524. [15]

Frank, E., Kupfer, D. J., Wagner, E. F., McEachran, A. B., & Cornes, C. (1991). Efficacy of interpersonal psychotherapy as a maintenance treatment of recurrent depression: Contributing factors. *Archives of General Psychiatry, 48,* 1053–1059. [16]

Frank, R. A. (2000). Tepid tastes. *Nature, 403,* 837–839. [3]

Frankenburg, W. K., Dodds, J. B., Archer, P., et al. (1992). *Denver II training manual.* Denver: Denver Developmental Materials. [9]

Franz, C. E., McClelland, D. C., & Weinberger, J. (1991). Childhood antecedents of conventional social accomplishment in midlife adults: A 36-year prospective study. *Journal of Personality and Social Psychology, 60,* 586–595. [9]

Fraser, A. M., Brockert, J. E., & Ward, R. H. (1995). Association of young maternal age with adverse reproductive outcomes. *New England Journal of Medicine, 332,* 1113–1117. [9, 10]

Frazer, A. (1997). Antidepressants. *Journal of Clinical Psychiatry, 58*(6, Suppl.), 9–25. [16]

Fredrikson, M., Annas, P., Fischer, H., & Wik, G. (1996). Gender and age differences in the prevalence of specific fears and phobias. *Behaviour Research and Therapy, 34,* 33–39. [15]

Freedman, J. L., & Fraser, S. C. (1966). Compliance without pressure: The foot-in-the-door technique. *Journal of Personality and Social Psychology, 4,* 195–202. [17]

Freeman, W. J. (1991). The physiology of perception. *Scientific American, 264,* 78–85. [3]

Frei, R., Begemann, E., & Willi, J. (2000). Catamnestic study of ecological brief therapy. *Psychother. Psychosom. Med. Psychol., 50,* 8335–8341. [16]

Freud, A. (1958). *Adolescence: Psychoanalytic study of the child* (Vol. 13). New York: Academic Press. [10]

Freud, A. (1966). *The ego and the mechanisms of defense* (rev. ed.). New York: International Universities Press. [14]

Freud, S. (1922). *Beyond the pleasure principle.* London: International Psychoanalytic Press. [6]

Freud, S. (1953a). The interpretation of dreams. In J. Strachey (Ed. and Trans.), *The standard edition of the complete psychological works of Sigmund Freud* (Vols. 4 and 5). London: Hogarth Press. (Original work published 1900). [4]

Freud, S. (1953b). Three essays on the theory of sexuality. In J. Strachey (Ed. and Trans.), *The standard edition of the complete psychological works of Sigmund Freud* (Vol. 7). London: Hogarth Press. (Original work published 1905). [14]

Freud, S. (1960). Psychopathology of everyday life. In J. Strachey (Ed. and Trans.), *The standard edition of the complete psychological works of Sigmund Freud* (Vol. 6). London: Hogarth Press. (Original work published 1901). [14]

Freud, S. (1961). The ego and the id. In J. Strachey (Ed. and Trans.), *The standard edition of the complete psychological works of Sigmund Freud* (Vol. 19). London: Hogarth Press. (Original work published 1923). [14]

Freud, S. (1962). *Civilization and its discontents* (J. Strachey, Trans.). New York: W.W. Norton. (Original work published 1930). [14]

Freud, S. (1963a). *An autobiographical study* (J. Strachey, Trans.). New York: W.W. Norton. (Original work published 1925). [14, 16]

Freud, S. (1963b). *A general introduction to psycho-analysis* (J. Riviere, Trans.). New York: Simon & Schuster. (Original work published 1920). [14, 16]

Freud, S. (1965). *New introductory lectures on psychoanalysis* (J. Strachey, Trans.). New York: W. W. Norton. (Original work published 1933). [14]

Frey, K. P., & Eagly, A. H. (1993). Vividness can undermine the persuasiveness of messages. *Journal of Personality and Social Psychology, 65,* 32–44. [17]

Frey-Hewitt, B., Vranizan, K. M., Dreon, D. M., & Wood, P. D. (1990). The effect of weight loss by dieting or exercise on resting metabolic rate in overweight men. *International Journal of Obesity, 14,* 327–334. [11]

Friedland, N., Keinan, G., & Regev, Y. (1992). Controlling the uncontrollable: Effects of stress on illusory perceptions of controllability. *Journal of Personality and Social Psychology, 63,* 923–931. [13]

Friedman, H. S., Tucker, J. S., Schwartz, J. E., Tomlinson-Keasey, C., Martin, L. R., Wingard, D. L., & Criqui, M. H. (1995). Psychosocial and behavioral predictors of longevity: The aging and death of the "Termites." *American Psychologist, 50,* 69–78. [10]

Friedman, J. M. (1997). The alphabet of weight control. *Nature, 385,* 119–120. [11]

Friedman, J. M. (2000). Obesity in the new millennium. *Nature, 404,* 632–634. [11]

Friedman, M. I., Tordoff, M. G., & Ramirez, I. (1986). Integrated metabolic control of food intake. *Brain Research Bulletin, 17,* 855–859. [11]

Friedman, M., & Rosenman, R. H. (1974). *Type A behavior and your heart.* New York: Fawcett. [13]

Fry, A. F., & Hale, S. (1996). Processing speed, working memory, and fluid intelligence. *Psychological Science, 7,* 237–241. [8]

Fujita, F., Diener, E., & Sandvik, E. (1991). Gender differences in negative affect and well-being: The case for emotional intensity. *Journal of Personality and Social Psychology, 61,* 427–434. [11]

Fuligni, A. J., & Stevenson, H. W. (1995). Time use and mathematics achievement among American, Chinese, and Japanese high school students. *Child Development, 66,* 830–842. [8]

Funnell, M. G., Corballis, P. M., & Gazzaniga, M. S. (2000). Insights into the functional specificity of the human corpus callosum. *Brain, 123,* 920–926. [2]

Fuster, J. M., Bodner, M., & Kroger, J. K. (2000). Cross-modal and cross-temporal association in neurons of frontal cortex. *Nature, 405,* 347–351. [2]

Fyer, A. J. (1993). Heritability of social anxiety: A brief review. *Journal of Clinical Psychiatry, 54*(12, Suppl.), 10–12. [15]

Gabrieli, J. D. E., Desmond, J. E., Demb, J. B., Wagner, A. D., Stone, M. V., Viadya, C. J., & Glover, G. H. (1996). Functional magnetic resonance imaging of semantic memory processes in the frontal lobes. *Psychological Science, 7,* 278–283. [6]

Gackenbach, J., & Bosveld, J. (1989, October). Take control of your dreams. *Psychology Today,* pp. 27–32. [4]

Gaertner, S. L., & Dovidio, J. F. (1986). The aversive form of racism. In J. F. Dovidio & S. L. Gaertner (Eds.), *Prejudice, discrimination, and racism* (pp. 61–89). San Diego, CA: Academic Press. [17]

Gaertner, S. L., Mann, J. A., Dovidio, J. F., & Murrell, A. J. (1990). How does cooperation reduce intergroup bias? *Journal of Personality and Social Psychology, 59,* 692–704. [17]

Gagnon, J. H, & Simon, W. (1973). *Sexual conduct: The social origins of human sexuality.* Chicago: Aldine. [12]

Galanter, M. (1993). *Network therapy for alcohol and drug abuse.* New York: Basic Books. [13]

Gallagher, M., & Rapp, P. R. (1997). The use of animal models to study the effects of aging on cognition. *Annual Review of Psychology, 48,* 339–370. [10]

Gallistel, C. R., & Gibbon, J. (2000). Time, rate, and conditioning. *Psychological Review, 107,* 289–344. [5]

Gallup, G., Jr. (1995). *The Gallup poll: Public opinion 1995.* Wilmington, DE: Scholarly Resources. [13]

Gallup, G., Jr., & Hugick, L. (1990). Racial tolerance grows, progress on racial equality less evident. *Gallup Poll Monthly,* No. 297, 23–32. [17]

Gallup, G., Jr., & Newport, F. (1990a). The battle of the bulge: Americans continue to fight it. *Gallup Poll Monthly,* No. 303, 23–34. [11]

Gallup, G., Jr., & Newport, F. (1990b). Belief in psychic and paranormal phenomena widespread among Americans. *Gallup Poll Monthly,* No. 299, 35–43. [3]

Gallup, G., Jr., & Newport, F. (1990c). Virtually all adults want children, but many of the reasons are intangible. *Gallup Poll Monthly,* No. 297, 8–22. [10]

Gallup, G., Jr., & Suarez, S. D. (1985). Alternatives to the use of animals in psychological research. *American Psychologist, 40,* 1104–1111. [1]
Galton, F. (1874). *English men of science: Their nature and nurture.* London: Macmillan. [8]
Galton, F. (1875). The history of twins as a criterion of the relative powers of nature and nurture. *Journal of the Royal Anthropological Institute, 5,* 391–406. [8]
Ganellen, R. J. (1996). Comparing the diagnostic efficiency of the MMPI, MCMI-II, and Rorschach: A review. *Journal of Personality Assessment, 67,* 219–243. [14]
Gannon, L., Luchetta, R., Rhodes, K., Paradie, L., & Segrist, D. (1992). Sex bias in psychological research: Progress or complacency? *American Psychologist, 47,* 389–396. [1]
Gao, J-H., Parsons, L. M., Bower, J. M., Xiong, J., Li, J., & Fox, P. T. (1996). Cerebellum implicated in sensory acquisition and discrimination rather than motor control. *Science, 272,* 545–547. [2]
Garavan, H., Morgan, R. E., Levitsky, D. A., Hermer-Vasquez, L., & Strupp, B. J. (2000). Enduring effects of early lead exposure: Evidence for a specific deficit in associative ability. *Neurotoxicology and Teratology, 22,* 151–164. [8]
Garcia, J., & Koelling, A. (1966). Relation of cue to consequence in avoidance learning. *Psychonomic Science, 4,* 123–124. [5]
Garcia-Segura, L. M., Azcojtia, I., & DonCarlos, L. L. (2001). Neuroprotection by estradiol. *Progress in Neurobiology, 62,* 29–60. [15]
Gardner, H. (1981, February). How the split brain gets a joke. *Psychology Today,* pp. 74–78. [2]
Gardner, H. (1983). *Frames of mind: The theory of multiple intelligence.* New York: Basic Books. [8]
Gardner, H., & Hatch, T. (1989). Multiple intelligences go to school: Educational implication of the theory of multiple intelligences. *Educational Researcher, 18*(8), 6. [8]
Gardner, L. I. (1972). Deprivation dwarfism. *Scientific American, 227,* 76–82. [9]
Gardner, R. A., & Gardner, B. T. (1969). Teaching sign language to a chimpanzee. *Science, 165,* 664–672. [7]
Garfield, C. (1986). *Peak performers: The new heroes of American business.* New York: Morrow. [7]
Garland, A. F., & Zigler, E. (1993). Adolescent suicide prevention: Current research and social policy implications. *American Psychologist, 48,* 169–182. [15]
Garma, L., & Marchand, F. (1994). Non-pharmacological approaches to the treatment of narcolepsy. *Sleep, 17,* S97–S102. [4]
Garmon, L. C., Basinger, K. S., Gregg, V. R., & Gibbs, J. C. (1996). Gender differences in stage and expression of moral judgment. *Merrill-Palmer Quarterly, 42,* 418–437. [10]
Garry, M., & Loftus, E. F. (1994). Pseudomemories without hypnosis. *International Journal of Clinical and Experimental Hypnosis, 42,* 363–373. [6]
Gartner, J., & Whitaker-Azimitia, P. M. (1996). Developmental factors influencing aggression: Animal models and clinical correlates. *Annals of the New York Academy of Sciences, 794,* 113–120. [17]
Gastil, J. (1990). Generic pronouns and sexist language: The oxymoronic character of masculine generics. *Sex Roles, 23,* 629–643. [7]
Gates, A. I. (1917). Recitation as a factor in memorizing. *Archives of Psychology, 40.* [6]
Gawin, F. H. (1991). Cocaine addiction: Psychology and neurophysiology. *Science, 251,* 1580–1586. [4]
Gazzaniga, M. S. (1970). *The bisected brain.* New York: Appleton-Century-Crofts. [2]
Gazzaniga, M. S. (1983). Right hemisphere language following brain bisection: A 20-year perspective. *American Psychologist, 38,* 525–537. [2]
Gazzaniga, M. S. (1989). Organization of the human brain. *Science, 245,* 947–952. [2]
Gazzaniga, M. S. (1997). Brain, drugs, and society. *Science, 275,* 459. [4]
Gazzaniga, M. S. (2000). Cerebral specialization and interhemispheric communication. *Brain, 123,* 1293–1326. [2]
Geary, D. C. (1996). Sexual selection and sex differences in mathematical abilties. *Behavioral and Brain Sciences, 19,* 229–284. [12]
Geen, R. G. (1984). Human motivation: New perspectives on old problems. In A. M. Rogers & C. J. Scheier (Eds.), *The G. Stanley Hall lecture series* (Vol. 4). Washington, DC: American Psychological Association. [11]
Geen, R. G. (1995). *Human motivation: A social psychological approach.* Pacific Grove, CA: Brooks/Cole. [11]
Geiselman, R. E., Haight, N. A., & Kimata, L. G. (1984). Context effects on the perceived physical attractiveness of faces. *Journal of Experimental Social Psychology, 20,* 409–424. [17]
Geiselman, R. E., Schroppel, T., Tubridy, A., Konishi, T., & Rodriguez, V. (2000). Objectivity bias in eye witness performance. *Applied Cognitive Psychology, 14,* 323–332. [6]
Genesee, F. (1994). Bilingualism. In V. S. Ramachandran (Ed.), *Encyclopedia of human behavior* (Vol. 1, pp. 383–393). San Diego, CA: Academic. [7]
George, M. S., Ketter, T. A., & Post, R. M. (1993). SPECT and PET imaging in mood disorders. *Journal of Clinical Psychiatry, 54*(11, Suppl.), 6–13. [15]
Gerbner, G., & Signorielli, N. (1990). *Violence profile, 1967 through 1988–1989. Enduring patterns.* Unpublished manuscript, Annenberg School of Communication, University of Pennsylvania, Philadelphia. [9]
Gergen, K. J., Gulerce, A., Lock, A., & Misra, G. (1996). Psychological science in cultural context. *American Psychologist, 51,* 496–503. [1]
Gervai, J., Turner, P. J., & Hinde, R. A. (1995). Gender-related behaviour, attitudes, and personality in parents of young children in England and Hungary. *International Journal of Behavioral Development, 18,* 105–126. [12]
Geschwind, N. (1979). Specializations of the human brain. *Science, 241,* 180–199. [2]
Geschwind, N., & Behan, P. O. (1982). Left handedness: Association with immune disease, migraine, and developmental learning disorders. *Proceedings of the National Academy of Sciences, 79,* 5097–5100. [2]
Getzels, J. W., & Csikszentmihalyi, M. (1976). *The creative vision: A longitudinal study of problem finding in art.* New York: Wiley. [8]
Gevins, A., Leong, H., Smith, M. E., Le, J., & Du, R. (1995). Mapping cognitive brain function with modern high-resolution electroencephalography. *Trends in Neurosciences, 18,* 429–436. [2]
Giacopassi, D., & Vandiver, M. (1999). University students' perceptions of tobacco, cocaine, and homicide fatalities. *American Journal of Drug and Alcohol Abuse, 25,* 163–172. [4]
Gibbons, A. (1991). Déjà vu all over again: Chimp-language wars. *Science, 251,* 1561–1562. [7]
Gibbs, W. W. (1996, August). Gaining on fat. *Scientific American, 275,* 88–94. [11]
Gibson, E., & Walk, R. D. (1960). The "visual cliff." *Scientific American, 202,* 64–71. [9]
Giedd, J. N., Rapoport, J. L., Garvey, M. A., Perlmutter, S., & Swedo, S. E. (2000). MRI assessment of children with obsessive-compulsive disorder or tics associated with streptococcal infection. *American Journal of Psychiatry, 157,* 2281–2283. [15]
Gilbert, D. T., & Malone, P. S. (1995). The correspondence bias. *Psychological Bulletin, 117,* 21–38. [17]
Giles, D. E., Jarrett, R. B., Biggs, M. M., Guzick, D. S., & Rush, A. J. (1989). Clinical predictors of recurrence in depression. *American Journal of Psychiatry, 146,* 764–767. [15]
Gillberg, M., Kecklund, G., Axelsson, J., & Åkerstedt, T. (1996). The effects of a short daytime nap after restricted night sleep. *Sleep, 19,* 570–575. [4]
Gilligan, C. (1982). *In a different voice: Psychological theory and women's development.* Cambridge, MA: Harvard University Press. [10]
Ginsberg, G., & Bronstein, P. (1993). Family factors related to children's intrinsic/extrinsic motivational orientation and academic performance. *Child Development, 64,* 1461–1474. [11]
Ginty, D. D., Kornhauser, J. M., Thompson, M. A., Bading, H., Mayo, K. E., Takahashi, J. S., & Greenberg, M. E. (1993). Regulation of CREB phosphorylation in the suprachiasmatic nucleus by light and a circadian clock. *Science, 260,* 238–241. [4]
Gladue, B. A. (1991). Aggressive behavioral characteristics, hormones, and sexual orientation in men and women. *Aggressive Behavior, 17,* 313–326. [12]

Glantz, L. A., & Lewis, D. A. (2000). Decreased dendritic spine density on prefrontal cortical pyramidal neurons in schizophrenia. *Archives of General Psychiatry, 57,* 65–73. [15]

Glass, D. C., & Singer, J. E. (1972). *Urban stress: Experiments in noise and social stressors.* New York: Academic Press. [13]

Glass, J., & Fujimoto, T. (1994). Housework, paid work, and depression among husbands and wives. *Journal of Health and Social Behavior, 35,* 179–191. [10]

Glassman, A. H. (1993). What is the relationship between depression and cigarette smoking? *Harvard Mental Health Letter, 10*(4), 8. [13]

Glazer, W. M., Morgenstern, H., & Doucette, J. T. (1993). Predicting the long-term risk of tardive dyskinesia in outpatients maintained on neuroleptic medications. *Journal of Clinical Psychiatry, 54,* 133–139. [16]

Gleaves, D. J. (1996). The sociocognitive model of dissociative identity disorder: A reexamination of the evidence. *Psychological Bulletin, 120,* 42–59. [15]

Glover, J. A., & Corkill, A. J. (1987). Influence of paraphrased repetitions on the spacing effect. *Journal of Educational Psychology, 79,* 198–199. [6]

Gluck, M. A., & Myers, C. E. (1997). Psychobiological models of hippocampal function in learning and memory. *Annual Review of Psychology, 48,* 481–514. [2, 6]

Godden, D. R., & Baddeley, A. D. (1975). Context-dependent memory in two natural environments: On land and underwater. *British Journal of Psychology, 66,* 325–331. [6]

Godden, D. R., & Baddeley, A. D. (1980). When does context influence recognition memory? *British Journal of Psychology, 71,* 99–104. [6]

Goh, V. H., Tong, T. Y., & Lee, L. K. (2000). Sleep/wake cycle and circadian disturbances in shift work: Strategies for their management—a review. *Annals of the Academy of Medicine Singapore, 29,* 90–96. [4]

Gökcebay, N., Cooper, R., Williams, R. L., Hirshkowitz, M., & Moore, C. A. (1994). Function of sleep. In R. Cooper (Ed.), *Sleep.* New York: Chapman & Hall. [4]

Gold, M. S. (1986). *800-cocaine* (rev.). Toronto: Bantam. [4]

Gold, M. S. (1994). The epidemiology, attitudes, and pharmacology of LSD use in the 1990s. *Psychiatric Annals, 24,* 124–126. [4]

Gold, P. W. (2000). The high cost of stress. In *Project on the decade of the brain* [On-line]. Available: lcweb.loc.gov/loc/brain/emotion/Gold.html [13]

Goldberg, J., True, W. R., Eisen, S. A., & Henderson, W. G. (1990). A twin study of the effects of the Vietnam War on posttraumatic stress disorder. *Journal of the American Medical Association, 263,* 1227–1232. [13]

Goldberg, L. R. (1993). The structure of phenotypic personality traits. *American Psychologist, 48,* 26–34. [14]

Goldberg, L. R., & Saucier, G. (1995). So what do you propose we use instead? A reply to Block. *Psychological Bulletin, 117,* 221–225. [14]

Goldberg, P. A. (1965). A review of sentence completion methods in personality. In B. I. Murstein (Ed.), *Handbook of projective techniques.* New York: Basic Books. [14]

Golden, J. (2000). "A tempest in a cocktail glass": Mothers, alcohol, and television. *Journal of Health Politics, Policy & Law, 25,* 473–498. [9]

Goldenberg, H. (1977). *Abnormal psychology: A social/community approach.* Monterey, CA: Brooks/Cole. [15]

Goldenberg, R. L., & Klerman, L. V. (1995). Adolescent pregnancy—another look. *New England Journal of Medicine, 332,* 1161–1162. [10]

Goldman, M. S. (1983). Cognitive impairment in chronic alcoholics: Some cause for optimism. *American Psychologist, 38,* 1045–1054. [13]

Goldsmith, H. H., Buss, A. H., Plomin, R., Rothbart, M. K., Thomas, A., Chess, S., Hinde, R. A., & McCall, R. B. (1987). Roundtable: What is temperament? Four approaches. *Child Development, 58,* 504–529. [9]

Goldstein, A., & Kalant, H. (1990). Drug policy: Striking the right balance. *Science, 249,* 1513–1521. [14]

Goldvarg, Y., & Johnson-Laird, P. N. (2000). Illusions in modal reasoning. *Memory and Cognition, 28,* 282–294. [7]

Goleman, D. (1979, November). Positive denial: The case for not facing reality. *Psychology Today,* pp. 13, 44–60. [13]

Goleman, D. (1995). *Emotional intelligence.* New York: Bantam. [8]

Goleman, D., Kaufman, P., & Ray, M. (1992). *The creative spirit.* New York: Dutton. [8]

Gómez, R. L., & Gerken, L. (2000). Infant artificial language learning and language acquisition. *Trends in Cognitive Sciences, 4,* 178–186. [9]

Gonzalez, R., Ellsworth, P. C., & Pembroke, M. (1993). Response biases in lineups and showups. *Journal of Personality and Social Psychology, 64,* 525–537. [6]

Goode, E. E. (1987, September 28). For a little peace of mine. *U.S. News & World Report,* pp. 98–102. [16]

Goodglass, H. (1993). *Understanding aphasia.* San Diego, CA: Academic Press. [2]

Goodwin, D. W. (1985). Alcoholism and genetics: The sins of the fathers. *Archives of General Psychiatry, 42,* 171–174. [13]

Goodwin, D. W. (1986). *Anxiety.* New York: Oxford University Press. [15]

Goodwin, G. M. (1996). How do antidepressants affect serotonin receptors? The role of serotonin receptors in the therapeutic and side effect profile of the SSRIs. *Journal of Clinical Psychiatry, 57*(4, Suppl.), 9–13. [16]

Gorman, C. (1996, Fall). Damage control. *Time* [Special Issue], 31–35. [2]

Gorman, E. M. (1991). Anthropological reflections on the HIV epidemic among gay men. *Journal of Sex Research, 28,* 263–273. [12]

Gormezano, I. (1984). The study of associative learning with CS-CR paradigms. In D. L. Alkon & J. Farley (Eds.), *Primary neural substrates of learning and behavioral change* (pp. 5–24). New York: Cambridge University Press. [5]

Gottesman, I. I. (1991). *Schizophrenia genesis: The origins of madness.* New York: W. H. Freeman. [15]

Gottesmann, C. (2000). Hypothesis for the neurophysiology of dreaming. *Sleep Research Online, 3,* 1–4. [4]

Gottfried, A. E., Fleming, J. S., & Gottfried, A. W. (1994). Role of parental motivational practices in children's academic intrinsic motivation and achievement. *Journal of Educational Psychology, 86,* 104–113. [11]

Gotthoffer, A. R. (1999). Localization of relevant consequences in anti-drinking and driving PSAs (public service announcements): A new approach to targeting underage college students. *Health Marketing Quarterly, 16,* 17–37. [17]

Gottman, J. (with Silver, N.). (1994). *Why marriages succeed or fail and how you can make yours last.* New York: Simon & Schuster. [10, 11]

Gough, H. (1987). *California Psychological Inventory: Administrator's Guide.* Palo Alto: Consulting Psychologists Press. [14]

Gould, E. R., Reeves, A. J., Graziano, M. S. A., & Gross, C. (1999). Neurogenesis in the neocortex of adult primates. *Science, 286,* 548. [2]

Gould, M. S., Fisher, P., Parides,, M., Flory, M., & Shaffer, D. (1996). Psychosocial risk factors of child and adolescent completed suicide. *Archives of General Psychiatry, 53,* 1155–1162. [15]

Graham, K. S., Simons, J. S., Pratt, K. H., Patterson, K., & Hodges, J. R. (2000). Insights from semantic dementia on the relationship between episodic and semantic memory. *Neuropsychologia, 38,* 313–324. [6]

Graham, S. (1992). "Most of the subjects were white and middle class": Trends in published research on African Americans in selected APA journals, 1970–1989. *American Psychologist, 47,* 629–639. [1]

Grant, B. F., & Dawson, D. A. (1998). Age at onset of alcohol use and its association with *DSM-IV* alcohol abuse and dependence: Results from the National Longitudinal Alcohol Epidemiologic Survey. *Journal of Substance Abuse, 9,* 103–110. [13]

Grant, B. F., Harford, T. C., Chou, P., Pickering, M. S., Dawson, D. A., Stinson, F. S., & Noble, J. (1991). Prevalence of DSM-III-R alcohol abuse and dependence: United States, 1988. *Alcohol Health & Research World, 15,* 91–96. [13]

Grbich, C. (1994). Women as primary breadwinners in families where men are primary caregivers. *Australian New Zealand Journal of Sociology, 30,* 105–118. [9]

Greden, J. F. (1994). Introduction Part III. New agents for the treatment of depression. *Journal of Clinical Psychiatry, 55*(2, Suppl.), 32–33. [2, 15]

Green, A. R., & Goodwin, G. M. (1996). Ecstasy and neurodegeneration: Ecstasy's long term effects are potentially more damaging than its acute toxicity. *British Medical Journal, 312,* 1493–1494. [4]

Green, B. L., Lindy, J. D., & Grace, M. C. (1985). Post-traumatic stress disorder: Toward DSM-IV. *Journal of Nervous and Mental Disorders, 173,* 406–411. [13]

Green, J. P., & Lynn, S. J. (2000). Hypnosis and suggestion-based approaches to smoking cessation: An examination of the evidence. *International Journal of Clinical Experimental Hypnosis, 48,* 195–224. [4]

Green, J. T., & Woodruff-Pak, D. S. (2000). Eyeblink classical conditioning: Hippocampal formation is for neutral stimulus associations as cerebellum is for association-response. *Psychological Bulletin, 126,* 138–158. [5]

Green, J., & Shellenberger, R. (1990). *The dynamics of health and wellness: A biopsychosocial approach.* Fort Worth: Holt, Rinehart & Winston. [13]

Green, L. R., Richardson, D. R., & Lago, T. (1996). How do friendship, indirect, and direct aggression relate? *Aggressive Behavior, 22,* 81–86. [17]

Green, R. (1985). Gender identity in childhood and later sexual orientation: Follow-up of 78 males. *American Journal of Psychiatry,* 142, 339. [12]

Green, R. (1987). *The "sissy boy syndrome" and the development of homosexuality.* New Haven: Yale University Press. [12]

Greenwald, A. G. (1992). New look 3: Unconscious cognition reclaimed. *American Psychologist, 47,* 766–779. [3, 13]

Greenwald, A. G., Spangenberg, E. R., Pratkanis, A. R., & Eskenazi, J. (1991). Double-blind tests of subliminal self-help audiotapes. *Psychological Science, 2,* 119–122. [3]

Greer, W. R. (1986, November 23). Violence against homosexuals rising, groups seeking wider protection say. *The New York Times,* p. 36. [12]

Gregory, R. J. (1996). *Psychological testing: History, principles, and applications* (2nd ed.). Boston: Allyn & Bacon. [8, 14]

Gregory, R. L. (1978). *Eye and brain: The psychology of seeing* (3rd ed.). New York: McGraw-Hill. [3]

Greist, J. H. (1992). An integrated approach to treatment of obsessive compulsive disorder. *Journal of Clinical Psychiatry, 53*(4, Suppl.), 38–41. [16]

Greist, J. H. (1995). The diagnosis of social phobia. *Journal of Clinical Psychiatry, 56*(5, Suppl.), 5–12. [15]

Griffith, R. M., Miyago, O., & Tago, A. (1958). The universality of typical dreams: Japanese vs. Americans. *American Anthropologist, 60,* 1173–1179. [4]

Griffitt, W., Nelson, J., & Littlepage, G. (1972). Old age and response to agreement-disagreement. *Journal of Gerontology,* 27, 269–274. [17]

Grinker, J. A. (1982). Physiological and behavioral basis for human obesity. In D. W. Pfaff (Ed.), *The physiological mechanisms of motivation.* New York: Springer-Verlag. [11]

Grochowicz, P., Schedlowski, M., Husband, A., King, M., Hibberd, A., & Bowen, K. (1991). Behavioral conditioning prolongs heart allograft survival in rats. *Brain, Behavior, and Immunity, 5,* 349–356. [5]

Grogger, J., & Bronars, S. (1993). The socioeconomic consequences of teenage childbearing: Findings from a natural experiment. *Family Planning Perspectives, 25,* 156–161. [10]

Gron, G., Wunderlich, A. P., Spitzer, M., Tomczrak, R., & Riepe, M. W. (2000). Brain activation during human navigation: Gender-different neural networks as substrate of performance. *Nature Neuroscience, 3,* 404–408. [2]

Gronfier, C., Luthringer, R., Follenius, M., Schaltenbrand, N., Macher, J. P., Muzet, A., & Brandenberger, G. (1996). A quantitative evaluation of the relationships between growth hormone secretion and delta wave electroencephalographic activity during normal sleep and after enrichment in delta waves. *Sleep, 19,* 817–824. [4]

Grossman, H. J. (Ed.). (1983). *Manual on terminology and classification in mental retardation.* Washington, DC: American Association on Mental Deficiency. [8]

Grossman, M., & Wood, W. (1993). Sex differences in intensity of emotional experience: A social role interpretation. *Journal of Personality and Social Psychology, 65,* 1010–1022. [11]

Grundy, S. M. (1999). The optimal ratio of fat to carbohydrate in the diet. *Annual Review of Nutrition, 19,* 325–341. [11]

Guéguen, N., & Pascual, A. (2000). Evocation of freedom and compliance: The "but you are free of . . ." technique. *Current Research in Social Psychology, 5,* 264–270. [17]

Guilford, J. P. (1967). *The nature of human intelligence.* New York: McGraw-Hill. [7, 8]

Guilleminault, C. (1993). 1. Amphetamines and narcolepsy: Use of the Stanford database. *Sleep, 16,* 199–201. [4]

Gunn, R. A., Montes, J. M., Toomey, K. E., Rolfs, R. T., Greenspan, J. R., Spitters, C. E., & Waterman, S. H. (1995). Syphilis in San Diego county 1983–1992: Crack cocaine, prostitution, and the limitations of partner notification. *Sexually Transmitted Diseases, 22,* 60–66. [12]

Gupta, D., & Vishwakarma, M. S. (1989). Toy weapons and firecrackers: A source of hearing loss. *Laryngoscope, 99,* 330–334. [3]

Gur, R. E., Cowell, P. E., Latshaw, A., Turetsky, B. I., Grossman, R. I., Amold, S. E., Bilker, W. B., & Gur, R. C. (2000). Reduced dorsal and orbital prefrontal gray matter volumes in schizophrenia. *Archives of General Psychiatry, 57,* 761–768. [15]

Gurin, J. (1989, June). Leaner, not lighter. *Psychology Today,* pp. 32–36. [11]

Gustavson, C. R., Garcia, J., Hankins, W. G., & Rusiniak, K. W. (1974). Coyote predation control by aversive conditioning. *Science, 184,* 581–583. [5]

Guthrie, J. P., Ash, R. A., & Bendapudi, V. (1995). Additional validity evidence for a measure of morningness. *Journal of Applied Psychology, 80,* 186–190. [4]

Guthrie, R. V. (1998). *Even the rat was white* (2nd ed.). Boston: Allyn & Bacon. [1]

Haaga, D. A. F., Dyck, M. J., & Ernst, D. (1991). Empirical status of cognitive theory of depression. *Psychological Bulletin, 110,* 215–236. [15]

Haas, E. M. (1992). *Staying healthy with nutrition: The complete guide to diet and nutritional medicine.* Berkeley, CA: Celestial Arts. [4]

Haber, R. N. (1980). How we perceive depth from flat pictures. *American Scientist, 68,* 370–380. [6]

Haberlandt, D. (1997). *Cognitive psychology* (2nd ed.). Boston: Allyn & Bacon. [1, 7, 8]

Hackel, L. S., & Ruble, D. N. (1992). Changes in the marital relationship after the first baby is born: Predicting the impact of expectancy disconfirmation. *Journal of Personality and Social Psychology, 62,* 944–957. [10]

Hager, W., Leichsenring, F., & Schiffler, A. (2000). When does a study of different therapies allow comparisons of their relative efficacy? *Psychother. Psychosom. Med. Psychol., 50,* 251–262. [16]

Haimov, I., & Lavie, P. (1996). Melatonin—a soporific hormone. *Current Directions in Psychological Science, 5,* 106–111. [4]

Häkkänen, H., & Summala, H. (1999). Sleepiness at work among commercial truck drivers. *Sleep, 23,* 49–57. [4]

Halaas, J. L., Gajiwala, K. S., Maffei, M., Cohen, S. L., Chait, B. T., Rabinowitz, D., Lallone, R. L., Burley, S. K., & Friedman, J. M. (1995). Weight-reducing effects of the plasma protein encoded by the obese gene. *Science, 269,* 543–546. [11]

Halford, G. S. (1989). Reflections on 25 years of Piagetian cognitive developmental psychology, 1963–1988. *Human Development, 32,* 325–327. [9]

Hall, C. S., & Van de Castle, R. L. (1966). *The content analysis of dreams.* New York: Appleton-Century-Crofts. [4]

Hall, G. S. (1904). *Adolescence: Its psychology and its relations to physiology, anthropology, sex, crime, religion, and education* (Vol. 1). New York: Appleton-Century-Crofts. [10]

Hall, J., Thomas, K. L., & Everitt, B. J. (2000). Rapid and selective induction of *BDNF* expression in the hippocampus during contextual learning. *Nature Neuroscience, 3,* 533–535. [5]

Hall, J. A. (1984). *Nonverbal sex differences.* Baltimore: Johns Hopkins University Press. [12]

Halligan, P. W., & Marshall, J. C. (1994). Toward a principled explanation of unilateral neglect. *Cognitive Neuropsychology, 11,* 167–206. [2]

Halmi, K. A. (1996). Eating disorder research in the past decade. *Annals of the New York Academy of Sciences, 789,* 67–77. [11]

Halpern, C. T., Joyner, K., Udry, J. R., & Suchindran, C. (2000). Smart teens don't have sex (or kiss much either). *Journal of Adolescent Health, 26,* 3213–3225. [8]

Halpern, D. F. (1992). *Sex differences in cognitive abilities* (2nd ed.). Hillside, NJ: Erlbaum. [12]
Halpern, D. F., & Coren, S. (1993). Left-handedness and life span: A reply to Harris. *Psychological Bulletin, 114,* 235–241. [2]
Hamer, D. H., Hu, S., Magnuson, V. L., Hu, N., & Pattatucci, A. M. L. (1993). A linkage between DNA markers on the X chromosome and male sexual orientation. *Science, 261,* 321–327. [12]
Hamilton, C. S., & Swedo, S. E. (2001). Autoimmune-mediated, childhood onset obsessive-compulsive disorder and tics: A review. *Clinical Neuroscience Research, 1,* 61–68. [15]
Hamilton, M. C. (1988). Using masculine generics: Does generic "he" increase male bias in the user's imagery? *Sex Roles, 19,* 785–789. [7]
Hamm, J. V. (2000). Do birds of a feather flock together? The variable bases for African American, Asian American, and European American adolescents' selection of similar friends. *Developmental Psychology, 36,* 209–219. [10]
Hammond, D. C. (1992). Hypnosis with sexual disorders. *American Journal of Preventive Psychiatry & Neurology, 3,* 37–41. [4]
Hanley, N. A., Hagan, D. M., Clement-Jones, M., Ball, S. G., Strachan, T., Salas-Cortés, L., McElreavey, K., Lindsay, S., Robson, S., Bullen, P., Ostre, H., & Wilson, D. I. (2000). *SRY, SOX9,* and *DAX1* expression patterns during human sex determination and gonadal development. *Mechanisms of Development, 91,* 403–407. [12]
Hannigan, J. H., & Armant, D. R. (2000). Alcohol in pregnancy and neonatal outcome. *Seminars in Neonatology, 5,* 243–254. [9]
Hansel, C. E. M. (1966). *ESP: A scientific evaluation.* New York: Charles Scribner's Sons. [3]
Hansel, C. E. M. (1980). *ESP and parapsychology: A critical reevaluation.* Buffalo, NY: Prometheus. [3]
Hare, R. D. (1970). *Psychopathy: Theory and research.* New York: Wiley. [15]
Hare, R. D. (1995, September). Psychopaths: New trends in research. *Harvard Mental Health Letter, 12*(3), 4–5. [15]
Harford, T. C., Parker, D. A., Grant, B. F., & Dawson, D. A. (1992). Alcohol use and dependence among employed men and women in the United States in 1988. *Alcoholism: Clinical and Experimental Research, 16,* 146–148. [13]
Hargadon, R., Bowers, K. S., & Woody, E. Z. (1995). Does counterpain imagery mediate hypnotic analgesia? *Journal of Abnormal Psychology, 104,* 508–516. [4]
Harkins, S. G., & Jackson, J. M. (1985). The role of evaluation in eliminating social loafing. *Personality and Social Psychology Bulletin, 11,* 456–465. [17]
Harkins, S. G., & Szymanski, K. (1989). Social loafing and group evaluation. *Journal of Personality and Social Psychology, 56,* 941–943. [17]
Harlow, H. F. (1950). Learning and satiation of response in intrinsically motivated complex puzzle performance by monkeys. *Journal of Comparative and Physiological Psychology, 43,* 289–294. [11]
Harlow, H. F. (1959). Love in infant monkeys. *Scientific American, 200,* 68–74. [9]
Harlow, H. F., & Harlow, M. K. (1962). Social deprivation in monkeys. *Scientific American, 207,* 137–146. [9]
Harlow, H. F., Harlow, M. K., and Suomi, S. J. (1971). From thought to therapy: Lessons from a primate laboratory. *American Scientist, 59,* 538–549. [9]
Harlow, J. M. (1848). Passage of an iron rod through the head. *Boston Medical and Surgical Journal, 39,* 389–393. [2]
Harlow, R. E., & Cantor, N. (1996). Still participating after all these years: A study of life task participation in later life. *Journal of Personality and Social Psychology, 71,* 1235–1249. [10]
Harris, J. (1998). *The nurture assumption.* New York: Free Press. [10]
Harris, L. J. (1993). Do left-handers die sooner than right-handers? Commentary on Coren and Halpern's (1991) "Left-handedness: A marker for decreased survival fitness." *Psychological Bulletin, 114,* 203–234. [2]
Harris, L. J., & Blaiser, M. J. (1997). Effects of a mnemonic peg system on the recall of daily tasks. *Perceptual and Motor Skills, 84,* 721–722. [6]
Harris, N. B. (1992). Sex, race, and experiences of aggression. *Aggressive Behavior, 18,* 201–217. [12]
Harris, R. A., Brodie, M. S., & Dunwiddie, T. V. (1992). Possible substrates of ethanol reinforcement: GABA and dopamine. *Annals of the New York Academy of Sciences, 654,* 61–69. [4]
Harrison, J. R., & Barabasz, A. F. (1991). Effects of restricted environmental stimulation therapy on the behavior of children with autism. *Child Study Journal, 21,* 153–166. [11]
Harrison, Y., & Horne, J. A. (2000). Sleep loss and temporal memory. *Journal of Experimental Psychology, 53,* 271–279. [4]
Hart, B., & Risley, T. R. (1992). American parenting of language-learning children: Persisting differences in family-child interactions observed in natural home environments. *Developmental Psychology, 28,* 1096–1105. [9]
Hart, D., Hofmann, V., Edelstein, W., & Keller, M. (1997). The relation of childhood personality types to adolescent behavior and development: A longitudinal study of Icelandic children. *Developmental Psychology, 33,* 195–205. [9]
Hartmann, E. L. (1973). *The functions of sleep.* New Haven: Yale University Press. [4]
Hartup, W. W. (1989). Social relationships and their developmental significance. *American Psychologist, 44,* 120–126. [9]
Hasselmo, M. E., & Bower, J. M. (1993). Acetylcholine and memory. *Trends in Neurosciences, 16,* 218–222. [2]
Hatfield, E., & Sprecher, S. (1986). *Mirror, mirror . . . The importance of looks in everyday life.* Albany, NY: State University of New York Press. [17]
Haught, P. A., Hill, L. A., Nardi, A. H., & Walls, R. T. (2000). Perceived ability and level of education as predictors of traditional and practical adult problem solving. *Experimental Aging Research, 26,* 89–101. [7]
Hauser, M. D. (1993). Right hemisphere dominance for the production of facial expression in monkeys. *Science, 261,* 475–477. [2]
Haut, M., Kuwabara, H., Leach, S., & Callahan, T. (2000). Age-related changes in neural activation during working memory performance. *Aging, Neuropsychology, and Cognition, 7,* 119–129. [10]
Hay, D. F. (1994). Prosocial development. *Journal of Child Psychology and Psychiatry, 35,* 29–71. [17]
Hayes, S. C., & Heiby, E. (1996). Psychology's drug problem: Do we need a fix or should we just say no? *American Psychologist, 51,* 198–206. [16]
Hayley, W. E., Roth, D. L., Coleton, M. I., Ford, G. R., West, C. A. C., Collins, R. P., & Isobe, T. L. (1996). Appraisal, coping, and social support as mediators of well-being in Black and White family caregivers of patients with Alzheimer's disease. *Journal of Consulting and Clinical Psychology, 64,* 121–129. [10]
Hebb, D. O. (1949). *The organization of behavior.* New York: John Wiley & Sons. [6]
Hecht, S., Shlaer, S., & Pirenne, M. H. (1942). *Journal of General Physiology, 25,* 819. [3]
Hedges, L. B., & Nowell, A. (1995). Sex differences in mental test scores, variability, and numbers of high-scoring individuals. *Science, 269,* 41–45. [12]
Hedley, L. M., Hoffart, A., Dammen, T., Ekeberg, O., & Friis, S. (2000). The relationship between cognitions and panic attack intensity. *Acta Psychiatrica Scandinavica, 102,* 300–302. [15]
Heikkinen, M., Aro, H., & Lönnqvist, J. (1993). Life events and social support in suicide. *Suicide and Life-Threatening Behavior, 23,* 343–358. [15]
Heimann, M., & Meltzoff, A. N. (1996). Deferred imitation in 9- and 14-month-old infants: A longitudinal study of a Swedish sample. *British Journal of Developmental Psychology, 14,* 55–64. [9]
Heinrich, R. K., Corbine, J. L., & Thomas, K. R. (1990). Counseling Native Americans. *Journal of Counseling and Development, 69,* 128–133. [16]
Held, R. (1993). What can rates of development tell us about underlying mechanisms? In C. E. Granrud (Ed.), *Visual perception and cognition in infancy* (pp. 75–89). Hillsdale, NJ: Erlbaum. [9]
Helgeson, V. S. (1994). Relation of agency and communion to well-being. Evidence and potential explanations. *Psychological Bulletin, 116,* 412–428. [12]
Hellige, J. B. (1990). Hemispheric asymmetry. *Annual Review of Psychology, 41,* 55–80. [2]
Hellige, J. B. (1993). *Hemispheric asymmetry: What's right and what's left.* Cambridge, MA: Harvard University Press. [2]
Hellige, J. B., Bloch, M. I., Cowin, E. L., Eng, T. L., Eviatar, Z., & Sergent, V. (1994). Individual variation in hemispheric asym-

metry: Multitask study of effects related to handedness and sex. *Journal of Experimental Psychology: General, 123,* 235-256. [2]

Hendin, H., & Haas, A. P. (1991). Suicide and guilt as manifestations of PTSD in Vietnam combat veterans. *American Journal of Psychiatry, 148,* 586-591. [13]

Hendler, J. (1994). High-performance artificial intelligence. *Science, 265,* 891–892. [7]

Henkel, L. A., Franklin, N., & Johnson, M. K. (2000). Cross-modal source monitoring confusions between perceived and imagined events. *Journal of Experimental Psychology: Learning, Memory, and Cognition, 26,* 321–335. [6]

Henley, N. M. (1973). Status and sex: Some touching observations. *Bulletin of the Psychonomic Society, 2,* 91–93. [17]

Henley, N. M. (1989). Molehill or mountain? What we know and don't know about sex bias in language. In M. Crawford & M. Gentry (Eds.), *Gender and thought: Psychological perspectives.* New York: Springer-Verlag. [7]

Hennessey, B. A., & Amabile, T. M. (1988). The conditions of creativity. In R. J. Sternberg (Ed.), *The nature of creativity: Contemporary psychological perspectives.* New York: Cambridge University Press. [8]

Hennevin, E., Hars, B., Maho, C., & Bloch, V. (1995). Processing of learned information in paradoxical sleep: Relevance for memory. *Behavioural Brain Research, 69,* 125–135. [4]

Henningfield, J. E., & Ator, N. A. (1986). *Barbiturates: Sleeping potion or intoxicant*? New York: Chelsea House. [4]

Henningfield, J. E., Hariharan, M., & Kozlowski, L. T. (1996). Nicotine content and health risks of cigars. *Journal of the American Medical Association, 276,* 1857–1858. [4]

Hensch, T. K., & Stryker, M. P. (1996). Ocular dominance plasticity under metabotropic glutamate receptor blockade. *Science, 272,* 554–557. [3]

Hepper, P. G., Shahidullah, S., & White, R. (1990). Origins of fetal handedness. *Nature, 347,* 431. [2]

Herbert, T. B., & Cohen, S. (1993). Depression and immunity: A meta-analytic review. *Psychological Bulletin, 113,* 472–486. [13]

Herek, G. M., & Capitanio, J. P. (1995). Black heterosexuals' attitudes toward lesbians and gay men in the United States. *Journal of Sex Research, 32,* 95–105. [12]

Herek, G. M., & Glunt, E. K. (1993). Interpersonal contact and heterosexuals' attitudes toward gay men: Results from a national survey. *Journal of Sex Research, 30,* 239–244. [12]

Herkenham, M. (1992). Cannabinoid receptor localization in brain: Relationship to motor and reward systems. *Annals of the New York Academy of Sciences, 654,* 19–32. [4]

Herman, L. (1981). Cognitive characteristics of dolphins. In L. Herman (Ed.), *Cetacean behavior.* New York: Wiley. [7]

Hernandez, L., & Hoebel, B. G. (1989). Food intake and lateral hypothalamic self-stimulation covary after medial hypothalamic lesions or ventral midbrain 6-hydroxydopamine injections that cause obesity. *Behavioral Neuroscience, 103,* 412–422. [11]

Herness, S. (2000). Coding in taste receptor cells: The early years of intracellular recordings. *Physiology and Behavior, 69,* 17–27. [3]

Herrnstein, R. J., & Murray, C. (1994). *The bell curve: Intelligence and class structure in American life.* New York: Free Press. [8]

Herron, J. (1980). *Neuropsychology of left-handedness.* New York: Academic Press. [2]

Hershenson, M. (1989). *The moon illusion.* Hillsdale, NJ: Erlbaum. [3]

Hertzog, C. (1991). Aging, information processing speed, and intelligence. In K. W. Schaie & M. P. Lawton (Eds.), *Annual Review of Gerontology and Geriatrics* (Vol. 11, pp. 55–79). [10]

Hertzog, C., Park, D. C., Morrell, R. W., & Martin, M. (2000). Ask and ye shall receive: Behavioural specificity in the accuracy of subjective memory complaints. *Applied Cognitive Psychology, 14,* 257–275. [6]

Hess, E. H. (1961). Shadows and depth perception. *Scientific American, 204,* 138–148. [3]

Hess, E. H. (1965). Attitude and pupil size. *Scientific American, 212,* 46–54. [3]

Hetherington, A. W., & Ranson, S. W. (1940). Hypothalamic lesions and adiposity in the rat. *Anatomical Record, 78,* 149–172. [11]

Hetherington, E. M., Stanley-Hagan, M., & Anderson, E. R. (1989). Marital transitions: A child's perspective. *American Psychologist, 44,* 303–312. [10]

Higbee, K. L. (1977). *Your memory: How it works and how to improve it.* Englewood Cliffs, NJ: Prentice-Hall. [6]

Higgins, A. (1995). Educating for justice and community: Lawrence Kohlberg's vision of moral education. In W. M. Kurtines & J. L. Gerwirtz (Eds.), *Moral development: An introduction* (pp. 49–81). Boston: Allyn & Bacon. [10]

Hilgard, E. R. (1975). Hypnosis. *Annual Review of Psychology, 26,* 19–44. [4]

Hilgard, E. R. (1979). Divided consciousness in hypnosis: Implications of the hidden observer. In E. Fromm & R. E. Shor (Eds.), *Hypnosis: Developments in research and new perspectives* (2nd ed.). Chicago: Aldine. [4]

Hilgard, E. R. (1986). *Divided consciousness: Multiple controls in human thought and action.* New York: Wiley. [4]

Hilgard, E. R. (1992). Dissociation and theories of hypnosis. In E. Fromm & M. R. Nash (Eds.), *Contemporary hypnosis research.* New York: Guilford. [4]

Hillebrand, J. (2000). New perspectives on the manipulation of opiate urges and the assessment of cognitive effort associated with opiate urges. *Addictive Behaviors, 25,* 139–143. [4]

Hinds, T. S., West, W. L., Knight, E. M., & Harland, B. F. (1996). The effect of caffeine on pregnancy outcome variables. *Nutrition Reviews, 54,* 203–207. [9]

Hines, M., & Green, R. (1991). Human hormonal and neural correlates of sex-typed behaviors. *Review of Psychiatry, 10,* 536–555. [12]

Hinton, G. E., Dayan, P., Frey, B. J., & Neal, R. M. (1995). The "wake-sleep" algorithm for unsupervised neural networks. *Science, 268,* 1158–1161. [7]

Hipwell, A. E., Goossens, F. A., Melhuish, E. C., & Kumar, R. (2000). Severe maternal psychopathology and infant–mother attachment. *Developmental Psychopathology, 12,* 2157–2175. [9]

Hirsch, J. (1997). Some heat but not enough light. *Nature, 387,* 27–28. [11]

Hirschfeld, M. A. (1995). The impact of health care reform on social phobia. *Journal of Clinical Psychiatry, 56*(5, Suppl.), 13–17. [15]

Hobson, J. A. (1988). *The dreaming brain.* New York: Basic Books. [4]

Hobson, J. A. (1989). *Sleep.* New York: Scientific American Library. [4]

Hobson, J. A. (1996, February). How the brain goes out of its mind. *Harvard Mental Health Letter, 12*(8), 3–5. [4]

Hobson, J. A. (2000). Sleep and cognition [On-line]. Available: http://www.websciences.org/worldsleep/cancun99/hobson.html [4]

Hobson, J. A., & McCarley, R. W. (1977). The brain as a dream state generator: An activation-synthesis hypothesis of the dream process. *American Journal of Psychiatry, 134,* 1335–1348. [4]

Hobson, J. A., & Stickgold, R. (1995). The conscious state paradigm: A neurological approach to waking, sleeping, and dreaming. In M. S. Gazzaniga (Ed.), *The cognitive neurosciences.* Cambridge, MA: MIT Press. [4]

Hobson, J. A., Stickgold, R., & Pace-Schott, E. F. (1998). The neuropsychology of REM sleep dreaming. *NeuroReport, 9,* R1–R4. [4]

Hocevar, D., & Bachelor, P. (1989). A taxonomy and critique of measurements used in the study of creativity. In J. A. Glover, R. R. Ronning, & C. R. Reynolds (Eds.), *Handbook of creativity.* New York: Plenum. [8]

Hodges, J. R., Graham, N., & Patterson, K. (1995). Charting the progression in semantic dementia: Implications for the organisation of semantic memory. *Memory, 3,* 463–495. [6]

Hodgins, S., Mednick, S. A., Brennan, P. A., Schulsinger, F., & Engberg, M. (1996). Mental disorder and crime: Evidence from a Danish birth cohort. *Journal of Personality and Social Psychology, 53,* 489–496. [17]

Hoebel, B. G., & Teitelbaum, P. (1966). Weight regulation in normal and hypothalamic hyperphagic rats. *Journal of Comparative and Physiological Psychology, 61,* 189–193. [11]

Hofstede, G. (1980). *Culture's consequences: International differences in work-related values.* Beverly Hills, CA: Sage. [14]

Hofstede, G. (1983). Dimensions of national cultures in fifty countries and three regions. In J. Deregowski, S. Dzuirawiec, and R. Annis (Eds.), *Explications in cross-cultural psychology.* Lisse: Swets and Zeitlinger. [14]

Hohagen, F. (1996). Nonpharmacological treatment of insomnia. *Sleep, 19,* S50–S51. [4]

Holden, C. (1986). Depression research advances, treatment lags. *Science, 233,* 723–726. [15]

Holden, C. (1991). New center to study therapies and ethnicity. *Science, 251,* 748. [16]

Holden, C. (1996). Sex and olfaction. *Science, 273,* 313. [3]

Holland, J. G., & Skinner, B. F. (1961). *The analysis of behavior.* New York: McGraw-Hill. [5]

Holloway, M. (1991). Rx for addiction. *Scientific American, 264,* 94–103. [4]

Holloway, M. (1994). Trends in women's health: A global view. *Scientific American, 271,* 76–83. [13]

Holmes, T. H., & Masuda, M. (1974). Life change and illness susceptibility. In B. S. Dohrenwend & B. P. Dohrenwend (Eds.), *Stressful life events: Their nature and effects.* New York: Wiley. [13]

Holmes, T. H., & Rahe, R. H. (1967). The social readjustment rating scale. *Journal of Psychosomatic Research, 11,* 213–218. [13]

Hoosain, Z., & Roopnarine, J. L. (1994). African-American fathers' involvement with infants: Relationship to their functioning style, support, education, and income. *Infant Behavior and Development, 17,* 175–184. [9]

Horgan, J. (1995, November). Gay genes, revisited. *Scientific American, 273,* 26. [12]

Horgan, J. (1996, December). Why Freud isn't dead. *Scientific American, 275,* 106–111. [16]

Horn, J. (1982). The aging of human abilities. In B. B. Wolman (Ed.), *Handbook of developmental psychology.* Englewood Cliffs, NJ: Prentice-Hall. [10]

Horn, J. C., & Meer, J. (1987, May). The vintage years. *Psychology Today,* pp. 76–90. [10]

Horn, J. L. (1982). The theory of fluid and crystallized intelligence in relation to concepts of cognitive psychology and aging in adulthood. In F. I. M. Craik & S. Trehub (Eds.), *Aging and cognitive processes* (pp. 201–238). New York: Plenum Press. [10]

Horne, J. (1992). Annotation: Sleep and its disorders in children. *Journal of Child Psychology and Psychiatry, 33,* 473–487. [4]

Horner, M. (1969, November). Fail: Bright women. *Psychology Today,* pp. 36–38, 62. [11]

Horney, K. (1937). *The neurotic personality of our time.* New York: W. W. Norton. [14]

Horney, K. (1939). *New ways in psychoanalysis.* New York: W. W. Norton. [14]

Horney, K. (1945). *Our inner conflicts.* New York: W. W. Norton. [14]

Horney, K. (1950). *Neurosis and human growth.* New York: W. W. Norton. [14, 15]

Horney, K. (1967). *Feminine psychology.* New York: W. W. Norton. [14]

Horvitz, L. A. (1997, November 10). Aromachologists nose out the secret powers of smell. *Insight on the News, 13,* pp. 36–37. [3]

Horwath, E., Lish, J. D., Johnson, J., Hornig, C. D., & Weissman, M. M. (1993). Agoraphobia without panic: Clinical reappraisal of an epidemiologic finding. *American Journal of Psychiatry, 150,* 1496–1501. [15]

Houlihan, D., Schwartz, C., Miltenberger, R., & Heuton, D. (1993). The rapid treatment of a young man's balloon (noise) phobia using in vivo flooding. *Journal of Behavior Therapy and Experimental Psychiatry, 24,* 233–240. [16]

Hovland, C. I., Lumsdaine, A. A., & Sheffield, F. D. (1949). *Experiments on mass communication.* Princeton, NJ: Princeton University Press. [17]

Howard, A. D., Feighner, S. D., Cully, D. F., Arena, J. P., Liberator, P. A., Rosenblum, C. I., et al. (1996). A receptor in pituitary and hypothalamus that functions in growth hormone release. *Science, 273,* 974–977. [2]

Hoyenga, K. B., & Hoyenga, K. T. (1993). *Gender-related differences: Origins and outcomes.* Boston: Allyn & Bacon. [12]

Hrushesky, W. J. M. (1994, July/August). Timing is everything. *The Sciences,* pp. 32–37. [4]

Hubel, D. H. (1963). The visual cortex of the brain. *Scientific American, 209,* 54–62. [3]

Hubel, D. H. (1995). *Eye, brain, and vision.* New York: Scientific American Library. [3]

Hubel, D. H., & Wiesel, T. N. (1959). Receptive fields of single neurons in the cat's striate cortex. *Journal of Physiology, 148,* 547–591. [3]

Hubel, D. H., & Wiesel, T. N. (1979). Brain mechanisms of vision. *Scientific American, 241,* 130–144. [3]

Hudson, J. I., Carter, W. P., & Pope, H. G., Jr. (1996). Antidepressant treatment of binge-eating disorder: Research findings and clinical guidelines. *Journal of Clinical Psychiatry, 57*(8, Suppl.), 73–79. [16]

Hudspeth, A. J. (1983). The hair cells of the inner ear. *Scientific American, 248,* 54–64. [3]

Huesmann, L. R., & Moise, J. (1996, June). Media violence: A demonstrated public health threat to children. *Harvard Mental Health Letter, 12*(12), 5–7. [17]

Huff, C. R. (1995). *Convicted but innocent.* Thousand Oaks, CA: Sage. [6]

Hug, T. E., Fitzgerald, K. M., & Cibis, G. W. (2000). Clinical and electroretinographic findings in fetal alcohol syndrome. *Journal of the American Association of Pediatric Opthalmology & Strabismus, 4,* 200–204. [9]

Hughes, J. R. (1992). Tobacco withdrawal in self-quitters. *Journal of Consulting and Clinical Psychology, 60,* 689–697. [13]

Hughes, R. J., & Badia, P. (1997). Sleep-promoting and hypothermic effects of daytime melatonin administration in humans. *Sleep, 20,* 124–131. [4]

Hugick, L. (1992). Public opinion divided on gay rights. *Gallup Poll Monthly,* No. 321, 2–6. [12]

Hull, C. L. (1943). *Principles of behavior.* New York: Appleton-Century-Crofts. [11]

Hull, M., Fiebich, B. L., Schumann, G., Lieb, K., & Bauer, J. (1999). Anti-inflammatory substances—a new therapeutic option in Alzheimer's disease. *Drug Discovery Today, 4,* 275–282. [10]

Hultsch, D. F., & Dixon, R. A. (1990). Learning and memory in aging. In J. E. Birren & K. W. Schaie (Eds.), *Handbook of the psychology of aging* (3rd ed., pp. 359–374). San Diego: Academic Press. [10]

Hummer, R. A., Rogers, R. G., Nam, C. B., & Ellison, C. G. (1999). Religious involvement and U.S. adult mortality. *Demography, 36,* 273–285. [13]

Hund-Georgiadis, M., & von Cramon, D. Y. (1999). Motor-learning-related changes in piano players and non-musicians revealed by functional magnetic-resonance sounds. *Experimental Brain Research, 125,* 417–425. [7]

Hunter, J. A., Reid, J. M., Stokell, N. M., & Platow, M. J. (2000). Social attribution, self-esteem, and social identity. *Current Research in Social Psychology, 5,* 97–125. [17]

Hurrell, R. M. (1997). Factors associated with regular exercise. *Perceptual and Motor Skills, 84,* 871–874. [13]

Hurvich, L. M., & Jameson, D. (1957). An opponent-process theory of color vision. *Psychological Review, 64,* 384–404. [3]

Huston, A. C., Donnerstein, E., Fairchild, H., Feshbach, N. D., Katz, P. A., Murray, J. P., Rubinstein, E. A., Wilcox, B. L., & Zuckerman, D. (1992). *Big world, small screen: The role of television in American society.* Lincoln: University of Nebraska Press. [17]

Hyde, J. S., & Linn, M. C. (1988). Gender differences in verbal ability: A meta-analysis. *Psychological Bulletin, 104,* 53–69. [1, 12]

Hyde, J. S., Fenema, E., & Lamon, S. J. (1990). Gender differences in mathematics performance: A meta-analysis. *Psychological Bulletin, 107,* 139–155. [12]

Hyman, A. (1983). The influence of color on the taste perception of carbonated water preparations. *Bulletin of the Psychonomic Society, 21,* 145–148. [3]

Hyman, I. E., Jr., & Pentland, J. (1996). The role of mental imagery in the creation of false childhood memories. *Journal of Memory and Language, 35,* 101–117. [6]

Hyman, I. E., Jr., Husband, T. H., & Billings, E. J. (1995). False memories of childhood. *Applied Cognitive Psychology, 9,* 181–197. [6]

Indian Health Service. (1988). *Indian health service chart series book.* Washington, DC: U.S. Department of Health and Human Services. [14]

Inglehart, R. (1990). *Culture shift in advanced industrial society.* Princeton, NJ: Princeton University Press. [10]

Inhelder, B. (1966). Cognitive development and its contribution to the diagnosis of some phenomena of mental deficiency. *Merrill-Palmer Quarterly, 12,* 299–319. [9]

International Food Information Council Foundation. (1998, July). *Everything you need to know about caffeine.* [4]

International Food Information Council Foundation. (2000). *Does caffeine cause dependence?* [4]

Intons-Peterson, M. J., & Fournier, J. (1986). External and internal memory aids: When and how often do we use them? *Journal of Experimental Psychology: General, 115,* 267–280. [6]

Intons-Peterson, M., & Roskos-Ewoldsen, B. (1989). Sensory-perceptual qualities of images. *Journal of Experimental Psychology: Learning, Memory, and Cognition, 15,* 188–199. [7]

Irwin, M., Mascovich, A., Gillin, C., Willoughby, R., Pike, J., & Smith, T. L. (1994). Partial sleep deprivation reduces natural killer cell activity in humans. *Psychosomatic Medicine, 56,* 493–498. [4]

Isabella, R. A., Belsky, J., & von Eye, A. (1989). Origins of infant-mother attachment: An examination of interactional synchrony during the infant's first year. *Developmental Psychology, 25,* 12–21. [9]

Isay, R. A. (1989). *Being homosexual: Gay men and their development.* New York: Farrar, Straus, & Giroux. [12]

Isenberg, D. J. (1986). Group polarization: A critical review and meta-analysis. *Journal of Personality and Social Psychology, 50,* 1141–1151. [17]

Ito, T. A., Miller, N., & Pollock, V. E. (1996). Alcohol and aggression: A meta-analysis on the moderating effects of inhibitory cues, triggering events, and self-focused attention. *Psychological Bulletin, 120,* 60–82. [17]

Iversen, L. L. (1996). Smoking . . . harmful to the brain. *Nature,* 382, 206–207. [4]

Izard, C. E. (1971). *The face of emotion.* New York: Appleton-Century-Crofts. [11]

Izard, C. E. (1977). *Human emotions.* New York: Plenum Press. [11]

Izard, C. E. (1990). Facial expressions and the regulation of emotions. *Journal of Personality and Social Psychology, 58,* 487–498. [11]

Izard, C. E. (1992). Basic emotions, relations among emotions, and emotion-cognition relations. *Psychological Review, 99,* 561–565. [11]

Izard, C. E. (1993). Four systems for emotion activation: Cognitive and noncognitive processes. *Psychological Review, 100,* 68–90. [11]

Jacklin, C. N. (1989). Female and male: Issues of gender. *American Psychologist, 44,* 127–133. [12]

Jacobs, G. H. (1993). The distribution and nature of colour vision among the mammals. *Biological Review, 68,* 413–471. [3]

Jacobs, J. E. (1991). Influence of gender stereotypes on parent and child mathematics attitudes. *Journal of Educational Psychology, 83,* 518–527. [12]

Jacobs, M. K., & Goodman, G. (1989). Psychology and self-help groups: Predictions on a partnership. *American Psychologist, 44,* 536–545. [16]

Jacobsen, P. B., Bovbjerg, D. H., Schwartz, M. D., Andrykowski, M. A., Futterman, A. D., Norton, L., & Redd, W. H. (1993). Formation of food aversions in cancer patients receiving repeated infusions of chemotherapy. *Behavior Research and Therapy 31,* 739–748. [5]

Jacobson, N., & Gottman, J. (1998). *Why men batter women: New insights into ending abusive relationships.* New York: Simon & Schuster. [17]

James, L. (1997, July 17). Aggressive driving and road rage: Dealing with emotionally impaired drivers. 105th Cong. (Testimony of Leon James). [13]

James, W. (1884). What is an emotion? *Mind, 9,* 188–205. [11]

James, W. (1890). *Principles of psychology.* New York: Holt. [1, 11]

Jamieson, D. W., & Zanna, M. P. (1989). Need for structure in attitude formation and expression. In A. R. Pratkanis, S. J. Breckler, & A. G. Greenwald (Eds.), *Attitude structure and function* (pp. 383–406). Hillsdale, NJ: Erlbaum. [17]

Jamison, K. R. (1995). Manic-depressive illness and creativity. *Scientific American, 272,* 62–67. [15]

Janis, I. L. (1982). *Groupthink: Psychological studies of policy decisions and fiascoes* (2nd ed.). Boston: Houghton Mifflin. [17]

Janowitz, H. D., & Grossman, M. I. (1950). Hunger and appetite: Some definitions and concepts. *Journal of the Mount Sinai Hospital, 16,* 231–240. [11]

Jarrold, C., Butler, D. W., Cottington, E. M., & Jimenez, F. (2000). Linking theory of mind and central coherence bias in autism and in the general population. *Developmental Psychology, 36,* 1126–1138. [9]

Jaskiewicz, J. A., & McAnamey, E. R. (1994). Pregnancy during adolescence. *Pediatrics in Review, 15,* 32–38. [10]

Jaynes, J. (1976). *The origin of consciousness and the breakdown of the bicameral mind.* Boston: Houghton Mifflin. [2]

Jefferson, J. W. (1995). Social phobia: A pharmacologic treatment overview. *Journal of Clinical Psychiatry, 56*(5, Suppl.), 18–24. [16]

Jefferson, J. W. (1996). Social phobia: Everyone's disorder? *Journal of Clinical Psychiatry, 57*(6, Suppl.), 28–32. [15]

Jefferson, J. W. (1997). Antidepressants in panic disorder. *Journal of Clinical Psychiatry, 58*(2, Suppl.), 20–24. [16]

Jeffrey, R. W., & French, S. A. (1996). Socioeconomic status and weight control practices among 20–45-year-old women. *American Journal of Public Health, 86,* 1005–1010. [11]

Jellinek, E. M. (1960). *The disease concept of alcoholism.* New Brunswick, NJ: Hillhouse Press. [13]

Jenike, M. A. (1990, April). Obsessive-compulsive disorder. *Harvard Medical School Health Letter, 15,* 4–8. [16]

Jenkins, J. H., & Karno, M. (1992). The meaning of expressed emotion: Theoretical issues raised by cross-cultural research. *American Journal of Psychiatry, 149,* 9–21. [16]

Jenkins, J. J., Jimenez-Pabon, E., Shaw, R. E., & Sefer, J. W. (1975). *Schuell's aphasia in adults: Diagnosis, prognosis, and treatment* (2nd ed.). Hagerstown, MD: Harper & Row. [2]

Jensen, A. R. (1985). The nature of the black-white difference on various psychometric tests: Spearman's hypothesis. *Behavioral and Brain Sciences, 8,* 193–263. [8]

Jernigan, T. L., Butters, N., DiTraglia, G., Schafer, K., Smith, T., Irwin, M., Grant, I., Schuckit, M., & Cermak, L. S. (1991). Reduced cerebral grey matter observed in alcoholics using magnetic resonance imaging. *Alcoholism: Clinical and Experimental Research, 15,* 418–427. [13]

Jeste, D. V. (1994). How does late-onset compare with early-onset schizophrenia? *Harvard Mental Health Letter, 10*(8), 8–9. [15]

Jimerson, D. C., Wolfe, B. E., Metzger, E. D., Finkelstein, D. M., Cooper, T. B., & Levine, J. M. (1997). Decreased serotonin function in bulimia nervosa. *Archives of General Psychiatry, 54,* 529–534. [11]

Jockin, V., McGue, M., & Lykken, D. T. (1996). Personality and divorce: A genetic analysis. *Journal of Personaliity and Social Psychology, 71,* 288–299. [14]

Johansson, P., Hallberg, M., Kindlundh, A., & Nyberg, F. (2000). The effect on opioid peptides in the rat brain, a chronic treatment with the anabolic androgenic steroid, nandrolone decanoate. *Brain Research Bulletin, 51,* 413–418. [12]

Johnson, D. L. (1989). Schizophrenia as a brain disease: Implications for psychologists and families. *American Psychologist, 44,* 553–555. [15]

Johnson, L. A. (1996, June 5). Eye witness: New ATM technology identifies a customer by the iris. *St. Louis Post-Dispatch,* p. C5. [3]

Johnson, M. P., Duffy, J. F., Dijk, D-J., Ronda, J. M., Dyal, C. M., & Czeisler, C. A. (1992). Short-term memory, alertness and performance: A reappraisal of their relationship to body temperature. *Journal of Sleep Research, 1,* 24–29. [4]

Johnson, S. C. (2000). The recognition of mentalistic agents in infancy. *Trends in Cognitive Sciences, 4,* 22–28. [9]

Johnson, W. G., Tsoh, J. Y., & Varnado, P. J. (1996). Eating disorders: Efficacy of pharmacological and psychological interventions. *Clinical Psychology Review, 16,* 457–478. [11]

Johnston, L. E., O'Malley, P. M., & Bachman, J. G. (1997). *National survey results on drug use from the Monitoring the Future Study, 1975–1996/97: Vol. 1. Secondary school students.* The University of Michigan Institute for Social Research; National Institute on Drug Abuse, 5600 Fishers Lane, Rockville, MD 20857; USDHHS, Public Health Service, National Institutes of Health. [4]

Johnston, L. E., O'Malley, P. M., & Bachman, J. G. (1999). Monitoring the Future national results on adolescent drug use [On-line]. Available: http://monitoringthefuture.org/data/999data/fig99_2.gif [4]

Johnston, L. E., O'Malley, P. M., & Bachman, J. G. (2001). *Monitoring the Future national results on adolescent drug use:*

Overview of key findings, 2000 (NIH Publication No. 01-4923). Rockville MD: National Institute on Drug Abuse. [1, 4]

Jonas, J. M., & Cohon, M. S. (1993). A comparison of the safety and efficacy of alprazolam versus other agents in the treatment of anxiety, panic, and depression: A review of the literature. *Journal of Clinical Psychiatry, 54*(10, Suppl.), 25–45. [16]

Jones, D. (1999). *Interpersonal perception.* New York: Freeman. [2]

Jones, E. E. (1976). How do people perceive the causes of behavior? *American Scientist, 64,* 300–305. [17]

Jones, E. E. (1986). Interpreting interpersonal behavior: The effects of expectancies. *Science, 234,* 41–46. [17]

Jones, E. E. (1990). *Interpersonal perception.* New York: Freeman. [17]

Jones, E. E., & Davis, K. E. (1965). A theory of correspondent inferences: From acts to dispositions. In L. Berkowitz (Ed.), *Advances in experimental social psychology* (Vol. 2, pp. 219–266). New York: Academic Press. [17]

Jones, E. E., & Nisbett, R. E. (1971). *The actor and the observer: Divergent perceptions of the causes of behavior.* New York: General Learning. [17]

Jones, H. E., Herning, R. I., Cadet, J. L., & Griffiths, R. R. (2000). Caffeine withdrawal increases cerebral blood flow velocity and alters quantitative electroencephalography (EEG) activity. *Psychopharmacology, 147,* 371–377. [4]

Jones, M. C. (1924). A laboratory study of fear: The case of Peter. *Pedagogical Seminary, 31,* 308–315. [5]

Jones, M. C., & Bayley, N. (1950). Physical maturing among boys as related to behavior. *Journal of Educational Psychology, 41,* 129–148. [10]

Jones, W. H., Chernovetz, M. E. O'C., & Hansson, R. O. (1978). The enigma of androgyny: Differential implications for males and females? *Journal of Consulting and Clinical Psychology, 46,* 298–313. [12]

Jopling, D. A. (2001). Placebo insight: The rationality of insight-oriented psychotherapy. *Journal of Clinical Psychology, 57,* 19–36. [16]

Jorgensen, M., & Keiding, N. (1991). Estimation of spermarche from longitudinal spermaturia data. *Biometrics, 47,* 177–193. [10]

Josephson, W. L. (1987). Television violence and children's aggression: Testing the priming, social script, and disinhibition predictions. *Journal of Personality and Social Psychology, 53,* 822–890. [17]

Joulain, M., Mullet, E., Lecomte, C., & Prevost, R. (2000). Perception of "appropriate" age for retirement among young adults, middle-aged adults, and elderly people. *International Journal of Aging and Human Development, 50,* 73–84. [10]

Joyce, P. R., & Paykel, E. S. (1989). Predictors of drug response in depression. *Archives of General Psychiatry, 46,* 89–99. [16]

Judd, C. M., Ryan, C. S., & Park, B. (1991). Accuracy in the judgment of in-group and out-group variability. *Journal of Personality and Social Psychology, 61,* 366–379. [17]

Judd, L. L., Akiskal, H. S., Zeller, P. J., Paulus, M., Leon, A. C., Maser, J. D., Endicott, J., Coryell, W., Kunovac, J. L., Mueller, T. I., Rice, J. P., & Keller, M. B. (2000). Psychosocial disability during the long-term course of unipolar major depressive disorder. *Archives of General Psychiatry, 57,* 375–380. [15]

Juliano, S. L. (1998). Mapping the sensory mosaic. *Science, 279,* 1653–1654. [2]

Julien, R. M. (1995). *A primer of drug action* (7th ed.). New York: W.H. Freeman. [4]

Jung, C. G. (1933). *Modern man in search of a soul.* New York: Harcourt Brace Jovanovich. [14]

Jung, C. G. (1953). *The psychology of the unconscious* (R. F. C. Hull, Trans.), *Collected works* (Vol. 7). Princeton, NJ: Princeton University Press. (Original work published 1917). [14]

Jung, C. G. (1961). *Memories, dreams, reflections* (R. Winston & C. Winston, Trans.). New York: Random House. [14]

Jung, C. G. (1966). *Two essays on analytical psychology* (R. F. C. Hull, Trans.). Princeton, NJ: Princeton University Press. [14]

Jusczyk, P. W., & Aslin, R. N. (1995). Infants' detection of the sound patterns of words in fluent speech. *Cognitive Psychology, 29,* 1–23. [9]

Kagan, J. (1996, October). Sanguine and melancholic temperaments in children. *Harvard Mental Health Letter, 13*(4), 4–6. [9]

Kagan, J. (1997). Temperament and the reactions to unfamiliarity. *Child Development, 68,* 139–143. [9]

Kagitcibasi, C. (1992). A critical appraisal of individualism-collectivism: Toward a new formulation. In U. Kim, H. C. Triandis, and G. Yoon (Eds.), *Individualism and collectivism: Theoretical and methodological issues.* Newbury Park, CA: Sage. [14]

Kahneman, D., & Tversky, A. (1984). Choices, values, and frames. *American Psychologist, 39,* 341–350. [7]

Kalb, C. (1997, August 25). Our embattled ears: Hearing loss once seemed a normal part of aging, but experts now agree that much of it is preventable. How to protect yourself. *Newsweek, 130,* 75–76. [3]

Kalish, H. I. (1981). *From behavioral science to behavior modification.* New York: McGraw-Hill. [5, 16]

Kamin, L. (1968). "Attention-like" processes in classical conditioning. In M. R. Jones (Ed.), *Miami symposium on the prediction of behavior: Aversive stimulation.* Miami: University of Miami Press. [5]

Kamin, L. J. (1995). Behind the curve [Review of *The Bell Curve: Intelligence and class structure in American life*]. *Scientific American, 272,* 99–103. [8]

Kanaya, Y., Nakamura, C., and Miyake, D. (1989). Cross-cultural study of expressive behavior of mothers in response to their five-month-old infants' different emotion expression. *Research and Clinical Center for Child Development Annual Report, 11,* 25–31. [11]

Kandel, D. B., & Davies, M. (1996). High school students who use crack and other drugs. *Archives of General Psychiatry, 53,* 71–80. [4]

Kane, J. M. (1996). Treatment-resistant schizophrenic patients. *Journal of Clinical Psychiatry, 57*(9, Suppl.), 35–40. [16]

Kanner, A. D., Coyne, J. C., Schaefer, C., & Lazarus, R. S. (1981). Comparison of two modes of stress measurement: Daily hassles and uplifts versus major life events. *Journal of Behavioral Medicine, 4,* 1–39. [13]

Kaplan, G. A., Wilson, T. W., Cohen, R. D., Kauhanen, J., Wu, M., & Salomen, J. T. (1994). Social functioning and overall mortality: Prospective evidence from the Kuopio Ischemic Heart Disease Risk Factor Study. *Epidemiology, 5,* 495–500. [13]

Kaplan, H. S. (1974). *The new sex therapy: Active treatment of sexual dysfunction.* New York: Brunner/Mazel. [12]

Karacan, I. (1988). Parasomnias. In R. L. Williams, I. Karacan, & C. A. Moore (Eds.), *Sleep disorders: Diagnosis and treatment* (pp. 131–144). New York: John Wiley. [4]

Karasek, R. A., & Theorell, T. (1990). *Healthy work.* New York: Basic Books. [13]

Karasu, T. B. (1990a). Toward a clinical model of psychotherapy for depression, I: Systematic comparison of three psychotherapies. *American Journal of Psychiatry, 147,* 133–147. [16]

Karasu, T. B. (1990b). Toward a clinical model of psychotherapy for depression, II: An integrative and selective treatment approach. *American Journal of Psychiatry, 147,* 269–278. [16]

Karau, S. J., & Williams, K. D. (1993). Social loafing; a meta-analytic review and theoretical integration. *Journal of Personality and Social Psychology, 65,* 681–706. [17]

Kareev, Y. (2000). Seven (indeed, plus or minus two) and the detection of correlations. *Psychological Review, 107,* 397–402. [6]

Karni, A., Tanne, D., Rubenstein, B. S., Askenasy, J. J. M., & Sagi, D. (1994). Dependence on REM sleep of overnight improvement of a perceptual skill. *Science, 265,* 679–682. [4]

Karp, B. I., Garvey, M., Jacobsen, L. K., Frazier, J. A., Hamburger, S. D., Bedwell, J. S., & Rapoport, J. L. (2001). Abnormal neurologic maturation in adolescents with early-onset schizophrenia. *American Journal of Psychiatry, 158,* 118–122. [15]

Karrer, T., & Bartoshuk, L. (1991). Capsaicin desensitization and recovery on the human tongue. *Physiological Behavior, 49,* 757–764. [3]

Kasch, F. W., Boyer, J. L., Schmidt, P. K., Wells, R. H., Wallace, J. P., Verity, L. S., Guy, H., & Schneider, D. (1999). Ageing of the cardiovascular system during 33 years of aerobic exercise. *Age and Ageing, 28,* 531–536. [10]

Kasper, S., Wehr, T. A., Bartko, J. J., Gaist, P. A., & Rosenthal, N. E. (1989). Epidemiological findings of seasonal changes in mood and behavior: A telephone survey of Montgomery County, Maryland. *Archives of General Psychiatry, 46,* 823–833. [15]

Kastenbaum, R. (1992). *The psychology of death.* New York: Springer-Verlag. [10]

Katon, W. (1996). Panic disorder: Relationship to high medical utilization, unexplained physical symptoms, and medical costs. *Journal of Clinical Psychiatry, 57*(10, Suppl.), 11–18. [15]

Katzell, R. A., & Thompson, D. E. (1990). Work motivation: Theory and practice. *American Psychologist, 45,* 144–153. [11]

Katzenberg, D., Young, T., Finn, L., Lin, L., King, D. P., Takahishi, J. S., & Mignot, E. (1998). A CLOCK polymorphism associated with human diurnal preference. *Sleep, 21,* 569. [4]

Kaufman, J. (1996). Teenage parents and their offspring. *Annals of the New York Academy of Sciences, 789,* 17–30. [10]

Kawachi, I., Colditz, G. A., Speizer, F. E., Manson, J. E., Stampfer, M. J., Willett, W. C., & Hennekens, C. H. (1997). A prospective study of passive smoking and coronary heart disease. *Circulation, 95,* 2374–2379. [13]

Kawanishi, Y., Tachikawa, H., & Suzuki, T. (2000). Pharmacogenomics and schizophrenia. *European Journal of Pharmacology, 410,* 227–241. [16]

Kay, S. A. (1997). PAS, present, and future: Clues to the origins of circadian clocks. *Science, 276,* 753–754. [4]

Kayumov, L., Zhdanova, I. V., & Shapiro, C. M. (2000). Melatonin, sleep, and circadian rhythm disorders. *Seminars in Clinical Neuropsychiatry, 5,* 44–55. [4]

Kazdin, A. E. (1999). Overview of research issues in clinical psychology. In P. C. Kendall, K. N. Butcher, & G. N. Holmbeck (Eds.), *Handbook of research methods in clinical psychology* (pp. 3–20). New York: Wiley. [1]

Kearney, M. (1984). A comparison of motivation to avoid success in males and females. *Journal of Clinical Psychology, 40,* 1005–1007. [11]

Keating, C. R. (1994). World without words: Messages from face and body. In W. J. Lonner & R. Malpass (Eds.), *Psychology and culture* (pp. 175–182). Boston: Allyn & Bacon. [11]

Keefauver, S. P., & Guilleminault, C. (1994). Sleep terrors and sleepwalking. In M. Kryger, T. Roth, & W. C. Dement (Eds.), *Principles and practice of sleep medicine* (pp. 567–573). Philadelphia: W.B. Saunders. [4]

Keesey, R. E. (1988). The body-weight set point. What can you tell your patients? *Postgraduate Medicine, 83,* 114–118, 121–122, 127. [11]

Keesey, R. E., & Powley, T. L. (1986). The regulation of body weight. *Annual Review of Psychology, 37,* 109–133. [11]

Kehoe, E. J. (2000). Extension of the CS past the US can facilitate conditioning of the rabbit's nictitating membrane response. *Behavioural Processes, 50,* 155–164. [5]

Keijsers, G. P., Schaap, C. P., & Hoogduin, C. A. (2000). The impact of interpersonal patient and therapist behavior on outcome in cognitive-behavior therapy. A review of empirical studies. *Behavior Modification, 24,* 264–297. [16]

Keith, S. J. (1993). Understanding the experience of schizophrenia. *American Journal of Psychiatry, 150,* 1616–1617. [15]

Keitner, G. I., Ryan, C. E., Miller, I. W., & Norman, W. H. (1992). Recovery and major depression: Factors associated with twelve-month outcome. *American Journal of Psychiatry, 149,* 93–99. [15]

Keller, H., Schlomerich, A., & Eibl-Eibesfeldt, I. (1988). Communication patterns in adult-infant interactions in western and non-western cultures. *Journal of Cross-Cultural Psychology, 19,* 427–445. [11]

Keller, M. B. (1989). Current concepts in affective disorders. *Journal of Clinical Psychiatry, 50,* 157–162. [16]

Kelly, J. J., Davis, P. G., & Henschke, P. N. (2000). The drug epidemic: Effects on newborn infants and health resource consumption at a tertiary perinatal centre. *Journal of Paediatric Child Health, 36,* 262–264. [9]

Kelly, S. J., Ostrowski, N. L., & Wilson, M. A. (2000). Gender differences in brain and behavior: Hormonal and neural bases. *Pharmacology, Biochemistry & Behavior, 64,* 655–664. [12]

Kelner, K. L. (1997). Seeing the synapse. *Science, 276,* 547. [2]

Kelso, W. M., Nicholls, M. E. R., Warne, G. L., & Zacharin, M. (2000). Cerebral lateralization and cognitive functioning in patients with congenital adrenal hyperplasia. *Neuropsychology, 14,* 370–378. [2]

Kendall-Tackett, K. A., Williams, L. M., & Finkehor, D. (1993). Impact of sexual abuse on children: A review and synthesis of recent empirical studies. *Psychological Bulletin, 113,* 164–180. [12]

Kendler, K. S., & Diehl, S. R. (1993). The genetics of schizophrenia: A current genetic-epidemiologic perspective. *Schizophrenia Bulletin, 19,* 261–285. [15]

Kendler, K. S., Gardner, C. O., & Prescott, C. A. (1997). Religion, psychopathology, and substance use and abuse: A multimeasure, genetic-epidemiologic study. *American Journal of Psychiatry, 154,* 322–329. [4]

Kendler, K. S., Gruenberg, A. M., & Kinney, D. K. (1994). Independent diagnoses of adoptees and relatives as defined by DSM-III in the provincial and national samples of the Danish Adoption Study of Schizophrenia. *Archives of General Psychiatry, 51,* 456–468. [15]

Kendler, K. S., Kessler, R. C., Walters, E. E., MacLean, C., Neale, M. C., Heath, A. C., & Eaves, L. J. (1995). Stressful life events, genetic liability, and onset of an episode of major depression in women. *American Journal of Psychiatry, 152,* 833–842. [15]

Kendler, K. S., MacLean, C., Neale, M., Kessler, R., Heath, A., & Eaves, L. (1991). The genetic epidemiology of bulimia nervosa. *American Journal of Psychiatry, 148,* 1627–1637. [11]

Kendler, K. S., Neale, M. C., Heath, A. C., Kessler, R. C., & Eaves, L. J. (1994). A twin-family study of alcoholism in women. *American Journal of Psychiatry, 151,* 707–715. [13]

Kendler, K. S., Neale, M. C., Kessler, R. C., Heath, A. C., & Eaves, L. J. (1992b). The genetic epidemiology of phobias in women. *Archives of General Psychiatry, 49,* 273–281. [15]

Kendler, K. S., Neale, M. C., Kessler, R. C., Heath, A. C., & Eaves, L. J. (1993). The lifetime history of major depression in women: Reliability of diagnosis and heritability. *Archives of General Psychiatry, 50,* 863–870. [15]

Kendler, K. S., Neale, M. C., MacLean, C. J, Heath, A. C., Eaves, L. J., & Kessler, R. C. (1993). Smoking and major depression: A causal analysis. *Archives of General Psychiatry, 50,* 36–43. [13]

Kendler, K. S., Walters, E. E., Truett, K. R., Heath, A. C., Neale, M. C., Martin, N. G., & Eaves, L. J. (1994). Sources of individual differences in depressive symptoms: Analysis of two samples of twins and their families. *American Journal of Psychiatry, 151,* 1605–1614. [15]

Kenrick, D. T., & Gutierres, S. E. (1980). Contrast effects and judgments of physical attractiveness: When beauty becomes a social problem. *Journal of Personality and Social Psychology, 38,* 131–140. [12]

Kessler, R. C., Kendler, D. S., Heath, A., Neale, M. C., & Eaves, L. J. (1992). Social support, depressed mood, and adjustment to stress: A genetic epidemiologic investigation. *Journal of Personality and Social Psychology, 63,* 257–272. [13]

Kessler, R. C., McGonagle, K. A., Zhao, S., Nelson, C. B., Hughes, M., Eshleman, S., Wittchen, H-U., & Kendler, K. S. (1994). Lifetime and 12-month prevalence of *DSM-III-R* psychiatric disorders in the United States: Results from the National Comorbidity Survey. *American Journal of Psychiatry, 51,* 8–19. [15]

Kessler, R. C., Stein, M. B., & Berglund, P. (1998). Social phobia subtypes in the National Comorbidity Survey. *American Journal of Psychiatry, 155,* 613–619. [15]

Kety, S. S., Wender, P. H., Jacobsen, B., Ingraham, L. J., Jansson, L., Faber, B., & Kinney, D. K. (1994). Mental illness in the biological and adoptive relatives of schizophrenic adoptees: Replication of the Copenhagen study in the rest of Denmark. *Archives of General Psychiatry, 51,* 442–455. [15]

Khachaturian, Z. S. (1997, July/August). Plundered memories. *The Sciences, 37,* 20–25. [10]

Kiecolt-Glaser, J. K., & Glaser, R. (1992). Psychoneuroimmunology: Can psychological interventions modulate immunity? *Journal of Consulting and Clinical Psychology, 60,* 569–575. [13]

Kiecolt-Glaser, J. K., Fisher, L. D., Ogrocki, P., Stout, J., Speicher, C. E., & Glaser, R. (1987). Marital quality, marital disruption, and immune function. *Psychosomatic Medicine, 49,* 13–34. [13]

Kiecolt-Glaser, J. K., Glaser, R., Gravenstein, S., Malarkey, W. B., & Sheridan, J. (1996). Chronic stress alters the immune response to influenza virus vaccine in older adults. *Proceedings of the National Academy of Science, 93,* 3043–3047. [13]

Kihlstrom, J. F. (1985). Hypnosis. *Annual Review of Psychology, 26,* 557–591. [4]

Kihlstrom, J. F. (1986). Strong inferences about hypnosis. *Behavioral and Brain Sciences, 9,* 474–475. [4]
Kihlstrom, J. F. (1995). The trauma-memory argument. *Consciousness and Cognition, 4,* 65–67. [6]
Kihlstrom, J. F., & Barnhardt, T. M. (1993). The self-regulation of memory: For better and for worse, with and without hypnosis. In D. M. Wegner & J. W. Pennebaker (Eds.), *Handbook of mental control.* Englewood Cliffs, NJ: Prentice Hall. [4]
Kilbride, J. E., & Kilbride, P. L. (1975). Sitting and smiling behavior of Baganda infants. *Journal of Cross-Cultural Psychology, 6,* 88–107. [9]
Kim, J. J., & Fanselow, M. S. (1992). Modality-specific retrograde amnesia of fear. *Science, 256,* 675–677. [6]
Kim, J. J., Mohamed, S., Andreasen, N. C., O'Leary, D. S., Watkins, L., Ponto, L. L. B., & Hichwa, R. D. (2000). Regional neural dysfunctions in chronic schizophrenia studied with positron emission tomography. *American Journal of Psychiatry, 157,* 542–548. [15]
Kim, K. H. S., Relkin, N. R., Lee, K-M., & Hirsch, J. (1997). Distinct cortical areas associated with native and second languages. *Nature, 388,* 171–174. [7]
Kim, S-G., Ugurbil, K., & Strick, P. L. (1994). Activation of a cerebellar output nucleus during cognitive processing. *Science, 265,* 949–951. [2]
Kimura, D. (1992). Sex differences in the brain. *Scientific American, 267,* 118–125. [12]
Kimura, D. (2000). *Sex and cognition.* Cambridge, MA: MIT Press. [12]
King, L. A., Walker, L. M., & Broyles, S. J. (1996). Creativity and the five-factor model. *Journal of Research on Personality, 30,* 189–203. [14]
King, N. J., Clowes-Hollins, V., & Ollendick, T. H. (1997). The etiology of childhood dog phobia. *Behaviour Research and Therapy, 35,* 77. [15]
Kingsbury, S. J. (1993). Brief hypnotic treatment of repetitive nightmares. *American Journal of Clinical Hypnosis, 35,* 161–169. [4]
Kingsbury, S. J. (1996, October). Prescriptions by psychologists. *Harvard Mental Health Letter, 13*(4), 8. [16]
Kington, R. S., & Smith, J. P. (1997). Socioeconomic status and racial and ethnic differences in functional status associated with chronic diseases. *American Journal of Public Health, 87,* 805–810. [13]
Kinnamon, S. C. (1988). Taste transduction: A diversity of mechanisms. *Trends in Neurosciences, 11,* 491–496. [3]
Kinnunen, T., Zamansky, H. S., & Block, M. L. (1994). Is the hypnotized subject lying? *Journal of Abnormal Psychology, 103,* 184–191. [4]
Kinomura, S., Larsson, J., Gulyás, B., & Roland, P. E. (1996). Activation by attention of the human reticular formation and thalamic intralaminar nuclei. *Science, 271,* 512–515. [2]
Kinon, B. J., & Lieberman, J. A. (1996). Mechanisms of action of atypical antipsychotic drugs: A critical analysis. *Psychopharmacology (Berl, 124,* 2–34. [4]
Kinsella, G., Prior, M. R., & Murray, G. (1988). Singing ability after right- and left-sided brain damage. A research note. *Cortex, 24,* 165–169. [2]
Kinsey, A. C., Pomeroy, W. B., & Martin, C. E. (1948). *Sexual behavior in the human male.* Philadelphia: W. B. Saunders. [12]
Kinsey, A. C., Pomeroy, W. B., Martin, C. E., & Gebhard, P. H. (1953). *Sexual behavior in the human female.* Philadelphia: W. B. Saunders. [12]
Kirkpatrick, B., Kopelowicz, A., Buchanan, R. W., & Carpenter, W., Jr. (2000). Assessing the efficacy of treatments for the deficit syndrome of schizophrenia. *Neuropsychopharmacology, 22,* 303–310. [16]
Kirsch, I., & Lynn, S. J. (1995). The altered state of hypnosis: Changes in the theoretical landscape. *American Psychologist, 50,* 846–858. [4]
Kitayama, S., & Markus, H. R. (2000). The pursuit of happiness and the realization of sympathy: Cultural patterns of self, social relations, and well-being. In E. Diener & E. M. Suh (Eds.), *Subjective well-being across cultures.* Cambridge, MA: MIT Press. [14]
Kitayama, S., Markus, H. R., & Kurokawa, M. (2000). Culture, emotion, and well-being: Good feelings in Japan and the United States. *Cognition and Emotion, 14,* 93–124. [11]
Kite, M. E., Deaux, K., & Miele, M. (1991). Stereotypes of young and old: Does age outweigh gender? *Psychology and Aging, 6,* 19–27. [17]
Klahr, D. (1992). Information-processing approaches to cognitive development. In M. H. Bornstein & M. E. Lamb (Eds.), *Developmental psychology: An advanced textbook,* 3rd ed. (pp. 273–335). Hillsdale, NJ: Erlbaum. [9]
Klatzky, R. L. (1980). *Human memory: Structures and processes* (2nd ed.). New York: W. H. Freeman. [6]
Klatzky, R. L. (1984). *Memory and awareness: An information-processing perspective.* New York: W. H. Freeman. [6]
Klein, D. N., Schwartz, J. E., Rose, S., & Leader, J. B. (2000). Five-year course and outcome of dysthymic disorder: A prospective, naturalistic follow-up study. *American Journal of Psychiatry, 157,* 931–939. [15]
Klein, D., Milner, B., Zatorre, R. J., Meyer, E., & Evans, A. C. (1995). The neural substrates underlying word generation: A bilingual functional-imaging study. *Proceedings of the National Academy of Science, 92,* 2899–2930. [7]
Klein, R. G. (1996). Comments on expanding the clinical role of psychologists. *American Psychologist, 51,* 216–218. [16]
Kleinman, A., & Cohen, A. (1997, March). Psychiatry's global challenge. *Scientific American, 276,* 86–89. [16]
Kleinmuntz, B., & Szucko, J. J. (1984). A field study of the fallibility of polygraph lie detection. *Nature, 308,* 449–450. [11]
Kleitman, N. (1960). Patterns of dreaming. *Scientific American, 203,* 82–88. [4]
Klerman, G. L., Weissman, M. N., Rounsaville, B. J., & Chevron, E. S. (1984). *Interpersonal therapy of depression.* New York: Academic Press. [16]
Klinger, E. (1987, October). The power of daydreams. *Psychology Today,* 36–44. [4]
Klinnert, M. D., Campos, J. J., Sorce, J. F., Emde, R. N., & Suejda, M. (1983). Emotions as behavior regulators: Social referencing in infancy. In R. Plutchik & H. Kellerman (Eds.), *Emotions in early development:* Vol. 2: *The emotions* (pp. 57–86). New York: Academic Press. [11]
Kluft, R. P. (1984). An introduction to multiple personality disorder. *Psychiatric Annals, 14,* 19–24. [15]
Kluft, R. P. (1992). Hypnosis with multiple personality disorder. *American Journal of Preventative Psychiatry & Neurology, 3,* 19–27. [4]
Kluft, R. P. (1993). Multiple personality disorder: A contemporary perspective. *Harvard Mental Health Letter, 10*(4), 5–7. [15]
Knecht, S., Deppe, M., Dräger, B., Bobe, L., Lohmann, H., et al. (2000). Language lateralization in healthy right-handers. *Brain, 123,* 74–81. [2]
Knight, G. P., Fabes, R. A., & Higgins, D. A. (1996). Concerns about drawing causal inferences from meta-analyses: An example in the study of gender differences in aggression. *Psychological Bulletin, 119,* 410–421. [12]
Knight, R. T. (1996). Contribution of human hippocampal region to novelty detection. *Nature, 383,* 256–259. [2]
Knisely, J. S., Barker, S. B., Ingersoll, K. S., & Dawson, K. S. (2000). Psychopathology in substance abusing women reporting childhood sexual abuse. *Journal of Addictive Diseases, 19,* 31–44. [4]
Knowles, E. S., & Condon, C. A. (2000). Does the rose still smell as sweet? Item variability across test forms and revisions. *Psychological Assessment, 12,* 245–252. [8]
Kobasa, S. (1979). Stressful life events, personality, and health: An inquiry into hardiness. *Journal of Personality and Social Psychology, 37,* 1–11. [13]
Kobasa, S. C., Maddi, S. R., & Kahn, S. (1982). Hardiness and health: A prospective study. *Journal of Personality and Social Psychology, 42,* 168–177. [13]
Koch, K. (1997, August 26). Experts say ignorance contributes to road rage. *CNN Interactive* [On-line]. Available: www.cnn.com [13]
Kochanska, G. (1993). Toward a synthesis of parental socialization and child temperament in early development of conscience. *Child Development, 64,* 325–347. [17]
Koenig, H. G., Cohen, H. J., Blazer, D. G., Pieper, C., Meador, K. G., Shelp, F., Goli, V., & DiPasquale, B. (1992). Religious coping and depression among elderly, hospitalized medically ill men. *American Journal of Psychiatry, 149,* 1693–1700. [13]
Kohlberg, L. (1966). A cognitive-developmental analysis of children's sex-role concepts and attitudes. In E. E. Maccoby (Ed.),

The development of sex differences (pp. 82–173). Stanford, CA: Stanford University Press. [12]

Kohlberg, L. (1968, September). The child as a moral philosopher. *Psychology Today*, pp. 24–30. [10]

Kohlberg, L. (1969). *Stages in the development of moral thought and action.* New York: Holt, Rinehart & Winston. [10]

Kohlberg, L. (1981). *Essays on moral development*, Vol. 1. *The philosophy of moral development.* New York: Harper & Row. [10]

Kohlberg, L. (1984). *Essays on moral development*, Vol. 2. *The psychology of moral development.* San Francisco: Harper & Row. [10]

Kohlberg, L. (1985). *The psychology of moral development.* San Francisco: Harper & Row. [10]

Kohlberg, L., & Gilligan, C. (1971). The adolescent as a philosopher: The discovery of the self in a postconventional world. *Daedalus, 100*, 1051–1086. [10]

Kohlberg, L., & Ullian, D. Z. (1974). In R. C. Friedman, R. M. Richart, & R. L. Vande Wiele (Eds.), *Sex differences in behavior* (pp. 209–222). New York: Wiley. [12]

Köhler, W. (1925). *The mentality of apes* (E. Winter, Trans.). New York: Harcourt Brace Jovanovich. [5]

Kohut, A., & DeStefano, L. (1989). Modern employees expect more from their careers: Job dissatisfaction particularly high among the young. *The Gallup Report*, No. 288, 22–30. [10]

Koivisto, M., & Revensuo, A. (2000). Semantic priming by pictures and words in the cerebral hemispheres. *Cognitive Brain Research, 10*, 91–98. [6]

Koltz, C. (1983, December). Scapegoating. *Psychology Today*, pp. 68–69. [17]

Kon, M. A., & Plaskota, L. (2000). Information complexity of neural networks. *Neural Networks, 13*, 365–375. [6]

Konishi, M. (1993). Listening with two ears. *Scientific American, 268*, 66–73. [3]

Kopelman, P. G. (2000). Obesity as a medical problem. *Nature, 404*, 635–643. [11]

Kopp, C. P., & Kaler, S. R. (1989). Risk in infancy: Origins and implications. *American Psychologist, 44*, 224–230. [9]

Korn, J. H., Davis, R., & Davis, S. F. (1991). Historians' and chairpersons' judgments of eminence among psychologists. *American Psychologist, 46*, 789–792. [1]

Korner, A. F., Zeanah, C. H., Linden, J., Berkowitz, R. I., Kraemer, H. C., & Agras, W. S. (1985). The relation between neonatal and later activity and temperament. *Child Development, 56*, 38–42. [9]

Kosslyn, S. M. (1975). Information representation in visual images. *Cognitive Psychology, 7*, 341–370. [7]

Kosslyn, S. M. (1983). *Ghosts in the mind's machine: Creating and using images in the brain.* New York: Norton. [7]

Kosslyn, S. M. (1988). Aspects of a cognitive neuroscience of mental imagery. *Science, 240*, 1621–1626. [7]

Kosslyn, S. M. (1994). *Image and brain: The resolution of the imagery debate.* Cambridge, MA: MIT Press. [7]

Kosslyn, S. M., Alpert, N. M., Thompson, W. L., Malijkovic, V., Weise, S. B., Chabris, C. F., Hamilton, S. E., Rauch, S. L., & Buoanno, F. S. (1993). Visual mental imagery activates topographically organized visual cortex: PET investigations. *Journal of Cognitive Neuroscience, 5*, 263–287. [7]

Kosslyn, S. M., & Ochsner, K. N. (1994). In search of occipital activation during visual mental imagery. *Trends in Neurosciences, 17*, 290–292. [7]

Kosslyn, S. M., & Sussman, A. L. (1995). Roles of imagery in perception: Or, there is no such thing as immaculate perception. In M. S. Gazzaniga (Ed.), *The cognitive neurosciences.* Cambridge, MA: MIT Press. [7]

Kosslyn, S. M., Thompson, W. L., Constantini-Ferrando, M. F., Alpert, N. M., & Spiegel, D. (2000). Hypnotic visual illusion alters color processing in the brain. *American Journal of Psychiatry, 157*, 1279–1284. [3]

Koutsky, L. A., et al. (1992). A cohort study of the risk of cervical intraepithelial neoplasia Grade 2 or 3 in relation to papillomavirus infection. *New England Journal of Medicine, 327*, 1272. [12]

Kozak, M. J., Foa, E. B., & McCarthy, P. R. (1988). Obsessive-compulsive disorder. In C. G. Last & M. Herson (Eds.), *Handbook of anxiety disorders* (pp. 87–108). New York: Pergamon Press. [15]

Krantz, D. S., Grunberg, N. E., & Baum, A. (1985). Health psychology. *Annual Review of Psychology, 36*, 349–383. [13]

Krantz, M. (1987). Physical attractiveness and popularity: A predictive study. *Psychological Reports, 60*, 723–726. [9]

Kranzler, H. R. (1996). Evaluation and treatment of anxiety symptoms and disorders in alcoholics. *Journal of Clinical Psychiatry, 57*(6, Suppl.). [15]

Kraus, S. J. (1995). Attitudes and the prediction of behavior: A meta-analysis of the empirical literature. *Personality and Social Psychology Bulletin, 21*, 58–75. [17]

Krause, N., Ingersoll-Dayton, B., Ellison, C. G., & Wulff, K. M. (1999). Aging, religious doubt, and psychological well-being. *The Gerontologist, 39*, 525–533. [10]

Kroll, N. E. A., Ogawa, K. H., & Nieters, J. E. (1988). Eyewitness memory and the importance of sequential information. *Bulletin of the Psychonomic Society, 26*, 395–398. [6]

Krosigk, M. von. (1993). Cellular mechanisms of a synchronized oscillation in the thalamus. *Science, 261*, 361–364. [2]

Krueger, J. M., & Takahashi, S. (1997). Thermoregulation and sleep: Closely linked but separable. *Annals of the New York Academy of Sciences, 813*, 281–286. [4]

Krueger, W. C. F. (1929). The effect of overlearning on retention. *Journal of Experimental Psychology, 12*, 71–81. [6]

Krupnick, J. L., Sotsky, S. M., Simmens, S., Moyer, J., Elkin, I., Watkins, J., & Pilkonis, P. A. (1996). The role of the therapeutic alliance in psychotherapy and pharmacotherapy outcome: Findings in the National Institute of Mental Health Treatment of Depression Collaborative Research Program. *Journal of Consulting and Clinical Psychology, 64*, 532–539. [16]

Kübler-Ross, E. (1969). *On death and dying.* New York: Macmillan. [10]

Kuczmarski, R. J., Flegal, K. M., Campbell, S. M., & Johnson, C. L. (1994). Increasing prevalence of overweight among U.S. adults: The National Health and Nutrition Examination Surveys, 1960 to 1991. *Journal of the American Medical Association, 272*, 205–211. [11]

Kuhl, P. K., Williams, K. A., Lacerda, F., Stevens, K. N., & Lindblom, B. (1992). Linguistic experience alters phonetic perception in infants by 6 months of age. *Science, 255*, 606–608. [9]

Kuhn, D. (1984). Cognitive development. In M. H. Bernstein & M. E. Lamb (Eds.), *Developmental psychology.* Hillsdale, NJ: Erlbaum. [9]

Kuhn, D. (1989). Children and adults as intuitive scientists. *Psychological Review, 96*, 674–689. [9]

Kuhn, D., & Lao, J. (1996). Effects of evidence on attitudes: Is polarization the norm? *Psychological Science, 7*, 115–120. [17]

Kuhn, D., Kohlberg, L., Langer, J., & Haan, N. (1977). The development of formal operations in logical and moral judgment. *Genetic Psychology Monographs, 95*, 97–188. [10]

Kukla, A. (1972). Foundations of an attributional theory of performance. *Psychological Review, 79*, 454–470. [11]

Kunda, Z., & Oleson, K. C. (1995). Maintaining stereotypes in the face of disconfirmation: Construction grounds for subtyping deviants. *Journal of Personality and Social Psychology, 68*, 565–579. [17]

Kunz, D., & Herrmann, W. M. (2000). Sleep-wake cycle, sleep-related disturbances, and sleep disorders: A chronobiological approach. *Comparative Psychology, 41*(2, Suppl. 1), 104–105. [4]

Kuperberg, G. R., McGuire, P. K., Bullmore, E. T., Brammer, M. J., Rabe-Hesketh, S., Wright, I. C., Lythgoe, D. J., Williams, S. C. R., & David, A. S. (2000). Common and distinct neural substrates for pragmatic, semantic, and syntactic processing of spoken sentences: An fMRI study. *Journal of Cognitive Neuroscience, 12*, 321–341. [7]

Kupersmidt, J. B., & Coie, J. D. (1990). Preadolescent peer status, aggression, and school adjustment as predictors of externalizing problems in adolescence. *Child Development, 61*, 1350–1362. [9]

Kupersmidt, J. B., Coie, J. D., & Dodge, K. A. (1990). Predicting disorder from peer social problems. In S. R. Asher & J. D. Coie (Eds.), *Peer rejection in childhood.* New York: Cambridge University Press. [9]

Kurdek, L. A., & Siesky, A. E. (1980). Sex-role self concepts of single divorced parents and their children. *Journal of Divorce, 3*, 249–261. [12]

La Berge, S. P. (1981, January). Lucid dreaming: Directing the action as it happens. *Psychology Today*, pp. 48–57. [4]

Lachnit, H., & Kimmel, H. D. (2000). Experimental manipulation of a unique cue in Pavlovian SCR conditioning with humans. *Biological Psychology, 53,* 105–129. [5]

Lalonde, R., & Botez, M. I. (1990). The cerebellum and learning processes in animals. *Brain Research Reviews, 15,* 325–332. [2]

Lalonde, R., & Botez-Marquard, T. (2000). Neuropsychological deficits of patients with chronic or acute cerebellar lesions. *Journal of Neurolinguistics, 13,* 117–128. [5]

LaMar, W. J., Gerberich, S. G., Lohman, W. H., & Zaidman, B. (1998). Work-related physical assault. *Journal of Occupational and Environmental Medicine, 40,* 317–324. [17]

Lamb, M. E. (1981). The development of father-infant relationships. In M. E. Lamb (Ed.), *The role of the father in child development.* New York: Wiley. [12]

Lamb, M. E. (1987). *The father's role: Cross-cultural perspectives.* Hillsdale, NJ: Erlbaum [9]

Lamb, M. E., & Elster, A. B. (1985). Adolescent mother-infant-father relationships. *Developmental Psychology, 21,* 768–773. [9]

Lambe, E. K., Katzman, D. K., Mikulis, D. J., Kennedy, S. H., & Zipursky, R. B. (1997). Cerebral gray matter volume deficits after weight recovery from anorexia nervosa. *Archives of General Psychiatry, 54,* 537–542. [11]

Lamberg, L. (1996). Narcolepsy researchers barking up the right tree. *Journal of the American Medical Association, 276,* 265–266. [4]

Lambert, G., Johansson, M., Agren, H., & Friberg, P. (2000). Reduced brain norepinephrine and dopamine release in treatment-refractory depressive illness. *Archives of General Psychiatry, 57,* 787–793. [15]

Lambert, W. E., Genesee, F., Holobow, N., & Chartrand, L. (1993). Bilingual education for majority English-speaking children. *European Journal of Psychology of Education, 8,* 3–22. [7]

Lamborn, S. D., Mounts, N. S., Steinberg, L., & Dornbusch, S. M. (1991). Patterns of competence and adjustment among adolescents from authoritative, authoritarian, indulgent, and neglectful families. *Child Development, 62,* 1049–1065. [9, 10]

Lamm, H. (1988). A review of our research on group polarization: Eleven experiments on the effects of group discussion on risk acceptance, probability estimation, and negotiation positions. *Psychological Reports, 62,* 807–813. [17]

Landis, C. A., Savage, M. V., Lentz, M. J., & Brengelmann, G. L. (1998). Sleep deprivation alters body temperature dynamics to mild cooling and heating, not sweating threshold in women. *Sleep, 21,* 101–108. [4]

Landry, D. W. (1997, February). Immunotherapy for cocaine addiction. *Scientific American, 276,* 42–45. [4]

Landy, D., & Sigall, H. (1974). Beauty is talent: Task evaluation as a function of the performer's physical attractiveness. *Journal of Personality and Social Psychology, 29,* 299–304. [17]

Lang, A. J., & Craske, M. G. (2000). Manipulations of exposure-based therapy to reduce return of fear: A replication. *Behaviour Research & Therapy, 38,* 1–12. [16]

Lang, A. R., Goeckner, D. J., Adesso, V. J., & Marlatt, G. A. (1975). Effects of alcohol on aggression in male social drinkers. *Journal of Abnormal Psychology, 84,* 508–518. [1]

Lange, C. G., & James, W. (1922). *The emotions* (I. A. Haupt, Trans.). Baltimore: Williams and Wilkins. [11]

Langer, E. J., & Rodin, J. (1976). The effects of choice and enhanced personal responsibility for the aged: A field experiment in an institutional setting. *Journal of Personality and Social Psychology, 34,* 191–198. [13]

Langevin, B., Sukkar, F., Léger, P., Guez, A., & Robert, D. (1992). Sleep apnea syndromes (SAS) of specific etiology: Review and incidence from a sleep laboratory. *Sleep, 15,* S25–S32. [4]

Langlois, J. H. (1985). From the eye of the beholder to behavioral reality: The development of social behaviors and social relations as a function of physical attractiveness. In C. P. Herman (Ed.), *Physical appearance, stigma, and social behavior.* Hillsdale, NJ: Erlbaum. [9]

Langlois, J. H., Kalakanis, L., Rubenstein, A. J., Larson, A., Hallam, M., & Smoot, M. (2000). Maxims or myths of beauty? A meta-analytic and theoretical review. *Psychological Bulletin, 126,* 390–423. [17]

Langlois, J. H., Ritter, J. M., Casey, R. J., & Sawin, D. B. (1995). Infant attractiveness predicts maternal behaviors and attitudes. *Developmental Psychology, 31,* 464–472. [17]

Langlois, J. H., Ritter, J. M., Roggman, L. A., & Vaughn, L. S. (1991). Facial diversity and infant preferences for attractive faces. *Developmental Psychology, 27,* 79–84. [17]

Langlois, J. H., & Roggman, L. A. (1990). Attractive faces are only average. *Psychological Science, 1,* 115–121. [17]

Lara, M. E., Leader, J., & Klein, D. N. (1997). The association between social support and course of depression: Is it confounded with personality? *Journal of Abnormal Psychology, 106,* 478–482. [13]

Latané, B., Williams, K., & Harkins, S. (1979). Many hands make light the work: The causes and consequences of social loafing. *Journal of Personality and Social Psychology, 37,* 822–832. [17]

Lattal, K. A., & Neef, N. A. (1996). Recent reinforcement-schedule research and applied behavior analysis. *Journal of Applied Behavior Analysis, 29,* 213–230. [5]

Lauber, J. K., & Kayten, P. J. (1988). Keynote address: Sleepiness, circadian dysrhythmia, and fatigue in transportation system accidents. *Sleep, 11,* 503–512. [4]

Laumann, E. O., Gagnon, J. H., Michael, R. T., & Michaels, S. (1994). *The social organization of sexuality.* Chicago: University of Chicago Press. [12]

Laurent, J., Swerdik, M., & Ryburn, M. (1992). Review of validity research on the Stanford-Binet Intelligence Scale: Fourth Edition. *Psychological Assessment, 4,* 102–112. [8]

Lavie, P., Herer, P., Peled, R., Berger, I., Yoffe, N., Zomer, J., & Rubin, A-H. (1995). Mortality in sleep apnea patients: A multivariate analysis of risk factors. *Sleep, 18,* 149–157. [4]

Lawson, W. B., Hepler, N., Holiday, J., et al. (1994). Race as a factor in inpatient and outpatient admissions and diagnosis. *Hospital & Community Psychiatry, 45,* 72–74. [16]

Lazar, T. A. (2000). Sexual differentiation of the brain. Akira Matsumoto (Ed.). *Trends in Neurosciences, 23,* 507. [12]

Lazarus, R. S. (1966). *Psychological stress and the coping process.* New York: McGraw-Hill. [13]

Lazarus, R. S. (1984). On the primacy of cognition. *American Psychologist, 39,* 124–129. [11]

Lazarus, R. S. (1991a). Cognition and motivation in emotion. *American Psychologist, 46,* 352–367. [11]

Lazarus, R. S. (1991b). Progress on a cognitive-motivational-relational theory of emotion. *American Psychologist, 46,* 819–834. [11]

Lazarus, R. S. (1993). From psychological stress to the emotions: A history of changing outlooks. *Annual Review of Psychology, 44,* 1–21. [13]

Lazarus, R. S. (1995). Vexing research problems inherent in cognitive-mediational theories of emotion—and some solutions. *Psychological Inquiry, 6,* 183–187. [11]

Lazarus, R. S., & DeLongis, A. (1983). Psychological stress and coping in aging. *American Psychologist, 38,* 245–253. [13]

Lazarus, R. S., & Folkman, S. (1984). *Stress, appraisal, and coping.* New York: Springer. [13]

Lebow, J. L., & Gurman, A. S. (1995). Research assessing couple and family therapy. *Annual Review of Psychology, 46,* 27–57. [16]

LeDoux, J. E. (1994). Emotion, memory, and the brain. *Scientific American, 270,* 50–57. [2]

LeDoux, J. E. (1995). Emotion: clues from the brain. *Annual Review of Psychology, 46,* 209–235. [2]

LeDoux, J. E. (1996). *The emotional brain: The mysterious underpinnings of emotional life.* New York: Simon & Schuster. [11]

LeDoux, J. E. (2000). Emotion circuits in the brain. *Annual Review of Neuroscience, 23,* 155–184. [2, 11]

Leger, D. (1994). The cost of sleep-related accidents: A report for the National Commission on Sleep Disorders Research. *Sleep, 17,* 84–93. [4]

Lehmann, H., Treit, D., & Parent, M. B. (2000). Amygdala lesions do not impair shock-probe avoidance retention performance. *Behavioral Neuroscience, 114,* 1107–1116. [5]

Leichtman, M. D., & Ceci, S. J. (1995). The effects of stereotypes and suggestions on preschoolers' reports. *Developmental Psychology, 31,* 568–578. [6]

Leigh, B. C., & Stall, R. (1993). Substance use and risky sexual behavior for exposure to HIV: Issues in methodology, interpretation, and prevention. *American Psychologist, 48,* 1035–1045. [12]

Leitenberg, H., & Henning, K. (1995). Sexual fantasy. *Psychological Bulletin, 117,* 469–496. [4, 12]
Leland, J. (1996, August 26). The fear of heroin is shooting up. *Newsweek,* pp. 55–56. [4]
Leland, J. (1997, Spring/Summer). The magnetic tube. *Newsweek* [Special Edition], pp. 89–90. [9]
Lenneberg, E. (1967). *Biological foundations of language.* New York: Wiley. [9]
Leon, M. (1992). The neurobiology of filial learning. *Annual Review of Psychology, 43,* 337–398. [9]
Lerman, D. C., & Iwata, B. A. (1996). Developing a technology for the use of operant extinction in clinical settings: An examination of basic and applied research. *Journal of Applied Behavior Analysis, 29,* 345–382. [16]
Lerman, D. C., Iwata, B. A. , Shore, B. A., & Kahng, S. W. (1996). Responding maintained by intermittent reinforcement: Implications for the use of extinction with problem behavior in clinical settings. *Journal of Applied Behavior Analysis, 29,* 153–171. [5]
Lester, B. M., Hoffman, J., & Brazelton, T. B. (1985). The rhythmic structure of mother-infant interaction in term and preterm infants. *Child Development, 56,* 15–27. [9]
Levav, I., Kohn, R., Golding, J. M., & Weissman, M. M. (1997). Vulnerability of Jews to affective disorders. *American Journal of Psychiatry, 154,* 941–947. [15]
LeVay, S. (1991). A difference in hypothalamic structure between heterosexual and homosexual men. *Science, 253,* 1034–1037. [12]
LeVay, S. (1993). *The sexual brain.* Cambridge, MA: MIT Press. [12]
LeVay, S., & Hamer, D. H. (1994). Evidence for a biological influence in male homosexuality. *Scientific American, 270,* 44–49. [12]
Levenson, R. W. (1992). Autonomic nervous system differences among emotions. *Psychological Science, 3,* 23–27. [11]
Levenson, R. W., Carstensen, L. L., & Gottman, J. M. (1993). Long-term marriage: Age, gender, and satisfaction. *Psychology and Aging, 8,* 301–313. [10]
Levenson, R. W., Ekman, P., & Friesen, W. (1990). Voluntary facial action generates emotion-specific autonomic nervous system activity. *Psychophysiology, 27,* 363–385. [11]
Levi, D. M., Klein, S. A., Sharmal, V., & Nguyen, L. (2000). Detecting disorder in spatial vision. *Vision Research, 40,* 75–95. [3]
Levine, C., Kohlberg, L., & Hewer, A. (1985). The current formulation of Kohlberg's theory and a response to critics. *Human Development, 28,* 94–100. [10]
Levine, W. C., Berg, A. O., Johnson, R. E., Rolfs, R. T., Stone, K. M., Hook, E. W., III, Handsfield, H. H., Holmes, K. K., Islam, M. Q., Piot, P., Brady, W. E., Schmid, G. P., and STD Treatment Guidelines Project Team and consultants. (1994). Development of sexually transmitted diseases treatment guidelines, 1993: New methods, recommendations, and research priorities. *Sexually Transmitted Diseases, 21*(2, Suppl.), S96–S101. [12]
Levinson, D. J. (with Darrow, C. N., Klein, E. B., Levinson, M. H., & McKee, B.) (1978). *Seasons of a man's life.* New York: Knopf. [10]
Levinson, D. J. (1986). A conception of adult development. *American Psychologist, 41,* 3–13. [10]
Levinthal, C. F. (1996). *Drugs, behavior, and modern society.* Boston: Allyn & Bacon. [4]
Levitt, A. G., & Wang, Q. (1991). Evidence for language-specific rhythmic influences in the reduplicative babbling of French- and English-learning infants. *Language and Speech, 34,* 235–249. [9]
Levitt, E. E., & Duckworth, J. C. (1984). Minnesota Multiphasic Personality Inventory. In D. J. Keyser & R. C. Sweetland (Eds.), *Test critiques* (Vol. 1, pp. 466–472). Kansas City: Test Corporation of America. [14]
Levy, G. D., & Carter, D. B. (1989). Gender-schema, gender constancy, and gender-role knowledge: The roles of cognitive factors in preschoolers' gender-role stereotype attributions. *Developmental Psychology, 25,* 444–449. [12]
Levy, G. D., Taylor, M. G., & Gelman, S. A. (1995). Traditional and evaluative aspects of flexibility in gender roles, social conventions, moral rules, and physical laws. *Child Development, 66,* 515–531. [12]
Levy, J. (1985, May). Right brain, left brain: Fact and fiction. *Psychology Today,* pp. 38–44. [2]
Levy, J., & Nagylaki, T. (1972). A model for the genetics of handedness. *Genetics, 72,* 117–128. [2]
Lévy, P., & Robert, D. (1996). From snoring to sleep apnea syndrome: Therapeutic approach. *Sleep, 19,* S55–S56. [4]
Lewinsohn, P. M., & Rosenbaum, M. (1987). Recall of parental behavior by acute depressives, remitted depressives, and nondepressives. *Journal of Personality and Social Psychology, 52,* 611–619. [6]
Lewis, C. E., Smith, D. E., Wallace, D. D., Williams, O. D., Bild, D. E., & Jacobs, D. R., Jr. (1997). Seven-year trends in body weight and associations with lifestyle and behavioral characteristics in Black and White young adults: The CARDIA study. *American Journal of Public Health, 87,* 635–642. [11]
Lewis, D. O., Pincus, J. H., Feldman, M., Jackson, L., & Bard, B. (1986). Psychiatric, neurological, and psychoeducational characteristics of 15 death row inmates in the United States. *American Journal of Psychiatry, 143,* 838–845. [17]
Lewis, M. (1995, January/February). Self-conscious emotions. *American Scientist, 83,* 68–78. [11]
Lewis-Fernández, R., & Kleinman, A. (1994). Culture, personality, and psychopathology. *Journal of Abnormal Psychology, 103,* 67–71. [16]
Leyens, J-P., Yzerbyt, V., & Olivier, C. (1996). The role of applicability in the emergence of the overattribution bias. *Journal of Personality and Social Psychology, 70,* 219–229. [17]
Lieberman, M. (1986). Self-help groups and psychiatry. *American Psychiatric Association Annual Review, 5,* 744–760. [16]
Liepert, J., Terborg, C., & Weiller, C. (1999). Motor plasticity induced by synchronized thumb and foot movements. *Experimental Brain Research, 125,* 435–439. [2]
Lilly, J. C. (1956). Mental effects of reduction of ordinary levels of physical stimuli in intact, healthy persons. *Psychiatric Research Reports, 5,* 1–5. [11]
Lindemann, B. (2000). A taste for umami. *Nature Neuroscience, 3,* 99–100. [3]
Lindenberger, U., Mayr, U., & Kliegl, R. (1993). Speed and intelligence in old age. *Psychology and Aging, 8,* 207–220. [10]
Linn, M. C., & Hyde, J. S. (1989). Gender, mathematics, and science. *Educational Researcher, 18,* 17–27. [12]
Linn, M. C., & Peterson, A. C. (1985). Emergence and characterization of sex differences in spatial ability: A meta-analysis. *Child Development, 56,* 1479–1498. [12]
Linn, R. L. (1982). Ability testing: Individual differences, prediction, and differential prediction. In A. K. Wigdor & W. R. Garner (Eds.), *Ability testing: Uses, consequences, and controversies* (Part II). Washington, DC: National Academy Press. [8]
Linszen, D. H., Dingemans, P. M., Nugter, M. A., Van der Does, J. W., Scholte, W. F., & Lenior, M. A. (1997). Patient attributes and expressed emotion as risk factors for psychotic relapse. *Schizophrenia Bulletin, 23,* 119–130. [16]
Linton, M. (1979, July). I remember it well. *Psychology Today,* pp. 80–86. [6]
Linville, P. W., Fischer, G. W., & Salovey, P. (1989). Perceived distributions of the characteristics of in-group and out-group members: Empirical evidence and a computer simulation. *Journal of Personality and Social Psychology, 57,* 165–188. [17]
Lipsey, M. W., & Wilson, D. B. (1993). The efficacy of psychological, educational, and behavioral treatment: Confirmation from meta-analysis. *American Psychologist, 48,* 1181–1209. [16]
Lipsitt, L. P. (1990). Learning processes in the human newborn: Sensitization, habituation, and classical conditioning. *Annals of the New York Academy of Sciences, 608,* 113–123. [9]
Lisetti, C. L., & Schiano, D. J. (2000). Automatic facial expression interpretation: Where human-computer interaction, artificial intelligence and cognitive science intersect. *Pragmatics & Cognition, 8,* 185–236. [11]
Lishman, W. A. (1990). Alcohol and the brain. *British Journal of Psychiatry, 156,* 635–644. [13]
Little, R. E., Anderson, K. W., Ervin, C. H., Worthington-Roberts, B., & Clarren, S. K. (1989). Maternal alcohol use during breast-feeding and infant mental and motor development at one year. *New England Journal of Medicine, 321,* 425–430. [9]
Litvack-Miller, W., McDougall, D., & Romney, D. M. (1997). The structure of empathy during middle childhood and its relationship to prosocial behavior. *Genetic, Social, & General Psychology Monographs, 123,* 303–324. [17]

Lizza, E. F., & Cricco-Lizza, R. (1990, October). Impotence—Finding the cause. *Medical Aspects of Human Sexuality, 24,* 30–40. [12]

Locke, E. A., & Latham, G. P. (1990). *A theory of goal setting and task performance.* Englewood Cliffs, NJ: Prentice-Hall. [11]

Locke, E. A., Shaw, K. N., Saari, L. M., & Latham, G. P. (1981). Goal setting and task performance: 1969–1980. *Psychological Bulletin, 90,* 125–152. [11]

Loeber, R., & Hay, D. (1997). Key issues in the development of aggression and violence from childhood to early adulthood. *Annual Review of Psychology, 48,* 371–410. [17]

Loehlin, J. C. (1992). *The limits of family influence: Genes, experience, and behavior.* New York: Guilford. [14]

Loehlin, J. C., Horn, J. M., & Willerman, L. (1989). Modeling IQ change: Evidence from the Texas Adoption Project. *Child Development, 60,* 993–1004. [8]

Loehlin, J. C., Horn, J. M., & Willerman, L. (1990). Heredity, environment, and personality change: Evidence from the Texas Adoption Project. *Journal of Personality, 58,* 221–243. [14]

Loehlin, J. C., Lindzey, G., & Spuhler, J. N. (1975). *Race differences in intelligence.* San Francisco: Freeman. [8]

Loehlin, J. C., Vandenberg, S., & Osborne, R. (1973). Blood group genes and Negro-White ability differences. *Behavior Genetics, 3,* 263–270. [8]

Loehlin, J. C., Willerman, L., & Horn, J. M. (1987). Personality resemblance in adoptive families: A 10-year follow-up. *Journal of Personality and Social Psychology, 53,* 961–969. [14]

Loehlin, J. C., Willerman, L., & Horn, J. M. (1988). Human behavior genetics. *Annual Review of Psychology, 39,* 101–133. [8, 14, 15]

Loftus, E. F. (1979). *Eyewitness testimony.* Cambridge, MA: Harvard University Press. [6]

Loftus, E. F. (1980). *Memory: Surprising new insights into how we remember and why we forget.* Reading, MA: Addison-Wesley. [6]

Loftus, E. F. (1984, February). Eyewitnesses: Essential but unreliable. *Psychology Today,* pp. 22–27. [6]

Loftus, E. F. (1993a). Psychologists in the eyewitness world. *American Psychologist, 48,* 550–552. [6]

Loftus, E. F. (1993b). The reality of repressed memories. *American Psychologist, 48,* 518–537. [6]

Loftus, E. F. (1997). Creating false memories. *Scientific American, 277,* 71–75. [6]

Loftus, E. F., & Hoffman, H. G. (1989). Misinformation and memory: The creation of new memories. *Journal of Experimental Psychology: General, 118,* 100–104. [6]

Loftus, E. F., & Klinger, M. R. (1992). Is the unconscious smart or dumb? *American Psychologist, 47,* 761–765. [14]

Loftus, E. F., & Loftus, G. R. (1980). On the permanence of stored information in the human brain. *American Psychologist, 35,* 409–420. [6]

Loftus, E. F., & Pickrell, J. (1995). The formation of false memories. *Psychiatric Annals, 25,* 720–725. [6]

London, E. D., Ernst, M., Grant, S., Bonson, K., & Weinstein, A. (2000). Orbitofrontal cortex and human drug abuse: Functional imaging. *Cerebral Cortex, 10,* 334–342. [4, 5]

Long, G. M., & Crambert, R. F. (1990). The nature and basis of age-related changes in dynamic visual acuity. *Psychology and Aging, 5,* 138–143. [10]

Lopez, J. C. (2000). Shaky memories in indelible ink. *Nature Reviews Neuroscience, 1,* 6–7. [6]

Lord, L. J., Goode, E. E., Gest, T., McAuliffe, K., Moore, L. J., Black, R. F., & Linnon, N. (1987, November 30). Coming to grips with alcoholism. *U.S. News & World Report,* pp. 56–62. [13]

Lorente, C., Cordier, S., Goujard, J., Aymé, S., Bianchi, F., Calzolari, E., De Walle, H. E. K., & Knill-Jones, R. (2000). Tobacco and alcohol use during pregnancy and risk of oral clefts. *American Journal of Public Health, 90,* 415–519. [9]

Lorenz, K. (1966). *On aggression.* New York: Harcourt, Brace, & World. [17]

Lotze, M., Montoya, P., Erb, M., Hulsmann, E., Flor, H., Klose, U., Birbaumer, N., & Grodd, W. (1999). Activation of cortical and cerebellar motor areas during executed and imagined hand movements: An fMRI study. *Journal of Cognitive Neuroscience, 11,* 491–501. [7]

Louderback, L. A., & Whitley, B. E., Jr. (1997). Perceived erotic value of homosexuality and sex-role attitudes as mediators of sex differences in heterosexual college students' attitudes toward lesbians and gay men. *Journal of Sex Research, 34,* 175–182. [12]

Lovelace, E. A., & Twohig, P. T. (1990). Healthy older adults' perceptions of their memory functioning and use of mnemonics. *Bulletin of the Psychonomic Society, 28,* 115–118. [10]

Lovett, S. B., & Flavell, J. H. (1990). Understanding and remembering: Children's knowledge about the differential effects of strategy and task variables on comprehension and memorization. *Child Development, 61,* 1842–1858. [9]

Lowell, B. B., & Spiegelman, B. M. (2000). Towards a molecular understanding of adaptive thermogenesis. *Nature, 404,* 652–660. [11]

Lubinsky, D., & Benbow, C. P. (1992). Gender differences in abilities and preferences among the gifted: Implications for the math science pipeline. *Current Directions in Psychological Science, 1,* 61–66. [12]

Lubman, D. I., Peters, L. A., Mogg, K., Bradley, B. P., & Deakin, J. F. (2000). Attentional bias for drug cues in opiate dependence. *Psychological Medicine, 30,* 169–175. [4]

Lucas, R. E., Diener, E., Grob, A., Suh, E. M., & Shao, L. (2000). Cross-cultural evidence for the fundamental features of extraversion. *Journal of Personality & Social Psychology, 79,* 452–468. [14]

Luchins, A. S. (1957). Experimental attempts to minimize the impact of first impressions. In C. I. Hovland (Ed.), *Yale studies in attitude and communication: Vol. 1. The order of presentation in persuasion* (pp. 62–75). New Haven, CT: Yale University Press. [17]

Lucio, E., Reyes-Lagunes, I., & Scott, R. L. (1994). MMPI-2 for Mexico: Translation and adaptation. *Journal of Personality Assessment, 63,* 105–116. [14]

Ludwig, A. M. (1995). *The price of greatness: Resolving the creativity and madness controversy.* New York: Guilford. [15]

Ludwig, A. M. (1996). Mental disturbance and creative achievement. *Harvard Mental Health Letter, 12*(9), 4–6. [15]

Lukeman, D., & Melvin, D. (1993). Annotation: The preterm infant: Psychological issues in childhood. *Journal of Child Psychology and Psychiatry, 34,* 837–849. [9]

Lummis, M., & Stevenson, H. W. (1990). Gender differences in beliefs about achievement: A cross-cultural study. *Developmental Psychology, 26,* 254–263. [12]

Lundgren, C. B. (1986, August 20). Cocaine addiction: A revolutionary new treatment. *St. Louis Jewish Light,* p. 7. [4]

Lusk, S. L., Ronis, D. L., & Kerr, M. J. (1995). Predictors of hearing protection use among workers: Implications for training programs. *Human Factors, 37,* 635–640. [3]

Lydiard, R. B., Brawman-Mintzer, O., & Ballenger, J. C. (1996). Recent developments in the psychopharmacology of anxiety disorders. *Journal of Consulting and Clinical Psychology, 64,* 660–668. [16]

Lykken, D. T. (1981). *A tremor in the blood: Uses and abuses of the lie detector.* New York: McGraw-Hill. [11]

Lykken, D. T. (1985). The probity of the polygraph. In S. M. Kassin & L. S. Wrightsman (Eds.), *The psychology of evidence and trial procedure.* Beverly Hills, CA: Sage. [11]

Lykken, D. T., Bouchard, T. J., Jr., McGue, M., & Tellegen, A. (1993). Heritability of interests: A twin study. *Journal of Applied Psychology, 78,* 649–661. [14, 17]

Lykken, D., & Tellegen, A. (1996). Happiness is a stochastic phenomenon. *Psychological Science, 7,* 186–189. [14]

Lynch, E. B., Coley, J. D., & Medin, D. L. (2000). Tall is typical: Central tendency, ideal dimensions, and graded category structure among tree experts and novices. *Memory and Cognition, 28,* 41–50. [7]

Lynn, S. J., Kirsch, I., Barabasz, A., Cardena, E., & Patterson, D. (2000). Hypnosis as an empirically supported clinical intervention: The state of the evidence and a look to the future. *International Journal of Clinical Experimental Hypnosis, 48,* 239–259. [4]

Lynn, S. J., & Nash, M. R. (1994). Truth in memory: Ramifications for psychotherapy and hypnotherapy. *American Journal of Clinical Hypnosis, 36,* 194–208. [4]

Lytton, H., & Romney, D. M. (1991). Parents' differential socialization of boys and girls: A meta-analysis. *Psychological Bulletin, 109,* 267–296. [12]

Lyvers, M. (2000). Cognition, emotion, and the alcohol–aggression relationship: Comment on Giancola. *Experimental Clinical Psychopharmacology, 8,* 612–617. [17]

Maccoby, E. E. (1992). The role of parents in the socialization of children: An historical overview. *Developmental Psychology, 28,* 1006–1017. [9]

Maccoby, E. E. (2000). Parenting and its effects on children: On reading and misreading behavior genetics. *Annual Review of Psychology, 51,* 1–27. [9]

Maccoby, E. E., & Jacklin, C. N. (1974a). *The psychology of sex differences.* Stanford, CA: Stanford University Press. [12]

Maccoby, E. E., & Jacklin, C. N. (1974b, December). What we know and don't know about sex differences. *Psychology Today,* pp. 109–112. [12]

Maccoby, E. E., & Jacklin, C. N. (1980). Sex differences in aggression: A rejoinder and reprise. *Child Development, 51,* 964–980. [12]

Maccoby, E. E., & Martin, J. A. (1983). Socialization in the context of the family: Parent-child interaction. In P. H. Mussen (Ed.), *Handbook of child psychology* (4th ed., Vol. 4). New York: John Wiley. [9]

MacLean, M. G., & Lecci, L. (2000). A comparison of models of drinking motives in a university sample. *Psychology of Addictive Behaviors, 14,* 83–87. [4]

Macrae, C. N., Milne, A. B., & Bodenhausen, G. V. (1994). Stereotypes as energy-saving devices: A peek inside the cognitive toolbox. *Journal of Personality and Social Psychology, 66,* 37–47. [17]

Madon, S., Jussim, L., & Eccles, J. (1997). In search of the powerful self-fulfilling prophecy. *Journal of Personality and Social Psychology, 72,* 791–809. [1]

Magee, J. C., & Johnston, D. (1997). A synaptically controlled, associative signal for Hebbian plasticity in hippocampal neurons. Science, 275, 209–213. [2]

Maguire, E. A., Gadian, D. G., Johnsrude, I. S., Good, C. D., Ashburner, J., Frackowiak, R. S. J., & Frith, C. D. (2000). Navigation-related structural change in the hippocampi of taxi drivers. *Proceedings of the National Academy of Science, 97,* 4398–4403. [2, 6]

Mahowald, M. W. (2000). What is causing excessive daytime sleepiness? Evaluation to distinguish sleep deprivation from sleep disorders. *Postgraduate Medicine, 107,* 108–110. [4]

Maier, S. F., & Laudenslager, M. (1985, August). Stress and health: Exploring the links. *Psychology Today,* pp. 44–49. [13]

Main, M., & Solomon, J. (1990). Procedures for identifying infants as disorganized/disoriented during the Ainsworth Strange Situation. In M. Greenberg, D. Cicchetti, & M. Cummings (Eds.), *Attachment in the preschool years: Theory, research, and intervention* (pp. 121–160). Chicago: University of Chicago Press. [9]

Maj, M. (1990). Psychiatric aspects of HIV-1 infection and AIDS. *Psychological Medicine, 20,* 547–563. [12]

Maj, M., Veltro, F., Pirozzi, R., Lobrace, S., & Magliano, L. (1992). Pattern of recurrence of illness after recovery from an episode of major depression: A prospective study. *Journal of Personality and Social Psychology, 62,* 795–800. [15]

Major, B., Schmidlin, A. M., & Williams, L. (1990). Gender patterns in social touch: The impact of setting and age. *Journal of Personality and Social Psychology, 58,* 634–643. [17]

Maldonado, P. E., Gödecke, I., Gray, C. M., & Bonhoeffer, T. (1997). Orientation selectivity in pinwheel centers in cat striate cortex. *Science, 276,* 1551–1555. [3]

Malkoff, S. B., Muldoon, M. F., Zeigler, Z. R., & Manuck, S. B. (1993). Blood platelet responsivity to acute mental stress. *Psychosomatic Medicine, 55,* 477–482. [13]

Maltz, W. (1991). *The sexual healing journey: A guide for survivors of sexual abuse.* New York: HarperCollins. [6]

Manton, K. G., Siegler, I. C., & Woodbury, M. A. (1986). Patterns of intellectual development in later life. *Journal of Gerontology, 41,* 486–499. [10]

Maratsos, M. (1983). Some current issues in the study of the acquisition of grammar. In P. H. Mussen (Ed.), *Handbook of child psychology* (Vol. 3). New York: Wiley. [9]

Maratsos, M., & Matheny, L. (1994). Language specificity and elasticity: Brain and clinical syndrome studies. *Annual Review of Psychology, 45,* 487–516. [2]

Marcus, G. F. (1996). Why do children say "breaked"? *Current Directions in Psychological Science, 5,* 81–85. [9]

Marcus-Newhall, A., Pedersen, W. C., Carlson, M., & Miller, N. (2000). Displaced aggression is alive and well: A meta-analytic review. *Journal of Personality & Social Psychology, 78,* 670–689. [17]

Marder, S. R. (1996a). Clinical experience with risperidone. *Journal of Clinical Psychiatry, 57*(9, Suppl.), 57–61. [16]

Marder, S. R. (1996b). Management of schizophrenia. *Journal of Clinical Psychiatry, 57*(3, Suppl.), 9–13. [16]

Mareschal, D. (2000). Object knowledge in infancy: Current controversies and approaches. *Trends in Cognitive Sciences, 4,* 408–416. [9]

Marín, G. (1994). The experience of being a Hispanic in the United States. In W. J. Lonner & R. Malpass (Eds.), *Psychology and culture* (pp. 23–27). Boston: Allyn & Bacon. [14]

Maris, C. L., Endriga, M. C., Speitz, M. L., Jones, K., & DeKlyen, M. (2000). Are infants with orofacial clefts at risk for insecure mother–child attachments? *Cleft Palate Craniofacial Journal, 37,* 3257–3265. [9]

Markovic, B. M., Dimitrijevic, M., & Jankovic, B. D. (1993). Immunomodulation by conditioning: Recent developments. *International Journal of Neuroscience, 71,* 231–249. [5]

Marks, G. A., Shatfery, J. P., Oksenberg, A., Speciale, S. G, & Roffwarg, H. P. (1995). A functional role for REM sleep in brain maturation. *Behavioral Brain Research, 69,* 1–11. [4]

Marks, I. (1987). The development of normal fear: A review. *Journal of Child Psychology and Psychiatry, 28,* 667–697. [9]

Marks, I. (1988). Blood-injury phobia: A review. *American Journal of Psychiatry, 145,* 1207–1213. [15]

Marks, I. M. (1972). Flooding (implosion) and allied treatments. In W. S. Agras (Ed.), *Behavior modification.* New York: Little, Brown. [16]

Marks, I. M. (1995). Advances in behavioral-cognitive therapy of social phobia. *Journal of Clinical Psychiatry, 56*(5, Suppl.), 25–31. [16]

Marlatt, G. A. (1983). The controlled-drinking controversy: A commentary. *American Psychologist, 38,* 1097–1110. [13]

Marlatt, G. A., & Rohsenow, D. J. (1981, December). The think-drink effect. *Psychology Today,* pp. 60–69, 93. [1]

Marmor, J. (Ed.). (1980). *Homosexual behavior: A modern reappraisal.* New York: Basic Books. [12]

Marshall, G. D., & Zimbardo, P. G. (1979). Affective consequences of inadequately explained physiological arousal. *Journal of Personality and Social Psychology, 37,* 970–988. [11]

Marshall, J. R. (1997a). Alcohol and substance abuse in panic disorder. *Journal of Clinical Psychiatry, 58*(2, Suppl.), 46–49. [15]

Marshall, J. R. (1997b). Panic disorder: A treatment update. *Journal of Clinical Psychiatry, 58,* 36–42. [15]

Marshall, R. D., Schneier, F. R., Fallon, B. A., Feerick, J., & Liebowitz, M. R. (1994). Medication therapy for social phobia. *Journal of Clinical Psychiatry, 56*(6, Suppl.), 33–37. [16]

Marshall, W. L., & Segal, Z. (1988). Behavior therapy. In C. G. Last & M. Hersen (Eds.), *Handbook of anxiety disorders* (pp. 338–361). New York: Pergamon. [16]

Marsiglio, W. (1993). Attitudes toward homosexual activity and gays as friends: A national survey of heterosexual 15- to 19-year-old males. *Journal of Sex Research, 30,* 12–17. [12]

Martikainen, P., & Valkonen, R. (1996). Mortality after the death of a spouse: Rates and causes of death in a large Finnish cohort. *American Journal of Public Health, 86,* 1087–1093. [10]

Martin, C. L. (1990). Attitudes and expectations about children and nontraditional gender roles. *Sex Roles, 22,* 151–155. [12]

Martin, C. L., & Little, J. K. (1990). The relation of gender understanding to children's sex-typed preferences and gender stereotypes. *Child Development, 61,* 1427–1439. [12]

Martin, C. L., Wood, C. H., & Little, J. K. (1990). The development of gender stereotype components. *Child Development, 61,* 1891–1904. [12]

Martin, F. N. (1994). *Introduction to audiology* (5th ed.). Englewood Cliffs, NJ: Prentice-Hall. [3]

Martin, J. T. (2000). Sexual dimorphism in immune function: The role of prenatal exposure to androgens and estrogens. *European Journal of Pharmacology, 405,* 251–261. [12]

Martin, S. K., & Eastman, C. I. (1998). Medium-intensity light produces circadian rhythm adaptation to simulated night-shift work. *Sleep, 21,* 154–165. [4]

Martinez, C. (1986). Hispanics: Psychiatric issues. In C. B. Wilkinson (Ed.), *Ethnic psychiatry* (pp. 61–88). New York: Plenum. [16]

Martinez, J. L., Jr., & Derrick, B. E. (1996). Long-term potentiation and learning. *Annual Review of Psychology, 47,* 173–203. [6]

Martinez-Taboas, A. (1991). Multiple personality in Puerto Rico: Analysis of fifteen cases. *Dissociation, 4,* 189–192. [15]

Martorano, S. C. (1977). A developmental analysis of performance on Piaget's formal operations tasks. *Developmental Psychology, 13,* 666–672. [10]

Masand, P., Popli, A. P., & Weilburg, J. B. (1995). Sleepwalking. *American Family Physician, 51,* 649–654. [4]

Masataka, N. (1996). Perception of motherese in a signed language by 6-month-old deaf infants. *Developmental Psychology, 32,* 874–879. [9]

Masland, R. H. (1996). Unscrambling color vision. *Science, 271,* 616–617. [3]

Maslow, A. H. (1970). *Motivation and personality* (2nd ed.). New York: Harper & Row. [14, 15]

Masters, J. C. (1981). Developmental psychology. *Annual Review of Psychology, 32,* 117–151. [9]

Masters, W. H., & Johnson, V. E. (1966). *Human sexual response.* Boston: Little, Brown [10, 12]

Masters, W. H., & Johnson, V. E. (1975). *The pleasure bond: A new look at sexuality and commitment.* Boston: Little, Brown. [12]

Masters, W. H., & Johnson, V. E. (1979). *Homosexuality in perspective.* Boston: Little, Brown. [12]

Mathew, R. J., & Wilson, W. H. (1991). Substance abuse and cerebral blood flow. *American Journal of Psychiatry, 148,* 292–305. [4]

Matlin, M. (1994). *Cognition* (3rd ed.). Fort Worth, TX: Harcourt. [8]

Matlin, M. W. (1989). *Cognition* (2nd ed.). New York: Holt, Rinehart & Winston. [6, 7]

Matlin, M. W., & Foley, H. J. (1997). *Sensation and perception* (4th ed.). Boston: Allyn & Bacon. [3]

Matsuda, L., Lolait, S. J., Brownstein, M. J., Young, A. C., & Bonner, T. I. (1990). Structure of a cannabinoid receptor and functional expression of the cloned CDNA. *Nature, 346,* 561–564. [4]

Matsunami, H., Montmayeur, J-P., & Buck, L. B. (2000). A family of candidate taste receptors in human and mouse. *Nature, 404,* 601–604. [3]

Matt, G. E., & Navarro, A. M. (1997). What meta-analyses have and have not taught us about psychotherapy effects: A review and future directions. *Clinical Psychology Review, 17,* 1–32. [16]

Mattay, V. S., Berman, K. F., Ostrem, J. L., Esposito, G., Van Horn, J. D., Bigelow, L. B., & Weinberger, D. R. (1996). Dextroamphetamine enhances "neural network-specific" physiological signals: A positron-emission tomography rCBF study. *Journal of Neuroscience, 16,* 4816–4822. [4]

Matthews, K. A. (1992). Myths and realities of the menopause. *Psychosomatic Medicine, 54,* 1–9. [10]

Matthews, K. A., Shumaker, S. A., Bowen, D. J., Langer, R. D., Hunt, J. R., Kaplan, R. M., Klesges, R. C., & Ritenbaugh, C. (1997). Women's health initiative: Why now? What is it? What's new? *American Psychologist, 52,* 101–116. [13]

Mauro, J. (1994, July/August). And Prozac for all. *Psychology Today,* pp. 44–48, 80–81. [16]

May, R. (1982). The problem of evil: An open letter to Carl Rogers. *Journal of Humanistic Psychology, 22,* 10–21. [14]

Mayer, J. D., Caruso, D., & Salovey, P. (2000). Emotional intelligence meets traditional standards for an intelligence. *Intelligence, 27,* 267–298. [8]

Mayer, J. D., & Salovey, P. (1993). The intelligence of emotional intelligence. *Intelligence, 17,* 433–442. [8]

Mayer, J. D., Salovey, P., & Caruso, D. R. (2000). Models of emotional intelligence. In R. J. Sternberg (Ed.), *Handbook of human intelligence* (2nd ed., pp. 396–420). New York: Cambridge University Press. [8]

Mayo Clinic. (1997, July). Coffee: What's the scoop on its health effects? *Mayo Clinic Health Letter.* [4]

Mazur, J. E. (1993). Predicting the strength of a conditioned reinforcer: Effects of delay and uncertainty. *Current Directions in Psychological Science,* 2(3), 70–74. [5]

McAdams, D. P. (1992). The five-factor model in personality: A critical appraisal. *Journal of Personality, 60,* 329–361. [14]

McAdams, D. P., de St. Aubin, E., & Logan, R. L. (1993). Generativity among young, midlife, and older adults. *Psychology and Aging, 8,* 221–230. [10]

McAneny, L. (1992). Number of drinkers on the rise again. *Gallup Poll Monthly,* No. 317, 43–47. [4]

McAnulty, R. D., & Burnette, M. M. (2001). *Exploring human sexuality: Making healthy decisions* (pp. 144-150). Boston: Allyn & Bacon. [9]

McCall, R. B. (1994). Academic underachievers. *Current Directions in Psychological Science, 3,* 15–19. [11]

McCann, U. D., Mertl, M., Eligulashvili, V., & Ricaurte, G. A. (1999). Cognitive performance in (+/-) 3,4–methylenedioxymethamphetamine (MDMA, "ecstasy") users: A controlled study. *Psychopharmacology, 143,* 417–425. [4]

McCarthy, P. (1989, March). Ageless sex. *Psychology Today,* p. 62. [10]

McCartney, K., Harris, M. J., & Bernieri, F. (1990). Growing up and growing apart: A developmental meta-analysis of twin studies. *Psychological Bulletin, 107,* 226–237. [8]

McClearn, G. E., Johansson, B., Berg, S., Pedersen, N. L., Ahern, F., Petrill, S. A., & Plomin, R. (1997). Substantial genetic influence on cognitive abilities in twins 80 or more years old. *Science, 276,* 1560–1563. [8]

McClelland, D. C. (1958). Methods of measuring human motivation. In J. W. Atkinson (Ed.), *Motives in fantasy, action and society: A method of assessment and study.* Princeton, NJ: Van Nostrand. [11]

McClelland, D. C. (1961). *The achieving society.* Princeton, NJ: Van Nostrand. [11]

McClelland, D. C. (1985). *Human motivation.* New York: Cambridge University Press. [11]

McClelland, D. C., & Pilon, D. A. (1983). Sources of adult motives in patterns of parent behavior in early childhood. *Journal of Personality and Social Psychology, 44,* 564–574. [11]

McClelland, D. C., Atkinson, J. W., Clark, R. W., & Lowell, E. L. (1953). *The achievement motive.* New York: Appleton-Century-Crofts. [11]

McClelland, J. L., McNaughton, B. L., & O'Reilly, R. C. (1995). Why there are complementary learning systems in the hippocampus and neocortex: Insights from the successes and failures of connectionist models of learning and memory. *Psychological Bulletin, 102,* 419–457. [6]

McConnell, J. V., Cutler, R. L., & McNeil, E. B. (1958). Subliminal stimulation: An overview. *American Psychologist, 13,* 229–242. [3]

McCormick, C. B., & Kennedy, J. H. (2000). Father–child separation, retrospective and current views of attachment relationship with father and self-esteem in late adolescence. *Psychological Reports, 86,* 827–834. [9]

McCourt, W. F., Gurrera, R. J., & Cutter, H. S. G. (1993). Sensation seeking and novelty seeking: Are they the same? *Journal of Nervous and Mental Disease, 181,* 309–312. [11]

McCrae, R. (1984). Situational determinants of coping responses: Loss, threat, and challenge. *Journal of Personality and Social Psychology, 46,* 919–928. [13]

McCrae, R. R. (1987). Creativity, divergent thinking, and openness to experience. *Journal of Personality and Social Psychology, 52,* 1258–1265. [8]

McCrae, R. R. (1993). Moderated analyses of longitudinal personality stability. *Journal of Personality and Social Psychology, 65,* 577–583. [14]

McCrae, R. R. (1996). Social consequences of experiential openness. *Psychological Bulletin, 120,* 323–337. [14]

McCrae, R. R., & Costa, P. T., Jr. (1987). Validation of the five-factor model of personality across instruments and observers. *Journal of Personality and Social Psychology, 52,* 81–90. [14]

McCrae, R. R., & Costa, P. T., Jr. (1990). *Personality in adulthood.* New York: Guilford. [10, 14]

McCrae, R. R., & Costa, P. T., Jr. (1997). Personality trait structure as a human universal. *American Psychologist, 52,* 509–516. [14]

McCrae, R. R., Costa, P. T., Jr., Ostendorf, F., Angleitner, A., Hrebickova, M., Avia, S. J., Sanchez-Bernardos, M. L., Kusdil, M. E., Woodfield, R., Saunders, P. R., & Smith, P. B. (2000). Nature over nurture: Temperament, personality, and life span development. *Journal of Personality & Social Psychology, 78,* 173–186. [14]

McCrae, R. R., Costa, P. T., Jr., Pedroso de Lima, M., Simoes, A., Ostendorf, F., Angleitner, A., Marusic, I., Bratko, D., Caprara, G. V., Barbaranelli, C., Chae, J. H., & Piedmont, R. L. (1999). Age differences in personality across the adult life span: Parallels in five cultures. *Developmental Psychology, 35,* 466–477. [14]

McCue, J. M., Link, K. L., Eaton, S. S., & Freed, B. M. (2000). Exposure to cigarette tar inhibits ribonucleotide reductase and blocks lymphocyte proliferation. *Journal of Immunology, 165,* 6771–6775. [13]

McCullough, M. E., Hoyt, W. T., Larson, D. B., Koenig, H. G., & Thoresen, C. (2000). Religious involvement and mortality: A meta-analytic review. *Health Psychology, 19,* 211–222. [13]

McDonald, C., & Murray, R. M. (2000). Early and late environmental risk factors for schizophrenia. *Brain Research Reviews, 31,* 130–137. [15]

McDonald, J. L. (1997). Language acquisition: The acquisition of linguistic structure in normal and special populations. *Annual Review of Psychology, 48,* 215–241. [7]

McDowell, C., & Acklin, M. W. (1996). Standardizing procedures for calculating Rorschach interrater reliability: Conceptual and empirical foundations. *Journal of Personality Assessment, 66,* 308–320. [14]

McGarvey, E. L., Clavet, G. J., Mason, W., & Waite, D. (1999). Adolescent inhalant abuse: Environments of use. *American Journal of Drug and Alcohol Abuse, 25,* 731–741. [4]

McGee, A-M., & Skinner, M. (1987). Facial asymmetry and the attribution of personality traits. *British Journal of Social Psychology, 26,* 181–184. [2]

McGlashan, T. H., & Fenton, W. S. (1992). The positive-negative distinction in schizophrenia: Review of natural history validators. *Archives of General Psychiatry, 49,* 63–72. [15]

McGlashan, T. H., & Hoffman, R. E. (2000). Schizophrenia as a disorder of developmentally reduced synaptic connectivity. *Archives of General Psychiatry, 57,* 637–648. [15]

McGue, M., Bouchard, T. J., Jr., Iacono, W. G., & Lykken, D. T. (1993). Behavioral genetics of cognitive ability: A life-span perspective. In R. Plomin & G. E. McClearn (Eds.), *Nature, nurture and psychology* (pp. 59–76). Washington, DC: American Psychological Association. [8]

McGue, M., Pickens, R. W., & Svikis, D. S. (1992). Sex and age effects on the inheritance of alcohol problems: A twin study. *Journal of Abnormal Psychology, 101,* 3–17. [13]

McGuinness, D. (1993). Gender differences in cognitive style: Implications for mathematics performance and achievement. In I. A. Penner, G. M. Batsche, H. M. Knoff, & D. L. Nelson (Eds.), *The challenge of mathematics and science education: Psychology's response.* Washington, DC: American Psychological Association. [12]

McGuire, P. K., Shah, G. M. S., & Murray, R. M. (1993). Increased blood flow in Broca's area during auditory hallucinations in schizophrenia. *Lancet, 342,* 703–706. [15]

McGuire, W. J. (1985). Attitudes and attitude change. In G. Lindzey & E. Aronson (Ed.), *Handbook of social psychology* (Vol. 2, 3rd ed.). New York: Random House. [17]

McHugh, P. R. (1993). Multiple personality disorder. *Harvard Mental Health Letter, 10*(3), 4–6. [15]

McInerney, F. (2000). "Requested death": A new social movement. *Social Science and Medicine, 50,* 137–154. [10]

McKellar, P. (1972). Imagery from the standpoint of introspection. In P. W. Sheehan (Ed.), *The function and nature of imagery* (pp. 36–63). New York: Academic Press. [7]

McKelvie, S. J. (1984). Relationship between set and functional fixedness: A replication. *Perceptual and Motor Skills, 58,* 996–998. [7]

McNally, R. J., & Shin, L. M. (1995). Association of intelligence with severity of posttraumatic stress disorder symptoms in Vietnam combat veterans. *American Journal of Psychiatry, 152,* 936–938. [13]

McNeil, T. F., Cantor-Graae, E., & Weinberger, D. R. (2000). Relationship of obstetric complications and differences in size of brain structures in monozygotic twin pairs discordant for schizophrenia. *American Journal of Psychiatry, 157,* 203–212. [15]

McReynolds, P. (1989). Diagnosis and clinical assessment: Current status and major issues. *Annual Review of Psychology, 40,* 83–108. [14]

Medina, J. H., Paladini, A. C., & Izquierdo, I. (1993). Naturally occurring benzodiazepines and benzodiazepine-like molecules in brain. *Behavioural Brain Research, 58,* 1–8. [16]

Mednick, S. A., & Mednick, M. T. (1967). *Examiner's manual, Remote Associates Test.* Boston: Houghton-Mifflin. [8]

Mednick, S. A., Brennan, P., & Kandel, E. (1988). Predisposition to violence. *Aggressive Behavior, 14,* 25–33. [17]

Medzerian, G. (1991). *Crack: Treating cocaine addiction.* Blue Ridge Summit, PA: Tab Books. [4, 5]

Meer, J. (1986, June). The age of reason. *Psychology Today,* pp. 60–64. [10]

Mehrabian, A. (1968, September). Communication without words. *Psychology Today,* pp. 53–55. [17]

Meichenbaum, D. (1977). *Cognitive behavior modification: An integrative approach.* New York: Plenum. [13]

Meier, R. P. (1991). Language acquisition by deaf children. *American Scientist, 79*(1), 60–70. [9]

Melamed, B. G., & Siegel, L. J. (1975). Reduction of anxiety in children facing hospitalization and surgery by use of filmed modeling. *Journal of Consulting and Clinical Psychology, 43,* 511–521. [16]

Mellet, E., Tzourio-Mazoyer, N., Bricogne, S., Mazoyer, B., Dennis, M., & Kosslyn, S. M. (2000). Functional anatomy of high-resolution visual mental imagery. *Journal of Cognitive Neuroscience, 12,* 98–109. [7]

Meltzer, H. (1930). Individual differences in forgetting pleasant and unpleasant experiences. *Journal of Educational Psychology, 21,* 399–409. [6]

Meltzer, H. Y., Rabinowitz, J., Lee, M. A., Cola, P. A., Ranjan, R., Findling, R. L., & Thompson, P. A. (1997). Age at onset and gender of schizophrenic patients in relation to neuroleptic resistance. *American Journal of Psychiatry, 154,* 475–482. [16]

Meltzoff, A. N. (1988a). Imitation of televised models by infants. *Child Development, 59,* 1221–1229. [9]

Meltzoff, A. N. (1988b). Infant imitation and memory: Nine-month-olds in immediate and deferred tests. *Child Development, 59,* 217–255. [9]

Meltzoff, A. N., & Kuhl, P. K. (1994). Faces and speech: Intermodal processing of biologically relevant signals in infants and adults. In D. J. Lewkowicz & R. Lickliter (Eds.), *The development of intersensory perception: Comparative perspectives* (pp. 335–369). Hillsdale, NJ: Erlbaum. [9]

Meltzoff, A. N., & Moore, M. K. (1977). Imitation of facial and manual gestures by human neonates. *Science, 198,* 75–78. [9]

Meltzoff, A. N., & Moore, M. K. (1989). Imitation in newborn infants: Exploring the range of gestures imitated and the underlying mechanisms. *Developmental Psychology, 25,* 954–962. [9]

Melzack, R., & Wall, P. D. (1965). Pain mechanisms: A new theory. *Science, 150,* 971–979. [3]

Melzack, R., & Wall, P. D. (1983). *The challenge of pain.* New York: Basic Books. [3]

Mendez, M. F., Chow, T., Ringman, J., Twitchell, G., & Hinkin, C. H. (2000). Pedophilia and temporal lobe disturbances. *Journal of Neuropsychiatry & Clinical Neurosciences, 12,* 171–176. [12]

Merckelbach, H., de Jong, P. J., Muris, P., & van den Hout, M. A. (1996). The etiology of specific phobias: A review. *Clinical Psychology Review, 16,* 337–361. [15]

Merskey, H. (1996). Ethical issues in the search for repressed memories. *American Journal of Psychotherapy, 50,* 323–335. [6]

Mertens, T. E., & Low-Beer, D. (1996). HIV and AIDS: Where is the epidemic going? *WHO Bulletin OMS, 74,* 121–128. [12]

Metter, E. J. (1991). Brain-behavior relationships in aphasia studied by positron emission tomography. *Annals of the New York Academy of Sciences, 620,* 153–164. [2]

Meyer, A. (1997, March/April). Patching up testosterone. *Psychology Today, 30,* 54–57, 66–70. [12]

Meyer, P. (1972). If Hitler asked you to electrocute a stranger, would you? In R. Greenbaum & H. A. Tilker (Eds.), *The challenge of psychology* (pp. 456–465). Englewood Cliffs, NJ: Prentice-Hall. [17]

Meyer-Bahlburg, H. F. L., Ehrhardt, A. A., Rosen, L. R., & Gruen, R. S. (1995). Prenatal estrogens and the development of homosexual orientation. *Developmental Psychology, 31,* 12–21. [12]

Michaels, J. W., Bloomel, J. M., Brocato, R. M., Linkous, R. A., & Rowe, J. S. (1982). Social facilitation and inhibition in a natural setting. *Replications in Social Psychology, 2,* 21–24. [17]

Middlebrooks, J. C., & Green, D. M. (1991). Sound localization by human listeners. *Annual Review of Psychology, 42,* 135–159. [3]
Miles, D. R., & Carey, G. (1997). Genetic and environmental architecture of human aggression. *Journal of Personality and Social Psychology, 72,* 207–217. [14, 17]
Miles, R. (1999). A homeostatic switch. *Nature, 397,* 215–216. [2]
Milgram, S. (1963). Behavioral study of obedience. *Journal of Abnormal and Social Psychology, 67,* 371–378. [17]
Milgram, S. (1965). Liberating effects of group pressure. *Journal of Personality and Social Psychology, 1,* 127–134. [17]
Miller, D. T., & Turnbull, W. (1986). Expectancies and interpersonal processes. *Annual Review of Psychology, 37,* 233–256. [17]
Miller, E. M. (2000). Homosexuality, birth order, and evolution: Toward an equilibrium reproductive economics of homosexuality. *Archives of Sexual Behavior, 29,* 11–34. [12]
Miller, G. A. (1956). The magical number seven, plus or minus two: Some limits on our capacity for processing information. *Psychological Review, 63,* 81–97. [6]
Miller, G. A., & Gildea, P. M. (1987). How children learn words. *Scientific American, 257,* 94–99. [9]
Miller, I. J., & Reedy, F. E., Jr. (1990). Variations in human taste bud density and taste intensity perception. *Physiological Behavior, 47,* 1213–1219. [3]
Miller, J. G., & Bersoff, D. M. (1992). Culture and moral judgment: How are conflicts between justice and interpersonal responsibilities resolved? *Journal of Personality and Social Psychology, 62,* 541–554. [10]
Miller, J. G., Bersoff, D. M., & Harwood, R. L. (1990). Perceptions of social responsibilities in India and in the United States: Moral imperatives or personal decisions? *Journal of Personality and Social Psychology, 58,* 33–47. [17]
Miller, L. (1988, February). The emotional brain. *Psychology Today,* pp. 34–42. [2]
Miller, L. (1989, November). What biofeedback does (and doesn't) do. *Psychology Today,* pp. 22–23. [5]
Miller, N. E. (1941). The frustration-aggression hypothesis. *Psychological Review, 48,* 337–342. [17]
Miller, N. E. (1985, February). Rx: Biofeedback. *Psychology Today,* pp. 54–59. [5]
Miller, N. S., & Gold, M. S. (1994). LSD and Ecstasy: Pharmacology, phenomenology, and treatment. *Psychiatric Annals, 24,* 131–133. [4]
Miller, S. A. (2000). Children's understanding of preexisting differences in knowledge and belief. *Developmental Review, 20,* 227–282. [9]
Miller, T. Q., Smith, T. W., Turner, C. W., Guijarro, M. L., & Hallet, A. J. (1996). A meta-analytic review of research on hostility and physical health. *Psychological Bulletin, 119,* 322–348. [13]
Miller, T. Q., Turner, C. W., Tindale, R. S., Posavac, E. J., & Dugoni, B. L. (1991). Reasons for the trend toward null findings in research on Type A behavior. *Psychological Bulletin, 110,* 469–485. [13]
Miller, W. C., Lindeman, A. K., Wallace, J., & Niederpruem, M. (1990). Diet composition, energy intake, and exercise in relation to body fat in men and women. *American Journal of Clinical Nutrition, 52,* 426–430. [14]
Millman, R. B., & Beeder, A. B. (1994). The new psychedelic culture: LSD, Ecstasy, "rave" parties and The Grateful Dead. *Psychiatric Annals, 24,* 148–150. [4]
Milner, B. (1966). Amnesia following operation on the temporal lobes. In C. W. M. Whitty & O. L. Zangwill (Eds.), *Amnesia* (pp. 109–133). London: Butterworth. [6]
Milner, B. (1970). Memory and the medial temporal regions of the brain. In K. H. Pribram & D. E. Broadbent (Eds.), *Biology of memory.* New York: Academic Press. [6]
Milner, B., Corkin, S., & Teuber, H. L. (1968). Further analysis of the hippocampal amnesic syndrome: 14-year follow-up study of H. M. *Neuropsychologia, 6,* 215–234. [6]
Mischel, W. (1966). A social-learning view of sex differences in behavior. In E. E. Maccoby (Ed.), *The development of sex differences* (pp. 56–81). Stanford, CA: Stanford University Press. [12]
Mischel, W. (1968). *Personality and assessment.* New York: Wiley. [14]
Mischel, W. (1973). Toward a cognitive social learning reconceptualization of personality. *Psychological Review, 80,* 252–283. [14]
Mischel, W. (1977). The interaction of person and situation. In D. Magnusson & N. S. Endler (Eds.), *Personality at the crossroads: Current issues in interactional psychology.* Hillsdale, NJ: Lawrence Erlbaum. [14]
Mistry, J., & Rogoff, B. (1994). Remembering in cultural context. In W. J. Lonner & R. Malpass (Eds.), *Psychology and culture* (pp. 139–144). Boston: Allyn & Bacon. [6]
Mitler, M. M., Aldrich, M. S., Koob, G. F., & Zarcone, V. P. (1994). Narcolepsy and its treatment with stimulants. *Sleep, 17,* 352–371. [4]
Mitler, M. M., Miller, J. C., Lipsitz, J. J., Walsh, J. K., & Wylie, C. D. (1997). The sleep of long-haul truck drivers. *New England Journal of Medicine, 337,* 755–761. [4]
Mitsis, E. M., Halperin, J. M., & Newcorn, J. H. (2000). Serotonin and aggression in children. *Current Psychiatry Reports, 2,* 95–101. [17]
Miyashita, Y. (1995). How the brain creates imagery: Projection to primary visual cortex. *Science, 268,* 1719–1720. [7]
Modestin, J. (1992). Multiple personality disorder in Switzerland. *American Journal of Psychiatry, 148,* 88–92. [15]
Moffitt, T. E., Caspi, A., Harkness, A. R., & Silva, P. A. (1993). The natural history of change in intellectual performance: Who changes? How much? Is it meaningful? *Journal of Child Psychology and Psychiatry, 34,* 455–506. [8]
Moldofsky, H., Gilbert, R., Lue, F. A., & MacLean, A. W. (1995). Sleep-related violence. *Sleep, 18,* 731–739. [4]
Molin, J., Mellerup, E., Bolwig, T., Scheike, T., & Dam, H. (1996). The influence of climate on development of winter depression. *Journal of Affective Disorders, 37,* 151–155. [15]
Money, J. (1987). Sin, sickness, or status? Homosexual gender identity and psychoneuroendocrinology. *American Psychologist, 42,* 384–399. [12]
Money, J., & Schwartz, M. (1977). Dating, romantic and nonromantic friendships, and sexuality in 17 early-treated adrenogenital females, aged 16–25. In P. A. Lee et al. (Eds.), *Congenital adrenal hyperplasia.* Baltimore: University Park Press. [12]
Monk, T. H. (1989). Circadian rhythms in subjective activation, mood, and performance efficiency. In M. H. Kryger, T. Roth, & W. C. Dement (Eds.), *Principles and practice of sleep medicine* (pp. 163–172). Philadelphia: W. B. Saunders. [4]
Montagu, A. (1962). *The humanization of man.* Cleveland: World. [9]
Montgomery, G. H., DuHamel, K. N., & Redd, W. H. (2000). A meta-analysis of hypnotically induced analgesia: How effective is hypnosis? *International Journal of Clinical Experimental Hypnosis, 48,* 138–153. [4]
Moore, D. W. (1993). Public polarized on gay issue. *Gallup Poll Monthly,* No. 331, 30–34. [12]
Moore-Ede, M. (1993). *The twenty-four hour society.* Reading, MA: Addison-Wesley. [4]
Moracco, K. E., Runyan, C. W., Loomis, D. P., Wolf, S. H., Napp, D., & Butts, J. D. (2000). Killed on the clock: A population-based study of workplace homicide, 1977–1991. *American Journal of Industrial Medicine, 37,* 629–636. [17]
Moraglia, G. (1994). C. G. Jung and the psychology of adult development. *Journal of Analytical Psychology, 39,* 55–75. [14]
Moran, M. G., & Stoudemire, A. (1992). Sleep disorders in the medically ill patient. *Journal of Clinical Psychiatry, 53*(6, Suppl.), 29–36. [4]
Morgan, C., Chapar, G. N., & Fisher, M. (1995). Psychosocial variables associated with teenage pregnancy. *Adolescence, 118,* 277–289. [10]
Morgan, C. D., & Murray, H. A. (1935). A method for investigating fantasies: The Thematic Apperception Test. *Archives of Neurology and Psychiatry, 34,* 289–306. [14]
Morgan, C. D., & Murray, H. A. (1962). Thematic Apperception Test. 530–545. In H. A. Murray et al. (Eds.), *Explorations in personality: A clinical and experimental study of fifty men of college age.* New York: Science Editions. [14]
Morgan, C. L. (1996). Odors as cues for the recall of words unrelated to odor. *Perceptual and Motor Skills, 83,* 1227–1234. [6]
Morgan, M. J. (1999). Memory deficits associated with recreational use of ecstasy (MDMA). *Psychopharmacology, 141,* 30–36. [4]
Morgan, R. E., Levitsky, D. A., & Strupp, B. J. (2000). Effects of chronic lead exposure on learning and reaction time in a visual discrimination task. *Neurotoxicology and Teratology, 22,* 337–345. [8]

Morin, C. M., & Wooten, V. (1996). Psychological and pharmacological approaches to treating insomnia: Critical issues in assessing their separate and combined effects. *Clinical Psychology Review, 16,* 521–542. [4]

Morley, J. E., & van den Berg, L. (Eds.). (2000). *Contemporary endocrinology* (No. 20). Totowa, NJ: Humana Press. [10]

Morris, J. S., Frith, C. D., Perrett, D. I., Rowland, D., Young, A. W., Calder, A. J., & Dolan, R. J. (1996). A differential neural response in the human amygdala to fearful and happy facial expressions. *Nature, 383,* 812–815. [2]

Morrison, A. M., & Von Glinow, M. S. (1990). Women and minorities in management. *American Psychologist, 45,* 200–208. [17]

Morrow, B. A., Roth, R. H., & Elsworth, J. D. (2000). TMT, a predator odor, elevates mesoprefrontal dopamine metabolic activity and disrupts short-term working memory in the rat. *Brain Research Bulletin, 52,* 519–523. [6]

Mościcki, E. K. (1995). Epidemiology of suicidal behavior. *Suicide and Life-Threatening Behavior, 25,* 22–31. [15]

Moscovitch, M., Behrmann, M., & Winocur, G. (1994). Do PETS have long or short ears? Mental imagery and neuroimaging. *Trends in Neurosciences, 17,* 292–294. [7]

Moser, D., & Dracup, K. (1996). Is anxiety early after myocardial infarction associated with subsequent ischemic and arrhythmic events? *Psychosomatic Medicine, 58,* 395–401. [13]

Motley, M. T. (1985). Slips of the tongue. *Scientific American, 253,* 116–127. [14]

Mourtazaev, M. S., Kemp, B., Zwinderman, A. H., & Kamphuisen, H. A. C. (1995). Age and gender affect different characteristics of slow waves in the sleep EEG. *Sleep, 18,* 557–564. [4]

Mui, A. C. (1992). Caregiver strain among black and white daughter caregivers: A role theory perspective. *The Gerontologist, 32,* 203–212. [10]

Mukerjee, M. (1997). Trends in animal research. *Scientific American, 276,* 86–93. [1]

Munroe, R. H., Shimmin, H. S., & Munroe, R. L. (1984). Gender role understanding and sex role preference in four cultures. *Developmental Psychology, 20,* 673–682. [12]

Muris, R., Steerneman, P., Merckelbach, H., & Meesters, C. (1996). The role of parental fearfulness and modeling in children's fear. *Behaviour Research and Therapy, 34,* 265–268. [5]

Murphy, E. (1989, July 13–27). Townshend. Tinnitus and rock & roll. *Rolling Stone,* pp. 101. [3]

Murray, D. W. (1995, July/August). Toward a science of desire. *The Sciences, 35,* 244–249 . [2]

Murray, H. (1938). *Explorations in personality.* New York: Oxford University Press. [11, 14]

Murray, H. A. (1965). Uses of the Thematic Apperception Test. In B. I. Murstein (Ed.), *Handbook of projective techniques* (pp. 425–432). New York: Basic Books. [14]

Murray, S. L., Holmes, J. G., & Griffin, D. W. (1996a). The benefits of positive illusions: Idealization and the construction of satisfaction in close relationships. *Journal of Personality and Social Psychology, 70*(1), 79–98. [10]

Murray, S. L., Holmes, J. G., & Griffin, D. W. (1996b). The self-fulfilling nature of positive illusions in romantic relationships: Love is not blind, but prescient. *Journal of Personality and Social Psychology 71*(6), 1155–1180. [10]

Mussen, P. H., & Jones, M. C. (1957). Self-conceptions, motivations, and interpersonal attitudes of late- and early-maturing boys. *Child Development, 28,* 243–256. [10]

Myers, D. A. (1992). *The pursuit of happiness: Discovering the pathway to fulfillment, well-being, and enduring personal joy.* New York: Avon. [11, 14]

Myers, D. G., & Bishop, G. D. (1970). Discussion effects on racial attitudes. *Science, 169,* 778–779. [17]

Myers, D. G., & Lamm, H. (1975). The polarizing effect of group discussion. *American Scientist, 63,* 297–303. [17]

Nader, K., Schafe, G. E., & Le Doux, J. E. (2000). Fear memories require protein synthesis in the amygdala for reconsolidation after retrieval. *Nature, 406,* 722–726. [6]

Nadon, R., Hoyt, I. P., Register, P. A., & Kilstrom, J. F. (1991). Absorption and hypnotizability: Context effects reexamined. *Journal of Personality and Social Psychology, 60,* 144–153. [4]

Naglieri, J. A., & Ronning, M. E. (2000). Comparison of White, African American, Hispanic, and Asian children on the Naglieri Nonverbal Ability Test. *Psychological Assessment, 12,* 328–334. [8]

Narrow, W. E., Regier, D. A., Rae, D. S., Manderscheid, R. W., & Locke, B. Z. (1993). Use of services by persons with mental and addictive disorders: Findings from the National Institute of Mental Health Epidemiologic Catchment Area Program. *Archives of General Psychiatry, 50,* 95–107. [15]

Nash, J. M. (1997, March 24). Gift of love. *Time,* pp. 80–82. [10]

Nash, M. (1987). What, if anything, is regressed about hypnotic age regression? A review of the empirical literature. *Psychological Bulletin, 102,* 42–52. [4]

Nash, M. R. (1991). Hypnosis as a special case of psychological regression. In S. J. Lynn & J. W. Rhue (Eds.), *Theories of hypnosis: Current models and perspectives* (pp. 171–194). New York: Guilford. [4]

Nash, M., & Baker, E. (1984, February). Trance encounters: Susceptibility to hypnosis. *Psychology Today,* pp. 18, 72–73. [4]

Nathan, P. E. (1992). Peele hasn't done his homework—again: A response to "Alcoholism, politics, and bureaucracy: The consensus against controlled-drinking therapy in America." *Addictive Behaviors, 17,* 63–65. [13]

Nathans, J. (1989). The genes for color vision. *Scientific American, 260,* 42–49. [3]

Nathans, J., Davenport, C. M., Maumenee, I. H., Lewis, R. A., Heitmancik, J. F., Litt, M., Lovrien, E., Weleber, R., Bachynski, B., Zwas, F., Klingaman, R., & Fishman, G. (1989). Molecular genetics of human blue cone monochromacy. *Science, 245,* 831–838. [3]

National Advisory Mental Health Council. (1995). Basic behavioral science research for mental health. *American Psychologist, 50,* 838–845. [11]

National Center for Health Statistics. (2000, June 23). Gonorrhea—United States, 1998. *MMWR Weekly, 49,* 538–542. [12]

National Center for Health Statistics. (2000). *Health, United States, 2000 with adolescent health chartbook* [On-line]. Available: http://www.cdc.gov/nchs/products/pubs/pubd/hus/hestatus.htm [9, 13]

National Institute of Mental Health. (1999a). Does this sound like you? [On-line]. Available: http://www.nimh.nih.gov/soundlikeyou.htm [15]

National Institute of Mental Health. (1999b). Facts about obsessive-compulsive disorder [On-line]. Available: http://www.nimh.nih.gov/anxiety/ocdfacts.cfm [15]

National Institute of Mental Health. (1999c). The invisible disease—depression [On-line]. Available: http://www.nimh.nih.gov/publicat/invisible.cfm [15]

National Institute of Mental Health. (2000). Bipolar disorder research at the National Institute of Mental Health: Fact sheet [On-line]. Available: http://www.nimh.nih.gov/publicat/bipolarresfact.cfm [15]

National Institute of Neurological Disorders and Stroke rt-PA Stroke Study Group. (1995). Tissue plasminogen activator for acute ischemic stroke. *New England Journal of Medicine, 333,* 1581–1587. [2]

National Research Council. (1993). *Losing generations: Adolescents in high risk settings.* Washington, DC: National Academy Press. [10]

National Safety Council. (1997). Accident facts. Chicago: Author. [13]

NBC Olympics. (1999). Jennifer Johnson Jordan. *Athlete Bios* [On-line]. Available: www.nbcolympics.com [10]

Nestadt, G., Samuels, J., Riddle, M., Bienvenu, O. J., III, Liang, K.-Y., LaBuda, M., Walkup, J., Grados, M., & Hoehn-Saric, R. (2000). A family study of obsessive-compulsive disorder. *Archives of General Psychiatry, 57,* 358–363. [15]

Needleman, H. L., Riess, J. A., Tobin, M. J., Biesecker, G. E., & Greenhouse, J. B. (1996). Bone lead levels and delinquent behavior. *Journal of the American Medical Association, 275,* 363–369. [17]

Neimark, E. (1975). Intellectual development during adolescence. In F. Horowitz (Ed.), *Review of child development research* (Vol. 4). Chicago: University of Chicago Press. [10]

Neimark, E. D. (1981). Confounding with cognitive style factors: An artifact explanation for the apparent nonuniversal incidence of formal operations. In I. Sigel, D. Brodzinsky, & R. Golinkoff (Eds.), *New directions in Piagetian research and theory.* Hillsdale, NJ: Erlbaum. [9]

Neimark, J., Conway, C., & Doskoch, P. (1994, September/October). Back from the drink. *Psychology Today,* pp. 46–53. [13]

Neisser, U. (1967). *Cognitive psychology.* New York: Appleton-Century-Crofts. [6]

Neisser, U., & Harsch, N. (1992). Phantom flashbulbs: False recollections of hearing the news about Challenger. In E. Winograd & U. Neisser (Eds.), *Affect and accuracy in recall: Studies of "flashbulb" memories* (pp. 9–31). New York: Cambridge University Press. [6]

Neisser, U., Boodoo, G., Bouchard, T. J., Jr., Boykin, A. W., Brody, N., Ceci, S. J., Halpern, D. F., Loehlin, J. C., Perloff, R., Sternberg, R. J., & Urbina, S. (1996). Intelligence: Knowns and unknowns. *American Psychologist, 51,* 77–101. [8]

Neitz, J., Neitz, M., & Kainz, M. (1996). Visual pigment gene structure and the severity of color vision defects. *Science, 274,* 801–804. [3]

Neitz, M., & Neitz, J. (1995). Numbers and ratios of visual pigment genes for normal red-green color vision. *Science, 267,* 1013–1016. [3]

Nelson, J. C. (1991). Current status of tricyclic antidepressants in psychiatry: Their pharmacology and clinical applications. *Journal of Clinical Psychiatry, 52,* 193–200. [16]

Nelson, J. C. (1997). Safety and tolerability of the new antidepressants. *Journal of Clinical Psychiatry, 58*(6, Suppl.), 26–31. [16]

Nelson, K. (1973). Structure and strategy in learning to talk. *Monographs of the Society for Research in Child Development, 38*(1–2, Serial No. 149). [9]

Nelson, M. D., Saykin, A. J., Flashman, L. A., & Riordan, H. J. (1998). Hippocampal volume reduction in schizophrenia as assessed by magnetic resonance imaging: A meta-analytic study. *Archives of General Psychiatry, 55,* 433–440. [15]

Nelson, W. L., Hughes, H. M., Katz, B., & Searight, H. R. (1999). Anorexic eating attitudes and behaviors of male and female college students. *Adolescence, 34,* 621–633. [11]

Neugarten, B. L. (1968). The awareness of middle age. In B. Neugarten (Ed.), *Middle age and aging* (pp. 93–98). Chicago: University of Chicago Press. [10]

Neugarten, B. L. (1982). Must everything be a midlife crisis? In T. H. Carr & H. E. Fitzgerald (Eds.), *Human development 82/83* (pp. 162–163). (Reprinted from *Prime Time,* February 1980, 45–48). Guilford, CT: Dushkin. [10]

Neumann, Y., Finaly, E., & Reichel, A. (1988). Achievement motivation factors and students' college outcomes. *Psychological Reports, 62,* 555–560. [11]

Neville, H. J., Bavelier, D., Corina, D., Rauschecker, J., Karni, A., Lalwani, A., Braun, A., Clark, V., Jezzard, P., & Turner, R. (1998). Cerebral organization for language in deaf and hearing subjects: Biological constraints and effects of experience. *Proceedings of the National Academy of Sciences, 95,* 922–929. [2]

Newcomb, A. F., Bukowski, W. M., & Pattee, L. (1993). Children's peer relations: A meta-analytic review of popular, rejected, neglected, controversial, and average sociometric status. *Psychological Bulletin, 113,* 99–128. [9]

Newcomb, M. D. (1997). Psychosocial predictors and consequences of drug use: A developmental perspective within a prospective study. *Journal of Addictive Diseases, 16,* 51–89. [4]

Newcomb, T. M. (1956). The prediction of interpersonal attraction. *American Psychologist, 11,* 575–587. [17]

Newell, A., & Simon, H. A. (1972). *Human problem solving.* Englewood Cliffs, NJ: Prentice-Hall. [7]

Newman, M., & Kaszniak, A. (2000). Spatial memory and aging: Performance on a human analog of the Morris Water Maze. *Aging, Neuropsychology, and Cognition, 7,* 86–93. [10]

Ng, S. H. (1990). Androcentric coding of *man* and *his* in memory by language users. *Journal of Experimental Social Psychology, 26,* 455–464. [7]

Ng, S. K. C., Hauser, W. A., Brust, J. C. M., & Susser, M. (1988). Alcohol consumption and withdrawal in new onset seizures. *New England Journal of Medicine, 319,* 665–672. [13]

Nguyen, P. V., Abel, T., & Kandel, E. R. (1994). Requirement of a critical period of transcription for induction of a late phase of LTP. *Science, 265,* 1104–1107. [6]

Ni, W., Constable, R. T., Menci, W. E., Pugh, K. R., Fulbright, R. K., & Shaywitz, S. E. (2000). An event-related neuroimaging study distinguishing form and content in sentence processing. *Journal of Cognitive Neuroscience, 12,* 120–133. [7]

Nicholl, C. S., & Russell, R. M. (1990). Analysis of animal rights literature reveals the underlying motives of the movement: Ammunition for counter offensive by scientists. *Endocrinology, 127,* 985–989. [1]

Nickerson, R. S., & Adams, M. J. (1979). Long-term memory for a common object. *Cognitive Psychology, 11,* 287–307. [6]

Nicol, S. E., & Gottesman, I. I. (1983). Clues to the genetics and neurobiology of schizophrenia. *American Scientist, 71,* 398–404. [15]

Nicotine dependence—Part I. (1997, May). *Harvard Mental Health Letter, 13*(11), 1–4. [4]

Nisbett, R. E., & Wilson, T. D. (1977). The halo effect: Evidence for unconscious alteration of judgments. *Journal of Personality and Social Psychology, 35,* 250–256. [17]

Nishimura, H., Hashikawa, K., Doi, K., Iwaki, T., Watanabe, Y., Kusuoka, H., Nishimura, T., & Kubo, T. (1999). Sign language "heard" in the auditory cortex. *Nature, 397,* 116. [2]

Niskar, A. S., Kieszak, S. M., Holmes, A., Esteban, E., Rubin, C., & Brody, D. J. (1998). Prevalence of hearing loss among children 6 to 19 years of age: The Third National Health and Nutrition Examination Survey. *Journal of the American Medical Association, 279,* 1071–1075. [3]

Nogrady, H., McConkey, K. M., & Perry, C. (1985). Enhancing visual memory: Trying hypnosis, trying imagination, and trying again. *Journal of Abnormal Psychology, 94,* 195–204. [4, 6]

Norcross, J. C., Prochaska, J. O., & Gallagher, K. M. (1989). Clinical psychologists in the 1980s: II. Theory, research, and practice. *Clinical Psychologist, 42,* 45–52. [16]

Nordström, P., Samuelsson, M., Åsberg, M., Träskman-Bendz, L., Åberg-Wistedt, A., Nordin, C., & Bertilsson, L. (1994). CSF 5-HIAA predicts suicide risk after attempted suicide. *Suicide and Life-Threatening Behavior, 24,* 1–9. [2]

Norris, F. H., & Kaniasty, K. (1996). Received and perceived social support in times of stress: A test of the social support deterioration deterrence model. *Journal of Personality and Social Psychology, 71,* 498–511. [13]

Norris, J. E., & Tindale, J. A. (1994). *Among generations: The cycle of adult relationships.* New York: Freeman. [10]

Novello, A. C. (1990). The Surgeon General's 1990 report on the health benefits of smoking cessation: Executive summary. *Morbidity and Mortality Weekly Report, 39* (No. RR–12). [4, 13]

Nowak, M. A., & McMichael, A. J. (1995). How HIV defeats the immune system. *Scientific American, 273,* 58–65. [12]

Noyes, R., Jr., Burrows, G. D., Reich, J. H., Judd, F. K., Garvey, M. J., Norman, T. R., Cook, B. L., & Marriott, P. (1996). Diazepam versus alprazolam for the treatment of panic disorder. *Journal of Clinical Psychiatry, 57,* 344–355. [16]

Noyes, R., Jr., Garvey, M. J., Cook, B. L., & Samuelson, L. (1989). Problems with tricyclic antidepressant use in patients with panic disorder or agoraphobia: Results of a naturalistic follow-up study. *Journal of Clinical Psychiatry, 50,* 163–169. [16]

Nutt, D. (2000). Treatment of depression and concomitant anxiety. *European Neuropsychopharmacology, 10* (Suppl. 4), S433–S437. [16]

Nutt, D. J., Lalies, M. D., Lione, L. A., & Hudson, A. L. (1997). Noradrenergic mechanisms in the prefrontal cortex. *Journal of Psychopharmacology, 11,* 163–168. [4]

Oatley, K., & Jenkins, J. M. (1992). Human emotions: Function and dysfunction. *Annual Review of Psychology, 43,* 55–85. [11]

O'Brien, C. P. (1996). Recent developments in the pharmacotherapy of substance abuse. *Journal of Consulting and Clinical Psychology, 64,* 677–686. [4]

O'Brien, E. (1996, May 30). Family Gallup has its hands on the pulse of America. *St. Louis Post-Dispatch,* p. 3G. [1]

Ochs, R. (1994, January 11). Cervical cancer comeback. *New York Newsday,* pp. 55, 57. [12]

Ochsner, K. N., & Kosslyn, S. M. (1994). Mental imagery. In V. S. Ramachandran (Ed.), *Encyclopedia of human behavior.* San Diego, CA: Academic. [7]

O'Connor, T. G., Rutter, M., Beckett, C., Keaveney, L., & Kreppner, J. M. (2000). The effects of global severe privation on cognitive competence: Extension and longitudinal follow-up. English and Romanian Adoptees Study Team. *Child Development, 71,* 376–390. [9]

O'Donohue, W., & Plaud, J. J. (1994). The conditioning of human sexual arousal. *Archives of Sexual Behavior, 23,* 321–344. [6, 12]

O'Heron, C. A., & Orlofsky, J. L. (1990). Stereotypic and non-stereotypic sex role trait and behavior orientations, gender identity, and psychological adjustment. *Journal of Personality and Social Psychology, 58,* 134–143. [12]

Ohzawa, I., DeAngelis, G. C., & Freeman, R. D. (1990). Stereoscopic depth discrimination in the visual cortex: Neurons ideally suited as disparity detectors. *Science,* 249, 1037–1041. [3]

Okazaki, S., & Sue, S. (2000). Implications of test revisions for assessment with Asian Americans. *Psychological Assessment, 12,* 272–280. [8]

Olds, D. L., Henderson, C. R., & Tatelbaum, R. (1994). Intellectual impairment in children of women who smoke cigarettes during pregnancy. *Pediatrics, 93,* 221–227. [9]

Olds, J. (1956). Pleasure centers in the brain. *Scientific American, 195,* 105–116. [2]

O'Leary, K. D., & Smith, D. A. (1991). Marital interactions. *Annual Review of Psychology, 42,* 191–212. [17]

Oliner, S. P., & Oliner P. M. (1988). *The altruistic personality: Rescuers of Jews in Nazi Europe.* New York: Free Press. [17]

Oliver, J. E. (1993). Intergenerational transmission of child abuse: Rates, research, and clinical implications. *American Journal of Psychiatry, 150,* 1315–1324. [17]

Oliver, M. B., & Hyde, J. S. (1993). Gender differences in sexuality: A meta-analysis. *Psychological Bulletin, 114,* 29–51. [12]

Omori, Y., & Miyata, Y. (1996). Eyeblinks in formation of impressions. *Perceptual and Motor Skills, 83,* 591–594. [17]

O'Neil, H. (2000, September 28). A perfect witness. *St. Louis Post-Dispatch,* p. A8. [6]

OnHealth WebMD. (2000, October). Eat twice as well, not twice as much. *OnHealth* [On-line]. Available: [9]

Orne, M. (1983, December 12). Hypnosis "useful in medicine, dangerous in court." *U.S. News & World Report,* pp. 67–68. [4]

Öst, L-G., & Westling, B. E. (1995). Applied relaxation vs. cognitive behavior therapy in the treatment of panic disorder. *Behavior Research and Therapy, 33,* 145–158. [16]

Ostrom, T. M., Carpenter, S. L., Sedikides, C., & Li, F. (1993). Differential processing of in-group and out-group information. *Journal of Personality and Social Psychology, 64,* 21–34. [17]

Otake, S., Gowdy, P. D., & Cicerone, C. M. (2000). The spatial arrangement of L and M cones in the peripheral human retina. *Vision Research, 40,* 677–693. [3]

Otto, M. W., Pollack, M. H., Sachs, G. S., Reiter, S. R., Meltzer-Brody, S., & Rosenbaum, J. F. (1993). Discontinuation of benzodiazepine treatment: Efficacy of cognitive-behavioral therapy for patients with panic disorder. *American Journal of Psychiatry, 150,* 1485–1490. [16]

Overmeier, J. B., & Seligman, M. E. P. (1967). Effects of inescapable shock upon subsequent escape and avoidance responding. *Journal of Comparative and Physiological Psychology, 67,* 28–33. [5]

Owens, J., Maxim, R., McGuinn, M., Nobile, C., Msall, M., & Alario, A. (2000). Television-viewing habits and sleep disturbance in school children. *Pediatrics, 104*(3), 27. [9]

Padian, N. S. et al. (1991). Female-to-male transmission of human immunodeficiency virus. *Journal of the American Medical Association, 266,* 1664–1667. [12]

Paikoff, R. L., & Brooks-Gunn, J. (1991). Do parent-child relationships change during puberty? *Psychological Bulletin, 110,* 47–66. [10]

Paivio, S. C., & Greenberg, L. S. (1995). Resolving "unfinished business": Efficacy of experiential therapy using empty-chair dialogue. *Journal of Consulting and Clinical Psychology, 63,* 419–425. [16]

Panksepp, J. (1992). A critical role for "affective neuroscience" in resolving what is basic about basic emotions. *Psychological Review, 99,* 554–560. [11]

Pappas, T. N., Melendez, R. L., & Debas, H. T. (1989). Gastric distension is a physiologic satiety signal in the dog. *Digestive Diseases and Sciences, 34,* 1489–1493. [11]

Park, K. A., & Waters, E. (1989). Security of attachment and preschool friendships. *Child Development, 60,* 1076–1081. [9]

Parke, R. D. (1977). Some effects of punishment on children's behavior–revisited. In E. M. Hetherington, E. M. Ross, & R. D. Parke (Eds.), *Contemporary readings in child psychology.* New York: McGraw-Hill. [5]

Parke, R. D., O'Leary, S. E., & West, S. (1972). Mother-father-newborn interaction: Effects of maternal mediation, labor and sex of infant. *Proceedings of the American Psychological Association, 7,* 85–86. [9]

Parker, J. G., & Asher, S. R. (1987). Peer relations and later personal adjustment: Are low-accepted children at risk? *Psychological Bulletin, 102,* 357–389. [9]

Parkinson, W. L., & Weingarten, H. P. (1990). Dissociative analysis of ventromedial hypothalamic obesity syndrome. *American Journal of Physiology, 259,* 829–835. [11]

Partinen, M. (1994). Epidemiology of sleep disorders. In M. Kryger, T. Roth, & W. C. Dement (Eds.), *Principles and practice of sleep medicine* (pp. 437–453). Philadelphia: W.B. Saunders. [4]

Partinen, M., Hublin, C., Kaprio, J., Koskenvuo, M., & Guilleminault, C. (1994). Twin studies in narcolepsy. *Sleep, 17,* S13–S16. [4]

Pascual-Leone, A., Dhuna, A., Altafullah, I., & Anderson, D. C. (1990). Cocaine-induced seizures. *Neurology, 40,* 404–407. [4]

Pastore, N. (1950). The role of arbitrariness in the frustration-aggression hypothesis. *Journal of Abnormal and Social Psychology, 47,* 728–731. [17]

Patterson, C. J. (1995). Sexual orientation and human development: An overview. *Developmental Psychology, 31,* 3–11. [12]

Patterson, D. R., & Ptacek, J. T. (1997). Baseline pain as a moderator of hypnotic analgesia for burn injury treatment. *Journal of Consulting and Clinical Psychology, 65,* 60–67. [4]

Pattison, E. M. (1982). The concept of alcoholism as a syndrome. In E. M. Pattison (Ed.), *Selection of treatment for alcoholics.* New Brunswick, NJ: Rutgers Center of Alcohol Studies. [13]

Paul, W. E. (1993). Infectious diseases and the immune system. *Scientific American, 269,* 90–99. [13]

Paulesu, E., McCrory, E., Fazio, L., Menoncello, N., Brunswick, N., Cappa, S. F., et al. (2000). A cultural effect on brain function. *Nature Neuroscience, 3,* 91–96. [7]

Paulus, P. B., Cox, V. C., & McCain, G. (1988). *Prison crowding: A psychological perspective.* New York: Springer-Verlag. [17]

Paunonen, S. V., & Jackson, D. N. (2000). What is beyond the big five? Plenty! *Journal of Personality, 68,* 821–835. [14]

Paunonen, S. V., Keinonen, M., Trzebinski, J., Forsterling, F., Grishenko-Roze, N., Kouznetsova, L., & Chan, D. W. (1996). The structure of personality in six cultures. *Journal of Cross-Cultural Psychology, 27,* 339–353. [14]

Pause, B. M., & Krauel, K. (2000). Chemosensory event-related potentials (CSERP) as a key to the psychology of odors. *International Journal of Psychophysiology, 36,* 105–122. [3]

Pavlov, I. P. (1960). *Conditioned reflexes: An investigation of the physiological activity of the cerebral cortex* (G. V. Anrep, Trans.). New York: Dover. (Original translation published 1927). [5]

Pedersen, D. M., & Wheeler, J. (1983). The Müller-Lyer illusion among Navajos. *Journal of Social Psychology, 121,* 3–6. [3]

Pederson, D. R., Moran, G., Sitko, C., Campbell, K., Ghesquire, K., & Acton, H. (1990). Maternal sensitivity and the security of infant-mother attachment: A Q-sort study. *Child Development, 61,* 1974–1983. [9]

Peek-Asa, C. (2001). Workplace violence in municipal occupations. *Occupational Medicine, 16,* 109–123. [17]

Peele, S. (1984). The cultural context of psychological approaches to alcoholism: Can we control the effects of alcohol? *American Psychologist, 39,* 1337–1351. [4]

Peele, S. (1992). Alcoholism, politics, and bureaucracy: The consensus against controlled-drinking therapy in America. *Addictive Behaviors, 17,* 49–62. [13]

Pelletier, L. G., & Vallerand, R. J. (1996). Supervisors' beliefs and subordinates' intrinsic motivation: A behavioral confirmation analysis. *Journal of Personality and Social Psychology, 71,* 231–240. [11]

Pen, C. L., Levy, E., Ravily, V., Beuzen, J. N., & Meurgey, F. (1994). The cost of treatment dropout in depression: A cost-benefit analysis of fluoxetine vs. tricyclics. *Journal of Affective Disorders, 31,* 1–18. [16]

Penfield, W. (1969). Consciousness, memory, and man's conditioned reflexes. In K. Pribram (Ed.), *On the biology of learning* (pp. 129–168). New York: Harcourt Brace Jovanovich. [6]

Penfield, W. (1975). *The mystery of the mind: A critical study of consciousness and the human brain.* Princeton, NJ: Princeton University Press. [6]

Penn, F. (1993, October 21). Cancer confusion: The risks and realities of human papilloma virus. *Manhattan Spirit,* pp. 14–15. [12]

Pennisi, E. (1997). Tracing molecules that make the brain-body connection. *Science, 275,* 930–931. [13]

Pepper, M. (1997). Road rage [On-line]. Available: http://www.drivers.com/cgi-bin [17]

Pepperberg, I. M. (1991, Spring). Referential communication with an African grey parrot. *Harvard Graduate Society Newsletter,* 1–4. [7]

Pepperberg, I. M. (1994a). Numerical competence in an African gray parrot (*Psittacus erithacus*). *Journal of Comparative Psychology, 108,* 36–44. [7]

Pepperberg, I. M. (1994b). Vocal learning in grey parrots (*Psittacus erithacus*): Effects of social interaction, reference, and context. *The Auk, 111,* 300–314 . [7]

Perls, F. S. (1969). *Gestalt therapy verbatim.* Lafayette, CA: Real People Press. [16]

Perls, T. T. (1995). The oldest old. *Scientific American, 272,* 70–75. [10]

Perrett, D. I., May, K. A., & Yoshikawa, S. (1994). Facial shape and judgements of female attractiveness. *Nature, 368,* 239–242. [17]

Pert, C. B., Snowman, A. M., & Snyder, S. H. (1974). Localization of opiate receptor binding in presynaptic membranes of rat brain. *Brain Research, 70,* 184–188. [2]

Perusse, L., Chagnon, Y. C., Weisnagel, J., & Bouchard, C. (1999). The human obesity gene map: The 1998 update. *Obesity Research, 7,* 111–129. [11]

Peskind, E. R. (1996). Neurobiology of Alzheimer's disease. *Journal of Clinical Psychiatry, 57*(14, Suppl.), 5–8. [10]

Peter, J. B., Bryson, Y., & Lovett, M. A. (1982, March/April). Genital herpes: Urgent questions, elusive answers. *Diagnostic Medicine,* pp. 71–74, 76–88. [12]

Peters, A., Leahu, D., Moss, M. B., & McNally, J. (1994). The effects of aging on area 46 of the frontal cortex of the rhesus monkey. *Cerebral Cortex, 6,* 621–635. [10]

Peterson, A. C. (1987, September). Those gangly years. *Psychology Today,* pp. 28–34. [10]

Peterson, A. C. (1988). Adolescent development. *Annual Review of Psychology, 39,* 583–607. [10]

Peterson, A. C., Compas, B. E., Brooks-Gunn, J., Stemmier, M., Ey, S., & Grant, K. E. (1993). Depression in adolescence. *American Psychologist, 48,* 155–168. [15]

Peterson, I. (1993). Speech for export: Automating the translation of spoken words. *Science News,* 144, 254–255 [7

Peterson, L. R., & Peterson, M. J. (1959). Short-term retention of individual verbal items. *Journal of Experimental Psychology, 58,* 193–198. [6]

Petitto, L. A., & Marentette, P. R. (1991). Babbling in the manual mode: Evidence for the ontogeny of language. *Science, 251,* 1493–1496. [9]

Petri, H. L. (1996). *Motivation: Theory, research, and applications* (4th ed.). Pacific Grove, CA: Brooks/Cole. [11]

Pettigrew, T. E. (1997). Generalized intergroup contact effects on prejudice. *Personality and Social Psychology Bulletin, 23,* 175–185. [17]

Petty, R. E., Wegener, D. T., & Fabrigar, L. R. (1997). Attitudes and attitude change. *Annual Review of Psychology, 48,* 609–647. [17]

Phillips, G. P., & Over, R. (1992). Adult sexual orientation in relation to memories of childhood gender conforming and gender nonconforming behaviors. *Archives of Sexual Behavior, 21,* 543–558. [12]

Phillips, G. P., & Over, R. (1995). Differences between heterosexual, bisexual, and lesbian women in recalled childhood experiences. *Archives of Sexual Behavior, 24,* 1–20. [12]

Phillips, K., Fulker, D. W., Carey, G., & Nagoshi, C. T. (1988). Direct marital assortment for cognitive and personality variables. *Behavioral Genetics, 18,* 347–356. [17]

Phillips, S. D., & Blustein, D. L. (1994). Readiness for career choices: Planning, exploring, and deciding. *The Career Development Quarterly, 43,* 63–75. [10]

Phillips, S. T., & Ziller, R. C. (1997). Toward a theory and measure of the nature of nonprejudice. *Journal of Personality and Social Psychology, 72,* 420–434. [17]

Piaget, J. (1960). *The child's conception of physical causality.* Patterson, NJ: Littlefield, Adams. [9]

Piaget, J. (1963a). *The child's conception of the world.* Patterson, NJ: Littlefield, Adams. [9]

Piaget, J. (1963b). *Psychology of intelligence.* Patterson, NJ: Littlefield, Adams. [9]

Piaget, J. (1964). *Judgment and reasoning in the child.* Patterson, NJ: Littlefield, Adams. [9]

Piaget, J. (1972). Intellectual evolution from adolescence to adulthood. *Human Development, 15,* 1–12. [10]

Piaget, J., & Inhelder, B. (1969). *The psychology of the child.* New York: Basic Books. [9, 10]

Pich, E. M., Pagliusi, S. R., Tessari, M., Talabot-Ayer, D., van Huijsduijnen, R. H., & Chiamulera, C. (1997). Common neural substrates for the addictive properties of nicotine and cocaine. *Science, 275,* 83–86. [4]

Pierrehumbert, B., Miljkovitch, R., Plancherel, B., Halfon, O., & Ansermet, F. (2000). Attachment and temperament in early childhood: Implications for later behavior problems. *Infant and Child Development, 9,* 17–32. [9]

Pigott, T. A. (1996). OCD: Where the serotonin selectivity story begins. *Journal of Clinical Psychiatry, 57*(6, Suppl.), 11–20. [15]

Pihl, R. O., Lau, M. L., & Assaad, J-M. (1997). Aggressive disposition, alcohol, and aggression. *Aggressive Behavior, 23,* 11–18. [4]

Pilcher, J. J., & Huffcutt, A. I. (1996). Effects of sleep deprivation on performance: A meta-analysis. *Sleep, 19,* 318–326. [4]

Pilcher, J. J., Lambert, B. J., & Huffcutt, A. I. (2000). Differential effects of permanent and rotating shifts on self-report sleep length: A meta-analytic review. *Sleep, 23,* 155–163. [4]

Pillemer, D. B. (1990). Clarifying the flashbulb memory concept: Comment on McCloskey, Wible, and Cohen (1988). *Journal of Experimental Psychology: General, 119,* 92–96. [6]

Pillow, D. R., Zautra, A. J., & Sandler, I. (1996). Major life events and minor stressors: Identifying mediational links in the stress process. *Journal of Personality and Social Psychology, 70,* 381–394. [13]

Pilowsky, T., Yirmiya, N., Arbelle, S., & Mozes, T. (2000). Theory of mind abilities of children with schizophrenia, children with autism, and normally developing children. *Schizophrenia Research, 42,* 2145–2155. [9]

Pinel, J. P. L. (2000). *Biopsychology* (4th ed.). Boston: Allyn & Bacon. [2]

Pinker, S. (1994). *The language instinct: How the mind creates language.* New York: Morrow. [7]

Pinquart, M., & Sörensen, S. (2000). Influences of socioeconomic status, social network, and competence on subjective well-being in later life: A meta-analysis. *Psychology and Aging, 15,* 187–224. [10]

Piot, P., & Islam, M. Q. (1994). Sexually transmitted diseases in the 1990s: Global epidemiology and challanges for control. *Sexually Transmitted Diseases, 21*(2, Suppl.), S7–S13. [12]

Pittenger, D. J. (1993). The utility of the Myers-Briggs Type Indicator. *Review of Educational Research, 63,* 467–488. [14]

Pitz, G. F., & Sachs, N. J. (1984). Judgment and decision: Theory and application. *Annual Review of Psychology, 35,* 139–163. [7]

Platt, R., Rice, P. A., & McCormack, W. M. (1983). Risk of acquiring gonorrhea and prevalence of abnormal adnexal findings among women recently exposed to gonorrhea. *Journal of the American Medical Association, 250,* 3205–3209. [12]

Plomin, R. (1989). Environment and genes: Determinants of behavior. *American Psychologist, 44,* 105–111. [8, 14]

Plomin, R. (1999). Genetics and general cognitive ability. *Nature, 402*(Suppl.), C25–C29. [8]

Plomin, R., & Dale, P. S. (2000). Genetics and early language development: A UK study of twins. In D. V. M. Bishop & L. B. Leonard (Eds.), *Speech and language impairment in children: Causes, characteristics, intervention and outcome.* Oxford: Oxford University Press. [8]

Plomin, R., & Daniels, D. (1987). Why are children in the same family so different from one another? *Behavioral and Brain Sciences, 10,* 1–60. [14]

Plomin, R., & Rende, R. (1991). Human behavioral genetics. *Annual Review of Psychology, 42,* 161–190. [8, 14]

Plomin, R., Chipuer, H. M., & Loehlin, J. C. (1990). Behavior genetics and personality. In L. A. Pervin (Ed.), *Handbook of personality theory and research* (pp. 225–243). New York: Guilford. [8, 9]

Plomin, R., DeFries, J. C., & Fulker, D. W. (1988). *Nature and nurture during infancy and early childhood.* New York: Cambridge University Press. [8]

Plomin, R., DeFries, J. C., McClearn, G. E., & Rutter, M. (1997). *Behavioral genetics* (3rd ed.). New York: Freeman. [8]

Plomin, R., Owen, M. J., & McGuffin, P. (1994). The genetic basis of complex human behaviors. *Science, 264,* 1733–1739. [8, 9, 14]

Plous, S. (1996). Attitudes toward the use of animals in psychological research and education: Results from a national survey of psychologists. *American Psychologist, 51,* 1167–1180. [1]

Plummer, D. L., & Slane S. (1996). Patterns of coping in racially stressful situations. *Journal of Black Psychology, 22,* 302–315. [13]

Polich, J. M., Armor, D. J., & Braiker, H. B. (1981). *The course of alcoholism: Four years after treatment.* New York: Wiley. [13]

Pollack, H., Lantz, P. M., & Frohna, J. G. (2000). Maternal smoking and adverse birth outcomes among singletons and twins. *American Journal of Public Health, 90,* 395–400. [9]

Pollack, M. H., & Otto, M. W. (1997). Long-term course and outcome of panic disorder. *Journal of Clinical Psychiatry, 58*(2, Suppl.), 57–60. [16]

Pollack, R. H. (1970). Müller-Lyer illusion: Effect of age, lightness contrast and hue. *Science, 179,* 93–94. [3]

Pontieri, F. C., Tanda, G., Orzi, F., & Di Chiara, G. (1996). Effects of nicotine on the nucleus accumbens and similarity to those of addictive drugs. *Nature, 382,* 255–257. [2, 4]

Poponoe, D., & Whitehead, B. D. (2000). Sex without strings, relationships without rings: Today's young singles talk about mating and dating [On-line]. Available: http://marriage.rutgers.edu/2000.htm [10]

Porrino, L. J., & Lyons, D. (2000). Orbital and medial prefrontal cortex and psychostimulant abuse: Studies in animal models. *Cerebral Cortex, 10,* 326–333. [4, 5]

Porte, H. S., & Hobson, J. A. (1996). Physical motion in dreams: One measure of three theories. *Sleep, 105,* 3329–3335. [4]

Porter, F. L., Porges, S. W., & Marshall, R. E. (1988). Newborn pain cries and vagal tone: Parallel changes in response to circumcision. *Child Development, 59,* 495–505. [9]

Posner, M. I. (1996, September). Attention and psychopathology. *Harvard Mental Health Letter, 13*(3), 5–6. [2]

Posner, M. I., & Raichle, M. E. (1995). Précis of *Images of Mind. Behavioral and Brain Sciences, 18,* 327–383. [7]

Postman, L., & Phillips, L. W. (1965). Short-term temporal changes in free recall. *Quarterly Journal of Experimental Psychology, 17,* 132–138. [6]

Potts, N. L. S., Davidson, J. R. T., & Krishman, K. R. R. (1993). The role of nuclear magnetic resonance imaging in psychiatric research. *Journal of Clinical Psychiatry, 54*(12, Suppl.), 13–18. [2]

Powell, K. E., Spain, K. G., Christenson, G. M., & Mollenkamp, M. P. (1986). The status of the 1990 objectives for physical fitness and exercise. *Public Health Reports, 101,* 15–21. [13]

Powell, L. H., Shaker, L. A., Jones, B. A., Vaccarino, L. V., Thoresen, C. E., & Pattillo, J. R. (1993). Psychosocial predictors of mortality in 83 women with premature acute myocardial infarction. *Psychosomatic Medicine, 55,* 426–433. [13]

Power, F. C., Higgins, A., & Kohlberg, L. (1989). *Lawrence Kohlberg's approach to moral education.* New York: Columbia University Press. [10]

Power, K. G., Sharp, D. M., Swanson, V., & Simpson, R. J. (2000). Therapist contact in cognitive behaviour therapy for panic disorder and agoraphobia in primary care. *Clinical Psychology & Psychotherapy, 7,* 37–46. [16]

Powlishta, K. K. (1995). Intergroup processes in childhood: Social categorization and sex role development. *Developmental Psychology, 31,* 781–788. [12]

Pratkanis, A. R. (1989). The cognitive representation of attitudes. In A. R. Pratkanis, S. J. Breckler, & A. G. Greenwald (Eds.), *Attitude structure and function* (pp. 71–93). Hillsdale, NJ: Erlbaum. [17]

Pratkanis, A. R., Eskenazi, J., & Greenwald, A. G. (1994). What you expect is what you believe (but not necessarily what you get): A test of the effectiveness of subliminal self-help audiotapes. *Basic and Applied Social Psychology, 15,* 251–276. [3]

Premack, D. (1971). Language in chimpanzees. *Science, 172,* 808–822. [7]

Premack, D., & Premack, A. J. (1983). *The mind of an ape.* New York: Norton. [7]

Prentice, A., & Goldberg, G. (1996). Maternal obesity increases congenital malformations. *Nutrition Reviews, 54,* 146–152. [9]

Preskorn, S. H. (1993). Pharmacokinetics of antidepressants: Why and how they are relevant to treatment. *Journal of Clinical Psychiatry, 54*(9, Suppl.), 14–34. [16]

Prien, R. F., & Kocsis, J. H. (1995). Long-term treatment of mood disorders. In F. E. Bloom & D. J. Kupfer (Eds.), *Psychopharmacology: The fourth generation of progress* (pp. 1067–1079). New York: Raven. [16]

Prigerson, H. G., Bierhals, A. J., Kasl, S. V., Reynolds, C. F., III, Shear, M. K., Day, N., Beery, L. C., Newsom, J. T., & Jacobs, S. (1997). Traumatic grief as a risk factor for mental and physical mortality. *American Journal of Psychiatry, 154,* 616–623. [13]

Prinz, P. N., Vitiello, M. V., Raskind, M. A., & Thorpy, M. J. (1990). Geriatrics: Sleep disorders and aging. *New England Journal of Medicine, 323,* 520–526. [4]

Provine, R. R. (1996, January/February). Laughter. *American Scientist, 84,* 38–45. [11]

Provins, K. A. (1997). Handedness and speech: A critical reappraisal of the role of genetic and environmental factors in the cerebral lateralization of function. *Psychological Review, 104,* 544–571. [2]

Pryke, S., Lindsay, R. C. L., & Pozzulo, J. D. (2000). Sorting mug shots: Methodological issues. *Applied Cognitive Psychology, 14,* 81–96. [6]

Pryor, J. (1994). Self-esteem and attitudes toward gender roles: Contributing factors in adolescents. *Australian Journal of Psychology, 46,* 48–52. [12]

Psychologists' pigeons score 90 pct. picking Picasso. (1995, May 7). *St. Louis Post-Dispatch,* p. 2A. [5]

Public Health Service. (1991). *Healthy people 2000: National health promotion and disease prevention objectives* [Summary]. (DHHS Publication No. PHS 91–50213). Washington, DC: U.S. Department of Health and Human Services. [13]

Pulvermüller, F., Mohr, B., Schleichert, H., & Veit, R. (2000). Operant conditioning of left-hemispheric slow cortical potentials and its effect on word processing. *Biological Psychology, 53,* 177–215. [5]

Putnam, F. W. (1989). *Diagnosis and treatment of multiple personality disorder.* New York: Guilford Press. [15]

Putnam, F. W. (1992). Altered states: Peeling away the layers of a multiple personality. *The Sciences, 32,* 30–36. [15]

Putnam, F. W., & Loewenstein, R. J. (1993). Treatment of multiple personality disorder: A survey of current practices. *American Journal of Psychiatry, 150,* 1048–1052. [15]

Putnam, F. W., Guroff, J. J., Silberman, E. K., Barban, L., & Post, R. M. (1986). The clinical phenomenology of multiple personality disorder: Review of 100 recent cases. *Journal of Clinical Psychiatry, 47,* 285–293. [15]

Putzke, J., Rickert, E., Duke, L., Marson, D., & Harrell, L. (2000). Differential automatic processing deficits in early stage Alzheimer's disease. *Aging, Neuropsychology, and Cognition, 7,* 112–118. [10]

Quadrel, M. J., Fischhoff, B., & Davis, W. (1993). Adolescent (in)vulnerability. *American Psychologist, 48,* 102–116. [10]

Quinn, T. C. (1994). Recent advances in diagnosis of sexually transmitted diseases. *Sexually Transmitted Diseases, 21*(2, Suppl.), S19–S27. [12]

Rachman, S. (1997). The conditioning theory of fear acquisition: A critical examination. *Behavior Research and Therapy, 15,* 375–387. [15]

Rachman, S. J., & Wilson, G. T. (1980). *The effects of psychological therapy* (2nd ed.). New York: Pergamon. [16]

Rahe, R. J., Meyer, M., Smith, M., Kjaer, G., & Holmes, T. H. (1964). Social stress and illness onset. *Journal of Psychosomatic Research, 8,* 35–44. [13]

Raichle, M. E. (1994). Visualizing the mind. *Scientific American, 270,* 58–64. [1, 2]
Raichle, M. E., Fiez, J. A., Videen, T. O., MacLeod, A. M., Pardo, J. V., Fox, P. T., & Petersen, S. E. (1994). Practice-related changes in human brain functional anatomy during nonmotor learning. *Cerebral Cortex, 4,* 8–26. [7]
Raine, A. (1996). Autonomic nervous system factors underlying disinhibited, antisocial, and violent behavior: Biosocial perspectives and treatment implications. *Annals of the New York Academy of Sciences, 794,* 46–59. [17]
Raloff, J. (1994). The great nicotine debate: Are cigarette recipes 'cooked' to keep smokers hooked? *Science News, 145,* 314–317. [4]
Raloff, J. (1996). Eyes possess their own biological clocks. *Science News, 149,* 245. [4]
Ralph, M. R. (1989, November/December). The rhythm maker: Pinpointing the master clock in mammals. *The Sciences, 29,* 40–45. [4]
Ramsay, D. S., & Woods, S. C. (1997). Biological consequences of drug administration: Implications for acute and chronic tolerance. *Psychological Review, 104,* 170–193. [4]
Randerath, W. J., Kroll, B., Schwickert, M., Gil, G., & Ruhle, K. H. (2000). Self-assessment by patients of impairment caused by obstructive sleep apnea syndrome. *Deutsche Medizinische Wochenschrift, 24,* 348–351. [4]
Randi, J. (1980). *Flim-flam: The truth about unicorns, parapsychology, and other delusions.* New York: Lippincott & Crowell. [3]
Rao, S. C., Rainer, G., & Miller, E. K. (1997). Integration of what and where in the primate prefrontal cortex. *Science, 276,* 821–824. [6]
Rapoport, D. M. (1996). Methods to stabilize the upper airway using positive pressure. *Sleep, 19,* S123–S130. [4]
Rapoport, J. L. (1989). The biology of obsessions and compulsions. *Scientific American, 260,* 83–89. [16]
Rasmussen, S. A., & Eisen, J. L. (1990). Epidemiology of obsessive compulsive disorder. *Journal of Clinical Psychiatry, 51*(2, Suppl.), 10–13. [15]
Rasmussen, S. A., Eisen, J. L., & Pato, M. T. (1993). Current issues in the pharmacologic management of obsessive compulsive disorder. *Journal of Clinical Psychiatry, 54*(6, Suppl.), 4–9. [15, 16]
Rate of births for teen-agers drops again. (1995, September 22). *The New York Times,* p. A18. [10]
Rathus, S. A., Nevid, J. S., & Fichner-Rathus, L. (2000). *Human sexuality in a world of diversity* (4th ed., pp. 216–217). Boston: Allyn & Bacon. [12]
Rauch, S. L., Jenike, M. A., Alpert, N. M., Baer, L., Breiter, H. C. R., Savage, C. R., & Fischman, A. J. (1994). Regional cerebral blood flow measured during symptom provocation in obsessive-compulsive disorder using oxygen 15–labeled carbon dioxide and positron emission tomography. *Archives of General Psychiatry, 51,* 62–70. [15]
Rauch, S. L., Savage, C. R., Alpert, N. M., et al. (1995). A positron emission tomographic study of simple phobic symptom provocation. *Archives of General Psychiatry, 52,* 20–28. [16]
Razoumnikova, O. M. (2000). Functional organization of different brain areas during convergent and divergent thinking: An EEG investigation. *Cognitive Brain Research, 10,* 11–18. [8]
Rechtschaffen, A. (1998). Current perspectives on the function of sleep. *Perspectives in Biology and Medicine, 41,* 359–390. [4]
Recklitis, C. J., & Noam, G. G. (1999). Clinical and developmental perspectives on adolescent coping. *Child Psychiatry and Human Development, 30,* 87–101. [10]
Reed, S., & Fischer, M. A. (1984, January 23). Adventure: Far from being over the hill, Hulda Crooks, at 87, is a real climber. *People Weekly,* pp. 88–90. [10]
Reinke, B. J., Ellicott, A. M., Harris, R. L., & Hancock, E. (1985). Timing of psychosocial changes in women's lives. *Human Development, 28,* 259–280. [10]
Reis, H. T., Wilson, I. M., Monestere, C., Bernstein, S., Clark, K., Seidl, E., Franco, M., Gioioso, E., Freeman, L., & Radoane, K. (1990). What is smiling is beautiful and good. *European Journal of Social Psychology, 20,* 259–267. [17]
Reite, M., Buysse, D., Reynolds, C., & Mendelson, W. (1995). The use of polysomnography in the evaluation of insomnia. *Sleep, 18,* 58–70. [4]
Reneman, L., Booij, J., Schmand, B., van den Brink, W., & Gunning, B. (2000). Memory disturbances in "Ecstasy" users are correlated with an altered brain serotonin neurotransmission. *Psychopharmacology, 148,* 322–324. [4]
Rensink, R. A. (2000). Seeing, sensing, and scrutinizing. *Vision Research, 40,* 1469–1487. [3]
Renzetti, C. M., & Curran, D. J. (1992). *Women, men, and society.* Boston: Allyn & Bacon. [17]
Rescorla, R. A. (1967). Pavlovian conditioning and its proper control procedures. *Psychological Review, 74,* 71–80. [5]
Rescorla, R. A. (1968). Probability of shock in the presence and absence of CS in fear conditioning. *Journal of Comparative and Physiological Psychology, 66,* 1–5. [5]
Rescorla, R. A. (1988). Pavlovian conditioning: It's not what you think it is. *American Psychologist, 43,* 151–160. [5]
Rescorla, R. A., & Wagner, A. R. (1972). A theory of Pavlovian conditioning: Variations in the effectiveness of reinforcement and nonreinforcement. In A. Black & W. F. Prokasy (Eds.), *Classical conditioning: II. Current research and theory.* New York: Appleton. [5]
Restak, R. (1988). *The mind.* Toronto: Bantam. [7]
Restak, R. (1993, September/October). Brain by design. *The Sciences,* pp. 27–33. [2]
Revelle, W. (1995). Personality processes. *Annual Review of Psychology, 46,* 295–328. [14]
Revensuo, A. (2000). The reinterpretation of dreams: An evolutionary hypothesis of the function of dreaming. *Behavioral & Brain Science, 23.* [4]
Reyner, A., & Horne, J. A. (1995). Gender- and age-related differences in sleep determined by home-recorded sleep logs and actimetry from 400 adults. *Sleep, 18,* 127–134. [4]
Reyner, L. A., & Horne, J. A. (1998). Evaluation of "in-car" countermeasures to sleepiness: Cold air and radio. *Sleep, 21,* 46–50. [4]
Rhéaume, J., & Ladouceur, R. (2000). Cognitive and behavioural treatments of checking behaviours: An examination of individual cognitive change. *Clinical Psychology & Psychotherapy, 7,* 118–127. [16]
Rhodes, N., & Wood, W. (1992). Self-esteem and intelligence affect influenceability: The medicating role of message reception. *Psychological Bulletin, 111,* 156–171. [17]
Rice, F. P. (1992). *Intimate relationships, marriages, and families.* Mountain View, CA: Mayfield. [10]
Rice, M. L. (1989). Children's language acquisition. *American Psychologist, 44,* 149–156. [9]
Rice, M. L., Huston, A. C., Truglio, R., & Wright, J. (1990). Words from "Sesame Street": Learning vocabulary while viewing. *Developmental Psychology, 26,* 421–428. [9]
Rice, P. L. (1987). *Stress and health: Principles and practice for coping and wellness.* Monterey, CA: Brooks/Cole. [13]
Rich, M., Woods, E. R., Goodman, E., Emans, S. J., & DuRant, R. H. (1998). Aggressors or victims: Gender and race in music video violence. *Pediatrics, 101*(Pt. 1), 669–674. [17]
Richardson, G. A., Hamel, S. C., Goldschmidt, L., & Day, N. L. (2000). Growth of infants prenatally exposed to cocaine/crack: Comparison of a prenatal care and a no prenatal care sample. *Pediatrics, 104*(2), 18. [9]
Richter, J., Eisenmann, M., & Richter, G. (2000). Temperament, character and perceived parental rearing in healthy adults: Two related concepts? *Psychopathology, 33,* 36–42. [9]
Richter, W., Somorjai, R., Summers, R., Jarmasz, M., Ravi, S., Menon, J. S., et al. (2000). Motor area activity during mental rotation studied by time-resolved single-trial fMRI. *Journal of Cognitive Neuroscience, 12,* 310–320. [7]
Rickels, K., Downing, R., Schweizer, E., & Hassman, H. (1993). Antidepressants for the treatment of generalized anxiety disorder. *Archives of General Psychiatry, 50,* 884–895. [16]
Rickels, K., Schweizer, E., Weiss, S., & Zavodnick, S. (1993). Maintenance drug treatment for panic disorder II. Short- and long-term outcome after drug taper. *Archives of General Psychiatry, 50,* 61–68. [16]
Riedel, G. (1996). Function of metabotropic glutamate receptors in learning and memory. *Trends in Neurosciences, 19,* 219–224. [2, 6]
Rimland, B. (1978). Inside the mind of the autistic savant. *Psychology Today, 12,* 69–80. [8]

Rinner, O., & Gegenfurtner, K. R. (2000). Time course of chromatic adaptation for color appearance and discrimination. *Vision Research, 40,* 1813–1826. [3]
Ritts, V., Patterson, M. L., & Tubbs, M. E. (1992). Expectations, impressions, and judgments of physically attractive students: A review. *Review of Educational Research, 62,* 413–426. [17]
Riva, D., & Giorgi, C. (2000). The cerebellum contributes to higher functions during development. *Brain, 123,* 1051–1061. [2]
Roan, S. (2000, March 6). Cyber analysis. *L.A. Times.* [16]
Roberts, B. W., & DelVecchio, W. F. (2000). The rank-order consistency of personality traits from childhood to old age: A quantitative review of longitudinal studies. *Psychological Bulletin, 126,* 3–25. [14]
Roberts, P., & Moseley, B. (1996, May/June). Fathers' time. *Psychology Today, 29,* 48–55, 81. [9]
Robertson, G. L. (1983). Thirst and vasopressin function in normal and disordered states of water balance. *Journal of Laboratory and Clinical Medicine, 101,* 351–371. [11]
Robertson, I. H., & Murre, J. M. J. (1999). Rehabilitation of brain damage: Brain plasticity and principles of guided recovery. *Psychological Bulletin, 125,* 544–575. [2]
Robins, C. J., & Hayes, A. M. (1993). An appraisal of cognitive therapy. *Journal of Consulting and Clinical Psychology, 61,* 205–214. [16]
Robins, R. W., Gosling, S. D., & Craik, K. H. (1999). An empirical analysis of trends in psychology. *American Psychologist, 54,* 117–128. [1]
Robinson, M. D. (2000). The reactive and prospective functions of mood: Its role in linking daily experiences and cognitive well-being. *Cognition and Emotion, 14,* 145–176. [11]
Roche, A. F., & Davila, G. H. (1972). Late adolescent growth in stature. *Pediatrics, 50,* 874–880. [10]
Rock, I., & Palmer, S. (1990). The legacy of Gestalt psychology. *Scientific American, 263,* 84–90. [5]
Rodin, J. (1981). Current status of the internal-external hypothesis for obesity: What went wrong? *American Psychologist, 36,* 361–372. [11]
Rodin, J. (1985). Insulin levels, hunger, and food intake: An example of feedback loops in body weight regulation. *Health Psychology, 4,* 1–24. [11]
Rodin, J. (1992, January/February). Body image. *Psychology Today,* pp. 56–60. [11]
Rodin, J., & Ickovics, J. R. (1990). Women's health: Review and research agenda as we approach the 21st century. *American Psychologist, 45,* 1018–1034. [13]
Rodin, J., & Salovey, P. (1989). Health psychology. *Annual Review of Psychology, 40,* 533–579. [13]
Rodin, J., & Wing, R. R. (1988). Behavioral factors in obesity. *Diabetes/Metabolism Reviews, 4,* 701–725. [11]
Rodin, J., Slochower, J., & Fleming, B. (1977). The effects of degree of obesity, age of onset, and energy deficit on external responsiveness. *Journal of Comparative and Physiological Psychology, 91,* 586–597. [11]
Rodin, J., Wack, J., Ferrannini, E., & DeFronzo, R. A. (1985). Effect of insulin and glucose on feeding behavior. *Metabolism, 34,* 826–831. [11]
Roediger, H. L., III, & McDermott, K. B. (1995). Creating false memories: Remembering words not presented in lists. *Journal of Experimental Psychology: Learning, Memory, and Cognition, 21,* 803–814. [6]
Roediger, H. L., III. (1980). The effectiveness of four mnemonics in ordering recall. *Journal of Experimental Psychology: Human Learning and Memory, 6,* 558–567. [6]
Roediger, H. L., III. (1991). They read an article? A commentary on the everyday memory controversy. *American Psychologist, 46,* 37–40. [6]
Roehrich, L., & Kinder, B. N. (1991). Alcohol expectancies and male sexuality: Review and implications for sex therapy. *Journal of Sex and Marital Therapy, 17,* 45–54. [4]
Roesch, S. C., & Amirkhan, J. H. (1997). Boundary condition for self-serving attributions: Another look at the sports pages. *Journal of Applied Social Psychology, 27,* 245–261. [17]
Rogers, C. R. (1951). *Client-centered therapy: Its current practice, implications, and theory.* Boston: Houghton Mifflin. [14, 16]
Rogers, C. R. (1959). A theory of therapy, personality, and interpersonal relationships, as developed in the client-centered framework. In S. Koch (Ed.), *Psychology: A study of a science, Vol. III. Formulations of the person and the social context* (pp. 184–256). New York: McGraw-Hill. [16]
Rogers, C. R. (1961). *On becoming a person: A therapist's view of psychotherapy.* Boston: Houghton Mifflin. [14, 15]
Rogers, C. R. (1977). The case of Mary Jane Tilden. In S. J. Morse & R. I. Watson, Jr. (Eds.), *Psychotherapies: A comparative casebook* (pp. 197–222). New York: Holt, Rinehart & Winston. [16]
Rogers, C. R. (1981). Notes on Rollo May. *Perspectives, 2*(1), 16. [14]
Rogoff, B., & Mistry, J. (1985). Memory development in cultural context. In M. Pressley & C. Brainerd (Eds.), *The cognitive side of memory development.* New York: Springer-Verlag. [6]
Roland, P. (1992). Cortical representation of pain. *Trends in Neurosciences, 15,* 3–5. [2]
Roland, P. E., & Gulyás, B. (1994). Visual imagery and visual representation. *Trends in Neurosciences, 17,* 281–287. [7]
Romach, M., Busto, U., Somer, G., et al. (1995). Clinical aspects of chronic use of alprazolam and lorazepam. *American Journal of Psychiatry, 152,* 1161–1167. [16]
Rombouts, S. A., Barkhof, F., Witter, M. P., & Scheltens, P. (2000). Unbiased whole-brain analysis of gray matter loss in Alzheimer's disease. *Neuroscience Letter, 285,* 231–233. [10]
Roorda, A., & Williams, D. R. (1999). The arrangement of the three cone classes in the living human eye. *Nature, 397,* 520–521. [3]
Rosch, E. H. (1973). Natural categories. *Cognitive Psychology, 4,* 328–350. [7]
Rosch, E. H. (1978). Principles of categorization. In E. H. Rosch & B. Lloyd (Eds.), *Cognition and categorization.* Hillsdale, NJ: Erlbaum. [7]
Rosch, E. H. (1987). Linguistic relativity. *Et Cetera, 44,* 254–279. [7]
Rose, R. J., Koskenvuo, M., Kaprio, J., Sarna, S., & Langinvainio, H. (1988). Shared genes, shared experiences, and similarity of personality: Data from 14,288 adult Finnish co-twins. *Journal of Personality and Social Psychology, 54,* 161–171. [14]
Rosekind, M. R. (1992). The epidemiology and occurrence of insomnia. *Journal of Clinical Psychiatry, 53*(6, Suppl.), 4–6. [4]
Rosen, R. C. (1996). Erectile dysfunction: The medicalization of male sexuality. *Clinical Psychology Review, 16,* 497–519. [12]
Rosen, R. C., & Leiblum, S. R. (1995). Treatment of sexual disorders in the 1990s: An integrated approach. *Journal of Consulting and Clinical Psychology, 63,* 877–896. [12]
Rosen, R. C., Rosekind, M., Rosevear, C., Cole, W. E., & Dement, W. C. (1993). Physician education in sleep and sleep disorders: A national survey of U.S. medical schools. *Sleep, 16,* 249–254. [4]
Rosenbluth, R., Grossman, E. S., & Kaitz, M. (2000). Performance of early-blind and sighted children on olfactory tasks. *Perception, 29,* 101–110. [3]
Rosenfeld, J. P. (1995). Alternative views of Bashore and Rapp's (1993) alternatives to traditional polygraphy: A critique. *Psychological Bulletin, 117,* 159–166. [11]
Rosengren, A., Tibblin, G., & Wilhelmsen, L. (1991). Self-perceived psychological stress and incidence of coronary artery disease in middle-aged men. *American Journal of Cardiology, 68,* 1171–1175. [13]
Rosenhan, D. L. (1973). On being sane in insane places. *Science, 179,* 250–258. [3]
Rosenthal, A. M. (1964). *Thirty-eight witnesses.* New York: McGraw-Hill. [17]
Rosenthal, N. E., Carpenter, C. J., James, S. P., Parry, B. L., Rogers, S. L. B., & Wehr, T. A.. (1986). Seasonal affective disorder in children and adolescents. *American Journal of Psychiatry, 143,* 356–358. [15]
Rosenthal, N. E., Sack, D. A., Carpenter, C. J., et al. (1985). Antidepressant effects of light in seasonal affective disorder. *American Journal of Psychiatry, 142,* 163–170. [15]
Rosenthal, R. (1973, September). The Pygmalion effect lives. *Psychology Today,* pp. 56–63. [1]
Rosenvinge, J. H., Matinussen, M., & Ostensen, E. (2000). The comorbidity of eating disorders and personality disorders: A meta-analytic review of studies published between 1983 and 1998. *Eating and Weight Disorders: Studies on Anorexia, Bulimia, and Obesity, 5,* 52–61. [11]
Rosenzweig, M. R. (1961). Auditory localization. *Scientific American, 205,* 132–142. [3]

Ross, C. A., Anderson, G., Fleisher, W. P., & Norton, G. R. (1991). The frequency of multiple personality disorder among psychiatric inpatients. *American Journal of Psychiatry, 148,* 1717–1720. [15]

Ross, C. A., Norton, G. R., & Wozney, K. (1989). Multiple personality disorder: An analysis of 236 cases. *Canadian Journal of Psychiatry, 34,* 413–418. [15]

Ross, J., Baldessarini, R. J., & Tondo, L. (2000). Does lithium treatment still work? Evidence of stable responses over three decades. *Archives of General Psychiatry, 57,* 187–190. [16]

Ross, J., & Lawrence, K. A. (1968). Some observations on memory artifice. *Psychonomic Science, 13,* 107–108. [6]

Rossellini, L. (2000, September 11). The sordid side of college sports. *U.S. News & World Report,* pp. 102–103. [17]

Rossi, A. F., Rittenhouse, C. D., & Paradiso, M. A. (1996). The representation of brightness in primary visual cortex. *Science, 273,* 1104–1107. [3]

Roth, T. (1996a). Management of insomniac patients. *Sleep, 19,* S52–S53. [4]

Roth, T. (1996b). Social and economic consequences of sleep disorders. *Sleep, 19,* S46–S47. [4]

Rothbaum, B. O., Hodges, L., Watson, B. A., Kessler, G. D., & Opdyke, D. (1996). Virtual reality exposure therapy in the treatment of fear of flying: a case report. *Behaviour Research and Therapy, 34,* 477–481. [16]

Rotter, J. B. (1966). Generalized expectancies for internal versus external control of reinforcement. *Psychological Monographs, 80*(1, Whole No. 609). [14]

Rotter, J. B. (1971, June). External control and internal control. *Psychology Today,* pp. 37–42, 58–59. [14]

Rotter, J. B. (1990). Internal versus external control of reinforcement: A case history of a variable. *American Psychologist, 45,* 489–493. [14]

Rotton, J., & Cohn, E. G. (2000). Violence is a curvilinear function of temperature in Dallas: A replication. *Journal of Personality & Social Psychology, 78,* 1074–1082. [17]

Rotton, J., Frey, J., Barry, T., Milligan, M., & Fitzpatrick, M. (1979). The air pollution experience and physical aggression. *Journal of Applied Social Psychology, 9,* 397–412. [17]

Rovee-Collier, C. (1990). The "memory system" of prelinguistic infants. *Annals of the New York Academy of Sciences, 608,* 517–576. [9]

Rowe, D. (1994). *The limits of family influence: Genes, experience, and behavior.* New York: Guilford. [14]

Rowe, D. C. (1987). Resolving the person-situation debate: Invitation to an interdisciplinary dialogue. *American Psychologist, 42,* 218–227. [14]

Rozin, P. (1996). Towards a psychology of food and eating: From motivation to module to model to marker, morality, meaning, and metaphor. *Current Directions in Psychological Science, 5,* 18–24. [11]

Rozin, P., & Zellner, D. (1985). The role of Pavlovian conditioning in the acquisition of food likes and dislikes. *Annals of the New York Academy of Sciences, 443,* 189–202. [5]

Rudd, M. D., Joiner, T., & Rajab, M. H. (1996). Relationships among suicide ideators, attempters, and multiple attempters in a young-adult sample. *Journal of Abnormal Psychology, 105,* 541–550. [15]

Rugg, M. D., Allan, K., & Birch, C. S. (2000). Electrophysiological evidence for the modulation of retrieval orientation by depth of study processing. *Journal of Cognitive Neuroscience, 12,* 664–678. [6]

Ruggero, M. A. (1992). Responses to sound of the basilar membrane of the mammalian cochlea. *Current Opinion in Neurobiology, 2,* 449–456. [3]

Ruggiero, K. M., & Taylor, D. M. (1997). Why minority group members perceive or do not perceive the discrimination that confronts them: The role of self-esteem and perceived control. *Journal of Personality and Social Psychology, 72,* 373–389. [17]

Rumsey, J. M., Nace, K., Donohue, B., Wise, D., Maisog, J. M., & Andreason, P. (1997). A positron emission tomography study of impaired word recognition and phonological processing in dyslexic men. *Archives of Neurology, 54,* 562–573. [7]

Rushton, J. P., Fulker, D. W., Neale, M. C., Nias, D. K. B., & Eysenck, H. J. (1986). Altruism and aggression: The heritability of individual differences. *Journal of Personality and Social Psychology, 50,* 1192–1198. [14, 17]

Russell, J. A. (1994). Is there universal recognition of emotion from facial expression? A review of the cross-cultural studies. *Psychological Bulletin, 115,* 102–141. [11]

Russell, J. A. (1995). Facial expressions of emotion: What lies beyond minimal universality? *Psychological Bulletin, 118,* 379–391. [11]

Russell, T. G., Rowe, W., & Smouse, A. D. (1991). Subliminal self-help tapes and academic achievement: An evaluation. *Journal of Counseling and Development, 69,* 359–362. [3]

Rutter, M. L. (1997). Nature-nuture integration: The example of antisocial behavior. *American Psychologist, 52,* 390–398. [15]

Ryan, M. (1997, July 6). She helps others to fight their way back. *Parade Magazine,* p. 10. [2]

Sackeim, H. A. (1992). The cognitive effects of electroconvulsive therapy. In W. H. Moos, E. R. Gamzu, & L. J. Thal (Eds.), *Cognitive disorders: Pathophysiology and treatment.* New York: Marcel Dekker. [16]

Sackeim, H. A., Luber, B., Katzman, G. P., Moeller, J. R., Prudic, J., Devanand, D. P., & Nobler, M. S. (1996). The effects of electroconvulsive therapy on quantitative electroencephalograms. *Archives of General Psychiatry, 53,* 814–824. [16]

Sackeim, H. A., Prudic, J., Devanand, D. P., Nobler, M. S., Lisanby, S. H., Peyser, S., Fitzsimons, L., Moody, B. J., & Clark, J. (2000). A prospective, randomized, double-blind comparison of bilateral and right unilateral electroconvulsive therapy at different stimulus intensities. *Archives of General Psychiatry, 57,* 425–434. [16]

Sadker, D., & Sadker, M. (1994). *Failing at fairness: How America's schools cheat girls.* New York: Scribner's. [12]

Salama, A. A. A., & England, R. D. (1990). A case study: Schizophrenia and tactile hallucinations, treated with electroconvulsive therapy. *Canadian Journal of Psychiatry, 35,* 86–87. [15]

Salgado, J. F. (1997). The five factor model of personality and job performance in the European community. *Journal of Applied Psychology, 82,* 30–43. [14]

Salovey, P., & Mayer, J. D. (1990). Emotional intelligence. *Imagination, cognition, and personality, 9,* 185–211. [8]

Salthouse, T. A. (1996). The processing-speed theory of adult age differences in cognition. *Psychological Review, 103,* 403–428. [10]

Salzinger, S., Feldman, R. S., Hammer, M., & Rosario, M. (1993). The effects of physical abuse on children's social relationships. *Child Development, 64,* 169–187. [9]

Sanbonmatsu, D. M., & Fazio, R. H. (1990). The role of attitudes in memory-based decision making. *Journal of Personality and Social Psychology, 59,* 614–622. [17]

Sandfur, G. D., Rindfuss, R. R., & Cohen, B. (Eds.). (1996). *American Indian demography and public health.* Washington, DC: National Academy Press. [13]

Sandou, F., Amara, D. A., Dierich, A., LeMeur, M., Ramboz, S., Segu, L., Buhot, M-C., & Hen, R. (1994). Enhanced aggressive behavior in mice lacking 5-HT1B receptor. *Science, 265,* 1875–1878. [2]

Sanes, J. N., & Donoghue, J. P. (2000). Plasticity and primary motor cortex. *Annual Review of Neuroscience, 23,* 393–415. [2]

Sanes, J. N., Donoghue, J. P., Thangaraj, V. Edelman, R. R., & Warach, S. (1995). Shared neural substrates controlling hand movements in human motor cortex. *Science, 268,* 1775. [2]

Sanfilippo, M., Lafargue, T., Rusinek, H., Arena, L., Loneragan, C., Lautin, A., Feiner, D., Rotrosen, J., & Wolkin, A. (2000). Volumetric measure of the frontal and temporal lobe regions in schizophrenia. *Archives of General Psychiatry, 57,* 471–480. [15]

Sanna, L. J., & Shotland, R. L. (1990). Valence of anticipated evaluation and social facilitation. *Journal of Experimental Social Psychology, 26,* 82–92. [17]

Sano, M., Ernesto, C., Thomas, R. G., Kauber, M. R., Schafer, K., Grundman, M., Woodbury, P., Growdon, J., Cotman, C. W., Pfeiffer, E., Schneider, L. S., & Thal, L. J. (1997). A controlled trial of selegiline, alpha-tocopherol, or both as treatment for Alzheimer's disease. *New England Journal of Medicine, 336,* 1216–1222. [10]

Sansavini, A., Bertoncini, J., & Giovanelli, G. (1997). Newborns discriminate the rhythm of multisyllabic stressed words. *Developmental Psychology, 33,* 3–11. [9]

Şar, V., Yargic, L. I., & Tutkun, H. (1996). Structured interview data on 35 cases of dissociative identity disorder in Turkey. *American Journal of Psychiatry, 153,* 1329–1333. [15]

Sarfati, Y. (2000). Deficit of the theory-of-mind in schizophrenia: Clinical concept and review of experimental arguments. *Canadian Journal of Psychiatry, 45,* 4363–4368. [9]

Sass, H., Soyha, M., Mann, K., & Zieglgänsberger, W. (1996). Relapse prevention by acamprosate: Results from a placebo-controlled study on alcohol dependence. *Archives of General Psychiatry, 53,* 673–680. [13]

Sateia, M. J., Doghramji, K., Hauri, P. J., & Morin, C. M. (2000). Evaluation of chronic insomnia. An American Academy of Sleep Medicine review. *Sleep, 23,* 243–308. [4]

Saudino, K. J., Plomin, R., & DeFries, J. C. (1996). Tester-rated temperament at 14, 20 and 24 months: Environmental change and genetic continuity. *British Journal of Developmental Psychology, 14,* 129–144. [9]

Sauter, S. L., Murphy, L. R., & Hurrel, J. J., Jr. (1990). Prevention of work-related psychological disorders: A national strategy proposed by the National Institute for Occupational Safety and Health (NIOSH). *American Psychologist, 45,* 1146–1158. [13]

Sauzeon, H., N'kaoua, B., Lespinet, V., Guillem, F., & Claverie, B. (2000). Age effect in recall performance according to the levels of processing, elaboration, and retrieval cues. *Experimental Aging Research, 26,* 57–73. [10]

Savage-Rumbaugh, E. S. (1986). *Ape language.* New York: Columbia University Press. [7]

Savage-Rumbaugh, E. S. (1990). Language acquisition in a nonhuman species: Implications for the innateness debate. *Developmental Psychology, 26,* 599–620. [7]

Savage-Rumbaugh, E. S. (1993). Language learnability in man, ape, and dolphin. In H. L. Roitblat, L. M. Herman, & P. E. Nachtigall (Eds.), *Language and communication: Comparative perspectives. Comparative cognition and neuroscience* (pp. 457–484). Hillsdale, NJ: Erlbaum. [7]

Savage-Rumbaugh, E. S., Sevcik, R. A., Brakke, K. E., & Rumbaugh, D. M. (1992). Symbols: Their communicative use, communication, and combination by bonobos (*Pan paniscus*). In L. P. Lipsitt & C. Rovee-Collier (Eds.). *Advances in infancy research* (Vol. 7, pp. 221–278). Norwood, NJ: Ablex. [7]

Savin-Williams, R. (1980). Dominance hierarchies in groups of middle to late adolescent males. *Journal of Youth and Adolescence, 9,* 75–85. [10]

Scarr, S., & Weinberg, R. (1976). The influence of "family background" on intellectual attainment. *American Sociological Review, 43,* 674–692. [8]

Scarr, S., Pakstis, A., Katz, S., & Barker, W. (1977). Absence of a relationship between degree of White ancestry and intellectual skills within a Black population. *Human Genetics, 39,* 69–86. [8]

Scarr, S., Webber, P. L., Weinberg, R. A., & Wittig, M. A. (1981). Personality resemblance among adolescents and their parents in biologically related and adoptive families. *Journal of Personality and Social Psychology, 40,* 885–898. [14]

Schab, F. R. (1990). Odors and the remembrance of things past. *Journal of Experimental Psychology: Learning, Memory, and Cognition, 16,* 648–655. [6]

Schachter, S., & Gross, L. P. (1968). Manipulated time and eating behavior. *Journal of Personality and Social Psychology, 10,* 98–106. [11]

Schachter, S., & Singer, J. E. (1962). Cognitive, social, and physiological determinants of emotional state. *Psychological Review, 69,* 379–399. [11]

Schaie, K. W. (1990). Late life potential and cohort differences in mental abilities. In M. Perlmutter (Ed.), *Late life potential* (pp. 43–61). Washington, DC: Gerontological Society. [10]

Schaie, K. W. (1993). Ageist language in psychological research. *American Psychologist, 48,* 49–51. [1]

Schaie, K. W. (1994). The course of adult intellectual development. *American Psychologist, 49,* 304–313. [10]

Schaie, K. W. (1995). *Intellectual development in adulthood: The Seattle Longitudinal Study.* New York: Cambridge University Press. [10]

Schaie, K. W., & Willis, S. L. (1996). *Adult development and aging* (4th ed.). New York: HarperCollins. [10]

Scheier, M. F., & Carver, C. S. (1985). Optimism, coping, and health: Assessment and implications of generalized outcome expectancies. *Health Psychology, 4,* 219–247. [13]

Scheier, M. F., & Carver, C. S. (1992). Effects of optimism on psychological and physical well-being: Theoretical overview and empirical update. *Cognitive Therapy and Research, 16,* 201–228. [13]

Scheier, M. F., Matthews, K. A., Owens, J., Magovern, G. J., Sr., Lefebvre, R. C., Abbott, R. A., & Carver, C. S. (1989). Dispositional optimism and recovery from coronary artery bypass surgery: The beneficial effects on physical and psychological well-being. *Journal of Personality and Social Psychology, 57,* 1024–1040. [13]

Scheier, M. F., Weintraub, J. K., & Carver, C. S. (1986). Coping with stress: Divergent strategies of optimists and pessimists. *Journal of Personality and Social Psychology, 51,* 1257–1264. [13]

Schenck, C. H., & Mahowald, M. W. (1995). A polysomnographically documented case of adult somnambulism with long-distance automobile driving and frequent nocturnal violence: Parasomnia with continuing danger as a noninsane automatism? *Sleep, 18,* 765–772. [4]

Schenck, C. H., & Mahowald, M. W. (2000). Parasomnias. Managing bizarre sleep-related behavior disorders. *Postgraduate Medicine, 107,* 145–156. [4]

Scher, M. S., Richardson, G. A., & Day, N. L. (2000). Effects of prenatal cocaine/crack and other drug exposure on electroencephalographic sleep studies at birth and 1 year. *Pediatrics, 105,* 39–48. [9]

Scherer, K. R., & Wallbott, H. G. (1994). Evidence for universality and cultural variation of differential emotion response patterning. *Journal of Personality and Social Psychology, 66,* 310–328. [11]

Scherer, K. R., Wallbott, H. G., & Summerfield, A. B. (1986). *Experiencing emotion: A cross-cultural study.* Cambridge, England: Cambridge University Press. [11]

Scheuffgen, K., Happé, F., Anderson, M., & Frith, U. (2000). High "intelligence," low "IQ"? Speed of processing and measured IQ in children with autism. *Developmental Psychopathology, 12,* 183–190. [8]

Schieber, M. H., & Hibbard, L. S. (1993). How somatotopic is the motor cortex hand area? *Science, 261,* 489–492. [2]

Schiff, M., & Lewontin, R. (1986). *Education and class: The irrelevance of IQ genetic studies.* Oxford, England: Clarendon. [8]

Schildkraut, J. J., Hirshfeld, A. J., & Murphy, J. M. (1994). Mind and mood in modern art, II: Depressive disorders, spirituality, and early deaths in the abstract expressionist artists of the New York school. *American Journal of Psychiatry, 151,* 482–488. [15]

Schiller, F. (1993). *Paul Broca: Explorer of the brain.* Oxford: Oxford University Press. [2]

Schlaug, G., Jäncke, L., Huang, Y., & Steinmetz, H. (1995). In vivo evidence of structural brain asymmetry in musicians. *Science, 267,* 699–700. [2]

Schmidt, G., & Weiner, B. (1988). An attributional-affect-action theory of behavior: Replications of judgments of helping. *Personality and Social Psychology Bulletin, 14,* 610–621. [17]

Schmitz, A. (1991, November). How to spot front-page fallacies. *Health,* pp. 43–45. [1]

Schneider, W., & Pressley, M. (1989). *Memory development between 2 and 20.* New York: Springer-Verlag. [9]

Schofield, J. W., & Francis, W. D. (1982). An observational study of peer interaction in racially mixed "accelerated" classrooms. *Journal of Educational Psychology, 74,* 722–732. [9]

Scholl, T. O., Heidiger, M. L., & Belsky, D. H. (1996). Prenatal care and maternal health during adolescent pregnancy: A review and meta-analysis. *Journal of Adolescent Health, 15,* 444–456. [10]

Schooler, N. R., Keith, S. J., Severe, J. B., Matthews, S. M., Bellack, A. S., Glick, I. D., Hargreaves, W. A., Kane, J. M., Ninan, P. T., Frances, A., Jacobs, M., Lieberman, J. A., Mance R., Simpson, G. M., & Woerner, M. G. (1997). Relapse and rehospitalization during maintenance treatment of schizophrenia: The effects of dose reduction and family treatment. *Archives of General Psychiatry, 54,* 453–463. [16]

Schou, M. (1997). Forty years of lithium treatment. *Archives of General Psychiatry, 54,* 9–13. [16]
Schreiber, F. R. (1973). *Sybil.* Chicago: Henry Regnery. [15]
Schreurs, B. G. (1989). Classical conditioning of model systems: A behavioral review. *Psychobiology, 17,* 145–155. [5]
Schuckit, M. A., Tipp, J. E., Bergman, M., Reich, W., Hesselbrock, V. M., & Smith, T. L. (1997). Comparison of induced and independent major depressive disorders in 2,945 alcoholics. *American Journal of Psychiatry, 154,* 948–957. [13]
Schulz, R., & Heckhausen, J. (1996). A life span model of successful aging. *American Psychologist, 51,* 702–714. [10]
Schulz, D. (1975). *A history of modern psychology* (2nd ed.). New York: Academic Press. [5]
Schuman, E. M., & Madison, D. V. (1994). Locally distributed synaptic potentiation in the hippocampus. *Science, 263,* 532–536. [6]
Schunn, C. D., & Dunbar, K. (1996). Priming, analogy, and awareness in complex reasoning. *Memory and Cognition, 24,* 271–284. [7]
Schwartz, D. L. (2000). Physical imagery: Kinematic versus dynamic models. *Cognitive Psychology, 38,* 433–464. [7]
Schwartz, G. E. (1982). Testing the biopsychosocial model: The ultimate challenge facing behavioral medicine? *Journal of Consulting and Clinical Psychology, 50,* 1040–1052. [13]
Schwartz, J. M., Stoessel, P. W., Baxter, L. R., Jr., Martin, K. M., & Phelps, M. E. (1996). Systematic changes in cerebral glucose metabolic rate after successful behavior modification treatment of obsessive-compulsive disorder. *Archives of General Psychiatry, 53,* 109–113. [16]
Schwartz, N. (1999). Self-reports: How the questions shape the answers. *American Psychologist, 54,* 93–105. [1]
Schwartz, R. H., & Miller, N. S. (1997). MDMA (Ecstasy) and the rave: A review. *Pediatrics, 100,* 705–708. [4]
Schwebke, J. R. (1991a, March). Gonorrhea in the '90s. *Medical Aspects of Human Sexuality, 24,* 42–46. [12]
Schwebke, J. R. (1991b, April). Syphilis in the '90s. *Medical Aspects of Human Sexuality, 25,* 44–49. [12]
Scott, J. (1996). Cognitive therapy of affective disorders: a review. *Journal of Affective Disorders, 37,* 1–11. [16]
Scott, S. K., Young, A. W., Calder, A. J., Hellawell, D. J., Aggleton, J. P., & Johnson, M. (1997). Impaired auditory recognition of fear and anger following bilateral amygdala lesions. *Nature, 385,* 254–257. [2]
Searles, J. S. (1988). The role of genetics in the pathogenesis of alcoholism. *Journal of Abnormal Psychology, 97,* 153–167. [13]
Sebald, J. (1981). Adolescents' concept of popularity and unpopularity comparing 1960 with 1976. *Adolescence, 16,* 187–192. [10]
Seeman, M., & Seeman, A. Z. (1992). Life strains, alienation, and drinking behavior. *Alcoholism: Clinical and Experimental Research, 16,* 199–205. [13]
Seeman, P. (2001). Antipsychotic drugs, dopamine receptors, and schizophrenia. *Clinical Neuroscience Research, 1,* 53–60. [16]
Segal, S. J., & Fusella, V. (1970). Influence of imaged pictures and sounds on detection of visual and auditory signals. *Journal of Experimental Psychology, 83,* 458–464. [7]
Segall, M. H. (1994). A cross-cultural research contribution to unraveling the nativist/empiricist controversy. In J. Lonner & R. Malpass (Eds.), *Psychology and culture* (pp. 135–138). Boston: Allyn & Bacon. [3]
Segall, M. H., Campbell, D. T., & Herskovitz, M. J. (1966). *The influence of culture on visual perception.* Indianapolis: Bobbs-Merrill. [3]
Seger, C. A., Desmond, J. E., Glover, G. H., & Gabrieli, J. D. E. (2000). Functional magnetic resonance imaging evidence for right-hemisphere involvement in processing unusual semantic relationships. *Neuropsychology, 14,* 361–369. [2]
Seidlitz, L., & Diener, E. (1993). Memory for positive versus negative life events: Theories for the differences between happy and unhappy persons. *Journal of Personality and Social Psychology, 64,* 654–664. [6]
Sejnowski, T. J. (1997). The year of the dendrite. *Science, 275,* 178–179. [2]
Seligman, M. E. P. (1970). On the generality of the laws of learning. *Psychological Review, 77,* 406–418. [5]
Seligman, M. E. P. (1972). Phobias and preparedness. In M. E. P. Seligman & J. L. Hager (Eds.), *Biological boundaries of learning.* Englewood Cliffs, NJ: Prentice Hall.
Seligman, M. E. P. (1975). *Helplessness: On depression, development and death.* San Francisco: Freeman. [5]
Seligman, M. E. P. (1990). *Learned optimism: How to change your mind and your life.* New York: Simon & Schuster. [8, 13, 14]
Seligman, M. E. P. (1991). *Learned optimism.* New York: Knopf. [5]
Seligman, M. E. P. (1995). The effectiveness of psychotherapy: The *Consumer Reports* Study. *American Psychologist, 50,* 965–974. [16]
Seligman, M. E. P. (1996). Science as an ally of practice. *American Psychologist, 51,* 1072–1079. [16]
Selkoe, D. J. (1997). Alzheimer's disease: Genotypes, phenotype, and treatments. *Science, 275,* 630–631. [10]
Selye, H. (1956). *The stress of life.* New York: McGraw-Hill. [13]
Selye, H. (1974). *Stress without distress.* Philadelphia: Lippincott. [13]
Sensky, T., Turkington, D., Kingdon, D., Scott, J. L., Scott, J., Siddle, R., O'Carroll, M., & Barnes, T. R. E. (2000). A randomized controlled trial of cognitive-behavioral therapy for persistent symptoms in schizophrenia resistant to medication. *Archives of General Psychiatry, 57,* 165–172. [16]
Serbin, L. A., & Sprafkin, C. (1986). The salience of gender and the process of sex-typing in three- to seven-year-old children. *Child Development, 57,* 1188–1209. [12]
Serdula, M. K., Collins, M. E., Williamson, D. F., Anda, R. F., Pamuk, E. P., & Byers, T. E. (1993). Weight control practices of U.S. adolescents and adults. *Annals of Internal Medicine, 119,* 667–671. [11]
Shaffer, D., Gould, M. S., Fisher, P., Trautman, P., Moreau, D., Kleinman, M., & Flory, M. (1996). Psychiatric diagnosis in child and adolescent suicide. *Archives of General Psychiatry, 53,* 339–348. [15]
Shapiro, J. P., & Schrof, J. M. (1995, February 27). Honor thy children. *U.S. News & World Report,* pp. 38–49. [9]
Shapiro, L. (1997, April 21). Is fat that bad? *Newsweek,* pp. 58–64. [11]
Sharp, D. M., Power, K. G., Simpson, R. J., & Swanson, V. (1996). Fluvoxamine, placebo, and cognitive behaviour therapy used alone and in combination in the treatment of panic disorder and agoraphobia. *Journal of Affective Disorders, 10,* 219–242. [16]
Sharp, D., Cole, M., & Lave, C. (1979). Education and cognitive development: The evidence from experimental research. *Monographs of the Society for Research in Child Development, 44*(1–2, Serial No. 178). [9]
Shatz, M. (1983). Communication. In P. H. Mussen (Ed.), *Handbook of child psychology* (Vol. 3). New York: Wiley. [9]
Shatz, M., & Gelman, R. (1973). The development of communication skills: Modifications in the speech of young children as a function of listener. *Monographs of the Society for Research in Child Development, 38*(5, Serial No. 152), 1–37. [9]
Shaw, D. W., & Thoresen, C. E. (1974). Effects of modeling and desensitization in reducing dentist phobia. *Journal of Counseling Psychology, 21,* 415–420. [16]
Shaw, J. I., & Steers, W. N. (2001). Gathering information to form an impression: Attribute categories and information valence. *Current Research in Social Psychology, 6,* 1–21. [17]
Shaw, J. S., III. (1996). Increases in eyewitness confidence resulting from postevent questioning. *Journal of Experimental Psychology: Applied, 2,* 126–146. [6]
Shaw, V. N., Hser, Y.-I., Anglin, M. D., & Boyle, K. (1999). Sequences of powder cocaine and crack use among arrestees in Los Angeles County. *American Journal of Drug and Alcohol Abuse, 25,* 47–66. [4]
Shaywitz, B. A., Shaywitz, S. E., Pugh, K. R., Constable, R. T., Skudlarski, P., Fulbright, R. K., Bronen, R. A., Fletcher, J. M., Shankweiler, D. P., Katz, L., & Gore, J. C. (1995). Sex differences in the functional organization of the brain for language. *Nature, 373,* 607–609. [12]
Shaywitz, S. E. (1996, November). Dyslexia. *Scientific American, 275,* 98–104. [2, 12]
Shear, M. K., & Weiner, K. (1997). Psychotherapy for panic disorder. *Journal of Clinical Psychiatry, 58*(2, Suppl.), 38–43. [15]
Sheehan, D. V. (1983). *The anxiety disease.* New York: Scribner's. [15, 16]

Sheehan, D. V., & Raj, A. B. (1988). Monoamine oxidase inhibitors. In C. G. Last & M. Hersen (Eds.), *Handbook of anxiety disorders* (pp. 478–506). New York: Pergamon. [16]

Shepard, R. J. (1986). Exercise in coronary heart disease. *Sports Medicine, 3,* 26–49. [13]

Shepard, R. N., & Metzler, J. (1971). Mental rotation of three-dimensional objects. *Science, 171,* 701–703. [7]

Shepperd, J. A. (1993). Productivity loss in performance groups: A motivation analysis. *Psychological Bulletin, 113,* 67–81. [11]

Sher, A. E., Schechtman, K. B., & Piccirillo, J. F. (1996). The efficacy of surgical modifications of the upper airway in adults with obstructive sleep apnea syndrome. *Sleep, 19,* 156–177. [4]

Sher, L. (2000). Memory creation and the treatment of psychiatric disorders. *Medical Hypotheses, 54,* 4628–4629. [6]

Sherbourne, C. D., Wells, K. B., & Judd, L. L. (1996). Functioning and well-being of patients with panic disorder. *American Journal of Psychiatry, 153,* 213–218. [15]

Sherif, M. (1956). Experiments in group conflict. *Scientific American, 195,* 53–58. [17]

Sherif, M. (1958). Superordinate goals in the reduction of intergroup conflict. *American Journal of Sociology, 63,* 349–358. [17]

Sherif, M., & Sherif, C. W. (1967). The Robbers' Cave study. In J. F. Perez, R. C. Sprinthall, G. S. Grosser, & P. J. Anastasiou, *General psychology: Selected readings* (pp. 411–421). Princeton, NJ: D. Van Nostrand. [17]

Sherman, C. (1994, September/October). Kicking butts. *Psychology Today,* 41–45. [4, 13]

Shimamura, A. P., Berry, J. M., Mangela, J. A., Rusting, C. L., & Jurica, P. J. (1995). Memory and cognitive abilities in university professors: Evidence for successful aging. *Psychological Science, 6,* 271–277. [10]

Shneidman, E. (1989). The Indian summer of life: A preliminary study of septuagenarians. *American Psychologist, 44,* 684–694. [8]

Shneidman, E. S. (1994). Clues to suicide, reconsidered. *Suicide and Life-Threatening Behavior, 24,* 395-397. [15]

Shoda, Y., & Mischel, W. (2000). Reconciling contextualism with the core assumptions of personality psychology. *European Journal of Personality, 14,* 407–428. [14]

Shoda, Y., Mischel, W., & Peake, P. K. (1990). Predicting adolescent cognitive and self-regulatory competencies from preschool delay of gratification. *Developmental Psychology, 26,* 978–986. [8]

Shulman, H. G. (1972). Semantic confusion errors in short-term memory. *Journal of Verbal Learning and Verbal Behavior, 11,* 221–227. [6]

Sia, T. L., Lord, C. G., Blessum, K. A., Ratcliff, C. D., & Lepper, M. R. (1997). Is a rose always a rose? The role of social category exemplar change in attitude stability and attitude-behavior consistency. *Journal of Personality and Social Psychology, 72,* 501–514. [17]

Siegler, R. S. (1991). *Children's thinking* (2nd ed.). Englewood Cliffs, NJ: Prentice-Hall. [9, 10]

Siegrist, J., Peter, R., Junge, A., Cremer, P., & Seidel, D. (1990). Low status control, high effort at work and ischemic heart disease: Prospective evidence from blue-collar men. *Social Science and Medicine, 31,* 1127–1134. [13]

Signorielli, N. (1990). Children, television, and gender roles: Messages and impact. *Journal of Adolescent Health Care, 11*(1), 50–58. [12]

Silva, C. E., & Kirsch, I. (1992). Interpretive sets, expectancy, fantasy proneness, and dissociation as predictors of hypnotic response. *Journal of Personality and Social Psychology, 63,* 847–856. [4]

Silveri, M. C., & Misciagna, S. (2000). Language, memory, and the cerebellum. *Journal of Neurolinguistics, 13,* 129–143. [5]

Simmons, R. G., Blyth, D. A., & McKinney, K. L. (1983). The social and psychological effects of puberty on white females. In J. Brooks-Gunn & A. C. Peterson (Eds.), *Girls at puberty: Biological and psychosocial perspectives.* New York: Plenum. [10]

Simon, H. A. (1974). How big is a chunk? *Science, 183,* 482–488. [6]

Simon, H. A. (1995). The information-processing theory of mind. *American Psychologist, 50,* 507–508. [7]

Simon, H. B. (1988, June). Running and rheumatism. *Harvard Medical School Health Letter, 13,* 2–4. [13]

Simon, L., Greenberg, J., & Brehm, J. (1995). Trivialization: The forgotten mode of dissonance reduction. *Journal of Personality and Social Psychology, 68,* 247–260. [17]

Simpson, S. (2000). Dyslexia: A developmental language disorder. *Child: Care, Health and Development, 26,* 355–380. [9]

Singer, J. L. (1975). Navigating the stream of consciousness: Research on daydreaming and related inner experiences. *American Psychologist, 30,* 727–738. [4]

Singer, J. L., & Singer, D. G. (1979, March). Come back, Mister Rogers, come back. *Psychology Today,* pp. 56–60. [9]

Singer, M. I., Miller, D. B., Guo, S., Flannery, D. J., Frierson, T., & Slovak, K. (1999). Contributors to violent behavior among elementary and middle school children. *Pediatrics, 104*(Pt. 1), 878–884. [17]

Singh, D. (1995a). Female judgment of male attractiveness and desirability for relationships: Role of waist-to-hip ratio and financial status. *Journal of Personality and Social Psychology, 69,* 1089–1101. [17]

Singh, D. (1995b). Female health, attractiveness, and desirability for relationships: Role of breast asymmetry and waist-hip ratio. *Ethology and Sociobiology, 16,* 445–481. [17]

Sivacek, J., & Crano, W. D. (1982). Vested interest as a moderator of attitude-behavior consistency. *Journal of Personality and Social Psychology, 43,* 210–221. [17]

Skarborn, M., & Nicki, R. (2000). Worry in pre-and post-retirement persons. *International Journal of Aging and Human Development, 50,* 61–71. [10]

Skiera, G., Petersen, D., Skalej, M., & Fahle, M. (2000). Correlates of figure-ground segregation in fMRI. *Vision Research, 40,* 2047–2056. [3]

Skinner, B. F. (1938). *The behavior of organisms.* New York: Appleton-Century-Crofts. [5]

Skinner, B. F. (1948a). "Superstition" in the pigeon. *Journal of Experimental Psychology, 38,* 168–172. [5]

Skinner, B. F. (1948b). *Walden two.* New York: Macmillan. [5]

Skinner, B. F. (1953). *Science and human behavior.* New York: Macmillan. [5, 14]

Skinner, B. F. (1957). *Verbal behavior.* New York: Appleton Century. [9]

Skinner, B. F. (1971). *Beyond freedom and dignity.* New York: Knopf. [5]

Skinner, B. F. (1988). The operant side of behavior therapy. *Journal of Behavior Therapy and Experimental Psychiatry, 19,* 171–179. [5]

Skrabalo, A. (2000). Negative symptoms in schizophrenia(s): The conceptual basis. *Harvard Brain, 7,* 7–10. [15]

Skuy, M., Taylor, M., O'Carroll, S., Fridjhon, P., & Rosenthal, L. (2000). Performance of black and white South African children on the Wechsler Intelligence Scale for Children—Revised and the Kaufman Assessment Battery. *Psychological Reports, 86,* 1727–1737. [8]

Slaby, R. G., Roedell, W. C., Arezzo, D., & Hendrix, K. (1995). *Early violence prevention.* Washington, DC: National Association for the Education of Young Children. [9]

Slawinski, E. B., Hartel, D. M., & Kline, D. W. (1993). Self-reported hearing problems in daily life throughout adulthood. *Psychology and Aging, 8,* 552–561. [10]

Slipp, S. (1999). From divergence to convergence in American psychoanalysis: The influence of Freud's background on the splitting of the psychoanalytic movement. *Journal of the American Academy of Psychoanalysis, 27,* 503–514. [14]

Slobin, D. (1972, July). Children and language: They learn the same all around the world. *Psychology Today,* pp. 71–74, 82. [9]

Slon, S. (1997, June). Night moves. *Prevention, 49,* 106–113. [4]

Smeaton, G., Byrne, D., & Murnen, S. K. (1989). The repulsion hypothesis revisited: Similarity irrelevance or dissimilarity bias? *Journal of Personality and Social Psychology, 56,* 54–59. [17]

Smith, C. (1995). Sleep states and memory processes. *Behavioural Brain Research, 69,* 137–145. [4]

Smith, D. (1982). Trends in counseling and psychotherapy. *American Psychologist, 37,* 802–809. [16]

Smith, K. H., & Rogers, M. (1994). Effectiveness of subliminal messages in television commercials: Two experiments. *Journal of Applied Psychology, 79,* 866–874. [3]

Smith, M. L., Glass, G. V., & Miller, T. I. (1980). *The benefits of psychotherapy.* Baltimore, MD: Johns Hopkins University Press. [16]

Smith, P. K. (1979). The ontogeny of fear in children. In W. Sluckin (Ed.), *Fears in animals and man* (pp. 164–168). London: Von Nostrand Reinhold. [9]

Smith, S. M. (1979). Remembering in and out of context. *Journal of Experimental Psychology: Human Learning and Memory, 5,* 460–471. [6]

Smith, S. M., Glenberg, A., & Bjork, R. A. (1978). Environmental context and human memory. *Memory & Cognition, 6,* 342–353. [6]

Snarey, J. R. (1985). Cross-cultural universality of social-moral development: A critical review of Kohlbergian research. *Psychological Bulletin, 97,* 202–232. [10]

Snarey, J. R. (1995). In communitarian voice: The sociological expansion of Kohlbergian theory, research, and practice. In W. M. Kurtines & J. L. Gerwirtz (Eds.), *Moral development: An introduction* (pp. 109–134). Boston: Allyn & Bacon. [10]

Snow, C. E. (1993). Bilingualism and second language acquisition. In J. B. Gleason & N. B. Ratner (Eds.), *Psycholinguistics.* Fort Worth, TX: Harcourt. [7, 8]

Snowden, J. S., Griffiths, H. L., & Neary, D. (1996). Semantic-episodic memory interactions in semantic dementia: Implications for retrograde memory function. *Cognitive Neuropsychology, 13,* 1101–1137. [6]

Snyder, F. (1971). Psychophysiology of human sleep. *Clinical Neurosurgery, 18,* 503–536. [4]

Sobell, M. B., & Sobell, L. C. (1978). *Behavioral treatment of alcohol problems.* New York: Plenum. [13]

Sobin, C., & Sackeim, H. A. (1997). Psychomotor symptoms of depression. *American Journal of Psychiatry, 154,* 4–17. [15]

Söderfeldt, B., Rönnberg, J., & Risberg, J. (1994). Regional cerebral blood flow in sign language users. *Brain and Language, 46,* 59–68. [2]

Soininen, H. S., & Riekkinen, P. J., Sr. (1996). Apolipoprotein E, memory and Alzheimer's disease. *Trends in Neurosciences, 19,* 224–228. [10]

Sokolov, E. N. (2000). Perception and the conditioning reflex: Vector encoding. *International Journal of Psychophysiology, 35,* 197–217. [3]

Soler, H., Vinayak, P., & Quadagno, D. (2000). Biosocial aspects of domestic violence. *Psychoneuroendocrinology, 25,* 721–739. [17]

Solms, M. (2000). Dreaming and REM sleep are controlled by different brain mechanisms. *Behavioral and Brain Sciences, 23*(6). [4]

Solomon, P. R., Blanchard, S., Levine, E., Velazquez, E., & Groccia-Ellison, M-E. (1991). Attenuation of age-related conditioning deficits in humans by extension of the interstimulus interval. *Psychology and Aging, 6,* 36–42. [5]

Solso, R. (1991). *Cognitive psychology* (3rd ed.). Boston: Allyn & Bacon. [7]

Spangler, D. L., Simons, A. D., Monroe, S. M., & Thase, M. E. (1996). Gender differences in cognitive diathesis-stress domain match: Implications for differential pathways to depression. *Journal of Abnormal Psychology, 105,* 653–657. [15]

Spangler, W. D. (1992). Validity of questionnaire and TAT measures of need for achievement: Two meta-analyses. *Psychological Bulletin, 112,* 140–154. [11]

Spanos, N. P. (1986). Hypnotic behavior: A social-psychological interpretation of amnesia, analgesia, and "trance logic." *Behavioral and Brain Sciences, 9,* 499–502. [4]

Spanos, N. P. (1991). A sociocognitive approach to hypnosis. In S. J. Lynn & J. W. Rhue (Eds.), *Theories of hypnosis: Current models and perspectives* (pp. 324–361). New York: Guilford. [4]

Spanos, N. P. (1994). Multiple identity enactments and multiple personality disorder: A sociocognitive perspective. *Psychological Bulletin, 116,* 143–165. [4, 15]

Spearman, C. (1927). *The abilities of man.* New York: Macmillan. [8]

Sperling, G. (1960). The information available in brief visual presentations. *Psychological Monographs: General and Applied, 74,* Whole No. 498, 1–29. [6]

Sperry, R. W. (1964). The great cerebral commissure. *Scientific American, 210,* 42–52. [2]

Sperry, R. W. (1968). Hemisphere deconnection and unity in conscious experience. *American Psychologist, 23,* 723–733. [2]

Spetch, M. L., Wilkie, D. M., & Pinel, J. P. J. (1981). Backward conditioning: A reevaluation of the empirical evidence. *Psychological Bulletin, 89,* 163–175. [5]

Spirito, A., Jelalian, E., Rasile, D., Rohrbeck, C., & Vinnick, L. (2000). Adolescent risk taking and self-reported injuries associated with substance use. *American Journal of Drug and Alcohol Abuse, 26,* 113–123. [4]

Spitz, R. A. (1946). Hospitalism: A follow-up report on investigation described in Volume I, 1945. *The Psychoanalytic Study of the Child, 2,* 113–117. [9]

Spitzer, M. W., & Semple, M. N. (1991). Interaural phase coding in auditory midbrain: Influence of dynamic stimulus features. *Science, 254,* 721–724. [3]

Spitzer, R. L., Gibbon, M., Skodol, A. E., Williams, J. B. W., & First, M. B. (1989). *DSM-III-R casebook.* Washington, DC: American Psychiatric Press. [15]

Spooner, A., & Kellogg, W. N. (1947). The backward conditioning curve. *American Journal of Psychology, 60,* 321–334. [5]

Sporer, S. L., Penrod, S., Read, D., & Cutler, B. (1995). Choosing, confidence, and accuracy: A meta-analysis of the confidence-accuracy relation in eyewitness identification studies. *Psychological Bulletin, 118,* 315–327. [6]

Sprecher, S., & Hatfield, E. (1996). Premarital sexual standards among U.S. college students: Comparison with Russian and Japanese students. *Archives of Sexual Behavior, 25,* 261–288. [12]

Sprecher, S., & Regan, P. C. (1996). College virgins: How men and women perceive their sexual status. *Journal of Sex Research, 33,* 3–15. [12]

Squire, L. R. (1992). Memory and the hippocampus: A synthesis from findings with rats, monkeys, and humans. *Psychological Review, 99,* 195–231. [2, 6]

Squire, L. R., Knowlton, B., & Musen, G. (1993). The structure and organization of memory. *Annual Review of Psychology, 44,* 453–495. [6]

Staal, W. G., Pol, H. E. H., Schnack, H. G., Hoogendoorn, M. L. C., Jellema, K., & Kahn, R. S. (2000). Structural brain abnormalities in patients with schizophrenia and their healthy siblings. *American Journal of Psychiatry, 157,* 416–421. [15]

Stage, K. B., Glassman, A. H., & Covey, L. S. (1996). Depression after smoking cessation: Case reports. *Journal of Clinical Psychiatry, 57,* 467–469. [13]

Stahl, S. M. (1997). Mental illness may be damaging to your brain. *Journal of Clinical Psychiatry, 58,* 289–290. [15]

Stahl, S. M. (1998). Basic psychopharmacology of antidepressants, part 1: Antidepressants have seven distinct mechanisms of action. *Journal of Clinical Psychiatry, 59*(4, Suppl.), 5–14. [16]

Stanovich, K. E. (1989). *How to think straight about psychology* (2nd ed.). Glenview, IL: Scott, Foresman. [14]

Stanton, M. E. (2000). Multiple memory systems, development and conditioning. *Behavioural Brain Research, 110,* 25–37. [5]

Stark, C. E., & Squire, L. R. (2000). Functional magnetic resonance imaging (fMRI) activity in the hippocampal region during recognition memory. *Journal of Neuroscience, 20,* 7776–7781. [6]

Stark, E. (1984, October). Answer this question: Responses: To sleep, perchance to dream. *Psychology Today,* p. 16. [4]

Stattin, H., & Magnusson, D. (1990). *Pubertal maturation in female development.* Hillsdale, NJ: Erlbaum. [10]

Stea, R. A., & Apkarian, A. V. (1992). Pain and somatosensory activation. *Trends in Neurosciences, 15,* 250–251. [2]

Steblay, N. M. (1992). A meta-analytic review of the weapon focus effect. *Law and Human Behavior, 16,* 413–424. [6]

Steffens, A. B., Scheurink, A. J., & Luiten, P. G. (1988). Hypothalamic food intake regulating areas are involved in the homeostasis of blood glucose and plasma FFA levels. *Physiology and Behavior, 44,* 581–589. [11]

Stein, A. H., & Friedrich, L. K. (1975). Impact of television on children and youth. In E. M. Hetherington (Ed.), *Review of child development research* (Vol. 5, pp. 183–256). Chicago: University of Chicago Press. [9]

Stein, M. B., & Kean, Y. M. (2000). Disability and quality of life in social phobia: Epidemiologic findings. *American Journal of Psychiatry, 157,* 1606–1613. [15]

Stein, M. B., Walker, J. R., & Forde, D. R. (1996). Public-speaking fears in a community sample: Prevalence, impact on functioning, and diagnostic classification. *Archives of General Psychiatry, 53,* 169–174. [15]

Stein-Behrens, B., Mattson, M. P., Chang, I., Yeh, M., & Sapolsky, R. (1994). Stress exacerbates neuron loss and cytoskeletal

pathology in the hippocampus. *Journal of Neuroscience, 14,* 5373–5380. [13]
Steinberg, L. (1990). Autonomy, conflict, and harmony in the family relationship. In S. S. Feldman & R. E. Glen (Eds.), *At the threshold: The developing adolescent.* Cambridge, MA: Harvard University Press. [10]
Steinberg, L. (1992). Ethnic differences in adolescent achievement: An ecological perspective. *American Psychologist, 47,* 723–729. [10]
Steinberg, L., Elman, J. D., & Mounts, N. S. (1989). Authoritative parenting, psychosocial maturity, and academic success among adolescents. *Child Development, 60,* 1424–1436. [9, 10]
Steinberg, L., Fegley, S., & Dornbusch, S. M. (1993). Negative impact of part-time work on adolescent adjustment: Evidence from a longitudinal study. *Developmental Psychology, 29,* 171–180. [10]
Steinberg, L., Lamborn, S. D., Darling, N., Mounts, N. S., & Dornbusch, S. M. (1994). Over-time changes in adjustment and competence among adolescents from authoritative, authoritarian, indulgent, and neglectful families. *Child Development, 65,* 754–770. [10]
Steinman, L. (1993). Autoimmune disease. *Scientific American, 269,* 106–114. [13]
Steinman, R. M., Pizlo, Z., & Pizlo, F. J. (2000). Phi is not beta, and why Wertheimer's discovery launched the Gestalt revolution. *Vision Research, 40,* 25–32. [3]
Steinmetz, J. E. (2000). Brain substrates of classical eyeblink conditioning: A highly localized but also distributed system. *Behavioural Brain Research, 110,* 13–24. [5]
Stelmack, R. M. (1990). Biological bases of extraversion: Psychophysiological evidence. *Journal of Personality, 58,* 293–311. [14]
Stemberger, R. T., Turner, S. M., Beidel, D. C., & Calhoun, K. S. (1995). Social phobia: An analysis of possible developmental factors. *Journal of Abnormal Psychology, 104,* 526–531. [15]
Stephan, K. M., Fink, G. R., Passingham, R. E., Silbersweig, D., Ceballos-Baumann, A. O., Frith, C. D., & Frackowiak, R. S. J. (1995). Functional anatomy of the mental representation of upper extremity movements in healthy subjects. *Journal of Neurophysiology, 73,* 373–386. [7]
Stephenson, M. T., & Witte, K. (1998). Fear, threat, and perceptions of efficiency from frightening skin cancer messages. *Public Health Review, 26,* 147–174. [17]
Steptoe, A. (2000). Stress, social support and cardiovascular activity over the working day. *International Journal of Psychophysiology, 37,* 299–308. [11, 13]
Steriade, M. (1996). Arousal: Revisiting the reticular activating system. *Science, 272,* 225–226. [2]
Stern, K., & McClintock, M. K. (1998). Regulation of ovulation by human pheromones. *Nature, 192,* 177–179. [3]
Stern, W. (1914). *The psychological methods of testing intelligence.* Baltimore: Warwick and York. [8]
Sternberg, R. J. (1985a). *Beyond IQ: A triarchic theory of human intelligence.* New York: Cambridge University Press. [8]
Sternberg, R. J. (1985b). Human intelligence: The model is the message. *Science, 230,* 1111–1118. [8]
Sternberg, R. J. (1986a). *Intelligence applied: Understanding and increasing your intellectual skills.* San Diego: Harcourt Brace Jovanovich. [8]
Sternberg, R. J. (1986b). A triangular theory of love. *Psychological Review, 93,* 119–135. [11]
Sternberg, R. J. (1987). Liking versus loving: A comparative evaluation of theories. *Psychological Bulletin, 102,* 331–345. [11]
Sternberg, R. J. (2000). The holey grail of general intelligence. *Science, 289,* 399–401. [8]
Sternberg, R. J., Wagner, R. K., Williams, W. M., & Horvath, J. A. (1995). Testing common sense. *American Psychologist, 50,* 912–927. [8]
Stevenson, H. W. (1992). Learning from Asian schools. *Scientific American, 267,* 70–76. [8]
Stevenson, H. W., Chen, C., & Lee, S. Y. (1993). Mathematics achievement of Chinese, Japanese, and American children: Ten years later. *Science, 259,* 53–58. [8]
Stevenson, H. W., Lee, S. Y., & Stigler, J. W. (1986). Mathematics achievement of Chinese, Japanese, and American children. *Science, 231,* 693–699. [8]
Stevenson, H. W., Lee, S. Y., Chen, C., Stigler, J. W., Hsu, C. C., & Kitamura, S. (1990). Contexts of achievement. *Monographs of the Society for Research in Child Development, 55*(1–2, Serial No. 221). [8]
Stevenson, M. R., & Black, K. N. (1988). Paternal absence and sex-role development: A meta-analysis. *Child Development, 59,* 793–814. [12]
Stewart, J. (2000). *Evolution's arrow: The direction of evolution and the future of humanity.* Canberra, Aust.: Chapman Press. [1]
Stewart, V. M. (1973). Tests of the "carpentered world" hypothesis by race and environment in America and Zambia. *International Journal of Psychology, 8,* 83–94. [3]
Stiff, J. B., Miller, G. R., Sleight, C., Mongeau, P. L., Garlick, R., & Rogan, R. (1989). Explanations for visual cue primacy in judgments of honesty and deceit. *Journal of Personality and Social Psychology, 56,* 555–564. [17]
Stone, E. F. (1986). Job scope–job satisfaction and job scope–job performance relationships. In E. A. Locke (Ed.), *Generalizing from laboratory to field settings* (pp. 189–206). Lexington, MA: Lexington Books. [11]
Stovall, K. C., & Dozier, M. (2000). The development of attachment in new relationships: Single subject analyses for 10 foster infants. *Developmental Psychopathology, 12,* 2133–2156. [9]
Strack, F., Martin, L. L., & Stepper, S. (1988). Inhibiting and facilitating conditions of facial expressions: A nonobtrusive test of the facial feedback hypothesis. *Journal of Personality and Social Psychology, 54,* 768–777. [11]
Strakowski, S. M., Lonczak, H. S., Sax, K. W., West, S. A., Crist, A., Mehta, R., & Thienhaus, O. J. (1995). The effects of race on diagnosis and disposition from a psychiatric emergency service. *Journal of Clinical Psychiatry, 56,* 101–107. [16]
Strassberg, Z. (2000). Interpretations of child emotion expressions and coercive parenting practices among adolescent mothers. *Social Development, 9*(1). [10]
Strauss, E., Spreen, O., & Hunter, M. (2000). Implications of test revisions for research. *Psychological Assessment, 12,* 237–244. [8]
Strawbridge, W. J., Cohen, R. D., Shema, S. J., & Kaplan, G. A. (1997). Frequent attendance at religious services and mortality over 28 years. *American Journal of Public Health, 87,* 957–961. [13]
Streissguth, A. P., Barr, H. M., Sampson, P. D., Darby, B. L., & Martin, D. C. (1989). IQ at age 4 in relation to maternal alcohol use and smoking during pregnancy. *Developmental Psychology, 25,* 3–11. [9]
Strentz, H. (1986, January 1). Become a psychic and amaze your friends! *Atlanta Journal,* p. 15A. [3]
Strickland, B. R. (1995). Research on sexual orientation and human development: A commentary. *Developmental Psychology, 31,* 137–140. [12]
Strobel, R. J., & Rosen, R. C. (1996). Obesity and weight loss in obstructive sleep apnea: A critical review. *Sleep, 19,* 104–115. [4]
Stroebe, M., & Schut, H. (1999). The dual process model of coping with bereavement: Rationale and description. *Death Studies, 23,* 197–224. [10]
Strome, M., & Vernick, D. (1989, April). Hearing loss and hearing aids. *Harvard Medical School Health Letter, 14,* pp. 5–8. [3]
Stromeyer, C. F., III. (1970, November). Eidetikers. *Psychology Today,* pp. 76–80. [6]
Stubbs, P. (2000). *Mental health care online.* [16]
Stuss, D. T., Gow, C. A., & Hetherington, C. R. (1992). "No longer Gage": Frontal lobe dysfunction and emotional changes. *Journal of Consulting and Clinical Psychology, 60,* 349–359. [2]
Suarez, M. G. (1983). Implications of Spanish-English bilingualism in the TAT stories. Unpublished doctoral dissertation, University of Connecticut. [16]
Sue, D. W. (1994). Asian-American mental health and help-seeking behavior: Comment on Solbert et al. (1994), Tata and Leong (1994), and Lin (1994). *Journal of Counseling Psychology, 41,* 292–295. [16]
Sue, D. W., & Sue, D. (1990). *Counseling the culturally different: Theory and practice.* New York: Wiley. [16]
Sue, S. (1999). Science, ethnicity, and bias: Where have we gone wrong? *American Psychologist, 54,* 1070–1077. [1]
Suedfeld, P. (1990). Restricted environmental stimulation and smoking cessation: A 15-year progress report. *International Journal of the Addictions, 25,* 861–888. [11]
Sullivan, A. D., Hedberg, K., & Fleming, D. W. (2000). Legalized physician-assisted suicide in Oregon—The second year. *New England Journal of Medicine, 342,* 598–604. [10]

Sullivan, E. V. (1977). A study of Kohlberg's structural theory of moral development: A critique of liberal social science ideology. *Human Development, 20,* 352–376. [10]

Sullivan, E. V., Deshmukh, A., Desmond, J. E., Lim, K. O., & Pfefferbaum, A. (2000). Cerebellar volume decline in normal aging, alcoholism, and Korsakoff's syndrome: Relation to ataxia. *Neuropsychology, 14,* 341–352. [2]

Sullivan, M. J. L., Bishop, S. R., & Pivik, J. (1995). The pain catastrophizing scale: Development and validation. *Psychological Assessment, 7,* 524–532. [3]

Sulloway, F. J. (1996). *Born to rebel: Birth order, family dynamics, and creative lives.* New York: Pantheon. [14]

Sulloway, F. J. (1997, September). Birth order and personality. *Harvard Mental Health Letter, 14*(3), 5–7. [14]

Sung, K-T. (1992). Motivations for parent care: The case of filial children in Korea. *International Journal of Aging and Human Development, 34,* 109–124. [10]

Super, C. W. (1981). Behavioral development in infancy. In R. H. Munroe, R. L. Munroe, & B. B. Whiting (Eds.), *Handbook of cross-cultural human development* (pp. 181–269). Chicago: Garland. [9]

Sussman, S., & Dent, C. W. (2000). One-year prospective prediction of drug use from stress-related variables. *Substance Use & Misuse, 35,* 717–735. [4]

Swaab, D. E., & Hofman, M. A. (1995). Sexual differentiation in the human hypothalamus in relation to gender and sexual orientation. *Trends in Neurosciences, 18,* 264–270. [12]

Swaffer, T., Hollin, C., Beech, A., Beckett, R., & Fisher, D. (2000). An exploration of child sexual abusers' sexual fantasies before and after treatment. *Sexual Abuse: A Journal of Research and Treatment, 2,* 61–68. [12]

Swain, I. U., Zelazo, P. R., & Clifton, R. K. (1993). Newborn infants' memory for speech sounds retained over 24 hours. *Developmental Psychology, 29,* 312–323. [9]

Swanson, L. W. (1995). Mapping the human brain: past, present, and future. *Trends in Neurosciences, 18,* 471–474. [2]

Swanson, N. G. (2000). Working women and stress. *Journal of the American Medical Womens Association, 55,* 276–279. [13]

Sweatt, J. D., & Kandel, E. R. (1989). Persistent and transcriptionally-dependent increase in protein phosphorylation in long-term facilitation of Aplysia sensory neurons. *Nature, 339,* 51–54. [6]

Swedo, S. E., Pietrini, P., Leonard, H. L., Schapiro, M. B., Rettew, D. C., Goldberger, E. L., Papoport, S. I., Rapoport, J. L., & Grady, C. L. (1992). Cerebral glucose metabolism in childhood-onset obsessive-compulsive disorder: Revisualization during pharmacotherapy. *Archives of General Psychiatry, 49,* 690–694. [15]

Swedo, S. E., Rapoport, J. L., Leonard, H., Lenane, M., & Cheslow, D. (1989). Obsessive-compulsive disorder in children and adolescents: Clinical phenomenology of 70 consecutive cases. *Archives of General Psychiatry, 46,* 335–341. [15]

Sweller, J., & Levine, M. (1982). Effects of goal specificity on means-end analysis and learning. *Journal of Experimental Psychology: Learning, Memory, and Cognition, 8,* 463–474. [7]

Swets, J. A. (1992). The science of choosing the right decision threshold in high-stakes diagnostics. *American Psychologist, 47,* 522–532. [3]

Symons, C. S., & Johnson, B. T. (1997). The self-reference effect in memory: A meta-analysis. *Psychological Bulletin, 121,* 371–394. [6]

Szymanski, K., & Harkins, S. G. (1987). Social loafing and self-evaluation with a social standard. *Journal of Personality and Social Psychology, 53,* 891–897. [17]

Takahashi, S., Matsuura, M., Tanabe, E., Yara, K., Nonaka, K., Fukura, Y., Kikuchi, M., & Kojima, T. (2000). Age at onset of schizophrenia: Gender differences and influence of temporal socioeconomic change. *Psychiatry and Clinical Neurosciences, 54,* 153–156. [15]

Takanishi, R. (1993). The opportunities of adolescence—research, interventions, and policy: Introduction to the special issue. *American Psychologist, 48,* 85–87. [10]

Talbot, J. D., Marrett, S., Evans, A. C., Meyer, E., Bushnell, M. C., & Duncan, G. H. (1991). Multiple representations of pain in human cerebral cortex. *Science, 251,* 1355–1358. [2]

Tamminga, C. A. (1996, Winter). The new generation of antipsychotic drugs. *NARSAD Research Newsletter,* pp. 4–6. [16]

Tamminga, C. A., & Conley, R. R. (1997). The application of neuroimaging techniques to drug development. *Journal of Clinical Psychiatry, 58*(10, Suppl.), 3–6. [2]

Tanda, G., Pontieri, F. E., & Di Chiara, G. (1997). Cannabinoid and heroin activation of mesolimbic dopamine transmission by a common μ1 opioid receptor mechanism. *Science, 276,* 2048–2050. [4]

Tanfer, K. (1994). Sex and disease: Playing the odds in the 1990s. *Sexually Transmitted Diseases, 21*(2, Suppl.), S65–S72. [12]

Tang, M-X., Jacobs, D., Stern, Y., Marder, K., Schofield, P., Gurland, B., Andrews, H., & Mayeux, R. (1996). Effect of oestrogen during menopause on risk and age at onset of Alzheimer's disease. *Lancet, 348,* 429–432. [10]

Tanner, J. M. (1961). *Education and physical growth.* London: University of London Press. [10]

Tanner, J. M. (1962). *Growth at adolescence* (2nd ed.). Oxford: Blackwell. [8, 10]

Tanner, J. M. (1990). *Fetus into man* (2nd ed.). Cambridge MA: Harvard University Press. [10]

Taylor, E. (1996, July / August). Peace Timothy Leary. *Psychology Today, 29,* 56–59, 84. [4]

Taylor, S. E. (1991). *Health psychology* (2nd ed.). New York: McGraw-Hill. [13]

Taylor, S. E., & Repetti, R. L. (1997). Health psychology: What is an unhealthy environment and how does it get under the skin? *Annual Review of Psychology, 48,* 411–447. [13]

Teasdale, J. D., & Fogarty, S. J. (1979). Differential effects of induced mood on retrieval of pleasant and unpleasant events from episodic memory. *Journal of Abnormal Psychology, 88,* 248–257. [6]

Tellegen, A., Lykken, D. T., Bouchard, T. J., Jr., Wilcox, K. J., Segal, N. L., & Rich, S. (1988). Personality similarity in twins reared apart and together. *Journal of Personality and Social Psychology, 54,* 1031–1039. [14]

Temmerman, M. (1994). Sexually transmitted diseases and reproductive health. *Sexually Transmitted Diseases, 21*(2, Suppl.), S55–S58. [12]

Templeton, R. D., & Quigley, J. P. (1930). The action of insulin on the motility of the gastrointestinal tract. *American Journal of Physiology, 91,* 467–474. [11]

Teng, E., Stefanacci, L., Squire, L. R., & Zola, S. M. (2000). Contrasting effects on discrimination learning after hippocampal lesions and conjoint hippocampal-caudate lesions in monkeys. *Journal of Neuroscience, 20,* 3853–3863. [6]

Terman, L. M. (1925). *Genetic studies of genius, Vol. 1: Mental and physical traits of a thousand gifted children.* Stanford, CA: Stanford University Press. [8]

Terman, L. M., & Oden, M. H. (1947). *Genetic studies of genius, Vol. 4: The gifted child grows up.* Stanford, CA: Stanford University Press. [8]

Terman, L. M., & Oden, M. H. (1959). *Genetic studies of genius, Vol. 5: The gifted group at mid-life.* Stanford, CA: Stanford University Press. [8]

Termine, N. T., & Izard, C. E. (1988). Infants' responses to their mother's expressions of joy and sadness. *Developmental Psychology, 24,* 223–229. [11]

Terrace, H. S. (1981). A report to an academy. *Annals of the New York Academy of Sciences, 364,* 115–129. [7]

Terrace, H. S. (1985). In the beginning was the "name." *American Psychologist, 40,* 1011–1028. [7]

Terrace, H. S. (1986). *Nim: A chimpanzee who learned sign language.* New York: Columbia University Press. [7]

Terry, W. S. (1988). Everyday forgetting: Data from a diary study. *Psychological Reports, 62,* 299–303. [6]

Tesch, S. A., & Whitbourne, S. K. (1982). Intimacy and identity status in young adults. *Journal of Personality and Social Psychology, 43,* 1041–1051. [10]

Tesser, A. (1993). The importance of heritability in psychological research: The case of attitudes. *Psychological Review, 100,* 129–142. [17]

Tew, J. D., Mulsant, B. H., Haskett, R. F., Prudic, J., Thase, M. E., Crowe, R. R., Dolata, D., Begley, A. E., Reynolds, C. F., III, & Sackeim, H. A. (1999). Acute efficacy of ECT in the treatment of major depression in the old-old. *American Journal of Psychiatry, 156,* 1865–1870. [16]

Thaler, R. (1980). Toward a positive theory of consumer choice. *Journal of Economic Behavior and Organization, 1,* 39–60. [7]

Tham, K., Borell, L., & Gustavsson, A. (2000). The discovery of disability: A phenomenological study of unilateral neglect. *American Journal of Occupational Therapy, 54,* 398–406. [2]

Thase, M. E., & Kupfer, D. J. (1996). Recent developments in the pharmacotherapy of mood disorders. *Journal of Consulting and Clinical Psychology, 64,* 646–659. [16]

Thase, M. E., Frank, E., Mallinger, A. G., Hammer, T., & Kupfer, D. J. (1992). Treatment of imipramine-resistant recurrent depression, III: Efficacy of monoamine oxidise inhibitors. *Journal of Clinical Psychiatry, 53*(1, Suppl.), 5–11. [16]

Thase, M. E., Simons, A. D., Cahalane, J. F., & McGeary, J. (1991). Cognitive behavior therapy of endogenous depression: Part 1: An outpatient clinical replication series. *Behavior Therapy, 22,* 457–467. [16]

Thigpen, C. H., & Cleckley, H. M. (1984). On the incidence of multiple personality disorder. *International Journal of Clinical and Experimental Hypnosis, 32,* 63–66. [15]

Thomas, A., Chess, S., & Birch, H. G. (1970). The origin of personality. *Scientific American, 223,* 102–109. [9]

Thomas, J. L. (1992). *Adulthood and aging.* Boston: Allyn & Bacon. [10]

Thompson, R. A. (2000). The legacy of early attachments. *Child Development, 71,* 145–152. [9]

Thompson, R. F., Swain, R., Clark, R., & Shinkman, P. (2000). Intracerebellar conditioning—Brogden and Gantt revisited. *Behavioural Brain Research, 110,* 2–11. [5]

Thompson, S. C., Sobolew-Shubin, A., Galbraith, M. E., Schwankovsky, L., & Cruzen, D. (1993). Maintaining perceptions of control: Finding perceived control in low-control circumstances. *Journal of Personality and Social Psychology, 64,* 293–304. [13]

Thorndike, E. (1898). Some experiments on animal intelligence. *Science, 7*(181), 818–824. [5]

Thorndike, E. L. (1970). *Animal intelligence: Experimental studies.* New York: Macmillan. (Original work published 1911). [5]

Thornhill, R., & Gangestad, G. W. (1994). Human fluctuating asymmetry and sexual behavior. *Psychological Science, 5,* 297–302. [17]

Thorpe, G. L., & Olson, S. L. (1990). *Behavior therapy: Concepts, procedures, and applications.* Boston: Allyn & Bacon. [16]

Thurstone, L. L. (1938). *Primary mental abilities.* Chicago: University of Chicago Press. [8]

Tiihonen, J., Hari, R., Naukkarinen, H., Rimon, R., Jousmaki, V., & Kajola, M. (1992). Modified activity of the human auditory cortex during auditory hallucinations. *American Journal of Psychiatry, 149,* 255–257. [15]

Tiihonen, J., Isohanni, M., Räsänen, P., Koiranen, M., & Moring, J. (1997). Specific major mental disorders and criminality: A 26-year prospective study of the 1966 northern Finland birth cohort. *American Journal of Psychiatry, 154,* 840–845. [17]

Tinkle, M. B. (1990). Genital human papillomavirus infection: A growing health risk. *Journal of Obstetric, Gynecologic, & Neonatal Nursing, 19,* 501–507. [12]

Tollefson, G. D., Rampey, A. H., Jr., Potvin, J. H., Jenike, M. A., Rush, A. J., Dominguez, R. A., Koran, L. M., Shear, M. K., Goodman, W., & Genduso, L. A. (1994). A multicenter investigation of fixed-dose fluoxetine in the treatment of obsessive-compulsive disorder. *Archives of General Psychiatry, 51,* 559–567. [16]

Tolman, E. C. (1932). *Purposive behavior in animals and men.* New York: Appleton-Century-Crofts. [5]

Tolman, E. C., & Honzik, C. H. (1930). Introduction and removal of reward, and maze performance in rats. *University of California Publications in Psychology, 4,* 257–275. [5]

Tomasello, M. (2000). The item-based nature of children's early syntactic development. *Trends in Cognitive Sciences, 4,* 156–163. [9]

Tomkins, S. (1962). *Affect, imagery, and consciousness: The positive effects* (Vol. 1). New York: Springer. [11]

Tomkins, S. (1963). *Affect, imagery, and consciousness: The negative effects* (Vol. 2). New York: Springer. [11]

Tondo, L., Baldessarini, R. J., Hennen, J., & Floris, G. (1998). Lithium maintenance treatment of depression and mania in bipolar I and bipolar II disorders. *American Journal of Psychiatry, 155,* 638–645. [16]

Torrey, E. F. (1983). *Surviving schizophrenia: A family manual.* New York: Harper & Row. [15, 16]

Torrey, E. F., & Bowler, A. (1990). Geographical distribution of insanity in America: Evidence for an urban factor. *Schizophrenia Bulletin, 16,* 591–604. [15]

Tosini, G., & Menaker, M. (1996). Circadian rhythms in cultured mammalian retina. *Science, 272,* 419–421. [4]

Toufexis, A. (1988, February 22). Older—but coming on strong. *Time,* pp. 76–79. [10]

Tourangeau, R., Smith, T. W., & Rasinski, K. A. (1997). Motivation to report sensitive behaviors on surveys: Evidence from a bogus pipeline experiment. *Journal of Applied Social Psychology, 27,* 209–222. [1]

Traverso, A., Ravera, G., Lagattolla, V., Testa, S., & Adami, G. F. (2000). Weight loss after dieting with behavioral modification for obesity: The predicting efficiency of some psychometric data. *Eating and Weight Disorders: Studies on Anorexia, Bulimia, and Obesity, 5,* 102–107. [11]

Travis, J. (1996). Brains in space. *Science News, 149,* 28–29. [2]

Tresemer, D. W. (1977). *Fear of success.* New York: Plenum. [11]

Triandis, H. C. (1994). *Culture and social behavior.* New York: McGraw-Hill. [11]

Triandis, H. C., McCusker, C., Betancourt, H., Iwao, S., Leung, K., Salazar, J. M., Setiadi, B., Sinha, J. B. P., Touzard, H., & Zaleski, Z. (1993). An etic-emic analysis of individualism and collectivism. *Journal of Cross-Cultural Psychology, 24,* 366–383. [14]

Trimble, J. E. (1994). Cultural variations in the use of alcohol and drugs. In W. J. Lonner & R. Malpass (Eds.), *Psychology and culture* (pp. 79–84). Boston: Allyn & Bacon. [4]

Triplet, R. G. (1992). Henry A. Murray: The making of a psychologist? *American Psychologist, 47,* 299–307. [14]

Triplett, N. (1898). The dynamogenic factors in pacemaking and competition. *American Journal of Psychology, 9,* 507–533. [17]

Trivedi, M. J. (1996). Functional neuroanatomy of obsessive-compulsive disorder. *Journal of Clinical Psychiatry, 57*(8, Suppl.), 26–36. [15, 16]

True, W. R., Rice, J., Eisen, S. A., Heath, A. C., Goldberg, J., Lyons, M. J., & Nowak, J. (1993). A twin study of genetic and environmental contributions to liability for posttraumatic stress symptoms. *Archives of General Psychiatry, 50,* 257–264. [13]

Tubbs, M. E., Boehne, D., & Dahl, J. G. (1993). Expectancy, valence, and motivational force functions in goal-setting research: An empirical test. *Journal of Applied Psychology, 78,* 361–373. [11]

Tueth, M. J. (2000). Exposing financial exploitation of impaired elderly persons. *American Journal of Geriatric Psychiatry, 8,* 104–111. [10]

Tulving, E. (1974). Cue-dependent forgetting. *American Scientist, 62,* 74–82. [6]

Tulving, E. (1989). Remembering and knowing the past. *American Scientist, 77,* 361–367. [6]

Tulving, E. (1995). Organization of memory: Quo vadis? In M. S. Gazzaniga (Ed.), *The cognitive neurosciences.* Cambridge, MA: MIT Press. [6]

Tulving, E., Schacter, D. L., McLachlan, D. R., & Moscovitch, M. (1988). Priming of semantic autobiographical knowledge: A case study of retrograde amnesia. *Brain and Cognition, 8,* 3–20. [6]

Tulving, E., & Thompson, D. M. (1973). Encoding specificity and retrieval processes in episodic memory. *Psychological Review, 80,* 352–373. [6]

Tuncer, A. M., & Yalcin, S. S. (2000). Multimedia and children in Turkey. *Turkish Journal of Pediatrics, 41*(Suppl.), 27–34. [9]

Turner, C. F., Danella, R. D., & Rogers, S. M. (1995). Sexual behavior in the United States, 1930–1990: Trends and methodological problems. *Sexually Transmitted Diseases, 22,* 173–190. [12]

Turner, J. C., Hogg, M. A., Oakes, P. J., Reicher, S. D., & Wetherell, M. S. (1987). *Rediscovering the social group: A self-categorization theory.* Oxford, England: Blackwell. [17]

Turner, T. J., & Ortony, A. (1992). Basic emotions: Can conflicting criteria converge? *Psychological Review, 99,* 566–571. [11]

Tversky, A. (1972). Elimination by aspects: A theory of choice. *Psychological Review, 79,* 281–299. [7]

Tversky, A., & Kahneman, D. (1973). Availability: A heuristic for judging frequency and probability. *Cognitive Psychology, 5,* 207–232. [7]

Tzschentke, T. M. (2001). Pharmacology and behavioral pharmacology of mesocortical dopamine system. *Progress in Neurobiology, 63,* 241–320. [15]

Ubell, E. (1996, September 15). Are you at risk? *Parade Magazine,* pp. 10–11. [12]

Uchino, B. N., Cacioppo, J. T., & Kiecolt-Glaser, J. K. (1996). The relationship between social support and physiological processes: A review with emphasis on underlying mechanisms and implications for health. *Psychological Bulletin, 119,* 488–531. [13]

Udry, J. R., Billy, J. O. G., Morris, N. M., Groff, T. R., & Raj, M. H. (1985). Serum androgenic hormones motivate sexual behavior in adolescent boys. *Fertility and Sterility, 43,* 90–94. [12]

Umberson, D., Wortman, C. B., & Kessler, R. C. (1992). Widowhood and depression: Explaining long-term gender differences in vulnerability. *Journal of Health and Social Behavior, 33,* 10–24. [10]

Underwood, B. J. (1957). Interference and forgetting. *Psychological Review, 64,* 49–60. [6]

Underwood, B. J. (1964). Forgetting. *Scientific American, 210,* 91–99. [6]

Unger, R. K., & Crawford, M. (1996). *Women and gender: A feminist psychology* (2nd ed.). New York: McGraw-Hill. [12]

Ungerleider, L. G. (1995). Functional brain imaging studies of cortical mechanisms for memory. *Science, 270,* 769–775. [6]

Ungerleider, S. (1992, July/August). Visions of victory. *Psychology Today,* pp. 46–53, 83. [7]

Updegraff, K. A., Crouter, A. C., Salehi-Isfahani, D., King, S. J., McHale, S. M., Rumsey, A., Tucker, C. J., & Jackson-Newsom, J. (2000). When does parents' differential treatment have negative implications for siblings? *Social Development, 9*(2). [10]

Urbano-Marquez, A., Estruch, R., Navarro-Lopez, F., Grau, J. M., Mont, L., & Rubin, E. (1989). The effects of alcoholism on skeletal and cardiac muscle. *New England Journal of Medicine, 320,* 409–415. [13]

U.S. Bureau of the Census. (1994). *Statistical abstract of the United States 1994* (114th ed.). Washington, DC: U.S. Government Printing Office. [10, 15]

U.S. Bureau of the Census. (1997). *Statistical Abstracts of the United States 1997* (117th ed.). Washington, DC: U.S. Government Printing Office. [10, 12, 14]

U.S. Bureau of the Census. (1999). *Statistical Abstracts of the United States 1999* (119th ed.). Washington DC: U.S. Government Printing Office. [15]

U.S. Bureau of the Census. (2000). Native resident population estimates of the United States by sex, race, and Hispanic origin. Population Estimates Program, Population Division [On-line]. Available: http://www.census.gov/population estimates/nation/nativity/nbtab003.txt [1, 13]

U.S. Department of Health and Human Services. (2000). *Reducing tobacco use: A report of the Surgeon General—executive summary.* Atlanta: Department of Health and Human Services, Centers for Disease Control and Prevention, National Center for Chronic Disease Prevention and Health Promotion, Office on Smoking and Health. [13]

Vaillant, G. E. (1977). *Adaptation to life.* Boston: Little, Brown. [10]

Vaillant, G. E. (1994). Ego mechanisms of defense and personality psychopathology. *Journal of Abnormal Psychology, 103,* 44–50. [14]

Valleroy, L. A., Harris, J. R., & Way, P. O. (1990). The impact of HIV infection on child survival in the developing world. *AIDS, 4,* 667–672. [12]

Van Cauter, E. (2000). Slow-wave sleep and release of growth hormone. *Journal of the American Medical Association, 284,* 2717–2718. [4]

Vandell, D. L., & Mueller, E. C. (1980). Peer play and friendships during the first two years. In H. C. Foot, A. J. Chapman, & J. R. Smith (Eds.), *Friendship and social relations in children.* New York: Wiley. [9]

van den Hout, M., & Merckelbach, H. (1991). Classical conditioning: Still going strong. *Behavioural Psychotherapy, 19,* 59–79. [5]

Van Eerde, W., & Thierry, H. (1996). Vroom's expectancy models and work-related criteria: A meta-analysis. *Journal of Applied Psychology, 81,* 575–586. [11]

van Elst, L. T., Woermann, F. G., Lemieux, L., Thompson, P. J., & Trimble, M. R. (2000). Affective aggression in patients with temporal lobe epilepsy. *Brain, 123,* 234–243. [17]

van Ijzendoorn, M. H., Moran, G., Belsky, J., Pederson, D., Bakermans-Kranenburg, M. J., & Kneppers, K. (2000). The similarity of siblings' attachments to their mother. *Child Development, 71,* 1086–1098. [9]

Van Lancker, D. (1987, November). Old familiar voices. *Psychology Today,* pp. 12–13. [2]

Vargha-Khadem, F., Gadian, D. G., Watkins, D. E., Connelly, A., Van Paesschen, W., & Mishkin, M. (1997). Differential effects of early hippocampal pathology on episodic and semantic memory. *Science, 277,* 376–380. [2, 6]

Vazdarjanova, A. (2000). Does the basolateral amygdala store memories for emotional events? *Trends in Neurosciences, 23,* 345–346. [5]

Veleber, D. M., & Templer, D. I. (1984). Effects of caffeine on anxiety and depression. *Journal of Abnormal Psychology, 93,* 120–122. [4]

Verhaeghen, P., Marcoen, A., & Goossens, L. (1993). Facts and fiction about memory aging: A quantitative integration of research findings. *Journal of Gerontology, 48,* 157–171. [10]

Vetulani, J., & Nalepa, I. (2000). Antidepressants: Past, present and future. *European Journal of Pharmacology, 405,* 351–363. [16]

Viemerö, V. (1996). Factors in childhood that predict later criminal behavior. *Aggressive Behavior, 22,* 87–97. [17]

Vilberg, T. R., & Keesey, R. E. (1990). Ventromedial hypothalamic lesions abolish compensatory reduction in energy expenditure to weight loss. *American Journal of Physiology, 258,* 476–480. [11]

Vincent, K. R. (1991). Black/white IQ differences: Does age make the difference? *Journal of Clinical Psychology, 47,* 266–270. [8]

Vincent, K. R. (1993, Fall). On the perfectibility of the human species: Evidence using fixed reference groups. *TCA Journal,* pp. 60–63. [8]

Vincent, M., & Pickering, M. R. (1988). Multiple personality disorder in childhood. *Canadian Journal of Psychiatry, 33,* 524–529. [15]

Viney, W. (1993). *A history of psychology: Ideas and context.* Boston: Allyn & Bacon. [1]

Vinokur, A., & Burnstein, E. (1978). Depolarization of attitudes in groups. *Journal of Personality and Social Psychology, 36,* 872–885. [17]

Visser, P. S., & Krosnick, J. A. (1998). Development of attitude strength over the life cycle: Surge and decline. *Journal of Personality & Social Psychology, 75,* 1389–1410. [17]

Vitousek, K., & Manke, F. (1994). Personality variables and disorders in anorexia nervosa and bulimia nervosa. *Journal of Abnormal Psychology, 103,* 137–147. [11]

Volkow, N. D., & Fowler, J. S. (2000). Addiction, a disease of compulsion and drive: Involvement of the orbitofrontal cortex. *Cerebral Cortex, 10,* 318–325. [4, 5]

Volkow, N. D., Wang, G-J., Fowler, J. S., Hitzemann, R., Angrist, B., Gatley, S. J., et al. (1999). Association of methylphenidate-induced craving with changes in right straito-orbitofrontal metabolism in cocaine abusers: Implications in addiction. *American Journal of Psychiatry, 156,* 19–26. [4]

Volkow, N. D., Wang, G.-J., Fischman, M. W., Foltin, R. W., Fowler, J. S., Abumrad, N. N., Vitkun, S., Logan, J., Gatley, S. J., Pappas, N., Hitzemann, R., & Shea, C. E. (1997a). Relationship between subjective effects of cocaine and dopamine transporter occupancy. *Nature, 386,* 827–830. [4]

Volkow, N. D., Wang, G.-J., Fowler, J. S., Logan, J., Gatley, S. J., Hitzemann, R., Chen, A. D., Dewey, S. L., & Pappas, N. (1997b). Decreased striatal dopaminergic responsiveness in detoxified cocaine-dependent subjects. *Nature, 386,* 830–833. [4]

Vollrath, M. (2000). Personality and hassles among university students: A three-year longitudinal study. *European Journal of Personality, 14,* 199–215. [14]

Von Dras, D. D., & Siegler, I. C. (1997). Stability in extraversion and aspects of social support at midlife. *Journal of Personality and Social Psychology, 72,* 233–241. [13]

Voyer, D., Voyer, S., & Bryden, M. P. (1995). Magnitude of sex differences in spatial abilities: A meta-analysis and consideration of critical variables. *Psychological Bulletin, 117,* 250–270. [12]

Vygotsky, L. S. (1986). *Thought and language* (A. Kozulin, Trans.). Cambridge, MA: MIT Press. (Original work published 1934). [9]

Wadden, T. A. (1993). Treatment of obesity by moderate and severe caloric restriction: Results of clinical research trials. *Annals of Internal Medicine, 119,* 688–693. [11]

Wadden, T. A., Vogt, R. A., Andersen, R. E., Bartlett, S. J., Foster, G. D., Kuehnel, R. H., Wilk, J., Weinstock, R., Buckenmeyer, P., Berkowitz, R. I., & Steen, S. N. (1997). Exercise in the treatment of obesity: Effects of four interventions on body composition, resting energy expenditure, appetite, and mood. *Journal of Consulting and Clinical Psychology, 65,* 269–277. [11]

Waid, W. M., Orne, E. C., & Orne, M. T. (1981). Selective memory for social information, alertness, and physiological arousal in the detection of deception. *Journal of Applied Psychology, 66,* 224–232. [11]

Wald, G. (1964). The receptors of human color vision. *Science, 145,* 1007–1017. [3]

Wald, G., Brown, P. K., & Smith, P. H. (1954). Iodopsin. *Journal of General Physiology, 38,* 623–681. [3]

Walker, D. (2000). Online therapy? Not yet. *CBS News.* New York: CBS. [16]

Walker, D., Greenwood, C., Hart, B., & Carta, J. (1994). Prediction of school outcomes based on early language production and socioeconomic factors. *Developmental Psychology, 65,* 606–621. [9]

Walker, L. (1989). A longitudinal study of moral reasoning. *Child Development, 60,* 157–166. [10]

Walker, L. E. (1999). Psychology and domestic violence around the world. *American Psychologist, 54,* 21–29. [17]

Wallach, H. (1985a). Learned stimulation in space and motion perception. *American Psychologist, 40,* 399–404. [3]

Wallach, M. A., & Wallach, L. (1983). *Psychology's sanction for selfishness: The error of egoism in theory and therapy.* New York: W. H. Freeman. [14]

Wallis, C. (1984, June 11). Unlocking pain's secrets. *Time,* pp. 58–66. [3]

Walster, E., & Walster, G. W. (1969). The matching hypothesis. *Journal of Personality and Social Psychology, 6,* 248–253. [17]

Walters, C. C., & Grusec, J. E. (1977). *Punishment.* San Francisco: Freeman. [5]

Ward, C. (1994). Culture and altered states of consciousness. In W. J. Lonner & R. Malpass (Eds.), *Psychology and culture* (pp. 59–64). Boston: Allyn & Bacon. [4]

Wark, G. R., & Krebs, D. L. (1996). Gender and dilemma differences in real-life moral judgment. *Developmental Psychology, 32,* 220–230. [10]

Warshaw, M. G., & Keller, M. B. (1996). The relationship between fluoxetine use and suicidal behavior in 654 subjects with anxiety disorders. *Journal of Clinical Psychiatry, 57,* 158–166. [16]

Wasserman, E. A. (1995). The conceptual abilities of pigeons. *American Scientist, 83,* 246–255. [7]

Wasserman, E. A., & Miller, R. R. (1997). What's elementary about associative learning? *Annual Review of Psychology, 48,* 573–607. [5]

Waterman, J., & Lusk, R. (1986). Scope of the problem. In K. MacFarlane et al. (Eds.), *Sexual abuse of young children: Evaluation and treatment* (pp. 3–14). New York: Guilford. [12]

Watson, J. B. (1913). Psychology as the behaviorist views it. *Psychological Review, 20,* 158–177. [1, 5]

Watson, J. B. (1919). *Psychology from the standpoint of a behaviorist.* Philadelphia: Lippincott. [5]

Watson, J. B. (1925). *Behaviorism.* New York: W. W. Norton. [5]

Watson, J. B., & Rayner, R. (1920). Conditioned emotional reactions. *Journal of Experimental Psychology, 3,* 1–14. [5]

Wayment, H. A., & Peplau, L. A. (1995). Social support and well-being among lesbian and heterosexual women: A structural modeling approach. *Personality and Social Psychology Bulletin, 21,* 1189–1199. [10]

Weale, R. A. (2000). Why we need reading-glasses before a zimmer-frame. *Vision Research, 40,* 1–8. [3]

Weaver, C. A., III. (1993). Do you need a "flash" to form a flashbulb memory? *Journal of Experimental Psychology: General, 122,* 39–46. [6]

Weaver, J. B., Masland, J. L., & Zillmann, D. (1984). Effect of erotica on young men's aesthetic perception of their female sexual partners. *Perceptual and Motor Skills, 58,* 929–930. [12]

Webb, W. (1995). The cost of sleep-related accidents: A reanalysis. *Sleep, 18,* 276–280. [4]

Webb, W. B. (1975). *Sleep: The gentle tyrant.* Englewood Cliffs, NJ: Prentice-Hall. [4]

Webb, W. B., & Campbell, S. S. (1983). Relationships in sleep characteristics of identical and fraternal twins. *Archives of General Psychiatry, 40,* 1093–1095. [4]

Weber, S. E. (1996). Cultural aspects of pain in childbearing women. *Journal of Obstetric, Gynecologic & Neonatal Nursing, 25,* 67–72. [3]

Webster, R. (1995). *Why Freud was wrong: Sin, science, and psychoanalysis.* New York: Basic Books. [14]

Wechsler, H., & Kuo, M. (2000). College students define binge drinking and estimate its prevalence: Results of a national survey. *Journal of American College Health, 49,* 57–64. [13]

Weekes, J. R., Lynn, S. J., Green, J. P., & Brentar, J. T. (1992). Pseudomemory in hypnotized and task-motivated subjects. *Journal of Abnormal Psychology, 101,* 356–360. [4]

Weeks, D. L., & Anderson, L. P. (2000). The interaction of observational learning with overt practice: Effects on motor skill learning. *Acta Psychologia, 104,* 259–271. [5]

Wehr, T. A., & Rosenthal, N. E. (1989). Seasonality and affective illness. *American Journal of Psychiatry, 146,* 829–839. [15]

Wehr, T. A., Jacobsen, F. M., Sack, D. A., et al. (1986). Phototherapy of seasonal affective disorder. *Archives of General Psychiatry, 43,* 870–875. [15]

Weigman, O., & van Schie, E. G. (1998). Video game playing and its relations with aggressive and prosocial behaviour. *British Journal of Social Psychology, 37*(Pt. 3), 367–378. [17]

Weinberg, R. A. (1989). Intelligence and IQ: Landmark issues and great debates. *American Psychologist, 44,* 98–104. [8]

Weinberger, M., Hiner, S. L., & Tierney, W. M. (1987). In support of hassles as a measure of stress in predicting health outcomes. *Journal of Behavioral Medicine, 10,* 19–32. [13]

Weiner, B. (1985). "Spontaneous" causal thinking. *Psychological Bulletin, 97,* 74–84. [17]

Weiner, B. (Ed.). (1974). *Achievement motivation and attribution theory.* Norristown, NJ: General Learning Press. [11]

Weiner, I. B. (1996). Some observations on the validity of the Rorschach Inkblot Method. *Psychological Assessment, 8,* 206–213. [14]

Weiner, I. B. (1997). Current status of the Rorschach Inkblot Method. *Journal of Personality Assessment, 68,* 5–19. [14]

Weingartner, H., Adefris, W., Eich, J. E., & Murphy, D. L. (1976). Encoding-imagery specificity in alcohol state-dependent learning. *Journal of Experimental Psychology: Human Learning and Memory, 2,* 83–87. [6]

Weiss, J. M. (1972). Psychological factors in stress and disease. *Scientific American, 226,* 104–113. [13]

Weissman, M. M., Bland, R. C., Canino, G. J., Faravelli, C., Greenwald, S., Hwu, H-G., Joyce, P. R., Karam, E. G., Lee, C-K., Lellouch, J., Lepine, J-P., Newman, S. C., Rubio-Stepic, M., Wells, J. E., Wickramaratne, P. J., Wittchen, H-U., & Yeh, E-K. (1996). Cross-national epidemiology of major depression and bipolar disorder. *Journal of the American Medical Association, 276,* 293–299. [15]

Weissman, M. M., Bland, R. C., Canino, G. J., Faravelli, C., Greenwald, S., Hwu, H-G., et al. (1997). The cross national epidemiology of panic disorder. *Archives of General Psychiatry, 54,* 305–309. [15]

Weissman, M. M., Bland, R. C., Canino, G. J., Greenwald, S., Hwu, H-G., Lee, C. K., Newman, S. C., Oakley-Browne, M. A., Rubio-Stipec, M., Wickramaratne, P. J., Wittchen, H-U., & Yeh, E-K. (1994). The cross national epidemiology of obsessive compulsive disorder. *Journal of Clinical Psychiatry, 55*(3, Suppl.), 5–10. [15]

Wells, D. L., & Hepper, P. G. (2000). The discrimination of dog odours by humans. *Perception, 29,* 111–115. [3]

Wells, G. L. (1993). What do we know about eyewitness identification? *American Psychologist, 48,* 553–571. [6]

Wells, G. L., Malpass, R. S., Lindsay, R. C., Fisher, R. P., Turtle, J. W., & Fulero, S. M. (2000). From the lab to the police station. A successful application of eyewitness research. *American Psychologist, 55,* 6581–6598. [6]

Wender, P. H., Kety, S. S., Rosenthal, D., et al. (1986). Psychiatric disorders in the biological and adoptive families of adoptive individuals with affective disorders. *Archives of General Psychiatry, 43,* 923–929. [15]

Wertheimer, M. (1912). Experimental studies of the perception of movement. *Zeitschrift fur Psychologie, 61,* 161–265. [3]

Wertheimer, M. (1958). Principles of perceptual organization. In D. C. Beardslee & M. Wertheimer (Eds.), *Readings in perception* (pp. 115–135). Princeton, NJ: D. Van Nostrand. [3]

Wertz, K., & Hermann, B. G. (2000). Large-scale screen for genes involved in gonad development. *Mechanisms of Development, 98,* 51–70. [12]

West, M. J., Coleman, P. D., Flood, D. G., & Troncoso, J. C. (1994). Differences in the pattern of hippocampal neuronal loss in normal ageing and Alzheimer's disease. *Lancet, 344,* 769–772. [2, 10]

West, R., Courts, S., Beharry, S., May, S., & Hajek, P. (1999). Acute effect of glucose tablets on desire to smoke. *Psychopharmacology, 147,* 319–321. [4]

Weström, L. V. (1994). Sexually transmitted diseases and infertility. *Sexually Transmitted Diseases, 21*(2, Suppl.), S32–S37. [12]

Wetter, M. W., Baer, R. A., Berry, T. R., Robison, L. H., & Sumpter, J. (1993). MMPI-2 profiles of motivated fakers given specific symptom information: A comparison to matched patients. *Psychological Assessment, 5,* 317–323. [14]

Wever, E. G. (1949). *Theory of hearing.* New York: Wiley. [3]

Wheeler, M. A., Stuss, D. T., & Tulving, E. (1997). Toward a theory of episodic memory: The frontal lobes and autonoetic consciousness. *Psychological Bulletin, 121,* 331–354. [6]

Whisenhunt, B. L., Williamson, D. A., Netemeyer, R. G., & Womble, L. G. (2000). Reliability and validity of the Psychosocial Risk Factors Questionnaire (PRFQ). *Eating and Weight Disorders: Studies on Anorexia, Bulimia, and Obesity, 5,* 1–6. [11]

Whitam, F. L., Diamond, M., & Martin, J. (1993). Homosexual orientation in twins: A report on 61 pairs and three triplet sets. *Archives of Sexual Behavior, 22,* 187–296. [12]

Whitbourne, S. K., Zuschlag, M. K., Elliot, L. B., & Waterman, A. S. (1992). Psychosocial development in adulthood: A 22-year sequential study. *Journal of Personality and Social Psychology, 63,* 260–271. [10]

White, D. P. (1989). Central sleep apnea. In M. H. Kryger, T. Roth, & W. C. Dement (Eds.), *Principles and practice of sleep medicine* (pp. 513–524). Philadelphia: W. B. Saunders. [4]

White, G. L., & Mullen, P. E. (1989). *Jealousy: Theory, research, and clinical strategies.* New York: Guilford. [11]

White, S. D., & DeBlassie, R. R. (1992). Adolescent sexual behavior. *Adolescence, 27,* 183–191. [10]

Whitehouse, D. (2000). Rats control robot arm with brain power alone [On-line]. Available: http://www.robotbooks.com/robot-rats.htm [7]

Whitehurst, G. J., Fischel, J. E., Caulfield, M. B., DeBaryshe, B. D., & Valdez-Menchaca, M. C. (1989). Assessment and treatment of early expressive language delay. In P. R. Zelazo & R. Barr (Eds.), *Challenges to developmental paradigms: Implications for assessment and treatment* (pp. 113–135). Hillsdale, NJ: Erlbaum. [9]

Whitley, B. E., & Kite, M. E. (1995). Sex differences in attitudes toward homosexuality: A comment on Oliver and Hyde (1993). *Psychological Bulletin, 117,* 146–154. [12]

Whitmore, D., Foulkes, N. S., & Sassone-Corsi, P. (2000). Light acts directly on organs and cells in culture to set the vertebrate circadian clock. *Nature, 404,* 87–91. [4]

Whorf, B. L. (1956). Science and linguistics. In J. B. Carroll (Ed.), *Language, thought, and reality: Selected writings of Benjamin Lee Whorf.* Cambridge, MA: MIT Press. [7]

Wickelgren, I. (1997). Getting a grasp on working memory. *Science, 275,* 1580–1582. [6]

Wicker, A. W. (1969). Attitudes versus action: The relationship of verbal and overt behavioral responses to attitude objects. *Journal of Social Issues, 25,* 41–78. [17]

Widiger, T. A., Frances, A., Spitzer, R. L., & Williams, J. B. W. (1988). The DSM-III-R personality disorders: An overview. *American Journal of Psychiatry, 145,* 786–795. [15]

Widom, C. S. (1989). Does violence beget violence? A critical examination of the literature. *Psychological Bulletin, 106,* 3–28. [5, 17]

Widom, C. S., & Maxfield, M. G. (1996). A prospective examination of risk for violence among abused and neglected children. *Annals of the New York Academy of Sciences, 794,* 224–237. [17]

Widom, C. S., & Morris, S. (1997). Accuracy of adult recollections of childhood victimization: Part 2. Childhood sexual abuse. *Psychological Bulletin, 9,* 34–46. [6]

Wiens, S., Mezzacappa, E. S., & Katkin, E. S. (2000). Heartbeat detection and the experience of emotions. *Cognition and Emotion, 14,* 417–427. [11]

Wierson, M., Long, P. J., & Forehand, R. L. (1993). Toward a new understanding of early menarche: The role of environmental stress in pubertal timing. *Adolescence, 28,* 13–24. [10]

Wierzbicka, A. (2000). The semantics of human facial expressions. *Pragmatics & Cognition, 8,* 147–184. [11]

Wiggins, J. S. (Ed.) (1996). *The five-factor model of personality: Theoretical perspectives.* New York: Guilford. [14]

Wilcox, D., & Hager, R. (1980). Toward realistic expectation for orgasmic response in women. *Journal of Sex Research, 16,* 162–179. [12]

Wilken, J. A., Smith, B. D., Tola, K., & Mann, M. (2000). Trait anxiety and prior exposure to non-stressful stimuli: Effects on psychophysiological arousal and anxiety. *International Journal of Psychophysiology, 37,* 233–242. [11]

Willems, P. J. (2000). Genetic causes of hearing loss. *New England Journal of Medicine, 342,* 1101–1109. [3]

Williams, G. C., Grow, V. M., Freedman, Z. R., Ryan, R. M., & Deci, E. L. (1996). Motivational predictors of weight loss and weight-loss maintenance. *Journal of Personality and Social Psychology, 70,* 115–126. [11]

Williams, K. D., & Karau, S. J. (1991). Social loafing and social compensation: The effects of expectations of co-worker performance. *Journal of Personality and Social Psychology, 61,* 570–581. [17]

Williams, K., Harkins, S. G., & Latané, B. (1981). Identifiability as a deterrent to social loafing: Two cheering experiments. *Journal of Personality and Social Psychology, 40,* 303–311. [17]

Williams, L. M. (1994). Recall of childhood trauma: A prospective study of women's memories of child sexual abuse. *Journal of Consulting and Clinical Psychology, 62,* 1167–1176. [6]

Williams, R. (1989, January/February). Curing Type A: The trusting heart. *Psychology Today,* pp. 36–42. [13]

Williams, R. (1993). *Anger kills.* New York: Times Books. [13]

Willoughby, J. C., & Glidden, L. M. (1995). Fathers helping out: Shared child care and marital satisfaction of parents of children with disabilities. *American Journal on Mental Retardation, 99,* 399–406. [9]

Willoughby, T., Wood, E., McDermott, C., & McLaren, J. (2000). Enhancing learning through strategy instruction and group interaction: Is active generation of elaborations critical? *Applied Cognitive Psychology, 14,* 19–30. [6]

Wills, T. A., & Cleary, S. D. (1996). How are social support effects mediated? A test with parental support and adolescent substance use. *Journal of Personality and Social Psychology, 71,* 937–952. [4]

Wills, T. A., McNamara, G., Vaccaro, D., & Hirky, A. E. (1996). Escalated substance use: A longitudinal grouping analysis from early to middle adolescence. *Journal of Abnormal Psychology, 105,* 166–180. [4]

Wilson, M. A., & McNaughton, B. L. (1993). Dynamics of the hippocampal ensemble code for space. *Science, 261,* 1055–1058. [2]

Wilson, T. D., Lindsey, S., & Schooler, T. Y. (2000). A model of dual attitudes. *Psychological Review, 107,* 101–126. [17]

Wilson, W., Mathew, R., Turkington, T., Hawk, T., Coleman, R. E., & Provenzale, J. (2000). Brain morphological changes and early marijuana use: A magnetic resonance and positron emission tomography study. *Journal of Addictive Diseases, 19,* 1–22. [4]

Wilton, M. M. M., Craig, W. M., & Pepler, D. J. (2000). Emotional regulation and display in classroom victims of bullying: Characteristic expressions of affect, coping styles and relevant contextual factors. *Social Development, 9*(2). [10]

Winch, R. F. (1958). *Mate selection: A study of complementary needs.* New York: Harper & Row. [17]

Wink, P., & Helson, R. (1993). Personality change in women and their partners. *Journal of Personality and Social Psychology, 65,* 597–605. [10]

Winograd, E. (1988). Some observations on prospective remembering. In M. M. Gruneberg, P. E. Morris, & R. N. Sykes (Eds.), *Practical aspects of memory: Current research and issues: Vol. 1* (pp. 348–353). Chichester, England: John Wiley & Sons. [6]

Winokur, G., Coryell, W., Keller, M., Endicott, J., & Akiskal, H. S. (1993). A prospective follow-up of patients with bipolar and primary unipolar affective disorder. *Archives of General Psychiatry,* 50, 457–465. [15]

Winson, J. (1990). The meaning of dreams. *Scientific American, 263,* 86–96. [4]

Wirz-Justice, A., Graw, P., Kräuchi, K., Sarrafzadeh, A., English, J., Arendt, J., & Sand, L. (1996) "Natural" light treatment of seasonal affective disorder. *Journal of Affective Disorders, 37,* 109–120. [15]

Witelson, S. F. (1985). The brain connection: The corpus callosum is larger in left-handers. *Science, 229,* 665–668. [2]

Wolfe, L. (1981). *The Cosmo report.* New York: Arbor House. [1]

Wolford, G., Miller, M. B., & Gazzaniga, M. (2000). The left hemisphere's role in hypothesis formation. *Journal of Neuroscience, 20,* 1–4. [8]

Wolpe, J. (1958). *Psychotherapy by reciprocal inhibition.* Stanford, CA: Stanford University Press. [16]

Wolpe, J. (1973). *The practice of behavior therapy* (2nd ed.). New York: Pergamon. [16]

Wolpe, J. (1981). Behavior therapy versus psychoanalysis: Therapeutic and social implications. *American Psychologist, 36,* 159–164. [16]

Wood, J. M., Nezworski, M. T., & Stejskal, W. J. (1996). The Comprehensive System for the Rorschach: A critical examination. *Psychological Science, 7,* 3–10. [14]

Wood, P. D. (1996). Clinical applications of diet and physical activity in weight loss. *Nutrition Reviews, 54,* S131–S135. [11]

Wood, W., Lundgren, S., Ovellette, J. A., Busceme, S., & Blackstone, T. (1994). Minority influence: A meta-analytic review of social influence processes. *Psychological Bulletin, 115,* 323–345. [17]

Wood, W., Rhodes, N., & Whelan, M. (1989). Sex differences in positive well-being: A consideration of emotional style and marital status. *Psychological Bulletin, 106,* 249–264. [10, 11]

Wood, W., Wong, F. Y., & Chachere, J. G. (1991). Effects of media violence on viewers' aggression in unconstrained social interaction. *Psychological Bulletin, 109,* 371–383. [5, 17]

Woods, S. C., & Gibbs, J. (1989). The regulation of food intake by peptides. *Annals of the New York Academy of Sciences, 575,* 236–243. [11]

Woodward, A. L., Markman, E. M., & Fitzsimmons, C. M. (1994). Rapid word learning in 13- and 18-month-olds. *Developmental Psychology, 30,* 553–566. [9]

Woody, E. Z., & Bowers, K. S. (1994). A frontal assault on dissociated control. In S. J. Lynn & J. W. Rhue (Eds.), *Dissociation: Clinical, theoretical and research perspectives* (pp. 52–79). New York: Guilford. [4]

Woody, E. Z., Drugovic, M., & Oakman, J. M. (1997). A reexamination of the role of nonhypnotic suggestibility in hypnotic responding. *Journal of Personality and Social Psychology, 72,* 399–407. [4]

Woolley, C. S., Weiland, N. G., McEwen, B. S., & Schwartzkroin, P. A. (1997). Estradiol increases the sensitivity of hippocampal CA1 pyramidal cells to NMDA receptor-mediated synaptic input: Correlation with dendritic spine density. *Journal of Neuroscience, 17,* 1848–1859. [6]

Word, C. O., Zanna, M. P., & Cooper, J. (1974). The nonverbal mediation of self-fulfilling prophecies in interracial interaction. *Journal of Experimental Social Psychology, 10,* 109–120. [17]

Worrel, J. A., Marken, P. A., Beckman, S. E., & Ruehter, V. L. (2000). Atypical antipsychotic agents: A critical review. *American Journal of Health System Pharmacology, 57,* 238–255. [16]

Wright, J. C., & Huston, A. C. (1983). A matter of form: Potentials of television for young viewers. *American Psychologist, 38,* 835–843. [9]

Wright, J. C., & Mischel, W. (1987). A conditional approach to dispositional constructs: The local predictability of social behavior. *Journal of Personality and Social Psychology, 53,* 1159–1177. [14]

Wright, S. C., Taylor, D. M., & Moghaddam, F. (1990). Responding to membership in a disadvantaged group: From acceptance to collective protest. *Journal of Personality and Social Psychology, 58,* 994–1003. [17]

Wu, C., & Shaffer, D. R. (1987). Susceptibility to persuasive appeals as a function of source credibility and prior experience with the attitude object. *Journal of Personality and Social Psychology, 52,* 677–688. [17]

Wurtman, R. J., & Wurtman, J. J. (1989). Carbohydrates and depression. *Scientific American, 260,* 68–75. [15]

Wyatt, H. J. (2000). A "minimum-wear-and-tear" meshwork for the iris. *Vision Research, 40,* 2167–2176. [3]

Yam, P. (1995a). Dangerous sex. *Scientific American, 272,* 10–12. [12]

Yam, P. (1995b). James Randi: A skeptically inquiring mind. *Scientific American, 273,* 34–35. [3]

Yanagita, T. (1973). An experimental framework for evaluation of dependence liability in various types of drugs in monkeys. *Bulletin of Narcotics, 25,* 57–64. [4]

Yapko, M. D. (1994). Suggestibility and repressed memories of abuse: A survey of psychotherapists' beliefs. *American Journal of Clinical Hypnosis, 36,* 163–171. [4]

Yarnold, B. M. (1996). Use of inhalants among Miami's public school students, 1992. *Psychological Reports, 79,* 1155–1161. [4]

Yazigi, R. A., Odem, R. R., & Polakoski, K. L. (1991). Demonstration of specific binding of cocaine to human spermatozoa. *Journal of the American Medical Association, 266,* 1956. [9]

Yonkers, K. A., & Hamilton, J. A. (1995, May). Do men and women need different doses of psychotropic drugs? *Harvard Mental Health Letter, 11*(11), 8. [16]

Young, S. J., Longstaffe, S., & Tenenbein, M. (1999). Inhalant abuse and the abuse of other drugs. *American Journal of Drug and Alcohol Abuse, 25,* 371–375. [4]

Zajonc, R. B. (1965). Social facilitation. *Science, 149,* 269–274. [17]

Zajonc, R. B. (1968). Attitudinal effects of mere exposure. *Journal of Personality and Social Psychology, Monographs Supplement, 9*(Pt. 2), 1–27. [17]

Zajonc, R. B. (1980). Feeling and thinking: Preferences need no inferences. *American Psychologist, 35,* 151–175. [11]

Zajonc, R. B. (1984). On the primacy of affect. *American Psychologist, 39,* 117–123. [11]

Zajonc, R. B., & Mullally, P. R. (1997). Birth order: Reconciling conflicting effects. *American Psychologist, 52,* 685–699. [8]

Zajonc, R. B., & Sales, S. M. (1966). Social facilitation of dominant and subordinate responses. *Journal of Experimental Social Psychology, 2,* 160–168. [17]

Zald, D. H., & Pardo, J. V. (2000). Functional neuroimaging of the olfactory system in humans. *International Journal of Psychophysiology, 36,* 165–181. [3]

Zamansky, H. S., & Bartis, S. P. (1985). The dissociation of an experience: The hidden observer observed. *Journal of Abnormal Psychology, 94,* 243–248. [4]

Zaragoza, M. S., & Mitchell, K. J. (1996). Repeated exposure to suggestion and the creation of false memories. *Psychological Science, 7,* 294–300. [6]

Zborowski, M. (1952). Cultural components in response to pain. *Journal of Social Issues, 8,* 16–30. [3]

Zeelenberg, M., van Dijk, W. W., Manstead, A. S. R., & van der Pigt, J. (2000). On bad decisions and disconfirmed expectancies: The psychology of regret and disappointment. *Cognition and Emotion, 14,* 521–541. [11]

Zentall, T. R., Sutton, J. E., & Sherburne, L. M. (1996). True imitative learning in pigeons. *Psychological Science, 7,* 343–346. [5]

Zhdanova, I. V., Wurtman, R. J., Morabito, C., Piotrovska, V. R., & Lynch, H. J. (1996). Effects of low oral doses of melatonin given 2–4 hours before habitual bedtime, on sleep in normal young humans. *Sleep, 19,* 423–431. [4]

Zhdanova, I., & Wurtman, R. (1996, June). How does melatonin affect sleep? *Harvard Mental Health Letter, 12*(12), 8. [4]

Zheng, C., Heintz, H., & Hatten, M. E. (1996). CNS gene encoding astrotactin, which supports neuronal migration along glial fibers. *Science, 272,* 417–421. [2]

Zilbergeld, B. (1986, June). Psychabuse. *Science, 86,* 48–52. [16]

Zimbardo, P. G. (1972). Pathology of imprisonment. *Society, 9,* 4–8. [17]

Zisook, S., Byrd, D., Kuck, J., & Jeste, D. V. (1995). Command hallucinations in outpatients with schizophrenia. *Journal of Clinical Psychiatry, 56*(10, Suppl.), 462–465. [15]

Zivin, J. A., & Choi, D. W. (1991). Stroke therapy. *Scientific American, 265,* 56–63. [2]

Zogg, W. (2000). Review of several different forms of psychotherapy in treatment of depression. *Ther. Umsch, 50,* 262–270. [16]

Zola, S. M., Squire, L. R., Teng, E., Stenfanacci, L., Buffalo, E. A., & Clark, R. E. (2000). Impaired recognition memory in monkeys after damage limited to the hippocampal region. *Journal of Neuroscience, 20,* 451–463. [6]

Zubin, J., & Spring, B. J. (1977). Vulnerability: A new view of schizophrenia. *Journal of Abnormal Psychology, 86,* 103–126. [15]

Zuckerman, M. (1979). *Sensation seeking: Beyond the optimal level of arousal.* Hillsdale, NJ: Erlbaum. [11]

Zuckerman, M., Miyake, K., & Hodgins, H. S. (1991). Cross-channel effects of vocal and physical attractiveness and their implications for interpersonal perception. *Journal of Personality and Social Psychology, 60,* 545–554. [17]

Zuger, B. (1990, August). Changing concepts of the etiology of male homosexuality. *Medical Aspects of Human Sexuality, 24,* 73–75. [12]

Zuwerink, J. R., & Devine, P. G. (1996). Attitude importance and resistance to persuasion: It's not just the thought that counts. *Journal of Personality and Social Psychology, 70,* 931–944. [17]

Glossary

absolute threshold: The minimum amount of sensory stimulation that can be detected 50% of the time.

accommodation: In vision, the action of the lens in changing shape as it focuses objects on the retina, becoming more spherical for near objects and flatter for far objects; in learning, the process by which existing schemas are modified and new schemas are created to incorporate new objects, events, experiences, or information.

acetylcholine (ah-SEET-ul-KOH-leen): A neurotransmitter that plays a role in learning, memory, and rapid eye movement (REM) sleep and causes the skeletal muscle fibers to contract.

acquired immune deficiency syndrome (AIDS): A devastating and incurable illness that is caused by HIV and progressively weakens the body's immune system, leaving the person vulnerable to opportunistic infections that usually cause death.

action potential: The sudden reversal of the resting potential, which initiates the firing of a neuron.

actor–observer effect: The tendency to attribute one's own behavior primarily to situational factors and the behavior of others primarily to internal or dispositional factors.

additive strategy: A decision-making approach in which each alternative is rated on each important factor affecting the decision and the alternative rated highest overall is chosen.

adolescence: The developmental stage that begins at puberty and encompasses the period from the end of childhood to the beginning of adulthood.

adolescent growth spurt: A period of rapid physical growth that peaks in girls at about age 12 and in boys at about age 14.

adoption method: A method researchers use to study the relative effects of heredity and environment on behavior and ability in children adopted shortly after birth, by comparing them with their biological and adoptive parents.

adrenal glands (ah-DREE-nal): A pair of endocrine glands that release hormones that prepare the body for emergencies and stressful situations and also release small amounts of the sex hormones.

aerobic exercise (ah-RO-bik): Exercise that uses the large muscle groups in continuous, repetitive action and increases oxygen intake and breathing and heart rates.

afterimage: The visual sensation that remains after a stimulus is withdrawn.

aggression: The intentional infliction of physical or psychological harm on another.

agoraphobia (AG-or-uh-FO-bee-uh): An intense fear of being in a situation from which immediate escape is not possible or in which help is not immediately available in case of incapacitating anxiety.

alarm stage: The first stage of the general adaptation syndrome, when there is emotional arousal and the defensive forces of the body are prepared for fight or flight.

alcohol: A central nervous system depressant.

algorithm: A systematic, step-by-step procedure, such as a mathematical formula, that guarantees a solution to a problem of a certain type if the algorithm is appropriate and is executed properly.

alpha wave: The brain wave associated with deep relaxation.

altered state of consciousness: A mental state other than ordinary waking consciousness, such as sleep, meditation, hypnosis, or a drug-induced state.

altruism: Behavior aimed at helping another, requiring some self-sacrifice and not designed for personal gain.

Alzheimer's disease (ALZ-hye-merz): An incurable form of dementia characterized by progressive deterioration of intellect and personality, resulting from widespread degeneration of brain cells.

amnesia: A partial or complete loss of memory resulting from brain trauma or psychological trauma.

amphetamines: A class of stimulants that increase arousal, relieve fatigue, improve alertness, and suppress the appetite.

amplitude: Measured in decibels, the magnitude or intensity of a sound wave, determining the loudness of the sound; the amplitude of a light wave affects the brightness of a visual stimulus.

amygdala (ah-MIG-da-la): A structure in the limbic system that plays an important role in emotion, particularly in response to aversive stimuli.

anal stage: Freud's second psychosexual stage (ages 1 or 1½ to 3 years), in which the child derives sensual pleasure mainly from expelling and withholding feces.

analogy heuristic: A rule of thumb that applies a solution that solved a problem in the past to a current problem that shares many similar features.

androgens: Male sex hormones.

androgyny (an-DROJ-uh-nee): A combination of the desirable male and female characteristics in one person.

anorexia nervosa: An eating disorder characterized by an overwhelming, irrational fear of being fat, compulsive dieting to the point of self-starvation, and excessive weight loss.

anterograde amnesia: The inability to form long-term memories of events occurring after a brain injury or brain surgery, although memories formed before the trauma are usually intact.

antidepressants: Drugs that are prescribed to treat depression and some anxiety disorders.

antipsychotic drugs: Drugs used to control severe psychotic symptoms, such as the delusions and hallucinations of schizophrenics; also known as neuroleptics or major tranquilizers.

antisocial personality disorder: A disorder marked by lack of feeling for others; selfish, aggressive, irresponsible behavior; and willingness to break the law, lie, cheat, or exploit others for personal gain.

anxiety: A general uneasiness or ominous feeling that may be associated with a particular object or situation or may be free-floating, not associated with anything specific.

anxiety disorders: Psychological disorders characterized by severe anxiety (e.g., panic disorder, phobias, general anxiety disorder, obsessive compulsive disorder).

aphasia (uh-FAY-zyah): A loss or impairment of the ability to understand or communicate through the written or spoken word, which results from damage to the brain.

apparent motion: The perception of motion when none is occurring (as in the phi phenomenon or in stroboscopic movement).

applied research: Research conducted to solve practical problems.

approach–approach conflict: A conflict arising from having to choose between desirable alternatives.

approach–avoidance conflict: A conflict arising when the same choice has both desirable and undesirable features.

aptitude test: A test designed to predict a person's achievement or performance at some future time.

archetype (AR-keh-type): Existing in the collective unconscious, an inherited tendency to respond in particular ways to universal human situations.

arousal: A state of alertness and mental and physical activation.

arousal theory: A theory suggesting that the aim of motivation is to maintain an optimal level of arousal.

artificial intelligence: Programming computer systems to simulate human thinking in solving problems and in making judgments and decisions.

assimilation: The process by which new objects, events, experiences, or information are incorporated into existing schemas.

association areas: Areas of the cerebral cortex that house memories and are involved in thought, perception, learning, and language.

attachment: The strong affectionate bond a child forms with the mother or primary caregiver.

attitude: A relatively stable evaluation of a person, object, situation, or issue.

attribution: An inference about the cause of one's own or another's behavior.

audience effects: The impact of passive spectators on an individual's performance.

audition: The sensation of hearing; the process of hearing.

authoritarian parents: Parents who make arbitrary rules, expect unquestioned obedience from their children, punish transgressions, and value obedience to authority.

authoritative parents: Parents who set high but realistic standards, reason with the child, enforce limits, and encourage open communication and independence.

automatic thoughts: Unreasonable and unquestioned ideas that rule a person's life and lead to depression and anxiety.

autonomy versus shame and doubt: Erikson's second stage (ages 1 to 3 years), when infants develop autonomy or shame based on how parents react to their expression of will and their wish to do things for themselves.

availability heuristic: A cognitive rule of thumb that says that the probability of an event or the importance assigned to it is based on its availability in memory.

aversion therapy: A behavior therapy in which an aversive stimulus is paired with an undesirable behavior until the behavior becomes associated with pain and discomfort.

avoidance–avoidance conflict: A conflict arising from having to choose between undesirable alternatives.

avoidance learning: Learning to avoid events or conditions associated with dreaded or aversive outcomes.

axon (AK-sahn): The slender, tail-like extension of the neuron that transmits signals to the dendrites or cell body of other neurons or to muscles or glands.

babbling: Vocalization of the basic speech sounds (phonemes), which begins between 4 and 6 months.

barbiturates: A class of addictive depressants used as sedatives, sleeping pills, and anesthetics; overdoses can cause coma or death.

basic emotions: Emotions that are found in all cultures, that are reflected in the same facial expressions across cultures, and that emerge in children according to their biological timetable; fear, anger, disgust, surprise, happiness, and distress are usually considered basic emotions.

basic research: Research conducted to advance knowledge rather than for its practical application.

basic trust versus basic mistrust: Erikson's first stage (ages birth to 1 year), when infants develop trust or mistrust based on the quality of care, love, and affection provided.

behavior modification: The systematic application of the learning principles of operant conditioning, classical conditioning, or observational learning to individuals or groups in order to eliminate undesirable behavior and/or encourage desirable behavior; also called behavior therapy.

behavior therapy: A treatment approach employing the principles of operant conditioning, classical conditioning, and/or observational learning theory to eliminate inappropriate or maladaptive behaviors and replace them with more adaptive responses.

behavioral genetics: The field of research that investigates the relative effects of heredity and environment on behavior and ability.

behavioral perspective: A perspective that emphasizes the role of environment in shaping behavior.

behaviorism: The school of psychology founded by John B. Watson that views observable, measurable behavior as the appropriate subject matter for psychology and emphasizes the key role of environment as a determinant of behavior.

beta wave (BAY-tuh): The brain wave associated with mental or physical activity.

binocular depth cues: Depth cues that depend on two eyes working together; convergence and binocular disparity.

binocular disparity: A binocular depth cue resulting from differences between the two retinal images formed of an object viewed at distances up to about 20 feet.

biofeedback: The use of sensitive equipment to give people precise feedback about internal physiological processes so that they can learn, with practice, to exercise control over them.

biological perspective: A perspective that emphasizes the role of biological processes and heredity as the key to understanding behavior.

biological sex: Physical and physiological status as male or female.

biological therapy: A therapy (drug therapy, ECT, or psychosurgery) that is based on the assumption that most mental disorders have physical causes.

biomedical model: A perspective that focuses on illness rather than on health, explaining illness in terms of biological factors without regard to psychological and social factors.

biopsychosocial model: A perspective that focuses on health as well as illness and holds that both are determined by a combination of biological, psychological, and social factors.

bipolar disorder: A mood disorder in which manic episodes alternate with periods of depression, usually with relatively normal periods in between.

bone conduction: The transmission of sound vibrations along the bones of the skull or face directly to the cochlea.

bottom-up processing: Information processing in which individual components or bits of data are combined until a complete perception is formed.

brainstem: The structure that begins at the point where the spinal cord enlarges as it enters the brain and that includes the medulla, the pons, and the reticular formation.

brightness: The dimension of visual sensation that is dependent on the intensity of light reflected from a surface and that corresponds to the amplitude of the light wave.

brightness constancy: The tendency to see an object as maintaining the same brightness regardless of differences in lighting conditions.

Broca's aphasia (BRO-kuz uh-FAY-zyah): An impairment in the physical ability to produce speech sounds, or in extreme cases an inability to speak at all; caused by damage to Broca's area.

Broca's area (BRO-kuz): The area in the frontal lobe, usually in the left hemisphere, that controls the production of speech sounds.

bulimia nervosa: An eating disorder characterized by repeated and uncontrolled episodes of binge eating, usually followed by purging, that is, self-induced vomiting and/or the use of large quantities of laxatives and diuretics.

burnout: The result of intense, unrelieved, and unmanaged job stress; a condition in which an individual becomes pessimistic, dissatisfied, inefficient on the job, and debilitated psychologically.

bystander effect: The fact that as the number of bystanders at an emergency increases, the probability that the victim will receive help decreases, and help, if given, is likely to be delayed.

California Psychological Inventory (CPI): A highly regarded personality test used to assess the normal personality.

Cannon–Bard theory of emotion: The theory that an emotion-provoking stimulus is transmitted simultaneously to the cortex, providing the feeling of an emotion, and to the sympathetic nervous system, causing the physiological arousal.

cardinal trait: Allport's name for a personal quality that is so strong a part of a person's personality that he or she may become identified with that trait.

case study: An in-depth study of one or a few individuals consisting of information gathered through observation, interview, and perhaps psychological testing.

catatonic schizophrenia (KAT-uh-TAHN-ik): A type of schizophrenia characterized by complete stillness or stupor and/or periods of great agitation and excitement; patients may assume an unusual posture and remain in it for long periods.

cell body: The part of the neuron that contains the nucleus and carries out the neuron's metabolic functions.

central nervous system (CNS): The brain and the spinal cord.

central trait: Allport's name for the type of trait that might be mentioned in an accurate letter of recommendation.

centration: A preoperational child's tendency to focus on only one dimension of a stimulus and ignore other dimensions.

cerebellum (sehr-uh-BELL-um): The brain structure that executes smooth, skilled body movements and regulates muscle tone and posture.

cerebral cortex (seh-REE-brul KOR-tex): The gray, convoluted covering of the cerebral hemispheres that is responsible for higher mental processes such as language, memory, and thinking.

cerebral hemispheres (seh-REE-brul): The right and left halves of the cerebrum, covered by the cerebral cortex and connected by the corpus callosum.

cerebrum (seh-REE-brum): The largest structure of the human brain, consisting of the two cerebral hemispheres connected by the corpus callosum and covered by the cerebral cortex.

chlamydia (klah-MIH-dee-uh): The most common bacterial STD found in both sexes, and one that can cause infertility in females.

chromosomes: Rod-shaped structures in the nuclei of body cells, which contain all the genes and carry all the hereditary information.

circadian rhythm (sur-KAY-dee-un): Within each 24-hour period, the regular fluctuation from high to low points of certain bodily functions.

circadian theory: The theory that sleep evolved to keep humans out of harm's way during the night and that sleepiness ebbs and flows according to a circadian rhythm.

classical conditioning: A learning process through which one stimulus comes to predict the occurrence of another stimulus and to elicit a response similar to or related to the response evoked by that stimulus.

clinical psychologist: A psychologist, usually with a PhD, whose training is in the diagnosis, treatment, or research of psychological and behavioral disorders.

co-action effects: The impact on a person's performance of the presence of others engaged in the same task.

cocaine: A type of stimulant that produces a feeling of euphoria.

cochlea (KOK-lee-uh): The snail-shaped, fluid-filled chamber in the inner ear that contains the hair cells (the sound receptors).

cognition: The mental processes that are involved in acquiring, storing, retrieving, and using information and that include sensation, perception, imagery, concept formation, reasoning, decision making, problem solving, and language.

cognitive developmental theory: A theory suggesting that when children realize their gender is permanent, they are motivated to seek out same-sex models and learn to act in ways considered appropriate for their gender.

cognitive dissonance: The unpleasant state that can occur when people become aware of inconsistencies between their attitudes or between their attitudes and their behavior.

cognitive map: A mental representation of a spatial arrangement such as a maze.

cognitive perspective: A perspective that emphasizes the role of mental processes that underlie behavior.

cognitive processes (COG-nuh-tiv): Mental processes such as thinking, knowing, problem solving, and remembering.

cognitive psychology: A specialty that studies mental processes such as memory, problem solving, decision making, perception, language, and other forms of cognition; often uses the information-processing approach.

cognitive therapy: A therapy designed to change maladaptive behavior by changing the person's irrational thoughts, beliefs, and ideas.

coitus (KOeh-tis): Penile-vaginal intercourse.

collective unconscious: In Jung's theory, the most inaccessible layer of the unconscious, which contains the universal experiences of humankind transmitted to each individual.

color blindness: The inability to distinguish some or all colors, resulting from a defect in the cones.

color constancy: The tendency to see an object as about the same color regardless of differences in lighting conditions.

compliance: Acting in accordance with the wishes, the suggestions, or the direct request of another person.

compulsion: A persistent, irresistible, irrational urge to perform an act or ritual repeatedly.

concept: A mental category used to represent a class or group of objects, people, organizations, events, situations, or relations that share common characteristics or attributes.

concrete operations stage: Piaget's third stage of cognitive development (ages 7 to 11 years), during which a child acquires the concepts of reversibility and conservation and is able to apply logical thinking to concrete objects.

conditioned reflex: A learned reflex rather than a naturally occurring one.

conditioned response (CR): That response that comes to be elicited by a conditioned stimulus as a result of its repeated pairing with an unconditioned stimulus.

conditioned stimulus (CS): A neutral stimulus that, after repeated pairing with an unconditioned stimulus, becomes associated with it and elicits a conditioned response.

conditions of worth: Conditions on which the positive regard of others rests.

cones: The receptor cells in the retina that enable humans to see color and fine detail in adequate light, but that do not function in dim light.

confederate: Someone who is posing as a participant in an experiment but is actually assisting the experimenter.

conformity: Changing or adopting an attitude or behavior to be consistent with the social norms of a group or the expectations of other people.

confounding variables: Any factors or conditions other than the independent variable that could cause observed changes in the dependent variable.

conscious (KON-shus): The thoughts, feelings, sensations, or memories of which a person is aware at any given moment.

consciousness: An awareness of one's own perceptions, thoughts, feelings, sensations, and external environment.

conservation: The concept that a given quantity of matter remains the same despite rearrangement or change in its appearance, as long as nothing is added or taken away.

consolidation: A physiological change in the brain that must take place for encoded information to be stored in memory.

consolidation failure: Any disruption in the consolidation process that prevents a permanent memory from forming.

consummate love: According to Sternberg's theory, the most complete form of love, consisting of three components—intimacy, passion, and decision/commitment.

contact hypothesis: The notion that prejudice can be reduced through increased contact among members of different social groups.

continuous reinforcement: Reinforcement that is administered after every desired or correct response; the most effective method of conditioning a new response.

control group: In an experiment, a group that is similar to the experimental group and is exposed to the same experimental environment but is not exposed to the independent variable; used for purposes of comparison.

controlled drinking: A behavioral approach to the treatment of alcoholism, designed to teach the skills necessary so that alcoholics can drink socially without losing control.

conventional level: Kohlberg's second level of moral reasoning, in which right and wrong are based on the internalized standards of others; "right" is whatever helps or is approved of by others, or whatever is consistent with the laws of society.

convergence: A binocular depth cue in which the eyes turn inward as they focus on nearby objects—the closer an object, the greater the convergence.

conversion disorder: A somatoform disorder in which a person suffers a loss of motor or sensory functioning in some part of the body; the loss has no physical cause but solves some psychological problem.

coping: Efforts through action and thought to deal with demands that are perceived as taxing or overwhelming.

cornea (KOR-nee-uh): The transparent covering on the front surface of the eyeball that bends light rays inward through the pupil.

corpus callosum (KOR-pus kah-LO-sum): The thick band of nerve fibers that connects the two cerebral hemispheres and makes possible the transfer of information and the synchronization of activity between them.

correlation coefficient: A numerical value that indicates the strength and direction of the relationship between two variables; ranges from +1.00 (a perfect positive correlation) to −1.00 (a perfect negative correlation).

correlational method: A research method used to establish the degree of relationship (correlation) between two characteristics, events, or behaviors.

crack: A form of cocaine that is smoked; the most potent and addictive form of cocaine.

crash: The feelings of depression, exhaustion, irritability, and anxiety that occur following an amphetamine, cocaine, or crack high.

creativity: The ability to produce original, appropriate, and valuable ideas and/or solutions to problems.

critical period: A period that is so important to development that a harmful environmental influence at that time can keep a bodily structure from developing normally or can impair later intellectual or social development.

critical thinking: The process of objectively evaluating claims, propositions, or conclusions to determine whether they follow logically from the evidence presented.

cross-sectional study: A type of developmental study in which researchers compare groups of participants of different ages on certain characteristics to determine age-related differences.

crowding: A subjective perception that there are too many people in a defined space.

crystallized intelligence: Aspects of intelligence, including verbal ability and accumulated knowledge, that tend to increase over the life span.

CT scan (computerized axial tomography): A brain-scanning technique involving a rotating X-ray scanner and a high-speed computer analysis that produces slice-by-slice, cross-sectional images of the structure of the brain.

culture-fair intelligence test: An intelligence test that uses questions that will not penalize those whose culture differs from that of the middle or upper classes.

dark adaptation: The eye's increasing ability to see in dim light, which results from regeneration of rhodopsin molecules from opsin and retinal in the rods and the dilation of the pupil.

decay theory: A theory of forgetting that holds that the memory trace, if not used, disappears with the passage of time.

decibel (DES-ih-bel): A unit of measurement of the intensity or loudness of sound based on the amplitude of the sound wave.

decision latitude: The degree to which employees have the opportunity to exercise initiative and use their skills to control their working conditions.

decision making: The process of considering alternatives and choosing among them.

declarative memory: The subsystem within long-term memory that stores facts, information, and personal life experiences; also called *explicit memory.*

deductive reasoning: Reasoning from the general to the specific, or drawing particular conclusions from general principles.

deep structure: The underlying meaning of a sentence.

defense mechanism: An unconscious, irrational means used by the ego to defend against anxiety; involves self-deception and the distortion of reality.

delta wave: The slowest brain-wave pattern, associated with Stage 3 sleep and Stage 4 sleep (deep sleep).

delusion: A false belief, not generally shared by others in the culture, that cannot be changed despite strong evidence to the contrary.

delusion of grandeur: A false belief that one is a famous person or a person who has some great knowledge, ability, or authority.

delusion of persecution: A false belief that a person or group is trying in some way to harm one.

dendrites (DEN-drytes): The branchlike extensions of a neuron that receive signals from other neurons.

denial: Refusing to acknowledge consciously the existence of danger or a threatening condition.

density: A measure referring to the number of people occupying a unit of space.

dependent variable: The variable that is measured at the end of an experiment and is presumed to vary as a result of manipulations of the independent variable.

depressants: A category of drugs that decrease activity in the central nervous system, slow down bodily functions, and reduce sensitivity to outside stimulation; also called "downers."

depth perception: The ability to see in three dimensions and to estimate distance.

descriptive research methods: Research methods that yield descriptions of behavior rather than causal explanations.

descriptive statistics: Statistics used to organize, summarize, and describe information gathered from actual observations.

developmental psychology: The study of how humans grow, develop, and change throughout the life span.

deviation score: A test score calculated by comparing an individual's score with the scores of others of the same age.

difference threshold: The smallest increase or decrease in a physical stimulus required to produce a difference in sensation that is noticeable 50% of the time.

diffusion of responsibility: The feeling among bystanders at an emergency that the responsibility for helping is shared by the group, so each person feels less compelled to act than if he or she alone bore the total responsibility.

directive therapy: An approach to therapy in which the therapist takes an active role in determining the course of therapy sessions and provides answers and suggestions to the patient.

discrimination: In classical conditioning, the learned ability to distinguish between similar stimuli so that the conditioned response occurs only to the original conditioned stimulus but not to similar stimuli; in social psychology, behavior, usually negative, directed toward others based on their gender, religion, race, or membership in a particular group.

discriminative stimulus: A stimulus that signals whether a certain response or behavior is likely to be followed by reward or punishment.

disorganized schizophrenia: The most serious type of schizophrenia, marked by inappropriate affect, silliness, laughter, grotesque mannerisms, and bizarre behavior.

displacement: In memory, the event that occurs when short-term memory is holding its maximum and each new item entering short-term memory pushes out an existing item; in behavior, substituting a less threatening object for the original object of an impulse.

display rules: Cultural rules that dictate how emotions should be expressed, and when and where their expression is appropriate.

dispositional attribution: Attributing a behavior to some internal cause, such as a personal trait, motive, or attitude; an internal attribution.

dissociative amnesia: A dissociative disorder in which there is a loss of memory of limited periods in one's life or of one's entire identity.

dissociative disorders: Disorders in which, under stress, one loses the integration of consciousness, identity, and memories of important personal events.

dissociative fugue (FEWG): A dissociative disorder in which one has a complete loss of memory of one's entire identity, travels away from home, and may assume a new identity.

dissociative identity disorder (DID): A dissociative disorder in which two or more distinct personalities occur in the same person, each taking over at different times; also called multiple personality.

divergent thinking: The ability to produce multiple ideas, answers, or solutions to a problem for which there is no agreed-on solution.

dominant gene: The gene that is expressed in the individual.

door-in-the-face technique: A strategy in which someone makes a large, unreasonable request with the expectation that the person will refuse but will then be more likely to respond favorably to a smaller request at a later time.

dopamine (DOE-pah-meen): A neurotransmitter that plays a role in learning, attention, and movement; a deficiency of dopamine is associated with Parkinson's disease, and an oversensitivity to it is associated with some cases of schizophrenia.

double-blind technique: An experimental procedure in which neither the participants nor the experimenter knows who is in the experimental or control groups until after the results have been gathered; a control for experimenter bias.

drive: A state of tension or arousal brought about by an underlying need, which motivates an organism to engage in behavior that will satisfy the need and reduce the tension.

drive-reduction theory: A theory of motivation suggesting that a need creates an unpleasant state of arousal or tension called a drive, which impels the organism to engage in behavior that will satisfy the need and reduce the tension.

drug tolerance: A condition in which the user becomes progressively less affected by the drug so that larger and larger doses are necessary to maintain the same effect.

DSM-IV: The *Diagnostic and Statistical Manual of Mental Disorders,* Fourth Edition, a manual published by the American Psychiatric Association, which describes about 290 mental disorders and their symptoms.

dyspareunia (dis-PAH-roo-nee-yah): A sexual pain disorder marked by genital pain associated with sexual intercourse, more comon in females than in males.

ego (EE-go): In Freudian theory, the rational, largely conscious system of personality, which operates according to the reality principle.

ego integrity versus despair: Erikson's stage for old age, when people look back on their lives with satisfaction or with major regrets.

eidetic imagery (eye-DET-ik): The ability to retain the image of a visual stimulus several minutes after it has been removed from view.

elaborative rehearsal: A technique used to encode information into long-term memory by considering its meaning and associating it with other information already stored in long-term memory.

electroconvulsive therapy (ECT): A treatment in which an electric current is passed through the brain, causing a seizure; usually reserved for severely depressed patients who are either suicidal or unresponsive to other treatment.

electroencephalogram (EEG) (ee-lek-tro-en-SEFF-uh-lo-gram): A record of brain-wave activity made by the electroencephalograph.

embryo: The developing human organism during the period (week 3 through week 8) when the major systems, organs, and structures of the body develop.

emotion: A feeling state involving physiological arousal, a cognitive appraisal of the situation arousing the state, and an outward expression of the state.

emotion-focused coping: A response aimed at reducing the emotional impact of the stressor.

emotional intelligence: A type of intelligence that includes an awareness of and an ability to manage one's own emotions, the ability to motivate oneself, empathy, and the ability to handle relationships successfully.

encoding: Transforming information into a form that can be stored in short-term or long-term memory.

encoding failure: A cause of forgetting resulting from material never having been put into long-term memory.

endocrine system (EN-duh-krin): A system of ductless glands in various parts of the body that manufacture and secrete hormones into the bloodstream or lymph fluids, thus affecting cells in other parts of the body.

endorphins (en-DOR-fins): Chemicals, produced naturally by the brain and the pituitary gland, that reduce pain and positively affect mood.

episodic memory (ep-ih-SOD-ik): The subpart of declarative memory that contains memories of personally experienced events.

estrogen (ES-truh-jen): A female sex hormone that promotes the secondary sex characteristics in females and controls the menstrual cycle.

evolutionary perspective: A perspective that focuses on how humans have evolved and adapted behaviors required for survival against various environmental pressures over the long course of evolution.

evolutionary psychology: The school of psychology that studies how humans' genetically inherited tendencies and dispositions influence a wide range of behaviors.

excitement phase: The first stage in the sexual response cycle, characterized by an erection in males and a swelling of the clitoris and vaginal lubrication in females.

exemplars: The individual instances of a concept that are stored in memory from personal experience.

exhaustion stage: The final stage of the general adaptation syndrome, occurring if the organism fails in its efforts to resist the stressor.

experimental group: In an experiment, the group that is exposed to the independent variable, or the treatment.

experimental method: The research method in which researchers randomly assign participants to groups and control all conditions other than one or more independent variables, which are then manipulated to determine their effect on some behavioral measure—the dependent variable in the experiment.

experimenter bias: A phenomenon that occurs when the researcher's preconceived notions in some way influence the participants' behavior and/or the interpretation of experimental results.

exposure and response prevention: A behavior therapy that exposes patients with obsessive compulsive disorder to stimuli generating increasing anxiety; patients must agree not to carry out their normal rituals for a specified period of time after exposure.

extinction: The weakening and often eventual disappearance of a learned response (in classical conditioning, the conditioned response is weakened by repeated presentation of the conditioned stimulus without the unconditioned stimulus; in operant conditioning, the conditioned response is weakened by withholding reinforcement).

extrasensory perception (ESP): Gaining awareness of or information about objects, events, or another's thoughts through some means other than the known sensory channels.

extrinsic motivation: The desire to perform an act to gain a reward or to avoid an undesirable consequence.

extroversion: The tendency to be outgoing, adaptable, and sociable.

facial-feedback hypothesis: The idea that the muscular movements involved in certain facial expressions trigger the corresponding emotions (for example, smiling makes one feel happy).

family therapy: Therapy involving an entire family, based on the assumption that an individual's problem is caused and/or maintained in part by problems within the family unit.

fat cells: Cells that serve as storehouses for liquefied fat in the body and that number from 25 to 35 billion in normal-weight individuals; with weight loss, they decrease in size but not in number.

feature detectors: Neurons in the brain that respond to specific features of a sensory stimulus (for example, to lines or angles).

female orgasmic disorder: The persistent inability of a woman to reach orgasm, or a delay in reaching orgasm despite adequate sexual stimulation.

female sexual arousal disorder: A sexual dysfunction in which a woman may not feel sexually aroused in response to sexual stimulation or may be unable to achieve or sustain an adequate lubrication-swelling response to sexual excitement.

fetal alcohol syndrome: A condition, caused by maternal alcohol intake during pregnancy, in which the baby is born mentally retarded, with a small head and facial, organ, and behavioral abnormalities.

fetus: The developing human organism during the period (week 9 until birth) when rapid growth and further development of the structures, organs, and systems of the body occur.

fight-or-flight response: A response to stress in which the sympathetic nervous system and the endocrine glands prepare the body to fight or flee.

figure-ground: A principle of perceptual organization whereby the visual field is perceived in terms of an object (figure) standing out against a background (ground).

five-factor theory: A trait theory that attempts to explain personality using five broad dimensions, each of which is composed of a constellation of personality traits.

fixation: Arrested development at a psychosexual stage occurring because of excessive gratification or frustration at that stage.

fixed-interval schedule: A schedule in which a reinforcer is given following the first correct response after a fixed period of time has elapsed.

fixed-ratio schedule: A schedule in which a reinforcer is given after a fixed number of correct responses.

flashback: The brief recurrence, occurring suddenly and without warning at a later time, of effects a person has experienced while taking LSD.

flashbulb memory: An extremely vivid memory of the conditions surrounding one's first hearing the news of a surprising, shocking, or highly emotional event.

flooding: A behavioral therapy used to treat phobias, during which clients are exposed to the feared object or event (or asked to imagine it vividly) for an extended period until their anxiety decreases.

fluid intelligence: Aspects of intelligence involving abstract reasoning and mental flexibility, which peak in the early 20s and decline slowly as people age.

foot-in-the-door technique: A strategy designed to secure a favorable response to a small request at first, with the aim of making the person more likely to agree later to a larger request.

formal concept: A concept that is clearly defined by a set of rules, a formal definition, or a classification system; an artificial concept.

formal operations stage: Piaget's fourth and final stage of cognitive development, characterized by the ability to apply logical thinking to abstract problems and hypothetical situations.

fovea (FO-vee-uh): A small area of the retina, 1/50 of an inch in diameter, that provides the clearest and sharpest vision because it has the largest concentration of cones.

framing: The way information is presented so as to emphasize either a potential gain or a potential loss as the outcome.

fraternal (dizygotic) twins: Twins, no more alike genetically than ordinary siblings, who develop after two eggs are released during ovulation and fertilized by two different sperm.

fraternal twins: Twins who are no more alike genetically than ordinary brothers and sisters; dizygotic twins.

free association: A psychoanalytic technique used to explore the unconscious by having patients reveal whatever thoughts or images come to mind.

frequency: Measured in the unit called the hertz, the number of sound waves or cycles per second, determining the pitch of the sound.

frequency distribution: An arrangement showing the numbers of scores that fall within equal-sized class intervals.

frequency polygon: A line graph that depicts the frequency or number of scores within each class interval in a frequency distribution.

frequency theory: The theory that hair cell receptors vibrate the same number of times as the sounds that reach them, thereby accounting for how variations in pitch are transmitted to the brain.

frontal lobes: The lobes that control voluntary body movements, speech production, and such functions as thinking, motivation, planning for the future, impulse control, and emotional responses.

frustration: Interference with the attainment of a goal, or the blocking of an impulse.

frustration–aggression hypothesis: The hypothesis that frustration produces aggression.

functional fixedness: The failure to use familiar objects in novel ways to solve problems because of a tendency to view objects only in terms of their customary functions.

functional MRI (fMRI): A brain-imaging technique that reveals both brain structure and brain activity.

functionalism: An early school of psychology that was concerned with how mental processes help humans and animals adapt to their environments.

***g* factor:** Spearman's term for a general intellectual ability that underlies all mental operations to some degree.

gate-control theory: The theory that the pain signals transmitted by slow-firing nerve fibers can be blocked at the spinal gate if fast-firing fibers get their messages to the gate first, or if the brain itself inhibits transmission of the pain messages.

gender (JEN-der): Psychological and sociocultural definition of masculinity or femininity based on the expected behaviors for males and females.

gender identity: One's sense of being a male or a female.

gender identity disorders: Disorders characterized by a problem accepting one's identity as male or female.

gender roles: Cultural expectations about the behavior appropriate to each gender.

gender typing: The process by which individuals acquire the traits, behaviors, attitudes, preferences, and interests that the culture considers appropriate for their gender.

gender-schema theory: A theory suggesting that young children are motivated to attend to and behave in ways consistent with gender-based standards and stereotypes of the culture.

general adaptation syndrome (GAS): The predictable sequence of reactions (alarm, resistance, and exhaustion stages) that organisms show in response to stressors.

generalization: In classical conditioning, the tendency to make a conditioned response to a stimulus similar to the original conditioned stimulus; in operant conditioning, the tendency to make the learned response to a stimulus similar to the one for which it was originally reinforced.

generalized anxiety disorder: An anxiety disorder in which people experience excessive anxiety or worry that they find difficult to control.

generativity versus stagnation: Erikson's stage for middle age, when people become increasingly concerned with guiding the next generation rather than stagnating.

genes: The segments of DNA that are located on the chromosomes and are the basic units for the transmission of all hereditary traits.

genital herpes (HER-peez): An STD caused by the herpes simplex virus (usually type 2) that results in painful blisters on the genitals; presently incurable, the infection usually recurs and is highly contagious during outbreaks.

genital stage: Freud's final psychosexual stage (from puberty on), in which for most people the focus of sexual energy gradually shifts to the opposite sex, culminating in the attainment of full adult sexuality.

genital warts: Growths that are caused by *human papillomavirus* (HPV), that often resemble cauliflower, and that are most often found in the genital and anal regions.

genitals (JEN-uh-tulz): The internal and external reproductive organs.

Gestalt (geh-SHTALT): A German word roughly meaning "form" or "pattern."

Gestalt psychology (geh-SHTALT): The school of psychology that emphasizes that individuals perceive objects and patterns as whole units and that the perceived whole is more than the sum of its parts.

Gestalt therapy: A therapy that was originated by Fritz Perls and that emphasizes the importance of clients' fully experiencing, in the present moment, their feelings, thoughts, and actions and taking personal responsibility for their behavior.

glial cells (GLEE-ul): Cells that help to make the brain more efficient by holding the neurons together, removing waste products such as dead neurons, making the myelin coating for the axons, and performing other manufacturing, nourishing, and cleanup tasks.

gonads: The sex glands; the ovaries in females and the testes in males.

gonorrhea (gahn-ah-REE-ah): An STD that, in males, causes a puslike discharge from the penis; if untreated, females can develop pelvic inflammatory disease and possible infertility.

group polarization: The tendency of members of a group, after group discussion, to shift toward a more extreme position in whatever direction they were leaning initially—either more risky or more cautious.

group therapy: A form of therapy in which several clients (usually 7–10) meet regularly with one or more therapists to resolve personal problems.

groupthink: The tendency for members of a very cohesive group to feel such pressure to maintain group solidarity and to reach agreement on an issue that they fail to weigh available evidence adequately or to consider objections and alternatives.

gustation: The sensation of taste.

habituation: A decrease in response or attention to a stimulus as an infant becomes accustomed to it.

hair cells: Sensory receptors for hearing, found in the cochlea.

hallucination: A sensory perception in the absence of any external sensory stimulus; an imaginary sensation.

hallucinogens (hal-LU-sin-o-jenz): A category of drugs, sometimes called psychedelics, that alter perception and mood and can cause hallucinations.

halo effect: The tendency to infer generally positive or negative traits in a person as a result of observing one or a few major positive or negative traits.

hardiness: A combination of three psychological qualities shared by people who can undergo high levels of stress yet remain healthy: a sense of control over one's life, commitment to one's personal goals, and a tendency to view change as a challenge rather than as a threat.

hassles: Little stressors that include the irritating demands and troubled relationships that can occur daily and that, according to Lazarus, cause more stress than do major life changes.

health psychology: The field concerned with the psychological factors that contribute to health, illness, and recovery.

heritability: An index of the degree to which a characteristic is estimated to be influenced by heredity.

heroin: A highly addictive, partly synthetic narcotic derived from morphine.

heuristic (yur-RIS-tik): A rule of thumb that is derived from experience and used in decision making and problem solving, even though there is no guarantee of its accuracy or usefulness.

higher-order conditioning: Conditioning that occurs when a neutral stimulus is paired with an existing conditioned stimulus, becomes associated with it, and gains the power to elicit the same conditioned response.

hippocampal region: A part of the limbic system, which includes the hippocampus itself (primarily involved in the formation of episodic memories) and its underlying cortical areas (involved in the formation of semantic memories).

hippocampus (hip-po-CAM-pus): A structure in the limbic system that plays a central role in the formation of long-term memories.

histogram: A bar graph that depicts the number of scores within each class interval in a frequency distribution.

HIV (human immunodeficiency virus): The virus that causes AIDS.

homeostasis: The tendency of the body to maintain a balanced internal state with regard to oxygen level, body temperature, blood sugar, water balance, and so forth.

homophobia: An intense, irrational hostility toward or fear of homosexuals.

hormone: A substance manufactured and released in one part of the body that affects other parts of the body.

hue: The property of light commonly referred to as color (red, blue, green, etc.), determined primarily by the wavelength of light reflected from a surface.

humanistic perspective: A perspective that emphasizes the importance of an individual's subjective experience as a key to understanding behavior.

humanistic psychology: The school of psychology that focuses on the uniqueness of human beings and their capacity for choice, growth, and psychological health.

hypnosis: A procedure through which one person, the hypnotist, uses the power of suggestion to induce changes in thoughts, feelings, sensations, perceptions, or behavior in another person, the subject.

hypoactive sexual desire disorder: A sexual dysfunction marked by little or no sexual desire or interest in sexual activity.

hypochondriasis (HI-poh-kahn-DRY-uh-sis): A somatoform disorder in which persons are preoccupied with their health and convinced they have some serious disorder despite reassurance from doctors to the contrary.

hypothalamus (HY-po-THAL-uh-mus): A small but influential brain structure that controls the pituitary gland and regulates hunger, thirst, sexual behavior, body temperature, and a wide variety of emotional behaviors.

hypothesis: A prediction about the relationship between two or more variables.

id (IHD): The unconscious system of the personality, which contains the life and death instincts and operates on the pleasure principle.

identical (monozygotic) twins: Twins with exactly the same genes, who develop after one egg is fertilized by one sperm, and the zygote splits into two parts.

identity versus role confusion: Erikson's fifth psychosocial stage, when adolescents need to establish their own identity and to form values to live by; failure can lead to an identity crisis.

illicit drug: An illegal drug.

illusion: A false perception of actual stimuli involving a misperception of size, shape, or the relationship of one element to another.

imagery: The representation in the mind of a sensory experience—visual, auditory, gustatory, motor, olfactory, or tactile.

imaginary audience: A belief of adolescents that they are or will be the focus of attention in social situations and that others will be as critical or approving as they are of themselves.

in-group: A social group with a strong sense of togetherness and from which others are excluded.

inappropriate affect: A symptom common in schizophrenia in which a person's behavior (including facial expression, tone of voice, and gestures) does not reflect the emotion that would be expected under the circumstances; for example, a person laughs at a tragedy or cries at a joke.

incentive: An external stimulus that motivates behavior (examples: money, fame).

independent variable: In an experiment, the factor or condition that the researcher manipulates in order to determine its effect on another behavior or condition known as the dependent variable.

inductive reasoning: A form of reasoning in which general conclusions are drawn from particular facts or individual cases.

industrial/organizational (I/O) psychologists: Psychologists who focus on the relationship between the workplace or organization and the worker.

industry versus inferiority: Erikson's fourth stage (ages 6 years to puberty), when children develop a sense of industry or inferiority based on how parents and teachers react to their efforts to undertake projects.

infantile amnesia: The relative inability of older children and adults to recall events from the first few years of life.

inferential statistics: Statistical procedures that allow researchers (1) to make inferences about the characteristics of the larger population from observations and measurements of a sample, and (2) to derive estimates of how much confidence can be placed in those inferences.

initiative versus guilt: Erikson's third stage (ages 3 to 6 years), when children develop a sense of initiative or guilt depending on how parents react to their initiation of play, their motor activities, and their questions.

innate: Inborn, unlearned.

inner ear: The innermost portion of the ear, containing the cochlea, the vestibular sacs, and the semicircular canals.

insight: The sudden realization of the relationship between elements in a problem situation, which makes the solution apparent.

insight therapy: Any type of psychotherapy based on the notion that psychological well-being depends on self-understanding.

insomnia: A sleep disorder characterized by difficulty falling or staying asleep, by waking too early, or by light, restless, or poor sleep.

instinct: An inborn, unlearned, fixed pattern of behavior that is characteristic of an entire species.

instinct theory: The notion that human behavior is motivated by certain innate tendencies, or instincts, shared by all individuals.

intelligence: An individual's ability to understand complex ideas, to adapt effectively to the environment, to learn from experience, to engage in various forms of reasoning, and to overcome obstacles through mental effort.

intelligence quotient (IQ): An index of intelligence originally derived by dividing mental age by chronological age and then multiplying by 100; now derived by comparing an individual's score with the scores of others of the same age.

interference: Memory loss that occurs because information or associations stored either before or after a given memory hinder the ability to remember it.

interpersonal therapy (IPT): A brief psychotherapy designed to help depressed people better understand and cope with problems relating to their interpersonal relationships.

intimacy versus isolation: Erikson's sixth psychosocial stage, when the young adult must establish intimacy in a relationship in order to avoid feeling a sense of isolation and loneliness.

intrinsic motivation: The desire to perform an act because it is satisfying or pleasurable in and of itself.

introversion: The tendency to focus inward; to be reflective, retiring, and nonsocial.

inventory: A paper-and-pencil test with questions about a person's thoughts, feelings, and behaviors, which can be scored according to a standard procedure.

James–Lange theory of emotion: The theory that emotional feelings result when an individual becomes aware of a physiological response to an emotion-provoking stimulus (for example, feeling fear because of trembling).

just noticeable difference (JND): The smallest change in sensation that a person is able to detect 50% of the time.

kinesthetic sense: The sense providing information about relative position and movement of body parts.

laboratory observation: A research method in which behavior is studied in a laboratory setting, where researchers can exert more control and take more precise measurements.

language: A means of communicating thoughts and feelings, using a system of socially shared but arbitrary symbols (sounds, signs, or written symbols) arranged according to rules of grammar.

latency period: The period following Freud's phallic stage (ages 5 or 6 years to puberty), in which the sex instinct is largely repressed and temporarily sublimated in school and play activities.

latent learning: Learning that occurs without apparent reinforcement but that is not demonstrated until sufficient reinforcement is provided.

lateral hypothalamus (LH): The part of the hypothalamus that acts as a feeding center and, when activated, signals an animal to eat; when the LH is destroyed, the animal refuses to eat.

lateralization: The specialization of one of the cerebral hemispheres to handle a particular function.

law of effect: Thorndike's law of learning, which states that connections between a stimulus and a response will be strengthened if the response is followed by a satisfying consequence and weakened if the response is followed by discomfort.

Lazarus theory of emotion: The theory that an emotion-provoking stimulus triggers a cognitive appraisal, which is followed by the emotion and the physiological arousal.

learned helplessness: The learned response of resigning oneself passively to aversive conditions, rather than taking action to change, escape, or avoid them; learned through repeated exposure to inescapable or unavoidable aversive events.

learning: A relatively permanent change in behavior, knowledge, capability, or attitude that is acquired through experience and cannot be attributed to illness, injury, or maturation.

left hemisphere: The hemisphere that controls the right side of the body, coordinates complex movements, and, in

95% of people, controls the production of speech and written language.

lens: The transparent structure behind the iris that changes shape as it focuses images on the retina.

levels-of-processing model: A model of memory as a single system in which retention depends on how deeply information is processed.

libido (lih-BEE-doe): Freud's name for the psychic or sexual energy that comes from the id and provides the energy for the entire personality.

life structure: Levinson's term for the basic pattern of one's life at any given time, including one's relationships and activities and the significance they have for the individual.

limbic system: A group of structures in the brain, including the amygdala and hippocampus, that are collectively involved in emotion, memory, and motivation.

linguistic relativity hypothesis: The notion that the language a person speaks largely determines the nature of that person's thoughts.

lithium: A drug used in bipolar disorder to control the symptoms in a manic episode and to even out the mood swings and reduce recurrence of future manic or depressive states.

lobotomy: A psychosurgery technique in which the nerve fibers connecting the frontal lobes to the deeper brain centers are severed.

locus of control: A concept used to explain how people account for what happens in their lives—people with an *internal* locus of control see themselves as primarily in control of their behavior and its consequences; those with an *external* locus of control perceive what happens to be in the hands of fate, luck, or chance.

long-term memory: The relatively permanent memory system with a virtually unlimited capacity.

long-term potentiation: A long-lasting increase in the efficiency of neural transmission at the synapses.

longitudinal study: A type of developmental study in which the same group of participants is followed and measured at different ages.

low-ball technique: A strategy to gain compliance by making a very attractive initial offer to get a person to agree to an action and then making the terms less favorable.

low-birthweight baby: A baby weighing less than 5.5 pounds.

LSD (lysergic acid diethylamide): A powerful hallucinogen with unpredictable effects ranging from perceptual changes and vivid hallucinations to states of panic and terror.

lucid dream: A dream during which the dreamer is aware of dreaming and is often able to influence the content of the dream while it is in progress.

lymphocytes: The white blood cells—including B cells and T cells—that are key components of the immune system.

mainstreaming: Educating mentally retarded students in regular rather than special schools by placing them in regular classes for part of the day or having special classrooms in regular schools.

major depressive disorder: A mood disorder marked by feelings of great sadness, despair, guilt, worthlessness, and hopelessness.

male erectile disorder: The repeated inability to have or sustain an erection firm enough for coitus; erectile dysfunction, or impotence.

male orgasmic disorder: A sexual dysfunction in which there is an absence of ejaculation, or in which ejaculation occurs only after strenuous effort over a prolonged period.

manic episode (MAN-ik): A period of extreme elation, euphoria, and hyperactivity, often accompanied by delusions of grandeur and by hostility if activity is blocked.

marijuana: A hallucinogen with effects ranging from relaxation and giddiness to perceptual distortions and hallucinations.

massed practice: Learning in one long practice session as opposed to spacing the learning in shorter practice sessions over an extended period.

matching hypothesis: The notion that people tend to have spouses, lovers, or friends who are approximately equivalent in social assets such as physical attractiveness.

maturation: Changes that occur according to one's genetically determined, biological timetable of development.

MDMA (Ecstasy): An amphetamine derivative that produces both stimulant and psychedelic effects and can cause permanent damage to the serotonin-releasing neurons.

mean: The arithmetic average of a group of scores; calculated by adding up all the single scores and dividing the sum by the number of scores.

means–end analysis: A heuristic strategy in which the current position is compared with the desired goal, and a series of steps are formulated and taken to close the gap between them.

measure of central tendency: A measure or score that describes the center, or middle, of a distribution of scores (example: mean, median, or mode).

median: The middle value or score when a group of scores are arranged from highest to lowest.

meditation (concentrative): A group of techniques that involve focusing attention on an object, a word, one's breathing, or body movement in order to block out all distractions, to enhance well-being, and to achieve an altered state of consciousness.

medulla (muh-DUL-uh): The part of the brainstem that controls heartbeat, blood pressure, breathing, coughing, and swallowing.

melatonin: A hormone secreted by the pineal gland that acts to reduce activity and induce sleep.

menarche (men-AR-kee): The onset of menstruation.

menopause: The cessation of menstruation, occurring between ages 45 and 55 and signifying the end of reproductive capacity.

mental retardation: Subnormal intelligence reflected by an IQ below 70 and by adaptive functioning severely deficient for one's age.

mental set: The tendency to apply a familiar strategy to the solution of a problem without carefully considering the special requirements of that problem.

mere-exposure effect: The tendency of people to develop a more positive evaluation of some person, object, or other stimulus with repeated exposure to it.

meta-analysis: A complex statistical procedure used to combine the results from many studies on the same topic in order to determine the degree to which a hypothesis can be supported.

metabolic rate (meh-tuh-BALL-ik): The rate at which the body burns calories to produce energy.

microelectrode: An electrical wire so small that it can be used either to monitor the electrical activity of a single neuron or to stimulate activity within it.

microsleep: A momentary lapse from wakefulness into sleep, usually occurring when a person has been sleep-deprived.

middle ear: The portion of the ear containing the ossicles, which connect the eardrum to the oval window and amplify the vibrations as they travel to the inner ear.

midlife crisis: A period of turmoil usually occurring in a person's 40s and brought on by an awareness of one's mortality; characterized by a reassessment of one's life and a decision to make changes, either drastic or moderate, in order to make the remaining years better.

Minnesota Multiphasic Personality Inventory (MMPI): The most extensively researched and widely used personality test; used to screen and diagnose psychiatric problems and disorders; revised as MMPI-2.

minor tranquilizer: A central nervous system depressant that calms the user.

mode: The score that occurs most frequently in a group of scores.

model: The individual who demonstrates a behavior or serves as an example in observational learning.

modeling: Another name for observational learning.

monocular depth cues (mah-NOK-yu-ler): Depth cues that can be perceived by only one eye.

mood disorders: Disorders characterized by extreme and unwarranted disturbances in feeling or mood.

morphemes: The smallest units of meaning in a language.

motivated forgetting: Forgetting through suppression or repression in order to protect oneself from material that is too painful, anxiety- or guilt-producing, or otherwise unpleasant.

motivation: The process that initiates, directs, and sustains behavior to satisfy physiological or psychological needs or wants.

motives: Needs or desires that energize and direct behavior toward a goal.

motor cortex: The strip of tissue at the rear of the frontal lobes that controls voluntary body movement.

MRI (magnetic resonance imaging): A diagnostic scanning technique that produces high-resolution images of the structures of the brain.

myelin sheath (MY-uh-lin): The white, fatty coating wrapped around some axons that acts as insulation and enables impulses to travel much faster.

Myers–Briggs Type Indicator (MBTI): An inventory for classifying personality types based on Jung's theory of personality.

naive subject: A person who has agreed to participate in an experiment but is not aware that deception is being used to conceal its real purpose.

naloxone: A drug that blocks the action of endorphins.

narcolepsy (NAR-co-lep-see): A serious sleep disorder characterized by excessive daytime sleepiness and sudden, uncontrollable attacks of REM sleep.

narcotics: A class of depressant drugs derived from the opium poppy and producing pain-relieving and calming effects.

natural concept: A concept acquired not from a definition but through everyday perceptions and experiences; a fuzzy concept.

naturalistic observation: A research method in which the researcher observes and records behavior in its natural setting, without attempting to influence or control it.

nature–nurture controversy: The debate concerning the relative influences of heredity and environment on development, intelligence, and other traits.

need for achievement (*n* Ach): The need to accomplish something difficult and to perform at a high standard of excellence.

negative correlation: A relationship between two variables in which an increase in one variable is associated with a decrease in the other variable.

negative reinforcement: The termination of an unpleasant stimulus after a response in order to increase the probability that the response will be repeated.

neodissociation theory of hypnosis: A theory proposing that hypnosis works by causing a split, or dissociation, between two aspects of consciousness that are ordinarily linked: the planning and the monitoring functions.

neonate: Newborn infant up to 1 month old.

neural networks: Computer systems that are intended to mimic the human brain.

neuron (NEW-ron): A specialized cell that conducts impulses through the nervous system and contains three major parts—a cell body, dendrites, and an axon.

neuroscience: A field that combines the work of psychologists, biologists, biochemists, medical researchers, and others in the study of the structure and function of the nervous system.

neurosis (new-RO-sis): An obsolete term for a disorder causing personal distress and some impairment in functioning but not causing loss of contact with reality or violation of important social norms.

neurotransmitter (NEW-ro-TRANS-mit-er): A chemical that is released into the synaptic cleft from the axon terminal of a sending neuron, crosses a synapse, and binds to appropriate receptor sites on the dendrites or cell body of a receiving neuron, influencing the cell either to fire or not to fire.

nightmare: A very frightening dream occurring during REM sleep.

nondeclarative memory: The subsystem within long-term memory that consists of skills acquired through repetitive practice, habits, and simple classically conditioned responses; also called *implicit memory.*

nondirective therapy: An approach in which the therapist acts to facilitate growth, giving understanding and support rather than proposing solutions, answering questions, or actively directing the course of therapy.

nonsense syllable: A consonant-vowel-consonant combination that does not spell a word; used to control for the meaningfulness of the material.

norepinephrine (nor-EP-ih-NEF-rin): A neurotransmitter affecting eating and sleep; a deficiency of norepinephrine is associated with depression.

normal curve: A symmetrical, bell-shaped frequency distribution that represents how scores are normally distributed in a population; most scores fall near the mean, and fewer and fewer scores occur in the extremes either above or below the mean.

norms: Standards based on the range of test scores of a large group of people who are selected to provide the bases of comparison for those who take the test later.

NREM dream: Mental activity occurring during NREM sleep that is more thoughtlike in quality than REM dreams are.

NREM sleep: Non–rapid eye movement sleep, consisting of the four sleep stages and characterized by slow, regular respiration and heart rate, an absence of rapid eye movements, and blood pressure and brain activity that are at a 24-hour low point.

olfaction (ol-FAK-shun): The sensation of smell; the process of smelling.

olfactory bulbs: Two matchstick-sized structures above the nasal cavities, where smell sensations first register in the brain.

olfactory epithelium: Two 1-square-inch patches of tissue, one at the top of each nasal cavity, which together contain about 10 million olfactory neurons, the receptors for smell.

operant conditioning: A type of learning in which the consequences of behavior are manipulated in order to increase or decrease that behavior in the future.

opponent-process theory: The theory that three classes of cells increase their firing rate to signal one color and decrease their firing rate to signal the opposing color (red/green, yellow/blue, white/black).

optic nerve: The nerve that carries visual information from the retina to the brain.

oral stage: Freud's first psychosexual stage (birth to 1 or 1½ years), in which sensual pleasure is derived mainly through stimulation of the mouth.

orgasm: The third phase in the sexual response cycle, marked by rhythmic muscular contractions and a sudden discharge of accumulated sexual tension.

out-group: A social group specifically identified by the in-group as not belonging.

outer ear: The visible part of the ear, consisting of the pinna and the auditory canal.

overextension: The act of using a word, on the basis of some shared feature, to apply to a broader range of objects than appropriate.

overlearning: Practicing or studying material beyond the point where it can be repeated once without error.

overregularization: The act of inappropriately applying the grammatical rules for forming plurals and past tenses to irregular nouns and verbs.

object permanence: The realization that objects continue to exist even when they can no longer be perceived.

observational learning: Learning by observing the behavior of others and the consequences of that behavior; learning by imitation.

obsession: A persistent, recurring, involuntary thought, image, or impulse that invades consciousness and causes great distress.

obsessive compulsive disorder (OCD): An anxiety disorder in which a person suffers from obsessions and/or compulsions.

occipital lobes (ahk-SIP-uh-tul): The lobes that contain the primary visual cortex, where vision registers, and association areas involved in the interpretation of visual information.

Oedipus complex (ED-uh-pus): Occurring in the phallic stage, a conflict in which the child is sexually attracted to the opposite-sex parent and feels hostility toward the same-sex parent.

panic attack: An attack of overwhelming anxiety, fear, or terror.

panic disorder: An anxiety disorder in which a person experiences recurrent unpredictable attacks of overwhelming anxiety, fear, or terror.

paranoid schizophrenia (PAIR-uh-noid): A type of schizophrenia characterized by delusions of grandeur or persecution.

paraphilia: A sexual disorder in which sexual urges, fantasies, and behavior generally involve children, other nonconsenting partners, nonhuman objects, or the suffering and humiliation of oneself or one's partner.

parapsychology: The study of psychic phenomena, including extrasensory perception (ESP).

parasympathetic nervous system: The division of the autonomic nervous system that is associated with relaxation and the conservation of energy and that brings the heightened bodily responses back to normal following an emergency.

parietal lobes (puh-RY-uh-tul): The lobes that contain the somatosensory cortex (where touch, pressure, temperature, and pain register) and other areas that are responsible for body awareness and spatial orientation.

partial reinforcement: A pattern of reinforcement in which some portion, rather than 100%, of the correct responses are reinforced.

partial-reinforcement effect: The greater resistance to extinction that occurs when a portion, rather than all, of the correct responses are reinforced.

participant modeling: A behavior therapy in which an appropriate response is modeled in graduated steps and the client attempts each step, encouraged and supported by the therapist.

pelvic inflammatory disease (PID): An infection in the female pelvic organs, which can result from untreated chlamydia or gonorrhea and can cause pain, scarring of tissue, and even infertility or ectopic pregnancy.

perception: The process by which sensory information is actively organized and interpreted by the brain.

perceptual constancy: The tendency to perceive objects as maintaining stable properties, such as size, shape, brightness, and color, despite differences in distance, viewing angle, and lighting.

perceptual set: An expectation of what will be perceived, which can affect what actually is perceived.

period of the zygote: The approximately 2-week-long period from conception to the attachment of the zygote to the uterine wall.

peripheral nervous system (PNS) (peh-RIF-er-ul): The nerves connecting the central nervous system to the rest of the body.

permeability (perm-ee-uh-BIL-uh-tee): The capability of being penetrated or passed through.

permissive parents: Parents who make few rules or demands and allow children to make their own decisions and control their own behavior.

person-centered therapy: A nondirective, humanistic therapy in which the therapist creates a warm, accepting climate, freeing clients to be themselves and releasing their natural tendency toward positive growth.

personal fable: An exaggerated sense of personal uniqueness and indestructibility, which may be the basis for adolescent risk taking.

personal space: An area surrounding each individual, much like an invisible bubble, that is considered to belong to the person and used to regulate the closeness of interactions with others.

personal unconscious: In Jung's theory, the layer of the unconscious containing all of the thoughts and experiences that are accessible to the conscious, as well as repressed memories and impulses.

personality: A person's characteristic patterns of behavior, thinking, and feeling.

personality disorder: A continuing, inflexible, maladaptive pattern of inner experience and behavior that causes great distress or impaired functioning and differs significantly from the patterns expected in the person's culture.

persuasion: A deliberate attempt to influence the attitudes and/or behavior of another.

PET scan (positron-emission tomography): A brain-imaging technique that reveals activity in various parts of the brain, based on the amount of oxygen and glucose consumed.

phallic stage: Freud's third psychosexual stage (ages 3 to 5 or 6 years), during which sensual pleasure is derived mainly through touching the genitals, and the Oedipus complex arises.

pheromones: Chemicals excreted by humans and other animals that act as signals to and elicit certain patterns of behavior from members of the same species.

phi phenomenon: An illusion of movement occurring when two or more stationary lights are flashed on and off in sequence, giving the impression that one light is actually moving from one spot to the next.

phobia (FO-bee-ah): A persistent, irrational fear of an object, situation, or activity that the person feels compelled to avoid.

phonemes: The basic speech sounds in any language that, when combined, form words.

physical drug dependence: A compulsive pattern of drug use in which the user develops a drug tolerance coupled with unpleasant withdrawal symptoms when the drug use is discontinued.

pituitary gland: The endocrine gland located in the brain and often called the "master gland," which releases hormones that control other endocrine glands and also releases a growth hormone.

place theory: The theory that sounds of different frequency or pitch cause maximum activation of hair cells at certain locations along the basilar membrane.

placebo (pluh-SEE-bo): Some inert substance, such as a sugar pill or an injection of saline solution, given to the control group in an experiment as a control for the placebo effect.

placebo effect: The phenomenon that occurs when a person's response to a treatment or response on the dependent variable in an experiment is due to expectations regarding the treatment rather than to the treatment itself.

plasticity: The ability of the brain to reorganize and compensate for brain damage.

plateau phase: The second stage of the sexual response cycle, during which muscle tension and blood flow to the genitals increase in preparation for orgasm.

pleasure principle: The principle by which the id operates to seek pleasure, avoid pain, and obtain immediate gratification.

polygraph: A device designed to detect changes in heart rate, blood pressure, respiration rate, and the skin conductance response that typically accompany the anxiety that occurs when a person lies.

population: The entire group that is of interest to researchers and to which they wish to generalize their findings; the group from which a sample is selected.

positive correlation: A relationship between two variables in which both vary in the same direction.

positive reinforcement: A reward or pleasant consequence that follows a response and increases the probability that the response will be repeated.

postconventional level: Kohlberg's highest level of moral reasoning, in which moral reasoning involves weighing moral alternatives; "right" is whatever furthers basic human rights.

posttraumatic stress disorder (PTSD): A prolonged and severe stress reaction to a catastrophic event or to chronic intense stress.

preconscious: The thoughts, feelings, and memories that a person is not consciously aware of at the moment but that may be brought to consciousness.

preconventional level: Kohlberg's lowest level of moral reasoning, based on the physical consequences of an act; "right" is whatever avoids punishment or gains a reward.

prejudice: Negative attitudes toward others based on their gender, religion, race, or membership in a particular group.

premature ejaculation: A chronic or recurring orgasmic disorder in which orgasm and ejaculation occur with little stimulation, before, during, or shortly after penetration and before the person desires it.

prenatal: Occurring between conception and birth.

preoperational stage: Piaget's second stage of cognitive development (ages 2 to 7 years), characterized by rapid development of language and thinking governed by perception rather than logic.

presbyopia (prez-bee-O-pee-uh): A condition, occurring in the mid- to late 40s, in which the lenses of the eyes no longer accommodate adequately for near vision, and reading glasses or bifocals are required for reading.

preterm infant: An infant born before the 37th week and weighing less than 5.5 pounds; a premature infant.

primacy effect: In memory, the tendency to recall the first items on a list more readily than the middle items; in social psychology the tendency for an overall impression of another to be influenced more by the first information that is received about that person than by information that comes later.

primary appraisal: An evaluation of the significance of a potentially stressful event according to how it will affect one's well-being—whether it is perceived as irrelevant or as involving harm or loss, threat, or challenge.

primary auditory cortex: The part of the temporal lobes where hearing registers in the cerebral cortex.

primary drive: A state of tension or arousal arising from a biological need; one not based on learning.

primary mental abilities: According to Thurstone, seven relatively distinct abilities that singly or in combination are involved in all intellectual activities.

primary reinforcer: A reinforcer that fulfills a basic physical need for survival and does not depend on learning.

primary sex characteristics: The internal and external reproductive organs; the genitals.

primary visual cortex: The area at the rear of the occipital lobes where vision registers in the cerebral cortex.

priming: The phenomenon by which an earlier encounter with a stimulus (such as a word or a picture) increases the speed or accuracy with which that stimulus or a related stimulus can be named at a later time.

proactive coping: Efforts or actions taken in advance of a potentially stressful situation to prevent its occurrence or to minimize its consequences.

problem-focused coping: A response aimed at reducing, modifying, or eliminating a source of stress.

problem solving: Thoughts and actions required to achieve a desired goal that is not readily attainable.

progesterone (pro-JES-tah-rone): A female sex hormone that plays a role in the regulation of the menstrual cycle and prepares the lining of the uterus for possible pregnancy.

projection: Attributing one's own undesirable thoughts, impulses, traits, or behaviors to others.

projective test: A personality test in which people respond to inkblots, drawings of ambiguous human situations, incomplete sentences, and the like, by projecting their own inner thoughts, feelings, fears, or conflicts onto the test materials.

prosocial behavior: Behavior that benefits others, such as helping, cooperation, and sympathy.

prospective forgetting: Forgetting to carry out some action, such as mailing a letter.

prototype: The example that embodies the most common and typical features of a concept.

proximity: Geographic closeness; a major factor in attraction.

psychiatrist: A medical doctor with a specialty in the diagnosis and treatment of mental disorders.

psychoactive drug: A drug that alters normal mental functioning—mood, perception, or thought; called a controlled substance if used medically.

psychoanalysis (SY-ko-ah-NAL-ih-sis): The term Freud used for both his theory of personality and his therapy for the treatment of psychological disorders; the unconscious is the primary focus of psychoanalytic theory, and the therapy uses free association, dream analysis, and analysis of resistance and transference to uncover repressed memories, impulses, and conflicts thought to cause psychological disorders.

psychoanalyst (SY-ko-AN-ul-ist): A professional, usually a psychiatrist, with special training in psychoanalysis.

psychoanalytic perspective (SY-ko-AN-il-IT-ik): A perspective initially proposed by Freud that emphasizes the importance of the unconscious and of early childhood experiences as the keys to understanding behavior and thought.

psycholinguistics: The study of how language is acquired, produced, and used, and how the sounds and symbols of language are translated into meaning.

psychological disorder: Mental processes and/or behavior patterns that cause emotional distress and/or substantial impairment in functioning.

psychological drug dependence: A craving or irresistible urge for a drug's pleasurable effects.

psychology: The scientific study of behavior and mental processes.

psychoneuroimmunology (sye-ko-NEW-ro-IM-you-NOLL-oh-gee): A field in which psychologists, biologists, and medical researchers study the effects of psychological factors on the immune system.

psychosexual stages: A series of stages through which the sexual instinct develops; each stage is defined by an erogenous zone that becomes the center of new pleasures and conflicts.

psychosis (sy-CO-sis): A severe psychological disorder, marked by loss of contact with reality and a seriously impaired ability to function.

psychosocial stages: Erikson's eight developmental stages through the life span, each defined by a conflict that must be resolved satisfactorily in order for healthy personality development to occur.

psychosurgery: Brain surgery to treat some severe, persistent, and debilitating psychological disorder or severe chronic pain.

psychotherapy: The treatment for psychological disorders that uses psychological rather than biological means and primarily involves conversations between patient and therapist.

puberty: A period of rapid physical growth and change that culminates in sexual maturity.

punishment: The removal of a pleasant stimulus or the application of an unpleasant stimulus, which tends to suppress a response.

random assignment: In an experiment, the assignment of participants to experimental and control groups by using a chance procedure, which guarantees that each has an equal probability of being placed in any of the groups; a control for selection bias.

random sample: A sample of subjects selected in such a way that every member of the population has an equal chance of being included in the sample; its purpose is to obtain a sample that is representative of the population of interest.

range: The difference between the highest score and the lowest score in a distribution of scores.

rational-emotive therapy: A directive, confrontational therapy developed by Albert Ellis and designed to challenge and modify the irrational beliefs thought to cause personal distress.

rationalization: Supplying a logical, rational, socially acceptable reason rather than the real reason for an action.

reaction formation: Denying an unacceptable impulse, often a sexual or aggressive one, by giving strong conscious expression to its opposite.

realistic conflict theory: The notion that prejudices arise when social groups must compete for scarce resources and opportunities.

reasoning: A form of thinking in which conclusions are drawn from a set of facts.

recall: A measure of retention that requires a person to remember material with few or no retrieval cues, as in an essay test.

recency effect: The tendency to recall the last items on a list more readily than those in the middle of the list.

receptors: Protein molecules on the dendrite or cell body of a neuron that will interact only with specific neurotransmitters.

recessive gene: A gene that will not be expressed if paired with a dominant gene but will be expressed if paired with another recessive gene.

reciprocal determinism: Bandura's concept that behavior, personal/cognitive factors, and environment all influence and are influenced by each other.

recognition: A measure of retention that requires a person to identify material as familiar, or as having been encountered before.

reconstruction: A memory that is not an exact replica of an event but has been pieced together from a few highlights, using information that may or may not be accurate.

reflex: An inborn, unlearned, automatic response (such as blinking, sucking, or grasping) to an environmental stimulus.

regression: Reverting to a behavior characteristic of an earlier stage of development.

rehearsal: The act of purposely repeating information to maintain it in short-term memory or to transfer it to long-term memory.

reinforcement: An event that follows a response and increases the strength of the response and/or the likelihood that it will be repeated.

reinforcer: Anything that strengthens a response or increases the probability that it will occur.

relearning method: Measuring retention in terms of the percentage of time or learning trials saved in relearning material compared with the time required to learn it originally; also called the savings method.

reliability: The ability of a test to yield nearly the same score when the same people are tested and then retested on the same test or an alternative form of the test.

REM dream: A type of dream having a dreamlike and storylike quality and occuring almost continuously during each REM period; more vivid, visual, and emotional than NREM dreams.

REM rebound: The increased amount of REM sleep that occurs after REM deprivation; often associated with unpleasant dreams or nightmares.

REM sleep: Sleep characterized by rapid eye movements, paralysis of large muscles, fast and irregular heart rate and respiration rate, increased brain-wave activity, and vivid dreams.

replication: The process of repeating a study with different participants and preferably a different investigator to verify research findings.

representative sample: A sample of participants selected from the larger population in such a way that important subgroups within the population are included in the sample in the same proportions as they are found in the larger population.

representativeness heuristic: A thinking strategy based on how closely a new object or situation is judged to resemble or match an existing prototype of that object or situation.

repression: Involuntarily removing from one's consciousness disturbing, guilt-provoking, or otherwise unpleasant memories so that one is no longer aware that a painful event occurred.

resistance: In psychoanalytic therapy, the patient's attempts to avoid expressing or revealing painful or embarrassing thoughts or feelings.

resistance stage: The second stage of the general adaptation syndrome, when there are intense physiological efforts to either resist or adapt to the stressor.

resolution phase: The final stage of the sexual response cycle, during which the body returns to an unaroused state.

resting potential: The membrane potential of a neuron at rest, about −70 millivolts.

restorative theory: The theory that the function of sleep is to restore body and mind.

reticular formation: A structure in the brainstem that plays a crucial role in arousal and attention and that screens sensory messages entering the brain.

retina: The layer of tissue at the back of the eye that contains the rods and the cones and onto which the incoming image is projected by the lens.

retinal image: The image of objects in the visual field projected onto the retina.

retrieval: The act of bringing to mind material that has been stored in memory.

retrieval cue: Any stimulus or bit of information that aids in the retrieval of particular information from long-term memory.

retrograde amnesia (RET-ro-grade): A loss of memory affecting experiences that occurred shortly before a loss of consciousness.

reuptake: The process by which neurotransmitter molecules are taken from the synaptic cleft back into the axon terminal for later use, thus terminating their excitatory or inhibitory effect on the receiving neuron.

reversibility: The realization that any change in the shape, position, or order of matter can be reversed mentally. A preoperational child's tendency to focus on only one dimension of a stimulus and ignore other dimensions.

right hemisphere: The hemisphere that controls the left side of the body and that, in most people, is specialized for visual-spatial perception and for interpreting nonverbal behavior.

rods: The light-sensitive receptors in the retina that allow humans to see in black, white, and shades of gray in dim light.

Rorschach Inkblot Method (ROR-shok): A projective test composed of 10 inkblots to which a test taker responds; used to reveal unconscious functioning and the presence of psychiatric disorders.

sample: The portion of any population that is selected for study and from which generalizations are made about the entire population.

saturation: The degree to which light waves producing a color are of the same wavelength; the purity of a color.

savant syndrome: A condition that allows an otherwise mentally retarded individual to perform an amazing mental feat or display a remarkable specific skill (such as computation, music, or art).

savings score: The percentage of time or learning trials saved in relearning material over the amount of time or number of learning trials required for the original learning.

scapegoating: Displacing aggression onto minority groups or other innocent targets not responsible for the frustrating situation.

Schachter–Singer theory of emotion: A two-stage theory stating that for an emotion to occur, there must be (1) physiological arousal and (2) an explanation for the arousal.

schedule of reinforcement: A systematic program for administering reinforcements that has a predictable effect on behavior.

schema: In memory, an integrated framework of knowledge and assumptions a person has about people, objects, or events, which affects how the person encodes and recalls information; in cognitive development, Piaget's term for a cognitive structure or concept used to identify and interpret information.

schizophrenia (SKIT-soh-FREE-nee-ah): A severe psychological disorder characterized by loss of contact with reality, hallucinations, delusions, inappropriate or flat affect, some disturbance in thinking, social withdrawal, and/or other bizarre behavior.

scientific method: The orderly, systematic procedures researchers follow as they identify a research problem, design a study to investigate the problem, collect and analyze data, draw conclusions, and communicate their findings.

seasonal affective disorder (SAD): A mood disorder in which depression comes and goes with the seasons.

secondary appraisal: An evaluation of one's coping resources prior to deciding how to deal with a stressful event.

secondary reinforcer: A neutral stimulus that becomes reinforcing after repeated pairings with other reinforcers.

secondary sex characteristics: Those physical characteristics that are not directly involved in reproduction but that develop at puberty and distinguish the mature male from the mature female.

sedentary lifestyle: A lifestyle that includes less than 20 minutes of exercise three times a week.

selection bias: The assignment of participants to experimental or control groups in such a way that systematic differences among the groups are present at the beginning of the experiment.

self-actualization: Developing to one's fullest potential.

self-efficacy: A person's belief in his or her ability to perform competently in whatever is attempted.

self-serving bias: The tendency to attribute personal successes to dispositional causes and failures to situational causes.

semantic memory: The subpart of declarative memory that stores general knowledge; a mental encyclopedia or dictionary.

semantics: The meaning or the study of meaning derived from morphemes, words, and sentences.

semicircular canals: Three fluid-filled tubular canals in the inner ear that provide information about rotating head movements.

senile dementia: A state of mental deterioration caused by physical deterioration of the brain and characterized by impaired memory and intellect and by altered personality and behavior; senility.

sensation: The process through which the senses pick up visual, auditory, and other sensory stimuli and transmit them to the brain; sensory information that has registered in the brain but has not been interpreted.

sensorimotor stage: Piaget's first stage of cognitive development (ages birth to 2 years), culminating with the development of object permanence and the beginning of representational thought.

sensory adaptation: The process of becoming less sensitive to an unchanging sensory stimulus over time.

sensory deprivation: A condition in which sensory stimulation is reduced to a minimum or eliminated.

sensory memory: The memory system that holds information coming in through the senses for a period ranging from a fraction of a second to several seconds.

sensory receptors: Specialized cells in the sense organs that detect and respond to sensory stimuli—light, sound, odors, etc.—and transduce (convert) the stimuli into neural impulses.

separation anxiety: The fear and distress shown by toddlers when their parent leaves, occurring from 8 to 24 months and reaching a peak between 12 and 18 months.

serial position effect: The tendency to remember the beginning and ending items of a sequence or list better than the middle items.

serotonin (ser-oh-TOE-nin): A neurotransmitter that plays an important role in regulating mood, sleep, aggression, and appetite; a serotonin deficiency is associated with anxiety, depression, and suicide.

set point: The weight the body normally maintains when one is trying neither to gain nor to lose weight; if weight falls below the normal level, appetite increases and metabolic rate decreases; if weight is gained, appetite decreases and metabolic rate increases to its original level.

sex chromosomes: The pair of chromosomes that determines the sex of a person (XX in females and XY in males), the primary and secondary sex characteristics, and other sex-linked traits.

sexual aversion disorder: A sexual desire disorder characterized by an aversion to or a desire to avoid genital contact with a sexual partner.

sexual dysfunction: A persistent or recurrent problem that causes marked distress and interpersonal difficulty and that may involve any or some combination of the following: sexual desire, sexual arousal, or the pleasure associated with sex or orgasm.

sexual orientation: The direction of one's sexual preference—toward members of the opposite sex (heterosexuality), toward one's own sex (homosexuality), or toward both sexes (bisexuality).

sexual response cycle: The four phases—excitement, plateau, orgasm, and resolution—that Masters and Johnson found are part of the human sexual response in both males and females.

sexually transmitted diseases (STDs): Infections that are spread primarily through intimate sexual contact.

shape constancy: The tendency to perceive an object as having a stable or unchanging shape regardless of differences in viewing angle.

shaping: An operant conditioning technique that consists of gradually molding a desired behavior (response) by reinforcing responses that become progressively closer to it.

short-term memory: The second stage of memory, which holds about seven (a range of five to nine) items for less than 30 seconds without rehearsal; working memory; the mental workspace a person uses to keep in mind tasks being thought about at any given moment.

signal detection theory: The view that detection of a sensory stimulus involves discriminating a stimulus from background "noise" and deciding whether the stimulus is actually present.

situational attribution: Attributing a behavior to some external cause or factor operating in the situation; an external attribution.

size constancy: The tendency to perceive an object as the same size regardless of changes in the retinal image.

Skinner box: A soundproof chamber with a device for delivering food and either a bar for rats to press or a disk for pigeons to peck; used in operant conditioning experiments.

sleep apnea: A sleep disorder involving periods during sleep when breathing stops and the person must awaken briefly in order to breathe; major symptoms are excessive daytime sleepiness and loud snoring.

sleep cycle: A cycle of sleep lasting about 90 minutes and including one or more stages of NREM sleep followed by a period of REM sleep.

sleep terror: A sleep disturbance in which a person partially awakens from Stage 4 sleep with a scream, dazed and groggy, in a panic state, and with a racing heart.

slow-wave sleep: Stage 3 and Stage 4 sleep; deep sleep.

social cognition: Mental processes that people use to notice, interpret, understand, remember, and apply information about the social world and that enable them to simplify, categorize, and order that world.

social facilitation: Any positive or negative effect on performance due to the presence of others, either as an audience or as co-actors.

social learning theory: A theory that explains the process of gender typing in terms of observation, imitation, and reinforcement.

social loafing: The tendency to put forth less effort when working with others on a common task than when working alone.

social motives: Motives acquired through experience and interaction with others.

social norms: The attitudes and standards of behavior expected of members of a particular group.

social phobia: An irrational fear and avoidance of social situations in which one might embarrass or humiliate oneself by appearing clumsy, foolish, or incompetent.

social psychology: The study of how the actual, imagined, or implied presence of others influences the thoughts, feelings, and behavior of individuals.

Social Readjustment Rating Scale (SRRS): Holmes and Rahe's stress scale, which ranks 43 life events from most to least stressful and assigns a point value to each.

social roles: Socially defined behaviors considered appropriate for individuals occupying certain positions within a group.

social support: Tangible support, information, advice, and/or emotional support provided in time of need by family, friends, and others; the feeling of being loved, valued, and cared for.

socialization: The process of learning socially acceptable behaviors, attitudes, and values.

sociocognitive theory of hypnosis: A theory suggesting that the behavior of hypnotized people is a function of their expectations about how a person behaves under hypnosis and their motivation to be good subjects.

sociocultural perspective: A perspective that emphasizes social and cultural influences on human behavior and stresses the importance of understanding those influences when interpreting the behavior of others.

somatoform disorders (so-MAT-uh-form): Disorders in which physical symptoms are present that are due to psychological rather than physical causes.

somatosensory cortex (so-MAT-oh-SENS-or-ee): The strip of tissue at the front of the parietal lobes where touch, pressure, temperature, and pain register in the cerebral cortex.

somnambulism (som-NAM-bue-lism): Sleepwalking that occurs during a partial arousal from Stage 4 sleep.

source traits: Cattell's name for the traits that make up the most basic personality structure and cause behavior.

specific phobia: A marked fear of a specific object or situation; a catchall category for any phobia other than agoraphobia and social phobia.

spinal cord: An extension of the brain, reaching from the base of the brain through the neck and spinal column, that transmits messages between the brain and the peripheral nervous system.

split-brain operation: An operation, performed in severe cases of epilepsy, in which the corpus callosum is cut, separating the cerebral hemispheres and usually lessening the severity and frequency of grand mal seizures.

spontaneous recovery: The reappearance of an extinguished response (in a weaker form) when an organism is exposed to the original conditioned stimulus following a rest period.

Stage 4 sleep: The deepest stage of NREM sleep, characterized by an EEG pattern of more than 50% delta waves.

standard deviation: A descriptive statistic reflecting the average amount that scores in a distribution deviate, or vary, from their mean.

standardization: Establishing norms for comparing the scores of people who will take a test in the future; administering tests using a prescribed procedure.

Stanford–Binet Intelligence Scale: An individually administered IQ test for those aged 2 to 23; Terman's adaptation of the Binet–Simon Scale.

state-dependent memory effect: The tendency to recall information better if one is in the same pharmacological or psychological (mood) state as when the information was encoded.

stereotypes: Widely shared beliefs about the characteristic traits, attitudes, and behaviors of members of various social groups (racial, ethnic, religious), including the assumption that the members of such groups are usually all alike.

stimulants: A category of drugs that speed up activity in the central nervous system, suppress appetite, and cause a person to feel more awake, alert, and energetic; also called "uppers."

stimulus (STIM-yu-lus): Any event or object in the environment to which an organism responds; plural is *stimuli.*

stimulus motives: Motives that cause humans and other animals to increase stimulation and that appear to be unlearned (examples: curiosity and the need to explore, manipulate objects, and play).

stimulus satiation (say-she-A-shun): A behavior modification technique that involves giving a patient so much of a stimulus that it becomes something the patient wants to avoid.

storage: The act of maintaining information in memory.

stranger anxiety: A fear of strangers common in infants at about 6 months and increasing in intensity until about 12½ months, and then declining in the second year.

stress: The physiological and psychological response to a condition that threatens or challenges a person and requires some form of adaptation or adjustment.

stressor: Any stimulus or event capable of producing physical or emotional stress.

stroke: The most common cause of damage to adult brains, arising when blockage of an artery cuts off the blood supply to a particular area of the brain or when a blood vessel bursts.

structuralism: The first formal school of psychology, aimed at analyzing the basic elements, or structure, of conscious mental experience through the use of introspection.

subjective night: The time during a 24-hour period when body temperature is lowest and when the biological clock is telling a person to go to sleep.

sublimation: Rechanneling sexual or aggressive energy into pursuits that society considers acceptable or admirable.

subliminal perception: Perceiving sensory stimulation that is below the absolute threshold.

subliminal persuasion: Sending persuasive messages below the recipient's level of awareness.

successive approximations: A series of gradual steps, each of which is more like the final desired response.

superego (sue-per-EE-go): The moral system of the personality, which consists of the conscience and the ego ideal.

suprachiasmatic nucleus (SCN): A tiny structure in the brain's hypothalamus that controls the timing of circadian rhythms; the biological clock.

surface structure: The literal words of a sentence that are spoken or written (or signed).

surface traits: Cattell's name for observable qualities of personality, such as those used to describe a friend.

surrogate: Substitute; someone or something that stands in place of someone or something else.

survey: A method in which researchers use interviews and/or questionnaires to gather information about the attitudes, beliefs, experiences, or behaviors of a group of people.

syllogism: A scheme for logical reasoning in which two statements known as premises are followed by a valid conclusion.

sympathetic nervous system: The division of the autonomic nervous system that mobilizes the body's resources during stress, emergencies, or heavy exertion, preparing the body for action.

synapse (SIN-aps): The junction where the axon of a sending neuron communicates with a receiving neuron across the synaptic cleft.

syntax: The aspect of grammar that specifies the rules for arranging and combining words to form phrases and sentences.

syphilis (SIF-ih-lis): An STD that progresses through three stages; if untreated, it can eventually be fatal.

systematic desensitization: A behavior therapy that is used to treat phobias and that involves training clients in deep muscle relaxation and then having them confront a graduated series of anxiety-producing situations (real or imagined) until they can remain relaxed while confronting even the most feared situation.

tactile: Pertaining to the sense of touch.

taste aversion: The dislike and/or avoidance of a particular food that has been associated with nausea or discomfort.

taste buds: Structures composed of 60 to 100 sensory receptors for taste.

telegraphic speech: Short sentences that follow a strict word order and contain only essential content words.

temperament: A person's behavioral style or characteristic way of responding to the environment.

temporal lobes: The lobes that contain the primary auditory cortex, Wernicke's area, and association areas for interpreting auditory information.

teratogens: Harmful agents in the prenatal environment, which can have a negative impact on prenatal development or even cause birth defects.

testosterone (tes-TOS-tah-rone): The most powerful androgen secreted by the testes and adrenal glands in males and by the adrenal glands in females; influences the development and maintenance of male sex characteristics and sexual motivation; associated with male aggressiveness.

thalamus (THAL-uh-mus): The structure, located above the brainstem, that acts as a relay station for information flowing into or out of the higher brain centers.

THC (tetrahydrocannabinol): The principal psychoactive ingredient in marijuana and hashish.

Thematic Apperception Test (TAT): A projective test consisting of drawings of ambiguous human situations, which the test taker describes; thought to reveal inner feelings, conflicts, and motives, which are projected onto the test materials.

theory of dissociated control: The theory that hypnosis is an authentic altered state of consciousness in which the control the executive function exerts over other subsystems of consciousness is weakened.

theory: A general principle or set of principles proposed to explain how a number of separate facts are related.

timbre (TAM-burr): The distinctive quality of a sound that distinguishes it from other sounds of the same pitch and loudness.

time out: A behavior modification technique used to decrease the frequency of undesirable behavior by withdrawing an individual from all reinforcement for a period of time.

token economy: A behavior modification technique that reinforces desirable behaviors with tokens that can be exchanged later for desired objects, activities, and/or privileges.

top-down processing: Application of previous experience and conceptual knowledge to recognize the whole of a perception and thus easily identify the simpler elements of that whole.

trait: A personal characteristic that is used to describe or explain personality.

trait theories: Theories that attempt to explain personality and differences between people in terms of their personal characteristics.

transduction: The process by which sensory receptors convert sensory stimuli—light, sound, odors, etc.—into neural impulses.

transference: An intense emotional reaction during psychoanalysis, when the patient displays feelings and attitudes toward the analyst that were present in a significant relationship in the past.

trial and error: An approach to problem solving in which one solution after another is tried in no particular order until an answer is found.

trial-and-error learning: Learning that occurs when a response is associated with a successful solution to a problem after a number of unsuccessful responses.

triangular theory of love: Sternberg's theory that three components—intimacy, passion, and decision/commitment—singly and in various combinations produce seven different kinds of love.

triarchic theory of intelligence: Sternberg's theory that there are three types of intelligence—componential (analytical), experiential (creative), and contextual (practical).

trichromatic theory: The theory of color vision suggesting that there are three types of cones, which are maximally sensitive to red, green, or blue, and that varying levels of activity in these receptors can produce all of the colors.

twin study method: Studying identical and fraternal twins to determine the relative effects of heredity and environment on a variety of characteristics.

Type A behavior pattern: A behavior pattern marked by a sense of time urgency, impatience, excessive competitiveness, hostility, and anger; considered a risk factor in coronary heart disease.

Type B behavior pattern: A behavior pattern marked by a relaxed, easygoing approach to life; not associated with coronary heart disease.

unconditional positive regard: Unqualified caring and nonjudgmental acceptance of another.

unconditioned response (UR): A response that is invariably elicited by the unconditioned stimulus without prior learning.

unconditioned stimulus (US): A stimulus that elicits a specific response without prior learning.

unconscious (un-KON-shus): For Freud, the primary motivating force of behavior, containing repressed memories as well as instincts and wishes that have never been conscious.

underextension: Restricting the use of a word to only a few, rather than to all, members of a class of objects.

uplifts: The positive experiences in life, which can neutralize the effects of many of the hassles.

vaginismus (VAJ-ah-NIZ-mus): A sexual pain disorder in which involuntary muscle contractions tighten and close the vagina, making intercourse painful or impossible.

validity: The ability of a test to measure what it is intended to measure.

variability: How much the scores in a distribution spread out, away from the mean.

variable-interval schedule: A schedule in which a reinforcer is given after the first correct response following a varying time of nonreinforcement based on an average time.

variable-ratio schedule: A schedule in which a reinforcer is given after a varying number of nonreinforced responses based on an average ratio.

ventromedial hypothalamus (VMH): The part of the hypothalamus that acts as a satiety center and, when activated, signals an animal to stop eating; when the VMH is destroyed, the animal overeats, becoming obese.

vestibular sense (ves-TIB-yu-ler): Sense that provides information about the body's movement and orientation in space through sensory receptors in the semicircular canals and the vestibular sacs, which detect changes in the movement and orientation of the head.

visible spectrum: The narrow band of electromagnetic waves, 380–760 nm in length, that are visible to the human eye.

visual cliff: An apparatus used to test depth perception in infants and young animals.

Weber's law: The law stating that the just noticeable difference (JND) for all the senses depends on a proportion or percentage of change in a stimulus rather than on a fixed amount of change.

Wechsler Adult Intelligence Scale (WAIS-III): An individual intelligence test for adults that yields separate verbal and performance (nonverbal) IQ scores as well as an overall IQ score.

Wernicke's aphasia: Aphasia that results from damage to Wernicke's area and in which the person's spoken language is fluent, but the content is either vague or incomprehensible to the listener.

Wernicke's area: The language area in the temporal lobe involved in comprehension of the spoken word and in formulation of coherent speech and written language.

withdrawal symptoms: The physical and psychological symptoms (usually the opposite of those produced by the drug) that occur when a regularly used drug is discontinued and that terminate when the drug is taken again.

work motivation: The conditions and processes responsible for the arousal, direction, magnitude, and maintenance of effort one puts forth in one's job.

working backwards: A heuristic strategy in which a person discovers the steps needed to solve a problem by defining the desired goal and working backwards to the current condition.

Yerkes–Dodson law: The principle that performance on tasks is best when the arousal level is appropriate to the difficulty of the task—higher arousal for simple tasks, moderate arousal for tasks of moderate difficulty, and lower arousal for complex tasks.

Name Index

Subject Index

Credits

Photos

2: Reuters/Mark Baker/Archive Photos; **3:** Jeff Greenberg/PhotoEdit; **6:** © Ron Chapple/FPG International/PictureQuest; **7:** Carlos Lopez-Barillas/Liaison Agency; **9:** Billy E. Barnes/PhotoEdit; **11:** © Pictor International/Pictor International Ltd./PictureQuest; **14:** © 1988 Warner Bros./Motion Picture and TV Archives; **20:** Tony Freeman/PhotoEdit; **21:** Steve Winter/ Black Star; **22:** David Young-Wolff/PhotoEdit; **25:** George Kraychyk/The Everett Collection; **29:** Reuters/Rose Prouser/Archive Photos; **34:** Jeff Greenberg/PhotoEdit; **40:** © Dr. Dennis Kunkel/Phototake; **42:** BioPhoto/Photo Researchers, Inc.; **47:** AP/Wide World Photos; **54:** A. Glauberman/Photo Researchers, Inc.; **58:** Reprinted with permission from Damasio, H., Grabowski, T., Frank, R., Galaburda, A. M., & Damasio, A. R: The return of Phineas Gage: Clues about the brain from a famous patient. *Science, 264:* 1102–1105. © 1994. American Association for the Advancement of Science. Photo courtesy of H. Damasio, Human Neuroanatomy and Neuroimaging Laboratory, Department of Neurology, University of Iowa. **59:** © Richard Gross/The Stock Market; **60:** AP/ Wide World Photos; **66:** Alexander Tsiaras/Photo Researchers, Inc.; **67L:** Berwyn MRI Center/Stone; **67R:** Dr. Michael Phelps and Dr. John Mazziotta; **67B:** Peter Menzel/Material World; **68:** AP/ Wide World Photos; **74:** Robert Brenner/PhotoEdit; **78:** © Copyright 2000 Stone; **81:** A. Ramey/Woodfin Camp & Associates; **83:** AP/ Wide World Photos; **84:** © Carolina Biological Supply Company/Phototake; **90L:** © Robert Harbison; **90R:** © Robert Harbison; **92:** AP/Wide World Photos; **95:** © Martin Rogers/Stock Boston; **96:** © G. Gardner/The Image Works; **98:** Omikron/Science Source/Photo Researchers, Inc.; **102:** Debbie Rogow/PhotoEdit; **104:** Gerard Vandeystadt/Photo Researchers, Inc.; **109:** Courtesy of Geotyme Enterprises; **110:** © 2000 Craig Tuttle/The Stock Market; **113:** © Richard Lord Ente/The Image Works; **122:** AP/ Wide World Photos; **127:** Charles Gupton/Stone; **128:** Russell D. Curtis/Photo Researchers, Inc.; **131:** © Esbin Anderson/The Image Works; **132:** AP/Wide World Photos; **137:** The Everett Collection; **141:** Louis Psihoyos/Matrix; **142:** The Next Best Thing Photo: Ron Batzdorff/The Everett Collection; **144:** Françoise Sauze/Science Photo Library/Photo Researchers, Inc.; **146:** Peter Schommartz/Liaison Agency; **149:** AP/ Wide World Photos; **153:** © David Austen/Stock Boston; **154:** R. Hutchings/PhotoEdit; **159:** © Pictor International/Pictor International Ltd./PictureQuest; **162:** © Peter Beck/The Stock Market; **165:** © Bettmann/CORBIS; **169:** Myrleen Ferguson/PhotoEdit; **171:** Archives of the History of American Psychology—University of Akron; **174:** Ed Kashi; **176:** Bill Aron/PhotoEdit; **180T:** © Nina Leen/TimePix; **180B:** AP/Wide World Photos; **184:** Chris Thomaidis/Stone; **185:** Jeff Greenberg/PhotoEdit; **191:** David Young Wolff/PhotoEdit; **193:** Will & Demi McIntyre/Photo Researchers, Inc.; **197T:** Myrleen Ferguson/PhotoEdit; **197B:** Edouard Berne/Stone; **198:** Photosynthesis Archives; **202:** Paul Conklin/PhotoEdit; **204:** AP/Wide World Photos; **207:** Kent Wood/Photo Researchers, Inc.; **211L:** Nicholas DeSciose/Photo Researchers, Inc.; **211R:** AP/Wide World Photos; **215:** Will Hart/PhotoEdit; **222:** Grantpix/Monkmeyer; **224:** James Shaffer/PhotoEdit; **226:** Nelson/Archive Photos; **227:** Reuters/Charles Platiau/Archive Photos; **229:** M & E Bernheim/Woodfin Camp & Associates; **232:** The Everett Collection; **235:** AP/Wide World Photos ; **244:** © Rob Lewine/The Stock Market; **249:** © Bill Greenblatt/Liaison Agency; **251T:** Jim Simncen/Stone; **251B:** Art Wolfe/Stone; **255:** © IAN HANNING/Impress/The Image Works; **262:** Barbara L. Johnson/Reuters/Archive Photos; **263:** Geoff Tompkinson/Science Photo Library/Photo Researchers, Inc.; **267:** © Stephanie Maze/Woodfin Camp & Associates; **268:** CNN/A & B Archives; **271:** Sidney/Monkmeyer; **273:** © Robert Harbison; **276:** © Vincent DeWitt/Stock Boston; **277T:** Jeffrey Foxx/Woodfin Camp & Associates; **277B:** Hank Morgan/Photo Researchers, Inc.; **280:** The Everett Collection; **281L:** Bernard Wolf/Monkmeyer; **281M:** Rafael Macia/Photo Researchers, Inc.; **281R:** B&C Alexander/Photo Researchers, Inc.; **282:** Archives of the History of American Psychology—University of Akron; **284:** Lew Merim/Monkmeyer; **292:** Porterfield/Chickering/Photo Researchers, Inc.; **294:** © Jonathan Barth/Liaison Agency; **296:** Peter Menzel/Material World; **298:** Collins/Monkmeyer; **303:** Kirk McCoy/Material World; **305:** © Robert Harbison; **308:** © George DiSario/The Stock Market; **309:** Bettmann/CORBIS; **311:** © E. Crews/The Image Works; **314T:** Francis Leroy/Photo Researchers, Inc.; **314M:** Lennart Nilsson/Bonniers; **314B:** Lennart Nilsson/Bonniers; **315:** George Steinmetz; **318T:** Courtesy of Dr. David Linton; **318B:** Enrico Ferorelli; **323:** © Martin Rogers/Stock Boston; **326:** David Young-Wolff/PhotoEdit; **328L:** Goodman/Monkmeyer; **328R:** Goodman/Monkmeyer; **333:** Frank Siteman/PhotoEdit; **338:** Robert E. Daemmrich/Stone; **340:** Cathlyn Melloan/Stone; **343:** Kate Connell/The Liaison Agency; **348:** AP/Wide World Photos; **349:** AP/Wide World Photos; **351:** David Young-Wolff/Stone; 353: © Nik Kleinberg/The Stock Market; **357:** © Paul Barton/The Stock Market; **360:** Mark Richards/PhotoEdit; **362:** Elizabeth Brooks/A & B Archives; **365:** © Bob Daemmrich/Stock Boston; **369:** Will and Demi McIntyre/Photo Researchers, Inc.; **371:** Ron Dalquist/Stone; **372:** Michael Newman/PhotoEdit; **374:** David Young-Wolff/PhotoEdit; **375:** Jalandoni/Monkmeyer; **378:** Blake Discher/CORBIS Sygma; **380:** Amy C. Etra/PhotoEdit; **384:** AP/Wide World Photos; **388:** © Anthony Neste; **390:** Courtesy McGill University; **392:** Prentice Hall, Inc.; **393:** Arthur Beck/Photo Researchers, Inc.; **395L:** AP/Wide World Photos; **395R:** AP/Wide World Photos; **399:** © 1993 ABC **H.L./Motion Picture & Television Archives; **400:** Tony Freeman/PhotoEdit; **402:** AP/Wide World Photos; **409:** © Richard Nowitz/Photo Researchers, Inc.; **412:** Reprinted by permission of the Human Interaction Laboratory/© Paul Ekman 1975; **413:** David Young-Wolff/PhotoEdit; **418:** © Dion Ogust/The Image Works; **424:** FPG International; **427:** Pater Cade/Stone; **433:** Richard Hutchings/Photo Researchers, Inc.; **436:** Blair Sietz/Photo Researchers, Inc.; **440:** © P. Watson/The Image Works; **442:** © Tom & DeAnn McCarthy/The Stock Market; **444:** Vanessa Vick/Photo Researchers, Inc.; **447:** © Bob Daemmrich/Stock Boston; **454:** AP/Wide World Photos; **457:** Lori Adamski Peek/Stone; **460:** David McNew/Liaison Agency; **463:** © Ted Spiegel/CORBIS; **466:** David Young-Wolff/Stone; **468:** © Robert Harbison; **470:** Mark Richards/PhotoEdit; **477:** David Tejada/Stone; **479:** © Paul S. Howell/Liaison Agency; **480:** Michael Newman/PhotoEdit; **484:** Tony Freeman/PhotoEdit; **487:** © L. Kolvoord/The Image Works; **489:** © Robert Harbison; **490:** Davis Barber/PhotoEdit; **494:** © Syracuse Newspapers/The Image Works; **497:** Archive Photos; **502:** Prettyman/PhotoEdit; **505:** Bettmann/CORBIS; **507L:** © Bob Daemmrich/Stock Boston; **507R:** Jim Cummins/FPG International; **511:** Andy Levin/Photo Researchers, Inc.; **513:** © John Eastcott/YVA Momatiuk/Stock Boston; **517:** Bettmann/CORBIS; **523:** Chris Arend/Stone; **525:** © Jose L. Pelaez/The Stock Market; **536 :** © Frank Siteman/Stock Boston; **539L:** © Robert Harbison; **539R:** © Dean Conger/CORBIS; **546:** Will Hart; **549:** © Abarno/The Stock Market; **550:** © J. Griffin/The Image Works; **555:** AP/Wide World Photos; **559:** AP/Wide World Photos; **561:** Spencer Grant/PhotoEdit; **563:** © Rob Crandall/Stock Boston; **570:** © Jose Pelaez/The Stock Market; **574:** Zigy Kaluzny/Stone; **577:** Bettmann/CORBIS; **579:** Michael Rougier/TimePix, Inc.; **581:** Will Hart; **582:** © Bob Daemmrich/Stock Boston; **588L:** Georgia Tech Telephoto; **588R:** Georgia Tech Telephoto; **593:** Leif Skoogfors/Woodfin Camp & Associates; **596:** Jonathan Nourak/Stone; **598:** J. Wilson/Woodfin Camp & Associates; **603:** Michael Newman/PhotoEdit; **605:** © Jose Pelaez/The Stock Market; **608:** © Rob Lewine/The Stock Market; **610:** Courtesy of Milgram Estate; **611:** © C. Gatewood/The Image Works; **615:** J. Christopher Briscoe/Photo Researchers, Inc.; **619:** William Vandevert/*Scientific American;* **629:** © Robert Harbison; **632:** Gary A. Conner/PhotoEdit; **634:** Paul Conklin/PhotoEdit; **637:** Dan Miller/Woodfin Camp & Associates; **639:** Baitel/Landmann/Liaison Agency; **644:** Gish/Monkmeyer

Text and Art

Chapter 1: Figure 1.3, p. 28: Buunk, B. P., Angleitner, A., Oubaid, V., & Buss, D. M. (1996), "Sex differences in jealousy in evolutionary and cultural perspective: Tests from the Netherlands, Germany, and the United States," *Psychological Science,* 1996, 7, pp. 359–363.

Chapter 2: Try It!, p. 63: Drawing from *The Origin of Consciousnes and the Breakdown of the Bicameral Mind* by J. Jaynes, 1976. Reprinted by permision of Houghton Mifflin Company.

Chapter 3: Figure 3.4, p. 88: http://www.hhmi.org/senses/b/b150.htm
Figure 3.8, p. 97: From John P. J. Pinel, *Biopsychology,* Fourth Edition. Copyright © 1999 by Allyn and Bacon. Reprinted by permission.
Figure 3.9, p. 98: From John P. J. Pinel, *Biopsychology,* Fourth Edition. Copyright © 1999 by Allyn and Bacon. Reprinted by permission.
Figure 3.10, p. 101: Reprinted from *Proceedings of the National Academy of Sciences,* Vol. 90, p. 3594, April 1993. Copyright 1993 National Academy of Sciences, U.S.A.
Figure 3.19, p. 113: Adapted from Gregory, R. L. *Eye and Brain: The Psychology of Seeing,* 3rd Edition. New York, McGraw-Hill, 1978.

Chapter 4: Figure 4.2, p. 134: http://wrair-www.army.mil/depts/behavbio/48sd.gif 301-295-7826
Figure 4.3, p. 148: http://monitoringthefuture.org/data/99data/fig99_1.gif

Chapter 5: Figure 5.4, p. 169: Pavlov, I. P. (1927). *Conditional Reflexes* (G. V. Anrep, Trans.). London: Oxford University Press.
Figure 5.7, p. 184: Margaret Gladback for Dan Todd, *Scientific American,* November, 1961, p. 96.
Figure 5.9, p. 196: From "Introduction and Removal of Reward and Maze Performance in Rats" by E. Tolman & C. H. Honzik, *University of California Publications in Psychology, 4,* 1930. Reprinted by permission of University of California Press.

Chapter 6: Opening vignette, pp. 203–204: *St. Louis Post Dispatch,* Thursday, Sept. 28, 2000, page A8, by Helen O'Neill. Reprinted with permission of The Associated Press.
Figure 6.3, p. 210: From "Short-term Retention of Individual Verbal Items" by L. R. Peterson & M. J. Peterson, *Journal of Experimental Psychology,* Vol. 58, 1959.
Try It!, p. 218: Drawing based on R. S. Nickerson & M. J. Adams, "Long-Term Memory for a Common Object," *Cognitive Psychology,* Vol. 11, p. 297, copyright © 1979 by Academic Press, reproduced by permission of the publisher.
Figure 6.8, p. 228: From R. N. Haber, "Eidetic Images Are Not Just Imaginary," *Psychology Today,* Vol. 14, 1980, p. 74. Copyright © 1980 (Sussex Publishers, Inc.)
Figure 6.13, p. 240: Adapted from G. H. Bower, "How to, uh, Remember," *Psychology Today,* 1973, pp. 63–70.

Chapter 7: Figure 7.1, p. 248: Reprinted with permission from R. N. Shepard & J. Metzler, "Mental Rotation of Three-Dimensional Objects," *Science,* Vol. 171 (2/19/71), p. 701+. Copyright 1971 by the American Association for the Advancement of Science.
Try It!, p. 260: From *Solve It! A Perplexing Profusion of Puzzles* by James F. Fixx. Copyright © 1978 by James F. Fixx. Used by permission of Doubleday, a division of Random House, Inc.
Figure 7.2, p. 268: From David Premack, "Language in Chimpanzees?" *Science,* Vol. 172, pp. 808–822. Copyright 1971 by the AAAS.

Chapter 8: Try It!, p. 288: Copyright Dept., www.iqtest.com, edg@iqtest.com
Figure 8.3, p. 289: From Ian J. Deary and Con Stough, "Intelligence and Inspection Time: Achievements, Prospects and Problems," *American Psychologist,* June 1996, Vol. 51, No. 6, pp. 599–608, Fig. 1. Copyright © 1996 by the American Psychological Association. Reprinted with permission.
Figure 8.6, p. 296: Illustration by Laurie Grace from "Learning from Asian Schools" by Harold W. Stevenson, *Scientific American,* December 1992, p. 73. Reprinted by permission of Laurie Grace.
Try It!, p. 299: From *Emotional Intelligence* by Daniel Goleman, copyright © 1995 by Daniel Goleman. Used by permission of Bantam Books, a division of Random House, Inc.
Figure 8.7, p. 301: Reprinted from *Neuropsychologia,* Volume 38, Issue 6: Ingegerd Carlsson, Peter E. Wend, and Jarl Risberg, "On the Neurobiology of Creativity Differences in Frontal Activity Between High and Low Creative Subjects," June 2000, with permission from Elsevier Science.

Chapter 9: Figure 9.4, p. 320: Taken in part from *Denver II Training Manual* by W. K. Frankenburg, J. Dodds, P. Archer, et al., 1992. Published by Denver Developmental Materials, Inc., Denver, CO. Reprinted by permission of W. K. Frankenburg.
Try It!, p. 329: Adapted from Laura E. Berk, *Development Through the Lifespan,* Second Edition, copyright © 2001 by Allyn & Bacon. Reprinted/adapted by permission.
Figure 9.5, p. 330: From Laura E. Berk, *Child Development,* Third Edition. Copyright © 1994 by Allyn and Bacon. Reprinted with permission.
Excerpted material, p. 340: Copyright © 1970 by The New York Times Company. Reprinted by permission. Excerpts from David Elkind, "Erik Erikson's Eight Ages of Man," *The New York Times* Magazine, April 5, 1970, pp. 87, 89, 90.

Chapter 10: Excerpted material, pp. 362, 363: Copyright © 1970 by The New York Times Company. Reprinted by permission. Excerpts from David Elkind, "Erik Erikson's Eight Ages of Man," *The New York Times* Magazine, April 5, 1970, pp. 87, 89, 90.

Chapter 12: Figure 12.1, p. 434: Illustrations by Jared Schneidman from "Sex Differences in the Brain" by Doreen Kimura, *Scientific American,* September 1992, pp. 120, 121. Reprinted by permission of the artist.
Figure 12.2, p. 436: U.S. Bureau of the Census and Bureau of Labor Statistics
Figure 12.4, p. 448: www.ama-assn.org
Try It!, p. 451: www.unspeakable.com
Try It!, p. 453: http://onhealth.webmd.com/home/interactives/conditions/188_02.asp
Apply It!, pp. 456–457: From Spencer A. Rathus, Jeffrey S. Nevid, & Lois Fichner-Rathus, *Human Sexuality in a World of Diversity,* Fourth Edition. Copyright © 1999 by Allyn and Bacon. Reprinted by permission.

Chapter 13: Table 13.1, p. 465: From Allen D. Kanner, James C. Coyne, C. Schaefer, and R. S. Lazarus, "Comparison of Two Modes of Stress Management: Daily Hassles and Uplifts Versus Major Life Events," *Journal of Behavioral Medicine, 4,* 1981, pp. 1–39.
Figure 13.3, p. 473: From "Personal Control and Stress and Coping Processes: A Theoretical Analysis" by Susan K. Folkman, *Journal of Personality and Social Psychology, 46,* 1984, pp. 839–852. Copyright 1984 by the American Psychological Association. Adapted by permission of the publisher and author.
Figure 13.4, p. 476: From Judith Green and Robert D. Shellenberger, *The Dynamics of Health and Wellness: A Biopsychosocial Approach,* Fig. 1.3. Copyright © 1991 by Holt, Rinehart and Winston, Inc.

Chapter 14: Figure 14.1, p. 498: Freud, S. *New Introductory Lectures on Psychoanalysis.* New York: Norton, 1965. Page 111. Found in David G. Myers, *Psychology,* Sixth Edition, Worth Publications.
Try It!, p. 510: Adapted from Cattell's *16PF® Fifth Edition Profile Sheet.* Copyright © 1993 by the Institute for Personality and Ability Testing, Inc., P.O. Box 1188, Champaign, IL, U.S.A. 61824-1188. Used with permission.

Chapter 15: Figure 15.1, p. 546: Daniel Weinberger, M.D. Clinical Brain Disorders Branch, Division of Intramural Research Programs, NIMH, 1990.
Figure 15.3, p. 550: "Cross-national epidemiology of major depression and bipolar disorder." Weissman, M. M., Bland, R. C., Canino, G. J., Faravelli, C., Greenwald, S., Hwu, H. G., Joyce, P. R., Karam, E. G., Lee, C. K., Lellouch, J., Lepine, J. P., Newman, S. C., Rubio-Stipec, M., Wells, J. E., Wickramaratne, P. J., Wittchen, H., and Yeh, E. K. *Journal of the American Medical Association,* 1996, July 24–31, 276: 4293–9.
Try It!, p. 557: National Institute of Mental Health, 1999

Chapter 17: Figure 17.7, p. 640: From "Crime in the United States," Federal Bureau of Investigation, 1999.